CORNERSTONE
BIBLICAL
COMMENTARY

General Editor
Philip W. Comfort
D. Litt. et Phil., University of South Africa;
Tyndale House Publishers;
Coastal Carolina University.

Consulting Editor, Old Testament
Tremper Longman III
PhD, Yale University;
Robert H. Gundry Professor of Biblical Studies, Westmont College.

Consulting Editor, New Testament
Grant Osborne
PhD, University of Aberdeen;
Professor of New Testament, Trinity Evangelical Divinity School.

Associate Editors
Jason Driesbach
MA, Biblical Exegesis and Linguistics, Dallas Theological Seminary;
Tyndale House Publishers.

Mark R. Norton
MA, Theological Studies, Wheaton Graduate School;
Tyndale House Publishers.

James A. Swanson
MSM, Multnomah Biblical Seminary;
MTh, University of South Africa;
Tyndale House Publishers.

CORNERSTONE
BIBLICAL
COMMENTARY

Leviticus
David W. Baker

Numbers
Dale A. Brueggemann

Deuteronomy
Eugene H. Merrill

GENERAL EDITOR
Philip W. Comfort

featuring the text of the
NEW LIVING TRANSLATION

TYNDALE HOUSE PUBLISHERS, INC. CAROL STREAM, ILLINOIS

Cornerstone Biblical Commentary, Volume 2

Visit Tyndale's exciting Web site at www.tyndale.com

Leviticus copyright © 2008 by David W. Baker. All rights reserved.

Numbers copyright © 2008 by Dale A. Brueggemann. All rights reserved.

Deuteronomy copyright © 2008 by Eugene H. Merrill. All rights reserved.

Designed by Luke Daab and Timothy R. Botts.

Library of Congress Cataloging-in-Publication Data

Cornerstone biblical commentary.
    p. cm.
  Includes bibliographical references and index.
  ISBN-13: 978-0-8423-3428-0 (hc : alk. paper)
  ISBN-10: 0-8423-3428-9 (hc : alk. paper)
  1. Bible—Commentaries. I. Baker, David W. II. Brueggemann, Dale A.
III. Merrill, Eugene H.

Printed in the United States of America

14	13	12	11	10	09	08
7	6	5	4	3	2	1

CONTENTS

Leviticus: David W. Baker
BA, Temple University;
MCS, Regent College:
MPhil, University of London;
PhD, University of London;
Professor of Old Testament and Semitic Languages at Ashland Theological Seminary.

Numbers: Dale A. Brueggemann
BA, Northwest Nazarene University;
MA, Westminster Theological Seminary;
PhD, Westminster Theological Seminary;
Director, Eurasia Education Services, Assemblies of God World Missions.

Deuteronomy: Eugene H. Merrill
BA, Bob Jones University;
MA, New York University;
MPhil, Columbia University;
PhD, Columbia University;
Distinguished Professor of Old Testament Studies at Dallas Theological Seminary;
Distinguished Professor of Old Testament Interpretation at the Southern Baptist
    Theological Seminary

GENERAL EDITOR'S PREFACE

The *Cornerstone Biblical Commentary* is based on the second edition of the New Living Translation (2007). Nearly 100 scholars from various church backgrounds and from several countries (United States, Canada, England, and Australia) participated in the creation of the NLT. Many of these same scholars are contributors to this commentary series. All the commentators, whether participants in the NLT or not, believe that the Bible is God's inspired word and have a desire to make God's word clear and accessible to his people.

This Bible commentary is the natural extension of our vision for the New Living Translation, which we believe is both exegetically accurate and idiomatically powerful. The NLT attempts to communicate God's inspired word in a lucid English translation of the original languages so that English readers can understand and appreciate the thought of the original writers. In the same way, the *Cornerstone Biblical Commentary* aims at helping teachers, pastors, students, and laypeople understand every thought contained in the Bible. As such, the commentary focuses first on the words of Scripture, then on the theological truths of Scripture—inasmuch as the words express the truths.

The commentary itself has been structured in such a way as to help readers get at the meaning of Scripture, passage by passage, through the entire Bible. Each Bible book is prefaced by a substantial book introduction that gives general historical background important for understanding. Then the reader is taken through the Bible text, passage by passage, starting with the New Living Translation text printed in full. This is followed by a section called "Notes," wherein the commentator helps the reader understand the Hebrew or Greek behind the English of the NLT, interacts with other scholars on important interpretive issues, and points the reader to significant textual and contextual matters. The "Notes" are followed by the "Commentary," wherein each scholar presents a lucid interpretation of the passage, giving special attention to context and major theological themes.

The commentators represent a wide spectrum of theological positions within the evangelical community. We believe this is good because it reflects the rich variety in Christ's church. All the commentators uphold the authority of God's word and believe it is essential to heed the old adage: "Wholly apply yourself to the Scriptures and apply them wholly to you." May this commentary help you know the truths of Scripture, and may this knowledge help you "grow in your knowledge of God and Jesus our Lord" (2 Pet 1:2, NLT).

PHILIP W. COMFORT
GENERAL EDITOR

ABBREVIATIONS

GENERAL ABBREVIATIONS

b.	Babylonian Gemara	Heb.	Hebrew	NT	New Testament
bar.	baraita	ibid.	*ibidem,* in the same place	OL	Old Latin
c.	*circa,* around, approximately	i.e.	*id est,* the same	OS	Old Syriac
		in loc.	*in loco,* in the place cited	OT	Old Testament
cf.	*confer,* compare			p., pp.	page, pages
ch, chs	chapter, chapters	lit.	literally	pl.	plural
contra	in contrast to	LXX	Septuagint	Q	Quelle ("Sayings" as Gospel source)
DSS	Dead Sea Scrolls	𝔐	Majority Text		
ed.	edition, editor	*m.*	Mishnah	rev.	revision
e.g.	*exempli gratia,* for example	masc.	masculine	sg.	singular
		mg	margin	*t.*	Tosefta
et al.	*et alli,* and others	ms	manuscript	TR	Textus Receptus
fem.	feminine	mss	manuscripts	v., vv.	verse, verses
ff	following (verses, pages)	MT	Masoretic Text	vid.	*videtur,* it seems
		n.d.	no date	viz.	*videlicet,* namely
fl.	flourished	neut.	neuter	vol.	volume
Gr.	Greek	no.	number	*y.*	Jerusalem Gemara

ABBREVIATIONS FOR BIBLE TRANSLATIONS

ASV	American Standard Version	NCV	New Century Version	NKJV	New King James Version
CEV	Contemporary English Version	NEB	New English Bible	NRSV	New Revised Standard Version
		NET	The NET Bible		
ESV	English Standard Version	NIV	New International Version	NLT	New Living Translation
GW	God's Word	NIrV	New International Reader's Version	REB	Revised English Bible
HCSB	Holman Christian Standard Bible				
		NJB	New Jerusalem Bible	RSV	Revised Standard Version
JB	Jerusalem Bible				
KJV	King James Version	NJPS	The New Jewish Publication Society Translation (*Tanakh*)	TEV	Today's English Version
NAB	New American Bible				
NASB	New American Standard Bible			TLB	The Living Bible

ABBREVIATIONS FOR DICTIONARIES, LEXICONS, COLLECTIONS OF TEXTS, ORIGINAL LANGUAGE EDITIONS

ABD *Anchor Bible Dictionary* (6 vols., Freedman) [1992]

ANEP *The Ancient Near East in Pictures* (Pritchard) [1965]

ANET *Ancient Near Eastern Texts Relating to the Old Testament* (Pritchard) [1969]

BAGD *Greek-English Lexicon of the New Testament and Other Early Christian Literature,* 2nd ed. (Bauer, Arndt, Gingrich, Danker) [1979]

BDAG *Greek-English Lexicon of the New Testament and Other Early Christian Literature,* 3rd ed. (Bauer, Danker, Arndt, Gingrich) [2000]

BDB *A Hebrew and English Lexicon of the Old Testament* (Brown, Driver, Briggs) [1907]

BDF *A Greek Grammar of the New Testament and Other Early Christian Literature* (Blass, Debrunner, Funk) [1961]

BHS *Biblia Hebraica Stuttgartensia* (Elliger and Rudolph) [1983]

CAD *Assyrian Dictionary of the Oriental Institute of the University of Chicago* [1956]

COS *The Context of Scripture* (3 vols., Hallo and Younger) [1997–2002]

DBI *Dictionary of Biblical Imagery* (Ryken, Wilhoit, Longman) [1998]

DBT *Dictionary of Biblical Theology* (2nd ed., Leon-Dufour) [1972]

DCH *Dictionary of Classical Hebrew* (5 vols., D. Clines) [2000]

DJD *Discoveries in the Judean Desert* [1955–]

DJG *Dictionary of Jesus and the Gospels* (Green, McKnight, Marshall) [1992]

DOTP *Dictionary of the Old Testament: Pentateuch* (T. Alexander, D.W. Baker) [2003]

DPL *Dictionary of Paul and His Letters* (Hawthorne, Martin, Reid) [1993]

EDNT *Exegetical Dictionary of the New Testament* (3 vols., H. Balz, G. Schneider. ET) [1990–1993]

GKC *Gesenius' Hebrew Grammar* (Gesenius, Kautzsch, trans. Cowley) [1910]

HALOT *The Hebrew and Aramaic Lexicon of the Old Testament* (L. Koehler, W. Baumgartner, J. Stamm; trans. M. Richardson) [1994–1999]

IBD *Illustrated Bible Dictionary* (3 vols., Douglas, Wiseman) [1980]

IDB *The Interpreter's Dictionary of the Bible* (4 vols., Buttrick) [1962]

ISBE *International Standard Bible Encyclopedia* (4 vols., Bromiley) [1979–1988]

KBL *Lexicon in Veteris Testamenti libros* (Koehler, Baumgartner) [1958]

LCL Loeb Classical Library

L&N *Greek-English Lexicon of the New Testament: Based on Semantic Domains* (Louw and Nida) [1989]

LSJ *A Greek-English Lexicon* (9th ed., Liddell, Scott, Jones) [1996]

MM *The Vocabulary of the Greek New Testament* (Moulton and Milligan) [1930; 1997]

NA[26] *Novum Testamentum Graece* (26th ed., Nestle-Aland) [1979]

NA[27] *Novum Testamentum Graece* (27th ed., Nestle-Aland) [1993]

NBD *New Bible Dictionary* (2nd ed., Douglas, Hillyer) [1982]

NIDB *New International Dictionary of the Bible* (Douglas, Tenney) [1987]

NIDBA *New International Dictionary of Biblical Archaeology* (Blaiklock and Harrison) [1983]

NIDNTT *New International Dictionary of New Testament Theology* (4 vols., C. Brown) [1975–1985]

NIDOTTE *New International Dictionary of Old Testament Theology and Exegesis* (5 vols., W. A. VanGemeren) [1997]

PGM *Papyri graecae magicae: Die griechischen Zauberpapyri.* (Preisendanz) [1928]

PG *Patrologia Graecae* (J. P. Migne) [1857–1886]

TBD *Tyndale Bible Dictionary* (Elwell, Comfort) [2001]

TDNT *Theological Dictionary of the New Testament* (10 vols., Kittel, Friedrich; trans. Bromiley) [1964–1976]

TDOT *Theological Dictionary of the Old Testament* (8 vols., Botterweck, Ringgren; trans. Willis, Bromiley, Green) [1974–]

TLNT *Theological Lexicon of the New Testament* (3 vols., C. Spicq) [1994]

TLOT *Theological Lexicon of the Old Testament* (3 vols., E. Jenni) [1997]

TWOT *Theological Wordbook of the Old Testament* (2 vols., Harris, Archer) [1980]

UBS[3] *United Bible Societies' Greek New Testament* (3rd ed., Metzger et al.) [1975]

UBS[4] *United Bible Societies' Greek New Testament* (4th corrected ed., Metzger et al.) [1993]

WH *The New Testament in the Original Greek* (Westcott and Hort) [1882]

ABBREVIATIONS FOR BOOKS OF THE BIBLE

Old Testament

Gen	Genesis	Judg	Judges	1 Chr	1 Chronicles
Exod	Exodus	Ruth	Ruth	2 Chr	2 Chronicles
Lev	Leviticus	1 Sam	1 Samuel	Ezra	Ezra
Num	Numbers	2 Sam	2 Samuel	Neh	Nehemiah
Deut	Deuteronomy	1 Kgs	1 Kings	Esth	Esther
Josh	Joshua	2 Kgs	2 Kings	Job	Job

Ps, Pss	Psalm, Psalms	Ezek	Ezekiel	Mic	Micah
Prov	Proverbs	Dan	Daniel	Nah	Nahum
Eccl	Ecclesiastes	Hos	Hosea	Hab	Habakkuk
Song	Song of Songs	Joel	Joel	Zeph	Zephaniah
Isa	Isaiah	Amos	Amos	Hag	Haggai
Jer	Jeremiah	Obad	Obadiah	Zech	Zechariah
Lam	Lamentations	Jonah	Jonah	Mal	Malachi

New Testament

Matt	Matthew	Eph	Ephesians	Heb	Hebrews
Mark	Mark	Phil	Philippians	Jas	James
Luke	Luke	Col	Colossians	1 Pet	1 Peter
John	John	1 Thess	1 Thessalonians	2 Pet	2 Peter
Acts	Acts	2 Thess	2 Thessalonians	1 John	1 John
Rom	Romans	1 Tim	1 Timothy	2 John	2 John
1 Cor	1 Corinthians	2 Tim	2 Timothy	3 John	3 John
2 Cor	2 Corinthians	Titus	Titus	Jude	Jude
Gal	Galatians	Phlm	Philemon	Rev	Revelation

Deuterocanonical

Bar	Baruch	1–2 Esdr	1–2 Esdras	Pr Man	Prayer of Manasseh
Add Dan	Additions to Daniel	Add Esth	Additions to Esther	Ps 151	Psalm 151
Pr Azar	Prayer of Azariah	Ep Jer	Epistle of Jeremiah	Sir	Sirach
Bel	Bel and the Dragon	Jdt	Judith	Tob	Tobit
Sg Three	Song of the Three Children	1–2 Macc	1–2 Maccabees	Wis	Wisdom of Solomon
Sus	Susanna	3–4 Macc	3–4 Maccabees		

MANUSCRIPTS AND LITERATURE FROM QUMRAN

Initial numerals followed by "Q" indicate particular caves at Qumran. For example, the notation 4Q267 indicates text 267 from cave 4 at Qumran. Further, 1QS 4:9-10 indicates column 4, lines 9-10 of the *Rule of the Community*; and 4Q166 1 ii 2 indicates fragment 1, column ii, line 2 of text 166 from cave 4. More examples of common abbreviations are listed below.

CD	Cairo Geniza copy of the *Damascus Document*	1QIsa^b	Isaiah copy ^{b}	4QLam^a	Lamentations
		1QM	*War Scroll*	11QPs^a	Psalms
		1QpHab	*Pesher Habakkuk*	11QTemple^{a,b}	*Temple Scroll*
1QH	*Thanksgiving Hymns*	1QS	*Rule of the Community*	11QtgJob	*Targum of Job*
1QIsa^a	Isaiah copy ^{a}				

IMPORTANT NEW TESTAMENT MANUSCRIPTS

(all dates given are AD; ordinal numbers refer to centuries)

Significant Papyri ($\mathfrak{P}$ = Papyrus)

$\mathfrak{P}$1 Matt 1; early 3rd
$\mathfrak{P}$4+$\mathfrak{P}$64+$\mathfrak{P}$67 Matt 3, 5, 26; Luke 1-6; late 2nd
$\mathfrak{P}$5 John 1, 16, 20; early 3rd
$\mathfrak{P}$13 Heb 2-5, 10-12; early 3rd
$\mathfrak{P}$15+$\mathfrak{P}$16 (probably part of same codex) 1 Cor 7-8, Phil 3-4; late 3rd
$\mathfrak{P}$20 James 2-3; 3rd
$\mathfrak{P}$22 John 15-16; mid 3rd
$\mathfrak{P}$23 James 1; c. 200
$\mathfrak{P}$27 Rom 8-9; 3rd
$\mathfrak{P}$30 1 Thess 4-5; 2 Thess 1; early 3rd
$\mathfrak{P}$32 Titus 1-2; late 2nd
$\mathfrak{P}$37 Matt 26; late 3rd
$\mathfrak{P}$39 John 8; first half of 3rd
$\mathfrak{P}$40 Rom 1-4, 6, 9; 3rd

𝔓45 Gospels and Acts;
early 3rd
𝔓46 Paul's Major Epistles (less
Pastorals); late 2nd
𝔓47 Rev 9-17; 3rd
𝔓49+𝔓65 Eph 4-5; 1 Thess
1-2; 3rd
𝔓52 John 18; c. 125
𝔓53 Matt 26, Acts 9-10;
middle 3rd

𝔓66 John; late 2nd
𝔓70 Matt 2-3, 11-12, 24; 3rd
𝔓72 1-2 Peter, Jude; c. 300
𝔓74 Acts, General Epistles; 7th
𝔓75 Luke and John; c. 200
𝔓77+𝔓103 (probably part of
same codex) Matt 13-14, 23;
late 2nd
𝔓87 Phlm; late 2nd

𝔓90 John 18-19; late 2nd
𝔓91 Acts 2-3; 3rd
𝔓92 Eph 1, 2 Thess 1; c. 300
𝔓98 Rev 1:13-20; late 2nd
𝔓100 James 3-5; c. 300
𝔓101 Matt 3-4; 3rd
𝔓104 Matt 21; 2nd
𝔓106 John 1; 3rd
𝔓115 Rev 2-3, 5-6, 8-15; 3rd

Significant Uncials

א (Sinaiticus) most of NT; 4th
A (Alexandrinus) most of NT;
5th
B (Vaticanus) most of NT; 4th
C (Ephraemi Rescriptus) most
of NT with many lacunae;
5th
D (Bezae) Gospels, Acts; 5th
D (Claromontanus), Paul's
Epistles; 6th (different MS
than Bezae)
E (Laudianus 35) Acts; 6th
F (Augensis) Paul's Epistles; 9th
G (Boernerianus) Paul's
Epistles; 9th

H (Coislinianus) Paul's
Epistles; 6th
I (Freerianus or Washington)
Paul's Epistles; 5th
L (Regius) Gospels; 8th
Q (Guelferbytanus B) Luke,
John; 5th
P (Porphyrianus) Acts—
Revelation; 9th
T (Borgianus) Luke, John; 5th
W (Washingtonianus or the
Freer Gospels) Gospels; 5th
Z (Dublinensis) Matthew; 6th
037 (Δ; Sangallensis) Gospels;
9th

038 (Θ; Koridethi) Gospels;
9th
040 (Ξ; Zacynthius) Luke; 6th
043 (Φ; Beratinus) Matt,
Mark; 6th
044 (Ψ; Athous Laurae)
Gospels, Acts, Paul's
Epistles; 9th
048 Acts, Paul's Epistles,
General Epistles; 5th
0171 Matt 10, Luke 22;
c. 300
0189 Acts 5; c. 200

Significant Minuscules

1 Gospels, Acts, Paul's Epistles;
12th
33 All NT except Rev; 9th
81 Acts, Paul's Epistles,
General Epistles; 1044
565 Gospels; 9th
700 Gospels; 11th

1424 (or Family 1424—a
group of 29 manuscripts
sharing nearly the same
text) most of NT; 9th-10th
1739 Acts, Paul's Epistles; 10th
2053 Rev; 13th
2344 Rev; 11th

f¹ (a family of manuscripts
including 1, 118, 131, 209)
Gospels; 12th-14th
f¹³ (a family of manuscripts
including 13, 69, 124, 174,
230, 346, 543, 788, 826,
828, 983, 1689, 1709—
known as the Ferrar group)
Gospels; 11th-15th

Significant Ancient Versions

SYRIAC (SYR)
syr^c (Syriac Curetonian)
Gospels; 5th
syr^s (Syriac Sinaiticus)
Gospels; 4th
syr^h (Syriac Harklensis) Entire
NT; 616

OLD LATIN (IT)
it^a (Vercellenis) Gospels; 4th
it^b (Veronensis) Gospels; 5th
it^d (Cantabrigiensis—the Latin
text of Bezae) Gospels, Acts,
3 John; 5th
it^e (Palantinus) Gospels; 5th
it^k (Bobiensis) Matthew, Mark;
c. 400

COPTIC (COP)
cop^bo (Boharic—north Egypt)
cop^fay (Fayyumic—central Egypt)
cop^sa (Sahidic—southern Egypt)

OTHER VERSIONS
arm (Armenian)
eth (Ethiopic)
geo (Georgian)

TRANSLITERATION AND NUMBERING SYSTEM

Note: For words and roots from non-biblical languages (e.g., Arabic, Ugaritic), only approximate transliterations are given.

HEBREW/ARAMAIC

Consonants

א	*aleph*	= '	מ, ם	*mem*	= *m*
ב, בּ	*beth*	= *b*	נ, ן	*nun*	= *n*
ג, גּ	*gimel*	= *g*	ס	*samekh*	= *s*
ד, דּ	*daleth*	= *d*	ע	*ayin*	= '
ה	*he*	= *h*	פ, פּ, ף	*pe*	= *p*
ו	*waw*	= *w*	צ, ץ	*tsadhe*	= *ts*
ז	*zayin*	= *z*	ק	*qoph*	= *q*
ח	*heth*	= *kh*	ר	*resh*	= *r*
ט	*teth*	= *t*	שׁ	*shin*	= *sh*
י	*yodh*	= *y*	שׂ	*sin*	= *s*
כ, כּ, ך	*kaph*	= *k*	ת, תּ	*taw*	= *t, th* (spirant)
ל	*lamedh*	= *l*			

Vowels

ַ	*patakh*	= *a*	ָ	*qamets khatuf*	= *o*
ַה	*furtive patakh*	= *a*	ֹ	*holem*	= *o*
ָ	*qamets*	= *a*	וֹ	*full holem*	= *o*
ָה	*final qamets he*	= *ah*	ֻ	*short qibbuts*	= *u*
ֶ	*segol*	= *e*	ֻ	*long qibbuts*	= *u*
ֵ	*tsere*	= *e*	וּ	*shureq*	= *u*
ֵי	*tsere yod*	= *e*	ֲ	*khatef patakh*	= *a*
ִ	*short hireq*	= *i*	ֳ	*khatef qamets*	= *o*
ִ	*long hireq*	= *i*	ְ	*vocalic shewa*	= *e*
ִי	*hireq yod*	= *i*	ַי	*patakh yodh*	= *a*

Greek

α	*alpha*	= *a*	ε	*epsilon*	= *e*
β	*beta*	= *b*	ζ	*zeta*	= *z*
γ	*gamma*	= *g, n (before* γ, κ, ξ, χ)	η	*eta*	= *ē*
			θ	*theta*	= *th*
δ	*delta*	= *d*	ι	*iota*	= *i*

κ	kappa	= k		τ	tau	= t
λ	lamda	= l		υ	upsilon	= u
μ	mu	= m		φ	phi	= ph
ν	nu	= n		χ	chi	= ch
ξ	ksi	= x		ψ	psi	= ps
ο	omicron	= o		ω	omega	= ō
π	pi	= p		ʼ	rough	= h (with
ρ	rho	= r (ῥ = rh)			breathing	vowel or
σ, ς	sigma	= s			mark	diphthong)

THE TYNDALE-STRONG'S NUMBERING SYSTEM

The Cornerstone Biblical Commentary series uses a word-study numbering system to give both newer and more advanced Bible students alike quicker, more convenient access to helpful original-language tools (e.g., concordances, lexicons, and theological dictionaries). Those who are unfamiliar with the ancient Hebrew, Aramaic, and Greek alphabets can quickly find information on a given word by looking up the appropriate index number. Advanced students will find the system helpful because it allows them to quickly find the lexical form of obscure conjugations and inflections.

There are two main numbering systems used for biblical words today. The one familiar to most people is the Strong's numbering system (made popular by the *Strong's Exhaustive Concordance to the Bible*). Although the original Strong's system is still quite useful, the most up-to-date research has shed new light on the biblical languages and allows for more precision than is found in the original Strong's system. The Cornerstone Biblical Commentary series, therefore, features a newly revised version of the Strong's system, the Tyndale-Strong's numbering system. The Tyndale-Strong's system brings together the familiarity of the Strong's system and the best of modern scholarship. In most cases, the original Strong's numbers are preserved. In places where new research dictates, new or related numbers have been added.[1]

The second major numbering system today is the Goodrick-Kohlenberger system used in a number of study tools published by Zondervan. In order to give students broad access to a number of helpful tools, the Commentary provides index numbers for the Zondervan system as well.

The different index systems are designated as follows:

TG Tyndale-Strong's Greek number   ZH Zondervan Hebrew number
ZG Zondervan Greek number   TA Tyndale-Strong's Aramaic number
TH Tyndale-Strong's Hebrew number   ZA Zondervan Aramaic number

So in the example, "love" *agapē* [TG26, ZG27], the first number is the one to use with Greek tools keyed to the Tyndale-Strong's system, and the second applies to tools that use the Zondervan system.

1. Generally, one may simply use the original four-digit Strong's number to identify words in tools using Strong's system. If a Tyndale-Strong's number is followed by a capital letter (e.g., TG1692A), it generally indicates an added subdivision of meaning for the given term. Whenever a Tyndale-Strong's number has a number following a decimal point (e.g., TG2013.1), it reflects an instance where new research has yielded a separate, new classification of use for a biblical word. Forthcoming tools from Tyndale House Publishers will include these entries, which were not part of the original Strong's system.

Leviticus

DAVID W. BAKER

INTRODUCTION TO
Leviticus

WHEN PEOPLE open their Bibles to read, or even for serious study, Leviticus is not usually the first place to which they turn. In fact, it is often the last. If any other biblical book is more removed from our experience, more different and even strange to twenty-first-century readers, it is hard to decide which book that might be. Therefore, before beginning to interpret Leviticus, it is necessary to think about why we should even bother in the first place. What actually makes Leviticus worth reading at all? There are three primary reasons to study Leviticus:

1. *Theological reasons.* Israel was not simply another people; they were the people of the First Testament (from among whom came Jesus and his disciples, who gave us the Second Testament). In order to appreciate and understand the latter, it is necessary to understand the former. Meaning comes from context, and the First Testament, including Leviticus, is the context of the latter. Various concepts and terms familiar to Jesus and his contemporaries were only familiar because they were introduced in Leviticus and have their background there. They were part of the cultural literacy of the period and formed an element of the knowledge reservoir upon which Jesus and the Gospel writers drew in their preaching, teaching, and writing. For example, the identification of Jesus as the "Lamb of God who takes away the sin of the world" (John 1:29) would be incomprehensible without Leviticus 4:32-35. And the unspeakable condition of a hemorrhaging woman coming into a crowd and touching someone (Mark 5:25-34) is not understood apart from Leviticus 15:25-27.

2. *Religious reasons.* Worship is an important matter of discussion in today's church, which is divided on this issue as well as many others concerning theology and practice. Questions are raised as to the how, who, where, when, and even the why of worship. There is also the question of whether worship must be a corporate, group exercise or whether it can equally, or even preferably, be individual, something between a person and God alone. Even more fundamentally, there is disagreement over what, in fact, worship is and what it is not.

For our purposes, we will understand worship to be service for God done by his people, since this reflects most accurately both the Hebrew and Greek terms that lie behind our English translations. This understanding as service is undoubtedly broader than what we usually assign to worship, but it is important since it highlights what we are called upon to do—namely to serve and to work—and not just how we should feel about God.

This background should shed some light on understanding the Old Testament book of Leviticus. Most Christians do not spend more time here than they have to, since the book appears distant, foreign to anything in our daily lives. Seeing it as a handbook for worship might make it a bit more understandable. For the ancient Israelite, including the Israelite priest, who instructed the people, Leviticus was the worship manual that answered many of the questions I have mentioned, especially those of who could worship, when, in what manner, and how people made themselves worthy or at least acceptable in God's sight so that they could worship. Rather than being a dead book of dead sacrifices, Leviticus is a living book of instruction about how to worship the living God and how to act as his living people. While we do not follow the same "how" in our worship procedures today, God still expects our worship to be holy and done on his terms. Thus, we can learn that much of Leviticus is applicable or adaptable to our own situation.

3. *Historical reasons.* Leviticus is a historical artifact, the product of a people who played a significant role in the history and religion of the ancient Near East. As historical evidence of who these people were and what they believed, Leviticus is worth studying. This is a subdiscipline of the study of history per se, namely the field of history of religion. Leviticus is a necessary source for understanding Israel, as the Qur'an is for understanding Iraq and the Gitas for appreciating India. All these are windows into other peoples, their culture, beliefs, and existence.

AUTHOR

The Hebrew title and the first verse of the book reflect the Israelite understanding that the primary author of Leviticus was the Lord himself. The first verse also names the recipient of the message: Moses. In the ancient Near Eastern context of the Old Testament, especially in Mesopotamia but also among the neighboring Canaanites, many written documents concluded with a colophon. This included material that we find near the front of our books today. These colophons could include the name of the composition, a summary of contents, the source of the copy, the scribe who copied the text, and the date when the copy was made. There are possibly two or three of these colophons in Leviticus, which will be discussed later (see comments at 7:35-36, 37-38; 27:34). For example, one includes a composition name ("instructions"), contents summary with the various sacrifice types (7:37), source (the Lord), scribe or transmitter (Moses), and date ("when he commanded," 7:38). In these biblical "colophons," we can see that Moses was functioning in the place of the scribe, accurately transmitting for the reader material from God, his source.

Mosaic authorship has been traditionally accepted for Leviticus and the entire Pentateuch. Unlike some of the other Pentateuchal books, Moses is never said to have written any of the material in Leviticus (see Exod 17:14; 24:4; 34:27; Deut 10:1; 31:9, 24); rather, throughout the book he receives God's oral revelation (1:1; 4:1; 5:14; 6:1, 8, 19, 24). Since the Enlightenment, people have questioned Mosaic involvement. Looking at Israelite history in conjunction with the contents of Leviticus, they have noted the particular relevance of the book to the priests. The most common argument has been that these functionaries came into their strongest period of authority in the Exile, and especially after the return from Babylonia. Since there was then no king to rule Israel, the priests were able to assume secular as well as civil authority. It was then, it has been argued, that the material most specifically relevant to them, called the "Priestly Document" (or "P" for short), was collected. Among numerous other problems with this proposal, it excludes any involvement of Moses in the affairs of the book.

A counter-swell of opinion has pointed out the antiquity of the laws and rituals found in this supposed P document, material which seems to have greatly predated the time of the Restoration and even the Exile. I have argued that the canonical character of the laws and rituals would point logically toward a life-setting back in the period of the wilderness wanderings, the picture of their composition as it is found in the biblical text itself (Baker 1987). Even in what are considered by many to be very early sources in the Pentateuch, the ritual procedure is assumed rather than explained (e.g., Gen 8:20; 22:2, 7-8, 13), presupposing its availability either in writing or as authoritative tradition to the author of these passages. The use of rituals recorded in Leviticus, according to pre-exilic texts, even outside of Israel (Num 23:15; 1 Kgs 18:38; 2 Kgs 3:27; 10:24) argues against the necessity of the P document being from the postexilic period.

DATE AND OCCASION OF WRITING

The biblical narrative places the events recorded in Leviticus at Mount Sinai (7:38) as part of God's revelation to his people through Moses. God not only gave his people the Ten Commandments (Exod 20), but also other laws concerning their civil and religious life. Leviticus continues these instructions. As such, it continues the material started in Exodus, which continues through Numbers 10. Though an exact date for the events is impossible to confirm, and therefore the subject of fierce debate, the middle of the second millennium BC fits the picture chronologically, and the Sinai wilderness, that section of land between the Gulf of Aqaba and what is now the Suez Canal, fits the picture geographically.

The occasion of writing is not mentioned, so suggestions must be tentative. Elsewhere I have contended that the type of prescriptive material found in Leviticus would have been a candidate for early recording in writing (Baker 1987). Since the material consists of foundational religious rituals for Israelite life and practice, it would have become fixed and authoritative upon its reception. While the first recipient generation under Moses and Aaron would hear the instructions, the need of documentation for future generations would soon become apparent.

AUDIENCE

The text of Leviticus indicates that it was directed toward "the people of Israel" (1:2). It was not exclusively for the common people, the clergy, the laity, or the rulers since all socioeconomic groups were addressed. Nobody is too poor (see 5:7), nobody is too powerful (see 4:22), nobody is too "religious" (see 4:3) to need the instructions found in this book.

Specifically, and most directly, the words were addressed to Moses, who was commissioned to pass the message on to another group (1:1-2; 4:1-2; 5:14; 6:1). In one case Aaron, Moses's brother, was addressed (10:8), and in one section both brothers were addressed together (11:1; 13:1; 14:33; 15:1-2a).

The inclusion of the book within the Pentateuch and the broader Old Testament canon shows that it had relevance and an audience beyond its first hearers. The transition from oral commission to written Scripture shows an awareness of its necessity for future generations of Jews, as well. Whether we like it or not—and the lack of preaching and teaching from Leviticus today seems to indicate that we don't—this book is also in our canon. Leviticus is God's Word to us in some way just as much as the Gospels. We also are an audience who must seek to determine the book's relevance to the church in our own times.

CANONICITY AND TEXTUAL HISTORY

There never seems to have been any discussion over the inclusion of Leviticus within the canon. Even within the scope of Scripture itself, the book was seen to contain authoritative instruction or canonical law. For example, Deuteronomy 24:8 refers explicitly to the laws of Leviticus 13:1–14:57, and the numerous occasions on which sacrifice is made in the former and latter prophets never prescribe detailed procedures, apparently relying on that information contained in Leviticus 1–7. I have also argued that these laws, at least, were available to those who brought their offerings to the Tabernacle in at least one written copy very soon after they were propagated and were not just in oral form (Baker 1987). In the case of such foundational laws for Israelite religious practice, relevant to both the priests and the people, a permanent record would have been necessary within the lifetime of those who received them at Sinai.

If this is the case, there was, of course, a long period of textual transmission between the time of the first writing and the Masoretic Text, which is the received Hebrew textual tradition after the tenth century AD, and also the basis of most modern translations. There are two main earlier witnesses to the text of Leviticus. The first is the Septuagint, a Greek translation done in Egypt. Its Pentateuch translation dates to the third century BC. The Samaritan Pentateuch, though currently available in manuscripts from the late medieval period, could have originated earlier, possibly dating from the second century BC. It was preserved by the community formed by the northern tribes of Israel and those with whom they intermarried after the Assyrian deportation of the northern kingdom in 722 BC.

The Qumran community, from the area of the Dead Sea, preserved texts from before the Christian period, providing Hebrew texts a millennium earlier than those of the Masoretes. They possessed texts related to each of the traditions mentioned, i.e., forebears of what we know as the Samaritan, Septuagint, and Masoretic text traditions. To date, some 16 texts and fragments of Leviticus from the Dead Sea vicinity have appeared in publication.

Unlike some of the biblical books, the textual traditions in Leviticus are very uniform, with few variations. Of these, even fewer make a difference to interpretation, and these will be discussed at the appropriate time. The consistency of the text could well reflect its nature as a canonical legal document which would not have been open to widespread alteration (Baker 1987).

LITERARY STYLE

The majority of Leviticus is prescriptive, detailing how different rituals and practices are to be carried out. It is presented in an impersonal manner because it is applicable to anyone who either cares or needs to perform the rituals. In Hebrew, this is done by use of the third person, "if one . . ." or "if a person . . ." In English, and in the NLT in particular, the impersonal second person is used, "if you . . ." This kind of material can be fairly dry, if the "you" referred to does not seem to be the "you" who is reading. We do a theological disservice to this book, and indeed any book of the Bible, if we read it in this way, however. This also is Scripture, and must, according to Paul (2 Tim 3:16), have something of profit for every "you" who is reading it.

The prescriptive texts are couched in a narrative framework. This presents some of the who, when, where, and how of the material. Unlike some contemporary ancient Near Eastern prescriptive documents that present laws and instructions by themselves, Leviticus shows the dynamics of how they were delivered to Moses and passed on to the people. The narrative framework shows that history is theologically significant. God meets his people in and through history, which is an important differentiation between the Judeo-Christian religion and others such as New Age or Eastern mysticism. There, present reality is often seen as something to be left behind or risen above. Leviticus shows how to live in God's world, not how to escape to some other world.

There are, in addition to prescriptive texts with a narrative framework, two short sections of historical narrative (10:1-7; 24:10-16), both showing in graphic terms the result of not following the prescriptions spelled out.

MAJOR THEMES

The unifying theme in Leviticus is personal and corporate holiness. The repeated command to "be holy because I am holy" (11:44-45; 19:2; 20:26; cf. 20:7) shows its importance. Words related to "holiness" occur over 150 times in the Hebrew text of the book. It is therefore appropriate to call Leviticus, or at least a portion of it, a "Holiness Code," as some scholars do.

This holiness theme is an organizing element for most of the book's material, but subthemes are also introduced and developed. One subtheme is sacrifice, which is detailed in the first seven chapters and used on numerous occasions throughout the book. Sacrifice maintained or reestablished a relationship with a holy God, which might have been breached through some defilement.

The offering of sacrifices needed trained and sanctified practitioners, so the priesthood was inaugurated and instructed, as described in chapters 8–10 and elsewhere in the book. The people also needed to know what unholy or unclean things they should be wary of. If a person came into contact with one of these things, purification was necessary before the person could worship God. These instructions appear in chapters 11–16, while chapters 17–27 deal with various actions and practices relating to holiness or the potential for its loss.

In the terminology of cultural anthropology, much of the book of Leviticus deals with the topic of ritual—observable aspects of Israel's religion. This could be another factor in making the book strange to many today, since many conservative Christians belong to traditions which enjoy freedom and spontaneity in worship rather than following a more liturgical format. Both spontaneity and order have much to offer the worship experience, and careful analysis would confirm that even the former has its own flow and expectations, and so is not entirely sponta-neous. Every tradition functions with its own ritual order, whether it is acknowl-edged or not, which deserves comparison and contrast to that presented in Leviticus.

Many Christians today practice the discipline of a "quiet time," a time set apart during the day for prayer and Bible reading, for a meeting with God and a reminder of his presence. For ancient Israel, reminders of the presence of God in their life as a nation and as individuals were also a daily thing, but it was by no means a quiet sep-aration from the regular aspects of life. Through the daily rituals of sacrifice and offering, a mixture of sight, sound, smell, touch, and taste, along with the God who controls life and death, blessing and judgment, was placed squarely in everyone's path every day. In symbol and reality, he was never far from anyone. Part of the reminder of this was not only the importance of the ritual in their day-to-day life, but also in the use of daily objects. The sacrifices were not some Shakespearean witch's brew that had secret ingredients that must be gathered with care. The cele-brations of God involved the daily things of the lives of these agricultural people— their animals, the birds from their rooftops and gardens, and the very food from their tables.

THEOLOGICAL CONCERNS

The presence and nature of Israel's God envelops Leviticus; his name appears from the first to the last verse (1:1; 27:34). The awareness of his presence continues from the book of Exodus. There God met his people at Mount Sinai and made them his people (Exod 19:6). He entered into a covenant relationship with them (Exod 24:3-8) and in-structed them as to how they should live within this relationship. These instructions continue through Leviticus and into Numbers. God's presence also continues, as shown by his words recorded in the book as well by the fact that many of the sacrifices mentioned are carried out "in the LORD's presence" (1:5, 11, etc.).

An important element of God's character, evident even in the first verse, is his self-revelation. He wants to speak, explaining what he finds pleasing and how a cor-rect relationship with him may be maintained or restored. Humanity is not left in ignorance, groping in the darkness, trying to please a God who hides himself. The detailed instructions take away the nagging fear as to whether one has gotten it right or not. God wants to be worshiped and served, and he makes his wishes known. Among these wishes is his overwhelming desire for holiness.

Holiness, the uniting theme of the book, is not just an arbitrary concept, but is required of God's people because it is one of the foundational characteristics of God himself. People are called to holiness because God is holy, as is often repeated throughout the book: "You must be holy because I, the LORD your God, am holy" (11:44-45; 19:2; 20:26; 21:8). God does not demand that his creatures, those made in his image (Gen 1:27), be something other than he is himself. He also does not make a demand that they are ultimately unable to meet, since in the final analysis, it is God himself who gives the holiness: "I make you holy," he says (20:8; 21:8, 15, 23; 22:9, 16, 32). Holiness, then, involves two parties, the worshiper, who fulfills the rituals required by God, and God, who accepts the offering and forgives (4:20, 26, 31). The second, Godward side of the equation is necessary to keep in mind, lest it appear that ritual is magic, compelling God to act through our control of him. The two-sided aspect of ritual reminds us that, in the midst of this book of law, God is a God of grace.

Even though God is gracious, breaking one's relationship with him, whether on purpose (through sin) or inadvertently, is a serious, even life-threatening business. God's love is strong, but so are his holiness and his justice. Wrongs cannot be simply ignored but must be dealt with. Sin does lead to judgment (10:1-7; 24:10-16). We are responsible for our actions and the logical consequences that flow from them. This is a doctrine that cannot be overemphasized today, since it has been so terribly diluted, not only in our society, but also in pulpits.

In the book of Leviticus, a view of the world is presented that is centered on God's holiness. God in his holiness is set apart, which is one of the core meanings of "holy." He cannot come into contact with anything that is not holy. This includes human beings, who, at their creation, were in God's image (Gen 1:27) and had an intimate and personal relationship with him (Gen 2). Through disobedience, humanity lost this relationship with the holy God (Gen 3). The ultimate goal of Scripture after Genesis 3, which is the very goal of all human history after the Fall, is to allow the divine–human relationship to be restored. This necessitates a restoration of human holiness because, even though humanity changed at the Fall, becoming unholy, God did not change, and still cannot abide unholiness in his presence. This restoration is in tension with a process that could be called "spiritual entropy," or a natural downward tendency toward sin, which is a result of the Fall. Human nature is now such that its natural tendency is to move toward disorder and unholiness, away from God and his order and purity, because the very human heart is evil (Jer 17:9). Even actions intended for good cannot produce the desired results because of the power of sin (Rom 7:14-20). Unholiness reigns in both attitude and action. Leviticus looks at how to counter this principle with its downward spiral. It provides the means, through ritual, to rectify the separation from God which resulted from the Fall. In one way, this reestablishes a pre-Fall spiritual principle, if you will—an original tendency in creation toward holiness and toward God. God, desiring an intimate relationship with his creation, made a way for his relationship to humans to be reestablished temporarily by restoring those who follow the rituals to a position of holiness, at least until the next unholy act or event brought separation again. This cyclical situation held until the permanent, sanctifying sacrifice was made by Jesus Christ (Heb 10:1-18).

The Old Testament, and Leviticus in particular, envisages a spiritual spectrum wherein the totally good, pure, and holy God is on one end, while evil, pollution, and vileness are on the other. The two ends of the spectrum are unable to be in contact with each other. Various biblical terms describe different positions on the spectrum. For example, Leviticus 10:10 uses some of these terms. According to this text, the priest is to "distinguish between what is [holy] and what is common, between what is ceremonially unclean and what is clean."

The spectrum, and the interrelationship between terms (adapted from Wenham 1979:26), may be portrayed as follows:

Positive Means	Sacrifice and water (moving toward holiness) →		
Positive Processes	Being cleansed		Being sanctified
Specrum of States	Unclean	Clean (but also ordinary, common)	Holy
Negative Processes	Being polluted		Being profaned
Negative Means	← Sin and infirmity (moving away from holiness)		

Most things start in the ordinary, normal, or common state and are clean. Being clean is synonymous with purity (*tahor* [TH2889, ZH3196]), as used to describe gold, for example (Exod 25:11). While this at times can be related to the presence of impurities and our concept of being dirty, it is not a question of sanitation, but rather of possessing elements that are unacceptable when in the presence of God. Uncleanness is a departure from the normal or clean in a direction away from holiness. Some animals are permanently unclean (ch 11). This permanent uncleanness is not contagious, that is, it cannot be passed on to anything else through mere physical contact; it is passed only through actual consumption (Wenham 1979:21). For example, while a camel is unclean, and thus unfit for consumption as food (11:4), it was still valued and used as a beast of burden (Gen 24; 31:34). This illustrates the important differentiation between uncleanness and sin or evil. One could say that all bad things are unclean, but not that all unclean things are bad. The unclean/clean distinction, in other words, is not a moral judgment, but a ritual one delineating whether something can approach the presence of God or not. The camel's uncleanness precludes its use for divine service.

Some things become unclean, or "polluted" temporarily. This move away from holiness (to the left in the figure) can be caused by sin (e.g., forbidden sexual relations, ch 18; see especially v. 24) or by natural infirmities or departures from the norm, which are not necessarily sinful in themselves (e.g., skin diseases; cf. ch 13). This is shown by the lower lines of the figure. That which is polluted in these ways is contagious and can pass uncleanness on to others, and therefore it is to be avoided. It cannot be repeated enough that becoming unclean is not solely a result of sin, and uncleanness does not necessarily reflect immorality. Some inadvertent bodily emissions, such as menstrual blood or nocturnal emissions, for example, as well as marital intercourse (ch 15), cause ritual impurity even though they are not morally reprehensible.

Part of the purpose of Leviticus is to discuss what leads to the left on the spectrum, what pollutes and profanes. This is to be avoided if at all possible. Sometimes such cannot be evaded, however, and Leviticus also gives procedures for cleansing, purifying, and sanctifying, allowing a move back toward holiness (to the right) on the spectrum. These means include sacrifices for sin (ch 5) or cleansing from contagious skin diseases (ch 14), shown at the top of the figure. In regards to the latter, it is vital to see that the texts are not therapeutic but relational. That is, there is no treatment given to cure the disease, some procedure with ointments or salves such as is found in some medical texts from Mesopotamia and among the Canaanites at Ugarit, for example. We do not have medical texts but theological texts—those showing how to restore a relationship with God by reestablishing purity rather than showing how to restore the body by reestablishing health.

The details of these matters will be elucidated below as we encounter them in the text. It is useful to remember, however, that spiritual entropy is the result of the Fall. God's ultimate goal is to abolish this entropy by destroying the restrictive distinction between sacred and profane, holy and common. While the sacred and common categories will remain, God will allow access by things in both categories into the sanctuary so that all in Jerusalem can be and serve in the presence of God. This is the goal expressed in Zechariah 14:20-21, where we are told: "On that day even the harness bells of the horses [themselves unclean animals; 11:1-8] will be inscribed with these words: HOLY TO THE LORD. And the cooking pots [archetypally common things in daily practice] in the Temple of the LORD will be as sacred as the basins used beside the altar. In fact, every cooking pot in Jerusalem and Judah will be holy to the LORD of Heaven's Armies. All who come to worship will be free to use any of these pots to boil their sacrifices. And on that day there will no longer be traders in the Temple of the LORD of Heaven's Armies." God's ultimate work on the day of the Lord will sanctify even those having blemish and deformity so they can worship God. For example, the eunuch who was once disallowed access to minister to God (cf. 21:20) one day will be sanctified (per the prophecy in Isa 56:3-7), a functioning member of the "kingdom of priests" (Exod 19:6). They, and even non-Israelites, will be welcome to worship (Isa 2:3). Praise be to God, for such are all of us, blemished and foreigners not only through the Fall, but also through our own sins—yet we are still offered salvation and sanctification by God!

OUTLINE

I. A Handbook for the People and the Priests (1:1–7:38)
  A. Commission (1:1-2)
  B. Instructions for the People about Offerings (1:3–6:7)
    1. Burnt offerings (1:3-17)
    2. Grain offerings (2:1-16)
    3. Peace offerings (3:1-17)
    4. Sin offerings (4:1–5:13)
    5. Guilt offerings (5:14–6:7)
  C. Instructions for the Priests about Offerings (6:8–7:34)
    1. Burnt offerings (6:8-13)
    2. Grain offerings (6:14-18)
    3. Grain offering for ordination of priests (6:19-23)
    4. Sin and guilt offerings (6:24–7:10)
    5. Peace offerings (7:11-34)
  D. Concluding Formulae (7:35-38)
    1. Conclusion of the priests' instructions (7:35-36)
    2. Conclusion of the handbook (7:37-38)
II. The Institution of the Priesthood (8:1–10:20)
  A. The Ordination of Priests (8:1-36)
  B. The First Service (9:1-24)
  C. The Sin of the Priests Nadab and Abihu (10:1-5)
  D. Instructions for Priests (10:6-15)
  E. A Dispute over Priestly Service (10:16-20)
III. Ceremonially Clean and Unclean Things (11:1–15:33)
  A. Animals (11:1-47)
    1. Land animals (11:1-8)
    2. Aquatic animals (11:9-12)
    3. Winged animals (11:13-23)
    4. Regulations concerning land animals (11:24-45)
    5. Summary (11:46-47)
  B. Childbirth (12:1-8)
  C. Surface Blemishes and Diseases (13:1–14:57)
    1. On skin (13:1-46)
    2. On fabric (13:47-59)
    3. Cleansing procedures (14:1-57)
  D. Genital Discharges (15:1-33)
    1. Abnormal male discharges (15:1-15)
    2. Normal male discharges (15:16-17)
    3. Marital intercourse (15:18)
    4. Normal menstruation (15:19-24)
    5. Abnormal menstruation (15:25-30)

COMMENTARY ON

Leviticus

◆ **I. A Handbook for the People and the Priests (1:1–7:38)**
   A. Commission (1:1-2)

The LORD called to Moses from the Tabernacle* and said to him, ²"Give the following
instructions to the people of Israel. When
you present an animal as an offering to the
LORD, you may take it from your herd of
cattle or your flock of sheep and goats.

1:1 Hebrew *Tent of Meeting;* also in 1:3, 5.

NOTES

1:1 In the MT the verse begins with the conjunction "and" (*waw* [TH2050.1, ZH2256]),
thereby joining the last verse of Exodus (Exod 40:38) with the first verse of Leviticus. As
such, one can read a continuing narrative from Exodus 40 to Leviticus 1. The continuity
is grammatical as well as literary, since the same characters, themes, and chronology
bridge Exodus and Leviticus.

1:2 *When you.* This is the contemporary American English indication of an unspecified
subject of a sentence. The Hebrew uses a third-person form, "one, a person" (indicating
any unnamed person), much like the British use the wording "when one." The actual
term used here (*'adam* [TH120, ZH132]) denotes a human being as distinct from both God
on the one hand and animals on the other. It was a general term, specifying neither male
nor female exclusively. It thus referred to all of the Israelites, whether male or female
(see 15:29), who could come to present sacrifices, bringing them near to God.

COMMENTARY

In Leviticus, God is primarily referred to by his personal name, Yahweh. The title
"LORD" is the traditional English rendition of the Hebrew "Yahweh," which was the
personal name of the God of Israel. From early in their history, the Israelites were
very serious about the fourth commandment against misusing God's personal
name (Exod 20:7; Deut 5:11). In order not to misapply it, they determined not to
utter it at all. Instead they read it as Adonai (Lord) or "the Name." Most English
translations still take this traditional approach, refusing to put "Yahweh" in the text.
Instead, they use "LORD," marking it as a distinctive divine name through the use of
special small-capital letters.

   Yahweh had called to Moses twice before using this same name—from the burning bush (Exod 3:4, 14-15) and from Mount Sinai (Exod 19:3). The continuity with

the previous two events in Exodus is shown by the "and" that begins Leviticus, though it is not translated in English translations (see note on 1:1). This is also shown by "the LORD" not being explicitly mentioned as the subject of the first verb of the book, only the second. These elements suggest a grammatical tie to the previous chapter—the last chapter of Exodus (Exod 40).

In Leviticus, God's revelation comes from the Tabernacle, the inner tent that contained the Holy Place and the Most Holy Place. Moses was never allowed into this dwelling place of God after he had it built (Exod 40:35). He, like the other Israelites, was only able to approach it as far as the outer court. Israel's God did not want his will to be secret, completely separate and hidden from those who might seek him. Rather, he revealed himself, calling out to his people rather than leaving them to guess at who he was and what he desired.

God revealed his will to Moses, who was to pass it along to Israel, since this section was most directly relevant to them (cf. 6:8-9a). God was separate from the people, being in the Tabernacle, while they could only remain outside. At the same time he was in their midst. The Tabernacle's place was in the middle of the camp, equidistant from all the people to allow equal access to the place of worship (Num 2:1–3:30). God expected their worship, giving all of them instructions for "when," not "if," they approached him with their gifts.

The individual people of Israel were to bring or present these gifts to the Lord, since, especially in Leviticus 1–3, the offerings were voluntary—true "presents" of love (though elsewhere they were part of the daily sacrificial practice of the nation as a whole; Num 28). They also were to have been at a cost to the offerer, that is, a sacrifice. In an agricultural society where wealth and the very maintenance of life were measured in livestock, these animal presents came from the very life necessities of the people. By comparison, have not our gifts to the Lord at times become trivialized and cheap, not costing us? Does money, which is the ordinary form which offerings take today, really cost anything to many in today's society? What would, in fact, be a sacrifice for those with abundant financial resources? Might not our time, our work, our service cost us more than cash in some cases?

Leviticus 1–7: A Reference Manual for Offering Sacrifices. The first seven chapters of Leviticus are a unit showing both the priests and the people how to offer sacrifices. However, it is too limiting to focus only on the "how" and thereby read these chapters as strictly functional and ritual texts (Mulholland 1985:83-93), though much of the material of the chapters themselves concern "how." This interpretation led not only Israel but also later readers into a complete misunderstanding of the text. Israel came to view the rituals as the initiating means by which they could enter into a relationship with God, when in fact the actions described were to result from an already existing relationship with God. They served to maintain the relationship spelled out in Exodus, not to establish it. Even the most well-known "ritual" or functional text, the Ten Commandments (Exod

20:3-17; Deut 5:6-21), does not provide ways to merit participation in God's covenant. The commandments were preceded by, and were the result of, the previous verse: "I am the LORD your God, who rescued you from the land of Egypt, the place of your slavery" (Exod 20:2; Deut 5:6). Prior to Israel's following any of God's requests, before they even knew them, they were already God's people and had been blessed by this relationship. The laws were then given as instruction on how to live within this covenant relationship with the greatest benefit for self, neighbor, and God himself.

Israel, as a nation, too often mistook the laws and rituals as an end in themselves, the opposite error to that mentioned in the last paragraph. Concentrating on the outward action of sacrifice without an inner commitment to the one receiving it was equally wrong for Israel. She thought that ritual functions of *doing* could replace a right relationship of *being* God's people (Mulholland 1985:95-105). God soundly condemned this attitude through his prophets (Jer 7; Amos 5:21-24). It was not that he did not desire the actions, since he was the one who set them up in the first place. It was rather that he wanted the attitude inspiring them to be the correct one; he wanted rejoicing instead of lifeless rote.

It is important to remember that meaning comes from context and that the geographical and historical context of Leviticus is the same as that of the Ten Commandments. Israel was still at Mount Sinai (7:38) and was just learning how to maintain its covenant relationship with God. The questions giving rise to chapters 1-7 were, What happens if I do something to endanger the relationship? Am I irrevocably separated from God? A motif of the book is holiness, and these chapters indicate how holiness, upon which an intimate relationship with God depends, might be regained if it was somehow lost, as it inevitably would be. Rather than being dead, stultifying rituals, they were gracious avenues of forgiveness.

It is also important to note chronological context. The sacrifices described here were not new, since offerings were mentioned from the beginning of the human race (e.g., Gen 4:3-4; 8:20-21; 22:2; Exod 18:12). Plans had been put in place for performing them earlier at Sinai (e.g., Exod 20:24; 24:5), but here they were presented in detail. These sacrificial regulations precede the installation ceremony for the priests (ch 8), so they had not yet begun their work, which started in Leviticus 9. Chapters 1-7 anticipate the idea that the specific priestly guild was an extension of the concept that the entire nation of Israel was a priesthood (Exod 19:6). Thus, the sacrifices and offerings brought by individual, non-priestly people as described in Genesis and Exodus were not replaced but supplemented by the provisions made here (cf. Goldingay 2003:416).

Both priest and offerer had obligations to meet and procedures to follow when coming with sacrifices into the presence of the Lord. Various aspects of these offerings are summarized in the following tables (adapted from LaSor, Hubbard, and Bush 1996:83).

MAJOR SACRIFICES

Name	Function	Material	Offerer's actions	Priest's actions	Disposal
'olah [TH5930, ZH6592] (lit., "going up"); [whole] burnt offering; holocaust; 1:3-17; 6:8-13; 7:8	Atonement	Bull, sheep, goat, bird; male; no defects	Bring; lay hand on head; slaughter; skin; cut up; wash animal	Sprinkle blood; build fire; burn offering	Completely burnt; hide saved for priest; bird crop and contents thrown on an ash heap to the east of the altar
minkhah [TH4503, ZH4966] (lit., "gift"); grain offering; present, meal, oblation; 2:1-16; 6:14-23; 7:9-10	Celebration	Choice flour, olive oil, incense, salt; roast grain	Bring material; pour oil; sprinkle incense	Take handful; burn on altar	Portion burnt; priests eat remainder
shelem [TH8002, ZH8968] (lit., "peace"); peace offering; communion, common, shared, fellowship, well-being; 3:1-17; 7:11-36	Rejoicing	Cattle, sheep	Bring animal; lay hand on offering; slaughter	Sprinkle blood; burn offering on altar	Organ fat, liver, kidneys burnt; meat eaten by priests and offerer
khatta'th [TH2403A, ZH2633] (lit., "sin"); sin offering; purification; 4:1-5:13; 6:24-30; 7:7; Num 15:22-31	Atone for unintentional sin	(a) High priest: bull, no defect; (b) Community: bull; (c) Leader: goat, male, no defect; (d) Citizen: sheep/goat, female, no defect; (e) Poor: young dove/pigeon; (f) Destitute: choice flour	Bring offering (all); lay hand on head (a-d); slaughter (a-d; leaders act for community in each step)	Place blood before inner curtain, on incense altar horns, at altar base; remove organ fat, kidneys, liver and burn these on altar (a-b); take the rest outside the camp; (f) burn	Organ fat, liver, kidneys burnt; remainder eaten by priests (c-f) or burnt (a-b)
'asham [TH817, ZH871] (lit., "guilt"); guilt offering; reparation; 5:14-6:7	Atonement	Ram, no defect, or cash equivalent	Bring offering; slaughter; restitution	Sprinkle blood; burn fat, kidneys, liver	Fat, kidneys, liver burnt; male priests eat rest

SECONDARY SACRIFICES (Subcategories of the Peace Offering).

Name	Function	Material	Offerer's actions	Priest's Actions	Disposal
todah [TH8426, ZH9343] (lit., "thanks"); thanksgiving offering; praise; 7:12-15	Give thanks	Same as peace offering (shelem [TH8002, ZH8968])	Same as peace offering, plus bread (leavened and unleavened), olive oil	Same as peace offering	Priest and offerer eat meat offered on the day offered and eat bread
neder [TH5088, ZH5624] (lit., "oath"); vow; votive; 7:16-17	Complete a vow	Same as peace offering	Same as peace offering	Same as peace offering	Priest and offerer eat meat offered on the day offered or the next day
nedabah [TH5071, ZH5607] (lit., "voluntary"); freewill offering; 7:16-17	Rejoicing	Same as peace offering	Same as peace offering	Same as peace offering	Same as vow

The layout of the text of Leviticus 1–7 is that of a reference manual, part addressed to the people (1:1–6:7) and part to the priests (6:8–7:38). It is divided into separate, easily discernable sections that could have been consulted depending on the kind of offering brought (burnt, grain, peace, sin, guilt) or what the material of the offering was (e.g., cattle, sheep, goats, or birds in ch 1) or who was bringing the offering (e.g., priest, nation, leader, or common citizen in ch 4). They were ordered according to whether the sacrifices were voluntary and spontaneous (chs 1–3) or required (chs 4–5). We don't have any of the original documents available, but we can surmise that each section and subsection probably started a new paragraph and that the key introductory words of each option might have been highlighted in red, as they were in some Aramaic (e.g., the Deir Alla Balaam inscription) and Egyptian (e.g., some coffin spells) texts (cf. also 4QNum[b] XIII 27, XV 16). This would have aided in quickly finding the section applicable to the offerer's particular needs. For reference purposes, the document was undoubtedly posted prominently at the entrance to the Tabernacle or near the altar to be readily consulted when necessary (Baker 1987).

◆ **B. Instructions for the People about Offerings (1:3–6:7)**
    1. Burnt offerings (1:3–17)

3"If the animal you present as a burnt offering is from the herd, it must be a male with no defects. Bring it to the entrance of the Tabernacle so you* may be accepted by the LORD. 4Lay your hand on the animal's head, and the LORD will accept its death in your place to purify you, making you right with him.* 5Then slaughter the young bull in the LORD's presence, and Aaron's sons, the priests, will present the animal's blood by splattering it against all sides of the altar that stands at the entrance to the Tabernacle. ⁶Then skin the animal and cut it into pieces. ⁷The sons of Aaron the priest will build a wood fire on the altar. ⁸They will arrange the pieces of the offering, including the head and fat, on the wood burning on the altar. ⁹But the internal organs and the legs must first be washed with water. Then the priest will burn the entire sacrifice on the altar as a burnt offering. It is a special gift, a pleasing aroma to the LORD.

¹⁰"If the animal you present as a burnt offering is from the flock, it may be either a sheep or a goat, but it must be a male with no defects. ¹¹Slaughter the animal on the north side of the altar in the LORD's presence, and Aaron's sons, the priests, will splatter its blood against all sides of the altar. ¹²Then cut the animal in pieces, and the priests will arrange the pieces of the offering, including the head and fat, on the wood burning on the altar. ¹³But the internal organs and the legs must first be washed with water. Then the priest will burn the entire sacrifice on the altar as a burnt offering. It is a special gift, a pleasing aroma to the LORD.

¹⁴"If you present a bird as a burnt offering to the LORD, choose either a turtledove or a young pigeon. ¹⁵The priest will take the bird to the altar, wring off its head, and burn it on the altar. But first he must drain its blood against the side of the altar. ¹⁶The priest must also remove the crop and the feathers* and throw them in the ashes on the east side of the altar. ¹⁷Then, grasping the bird by its wings, the priest will tear the bird open, but without tearing it apart. Then he will burn it as a burnt offering on the wood burning on the altar. It is a special gift, a pleasing aroma to the LORD.

1:3 Or *it.* **1:4** Or *to make atonement for you.* **1:16** Or *the crop and its contents.* The meaning of the Hebrew is uncertain.

NOTES

1:9 *special gift.* This term (*'isheh* [TH801, ZH852]) is difficult. It has most commonly been interpreted in association with the similar word for "fire." This whole offering was burnt, but not all offerings described by this term were burnt (e.g., the drink or wine offering, 23:37; Exod 29:41; Num 15:10). Also, not every burnt offering was described by the term (cf. sin and guilt offerings, 4:1-6:7). In 3:5, the term is placed immediately next to the word for fire, which would make a meaning such as "made by fire" redundant. A study of the same form in other Semitic languages suggests a meaning of "[food] gift" (Milgrom 1991:161-162; Hartley 1992:22), or special offering, which fits better into most of the contexts where the word is used. This term is commonly associated with the phrase "a pleasing aroma to the LORD."

a pleasing aroma to the LORD. The phrase concerns an odor, the smell of the smoke which arose to God. Some translations see it as calming God, settling his anger ("soothing odour," NEB; cf. the Heb. of 1 Sam 26:19). It reached God from Noah after the Flood and is presented as part of what convinced him to never again bring such widespread destruction on the earth (Gen 8:21-22). The suggested soothing function is problematic, since the phrase only occurs once in association with a sin offering (4:31), which seeks to receive God's pardon. The other sacrifices with which it was used (burnt, grain, fellowship) were not generally for this purpose. Others see the act as bringing God delight (NLT, NIV; NIDOTTE 3.1071).

1:10 *goat.* A male goat was much rarer among burnt offerings than was a sheep (22:19; Num 28:30).

1:11 *on the north side of the altar.* The exact location of the slaughter is more specific here than in the other two cases (1:5, 15 [different verb]). It was still in the Lord's presence (1:5), but on the north or right side of the altar as one entered the Tabernacle.

1:14 *a turtledove or a young pigeon.* They are both members of the dove family, which was common in the area of Israel (Isa 60:8). Two species, *Columba livia* and *Streptopelia decaocto*, were domesticated, possibly for both food and sacrificial purposes, though when this took place is unknown. Undomesticated birds were probably also accepted for sacrifice.

1:16 *remove the crop.* The organ called the "crop" is the enlargement of the gullet in birds, and so equivalent to the animal intestines (1:9, 13).

and the feathers. This is the reading preferred by the LXX and most early rabbinic interpreters. Others (Targum, Syriac, TEV; cf. HALOT 1.683) understand the last word as "excrement" or the matter found in the crop rather than feathers, which would fit the context since this unclean material would have been unsuitable for offering (see commentary on 1:9).

ashes. The Hebrew word here is not the regular word for ashes (*'eper* [TH665, ZH709]) but one for ashes soaked by the dripped fat (*deshen* [TH1880, ZH2016]), which was the special part of each meat offering dedicated to God alone. Since these ashes were special, they needed special handling (4:12). The word is used elsewhere for the choicest and the best (Job 36:16; Ps 63:5; Isa 30:23).

COMMENTARY

The first part of Leviticus was directed toward the people who were bringing offerings to the Tabernacle, instructing them what to bring as demanded by different occasions for sacrifice. All could come to sacrifice. Both men and women had equal access to the courtyard, the altar, and the rituals done there (12:6; 15:29); this stands in contrast to the later Herodian Temple, which had a separate "Court of Women." All were invited to participate, and all were also enabled to do so. There were offerings affordable not only to the wealthy (the bull; 1:3-9) and the middle class (one of the flock; 1:10-13), but also to the poor (birds; 1:14-17). No one was exempt from coming. Whether high priest or leaders, common citizens or the destitute, none could reestablish a damaged relationship with God apart from the means he provides in these chapters.

The whole burnt offerings, addressed in this section, were the most important in Israel. They were offered daily (Num 28:3; cf. 2 Kgs 16:15; 1 Chr 16:40), and they were the first offering of any of the weekly (Sabbath) or annual festivals (Passover, Harvest, Trumpets, Day of Atonement, Shelters—see ch 23; Num 28:4–29:40), as well as on special occasions such as finishing the Tabernacle (Exod 40:29), preparing for war (1 Sam 7:9-10), or bringing the Ark up to Jerusalem (2 Sam 24:22). The whole burnt offering seems to have become the offering par excellence, since the writer of Chronicles calls the bronze altar "the altar of burnt offering" (1 Chr 21:29; 22:1; 2 Chr 29:18), even though all of the offerings in Leviticus 1–7 were burnt on that same altar. The first offering, a sacrifice of a bull, is presented in more detail than the others since some of the details, such as the location of the altar (1:5) and building the fire (1:7), would be assumed from here on in the text and would not need repeating.

"Burnt offering" (1:3) is a single word in Hebrew (*'olah* [TH5930, ZH6592]), which has the root meaning of "going up," since the complete flesh of the offering went up in smoke toward God, with none of it remaining. While many other offerings involved burning, the difference here is the relative completeness of the act—all that remained was the skin (for the priest's use; 7:8), or, in the case of a bird, the crop, which was cast aside (1:16). It is specifically called a *"whole* burnt offering" in 1 Samuel 7:9 (see Ps 51:19).

Adult male animals were the rule for the whole burnt offering, though others were used elsewhere—for example, a cow was acceptable for a peace offering (3:1; cf. Num 19:2), also a calf (9:3; Deut 21:3), and a bull (9:4). Since far fewer males were necessary to maintain the herd or flock size, male animals were more dispensable. Each of these must have had no physical defects since God demands the best (see 1:3; 3:1, 6). This was necessary for both sacrifice and sacrificer to be accepted or shown favor by God, which was the goal of the burnt offering (22:19-20; Jer 6:20) and peace offering (19:5; 22:21), but is not mentioned of the sin and guilt offerings, which have different functions (see below), though it shares with these two the function of atonement.

A person entering the Tabernacle court first encountered the altar, which was just inside the gate. A perpetual fire burned on it, welcoming worshipers to approach the Lord much as a warm hearth welcomes weary travelers. The animals were brought here and sacrificed, in plain view not only of the priests, but of other worshipers and others passing by the Tabernacle entrance. This aspect of Israelite worship was thus a public proclamation of devotion to God.

Laying one's hand on the sacrifice (*samak* [TH5564, ZH6164]; 1:4) is perhaps better understood as pressing with some force (cf. Judg 16:29) in contrast to doing so without pressure, as one did while imparting a blessing (cf. *shith* [TH7896, ZH8883]; Gen 48:14). One hand is mentioned here, in contrast to the scapegoat ritual (16:21; cf. *b. Menahot* 93a), where two are mentioned. There are several suggested understandings of the act's significance. The most likely understands the laying on of hands as indicating a substitute, as discussed below. Laying on of hands as an indication of ownership, as some suggest, seems redundant since the offerer had personally brought the animal. Another suggestion is transference, passing sin or guilt onto the animal, much as one might pass on a blessing (Gen 48:14-16). This suggestion is unlikely since the animal would then have been defiled and not have been allowed to touch the altar.

Whichever reason is accepted, the action is done to "make atonement" (1:4, NLT mg). This translates the term *kapar* [TH3722, ZH4105], which has a range of possible meanings. The basic meaning of the verb is "to rub," originally "to smear, rub on" (Gen 6:14), then "to rub, wipe, clean off," or "to clean, purify." The material with which this was done was usually blood, which was applied ritually to wipe off any impurities (4:20, 26, 31, 35; for oil, cf. 14:18), almost like a spiritual detergent. The purifying material itself must not become polluted because it would come directly into contact with the altar. There is a further meaning of the verb—namely, "to substitute for, be a ransom for," which is not rare in the Old Testament (e.g., Exod 30:12-16; Num 35:31-33). Finally, the verb could mean "to atone for," itself containing many of the elements of meaning included in the earlier discussion, since sin was carried away at the cost of shed blood. Atonement was only rarely associated with the burnt offering

(16:24; Job 1:5; 42:8). Though sin is not specifically mentioned in this connection, the verb could imply it, as it was part of the context of the burnt offering elsewhere (Job 1:5). (See the fuller discussion in the comments on 5:6.)

The offerer was intimately involved in the sacrificial process, which was appropriate because the offering was to serve as a substitute, taking the place of the offerer. Other examples of this include the Levites replacing the firstborn of the other tribes as dedicated to the service of God (Num 8:10). This interpretation of the relationship between the animal and the offerer is supported by Genesis 22:13, where the ram provided by God served as a substitute for Abraham to sacrifice "in place of" Isaac. Here the animal was taking the place of, and receiving the death deserved by, the offerer, as he showed by laying his hand on its head.

Transference of authority or power is a subcategory of this interpretation. A medieval monarch did this through the ritual of knighthood, and some today lay hands on the ordinand at ordination services. The person so acting indicates that the recipient of the action is a substitute for him, having some of the authority or power which he exercises.

Physical contact with the animal shows that there was no worship by proxy or at a safe distance. The worshiper personally carried out over half of the ritual steps, more than the priest did. This personal involvement is an immediate reminder of the life taken in the sacrifice, since its blood would literally have been on their hands. Blood was the life-giving element dedicated to God alone and could not be used for human consumption (17:10-14). Only the sanctified priests could use it, and only as part of the ritual. This life element was returned to God, its giver, by the priest's sprinkling, not burning, it on behalf of the offerer on the altar. Active, direct involvement of this kind precluded distancing oneself. Sacrifice cost a life, and this life was to be taken by the offerer. It was a substitute for his or her own life.

Since dirt or physically unclean matter could not be allowed to contaminate the altar, the internal organs, including the stomach and intestines (but not the liver and kidneys; Exod 29:13, 22), needed to be cleaned of partially digested matter, which could not be part of the offering. The legs, most probably the shins or lower section below the knee joint, which would have been literally as well as ritually unclean, were washed with water.

All of the previous steps were preparatory. The animal only became an offering when reduced to smoke. This burning of the offered material was the only common element of all of the offerings here in Leviticus. Sacrificial loss of life was found in most, along with manipulation of blood, but neither of these were evident in the grain offering (ch 2), which was just as efficacious as all of the others. Therefore, the burning, rendering all or part of the sacrifice into smoke, which in its turn ascends to God, is a central element for understanding Hebrew sacrifice. In anthropomorphic terms, the text says that God smells the aroma of the sacrificial smoke and finds it very pleasing. This description is common for the burnt offering (e.g., 1:9, 13, 17; Exod 29:18), grain offering (e.g., 2:2, 9, 12), and peace offering (e.g., 3:5, 16; Exod 29:25), but only occurs once in relation to the sacrifices made to seek pardon for sin

(4:31). The offering found favor with God, and he accepted it (1:4), as he did when Noah presented such an offering immediately after the Flood (Gen 8:20-21). It's almost as if it reminded God of his love for his people and attracted his attention to their worship of him (cf. Num 23:3).

The second permissible burnt offering was a male sheep (1:10-13). These were more commonly offered than bulls since they were more affordable. Even the affluent would have more of them in their possession (cf. Job 1:3). These, the most common domesticated animal for ancient Israel, were a reminder of a principle later exemplified by Brother Lawrence in the seventeenth century: Practicing and celebrating the presence of God in worship and service is of everyday stuff. It is not something esoteric, hidden, and inaccessible. Even in the ordinary, God is pleased to receive worship.

The ritual procedures for the sheep and goats were very similar to those for a bull. The lack of mention of laying on of hands (1:4) has led some to suggest this as particular to the bull, though I have suggested that its mention once applies to all three offering types. This omission was not unique, since three of the other necessary steps listed for the bull (slaughter, stoking the fire, and arranging wood) are not mentioned here either. This is further evidence that Leviticus 1–7 served as a reference document rather than a detailed description, since the missing steps were supplied from the written text posted for the offerer's consultation (Baker 1987).

A bird was the third category of offering (1:14-17). This offering would have been within the economic reach of almost everyone, since wild birds could have been caught with only the cost of time. If the wild birds were acceptable, this is the only instance where nondomesticated creatures could have been sacrificed. Here a choice is specifically allowed, though a choice is also implicit in the flock offering, where either a sheep or goat could have been offered. God is often more flexible than we give him credit for (see Num 9:10 and 2 Chr 30:17-20). The birds are not explicitly required to have been without blemish (1:3, 10). This also could have been presumed from the previous two instructions, or it could have been less important or more difficult to monitor, due to the covering of feathers. There is no mention of the laying on of hands either, since they would have been presented by the hand of the offerer—unlike the other, larger animals, which were probably led by a rope.

The offerers played a less active role in this offering. The priest was the one who performed the ritual tasks mentioned (slaughter and blood sprinkling, the equivalent of skinning and cutting it up and burning it), possibly because birds were small enough that their proper handling required some skill. Each person, however, still had to bring their own offering. It was up to the offerer to make the decision, to select and approach God with something, which, while not expensive, was still valuable. God, who provides life itself and all the necessities for sustaining it, received the things given from these potential food items as a gift.

What can we take from this chapter that will help us in our worship? First, we can see that in the entire chapter, there is no explicit gradation of acceptability or honor for the offerings—that is, the bull is not better than the bird. All were welcomed by

God; all were equally pleasing to him (1:9, 13, 17). Psalm 69:30-31 indicates that prayer and praise from a truly worshipful heart are preferable to the sacrifice of animals—presumably sacrifice from a lukewarm heart. This permits even the truly destitute, those without access to any of the acceptable animal sacrifices, to be able to worship. Offering was made from love and gratitude; it was a matter of worshiping God rather than competing with one's neighbor. Second, the ritual steps listed in the chapter were most probably not exhaustive. In particular, it would be surprising if the rituals were accomplished in complete silence. Most likely there were prayers and hymns that accompanied various ritual steps. We have the "video" portion of the proceedings (if you will), while the "audio" could well have been provided by some of the psalms mentioning the burnt offering (see Pss 20:3; 66:13, 15). Third, all of the five senses would have been actively stimulated in the proceedings mentioned here and in the next chapters. There would have been a commotion of animals and people for eye and ear, the smell of animals and blood, the feel of the hand on the animal and its slaughter, and the taste of the offerer's portion of some of the sacrifices. The whole being, not just the intellect, would have been caught up in this celebration of worship for the God who held life itself in his hand, who gave blessings and heard prayers, and who even smelled the scent of his people's worship.

Is not our contemporary worship too often more cerebral than sensory, thinking about God rather than celebrating him? Sound doctrine and belief are necessary and proper, but so is physical jubilation. We need to consider the senses, the visual in architecture, art, and pageantry; the sound of music, oral prayer, and praise; the smell, taste, and feel of the communion loaf and cup, the handclasp, and the kiss.

In conclusion, we need to consider the significance of the burnt offering as presented in the New Testament. The burnt offering is referred to only twice in the New Testament, in each case being replaced by something better—in Mark 12:33, by complete love for God, and in Hebrews 10:6-8, by the obedience of Jesus Christ. Obedience is better than sacrifice (1 Sam 15:22). The epitome of obedience in the New Testament was Jesus Christ in his life and in his death on the cross. In this act he gave his life, shed his blood, and acted as a whole burnt offering, fulfilling his description as "the Lamb of God who takes away the sin of the world" (John 1:29, 36). He exhibited the perfection and lack of blemish required for a sacrifice (Heb 9:14; 1 Pet 2:22) and ransomed people from their sins (Mark 10:45; 1 Pet 1:18-19). He was acceptable and pleasing to God (Matt 3:17), a sweet smell to God (Eph 5:2).

In the Old Testament, an offering itself was not a thing of power, not magical stuff that would necessarily and by its own might bring results. It was to be prompted by love, an act of willing obedience. Christ's death was a sweet fragrance to God (Eph 5:2). If our spiritual sacrifices don't have this motivation, they are without effect, a stench rather than a fragrance to the God toward whom they are directed (cf. 1 Sam 15; Amos 5:21-24). These sacrifices symbolized the offerer's being sacrificed to God. This is implied in Romans 12:1, where a more general term for "sacrifice" is used. God desires lives working, serving, worshiping him, rather than dead animals. Atonement was a serious business: It cost a life. This life was lost on behalf of the offerer, and it was also taken by the offerer's hand (1:5, 11; cf. Isa 53:4-7). In the Old Testament, this was done daily and also at special occasions (Num 28–29), since it was at heart a symbolic act. By contrast, according to the New Testament, the sacrifice of Jesus Christ was effective in bringing complete and actual atonement, and so it was necessary only once (Heb 10:1-10).

◆   ## 2. Grain offerings (2:1-16)

"When you present grain as an offering to the LORD, the offering must consist of choice flour. You are to pour olive oil on it, sprinkle it with frankincense, ²and bring it to Aaron's sons, the priests. The priest will scoop out a handful of the flour moistened with oil, together with all the frankincense, and burn this representative portion on the altar. It is a special gift, a pleasing aroma to the LORD. ³The rest of the grain offering will then be given to Aaron and his sons. This offering will be considered a most holy part of the special gifts presented to the LORD.

⁴"If your offering is a grain offering baked in an oven, it must be made of choice flour, but without any yeast. It may be presented in the form of thin cakes mixed with olive oil or wafers spread with olive oil. ⁵If your grain offering is cooked on a griddle, it must be made of choice flour mixed with olive oil but without any yeast. ⁶Break it in pieces and pour olive oil on it; it is a grain offering. ⁷If your grain offering is prepared in a pan, it must be made of choice flour and olive oil.

⁸"No matter how a grain offering for the LORD has been prepared, bring it to the priest, who will present it at the altar.

⁹The priest will take a representative portion of the grain offering and burn it on the altar. It is a special gift, a pleasing aroma to the LORD. ¹⁰The rest of the grain offering will then be given to Aaron and his sons as their food. This offering will be considered a most holy part of the special gifts presented to the LORD.

¹¹"Do not use yeast in preparing any of the grain offerings you present to the LORD, because no yeast or honey may be burned as a special gift presented to the LORD. ¹²You may add yeast and honey to an offering of the first crops of your harvest, but these must never be offered on the altar as a pleasing aroma to the LORD. ¹³Season all your grain offerings with salt to remind you of God's eternal covenant. Never forget to add salt to your grain offerings.

¹⁴"If you present a grain offering to the LORD from the first portion of your harvest, bring fresh grain that is coarsely ground and roasted on a fire. ¹⁵Put olive oil on this grain offering, and sprinkle it with frankincense. ¹⁶The priest will take a representative portion of the grain moistened with oil, together with all the frankincense, and burn it as a special gift presented to the LORD.

NOTES

2:1 you. In this chapter, a different but synonymous word (*nepesh* [TH5315, ZH5883]) is used instead of *'adam*, which occurred in 1:2 (see note). Each includes both men and women (see Num 5:6-7) and is rendered with second-person forms in the NLT.

2:14 the first portion of your harvest. The word *bikkurim* [TH1061, ZH1137] indicates something given at the beginning and is often translated as "firstfruits." Milgrom (1991:190-191) suggests that there was a distinction between this term, indicating that which was first ripe or first harvested (rendered "first crops" in Num 18:13), and the term used in Num 18:12 (rendered "harvest gifts"), indicating that which was first processed.

fresh grain. This was crushed or ground fresh ears of grain, usually barley (Exod 9:31), but here it is possibly ripening wheat. The descriptive word translated as "fresh" in the NLT is related to the name Carmel, an area that produces lush, rich crops due to abundant water (Amos 1:2), indicating the choice nature of this offering.

COMMENTARY

The next offerings to Yahweh were no farther away than the breakfast table. He desired a gift from the very bread of life, which was originally a gift from him in the form of grain. The grain was reworked, processed by human hands, and returned to God. These gifts implied the hospitality that was, and still is, part of Near Eastern life—the notion that "what I have, I am pleased to share with you" (cf. Gen 18:6; Kidner 1971:6). We all like to share a meal with a friend, and God was more than that: He was Israel's covenant partner. The major difference between this sacrifice and the previous was that here there was no blood shed, and as a result, there was no atonement (1:4; Heb 9:22). Since grain offerings regularly followed the burnt offering in daily rituals (Num 28), they follow it here in the written description. It became representative of those types of offering that did not require blood (Heb 10:5).

A grain offering was a gift from any of the people, male or female, to Yahweh as covenant Lord and King (2:1-3). Very frequently it accompanied the burnt offerings or peace offerings. The term "grain offering" (*minkhah* [TH4503, ZH4966]; 2:1) is ambiguous in the Old Testament. It first referred to both animal and vegetable sacrifices (Gen 4:3-5), and at other times it indicated offerings of meat (1 Sam 2:12-17), mixed meat and bread (Judg 6:18-20), incense (Num 16:15-17), and offerings in general (1 Chr 16:29; Ps 96:8; Zeph 3:10). In fact, in one eschatological passage the term refers to human beings who would be an offering to Yahweh (Isa 66:20). At other times, including the passage in Leviticus 2, it designated offerings of grain (9:4, 17; 14:10, 20, 31; Num 15:1-10). In nonreligious contexts, the term spoke of a gift, often to someone who was being honored (Gen 33:10), such as a king (1 Sam 10:27; 1 Kgs 10:25; 2 Chr 17:5), or tribute, an expected or enforced "gift" (Judg 3:15-18; 2 Sam 8:2). "Gift" seems to have been the basic meaning, becoming more specific if used in a religious or in a sociopolitical context (NIDOTTE 2.978-990). Here it was a gift in appreciation and worship of God.

Most of the ingredients were ordinary, from the daily stuff of life. They are listed in the first verse. Choice flour came from wheat (Exod 29:2) and not barley, the other main grain of the area. (According to 2 Kgs 7:16, the value of wheat was double that of barley.) Olive oil was obtained by crushing, pressing, or grinding the olives. It was a staple part of Israel's diet (1 Kgs 17:12-16) as well as part of its rituals. It was a part of sacrifices such as this, though never offered on its own, and was also used for purification through anointing (see commentary on 8:10-13). The exception to common household products was the incense. It was made of a tree resin available to Israel only through trade with its source areas in southern Arabia (Jer 6:20) and Somalia. It was transported in dried form and was used not only with grain offerings (Neh 13:5, 9; Isa 43:23; Jer 17:26) but was also burnt on the inner incense altar (Exod 30:7-8, 34-36) to provide a sweet odor. It was very costly since it was imported.

Only a part of the offering was burnt, in contrast to the completely destroyed offerings of chapter 1. This was called a token portion since only a part, or token, of the whole was burnt. The Hebrew word ('azkarah [TH234, ZH260], 2:9) involves "remembrance," though what was remembered is debated. Some suggest it was the goodness of God, especially in his provision of food, or that it serves as a prod to God to remember the offerer (Hartley 1992:30). More likely it was a reminder that this was just a token of all the offering, which in fact belonged completely to God (Milgrom 1991:182). The remainder was given to the priests for their use, since they were to be provided for from the people's gifts instead of having to raise their own food (Num 18:8-32; cf. Deut 18:1-4). Just because they were dedicating themselves to God's work, they should not miss out on his goodness. This has serious implications for today's full-time religious workers, who are often expected by their congregations to exemplify sacrificial poverty rather than enjoying God's providential bounty (see Luke 10:7; 1 Cor 9:3-14).

Different types of grain offerings receive detailed discussion in this passage, though the ritual actions of the offerings themselves remained constant (2:4-16). Bread made without any yeast (*matsah* [TH4682, ZH5174], 2:4) was the unleavened bread similar to that made by Israel when they had to leave Egypt quickly, not having time for their bread to rise (Exod 12:8, 15). It could not be made with leaven, a fermenting agent that helped bread to rise. No reason is given here for its exclusion, though numerous suggestions have been supplied by commentators. Most probably it was excluded since its processes include fermentation, a type of spoilage that would not fit in with the perfection required of sacrifices. In later Jewish and Christian interpretation (Matt 16:6; 1 Cor 5:6-7; Gal 5:9), leaven often symbolized humanity's sinful nature, a nature that had the propensity to spread to whatever it contacted. The one exception to this appears in Jesus' parable of the Kingdom of God, where leaven symbolizes the secret, effective spread of the gospel (Matt 13:33; Luke 13:21).

Honey (2:11) was rarely taken from beehives (cf. Judg 14:8-9); in the Old Testament, the word most often refers to the sweetening nectar from fruit, an agricultural product (2 Chr 31:5; cf. Deut 8:8). It was banned along with yeast. While it is said in many verses that honey is a blessing (20:24; Gen 43:11; Deut 32:13; Prov 16:24), its prohibition here was possibly because of its tendency to ferment quickly (Ross 2002:105). Yeast, but not honey, was allowed rarely for certain offerings, such as those presented at the Harvest Festival (23:17; see also 7:13), a special time of thanksgiving for God's faithful provision.

Salt (lit., "salt of God's covenant") was necessary for all of these offerings. It was a natural preservative, especially important in a temperate climate without refrigeration. It was an appropriate symbol for the binding, nondegenerating keeping of a covenant (Num 18:19; 2 Chr 13:5). Salt is also not destroyed by fire, another possible symbolic reason for its inclusion. A covenant was a binding agreement between two parties, often in the political sphere. A great king would often enter a suzerain-vassal covenant with several minor rulers, who would obey him and support him with taxes, conscripted soldiers, and so forth. The relationship between God and his people Israel was very often presented as a covenant, and this salt reminded the people of it.

The details of different ways of preparing the grain were given because it is human nature for people to wriggle their way out of any obligation that might cost them something. All the regular ways meal was prepared were covered, and just in case something was left out, the summary statement (2:8) covers them as well.

The grain offerings were a constant reminder that everything in life is a gift from God and must be offered back to him. This involves offering one's entire resources and being (Rom 12:1-2) and sharing resources with God's ministers, a requirement that should be expanded to everyone in need. We should share with others the abundance God has shared with us (Heb 13:15-16).

◆   ## 3. Peace offerings (3:1-17)

"If you present an animal from the herd as a peace offering to the LORD, it may be a male or a female, but it must have no defects. ²Lay your hand on the animal's head, and slaughter it at the entrance of the Tabernacle.* Then Aaron's sons, the priests, will splatter its blood against all sides of the altar. ³The priest must present part of this peace offering as a special gift to the LORD. This includes all the fat around the internal organs, ⁴the two kidneys and the fat around them near the loins, and the long lobe of the liver. These must be removed with the kidneys, ⁵and Aaron's sons will burn them on top of the burnt offering on the wood burning on the altar. It is a special gift, a pleasing aroma to the LORD.

⁶"If you present an animal from the flock as a peace offering to the LORD, it may be a male or a female, but it must have no defects. ⁷If you present a sheep as your offering, bring it to the LORD, ⁸lay your hand on its head, and slaughter it in front of the Tabernacle. Aaron's sons will then splatter the sheep's blood against all sides of the altar. ⁹The priest must present the fat of this peace offering as a special

gift to the LORD. This includes the fat of the broad tail cut off near the backbone, all the fat around the internal organs, ¹⁰the two kidneys and the fat around them near the loins, and the long lobe of the liver. These must be removed with the kidneys, ¹¹and the priest will burn them on the altar. It is a special gift of food presented to the LORD.

¹²"If you present a goat as your offering, bring it to the LORD, ¹³lay your hand on its head, and slaughter it in front of the Tabernacle. Aaron's sons will then splatter the goat's blood against all sides of the altar. ¹⁴The priest must present part of this offering as a special gift to the LORD. This includes all the fat around the internal organs, ¹⁵the two kidneys and the fat around them near the loins, and the long lobe of the liver. These must be removed with the kidneys, ¹⁶and the priest will burn them on the altar. It is a special gift of food, a pleasing aroma to the LORD. All the fat belongs to the LORD.

¹⁷"You must never eat any fat or blood. This is a permanent law for you, and it must be observed from generation to generation, wherever you live."

3:2 Hebrew *Tent of Meeting;* also in 3:8, 13.

NOTES

3:1 If. This is the same Hebrew term (*'im* [TH518, ZH561]) as in 1:3 and shows that both chapters are subtypes of the animal sacrifices of 1:2. Often the main category in a conditional discussion (the first, main "if" clause) opens with a different word for "if" (*ki* [TH3588, ZH3954]) found in 1:2, with subcategories marked by *'im* (e.g., 1:3, 14; 2:7).

you. This reflects a third-person indefinite construction (see notes on 1:2; 2:1), referring to the same kind of unidentified worshiper, whether male or female, as in 1:2.

3:4 loins. This appears to be best translated as "sinews" based on comparison with other Semitic languages (Milgrom 1991:207; Hartley 1992:40).

lobe of the liver. This is probably the small projection from the liver (*lobus caudatus*), lying very near the right kidney.

3:9 broad tail. This was a technical term for the very fatty tail, weighing up to 15 pounds, of a kind of sheep common in Israel (Hartley 1992:40). Its fat, like all the rest, was dedicated to God.

3:11 food. This is the general Semitic word for food (Gen 3:19; 18:5) and at times refers to the staple food of the society in which it was used.

3:17 permanent law. This derives from a word indicating inscribing into stone. While not implying that it was written when Moses received it, the phrase would indicate that the obligation was not just for Moses's generation.

COMMENTARY

Like the earlier whole burnt offerings (ch 1), peace offerings are animal sacrifices. Unlike them, however, not all the animal was burnt. Instead, after a portion was burnt on the altar as an offering to God, the remainder was eaten by the worshiper (7:11-21) so that both the worshiper and the one worshiped could celebrate the feast together.

"Peace offering" represents two Hebrew words: The first Hebrew word, translated as "offering" (*zebakh* [TH2077, ZH2285]), designated flesh offerings (Exod 12:27; 34:25; Deut 18:3) in general but was often used with the next word (*shelamim* [TH8002, ZH8968]), whose meaning is much debated. Traditionally regarded as relating to *shalom* [TH7965, ZH8934] (peace), it has long been translated "peace offering" (KJV, RSV, NLT). The related term, meaning "well-being," has led some to translate it as "well-being offering" (Harrison 1980:56; Hartley 1992:33; Milgrom 1991:217). The only use of the term in the singular (Amos 5:22) could support this view. Because the offering was "shared" with God, "communion sacrifice" has also been suggested (JB; NIDOTTE 4.135; cf. HALOT 1537).

There are significant differences between this and the previous two sacrifices, though all three were made by choice, not by command. Once atonement had been made and thanks given through the burnt and grain offerings, the offerer could enjoy the presence of God, so this sacrifice might be viewed as a goal toward which the first two were reaching. Also, unlike the burnt offering, female animals were accepted as well as males (cf. 1:3, 10), and there were no age restrictions—other indications of the openness of this sacrifice. Some suggest that the inclusion of female animals here is significant, since the females could be seen as more valuable than their male counterparts, and since they produced not only milk but also the next generation. Thus, more of them were needed than male animals (see Gen 32:15-16; Ruane 2005). It is more likely that female animals are included since the offering itself is not as restrictive as the previous two: Rather than going completely to God, like the burnt offering, or to God and the priests, like the grain offering, this one was partly eaten by the offerer (see Deut 12:7).

There were three occasions for this offering as mentioned in 7:11-18 (see comments there): thanksgiving (7:12, 15), fulfillment of a vow, or spontaneous freewill (7:16). In this celebration of peace and fellowship, there was communion between God, priest (7:34), and offerer (7:15-16, 19; Deut 12:7), all of whom shared the meal. Such table fellowship was not for strangers and enemies, but for those who had established a close, even covenantal relationship (see Gen 14:18; 31:54; Exod 24:11). Since animals were economically important, representing a sizable portion of one's disposable wealth, slaughtering and eating them were not part of daily life. This contrasts with the meat that forms a regular part of the diet of many in the developed world today. When meat was eaten in Israel, it was an event to be joyfully shared with friends and family (cf. Exod 12:4), and in this case, with one's God. The national joy was shown by the mass celebration accompanying this offering when Solomon completed building the Temple (1 Kgs 8:62-66).

The fact that the liver of the offering was reserved for God is significant, especially when compared with the practices of Israel's polytheistic neighbors in Canaan and Mesopotamia. There, specialist religious functionaries called "diviners" would look for messages from the gods by examining omens, much like people today consult tarot cards and horoscopes, or read tea leaves. In Mesopotamia, an often-consulted source was the entrails of animals, with the liver being the organ of choice. The diviner searched it for abnormalities and made predictions based on any found therein. This sort of divine consultation was an abomination to God and therefore banned in Israel (Deut 18:10-12). Since at least part of the liver was dedicated to God and destroyed by burning, Israel could not be led astray into this kind of pagan practice, since the main "tool of the trade" had been dedicated to God.

A special, permanent restriction was placed upon the consumption of blood and fat (3:17). Blood, so obviously associated with life (17:11), was God's alone. The prohibition against consuming blood is well known today through the Jewish kosher regulations. Fat does not refer to the marbling in meat that was closely integrated with it, but rather the layers under the skin and surrounding the entrails and organs that can be easily peeled off, called "suet" in English. It was a choice part of the animal (Gen 45:18). The reason for the ban against eating fat is not clear (7:22-25), though possibly its special, choice character made it especially appropriate as a gift to God. Such a lack of explanation for divine requirements is not rare. If God is viewed as a gracious Creator who knows how his creation operates best for all concerned, then his commands can and should be simply accepted, even if their purpose is obscure—this Adam and Eve discovered to their cost and ours (Gen 2:17; 3:1-24; Rom 5:12).

Since the peace offering was not made for atonement, it could be viewed as the joyful response to atonement already won and a relationship made whole. God still wants Christians' celebratory thanksgiving, not through animal sacrifice, but through other things important for life, our very bodies (Rom 12:1) or our time, one of today's most precious commodities. Furthermore, the communal aspect of the feasting celebrated in this sacrifice finds parallel in Christian communion. There, reconciled friends enjoy a meal of flesh (= bread) and blood (= wine; John 6:51-58; 1 Cor 11:23-26).

Though blood was banned in Leviticus, it is required in symbolic form as part of Christian communion. Both communion elements give life (cf. 17:11). The Old Testament shows that life in the form of bread and blood must be returned to God, who is its source, but the New Testament shows that he gives life back to his human creatures through these same symbols. The blood of the new covenant should remind Christians of the blood of the old covenant—blood Moses sprinkled on the people (Exod 24:8) and blood that was taken from both burnt and peace offerings (3:5). The act that communion symbolizes (Christ's death on the cross) was the ultimate peace and atonement offering and is what finally brings people into a state of peace through being in a right relationship with God.

◆ 4. Sin offerings (4:1–5:13)

Then the LORD said to Moses, [2]"Give the following instructions to the people of Israel. This is how you are to deal with those who sin unintentionally by doing anything that violates one of the LORD's commands.

[3]"If the high priest* sins, bringing guilt upon the entire community, he must give a sin offering for the sin he has committed. He must present to the LORD a young bull with no defects. [4]He must bring the bull to the LORD at the entrance of the Tabernacle,* lay his hand on the bull's head, and slaughter it before the LORD. [5]The high priest will then take some of the bull's blood into the Tabernacle, [6]dip his finger in the blood, and sprinkle it seven times before the LORD in front of the inner curtain of the sanctuary. [7]The priest will then put some of the blood on the horns of the altar for fragrant incense that stands in the LORD's presence inside the Tabernacle. He will pour out the rest of the bull's blood at the base of the altar for burnt offerings at the entrance of the Tabernacle. [8]Then the priest must remove all the fat of the bull to be offered as a sin offering. This includes all the fat around the internal organs, [9]the two kidneys and the fat around them near the loins, and the long lobe of the liver. He must remove these along with the kidneys, [10]just as he does with cattle offered as a peace offering, and burn them on the altar of burnt offerings. [11]But he must take whatever is left of the bull—its hide, meat, head, legs, internal organs, and dung—[12]and carry it away to a place outside the camp that is ceremonially clean, the place where the ashes are dumped. There, on the ash heap, he will burn it on a wood fire.

[13]"If the entire Israelite community sins by violating one of the LORD's commands, but the people don't realize it, they are still guilty. [14]When they become aware of their sin, the people must bring a young bull as an offering for their sin and present it before the Tabernacle. [15]The elders of the community must then lay their hands on the bull's head and slaughter it before the

LORD. [16]The high priest will then take some of the bull's blood into the Tabernacle, [17]dip his finger in the blood, and sprinkle it seven times before the LORD in front of the inner curtain. [18]He will then put some of the blood on the horns of the altar for fragrant incense that stands in the LORD's presence inside the Tabernacle. He will pour out the rest of the blood at the base of the altar for burnt offerings at the entrance of the Tabernacle. [19]Then the priest must remove all the animal's fat and burn it on the altar, [20]just as he does with the bull offered as a sin offering for the high priest. Through this process, the priest will purify the people, making them right with the LORD,* and they will be forgiven. [21]Then the priest must take what is left of the bull and carry it outside the camp and burn it there, just as is done with the sin offering for the high priest. This offering is for the sin of the entire congregation of Israel.

[22]"If one of Israel's leaders sins by violating one of the commands of the LORD his God but doesn't realize it, he is still guilty. [23]When he becomes aware of his sin, he must bring as his offering a male goat with no defects. [24]He must lay his hand on the goat's head and slaughter it at the place where burnt offerings are slaughtered before the LORD. This is an offering for his sin. [25]Then the priest will dip his finger in the blood of the sin offering and put it on the horns of the altar for burnt offerings. He will pour out the rest of the blood at the base of the altar. [26]Then he must burn all the goat's fat on the altar, just as he does with the peace offering. Through this process, the priest will purify the leader from his sin, making him right with the LORD, and he will be forgiven.

[27]"If any of the common people sin by violating one of the LORD's commands, but they don't realize it, they are still guilty. [28]When they become aware of their sin, they must bring as an offering for their sin a female goat with no defects. [29]They must lay a hand on the head of the sin offering and slaughter it at the place where burnt offerings are slaughtered. [30]Then the priest will dip his finger in the blood and put it on the horns of the altar for burnt offerings. He will pour out the rest of the blood at the base of the altar. [31]Then he must remove all the goat's fat, just as he does with the fat of the peace offering. He will burn the fat on the altar, and it will be a pleasing aroma to the LORD. Through this process, the priest will purify the people, making them right with the LORD, and they will be forgiven.

[32]"If the people bring a sheep as their sin offering, it must be a female with no defects. [33]They must lay a hand on the head of the sin offering and slaughter it at the place where burnt offerings are slaughtered. [34]Then the priest will dip his finger in the blood of the sin offering and put it on the horns of the altar for burnt offerings. He will pour out the rest of the blood at the base of the altar. [35]Then he must remove all the sheep's fat, just as he does with the fat of a sheep presented as a peace offering. He will burn the fat on the altar on top of the special gifts presented to the LORD. Through this process, the priest will purify the people from their sin, making them right with the LORD, and they will be forgiven.

CHAPTER 5

"If you are called to testify about something you have seen or that you know about, it is sinful to refuse to testify, and you will be punished for your sin.

[2]"Or suppose you unknowingly touch something that is ceremonially unclean, such as the carcass of an unclean animal. When you realize what you have done, you must admit your defilement and your guilt. This is true whether it is a wild animal, a domestic animal, or an animal that scurries along the ground.

[3]"Or suppose you unknowingly touch something that makes a person unclean. When you realize what you have done, you must admit your guilt.

⁴"Or suppose you make a foolish vow of any kind, whether its purpose is for good or for bad. When you realize its foolishness, you must admit your guilt.

⁵"When you become aware of your guilt in any of these ways, you must confess your sin. ⁶Then you must bring to the LORD as the penalty for your sin a female from the flock, either a sheep or a goat. This is a sin offering with which the priest will purify you from your sin, making you right with the LORD.*

⁷"But if you cannot afford to bring a sheep, you may bring to the LORD two turtledoves or two young pigeons as the penalty for your sin. One of the birds will be for a sin offering, and the other for a burnt offering. ⁸You must bring them to the priest, who will present the first bird as the sin offering. He will wring its neck but without severing its head from the body. ⁹Then he will sprinkle some of the blood of the sin offering against the sides of the altar, and the rest of the blood will be drained out at the base of the altar. This is an offering for sin. ¹⁰The priest will then prepare the second bird as a burnt offering, following all the procedures that have been prescribed. Through this process the priest will purify you from your sin, making you right with the LORD, and you will be forgiven.

¹¹"If you cannot afford to bring two turtledoves or two young pigeons, you may bring two quarts* of choice flour for your sin offering. Since it is an offering for sin, you must not moisten it with olive oil or put any frankincense on it. ¹²Take the flour to the priest, who will scoop out a handful as a representative portion. He will burn it on the altar on top of the special gifts presented to the LORD. It is an offering for sin. ¹³Through this process, the priest will purify those who are guilty of any of these sins, making them right with the LORD, and they will be forgiven. The rest of the flour will belong to the priest, just as with the grain offering."

4:3 Hebrew *the anointed priest;* also in 4:5, 16.   4:4 Hebrew *Tent of Meeting;* also in 4:5, 7, 14, 16, 18. 4:20 Or *will make atonement for the people;* similarly in 4:26, 31, 35.   5:6 Or *will make atonement for you for your sin;* similarly in 5:10, 13, 16, 18.   5:11 Hebrew ¹/₁₀ *of an ephah* [2.2 liters].

NOTES

4:2 *commands.* This term (*mitswah* [TH4687, ZH5184]), best known to contemporary readers through the name of the common Jewish custom called a bar mitzvah, refers in Leviticus to religious or cultic commands and at times to the entire book (27:34; NIDOTTE 2.1070). These commands dealt with breaches of Israel's covenant with God, emphasizing him as the wronged party.

4:7 *horns.* These were projections or knobs on each corner of the altar top. In the ancient Near East they represented the god, who was often portrayed with a horned headdress, in power and might. Israel's God had no physical representation of his being, but the horns could still be a reminder of his power. They also served as a point of asylum or sanctuary later in Israel's history (1 Kgs 1:50).

altar for fragrant incense. This was the smaller gold altar in the inner Tabernacle chamber, the Holy Place (Exod 30:1-10; 37:25-28), where access was restricted to priests.

4:12 *ceremonially clean.* This cleanness does not necessarily involve physical dirt, but describes things ritually or theologically pure and able to be used in the worship and service of God (10:10). Since the material taken here was part of a sacrifice to God, even though it was removed from the Tabernacle (the regular place associated with sacrifice), it had to be pure.

4:14 *an offering for their sin.* This phrase is related to a Hebrew root (*khatta'* [TH2398, ZH2627]) which means "to fail, err, sin" and in another form means "to remove sin, purify." The noun thus could refer to the sin itself, the offering that purified from that sin, or the animal used for this offering. In 4:3, the first two meanings are evident, since the priest was to bring an offering because of his sin. Sin necessitates the sacrifice in this section of Leviticus, but a number of precipitating events elsewhere (e.g., chs 12–15) involve natural bodily functions, such as menstruation, childbirth, sexual intercourse, and death, which do not break any of God's commands. Thus, calling these "sin offerings" can lead to misunderstanding. Today we usually understand sin as something that is morally wrong and to be condemned, but there is no moral demeaning of these functions mentioned. A translation as "purification offering" has been suggested (Hartley 1992:55-57; Milgrom 1991:253-254; Wenham 1979:88-89) and describes more positively the function of the sacrifice.

4:22 leaders. The word *nasi'* [TH5387, ZH5954] signifies a chief, "one who is elevated" (the root meaning of the term) over the family unit, clan (Num 3:24; 7:2), or nation (Num 10:3-4).

4:27 common people. The common folk also include other priests and the Levites, servants of the Tabernacle.

5:1 *you will be punished for your sin.* By refusing to do what he was expected to do, he was guilty of wrongdoing and would receive the logical consequences of his action.

COMMENTARY

This new literary section starts with another narrative introduction (cf. 1:1; 6:1). The sin offerings are theologically different from those mentioned before, which involve voluntary celebration and worship of God. The sin offerings are required of those wanting to repair a relationship with God that has been broken by sin or some other means. Everyone, from high to low, was required to bring these offerings, and the common person was enabled to do so by the provision of options at various levels of cost (4:27-35; 5:5-13). There was something that everyone, no matter how destitute, would be able to afford.

In descriptions of sacrifices, the sin offering precedes the freewill offerings (e.g., 8:14), even though it was listed after them in this prescriptive passage. Before one could rejoice in God, one needed to be purified so that contact with him was possible. Repentance and forgiveness were prerequisites for peace (Ps 51:16-19).

Israel, like most societies, had numerous legal requirements, some obvious and some obscure. It was not difficult in the course of daily existence to cross over one of these legal boundaries without even being aware that the boundary was there. The sin offering was established to deal with this sort of inadvertent or unintentional wrongdoing (5:17). This could be doing something without knowing it was wrong (1 Sam 14:27-28; 26:21 [cf. KJV]; Ps 19:12), or doing a wrong by accident (e.g., involuntary manslaughter; Deut 19:4-5). In either case, the actor was not aware that a sin was being committed, in contrast to a premeditated act (see Num 15:22-31, where unwitting and purposeful are contrasted). This offering was not for a wrong perpetrated in brazen disregard for laws well known to the wrongdoer ("with a high hand"; Num 15:30; e.g., 1 Sam 2:16-17).

Ignorance was no excuse, and when any wrongdoer, no matter the place of the offender in society, learned of the error, these steps were to be taken in order to make atonement for the sin. This was necessary because the lapse made the offender "guilty"—the same term used to name the next set of sacrifices (5:14–6:7).

Guilt is the objective state of being in the wrong. It was a legal term denoting culpability, not a psychological term describing any feeling of shame or remorse, as is clear from this passage. Here the offender was in the wrong but did not *feel* guilt because the sin was not known.

The offerings are ordered by the "profile" of the sinner. Those with a "higher profile" as regards the effect their sin had on others are listed first. The anointed priest (4:3-12; Exod 30:22-33), a phrase that could refer to any of the priests who were sons of Aaron, most probably indicates the high priest, the priest par excellence, the chief representative of the people before God (e.g., 16:11-15), whose actions affected the entire nation (cf. Num 35:25). If priests sinned and were unable to perform their sacred duties, they would be depriving everyone else of access to forgiveness, since there would be no one to perform the offering rituals on their behalf. They had to attend to their own sins first (4:3). They were not exempt from ritual requirements.

The nation itself could also be guilty of inadvertent wrongdoing (4:13), a fact that should make Western individualists take note. Sin was not simply personal, but was also a corporate responsibility. The actions we perform "in the privacy of our own home" have national implications since, for example, in the case of adultery, a sin that is by its nature private and between "two consenting adults," tears apart the family, the very foundation of a society. Both the priest and the people were to bring a costly bull. In this chapter, the national guilt and restoration seemed to be necessitated by the sin of the high priest as its representative, since his sin made them guilty (4:3; cf. Heb 7:27-28). Therefore, the rituals for priest and people would be one, the actions being the same, and the forgiveness won for the people (4:2) would also apply to the priest, who enjoyed no separate declaration of forgiveness (Milgrom 1991:241).

The purpose of these sacrifices was to repair a breach of relationship between God and people. This rectification or reconciliation ("at-one-ment") was what the priest did through his deeds, most specifically his manipulation of the blood. Placing the blood on the altar rather than on the worshiper indicated that the altar (representing the entire Tabernacle because it was the only instrument to which the people had direct access) had been contaminated by an undesirable action or event and needed to be cleansed or purified (Heb 9:23). After the sanctuary had been restored through the actions of the priest and the offerer, then God's action was to forgive (4:26, 31; Num 15:25).

Civil leaders were held accountable to the lesser cost of a male goat (4:22-25), while the members of the citizenry were to bring a female goat (4:28) or sheep (4:32; 5:6), or, if very poor, two birds (5:7) or even some flour (5:11). No one was excluded from taking responsibility for an action, no matter their social position, and no one was precluded from taking this responsibility, no matter their economic position. Access to God was necessary for and available to everyone.

The sacrifice for a citizen's sin was the only place in prescriptive texts where a female sacrifice was demanded rather than allowed (5:6; Num 15:27). Some suggest that this allowed them to bring animals of less value than those required of people in a higher social position (see Wenham 1979:100), but I argued in the discussion of Leviticus 3 that this relative value does not seem to be the case; rather, this sacrifice is simply more open than some of the others discussed (see Milgrom 1991:252). On the economic front, however, common folk, with smaller herds, would likely keep more female animals since the females have more immediate economic benefit through provision of milk as well as offspring, which provide meat and hides. It is suggested that the wealthy, having several male animals, would be able to sacrifice a male more easily than a poor person, who may have had only one male. The poor, if forced to sacrifice a male, would lose all breeding capability (Milgrom 1991:252). Alternatively, the reason could be sociological rather than economic since males, human and animal, were considered greater symbols of power and prestige, even if not of actual economic worth. So those in positions of power had to bring a male goat (Ruane 2005).

In the rituals described, it was not in the first instance the wrongdoer who was purified, but rather the sanctuary (8:15), which became polluted through the actions of those who came to it. God in his holiness could not abide ritual uncleanness, even if it was inadvertent. It was not physical but spiritual dirt that was the problem. This had to be washed away, usually by the blood of the sacrifices, though for the most impoverished, grain was used, so no blood was shed (cf. Heb 9:22). The high priest, having greater access to God, was the only one able to pass through the Holy Place, past the veil, and into the Most Holy Place (ch 16). For him, the inner curtain, the incense altar, and the outside altar for burnt offerings needed to be cleansed, as they were for the nation as a whole, on whose behalf he entered into the inner sanctum. Other individuals needed only to cleanse the burnt offering altar with their sacrifice in order to be forgiven and have their relationship with God restored.

The priest applied the blood of the sacrifice to the horns of the altar of burnt offering. The horns were an important part of Israelite life and worship. Daubing them with blood was necessary for cleansing from sin, and grasping them provided a place of sanctuary (1 Kgs 1:50-51). Cutting them off would thus be a severe punishment (Amos 3:14), meaning that the Israelite would have no possibility of forgiveness and also no place of refuge. They would truly be without hope.

The beginning of chapter five addresses the kind of actions that might have led to the need for a sin offering. Since no complete list of wrongs requiring the atonement of these sacrifices was possible, representative sins were listed. They are sins of omission, wrongs committed by not doing something rather than by doing it. Also, not all of them were inadvertent, indicating that, while this chapter continues the topic of sin offerings (5:6-13), it also slightly modifies the category of wrongs. Here some of the sinful acts were done purposefully (cf. 4:2, 13, 22, 27). Those who observed something relevant to a case but did not come forward with the evidence when it was publicly requested skewed the decision in the case due to incorrect or incomplete evidence. This was not lying under oath (6:5), but was rather refusing to provide the whole truth. It appears that a civic responsibility was expected of Israel far above that practiced by many today who do not want to get involved (cf. Jas 4:17).

Inadvertently touching an unclean object, whether human (12:1–13:46; 14:1-32; 15:1-33) or something else (13:47-59; 14:33-57), transferred its ritual pollution, even if the contact was not conscious. Atonement needed to be made for it. "Ceremonial uncleanness" (5:2) is a technical religious term for something or someone defiled, which therefore could not come into the presence of a holy God (Isa 6:5). God is at the extreme opposite end of the unclean–clean spectrum from pollution. The idea has nothing to do with physical dirt but speaks of theological or religious contamination. In nonreligious, social contexts it also means defilement, as when it describes Dinah's defilement as a result of being raped (Gen 34:5, 13). Specific types of animal and human uncleanness are elaborated later (chs 11–15). This regulation makes the episode of the woman with the constant bleeding (Mark 5:25-34) even more remarkable, since Jesus did not shrink in disgust at contact with an unclean person. Purification rather than pollution was transmitted, a very rare occurrence (6:18; Exod 29:37 are among the few other examples; cf. Hag 2:10-14). In our modern awareness of the potentially life-threatening danger of physical contaminants such as tainted blood, it is necessary to remember that there are matters of impurity that also endanger spiritual life.

The person who inadvertently touched uncleanness was also guilty (5:3). The root of the Hebrew word for "guilt" ('asham) has a range of meanings, with both an action and its consequence identified by the same term. The verb 'asham [TH816, ZH870] indicates the process of one's becoming guilty. The noun 'asham [TH817, ZH871] could indicate the guilt itself or the guilt offering, which in effect was a penalty or reparation to get rid of the guilt. Finally, rash, unthinking, and ill-advised actions (5:4; cf. Num 30:6; Ps 106:33) had results that needed to be made right. Oaths were not condemned here, but rather their nonfulfillment for whatever reason. Giving one's word placed one's honor at stake and should not be taken lightly.

Since the sins described in 5:1-4 were at times inadvertent violations (4:2), the wrongdoer needed to be made aware of the wrongdoing before being able to confess. Then he had to publicly acknowledge the wrong done in any of the above instances (see 16:21; Num 5:7; Dan 9:4-20). Recognition and acceptance of responsibility were necessary before steps could be taken to make things right. Rectification was brought about through a penalty (5:6), a term related to the word translated "guilt" in 4:3. Wrongdoing brought a cost to the one wronged, and restoration of purity meant a cost also for the wrongdoer. This could only be offered through the priest. For those with fewer financial resources, two birds were allowed, one each for the sin and burnt offerings. Although it is not explicit in the case of the other animals brought for a sin offering, a supplemental burnt offering could be implied for them as well. The details for the former were provided, since it involved new regulations, but the latter had already been explained (1:14-17) and only needed to be referred to. A final option for the truly impoverished was a sin offering of flour, a portion of which was burnt, with the rest going to the officiating priest, as would the meat from the sheep or goat (6:26). After these ceremonies were performed by the priest, forgiveness was granted.

The blood of the sin offering brought purification to the sanctuary, which was affected by the sins of the people (Heb 9:23). The offering needed to be preceded by repentance and confession. (Elsewhere confession was tied to laying hands on the offering; 16:21.) Without confession, there would have been no forgiveness; a mere dead ritual would not have worked. The procedure is the same today, with the same three steps—confession, payment, forgiveness—only now the middle step was taken by God himself in the person of his Son. Jesus' blood (1 Pet 1:2) makes cleansing available for everyone who acknowledges and confesses their sin (1 John 1:7-9).

In the Old Testament, the physical sanctuary was purified through the shed blood of the animal; for the Christian it is the metaphorical temple, the believers themselves (1 Cor 6:19), who are purified through Christ's blood. The writer of Hebrews (Heb 9–10) unpacked the significance of the sin offering most completely. The high priest had to bring the blood of animals inside the sanctuary to represent both himself (4:3) and the people (Heb 9:7) through the sin offering. When Jesus, the new high priest, came for this offering, it only needed to be done once (Heb 9:25; 10:1-18), and it was with his own blood, himself becoming the sacrifice. In fact, he is mentioned as fulfilling the role of both the burnt (see ch 1) and sin offerings (Heb 10:9-10). This shed blood was needed for humans to receive forgiveness. The sanctuary, which needed regular purification because the people regularly sinned, was simply a representative of the true temple, which was not that of Solomon or Herod, but rather the one in heaven, which Jesus entered and purified. Through his sin offering, we have become the promised kingdom of priests (Exod 19:6), and high priests at that, since, having been purified, we are invited to enter right into the sanctuary (Heb 10:22).

◆   ## 5. Guilt offerings (5:14–6:7)

¹⁴Then the LORD said to Moses, ¹⁵"If one of you commits a sin by unintentionally defiling the LORD's sacred property, you must bring a guilt offering to the LORD. The offering must be your own ram with no defects, or you may buy one of equal value with silver, as measured by the weight of the sanctuary shekel.* ¹⁶You must make restitution for the sacred property you have harmed by paying for the loss, plus an additional 20 percent. When you give the payment to the priest, he will purify you with the ram sacrificed as a guilt offering, making you right with the LORD, and you will be forgiven.

¹⁷"Suppose you sin by violating one of the LORD's commands. Even if you are unaware of what you have done, you are guilty and will be punished for your sin. ¹⁸For a guilt offering, you must bring to the priest your own ram with no defects, oryou may buy one of equal value. Through this process the priest will purify you from your unintentional sin, making you right with the LORD, and you will be forgiven. ¹⁹This is a guilt offering, for you have been guilty of an offense against the LORD."

CHAPTER 6

¹*Then the LORD said to Moses, ²"Suppose one of you sins against your associate and is unfaithful to the LORD. Suppose you

cheat in a deal involving a security deposit, or you steal or commit fraud, ³or you find lost property and lie about it, or you lie while swearing to tell the truth, or you commit any other such sin. ⁴If you have sinned in any of these ways, you are guilty. You must give back whatever you stole, or the money you took by extortion, or the security deposit, or the lost property you found, ⁵or anything obtained by swearing falsely. You must make restitution by paying the full price plus an additional 20 percent to the person you have harmed. On the same day you must present a guilt offering. ⁶As a guilt offering to the LORD, you must bring to the priest your own ram with no defects, or you may buy one of equal value. ⁷Through this process, the priest will purify you before the LORD, making you right with him,* and you will be forgiven for any of these sins you have committed."

5:15 Each shekel was about 0.4 ounces or 11 grams in weight.   **6:1** Verses 6:1-7 are numbered 5:20-26 in Hebrew text.   **6:7** Or *will make atonement for you before the Lord.*

NOTES

5:15 *sanctuary shekel.* A shekel is a weight indication, which appears to refer to a special standard use for sanctuary functions (see note on 27:25). Sometimes when the phrase was used, a more precise measurement was also given (Exod 30:13; Num 3:47; 18:16), indicating that it needed clarification since it was not the customary shekel. The weight was about 11 to 13 grams per shekel.

6:1-7 [5:20-26] The versification of ch 6 is different in the Hebrew text than in the English translations. Leviticus 5:20-26 in the Hebrew text corresponds to 6:1-7 in the English, and 6:1-23 in the Hebrew text corresponds to 6:8-30 in the English (see NLT mg). The Hebrew text has the more logical versification because 6:1-7 [5:20-26] discusses the same kind of offering as ch 5, while 6:8 [1] begins the discussion of the burnt offering. Both numbering systems were added much later to an already existing text.

COMMENTARY

This section (5:14–6:7) addresses the guilt offering, a second type of sacrifice occasioned by unintentional wrongdoing—this time by an individual worshiper. This offering is similar to the sin offering (see 7:7), though for the sin offering corporate wrong was included, different animals were used, and the blood manipulation varied (4:1–5:13). The main difference between the two was that the offerer not only brought an animal for sacrifice, but usually had to pay an additional, financial penalty in order to be forgiven. This payment apparently compensated for losses deriving from the sin.

The guilt offering was a rectification for actions taken against the wishes of God (Num 5:6; Josh 22:31) including using something promised to him in a way not allowed (Josh 22:20; 1 Chr 2:7) or marrying pagan wives (Ezra 9:2, 4), which also overstepped the bounds of what was right for the nation reserved for a relationship with God (Neh 13:27). In what could be considered more of a civil case, the term "guilt" involved a suspected violation of marriage vows of fidelity (Num 5:12, 27), so the general meaning of "guilt" in this situation would be a willful breach of established and understood covenant expectations. Guilt offerings atoned for these by not only making matters right with God, but also providing compensation for the loss.

Loss to God himself was first addressed, where sacred property was affected (5:16). Set apart for God alone, this property could also be transferred to others such as the priests. There was a considerable amount of this reserved property in Israel. Included were the sacred place par excellence, the Tabernacle and later the Temple, known in Hebrew as the "Holy Place" (often translated as "sanctuary"; Exod 25:8), with its inner room, the Most Holy Place (Exod 26:33); the holy implements—the altar (Exod 40:10), the Ark, and other furniture sanctified for use in the Tabernacle (Exod 30:26-29; Num 4:4); other, non-fixed things such as the priestly clothes used on ritual occasions (Exod 28:2), the bread (24:9) and incense (Exod 30:36) kept at the shrine, the anointing oil (Exod 30:32), and also the sacrifices themselves discussed in these chapters.

All of the sacrifices mentioned in these chapters were holy, though the peace offerings were not called "holy" in these chapters (but see 19:5-8). Holiness extends beyond the sanctuary precincts, however. The landholdings of the priests and Levites were holy, set apart for their sole use (Ezek 45:4-5; 48:13-14). Plunder, including weapons, that was dedicated to God and destined for use in the sanctuary was also holy, even if not yet stored there (2 Sam 8:10-11; 1 Kgs 14:26-27), as were the firstfruits of the harvest (Num 18:12-13) and the tithe (27:30-33). People, namely the priests (1 Chr 23:13) and Levites (2 Chr 23:6), were also holy, and their person or position was not to be usurped. The term was used even more broadly, since the entire Israelite camp was holy (Deut 23:14), which was the reason why unclean people such as lepers were to be sent away from it (Num 5:2-3). Finally, all of God's people were holy (Exod 19:6; cf. 1 Pet 2:9), and it was to this holiness which Leviticus repeatedly called them (11:44-45; 19:2; 20:7-26; cf. 1 Pet 1:16).

It is not clear from this passage what kind of infringement on the holy was in view, though it was something that caused economic loss. Possibly what was implied was withholding a required tithe or offering or otherwise encroaching on the property rightfully belonging to the priests or Levites, and thus to God (cf. Mal 3:8-9). Whatever it was, it crossed an established boundary into someone else's territory, hence a "trespass," as this wrong is called in KJV. This also seems to be the essence of the next sub-case (5:17-19), though there, the trespass seems not to include usurpation, since no restitution was called for. It appears here that God alone knew the exact wrong, so atonement was necessary but no compensation was possible since no amount could be determined. It was the lack of exact knowledge that was the only distinguishing mark between this and the sin offering (4:2, 13, 22, 27). It was a grace to have this sacrifice available, allowing guilt to be removed and to not live with constant fear in one's heart (Ps 19:12; Jer 17:9).

The requirement was called a guilt offering (4:3; 5:2) and could refer to the penalty required, a repayment, though not one of money ("reparation"; Milgrom 1991:319; Hartley 1992:72; cf. NIV) or the offering (NRSV), which would itself also be a penalty paid for wrong (5:15). Some interpret the verse as indicating that one was able to pay a financial penalty in place of an animal sacrifice (cf. 2 Kgs 12:16), with the priest either evaluating the wrong done and assessing a penalty amount

(Milgrom 1991:326-327) or evaluating the value of the ram and accepting its equivalent in cash instead of in kind, which would then be used to purchase the ram
(Speiser 1967:128; Wenham 1979:107). This interpretation is problematic, since
atonement was effected by blood manipulation and not money. The next verse
seems best to indicate that a ram was offered. The context could suggest that the
evaluation was to determine the value of the ram so that an additional twenty
percent of that value could supplement the animal sacrifice as compensation for the
wrong suffered (5:16).

Leviticus 6:1-7 indicates that defrauding one's neighbor or trespassing into misuse
of goods belonging to him also necessitated the guilt offering. This could take three
forms. First, it was fraudulent to misappropriate a security deposit, not returning
something "placed in the hand" for a limited time. The translation "security deposit"
indicates a technical performance bond, but the something "placed in the hand" may
have simply been a valuable to be looked after. Milgrom (1991:335), based on rabbinical discussion, suggests "investment" or "partnership," though this cannot be proved
on biblical grounds. The second form of fraud addressed could be translated "stealing" or "robbery," as Milgrom (1991:335-336) suggests, since the Hebrew implies
actual force is used in this crime. The third example is extortion, which also involved
force, taking advantage of the weak, whether poor (Prov 14:31), widowed, or
orphaned (Ezek 22:7) by subjecting them to tyranny (Isa 54:14, NIV). The claim that
this was acquisition in ways that were legal but immoral (Milgrom 1991:337; Hartley
1992:83) does not seem to fit the evidence. Extortion as a technical term indicates illegal activity (see, for example, its use associated with dishonest scales in Hos 12:7).

In the above cases there could be no lack of knowledge: The act was intentional
(see 5:15). As well as bringing atonement before God through the expensive offering of a ram, the guilty party had to recompense in full plus 20 percent to satisfy the
injured party. The high cost of the entire procedure would most likely deter the
person from trying the same thing again.

Israel did not have an unhealthy view that placed the sacred and secular in mutually exclusive spheres. While the sacred and secular are distinct, that is the result of
human sin (Gen 3), not of creation. The ultimate goal of history is to break down
this distinction, so that all things may be holy (Zech 14:20-21; cf. Eph 2:14). A strict
splitting of the two spheres was as unhealthy for Israel as it is for us, in that it
becomes easy to think that what I do in the "secular" sphere does not touch my relationship with God, for example, the thought that I can do whatever I feel like in
business, but can still come glibly to worship God. This approach is denied implicitly by the melding of sacred and secular in the Ten Commandments (Exod 20; Deut
5) and the other Israelite law codes. It was explicitly condemned by the prophets, as
when Amos said that the vertical relationship—worship of God—was impossible
without the horizontal—justice and righteousness in dealing with one's neighbor
(see especially Amos 5:21-24). Jesus himself taught that the vertical was hindered if
the horizontal was broken, and he instructed the worshiper to make the necessary
amends no matter who was ultimately at fault (Matt 5:23-24; 18:15). Among other

important implications of this truth is that there was no distinction in Israel between a crime (a civil, "secular" wrong) and a sin (a wrong against the "sacred"). When a person harms another, he also attacks God.

The sacrifice called for here was a ram, whose blood was applied to the altar, bringing atonement. The meat was for the priests (7:6-7). In one instance, the "Suffering Servant" passage in Isaiah 53:10, a human life was sanctioned by God as a guilt offering. Though blood is not mentioned in the Isaiah passage, it is implied in the mention of slaughter and death (Isa 53:7-8). The New Testament applies this language to the blood of Jesus, who takes away the sin of the world (Eph 2:13; Heb 9:14; 12:24; 13:12; 1 Pet 1:2, 19; 1 John 1:7; Rev 1:5; cf. John 1:29). Through it, transgressions between neighbors and between people and God are atoned for. Jesus made full compensation at no cost to the trespasser. Unrestricted worship and fellowship have been restored.

◆   ## C. Instructions for the Priests about Offerings (6:8–7:34)
1. Burnt offerings (6:8–13)

⁸*Then the LORD said to Moses, ⁹"Give Aaron and his sons the following instructions regarding the burnt offering. The burnt offering must be left on top of the altar until the next morning, and the fire on the altar must be kept burning all night. ¹⁰In the morning, after the priest on duty has put on his official linen clothing and linen undergarments, he must clean out the ashes of the burnt offering and put them beside the altar. ¹¹Then he must take off these garments, change back into his regular clothes, and carry the ashes outside the camp to a place that is ceremonially clean. ¹²Meanwhile, the fire on the altar must be kept burning; it must never go out. Each morning the priest will add fresh wood to the fire and arrange the burnt offering on it. He will then burn the fat of the peace offerings on it. ¹³Remember, the fire must be kept burning on the altar at all times. It must never go out.

6:8 Verses 6:8-30 are numbered 6:1-23 in Hebrew text.

NOTES
6:9 [2] *on top of the altar.* Lit., "on the hearth, on the altar." The hearth would be the place on the top of the altar where the red-hot coals would have rested (Ps 102:3; Isa 33:14), as opposed to the horns or sides of the altar, which were used in other ritual activities.

6:10 [3] *linen.* This fabric made from flax fibers breathes well, allowing the officiating priest to keep from perspiring (Ezek 44:18).

COMMENTARY
The earlier chapters of Leviticus detailed the who, when, and how as well as the results of the sacrifices. These chapters were directed toward all Israel (1:2; 4:2), providing a handbook mainly for the laity, with ritual actions required of priest and people. This handbook is followed by instructions concerning what was to be done with the sacrificial material once the sacrifice itself had been performed. Both the priests (6:9) and the nation as a whole (7:23, 29) had responsibilities, though the

main actors and the direct beneficiaries were the priests. There is also additional ritual information for the priests not included in the previous chapters, so these chapters were their ritual handbook. Any repetition between 1:1–6:7 and this section is due to the material's relevance to two different audiences.

The section begins with Moses being told to pass God's revelation along to Aaron and his sons (6:8-9), who soon would be the Israelite priesthood (ch 8). The nature of what he was to pass along is described as "instructions" (*torah* [TH8451, ZH9368]), coming from the same Hebrew word used to describe the Pentateuch, the law of Moses (Deut 4:8; Josh 1:8; 8:34; Neh 8:14). This *torah* was not restricted to ritual instruction, as it is in this verse, nor is it a negative description of restrictive practices, as we often seem to view the word "law" today. Rather, it concerns all aspects of teaching coming from God (Prov 6:23; Mal 2:7-8), the Creator of the universe, on how to live as part of his creation to the greatest advantage (cf. Prov 29:18, NIV).

In addition to the occasional burnt offerings brought by individual Israelites, there were also daily sacrifices offered morning and evening. These were burnt offerings and grain offerings for the people as a whole (Exod 29:38-46; Num 28:1-8). The daily evening sacrifice is the subject of 6:9 (cf. 2 Kgs 16:15; Ezra 9:4-5; Dan 9:21). The daily morning ritual is mentioned elsewhere as a reminder for God's people to spend time in prayer and communion with God (cf. Ps 5:3), who not only wants to provide atonement for his people but take care of all their needs (see Ps 103:3-6).

Since the burnt offering was dedicated in its entirety to God, further details were provided to make sure this took place correctly. All that was burnable must be consumed, so the fire was kept blazing perpetually, and the sacrifice itself was to be on the altar long enough to be incinerated. Even the hottest fire could not destroy everything, so the remaining ashes needed to be treated appropriately. The glow of the perpetual fire and the constantly rising smoke would have reminded Israel of the perpetual need for atonement and its constant availability. This knowledge was to stimulate perpetual worship.

The translation "hearth" (NASB, NIV, NRSV) instead of "altar" (see note on 6:9) is appropriate since it, like that of many households of times gone by, would have had a fire constantly burning to welcome visitors and family members. God, too, "kept a light on" for his people. It was to burn day and night (cf. 24:1-2, regarding the constantly burning lamp within the sanctuary), necessitating a commitment of the people to provide wood for the fire, either directly, as probably would have happened while in the wilderness, or through a tax for sanctuary support (Neh 10:32-39). For Christians, this serves as a good reminder of the constant presence of God with us through the Spirit. Unlike the presence of the Spirit in the Old Testament, which came upon people (1 Sam 10:10; 16:13) and then could depart (1 Sam 16:14), God's presence is permanently with all believers through the Holy Spirit (Matt 28:20; Acts 2:4).

The priests were reminded of the sacredness of the place and their duty by wearing special clothes (Exod 28:39-42), which, besides being visually distinct from their daily garb, would be cooler in proximity to the burning altar (Ezek 44:15-19).

In the worship of the Lord, form and function are both important. Also, in the service of God, no task, even cleanup, is trivial; everything is sacred and requires care and diligence (cf. 1 Cor 12:21-25).

◆ ## 2. Grain offerings (6:14-18)

14"These are the instructions regarding the grain offering. Aaron's sons must present this offering to the LORD in front of the altar. 15The priest on duty will take from the grain offering a handful of the choice flour moistened with olive oil, together with all the frankincense. He will burn this representative portion on the altar as a pleasing aroma to the LORD. 16Aaron and his sons may eat the rest of the flour, but it must be baked without yeast and eaten in a sacred place within the courtyard of the Tabernacle.* 17Remember, it must never be prepared with yeast. I have given it to the priests as their share of the special gifts presented to me. Like the sin offering and the guilt offering, it is most holy. 18Any of Aaron's male descendants may eat from the special gifts presented to the LORD. This is their permanent right from generation to generation. Anyone or anything that touches these offerings will become holy."

6:16 Hebrew *Tent of Meeting;* also in 6:26, 30.

NOTES
6:18 [11] *these offerings.* Lit., "them." This must refer to more than the singular grain offering. Likely, it refers to the priestly food portions of the guilt and sin offerings as well as the grain offering, to which the latter is compared in 6:10 (cf. Ezek 46:20).

COMMENTARY
Further regulations were needed for the grain offering. What is presented here is just one of the possible preparation options, namely that of the unbaked flour (cf. 2:1-3). This could represent all of the other grain offerings listed in chapter 2 as well. There it was simply stated that the unburned portion of grain was given to the priest for food (2:3, 10). Here they received further directions on preparation. This offering was usable in part by the male priests, since only they performed the ritual acts and regularly worked in the Tabernacle precincts. It was still "most holy," dedicated in the first instance to God, as were the sin (6:25) and guilt (7:5-6) offerings. If baked, it could still be only without yeast since leaven, with its fermentation process, was forbidden for the grain offering (2:11), and this was a portion of that same offering. Leaven could not be used by the priests even after control and use of the offering had passed over to them. It was also to be eaten in a special, sacred place. The sin offering was to be disposed of in a "place outside the camp that is ceremonially clean" (4:12), while the priestly portion was to be eaten in a sacred or holy place within the Tabernacle precinct. Since it was among the "most holy" things, it had to stay in a holy, not just clean, environment. There could have been a smaller dining area within the courtyard of the Tabernacle, but the Hebrew most naturally indicates that the holy place and the court are identical. This could have been eaten anywhere within it, just not taken outside into the camp itself.

Priestly use of portions of the offerings was a grace from God, not a right to be expected and exploited (contra the view of some officiants, 1 Sam 2:12-17). This is still important today for those who receive provision from gifts given to God. Clergy or professional religious workers need to be mindful of "whose we are and whom we serve," and also through whose grace we receive provision. Paul exemplifies the correct attitude in his thankfulness to God for the gifts he received through the Philippians (Phil 4:18). Their gift, while not of grain, was still viewed as a sweet-smelling sacrifice.

This offering involves one of the rare instances where ritual purity was transmitted by contact with something (6:18, 27; Exod 29:37; 30:26-29; Ezek 44:19; 46:20; cf. also Mark 5:24-34). More commonly, contamination was passed on through contact (e.g., 11:33-40; 15:3-12, 19-27; cf. Hag 2:12-13).

◆   ## 3. Grain offering for ordination of priests (6:19–23)

[19]Then the LORD said to Moses, [20]"On the day Aaron and his sons are anointed, they must present to the LORD a grain offering of two quarts* of choice flour, half to be offered in the morning and half to be offered in the evening. [21]It must be carefully mixed with olive oil and cooked on a griddle. Then slice* this grain offering and present it as a pleasing aroma to the LORD. [22]In each generation, the high priest* who succeeds Aaron must prepare this same offering. It belongs to the LORD and must be burned up completely. This is a permanent law. [23]All such grain offerings of a priest must be burned up entirely. None of it may be eaten."

6:20 Hebrew *1/10 of an ephah* [2.2 liters].   **6:21** The meaning of this Hebrew term is uncertain.   **6:22** Hebrew *the anointed priest.*

NOTES

6:20 [13] *anointed.* The Hebrew here is the verb form of the well-known Hebrew title "Messiah" (*mashiakh* [TH4899, ZH5431]) and is parallel to the verb form of the Greek *Christos* [TG5547, ZG5986]. Both Messiah and Christ mean "anointed one." The anointing was done with oil to symbolize the elevation of the person to a new position such as priest or king (2 Sam 5:3).

a grain offering. Though not mentioned in the NLT, the grain offering mentioned in this verse is called a "continual" or "perpetual" possession of God. This refers either to continuous actions (6:13; Exod 27:20); regular, daily events (Num 4:16); or a regular event that had no fixed frequency, such as the inauguration of a new high priest, which fits this context. Since there was an ordination offering for priests elsewhere (ch 8), which had differences from this, it appears more likely that this is a daily priestly offering (Levine 1989:39; Milgrom 1991:399), starting on the day when a priest is anointed (Wenham 1979:122).

COMMENTARY

Many significant events in life, such as births, graduations, weddings, and promotions are marked by specific rituals in order to set the event apart from the mundane and ordinary. This passage depicts the special transition day for a priest when he moved from being common and ordinary to being set apart for the service of God (10:10). One of the regular grain offerings (2:5-6) was used for this special event.

This grain offering was different from the sacrifices explained in earlier chapters (cf. also 16:6, 11) because this grain offering was to be completely consumed by fire. When the priest performed rituals for other Israelites, some of the sacrificial material was for his personal or clan use, but this luxury was not available when he was sacrificing on his own behalf (Heb 5:3; 7:27). Everything was to be given to God by burning it completely. This would save the priest from a conflict of interest that would arise if he could "have his sacrifice and eat it, too."

◆   ## 4. Sin and guilt offerings (6:24–7:10)

²⁴Then the LORD said to Moses, ²⁵"Give Aaron and his sons the following instructions regarding the sin offering. The animal given as an offering for sin is a most holy offering, and it must be slaughtered in the LORD's presence at the place where the burnt offerings are slaughtered. ²⁶The priest who offers the sacrifice as a sin offering must eat his portion in a sacred place within the courtyard of the Tabernacle. ²⁷Anyone or anything that touches the sacrificial meat will become holy. If any of the sacrificial blood spatters on a person's clothing, the soiled garment must be washed in a sacred place. ²⁸If a clay pot is used to boil the sacrificial meat, it must then be broken. If a bronze pot is used, it must be scoured and thoroughly rinsed with water. ²⁹Any male from a priest's family may eat from this offering; it is most holy. ³⁰But the offering for sin may not be eaten if its blood was brought into the Tabernacle as an offering for purification* in the Holy Place. It must be completely burned with fire.

CHAPTER 7

¹These are the instructions for the guilt offering. It is most holy. ²The animal sacrificed as a guilt offering must be slaughtered at the place where the burnt offerings are slaughtered, and its blood must be splattered against all sides of the altar. ³The priest will then offer all its fat on the altar, including the fat of the broad tail, the fat around the internal organs, ⁴the two kidneys and the fat around them near the loins, and the long lobe of the liver. These are to be removed with the kidneys, ⁵and the priests will burn them on the altar as a special gift presented to the LORD. This is the guilt offering. ⁶Any male from a priest's family may eat the meat. It must be eaten in a sacred place, for it is most holy.

⁷"The same instructions apply to both the guilt offering and the sin offering. Both belong to the priest who uses them to purify someone, making that person right with the LORD.* ⁸In the case of the burnt offering, the priest may keep the hide of the sacrificed animal. ⁹Any grain offering that has been baked in an oven, prepared in a pan, or cooked on a griddle belongs to the priest who presents it. ¹⁰All other grain offerings, whether made of dry flour or flour moistened with olive oil, are to be shared equally among all the priests, the descendants of Aaron.

6:30 Or *an offering to make atonement.*   7:7 Or *to make atonement.*

NOTES

7:8 *burnt offering.* Lit., "burnt offering for a person." The Hebrew indicates that the priest would be making the offering on behalf of someone else. If he did this on his own behalf, the entire sacrifice would need to be burned as was the case in 6:23, 30.

the priest may keep the hide. This was valuable payment for the priest, one of longer-lasting value than the meat, which needed to be quickly eaten.

COMMENTARY

In the first paragraph of this section (6:24-30) further details are provided for the sin (4:1–5:13) and guilt (5:14–6:7) offering rituals. These are details related to the priestly officiant who needed to take care that the offering's sanctity was protected. This passage indicates that Leviticus 1–7 was designed to be a reference manual, since it cross-references the previously detailed burnt offering (6:25; 7:2; cf. 1:11).

The priests were able to eat part of the sacrifice, except when the sin offering was given on behalf of the entire nation (6:30), of which they were a part. In that case, the entire sacrifice was burnt (cf. 6:23). Things touching the sacrifice or its blood became holy and were to be specially treated before they could be reused. Items that could be were thoroughly washed (cf. Mark 7:4), while unfired pottery, which was porous and thus absorbed things cooked in it, needed to be destroyed.

The second paragraph of this section (7:1-10) provides a summary list of the priests' portions from each of the offerings that have been mentioned since 6:8. It gives some new information, since disposal of the burnt offering's hide was not previously mentioned, nor that of the grain offering apart from the raw flour mixed with oil (6:15). Since these offerings were so frequent, occurring daily (Num 28:3), the priests would have been very rich in hides (Milgrom 1991:411). The reason for the distinction in use between cooked and uncooked grain is not clear. To say that only the officiating priest could eat of the cooked grain is contrary to 2:10. Milgrom (1991:412) suggests that this was an indication that the officiant could distribute this portion among his fellows.

All in all, this section teaches us that priests were dependent on the offerings of the people for their livelihood. This teaching is supported in the Old Testament (Deut 25:4) and in the New Testament by Jesus and by Paul (Luke 10:7; 1 Tim 5:18). The servant of God is worthy of his wages.

◆   5. Peace offerings (7:11-34)

[11]"These are the instructions regarding the different kinds of peace offerings that may be presented to the LORD. [12]If you present your peace offering as an expression of thanksgiving, the usual animal sacrifice must be accompanied by various kinds of bread made without yeast—thin cakes mixed with olive oil, wafers spread with oil, and cakes made of choice flour mixed with olive oil. [13]This peace offering of thanksgiving must also be accompanied by loaves of bread made with yeast. [14]One of each kind of bread must be presented as a gift to the LORD. It will then belong to the priest who splatters the blood of the peace offering against the altar. [15]The meat of the peace offering of thanksgiving must be eaten on the same day it is offered. None of it may be saved for the next morning.

[16]"If you bring an offering to fulfill a vow or as a voluntary offering, the meat must be eaten on the same day the sacrifice is offered, but whatever is left over may be eaten on the second day. [17]Any meat left over until the third day must be completely burned up. [18]If any of the meat from the peace offering is eaten on the third day, the person who presented it will not be accepted by the LORD. You will receive no credit for offering it. By then the meat will be contaminated; if you eat it, you will be punished for your sin.

¹⁹"Meat that touches anything ceremonially unclean may not be eaten; it must be completely burned up. The rest of the meat may be eaten, but only by people who are ceremonially clean. ²⁰If you are ceremonially unclean and you eat meat from a peace offering that was presented to the LORD, you will be cut off from the community. ²¹If you touch anything that is unclean (whether it is human defilement or an unclean animal or any other unclean, detestable thing) and then eat meat from a peace offering presented to the LORD, you will be cut off from the community."

²²Then the LORD said to Moses, ²³"Give the following instructions to the people of Israel. You must never eat fat, whether from cattle, sheep, or goats. ²⁴The fat of an animal found dead or torn to pieces by wild animals must never be eaten, though it may be used for any other purpose. ²⁵Anyone who eats fat from an animal presented as a special gift to the LORD will be cut off from the community. ²⁶No matter where you live, you must never consume the blood of any bird or animal. ²⁷Anyone who consumes blood will be cut off from the community."

²⁸Then the LORD said to Moses, ²⁹"Give the following instructions to the people of Israel. When you present a peace offering to the LORD, bring part of it as a gift to the LORD. ³⁰Present it to the LORD with your own hands as a special gift to the LORD. Bring the fat of the animal, together with the breast, and lift up the breast as a special offering to the LORD. ³¹Then the priest will burn the fat on the altar, but the breast will belong to Aaron and his descendants. ³²Give the right thigh of your peace offering to the priest as a gift. ³³The right thigh must always be given to the priest who offers the blood and the fat of the peace offering. ³⁴For I have reserved the breast of the special offering and the right thigh of the sacred offering for the priests. It is the permanent right of Aaron and his descendants to share in the peace offerings brought by the people of Israel.

NOTES

7:14 *presented as a gift to the LORD.* This offering, called "a gift" (*terumah* [TH8641, ZH9556]), was previously thought by translators and commentators to be something physically raised up to God as part of the ritual ("heave offering," KJV). It has now been shown through comparative language study that it is understood as a gift or contribution (cf. NASB, NIV, NRSV).

7:18 *contaminated.* This is a term used of consecrated meat that had passed its "use-by" date (19:7; the same word is used in Isa 65:4 and Ezek 4:14); the verb to which it is related means "to rot" (Wenham 1979:124). It is a different term than simple ceremonial uncleanness (see commentary on 5:2).

7:21 *an unclean animal or any other unclean, detestable thing.* The Hebrew has "unclean four-legged animals" (see "land animals" in 11:2) and "unclean abominable things," for which some manuscripts read "swarming creatures" (a one-letter difference in Hebrew; cf. Gen 1:20). This prohibition anticipates the fuller discussion in ch 11.

7:30 *lift up the breast as a special offering.* The term *tenupah* [TH8573, ZH9485] was translated as "wave offering" in KJV because the verb (*nup* [TH5130, ZH5677]) indicates brandishing or moving something back and forth (2 Kgs 5:11; Isa 10:15). The actual priestly actions are unknown, though we do have illustrations from Mesopotamia of what appear to be drink offerings lifted up to a god.

7:32 *right thigh.* The thigh may have been given special honor due to its proximity to the reproductive organs, which symbolize continuity of life (Péter-Contesse and Ellington 1990:104). The right could have been chosen due to its relative strength and dominance in most people (see 8:23-26).

COMMENTARY

This section introduces three subcategories of peace offerings for different occasions of celebration, though not all of the details are clear. More description concerning the occasions is provided here than there is in chapter 3, which deals with the offering material. A major element is the quickness with which the offering must be eaten. As already mentioned (see ch 3 and discussion there), the peace offering was a special time of joyful communion between the offering priest, God, and the offerer, since the latter was able to eat part of it (7:11-15). Since the priestly portion is singled out in 7:14, and God's portions in 3:3-4, 9-10, and 14-15, this means the offerer was the one who partook of the remainder.

This thanksgiving sacrifice was presented as a spontaneous response to a beneficial, though here unspecified, action by God (cf. 2 Chr 29:30-33; Jer 17:26). It was a gift to God (*terumah* [TH8641, ZH9556]) given at a worshiper's own free will (Exod 25:2). In addition to bread, it could also be money (Exod 35:24), the thigh of a peace offering (7:32), a cake (Num 15:19-20), or Israel's tithes (Num 18:24, 26). The offering was accompanied by a baked grain offering (cf. 2:4), a similar practice to that followed at the priestly dedication (8:26-28) and at the completion of a Nazirite vow (Num 6:15, 19). Each of these three cases celebrates a special closeness to God. The inclusion of yeast bread distinguished this from the regular grain offering, where yeast was banned (2:5, 11; cf. 7:12).

The vow referred to in 7:16-21 was made when a person promised to do something if God answered a prayer (cf. 27:2; 2 Sam 15:7-8; Prov 7:14; cf. Gen 28:18-22; 1 Sam 1:11, 25-28). A freewill offering (22:21, 23) was a spontaneous offering of celebration arising from the heart of the worshiper (Exod 35:29). Later in Israel's existence a whole burnt offering could be called a freewill offering (Ezek 46:12), as could a financial gift (Ezra 8:28).

Vow fulfillment and freewill offerings differed from the thanksgiving offering in that they did not include the grain offering and that they could be eaten within two days, while the thanksgiving offering must be eaten on the day of the sacrifice. This haste in eating could have been for health considerations, since preservation and storage were a problem (cf. Exod 16:20). It could also force the offerer to share his celebration with others, making his communion circle wider since he would not be able to eat it all himself within the allotted time.

Whatever the reason for not delaying consumption, a wrong step here was serious since it not only invalidated the sacrifice but also brought judgment upon the wrongdoer. This person would have to take personal responsibility for the action (7:18, cf. 5:1), which included being "cut off from the community" (7:20-21; cf. Gen 17:14). This expression is used only of wrongs punishable by God (see Milgrom 1991:458 for a list, 457-460 for a discussion). It is considered by some to be a euphemism for death (Wenham 1979:242). This would fit in some cases, as when people who committed forbidden sexual relationships are said to be punished by being cut off from the community and then said to die—the terms are used interchangeably (cf. 20:17-18 with numerous other verses in that chapter). Even more severe is an understanding that being cut off also involved bringing the family line of the wrongdoer to an end (Milgrom 1991:459). Another interpretation is that the person was banished, separated from the people, which could find support in the alternative forms "be cut off from the people" and "from among the people" (20:3, 6, 17), the latter indicating separation. One could also be cut off from God's presence (22:3), or at least from his blessing. Since we accept that God is omnipresent, it would not be possible to be actually removed from his presence, unless what is meant is disallowing access to the special place of his presence, the Israelite shrine or the camp itself. In Leviticus, coming to God regularly signifies coming to the Tabernacle (1:2-3), so separation from him could also be understood as banishment from Tabernacle worship. Whatever it meant, it was especially serious for a people where family and community were central to one's existence.

The modern West seems to operate under the illusion that "we can go it alone," a sentiment that goes against God's creation of humanity in need of community (Gen 2:18). While many live today separated from family and close relationships, it is surely at a cost. Ostracism and shunning were also used as a means of punishment in the early church (Matt 18:15-20). There, as in the Leviticus situation, restoration of a repentant wrongdoer rather than his irremediable punishment was the ultimate goal.

In 7:22-27, further instructions are given as to what was impermissible to eat. This parenthetical section is connected with the previous passage in that it arises from the discussion of what was permissible for the priests to eat from the offerings. Instructions about eating, therefore, were extended by association to any occasion for eating meat by anyone. As such, Moses was instructed to pass along God's revelation, which concerned all the people (cf. 1:2) and not just the priests (cf. 6:25). Meat consumption would have been a luxury for most Israelites were it not for the peace or fellowship offerings. Regulations for their use were given in discussion of that offering (7:11-21), but further elaboration came here, applying to any meat, wherever it might be consumed. Fat and blood were prohibited earlier in the context of the peace offering (3:17). While the wording there seems to be for a universal ban, this becomes detailed and even more explicit here. The detail includes various sources of animal fat, a more widespread ban as to location (not only at the sanctuary but also at home, again breaking down sacred/secular boundaries), and also the consequent punishment.

Eating the fat of sacrificial animals and those unsuitable for sacrifice due to blemish was banned, though not so for other household uses, such as lamp oil or for polishing. Apparently the fat of other animals permissible for eating could be consumed (see Deut 12:20-25), since only consumption of their blood was specifically prohibited (Milgrom 1991:427).

Following the parenthetical instructions regarding fat and blood (7:22-25), requirements for the peace offering were picked up from 7:11-21. The instructions continued to be directed to all of Israel, who were told to provide for the support of the priests. These instructions indicate that personal involvement was required for the offerer (cf. 1:4; 3:2, 8, 12), who symbolically handed the breast, a choice cut of meat, to God by lifting it up (7:30). This offering could involve flesh (Exod 29:26), grain (23:15, 17), mixed offerings of flesh and grain (Exod 29:24; Num 6:19-20), money (Exod 38:24), and even the dedication of people (Num 8:11, 13). The latter case in particular indicates that any "lifting up" was symbolic of presentation to God, though it could also indicate literal lifting. The breast and the other prime cut, the thigh (1 Sam 9:23-24), became the property of the officiating priests. It is good to note that the Lord's servants, who were also servants of the people in ministering to them, were not given the dregs and leftovers, but choice cuts, the desirable portions.

◆　　**D. Concluding Formulae (7:35-38)**
　　　1. Conclusion of the priests' instructions (7:35-36)

³⁵This is their rightful share. The special gifts presented to the LORD have been reserved for Aaron and his descendants from the time they were set apart to serve the LORD as priests. ³⁶On the day they were anointed, the LORD commanded the Israelites to give these portions to the priests as their permanent share from generation to generation."

NOTES

7:35 share. This word occurs only here and in Num 18:8, where it is vocalized differently. The root is the same as "anoint" (7:36), which has led to difficulty in interpretation (see Vulgate, KJV, ASV), but other Semitic languages have a word of the same root meaning "measure out" (Milgrom 1991:433; Hartley 1992:101). The idea of a measured portion fits well in this context, and there is a bit of wordplay with the homonymous root in this and the next verses.

COMMENTARY

Many ancient Near Eastern documents have a concluding formula called a colophon that summarizes the document and provides information about it (Baker 1986). It is possible that remnants of two colophons conclude this text, one ending the portion concerning priestly instructions (6:8–7:34), and the other the entire passage dealing with sacrifices and offerings (1:1–6:7, or possibly 1:1–7:34). It is unclear why there are two apparent colophons here, with none closing other subsections of these chapters. As it stands, they draw this section to a close as a self-contained unit before turning to other items that were more strictly relevant to the priests. No other such compound colophons are known from ancient Near Eastern sources.

Ancient Near Eastern colophons included several pieces of information and were somewhat similar to the material included at the front of the modern book (Baker 1986:48). While 7:37-38 follows the form of the colophon more closely (see commentary on those verses), there could also be one in 7:35-36. These verses contain the summarizing pronoun "this," a description of the text subject ("their ... share," 7:35a), the source person ("the LORD," 7:36a), the copyright date described in two ways ("from the time they were set apart," 7:35; "on the day they were anointed," 7:36), the literary genre or text type (lit., "this regulation," 7:36c), and the importance of preserving the command in writing ("from generation to generation," 7:36).

More general notes to the people as a whole included in this section were prompted by word or thought association (7:22-27) or refer mainly to the priests (7:28-34). Its genre as an eternal regulation (cf. 6:18) indicates its importance and the necessity for preserving it. This was in one way a canonical statement, an indication that the words became authoritative "Scripture" as soon as they were received, and their commitment to writing would logically follow soon after, at the latest within the lifetime of those receiving these instructions (Baker 1987). The source or "author" was Yahweh himself, and the material dated from the consecration of the priests by anointing (ch 8).

◆   ## 2. Conclusion of the handbook (7:37-38)

37These are the instructions for the burnt offering, the grain offering, the sin offering, and the guilt offering, as well as the ordination offering and the peace offering.

38The LORD gave these instructions to Moses on Mount Sinai when he commanded the Israelites to present their offerings to the LORD in the wilderness of Sinai.

NOTES
7:38 *wilderness of Sinai.* This is the land surrounding the mountain Moses had climbed to meet with God (Exod 19:1-2).

COMMENTARY
This colophon includes many significant elements. Its genre ("instructions," 6:25) is applied to the contents of the chapters with subsections identified by the offering names. The source or "author" is again Yahweh, but this time the scribe, Moses, is mentioned, as is the place where they were received (Mount Sinai, in the wilderness of Sinai). The date is also supplied.

There are several indicators that this colophon, and the section it describes, are very old. First, a colophon within the body text such as we find in Leviticus was rare, since ordinarily it came at the end of a document. This could be taken to indicate that these chapters were earlier than the ending of the book of Exodus, though the subject of the chapters fits more closely with what follows than with what precedes. Alternatively, the unit could well have circulated independently and been incorporated as a whole, including colophon, into the rest of Leviticus at a later date.

Another indication of age for both the passage and the colophon—and also of the care with which the scribes transmitted the text—is the inclusion of the "ordination offering" within the list of sacrifices (7:37). The name for this offering (*millu'im* [TH4394, ZH4854]; lit., "filling") is not used anywhere in the text of Leviticus 1:1–7:36 that we now have. It occurs in Exodus 29:22, 26-27, 31, 34 and in Leviticus 8:22-33. A reference in this verse without an identifiable referent could have arisen due to the title "ordination offering" having dropped from a previous section in the text, possibly from 6:19-23, at some time during its transmission. The NLT editors seem to take this position, since they give this heading to that section, even though the term is not in the text itself. Another possibility is that there was another complete ritual description for a separate ordination offering. This entire description could have totally dropped out of the text and so become unavailable to us. Or it could have been moved elsewhere (some suggest that what was originally here has moved to Exod 29). Either of these scenarios indicates that the colophon was ancient in its original composition, as is the text it describes, which predated the time when the name or section connected to "ordination" dropped out or moved. It is most likely that it was an integral part of the section when it was originally penned. This shows that the scribes were very careful to transmit exactly what they had in their possession. They could not take it upon themselves to alter the text, even though it was clear that something was missing here, and they could, if they so chose, have easily left out the name of this one missing offering. This extreme care in transmitting (not adding to or correcting an obviously flawed text) is evident elsewhere as well. Just one example of this is 1 Samuel 13:1, where several words have been lost but the ancient scribes passed along the flawed text before them rather than attempting to reconstruct it, as most modern translators do (see NLT and its footnotes). Since these scribes were charged with preserving and transmitting the very words of God, the scribes saw their task as being theologically significant, and not just a job—they did not think it within their right to suggest what a text might have said prior to its being in some way damaged in transmission. This extreme care supports the confidence with which readers today can read the biblical text.

◆ II. The Institution of the Priesthood (8:1–10:20)
   A. The Ordination of Priests (8:1-36)

Then the LORD said to Moses, ²"Bring Aaron and his sons, along with their sacred garments, the anointing oil, the bull for the sin offering, the two rams, and the basket of bread made without yeast, ³and call the entire community of Israel together at the entrance of the Tabernacle.*"

⁴So Moses followed the LORD's instructions, and the whole community assembled at the Tabernacle entrance. ⁵Moses announced to them, "This is what the LORD has commanded us to do!" ⁶Then he presented Aaron and his sons and washed them with water. ⁷He put the official tunic on Aaron and tied the sash around his waist. He dressed him in the robe, placed the ephod on him, and attached the ephod securely with its decorative sash. ⁸Then Moses placed the chestpiece on Aaron and put the Urim and the Thummim inside it. ⁹He placed the turban on Aaron's head and attached the gold medallion—the badge of holiness—to the front of the turban, just as the LORD had commanded him.

¹⁰Then Moses took the anointing oil and anointed the Tabernacle and everything in it, making them holy. ¹¹He sprinkled the oil on the altar seven times, anointing it and all its utensils, as well as the washbasin and its stand, making them holy. ¹²Then he poured some of the anointing oil on Aaron's head, anointing him and making him holy for his work. ¹³Next Moses presented Aaron's sons. He clothed them in their tunics, tied their sashes around them, and put their special head coverings on them, just as the LORD had commanded him.

¹⁴Then Moses presented the bull for the sin offering. Aaron and his sons laid their hands on the bull's head, ¹⁵and Moses

slaughtered it. Moses took some of the blood, and with his finger he put it on the four horns of the altar to purify it. He poured out the rest of the blood at the base of the altar. Through this process, he made the altar holy by purifying it.* ¹⁶Then Moses took all the fat around the internal organs, the long lobe of the liver, and the two kidneys and the fat around them, and he burned it all on the altar. ¹⁷He took the rest of the bull, including its hide, meat, and dung, and burned it on a fire outside the camp, just as the LORD had commanded him.

¹⁸Then Moses presented the ram for the burnt offering. Aaron and his sons laid their hands on the ram's head, ¹⁹and Moses slaughtered it. Then Moses took the ram's blood and splattered it against all sides of the altar. ²⁰Then he cut the ram into pieces, and he burned the head, some of its pieces, and the fat on the altar. ²¹After washing the internal organs and the legs with water, Moses burned the entire ram on the altar as a burnt offering. It was a pleasing aroma, a special gift presented to the LORD, just as the LORD had commanded him.

²²Then Moses presented the other ram, which was the ram of ordination. Aaron and his sons laid their hands on the ram's head, ²³and Moses slaughtered it. Then Moses took some of its blood and applied it to the lobe of Aaron's right ear, the thumb of his right hand, and the big toe of his right foot. ²⁴Next Moses presented Aaron's sons and applied some of the blood to the lobes of their right ears, the thumbs of their right hands, and the big toes of their right feet. He then splattered the rest of the blood against all sides of the altar.

²⁵Next Moses took the fat, including the fat of the broad tail, the fat around the internal organs, the long lobe of the liver, and the two kidneys and the fat around them, along with the right thigh. ²⁶On top

of these he placed a thin cake of bread made without yeast, a cake of bread mixed with olive oil, and a wafer spread with olive oil. All these were taken from the basket of bread made without yeast that was placed in the LORD's presence. ²⁷He put all these in the hands of Aaron and his sons, and he lifted them up as a special offering to the LORD. ²⁸Moses then took all the offerings back from them and burned them on the altar on top of the burnt offering. This was the ordination offering. It was a pleasing aroma, a special gift presented to the LORD. ²⁹Then Moses took the breast and lifted it up as a special offering to the LORD. This was Moses' portion of the ram of ordination, just as the LORD had commanded him.

³⁰Next Moses took some of the anointing oil and some of the blood that was on the altar, and he sprinkled them on Aaron and his garments and on his sons and their garments. In this way, he made Aaron and his sons and their garments holy.

³¹Then Moses said to Aaron and his sons, "Boil the remaining meat of the offerings at the Tabernacle entrance, and eat it there, along with the bread that is in the basket of offerings for the ordination, just as I commanded when I said, 'Aaron and his sons will eat it.' ³²Any meat or bread that is left over must then be burned up. ³³You must not leave the Tabernacle entrance for seven days, for that is when the ordination ceremony will be completed. ³⁴Everything we have done today was commanded by the LORD in order to purify you, making you right with him.* ³⁵Now stay at the entrance of the Tabernacle day and night for seven days, and do everything the LORD requires. If you fail to do this, you will die, for this is what the LORD has commanded." ³⁶So Aaron and his sons did everything the LORD had commanded through Moses.

8:3 Hebrew *Tent of Meeting;* also in 8:4, 31, 33, 35.   8:15 Or *by making atonement for it;* or *that offerings for purification might be made on it.*   8:34 Or *to make atonement for you.*

NOTES

8:7 *ephod*. The appearance of the ephod is unclear, as is indicated by scholars' inability even to translate the term confidently into English. Thus, the word is usually transliterated "ephod," as here in the NLT.

8:8 *Urim and the Thummim*. Like "ephod," these are transliterations rather than translations. These were part of the official clothing of the high priest. Their exact nature is so unclear that the two words are not really translated even in the LXX. Instead, the LXX interprets them as "Revelation and Truth" from the root ideas of the Hebrew *'urim* [TH224, ZH242] (lights) and *tummim* [TH8550, ZH9460] (perfections). They were small objects stored inside the chestpiece (Exod 28:30). They were probably small stones or other objects that could be thrown, something like dice or lots (e.g., 16:8; Matt 27:35). They were used for oracles, directions received from God regarding choices to be made (Num 27:21; 1 Sam 28:6).

8:9 *turban . . . the gold medallion—the badge of holiness*. The purpose of the turban is not explained, apart from it being the bearer of a gold medallion (*tsits* [TH6731, ZH7488]), also called "the badge of holiness." Words related to the root *tsuts* [TH6692, ZH7437] are translated "flower" in other passages (Num 17:8; Isa 40:6-8), so the medallion was possibly flower shaped or decorated with flower motifs.

8:10 *making them holy*. Or "setting them apart" (*qadash* [TH6942, ZH7727]). An equivalent English term is "sanctify." This meant to remove from common, everyday use and reserve for special, divine use (e.g., Gen 2:3), such as use at the sanctuary (1 Kgs 9:3). This could include both things and people, such as holy bread that could be eaten only by holy soldiers (1 Sam 21:4-5).

8:11 *altar . . . washbasin*. Special mention is made of the altar, on which the sacrifices would soon be made, and of the washbasin. This was the bronze water container that stood between the burnt offering altar and the door of the Tabernacle proper (Exod 30:18). The priests were to wash their hands and feet with water from this basin before ministering in the Tabernacle. The washbasin, made holy in this verse, might have been what was used for the preparatory washing for this ceremony (8:6).

8:23 *right ear . . . right hand . . . right foot*. Owing to the preponderance of right-handedness, right seems to be the favored side in numerous contexts. It was the place of special blessing (Gen 48:13-18), symbolizing God's power (Exod 15:6, 12; Ps 118:15; cf. Matt 27:29), and was a special place of honor and assistance (2 Kgs 12:9; Isa 63:12; Matt 25:33-34; 26:64). The right hand was extended in greeting (2 Sam 20:9) and raised in joy (Ps 89:42, KJV). Its prominence is also shown in the biblical stock pair "right and left," in which the right always precedes. This precedence carried over into priestly ritual (see 7:32-33; 14:14-28).

8:33 *ordination ceremony*. Lit., "filling," and the ceremony consisted of literally "filling the hand." This usually indicated ordination of the priesthood (Exod 28:41) or the Levites (Exod 32:29; Num 3:3). From the OT it is not clear what filled the hand, though sacrificial material had been placed in the priest's hands during this ceremony (8:27). In Akkadian, the language of neighboring Mesopotamia (present-day Iraq), the same term was used in a ceremony where a king was installed and a scepter placed in his hands (Milgrom 1991:539).

COMMENTARY

Following the general instructions on how the ritual system of sacrifice and offering was to work (chs 1-7), there comes a section on how to prepare the personnel who would make it all happen. The best-laid plans in business or the church cannot come to adequate fruition without someone prepared and equipped to carry it all out. In the case of Israel, these trained people were the priests, the descendants of Aaron, whom God had already set aside for this job. (See Exod 28–29, where there are many similarities to the rituals found here.)

Chapters 8–10 appear to form a narrative in the midst of a record of regulations. It is not the case, however, that stories interrupted laws, but rather the reverse. The story of slavery, the Exodus, and a national covenant with God was the setting in which the laws were revealed. Rather than the laws being simply a list of regulations with no context, the stories show the circumstances that gave birth to the laws, providing living flesh and sinews to the legal bones. It is important to remember, both in the case of God's dealing with his people in the past, as well as with his people today, that God first encounters his people in history, and only after a relationship has been established are the expectations derived from the relationship presented. Expectations follow encounter.

Early in human history, people were able to bring their own gifts and offerings directly to God, building their own altars and performing the rituals themselves (e.g., Cain and Abel, Gen 4:3-4; Noah, Gen 8:20-21; Abraham, Gen 12:7-8; 22:9; Isaac, Gen 26:25; Jacob, Gen 33:20; 35:1, 3), a practice that never completely disappeared (e.g., Gideon, Judg 6:25-27; David, 2 Sam 6:13; Elijah, 1 Kgs 18:30-38). While the involvement of individuals in the ritual process never disappeared, a special, skilled class, consisting of the priests and their assistants the Levites, took over the formal functions of the sacrificial system. Their official involvement was particularly associated with Israelite shrines, which were frequented by many worshipers and so involved numerous sacrifices (e.g., the Tabernacle in Exodus and Leviticus; Shiloh, 1 Sam 2:12-14; the Temple in Jerusalem, 2 Chr 29:20-24; DOTP 646-655; cf. 1 Kgs 12:31-32). Recent archaeological finds at Emar in Syria include texts that provide interesting parallels to the biblical priestly installation service in a Syrian installation of a priestess (Fleming 1992). Parallels include anointing with oil (8:12, 30), sacrificing sheep (8:18-29), the use of baked goods in the ceremonies (8:26-29), all in a ritual involving several different kinds of sacrifices whose main events cover seven days (8:35). The purpose and result of both rituals was sanctification, making the priest holy (8:10-12, 15, 30).

Leviticus 8:1-3 begins a new section wherein God reveals a new set of instructions to Moses (cf. similar section breaks, e.g., 1:1; 4:1; 5:14; 6:1, 8). Here the priests are designated and set apart as a special group within the nation of Israel in a public ceremony to which the entire population was invited. Everyone was to witness this consecration of a group that would represent them very directly in their later encounters with God. All the necessary material was gathered together ahead of time. This included the animals used in these offerings—a bull and two rams, which were among the more expensive offerings available.

Moses obeyed God's instructions and then passed his instructions on to the people, since this was a new ceremony they had never before experienced (8:4-9). This showed good leadership. The first ceremonial step, prior even to putting on their new clothes, was for the priests to be washed with water, removing any spiritual, as well as physical, dirt or uncleanness (14:8; 15:1-33; John 13:8). Unless one is clean, putting on clean clothes will not give the desired effect.

Not only would the priests stand out from their country folk through the ritual tasks they performed, they would also be different in their garb. This included not only the innermost undergarments, but the whole uniform, including the accompanying accessories. Today, as in the days of the Israelites, some people and professions, such as police officers and clerics, are set apart and identified by their special clothing.

The tunic (8:7), which became an object of value (Ezra 2:69; Neh 7:70, 72, where it is translated as "robe"), was made of fine linen (Exod 28:39; 39:27). It was the innermost priestly garment, itself covered by an outer robe or cloak. The sash was embroidered (Exod 28:39) with blue, purple, and scarlet thread (Exod 39:29). The blue, single-piece, woven, woolen robe (Exod 28:31-32) had a hole in the center for the head. The decorative sash was different from that mentioned earlier in the verse, which was to secure the innermost garment.

The under and outer robes are easy to visualize, but not so the ephod (see note on 8:7) It, like the sash, was fine linen, a very special cloth (cf. Rev 19:8), intricately worked with gold thread interwoven with blue, purple, and scarlet. It appears to have been a two-piece garment, joined at the shoulders and open at the sides, something like some coats of chain mail (Exod 28:6-7). A less elaborate model seems to have been worn by priests and sanctuary assistants (1 Sam 2:18; 22:18; 2 Sam 6:14) as if it were a recognized uniform of office. Something with the same name was also associated with receiving divine revelation (1 Sam 23:6, 9; Hos 3:4). In 1 Samuel 23, it was associated with a priest, but apparently was not regularly worn, since its presence needed to be specifically requested.

The chestpiece (8:8) was an added element placed outside the clothing. Made of the same material as the ephod (Exod 28:15), it was doubled over and contained 12 semiprecious stones, representing the 12 Israelite tribes (Exod 28:16-21). It also was involved in decision making (Exod 28:15) and was fastened to the ephod by gold cords. Possibly since it and the ephod were a unit, the revelatory function of the ephod was really that of the chestpiece, with the name "ephod" signifying both used together. The actual means of divine revelation were the Urim and the Thummim ('urim [TH224, ZH242] and tummim [TH8550, ZH9460]), which again are not well enough understood to be adequately translated (see note on 8:8). They were held by the chestpiece (Exod 28:30) and were useful in some way to make decisions (Num 27:21). Exactly how they worked is unknown; some have suggested that there were two items indicating a positive or negative response, like a modern computer with its open or closed circuits. Others suggest there were numerous items with the letters of the alphabet spelling out the revelation given (Milgrom 1991:507-511). All of these suggestions are intriguing, but none is certain.

The turban (8:9) was a linen cloth wrapped around (16:4) the top of the head of priests (Exod 28:39) or rulers (Ezek 21:26). It had a medallion with a surface for writing a short inscription describing it and its wearer as "HOLY TO THE LORD" (Exod 28:36-37). The medallion was fastened to the turban with a purplish-blue cord.

The priest was thus decked out to assume his new job, but not quite "from head to toe," because there is no mention of any foot covering. Since the priest was to minister in the Tabernacle sanctuary, which was a portable piece of holy space, he could not wear shoes, similar to Moses at the burning bush (Exod 3:2-5). This is in contrast to the armor of God, typified in Ephesians 6:10-18, where shoes are necessary since the warrior would go forth for ministry and conflict from the sacred place into the world.

Moses, as God's delegate and representative (8:1-4), took an active role not only in the preparatory rituals, but also in the ordination service itself (8:22-30). After the Israelite cultic practices were formally established in conjunction with the Tabernacle under the auspices of the priesthood itself, Moses could no longer perform some of these same functions since he was not a priest (see Exod 40:35). With formalization often comes a diminution of freedom.

The actual consecration of the priests took place with the use of anointing oil (8:10-13). The anointing oil was specially prepared in order to sanctify the Tabernacle and its contents and those who would serve in it, and the oil could only be used for that purpose. Misuse or inappropriate mixing of the oil was severely punished (Exod 30:23-33). The act of anointing was performed by applying this special oil either by smearing (the basic meaning of the verb *mashakh* [TH4886, ZH5417]) or pouring it on an object such as the Tabernacle and its contents here (Gen 31:13; Exod 30:26-29; Num 7:1).

In addition to objects, people such as the priests could also be anointed, setting them apart or consecrating them for a specific function. This could be in order to rule the people (1 Sam 9:16; 16:12-13) or to serve God in some other way. In this case, it was a group of people set apart from regular daily work for special service to God (Exod 28:41). In other instances, though not mentioned here, anointing, which prepared one for ministry, was also accompanied by the coming of God's Spirit, who empowered for ministry (a king in 1 Sam 10:1-6 and 16:13; a prophet in Isa 61:1-2).

Though the priests were correctly dressed and had been set apart through anointing, they could not yet represent the nation before God until they were purified through a sin offering (4:1–5:13; Exod 29:10-14) made on their behalf. It is easy to forget that it is not the position that sets the person apart for service. The law also applied to leaders, who needed to show in character, commitment, and, in the case of the priests, ritual "cleanliness," that they had been made fit for God's service. Too often in the church, and the wider society, leaders feel that their position and power do not require accompanying purity. This is damaging not only to the individual leaders, but also to those they lead, whether their family, congregation, corporation, or country.

Prior to the priestly purification, the altar also needed cleansing, since it was the instrument used to give this cleansing to Aaron and his sons (4:7, 18-19, 25-26, 30-31, 34-35). The altar was set apart as holy, using the same Hebrew root as for the sin offering (see note on 4:14). Here it was the altar, rather than the offerer, that was sanctified, though it was the offerer's contaminating behavior that necessitated the purification.

As well as being purified, the priests needed to be made right with God, which was the function of the burnt offering (8:18-21). They identified with the offering by touching it, and were forbidden from receiving any physical advantage from eating it (cf. 6:26) since it was an offering done on their behalf. Moses carried out the actual sacrifice according to the already established procedure (1:10-13). Aaron and his sons needed to mend any breach between themselves and God, whom they represented and to whom they were to bring offerings on behalf of the people.

After all the preliminary purification preparations had been completed, it was time for the ministers themselves to be consecrated for divine service (8:22-24). The priests were those charged with performing Israelite rituals, but since they had not yet been consecrated for the task, Moses had to step in. As a prophet par excellence (Deut 18:15; 34:10), he anointed the priests for religious service just as later prophets did the same for royal service (e.g., Saul and David in 1 Sam 10:1; 16:13; Jehu in 2 Kgs 9:6). The new priests then could take over these ritual functions for the people.

This second animal sacrifice was similar to the sin and fellowship offerings since the unburned remains could be eaten (6:26; 7:14-18; 8:31). The first element of the ritual involved the manipulation of the blood. In the regular offerings, the blood was applied to the altar. For the sin offering, this was done in order to purify it for God's service (Exod 29:36; Ezek 43:26). This was done to the altar here also, but unlike the other offerings, the priest himself also received an anointment of blood, on three appendages on the right side of the body. He also was purified in preparation for service. This was a reminder that, though he was among a select group of people, he was still just an instrument in God's hand. Both inanimate altar and human priest needed the same purification and could, through this purification and not through their own merit or skill, be of service to God.

The earlobe, thumb, and big toe probably symbolize the entire body of the purified priest, since the ritual was to make him completely fit for service, not just the body parts directly daubed. There was most likely a reason why these particular body parts and not others were chosen. Perhaps they allegorically represent their functions: hearing God, serving him, and going where he calls (Ross 2002:213), though any such interpretation is speculative.

According to 8:25-30, other previously established sacrifices were also incorporated into the priestly ordination, including the peace offering with its fat, breast, and thigh (8:25; cf. 3:9-10; 7:30-33) and the grain offering with its bread (8:26; cf. 2:4-5; 7:12). Moses gave portions of all of these except the breast to the priests, who raised them up as an offering to God before they were completely burned on the altar. The breast was not raised by them, but by Moses, who raised it to God and received it back from him. Moses's position in the procedure seems to be ambiguous, since he was only a temporary priest. He did not receive the right thigh for his own personal use (8:28), though it was customary for that part of the fellowship offering to go to the officiating priest (7:32-33).

By means of all of these steps, in addition to the final sprinkling with anointing oil and blood from the altar, the priests were made fit for service—their sins having been atoned for. It was most regularly just oil that was used for this anointing (Exod 30:22-30), but here blood was used as well. This was taken from the altar and not directly from the slaughtered animal since contact with the altar itself had first sanctified the blood (Exod 29:37), which now sanctified those things, both people and uniforms, sprinkled by it (cf. 16:14-19; Milgrom 1991:533-534).

According to the last paragraph (8:31-36), Aaron and the other priests were able to eat the parts of the sacrifices that had not been completely burnt by fire and were left over, fulfilling the previously given command to do so (7:6). This command is given here in the form of a quotation (8:31b), but the exact words do not occur elsewhere, indicating either that a paraphrase was acceptable as a quote, or that some of the original ritual instruction has not been preserved in the text now before us (cf. comments on 7:37). Anything left over needed to be destroyed. This referred specifically to things remaining until the next day, since keeping the offered food for this long was not allowed (7:15; Exod 29:34).

For the first time, the passage indicates that the entire ritual lasted a total of seven days (8:33; cf. Exod 29:30, 35-37). It appears best to understand the rituals of the first day as having been repeated throughout the seven-day period as in other ordination and dedication events (cf. Exod 29:35-37; Ezek 43:25-26), rather than just happening once, with nothing to do but wait for the remaining six days. Seven days were associated with several other ritual contexts, including the period between healing from a discharge or skin disease and being pronounced clean (14:8-9; 15:13-14, 28-29). They also mark other important transitions in human life, including birth, marriage, and death (12:2; Gen 29:27-28; 50:10; Num 19:11, 14, 16 respectively), as well as festivals such as Unleavened Bread (23:6; Exod 23:15; 34:18) and Shelters (23:34; see Exod 23:16 mg; 34:22 mg). Another passage that might shed some light on the seven-day period is Exodus 22:29b-30 (cf. Lev 22:27), in which the firstborn Israelite males and sacrificial animals dedicated for God's service were to stay for seven days with their mothers before being placed into his service. The priestly preparation could be understood as a time of maturation for service.

The priests were to remain at their post, at the entryway to the sanctuary, at all times, fulfilling all the requirements laid out (8:35). If not, they would die—a severe penalty showing the seriousness of the offense. This term is not ambiguous, as was the alternative formulation "be cut off from the community" (7:20).

Similar rites for ordination and induction of priests are known elsewhere in the ancient Near East. During the thirteenth century BC in the town of Emar on the Euphrates in Syria, there were nine-day rituals for dedicating priestesses. They included seven days of offering (cf. 8:33), part of which was eaten by the participants (Fleming 1992:150-156), and two separate times of anointing (ibid., 174-179), just like for Aaron (8:12, 30). The priestess would be dressed and adorned with special clothing, including special turbans (Fleming 1992:153, 156; cf. 8:9).

Part of the function of the ceremony was sanctification of the priestess (Fleming 1992:158-162; cf. 8:10-12, 15, 30). An aspect of the Syrian ritual not mentioned in the Leviticus text, though it was most likely a part of the Israelite priestly installation, was the accompaniment of parts of the rituals by singers (Fleming 1992:152, 154, 157, 158). Among the Hittites, in what is now Turkey, there were rites inducting new deities that lasted a period of seven days (Kitchen 2003:280).

Finally, this chapter has significance for the New Testament and is relevant for life today. The writer of the Epistle to the Hebrews spent much space discussing the office of priest and the sacrificial system (Heb 4:14–10:22). The priests themselves were not without sin and therefore needed to receive atonement if they were to serve God, in the same way that all people do (1 John 1:7). In contrast, the book of Hebrews shows Jesus as not needing sacrifices on his own behalf, but rather that he was himself the sacrifice for others (Heb 7:11-28; cf. 1 John 1:8-9). He is the perfect, archetypical high priest (Heb 4:14-16; 8:1-6), who can minister on behalf of the people without impediment.

Physical anointing with oil is integral to ordination for ministry in some Christian traditions, but divine anointing by the Holy Spirit must be a prerequisite to all ministry (2 Cor 1:21-22), since the Spirit is the enabler for any ministry (1 Cor 12:28). The priest's task was not for his own benefit, but rather it was a means to an end, which was the representation of the people before God, helping them attain, through the working of the Spirit, the holiness necessary to perform their own tasks of worship and service. Paul indicated that this enabling role, through teaching and preparation of people for ministry rather than through rites of sanctification per se, is still that of Christian ministers today (Eph 4:11-13).

◆   B. The First Service (9:1-24)

After the ordination ceremony, on the eighth day, Moses called together Aaron and his sons and the elders of Israel. [2]He said to Aaron, "Take a young bull for a sin offering and a ram for a burnt offering, both without defects, and present them to the LORD. [3]Then tell the Israelites, 'Take a male goat for a sin offering, and take a calf and a lamb, both a year old and without defects, for a burnt offering. [4]Also take a bull* and a ram for a peace offering and flour moistened with olive oil for a grain offering. Present all these offerings to the LORD because the LORD will appear to you today.' "

[5]So the people presented all these things at the entrance of the Tabernacle,* just as Moses had commanded. Then the whole community came forward and stood before the LORD. [6]And Moses said, "This is what the LORD has commanded you to do so that the glory of the LORD may appear to you."

[7]Then Moses said to Aaron, "Come to the altar and sacrifice your sin offering and your burnt offering to purify yourself and the people. Then present the offerings of the people to purify them, making them right with the LORD,* just as he has commanded."

[8]So Aaron went to the altar and slaughtered the calf as a sin offering for himself. [9]His sons brought him the blood, and he dipped his finger in it and put it on the horns of the altar. He poured out the rest of the blood at the base of the altar. [10]Then

he burned on the altar the fat, the kidneys, and the long lobe of the liver from the sin offering, just as the LORD had commanded Moses. ¹¹The meat and the hide, however, he burned outside the camp.

¹²Next Aaron slaughtered the animal for the burnt offering. His sons brought him the blood, and he splattered it against all sides of the altar. ¹³Then they handed him each piece of the burnt offering, including the head, and he burned them on the altar. ¹⁴Then he washed the internal organs and the legs and burned them on the altar along with the rest of the burnt offering.

¹⁵Next Aaron presented the offerings of the people. He slaughtered the people's goat and presented it as an offering for their sin, just as he had first done with the offering for his own sin. ¹⁶Then he presented the burnt offering and sacrificed it in the prescribed way. ¹⁷He also presented the grain offering, burning a handful of the flour mixture on the altar, in addition to the regular burnt offering for the morning. ¹⁸Then Aaron slaughtered the bull and the ram for the people's peace offering. His sons brought him the blood, and he splattered it against all sides of the altar. ¹⁹Then he took the fat of the bull and the ram—the fat of the broad tail and from around the internal organs—along with the kidneys and the long lobes of the livers. ²⁰He placed these fat portions on top of the breasts of these animals and burned them on the altar. ²¹Aaron then lifted up the breasts and right thighs as a special offering to the LORD, just as Moses had commanded.

²²After that, Aaron raised his hands toward the people and blessed them. Then, after presenting the sin offering, the burnt offering, and the peace offering, he stepped down from the altar. ²³Then Moses and Aaron went into the Tabernacle, and when they came back out, they blessed the people again, and the glory of the LORD appeared to the whole community. ²⁴Fire blazed forth from the LORD's presence and consumed the burnt offering and the fat on the altar. When the people saw this, they shouted with joy and fell face down on the ground.

9:4 Or *cow;* also in 9:18, 19.   9:5 Hebrew *Tent of Meeting;* also in 9:23.   9:7 Or *to make atonement for them.*

NOTES

9:4 *the LORD will appear.* The verbal form in Hebrew (*nir'ah* [TH7200, ZH8011], Niphal) indicates that God would "allow himself to be seen," in the form of holy fire (9:24), as he did earlier at Sinai (Exod 20:18). Elsewhere God appeared in his dazzlingly glorious presence (Exod 24:17; Num 16:19, 42) as a pillar of cloud (Deut 31:15) or as an angel (Judg 6:12; 13:3). His glory is the outward, visible manifestation of his being, which in itself evokes reverence and fear from those who see it (Isa 6:3-5). Ezekiel was so awestruck that he could not bring himself to state that he even saw God's presence, saying instead that he saw (lit.) "the appearance of the likeness of the glory of the LORD" (Ezek 1:28).

9:9, 12, 18 *brought him the blood.* This verbiage might lead the reader astray because the blood of the slaughtered animal was not brought from some other location to Aaron. Rather, the blood was passed over to Aaron in the bowl or basin into which it had been poured (Exod 24:6; 27:3; Num 4:14).

9:20 *burned them.* This pronominal reference is ambiguous in the NLT. In the Hebrew it clearly refers only to the fat and not to the breast; the latter remained and was subsequently lifted up by Aaron (9:21).

9:22 *raised his hands.* This is an action done in prayer (Pss 28:2; 134:2; Hab 3:10) or blessing (here and Luke 24:50), which must be differentiated from raising one hand. The latter could indicate a threat (2 Sam 18:28; 20:21; cf. Ps 10:12), or an oath (Exod 6:8), showing the importance of both context and parallel forms in order to determine meaning, which must be determined not only for words but also for actions.

COMMENTARY

Once the priests were prepared and dedicated, they could perform the first public ritual acts. It was for this event of public service, and what it foreshadowed for the rest of Israel's history, that the previous rituals had been preparing. The center of attention of this chapter is the altar, the focus of the rituals (9:7-14, 17-20) and the place of the fiery appearance of God himself (9:24).

Moses, who had to perform the ritual acts of priestly ordination himself, now delegated the ceremonies into the hands of the priests. They stepped in as representatives of and ministers for the people. As soon as possible after the completion of their installation, the priests set to work under Moses's direction (9:1-5).

This was the eighth day, the day after the seven-day priestly ritual, when the people (9:3, 5) were allowed to bring their offerings through the agency of the duly ordained priests for public worship (Ezek 43:27). This numbered day became an important part of other aspects of Israelite ritual, including the dedication of the firstborn to God (Exod 22:29-30), circumcision (12:3), purification of one suffering from a skin disease (14:10) or from a bodily discharge (15:14, 29), the age of sacrificial animals (22:27), the conclusion of the Feast of Shelters (23:36, 39), and purification of a defiled Nazirite (Num 6:10; 29:35).

This time the rituals were not only for the priests, but for the entire nation, which was represented by the elders, who joined the priests when they received their instructions. While the priests may have been clothed differently and had a different function in society than other leaders and the people, they were also part of the people, as they symbolized by standing shoulder to shoulder with the elders, the people's representatives.

The first sacrifices were for the priests themselves (9:2). The sacrifice for sin was a young bull (lit., "calf," in contrast to the bull called for elsewhere; see 4:3; 8:2; 16:3) and for a burnt offering a ram (cf. 8:18; 16:3). While they had been purified as part of their consecration service (ch 8), that was a private function; this was their first public ministry. So the public sacrifices needed to be made as acknowledgment that they also were under the law.

The result of the complex of offerings was not presented in the same terms previously given in Leviticus. There was no mention in 9:4 of atonement (see 9:7), but of something even more basic, the very reason why atonement was desired. This was the actual presence of Yahweh himself, whose appearance was promised here. On the very day that these rituals were done, God would appear. God had previously appeared on Sinai (Exod 24:17) and also at the inauguration of the Tabernacle (Exod 40:34-38). In those instances, as in this case, it was God's "glory" that appeared (see 9:6, 23, 24). God's glory was said to fill the Tabernacle, entry to which was restricted to the priests, even Moses being denied access to witness it (Exod 40:34-35; cf. 1 Kgs 8:11). What was available only to the few would now be experienced by all the people: The Tabernacle entrance and forecourt by the altar would become Mount Sinai, the mountain and meeting place of God, for God's people. At Sinai the people begged Moses to represent them before God rather than being in his presence and beholding God themselves (Exod 20:18-21; Deut 5:5). God granted their request by giving them intermediaries such as Moses, but at times he still let his glory shine more broadly for the people to see, even if from afar (e.g., Exod 24:17; Num 14:10). Such physical manifestations of the invisible God were powerful indeed, driving those who beheld them to a realization of their own inadequacy (e.g., Isa 6:1-5). God's ultimate goal is for everyone, Israelite and Gentile, to be able to see God's glory up close and personal, as it is here in Leviticus, and to worship him as the Glorious One, even to the point of sharing in his glory (Isa 35:2; 40:5; Hab 2:14; 1 John 3:2).

In preparation for this glorious occasion, the people brought offerings on their own behalf (9:5-7). The first mentioned was a sin offering of a goat, following the prescription for a goat (found in Num 15:24) rather than that for a bull (4:14). The male goat was the sin offering for a leader of Israel according to 4:22-26, although on the Day of Atonement (16:5, 15) and in Numbers 15:24 it is the sin offering for the people. No note was made of the discrepancy. The leaders were part of the people, and it might have been necessary to bring the highest relevant sacrifice for all those involved, though it seems that the leaders and priests had already brought the bull, according to 9:2.

The people also brought two animals for burnt offerings, following the practice for public festivals (Num 28–29) rather than the more regular form in chapter 1, where one or the other animal was to be brought; two animals for a peace offering, a bull (see 4:10; 7:23, though a bull is not mentioned in ch 3) and a ram (calling for a more restricted offering as regards gender and age than that allowed according to 3:6-7), and finally a grain offering (7:10). In other words, every offering type mentioned in the priestly handbook (chs 1–7) was included in this premier ritual event, except for the guilt offering. Since the latter was more individual in character, as shown by its particular financial reparations, it alone among the offerings was inappropriate for a public context.

A detailed, step-by-step description shows how Aaron followed Moses's instructions to the letter (9:8-14). Even though he was the high priest, he was still under the authority of the messenger who had heard directly from God. Aaron first atoned for his own sins and those of the priests (cf. 4:3-12). Leaders need to take care of their own relationship with God before they can adequately lead others (cf. Acts 20:28). The only departure here from the original instructions in 4:4, 15, 24 is the lack of mention that hands were laid on the sacrifice, which was assumed not only for Aaron, but also for the elders as representatives of the people (9:1). Blood, fat, flesh, and hide were disposed of as described for a sin offering, with a reference (9:10) given to the "priestly handbook" (cf. 4:7-12) for the actual procedures. The same detail, without reference to the previous instructions, follows for the burnt offering (1:3-9). The fat disposal was not reiterated here (cf. 1:8), though it would be included with "the rest" in 9:14.

After taking care of their own sacrificial needs, the priests could now attend to the needs of the rest of the population (9:15-21). The author in several instances referred back to previously mentioned acts and therefore did not need to provide repetitious detail. The priests offered sin offerings for the people (referring back to 9:8-11 and presupposing ch 4) as well as their burnt offering (referring back to 1:3-13 for procedures, though the actual young animals were not mentioned there, but were those used for the festivals, Num 28–29), and grain offerings (referring back to ch 2 and also referring to a daily, morning burnt offering only mentioned in Exod 29:38-40). More detail was given for the peace offerings (ch 3), with the manipulation of the breast and thigh detailed in 7:30-34, to which reference is made (9:21).

Ritual actions were accompanied by ritual words, even though they usually were not quoted or even mentioned. In 9:22, the words are described as a blessing that Aaron made over the people. He did this from an elevated position beside the altar, where he had been officiating, so that he could see the people at the Tabernacle entrance, and also so that all those in attendance could see him and be part of this ceremony as well (cf. Neh 8:4). Moses and Aaron pronounced a second blessing when the two exited the Tabernacle, which they had entered for an unspecified reason, though it was most likely for prayer (cf. 1 Kgs 8:14-61; Milgrom 1991:588).

This was followed by a visible manifestation of God's glory in the form of fire, a sign of his approval and acceptance of the ceremonies just completed. Fire, often in the form of lightning, was a common demonstration of the presence of God (Exod 19:16-18; 1 Kgs 18:38; Job 1:16). Fire also accompanied and guided Israel and its shrine throughout its wandering in the wilderness (Exod 40:38; Num 9:18). Divine fire in whatever form caused the instant consumption of the offering, in contrast to its regular, slow burning.

As a natural, automatic reaction to such a powerful physical force, the people fell down. This was at times a sign of honor to a powerful being, whether human or divine (Judg 13:20; 2 Sam 9:6; 1 Kgs 18:39). Here it was accompanied by joyful praise that the people offered to God (cf. 2 Chr 7:3). The people could not keep silent before a God who responded to their worship, so they joined their voices to those of the priests (9:24). God can and should be approached at times in stillness (Ps 46:10), but exuberance can also be appropriate. Everyone, young and old, male and female, was represented by the priests and leaders in the rituals; they each witnessed God's response, and each responded appropriately in worship.

While spiritual encounters with God can be individual and private, simple and serene, there is also an appropriate time for communal celebration and ceremony. These are not an end in themselves, however, but a means of worship and an opportunity to meet with God. Corporate encounters with the Creator and Lord of the universe, which are predicated on personal cleansing and holiness (2 Cor 7:1), should fill the worshipers with awe and wonder (Acts 2:43; Rev 11:16).

This chapter provides several parallels to Christian doctrine and experience, especially as written in the book of Romans. Ross (2002:229) highlights the correlations between these ceremonies and Paul's structure of his argument in Romans. Creation starts in a state of sin and a need for atonement (Rom 1–2), the same state in which Aaron and his sons were at the start of the chapter. To bring about atonement, making creation right with God, God provided the cleansing sacrifice of his Son (Rom 3) as he did with the sin and burnt offerings for the priests (9:7). Christ's sacrifice needs to be accompanied by personal faith, not simply dead ritual (Rom 5), just as the people and the priests had to be personally involved in these purification sacrifices in Leviticus. Being identified with the sacrifice and death of Christ (Rom 6), as the people were identified with the sacrifices they brought, we should not live in sin any longer. This was one of the things that had caused the lack of purity among the Israelites and their priests and needed to be put right through this ceremony. Though we do sin (Rom 7), as did Israel, the one sacrifice was sufficient and does not require repetition since the Holy Spirit enables proper life and practice (Rom 8); this is in contrast to the Israelite sacrifices, which needed to be repeated as necessary. After showing how God had worked through the history of Israel, joining the church to his Old Testament people (Rom 9–11), Paul urges that the appropriate response of the believers—in correlation to those present at the ceremony in Leviticus—is to offer themselves to God (Rom 12) and live all of life in light of their reconciliation with God (Rom 13–16). This would have been the ideal goal for Israel: to live permanently in a close covenant relationship with God, maintaining their purity. For the people of Israel, this did not take place; because of sin, the sacrificial arrangements for restoration needed to be made. For us as Christians, the permanent condition of purity also is jeopardized by our sins, for which the perfect and final sacrificial arrangements have already been made.

◆   ## C. The Sin of the Priests Nadab and Abihu (10:1-5)

Aaron's sons Nadab and Abihu put coals of fire in their incense burners and sprinkled incense over them. In this way, they disobeyed the LORD by burning before him the wrong kind of fire, different than he had commanded. ²So fire blazed forth from the LORD's presence and burned them up, and they died there before the LORD.

³Then Moses said to Aaron, "This is what the LORD meant when he said,

'I will display my holiness
    through those who come near me.

I will display my glory
    before all the people!' "

And Aaron was silent.

⁴Then Moses called for Mishael and Elzaphan, Aaron's cousins, the sons of Aaron's uncle Uzziel. He said to them, "Come forward and carry away the bodies of your relatives from in front of the sanctuary to a place outside the camp." ⁵So they came forward and picked them up by their garments and carried them out of the camp, just as Moses had commanded.

NOTES

10:3 *display my holiness . . . my glory.* God's glory was to be displayed through the holiness of those who were near him (Ezek 42:13; 43:19), the priests ministering in his name.

10:4 *sanctuary.* This could refer to the Most Holy Place (16:2, 23), which would mean that the two priests had brought their "foreign fire" far into the Tabernacle precinct. It can also mean the tent or the Tabernacle courtyard (6:30; 10:18; Exod 28:29), but even that place was holy, so inappropriate things or people had no place there.

COMMENTARY

Chapter 10 is a self-contained unit arranged as a chiastic structure. In a chiasm, the first and last elements are similar, as are the second and next to last, and so on. The key element in such a construction is usually at the middle—the target at which the arrow is aimed. For Leviticus 10, it works out as follows:

A. Brothers sin and are punished (10:1-5)
   B. Moses instructs the priests (10:6-7)
      C. Yahweh instructs Aaron (10:8-11)
   B'. Moses instructs the priests (10:12-15)
A'. Brothers sin and are forgiven (10:16-20)

A unique feature of this chapter—in contrast with the rest of Leviticus, which is largely a presentation of regulations—is that it has two narratives, stories of those who chose to take their own path in opposition to what was required by God (see also 24:10-23). In both cases, two of Aaron's sons, members of the priestly family, erred in the practices that had just been delivered to the people. This occurred right in the middle of carrying out the offerings described in chapter 9, on the first day after the weeklong ordination ceremony. As soon as the commands had come from Moses's lips, they were broken (cf. Exod 32). The sacrifices had been prepared and offered (9:15-21), but the priests had not yet eaten their portions (10:12-20; cf. 6:16-18, 26-29; 7:31-34) when the events of this chapter took place. Though they had just been consecrated along with their father, Aaron, and their younger brothers, Eleazar and Ithamar (Exod 6:23), Nadab and Abihu were not careful in their religious practices. They broke God's commands at the very time these were first publicly carried out. Having witnessed the fall of God's holy fire, which consumed the acceptable sacrifices (9:24), they now experienced it firsthand, when it consumed them as unacceptable sacrificers.

Though the exact nature of Nadab and Abihu's wrongdoing is debated, it clearly involved burning incense. Incense was supposed to be burnt on the inner incense altar (Exod 30:1, 34-36; 40:5), and it was also used with the grain offering (ch 2; cf. also Aaron burning it in the Holy Place during the special Day of Atonement, 16:12-13). It was to be burned by the priests in a specified manner, namely on the altar, and this was not done with incense burners (lit., "pans"; "trays" in the NLT). These did have a part in Israelite ritual (Exod 25:38; Num 4:9), but they had nothing to do with incense anywhere in previous texts in Leviticus (cf. 16:12). This indicates that a practice was done that was outside the divinely delivered regulations of chapters 1–9, as the last part of 10:1 indicates. In addition, incense was commonly used in pagan worship (e.g., 1 Kgs 3:3), so this offense might even have involved the introduction of a pagan rite into the worship of Yahweh (cf. 26:30). In this and the episode of Korah's rebellion (Num 16), Milgrom (1991:597) points out that the incense burners are stated to belong to the wrongdoer, indicating the use of personal, nonsacred implements for sacred service, something that was not allowed. Any of these possibilities—sacrificing in ways other than those specified in chapters 1–9, using pagan practices, using personal property in a sacrificial context, or a combination of them—could explain why Nadab and Abihu's wrong is described as being a "wrong kind of fire" (better translated by Milgrom as "unauthorized fire"). It did not follow God's wishes as regards either the pans or the fire used.

Yahweh responded in the same way he responded to the acceptable offerings in chapter 9, but with reverse effect. There he sent forth his holy fire to consume the good offerings (9:24); here it blazed from the same location to consume the evil offerers along with their unholy fire. The joy of acceptance was replaced by the silence of death.

Moses then gave Aaron a theological explanation of what had just transpired before the shocked eyes of Israel (10:3). The saying in 10:3 is said to have come from Yahweh himself, but it is not a quote from any existing biblical text, so this could indicate an immediate response from God to this very event (Milgrom 1991:600). God, being holy, cannot come into contact with that which is unholy. The nature of his holiness is reflected by those who claim ability to come before him, whether in truth, such as the purified priests, or in error, such as this unworthy pair of brothers. Those who claim to represent him could, in fact, bring disrepute if they themselves were disreputable.

The unclean bodies of Nadab and Abihu had to be disposed of, but the priests who were in the midst of their dedication ceremony could not become ceremonially unclean by doing so (21:11; 22:4). More distant family members took the responsibility, not touching the bodies themselves lest they, too, become unclean.

◆   ## D. Instructions for Priests (10:6-15)

⁶Then Moses said to Aaron and his sons Eleazar and Ithamar, "Do not show grief by leaving your hair uncombed* or by tearing your clothes. If you do, you will die, and the LORD's anger will strike the whole community of Israel. However, the rest of the Israelites, your relatives, may mourn because of the LORD's fiery destruction of Nadab and Abihu. ⁷But you must not leave the entrance of the Tabernacle* or you will die, for you have been anointed with the LORD's anointing oil." So they did as Moses commanded.

⁸Then the LORD said to Aaron, ⁹"You and your descendants must never drink wine or any other alcoholic drink before going into the Tabernacle. If you do, you will die. This is a permanent law for you, and it must be observed from generation to generation. ¹⁰You must distinguish between what is sacred and what is common, between what is ceremonially unclean and what is clean. ¹¹And you must teach the Israelites all the decrees that the LORD has given them through Moses."

¹²Then Moses said to Aaron and his remaining sons, Eleazar and Ithamar, "Take what is left of the grain offering after a portion has been presented as a special gift to the LORD, and eat it beside the altar. Make sure it contains no yeast, for it is most holy. ¹³You must eat it in a sacred place, for it has been given to you and your descendants as your portion of the special gifts presented to the LORD. These are the commands I have been given. ¹⁴But the breast and thigh that were lifted up as a special offering may be eaten in any place that is ceremonially clean. These parts have been given to you and your descendants as your portion of the peace offerings presented by the people of Israel.

¹⁵You must lift up the thigh and breast as a special offering to the LORD, along with the fat of the special gifts. These parts will belong to you and your descendants as your permanent right, just as the LORD has commanded."

10:6 Or by uncovering your heads.   10:7 Hebrew Tent of Meeting; also in 10:9.

NOTES

10:6 by leaving your hair uncombed. This is the same verb (*para'* [TH6544/A, ZH7277]) that is translated as "get completely out of control" in Exod 32:25. Disheveled hair was a sign of mourning.

by tearing your clothes. A different verb from this is used in most cases (*qara'* [TH7167, ZH7973]; cf. Gen 37:29, 34; 2 Sam 3:31; Job 1:20). This verb (*param* [TH6533, ZH7268]) is used of the consecrated high priest (21:10), who must not do it, and, at the opposite end of the spectrum of holiness, also of the person suffering from a skin disease (13:45), who must have torn clothes and disheveled hair.

COMMENTARY

The priests needed specific instruction on how they were to behave in light of these unparalleled events. Moses delivered God's instruction here and in 10:12-15, in contrast to Yahweh's speaking directly to Aaron in 10:8-11.

Moses told the high priest, Aaron, that he could not take part in the burial of his sons or even partake in the customary mourning practices of making oneself disheveled (10:6-7; cf. 13:45; 21:10-12). This was left to other family members, since priests other than the high priest could aid in burying their own kin (21:1-4). It is unclear why the brothers of the dead were not called upon to bury them. Perhaps being in the direct line of the high priest and also having been anointed with him (Num 3:3-4) placed some of his restrictions upon them as well. Since they were still on "active duty," they needed to preserve their purity in order to be able to continue to perform the needed rituals (10:7). Possibly their own missteps at the end of this chapter (10:16-18) could have made them inappropriate mourners for others who had done similar things. The dead bodies, being unclean, were removed from the camp; though once set apart for God's service, they were now unworthy of being in his presence and were taken to the same place as the useless parts of sacrificial animals (4:12).

According to 10:8-11, Yahweh addressed Aaron directly (cf. Exod 4:27; Num 18:1, 8), without speaking through Moses as he did elsewhere (cf. 9:2, 7; 10:3, 6, 12, 16). His message concerned drinking alcohol, specifically wine. Wine (*yayin* [TH3196, ZH3516]) was a common alcoholic drink of the area made from grapes; this stood in contrast to Abram's home country of Mesopotamia, where beer was common. All alcoholic beverages were being prohibited here, since the ban also included a more general term for intoxicants (*shekar* [TH7941, ZH8911]).

A message about alcohol prohibition is difficult to fit into this textual position, causing some to suggest that the chapter is a mixture of different pieces from different times and occasions (Milgrom 1991:611). The discussion is not a complete interruption, however, since it is tied with the preceding passage on the issue of the threat of death (10:6). Possibly its inclusion here points to Nadab and Abihu's being drunk when they sinned, but this is not mentioned in our passage. Probably the best explanation is derived from a careful reading of the text before us, which permanently bans alcohol consumption prior to ministering before the Lord. This was not a general, complete prohibition of priestly alcohol consumption. It rather spelled out a specific aspect of priestly ministry, the ability to differentiate between different elements or categories (Gen 1:4; Exod 26:33), in this case distinguishing between the sacred and the common, which was jeopardized by inebriation. This ability to make distinctions is one of the central thrusts of this entire book (cf. 11:44-45; 20:7) and was to be taught by them to the people (11:47). When intoxicated, one's judgment is blurred, and if that judgment involved the very nature of what is appropriate for divine service and what is not, disaster could result (cf. Isa 28:7). This lack of discernment, whether induced by alcohol or not, caused Nadab and Abihu's deaths. There could also have been an element of pagan religious practice condemned here. Canaanite worshipers at times sought to leave their normal state of mind in order to commune with their gods (see 1 Kgs 18:26-29), but clearheadedness was required of all worshipers of Yahweh (1 Sam 1:13-15).

Yahweh then told Aaron that it was the task of the priests to teach the law of Moses to all of Israel (10:11; cf. Deut 17:10-11; 24:8; 2 Kgs 12:2; Ezek 44:23). The law was not for their sole benefit as priests, but was entrusted to them to transmit to the people, who were the ultimate audience of God's revelation.

The last paragraph of this section (10:12-15) pertains to the completion of the rituals for the eighth day (9:1), which had been interrupted by the episode with Nadab and Abihu. Moses reminded the officiating priests, Aaron and his two surviving sons (Exod 6:23), that there were further steps to take in order to complete the grain offerings (2:3; 7:10; 9:17) and peace offerings (7:30-34; 9:21)—namely, the consumption of the offerings by the priests. The sacrifice was incomplete if only the portion presented directly to God had been consumed; the entire sacrifice needed to be treated appropriately, according to God's instructions. The priestly food was sanctified, so it could not be eaten just anywhere. The cereal must be eaten within the Tabernacle court, identified here as being "beside the altar" (10:12) and "a sacred place" (10:13; cf. 6:16), while the meat could be eaten in any place that was not impure, within or outside the sanctuary. The difference between the two might have been in the designation of the grain offering as "most holy" (2:3; 6:17), a phrase not used to describe the peace offering.

◆   ## E. A Dispute over Priestly Service (10:16-20)

¹⁶Moses then asked them what had happened to the goat of the sin offering. When he discovered it had been burned up, he became very angry with Eleazar and Ithamar, Aaron's remaining sons. ¹⁷"Why didn't you eat the sin offering in the sacred area?" he demanded. "It is a holy offering! The LORD has given it to you to remove the guilt of the community and to purify the people, making them right with the LORD.* ¹⁸Since the animal's blood was not brought into the Holy Place, you

should have eaten the meat in the sacred area as I ordered you."

¹⁹Then Aaron answered Moses, "Today my sons presented both their sin offering and their burnt offering to the LORD. And yet this tragedy has happened to me. If I had eaten the people's sin offering on such a tragic day as this, would the LORD have been pleased?" ²⁰And when Moses heard this, he was satisfied.

10:17 Or *to make atonement for the people before the LORD.*

NOTES

10:17 the LORD has given it to you to remove the guilt of the community. This can be interpreted in several ways. It may indicate that: (1) The priests received the meat in exchange for performing the sin-offering ritual for the people (6:26; 9:15; Milgrom 1991:623). Moses's anger would necessitate that the regulation of 6:26 would be violated if the sacrifice were burnt rather than eaten. (2) The purpose of giving the meat to the priest was to remove the people's guilt and by not eating it, the guilt had not been removed. (3) The meat of the sin offering was seen as actually absorbing the guilt, which would have passed on to the priest, being borne by him, when he ate it (Kiuchi 1987:47; Milgrom 1991:624-625). But assuming guilt by eating is not known elsewhere in the Bible or in the ancient Near East. Also, the offering was "most holy" (6:25; 10:17; cf. 10:12), arguing against its being tainted by guilt. Though the Hebrew is difficult, the context of 10:18 would argue for the first interpretation.

10:18 as I ordered you. This refers to the instruction in 6:30, which says that burning only follows blood being taken into the Tabernacle, which was not done in this case.

COMMENTARY

In the middle of all the confusion of sin and punishment on this tragic eighth day (cf. 9:1), along with the needed clarification of ritual expectations, something else had gone wrong, this time involving the two remaining sons of Aaron (10:12). The people's sin offering of a goat had been brought as it was supposed to be (9:3), but in the confusion, it had been completely burned instead of being partly eaten by the priests in the manner that was required (6:26, 29). Moses was angry due to the breach of the commandment so soon after it had been given, but possibly also since, if the same punishment was to be given to the two younger brothers as their older brothers had received, that would be the quick end of the entire priestly line of Aaron! The passage reads as if the purpose of the sacrifice—atonement for the people—might have been placed in jeopardy because of their lack of diligence.

Part of Moses's rationale in confronting Aaron regarded the fact that the blood had not been brought into the sanctuary (10:18). This would have been necessary if the offering were for the priests or the nation as a whole (4:5, 16). Such use of blood would have disallowed the sacrifice from priestly consumption (6:30), but otherwise, as in this case, they were required to eat the rest of the offering.

Aaron provided a defense for his remaining sons. He reminded Moses that he, and by implication, all four of his sons, who had assisted him, had already brought their own sacrifices that day (9:8-14). In spite of that, judgment had fallen (10:2), and Aaron questioned whether bringing the sacrifice to a conclusion through eating it as required would have made everything right. Since the entire priesthood was new at this point, never having sacrificed before, and was faced with the deadly results that could follow a mistake, Aaron was justifiably concerned. Perhaps Aaron was aware that the people's sin offering, which did allow eating, had become one for the priests as well, since it would have needed to atone for Nadab and Abihu's sins, and was therefore not to be eaten after all (6:30). He might also have deemed the sacrifices invalid, having been presented by invalid officiants. By not eating it, he averted yet another sin. Whatever the exact nature of Aaron's explanation, it was acceptable to Moses and, by implication, to God, since punishment did not follow. Grace superseded law, even though the nature of both is obscure here.

The entire chapter, while puzzling and disturbing, has several contemporary applications. Religious leaders are not above the law, as some today seem to think. They are in fact held to a higher standard than those they lead (Luke 12:48; Jas 3:1). It is important for them to act with understanding, not only of what is expected of them, but also of the possible ramifications of their actions. Leaders in the church and society find it hard to act as private citizens, since too often their actions and statements are viewed as reflecting the institution they lead rather than their own stance. Extreme care needs to be taken in deciding what a leader does and says.

In the circumstances of chapter 10, unreflective actions could have resulted in serious consequences for the entire nation. Aaron and his younger sons responded to the call for a greater dedication to God's expectations than to the emotional calls of family. While their emotions were human and very real, grief and mourning had to be set aside in order to continue ministry on behalf of the people. Family relationships are of high priority, but they come after the relationship with God (cf. Matt 8:21-22; Luke 14:26).

Alcohol use is not banned here or anywhere else in Scripture, but it must be used appropriately. It is a gift from God, if used properly (Deut 11:13-15; 32:12-14; Ps 104:15; John 4:46; 1 Tim 5:23), but overuse resulting in intoxication can be a perversion of God's good gift (Prov 20:1; 23:31-32; Isa 28:7; Eph 5:18; cf. Gen 19:32). It has a place in celebration (Gen 43:34; Deut 14:26) but can be harmful if used where there is a need for discerning service. Leaders must show temperance in its use, as in all things (1 Tim 3:3, 8).

◆ III. Ceremonially Clean and Unclean Things (11:1–15:33)
A. Animals (11:1–47)
1. Land animals (11:1-8)

Then the LORD said to Moses and Aaron, [2]"Give the following instructions to the people of Israel.

"Of all the land animals, these are the ones you may use for food. [3]You may eat any animal that has completely split hooves and chews the cud. [4]You may not, however, eat the following animals* that have split hooves or that chew the cud, but not both. The camel chews the cud but does not have split hooves, so it is ceremonially unclean for you. [5]The hyrax* chews the cud but does not have split hooves, so it is unclean. [6]The hare chews the cud but does not have split hooves, so it is unclean. [7]The pig has evenly split hooves but does not chew the cud, so it is unclean. [8]You may not eat the meat of these animals or even touch their carcasses. They are ceremonially unclean for you.

11:4 The identification of some of the animals, birds, and insects in this chapter is uncertain.   11:5 Or coney, or rock badger.

NOTES

11:2 *land animals.* This phrase represents the word *khayyah* [TH2416/B, ZH2651], which designates living creatures, animals in general (Gen 9:5), and a second word, *behemah* [TH929, ZH989], which further defines the animals as living on the land and excludes swimming (11:9-12) or winged (11:13-23) creatures. Milgrom's translation "quadruped" was well chosen, since the term included both domestic and wild, large and small, all of which were included here (1991:643).

11:8 *touch their carcasses.* The carcasses here must be from animals that die from natural causes, not those slaughtered or sacrificed (11:39). Unacceptable animal carcasses are always referred to by the Hebrew word used here (*nebelah* [TH5038, ZH5577]) and always pollute (Milgrom 1991:653-654).

COMMENTARY

The last section (8:1–10:20) introduced some actions that ceremonially defiled those who practiced them, making them susceptible to death should they enter into the sanctuary in their unclean condition. The narration will be picked up chronologically in chapter 16. In the interim, there is a textual parenthesis where other actions causing ceremonial uncleanness are discussed. These actions could also result in death if the correct purification rites were not performed (15:31).

Holiness did not pertain only to the sanctuary with respect to how one worshiped or what one did in some sacred place, though there were examples of unholy actions in this context in the last chapter. Holiness has to do with how we interact with the everyday things of life, what we do at home, at work, or at play. Part of the priestly mandate was to distinguish between things that were holy and those that were not, between the clean and the unclean (10:10). The Israelites were given practical guidance as to how that might be accomplished in matters of food (ch 11), childbirth (ch 12), skin disease and mildew (chs 13–14), and discharges from the human body (ch 15). These naturally led to what follows (ch 16, the Day of Atonement)—namely, an explanation on how to bring purification from things like these that brought defilement (16:16). Israel did not suffer from the religious schizophrenia that seems to characterize many people today, seeing "church" or "Sunday" things separately from everything else. How Israel behaved "in the world" directly affected their relationship with God.

In reading this section, and indeed the entire book of Leviticus, we should remember that this was mainly a procedural manual, explaining *how* to do different things. It did not always explain *why* things were done this way, though sometimes it did. Therefore, many of the explanations given below as to why some things were acceptable and some were not are very tentative and disputed (see Ross 2002:251-255 for a discussion with various interpretations that have been offered). The animals listed are only those that were prohibited. The more commonly encountered animals that were permissible for eating, namely those also available for sacrifice, did not need mentioning.

Another difficulty concerns precise identification of various animals. Even though the geographical area of Israel was relatively small (the area settled by the 12 tribes was only about the size of the state of New Jersey or half the size of Denmark), it had numerous species and subspecies of animals, reptiles, birds, and fish. Following climatic and other changes, the animal population has changed, with some species dying out (there are no more native lions and bears in Israel today) and others being introduced (horses were brought into the area by Solomon from the Egyptians and Hittites). Adding to this is the difficulty of Hebrew vocabulary. Leviticus is not an exhaustive catalog of Near Eastern flora and fauna, so we cannot distinguish all of the animals in relation to others of their kind. Also, since the meaning of words comes from context and the only context we have for numerous animal identifications is a list where they occur with other obscure animal terms, many of the translations used in the various English versions, including the NLT, are tentative.

Laws concerning Land Animals. Early in Israel's history, as the people wandered in the wilderness and settled into the new land, they had much to do with animals. The animals supplied most of what was essential to the life of the community, including food, clothing, and shelter. Although all were God's creation (Gen 1:21, 25), different animals had different functions in the life of the nation. Some were suitable for human consumption and some were not. Of course, the most important animals for the Israelite economy were the land animals, since Israel was not a major seafaring nation. They raised domestic animals for meat, milk, and hides and also had frequent contact with wild animals. This category, being of primary importance, comes first (11:1-8).

In this first section, we learn that both Moses and Aaron received instruction from God. Moses was Israel's leader, and Aaron had the priestly task of distinguishing between the clean and unclean (10:10) and teaching the people (10:11). Here the distinction concerned a most basic human necessity—food, what was permissible to eat and what was not. The criteria did not include fat content or nutritional value, as they might if one were compiling such a list today. Rather, the criteria pertains to physical form (having hooves, horny coverings over the end of the feet, which are split—in two parts according to Deut 14:6, though that was not mentioned here) and eating habits (chewing the cud). The animals prohibited for food were inherently unclean, but their pollution was only transmitted through ingesting them, not by mere physical contact.

The law was simply presented, with no examples of allowable animals. The audience was already aware of the edible sacrificial animals, since they had been the subject of discussion up to this point in the book. Other, non-sacrificial animals also fit the criteria (seven more are included in Deut 14:4-5). These were game animals, which were less common than the sacrificial animals. Possibly they were omitted here since only the simple regulation and some well-known examples were necessary to make it clear to the people what was allowed. They were more in need of instruction concerning the unacceptable. It has been suggested that clean animals are among those "normal" to the Israelites, regularly brought as sacrifice and so also available for regular consumption (Wenham 1979:20; Douglas 2000:137-151). The strange and unfamiliar were forbidden. Means of locomotion also seems to play into the clean/unclean distinction, with cleanness associated with land animals that have no direct skin contact with the ground; the ground had been cursed by God through the actions of the serpent, who seduced the first humans, and creeping, ground-touching animals are unclean (Gen 3; Kiuchi 2007:204-207).

Four animals are mentioned as examples of the unacceptable, along with the criteria they lacked. Three appear to chew their cud but have no true hoof. Camels, evident in texts and through archaeology from the early second millennium BC on (Kitchen 2003:339), were used for long-range transportation and travel (Gen 24; 31:17; 1 Kgs 10:2), mainly by non-Israelites who lived in desert areas (e.g., Gen 37:25; 1 Sam 15:3; Jer 49:29). They could be used by Israel for their milk and hair, but not their flesh. Rock badgers, or hyraxes, were wild and lived in the mountain crags (Ps 104:18). They had thick nails instead of hooves and thoroughly worked their food when eating, though without regurgitating it. Two species of hare were found in Israel, one in inhabited places and another in barren places (Milgrom 1991:648). The hare lived above the ground, as distinct from a "rabbit" (NIV, NASB), which burrowed and worked its food like the rock badger, neither of which had hooves. The fourth animal, the pig, was excluded not for the hooves, which it had, but for lack of cud-chewing, since it is an omnivore, eating almost anything except grass. Pigs, which were abhorrent in Israel (Prov 11:22; Isa 66:3, 17), were used in neighboring pagan rituals, mainly in sacrifices directed to the underworld deities (Milgrom 1991:651-652; ABD 6.1131-1133). There seem to have been elements of that same practice in some of the popular religions in Israel as well (cf. Isa 65:4-5). The pig was possibly banned so that the Israelites could distinguish themselves from those who carried out unacceptable religious practices, including the Philistines, who ate pork (King and Stager 2001:119; cf. 2 Macc 6:18). This distinctiveness from pagan practices of her neighbors could well have been one of the reasons for these laws (cf. John 4:9). Pigs could be raised, possibly for sale (Matt 8:30), just not consumed (Isa 66:17). Today in Israel some farmers raise pigs, but keep them on cardboard or raised platforms so they have no direct contact with the land. The flesh of the butchered animal could not be eaten, nor could their dead bodies even be touched (cf. 11:24-28), lest impurity be transmitted. Jewish dietary or kosher laws continued and developed during the intertestamental period, with many Jews choosing death over consumption of unclean animals (1 Macc 1:62-63; 2 Macc 6:18). In the New Testament period, the Pharisees were very particular about food purity and eating practices (Mark 7:1-15; Smith 2003:150-152), practices which Jesus himself may have followed as part of Jewish tradition, but not in a manner to exclude anyone from the worship of God.

◆   ## 2. Aquatic animals (11:9-12)

9"Of all the marine animals, these are ones you may use for food. You may eat anything from the water if it has both fins and scales, whether taken from salt water or from streams. 10But you must never eat animals from the sea or from rivers that do not have both fins and scales. They are detestable to you. This applies both to little creatures that live in shallow water and to all creatures that live in deep water. [11]They will always be detestable to you. You must never eat their meat or even touch their dead bodies. [12]Any marine animal that does not have both fins and scales is detestable to you.

NOTES

11:9 *marine animals.* This is better translated as "aquatic animals" since they are not only from the sea but also from freshwater sources.

11:10 *detestable.* These animals are detestable not due to personal taste but because they are an "abomination" (KJV), things that could not be eaten.

COMMENTARY

Creatures inhabiting the water are presented second in this legal discussion, followed by those with wings. This arrangement follows the creation order as presented in Gen 1:20-21. Water creatures acceptable for eating must have both fins and scales (Deut 14:9; cf. Ezek 29:4). These are fish that move "normally." It didn't matter where the creatures were found, in fresh or salt water. These points are hammered home, repeated several times in the passage in positive (11:9) and negative (11:10-12) forms. The distinction made between shallow- and deepwater creatures (11:10) is uncertain, since the Hebrew had rather two categories that could be literally translated "water swarmers" and other "living creatures which are in the water" (cf. Gen 1:20, where the two are combined into one phrase, "swarmers, living creatures"). While the distinction was known to the original hearers, it is unclear to us today. It was not a distinguishing factor in food selection, but rather a comprehensive marker—that is, everything from the water, no matter what its other characteristics might be, should only be judged through scales and fins. Therefore, most fish were included, but shellfish and mollusks, which also have direct contact with the earth (as did the unclean animals mentioned earlier), were excluded.

Israel itself was not a seagoing people and had little contact with seafood, since the sea immediately adjacent to their territory was deficient in sea life due to lack of aquatic nutrients (Milgrom 1991:660-661). Fish types were not identified at all in the Old Testament, though fishing had become a means of livelihood by the time of Jesus (cf. Matt 4:18, 21; Mark 1:16; Luke 5:1-10). This could well have been the reason why individual types are not mentioned here as they are for the other two categories: The Israelites simply didn't know enough about them.

◆ ## 3. Winged animals (11:13-23)

[13]"These are the birds that are detestable to you. You must never eat them: the griffon vulture, the bearded vulture, the black vulture, [14]the kite, falcons of all kinds, [15]ravens of all kinds, [16]the eagle owl, the short-eared owl, the seagull, hawks of all kinds, [17]the little owl, the cormorant, the great owl, [18]the barn owl, the desert owl, the Egyptian vulture, [19]the stork, herons of all kinds, the hoopoe, and the bat.

²⁰"You must not eat winged insects that walk along the ground; they are detestable to you. ²¹You may, however, eat winged insects that walk along the ground and have jointed legs so they can jump ²²The insects you are permitted to eat include all kinds of locusts, bald locusts, crickets, and grasshoppers. ²³All other winged insects that walk along the ground are detestable to you.

NOTES

11:21 *walk along the ground.* Lit., "walk on all fours," perhaps better rendered as "scuttle."

COMMENTARY

The last category of inedible animals includes winged animals, both birds (11:13-19) and insects (11:20-23). Since these were a more common element of Israel's daily existence than fish, various species were named. Albeit, modern interpreters are unsure exactly what species are referred to by many of the Hebrew terms. No general category distinguished between acceptable and unacceptable birds. There was simply a list of 20 of the latter. The rabbis suggest that there was no corresponding list of allowable birds, since it would have been much too long. Included in it would have been the pigeon and turtledove, the sacrificial birds (e.g., 1:14 and elsewhere). Unlike the unclean members of the previous categories, uncleanness was not spread through touching birds, only through eating them.

For centuries, people have tried to determine what the unclean birds have in common, perhaps being eaters of carrion or live flesh. The matter has not yet been adequately resolved in such a way as to provide criteria that exclude only those listed and no other birds and also include all listed members.

Insects, however, are categorized by their means of locomotion. Since they were winged, the natural means of locomotion would have been flying. Those that did not do so, but rather walked on the ground, must be avoided, possibly as being unnatural. One exemption was those with extra legs that allow them to hop or jump, being airborne for at least some of the time. Four of these were identified as being permitted: locusts, bald locusts, crickets, and grasshoppers (cf. Matt 3:4; Mark 1:6). All others were denied.

◆   ## 4. Regulations concerning land animals (11:24-45)

²⁴"The following creatures will make you ceremonially unclean. If any of you touch their carcasses, you will be defiled until evening. ²⁵If you pick up their carcasses, you must wash your clothes, and you will remain defiled until evening.

²⁶"Any animal that has split hooves that are not evenly divided or that does not chew the cud is unclean for you. If you touch the carcass of such an animal, you will be defiled. ²⁷Of the animals that walk on all fours, those that have paws are unclean. If you touch the carcass of such an animal, you will be defiled until evening. ²⁸If you pick up its carcass, you must wash your clothes, and you will remain defiled until evening. These animals are unclean for you.

²⁹"Of the small animals that scurry along the ground, these are unclean for you: the mole rat, the rat, large lizards of all kinds, ³⁰the gecko, the monitor lizard,

the common lizard, the sand lizard, and the chameleon. ³¹All these small animals are unclean for you. If any of you touch the dead body of such an animal, you will be defiled until evening. ³²If such an animal dies and falls on something, that object will be unclean. This is true whether the object is made of wood, cloth, leather, or burlap. Whatever its use, you must dip it in water, and it will remain defiled until evening. After that, it will be ceremonially clean and may be used again.

³³"If such an animal falls into a clay pot, everything in the pot will be defiled, and the pot must be smashed. ³⁴If the water from such a container spills on any food, the food will be defiled. And any beverage in such a container will be defiled. ³⁵Any object on which the carcass of such an animal falls will be defiled. If it is an oven or hearth, it must be destroyed, for it is defiled, and you must treat it accordingly.

³⁶"However, if the carcass of such an animal falls into a spring or a cistern, the water will still be clean. But anyone who touches the carcass will be defiled. ³⁷If the carcass falls on seed grain to be planted in the field, the seed will still be considered clean. ³⁸But if the seed is wet when the carcass falls on it, the seed will be defiled.

³⁹"If an animal you are permitted to eat dies and you touch its carcass, you will be defiled until evening. ⁴⁰If you eat any of its meat or carry away its carcass, you must wash your clothes, and you will remain defiled until evening.

⁴¹"All small animals that scurry along the ground are detestable, and you must never eat them. ⁴²This includes all animals that slither along on their bellies, as well as those with four legs and those with many feet. All such animals that scurry along the ground are detestable, and you must never eat them. ⁴³Do not defile yourselves by touching them. You must not make yourselves ceremonially unclean because of them. ⁴⁴For I am the LORD your God. You must consecrate yourselves and be holy, because I am holy. So do not defile yourselves with any of these small animals that scurry along the ground. ⁴⁵For I, the LORD, am the one who brought you up from the land of Egypt, that I might be your God. Therefore, you must be holy because I am holy.

NOTES

11:32 *cloth*. This is not limited to "garments" (a common translation of the word *beged* [TH899/A, ZH955]; Gen 28:20; Isa 59:6; Ezek 18:7), but also includes other fabric items (Num 4:6-13; 1 Sam 19:13).

***burlap*.** This is understood as a coarser cloth made of goat hair, based on the parallel passage in Num 31:20.

11:33 *clay pot*. This kind of pot would be turned and fired but not glazed, so it was quite porous. The impurity, like any liquid within the pot, would be absorbed and could not be removed.

11:35 *oven*. Since this was where things were baked, it was important to keep the inside pure. The material from which the oven was constructed is not mentioned in the Hebrew, but clay and mud were common materials.

***hearth*.** The grammatical number of the Hebrew form is dual, designating a pair of something. Archaeologists have found a stove with openings for two pots to boil simultaneously (Milgrom 1991:679), a possible explanation of the dual form.

11:36 *cistern*. This is a man-made water storage pit (the same Hebrew word is used in Exod 21:33; Ps 7:15; Isa 51:1; Jer 2:13) dug into rock but often still very porous unless sealed.

11:37 *seed grain*. This was grain that would be used to plant the next crop rather than eaten.

11:41 *animals that scurry along the ground.* This is in distinction from those that scurry or swarm in the water (11:9-12) or air (11:20-23). Rodents, snakes, lizards, and insects would be included here.

11:42 *bellies.* This word (*gakhon* [TH1512, ZH1623]) contains the middle letter of the Pentateuch in the Masoretic Text (it is a Waw, represented by the *o* in *gakhon*), a letter that was written larger than the surrounding letters in many Hebrew mss.

11:43 *defile yourselves.* The defilement here is contaminated through eating (11:10). Milgrom (1991:684) points out that the word "self" could also be more specifically translated "throat," which was the part of the body directly affected by eating (see Hebrew text at Num 21:5; Isa 5:14).

11:44 *You must . . . be holy.* In context, this means to keep oneself from things that pollute and profane, as in 11:43.

COMMENTARY

The previous discussion concerned which creatures were acceptable to eat or the carcass of which it was permissible or impermissible to touch. These laws provide greater detail regarding unclean land animals. The commands pertain first of all to the unclean animals, with religious impurity befalling the one who touched them, lasting until night fell. The clothes of one who carried a carcass needed to be washed, probably since this was an action that involved sustained contact with the dead. One would assume that not only here but throughout the rest of the chapter, whenever a carcass was even touched, the person would also need to wash at least the hands, if not the entire body (cf. 17:15; 22:6).

Uncleanness was not transmitted only through intentional contact, however, but also through unintentional contact, as when the dead body of a small animal falls onto or into another object. Some things were able to be purified after being washed by completely immersing them in water (11:32; cf. Jer 13:1), even though they came into contact with a dead animal. This includes items of cloth and wood, the former being easily washed and the latter being not very porous over the short term. Clay items, being more porous, became unusable after any contact with an unclean animal, whether dead or alive, and needed to be destroyed by breaking them so they could not be reused (11:33; cf. 6:28; 15:12). This pollution also carried over to any of its liquid contents or anything in which it was heated. Fixed, non-portable water holders such as natural springs (e.g., 1 Kgs 18:5; Isa 41:18; Hos 13:15) and hand-hewn cisterns (e.g., Exod 21:33; Deut 6:11) did not suffer pollution of their contents from an unclean carcass. Dry seed grain was also unaffected, since it was not for human consumption but for planting. If it was moist, however, it became tainted and unusable. Here the dual nature of water is evident: It is the means of purification (11:32) while also being the means of access of pollution (cf. the dual character of the water of Noah's flood, which was at the same time the means of death, drowning all life, and the means of life, floating the ark).

Clean, permissible animals also carried ceremonial uncleanness if they died from natural causes (in contrast to slaughter for sacrifice [17:3-7] or being killed by a hunter [17:13-14]). They were not forbidden as food, but those contacting them were to remain unclean until the evening (11:39). This had implications for such folks as shepherds, who raised large flocks for the sacrificial needs of the people (see Num 28–29 and especially 1 Kgs 8:63 for the large number of sacrificial sheep used). Large flocks would likely have had frequent enough animal deaths that shepherds would have been, due to their vocation as well as other factors, regularly in a state of uncleanness and would not have been allowed to offer the very animals that were in their charge. This makes it even more significant that the first announcement of the birth of Jesus came to these people at the margins of society (Luke 2:8-20), who couldn't go to the Temple; instead, the Temple came to them.

Finally, a general prohibition was made against small, scurrying creatures of three different types: legless, four-legged, and many-legged. All were "detestable," which distinguishes them from the eight identified members of this general group mentioned above (11:29-30), which are designated only as "unclean." The importance of this section was heightened by God's double self-declaration of holiness, which previous sections of the chapter did not include. In light of his holy character (19:2; 20:26) and his actions in saving Israel from Egyptian slavery (26:13; Josh 24:17; 2 Kgs 17:7) so that he could have a special relationship with them as their God (26:12; Exod 6:7; 16:12), they needed to respond.

Their response was presented in negative (avoid contamination) and positive (be holy) terms. Israel's response to God's saving grace needed to be shown in action and ethics, which involved keeping these regulations as well as the wider law (Num 15:40). It was the same motivation of grace, exemplified by being freed from Egypt, which prompted Israel to respond by basing her personal and national existence on the Ten Commandments (Exod 20:2; Deut 5:6).

◆   ## 5. Summary (11:46-47)

46"These are the instructions regarding land animals, birds, marine creatures, and animals that scurry along the ground. 47By these instructions you will know what is unclean and clean, and which animals may be eaten and which may not be eaten."

COMMENTARY

The chapter concludes with a summary of its contents and purpose. The text tells us that these were "instructions" (*torah* [TH8451, ZH9368], 11:46), a term used of the Mosaic law in general and as the Jewish name for the Pentateuch itself. This term was also used of regulations elsewhere in Leviticus (6:9 [2], 14 [7], 25 [18]; 7:1, 7, 11, 37). The purpose, to help Israelites in distinguishing (cf. Gen 1:4, 6, 7, 14, 18) clean and unclean, was given an immediately practical bent by showing what was allowed for eating and what was not. This type of differentiation, though between different categories, was the task of God himself in Genesis 1 and of his ministerial representatives, the priests, here in Leviticus (10:10).

These instructions were given to a specific people, Israel, in their wanderings in the wilderness and for a specific context: settling into the land of Canaan among a group of pagan neighbors. They are set into Israel's story (11:1-2) and are not presented as universal guidelines for every person in the world. However, they almost split the church very soon after it was born. The council of Jerusalem (Acts 15) included some eating restrictions in their conclusions regarding fellowship inclusion of Gentiles into the family of God along with their fellow Jews, who still observed regulations concerning the clean and the unclean. Though Jesus made this distinction regarding food and its polluting potential moot (Matt 15:17-20; Mark 7:19; cf. Col 2:16), some Jewish believers were making it a touchstone of true faith (Gal 2:11-14). For the Jerusalem council (Acts 15:20), the criteria were different than those mentioned here. There, eating blood was banned (see 7:26-27), as were strangled animals—those from which the blood had not been drained. Animals sacrificed in pagan rites were also not allowed, a matter also discussed by Paul (1 Cor 8). None of these criteria were mentioned in chapter 11.

The focus had shifted in Paul's writings from any pollution intrinsic to the food itself to the person who consumes it. There is, in Christian life, a need to distinguish between acceptable and unacceptable practices. Those mentioned by Paul are not fixed, absolute categories, however, but change according to the maturity of the person involved and according to the personal and cultural context in which a person is acting. Like children who need carefully set and explained boundaries when they are young, strictly defined rules of conduct are necessary for those beginning their walk in the family of God. As one matures, so does the awareness that all is from God's hand, and that purity of external things depends on the purity of the person (Titus 1:15), though there are some (e.g., idolatry and prostitution) that are never acceptable.

Peter was made aware of this changing outlook on the acceptable and unacceptable in his vision at Joppa, where God overturned the regulations given here in chapter 11 (Acts 10:9-16; 11:1-10). He did not acquiesce at the first hearing of this change, however, since it was an approach to food that had been ingrained for generations. He only made the change after God had specifically urged him three times.

◆ B. Childbirth (12:1-8)

The LORD said to Moses, "Give the following instructions to the people of Israel. ²If a woman becomes pregnant and gives birth to a son, she will be ceremonially unclean for seven days, just as she is unclean during her menstrual period. ³On the eighth day the boy's foreskin must be circumcised. ⁴After waiting thirty-three days, she will be purified from the bleeding of childbirth. During this time of purification, she must not touch anything that is set apart as holy. And she must not enter the sanctuary until her time of purification is over. ⁵If a woman gives birth to a daughter, she will be ceremonially unclean for two weeks, just as she is unclean during her menstrual period. After waiting sixty-six days, she will be purified from the bleeding of childbirth.

⁶"When the time of purification is completed for either a son or a daughter, the woman must bring a one-year-old lamb for a burnt offering and a young pigeon or turtledove for a purification offering. She must bring her offerings to the priest at the entrance of the Tabernacle.* ⁷The priest will

then present them to the LORD to purify her.* Then she will be ceremonially clean again after her bleeding at childbirth. These are the instructions for a woman after the birth of a son or a daughter.

⁸"If a woman cannot afford to bring a lamb, she must bring two turtledoves or two young pigeons. One will be for the burnt offering and the other for the purification offering. The priest will sacrifice them to purify her, and she will be ceremonially clean."

12:6 Hebrew *Tent of Meeting.* 12:7 Or *to make atonement for her;* also in 12:8.

NOTES

12:2 son. Lit., "a male." The term *zakar* is suggested to be etymologically related to other Semitic words for "male" and "phallus" (BDB 271; HALOT 270).

12:5 daughter. Lit., "female," (*neqebah* [TH5347, ZH5922], the same root as "hole, to pierce," here in reference to the female genitalia; BDB 666; HALOT 719; *naqab* [TH5344, ZH5918]).

COMMENTARY

The continued existence of an individual depends on food and drink, the subject of chapter 11. The continued existence of a people also depends on subsequent generations, the subject of the present chapter. Since childbirth was not only a significant event in a family's life but also an event fraught with danger for mother and baby (Gen 35:16-19; 1 Sam 4:19-20), it is understandable that it is a matter of legal interest as well as a situation in which any protection possible, whether physical or ceremonial, might be sought. The regulations here are directed only toward the mother; there is no explicit mention of the father anywhere in the chapter. Ritual expectations varied according to whether the baby was a boy or a girl.

According to the opening verses (12:1-2), Yahweh continued to speak through his servant Moses to the people (4:1; 5:14; 6:1, 8, 19, 25; 7:22, 28; 8:1). Yahweh spoke concerning any woman who "becomes pregnant and gives birth to a son." The verb for "becoming pregnant" ("brings forth or produces seed") was used only rarely concerning human reproduction (*zara'* [TH2232, ZH2445]; cf. Num 5:28; Nah 1:14). The reason for this particular use lies in the focus in this passage on the "seed" or fruit of the pregnancy, the baby produced, rather than the state of pregnancy itself. This verb was used in place of the verb more commonly used to denote becoming pregnant (*harah* [TH2029, ZH2225]). No father is specifically mentioned here, though biologically the "seed" is supplied by the male, and the noun almost always applies to the father in the Old Testament.

When the baby was a boy, the birthing process left the mother ceremonially unclean for a week. This was compared to the uncleanness a woman had as a result of her monthly menstrual period (12:2). The impurity associated with the menstrual blood flow is not discussed until 15:19-24, though knowledge of its regulations must have been well-known prior to their being written down in Leviticus. There must have been a correspondence between childbirth impurity and the length of impurity through menstrual bleeding, though no mention of her bleeding at childbirth is made here, so it is unclear if it was the blood that caused uncleanness. In her uncleanness, anything she touched would also become unclean for a week, which must also be what was understood, though not stated, here.

Nowhere in the passage is there any indication of what, besides the passage of time, marked the end of this period of uncleanness. Probably there was a ritual washing for the woman on the seventh day, even though it is not explicitly mentioned, since such a washing marked the end of many such periods (e.g., 11:25, 28, 40; 15:1-33). Another washing probably concluded the 40- or 80-day period as well.

The instructions then focus on the baby boy (12:3), who was to be circumcised (lit., "circumcise the foreskin of his penis"; cf. Gen 17:14, 24-25). This common practice among Israel's neighbors (Jer 9:25-26) was a premarriage preparation rite (Milgrom 1991:747). For Israel it symbolized the special relationship Abraham and his descendants had with their covenant God (Gen 17:1-27). This symbolism, as well as the timing (to an infant on its eighth day of life), distinguished this practice from that of the neighboring peoples. Those who did not undergo the rite were not able to participate in covenant celebration events (Exod 12:43-49; Josh 5:2-10).

Then the instructions reverted to the mother (12:4), who was to wait an additional 33 days (a total of 40 days since the actual childbirth) to be purified. Here there was specific mention of her bleeding in association with the impurity, an element lacking in 12:2. The blood was literally called "blood of purity," since blood itself cleanses (16:19), only causing pollution if eaten (7:26-27; 17:10-12) or shed improperly (Num 35:33-34). It was this afterbirth blood, or "lochia," not the baby itself, that caused the uncleanness: "For the first few days after delivery this discharge is bright red, then it turns brown and later becomes paler. It may last from two to six weeks. Because the first phase of lochia resembles the menstrual discharge, it is consistent for the woman to be treated as contagiously unclean as she is when she menstruates" (Wenham 1979:188). The wording thus indicated that there were two stages. In the first, she was unclean, and her uncleanness polluted anything with which she had contact. During the second stage, there was no more polluting influence, but she still could not come into contact with the holy, whether a holy object or a holy place. That she was not allowed access to the sacred place now, in her state of impurity, indicates that she could enter there under ordinary circumstances in order to bring her own sacrifices. This confirms that the offerers in chapters 1–7, though described there using grammatically masculine forms, also included women.

At the birth of a girl, uncleanness was of a similar type, though the time period of the two stages was double those of a boy (12:5). We are not told in the Bible why there was this difference, though the practice is found in many societies around the world (Milgrom 1991:750-751). A lack of clear evidence has not stopped many explanations by commentators, though none can be sure (see Ross 2002:271-272). Some reasons are biological, such as the fact that some baby girls, under the influence of the mother's hormones associated with the bleeding at birth, also experience vaginal bleeding at birth. The uncleanness was thus not doubled because of any difference for the mother, but because there were two individuals who were bleeding, the mother and the daughter. Other explanations are sociological, claiming that the female showed "cultic inferiority" to the male and so purification needed to be twice as long (Noth 1965:97). This runs counter to the relative equality of the sexes at creation (see Gen 1, where both are created in God's image and given the same charge to look after the earth) and also to the logic of other scriptural passages. This proposed logic that the inferior produced greater impurity and required a longer purification process would indicate that a human, whose corpse polluted for seven days (Num 19:14-16), was inferior to an animal, which only polluted until the evening (11:39). If one acknowledges the superiority of human to animal, this proposed logic would also demand that the female was superior to the male!

Whatever the sex of the baby, when the purification period was over, the mother brought her sacrifices to the sanctuary (12:6-7). The order in which they are listed follows that in chapters 1-5 (burnt, then purification offerings), rather than the order in which they were actually performed (purification, then burnt offerings; 8:14-21). These sacrifices were not to gain purity for the mother, since it had already been achieved according to the text, possibly through either the passage of time or the implied washing. The traditional English name for the second offering as one for sin (e.g., KJV, NIV) is clearly inappropriate, since childbirth and blood flow are natural, not sinful, events. Provision was made for people from different economic classes to bring their offerings. Those who could afford a lamb for a burnt offering should do so (1:10), but a bird was also acceptable (12:8; cf. 1:14), as it was for the sin offering (12:6; cf. 5:7). As a result of the sacrifice performed on her behalf by a priest, she could again come into contact with that which was holy. Her purification (*taher* [TH2891, ZH3197]) from physical uncleanness is distinguished from forgiveness needed for moral sin (*salakh* [TH5545, ZH6142]; see 4:20, 26, 31, 35), since different verbs are used (Milgrom 1991:760).

There might be a reference to these practices in 1 Samuel 1, where Hannah did not join her husband, Elkanah, in the annual journey to the shrine for sacrifice (1 Sam 1:22). While it is not so stated in the text, and there is not a clear timeline between the birth and the journey, it could be that she was still in the 33-day period of uncleanness. In the New Testament, Jesus was circumcised and named eight days after his birth (Luke 2:21; the giving of a name is not mentioned in conjunction with the events in ch 12). Then he was later presented at the Temple, after the purification of mother and son (Luke 2:22), for this would have been the first opportunity for Jesus' mother to have been able to present herself there. She also presented the expected sacrifices (12:6-8; Luke 2:23-24).

◆ ## C. Surface Blemishes and Diseases (13:1–14:57)
   ### 1. On skin (13:1–46)

The LORD said to Moses and Aaron, ²"If anyone has a swelling or a rash or discolored skin that might develop into a serious skin disease,* that person must be brought to Aaron the priest or to one of his sons.* ³The priest will examine the affected area of the skin. If the hair in the affected area has turned white and the problem appears to be more than skin-deep, it is a serious skin disease, and the priest who examines it must pronounce the person ceremonially unclean.

⁴"But if the affected area of the skin is only a white discoloration and does not

appear to be more than skin-deep, and if the hair on the spot has not turned white, the priest will quarantine the person for seven days. ⁵On the seventh day the priest will make another examination. If he finds the affected area has not changed and the problem has not spread on the skin, the priest will quarantine the person for seven more days. ⁶On the seventh day the priest will make another examination. If he finds the affected area has faded and has not spread, the priest will pronounce the person ceremonially clean. It was only a rash. The person's clothing must be washed, and the person will be ceremonially clean. ⁷But if the rash continues to spread after the person has been examined by the priest and has been pronounced clean, the infected person must return to be examined again. ⁸If the priest finds that the rash has spread, he must pronounce the person ceremonially unclean, for it is indeed a skin disease.

⁹"Anyone who develops a serious skin disease must go to the priest for an examination. ¹⁰If the priest finds a white swelling on the skin, and some hair on the spot has turned white, and there is an open sore in the affected area, ¹¹it is a chronic skin disease, and the priest must pronounce the person ceremonially unclean. In such cases the person need not be quarantined, for it is obvious that the skin is defiled by the disease.

¹²"Now suppose the disease has spread all over the person's skin, covering the body from head to foot. ¹³When the priest examines the infected person and finds that the disease covers the entire body, he will pronounce the person ceremonially clean. Since the skin has turned completely white, the person is clean. ¹⁴But if any open sores appear, the infected person will be pronounced ceremonially unclean. ¹⁵The priest must make this pronouncement as soon as he sees an open sore, since open sores indicate the presence of a skin disease. ¹⁶However, if the open sores heal and turn white like the

rest of the skin, the person must return to the priest ¹⁷for another examination. If the affected areas have indeed turned white, the priest will then pronounce the person ceremonially clean by declaring, 'You are clean!'

¹⁸"If anyone has a boil on the skin that has started to heal, ¹⁹but a white swelling or a reddish white spot develops in its place, that person must go to the priest to be examined. ²⁰If the priest examines it and finds it to be more than skin-deep, and if the hair in the affected area has turned white, the priest must pronounce the person ceremonially unclean. The boil has become a serious skin disease. ²¹But if the priest finds no white hair on the affected area and the problem appears to be no more than skin-deep and has faded, the priest must quarantine the person for seven days. ²²If during that time the affected area spreads on the skin, the priest must pronounce the person ceremonially unclean, because it is a serious disease. ²³But if the area grows no larger and does not spread, it is merely the scar from the boil, and the priest will pronounce the person ceremonially clean.

²⁴"If anyone has suffered a burn on the skin and the burned area changes color, becoming either reddish white or shiny white, ²⁵the priest must examine it. If he finds that the hair in the affected area has turned white and the problem appears to be more than skin-deep, a skin disease has broken out in the burn. The priest must then pronounce the person ceremonially unclean, for it is clearly a serious skin disease. ²⁶But if the priest finds no white hair on the affected area and the problem appears to be no more than skin-deep and has faded, the priest must quarantine the infected person for seven days. ²⁷On the seventh day the priest must examine the person again. If the affected area has spread on the skin, the priest must pronounce that person ceremonially unclean, for it is clearly a serious skin disease. ²⁸But if the affected area has not

changed or spread on the skin and has faded, it is simply a swelling from the burn. The priest will then pronounce the person ceremonially clean, for it is only the scar from the burn.

²⁹"If anyone, either a man or woman, has a sore on the head or chin, ³⁰the priest must examine it. If he finds it is more than skin-deep and has fine yellow hair on it, the priest must pronounce the person ceremonially unclean. It is a scabby sore of the head or chin. ³¹If the priest examines the scabby sore and finds that it is only skin-deep but there is no black hair on it, he must quarantine the person for seven days. ³²On the seventh day the priest must examine the sore again. If he finds that the scabby sore has not spread, and there is no yellow hair on it, and it appears to be only skin-deep, ³³the person must shave off all hair except the hair on the affected area. Then the priest must quarantine the person for another seven days. ³⁴On the seventh day he will examine the sore again. If it has not spread and appears to be no more than skin-deep, the priest will pronounce the person ceremonially clean. The person's clothing must be washed, and the person will be ceremonially clean. ³⁵But if the scabby sore begins to spread after the person is pronounced clean, ³⁶the priest must do another examination. If he finds that the sore has spread, the priest does not need to look for yellow hair. The

infected person is ceremonially unclean. ³⁷But if the color of the scabby sore does not change and black hair has grown on it, it has healed. The priest will then pronounce the person ceremonially clean.

³⁸"If anyone, either a man or woman, has shiny white patches on the skin, ³⁹the priest must examine the affected area. If he finds that the shiny patches are only pale white, this is a harmless skin rash, and the person is ceremonially clean.

⁴⁰"If a man loses his hair and his head becomes bald, he is still ceremonially clean. ⁴¹And if he loses hair on his forehead, he simply has a bald forehead; he is still clean. ⁴²However, if a reddish white sore appears on the bald area at the top or back of his head, this is a skin disease. ⁴³The priest must examine him, and if he finds swelling around the reddish white sore anywhere on the man's head and it looks like a skin disease, ⁴⁴the man is indeed infected with a skin disease and is unclean. The priest must pronounce him ceremonially unclean because of the sore on his head.

⁴⁵"Those who suffer from a serious skin disease must tear their clothing and leave their hair uncombed.* They must cover their mouth and call out, 'Unclean! Unclean!' ⁴⁶As long as the serious disease lasts, they will be ceremonially unclean. They must live in isolation in their place outside the camp.

13:2a Traditionally rendered *leprosy*. The Hebrew word used throughout this passage is used to describe various skin diseases. 13:2b Or *one of his descendants.* 13:45 Or *and uncover their heads.*

NOTES

13:2 *skin disease.* Numerous English versions present the disease as leprosy (KJV, NASB, NRSV; cf. LXX), but the symptoms do not correspond to those of Hansen's disease, which exhibits loss of sensation caused by bacterial infection. Nor does "leprosy" affect clothing or buildings, as did this affliction (13:47-58; 14:33-53). For this reason, the NLT avoids the rendering "leprosy" (see NLT mg), and instead uses "serious skin disease." Actually, a number of different conditions are probably included within the meaning of the single Hebrew term *tsara'ath* [TH6883, ZH7669] and its verbal form *tsara'* [TH6879, ZH7665]). There is no English term that covers all the symptoms found here, as is apparent from the NLT's translation of the term as both "skin disease" and "mildew" (13:47, 49). The closest might be to simply call them all "visible blemishes."

13:4 *seven days.* A seven-day period is noted elsewhere in conjunction with religious acts: 8:33, 35; 12:2; often in ch 13; 14:8-9; 15:13, 19, 24, 28; 23:3, 6; cf. 23:18; 25:4, 8. This period of quarantine was to guard against the spread of infection and was not a form of banishment (cf. Num 12:14-15, where the same term is sometimes erroneously interpreted as banishment, which goes beyond the evidence; cf. 2 Kgs 15:5; 2 Chr 26:21).

13:10 open sore. Lit., "raw [living] flesh" (cf. 1 Sam 2:15) or ulcer, which would be contagious due to oozing blood or other discharge (see ch 15).

13:30 scabby sore. The term *neteq* [TH5424, ZH5999] comes from a verb meaning "pull, tear away" (cf. the castrated animal in 22:24) because either the hair (Milgrom 1991:793) or skin or scab (Hartley 1992:192) was torn away. Some suggest that this points to psoriasis, eczema (ibid.), or ringworm (Harrison 1980:144).

13:40-42 bald. Hebrew has two separate words for balding. The first (*qereakh* [TH7142, ZH7944]) refers to ordinary baldness on the crown or top of the head (2 Kgs 2:23), while the second (*gibbeakh* [TH1371, ZH1477]) indicates a bald forehead, which is also natural and not disease related. Since the Hebrew words translated "the top or back of his head" in 13:42 are related to the two types of baldness mentioned in 13:40-41, the phrase would be clearer if rendered as "front or back."

COMMENTARY

Blemishes were considered a departure from the norm and needed to be eradicated or otherwise handled wherever they occurred, since the blemished people could not come into contact with anything sacred and could spread their contamination. This section deals with the diagnosis of such blemishes in the form of a scaly disease of the skin that could affect not only people but also other materials. This is not a section dealing with cures—explaining what to do to get rid of the affliction; rather it tells how to determine if the contagious stage of infection had passed. In other words, this section is not instruction for a doctor as healer but for a priest as diagnostician (10:10). This is accentuated by God's speaking only to Moses, as the nation's leader, and Aaron, the leader of the priests (13:1). The content was not to be passed on to the Israelites, as much of the other legislation was (1:2; 11:2; 12:1; 15:1-2; 17:2; 18:2). In other situations the common person played an active role, but here there needed to be expert involvement lest a misdiagnosis be made and the uncleanness spread.

The terminology used in this section is technical, and since there is no other discussion of the topic in the Bible, much of it is very uncertain. The context can indicate some of the content of the terms, but specific nuances often need to be provided by the translator, with no certainty of accuracy. Similar terminology from the ancient Near Eastern environment of Old Testament times, as well as modern medical understanding, can help to some extent, but much is still only tentatively understood.

Contamination of the human body was of primary importance since it was people who entered the holy sanctuary in order to worship (see Rev 21:27). Since there are a number of skin conditions affecting people, numerous options are presented, with various diagnostic procedures to be followed, some lasting a period of time. The ailments listed here fall into several categories: those involving rashes or discoloration (13:2-17), boils (13:18-23), burns (13:24-28), and those affecting the hairy parts of the head (13:29-44).

The first three conditions (13:1-17) seem to have involved a discoloring shininess on the skin that needed to be checked to see if it was mild, only affecting the surface of the skin of the body, or more severe, extending deeper into the epidermis. These could affect anyone, regardless of sex or age. When such a problem was noted, either by the sufferer or someone else, it needed to be reported. Then the person needed to come to any of the priests (cf. Luke 17:14), who would carefully inspect the area for white color, possibly caused by the flaky skin, and for the visible depth of the infection. If it had these, it was recognized and categorized by the priest as something that had caused uncleanness. If the diagnosis was unsure, a seven-day quarantine in an unspecified place was necessary (13:4). This was to protect others from contact with the person if they might be contagious. No treatment was specified, since the wait was only for diagnosis. The initial wait was a week. If no change was visible after the wait, a second week of quarantine was imposed (13:5). If the condition had improved or remained the same, the priest diagnosed that it was not serious, and he would recognize the person as being clean and able to participate fully in community life after washing his clothes, and presumably his body as well (cf. 11:25, 32). If at any of these inspections, or even a later one, the infection had spread, the person was declared unclean, and more serious steps were to be followed as spelled out in 14:1-32. This was also true if the initial inspection showed a more serious occurrence having an open sore (see note on 13:10). The latter was immediately recognizable as being "chronic" (13:11; cf. "long time" in Deut 4:25) and needed no further inspections.

If the entire body was affected but was white due to the peeling of the scaly skin, the priest made the diagnosis of "clean"; the person was whole because the skin was no longer oozing, and the person was able to engage in the full life of the community (13:12-13). Open sores could bring the opposite diagnosis and result, unless and until they healed (13:14-17).

The next case (13:18-23) pertains to a boil (a "burning" sore in other Semitic languages), caused by an infected skin pore that became inflamed. These were at times sent by God (Exod 9:9-11; Deut 28:27, 35) or Satan (Job 2:7). Special attention was needed if the affected place became a reddish white spot, where the red is emphatic in Hebrew, "bright red." It required inspection by the priest, being diagnosed and handled as with the previous cases (13:4-5), though with only a single seven-day quarantine period. Like the discoloration in 13:6, the redness would fade as healing progressed. If not, the person was declared infected and unclean.

The next case deals with burns (13:24-28). Since fire was used for cooking, heat, and lighting in the Israelite home, accidental burns were probably relatively common. The text specifies what a burn looked like if it had some kind of secondary infection. This also needed inspection and diagnosis in the same way as a boil.

Following these matters, attention is given to the head and its hair, the scalp and beard areas (13:29-37, 40-44). Both men and women were specifically included here. Inspection and diagnosis parallels that already described in 13:2-8. Here a diagnostic element was the hair's turning yellow, rather than white, as in previous cases (13:20-21, 25-26). This different color made it diagnostic of a different form of "scabby sore" (infection). In Israel, black hair was normal and therefore uninfected. Sumerian and Akkadian literature referred to foreigners, especially those from this area of Syria-Palestine, as the "black-headed people," indicating that this may have been the general, but not exclusive, hair color. The present text means that signs of normalcy had not yet returned. Two seven-day quarantines and washing were also prescribed for this case.

A brief discussion (13:38-39) about another bodily anomaly interrupts the discussion of the head, possibly because it, too, concerned either a man or woman (cf. 13:29). The Hebrew suggests numerous affected areas that necessitate inspection and diagnosis. Only a positive diagnosis was mentioned for those that did not have the sheen of previously mentioned sores. One would assume that a more serious finding would have again resulted in being declared unclean. These symptoms have been identified as indicating *leukoderma* or *vitiligo*, which have patches of unpigmented skin (Hulse 1975:95; Milgrom 1991:800), or even herpes simplex, which produces numerous small blisters (Harrison 1980:145).

The final symptom pertains to male hair loss, which at times occurs naturally (13:40-44), not due to any skin disease that might cause him to go bald, such as the infection in 13:30. However, if there was a sore accompanying the baldness, and if it was reddish-white, the color identified it as abnormal (cf. 13:19) and contagious. As such, it was pronounced unclean by the priest.

This section closes with regulations regarding the actions to be taken by those who were diagnosed as unclean because of any of the preceding ailments (13:45-46). They were to show grief (cf. 10:6) because of their condition and also cover their mouth (lit., "mustache;" cf. 2 Sam 19:24 [25]; Ezek 24:17, NASB) as a sign of shame and disgrace (Mic 3:7) or mourning (Ezek 24:17, 22). This covering was probably done with the cloak (cf. 1 Sam 28:14; Ps 109:19, where the same verb appears); as such, the entire mouth would be covered. Alternatively, if, as the rabbis suggested, the cloak was lowered over the head (Milgrom 1991:803), the entire face would be covered. The rabbis suggest that this was to prevent the contagion passing on through the breath. The infected person also had to warn others not to get near them by calling out that they were unclean. This lasted as long as the impurity lasted, which implied that if there was any visible change in symptoms, the person could go back to the priest for another inspection.

The sufferer had to live apart from others, staying outside the camp while they were on the march in the Sinai wilderness or outside the city or village when they settled in the land, apparently in separation even from people with other contaminations (13:46), but not from those contaminated in the same way (see 2 Kgs 7:3-10; Mark 1:45; Luke 17:11-19, where groups of sufferers from contagious skin diseases lived together; see Milgrom 1991:805). This separation was not because they might be contagious, which was not mentioned anywhere in the passage. Rather, it was because they were unclean, and contact with them would have passed the ceremonial uncleanness on to others, defiling the holy camp where God dwelt (see Num 5:2-3).

Victims of such afflictions undoubtedly included people from every social class. The main cases cited in the Old Testament involve people of some importance. The Syrian military commander Naaman was a sufferer of an unspecified skin disease (using the general term applied to most of the maladies in this chapter; 2 Kgs 5), as was the Judean King Hezekiah, who had a terminal boil (2 Kgs 20:1-7). Neither episode records the priestly, religious aspect of the disease, but rather their treatment, which is not found in chapter 13. King Uzziah of Judah also suffered from skin disease sent as a punishment from God (2 Chr 26:19-20). As a result, he was unable to take part in Temple functions and had to live the rest of his life in quarantine (cf. Miriam, Moses's sister in Num 12:10-15).

None of these symptoms are said to arise from any moral flaw or sin, so it is going too far to blame them on an immoral condition or action (see John 9:2). This is made clear in the next section, where similar blemishes affect fabric of different kinds, which is morally neutral and whose owners did not need to take any cleansing steps themselves. This indicates that their own person was not contaminated in any way, nor was it seen as causing the contamination of their belongings. Illness, including skin diseases such as these, could come because of God's punishment (Num 12:10-12; 2 Chr 26:19-21) but were not necessarily anything more than a result of human mortality after the Fall. We are all subject to death (Gen 2:17; 3:19; 2 Cor 4) and disease, including degenerative skin diseases, where the body actually wastes away.

◆   2. On fabric (13:47-59)

47"Now suppose mildew* contaminates some woolen or linen clothing, 48woolen or linen fabric, the hide of an animal, or anything made of leather. 49If the contaminated area in the clothing, the animal hide, the fabric, or the leather article has turned greenish or reddish, it is contaminated with mildew and must be shown to the priest. 50After examining the affected spot, the priest will put the article in quarantine for seven days. 51On the seventh day the priest must inspect it again. If the contaminated area has spread, the clothing or fabric or leather is clearly contaminated by a serious mildew and is ceremonially unclean. 52The priest must burn the item—the clothing, the woolen or linen fabric, or piece of leather—for it has been contaminated by a serious mildew. It must be completely destroyed by fire.

53"But if the priest examines it and finds that the contaminated area has not spread in the clothing, the fabric, or the leather, 54the priest will order the object to be washed and then quarantined for seven more days. 55Then the priest must examine the object again. If he finds that the contaminated area has not changed color after being washed, even if it did not spread, the object is defiled. It must be completely burned up, whether the contaminated spot* is on the inside or outside. 56But if the priest examines it and finds that the contaminated area has faded after being washed, he must cut the spot from the clothing, the fabric, or the leather. 57If the spot later reappears on the clothing, the fabric, or the leather article, the mildew is clearly spreading, and the contaminated object must be burned up. 58But if the spot disappears from the clothing, the fabric, or the leather article after it has been washed, it must be washed again; then it will be ceremonially clean.

59"These are the instructions for dealing with mildew that contaminates woolen or linen clothing or fabric or anything made of leather. This is how the priest will determine whether these items are ceremonially clean or unclean."

13:47 Traditionally rendered *leprosy*. The Hebrew term used throughout this passage is the same term used for the various skin diseases described in 13:1-46.   13:55 The meaning of the Hebrew is uncertain.

NOTES

13:59 *These are the instructions.* The section closes with its own summary (cf. 11:46-47), indicating that this small section (13:47-59) was a self-contained unit. It is called an "instruction" (cf. 6:9, 14, 25; 7:1, 7, 11, 37; 11:46; 12:7) for the work of the priest.

COMMENTARY

Cloth and other kinds of fabrics could also be affected by discoloration and infection by outside agents, especially dry rot and mildew. These are stimulated by the heat in the semitropical Middle East. Visually, the effects of such things appeared similar to those that could happen to human skin, through color change and unnatural deposits or flaking and peeling. They underwent diagnostic procedures similar to those of humans showing surface abnormalities.

Wool and linen were the most common material for clothing fabric, and the terms seem often to be used together to indicate all fabrics (Deut 22:11; Prov 31:13). The former was an animal product, from a sheep (Deut 18:4; 2 Kgs 3:4) or goat (1 Sam 25:2; see King and Stager 2001:147-148). The latter derives from the plant flax, grown especially in Egypt (Exod 9:31; Prov 7:16; Isa 19:9) but also in Israel (Josh 2:6; Gezer calendar, COS 2.85:222; see King and Stager 2001:148-152). Leather or skin, another by-product of the domestication of animals, was tanned and used especially for footwear but also for clothing and water bags (11:32; Gen 3:21; 21:14; 2 Kgs 1:8).

The diagnostic feature on fabric was a color change, to red or green, which in Hebrew are given an intensive form (cf. 13:19), so the colors were bright. If a color change occurred, the priest was consulted, and he quarantined the object for up to two weeks. Since fabric did not have the natural healing properties of living flesh, once the condition was diagnosed as being malignant and the fabric contaminated, the object needed to be completely disposed of by fire. After the first period of quarantine, if the condition had not spread, the material was washed to remove the stains. This had to result in the disappearance of the symptoms or else the fabric was considered unclean. A faded spot was to be cut out, but the material could still be used if there was no recurrence. Presumably the object needed washing again, even though the text did not mention this step, since this had to be done to an object from which the mark completely disappeared. This time the washing was not for treatment, but for ceremonial purification. No mention is made in the chapter of the defiling power of those items or of people contaminated by such abnormalities.

◆   3. Cleansing procedures (14:1-57)

And the LORD said to Moses, ²"The following instructions are for those seeking ceremonial purification from a skin disease.* Those who have been healed must be brought to the priest, ³who will examine them at a place outside the camp. If the priest finds that someone has been healed of a serious skin disease, ⁴he will perform a purification ceremony, using two live birds that are ceremonially clean, a stick of cedar,* some scarlet yarn, and a hyssop branch. ⁵The priest will order that one bird be slaughtered over a clay pot filled with fresh water. ⁶He will take the live bird, the cedar stick, the scarlet yarn, and the hyssop branch, and dip them into the blood of the bird that was slaughtered over the fresh water. ⁷The priest will then sprinkle the blood of the dead bird seven times on the person being purified of the skin disease. When the priest has purified the person, he will release the live bird in the open field to fly away.

⁸"The persons being purified must then wash their clothes, shave off all their hair, and bathe themselves in water. Then they will be ceremonially clean and may return to the camp. However, they must remain outside their tents for seven days. ⁹On the seventh day they must again shave all the hair from their heads, including the hair of the beard and eyebrows. They must also wash their clothes and bathe themselves in water. Then they will be ceremonially clean.

¹⁰"On the eighth day each person being purified must bring two male lambs and a one-year-old female lamb, all with no defects, along with a grain offering of six quarts* of choice flour moistened with olive oil, and a cup* of olive oil. ¹¹Then the officiating priest will present that person for purification, along with the offerings, before the LORD at the entrance of the Tabernacle.* ¹²The priest will take one of the male lambs and the olive oil and present them as a guilt offering, lifting them up as a special offering before the LORD. ¹³He will then slaughter the male lamb in the sacred area where sin offerings and burnt offerings are slaughtered. As with the sin offering, the guilt offering belongs to the priest. It is a most holy offering. ¹⁴The priest will then take some of the blood of the guilt offering and apply it to the lobe of the right ear, the thumb of the right hand, and the big toe of the right foot of the person being purified.

¹⁵"Then the priest will pour some of the olive oil into the palm of his own left hand. ¹⁶He will dip his right finger into the oil in his palm and sprinkle some of it with his finger seven times before the LORD. ¹⁷The priest will then apply some of the oil in his palm over the blood from the guilt offering that is on the lobe of the right ear, the thumb of the right hand, and the big toe of the right foot of the person being purified. ¹⁸The priest will apply the oil remaining in his hand to the head of the person being purified. Through this process, the priest will purify* the person before the LORD.

¹⁹"Then the priest must present the sin offering to purify the person who was cured of the skin disease. After that, the priest will slaughter the burnt offering ²⁰and offer it on the altar along with the grain offering. Through this process, the priest will purify the person who was healed, and the person will be ceremonially clean.

²¹"But anyone who is too poor and cannot afford these offerings may bring one male lamb for a guilt offering, to be lifted up as a special offering for purification. The person must also bring two quarts* of choice flour moistened with olive oil for the grain offering and a cup of olive oil. ²²The offering must also include two turtledoves or two young pigeons, whichever the person can afford. One of the pair must be used for the sin offering and the other for a burnt offering. ²³On the eighth day of the purification ceremony, the person being purified must bring the offerings to the priest in the LORD's presence at the entrance of the Tabernacle. ²⁴The priest will take the lamb for the guilt offering, along with the olive oil, and lift them up as a special offering to the LORD. ²⁵Then the priest will slaughter the lamb for the guilt offering. He will take some of its blood and apply it to the lobe of the right ear, the thumb of the right hand, and the big toe of the right foot of the person being purified.

²⁶"The priest will also pour some of the olive oil into the palm of his own left hand. ²⁷He will dip his right finger into the oil in his palm and sprinkle some of it seven times before the LORD. ²⁸The priest will then apply some of the oil in his palm over the blood from the guilt offering that is on the lobe of the right ear, the thumb of the right hand, and the big toe of the right foot of the person being purified. ²⁹The priest will apply the oil remaining in his hand to the head of the person being purified. Through this process, the priest will purify the person before the LORD.

³⁰"Then the priest will offer the two turtledoves or the two young pigeons, whichever the person can afford. ³¹One of them is for a sin offering and the other for a burnt offering, to be presented along with the grain offering. Through this process, the priest will purify the person before the LORD. ³²These are the instructions for purification for those who have recovered from a serious skin disease but who cannot afford to bring the offerings normally required for the ceremony of purification."

³³Then the LORD said to Moses and Aaron, ³⁴"When you arrive in Canaan, the land I am giving you as your own possession, I may contaminate some of the houses in your land with mildew.* ³⁵The owner of such a house must then go to the priest and say, 'It appears that my house has some kind of mildew.' ³⁶Before the priest goes in to inspect the house, he must have the house emptied so nothing inside will be pronounced ceremonially unclean. ³⁷Then the priest will go in and examine the mildew on the walls. If he finds greenish or reddish streaks and the contamination appears to go deeper than the wall's surface, ³⁸the priest will step outside the door and put the house in quarantine for seven days. ³⁹On the seventh day the priest must return for another inspection. If he finds that the mildew on the walls of the house has

spread, ⁴⁰the priest must order that the stones from those areas be removed. The contaminated material will then be taken outside the town to an area designated as ceremonially unclean. ⁴¹Next the inside walls of the entire house must be scraped thoroughly and the scrapings dumped in the unclean place outside the town. ⁴²Other stones will be brought in to replace the ones that were removed, and the walls will be replastered.

⁴³"But if the mildew reappears after all the stones have been replaced and the house has been scraped and replastered, ⁴⁴the priest must return and inspect the house again. If he finds that the mildew has spread, the walls are clearly contaminated with a serious mildew, and the house is defiled. ⁴⁵It must be torn down, and all its stones, timbers, and plaster must be carried out of town to the place designated as ceremonially unclean. ⁴⁶Those who enter the house during the period of quarantine will be ceremonially unclean until evening, ⁴⁷and all who sleep or eat in the house must wash their clothing.

⁴⁸"But if the priest returns for his inspection and finds that the mildew has not reappeared in the house after the fresh plastering, he will pronounce it clean because the mildew is clearly gone. ⁴⁹To purify the house the priest must take two birds, a stick of cedar, some scarlet yarn, and a hyssop branch. ⁵⁰He will slaughter one of the birds over a clay pot filled with fresh water. ⁵¹He will take the cedar stick, the hyssop branch, the scarlet yarn, and the live bird, and dip them into the blood of the slaughtered bird and into the fresh water. Then he will sprinkle the house seven times. ⁵²When the priest has purified the house in exactly this way, ⁵³he will release the live bird in the open fields outside the town. Through this process, the priest will purify the house, and it will be ceremonially clean.

⁵⁴"These are the instructions for dealing

with serious skin diseases,* including scabby sores; ⁵⁵and mildew,* whether on clothing or in a house; ⁵⁶and a swelling on the skin, a rash, or discolored skin. ⁵⁷This procedure will determine whether a person or object is ceremonially clean or unclean.

"These are the instructions regarding skin diseases and mildew."

14:2 Traditionally rendered *leprosy;* see note on 13:2a.   **14:4** Or *juniper;* also in 14:6, 49, 51.   **14:10a** Hebrew *3/10 of an ephah* [6.6 liters].   **14:10b** Hebrew *1 log* [0.3 liters]; also in 14:21.   **14:11** Hebrew *Tent of Meeting;* also in 14:23.   **14:18** Or *will make atonement for;* similarly in 14:19, 20, 21, 29, 31, 53.   **14:21** Hebrew *1/10 of an ephah* [2.2 liters].   **14:34** Traditionally rendered *leprosy;* see note on 13:47.   **14:54** Traditionally rendered *leprosy;* see note on 13:2a.   **14:55** Traditionally rendered *leprosy;* see note on 13:47.

NOTES

14:4 *live birds.* The birds were to be "living," which could seem redundant since all sacrificial animals were alive when brought as a sacrifice. Milgrom (1991:832) translates the word *khayyoth* [TH2416A, ZH2645] (living) as "wild" (thus, "wild birds") since one needed to fly away from the camp, but this seems to lay too much burden on a single word that did not have this meaning elsewhere.

14:6 *scarlet yarn.* The phrase *sheni hatola'ath* [TH8438A, ZH9357] means "red of the worm," indicating the particular color of dye produced from the cochineal worm.

14:30 *the priest will offer the two turtledoves or the two young pigeons.* The bird ritual is alluded to twice more in Scripture by mention of its key elements (such as hyssop), once in conjunction with the red heifer in Num 19:6, and once in Ps 51:7, where the psalmist seeks purification (*taher* [TH2891, ZH3197]; cf. also *taharah* [TH2893, ZH3200] in 14:32), which is the result of the bird sacrifice (14:2, 4, 7, 8).

14:34 *the land I am giving you . . . I may contaminate.* The word *natan* [TH5414, ZH5989] is used twice here, translated "give" and "contaminate." As God would give the land, he would also contaminate, or "give" mildew.

mildew. This is the same Hebrew expression translated in 14:3 as "skin disease" (*nega' tsara'ath* [TH5061/6883, ZH5596/7669]). The Hebrew indicates that what was visible was "something like mildew," since it had not yet been actually diagnosed.

COMMENTARY

The natural reaction concerning something or someone who had been rendered ceremonially unclean would have been "What do I do now? Is this condition permanent?" These questions are addressed in chapter 14 in the form of instructions (13:59; 14:1) concerning, first, those that affected people (14:2-32, with special provision for the poor in 14:21-32) and then those affecting houses (14:33-53). The latter are not mentioned in chapter 13, and so the passage here also includes discussion of diagnosis. The question of unclean fabrics (13:47-59) is not addressed here. The chapter concludes (14:54-57) with a summary that closes chapters 13–14.

People needed to undergo three ceremonial stages, one when they found themselves healed (14:2-8), the second on the seventh day after that (14:9), and the third on the eighth day (14:10-32). The first of these ceremonies was also used for houses that had been found free from contamination (14:48-53). The purpose of these was to restore the person to the community from which he or she had been separated by uncleanness. This restoration was shown by the first set of rituals taking place outside the camp, with those of days seven and eight being inside the camp.

Cleansing for People (14:1-32). This chapter begins with the Lord addressing Moses, with no mention of Aaron or the priests (cf. 11:1; 13:1), even though they had a significant role to play in the procedures. The instructions were directed to those previously pronounced unclean by a priest according to the procedures in chapter 13. They included no medical instructions for healing since this was a religious and ceremonial text rather than a therapeutic one. We can assume that Israel had treatments for skin ailments (see King and Stager 2001:78-84), but no specific regimens are listed here. Prayer for healing also played an important role in Israel (2 Kgs 20:5; 2 Chr 30:18-20; Pss 6:2; 30:2).

As the priest had diagnosed the ailment in chapter 13, so he needed to recognize the restoration of wholeness. There was no mention of those who were still infected, since they would be covered under the regulations of chapter 13 and would presumably have had to wait a longer period until it appeared that they were in fact healed. There is also no mention of how often this might need to take place. Since those concerned had not as yet been actually declared clean, they could not enter the camp (13:46). Once they were found to be healed, two things happened to them: (1) They were no longer described in relation to their disease (13:44-45; 14:2-3) but in relation to their healing (14:4; see 14:7, "the person being purified"; the Hebrew behind this expression occurs 12 times in this chapter; Milgrom 1991:832), and (2) they could start the ritual purification process.

The ceremony involved four elements: two birds, cedar wood, scarlet yarn, and a hyssop branch. In order to be used in a purification ceremony, the birds had to be pure (not among those listed in 11:13-19). Two specific birds were used in sacrifices, turtledoves and pigeons (1:14; 5:7). These were apparently included among those that could be brought, but others were allowed as well, indicating that the two birds here were not serving as either a whole or sin offering. Cedar was a common wood for building, due to its imperviousness to rot. Its red color fits well into this context where red blood plays such a prominent role, as did the scarlet cloth (see note on 14:6). Hyssop was used elsewhere for dipping and sprinkling liquids (Exod 12:22; Num 19:6, 18; John 19:29; Heb 9:19). It was probably sweet marjoram, a popular herb.

The first bird was slaughtered, not sacrificed as a burnt offering (cf. 1:15, where its head was wrung off, which was not the case here). Its blood was captured in a clay pot along with "fresh water," (literally "living" or running, water) from a spring or stream (cf. 2 Kgs 5:10), rather than stagnant, still, or "dead" water such as from a well or cistern. The remaining bird and the other three elements were dipped into the blood–water mixture, which was then sprinkled seven times on the healed person. Sevenfold sprinkling was common in Israelite purification rites (see 4:6; 8:11; 16:19; cf. Exod 24:8, where blood was sprinkled, but no mention made as to how often) and also occurred among her neighbors in Mesopotamia (Milgrom 1991:839). The exact significance and effect of the act is unclear, but it did move the process along toward purification, though that was not completed until more cleansing happened (14:8).

Verse 7 ends with the priest releasing the second bird into the open fields. No reason for this action is given, just as none is provided for many of the ceremonies in Leviticus. Some see the bird as carrying upon itself the impurities of the unclean person, much like the scapegoat carries the sin according to 16:8, 22 (Milgrom 1991:832-834, 840). If this was the case and the impurity was completely removed, there would be no apparent reason why the person still had to wash (14:8). Also, the parallel between goat and bird is not exact, since the former was sent into the wilderness (16:10, 21-22), an uninhabited area (cf. Job 38:26), while the latter was released to the fields, usually indicating the cultivated areas in the vicinity of habitation (cf. Num 20:17, where they are associated with vineyards and wells, both signs of civilization). Others see the release of the bird from captivity into the open land as symbolizing the release of the unclean person from his condition of uncleanness, allowing him entrance again into his natural environment of the community (Wenham 1979:208-209; Ostrer 2003:348-363). It was thus a picture of newly gained freedom.

The ceremony concluded with the persons laundering their clothes just like those who had become contaminated through contact with a corpse (11:25, 28, 40); this had been done previously in the diagnostic process (13:6, 34). They also had to shave off all hair, including that of the infected area, which was previously left unshaven (13:33), and then bathe completely, which was also the final ritual act of the priests before they could put on their official ministerial clothing (8:6; 16:4). This was also the final act of this ritual, and the person was now purified enough to be able to return to the community.

The entire purification process was not complete, however, since further steps were needed seven and eight days later. While the person was allowed access into the camp itself, they were still not allowed to enter their tent, apparently lest they touch someone or something pure. This period of contact uncleanness parallels that of the new mother of a baby boy (12:2), a man with a discharge (15:13), a menstruating woman (15:19), or one who touched a human corpse (Num 19:11). After seven days, the person performed purification acts without the aid of a priest. The person again completely shaved. This text gives more specific detail than in the previous shaving instructions, specifying not only all head hair, but also all the rest of the body hair. None could be missed. The person must again launder clothes and completely bathe, though it is not clear why the order of events was different here than it was a week earlier. This resulted in a further stage of purity, at which time the person could reenter the tent in which they had lived, though total ceremonial purity had still not happened.

The culminating ceremonies took place on the eighth day with participation of both priest and purified person in order for the latter to be completely restored to the community and to God. The instructions in 14:8-10 presuppose reference to chapters 1-5, since detailed instruction for individual sacrifices are not given here. Three lambs were brought: One female for a purification or sin offering (cf. 4:27-35, where a female was only brought for the sin of a member of the community) and two males for guilt (5:15) and burnt (1:10) offerings. The female was specified as being a yearling, so we should assume that the same also held for the male lambs (9:3; 12:6; 23:12, 18). A grain offering (ch 2) of flour mixed with olive oil (cf. 2:5; Num 15:4) was also provided, along with another measure of unmixed oil for anointing. Three-tenths of an *'epah* [TH374, ZH406] of flour (around six quarts) was required (14:10), even though only one-tenth was needed for a grain offering (6:20 [13]). This suggests that the other two-tenths were grain offerings that accompanied the animal sacrifices, following a practice mentioned in Numbers 15:3-4 but not recorded in Leviticus 2.

Leviticus 14:11-20 gives the order of service for the purification ceremony, which took place at the Tabernacle entryway, a regular spot for such ceremonies since it was where the altar was (1:3; 3:2; 4:4; 8:3-4; 12:6; 15:14; 16:7). First came the guilt offering, following the instructions of 7:1-7 as regards both procedure and disposal of the sacrificed animal, but with some variants. Here the entire animal, along with the oil, was raised to God, while elsewhere such a thing was done only for part of a peace offering (7:30) or priestly dedication offering (8:26-29). Both animal and oil were thus specially consecrated. Some of the blood of the lamb was daubed in a pattern similar to that of the priestly ordination ceremony (8:23-24). Unlike that event, however, some of the oil was then daubed over the blood (cf. 8:30, where blood and oil were mixed in the dedication ceremony). The oil was first dedicated to God by the priest dipping his finger into it and sprinkling it toward the Tabernacle seven times (cf. Num 19:4, where blood was dedicated to God in the same way). The remaining oil was applied to the offerer's shaved head like the dedicatory oil that had been applied to Aaron's head (14:18, 29; cf. 8:12). All of this was done in case the person had somehow violated some of God's holy things (cf. 5:15). Such a violation needed to be made right before the other sacrifices could be brought (Milgrom 1991:856-857).

After this, the other three offerings could be brought: the sin offering (cf. 4:32-35, better called a purification offering since there was no indication that these skin diseases were identified as deriving from sin), the burnt offering (cf. 1:10-13), and the grain offering (cf. ch 2). As a result of all these sacrifices, the person was again allowed access to God, who could have no contact with any uncleanness—the person had been completely purified from any ceremonial contamination caused by the disease. This reinstituted not only access to the camp and to the dwelling place, but to the sanctuary itself. The person was now completely restored to the community and could join Israel in worship.

While everyone in the land, from king to commoner, might contract a skin disease requiring purification, not everyone was rich enough to be able to bring three lambs. Thus, 14:21-32 provides an alternative for poor folk who also wanted to rejoin the community in worship and service. They still had to bring a male yearling lamb for the primary guilt offering, as well as the same amount of oil, but could replace the other two lambs with sacrificial birds for the sin and burnt offerings and provide less flour for the grain offering. The implication is that the turtledove was more valuable than the young pigeon, possibly because it was mature. Nonetheless, pigeons would also do. The same ritual processes were followed for the poor person's sacrifices, with the same results as there were for those with greater economic resources—restoration to God and community. God did not want to exclude any-one from his community.

For Christians, members of the new community of God, purification was made once and for all by the blood of Jesus Christ. He went "outside the city gates" (Heb 13:12; see Lev 14:3) to die, identifying with the outcast. The priest had to go out there to start the purification process, but its ultimate goal was to bring the outcast back in for sacrifices of purification and restoration. As the two birds fulfilled roles on behalf of the sufferer, so Christ died on behalf of those suffering from sin (2 Cor 5:14). He, as the Suffering Servant of Isaiah 53:10, was a guilt offering that makes us right with God (Rom 3:25; 1 John 2:2; 4:10; cf. Heb 2:17, where Jesus is said to be the priest bringing atonement) and brings purification (Titus 2:14). Christians are purified through the sprinkling of blood (1 Pet 1:2), and pure water was provided by Christ our priest (Heb 10:22).

As such, the technical, apparently dry description of long-dead Israelite practices was a fertile bed from which germinated the expression of many of the founda-tional Christian doctrines of sin, falling from grace, and restoration through Christ, who was not only our sacrifice but also our priest. Jesus went beyond the priestly role of diagnosis; he healed those with skin diseases and other afflictions (Matt 4:23-24; Luke 17:11-19). Finally, at his death he provided the sacrifice needed to atone for sin. Though that was its primary function (1 John 2:2); it also served to restore ceremonial purity (e.g., Heb 10:22). Christ's sacrifice accomplished atone-ment and restoration by fulfilling a number of the Levitical sacrifices at one time.

Cleansing for Houses (14:33-53). This passage is anticipatory as presented here in Leviticus. The setting for the reception of these laws is toward the beginning of Israel's wilderness wanderings, after the exodus from Egypt and while the people were still at Mount Sinai (7:38). They lived in tents (cf. 14:8) since they were a people on the move. The focus here, however, jumps forward to the period of the nation's settle-ment in Canaan (14:34). This was the land previously promised to the patriarchs (Gen 12:1; 15:7; 17:8) and the nation of Israel (25:38; Exod 3:8; 6:4), to which they would be on their way when they departed from Sinai. Some laws such as these would take effect only upon settlement in the land (see 19:23; 23:10; 25:2; Num 15:2; 33:51; 35:10). This law started from an existing situation, that of people unclean through contamination, and was applied to a new situation that the people would face when they settled in permanent houses in the land they were about to seize.

Buildings could also suffer from surface abnormalities and fungal growths such as dry rot and mildew, which at times resembled skin diseases in humans. This con-dition could easily spread, damaging the integrity of the fabric of the structure in which it occurred and, if severe enough, destroying it for safe use. Since this was not encountered in earlier discussion in Leviticus, the writer presented here both the diagnosis and purification prescriptions. The latter relied on the ceremonies for the purification of people just discussed (14:2-32) and also the diagnostic passages, especially for cloth, in chapter 13.

After the owner reported his suspicions to the priest, and before the priest made his actual diagnosis, the house was emptied so that none of its contents would become unclean if the house was found to be infected (14:36). This indicates that diagnosis was not retroactive. That is, until something was declared unclean by the priest, it was in reality not unclean, so it would not "infect" anything else. The priest, who had the role of distinguishing clean and unclean, thus served the same role as today's baseball umpire, since a pitch is neither a ball nor a strike until he says what it is.

The priest then inspected the house for color and depth of contamination. If there was either pitting below the surface or green or red discoloration (cf. the infected cloth in 13:49), the house needed to be quarantined for a week, just like the person (13:4, 21, 26, 31) or fabric (13:50) suspected of infection. If, after the week, the diagnosis was that it was mildew, the infected area was to be removed just like the infected fabric spot (13:56). While fabric could be burnt to prevent recurrence or spread of infection, the infected stone and all of the house's inside plaster, which needed to be scraped off, could not be completely destroyed with fire. These things needed to be disposed of in a special place, away from where the people lived. This was an important step because people of that time often reused building material for new construction. They must be prevented from reusing contaminated material. This disposal spot was called an "unclean place," so it was not the same place where the remains of the animal sacrifices were to be taken, since that was a "holy place" (4:12; Num 19:9). Both locations were to be away from contact with people, but for opposite reasons, the latter due to its holiness and the former due to its contamination. The house was then to be repaired by reapplying plaster over the stone core of the wall.

The next section (14:43-47) looks further down the road to a time of possible reinfection. If the infection reappeared some time later, another inspection was called for. This probably refers to any time subsequent to the first diagnosed infection (cf. 13:7-8, where the same possible recurrence of skin disease was discussed). If reinfection was present, the entire structure needed to be destroyed and removed from where people lived. People needed to avoid the house under quarantine, and by implication, that which had been declared infected, lest they also become ceremonially unclean. This uncleanness lasted for the daylight period just like it did for one who contacted an animal's carcass (11:24). Simply entering the building caused contamination, so one assumes that touching it did as well, and more prolonged contact such as eating or sleeping in it required laundering one's clothes, which would have become unclean just like those of one who carried a carcass (11:25, 28).

The next section (14:48-53) pertains to the alternate finding of the priest to that in 14:39-42—that is, an "innocent" verdict. If there was no sign of infection after the rebuilding, the priest pronounced the house ceremonially clean (cf. 13:6). He then performed a purification ceremony with birds, cedar, cloth, and hyssop, just like the one done for skin disease (14:4-7), except for the addition of the birds being sent away from the town, since the context had changed from the wilderness to Canaan. Here there was no mention of the other elements needed for the one found clean of skin disease, namely washing, shaving, and the guilt, purification ("sin"), and grain offerings. The bird ceremony was enough to purify or decontaminate the house (Milgrom 1991:879). There is no indication of any personal impact on the owner, and no moral guilt of any kind, since he did not have to bring any of these sacrifices for personal restoration. When the steps were all completed, the house was declared clean and fit for reoccupation.

God's law was not static, but dynamic, changing to meet new situations as they arose. In this case, it anticipated a change among his people from being wanderers to settlers who would face new circumstances and so would need tools and procedures to face these new things. God didn't change his approach to a situation, but was ready to approach changing situations. This is similar to what preachers do in their sermons. They do not usually simply repeat the biblical text verbatim, but provide comment and contemporary application so their congregants can see that it is still relevant to them in their new context.

The final section (14:54-57) summarizes all of chapters 13–14, which are described as "instructions," or what we would call procedural guidelines, for dealing with surface abnormalities, some of which, though not all, are listed. The purpose as stated is to be diagnostic rather than therapeutic, recognizing uncleanness rather than bringing about wellness (14:57). The summary forms an inclusion, in which the first and last elements parallel each other, showing that the unit is self-contained.

God in his grace wants to have a relationship with all of his people, something that was not possible if someone was unclean. God had made numerous means available to those who had become unclean for various reasons, and here he provided one more, touching again on areas over which the person had no control. He also saw that a person needed not only physical and spiritual fellowship, which could be damaged through uncleanness, but also economic security. While Israel's economic livelihood when they occupied the land was agriculturally based, giving land and seed and flocks special importance, loss of a house was also a severe economic blow, even if it could be rebuilt (see 27:14-15 for a discussion of the value of a house as an offering to God). This valuable part of a person's estate could be lost if the home was affected by mildew, so steps were taken to see that it could be restored to his use as well.

◆   ## D. Genital Discharges (15:1-33)
1. Abnormal male discharges (15:1-15)

The LORD said to Moses and Aaron, [2]"Give the following instructions to the people of Israel.

"Any man who has a bodily discharge is ceremonially unclean. [3]This defilement is caused by his discharge, whether the discharge continues or stops. In either case the man is unclean. [4]Any bed on which the man with the discharge lies and anything on which he sits will be ceremonially unclean. [5]So if you touch the man's bed, you must wash your clothes and bathe yourself in water, and you will remain unclean until evening. [6]If you sit where the man with the discharge has sat, you must wash your clothes and bathe yourself in water, and you will remain unclean until evening. [7]If you touch the man with the discharge, you must wash your clothes and bathe yourself in water, and you will remain unclean until evening. ⁸If the man spits on you, you must wash your clothes and bathe yourself in water, and you will remain unclean until evening. ⁹Any saddle blanket on which the man rides will be ceremonially unclean. ¹⁰If you touch anything that was under the man, you will be unclean until evening. You must wash your clothes and bathe yourself in water, and you will remain unclean until evening. ¹¹If the man touches you without first rinsing his hands, you must wash your clothes and bathe yourself in water, and you will remain unclean until evening. ¹²Any clay pot the man touches must be broken, and any wooden utensil he touches must be rinsed with water.

¹³"When the man with the discharge is healed, he must count off seven days for the period of purification. Then he must wash his clothes and bathe himself in fresh water, and he will be ceremonially clean. ¹⁴On the eighth day he must get two turtledoves or two young pigeons and come before the LORD at the entrance of the Tabernacle* and give his offerings to the priest. ¹⁵The priest will offer one bird for a sin offering and the other for a burnt offering. Through this process, the priest will purify* the man before the LORD for his discharge.

15:14 Hebrew *Tent of Meeting;* also in 15:29.   15:15 Or *will make atonement for;* also in 15:30.

NOTES
15:2 *any man.* This specifically refers to a male (contrast note on 1:2), since females are discussed later.

bodily discharge. This person had a discharge or flow (cf. the use of the same word in a different, non-bodily context in 20:24; Isa 48:21) of some kind. The discharge was described as literally coming "from his flesh," which the NLT translates as "bodily." This seems too broad for the context, since a bodily discharge could include pus from wounds or sores, which are included in chs 13–14. Since ch 15 is concerned in all other instances with genital discharges, this is undoubtedly also meant here.

15:11 *rinsing.* This meant that the water was moving, not just standing in a container, in order to carry the impurity away rather than simply soaking in it. An example is the difference between a shower and a bath (6:28; Ezek 13:11 [cf. "heavy rainstorm," NLT]). The NT speaks of the practice of washing hands to remove impurity (Mark 7:3-4).

COMMENTARY
One might expect this chapter to follow immediately after chapter 12, which also dealt with genital discharges. Milgrom (1991:905) notes that the present order reflects the duration and complexity of the necessary processes for purification (a function of time and all necessary rituals), with the longer ones (ch 12 gives 40–80 days) moving toward those that are shorter (chs 13–14 give 8 days; ch 15 gives 8–1 day[s]).

The previous section addresses contaminations that affected the surface of the body, of fabrics, or of houses (chs 13–14). These were visible and public, and priests played a major role. This chapter concerns uncleanness that arose from within the body and involved private, intimate matters that were self-diagnosed by the person involved, not by the priest. There needed to be an element of trust that the members of Israelite society would be forthcoming with problems in this area.

The chapter is divided into four sections, which are laid out with structural symmetry as a chiasm (see the introduction to ch 10) in this form:

A. Introduction (15:1-2a)
  B. Abnormal male discharges (15:2b-15)
    C. Normal male discharges (15:16-17)
      D. Marital intercourse, affecting male and female (15:18)
    C'. Normal female discharges (15:19-24)
  B'. Abnormal female discharges (15:25-30)
A'. Summary (15:31-33)

As with the circumstances in the previous section, there was no blame attached to these natural phenomena since they are in no way identified as resulting from sin. They were viewed as part of the course of human life in which there is potential for new life and vitality through the unfertilized egg and motile sperm—but the potential of these two elements is not always realized (as when the egg or sperm are expelled unused), and the result is a month of sterility (according to the woman's cycle) and the loss of a potential life. By association with the latter circumstances, these phenomena caused ceremonial impurity. Since what was holy could only be in contact with wholeness and vitality, impurity caused by such discharges must be removed before the person could be restored to the community of Israel and of God.

The instructions were delivered to Moses and Aaron because there needed to be some priestly involvement in the process (15:14-15, 29-30). Since most of the responsibility lay on the person concerned, the instructions were also to be transmitted to all Israelites (lit., "sons of Israel"; incidentally, this is a clear indication that the word "son" had a wider connotation than simply an immediate male descendant, since females were also specifically included here within this term; cf. 1:2).

The chapter begins with a discussion about a male's bodily discharge (see note on 15:2). This discharge must have been something besides semen, since that would be covered in 15:16. This discharge was abnormal and was almost certainly caused by a form of gonorrhea, possibly urinary bilharzia (Milgrom 1991:907) or something else that would cause the release of pus or mucus from the penis. This abnormality, whether chronic or an isolated case, caused the man to be ceremonially unclean and unable to partake fully in community life.

This uncleanness was contagious and could be transmitted to anything the man slept or sat or rode upon (that is, things underneath the one with the flow), or to anyone who touched him (15:4-11). And this could then be transmitted secondarily to anyone who touched any of these things. The one who became unclean through touching needed to go through a laundering and bathing process similar to that for those who became unclean through skin disease (14:8-9) or through contact with animal carcasses (11:25, 28, 40), though in the latter case bathing was implied rather than stated. This case must be more infectious than the other two, however, since there was no mention of the possibility of secondary infection with those two. The person had to wait until night fell before purity was restored, which happened without any special sacrifices.

Uncleanness could also be transmitted through saliva (15:8), which, when spat upon someone in other contexts, was a sign of dislike or disdain (Num 12:14; Deut

25:9; Matt 26:67; 27:30) but was not said to pollute. One with a discharge, however, was unclean in all of his bodily fluids, which could transmit his uncleanness. They did not necessarily have to do so, however, since the person with the discharge could wash his hands (15:11), which had probably come into contact with the genitals, and this would have stopped any contamination, at least temporarily.

This applied to almost everything he touched (not just a person, as in NLT, NIV, NASB, KJV) except clay pots (cf. 6:28 [21]; 11:33-35), which were porous and absorbed impurity. As such, they had to be destroyed (15:12a). Wooden implements, being less porous than clay, needed only to be washed (15:12b). This temporary stop to transmitting uncleanness was important, since the man would not have to live outside the camp (like others who were unclean) as long as he was careful and kept his hands clean.

Only after the man saw that his discharge had cleared up did the priest become involved. The man waited a week afterward, like the person who had a skin disease, still retaining his impurity since he had not yet performed the ceremonies that the diseased person did on the first day (14:8; see Milgrom 1991:922), but he did so on the seventh day (15:13). The following day he came to the priest at the Tabernacle, bringing the birds for a purification offering ("sin offering"; 15:15) and a burnt offering, like the new mother (12:8) and the person with a skin disease (14:22) did. Following all of these steps, he was declared pure (15:13-15).

◆   ## 2. Normal male discharges (15:16-17)

¹⁶"Whenever a man has an emission of semen, he must bathe his entire body in water, and he will remain ceremonially unclean until the next evening.* ¹⁷Any clothing or leather with semen on it must be washed in water, and it will remain unclean until evening.

15:16 Hebrew *until evening*; also in 15:18.

NOTES
15:16 *an emission of semen.* This refers to ejaculation, lit., "outpouring of seed." This included either an involuntary nocturnal emission (cf. Deut 23:10, where a different term is used) or sexual intercourse.

COMMENTARY
The instructions then addressed a man's ejaculation, whether involuntarily or voluntarily. These instructions do not pertain to abnormal discharge from the penis (as in 15:2b-15), but normal discharge. Nonetheless, this normal discharge rendered the man ceremonially unclean so that he could not take part in eating sanctified food (7:20). It was not considered in any way a sin, since it only required that he bathe completely and await evening before he could again come into contact with the holy. One assumes, though it is not stated in the Hebrew, that if the event happened at night, the uncleanness lasted until the following dusk, as indicated by the NLT in 15:16.

Clothing or leather was rendered unclean for the same period if they came into contact with the semen. These items must have been his bedclothes and bedding, and this involved a nocturnal emission, since no sexual partner is mentioned here (see 15:18). They, too, were laundered.

◆ 3. Marital intercourse (15:18)

18After a man and a woman have sexual intercourse, they must each bathe in water, and they will remain unclean until the next evening.

NOTES
15:18 *a man and a woman have sexual intercourse.* This verse is structurally transitional in the chapter, switching over from an interest in the male (15:2b-17) to the female (15:19-30). It serves as sort of a hook, tying the two together; in the Hebrew the verse starts with the woman, the subject of the following passage, and only then mentions the man, the subject of the preceding. It also relates to the preceding context through mention of semen and not of blood, the subject of the next section.

COMMENTARY
The subject turns to heterosexual intercourse, using the common euphemism of a man who "lies with" a woman (cf. Gen 26:10; Ezek 23:8). After this act, both partners were to bathe and would remain ceremonially unclean until evening. This is a natural extension of the previous case of the man with an ejaculation, since, again, what came into contact with the semen, in this case his sexual partner, had the same result and subsequently needed the same remedy of washing and awaiting evening. This indicates that if a person was required to participate in public worship at the sanctuary, intercourse the previous night had to be avoided (cf. Exod 19:15; 1 Sam 21:4).

◆ 4. Normal menstruation (15:19-24)

19"Whenever a woman has her menstrual period, she will be ceremonially unclean for seven days. Anyone who touches her during that time will be unclean until evening. 20Anything on which the woman lies or sits during the time of her period will be unclean. 21If any of you touch her bed, you must wash your clothes and bathe yourself in water, and you will remain unclean until evening. 22If you touch any object she has sat on, you must wash your clothes and bathe yourself in water, and you will remain unclean until evening. 23This includes her bed or any other object she has sat on; you will be unclean until evening if you touch it. 24If a man has sexual intercourse with her and her blood touches him, her menstrual impurity will be transmitted to him. He will remain unclean for seven days, and any bed on which he lies will be unclean.

NOTES
15:19 *menstrual period.* Lit., "discharge of blood" (cf. 15:2), addressing here the monthly menstrual cycle, though the term used for the discharge could also apply to abnormal flows, as in the next text section.

15:24 bed. Lit., "place of lying down"; it could indicate a mat or couch (2 Sam 4:11; 11:2; 17:28). Since it was a place for reclining where intercourse could take place, the word "bed" became a metaphor for the act itself (Gen 49:4).

COMMENTARY

The chapter opened with the case of a male who had a discharge or flow (15:2) and now continues with a female who had a similar discharge, only this time of blood rather than mucus. As males have a normal flow of semen from their genital organs, so females have a flow of blood during their monthly menstrual cycle. Contact with menstrual blood rendered things ceremonially unclean in the same way as contact with semen.

This ceremonial uncleanness lasted for a week, in contrast to the male's semen flow, which rendered him unclean until the next evening (15:16). It is unclear whether the seven days were a total for the uncleanness, corresponding approximately to the total time of menstrual blood flow, or whether it started at the cessation of that flow. There is no mention here as to what restored her ceremonial cleanness, but she most likely had to bathe (see 2 Sam 11:4) since the male had to bathe after his shorter period of impurity (15:16). The male also had to bathe a week after healing from an abnormal discharge (15:13), as did anyone who touched a human corpse (Num 19:19). The cleansing was not mentioned in three cases of female uncleanness: (1) here, (2) after childbirth (ch 12), and (3) with an abnormal blood flow (15:28). In both the latter case (15:27) and this one, secondary contamination had to be washed off, so surely the primary contamination would have been as well, since it would cause impurity. Secondary contamination came through clothing and bedding that would have come into direct contact with the menstrual blood as it did from the male abnormal flow (15:4). Anyone so affected also needed to bathe and launder his or her clothes (15:5-6).

Anyone who touched the menstruating woman would be unclean. But unlike the male who had to wash his hands before touching anything, this was not mentioned for the woman. One therefore assumes that her touch did not contaminate and that she was able to remain at home and carry out most of her regular duties, as long as someone did not touch her (Milgrom 1991:936). It is difficult to see the difference between someone touching her, which transmitted uncleanness, and her touching something else, which did not. Perhaps what a person could not touch was the contaminating blood, which did transmit uncleanness to bedding, rather than the woman's body, which did not transmit contamination. This also explains the transmission of uncleanness to a sexual partner, who would contact not only her body but also her blood. As a result, he would be under the same regulations as she was (15:19-23).

◆   5. Abnormal menstruation (15:25-30)

[25]"If a woman has a flow of blood for many days that is unrelated to her menstrual period, or if the blood continues beyond the normal period, she is ceremo-

nially unclean. As during her menstrual period, the woman will be unclean as long as the discharge continues. ²⁶Any bed she lies on and any object she sits on during that time will be unclean, just as during her normal menstrual period. ²⁷If any of you touch these things, you will be ceremonially unclean. You must wash your clothes and bathe yourself in water, and you will remain unclean until evening.

²⁸"When the woman's bleeding stops, she must count off seven days. Then she will be ceremonially clean. ²⁹On the eighth day she must bring two turtledoves or two young pigeons and present them to the priest at the entrance of the Tabernacle. ³⁰The priest will offer one for a sin offering and the other for a burnt offering. Through this process, the priest will purify her before the LORD for the ceremonial impurity caused by her bleeding.

NOTES

15:25-30 This portion of ch 15 brings the discussion of discharges itself to a conclusion, in accord with the internal chiastic structure pointed out in the commentary on 15:1-15. Having dealt with issues pertaining to male abnormal discharges, male normal discharges, heterosexual intercourse, female normal discharges, the discussion now moves to female abnormal discharges.

COMMENTARY

Women sometimes experience abnormal blood flow at times other than their monthly cycle or for longer periods than are customary. These times required extra ceremonial steps, which correspond to those of the male with an abnormal flow. The female's flow was specifically identified, unlike that of the male (15:2)—it was a flow of blood. This, therefore, continues the topic of the previous verses. Two departures from the normal menstruation are listed, one concerning duration and the other timing. The first is a blood flow of extraordinary duration. No specific duration is mentioned, so it could last from days to years (cf. Matt 9:20; Mark 5:25; Luke 8:43). The other is a departure from the ordinary cycle, which generally revolves every 28 days. In both cases, her discharge is designated impure, something not said of the blood of either the regular menstrual cycle or of childbirth (ch 12). She was also impure and could transmit contamination like she could during her monthly period. Those contacting the transmitted, secondary uncleanness (undoubtedly including touching the woman herself, though that is unstated; cf. 15:19) were to bathe, launder, and wait until the next evening, as they did for such contact during regular menstruation.

No mention is made of any healing steps that might have aided the woman, since the text is concerned with ceremonial cleanness rather than physical wellness. Whenever and however healing might take place, the woman would become clean after the same seven-day wait (and implied bathing and laundering; 15:13) that she would have observed after her regular period. Then, on the eighth day, she was expected to bring the same two birds and have the same sacrifices performed on her behalf by the priest as the male with an abnormal discharge, with the same purifying results (15:14-15). These sacrifices were not required for either gender when the genital discharges were normal; it was only in abnormal circumstances, with increased defilement, that extraordinary purification must take place.

This discussion of abnormal blood flow casts light on the episode of the woman with constant bleeding told in the synoptic Gospels (Matt 9:20-22; Mark 5:24b-34; Luke 8:42b-48). Since the Mark passage has the most detail, it will be the object of comparison. The scene is set by mentioning a large, pressing crowd that would have touched Jesus, but also anyone who approached him. In this case it was a woman who was said to have had an abnormal blood flow that had lasted 12 years, so she would have been under the regulations of these verses in Leviticus 15. All who touched her would have become defiled, including those in the jostling crowd and Jesus himself. She was undoubtedly a pious woman who wanted to be able to worship again at the Temple. Even more so, she wanted to restore normal human contact, which she had been deprived of due to the contamination she could transmit. Her deeply felt lack in these areas was highlighted by her willingness to pay whatever she had for a cure, but to no avail. Since she knew that she was a contaminant, she did not approach Jesus directly, like others did (e.g., Matt 4:24; 21:14), but instead secretly touched his robe and then sought to slip away.

Though she was immediately healed through contact with Jesus, her seven-day wait and necessary sacrifices had not yet happened, so she still did not want either Jesus or the crowd to know she had been there. Jesus, wanting to teach the crowd, his disciples, and the woman, did not allow this to happen, but called her out. When she confessed what she had done, probably much to the horror of the crowd, he blessed her. Though not stated in the text, I would also think he reached out to touch her as he gave the blessing (cf. Mark 10:16; Luke 18:15), perhaps the first human contact she had experienced in 12 years.

◆ 6. Summary (15:31-33)

31"This is how you will guard the people of Israel from ceremonial uncleanness. Otherwise they would die, for their impurity would defile my Tabernacle that stands among them. 32These are the instructions for dealing with anyone who has a bodily discharge—a man who is unclean because of an emission of semen 33or a woman during her menstrual period. It applies to any man or woman who has a bodily discharge, and to a man who has sexual intercourse with a woman who is ceremonially unclean."

NOTES

15:31 *guard the people.* The verb is *nazar* [TH5144, ZH5692], meaning "separate from." A good example of those who separated themselves to God and from impurity were the Nazirites, whose name was derived from the verb here translated "guard" ("separate from"; Num 6:2-12).

COMMENTARY

Ceremonial cleanness was very important to Israel, since without it, a person could not approach God in worship and service. Holiness characterizes God, and only the holy can approach him. So impurity needed to be guarded against. The regulations showed Israel how uncleanness could be avoided or purity restored. It is debatable as to which ceremonial uncleanness was referred to in 15:31, whether all of chapters 11–15 or just chapter 15. The latter is most likely, since the summary statement of 15:32 clearly pertains to chapter 15, and it was not the practice to have a more general summary precede a more specific one (cf. 7:35-36, which refers to 6:8–7:34, while 7:37-38 refers to 1:1–7:36). If so, the uncleanness caused by genital discharge was quite serious, since it could affect everyone in the nation. If unattended, it could pollute the Tabernacle, the very sanctuary of God himself, since those affected would approach the Tabernacle in an unclean state (cf. Num 5:1-4), resulting in death by the hand of the holy God (cf. 22:9). This divine capital punishment tied this section of laws to the punishment of Nadab and Abihu, which brackets these chapters (10:2; 16:1).

The passage concludes with a summary of what was previously discussed, using the same descriptive term "instructions" that was used to characterize the regulations concerning unclean food (11:46), childbirth (12:7), skin disease (14:2, 32, 57), and infected houses (14:54-55, 57). The instructions of chapter 15 concern the issue of discharge, with subcategories of those affected by genital discharge: a man with a semen emission (15:32; 15:16-18, including two of our categories in one term— normal male discharge and marital intercourse), a woman with a normal menstrual period (15:33; 15:19-23), a male or female's other discharge (presumably the abnormal ones discussed in 15:2-15, 25-30, since normal discharges had just been mentioned), and finally a male who had sexual relations with a menstruating woman (15:24). The order of the summary seems to move from normal events (the center of the chiastic structure outlined in the commentary on 15:1-15) to abnormal events (on the periphery of the chiasm). The last element (intercourse with a menstruating woman) in its present location is peculiar, however, since it appears as if it would fit more naturally one stage earlier, as part of the section on normal menstruation.

An important question is, Why did semen and menstrual blood, so associated with new life and the continuation of the species, bring ceremonial uncleanness? No reason arises directly from the text itself, so expositors and commentators have felt a fairly free interpretational rein. Sexuality and childbirth were viewed as mysterious and at times dangerous in many societies, since they were boundary events between life and death. There is no evident fear of sexuality in the Old Testament; it is something to be enjoyed and celebrated in its correct expression (cf. Gen 2:23-25; Prov 5:15-19; Song of Songs), though its misuse was warned against (cf. numerous laws prohibiting rape and adultery; Prov 5:1-14, 20).

Wenham (1979:224) suggests that this chapter helped maintain the correct sexual parameters. It would mainly be younger, unmarried women who would have had a regular menstrual cycle due to societal practices of early marriage, frequent pregnancy, and lengthened periods of breast feeding. These regulations would have inhibited sexual contact if the men involved knew that the resulting uncleanness would preclude worship and also could result in death.

Milgrom's (1991:1002-1004) interpretation picks up on the life/death polarity as an explanation not only of this chapter but also of those concerning skin disease (chs 13–14). For Israel, as for all humans, life is precious and death is feared. The

former is associated with good and the latter with destruction and evil, so guidelines were provided to support the one and thwart the other (e.g., Deut 30:15-20).
Life and wholeness are desired, so its symbols (e.g., flowing, "living" water) and
progenitors (e.g., marriage, semen) are, if not labeled "good," at least not in themselves impure, in contrast to death and its harbingers. Among the latter would be
corpses and skin disease, which resembles death (Num 12:12) and, if virulent and
untreated, could lead to death. Blood is at an interesting cusp between life and
death. In its proper place, circulating through the body, it is life (Gen 9:4), and
when shed in divinely ordained sacrifice, it could purify and promote life (17:11).
When violently or illegally shed, however, it is related to death and a pollutant
(17:4; Gen 9:6; Num 35:33; Ezek 23:45). These chapters allow for life and holy service to continue through purifying anything that might have been polluted through
contact with something marginal between life and death.

◆ IV. Day of Atonement: Purifying the Tabernacle (16:1-34)
A. Introduction (16:1)

The LORD spoke to Moses after the death
of Aaron's two sons, who died after they
entered the LORD's presence and burned
the wrong kind of fire before him.

NOTES

16:1 The actual order of presentation in the Hebrew of this chapter is quite choppy, jumping
back and forth between the different offerings and animals. A visual presentation of the order,
showing the material topically by means of numbers and alignment, is presented below.
Each topic is aligned and numbered similarly (e.g., 1 pertains to Aaron's sin offering, while
3 pertains to the people's sin offerings), while comments pertaining to washing and clothes
are enclosed in brackets ([]) and the overall order of lines follows the order of the verses.

1. Bull for Aaron's sin offering brought (16:3)
    2. Ram for Aaron's burnt offering brought (16:3)
    [Aaron washes and dresses (16:4)]
        3. Two goats for the people's sin offering brought (16:5)
        4. Ram for the people's burnt offering brought (16:5)
1a. Aaron's bull presented (16:6)
        3a. Goats for sin offering brought and selected (16:7-8)
        3b. Goat for sin offering presented, other goat kept alive (16:9-10)
1b. Aaron's bull slaughtered (16:11-14)
        3c. Goat for people's sin offering slaughtered (16:15-17)
1c. and   3d. Bull and goat blood smeared on altar (16:18-19)
        3e. Live goat sent away (16:20-22)
        [Aaron undresses, washes, and dresses (16:23-24a)]
    2a. Ram for Aaron's burnt offering sacrificed (16:24b)
            4a. Ram for the people's burnt offering sacrificed (16:24c)
1d. and   3f. Sin offering fat burnt (16:25)
        [Live goat attendant launders his clothes and washes himself (16:26)]
1e. and   3g. Disposal of sin offerings outside the camp (16:27)
        [Attendant launders his clothes and washes himself (16:28)]

From this structure, several things are clear. Purification from sin was central in the chapter, both quantitatively and structurally. The number of references to it is larger than to any other element, not only to the various sin offerings (mentioned 12 times, and bracketing the passage, occurring at each end of it) but also to the physical laundering and washing (mentioned 4 times). The structural center is the people's sin or purification offerings (points 3c-3e), which seem to be the theological focus of the events as well, since it was this aspect that was to be carried on each year (16:30, 34). The burnt offerings, mentioned 4 times, are of secondary importance structurally.

COMMENTARY

Chapter 16 begins by establishing its addressee. Moses was the sole recipient of this message (cf. 8:1); he was responsible to relay the instructions to his brother Aaron, the high priest, the one who needed to respond. The chapter also establishes the timing of the passage in the narrative, which was precipitated by the death of Aaron's two eldest sons when they approached Yahweh in the wrong way (10:1-2).

Chapter 16 is linked narratively to chapter 10, and it logically follows chapters 1–15. Chapter 10 describes in narrative form the illegal actions of Nadab and Abihu, Aaron's sons. These acts had desecrated the sanctuary. This led to legal instructions concerning other desecrating acts and events, which were detailed in chapters 11–15, along with the ceremonies needed to purify the offenders and the sanctuary. What was supposed to happen when this kind of willful desecration took place, especially if it was caused by the priests themselves? Chapter 16, a composite of narrative and legal material, returns specifically to the events in chapter 10, warning against any repetition of unlawful entry into the sanctuary (16:1) and describing the purification necessary to restore the sanctity that had been lost. The instructions for Aaron had detailed what he was to do for his own preparation (16:2-5) and for a ceremony to sanctify himself (16:6-14) and the people (16:15-19) from this defilement, along with other special purification instructions (16:20-28). These regulations were then established in perpetuity, so the cleansing could be performed annually on behalf of the people, the sanctuary, and the priests (16:29-34). Since during the course of time, contamination accumulated, this event was established to allow the people to perform what we would do for a "spring cleaning" for the early part of a new year, though for Israel the religious year began in the fall (see the discussion at 23:23-25). Using a modern analogy, this was to reformat a hard drive which had become corrupt and needed restoration to its original state. This annual event was later called the "Day of Atonement," as chapter 16 is often headed in English Bible versions. This name for the day is actually not given until later (e.g., 23:27-28; 25:9) and is not mentioned in the passage itself, though Hebrew terms related to "atone" (*kapar* [TH3722, ZH4105]) occur 23 times in the chapter.

◆　B. Warning and Preparations (16:2-5)

2The LORD said to Moses, "Warn your brother, Aaron, not to enter the Most Holy Place behind the inner curtain whenever he chooses; if he does, he will die. For the

Ark's cover—the place of atonement—is there, and I myself am present in the cloud above the atonement cover.

³"When Aaron enters the sanctuary area, he must follow these instructions fully. He must bring a young bull for a sin offering and a ram for a burnt offering. ⁴He must put on his linen tunic and the linen under-garments worn next to his body. He must tie the linen sash around his waist and put the linen turban on his head. These are sacred garments, so he must bathe himself in water before he puts them on. ⁵Aaron must take from the community of Israel two male goats for a sin offering and a ram for a burnt offering.

NOTES

16:2 *the place of atonement.* Or "the atonement cover," known traditionally as the "mercy seat" (*kapporeth* [TH3727, ZH4114]). The word for "atonement" (*kapar* [TH3722, ZH4105]) and its derivatives occur 23 times in this chapter.

COMMENTARY

Aaron's sons were punished for entering a location open to them as priests when they came in an unacceptable manner (10:1-2). Moses was instructed to pass on a warning to Aaron lest he do the same thing in entering the Most Holy Place. This was the very innermost part of the shrine itself and was *the* Holy Place par excellence. Only in this chapter is this part of the Tabernacle called the Holy Place (16:2, 16, 17, 20, 23, 27—see NASB, KJV; many modern translations render "Most Holy Place" in these verses to avoid confusion). Elsewhere it is called the "Holy of Holies" (cf. Exod 26:33, 34; 1 Kgs 6:16; 7:50; NLT, "Most Holy Place"), and the term used here usually refers to the Holy Place, the chamber just outside the Most Holy Place (Exod 26:33; see diagram on p. 253). This special use of the term here is confirmed by the description of the location as inside the inner curtain, the thick cloth divider between the two rooms within the tent (16:12, 15; cf. Exod 26:31-33; Num 18:7). Since this was the most sacred of places, entry was not determined by the visitor (the high priest), but rather by the host (Yahweh himself). The Tabernacle and priesthood were new at this stage in the life of Israel, so procedures were being established so that matters might be regulated rather than carried out *ad hoc*.

The present location of this warning in Leviticus is logically appropriate. The crisis of Aaron's sons' sins necessitated immediate resolution, which was provided by the precedent established here. The instruction was also given in time for the annual ceremony with which the chapter closes. Inappropriate entry led to their death (10:2); the same warning applied to Aaron if he misbehaved in a similar fashion.

Inside the Most Holy Place was the Ark, the cover of which was called the "atonement cover" or, more traditionally, the "mercy seat" (Exod 26:34; NLT, "the place of atonement"). Made of solid gold with two facing cherubs, one at each end, it covered the hollow Ark of the Covenant (Exod 25:17-22). The appearance of God's very presence was also said to reside over this cover in the form of "the cloud." This could have been the cloud of smoke and fire that filled the Tabernacle upon its completion (Exod 40:34-35) and led Israel through the wilderness (Exod 40:36-38). But the very public nature of this cloud in Exodus would argue against its appearance here in a context of hiddenness and exclusivity. The only other appearance of a "cloud" in the context was the smoke from the incense Aaron burned before the Ark (16:13). This sacred object was doubly obscured, by the veil and also by the smoke.

In order to enter the Most Holy Place, Aaron had strict preparations to make. First he needed to gather two animals for his own sacrifices: a bull for a sin or purification offering (4:3-12) and a ram for a burnt offering (1:10-13). He needed also to prepare special, high-priestly clothing, putting it on after he had bathed his entire body, not just his hands and feet as in ordinary sanctuary service (16:4; Exod 30:19-21). These were simpler garments than those described in his ordination (8:7-9), made of linen (cf. 6:10), without embroidery or other decoration and also without the accessories like the ephod, breastplate, and badge. Though simple, and of a type that could be worn by any Israelite (see 13:47-48; Deut 22:11), they were sacred, set apart for this special function rather than by any intrinsic holiness. The fancier, official uniform was put on later in the ceremony (16:24). Aaron also gathered two goats for a sin offering (following 9:3) and a ram for a burnt offering (cf. 1:10-13).

This passage shows that nobody is above the law. Everyone was accountable to established standards, even if, like Aaron himself, he was the leader of the priests, who were supposed to teach and regulate these standards. Some in politics, business, and the church have forgotten this, and if they have not physically died, their ministry and their personal integrity have received a mortal wound.

In any enterprise, planning and preparation are vital for a successful outcome, as Aristotle noted when he said "well begun is half done." A lack of both led to the deaths of Aaron's sons and is also the death of many a project today in both business and the church. Guidelines, with careful details, were presented here so that the act of service might not again go awry.

◆   ## C. Purification Ceremonies (16:6-28)
1. For Aaron (16:6-14)

[6]"Aaron will present his own bull as a sin offering to purify himself and his family, making them right with the LORD.* [7]Then he must take the two male goats and present them to the LORD at the entrance of the Tabernacle.* [8]He is to cast sacred lots to determine which goat will be reserved as an offering to the LORD and which will carry the sins of the people to the wilderness of Azazel. [9]Aaron will then present as a sin offering the goat chosen by lot for the LORD. [10]The other goat, the scapegoat chosen by lot to be sent away, will be kept alive, standing before the LORD. When it is sent away to Azazel in the wilderness, the people will be purified and made right with the LORD.*

[11]"Aaron will present his own bull as a sin offering to purify himself and his family, making them right with the LORD. After he has slaughtered the bull as a sin offering, [12]he will fill an incense burner with burning coals from the altar that stands before the LORD. Then he will take two handfuls of fragrant powdered incense and will carry the burner and the incense behind the inner curtain. [13]There in the LORD's presence he will put the incense on the burning coals so that a cloud of incense will rise over the Ark's cover—

the place of atonement—that rests on the Ark of the Covenant.* If he follows these instructions, he will not die. ¹⁴Then he must take some of the blood of the bull, dip his finger in it, and sprinkle it on the east side of the atonement cover. He must sprinkle blood seven times with his finger in front of the atonement cover.

16:6 Or *to make atonement for himself and his family;* similarly in 16:11, 17b, 24, 34.   16:7 Hebrew *Tent of Meeting;* also in 16:16, 17, 20, 23, 33.   16:10 Or *wilderness, it will make atonement for the people.* 16:13 Hebrew *that is above the Testimony.* The Hebrew word for "testimony" refers to the terms of the LORD's covenant with Israel as written on stone tablets, which were kept in the Ark, and also to the covenant itself.

NOTES

16:8 *cast.* Lit., "give" or "set." Almost all modern translations use "cast" here; lots are most commonly said to be "cast" or "thrown" in order to make a decision (Josh 18:6; Isa 34:17; Joel 3:3 [4:3]; Obad 1:11). Here, however, the wording indicates that the decision was already made (i.e., the lots had been "cast"), and the instruction was to place the appropriate lots directly on the two animals in order to identify which was which.

cast sacred lots. Possibly through use of pebbles of different colors (as with Arabic *garal;* cf. BDB 174) or tablets with identifying labels (Milgrom 1991:1019-1020), lots were used to determine between two options such as yes or no, left or right, or, in this case "for [sacrificing to] Yahweh" or "for [sending to] Azazel" (cf. Neh 11:1; Jonah 1:7). They could be the same as the Urim and Thummim, which were also used as a means of determining God's will (Num 27:21).

16:8-10 *to the wilderness of Azazel . . . Azazel in the wilderness.* The meaning of the term "Azazel" is much debated (see ABD 1.536-537; Milgrom 1991:1020-1021). Since word meanings come from the contexts in which they are used, and this chapter contains the only four uses of the term in the OT (16:8, 10 [twice in Heb.], 26), any understanding must start from this chapter. Since the first goat was dedicated to a deity, one suggestion is that the other was as well and that Azazel was some desert demon (17:7; see *1 Enoch* 8:1; 9:6; 10:4-8), the desert wilderness being a haunt of such beings (e.g., Isa 13:21-22; 34:14; Matt 12:43; Rev 18:2). A second possibility is that Azazel was a geographical term for a desert region (see 16:10, which literally reads "to Azazel, to the desert," and 16:21-22, where the goat goes to the wilderness, also called in 16:22 "a desolate land"). The NLT seems to translate with this in mind. These two interpretations could in fact be related, with the habitation of the demon either becoming the demon's identification (such as a Moabite coming from Moab) or the two becoming interchangeable, such as the equivalent colloquialisms "go to hell" and "go to the devil." The identification of place with person is known elsewhere (cf. Matt 5:34-35; 23:16-22), including the phrase "the Kingdom of Heaven," which is used in Matthew in place of "the Kingdom of God" used by the other Evangelists (cf. Matt 3:2 and Mark 1:15). A third option is that instead of the preposition *le-* [TH3807.1, ZH4200], which governs Azazel, being one of direction or ownership ("*to/for* Azazel"), it could describe its *function as* a goat that carries away the sins of others, though the etymological background of "Azazel" (*'aza'zel* [TH5799, ZH6439]) is unknown. This is the preferred interpretation of some of the earlier versions and is followed in some modern versions (LXX, Vulgate, KJV, NASB, NIV). Since demonic worship was banned for Israel (17:7; Deut 32:16-17; Ps 106:34-39), and this goat, too, was presented "before the LORD" (16:10), the first interpretation is doubtful, though the other two have merit. Whichever interpretation is correct, the important point in this passage is that the goat was far removed from the camp of Israel.

16:12 *powdered incense.* This was made by mixing frankincense (cf. 2:1) with three ingredients: a gum-resin from a member of the fennel family, another called storax, which was a tree derivative, and a kind of seashell (Milgrom 1991:1027-1028). Cf. Exod 30:34-35.

16:13 *the Ark of the Covenant.* Lit., the cover is said to be "on the testimony," a technical term for the covenant tablets stored in the Ark (Exod 25:21). The word "testimony" became a surrogate term for the Ark itself (e.g., Exod 16:34; 27:21, RSV).

COMMENTARY

Priests, even the high priest, could be separated from God. Such a breach of relationship had to be made right before one could perform sacred duties on behalf of someone else (Heb 5:3; 7:27). For example, this is evident in 2 Chronicles 30–31, where a lack of diligence in this area on the part of the priests delayed the people's worship.

Aaron's presentation of his bull for a sin offering was mentioned twice with identical terms in both cases (16:6, 11). It was to bring purification or atonement, the first of its 16 uses in the chapter, which was also given as the function of most of the purifications from sin in chapter 4 (4:20, 26, 31, 35). This function was also given to the sacrifice whose blood was brought into the Tabernacle (6:30), of which this was an example (16:14). Even though the high priest was the only one actively involved in the offering, he acted for his kin as well. But before providing detail about the bull, there is a digression about the two goats. They both were brought into the Tabernacle courtyard at the entry to the tent, since God needed to show his choice regarding their disposal. One would be used for a regular sin offering for the people (16:15), and the other would play a special sin-bearing role (16:20-22). God indicated his selection through lots, a mechanical means of divine revelation (see note on 16:8).

The first goat was Yahweh's, an understandable designation since it would be slaughtered and offered to him (16:15). The second was designated simply as "for Azazel" (see notes on 16:8 and 16:8-10). Yahweh's goat was brought by the priest to serve as a purification offering for the people. According to the procedure of 4:28, the people were to bring their own offering for inadvertent sin, but since this case involved active rebellion (16:16, 21), it was therefore more severe (Num 15:30-31), and so the people needed the priest to act on their behalf. In contrast to this goat and Aaron's bull, which were to be slaughtered (16:11, 15), the second goat was kept alive, since it had a different, non-sacrificial purpose.

Leviticus 16:11-14 picks up again from 16:6. Aaron's purification offering was brought and actually slaughtered (it still presupposes the prescription in ch 4). He took the blood from his own bull and, going inside the Most Holy Place, sprinkled it seven times before the cover of the Ark. As the high priest, he was the only one who had this access and could manipulate the blood here, since in other cases it was sprinkled on the outside of the separating veil (4:6, 17). Although the purpose is not stated here, it must have been to purify the cover from any contamination it had suffered as a result of his sins since some of the same blood applied to the altar purified it (16:18-19).

Before he could enter the inner sanctuary to perform the blood ceremony, he needed to burn incense there. This was regularly burned on the incense altar outside the veil (Exod 30) as part of the purification offering (4:7), but the inner area served almost as the high priest's private sanctuary where he performed rituals on his own behalf. Special, fragrant incense (see note on 16:12) was used for special occasions (Exod 37:29), instead of regular incense such as that brought by Aaron's two sons (10:1; cf. numerous times in Num 7 and 16). Since there was no fire or altar inside the Most Holy Place, Aaron had to gather fire in a burner or censer (10:1; Num 16:6, 46) from the golden incense altar just outside or else from the outer, bronze altar, along with the incense, which was itself placed on the coals once inside. Its smoke billowed up like a cloud, covering and perhaps obscuring the atonement cover. The cloud was important for the passage since God himself was present in it (16:2). He must be approached correctly or else Aaron would die as his sons had.

◆   ## 2. For the people (16:15-19)

¹⁵"Then Aaron must slaughter the first goat as a sin offering for the people and carry its blood behind the inner curtain. There he will sprinkle the goat's blood over the atonement cover and in front of it, just as he did with the bull's blood. ¹⁶Through this process, he will purify* the Most Holy Place, and he will do the same for the entire Tabernacle, because of the defiling sin and rebellion of the Israelites. ¹⁷No one else is allowed inside the Tabernacle when Aaron enters it for the purification ceremony in the Most Holy Place. No one may enter until he comes out again after purifying himself, his family, and all the congregation of Israel, making them right with the LORD.

¹⁸"Then Aaron will come out to purify the altar that stands before the LORD. He will do this by taking some of the blood from the bull and the goat and putting it on each of the horns of the altar. ¹⁹Then he must sprinkle the blood with his finger seven times over the altar. In this way, he will cleanse it from Israel's defilement and make it holy.

16:16 Or *make atonement for;* similarly in 16:17a, 18, 20, 27, 33.

NOTES
16:15 *slaughter the first goat as a sin offering for the people and carry its blood behind the inner curtain.* This wording is nearly repeated by the writer of Hebrews in describing how Jesus, as a sacrifice for sin, took his own blood into the Most Holy Place, heaven itself (cf. Heb 9:11-12).

COMMENTARY
Having purified himself from any contamination that might have stopped him from ministering in the presence of God, Aaron could now do his job as priest, representing the people before God. He could now purify them as well as the altar.

One of the people's goats had already been chosen for their purification offering (16:9). Aaron killed it and took its blood inside the Most Holy Place on the people's behalf, just as he had previously done on his own behalf with the bull's blood (to which reference is made in Heb 13:11). The purpose of this was to purify not only the inner sanctuary but also the Tabernacle as a whole from any uncleanness that might have resulted from any of the things described in chapters 10–15 and from any rebellious sins of open defiance and treachery against God the people might have committed (cf. Gen 50:17; 1 Kgs 12:19; 2 Kgs 1:1). This showed that wrong-doing not only affected them but also contaminated the sanctuary itself. This purification was done by taking some of the sanctified blood that he had taken inside the Most Holy Place and dabbing it on the horns of the burnt offering altar to purify it from any past contamination (16:18-19; cf. Exod 29:37) and then sprinkling it on the altar to sanctify it again, restoring its holiness for future service.

Aaron had to be alone when he was in the Tabernacle proper. No other priest, the only ones allowed inside the sanctuary, could assist him. This would prevent a repetition of what had happened to his sons. Furthermore, this was such an important ceremony for the nation that only the one who was sure to be pure (since he had just performed his own purification ceremony) could take part. This is paralleled in the New Testament, where it is said that our high priest, Jesus, is pure—through his own sanctity rather than through any sacrifice (Heb 7:26; 1 Pet 2:22). It is he and he alone who is our intermediary (1 Tim 2:5).

The book of Hebrews brings out numerous parallels between the death of Christ and the purification ritual. Aaron was able to enter the Most Holy Place through the merit of the sanctified blood (16:14), but Jesus Christ was able to enter there on the merit of his own purifying blood (Heb 9:12). He only needed to do this once, not on the annual basis required for the Day of Atonement since its purification was only temporary (16:34; Heb 10:1, 3-4).

◆   ## 3. Special purification offering (16:20-22)

20"When Aaron has finished purifying the Most Holy Place and the Tabernacle and the altar, he must present the live goat. 21He will lay both of his hands on the goat's head and confess over it all the wickedness, rebellion, and sins of the people of Israel. In this way, he will trans- fer the people's sins to the head of the goat. Then a man specially chosen for the task will drive the goat into the wilderness. 22As the goat goes into the wilderness, it will carry all the people's sins upon itself into a desolate land.

NOTES

16:22 *a desolate land.* The "desolate" place was literally a place "cut off" (*gezerah* [TH1509, ZH1620]; cf. the verb *gazar* [TH1504, ZH1615])—that is, it was separated so that the goat with its accompanying sin would never return to the Israelite camp. While the text does not say that the goat itself was unclean, it carried the impurities of the people and so also must live "outside the camp" (cf. Num 5:3).

COMMENTARY

When all of the sanctuary and its implements had been cleansed, Aaron turned his attention to the remaining goat, which had been chosen by God to be "for Azazel" (16:8). Standing outside the Tabernacle (16:7), and thus in sight of all of the people, Aaron laid both of his hands on the goat's head and made confession. The laying on of hands was a part of the burnt offering of a bull (1:4), the peace offering of a bull (3:2), and also the bull purification offering for sin (4:4, 15, 24, 29, 33; 8:14), but this case was different. In those, only one of the priest's hands was used, while here both of the high priest's hands were specified. This special action indicated that this goat was not a sacrifice in the same way that the other animals were. In some cases, a two-handed gesture such as this transferred something from one party to the other (see Num 27:23; Deut 34:9, Moses transferring his authority to Joshua), and this could be such a transference of the sins to the goat (so NLT). Transference was not always evident, however (see 24:14, where it is an indication of the guilty party).

Confession was an oral acknowledgment of wrongdoing and was done as part of the sin (5:5) and guilt (cf. Num 5:7) offering ceremonies. The use of "confess" indicates that the ceremonies here in this chapter, and most probably all of those in the book, were not done in silence. While we do not have any actual words recorded, there were probably prayers and other words that accompanied most of the ceremonies. As people looking in on the life of ancient Israel, we often have only "video" of their lives (i.e., descriptions of the visual aspects) and lack much of the "audio." This verse helps us understand at least the content, if not the actual wording, of what might have been said. The Mishnah (*m. Yoma* 6:2) suggests the wording was "O Lord, your people, the house of Israel, have committed iniquity, transgressed, and sinned before you. O, by the Lord, grant atonement, I pray, for the iniquities and sins that your people the house of Israel have committed and transgressed and sinned before you, as it is written in the Torah of your servant Moses: 'For on this day shall atonement be made for you to purify you from all of your sins; thus you shall become pure before the Lord' [16:30]."

Three things were confessed: wickedness, rebellion, and sin. The first term (Heb., 'awon [TH5771, ZH6411]) appears to have been the most general and also the most significant for this occasion since it is the only one of the three mentioned in the description of the results of the event (16:22, cf. "sin," NLT). It was also the term most frequently found first in lists of different types of wrongdoing. The sin offering was made to remove its guilt (5:1; 10:17). All of the people, including the priests, would have heard this confession and, presumably, assented to its truthfulness. All of these confessed sins would now be associated with the goat, which was sent to a distant, desolate place without Israelite inhabitants (cf. Deut 32:10; Job 38:26; Jer 17:6), carrying their sins with it.

Contemporary application of this part of the ceremony is clear at several levels, even though it is not physically enacted today. Confession of wrongdoing is necessary for forgiveness and a restored relationship with God or one's fellows (1 John 1:9-10). While different traditions handle the public confession of private sins in different ways, it is entirely appropriate and necessary, if the sins are corporate, to confess them in a corporate context. For the Christian, wrongdoings were also carried by another, but not a goat—rather, a Lamb (John 1:29), who suffered for all of our sins (Isa 53:6; Heb 9:28). The Lamb of God, Jesus Christ, was not unclean in himself, but he took on the sins of others (2 Cor 5:21; 1 Pet 2:24).

◆   4. Concluding acts (16:23-28)

23"When Aaron goes back into the Taber-nacle, he must take off the linen gar-ments he was wearing when he entered the Most Holy Place, and he must leave the garments there. 24Then he must bathe himself with water in a sacred place, put on his regular garments, and go out to sacrifice a burnt offering for himself and a burnt offering for the people. Through this process, he will purify himself and the people, making them right with the LORD. 25He must then burn all the fat of the sin offering on the altar.

26"The man chosen to drive the scape-goat into the wilderness of Azazel must wash his clothes and bathe himself in water. Then he may return to the camp. 27"The bull and the goat presented as sin offerings, whose blood Aaron takes into the Most Holy Place for the purifica-tion ceremony, will be carried outside the camp. The animals' hides, internal organs, and dung are all to be burned. 28The man who burns them must wash his clothes and bathe himself in water before return-ing to the camp.

NOTES
16:26 *into the wilderness of Azazel.* See note on 16:8-10.

COMMENTARY
After the required sin offerings for Aaron and the people, the voluntary offerings (burnt offerings in this case) could be brought. The brief description of these and the disposal of the remnants of the offerings conclude the description of this special ceremony.

Aaron had donned special clothing for the special ceremony (16:4), which he had worn up to this stage in the ceremony. Since this part was finished, these clothes needed to be removed and left inside the Tabernacle because they were especially holy (16:23). Although not stated in the text, one assumes that they were laundered since Aaron had to bathe himself and the two actions are associated elsewhere (14:8-9)—blood-stained clothes would not have been left unwashed. Milgrom sug-gests that leaving the clothing and washing the entire body was not done to remove uncleanness because that had just been done by the previous ceremonies. Rather, it was to remove the "superholiness" brought on by being in the Most Holy Place (1991:1048-1049). This would be similar to the special radiance Moses received when he was in God's presence on Sinai, something that terrified the people (Exod 34:29-30). If this was the reason, the two washings that bracketed the special cere-monies were for two different purposes, the first to remove impurity (16:4) and the second to remove "superholiness."

Bathing probably took place in the courtyard, outside the Tabernacle proper ("a sacred place"; 6:16, 26), where Aaron also put on his regular priestly clothing again (8:7-9). He then could conclude the sacrifices by bringing his and the people's burnt offerings, which had been set aside earlier (16:3-5). Since details of the pro-cess are recorded in 1:10-13, they did not need to be listed here. The purpose of this offering was to restore a right relationship between God and his people. As a final step, the fat, which had been separated from the sin or purification offerings (4:8, 19, 31, 35), was burnt.

While the priest's role was finished, there were still some details to be looked after. The man who had led the goat outside the camp (16:21) was still out there and needed to wash and launder his clothes before he could return (16:26). This was also necessary for the person who disposed of the unburned remnants of the sin offerings (16:28; on the disposal, see 4:11-12, 21). The entire ceremony was now complete, with the sanctuary and its contents, the camp and the people, purified from contamination and able to worship as a community and to serve God.

◆   ## D. Perpetuating the Day (16:29-34)

²⁹"On the tenth day of the appointed month in early autumn,* you must deny yourselves.* Neither native-born Israelites nor foreigners living among you may do any kind of work. This is a permanent law for you. ³⁰On that day offerings of purification will be made for you,* and you will be purified in the LORD's presence from all your sins. ³¹It will be a Sabbath day of complete rest for you, and you must deny yourselves. This is a permanent law for you. ³²In future generations, the purification* ceremony will be performed by the priest who has been anointed and ordained to serve as high priest in place of his ancestor Aaron. He will put on the holy linen garments ³³and purify the Most Holy Place, the Tabernacle, the altar, the priests, and the entire congregation. ³⁴This is a permanent law for you, to purify the people of Israel from their sins, making them right with the LORD once each year."

Moses followed all these instructions exactly as the LORD had commanded him.

16:29a Hebrew *On the tenth day of the seventh month.* This day in the ancient Hebrew lunar calendar occurred in September or October.   16:29b Or *must fast;* also in 16:31.   16:30 Or *atonement will be made for you, to purify you.*   16:32 Or *atonement.*

NOTES

16:29 *tenth day of the appointed month in early autumn.* The date for the annual ceremony was "in the seventh month, the tenth of the month" (see NLT mg). Israel used a lunar calendar of 29-30 days per month, making it differ from our calendar by about 11 days per year. There is, therefore, no fixed correspondence to our calendar today, much like our Easter and Thanksgiving, which are on different dates each year. The first month was associated with Passover, which occurs in the spring (23:5; Exod 12:2); the seventh month, called Ethanim (1 Kgs 8:2; Babylonian Tishri), occurred in the fall (September/October).

a permanent law. Three times this ceremony is called "a permanent law" (16:29, 31, 34), two of these—in the original word order—bracketing the establishment section (16:29, 31).

COMMENTARY

Personal and corporate impurity was a perpetual problem that needed a permanent solution. The solution was provided by establishing an annual ceremony. Since this ceremony was for all of Israel, they were addressed directly (16:29) instead of receiving the word secondhand through Moses and Aaron. Structurally, the passage begins by establishing the permanent rite (16:29-31) and then goes on to describe its ritual and function (16:32-34a), with a concluding historical note (16:34b).

This ceremony involved a period of self-denial, not only from food (though that was undoubtedly included), for which there was a separate Hebrew word, but from other amenities as well. The Aramaic Targum called Pseudo-Jonathan includes refraining "from food, drink, and from enjoying bathing, and from anointing, and from sexual intercourse" (cf. 2 Sam 12:16-20). All work was also to be avoided in what was called a "Sabbath day of complete rest." While not an actual Sabbath day, it was literally a "Sabbath's Sabbath" (used also of the Sabbath itself in 23:3 and the land's Sabbath year in 25:4), indicating a special day when all work must cease. This applied to everyone living in the land, since anyone who sinned, whether Israelite or not, brought pollution (Num 15:29-30; cf. Lev 17:8-15; 18:26; 20:2; 24:16).

There is purposeful repetition in the structure of the Hebrew text, which forms a chiasm (Milgrom 1991:1057). The NLT has changed the order of some elements for stylistic reasons, but the order of the Hebrew can be shown as follows:

A. Permanent law [with date] (16:29a)
   B. Deny selves (16:29b)
      C. No work (16:29c)
         D. Purification gained (16:30)
      C'. Sabbath of complete rest (16:31a)
   B'. Deny selves (16:31b)
A'. Permanent law (16:31c)

This layout shows that the central element described the actions and results desired for the ceremony: purification from all sins and restoration to a relationship with God. This resulted for everyone if they followed the ceremonies of the chapter and ceased from all work.

There might have been a misunderstanding that this result followed from self-denial alone and that these regulations held only for Aaron and not for later high priests. Neither of these was the case, as shown in this description of the ritual and its function. Those who succeeded Aaron by sharing in his ordination and in the anointing ceremony of chapter 8 were to perform all of the actions of 16:2-28, not just the self-denial. This was their permanent law, and it was to be performed annually (16:29; cf. Heb 9:7). Aaron followed God's command, which was given through Moses (16:2). Aaron was able to purify the nation from the defilement brought by the sins of his sons, and through this, to establish a precedent for the same purification to be reenacted every year.

To this day, the Day of Atonement (Yom Kippur, or Yom Hakippurim) plays a significant role in the religious calendar of the Jewish people. It remains a solemn day of introspection and prayer, a day for repenting of sins committed during the previous year. On this day, Jews are to refrain from eating, drinking, sex, and working, among other things. Unlike other festivals such as Hanukkah, Purim, and Sukkoth, where there is feasting and merrymaking, on Yom Kippur there is to be fasting from sundown (when the following day begins in Hebrew tradition) to sunset of the day itself. The day is important theologically because it provides an opportunity to reflect not only on human frailty and sinfulness, but also on the abundance of divine grace and forgiveness.

The New Testament shows that the blood of Christ shed at his death has made the ceremony of Yom Kippur unnecessary. In addition to the effect of Christ's blood mentioned already, it became no longer necessary for the high priest alone to enter behind the curtain into the Most Holy Place (16:12, 15). The curtain was ripped in two (Matt 27:51; Mark 15:38; Luke 23:45), providing continual access to everyone who has been purified by his blood. Now indeed everyone is a full member of a "kingdom of priests" since they are all ceremonially holy (Exod 19:6; 1 Pet 2:9; Rev 1:6) and can join the community in the worship and service of God.

◆ **V. Code for Daily Holy Living (17:1–27:34)**
   A.   Holiness of Blood (17:1-16)

Then the LORD said to Moses, ²"Give the following instructions to Aaron and his sons and all the people of Israel. This is what the LORD has commanded.

³"If any native Israelite sacrifices a bull* or a lamb or a goat anywhere inside or outside the camp ⁴instead of bringing it to the entrance of the Tabernacle* to present it as an offering to the LORD, that person will be as guilty as a murderer.* Such a person has shed blood and will be cut off from the community. ⁵The purpose of this rule is to stop the Israelites from sacrificing animals in the open fields. It will ensure that they bring their sacrifices to the priest at the entrance of the Tabernacle, so he can present them to the LORD as peace offerings. ⁶Then the priest will be able to splatter the blood against the LORD's altar at the entrance of the Tabernacle, and he will burn the fat as a pleasing aroma to the LORD. ⁷The people must no longer be unfaithful to the LORD by offering sacrifices to the goat idols.* This is a permanent law for them, to be observed from generation to generation.

⁸"Give them this command as well. If any native Israelite or foreigner living among you offers a burnt offering or a sacrifice ⁹but does not bring it to the entrance of the Tabernacle to offer it to the LORD, that person will be cut off from the community.

¹⁰"And if any native Israelite or foreigner living among you eats or drinks blood in any form, I will turn against that person and cut him off from the community of your people, ¹¹for the life of the body is in its blood. I have given you the blood on the altar to purify you, making you right with the LORD.* It is the blood, given in exchange for a life, that makes purification possible. ¹²That is why I have said to the people of Israel, 'You must never eat or drink blood—neither you nor the foreigners living among you.'

¹³"And if any native Israelite or foreigner living among you goes hunting and kills an animal or bird that is approved for eating, he must drain its blood and cover it with earth. ¹⁴The life of every creature is in its blood. That is why I have said to the people of Israel, 'You must never eat or drink blood, for the life of any creature is in its blood.' So whoever consumes blood will be cut off from the community.

¹⁵"And if any native-born Israelites or foreigners eat the meat of an animal that died naturally or was torn up by wild animals, they must wash their clothes and bathe themselves in water. They will remain ceremonially unclean until evening, but then they will be clean. ¹⁶But if they do not wash their clothes and bathe themselves, they will be punished for their sin."

17:3 Or cow.   17:4a Hebrew *Tent of Meeting;* also in 17:5, 6, 9.   17:4b Hebrew *will be guilty of blood.*
17:7 Or *goat demons.*   17:11 Or *to make atonement for you.*

NOTES

17:2 instructions. Lit., "word," a term used previously to describe the priestly dedication procedure (8:5) and the priestly offerings that began their ministry (9:6). Moses was delegated to pass on God's instructions not only to the priests, who were the main audience of chs 1–16, but also to "all" the Israelite males (including the priests—see 21:24; 22:18).

all the people. Lit., "every man." Though this could include females (cf. 24:15), it is here most likely restricted to males (cf. 15:2) since animal slaughter and hunting (17:8, 10, 13) in Israel would have been tasks for the male.

17:3-4 If . . . [then] that person will be as guilty as a murderer. The chapter includes numerous prohibitions against various activities. Rather than being in the form of an imperative, "don't do X or Y" (e.g., Exod 20:3-17), they are usually presented in the form of a case with its consequences, "if anyone does X or Y, then Z will happen" (e.g., Exod 21:2-11). Since the development of such case laws followed the actual event, the matters addressed here must have been real-life issues for the Israelites.

17:7 be unfaithful. Lit., "go after them like prostitutes," a metaphor for Israel breaking her covenantal "wedding vows" made at Mount Sinai.

17:10 eats or drinks. The Hebrew simply has "eats," probably referring to eating meat from which blood had not been properly drained (see 7:26-27; Gen 9:4; Deut 12:16, 23; 15:23; 1 Sam 14:32-34).

COMMENTARY

The first 16 chapters dealt with the large issues of sacrifice and purity for the people and sanctuary of Israel. The main actors were the priests, who were professionally involved in the subject. The rest of the book turns to more practical applications of these major themes to individual lives and situations. One could say that the first part of the book asks "How do those who are ceremonially impure regain their purity?" while the second asks "How do we live holy lives to keep from becoming impure in the first place?" Rooker (2000:42) suggests a two-part structure of doctrine and application similar to that of some New Testament books like Romans (1–11, 12–16) and Ephesians (1–3, 4–6). Wenham (1979:5) observes that chapters 1–16 concern Israel being a "kingdom of priests," while chapters 17–27 pertain to Israel being a "holy nation" (Exod 19:6).

However, it must be observed that these laws were not directed only to Israel. Foreign residents were mentioned as being bound by prohibitions against drinking blood (17:8-16), and the mention of Canaan and Egypt as negative examples of sexual practices that were to be avoided (18:3, 24-27) would indicate that a number of these regulations are universal (see, for example, Amos 1:3–2:3, where Israel's neighbors are held accountable for actions they would likely have judged inhumane if done to them, just as Israel and Judah are accountable to their own covenant obligation in Amos 2:4-12).

This has serious implications for contemporary reflection and application of the Levitical laws in church and society. The excuse that some expectations were for Israel alone or were applicable only during the period of the Old Testament, is too simplistic. This concerns a key problem for Old Testament study, the relationship between the Testaments, and the relevance of the Old Testament to a Christian. While contemporary Christians do not perform animal sacrifice, the concepts of holiness, purity, and a relationship with God that underlie these ceremonies are still relevant to them. We too often seem to take the wrong view of the laws in the Old Testament—and in the New, for that matter. Rather than asking, "What is the minimum that I can get away with?" (seeking to find which laws we can jettison), it would better serve those who claim the inspiration, authority, and usefulness of the entire Bible to ask, "In what ways can I keep the whole law, not as a means of salvation, but as a way of holy living?"

Many scholars call this section (chs 17–26) the "Holiness Code" and think it was originally separate from the first part of the book. This is based on its distinct structure and vocabulary (Milgrom 2000:1319-1332). Holiness is indeed central, but it is important in the first half of the book as well. In the Holiness Code (chs 17–26) there are 69 occurrences of words deriving from the Hebrew word for "be holy" (*qadash* [TH6942, ZH7727]), which is a significant number. Yet it should be noted that the non–Holiness Code section (chs 1–16, 27) contains 82 words from this root. Based solely on this small sampling, there is no compelling reason to see the two parts as separate, since there is much in vocabulary, theme, and structure uniting them.

Since blood played an important part in the Israelite sacrificial system, God was jealous that it not be misused, especially in the worship of any foreign gods (17:7). It had been deemed special from very early in human history (Gen 9:4-6). Though the regulations presented here seem to cover a gamut of topics, all of them were united by the presence of blood. This includes blood shed when slaughtering animals and also blood that might be used as food. Care was called for in the former and avoidance in the latter.

When Israel became settled in the land, agriculture would increase in importance, but as a people on the move after the Exodus and prior to their entry into the land, domesticated animals played a more important role in the social and economic life of Israel (Exod 12:38). Animals provided much of their food (through milk—e.g., Gen 18:8—and to a lesser extent the meat, Gen 27:9) and clothing (through the hair and skin). They were also an important part of Israel's religious life through the sacrificial system, as shown already in this book. A person's wealth was often indicated in terms of animals owned (e.g., Gen 12:16; 13:2, 5; Deut 8:13; Job 1:3; 42:12). Regulations showed the people how to deal with various aspects of their use and ownership (e.g., 27:32; Exod 21:28–22:4, 31).

Animals to Be Sacrificed (17:3-7). The first instruction (17:3-7) concerns three domesticated animals that were used as sacrifices: cattle (cf. 4:10; 9:4, 18, 19), sheep (cf. 1:10; 3:7; 4:35), and goats (cf. 1:10; 3:12; 4:23; 5:6; 9:3; 16:5). They were mentioned together in an earlier ban on eating fat (7:23). The action involved is set clearly in the context of the wilderness wanderings, since it refers to "the camp." This is unlike other regulations, which had their focus on life as it would be when the people were settled in the land (e.g., harvest festivals, 23:9-22; selling real estate, 25:23-34). What exactly was being regulated here is debated on several levels. The verb "sacrifice" could mean "slaughter for sacrifice" (1:5, and commonly in Leviticus; Gen 22:10), but it could also refer to non-sacrificial slaughtering (e.g., Gen

37:31; Num 11:22). So it is unclear whether one was banned just from making sacrifices anywhere besides the Tabernacle, an option taken by NLT (17:3), or whether all slaughter of these animals was to be done at the Tabernacle, thereby making all slaughter of animals a ceremonial, sacrificial event—specifically, a peace offering (Wenham 1979:241; Milgrom 2000:1452). Going even further, these animals, while not comprising the totality of edible domesticated animals, could be understood as representing all such animals, so this could be a ban on all secular slaughter of any domesticated animal at all.

The first option can be seen as a law to prevent any sacrifice to a pagan deity, but this could be redundant depending on the interpretation of 17:8-9. The latter options would have the same effect, but would go even further. Conducting all slaughter at the Tabernacle could work in this wilderness context, where animal slaughter for food would have been minimal, since the animals were precious and would not have been squandered as food. This lack of meat led to complaints to Moses (Exod 16:1-13). In this context, and with the geographical unity of the people as they were on the march, such a regulation could have been followed. But it is not realistic to expect that this could have been followed after the people had settled throughout the land of Israel since such a frequent recourse to the Tabernacle or Temple would not have been practical. There is no mention of this restrictive practice in the context of the settlement—in fact, slaughter away from the Tabernacle was allowed, according to Deuteronomy 12:15 and 21.

Another egregious misuse of sacrifice was bringing it to foreign gods, which was unfaithfulness (see note on 17:7). The specific gods mentioned were apparently deities worshiped in the Sinai in the form of a goat, denoted by a different term than that used for the animal acceptable for Israelite sacrifice (17:3). These would have been like the classical satyrs (2 Chr 11:15; Isa 13:21; 34:14, RSV). Multiple altars plagued Israel during the period of the monarchy (e.g., 1 Kgs 11:7-8; 12:32-33; Hos 8:11).

The penalty for misuse was severe, no matter which interpretation is followed. The wrong is literally identified as shedding blood, which is also used to describe murder (Gen 9:5-6; 37:22, RSV). This was a completely unacceptable practice (Num 35:33), and the one who did this thing would be as guilty as if he had killed a person. Like those who deliberately sinned, the person must be punished by God himself, either by banishment or by execution (see the discussion of "cut off from the community" in 7:20). Also, if the blood was used in an unacceptable way, it would not be available for its desired purpose—that is, to bring back spiritual life through atonement just as it gave physical life to the body (17:11).

Prohibited Sacrifices (17:8-9). The next prohibition expanded to include resident foreigners as well as Israelites. Two offerings were identified, the burnt offering (ch 1) and the peace, or fellowship, offering (ch 3), the latter being the only offering in chapters 1-7 called a "sacrifice" (3:1, RSV). It could have been only these two that were banned if not presented at the sanctuary, or the latter term could be more general, including all sacrifices. Since the context of the chapter focuses on blood, at least all of the blood sacrifices, which would include also the sin offerings (4:1-5:13) and guilt offerings (5:14–6:7), must have been intended. These "go up" to God, in whole (burnt offering) or in part (peace offering; 3:5). Though the sanctuary was to be the location of the sacrifices, what was more important was that they be directed to Yahweh, the God of Israel, and not some pagan deity. This carries on from the previous instructions, applying now unambiguously to sacrifice.

Prohibition against Eating Blood (17:10–12). Israel and everyone living among her people were twice prohibited from ingesting blood from any source, whether a sacrifice or regular slaughter. This is once stated in the form of case law (17:10) and once as a prohibition (17:12). The frequency of the prohibition here and elsewhere shows that it was central to the Israelite belief system. The penalty highlighted this importance, since it was stated more forcefully than previously. Not only would the wrongdoer be banished, but God himself would turn against him (17:10; cf. 26:17). If Israel, or those who had identified with her by residing in her midst, turned to another who was not their God, breaking covenant with Yahweh, God would treat them as actually being who they were acting like: those who were not Israelites or followers of Yahweh.

The regulations are strict because blood is vitally important to God and to people. Thus, God gave a statement concerning the nature and function of blood: It is life (17:11, 14; Gen 9:4). This is true on two levels, the biological and the theological. Biologically, flowing blood keeps the flesh alive by providing oxygen and nutrients. Its loss leads to death (cf. the discussion of blood and life in ch 12); refraining from eating it honored life's sanctity (Gen 9:4-6). Theologically, blood shed in sacrifice (here described as being "on the altar") purified the altar from contamination, which could lead to separation and death; it brought the person back to God, the source of all life. It served as a person's ransom (cf. Exod 30:12-16), taking the place of the offerer's own life. Though the people brought the sacrifices to God, it was he who initiated the entire sacrificial system ("I have given you the blood"; 17:11) in order to allow them to restore a relationship they had broken. This proclamation turned the perception of the sacrificial system on its head. It was not a duty demanded of Israel, but a privilege afforded to Israel. For both of these reasons, biological and theological, blood consumption was banned for Israel.

Blood was important to the early church, as well, since the shed blood of Christ allows believers to join the family of God through forgiveness (Heb 9:22). Its literal consumption was not condoned by the early leaders (Acts 15:29); its prohibition was most probably given as a concession so as not to offend Jewish members of the early church (Wenham 1979:247). However, drinking Christ's metaphorical blood at communion has profound theological symbolism for the Christian (1 Cor 11:23-26; cf. John 6:54), something not to be misused any more than the blood in the Old Testament (Heb 10:29).

Hunting Practices (17:13–14). Attention had been reserved up to this point to domesticated animals, but what of wild creatures that were still edible according to the laws of chapter 11? Was blood from one of them any different? Game was a source of food (e.g., Gen 25:27; 27:3), so its treatment also needed consideration.

Israel, and those living among her population, could hunt, kill, and eat animals and birds not on the prohibited list (ch 11). These included gazelle and deer (Deut 12:15, 22; 1 Kgs 4:23) as well as others (Deut 14:5). Their meat was acceptable for the table, but it still needed to be treated like any other, with the blood drained onto the ground and buried so there would be no danger of its being misused, either by eating it (17:10-12) or using it for sacrifice. Milgrom points out archaeological evidence of bones near altars, indicating that some of these animals, along with some of the unclean animals noted in chapter 11, were sacrificed outside of the central Israelite shrine in Jerusalem (2000:1480-1481). This perhaps indicates an unofficial religious practice or at the least gives a reason why this regulation was needed.

In another aside to Moses (17:14), God explained again the nature of blood (cf. 17:11), showing that it applied to every creature, whether sacrificial or not. No blood of any kind from any source could be misused, or there would be punishment.

Found Meat (17:15-16). A final case concerned meat from an edible animal that died on its own or was killed by another animal. As this follows the regulation concerning game, game animals could also be meant here (Wenham 1979:245), though all permissible meat was probably meant, since domesticated animals must also have died naturally at times and could have been eaten. Their blood was drained and buried, in conformity with the last law, even though this was not specifically mentioned. Eating would have made the eater impure, and he therefore had to launder, bathe, and wait, as described in 11:39-40 (see discussion there). If not, the person would suffer unspecified consequences. Since purity was required to be able to approach God, at the least an unresponsive person would be deprived of access to the sanctuary. Since there was no response, punishment was inevitable.

◆ B. Holiness of Sex (18:1-30)

Then the LORD said to Moses, ²"Give the following instructions to the people of Israel. I am the LORD your God. ³So do not act like the people in Egypt, where you used to live, or like the people of Canaan, where I am taking you. You must not imitate their way of life. ⁴You must obey all my regulations and be careful to obey my decrees, for I am the LORD your God. ⁵If you obey my decrees and my regulations, you will find life through them. I am the LORD.

⁶"You must never have sexual relations with a close relative, for I am the LORD.

⁷"Do not violate your father by having sexual relations with your mother. She is your mother; you must not have sexual relations with her.

⁸"Do not have sexual relations with any of your father's wives, for this would violate your father.

⁹"Do not have sexual relations with your sister or half sister, whether she is your father's daughter or your mother's daughter, whether she was born into your household or someone else's.

¹⁰"Do not have sexual relations with your granddaughter, whether she is your son's daughter or your daughter's daughter, for this would violate yourself.

¹¹"Do not have sexual relations with your stepsister, the daughter of any of your father's wives, for she is your sister.

¹²"Do not have sexual relations with your father's sister, for she is your father's close relative.

¹³"Do not have sexual relations with your mother's sister, for she is your mother's close relative.

¹⁴"Do not violate your uncle, your father's brother, by having sexual relations with his wife, for she is your aunt.

¹⁵"Do not have sexual relations with your daughter-in-law; she is your son's wife, so you must not have sexual relations with her.

¹⁶"Do not have sexual relations with your brother's wife, for this would violate your brother.

¹⁷"Do not have sexual relations with both a woman and her daughter. And do not take* her granddaughter, whether her son's daughter or her daughter's daughter, and have sexual relations with her. They are close relatives, and this would be a wicked act.

¹⁸"While your wife is living, do not marry her sister and have sexual relations with her, for they would be rivals.

¹⁹"Do not have sexual relations with a woman during her period of menstrual impurity.

²⁰"Do not defile yourself by having sexual intercourse with your neighbor's wife.

²¹"Do not permit any of your children to be offered as a sacrifice to Molech, for you must not bring shame on the name of your God. I am the LORD.

²²"Do not practice homosexuality, having sex with another man as with a woman. It is a detestable sin.

²³"A man must not defile himself by having sex with an animal. And a woman must not offer herself to a male animal to have intercourse with it. This is a perverse act.

²⁴"Do not defile yourselves in any of these ways, for the people I am driving out before you have defiled themselves in all these ways. ²⁵Because the entire land has become defiled, I am punishing the people who live there. I will cause the land to vomit them out. ²⁶You must obey all my decrees and regulations. You must not commit any of these detestable sins. This applies both to native-born Israelites and to the foreigners living among you.

²⁷"All these detestable activities are practiced by the people of the land where I am taking you, and this is how the land has become defiled. ²⁸So do not defile the land and give it a reason to vomit you out, as it will vomit out the people who live there now. ²⁹Whoever commits any of these detestable sins will be cut off from the community of Israel. ³⁰So obey my instructions, and do not defile yourselves by committing any of these detestable practices that were committed by the people who lived in the land before you. I am the LORD your God."

18:17 Or *do not marry.*

NOTES

18:2 *I am the LORD your God.* God identified himself by his personal name, Yahweh, and stated that he had a relationship with the people of Israel as "your God," not only here, but 21 times before the end of the book, three of which are in this chapter (see 18:2, 4, 30). The present chapter also includes three additional statements of God's personal name using the shorter form "I am Yahweh" (18:5-6, 21). This identification of God's name and relationship to Israel is significant because it brackets the entire chapter (18:2, 30).

18:5 *If you obey my decrees and my regulations, you will find life through them.* Paul used this in his argument against seeing regulations on their own as leading to life (Gal 3:12, 21); regulations are only life-giving if they are based on faith in a covenant God, not based on the deeds themselves.

18:6 *You must never have.* The prohibitions are directed literally to "every man," specifically referring to males (cf. the Hebrew of 15:2; 17:3). It is written in the second person, to a "you," who was probably the head of the family unit, since he would have had it within his power to initiate these relationships and so would have appropriately been commanded to desist. To one who could not initiate, it would be illogical to deliver a command to stop.

sexual relations. This is described in Hebrew by two euphemisms, or polite ways to discuss private matters. In English, we also use euphemisms for sexual relationships—for example, "to sleep with someone." The euphemism in Hebrew is formed from two verbs: "to approach" (*qarab* [TH7126, ZH7928]) in order "to expose" (*galah* [TH1540, ZH1655]) nakedness. "Approach" in this Hebrew form could even by itself indicate a sexual encounter (18:14; 20:16; Gen 20:4; Deut 22:14; cf. Lev 18:19; 20:16). This is made more specific in this chapter by stating the purpose of the encounter through the term "uncover," with which it was used as a synonym (18:14). The term for "nakedness" stands for the person's sexual organs and usually carries a connotation of shame and unacceptability, which was always the case if they were "exposed" (Ezek 16:36-37; 22:10; 23:10, 18). The verses in Ezekiel indicate the action did not specifically indicate a sexual encounter with near relatives (contra Ross 2002:346). If the phrase did only specify sex with near relatives, the next phrase in Leviticus ("with a close relative") would be redundant since that would have been implied in the Hebrew verb and not spelled out as it is here.

a close relative. Lit., "any flesh of his flesh" (*kol-she'er basaro* [TH7607/1320, ZH8638/1414]), a term much like our "flesh and blood." Cf. 21:2-3.

18:7 *Do not violate your father by having sexual relations with your mother.* Lit., "The nakedness of your father and the nakedness of your mother you shall not uncover." What did the father have to do with prohibiting sex with the mother? It must be significant because it also occurs in another prohibition (18:8 [stepmother; cf. 20:11]). On several other occasions, the husband of the woman in a banned relationship is mentioned in a similar context (18:14 [aunt; cf. 20:20], 16 [sister-in-law; cf. 20:21]), so the Hebrew form is significant, and numerous interpretations have been given (e.g., Milgrom 2000:1536-1537 offers nine). It appears that a violation of one's mother was at the same time a violation of one's father, even though the sexual act was only with one of them. The two were one "flesh" (Gen 2:24; Wenham 1979:255), the term which in 18:6 was used to summarize all banned sexual relationships. The law functions "to classify all the following incestuous unions as either a violation of one's father or of one's mother" (Hartley 1992:287), and it also allows inclusion in the following regulations of not only those related by blood but also those related by marriage (Milgrom 2000:1537).

18:9 *your sister or half sister.* Lit., "your sister, the daughter of your father or the daughter of your mother." The implication of the Hebrew is that the "sister" spoken of here is in fact a half sister. The full sister is not mentioned individually in the passage, but rather implied as a "close relative" in 18:6.

18:17 *do not take her granddaughter.* Cf. NLT mg. Rather than "uncovering nakedness" (see note on 18:6), the verb is "take" (*laqakh* [TH3947, ZH4374]), often associated with marriage if a "wife" was taken (e.g., Gen 4:19; 25:1), but not necessarily so, if no "wife" is mentioned (e.g., Gen 20:2).

18:20 This verse is a rewording of one of the Ten Commandments (Exod 20:14; cf. Deut 5:18), though it focuses on the male initiator rather than two consensual parties.

18:21 *permit . . . to be offered as a sacrifice.* Lit., "to give in order to cause to pass through/over." This is an awkward clause used of turning over or dedicating someone or something to a pagan deity. It was usually "children" (seed, offspring—either male or female; cf. Jer 32:35) who were turned over. Once it is said that they were literally "passed through fire" (2 Kgs 23:10). The present verse points to pagan religious practices, even those of child sacrifice, being followed by Israel often enough to require special prohibition.

18:23 *perverse*. It is unclear how this term (*tebel* [TH8397, ZH9316]) differs from other judg-mental terms in this chapter. Most likely it comes from the word *balal* [TH1101, ZH1176], meaning "to mix" (Wenham 1979:260), which is appropriate here since the act crosses the creation boundaries between species.

COMMENTARY

Maintaining a relationship with God and restoring such a relationship, which might have been jeopardized through impurity, are concerns of the book of Leviti-cus. This chapter explores another type of relationship: sexual relations between humans, which also impacted a person's relationship with God. The structure of the chapter shows a deliberate contrast between God and his standards, which open and close the chapter (18:1-2, 30d), and pagans and their practices (18:3-30)—with general commands prohibiting their practices (18:3, 30b) bracketing specific examples.

Avoiding Pagan Practices (18:1-5). Yahweh warned Moses against following the pagan practices of Israel's "host" countries: Egypt, where she lived before the Exo-dus, and Canaan, into whose land she would soon be entering. The nature of the forbidden practices was not spelled out, but the following context dealt with forbid-den sexual relationships, namely relations between near relatives, or incest. The prohibited actions most probably also involved similar sexual activities.

The instructions in this chapter flowed from Yahweh through Moses to the peo-ple. Aaron was not mentioned as having any part, since the subject concerned pri-vate sexual relationships that would not have any priestly concern. Purification after sexual intercourse simply demanded that the parties involved wash and wait until evening (15:18), with no priestly involvement necessary.

The primary reason given for stipulating instructions concerning sexual relations was that it stemmed from God's self-identity and stated relationship with Israel—the same reason given as to why Israel should obey the Ten Commandments (Exod 20:2; Deut 5:6). God's covenant name, Yahweh, was used, and the covenant rela-tionship he shared with Israel was thereby highlighted (see note on 18:2). Because of this relationship, which was to be exclusive according to the first of the Ten Com-mandments (Exod 20:3; Deut 5:7), they were to avoid any of the practices of the followers of pagan gods.

Egypt and Canaan were the regions where Israel lived prior to the Sinai setting of Leviticus (18:3; 25:38; Exod 6:5; 12:40-41), and Canaan was where they would be going in the future (14:34; Exod 6:4). Thus they were the most immediate outside influences on the Israelites. Their deeds and way of life, the "statutes" or customs by which they oriented their existence, were not to be models for Israel. In contrast, Yahweh's regulations (the same word as the "way of life" in 18:3) were to be fol-lowed. These included not only the civil laws of Israel as a nation, but also the ritual prescriptions of Israel as God's followers, as were recorded in this book (5:10; 9:16).

Egypt was known to Ezekiel as being sexually voracious (Ezek 16:26; 23:3, 19-21), and individuals from there, though not necessarily the nation as a whole, were pictured as lusty (Gen 12:10-16; 39:6b-13). Marriages between relatives were also common in Egypt, among both royalty and commoners (Milgrom 2000:1518-1519). Egypt was not the main subject, however, since Canaan was the primary counterexample to Israelite practice in this chapter (18:3, 24, 26, 27, 30). Canaan was cursed due to the sin of his father, Ham (Gen 9:25), the nature of which sin is unclear, though some take it as being a sexual impropriety, possibly homosexuality. Homosexuality was known among the Canaanites (Gen 19:5-8), as were other sexual evils (20:23); some in Israel practiced homosexuality as well (cf. Judg 19:22-26). This is prohibited in this chapter (18:22).

The opening section closes with positive motivation for keeping the directions of God: They bring life and prosperity, in contrast to unacceptable practices, which would bring death and destruction (18:29; cf. Deut 28:1-14; 30:6, 15; see note on 18:5).

Prohibited Relationships (18:6-23). While sexuality was affirmed in the right context (cf. Gen 2:24; Song of Songs), it could also be perverted. Judging from contemporary practices and the presence of two separate lists of sexual prohibitions in Leviticus (see also 20:9-21), it seems that such behaviors were well-known in Israel and needed regulation. Sexuality was part of some Canaanite religious practices (e.g., Num 25), but had no place as part of Israelite religion (cf. Exod 19:15). The family is foundational to the continued existence of a society, and anything that endangers it threatens the society itself. Marriage, and a committed sexual relationship, were covenantal (see Gen 2:24); by its nature, a covenant is something to be protected and nurtured. These regulations indicate areas in which the relationship was unlawful, non-covenantal, and banned. All societies have some regulation of sexual relationships, whether taboos regarding homosexuality, incest, bestiality, or pedophilia, which are viewed as detrimental to the social structure.

As well as providing legal and theological insight into ancient Israel, this passage also opens a window into the social structure of God's people. Since laws were generally unnecessary if the act they regulated was impossible or unheard of, the wrongs banned were probably commonly found within Israel, at least at some time in their history. The partners involved would at times have been together in situations making sexual relationships possible. Through the family relationships mentioned in this chapter, it is possible to diagram the membership of the extended family, the "father's house" (*beth-'ab* [TH1004/1, ZH1074/3]; e.g., Num 3:24; Isa 3:6), a unit of three to five generations whose members lived in proximity to each other, most frequently in separate accommodations surrounding a common central courtyard (King and Stager 2001:39-40; Perdue 1997:13-21, 51-52). The ban was on sexual relationships with "a close relative" (see note on 18:6). This includes those in what we would view as both the immediate and extended family (25:49). Wenham views this as a discussion of forbidden marriages (1979:253) because Israelites looked for marriage partners from among their own tribal families (Gen 24; Num 36) and frowned upon marrying foreigners (Deut 7:3). These regulations protected marriages from being between relatives who were too close, though still allowing intermarriage between first cousins. Ancient Israel was much more conservative sexually than Western societies are today, and most Israelite sexual activity would have been within the bonds of marriage, unlike today, but Wenham's seems to be too narrow a reading of our chapter, which is best seen as covering any sexual activity, whether protected by marriage or not.

Many have been puzzled by the fact that there is no mention of either one's full sister or daughter in the regulations that follow (see note on 18:9). It cannot be assumed that these relationships were already regarded as taboo by everyone, at least if one goes by the all-too-common incestuous relationships of our day. These relationships were included, however, within the "close relative" category, as 21:2-3 clearly shows in reference to the nuclear, blood family.

The reason given for this ban is simply Yahweh's self-identification (cf. 18:2). He is the only one who would have authority over the family head during Israel's wilderness wandering, since there was as yet no other authority such as a king, and so accountability would have been only to God (Milgrom 2000:1536).

The regulations were arranged from nearer to more distant relationships, starting with the person's closest kin (including his mother, 18:7; his stepmother, 18:8; his half sister, 18:9, 11; his granddaughter, 18:10), followed by those of his parents (his aunts by blood, 18:12-13, or marriage, 18:14), those related to him through marriage (his daughter-in-law, 18:15; his sister-in-law, 18:16), and relatives from his wife's family (her daughter [his stepdaughter], 18:17a; her granddaughter [his step-granddaughter], 18:17b; her sister [his sister-in-law], 18:18). The section concludes with several other condemned Canaanite practices, some involving sexual relationships—with a menstruating woman (18:19), with someone else's wife (18:20), with someone of the same gender (18:22), and with animals (18:23).

The first regulation concerns the person's mother, meaning the natural, birth mother (18:7). Sexual relations with her were banned (see note on 18:7). The second regulation concerns having sexual relations with any one of the wives belonging to one's father (18:8). The command may also extend to concubines (Milgrom 2000:1538). In Israel, a man could have more than one wife at the same time. Examples of this are found throughout the Old Testament: Abraham with a wife and two concubines (Gen 16; 25:1-2); Esau with five wives (Gen 26:34; 36:2; 28:9); Jacob marrying Leah and Rachel (Gen 29:16-30) and also having two concubines (Gen 30); Gideon with "many wives" (Judg 8:30); Samuel's father, Elkanah, with two wives (1 Sam 1:2); David with at least seven wives (1 Sam 18:17-30; 25:38-43; 2 Sam 3:2-5; 5:13); Solomon with 1,000 wives and concubines (1 Kgs 3:1; 11:3); and Rehoboam with 18 wives (2 Chr 11:21). Leviticus 18:8 prohibited sexual relations between a man and another of his father's wives, whether his own mother was still alive (an instance of polygamy) or already dead. Doing so was a violation of the father, as a blood relative, but not of her, as one who was related to the son only by marriage. This prohibition was broken several times, always with unfortunate results—for people such as Reuben, who consequently lost his firstborn status (Gen 35:22; cf. Gen 30:4; 49:4); Absalom, who unsuccessfully tried to overthrow his father David (2 Sam 16:21-22); and Adonijah, who tried to usurp Solomon's throne (1 Kgs 2:13-25).

One's sister, whether a full sister or a half sister, was also outside the bounds (18:6, 9-10). If she were the daughter of the man's father, she would be part of the "father's house" through birth into it and would also live nearby, but if she was a half sister on the mother's side, she could have lived elsewhere, born into a different "father's house" (see the example of Tamar, who in Gen 38:11 returned to her original "father's house"). Both were covered by the regulation, being blood relatives of either the father or the mother. A man's direct blood descendant, his granddaughter, was also forbidden since he would be violating himself—that is, his own bloodline. As head of the household, the patriarch had the responsibility to protect the virtue of those in his family group, not taking advantage of them, nor letting others do so (see Gen 34, where Jacob didn't fulfill this role).

The final close relative mentioned is a stepsister through another relationship of a wife of the man's father (18:11), following on from 18:8 (20:11; Gen 37:2; Deut 22:30; 27:20). She had no blood tie personally to the man, since the nakedness of neither the mother nor father was mentioned. She was "born into" the father's family (cf. 18:9), that is, his clan, but not his actual physical household (since "house" is missing from the phrase; Milgrom 2000:1542). In spite of there being no biological blood relationship with the man, since she was fully of his father's clan, she was still banned, as was his sister, who was banned in 18:9.

The prohibition was stretched even one step further, moving from blood-related (18:12-13) to marriage-related aunts (18:14). Such a relationship would violate the uncle through the father's side (20:20). He himself would be a blood relative to the man, though his wife would only be related through marriage. An aunt by marriage through the mother's side was not mentioned. She could have been assumed to have been banned and so not mentioned, or, more likely, she, being doubly removed from the line of the father, was considered too far removed to be incest. She was not the "mother's close relative" (18:13), like the previous two aunts were. Milgrom (2000:1544) also notes that the paternal uncle played an important part in the family in other contexts, which is possibly the reason why he is mentioned here.

Moving further away in kinship to those outside the direct blood line, two prohibitions were given concerning females related through marriage (18:15-16). A daughter-in-law was one married, not born, into the family (see Gen 11:31; Ruth 1:6), from the perspective of the preceding generation. However, the same term referred to a "bride," from the perspective of her own generation (Song 4:8-12; Isa 61:10). To specify which of these was meant, she is described as the son's wife. Judah unwittingly broke this sanction when he had intercourse with the wife of two of his sons (Gen 38:11-18), though he did not suffer execution as the law would later stipulate (20:12). A sister-in-law who was married to one's brother, rather than one married to a brother-in-law, was also protected. Approaching her would violate the relationship she had with one's brother. Presumably this law held during the brother's life, since his death, if he was childless, would have required a levirate marriage—that is, the brother of the deceased would be expected to marry the widow in order to father a son to carry on his brother's line (Deut 25:5-10). The present law could have been the norm, with the levirate exception only allowed under that circumstance and for that single purpose.

A further step away from the bloodline moved to the family relationship established between the man and a woman when they entered into a relationship with each other (18:17-18). Many relationships were prohibited between him and those on her side of the family, firstly her daughter, then her granddaughter. Neither were said to be related to the man by blood, so marriage or a sexual relationship with either the woman or her daughter would not have violated any of these laws. This law banned a relationship with both simultaneously. If a man was married to one of these two and she died, a relationship with the other was not banned in this chapter, since there was no mention of banning a mother-in-law (but see Deut 27:23) or a stepdaughter (Milgrom 2000:1546). With the death of the first wife, neither of these relationships would still be in place.

The second half of 18:17 picks up from the first, looking to the next generation, a granddaughter who was not related biologically to the head of household, but would have lived in his family unit. A blood granddaughter is covered in 18:10, but this law gave further protection to one who had entered into the care of the family unit. She was considered one flesh (see 18:6, 12-13) with her grandmother, his wife, and so inviolate. The form had changed here, as had the wording (see note on 18:17). Another difference was a lack of mention of a motive that the woman was a relative. Instead there was a moral evaluation, that the relationship was "a wicked act," something completely abhorrent to ordinary sensibilities, usually referring to a sexual perversion (e.g., 19:29; 20:14; Judg 20:6; Jer 13:27). It appears, based on form and vocabulary, that the laws here were added to those already listed from a different source, though they were well integrated into this context through cross-references and the shared topic of sexual relationships.

The next prohibition, in 18:18, commands "do not take" (the same verb as in 18:17; see note) into a sexual relationship both a woman as wife and simultaneously her sister as a second wife while the first was still alive. This brings to bear elements of several previous prohibitions against relationships with two related women (18:17): There is a time element (cf. 18:19), and a sister is involved (cf. 18:12-13). Her sister became as the man's own sister, and was therefore unapproachable, at least until his wife should die. The two sisters would be rivals. The word "rivals" translates a Hebrew root (*tsarar* [TH6887/A/B, ZH7674/7675]; cf. also *tsarah* [TH6869/A, ZH7650/7651]) with two different but related meanings: "take a second, or rival, wife" (cf. 1 Sam 1:6), and "trouble, oppression, or antagonism" (cf. Num 10:9; Pss 54:7; 138:7). That the first could lead to the second was clear from the situation of Jacob, who married both Leah and Rachel, two sisters (Gen 29:26-35; 30:1-2, 14-24), with much anguish on all sides as a result. The sisters vied for place and honor in the same household—imagery also found in the prophets (Isa 11:13).

The remaining restrictions (18:19-23) were more mixed, many involving sexual relations, but not in incestuous contexts. A woman who was unclean from her monthly menstrual cycle of bleeding was earlier said to be ceremonially unclean (15:19), and the uncleanness was passed on to any sexual partner through contact with her menstrual blood (15:24). Therefore, a man was not allowed to approach her for sexual relations (18:19). Marriage was not mentioned, so this was a general prohibition for within the marriage relationship and outside of it. Though not highlighted here, the penalty imposed for this violation (20:18) indicates that this was viewed as a serious offense.

Adultery—that is, illicit intercourse with a woman married to someone else—was prohibited. She was the wife of someone of the same clan, a neighbor (6:2; 19:11, 15, 17; 24:19; 25:14, 15, 17), but not of the same "father's house," so she did not come under the previous prohibitions. She and her husband were still worthy of respect for their personal rights, even though she was not a blood relative.

The next prohibition against child sacrifice to Molech seems to have been of a different category than the others, which dealt with sexual matters. Molech (see 20:2-5) was a pagan Canaanite deity associated with the afterlife and the underworld (Milgrom 2000:1770-1771). The context of the surrounding regulations suggests that there was some sexual element involved in this as well, though this could be metaphorical rather than physical adultery (cf. 20:5 and the discussion there; Day 1989:22-24). Some of the later prophets (e.g., Hosea) used the metaphor of sexual unfaithfulness to point toward covenant unfaithfulness, turning away from God to another "partner." This wrong not only affected the perpetrator and his partners, as did previous wrongs in the chapter, but it also affected God himself by desecrating his holy name, making the holy common and so destroying the boundaries between the holy and profane, which the priests were to guard (10:10). Apparently the people were mixing up Yahweh and Molech, either using God's name in the pagan rituals (Milgrom 2000:1560), or thinking that they were one and the same God, and that by worshiping Molech they were in fact worshiping Yahweh. This is found also in Hosea, where Baal and Yahweh were being confused in people's minds, something that God could not allow (Hos 2). Israel's God was being treated as no god when another was allowed to take his place. The prohibition concluded with a reminder of who it was who was speaking, Yahweh and not any other god (18:21). He also was the one who would enforce the prohibitions.

Interest then turned away from illicit male–female sexual relations and metaphorical relations between Israel and a foreign god to even more extreme behaviors, male homosexual intercourse and bestiality (18:22-23). Male homosexuality, or sodomy, so named after Sodom, where this act of anal intercourse was practiced (Gen 19:5; cf. Judg 19:22), was literally "lying with a male in the manner of a female." (Female homosexuality did not enter into consideration here or elsewhere in the Old Testament, perhaps because no semen, with its life potential, was wasted; Milgrom 2000:1568.) The lack of a single term for the activity could show its foreignness in Israel. The act was called detestable, an abomination that was morally repugnant (a term picked up more fully in the summary of this chapter and will be discussed there). The only individual wrongdoing described by this word in this chapter is homosexuality (cf. 20:13). No explanation is given as to why this ban might be in place. Milgrom (2000:1565-1568) suggests that the ban, and this whole chapter, has to do with procreation. Babies potentially born of the various sexual acts mentioned in this chapter would be illegitimate, or destroyed in the case of Molech offerings, or nonexistent in the case of homosexuality or bestiality. Life is God's ideal and also his mandate when he delegated humanity to fill the earth (Gen 1:28; 9:1), and these last two cases waste the opportunity to do this. (For further comment on homosexuality, see DOTP 747-749.)

Paul was consistent with this law in his condemnation of homosexuality, expanding it to add female homosexuality to the male act described here (Rom 1:24-27; cf. 1 Cor 6:9; 1 Tim 1:10). He saw it as a result of turning one's back on God to pagan deities and practices, even as chapter 18 is based on Canaanite and Egyptian precedents. Paul seems to have even expanded the argument, not basing it only on Israelite law, but on homosexuality's being unnatural, going against a creational ordering of things.

Bestiality involves sexual union between a human and an animal (18:23; cf. Exod 22:19). For the male, the terms used for the acts were the same as with a neighbor's wife (18:20), and with the same result, moral defilement. A woman (18:23) is said to offer herself voluntarily, literally "stand before a male animal in order to mate with it," though the masculinity of the animal is assumed, not stated in the Hebrew. Such intercourse is a terrible perversion. In Genesis 1, animals were created "according to their kinds" (Gen 1:24-25, RSV), suggesting exclusive boundaries between each and between them and other parts of creation, including humanity, which was created next. Also, the man's response to the created woman (Gen 2:23) indicates that in her he saw something appropriate to him, which he had not found in relation to the previously created animals (Gen 2:19-20). Unnatural mixtures are condemned elsewhere as well (19:19; Deut 22:5, 9-11; 2 Cor 6:14).

Anyone familiar with the Old Testament story, especially the book of Genesis, knows that on numerous occasions the actions banned in this chapter were practiced without condemnation by some important people in Israel's history. Abraham married a half sister (18:9; Gen 20:12) and was ready to perform child sacrifice (18:21; Gen 22). Lot had children by his daughters (Gen 19:30-38). Jacob married two sisters (18:18; Gen 29:14-30). Judah had intercourse with the wife of his sons (18:15; Gen 38:18). And Moses's mother was his father's aunt (18:12; Exod 6:20). Carmichael (1997) proposes that the laws in chapters 18-20 were written as a response to this kind of patriarchal story, though that questions the historical integrity of the narrative framework of the chapter. It is clear from the lack of condemnation of these actions in the patriarchal stories or even later, after chapter 18 was written, that the laws of Leviticus were not retroactive (cf. 14:36 and comments).

Unlike contemporary proponents of freedom for any and every sexual expression, an Israelite was unable to say that what happened in the privacy of one's own home between consenting adults harmed no one and was thus okay. All of these acts listed were condemned, with rationales provided for many. For Israel, there was an objective morality presented by God through Moses so that such relationships or actions were not just left up to one's own whim or proclivities.

Consequences for Violating the Laws (18:24–30). Thus far, the chapter has given no penalties for breaking any of the individual prohibitions (cf. 20:21). In the summary of 18:24-30, severe consequences are spelled out. The audience is urged to avoid all of the things listed since they would defile those who did them, just as much as touching an animal carcass did (5:2). For Israel, defilement resulted in exclusion from God's presence, and even the pagan predecessors of Israel in the land were held accountable and would lose the land because of their moral uncleanness, including sexual misdeeds such as those listed (cf. 18:2). Not just the people were affected, however, but the land itself became polluted by sexual sins just like it did by the blood of murder victims (Num 35:33-34; Milgrom 2000:1579).

The writer drew a clear picture of what would happen, one everyone could understand. If you eat rotten food, it could make you violently ill. So the land became ill enough to vomit those evil practitioners out of it, whether the Canaanites for what they had done or the Israelites if they should do any of these banned things (18:28). Just because God had entered into a special covenant relationship with Israel would be no excuse for them to exercise abominable practices. They also were liable to punishment. The great fish did the same to Jonah, vomiting him out to a place of safety (Jonah 2:10), but here the land would vomit Israel from a place of safety to one of jeopardy, outside the care of their God in their promised land. They would be exiled and their place taken by others.

To avoid this dire penalty, Israel, who had not yet even reached their promised land, and those who might be residing with them in the land and therefore under many of Israel's laws (e.g., Exod 12:48-49; cf. Lev 19:23-24) were reminded that they must keep, not break, these laws. A summary description of all of the prohibited activities in the chapter is that they are detestable (cf. 18:23). The term indicates the repugnance that one feels for things that are physically foul and turn one's stomach (e.g., Ps 107:18), or else are psychologically distasteful because they run completely against one's moral sensibilities. Ingrained by one's background and upbringing, it would be a feeling of natural revulsion. Since Israel was steeped in its covenant with God, living in the light of its teaching day in and day out (cf. Deut 6:7), this gut reaction would have arisen when faced with a serious breach of that covenant. This indicates the seriousness with which the writer took these wrongs in general, and homosexuality in particular, since it was the only individual wrong given this description (18:22; 20:13).

The pre-Israelite Canaanites were used as a negative model for Israel, exhibiting behavior they were to avoid if they wanted to avoid the same punishment. If Israel was found to contain practitioners of these things, the nation would be exiled, and the individual practitioners would receive personal punishment in the form of being cut off from the people and clan to which they belonged, just like the person who illegally slaughtered or consumed blood (17:4, 10).

The chapter closes with a reiteration of its opening injunctions (18:4, 5): Keep God's commands (18:26). It also adds the negative: Avoid defiling actions. The people had before them a negative example and a positive exhortation. Which would they choose? In order to help their decision, God reminded them, as he also had at the outset, of whom they were dealing with: Yahweh himself, the Creator of the universe and their own covenant God.

In closing, it should be noted that many of the sexual prohibitions listed here were also banned in the New Testament (Matt 15:19; Rom 13:9; 1 Cor 5:1-5; 10:14; 1 Pet 4:3), and some prohibitions were even intensified (e.g., adultery, Matt 5:27-28). This is uncomfortable for some in the church, since in Western culture "tolerance" has become a watchword. It was the tolerance of pagan practices that was a threat to Israel's national existence, and one must be very careful today that such tolerance for fear of offending does not lead to an even greater offense (Gal 5:7-11), allowing death to come because the church did not take a biblically sanctioned stand. If God created the universe and established how it should run in a manner that would provide the most benefit to its inhabitants, and even revealed how best to live in it through the "owner-operator's manual" of his revelation, it behooves us to take his guidelines very seriously. It is also important to remember the purposes of these regulations: They were not given to limit personal freedom but to expand personal holiness.

◆ C. Holiness of Personal Conduct (19:1-37)

The LORD also said to Moses, ²"Give the following instructions to the entire community of Israel. You must be holy because I, the LORD your God, am holy.

³"Each of you must show great respect for your mother and father, and you must always observe my Sabbath days of rest. I am the LORD your God.

⁴"Do not put your trust in idols or make metal images of gods for yourselves. I am the LORD your God.

⁵"When you sacrifice a peace offering to the LORD, offer it properly so you* will be accepted by God. ⁶The sacrifice must be eaten on the same day you offer it or on the next day. Whatever is left over until the third day must be completely burned up. ⁷If any of the sacrifice is eaten on the third day, it will be contaminated, and I will not accept it. ⁸Anyone who eats it on the third day will be punished for defiling what is holy to the LORD and will be cut off from the community.

⁹"When you harvest the crops of your land, do not harvest the grain along the edges of your fields, and do not pick up what the harvesters drop. ¹⁰It is the same with your grape crop—do not strip every last bunch of grapes from the vines, and do not pick up the grapes that fall to the ground. Leave them for the poor and the foreigners living among you. I am the LORD your God.

¹¹"Do not steal.

"Do not deceive or cheat one another.

¹²"Do not bring shame on the name of your God by using it to swear falsely. I am the LORD.

¹³"Do not defraud or rob your neighbor.

"Do not make your hired workers wait until the next day to receive their pay.

¹⁴"Do not insult the deaf or cause the blind to stumble. You must fear your God; I am the LORD.

¹⁵"Do not twist justice in legal matters by favoring the poor or being partial to

the rich and powerful. Always judge people fairly.

¹⁶"Do not spread slanderous gossip among your people.*

"Do not stand idly by when your neighbor's life is threatened. I am the LORD.

¹⁷"Do not nurse hatred in your heart for any of your relatives.* Confront people directly so you will not be held guilty for their sin.

¹⁸"Do not seek revenge or bear a grudge against a fellow Israelite, but love your neighbor as yourself. I am the LORD.

¹⁹"You must obey all my decrees.

"Do not mate two different kinds of animals. Do not plant your field with two different kinds of seed. Do not wear clothing woven from two different kinds of thread.

²⁰"If a man has sex with a slave girl whose freedom has never been purchased but who is committed to become another man's wife, he must pay full compensation to her master. But since she is not a free woman, neither the man nor the woman will be put to death. ²¹The man, however, must bring a ram as a guilt offering and present it to the LORD at the entrance of the Tabernacle.* ²²The priest will then purify him* before the LORD with the ram of the guilt offering, and the man's sin will be forgiven.

²³"When you enter the land and plant fruit trees, leave the fruit unharvested for the first three years and consider it forbidden.* Do not eat it. ²⁴In the fourth year the entire crop must be consecrated to the LORD as a celebration of praise. ²⁵Finally, in the fifth year you may eat the fruit. If you follow this pattern, your harvest will increase. I am the LORD your God.

²⁶"Do not eat meat that has not been drained of its blood.

"Do not practice fortune-telling or witchcraft.

²⁷"Do not trim off the hair on your temples or trim your beards.

²⁸"Do not cut your bodies for the dead, and do not mark your skin with tattoos. I am the LORD.

²⁹"Do not defile your daughter by making her a prostitute, or the land will be filled with prostitution and wickedness.

³⁰"Keep my Sabbath days of rest, and show reverence toward my sanctuary. I am the LORD.

³¹"Do not defile yourselves by turning to mediums or to those who consult the spirits of the dead. I am the LORD your God.

³²"Stand up in the presence of the elderly, and show respect for the aged. Fear your God. I am the LORD.

³³"Do not take advantage of foreigners who live among you in your land. ³⁴Treat them like native-born Israelites, and love them as you love yourself. Remember that you were once foreigners living in the land of Egypt. I am the LORD your God.

³⁵"Do not use dishonest standards when measuring length, weight, or volume. ³⁶Your scales and weights must be accurate. Your containers for measuring dry materials or liquids must be accurate.* I am the LORD your God who brought you out of the land of Egypt.

³⁷"You must be careful to keep all of my decrees and regulations by putting them into practice. I am the LORD."

19:5 Or it.   19:16 Hebrew Do not act as a merchant toward your own people.   19:17 Hebrew for your brother.   19:21 Hebrew Tent of Meeting.   19:22 Or make atonement for him.   19:23 Hebrew consider it uncircumcised.   19:36 Hebrew Use an honest ephah [a dry measure] and an honest hin [a liquid measure].

NOTES

19:3 show great respect. The word yare' [TH3372, ZH3707] is often translated "fear," not necessarily with the idea of terror or horror, but rather of awe in the presence of majesty and power. This is the same term that characterizes one's attitude toward God himself (19:14, 32). Parents were thus viewed as being extremely important in Israelite family relationships.

19:4 This verse rewords the first two of the Ten Commandments (Exod 20:3-6) and closes with the same motive that began the Ten (Exod 20:2).

19:11 *Do not deceive or cheat.* Milgrom (2000:1631) helpfully describes the difference between the two verbs: "[Deceive] refers to the desire to keep what you unlawfully have; you therefore *deny* that it belongs to someone else. [Cheat (better rendered as 'lie'; cf. 6:3, 5)] refers to the desire to want something that belongs to someone else; that is, you *affirm* that it belongs to you. The difference, then, was that in the former you deny a *truth;* in the latter, you affirm a *lie."*

19:15 *twist justice.* Lit., "[do] injustice," a word for "wrong," which is an antonym of "good" (e.g., Ps 37:1-3) and numerous other positive and desired terms (Milgrom 2000:1642).

19:16 *Do not spread slanderous gossip among your people.* "Gossip" (*rakil* [TH7400, ZH8215]) indicates words that can harm the one about whom they are spoken. The NLT's "slanderous gossip" implies lies or half-truths, though the term *rakil* could also refer to information told in confidence (Prov 11:13). The alternative translation in the NLT mg reads: "Do not act as a merchant toward your own people." "Act as a merchant" is derived from another form of the same Hebrew root (*rakal* [TH7402, ZH8217]) having this meaning (e.g., 1 Kgs 10:15; Neh 13:20). The context in Leviticus points to this being a reprehensible action, and honest trade is not condemned, though dishonesty is (e.g., 19:35; Deut 25:16; Hos 12:7). It is perhaps dishonest business practices being condemned here (cf. 19:13). English translations more generally follow the translation used in the main NLT text, as there are other verses that use this term where perverse words rather than perverted business ethics are clearly in view (Prov 11:13; Jer 9:4; Ezek 22:9).

Do not stand idly by when your neighbor's life is threatened. Lit., they were prohibited to "stand on the blood of your companion." Wenham (1979:268) interprets this as being a further point from the legal system meaning to stand as witness in a capital case against someone in court.

19:28 *tattoos.* This word (*qa'aqa'* [TH7085, ZH7882]) occurs only here in the OT, so an exact meaning is unsure. The context allies it with other practices involving the dead, though writing God's name on one's hand could signify allegiance to him (Isa 44:5). This might refer to a pagan practice of dedication to another god, unacceptable for Israel (Milgrom 2000:1695).

COMMENTARY

This chapter is theologically central to the book of Leviticus, having holiness as its focus. It is bracketed on each side by regulations concerning sexual holiness (ch 18) and penalties for breaking these sexual regulations (ch 20). Before specifying the penalties, however, the book lists numerous additional instructions. These are a mixture of laws, several of which are also found elsewhere, including some among the Ten Commandments. For the people, these were practical examples of how holiness should work out in real life.

The regulations are in a number of different grammatical forms: jussives, indicating expectation ("you will certainly . . ."); imperatives ("do A"); strong negative imperatives ("never do B"); negative exhortations ("don't do C") and case law ("when E happens, do F"). These laws and their forms are identified in the following chart.

REGULATION	GRAMMATICAL FORM	OTHER REFERENCES
Be holy (19:2)	Jussive	11:44, 45; 20:26
Honoring parents (19:3a)	Jussive	= fifth commandment (cf. Exod 20:12; Deut 5:16
Keeping Sabbath (19:3b)	Jussive	= fourth commandment (cf. 26:2; Exod 20:9-11; 31:13; Deut 5:12-15)
Following idols (19:4a)	Negative exhortation	= first commandment (cf. 26:1; Exod 20:3; Deut 5:7)
Making idols (19:4b)	Negative imperative	= second commandment (cf. Exod 20:4-5; 34:17; Deut 5:8-10)
Proper peace offering (19:5)	Case	3:1-17
Eating peace offering (19:6-8)	Case	7:16-18
Harvesting crops (19:9-10)	Case	23:22
Stealing (19:11a)	Negative imperative	= eighth commandment (cf. Exod 20:15; Deut 5:19)
Lying (19:11b; cf. 19:16a)	Negative imperative	= ninth commandment (cf. Exod 20:16; Deut 5:20)
Cheating (19:11c)	Negative imperative	
Misusing God's name (19:12)	Negative imperative	= third commandment (cf. Exod 20:7; Deut 5:11)
Fraud (19:13a)	Negative imperative	6:1-4; Deut 24:14
Robbery (19:13b)	Negative imperative	Prov 22:22
Withholding wages (19:13c)	Negative imperative	
Disrespect of infirm (19:14a, b)	Negative imperative	
Respect God (19:14c)	Imperative	19:32c; 25:17, 36, 43
Perverting justice (19:15)	Negative imperative	19:35
Slander (19:16a)	Negative imperative	
Apathy to danger (19:16b)	Negative imperative	
Hatred (19:17a)	Negative imperative	
Confrontation (19:17b)	Emphatic Jussive	
Revenge, grudge (19:18a, b)	Negative imperative	
Love neighbor (19:18c)	Imperative (cf. Waltke and O'Connor 1990:529)	
Obey laws (19:19a)	Jussive	19:37; 18:4; 20:8, 22; 25:18
Mixtures (19:19b, c, d)	Negative imperative	18:23; 20:16; Deut 22:9

REGULATION (CONT.)	GRAMMATICAL FORM (CONT.)	OTHER REFERENCES (CONT.)
Sex with slave girl (19:20-22)	Case	
Fallow fruit trees (19:23-25)	Case	
Eating blood (19:26a)	Negative imperative	17:10-12, 14
Fortune-telling (19:26b)	Negative imperative	
Witchcraft (19:26c)	Negative imperative	
Trimming hair and beard	Negative imperative	(19:27)
Self-mutilation for the dead (19:28a)	Negative imperative	21:5
Tattooing (19:28b)	Negative imperative	
Defiling daughter (19:29a)	Negative exhortation	
Keep Sabbath (19:30a)	Jussive	
Respect sanctuary (19:30b)	Jussive	26:2
Following mediums (19:31)	Negative exhortation	20:6, 27
Respect elders (19:32a, b)	Jussive	
Respect God (19:32c)	Jussive	19:14c; 25:17, 36, 43
Exploiting foreigner (19:33)	Case	
Respect foreigner (19:34)	Jussive	
Dishonest measurements (19:35)	Negative imperative	19:15a
Accurate measurements (19:36a)	Jussive	
Keep commands (19:37a, b)	Jussive	

In this new section Moses is commanded by God to direct the regulations to everyone in Israel, highlighting the entire congregation or community. The term "congregation of Israel" has not been used previously in this context in Leviticus, though it is in other key places in the life of Israel: preparation for the first Passover (Exod 12:3), provision of meat and manna (Exod 16:9), and instructions for the Sabbath and making the Tabernacle (Exod 35:1, 4). In this important situation for Israel, a key point in the book, there is a strong emphasis that all who were able to respond—men, women, and children (e.g., Exod 16:1)—must hear the word being spoken. This is strengthened through the use of plural verbs, since each individual was to take to heart and put into practice the directives that follow.

The starting point for the chapter is a key refrain for the entire book (cf. 11:44-45; 20:26) and for the continued life of Israel in relationship with her God: The people should be holy because God is holy. His holy nature was a given for his people (John 17:11; Rev 4:8; cf. Mark 1:24; Acts 3:14), just like theirs should be (Heb 12:10, 14). The Hebrew word order of the command to be holy in 19:2 emphasizes holiness by placing it at the beginning of each part of the sentence: "Holy shall you be, for holy I am." The people were reminded of the need to be separate from any contamination and set apart for a divine purpose because they were the people of God, and this holiness is what characterizes God himself. It is his very nature. The people were to be different from their neighbors and not associate themselves with any other god (20:26). The following laws, as well as those already listed, provide concrete examples of holiness in daily life. Some of the laws concern things best avoided, while others concern things encouraged. Holiness is not simply a "don't do" list, but also involves what one is and does.

An awareness of God's special relationship with Israel also permeates this chapter in the expression, "I am the LORD your God," which occurs seven times (19:3, 4, 10, 25, 31, 34, 36), in addition to the shorter divine self-identification "I am Yahweh," which occurs eight times (19:12, 14, 16, 18, 28, 30, 32, 37). The longer form of this expression opens the Ten Commandments (Exod 20:2; Deut 5:6). This is not only a statement of relationship, but also of exclusivity: "I and I alone am your God." It is the positive statement of what the first of the Ten Commandments states in negative form ("You must not have any other god but me"), implying a statement like "Because I, Yahweh, am your God, you need no other god" (Exod 20:2-3). Because of the exclusive relationship Israel had with God, the people are reminded of their primary covenant commitment a total of 16 times throughout the chapter, from beginning to end.

The regulations begin with two of the Ten Commandments, but in reverse order: parents and Sabbath (19:3). The first is a positive statement of the desired relationship with one's parents, in counterpoint to the negative imperative concerning a perverted relationship with a parent that began the last chapter (18:7). Parents, rather than being the object of sexual desire, were to be the object of one's respect or reverence (cf. Eph 6:1; Col 3:20). The respect and obedient care for one's parents as authority figures and as lifegivers was expected. The order of the parents was reversed from that found in the Ten Commandments (Exod 20:12; Deut 5:16), perhaps to highlight and give special honor to the mother, the parent who would have been most directly violated in 18:7. It is this command, the pivotal one among the Ten Commandments between those directed toward God (commands 1-4) and those directed toward one's fellow humans (commands 6-10), that is remembered first in this chapter.

The last of the God-directed commandments follows: ritually observing the Sabbath day. No details are given here as to what this means; it is assumed that the requirements were already known from the Ten Commandments themselves and other instructions regarding not working (Exod 16:25-30; 31:12-17; 35:2-3; Num 15:32-36). God reidentified himself as the author of the regulation, the one who would enforce it if broken, and also the model for resting on this seventh day (Gen 2:3; Exod 20:11).

The people were commanded not to seek idols, worthless and powerless substitutes for God (26:1; Ps 96:5), for any kind of help (Acts 15:20; 1 Cor 10:14). And the people were forbidden to make idolatrous statues from metal like the golden calf (Exod 34:17). These would have been formed by pouring melted metal into a mold or over a wooden frame (King and Stager 2001:167-170). It was not that images made from melted metal were bad in themselves, since God allowed such images in his own service (Exod 25:18; Num 21:6-9; cf. Gen 1:26). One needed to take care, however, that they were not used in worship of another god (cf. 2 Kgs 18:4; Matt 6:24).

The details for peace offerings were given earlier (ch 3), including directions on how they were to be eaten (7:11-21), with the details here taken from 7:16-18. These earlier directions are here assumed and referred to, marked by the NLT as doing things "properly" (19:5). Milgrom (2000:1616) points out that the single difference from the earlier passage was that here the result of misuse was to defile that which was holy, the food. Being the only holy material with which the laypeople would come into contact, even as far as being able to take it home, it would be too easy to pollute it through lack of care. This made useless the reason for performing sacrifice in the first place, ruined the opportunity to follow the first, foundational command of this chapter (19:2), and destroyed the very purpose for the book of Leviticus itself. Since the potential desecration was so great, so was the punishment (7:20). Paul also addressed a concern with eating sacrificial food, but it concerned food offered to pagan gods, which he banned only if eating it would cause someone a theological problem (1 Cor 10:23-33). Christians also partake of food that represents part of a sacrifice in the Communion meal, eating the body of Christ (1 Cor 11:23-24). Wrongfully eating it could also have severe consequences (1 Cor 11:27-30).

The regulations then address agricultural issues (19:9-10), something we would view as completely separate from the preceding "religious" laws. That is not the case, since even the Ten Commandments mixed "religious" and "secular." This law anticipated a settled life for the people in the land, since it would have had no relevance for a people on the move in the Sinai wilderness. A fixed location was necessary for grain to be planted and harvested, and an even longer period was required for vineyards to be prepared, planted, tended, and harvested (cf. Isa 5:2). When grain was ripe, it would have been an easy task to manually cut every stalk and then have the harvesters go back over the fields to collect every last grain that had fallen. The grape harvest could also have been completely brought into the owner's vats. This was not to be done (23:22), since landowners needed a wider social perspective than simply their own self-interest. Apparently, at least two social groups were not landowners, and thus could not provide for their needs from their own resources. Those who were dependent were the poor (Exod 22:25) and the foreign residents of the land. This food source was to be left for them to enjoy (cf. Ruth 2:2-3). These regulations, as all in this chapter, were spoken and enforced by Israel's God, who had a special place in his heart for the poor and unfortunate.

Further ethical commands follow. The prohibition against stealing reflects the eighth commandment, here stated in the plural rather than the singular as in Exodus (cf. Rom 13:9). This fits with the preceding (*"your* harvest," 19:9; *"your* God,"

19:10) and following contexts, where the plural is used. The logic of the order of this command following the preceding one could indicate that depriving the poor of food was an example of theft. Here the taking was done in secret (e.g., Gen 31:19; 44:8) rather than by force (cf. 19:13).

The next two clauses describe telling an untruth and cheating someone (see note on 19:11). Both of these deprive someone of something just as much as if it were stolen from them. The person hurt in each case is a neighbor (18:20; 19:15, 17), one whose best interests should be a concern (cf. Col 3:9). Lying, and deprivation by means of lying, are the subject of a prohibition against false oaths using God's name (19:12). The oath was to claim something was true, and this claim was strengthened by associating it with God's name, calling him as witness to its truth-fulness and judge if it were false (cf. 1 Sam 3:17; 14:44; 2 Sam 3:35). If the claim was in fact a lie, that not only ruined the reputation of the one who swore, but also of the one whose name and honor were called upon as witness. The name of the holy God was desecrated and made common in the same way as if a pagan god were worshiped (cf. 18:21). This is a different wrong than those mentioned in the previ-ous verse, since it deprives God rather than one's fellow Israelite. This was still a problem in New Testament times, with people making false oaths and invoking God (Matt 5:33-36; 23:16-22; Jas 5:12). Today a false oath before God, shown by laying one's hand on a Bible in court, is a civil felony and severely punished.

The next verse (19:13) involves three kinds of deprivation that were not done in secret like those of 19:11-12. The first is taking from someone who was weaker and unable to defend themselves against the exploitation—closer to what we would call extortion than fraud (cf. Deut 24:14; 1 Sam 25:4-13). The next two verbs could be understood as subcategories of this more general term for forceful deprivation: rob-bery and withholding earned wages (6:2, 3; Gen 31:31; Isa 10:2). Two parties are protected here, the neighbor against exploitation and robbery and hirelings against wage withholding. Day laborers were Israelite or foreign workers hired for a brief period, and they expected payment by the evening (Deut 24:14-15) or at least, as in this verse, the following morning. They did not have any financial cushion, since they did not have regular employment and were consequently dependent on receiv-ing their wages quickly.

Two other helpless groups could be robbed, not of physical resources, but of their dignity (19:14). The deaf and blind were especially vulnerable in the areas of their disabilities, and abuse of them in these two areas was prohibited. Since the deaf could not hear what was being said about them, they were vulnerable to insult, of being lightly or disparagingly spoken of, or cursed. Doing such a thing to one's parents was punishable by death (20:9) since it was contrary to the honor and respect that was their due (19:3). This was not due only to one's parents, but to all of one's fellows. The blind could not see and so were prone to tripping if something was in their way. Purposefully putting something in their path was very cruel (cf. Deut 27:18).

Attention then turned from deprivation of property or dignity on a personal level to depriving someone of a fair decision in the legal sphere (19:15). The general rule was not to pervert justice, with two subcategories indicating ways in which it could be skewed, depending on the social location of those who stood before the judge. Justice could be perverted in two opposite directions: On the one hand, those who are weak, poor, and inconsequential in the eyes of society and thus at the bottom of the ladder (Exod 30:15; Judg 6:15) must not receive unwarranted special treatment by the judge, raising them above what they deserve simply because they are poor. On the other hand, those esteemed by society, far up the socioeconomic ladder (lit., "great"), are not to be preferred by the legal system only on the basis of status. Justice must be blind, not noticing the "who" (the identity of defendant or plaintiff), but the "what" (the merits of the case itself). Rather than perversion, there needs to be fairness or righteousness (19:36), equality for all of one's kin who come before the law.

One's reputation could also be stolen by "slanderous gossip" (19:16), spreading abroad what was entrusted in confidence (Prov 11:13; 20:19). Travel became more restricted when the people settled in the land, and all of the people were moving as a group in the wilderness, so a person's social circle was very small. Spreading such gossip to anyone would likely soon spread it among the entire group, ruining a reputation throughout the community.

The second restriction (see note on 19:16, "Do not stand idly by") concerns slanderous gossip that led to false charges being brought and proved so that the life of the accused was in jeopardy. If that was so, one could not stand by and let this miscarriage take place (Milgrom 2000:1645). Malicious or loose talk could have deprived someone of their very life.

The next two verses (19:17-18) belong together because they begin and end with polar opposite verbs: "hate" and "love." The former was forbidden, using a negative form, while the latter was commanded. The ones to whom these verbs are directed are described in two ways, literally as "the brother" and "the neighbor." Two other terms occur in these verses indicating those in relationship: one's "people" (cf. Hebrew of 19:11, 15), and "a fellow Israelite" (19:18). While the term "brother" could indicate an immediate male sibling, it probably was used of members of the wider kinship group comprising the Israelite nation as a whole. While also united by ancestry, the nation was more immediately joined by a mutual covenant relationship with God. This was also evident in the two verbs, which were also covenant terms: "Love" means to live in covenant relationship with someone, while "hate" means to break covenant relationship.

Rather than showing animosity for a neighbor and hauling him to court, the Israelite who had been offended was to go directly to him personally and sort out the situation between them, lest the person go astray into sin (Prov 10:17; cf. 1 Cor 6:1, 6). This concept was picked up also in the New Testament, where reconciliation after personal animosity should first be done person to person (Matt 18:15-17). A reestablished relationship rather than a repudiated one is expected of covenant partners. A cause of hatred is revenge and grudge bearing, which leads to stewing in one's rage without any positive and restorative outcome (Eph 4:26). But rather than feeling or acting against a covenant partner, love must be shown through actions of love (e.g., Deut 10:18-19; Matt 7:2; Rom 13:8-10).

The nature of this love is to "love your neighbor as yourself" (19:18). This has several possible interpretations (Milgrom 2000:1655-1666). One suggestion is that one should love because the other was "like yourself," i.e., an Israelite, one of your clan, and so is worthy of love. This would fit the context in which this kinship relationship is highlighted. If so, the new teaching brought out by Jesus in the story of the "Good Samaritan" (Luke 10:25-37) is that we need to greatly widen what our understanding of kinship is and who deserves our love. Another approach is to see "like yourself" modifying the verb "love": You should treat the other with the love resulting in good benefits for your neighbor as you hope to be beneficially loved yourself. This also fits a covenant context in that it compares the benefit you expect from the covenant with what you should expect for everyone else in the covenant. It also fits the immediate context, since revenge and grudges are not desired either for self or for the other, so they need to be avoided.

This love command is well represented in the New Testament (Matt 5:43; 19:19; 22:39; Mark 12:31, 33; Luke 10:27; Rom 13:9; Gal 5:14; Jas 2:8). It is also probably among the best-known biblical sayings to the person on the street, who may not know that it is biblical, or even less that it originated in Leviticus! The love command is central to life in human community and is more important than sacrifice (Mark 12:33), but its frequent repetition indicates that it is very hard to really learn and put into practice. In order to aid in its understanding, the writer placed it in chapter 19, surrounded by some examples of how this command could be actualized in real-life circumstances.

A command to obedience in 19:19 ("you must obey all my decrees") marks a transition in the chapter (cf. 19:3, 30), with a very similar command closing it (19:37). The decrees referred to could be both the preceding and following admonitions, serving as a fulcrum and turning point between how one deals with one's fellows (19:3-18) and how one deals with one's possessions (19:19b-36). Both concern holiness because, for a follower of God, all is to be sacred.

Mixing different kinds of the same thing in inappropriate ways is the first concern (19:19b). Three areas of daily life are addressed: animals and their breeding, planting crops, and weaving cloth. The animals are not to be interbred with other species, just as humans are not to have intercourse with animals (18:23). Holiness relates to purity, which interspecies breeding destroys (cf. Gen 1:24-25, "of the same kind"). A similar section in Deuteronomy (Deut 22:9-11) forbids different animals working together rather than interbreeding. If sacrificial animals are the subject here, the interbreeding of horses and donkeys to produce mules, which only appear later in the history of Israel (e.g., 2 Sam 13:29; 18:9), was not of concern, since neither were allowed for sacrifices. This law could have been put in place in order to stop interbreeding between acceptable sacrificial animals and those that were not, lest the offspring, though unacceptable for that purpose, be inadvertently used for sacrifices. More likely this prohibits any animal interspeciation.

Plants were not to be intersown (cf. Deut 22:9, where the subject was the vine-yard rather than the field). On a practical level, the resulting mixture would be hard to separate at harvest, so it was better to keep them separate from the beginning (cf. Matt 13:24-30, where the subject is good plants and weeds). On a symbolic level, these banned mixtures symbolize the holiness of God's covenant people, who are to keep themselves separate from their pagan neighbors, maintaining the demarca-tion between clean and unclean as regards people. Clothing made from two differ-ent fabrics, most probably wool and linen (13:47-48; Deut 22:11), was also banned, except, apparently, for the priest, whose ephod (Exod 28:6; 39:2) and breastplate (Exod 28:15; 39:8) were of mixed material. The curtains of the Taberna-cle were also of mixed material (Exod 26:1), which shows that the ban was not uni-versal, involving all cloths. Milgrom suggests that it was restricted to laity, with mixtures being permissible for the divine realm (2000:1660).

Another forbidden mixing was sexual, between a man and a slave girl who was engaged to someone else (19:20). She could also be a concubine (see Gen 16, where the same term described Hagar), so the wrong was not in the sexual rela-tionship *per se*, but that she was betrothed (engaged) when it happened. Appar-ently a betrothal bride-price had already been paid to her master, which would now be forfeit since the girl was no longer desirable for marriage. The master would have had to return this to the intended husband, and now needed compen-sation for his loss. If she had been an engaged free girl, this would have been con-sidered adultery, and the violator would be liable to capital punishment (Deut 22:23-27), but this was stated not to hold in this case. Aside from the monetary penalty, the man needed also to bring a guilt offering (5:14–6:7), which implies the man's special offense against God, and thus against holiness. He therefore had steps to take to make things right with God and man. This explains this law's inclusion in this chapter, even though both form and content are different from other verses here.

The regulations then turned to agricultural issues, this time fruit trees, anticipat-ing Israel's settlement in the land. The fruit crop of the first three years was to be avoided, treated as if it were "uncircumcised" or unacceptable for an Israelite. In the fourth year, the first mature crop was God's and was specifically forbidden to the owner (in contrast to Num 18:12-13). There was to be joyful celebration for the crop, though the joy was not from its consumption, since that did not happen until the following, fifth year. Then the produce belonged to the people. God's self-identification formula ("I am the LORD your God") brings this section to a close before resuming a set of negative commands.

Seven prohibitions follow, all dealing with aspects of death. The first (19:26a) could be a repeated prohibition against eating blood (3:17; 7:26-27; 17:10-12), though the context suggests another interpretation. The next two prohibitions (19:26b) are against occult practices that seek messages from the gods by divination (e.g., Gen 44:5, 15) and soothsaying (Isa 2:6; 57:3), both condemned elsewhere (Deut 18:10; 2 Kgs 21:6; 2 Chr 33:6; Mic 5:12). Some suggest that a pagan ritual involved pouring blood onto the ground to call forth the divine (Hartley 1992:320; Milgrom 2000:1685-1686), fitting with the other two banned practices. These kinds of practices were common among Israel's neighbors seeking divine guidance through such things as throwing lots (1 Sam 14:42-43) or arrows, inspecting the entrails of slaughtered animals (Ezek 21:21; see Lev 3:4 and comments), or consulting the dead (necromancy; see 19:31; 1 Sam 28:9; Isa 8:19; 19:3; 29:4). They were all banned for Israel, not because they themselves were unacceptable (cf. Gen 44:5; 1 Sam 14:9-10), except for necromancy (20:27), but rather because the practitioners were consulting gods other than Yahweh.

A mourning practice was trimming one's hair or beard and slashing one's body (Deut 14:1; Jer 41:5; 47:5; 48:37; Ezek 44:20). Tattooing one's body was also illegal (see note on 19:28). These were pagan rites practiced by the Moabites and Canaanites (1 Kgs 18:28; Isa 15:2; Jer 48:37) and were not acceptable for Israel. Yahweh is a God of life, and rituals of death are not becoming for his followers, nor are rituals directed toward any other god.

It was against God's commands for a father to have his daughter engage in prostitution (19:29). The Hebrew indicates that this was not a choice she made, but one made by her father, most probably for his own monetary gain rather than hers. In this chapter that urges holiness, a parent, who was given responsibility over children, caused his daughter's defilement or degradation, exploiting her so she was unable to experience holiness. The people of the land would also be polluted (Jer 3:2) by engaging in these and similar disgraceful acts (cf. 18:17; Judg 20:6).

Special times and places for encountering God were to be protected (19:30). The Sabbath was a time of rest that must be observed, reiterating the chapter's opening commands (19:3; cf. 23:3). It is given first priority, since it was initiated first by God (Gen 2:2) and included among the Ten Commandments (Exod 20:8-11; Deut 5:12-15). Here it is expanded to also include the Tabernacle, the special holy place to be respected and revered ("fear") in the same way one should treat parents (19:3) and God himself (19:14, 32). Holy encounters in space and time with Yahweh needed to be protected from defilement.

Necromancy, consulting the dead for advice (cf. 19:26) was specifically forbidden (19:31), since Israel's God did not reveal himself through mediums and spiritualists (cf. 20:6, 27; Deut 18:11), but through his prophets. Israel should not turn to them any more than to idols, but rather they should turn to God, who had a special, living relationship with Israel.

One's elders, those with gray hair (cf. Deut 32:25; Hos 7:9, NASB), were to be treated respectfully (19:32), just as one respected one's parents (19:3) and God himself. Standing to show respect was an Israelite practice (e.g., Job 29:7-8), as it was in an earlier day in North America and still is in some areas. The actual action is not the focus here, but rather that due honor be shown. The elderly and disabled deserve proper treatment even though they are unable to enforce it. God is able to do so, however.

While the nation of Israel was united by kinship and covenant, foreigners had lived among them from the outset and shared some of their rights and privileges (Exod 12:38; 20:10; cf. Lev 16:29; 17:8, 10, 12, 13; 18:26; 19:10). They were practically without power, like the elderly and infirm mentioned above. This unexpected benevolence was due to Israel's having previously been in the same place—foreigners in Egypt (Exod 20:10; 22:21; 23:9). Foreigners were not to be mistreated any more than one would mistreat one's kin (19:33-34). Rather, Israel was to "love" the stranger with the same kinship and covenantal love they were to show their neighbor (19:18; cf. Luke 10:25-37). This is not an emotional response, but rather a practical one for those without natural rights in a foreign country.

A very practical example of potential exploitation closes the chapter (19:35-36a). Since merchants were the ones who measured out their wares, inaccurate measures would have been a tempting and simple fraud (Deut 25:13-16). To do so, however, was "twisting justice" (cf. 19:15, which these verses expand upon), so all measures must be accurate (lit., "righteous"). Since Israel did not have inspectors, the people themselves were responsible for honesty in the balancing scales (Jer 32:10), their weights (lit., "stones"; 2 Sam 14:26; Mic 6:11), and their dry (5:11; 6:20) and wet (23:13; Exod 29:40) measures. Holiness was to be lived out even in the very commonplace aspects of life.

The chapter concludes with motivation for keeping the holiness regulations listed in it (19:37). This motivation comes from God, who had redeemed Israel from Egypt (25:38; 26:13; Num 15:41). This is practically verbatim the motivation God had given to the people for keeping the Ten Commandments (Exod 20:2; Deut 5:6). This unmerited grace on the part of God toward a people who had not as yet had the opportunity to fulfill the obligations of the covenant was to motivate Israel to act likewise. They also needed to show grace, not only to those who were without personal power but in all of life's relationships. Israel was not to permit the unacceptable practices of the Egyptians (18:2), but rather to emulate what God had done for them in Egypt.

What should a Christian's response be to such laws as these? In most societies, some of the practices, such as slavery, have been long abolished (although there is still a large, underground trade in slaves for the sex industry and for use as undocumented workers all over the world, including North America; Baker 2006:130-131). The principles of how one should or should not treat those over whom one has control are still valid, however. In most discussions of Old Testament law and its applicability to the Christian, an ethical minimalism seems to be the preferred approach: How much of the law can I get away with avoiding? Since laws in Israel were often established to protect those who were without a protector and were also formulated to reflect the way that the ordered universe of a creator God would work best, we should likely take another approach to the law. It is not a question of What do I have to do to get God to love me? That is the wrong question. God loves before obedience, as he showed Israel (Exod 20:2). A better question might be, How can I live my life so as to apply as many of God's directions as possible, especially in ways of helping my sister and brother?

◆ D. Penalties for Unholiness (20:1-27)

The LORD said to Moses, ²"Give the people of Israel these instructions, which apply both to native Israelites and to the foreigners living in Israel.

"If any of them offer their children as a sacrifice to Molech, they must be put to death. The people of the community must stone them to death. ³I myself will turn against them and cut them off from the community, because they have defiled my sanctuary and brought shame on my holy name by offering their children to Molech. ⁴And if the people of the community ignore those who offer their children to Molech and refuse to execute them, ⁵I myself will turn against them and their families and will cut them off from the community. This will happen to all who commit spiritual prostitution by worshiping Molech.

⁶"I will also turn against those who commit spiritual prostitution by putting their trust in mediums or in those who consult the spirits of the dead. I will cut them off from the community. ⁷So set yourselves apart to be holy, for I am the LORD your God. ⁸Keep all my decrees by putting them into practice, for I am the LORD who makes you holy.

⁹"Anyone who dishonors* father or mother must be put to death. Such a person is guilty of a capital offense.

¹⁰"If a man commits adultery with his neighbor's wife, both the man and the woman who have committed adultery must be put to death.

¹¹"If a man violates his father by having sex with one of his father's wives, both the man and the woman must be put to death, for they are guilty of a capital offense.

¹²"If a man has sex with his daughter-in-law, both must be put to death. They have committed a perverse act and are guilty of a capital offense.

¹³"If a man practices homosexuality, having sex with another man as with a woman, both men have committed a detestable act. They must both be put to death, for they are guilty of a capital offense.

¹⁴"If a man marries both a woman and her mother, he has committed a wicked act. The man and both women must be burned to death to wipe out such wickedness from among you.

¹⁵"If a man has sex with an animal, he must be put to death, and the animal must be killed.

¹⁶"If a woman presents herself to a male animal to have intercourse with it, she and the animal must both be put to death. You must kill both, for they are guilty of a capital offense.

¹⁷"If a man marries his sister, the daughter of either his father or his mother, and they have sexual relations, it is a shameful disgrace. They must be publicly cut off from the community. Since the man has violated his sister, he will be punished for his sin.

¹⁸"If a man has sexual relations with a woman during her menstrual period, both of them must be cut off from the community, for together they have exposed the source of her blood flow.

¹⁹"Do not have sexual relations with your aunt, whether your mother's sister or your father's sister. This would dishonor a close relative. Both parties are guilty and will be punished for their sin.

²⁰"If a man has sex with his uncle's wife, he has violated his uncle. Both the man and woman will be punished for their sin, and they will die childless.

²¹"If a man marries his brother's wife, it is an act of impurity. He has violated his brother, and the guilty couple will remain childless.

²²"You must keep all my decrees and regulations by putting them into practice; otherwise the land to which I am bringing you as your new home will vomit you out. ²³Do not live according to the customs of the people I am driving out before you. It is because they do these shameful things that I detest them. ²⁴But I have promised you, 'You will possess their land because I will give it to you as your possession—a

land flowing with milk and honey." I am the LORD your God, who has set you apart from all other people.

²⁵"You must therefore make a distinction between ceremonially clean and unclean animals, and between clean and unclean birds. You must not defile yourselves by eating any unclean animal or bird or creature that scurries along the ground. I have identified them as being unclean for you. ²⁶You must be holy because I, the LORD, am holy. I have set you apart from all other people to be my very own.

²⁷"Men and women among you who act as mediums or who consult the spirits of the dead must be put to death by stoning. They are guilty of a capital offense."

20:9 Greek version reads *Anyone who speaks disrespectfully of.* Compare Matt 15:4; Mark 7:10.

NOTES

20:2 *Molech.* This god was a pagan Canaanite deity associated with the afterlife and the underworld (Milgrom 2000:1770-1771).

20:7 This verse repeats the words of 11:44a in a different order but to the same effect; it is also essentially repeated in 20:26. It is a reminder for Israel to separate from other deities that were not truly gods and to be devoted to Yahweh, Israel's God.

20:10 *commits adultery.* The technical term "commit adultery" (*na'ap* [TH5003, ZH5537]) is used here but not elsewhere in Leviticus. It is found in the Ten Commandments (Exod 20:14; Deut 5:18).

20:17 *shameful disgrace.* This phrase translates an unusual use of the word *khesed* [TH2617/A, ZH2875/6], which in almost every other instance means "grace, kindness, covenant love," a positive thing rather than what it is here. A useful suggestion is that it had at its basis the strong, binding love that should be exhibited between family members and was extended in meaning to covenant relationships and those between friends. If this chaste love overstepped into sexual incest, it became an abomination, an illicit "family love."

20:22 *You must keep all my decrees.* The chapter's tone changes from an impersonal address ("anyone"; 20:9) to a direct address to the Israelites.

COMMENTARY

Leviticus 18–19 presented numerous regulations regarding holy living for the people of God. Now the next logical question is answered: What happens if someone breaks one of these regulations? This separation of command and punishment was not rare. The Ten Commandments are generally in this form. For example, the first command against having other gods (Exod 20:3) was fleshed out in Exodus 22:20; 23:13, while the penalty was given in Deuteronomy 17:2-7. In chapter 20 punishments are described for 15 of the previously prohibited acts, so back references are frequent.

The chapter has a well-laid-out literary structure. After the introduction (20:1), it forms a chiasm, which looks like this:

A. Pagan religious practices, including necromancy (20:2-6)
   B. Be holy (20:7)
      C. Obey (20:8)
         D. Punishment for sins against people (20:9-21)
      C'. Obey (20:22-24)
   B'. Be holy (20:25-26)
A'. Pagan religious practices, particularly necromancy (20:27)

The structure shows that holiness looks in two directions: one's actions towards God, which is the outside boundary of the chapter, and one's actions toward humans, the center of the chapter.

The chapter begins with the Lord telling Moses that he is to pass the divine instructions along to "native Israelites and to the foreigners living in Israel" (20:2; cf. 19:33-34). The first instruction addresses the issue of breaking the first commandment (Exod 20:3) and the sixth (Exod 20:13). In particular, God spoke against the worship of Molech (see note on 18:21; 1 Kgs 11:7; van der Toorn 1999:581-585), who is probably to be identified with the god Milcom, who was worshiped by Israel's neighbors to the east, the Ammonites (1 Kgs 11:5, 33; 2 Kgs 23:13; van der Toorn 1999:575-576). The two names seem to be variants referring to the same deity.

Breaking the first covenant commandment against worshiping other gods (Exod 20:3) and the sixth against murder (Exod 20:13) were both capital offenses (Exod 21:14; Num 35:31; Deut 17:2-7), and execution was to be carried out by native Israelites (20:2, 27). This was done by throwing stones at the guilty party until they were dead (20:2; cf. Num 14:10). This brought home to everyone the seriousness not only of the wrong, but also of its punishment, since the community itself had a hand in the execution. Since the corporate existence of the nation was threatened by turning against God, their covenant partner, the punishment was also carried out corporately. God also brought punishment, actively cutting off the person's line from the house of Israel (20:5; cf. 7:20-21, where this is stated as a passive, without the mention of God as the agent).

This sin could not be covered up by the nation since it went against the very foundations of their national covenant. If they didn't take the required steps to address the issue, God would take the matter completely into his own hands, with both the sinner and his extended family. This would serve as a safeguard for the committed relationship between Yahweh and his partner, Israel, a relationship that did not allow for any other partners, whether Molech or the spirits to whom mediums and spiritists turned (20:6; cf. 19:31; Deut 18:11). Turning to other gods was prostitution on a spiritual level. Yahweh allowed no paramours (cf. 18:21), nor did he allow one to go behind his back for spiritual guidance (cf. 1 Sam 28:3-19).

God reminded the Israelites to separate from other "deities," which were not gods, and be devoted solely to him (20:7). The way to holiness is found in the decrees given by God, who gave not only the expectation of holy living, but also the means for holy living (20:8). They were not to be a memorial but a lifestyle. Obedience to God's expectations was to be a way of life.

Honoring one's parents (20:9) acknowledges their high value, while dishonoring them (or cursing, another meaning of the term) demeans them, making them small and inconsequential (Exod 21:17; Deut 21:18-21; Matt 15:4; Mark 7:10). This is the primary human relationship, at least until marriage, and it is to be maintained lest all society be in danger of disintegrating. Dishonoring a parent was therefore a capital offense, punishable by death, most probably by stoning (20:2; Deut 21:18-21).

Any illicit sexual relationship outside the marital bounds was unacceptable (20:10). It might involve a sexual relationship between two people who were married, but not to each other. Both were breaking an exclusive, covenantal relationship, and the death penalty was required for both parties (cf. John 8:4-5). The same held for a sexual relationship with one's stepmother (18:7-8) or daughter-in-law (20:12), and also presumably for one's own mother, full daughter, and full sister (cf. 20:17, a half sister). The latter, being even closer in relation than those listed, would have been implied and understood by all who heard these laws. Both parties were to be executed (20:12).

Male homosexuality was called "detestable" (20:13) and received the same punishment for both parties, there being no distinction between the passive and dominant participants. The same holds for one who married both a mother and her daughter (20:14) and participants in bestiality, whether male or female (20:15-16). Sex with mother and daughter had previously been banned (18:17), but here actual marriage was entered into (Gen 4:19; 12:19), attempting to institutionalize the sexual relationship, at least as a common-law marriage. This could not be done, so each party was subject to execution. The threesome was to be burnt (20:14) for engaging in this wickedness (18:17). All three are mentioned since a marriage with either woman alone would have been permitted; the sin only arose when the other was married at the same time.

Several other cases of sexual misconduct did not involve human punishment; it was left to the hands of God (20:17-19; see commentary on 7:20). These included a man marrying a half sister (cf. 18:9); engaging in sexual activity with a woman suffering from bleeding, not only during her normal menstrual flow (cf. 12:1-2; 18:19), but at any time when she had a genital discharge (ch 15); or having sex with one's aunt related by blood (cf. 18:12-13). Those involved in the first two cases were to be cut off (20:17-18), while the latter would be punished in some unexplained way. The command in 20:19 is the only of these laws formulated as a simple imperative ("do not . . .") rather than a case law ("if . . . then"). It stands in a middle ground, having its own form and the stated punishment standing between the punishment of God cutting off the offenders (20:17-18) and the family line being cut off through childlessness (20:20-21).

Having a sexual relationship with an aunt by marriage (20:20; cf. 18:14) or marrying a sister-in-law (20:21; cf. 18:16), presumably after the death of the brother to whom she was originally married, would result in lack of any further offspring for either partner of the union. This was a serious penalty since children were viewed as a divine blessing (Ruth 4:11-12; Ps 127:3) and were necessary in a society that did not have any retirement or social security system. Children were responsible for looking after their aged parents even as far as burying them after death (Gen 50:1-14), so their lack left people in difficult circumstances.

The importance of children is highlighted in the one exception to the law against marrying a sister-in-law, the practice known as levirate marriage in which a brother would marry his brother's wife if he died without any offspring (Deut 25:5-10;

cf. Gen 38:8). This was done in order to continue the bloodline of the deceased, since the first son born to this union was legally considered that of the dead brother. In this case, the continuity of the line, not having the deceased "cut off" from the nation of Israel, takes precedence over this prohibited marriage.

Building on 20:8, which says "Keep all [God's] decrees by putting them into practice," Moses reminded the audience of their obligations to God. Failure to meet these would cause the land itself to expel them just as it would do to those Canaanites who lived there before Israel came (20:22-23). These prohibited acts were as disgusting to God as Canaan's were (cf. Gen 27:46). Since the setting for these laws is with Israel still in the wilderness before entering and settling in the land, breaking God's regulations could jeopardize the promise (Gen 12:1) even before the nation was able to fulfill it. In contrast to the negative outcome of disobedience, obedience would lead to the fulfillment of God's promise of Israel inheriting the land (cf. Gen 15:7; 28:4), which he himself would give them. The land is described as "flowing with milk and honey" (20:24)—the rich, natural foods that characterize the Promised Land (e.g., Exod 3:8). Israel, who was wandering in the wilderness without food to their liking, would be wonderfully fed in the land if they obeyed and lived as God's holy people.

In light of this call to holiness, the distinction between holy and unholy is the subject of the next two verses (20:25-26). These verses return to chapter 11 and its concern with animals and birds acceptable to eat. Since God showed discernment from the moment of creation (cf. Gen 1:4-7), as well as in the election of his people (20:24), so must his people show the same in their lives. Rather than becoming unclean through eating unacceptable animals (see 11:10), they were to maintain their holiness so they could continue the sacred relationship with God that he had established with them. The chapter concludes as it began, condemning pagan worship, repeating the penalty for mediums and spiritists (20:27). In 20:6, a divine retribution is described, while here it is the community who must take action by stoning the guilty party.

The Christian's response to the punishments mandated for these wrongs is a vexing one, especially as regards capital punishment. Since the wrongful actions were serious, an appropriate response was required, not only for the message that such a response brings to the society, but also because such a response actually honors the wrongdoer: Their actions are treated as important enough to demand a response (see Lewis 1970). Nonetheless, an important distinction must be drawn between Israelite society and our own. Israel was a covenant people, and everyone at Mount Sinai was a member, either through birth or by association, of that people. Upon entering into the land, the people became a city-state, a physical, political entity. Everyone within it was under the same expectations and open to the same punishments if they were not met. For an egregious sin against the state and its laws, physical execution was called for. Today the church is a "spiritual state" that exists in the midst of a pluralistic society, where not all, or in some places, not even most, of the population has any connection with the covenant. It is not theirs, so the obligation and punishments are not theirs either. The church does not exact physical execution for egregious sins for which there is no repentance, but instead responds on a spiritual level, separating herself from the wrongdoer through excommunication. Much of the Old Testament legal material (e.g., many of the Ten Commandments) provides universal guidelines that are applicable everywhere and for all time, serving as a foundation on which any civil society is built. It needs to be stated that the Ten Commandments do not include the punishments for violation, which are detailed elsewhere (e.g., Deut 17:2-7).

◆   E. Holiness of Priests (21:1–22:16)

The LORD said to Moses, "Give the following instructions to the priests, the descendants of Aaron.

"A priest must not make himself ceremonially unclean by touching the dead body of a relative. ²The only exceptions are his closest relatives—his mother or father, son or daughter, brother, ³or his virgin sister who depends on him because she has no husband. ⁴But a priest must not defile himself and make himself unclean for someone who is related to him only by marriage.

⁵"The priests must not shave their heads or trim their beards or cut their bodies. ⁶They must be set apart as holy to their God and must never bring shame on the name of God. They must be holy, for they are the ones who present the special gifts to the LORD, gifts of food for their God.

⁷"Priests may not marry a woman defiled by prostitution, and they may not marry a woman who is divorced from her husband, for the priests are set apart as holy to their God. ⁸You must treat them as holy because they offer up food to your God. You must consider them holy because I, the LORD, am holy, and I make you holy.

⁹"If a priest's daughter defiles herself by becoming a prostitute, she also defiles her father's holiness, and she must be burned to death.

¹⁰"The high priest has the highest rank of all the priests. The anointing oil has been poured on his head, and he has been ordained to wear the priestly garments. He must never leave his hair uncombed* or tear his clothing. ¹¹He must not defile himself by going near a dead body. He may not make himself ceremonially unclean even for his father or mother. ¹²He must not defile the sanctuary of his God by leaving it to attend to a dead person, for he has been made holy by the anointing oil of his God. I am the LORD.

¹³"The high priest may marry only a virgin. ¹⁴He may not marry a widow, a woman who is divorced, or a woman who has defiled herself by prostitution. She must be a virgin from his own clan, ¹⁵so that he will not dishonor his descendants among his clan, for I am the LORD who makes him holy."

¹⁶Then the LORD said to Moses, ¹⁷"Give the following instructions to Aaron: In all future generations, none of your descendants who has any defect will qualify to offer food to his God. ¹⁸No one who has a defect qualifies, whether he is blind, lame, disfigured, deformed, ¹⁹or has a broken foot or arm, ²⁰or is hunchbacked or dwarfed, or has a defective eye, or skin sores or scabs, or damaged testicles. ²¹No descendant of Aaron who has a defect may approach the altar to present special gifts to the LORD. Since he has a defect, he may not approach the altar to offer food to his God. ²²However, he may eat from the food offered to God, including the holy offerings and the most holy offerings. ²³Yet because of his physical

defect, he may not enter the room behind the inner curtain or approach the altar, for this would defile my holy places. I am the LORD who makes them holy."

²⁴So Moses gave these instructions to Aaron and his sons and to all the Israelites.

CHAPTER 22

The LORD said to Moses, ²"Tell Aaron and his sons to be very careful with the sacred gifts that the Israelites set apart for me, so they do not bring shame on my holy name. I am the LORD. ³Give them the following instructions.

"In all future generations, if any of your descendants is ceremonially unclean when he approaches the sacred offerings that the people of Israel consecrate to the LORD, he must be cut off from my presence. I am the LORD.

⁴"If any of Aaron's descendants has a skin disease* or any kind of discharge that makes him ceremonially unclean, he may not eat from the sacred offerings until he has been pronounced clean. He also becomes unclean by touching a corpse, or by having an emission of semen, ⁵or by touching a small animal that is unclean, or by touching someone who is ceremonially unclean for any reason. ⁶The man who is defiled in any of these ways will remain unclean until evening. He may not eat from the sacred offerings until he has bathed himself in water. ⁷When the sun goes down, he will be ceremonially clean again and may eat from the sacred offer-ings, for this is his food. ⁸He may not eat an animal that has died a natural death or has been torn apart by wild animals, for this would defile him. I am the LORD.

⁹"The priests must follow my instructions carefully. Otherwise they will be punished for their sin and will die for violating my instructions. I am the LORD who makes them holy.

¹⁰"No one outside a priest's family may eat the sacred offerings. Even guests and hired workers in a priest's home are not allowed to eat them. ¹¹However, if the priest buys a slave for himself, the slave may eat from the sacred offerings. And if his slaves have children, they also may share his food. ¹²If a priest's daughter marries someone outside the priestly family, she may no longer eat the sacred offerings. ¹³But if she becomes a widow or is divorced and has no children to support her, and she returns to live in her father's home as in her youth, she may eat her father's food again. Otherwise, no one outside a priest's family may eat the sacred offerings.

¹⁴"Any such person who eats the sacred offerings without realizing it must pay the priest for the amount eaten, plus an additional 20 percent. ¹⁵The priests must not let the Israelites defile the sacred offerings brought to the LORD ¹⁶by allowing unauthorized people to eat them. This would bring guilt upon them and require them to pay compensation. I am the LORD who makes them holy."

21:10 Or *never uncover his head.*   22:4 Traditionally rendered *leprosy;* see note on 13:2a.

NOTES

21:1-2 *the dead body of a relative. The only exceptions are his closest relatives.* A broad prohibition against contact with one's deceased kin (lit., "people group, nation," one's covenant community) opens the case, but an allowance was given for close relatives, one's "flesh and blood," as one might say in English idiom (see 18:6).

21:6 *food for their God.* Sacrifice was called "food of their God," a term that is not very frequent in the OT (cf. 3:11, 16; 22:25; Num 28:2), lest it be thought that God needed to be fed in the same way other deities needed food (e.g., from Mesopotamia, COS 1.132:460; ANET 332.210, 280; 339.23; 343-345; cf. 95.155-166). The food, a necessity to sustain the life of the offerer, is dedicated to God, though not for his sustenance, as was the view among Israel's neighbors.

21:12 I am the LORD. The section concerning contact with the dead is brought to a close by the identification formula, which also indicates the seriousness of the regulations.

21:17 defect. This was an imperfection, whether natural or due to injury (24:19-20), that precluded animals (22:20-21; Num 19:2) and people from direct service to God.

21:18 disfigured. This may have been a birth defect (NIDOTTE 5.277) such as a cleft palate.

deformed. The word suggests that one was stretched or lopsided in some way, though it and the last term are obscure, not having sufficient context to warrant a definite interpretation.

21:20 dwarfed. This means either exceptionally short or thin and spindly.

defective eye. This possibly could be spotted or having mixed color (Levine 1989:146)—based on a cognate Akkadian term, *balalu* (CAD 2.41).

skin sores or scabs. These would fester and run (cf. NIV), suggesting a skin condition such as eczema (22:22).

testicles. This noun (*'eshek* [TH810, ZH863]) is unique in the OT, but known from other Semitic languages (Akk., *ishku,* CAD 7.250-251; cf. Deut 23:1).

22:2 to be very careful. This translation fits this context, though the verb *nazar* [TH5144, ZH5692] usually indicates separation or dedication to God (see the related term "Nazirite" in Num 6:1-21).

22:3 Give them the following instructions . . . if any of your descendants. Regulations regarding ritual purity were given to Moses to pass along to the priests ("them"), who were then addressed directly as "you."

22:9 The priests must follow my instructions. . . . Otherwise they will be punished. Punishment followed breaking God's "instruction," a term that is singular in the Hebrew and most likely refers only to 22:8.

22:10 No one outside a priest's family. Lit., a "stranger, foreigner," someone whose consumption would be illegitimate (10:1). This could refer to a foreigner (Jer 5:19; 51:51), but in this context it refers to someone outside of the priestly clan or family, a layperson to whom the food was not available (Milgrom 2000:1861; cf. comment on 21:22).

guests and hired workers. Lit., "a resident of a priest and a hireling." Milgrom (2000:1861) suggests, against most translations, that this was one category, a resident hireling, instead of two different figures. The singular verb supports this, and the conjunction "and" would then be best read as explanatory, "a resident of a priest, that is, a hireling," where the clearer second term defines the obscure first term (see Baker 1980:129-136).

COMMENTARY

Leviticus 17–20 contains instructions to all Israelites, priests and laity alike. The next chapter and a half (21:1–22:16) specifically address the priests on matters of holiness, while the last half of chapter 22 (vv. 17-33) includes all Israel in the instructions. The chapters are united by their concern for things specifically dedicated to the service of God, the priests themselves and the sacrifices they manipulated on behalf of the people. While everyone had standards of holiness that they were to maintain as the people of God, those directly serving him and coming into closer proximity to his sanctuary were held to a higher standard (cf. Luke 12:48). This distinction between priest and laity, acceptable and unacceptable animals for sacrifice should only be understood as provisional, accommodating the situation at that time and not as permanent and ideal. Part of this accommodation can be seen in the division of the laws between the ideal (20:1-16), which were stated in absolute terms with no exceptions, and the actual (20:17-23), where grace is given. Only the pure could officiate, but all in the tribe could benefit.

All of Israel was to be a "kingdom of priests" and a "holy nation" (Exod 19:6; 1 Pet 2:9), and everything, from animals previously unacceptable for sacrifice to common household utensils, would be "HOLY TO THE LORD" (Zech 14:20-21). National priesthood preceded the selection of a particular group as priests (Exod 19:6, 22), so these purity regulations could be seen as having a wider, national application beyond their original recipients, the Aaronic priests. All the laws should be seen as positive, given in order that one might be able to move toward greater levels of holiness so as to be able to have the personal fellowship with God that was enjoyed by the first humans in the Garden (Gen 1-2).

The chapters are divided into five discrete sections by new introductory formulae, where Yahweh addresses Moses. The sections are arranged in a chiasm (Milgrom 2000:1792), starting and ending with the same theme:

A. Priests and their family relationships (21:1-15)
  B. Priestly defects (21:16-24)
    C. Protecting the sacred offerings (22:1-16)
  B'. Animal defects (22:17-25)
A'. Animals and their family relationships (22:26-28)

The arrangement reverses that of the beginning chapters of Leviticus. There attention is first drawn to the animals for sacrifice (chs 1-7) and then to the priests (chs 8-10).

Chapter 21 begins with the Lord telling Moses to pass along instructions to the priests (21:1; cf. 6:8-9, 24-25). These priests were "sons of Aaron," which included not only the regular priesthood (21:2b-9) but also the high priest (21:10-15). The first instruction concerns contact with a dead person. Contact with a dead animal passed on ceremonial uncleanness (5:2; 11:24, 39) and even more so contact with a human corpse (21:1b; cf. Num 5:2; 6:6; 9:10). Since priests were charged with approaching the holy God, they in particular were to guard against anything that would hinder their doing so.

The priests were not allowed to touch the corpse of anyone in the covenant community except a close family member (see note on 21:1-2). These close family members were blood relatives who lived in the same extended household, including father, mother, children, brother, and young, marriageable sister (cf. 21:14; Gen 24:16). Since she was unmarried, she still resided in her father's household, which she would have left upon marriage. A married sister was excluded from this list by the delimitation of the unmarried sister. The rabbis understood that a priest was unable to bury his own wife. She was not related by blood, as those in 21:3 with whom he could have contact, but only through marriage. This would leave her among those mentioned in 21:1, and thus unable to be touched upon death (Levine 1989:142). Arguing against this position is the fact that a spouse becomes "one flesh" with her husband through marriage (Gen 2:24). While a priest could touch these family members in their death, he would do so at the cost of ceremonial uncleanness, losing the sanctity necessary to perform his duties.

Mourning rituals were also banned for a priest (21:5-6). These included purposefully making bald patches on the head (Deut 14:1; Isa 3:24), shaving off part of the beard (Isa 15:2), and cutting the body (Jer 48:37). There was apparently no exemption here for close family. It was likely that these were acts of pagan mourning practice (cf. 19:27-28) and therefore unsuitable for ministers of Yahweh. Since the animal sacrifices the priests were to offer were to be without blemish (1:3, 10, etc.), it follows that the officiating priest should be as well. As holiness was to characterize the laity (20:26), so it should characterize the priesthood, since they had even closer physical proximity to God in his sanctuary in bringing sacrifices to him.

The relationship of priests to sacrifice was also given as a motive for selectivity in marriage partners (21:7-8). They were forbidden to marry either a prostitute (cf. Hos 1:2), who was defiled by her indiscriminate sexual encounters, or a divorcée—literally one who was "driven away" (Deut 24:1-4)—who was unable to keep her original vows of commitment, though through no fault of her own: Since it was the man who initiated divorce proceedings (Deut 24:1-3), the woman might find herself divorced not by her own choosing. Milgrom (2000:1807) suggests that the term for "defiled" (v. 7) indicates a third case of forbidden partner, one who had been raped. In order to ensure the paternity of any child born from a union with a priest, these women, who had experienced previous sexual contact, even though not always by their own volition, were excluded from marriage to a priest. The holiness of the priest and his reputation in the community, or perhaps even more the purity of his line, were being protected, since in each of these cases he would have been unsure of the paternity of offspring. The regulations were directed toward the nation as a whole, rather than just to the priests themselves. It was incumbent upon the congregation to make sure that their ministers maintained their own sanctity.

There was also a law concerning a priest's daughter involved in prostitution (21:9), or perhaps just engaged in premarital sex (Milgrom 2000:1810; cf. Gen 38:24; Judg 15:6). The demands on the life and family of a leader were higher than those on the led (cf. 1 Tim 3:4, 12; Titus 1:6). A promiscuous daughter not only desecrated herself, but also brought dishonor on the family, including her father. Sons engaging in sin led to similar consequences (1 Sam 2:12-25), so this was not a charge directed only against women. The penalty was severe and uncommon: execution by burning for the promiscuous daughter (21:9), and, possibly by implication, for such sons as well. In Leviticus, this death was reserved for Aaron's sons (10:2) or for the partners in a mother–daughter marriage with a man (20:14). It was also the fate of objects contaminated beyond restoration (13:52), indicating the seriousness with which this trespass was viewed. Sexual sins were punished by stoning (Deut 22:21, 24), which would suggest that the person was first stoned and then burnt, making proper burial impossible.

The instructions then addressed the high priest, who was held to an even higher standard than regular priests (21:10). He was distinguished from them by receiving anointing oil on his head (8:12), while his sons received it only on their clothing (8:30), and also by his special uniform (8:7-9). His contact with the dead was even more restricted than it was for others. They could not shave their hair or beard in mourning (21:5), while he could not even show less drastic indications of mourning—that is, he could not let the hair hang free without the priestly head covering or tear his special clothes (cf. 10:6). While ordinary priests could attend to the dead body of their closest kin (21:1-2), the high priest could not even be in the presence of a corpse (cf. Num 6:6-7), even that of his closest blood relatives, his parents (cf. Luke 9:59-60). This shows a gradation of sanctity, moving from common folk, who could tend their own dead, through the priests, who could only attend to their near kin, to the high priest, who could not approach the dead. This parallels the access to the sanctuary—with commoners able to enter the outer court, the priests into the Holy Place, and only the high priest into the Most Holy Place. The high priest's movements seem to have been restricted to the holy sanctuary in the case of a funeral (21:12). He was not permitted to join the funeral cortege (10:7), though he could leave on other occasions (see 8:31). At all times he needed to protect his sanctification and also that of the sanctuary in which he served.

Marriage restrictions were stricter for the high priest than they were for the priesthood as a whole (21:13-15). They could not marry a prostitute or divorcée (21:7), while to the high priest's restrictions was added a widow (cf. Ezek 44:22, where a priest could marry the widow of a priest). He was only allowed to marry a young virgin (21:13; cf. 21:3) who was an Israelite (Ezek 44:22), though possibly only a girl from the priestly clan was acceptable. She was to be uniquely his as he was uniquely God's. Whereas in 21:9 promiscuity brought stigma against the father, here a marriage outside of the specified bounds would stigmatize and pollute the descendant children. Since it was God who sanctified the high priest and his family line in the first place, it was unacceptable to jeopardize that by deliberately breaching marriage restrictions.

Following these instructions to the high priest, a new section opens concerning the general priesthood of Aaron and his descendants (21:16-23). While the previous laws in the chapter had to do with relationships, these regulations concern the actual physical being of the priests themselves. They must be free of bodily blemishes of any kind. The nature of some of the defects is uncertain. Most were readily visible, except the last. These shortcomings disallowed a priest from officiating at the sanctuary by bringing sacrifices to God. He was still a priest, however, since he could eat from the priestly portion of the sacrifices that were manipulated by his priestly brothers (cf. 6:26 [19], 29; 7:6-10, 14, 31-36). He himself had not become impure, since the priestly portion was only to be eaten in a pure place where he could not go if he had become unclean. Wrongful approach to the holy places of God would desanctify them, which must be avoided at all costs. This was because God himself had sanctified them in the first place by his presence (Exod 29:43-44), which would then have to depart in the face of unholiness.

Moses passed on the message from God to all who were to receive it, Aaron the high priest (21:17), the priests (21:1), and the Israelites. Since the latter are not mentioned previously in this chapter (cf. 22:18), 21:24 could be a conclusion for the unit of chapters 20–21. However, the community had responsibility in chapter 21 (see comments on 21:7-8), so this summary could be restricted to this chapter, making the role of the people more explicit than it was from any of the specific audience indicators in the chapter itself. All the Israelites needed to be aware of the expectations placed upon their leaders in order to hold them accountable, since their own ability to worship God through sacrifice was predicated on the ability of the priests to perform their sacrificial functions.

Chapter 22 introduces a new commission—from God to the priests through Moses. Rather than addressing priestly interpersonal relationships (21:1-15) or their physical wholeness (21:16-23), attention was given specifically to all of the Israelites' offerings, here called "sacred gifts." Since priests served as intermediaries between people and God, they were to be "very careful" with their responsibilities lest they damage God's reputation, embodied in his name, "Yahweh" (22:1-2).

If any among the priests was found to be ceremonially unclean when approaching with the offerings for God, he would be cut off from the presence of God (22:3; cf. 7:20). From the following verses, it can be seen that these were temporary conditions of impurity rather than a permanent state, which would presumably have permanently banned a priest from approaching God. Since this was a case of a qualified priest becoming disqualified, constant vigilance regarding purity was necessary. Being excluded from God's presence not only disallowed continued ministry (he could no longer "stand before the LORD"; Deut 10:8), but also meant the end of his line at the hand of God himself (cf. 20:3).

Specific causes of impurity are stated earlier, but here they are gathered into one place (22:4-7). They included skin disease (cf. 13:44-45), abnormal genital discharge (cf. 15:2), corpse contamination (cf. 21:1; Num 5:2), ejaculation (cf. 15:16), and impurity caused by touching a small animal (lit., "creeping thing," 11:29-31, indicating that it was the dead animal that must not be touched), or an unclean person (cf. 5:3). This is a reprise of 7:21, where eating the peace offering while defiled by many of these same things is said to bring the same result. Uncleanness from these things lasted from one day (cf. 11:31; 15:16) to seven days (cf. 13:33-34; 15:13), and the uncleanness was purified through washing (cf. 14:8-9; 15:1-33) and waiting until sundown. Only after the ritual cleansing could the priest eat from the sacrificial food. Since it is not mentioned, regular, non-sacrificial food would have been allowed in the meantime.

An additional dietary restriction, though not linked to sacrificial food, concerned meat that had not been properly slaughtered (22:8). Since this was a voluntary defilement, unlike those just listed, it should not be contracted by a priest. If he did, he was liable to punishment by God himself (see note on 22:9). The section closes with a reminder that priestly sanctification comes from God himself. Thus, treating such important things lightly, or with contempt, could make one liable to punishment (22:9; cf. Matt 5:19).

The instructions then turned again to sacrificial food, which was not only to be protected from encroachment by an impure priest, but also from others (22:10-16). It was a privilege for the priesthood and a necessity for their survival, since they did not own agricultural lands. Any misuse directly affected their livelihood. Outside of the priesthood itself, there were two categories identified: those who were not allowed to eat and those who were. The first term in the former category was the broadest, including within it those who follow (see note on 22:10). The outsiders were temporary laborers, not members of a household such as slaves (and their children), who had been purchased and thus were considered part of the priest's family (22:11).

Marriage practice in ancient Israel was that a woman who married would go live with her husband's family, being now dependent on them (e.g., Gen 24:1-67; 31:17-18; cf. Lev 21:3). No longer under the authority or obligation of her priestly father's family, she was no longer eligible for its provisions from the sacrificial food; she had become a "layperson." If her marriage ended through divorce (cf. 21:14) or death (cf. 21:11) and she was childless and therefore did not have the support network children were supposed to provide for her needs, and then consequently returned to her parental home (Gen 38:11; Ruth 1:8-14), she would again be eligible for support from the sacrificial food. She was no longer a "layperson" in terms of the restricted eating legislation. The prohibition against wrongful eating was repeated (22:13), closing out this small unit, while also providing a transition to the next unit.

What happened if one of the prohibited parties did eat sacrificial food by mistake (22:14; cf. 4:2, 22, 27; 5:15)? There was no ceremonial cost to the eater in that he was not defiled, but the sacrificial food was. He needed to pay the worth of the food eaten plus a penalty of 20 percent (cf. 5:16), which became the property of the priest. It was the priestly responsibility to make sure this defilement didn't happen (22:15). The passage then ends just like the last one did (22:9), with a reminder that Yahweh was active in the process of sanctifying the priests, so they must also take care not to allow desecration of what was holy.

◆   ## F. Holiness of Sacrifices (22:17-33)

¹⁷And the LORD said to Moses, ¹⁸"Give Aaron and his sons and all the Israelites these instructions, which apply both to native Israelites and to the foreigners living among you.

"If you present a gift as a burnt offering to the LORD, whether it is to fulfill a vow or is a voluntary offering, ¹⁹you* will be accepted only if your offering is a male animal with no defects. It may be a bull, a ram, or a male goat. ²⁰Do not present an animal with defects, because the LORD will not accept it on your behalf.

²¹"If you present a peace offering to the LORD from the herd or the flock, whether it is to fulfill a vow or is a voluntary offering, you must offer a perfect animal. It may have no defect of any kind. ²²You must not offer an animal that is blind, crippled, or injured, or that has a wart, a skin sore, or scabs. Such animals must never be offered on the altar as special gifts to the LORD. ²³If

a bull* or lamb has a leg that is too long or too short, it may be offered as a voluntary offering, but it may not be offered to fulfill a vow. ²⁴If an animal has damaged testicles or is castrated, you may not offer it to the LORD. You must never do this in your own land, ²⁵and you must not accept such an animal from foreigners and then offer it as a sacrifice to your God. Such animals will not be accepted on your behalf, for they are mutilated or defective."

²⁶And the LORD said to Moses, ²⁷"When a calf or lamb or goat is born, it must be left with its mother for seven days. From the eighth day on, it will be acceptable as a special gift to the LORD. ²⁸But you must

not slaughter a mother animal and her offspring on the same day, whether from the herd or the flock. ²⁹When you bring a thanksgiving offering to the LORD, sacrifice it properly so you will be accepted. ³⁰Eat the entire sacrificial animal on the day it is presented. Do not leave any of it until the next morning. I am the LORD.

³¹"You must faithfully keep all my commands by putting them into practice, for I am the LORD. ³²Do not bring shame on my holy name, for I will display my holiness among the people of Israel. I am the LORD who makes you holy. ³³It was I who rescued you from the land of Egypt, that I might be your God. I am the LORD."

22:19 Or *it.*   22:23 Or *cow.*

NOTES

22:22 *injured.* This refers to a broken bone.

22:24 *damaged.* This is a translation of two adjectival forms: "squeezed, crushed" (cf. Ezek 23:3) or "squashed, pulverized" (cf. Deut 9:21).

castrated. This could result from two different means, being torn off (cf. Judg 16:9) or cut off (Exod 4:25; cf. Deut 23:1 [2])

22:24-25 *You must never do this in your own land, and you must not accept such an animal from foreigners.* The NLT presents the ban being on offering such damaged animals in Israel ("your land"), even if obtained from a foreigner. The restriction could be narrower, banning gelding of any unacceptable animal (Wenham 1979:295). The NLT's interpretation is preferred since only sacrifice was under discussion.

COMMENTARY

In 22:17 a new subsection begins with a new messenger formula, this time directing Moses not only to pass the word along to Aaron and the priests (cf. 22:2) but also to all those living in Israel. Previously the concern had been with the suitability of the priesthood for bringing sacrifices. The new concern was the suitability of the animals brought for sacrifice. It would be human nature to try to offer substandard animals that might not be usable in other ways (cf. Mal 1:8), and this was to be prevented. This was relevant to everyone in the land, whether a physical descendant of Israel or one who had taken up more temporary residence there, since everyone could make offerings to God (17:8). The list of addressees provided several levels of safeguard against improper animals: The people themselves, when they brought the animal, needed to check its suitability, and the priests also needed to check it when it was brought to the sanctuary. The writer of Hebrews picked up this theme in speaking of the blood of the unblemished Christ (Heb 9:14).

The first "offering" is a burnt offering (ch 1) brought for either of two reasons: either as a response to a vow that had been made or as a gift of one's free will. These were voluntary rather than mandatory purification offerings (cf. 1:4, where this was another function of a burnt offering), which were not mentioned in this chapter. If voluntary offerings needed perfect animals (and perfect priests), it can be assumed that the same expectations held for purification or sin offerings. Each offering was brought for a purpose; some result was desired. It was vital that the offering be acceptable, thereby fulfilling its goal. Since the offerings here were not required, their acceptance was not certain (though any offering could be rejected if brought inappropriately; Mal 1:8). Anything potentially standing in the way of acceptance was to be taken care of.

Each animal had to meet three criteria before it could be accepted. It was to be (1) completely free from blemish, (2) male, and (3) from the cattle, sheep, or goats. All three of these criteria are also mentioned in chapter 1 (1:3, 10). The option of offering a bird was not allowed for a voluntary offering, though it was acceptable for purification (1:14-17).

The peace offering (22:21) was also voluntary and was also to be free from blemish or defect (cf. 21:17-18). Its gender was unspecified, but it could be a cow, sheep, or goat. The list of 12 disqualifying defects corresponds in number to those disqualifying a priest from service (21:18-20), with several identical terms in both lists and most others similar in meaning as far as we can determine. All would be clearly visible, as were most of those for priests. Some of the defects completely disqualified the animal for any sacrifice, while other defects meant that certain animals could be used in some cases (such as a freewill offering, which was spontaneous) but not in others (such as a vow, which involved planning and so one could avoid a blemished animal; Milgrom 2000:1879).

Leviticus 22:26-28 presents a new subsection wherein God instructs Moses. There is no mention of relaying the teaching to others, though its subject matter relates to all of Israel (cf. 22:18). People must have sought other ways to lower the cost of offerings, in this case by bringing very young animals that would not as yet have cost anything for feed and care. Animals must be at least a week old (cf. Exod 22:30), with indications that yearlings were preferred (e.g., 9:3; 12:6). A mother animal could not be sacrificed on the same day as her offspring (cf. Deut 22:6), though no reason was given. Some suggest that both of these restrictions were for humanitarian reasons, but it is not clear that there was any concern for animal feelings. And it is not clear how their feelings would be eased by their living together for a week or by the related animals being killed on subsequent days. Any suggested motivation for either restriction is speculative.

Two final regulations touch on voluntary sacrifices (22:29-30). A thanksgiving offering was a subcategory of the peace offering (7:12, 13, 15), which for some reason was separated for special mention here. Milgrom (2000:1885) suggests that the placement of these two verses here was to bring to a close the section of chapters 19–22, which opens with another set of regulations concerning the peace offering (19:5-6). For a thanksgiving offering to be acceptable, it could not remain until the day after it was offered but needed to be eaten, or otherwise disposed of, on the day of sacrifice (7:15).

The conclusion brings the chapter to a close (22:31-33), repeating a concern for the honor of God's name (cf. 22:2). It also brings the section begun in chapter 19 to a close, reiterating the holiness of God, which was the motivation for keeping all of the intervening regulations (19:2). In 19:2, an expectation of holiness is given, while here it is said that God himself brings the sanctification. There is a divine–human partnership in the journey toward holiness. The God who promised is the same who had already acted for the salvation of the people by bringing them out of their Egyptian bondage (11:45; 19:36) so that he could have this partnership. He was Yahweh, their God. Would they live in the holiness he had shown them so that they might be his partners?

◆   G. Holiness of Festivals (23:1-44)
    1. Introduction and Sabbath (23:1-4)

The LORD said to Moses, ²"Give the following instructions to the people of Israel. These are the LORD's appointed festivals, which you are to proclaim as official days for holy assembly.

³"You have six days each week for your ordinary work, but the seventh day is a Sabbath day of complete rest, an official day for holy assembly. It is the LORD's Sabbath day, and it must be observed wherever you live.

⁴"In addition to the Sabbath, these are the LORD's appointed festivals, the official days for holy assembly that are to be celebrated at their proper times each year.

NOTES

23:2 *festivals.* A calendar of religious ceremonies was found at the thirteenth-century BC site of Emar in Syria (Fleming 2000:141-195). Each of its ceremonies consisted of three elements, as we find in the text of Leviticus: (1) a procession (cf. the "holy assembly," 23:2 and 10 further times in ch 23); (2) offerings presented (cf. "special gifts," 23:8 and seven further times), and (3) the assignment of some of the offering for the people involved in the ceremony (Fleming 2000:149; cf. 23:20 and provisions in the regulations for various offerings mentioned in the chapter in 6:16-18, 26, 29; 7:6-10, 14-16, 32-36). Israel was not alone in celebrating the divine–human interaction at periodic intervals in her national life.

23:3 *the seventh day is a Sabbath day of complete rest.* The seventh day had an ominous connotation in Mesopotamia (Cohen 1993:391), the homeland of the forefather of Israel (Gen 11:27-31), but it had none of the sacred characteristics as described in the OT.

23:4 *at their proper times each year.* The festivals were to be celebrated at times indicated as appropriate by the lunar cycle (Ps 104:19).

COMMENTARY

This section pertains to the cyclic festivals appointed by God for his people, Israel. The Sabbath is the most frequent holiday and one that is essentially different from the other festivals. The annual festivals follow, divided into two main sections: spring (23:5-22) and autumn (23:23-43) festivals. Further subdivisions are shown by formulas of God commissioning Moses for all except the first section, which had its own introduction: Passover and Unleavened Bread (23:5-8), Firstfruits

(23:9-14) and Harvest (23:15-22), Trumpets (23:23-25), Day of Atonement (23:26-32), and Shelters (23:33-43). These festivals had strong ties to Israel's history and also to the land; some had an agricultural background. They transcended these roots, however, and because they provided an opportunity for God's people to encounter God even when the consecrated priesthood and Tabernacle or Temple were no longer available.

Chapter 23 begins with the common messenger formula opening the chapter. The Lord instructed Moses to pass along his message directly to the people, bypassing the priests (cf., e.g., 22:1-2, 17-18). These were public, national festivals for all those who made up Israel, not just for the priests, even though the priests did play an important part in them. The subject is the "appointed festivals," those that fall at fixed intervals during the lunar cycle of the year, which had been fixed since creation (Gen 1:14). The festivals were said to be "the LORD's" in the sense that he was their focus and honoree. Since they were his, they were holy occasions, as described often in the chapter (23:2, 3, 4, 7, 8, 21, 24, 27, 35, 36, 37). They were announced or determined by the Israelites themselves in that the people in this period operated on a lunar calendar, which had shorter months than a solar calendar. Periodically an additional, thirteenth month needed to be inserted into the year to bring the lunar calendar into alignment with the agricultural cycle. It was therefore more complicated than looking at a wall calendar to figure out when the festivals fell each year.

The first and most frequent of the periodic events was the Sabbath, which occurs every seven days, at a time fixed by God since creation (Gen 2:2) and not by the Israelites. It was to be marked by completely stopping all work (16:31; 25:4; Exod 31:15; 35:2) and the people assembling together. The exact nature of these Sabbath gatherings is unclear, since they are not mentioned elsewhere. Its importance is highlighted by Milgrom (2001:1960), who writes, "The Sabbath is the only holiday commanded in the Decalogue (Exod 20:8-11) and the only command grounded in creation (Exod 20:11). It is mentioned by all sources and genres: prophecy (Isa 56:2-6; Jer 17:21-27), history (2 Kgs 11:5-9), poetry (Ps 92:Title; Lam 2:6), narrative (2 Kgs 4:23; Neh 13:15-22), and law (Exod 23:12; Neh 10:32-34)."

This rest from work was not just for native Israelites but also for foreign residents and even livestock (Exod 20:10). It was not only to be observed in the land itself, but wherever they might find themselves residing in the future, whether inside the land or outside it. It was the holiday that not only focused upon God, but was also enjoyed and blessed by him (Gen 2:2-3). Unlike most of the other festivals, which involved the sacrificial system, the Sabbath could still be fully observed after the destruction of the Temple. Its importance as a special day continued into the New Testament period, even among Jews outside of Israel (Matt 24:20; Mark 1:21; 6:2; 15:42; 16:1; Acts 13:14; 15:21; 16:13; 17:2; 18:4; Col 2:16). There was frequent conflict between Jesus and the Jewish authorities as to what the exact nature of the day was (Matt 12:1-4; Mark 3:1-6; John 5:1-15; 7:21-24).

The following chart presents a summary of the holidays.

NAME	TIME	SEASON	LENGTH	PURPOSE	REFERENCES
Sabbath	Weekly		1 day	Rest; salvation	Exod 20:8-11 (cf. Gen 2:2-3); Num 28:9-10; Deut 5:12-15
Passover (Good Friday)	14th day, 1st month	Spring	1 day	Celebrating salvation	Exod 12; Num 28:16-25; Deut 16:1-8; 2 Kgs 23:21; Ezra 6:19; Matt 20:18; 26:2, 17-19; Luke 2:41; John 2:13, 23; 4:45; 6:4; 11:55-57; 12:1; 13:1; 19:14; Acts 12:4; 1 Cor 5:7; Heb 11:28
Unleavened Bread (Easter)	15th day, 1st month	Spring	7 days	Historical remembrance; removing leaven; pilgrimage festival	Exod 12:17-20; 13:7; 23:15; 34:18; Deut 16:16; 2 Chr 30:13; Ezra 6:22; Matt 26:17; Mark 14:1; Acts 12:3; 20:6
Firstfruits		Spring	1 day (50 days?)	Grain harvest beginning celebration; conjoined with next festival	Exod 23:16; 34:22
Harvest (Weeks; Day of New Grain; Pentecost)	3rd month	Spring	1 day	Grain harvest ending cele-bration; pilgrimage festival	Exod 23:16; 34:22; Num 28:26-31; Deut 16:9-12; Acts 2; 20:16; 1 Cor 16:8
Trumpets	1st day, 7th month	Autumn (Sept/Oct)	1 day	Civil New Year? (Hartley 1992:383); reminder	Num 29:1-6
Day of Atonement (Yom Kippur; Fast)	10th day, 7th month	Autumn (Sept/Oct)	1 day	Atonement for sin	16:1-34; 25:9; Num 29:7-11; Acts 27:9
Shelters (Booths, Tabernacles, Succoth; Ingathering; Feast)	15th day, 7th month	Autumn (Sept/Oct)	7 + 1 days	Grape and summer fruit harvest; pilgrimage festival	Exod 34:22; Num 29:12-38; Deut 16:13-17; 1 Kgs 8:2, 65; Ezra 3:4; Neh 8:15; Zech 14:16-19; John 7

◆   ## 2. Passover and Unleavened Bread (23:5-8)

⁵"The LORD's Passover begins at sundown on the fourteenth day of the first month.* ⁶On the next day, the fifteenth day of the month, you must begin celebrating the Festival of Unleavened Bread. This festival to the LORD continues for seven days, and during that time the bread you eat must be made without yeast. ⁷On the first day of the festival, all the people must stop their ordinary work and observe an official day for holy assembly. ⁸For seven days you must present special gifts to the LORD. On the seventh day the people must again stop all their ordinary work to observe an official day for holy assembly."

23:5 This day in the ancient Hebrew lunar calendar occurred in late March, April, or early May.

NOTES
23:5 Passover. This is its only mention in Leviticus. The name (*pesakh* [TH6453, ZH7175]) is drawn from a root that designates either God's "skipping" Israel's firstborn on the night when Egypt's firstborn were killed (Exod 11) or his "protection" of them (Isa 31:5; Milgrom 2001:1970-1971).

sundown. Lit., "between the two evenings"—these are the times of the sun setting and darkness falling.

23:6 Festival of Unleavened Bread. This was a time when no yeast could be used (2:4). It also commemorated Israel's release from Egypt (Exod 12:14-20).

This festival. The term for "festival" (*khag* [TH2282, ZH2504]) is related to the Arabic word *hajj*, which today denotes the annual Muslim pilgrimage to Mecca.

COMMENTARY
Two festivals fall in the first month of the older Israelite calendar (March–April; see commentary on 23:24): Passover in celebration of God's acts in delivering Israel from Egyptian slavery (see Exod 12) and Unleavened Bread in celebration of the start of the barley harvest, the earliest of the grains to ripen (Exod 9:31). This calendar period corresponded to the time of the Exodus (Exod 23:15; 34:18; Num 28:17-25), from which the Israelite months were counted and thereby became the first month of the year. It also marked the change from rainy to dry season.

Passover is simply noted without details, which can be found in Exodus 12–13. It was in the first month, elsewhere called "Abib" (March–April; Exod 13:4; 23:15; 34:18; Deut 16:1), the month of new grain (cf. 2:14), which was later renamed "Nisan" (Neh 2:1; Esth 3:7; modern Jewish calendars). Passover was to be held on the fourteenth of the month, the date of the original Passover celebration (Exod 12:6). It became closely linked with the next listed Feast of Unleavened Bread, with later texts using the names and lengths of the celebrations interchangeably (2 Chr 30:13, 21; Ezra 6:22; Ezek 45:21).

A glance at the chart above indicates that it was one of the more significant festivals in Israel and also in the early church, based on the number of times it was referred to. The reason for the relative silence concerning it in Leviticus is unclear. It had special significance in relation to the life and ministry of Jesus, the Passover lamb (John 19:36, citing Exod 12:46; cf. 1 Cor 5:7). The period was closely tied to Jesus' passion (John 19:14), with the Last Supper apparently being a Passover meal (Matt 26:17).

On the following day in this "new grain" month, the Festival of Unleavened Bread began (Exod 12:15-20). It was one of three religious celebrations called a "festival"; the others were those of Harvest (Weeks) and Shelters (Tabernacles), pilgrimage feasts when all the people should come to celebrate in Jerusalem (Exod 23:15-16; 34:18-22; Deut 16:16). The Jews celebrated for a week with special observations, including communal gatherings involving a complete cessation from all work (cf. the discussion of Sabbath in the commentary on 23:1-4), held on the first and last days. The communal aspect stands in contrast to the private, family setting of Passover, which was and still is celebrated in the home (Exod 12:3-7).

The menu during this period was special, with the only bread being unleavened (Deut 16:3-4, 8). Therefore, it would have been flat, non-rising bread. No explanation of the practice was given here, showing that this passage presumed the explanation for not using yeast found in Exodus 12:39: The people were driven out quickly and left during the night, before yeast had been added to the dough. This would indicate that the regular practice was to make bread in the evening and let it rise overnight before it was baked to be fresh in the morning.

Work was to cease on days one and seven, but not completely as on the Sabbath. Light work, such as meal preparation (Exod 12:16) and farm chores, were not banned. This would have allowed life to continue, though at a reduced pace. After all, the people had to eat, and the animals had to be tended and milked. Special offerings were also offered (cf. 23:13, 18, 25, 27, 36). They were not explained here, but are detailed in Numbers 28:19-24: 10 burnt offering animals, a grain offering (cf. 23:18), and a sin offering in addition to the regular daily sacrifices. The amount of material offered each day was an indication of why the Festival of Unleavened Bread was national and public rather than individual and private, since few private citizens would have been able to afford such a cost on their own.

◆   ## 3. Firstfruits (23:9-14)

9Then the LORD said to Moses, 10"Give the following instructions to the people of Israel. When you enter the land I am giving you and you harvest its first crops, bring the priest a bundle of grain from the first cutting of your grain harvest. 11On the day after the Sabbath, the priest will lift it up before the LORD so it may be accepted on your behalf. 12On that same day you must sacrifice a one-year-old male lamb with no defects as a burnt offering to the LORD. 13With it you must present a grain offering consisting of four quarts* of choice flour moistened with olive oil. It will be a special gift, a pleasing aroma to the LORD. You must also offer one quart* of wine as a liquid offering. 14Do not eat any bread or roasted grain or fresh kernels on that day until you bring this offering to your God. This is a permanent law for you, and it must be observed from generation to generation wherever you live.

23:13a Hebrew 2/10 of an ephah [4.4 liters]; also in 23:17.   23:13b Hebrew 1/4 of a hin [1 liter].

NOTES

23:10 *you harvest its first crops.* Barley was the first grain harvested (Exod 9:31-32; Ruth 1:22; 2:23; ANET 321). Though it was milled, it was too coarse for fine flour, so it was used mainly to make unleavened bread and cakes (see 2 Kgs 4:42; Ezek 4:12; ABD 1.777; DOTP 24-25). In Egypt and Mesopotamia it was used to make beer. Wine was the drink of choice in Israel.

23:11 *lift it up.* This lifting happened either by raising it straight up (NLT, NRSV) or waving it back and forth (KJV, NIV) before God (see note on 7:30).

COMMENTARY

The phrase "the LORD said to Moses," again marks a new textual section (23:9-22). The instructions were to be passed on to all Israel as before. This section concerns two single-day harvest festivals. Two grain harvest festivals, the first for the barley and the second for wheat, were addressed together and given a single introduction. This was due not only to their similar nature as harvest festivals, but also because the timing of the second depends on that of the first, tying them together chrono-logically. In fact, they could be viewed as one harvest festival complex and not two completely separate occasions. They both concern grain harvest, and it was only at the end of the description of the second that the common proclamation of a holy assembly was given (see DOTP 303). The harvest festivals celebrate the annual pro-vision of nourishment from God and the release from the scarcity of winter.

Both harvest festivals presuppose settlement in the land of Israel (cf. 14:34; 19:23; 25:2), which was a gift from God. A people wandering in the wilderness would not have been able to stay in one place long enough to be able to plant and reap crops. By contrast, a fixed living place was not necessary for the previous two special celebrations, which were by their nature movable feasts. From the first crop of barley (see note on 23:10), a sheaf of the first grain cutting was to be brought as an offering to God and raised before him at a sanctuary by a priest. Since God cre-ated all things, everything belongs to him, but this token portion dedicated to him represented the entire crop and allowed the people to use the remainder of the har-vest for their own needs. It was given not only as a token of thanks, but also as a prayer that God might bless the harvest of which this was representative.

The exact date of the festival of the firstfruits of the barley harvest is debated. It was to be literally "on the day after the Sabbath" (23:11, 15-16), but which Sab-bath? It could not be the one mentioned in 23:3, which occurs every week. It could be the Sabbath following the fifteenth day of the first month, the beginning of the celebration of the Unleavened Bread festival (ABD 4.317), so the events here would have happened during the Unleavened Bread festival (Ross 2002:415). This would result in the celebration of both festivals at the same time. It could refer to the seven-day period of relative rest (a weeklong Sabbath) during the Unleavened Bread cele-bration and therefore would start the day after this finished (Milgrom 2001:2056-2063). The latter seems preferable, not necessarily because the entire week was a Sabbath, but because the seventh day was such, with its complete cessation from work (23:8), even if it didn't fall on the Sabbath.

Three offerings accompanied the grain sheaf (23:11-13): a burnt offering of a per-fect male yearling lamb (1:10-13), a grain offering of flour and olive oil (2:14-16, including frankincense, which is not mentioned here), and a drink offering of wine.

The last, not described elsewhere in Leviticus, was poured out on the ground in dedication to God and was not for human consumption (cf. Gen 35:14; 2 Sam 23:16). This amount of material would have been within the ability of a family to bring, in contrast to the larger quantities required for the previous and next celebrations.

None of the harvested grain at any stage of its development cycle could be eaten by the people before the token portion, with its accompanying sacrifices, was offered to God. This included the final stage, in which mature barley could be ground into bread flour; the preceding stage with unprocessed kernels (2:14; 2 Kgs 4:42; Matt 12:1; Mark 2:23; Luke 6:1); or the earliest stage, when the immature kernels needed to be roasted (Ruth 2:14; 1 Sam 17:17). None could eat before God was served. This was not just a one-time celebration, but an annual and perpetual one (cf. 7:36) in every place the Israelites might find themselves residing long enough to plant and harvest crops (cf. 3:17; 23:21).

While not referring specifically to this festival, firstfruits were significant in the New Testament. Paul used it to represent the portion of the Spirit that we now enjoy and that has yet to reach eschatological fullness (Rom 8:23). He also used it in discussing the relationship between Jews (the firstfruits) and Gentiles (Rom 11:16, RSV). Christ as the firstfruits from death gives hope to his followers that they also will share in resurrection (1 Cor 15:20-23). Salvation was given to humans as a token, a firstfruits, of what would ultimately happen to all of God's creation (Jas 1:18; cf. 2 Thess 2:13; Rev 14:3).

◆   ## 4. Harvest (23:15-22)

15"From the day after the Sabbath—the day you bring the bundle of grain to be lifted up as a special offering—count off seven full weeks. 16Keep counting until the day after the seventh Sabbath, fifty days later. Then present an offering of new grain to the LORD. 17From wherever you live, bring two loaves of bread to be lifted up before the LORD as a special offering. Make these loaves from four quarts of choice flour, and bake them with yeast. They will be an offering to the LORD from the first of your crops. 18Along with the bread, present seven one-year-old male lambs with no defects, one young bull, and two rams as burnt offerings to the LORD. These burnt offerings, together with the grain offerings and liquid offerings, will be a special gift, a pleasing aroma to the LORD. 19Then you must offer one male goat as a sin offering and two one-year-old male lambs as a peace offering.

20"The priest will lift up the two lambs as a special offering to the LORD, together with the loaves representing the first of your crops. These offerings, which are holy to the LORD, belong to the priests. 21That same day will be proclaimed an official day for holy assembly, a day on which you do no ordinary work. This is a permanent law for you, and it must be observed from generation to generation wherever you live.*

22"When you harvest the crops of your land, do not harvest the grain along the edges of your fields, and do not pick up what the harvesters drop. Leave it for the poor and the foreigners living among you. I am the LORD your God."

23:21 This celebration, called the Festival of Harvest or the Festival of Weeks, was later called the Festival of Pentecost (see Acts 2:1). It is celebrated today as Shavuot (or Shabuoth).

NOTES

23:15 *count off seven full weeks.* The next festival (cf. Num 28:26-31; Deut 16:9-10) was carefully tied in time to the barley harvest festival (the firstfruits mentioned in 23:10), falling seven full weeks (lit., "seven Sabbaths") plus one day (= 50 days) after it finished. This accounts for two names by which it was identified: "weeks" (Exod 34:22; Num 28:26; Deut 16:9-10, 16) and "Pentecost" (meaning "50"; Acts 2:1; 20:16; 1 Cor 16:8; Tob 2:1; 2 Macc 12:31-32). It was also identified as "Harvest" (Exod 23:16) and "Firstfruits" (23:17; Num 28:26, KJV). It was described as "new offering of grain," additional to the barley harvest grain, which was the "old offering." It was the second of the annual pilgrimage feasts (cf. Exod 23:16; Acts 2:1, 5), though it was not so designated in this chapter.

23:20 *loaves representing the first of your crops.* Lit., "bread of the firstfruits." The function of this bread was to symbolically represent the entire crop.

COMMENTARY

The second festival for grain harvest, also known as the Festival of Weeks and Pentecost (cf. 23:21 mg) is chronologically tied to the first and is included in the same introduction (23:9-10a). It celebrates the wheat harvest, which along with various other sacrifices, was presented to the God of the harvest. One could even view this and the last festival as a single, 50-day harvest festival complex.

The grain of this harvest was wheat, which ripened later than barley (ANET 321). It was to be prepared at home and then presented at a sanctuary by lifting it before God. It was not in the form of a sheaf of grain (cf. 23:10), but the finished product as it would have been consumed by the people: two loaves of bread (23:17). Their prescribed weight can be read in two ways: either they were each made with four quarts of flour (cf. 24:5), or they both together used that much flour. They were made of fine flour with yeast, but there is no mention of incense or oil. Since they were yeast bread, they were not a grain offering (cf. 2:11; 6:16-17) but rather a form of thanksgiving offering (7:13) called "firstfruits" (23:20, KJV; cf. 2:14), coming from the first of the wheat crop and representing the entire crop as offered to God (cf. Rom 11:16). These loaves, prepared and presented by individual Israelites at a sanctuary, would then have become part of a communal celebration with accompanying special offerings: (1) burnt offerings consisting of seven yearling lambs (23:12; cf. 1:10-13; Num 28:27), one bull (1:3-9; contrast two in Num 28:27), and two rams (one in Num 28:27), which themselves would be accompanied by a grain offering and drink offerings; (2) a sin offering of a male goat; and (3) two male yearling lambs for a peace offering (more specific in gender, age, and breed than the general regulations in 3:6-11).

Specific directions for the priests follow (23:20). A priest took the peace offering lambs, along with the two bread loaves, and raised them to God as an offering (cf. 23:11). Probably only a part of the meat was treated in this way, based on the instructions in 7:30 and the physical difficulty in handling two entire lambs like this. The officiating priest could then eat them himself (cf. 7:31-35). This was necessary for his livelihood, since a priest could not own land and raise his own crops, and therefore was dependent on sacrifices. The entire nation had obligations, as well, only these were of avoidance rather than action. They could do no laborious work (23:21) but were to gather together as a community (cf. 23:2). This, too, held in all places for all time (23:14).

The author then added a general harvesting law, which had been given earlier (cf. 19:9-10). Some of the harvested grain was not for the benefit of its owner, but for the poor, who did not have their own fields but also needed to be able to rejoice in God's bounty (cf. Heb 13:15-16). Since grapes do not ripen until later in the season than the barley and wheat harvests, no mention of them was made.

The New Testament carries forward several motifs from this passage. Firstfruits not only indicates an offering for God but also Christians themselves, who are the firstfruits of the work of the Holy Spirit in anticipation of all of creation being made new (Rom 8:23; Jas 1:18; Rev 14:4). The first part of the harvest was a sign of hope for its completion, as the resurrected Christ is a sign of hope for resurrection for those who follow him (1 Cor 15:20, 23). The festival was also historically significant in the New Testament in that it was the occasion for Peter's Pentecostal sermon (Acts 2:1-47), which involved a celebration of receiving the blessing of God's outpoured Spirit.

◆   5. Trumpets (23:23-25)

²³The LORD said to Moses, ²⁴"Give the following instructions to the people of Israel. On the first day of the appointed month in early autumn,* you are to observe a day of complete rest. It will be an official day for holy assembly, a day commemorated with loud blasts of a trumpet. ²⁵You must do no ordinary work on that day. Instead, you are to present special gifts to the LORD."

23:24 Hebrew *On the first day of the seventh month.* This day in the ancient Hebrew lunar calendar occurred in September or October. This festival is celebrated today as Rosh Hashanah, the Jewish new year.

COMMENTARY

A new section of autumn festivals begins with Trumpets (cf. Num 29:1-6). The name of this festival, the Festival of Trumpets, was not included in the Hebrew text, which simply says it is to be marked by loud blasts. The type of instrument making the noise is not given, though it is generally understood to be a trumpet that was made from a ram's horn (cf. 25:9; Ps 81:3). Such blasts were signals—for example, in the case of maneuvers of large groups of people (Num 10:3-6) in war (Josh 6:5, 20; Amos 1:14) and also in celebration (1 Sam 4:5-6).

It was held on a specific day and was marked negatively by refraining from work (23:39) and positively by being a memorial for the people (cf. Num 10:10, where the reminder is for God), though there is no indication of what was being memorialized, except as a reminder to celebrate the festival itself by gathering together as a community. Special gifts were also brought (see comments on 23:8).

There are at least two "new year's" celebrations in the Old Testament. The earliest, the beginning of the new nation, is associated with the exodus from Egypt in the spring of the year (Exod 12:2). Here in Leviticus is a later (see Ezek 40:1), religious new year celebrated in the autumn (the seventh month, September/October on the Western calendar) and called Rosh Hashanah, "the head of the year."

◆   6. Day of Atonement (23:26-32)

²⁶Then the LORD said to Moses, ²⁷"Be careful to celebrate the Day of Atonement on the tenth day of that same month—nine days after the Festival of Trumpets.* You must observe it as an official day for holy assembly, a day to deny yourselves* and present special gifts to the LORD. ²⁸Do no work during that entire day because it is the Day of Atonement, when offerings of purification are made for you, making you right with* the LORD your God. ²⁹All who do not deny themselves that day will be cut off from God's people. ³⁰And I will destroy anyone among you who does any work on that day. ³¹You must not do any work at all! This is a permanent law for you, and it must be observed from generation to generation wherever you live. ³²This will be a Sabbath day of complete rest for you, and on that day you must deny yourselves. This day of rest will begin at sundown on the ninth day of the month and extend until sundown on the tenth day."

23:27a Hebrew *on the tenth day of the seventh month;* see 23:24 and the note there. This day in the ancient Hebrew lunar calendar occurred in September or October. It is celebrated today as Yom Kippur.   23:27b Or *to fast;* similarly in 23:29, 32.   23:28 Or *when atonement is made for you before.*

NOTES

23:27 Day of Atonement. Heb., *yom hakippurim* ("day of atonements"). The Hebrew for "Atonement" here is the plural *kippurim* [TH3725, ZH4113] (from the verb *kapar* [TH3722, ZH4105]). In the singular, this phrase is transliterated "Yom Kippur," the name of the Jewish holiday better known to English speakers. The importance of this day for understanding the NT was discussed at the conclusion of ch 16. This day was referred to as "the fast" in the story of Paul's trip to Rome (Acts 27:9, cf. NLT mg).

COMMENTARY

The Day of Atonement (Num 29:7-11) was necessitated in the first instance by the sin of Aaron's sons (ch 10) and is described in detail in chapter 16, where it was established as a permanent practice (16:29-34) in order to bring about atonement with God (16:30). Here is the first time that it is actually named (23:27). This description adds some penalties that would happen if it were not kept as it was supposed to be.

God's revelation to Moses concerning the Day of Atonement follows the pattern already established in the chapter (23:1, 9, 23, 33), but without specifying that it be relayed to Israel (23:2, 10, 24, 34). The date of the Day of Atonement was given in reference to that of the Festival of Trumpets; it was in the same month, but on the tenth day. In contrast to the joy of Trumpets, this day was very somber. Its ritual was made up of four elements: a community assembly (23:27), self-denial (23:29), special offerings to God (23:27), and a complete cessation of work (23:28). It was the self-denial of food and other elements of life such as sexual intimacy (cf. Num 30:13; Ps 35:13; Isa 58:3, 5) that distinguished this from other festivals that contain some or all of the other elements. All of these elements were to be carefully observed because on this day purification for the nation's sins for the past year was being made. From the passage itself it can be ascertained that these four elements brought about this purification.

Not obeying would result in the end of the wrongdoer, his total annihilation (cf. Esth 9:5), and any kind of work at all done on the day would have the same result (23:29-32). The latter seems to have been taken even more seriously on this day than the others since work was banned twice in this passage, not for the purpose of relaxation but to be a sacred time set apart for worship of God (NIDOTTE 5.1159). The entire day was designated as a permanent and universal regulation (cf. 23:14).

◆   ## 7. Shelters (23:33-44)

³³And the LORD said to Moses, ³⁴"Give the following instructions to the people of Israel. Begin celebrating the Festival of Shelters* on the fifteenth day of the appointed month—five days after the Day of Atonement.* This festival to the LORD will last for seven days. ³⁵On the first day of the festival you must proclaim an official day for holy assembly, when you do no ordinary work. ³⁶For seven days you must present special gifts to the LORD. The eighth day is another holy day on which you present your special gifts to the LORD. This will be a solemn occasion, and no ordinary work may be done that day.

³⁷("These are the LORD's appointed festivals. Celebrate them each year as official days for holy assembly by presenting special gifts to the LORD—burnt offerings, grain offerings, sacrifices, and liquid offerings—each on its proper day. ³⁸These festivals must be observed in addition to the LORD's regular Sabbath days, and the offerings are in addition to your personal gifts, the offerings you give to fulfill your vows, and the voluntary offerings you present to the LORD.)

³⁹"Remember that this seven-day festival to the LORD—the Festival of Shelters—begins on the fifteenth day of the appointed month,* after you have harvested all the produce of the land. The first day and the eighth day of the festival will be days of complete rest. ⁴⁰On the first day gather branches from magnificent trees*—palm fronds, boughs from leafy trees, and willows that grow by the streams. Then celebrate with joy before the LORD your God for seven days. ⁴¹You must observe this festival to the LORD for seven days every year. This is a permanent law for you, and it must be observed in the appointed month* from generation to generation. ⁴²For seven days you must live outside in little shelters. All native-born Israelites must live in shelters. ⁴³This will remind each new generation of Israelites that I made their ancestors live in shelters when I rescued them from the land of Egypt. I am the LORD your God."

⁴⁴So Moses gave the Israelites these instructions regarding the annual festivals of the LORD.

23:34a Or *Festival of Booths,* or *Festival of Tabernacles.* This was earlier called the Festival of the Final Harvest or Festival of Ingathering (see Exod 23:16b). It is celebrated today as Sukkot (or Succoth). 23:34b Hebrew *on the fifteenth day of the seventh month;* see 23:27a and the note there. 23:39 Hebrew *on the fifteenth day of the seventh month.* 23:40 Or *gather fruit from majestic trees.* 23:41 Hebrew *the seventh month.*

NOTES

23:34 *Give the following instructions to the people.* God's revelation formula directed Moses to again pass the message concerning this festival along to all the Israelites (cf. 23:2, 10, 24).

23:38 *personal gifts.* These were gifts that had an element of personal choice (Gen 25:6; Deut 16:17), rather than being narrowly prescribed as was the case for the periodic sacrifices.

23:39 Remember. Lit., "surely." The same word (*'ak* [TH389, ZH421]) is used to introduce the section on the Day of Atonement, translated there as "Be careful" (23:27).

23:40 branches. The Hebrew, followed by numerous English versions, reads "fruit" (*peri* [TH6529, ZH7262]), possibly the olive (Neh 8:15) or the citron (suggested by the rabbis).

COMMENTARY

The last of the annual festivals mentioned here is known by several different names: (1) "Shelters" (NLT), "Booths" (NASB, NRSV), or "Tabernacles" (Vulgate, KJV, NIV), all derived from the Hebrew name, which is *sukkoth* [TH5521, ZH6109] (Num 29:12-39), a reminder of the Exodus and the accommodations available to Israel during their wandering in the wilderness; (2) "Ingathering" or "Final Harvest" (Exod 23:16; 34:22), relating it to the agricultural calendar (this passage and Deut 16:13-15 use the first name in conjunction with agriculture), especially celebrating the harvest from the grape vine and olive trees; and (3) simply "the festival" (1 Kgs 8:2, 65; 12:32; 2 Chr 7:8-9; Neh 8:14; Ezek 45:25; John 7:37). It was the third pilgrimage festival (see comments on 23:6). It brought the festival calendar to a close in a manner similar to how it opened, with a multiday celebration (23:6-8).

This was the third festival in the seventh month of the Israelite year and the third pilgrimage feast in which people were expected to present themselves at the sanctuary. The festival lasted for a week (e.g., Num 9:12; Deut 16:13), with a special day added at its end. The first day was a special community gathering without any heavy labor. On each of the seven days, special sacrifices were brought (see note on 23:38). These are not spelled out here, but Numbers 29:13-34, which provides much more detailed information, indicates that on each of the seven days there were sacrifices of 2 rams, 14 male yearling lambs, and a number of bulls starting at 13 on the first day and decreasing by one for each of the seven days of the festival. These were each accompanied by their own grain and drink offerings.

The eighth day was an additional special day added to the end of the weeklong Shelters festival. It was another community gathering without hard labor and with the special offerings. It was distinguished from the other festival days by a different title: "solemn occasion" (23:36; cf. Deut 16:8, where the last day of Passover is given this same description in Hebrew, "holy day" in NLT). As such, it appears to have been added to an original weeklong celebration.

A summary in 23:37-38 draws the description of the annual festivals to a close. It calls them "appointed festivals," a reiteration from the introduction in 23:4. The summary mentions burnt, grain, and drink offerings, as well as "sacrifices," most probably the peace offerings of the Harvest (23:19), and possibly also the lamb offered on Passover (Exod 12:3-5, though not mentioned in ch 23; Milgrom 2001:2033). No mention is made of the sin offering or the accompanying grain offerings. These sacrifices were made on each special festival day (23:8, 13, 18, 25, 27, 36). Lest people think these special gifts should replace the customary Sabbath offerings or could take the place of any voluntary offering they might have made, they were reminded that these were a different category, and so they were in addition to, rather than in place of, these other offerings.

At the end of this section (23:39-43), the author added further explanation and expectations for the Festival of Shelters. It is unclear why the material was added after the concluding summary in 23:37-38, since it contains information necessary for understanding the nature of the festival. The further explanation dates the festival in the same words used previously (23:34), with the additional information that it would fall after the harvest of the land had been brought in. The first day of the seven-day festival and the supplemental eighth day are here designated as being for "complete rest" (23:39), a different designation for the days than that used earlier (23:35-36).

Tree branches from several species were to be used in the celebration. The all-encompassing term is probably the first stated—"branches from magnificent trees" (23:40)—of which three examples follow: palm fronds, leafy branches from unspecified trees, and willow (or poplar) branches. No use of these is specified here, except that the people should have them for the joyful celebration for a week. The context suggests that they were used to make the "little shelters" (23:42; see Neh 8:15-16), though they could have been used for other celebratory purposes (Ps 118:26-27, RSV; cf. Palm Sunday, Matt 21:8-9).

The perpetual nature of the weeklong festival in the seventh month is reiterated, though no mention of its geographical universality is given (cf. 23:3, 14, 21, 31). Part of the reason for the continued observance of the celebration was to be a reminder to the people of their exodus. The reminder was intensified by the people's living in temporary shelters or booths (cf. Isa 1:8; Jonah 4:5), probably a simple roof covering on poles. The event being commemorated was Israel's wandering in the wilderness (cf. Exod 16:32), where they also had no permanent home, though the word "shelter" was not used in the biblical account of this event. It was, however, reflected in the first stopping point on the journey (Succoth, Exod 12:37). The reminder was most probably not of the hardship of the past, but of their salvation from slavery.

This living arrangement was commanded only for Israelite natives (23:42), though presumably the foreigner (cf. 23:22) could do so as well, since they could, but were not required to, observe other Israelite ceremonial practices (17:8, 10, 12, 13, 15; 18:26; 20:2; 22:18). The people's savior in this event was Yahweh himself (cf. Exod 7:4-5; 12:41-42; 16:6; 20:2). This celebration of liberation, with its unique camping experience, would eventually become part of the eschatological life of all peoples (Zech 14:16-19). It is still among the favorites for Jewish children.

◆   H. Holiness of Sacred Foods (24:1-9)

The LORD said to Moses, ²"Command the people of Israel to bring you pure oil of pressed olives for the light, to keep the lamps burning continually. ³This is the lampstand that stands in the Tabernacle, in front of the inner curtain that shields the Ark of the Covenant.* Aaron must keep the lamps burning in the LORD's presence all night. This is a permanent law for you, and it must be observed from generation to generation. ⁴Aaron and the priests must tend the lamps on the pure gold lampstand continually in the LORD's presence.

⁵"You must bake twelve loaves of bread from choice flour, using four quarts* of flour for each loaf. ⁶Place the bread before the LORD on the pure gold table, and arrange the loaves in two rows, with six loaves in each row. ⁷Put some pure frankincense near each row to serve as a representative offering, a special gift presented to the LORD. ⁸Every Sabbath day this bread must be laid out before the LORD. The bread is to be received from the people of Israel as a requirement of the eternal covenant. ⁹The loaves of bread will belong to Aaron and his descendants, who must eat them in a sacred place, for they are most holy. It is the permanent right of the priests to claim this portion of the special gifts presented to the LORD."

24:3 Hebrew *in the Tent of Meeting, outside the inner curtain of the Testimony;* see note on 16:13.
24:5 Hebrew *²/10 of an ephah* [4.4 liters].

NOTES

24:4 *Aaron and the priests.* This is the subject implied by the LXX, which reads "You [plural] must tend the lamps." The MT reads "He must tend the lamps," implying Aaron alone as the subject.

24:5-8 This section has numerous points of continuity with the previous section (24:2-4). Both involve foodstuffs (olive oil and bread) that were provided by the people (though in the second instance the bread was made first by Moses [v. 5, with a sg. verb for "bake"] and subsequently by the people [v. 8]); both concern an arrangement (24:4, which has the word "tend"; 24:6, 8—all using the same Hebrew root) of implements of pure gold inside the sanctuary; both regulations were permanent.

COMMENTARY

This chapter has its own single-heading formula, but falls into two distinct parts based on content: food that was used in the sanctuary (24:2-9) and the treatment of a blasphemer (24:10-23). The first section continues the discussion concerning public religious ceremony started in chapter 23, but the latter is a completely different subject. It is not clear why these two elements were included in the same section, since they not only differ in content but also in literary genre, the first being legal and the second being narrative, with a legal section imbedded in it (24:17-22).

Chapter 24 begins with the notification that Moses received another revelation from God, which he was to pass on to Israel. This was not just something told to them (as in 23:2, 10, 24, 34, 44; 25:2); it was commanded of them (24:1-2). Just as the festivals were to be permanent reminders to Israel of God's acts and provision, so a light was to burn perpetually, day and night, in the sanctuary in Yahweh's presence. The Lord commanded this to be a permanent regulation. The law was practically a word-for-word repetition of Exod 27:20-21: There Moses was told that he would pass these regulations on to the people, and here he did so.

The oil was pressed from olives and was to be especially pure—something not necessary for the oil used with sacrifices (e.g., 2:1) or in anointing (e.g., 8:2). It was used in the Tabernacle's golden lamp, which was in front of the veil separating the two inner parts of the sanctuary (4:6; 16:2; Exod 25:31-39; 37:17-24; 40:25-26). Since the flame burned at all times (Exod 30:7-8; 1 Sam 3:3), it needed pure oil to lessen the smoke and soot (Milgrom 2001:2086; see Exod 27:20). Aaron and the priests had to care for the lamp as a perpetual task, while the job of the people was to provide the oil.

Each week, for every Sabbath, Israel was to bake 12 loaves of wheat bread from fine flour, each using four quarts of flour. These were either the same size as the Harvest Festival loaves or double them in size, depending on the interpretation of 23:17 (see comments). They were arrayed in two rows on the gold-covered table inside the sanctuary, also in front of the inner curtain according to its description in Exodus (Exod 25:23-30; 37:10-16; 40:22-23), where it was called "the Bread of the Presence." When purified frankincense, an aromatic resin (2:1, 15; 5:11), was sprinkled nearby, it became a special representation.

The bread loaves were rotated every week on the Sabbath (cf. 2 Kgs 11:5) in perpetuity as a reminder and part of the eternal covenant God had established with his people. The people were to supply the loaves beyond this first instance, when Moses was to bring them. Though not burnt, the loaves did not go to waste, since they became the property of the priests as their perpetual portion. They could eat them in the holy Tabernacle courtyard (cf. 6:9). Although not mentioned here, the bread seems also to have been available on an *ad hoc* basis under exceptional circumstances to others who were ceremonially clean and able to approach the sanctuary (cf. David in 1 Sam 21:4-6, though it appears David ate it outside the Tabernacle precincts). This played a significant economic role in the maintenance of the Israelite religious system, since it supplied a necessary part of the priestly provisions. This was necessary since they could not own and work their own land to raise crops.

◆   I. More Penalties for Unholiness (24:10-23)

[10]One day a man who had an Israelite mother and an Egyptian father came out of his tent and got into a fight with one of the Israelite men. [11]During the fight, this son of an Israelite woman blasphemed the Name of the LORD* with a curse. So the man was brought to Moses for judgment. His mother was Shelomith, the daughter of Dibri of the tribe of Dan. [12]They kept the man in custody until the LORD's will in the matter should become clear to them.

[13]Then the LORD said to Moses, [14]"Take the blasphemer outside the camp, and tell all those who heard the curse to lay their hands on his head. Then let the entire community stone him to death. [15]Say to the people of Israel: Those who curse their God will be punished for their sin. [16]Anyone who blasphemes the Name of the LORD must be stoned to death by the whole community of Israel. Any native-born Israelite or foreigner among you who blasphemes the Name of the LORD must be put to death.

[17]"Anyone who takes another person's life must be put to death.

[18]"Anyone who kills another person's animal must pay for it in full—a live animal for the animal that was killed.

[19]"Anyone who injures another person must be dealt with according to the injury inflicted—[20]a fracture for a fracture, an eye for an eye, a tooth for a tooth. Whatever anyone does to injure another person must be paid back in kind.

[21]"Whoever kills an animal must pay for it in full, but whoever kills another person must be put to death.

[22]"This same standard applies both to native-born Israelites and to the foreigners living among you. I am the LORD your God."

[23]After Moses gave all these instruc-

tions to the Israelites, they took the blasphemer outside the camp and stoned him

to death. The Israelites did just as the
LORD had commanded Moses.

24:11 Hebrew *the Name;* also in 24:16b.

NOTES

24:19 *who injures another person.* Lit., "causing a blemish to someone," identified here as
either a neighbor (24:19; cf. 18:20) or more broadly as "any human" (24:17).

24:20 *a fracture for a fracture, an eye for an eye, a tooth for a tooth.* The technical name
for this kind of case is *lex talionis,* popularly referred to as "an eye for an eye."

COMMENTARY

A story of a man's sin interrupts the regulations concerning sacred times, spaces,
and objects. It describes an incident when the holy name of God himself was
besmirched, calling for some kind of action. This was the occasion to establish a
case law, which itself led to the record of several similar regulations. It follows a pattern only found once elsewhere in Leviticus, the narrative of the punishment of
Aaron's sons and the regulations that arose from their misdeeds (chs 10, 16). These
both show the close bond between the stories of the people and the laws relating to
them, showing real-life application and refinement of law (see also Num 27:1-11
and 36:1-12). A law devoid of context was rare indeed.

Since an event took place in the life of Israel that was without precedent, the people had to await a new revelation from God as to how it should be handled. It
involved a man who was half-Israelite, the son of an Israelite mother and an Egyptian father. The father was likely to have been either one of the non-Israelites who
went with Israel when they left Egypt at the Exodus (Exod 12:38), or else he could
have fathered the boy while Israel was still in Egypt. The man came out, presumably
from his tent, and got into a fight, two Israelites against each other, an event that
would remind hearers of the story from Moses's own life when he went out and saw
a fight between two Israelites (Exod 2:13). The contrast between the two events is
clear: Moses stood up for the right, while this fellow was in the wrong. He misused
"the Name"—the name of God himself (Deut 28:58)—when he cursed God (Exod
22:28; cf. 2 Kgs 2:24, where God's name was used to curse someone else). In both of
these ways, the commandment against misusing God's name (Exod 20:7; Deut
5:11) would have been broken, so this was a serious matter.

Since the situation was new and the appropriate response to this incident was
unclear, the man was placed in temporary confinement until God's direction could
be clarified. It was not uncommon to await such divine direction when new situations arose. For example, this was the case with the daughters of Zelophehad (Num
27:5; 36:5), where a specific revelation from God was needed before a new legal
precedent could be established. The question here was apparently not what penalty
should come on the man, since death was the regular response to such things (cf.
1 Kgs 21:10, 13; Matt 26:65-66; Acts 6:11–7:58). Rather, the question was whether a
half-Israelite was as liable as a full-blooded one.

When God's answer came to Moses, it was not good news for the wrongdoer. He was to be taken from the camp, since its ceremonial purity needed protection because God's sanctuary was there. Those who heard the curse were to take personal action against the man who had wrongly spoken the words (cf. 5:1), having to press both hands onto his head, either to identify him as the sinner or to pass back to him any contamination they might have received in the simple act of hearing. Then they and the entire community of Israel were to execute the man by throwing stones at him until he was dead, a punishment associated with serious encroachment upon what was sacred (see 20:2, 27; Exod 19:13; Num 15:35-36). Since the entire nation could be compromised by such an action, the entire nation had to take active steps to punish it.

Following this, God told Moses to give Israel seven regulations, stating that the decision he had made concerning the blasphemer was not just for this instance alone. The first two relate to the immediate case (24:15-16). Those cursing God were to receive the consequences for their own sin—that is, they and they alone would receive an unspecified punishment, and not their family as well, as was sometimes the case (Num 16). Secondly, in any and every case where someone, Israelite or not, misused God's name in such a way, they were to suffer the same death penalty. The very continuation of Israel as a nation was in jeopardy if they did not adequately punish a breach of one of their foundational ordinances against misusing God's name. As their national life was subject to forfeit by the sin, the sinner's own life was considered forfeit.

The same correspondence of punishment to crime just noted held for the next series of five cases as well (24:17-21). Wenham (1979:312) notes that the previous regulation plus these five form a chiastic pattern:

A. Native or foreigner (24:16)
   B. Killing a person (24:17)
      C. Killing an animal (24:18)
         D. Injury for injury (24:19)
         D'. Injury for injury (24:20)
      C'. Killing an animal (24:21a)
   B'. Killing a person (24:21b)
A'. Native or foreigner (24:22)

The first case involves someone striking any person (Israelite or not), resulting in death (Num 35:30; Deut 19:6, 11). Since this person caused a death, he would have to die as his punishment (24:18; Exod 21:23; 2 Kgs 10:24). The second, lesser case involves someone mortally striking an animal. The necessary response was literally to "make it good," making sure that the life of the dead beast was made up for by a living one, which the killer gave to the dead animal's owner. Milgrom suggests that monetary payment would also suffice (2001:2122).

The next, central case in the pattern involves injury. These injuries (lit., "blemishes"—see note on 24:19) not only had physical results, but also barred the injured person from bringing offerings to God (21:18-21). Whatever the person inflicted on another could be inflicted on him, whether damage to a bone, an eye, or a tooth. In another place where this same regulation was given, "a life for a life" is also included (Exod 21:23-24). It was not stated here because it was covered in the preceding and following verses. Also, death was not a "blemish," so it did not fit with the other injuries listed. The last two laws (24:21) repeat the first two (24:17-18).

These laws appear to be barbaric in that they stipulate that even accidents causing injury would result in the person who caused them being maimed. While this might lead to more care that accidents not happen, that did not appear to be the purpose of these laws. It is helpful to read them in the light of their environment in the ancient Near East. In Mesopotamia, there were a number of similar *lex talionis* laws (COS 2.131:348 §196, 200, 203, 209-210). Some of these laws, however, permitted a disproportionate punishment. For example, when a slave struck someone of a higher class, he lost his ear (COS 2.131:348 §205). The biblical laws were thus tempering possible overreaction. The Hebrew could also be read as granting permission rather than giving a strict command: "may be paid back" rather than "must be paid back." If a person was injured in Israel, he could demand a comparable fate for the other, but could not demand more than what was commensurate and could show grace by demanding less.

The regulations close with a reminder that they applied to everyone living in the land, no matter their ethnic origin (24:16), followed by a concluding formula of who was speaking. The narrative picked up again after the legal insertion, concluding with Moses and the people fulfilling the requirements given by God.

The episode clearly points out the sanctity of the name of God, which represents the totality of who he is (Exod 3:13-15; 6:2-9; 34:4-7). As the creator and sustainer of the universe, he is worthy of due honor and respect. Blasphemy, like slander, tends to demean the subject, and this is not at all appropriate for God. It is considered a serious offence in the New Testament (Matt 12:31; Mark 2:7; John 10:33; Rev 13:6), and it was the charge (albeit a false one) brought against Jesus by the Jewish leaders in order to justify his execution (Matt 26:55-56).

◆ J. Holy Living in the Land (25:1-55)
     1. Holiness of the Sabbath year (25:1-7)

While Moses was on Mount Sinai, the LORD said to him, 2"Give the following instructions to the people of Israel. When you have entered the land I am giving you, the land itself must observe a Sabbath rest before the LORD every seventh year. 3For six years you may plant your fields and prune your vineyards and harvest your crops, 4but during the seventh year the land must have a Sabbath year of complete rest. It is the LORD's Sabbath. Do not plant your fields or prune your vine-yards during that year. 5And don't store away the crops that grow on their own or gather the grapes from your unpruned vines. The land must have a year of complete rest. 6But you may eat whatever the land produces on its own during its Sabbath. This applies to you, your male and female servants, your hired workers, and the temporary residents who live with you. 7Your livestock and the wild animals in your land will also be allowed to eat what the land produces.

NOTES

25:4 *during the seventh year the land must have a Sabbath year of complete rest.* The people of Emar (Syria) in the thirteenth century BC celebrated a major festival lasting seven days (cf. Unleavened Bread, 23:6; Shelters, 23:39), starting on the fifteenth of the month (cf. Unleavened Bread, 23:6; Shelters, 23:34, 39) every seven years (Fleming 2000:48-140). Rather than enforcing and celebrating a cessation from work, the festival in Emar celebrated the place of Dagan (also called Dagon) as the head of their pantheon (Fleming 2000:91). So the periodicity but not the function finds parallel in Israel.

COMMENTARY

Holiness is wider than religious observance—how one relates vertically with one's God: It encompasses all of life, including how one relates horizontally, living justly and in harmony with one's fellow human beings and with the earth itself. This chapter discusses occasions when these aspects of life were given singular consideration, a special sabbatical year (25:2b-7) and a Year of Jubilee (25:8-22). Both of these events had a theological motivation, but they also had economic and social ramifications for Israel. They are here followed by other socioeconomic regulations regarding property ownership (25:23-34) and the treatment of slaves and debtors (25:35-55). In Israel, both religious law and personal ethics were everyday parts of life.

God set aside one day a week as a Sabbath of rest for Israel (23:3), as it had been for God himself (Gen 2:1-4a). Here this rest is expanded to provide a rest for the land itself, and secondarily for the people. This not only allowed people and pasture to be renewed, but it was a strong reminder of the ultimate source of one's sustenance; humanity did not live by the produce of their own hands alone, but through the provision of God (Luke 4:4).

The first verse of the chapter reminds the reader of the geographical location of God's revelation: The people were still at Mount Sinai, having arrived there after the exodus from Egypt (Exod 19:1). Moses, whom God was directing to pass his revelation on to Israel, was himself still up on the mountain (7:38; 26:46; 27:34). This section, therefore, is actually presenting material given before the material in chapters 8–24, which is a record of events that happened after Moses had come down from the mountain (see 8:4). Interpreters debate why the chapter was recorded here, out of time sequence. We cannot be certain, but since the previous chapter concerned special times in the life of Israel, the special times recorded here naturally follow.

The words given to Moses anticipate settlement in the land, rather than viewing it as an accomplished fact (also 14:34; 19:23; 23:10). In other words, the land is the subject of the passage (25:1-7). The land was to be granted a cessation from work in the same way as humans (19:3, 30; 23:3), and in honor of God, who himself rested (Gen 2:2). This event seems to bundle all of God's creation, including the inanimate earth, into his day of rest, just as humans and animals were included in other similar passages (cf. Exod 20:10).

The nature of this Sabbath was explained in contrast to the rest of Israelite life in the land, which revolved around agriculture. This life was to proceed normally, with the annual cycle of planting grain in the fields, which took place in late fall or winter (DOTP 24-25), tending the grape vines in early summer prior to their harvest, and harvesting all crops as they ripened at various times throughout the year. This was the regular pattern to follow for six years, but the seventh year was to be set aside as a "rest" year. It was designated a Sabbath, not only for the earth (cf. 23:3), which was allowed to renew itself, but also for God. In this seventh year, planting and pruning were banned. This could technically allow for other agricultural activities to continue unabated, thus fulfilling the letter of the law. The spirit of the law, however, was to provide complete rest, a total fallow year, so the two listed activities were probably symbolic of the entire enterprise of agricultural farming: It all should cease.

Planted crops often produced a second crop from seed that fell before the harvest or otherwise remained after the harvest (e.g., 19:9-10). Fruit trees and vines would also produce, though they were not pruned. Even this could not be harvested for storage or for sale during this seventh year. It could be used for daily food for all of Israel, which, in the case of this provision, included not only free Israelites, but also their servants, hired hands, and those who were temporarily resident in the land, as well as the animals that might graze in their fields. Divine ownership of all the land took precedence over the rights of individual Israelite owners, for God was making all land and its produce public property. God's provision, even without the direct intervention of human labor, would continue; this grace was universal, blessing not only those who followed his wishes but also those who did not (cf. Matt 5:45).

It is unclear whether the Sabbath year was ever carried out in actual practice. This might be hinted at in several passages (2 Kgs 19:29; Isa 37:30), but the exile of Israel from her land is framed in terms of allowing the land to enjoy the Sabbath Israel had neglected to provide (26:43; 2 Chr 36:21; 1 Macc 6:49, 53).

◆   ## 2. Holiness of the jubilee year (25:8-22)

8"In addition, you must count off seven Sabbath years, seven sets of seven years, adding up to forty-nine years in all. 9Then on the Day of Atonement in the fiftieth year,* blow the ram's horn loud and long throughout the land. 10Set this year apart as holy, a time to proclaim freedom throughout the land for all who live there. It will be a jubilee year for you, when each of you may return to the land that belonged to your ancestors and return to your own clan. 11This fiftieth year will be a jubilee for you. During that year you must not plant your fields or store away any of the crops that grow on their own, and don't gather the grapes from your unpruned vines. 12It will be a jubilee year for you, and you must keep it holy. But you may eat whatever the land produces on its own. 13In the Year of Jubilee each of you may return to the land that belonged to your ancestors.

14"When you make an agreement with your neighbor to buy or sell property, you must not take advantage of each other. 15When you buy land from your neighbor, the price you pay must be based on the number of years since the last jubilee. The seller must set the price by taking into account the number of years remaining until the next Year of Jubilee. ¹⁶The more years until the next jubilee, the higher the price; the fewer years, the lower the price. After all, the person selling the land is actually selling you a certain number of harvests. ¹⁷Show your fear of God by not taking advantage of each other. I am the LORD your God.

¹⁸"If you want to live securely in the land, follow my decrees and obey my regulations. ¹⁹Then the land will yield large crops, and you will eat your fill and live securely in it. ²⁰But you might ask, 'What will we eat during the seventh year, since we are not allowed to plant or harvest crops that year?' ²¹Be assured that I will send my blessing for you in the sixth year, so the land will produce a crop large enough for three years. ²²When you plant your fields in the eighth year, you will still be eating from the large crop of the sixth year. In fact, you will still be eating from that large crop when the new crop is harvested in the ninth year.

25:9 Hebrew *on the tenth day of the seventh month, on the Day of Atonement;* see 23:27a and the note there.

NOTES

25:8 *you must count off seven Sabbath years, seven sets of seven years, adding up to forty-nine years in all.* The time frame of this particular event was meticulously described in several ways in order to tie it in with the sabbatical year. This is very similar to the calculation formula for the Festival of Harvest (23:15), when periods of seven were counted in relation to a Sabbath. The period determined by the sabbatical year cycle is 49 years.

25:10 *return to the land . . . return to your own clan.* The nature of the release is illuminated by the same word which occurs in Akkadian (*duraru*), a sister language to Hebrew that was used in what is now Iraq, formerly Assyria and Babylonia. This word conveys a concept derived from Sumerian, an earlier language of the area, meaning "returning to the mother" (Milgrom 2001:2167). The concept here paralleled this, a return to family roots of land (place) and kin (people).

25:22 *When you plant your fields in the eighth year, you will still be eating from the large crop of the sixth year.* Difficulties arise with placing the jubilee year into this equation along with the Sabbath year because it speaks of planting in "the eighth year," which would be the jubilee year (when it occurred). If the harvest of the sixth year needed to last through a planting-reaping cycle of the Sabbath year (year 7) and again through a cycle of the jubilee year (year 8), one could only sow again in year 9 and reap in year 10. Planting in year 8 was not allowed if that was the jubilee year (25:11). It is possible, therefore, that this section refers back to the regulations concerning the Sabbath year (25:2-7) with no reference here to the jubilee.

COMMENTARY

The weekly Sabbath was extended and amplified in the sabbatical year (25:2-7), and the concept was here amplified again to a Sabbath of Sabbath years, a sevenfold multiplication of the seven-year period. The forty-ninth year would be a regular sabbatical year, but the following, fiftieth year was freedom not only for the land but also for others who were in bondage, socially or economically. The passage contains within it a subsection dealing with various aspects of real estate repurchase (25:23-34) and the humane treatment of slaves and the poor (25:35-55), both of which were impacted by the jubilee regulations. Theology and socioeconomic policy were strongly intertwined because God is both Creator and sustainer.

The actual period for the jubilee year came in the fiftieth year, after a full sabbatical year was celebrated in the forty-ninth year. The year itself started on a very significant day, the Day of Atonement, which fell on the tenth day of the seventh month (16:29-34; 23:27-32). There is no mention as to why this day in particular marked the beginning, but it highlighted the importance of that national day of cleansing from sin. Freedom from the impurity of sin would be a theologically significant parallel to the economic and social freedom so important in this fiftieth year. To particularly mark that day, everyone living in the land of Israel was to hear the loud blast of the ram's horn, the sound that also marked the constitution of Israel as a nation: God's meeting with Moses on Mount Sinai (Exod 19:16, 19; 20:18). It also signaled other important occasions (e.g., Judg 3:27; 1 Sam 13:3; 2 Sam 6:15; 15:10).

Like the holy Sabbath (Exod 20:8, 11; Deut 5:12), this special fiftieth year was sanctified—set apart as a special, holy period. Part of what was proclaimed by the loud trumpets was freedom or release of land (Ezek 46:17), such as prisoners or slaves might experience upon their release (Isa 61:1; Jer 34:8-9). Those who had lost any family real estate through sale or debt were able to return and reclaim it (see note on 25:10), with the implication that the debt had been met or forgiven. In Deuteronomy, this release from debt is part of the sabbatical every seven years, rather than the fiftieth year (Deut 15:1-5).

The year is called a "jubilee" (the English word coming from *yobel* [TH3104, ZH3413]), a term most likely deriving from the ram's horn trumpet used to usher in the day (25:9). Its release also extended to the land itself, which, as in the Sabbath year (25:4-5), was to be free from agricultural working. Tasks leading to agricultural production were banned, but gathering simply for food was again allowed (25:6). Foreign-born slaves were exempt from these provisions of release (25:44-46); they were not considered on this occasion as being part of Israel.

The jubilee year, with its restoration of ancestral land to the original owners, had implications for land-sale agreements with one's fellow Israelite (25:14-17). These were in reality not sale but lease arrangements. One was not buying the land, but only the use of it and its produce—and that only until the time of the next jubilee, at which time the leasehold would be removed. Since this was the case, one must not cheat or take unfair advantage of others when arranging the price. This was to be determined by the owner on the basis of how many years since the previous jubilee. This would determine how many years remained until the next jubilee. Since there was one crop per year, in actuality the negotiations concerned how many crop harvests one might be able to benefit from before the land was returned to its original owner at the next jubilee. The ban on taking unfair advantage most immediately pertained to the jubilee but held for all situations where one could misuse the poor and disadvantaged (e.g., 19:33; Exod 22:21; Deut 23:15-16). By treating one's fellows fairly, looking after their interests, one showed Yahweh great respect.

Leviticus 25:18-21 returns to the issue of letting the land lie fallow. What would motivate Israelites to treat the land in this way? On what food would they be able to survive for this extended period? God reminded the people that security and plenty did not come from their agricultural efforts, but from their religious ones. Security and satiety came not from working their land but from worshiping their God and obeying him. Submission to God's directives would supply food for the larder, even in a Sabbath year, when no planting or harvesting was permitted (25:4-5; 26:10).

Both the Sabbath and jubilee years provide an interesting foil to the harvest festivals of the previous chapter. These were joyful times of thanksgiving for the nourishment of a good harvest supplied from the hand of God. These two years took the message a major step forward, reminding the people that it was not in reality the harvest that was the source of national and personal life, since there would be no harvest for a year or longer. The actual source of life was a God who was not only the God of the harvest but was also God, the provider, when there was no harvest (Hab 3:17-18).

◆   ## 3. Redemption of property (25:23-34)

23"The land must never be sold on a permanent basis, for the land belongs to me. You are only foreigners and tenant farmers working for me.

24"With every purchase of land you must grant the seller the right to buy it back. 25If one of your fellow Israelites falls into poverty and is forced to sell some family land, then a close relative should buy it back for him. 26If there is no close relative to buy the land, but the person who sold it gets enough money to buy it back, 27he then has the right to redeem it from the one who bought it. The price of the land will be discounted according to the number of years until the next Year of Jubilee. In this way the original owner can then return to the land. 28But if the original owner cannot afford to buy back the land, it will remain with the new owner until the next Year of Jubilee. In the jubilee year, the land must be returned to the original owners so they can return to their family land.

29"Anyone who sells a house inside a walled town has the right to buy it back for a full year after its sale. During that year, the seller retains the right to buy it back. 30But if it is not bought back within a year, the sale of the house within the walled town cannot be reversed. It will become the permanent property of the buyer. It will not be returned to the original owner in the Year of Jubilee. 31But a house in a village—a settlement without fortified walls—will be treated like property in the countryside. Such a house may be bought back at any time, and it must be returned to the original owner in the Year of Jubilee.

32"The Levites always have the right to buy back a house they have sold within the towns allotted to them. 33And any property that is sold by the Levites—all houses within the Levitical towns—must be returned in the Year of Jubilee. After all, the houses in the towns reserved for the Levites are the only property they own in all Israel. 34The open pastureland around the Levitical towns may never be sold. It is their permanent possession.

NOTES

25:23 *the land belongs to me*. Since God was the actual landowner, and Israel was simply his tenant, land tenure was not secure unless Israel fulfilled his wishes. If tenants were unworthy, they could lose their land (cf. Isa 5:8, 13) and be replaced by others. This was what God did at the Exile; he sent Israel and Judah to other lands (2 Kgs 25:8-21), while he resettled strangers in their place. Through his grace he restored the land to them (Ezra 1:1-8).

COMMENTARY

Property transactions are the subject of 25:23-34 (cf. 25:14-17). A general regulation was presented first, followed by various different scenarios. The underlying
principle regarding property is that Yahweh, the creator of all things, including the
land (or the earth; cf. Gen 1:1), was the one who gave it to Israel in the first place
(Gen 12:1; 15:7) and is the ultimate landowner. Everything belongs in his holdings,
not just the land of Canaan, in which Israel would soon settle (Exod 9:29; Deut
10:14). Therefore, land distribution and allocation were in his control (cf. Num
34:16-29; Josh 13:8–21:45, with frequent mention of Yahweh's guidance in the
division) and were therefore theological rather than purely socioeconomic con-
structs. His rights, rather than those of any human landowner, were the concern of
these regulations.

His first statement was that he never would relinquish his ownership of the land,
so there would be no permanent sale by an Israelite, since the land was not his to
dispose of in this way. The loss of land, even if only until the next jubilee year, was
serious indeed. Should a person become a slave through debt and loss of land, that
person would be provided for by his owner (e.g., 22:11). Should freedom from slavery be possible, however, the free person would still be deprived not just of the land,
but of its produce, which would have provided the necessities of life, made the people self-sufficient, and kept them out of slavery. Since there was no state-funded
unemployment or social security system in ancient Israel, landless people and their
families, as well as widows and orphans, were left to the mercies of their not-always-
merciful neighbors. They were the same as those others who were unable to acquire
their own land—namely, foreigners and renters.

It was precisely to make provision for these unfortunates that Yahweh declared
himself the one championing their cause, being their provider, husband, and father,
and so, in a way, mandating a theological system of unemployment and social security (Deut 10:18; 14:28-29; 24:19-21; 26:12-15). The problem would become more
widespread if land was allowed to be sold outside of one's tribe. Individual Israelites would be expected to care for their own kin. But if the means of agricultural production were taken from the tribe by the hands of a few wealthy landowners, tribal
existence itself could have been jeopardized.

Israel's landlord and master was God. He would not only provide for the unfortunate, but also provide a motive for Israel to treat their own slaves and other poor
people well (cf. Deut 5:15; 15:15; 24:18, 22). One way to prevent permanent separation from the land was through its release at jubilee. Another was granting the
seller the opportunity to buy the land back at some time between jubilee years
(25:24).

The next verses (25:25-28) provide regulations for how this last point of redemption, or repurchase, was to be worked out. The first case involved an impoverished
Israelite who was unable to provide for himself and his family. He could either sell
himself or his family into slavery (25:39), or he could sell some or all of his land.
Since these were such serious and far-reaching options, steps were made to stop

them from being implemented in a way that might bring permanent damage to a family and ultimately to society itself. The first step toward protecting property from completely leaving a family's control was to have the portion of it that had been sold purchased back by a close relative, called a family redeemer (cf. Ruth 2:20; 4:1-14). There is no mention of what the redeemer would then do. He might have immediately returned the land to its original owner, though this is not mentioned (cf. 25:27). More likely he enjoyed the use of the land's produce until the next jubilee (25:14-16). This allowed him to recover at least some of his expenses.

Another possibility, if there was no near redeemer, was that the slave had gathered enough personal resources to redeem it, or buy it back, himself. He would not need to match the full sale price, or any increase in value such as we expect in real estate transactions today. Rather, following the principle established for the jubilee, the price was calculated on the number of harvests the buyer enjoyed and the potential harvests until the next jubilee. After making this payment, he could return home and start providing for himself and his family from his own labors. If neither of these options worked out, there was still hope, because the jubilee regulation was still in effect. Upon the fiftieth year (which might still have been decades away, depending on when the property was sold), the property would return to the original owner or his family.

A variant of the sale of property concerned the sale of houses rather than agricultural land (25:29-31). This reflected a different stage in the socioeconomic development of Israel. At the time pictured at the writing of these laws, Israel was wandering in the wilderness and had no land. When they arrived in the land, most would have lived on the land as farmers, but some lived in small, unwalled villages and farmed just outside the town limits. As farmers began to produce more than they and their families needed for survival, they could sell their produce to those who would have been free to live in larger towns and engage in work unrelated to agriculture. These three different social situations were reflected in the laws. The jubilee was necessary to protect the livelihood of those farmers who lived and depended directly on their land. Houses in walled cities did not fit into this category, since they did not produce any agricultural capital. They seem to be the property of the individual and not of the clan or tribe, and were thus treated differently. A house could be sold, apparently at the choice of its owner, since no forced sale through poverty was mentioned. The owner retained the right to buy it back or redeem it, if he so chose, for one calendar year. The price, though not specified, must have been in relation to the sale price, since, unlike the land, which was paid for based on potential harvests, the house had no income-producing potential on which to calculate a price. If not repurchased, it became the permanent property of the new owner and did not revert at jubilee. It did not need to be protected since its sale had no long-term negative potential.

Smaller villages did not have protective walls, so they would have depended for protection in case of attack on nearby, larger walled towns with which they were associated (cf. Deut 2:23; Josh 19:8; 1 Chr 4:33). They were surrounded by agricultural land (cf. Neh 11:25) and were considered agricultural for the purpose of sale. Therefore, they fell under the regular redemption and jubilee regulations.

Landholdings belonging to Levites fell into yet a different category, so they needed special regulations (25:32-34). They were not allowed to own land in the same way as other Israelites (Num 18:23; 26:62) because their job was to look after the sanctuary, not to farm (Num 3:5-10). When settled in the land, they received 48 walled towns for themselves, in addition to the surrounding pastureland for their livestock (Num 35:1-8; Josh 21), but no agricultural land. If they sold a house, they were always allowed to buy it back; it did not have the one-year restriction (25:30). If it was redeemed by a fellow Levite (the close relative, 25:26), it did not become his perpetual property, but would revert to the original owner at jubilee. This was their holding from the property given by God, its owner (25:23), just as the rest of Israel had their own holdings. The surrounding pastureland, defined in Numbers 35:4-5, was never allowed to be sold, since it was not the property of an individual, but was common land for use of all the town residents.

◆ 4. Redemption of the poor and slaves (25:35-55)

35"If one of your fellow Israelites falls into poverty and cannot support himself, support him as you would a foreigner or a temporary resident and allow him to live with you. 36Do not charge interest or make a profit at his expense. Instead, show your fear of God by letting him live with you as your relative. 37Remember, do not charge interest on money you lend him or make a profit on food you sell him. 38I am the LORD your God, who brought you out of the land of Egypt to give you the land of Canaan and to be your God.

39"If one of your fellow Israelites falls into poverty and is forced to sell himself to you, do not treat him as a slave. 40Treat him instead as a hired worker or as a temporary resident who lives with you, and he will serve you only until the Year of Jubilee. 41At that time he and his children will no longer be obligated to you, and they will return to their clans and go back to the land originally allotted to their ancestors. 42The people of Israel are my servants, whom I brought out of the land of Egypt, so they must never be sold as slaves. 43Show your fear of God by not treating them harshly.

44"However, you may purchase male and female slaves from among the nations around you. 45You may also purchase the children of temporary residents who live among you, including those who have been born in your land. You may treat them as your property, 46passing them on to your children as a permanent inheritance. You may treat them as slaves, but you must never treat your fellow Israelites this way.

47"Suppose a foreigner or temporary resident becomes rich while living among you. If any of your fellow Israelites fall into poverty and are forced to sell themselves to such a foreigner or to a member of his family, 48they still retain the right to be bought back, even after they have been purchased. They may be bought back by a brother, 49an uncle, or a cousin. In fact, anyone from the extended family may buy them back. They may also redeem themselves if they have prospered. 50They will negotiate the price of their freedom with the person who bought them. The price will be based on the number of years from the time they were sold until the next Year of Jubilee—whatever it would cost to hire a worker for that period of time. 51If many years still remain until the jubilee, they will repay the proper proportion of what they received when they sold themselves. ⁵²If only a few years remain until the Year of Jubilee, they will repay a small amount for their redemption. ⁵³The foreigner must treat them as workers hired on a yearly basis. You must not allow a foreigner to treat any of your fellow Israelites harshly. ⁵⁴If any Israelites have not been bought back by the time the Year of Jubilee arrives, they and their children must be set free at that time. ⁵⁵For the people of Israel belong to me. They are my servants, whom I brought out of the land of Egypt. I am the LORD your God.

NOTES

25:35 *allow him to live with you.* This should not be understood as permitting him to move into the house, which would have been rendered by a different Hebrew verb (*yashab* [TH3427, ZH3782], "to remain, dwell"). The term used here (*khayah* [TH2421, ZH2649]) should rather be rendered in this passage "allow him to stay alive."

25:48-49 *They may be bought back by a brother, an uncle, or a cousin. In fact, anyone from the extended family may buy them back.* Representative examples of these relatives were listed in order from closer to more distant: brother, uncle, uncle's son (cousin), anyone else from his own family (cf. 18:6). No father is mentioned since, if the son owned the land, it would have been his inheritance from his father, who thus would be dead. No son is mentioned, since he would have been enslaved along with his father and would not have the means to redeem.

COMMENTARY

Property was not the only thing that could be encumbered through debt and poverty. People could be so encumbered as well. Once poverty led to the depletion of family landholdings, the next step was destitution, depending on the goodwill of others (25:35-38). If insufficient provision was found to care for the family through this, the only thing left was for an Israelite to sell his family or himself into slavery (25:39-55). Being in God's image, the destitute and slave also had some rights and could not be exploited at the will of their owners or employers. Regulations governing their treatment provided them the privileges of jubilee freedom enjoyed by their fellow Israelites, as well as by the land itself.

The situation outlined in 25:35-37 is that poverty could force a landholder to sell part of his land in order to pay for food for his family (25:25). If further crop failure made this necessary again, he would have had to sell all of his land to meet his debt and would then have nothing to provide for his living. The law to support such a person and not charge him interest was directed to the one who had helped him meet his needs by purchasing (leasing) the land for its potential crops. He had a responsibility to provide the means for the poor person to maintain his life. This indicates that one's financial means are not one's own, but God's, to be used at his direction just as were one's fields and crops (19:9-10; 23:22).

The action the landowner was to take can be read in two ways. The new owner could be called upon to maintain and support him, looking after him as one would have looked after a hired laborer (so most English translations), though no mention is made anywhere else of providing hired laborers with interest-free loans.

Another possibility is that the poor man became like a hired laborer to his creditor, allowed to live under his authority, working for him—with his wages being credited against his accrued debt (Milgrom 2001:2206-2209), much like an indentured servant. The debt was to be fixed; no interest could be charged against it, driving him further and further into debt (Exod 22:25; Deut 23:20-21), nor could the provisions the new landowner provided to him be sold to him at a profit (cf. Neh 5:1-3). An Israelite was not to gain an advantage at the cost of another Israelite's suffering. Treating one's fellow Israelite in a helpful way like this was one means of showing proper respect for God, who would himself step in to support a person who might be wronged in this area (25:37). Yahweh had saved Israel by bringing them out of Egypt (25:42, 55). He did this to provide for their physical needs by giving them the land of Canaan and its yield, and in response, Israelite creditors must also provide for the needs of their debtors (25:38).

An economic spiral of poverty could lead through a loss of land to a loss of freedom (25:39-43): As a last resort, a destitute Israelite could sell himself and his family into servitude to the creditor. They were still Israelites, however, and were afforded rights. These included not being treated simply like chattel, property completely under the control of the owner, but like hired laborers. As such they received wages, which they used to pay off their debt. Even if not completely repaid, the servant and his family were freed at jubilee and allowed to return to their original land, which reverted to the family at jubilee (25:10, 13). Thus, Israelites were not to become slaves to their creditors but rather hired hands. This was the ideal, which was not always evident in practice, where Israelites were actually enslaved with the loss of everything they had (cf. Exod 22:25; Deut 24:6, 10-13).

The reason they were not to be counted as actual slaves was that they, and all of Israel, were the slaves of God since he redeemed them from slavery in Egypt (Exod 6:6; 15:13; Deut 13:5), and they were his to command as he would. The exodus from Egypt had not won their freedom, but a new master, Yahweh (Goldingay 2003:380). There was not only a restriction on slavery, but also on the kind of treatment with which an Israelite could treat his fellow. Cruelty was not allowed (25:46, 53). If they did treat them so, they would be no better than their Egyptian masters who had so treated them (Exod 1:13-15). Once again, the way one treats fellow human beings reflects one's attitude toward God himself (25:17, 36; 19:14, 32).

Non-Israelites in service to another were treated differently than Israelites (25:44-46). They are the only ones actually called "slaves" in this chapter (though Israelites were called this in other passages, e.g., Exod 21:5-7), a term twice denied of Israelites in relation to anyone besides God (25:39, 42; cf. 25:55). Those bought either from neighboring countries or from among the non-Israelites living in the land did not have the rights of periodic release at jubilee since they were not debt-slaves but actual property, which could be bought, sold, and inherited. This was in marked contrast to Israelites, whose harsh treatment was again banned, suggesting that such treatment might be permissible for non-Israelites, though even they were also in God's image and had rights as human beings (24:22).

Slavery was common among all of Israel's neighbors, but the Old Testament laws served to curb some of the abuses this practice could entail. They do not establish slavery but recognize its existence and seek to regulate it. All people are created in God's image and are worthy of respect and dignity, so some of the laws needed to address the real situation (slavery existed) rather than the ideal (there should be no slaves). Paul carried this concept forward yet another step, not only saying that there should be no ultimate distinction between Israelites and non-Israelites when it came to slavery and service, but that there should no longer be any difference at all in an equitable society between a slave and a free person (Gal 3:28)—i.e., that ultimately there should be no slavery (see Swartley 1983:31-64; Webb 2001).

Since both Israelites and the foreigners living in the land had opportunity to prosper, some of the foreigners did do so and could gain control over impoverished Israelites (25:47). This situation was different than the last case. The Israelite was granted the same rights no matter who his master was, whether another Israelite (25:35-43) or a foreigner. The options open in this case were quite similar to those available when land was sold (25:15-28). The Israelite could be bought back, or redeemed, by a close relative who would pay the debt (25:48). The person in servitude could earn sufficient funds (25:53) to buy himself back by paying off his accrued debt (25:26). The price paid was calculated in a way similar to that for redeeming land. The land price was according to how many harvests there were until the next jubilee (25:27), and the price of the human was calculated on how much it would cost to hire a day laborer to do the work he would have done if he had stayed in service, which was calculated on an annual basis. The price would be raised or lowered depending on how long it would be until the next jubilee (cf. 25:16), when the debt-worker and his family needed to be released (25:28, 40) if they had not been redeemed before that time. They also could not be mistreated (25:43, 46). Both land and person were God's possession (25:23, 42), so only their produce and not their person was sold.

These two events, the Sabbath and jubilee years, show that God has interest not only in religious ceremony, but also in environmental and economic matters. The land is under the charge and care of humanity (Gen 1:28), but they could not indiscriminately rape it for their own selfish advantage. People were also not a commodity for exploitation. Part of human dignity is the ability to provide for oneself, even if only through laborious toil (cf. Gen 3:17-19). These verses provided the means to prevent or reverse a state of human or environmental abuse. The redistribution of land (capital) and freeing of slaves would have done much to prevent the alienation of the worker from the means of production, an idea based on the way God structured his creation, giving humanity earth's bounty but also the responsibility for its care. Particularly in an agricultural society, the loss of land could lead to social and individual distress. Protection of life and dignity through a shared distribution of wealth was also known and practiced in the early church at Jerusalem (Acts 2:44-45), though not in relation to any actual Year of Jubilee. This might sound radical and unheard of in much of today's church, but its implementation in Acts seems to have been a catalyst for many becoming members of the church every day. Could there be a causal link between the two, which the church today should take into consideration? The church needs to give greater thought to its economic responsibilities in addition to, and as part of, its theological ones.

◆ K. Holiness: Blessings and Punishment (26:1-46)
1. Blessings of obedience (26:1-13)

"Do not make idols or set up carved images, or sacred pillars, or sculptured stones in your land so you may worship them. I am the LORD your God. ²You must keep my Sabbath days of rest and show reverence for my sanctuary. I am the LORD.

³"If you follow my decrees and are careful to obey my commands, ⁴I will send you the seasonal rains. The land will then yield its crops, and the trees of the field will produce their fruit. ⁵Your threshing season will overlap with the grape harvest, and your grape harvest will overlap with the season of planting grain. You will eat your fill and live securely in your own land.

⁶"I will give you peace in the land, and you will be able to sleep with no cause for fear. I will rid the land of wild animals and keep your enemies out of your land. ⁷In fact, you will chase down your enemies and slaughter them with your swords. ⁸Five of you will chase a hundred, and a hundred of you will chase ten thousand! All your enemies will fall beneath your sword.

⁹"I will look favorably upon you, making you fertile and multiplying your people. And I will fulfill my covenant with you. ¹⁰You will have such a surplus of crops that you will need to clear out the old grain to make room for the new harvest! ¹¹I will live among you, and I will not despise you. ¹²I will walk among you; I will be your God, and you will be my people. ¹³I am the LORD your God, who brought you out of the land of Egypt so you would no longer be their slaves. I broke the yoke of slavery from your neck so you can walk with your heads held high.

NOTES

26:1-2 The Ten Commandments formed the "Bill of Rights" of Israel's constitution—its foundation. This chapter begins with three of the first four commandments, those relating to the obligations Israel had toward God, their owner and covenant Lord (see Exod 20:2-5).

26:3-4 *If you follow my decrees and are careful to obey my commands, [then] I will send you the seasonal rains.* The passage begins with a brief conditional clause ("if"), which is followed by a lengthy result statement ("then I will send you . . .") that extends to 26:13. The following promises would result if God's decrees and commands were carefully kept as a pattern of life (lit., "walking" in them; cf. Deut 8:6; 28:9; 1 John 1:6-7). Which decrees and commands are being referred to is not clear. This could be a reference just to 26:1-2, to the Sabbath and jubilee laws of ch 25, or to the entire book of Leviticus. The latter is preferable, since only the term "decree" is used of ch 25, while both terms are used of numerous elements within the book as a whole (see 3:17; 4:2, 13, 22, 27, etc.). Leviticus 26:1-2 could also be seen as representing the entire book, since its subject, holiness, concerned the divine–human relationship, of which these two verses provide representative examples.

26:5 *securely.* The term *betakh* [TH983, ZH1055] can apply to military (Deut 12:10) as well as economic security, the latter of which better fits the context here (cf. 25:18-19; Judg 18:7-8, where both meanings seem to apply).

COMMENTARY

The structure of the chapter is deliberate, highlighting the Israelite covenant with God. The chapter closes with mention of the ancestral, patriarchal covenant (26:45) and opens with reference to three of the Ten Commandments (26:1-2), the foundational element of the covenant with Moses. The term "covenant," referring to the original family covenant (Gen 12:1-3), which was nationalized at Mount Sinai to include all of Israel (Exod 19:5; 24:7-8), occurs a total of eight times in this chapter (26:9, 15, 25, 42 [three times], 44, 45).

Unlike most other text sections in Leviticus, this chapter does not begin with any of the regular introductory formulas. The preceding chapter was set apart from what followed, however, by its concluding formula (25:55). The structure of this chapter, which forms an inclusion, a structure that begins and ends with the same element (here, the self-identification of the speaker, 26:1, 45), also sets it apart from its context.

God placed numerous expectations on his people so that they could maintain or regain holiness as needed, which was a prerequisite for them to be able to approach him in worship. These expectations had been recounted in the previous chapters of Leviticus. This chapter describes both the blessings and benefits that would follow if the expectations were met (26:3-13) and also the punishments and grief that would follow if they were not met (26:14-43). These expectations were part of God's covenant with his people (26:44-45), and there are parallels with other lists of covenant blessings and curses, not only in content, but also in structure. It seems to be human nature that, while a carrot is useful for attracting God's people to obedience, there is more need for the stick to be applied when they are disobedient. This is shown in covenant contexts, where there was less need for blessings for keeping the covenant, which were often fewer (Deut 28:1-14), than for curses for breaking it, which were more (Deut 28:15-68; Josh 24:20), since the latter was a more likely scenario. Prophets regularly referred to these blessing and curses when they were preaching blessing or doom to Israel or the nations. Some examples of this will be cited in the following comments.

The first command (26:1), organized in several sections with three separate verbs describing prohibited actions, forbids worshiping idols (cf. 19:4)—an allusion to the first and second of the Ten Commandments (Exod 20:3; Deut 5:7); it also forbids making physical emblems of the divine—an allusion to the second (Exod 20:4-5a; Deut 5:8-9a). The reason that these things were banned was that Israel needed no other deity, since Yahweh himself was their God, as he reminded them before he gave them the Ten Commandments (Exod 20:2; Deut 5:6). Milgrom (2001:2280) suggests that there was no ban here on physical representations of foreign gods, which would have been covered by the first command, but rather a ban against making physical representations of Yahweh himself (Deut 4:15-18). Any physical representation of Yahweh would not only be insufficient, but potentially diminishing to the "otherness" of the divine.

The Sabbath was to be observed as regulated (26:2)—an allusion to the fourth commandment (Exod 20:8-11; Deut 5:12-15). Holy time must be protected. Israel must also treat the holy space, the sanctuary (19:30), with the same reverence and respect due to God himself (19:14, 32). The latter was not a reference to the Ten Commandments, but did allude to several places in Leviticus where its sanctity could be compromised by improper acts (12:4; 20:3; 21:12, 23). It is not clear why all of the first four of the Ten Commandments were not included here, though they, like all the instructions in these two verses, were to regulate the divine–human relationship rather than the human–human relationships of the following commandments.

Blessings of Obedience. The blessings in this section are cast in the form of promises made by God (cf. e.g., Gen 12:2-3), in which he fulfills his covenant promises to Israel. The blessings are divided into five sections (26:4-5, 6, 7-8, 9-10, 11-12), culminating with the most important: the presence of God himself among his people. They are bracketed by an introduction (26:3) and conclusion (26:13).

The first of God's promises concerns various aspects of agricultural plenty (26:4-5), all of which would follow the first blessing mentioned: much-needed rain at its regular time and season (Deut 28:12; Hos 6:3; Joel 2:23). Unlike Egypt, which depended upon the Nile for its water supply, and Mesopotamia, which used irrigation, Israel, while blessed with some streams (Deut 8:7), was largely dependent upon rainfall that needed to fall at certain times during the year to aid in plowing, planting, and crop growth (Deut 11:14; Ezek 34:26; DOTP 22). If the rain fell, field and tree would yield produce and fruit (cf. Ps 67:6; Ezek 34:27; Zech 8:12).

The various harvests were generally at different times during the year, depending on when the crop ripened. This is shown most clearly by the Gezer calendar, an agricultural calendar from the tenth century BC that is among the oldest examples of Hebrew text available today. It reads, "Two months of ingathering [olives]/two months of sowing [cereals]/two months of late sowing [legumes and vegetables], a month of hoeing weeds [for hay], a month of harvesting barley, a month of harvesting [wheat] and measuring [grain], two months of grape harvesting, a month of ingathering summer fruit" (ABD 1.97). With the promised good rainfall, each harvest would be so plentiful that one harvest would run into the next instead of having the ordinary gap between (cf. Amos 9:13). The provision of food, so necessary for human survival, would not only be sufficient but bountiful (Joel 2:19). There would also be national security (25:18-19; Jer 32:36-37; Ezek 28:26; Zech 14:11), at least on the economic level (26:4-5; see note on 26:5).

Economic security led to the promise of peace (26:6-8). This was to be on three levels: no internal threats, which would make one lose sleep through worry about possible human violence (Hos 2:18); freedom from worry over dangerous wild animals (Ezek 34:28; cf. Judg 14:5; 1 Sam 17:34-35; 1 Kgs 13:24-25; 2 Kgs 2:24); and no incursions from outside by marauding bands. Israel would also be able to take the offense in armed combat through the use of their own swords, with which they would rout and destroy the enemy. A small Israelite troop would be able to best a much larger contingent of the enemy (Deut 28:7).

Human and agricultural reproduction would flourish due to God's good favor (26:9). God himself would bring about the fulfillment of his command to the first couple, to "be fruitful and multiply" (Gen 1:28; 9:1, 7). Through this he would fulfill or follow through on the covenant promises he made, first to Noah, for security from fear (Gen 9:11), and then to the patriarchs, for increase of descendants (Gen 12:2; 17:6, 7, 20; 26:4, 24; 28:3; 35:11; 48:4). Agricultural produce would be so plentiful (26:4-5) that even the increased number of Israelites would not be able to eat it before the next crop came in.

God also promised that his very presence would be with his people in their sanctuary and in their worship (26:11-12). Stated in negative terms, he would not treat them with abhorrence and disgust (cf. 26:30, 44; Jer 14:19). God's presence is positively described in terms of walking to and fro among humanity as he had done at the very beginning of human existence (Gen 3:8; cf. Deut 23:14; 2 Sam 7:7) and as his presence will be in the new Jerusalem (Rev 21:3). He would walk with his people if they would walk with him (26:3). God was establishing the relationship that he had promised his covenant people.

The certainty of these promises was assured in two ways (26:13): (1) by identifying Yahweh himself as the speaker in a clause already quite familiar (e.g., 11:44; 18:2, 4, 30), and (2) by reminding Israel of the great deeds that God had already done for them, bringing her out from Egyptian slavery. This event is broken down into three separate acts: (1) releasing them from Egyptian slavery (Exod 20:2); (2) breaking the yoke—a wooden bar joining two draft animals together, here a symbol of harsh servitude (Deut 28:48; Ezek 34:27); and (3) allowing them to once again walk upright rather than being bowed down under their yoke.

God is communicating that he, not any other deity, is Israel's God; he brought Israel out from Egyptian ownership, so now he owns them. The people were Egypt's slaves, but now they are free because he removed the yoke that bowed them down.

◆   ## 2. Punishments for disobedience (26:14-39)

¹⁴"However, if you do not listen to me or obey all these commands, ¹⁵and if you break my covenant by rejecting my decrees, treating my regulations with contempt, and refusing to obey my commands, ¹⁶I will punish you. I will bring sudden terrors upon you—wasting diseases and burning fevers that will cause your eyes to fail and your life to ebb away. You will plant your crops in vain because your enemies will eat them. ¹⁷I will turn against you, and you will be defeated by your enemies. Those who hate you will rule over you, and you will run even when no one is chasing you!

¹⁸"And if, in spite of all this, you still disobey me, I will punish you seven times over for your sins. ¹⁹I will break your proud spirit by making the skies as unyielding as iron and the earth as hard as bronze. ²⁰All your work will be for nothing, for your land will yield no crops, and your trees will bear no fruit.

²¹"If even then you remain hostile toward me and refuse to obey me, I will inflict disaster on you seven times over for your sins. ²²I will send wild animals that will rob you of your children and destroy your livestock. Your numbers will dwindle, and your roads will be deserted.

²³"And if you fail to learn the lesson and continue your hostility toward me, ²⁴then I myself will be hostile toward you. I will personally strike you with calamity seven times over for your sins. ²⁵I will send armies against you to carry out the curse of the covenant you have broken. When you run to your towns for safety, I will send a plague to destroy you there, and you will be handed over to your enemies. ²⁶I will destroy your food supply, so that ten women will need only one oven to bake bread for their families. They will ration your food by weight, and though you have food to eat, you will not be satisfied.

²⁷"If in spite of all this you still refuse to listen and still remain hostile toward me, ²⁸then I will give full vent to my hostility. I myself will punish you seven times over for your sins. ²⁹Then you will eat the flesh of your own sons and daughters. ³⁰I will destroy your pagan shrines and knock down your places of worship. I will leave your lifeless corpses piled on top of your lifeless idols,* and I will despise you. ³¹I will make your cities desolate and destroy your places of pagan worship. I will take no pleasure in your offerings that should be a pleasing aroma to me. ³²Yes, I myself will devastate your land, and your enemies who come to occupy it will be appalled at what they see. ³³I will scatter you among the nations and bring out my sword against you. Your land will become desolate, and your cities will lie in ruins. ³⁴Then at last the land will enjoy its neglected Sabbath years as it lies desolate while you are in exile in the land of your enemies. Then the land will finally rest and enjoy the Sabbaths it missed. ³⁵As long as the land lies in ruins, it will enjoy the rest you never allowed it to take every seventh year while you lived in it.

³⁶"And for those of you who survive, I will demoralize you in the land of your enemies. You will live in such fear that the sound of a leaf driven by the wind will send you fleeing. You will run as though fleeing from a sword, and you will fall even when no one pursues you. ³⁷Though no one is chasing you, you will stumble over each other as though fleeing from a sword. You will have no power to stand up against your enemies. ³⁸You will die among the foreign nations and be devoured in the land of your enemies. ³⁹Those of you who survive will waste away in your enemies' lands because of their sins and the sins of their ancestors.

26:30 The Hebrew term (literally *round things*) probably alludes to dung.

NOTES

26:14-15 *if you do not listen . . . refusing to obey my commands.* The list of punishments, like that of the blessings in 26:3, also begins with conditions, only there are three of them instead of just one. (The NLT does not mark all these conditions with "if" but groups them together.) The one condition of the blessing section does however contain three elements marked by three verbs.

26:16 *I will punish you.* As a consequence of Israel's disobedience, twice refusing to "do," God himself would respond by "doing" to Israel (lit., "moreover I myself will do this to you"). This serves as an introduction to the following list of consequences to disobedience.

26:21, 23, 24 *remain hostile.* Lit., "walking with X in hostile opposition." "Be hostile" (26:24) and "continue your hostility" (26:23) translate this same idea.

I will inflict disaster on you seven times over for your sins. Refusal to live in God's decrees would increase the punishment to sevenfold "disaster" (lit., "blow" or "plague").

26:26 *destroy your food supply.* Lit., "break the staff of food" on which they would lean for support (see Ezek 4:16; 5:16; 14:13).

26:30 *shrines.* Lit., "sanctuaries." In the Pentateuch, this term is used mainly of the sanctuary of Yahweh (cf. Exod 15:17; Num 19:20), which God at times called "my sanctuary"

(26:2; cf. 19:30; 20:3). This was a deliberate contrast between "my sanctuary," which was legitimate since Yahweh was the one worshiped there, and "your sanctuaries," which were illegitimate since they were Israel's but not God's, implying that they were in fact pagan shrines.

COMMENTARY

Like the promised blessings, the punishment list is divided into five sections (26:16b-17, 18-20, 21-22, 23-26, 27-39), all except the first opened by a conditional indicator ("and if . . .") and each increasing in intensity, as well as in length. These punishments show correspondence with the five promise sections, as noted in the comments below. This section indicates that God fulfilled his covenant promises, not for blessing, but for the opposite, since Israel had not fulfilled her obligations.

The first condition involves not listening to God, which is explained as not doing the commandments (26:14; cf. 26:3c). The second involves rejecting or refusing his decrees (26:15a; cf. 26:3a). The third is despising God's regulations or judgments decided in case law, in contrast to how God would treat Israel as a nation (26:15b). This has no parallel in the preceding section, though it is also explained as entailing not doing God's commands (26:15b). All of these acts of disobedience were a breach of the covenant God had just promised to fulfill (26:9), though here the Sinai covenant with its stipulations was meant by "covenant" rather than the covenants of blessing with Noah and the patriarchs. The conditionality of this and the next sections indicate that grace was still possible, since the "if" did not need to be realized except by the choice of the people (26:21, 23, 27).

If Israel disobeyed, Israel would be visited by blind panic or confusion and by dread disease, which would endanger their life (26:16a; cf. Deut 28:22, 60-61), wearing out their eyes by looking for relief that would not come (26:16b; Deut 28:28, 32; Lam 4:17). Instead of abundant produce (26:4-5), their sowing would be in vain because any harvest would be scavenged by marauding enemies (26:16c). Instead of turning his favor on Israel (26:9), God would turn it away, leaving them in their enemies' power. Rather than routing their enemy with a few (26:7-8), Israel would suffer defeat, retreating in panic for no cause (26:17). Rather than living under a God of blessing (26:11-12), they would suffer domination by antagonists (26:17).

These punishments for sinful disobedience were for the purpose of discipline (26:18-20), intending to drive the people back to obedience—as is clear in this section, which continues the litany, ratcheting up the intensity of punishment sevenfold if the people still would not listen. Instead of breaking the slave's yoke (26:13), God would break Israel's pride in thinking that any of the promised blessings had anything to do with her own accomplishments. They would see that it was God who had provided the plentiful harvests since he would now withhold them. He would do this by making the sky impermeable like iron, not letting the rain get through the sky. This would make the dry ground so hard that the plow and germinating seed would not be able to pierce it (26:19; cf. Deut 28:23; Amos 4:7). All the energy

Israel used in trying to grow crops and tend fruit trees, rather than leading to bumper yields (26:4), would be fruitless, producing nothing (26:20; cf. Deut 11:17; 28:38-40).

Increased disobedience would increase God's punishment sevenfold. Instead of being free from predators (26:6), God would send them against Israel, causing loss of children and livestock (26:22). Instead of having their people increase (26:9), they would be diminished through these predators. If the discipline proved yet ineffective, the pressure would continue to mount, with God responding in kind, "walking in hostile opposition" (see note on 26:21) to Israel, noting that the blow that would befall them came directly from him (26:24). Instead of freedom from warfare (26:6), God would bring destruction by a vengeful sword to destroy Israel for breaking the Sinai covenant (26:24-25). Israel would not be able to hide, even if they went to their fortified cities (26:25; cf. Deut 28:52; 2 Chr 12:5; Jer 4:5). They were still vulnerable to a plague walls could not keep out (26:25). If Israel did not keep the stipulations of the covenant that set it apart for God from other nations, it would be treated just as if it were one of the pagan nations.

One-third of the triad of calamities was famine (26:26; cf. Jer 34:17; Ezek 6:11; Amos 4:6), which would follow when God cut off the food supply. Several examples illustrate the extent of the famine. In an analogy similar to one found elsewhere in the ancient Near East (Milgrom 2001:2314), 10 women, each of whom would have needed her own cooking facilities in normal times, would have so little to bake that a single oven would be sufficient. Even if someone were able to bring them material with which to bake, it would need to be rationed, though there still would be at least some still available. Rather than the promised plenty (26:5), there would not be sufficient bread to make one full (cf. Hos 4:10; Mic 6:14).

One final level of punishment was prepared for Israel if she stayed unrepentant (26:27-39). All other food having been exhausted, Israel would resort to cannibalism—Israelites eating their own children (26:29; cf. Deut 28:53-57; 2 Kgs 6:28-29; Ezek 5:10). Instead of God's living in their midst in his sanctuary (26:11), he would destroy the pagan sanctuaries and implements they had made to replace him with other gods (26:30a; cf. 2 Chr 14:4-5; 34:7; Ezek 6:3). Rather than bringing life, the "corpses" of the lifeless pagan idols would be covered by the corpses of the Israelites who had turned to worship them (26:30b; cf. Deut 28:26; Ezek 6:3-6; Amos 8:3). Yahweh would treat his people with the contempt they deserved, something he promised not to do to the obedient (26:11).

Israel's own cities would become ruins (26:33), its sanctuaries emptied (26:22, 43), and the pleasing odor of her sacrifices no longer acceptable. While loss of habitation was serious, the latter two punishments were theologically more significant. First, the sanctuary was the place where the people were to meet God. Second, among the sacrifices whose aroma needed to be appreciated by God for them to be accepted was the sin offering (4:31). If it were no longer acceptable, forgiveness would no longer be possible, and a correct relationship between the people and God could no longer be restored.

As a final punishment, God promised not only to leave the shrines empty, but also the land itself. Exile such as this was a common punishment for breaking covenant (Deut 28:36, 37, 64; Hos 9:3). The punishment was carried out in the two exiles of the Israelites from Israel in 722 BC and from Judah in 586 BC. Rather than being driven away (26:7), now Israel's enemies would settle in the land as Israel would be resettled among their enemies (26:36). This reflected a practice of the Assyrians and Babylonians by which they dispossessed peoples from one place and replaced them with the dispossessed from other places. The practice, they felt, would cut down on rebellion among conquered peoples since they would not be in their own lands and would find it harder to organize a rebellion.

Israel would be dispersed abroad and not allowed to return by force of its captors' military might (26:33; cf. Jer 19:15). The land and cities would suffer the fate mentioned already in 26:31-32. The reason given for this exile was presented in theological rather than sociopolitical terms (26:34). The land was supposed to benefit from lying fallow during the periodic Sabbath years (25:2-7)—there is no record of Israel's ever observing the jubilee year until God helped them do so through the Exile (2 Chr 36:21). The motivation here seems to be one of compensatory damages for the land; since it was neglected, it needed to be repaid for its losses. While the land was ruined and lying empty, it would be able to enjoy an enforced rest with the people gone.

The people who survived the sword (26:33; cf. Deut 28:62) long enough to live in exile would be psychologically demoralized and fainthearted. Rather than seeing the enemy flee in terror before them (26:8), the Israelites would become so skittish that the smallest unexpected sound would drive them to panic (26:36). Their terror would be such that they clambered over each other to make their escape, even though there was no actual enemy in pursuit. Those who would have been able to walk with head raised high (26:13) would not be able to stand before the enemy. In fact, they would die, not to finally "rest with their fathers," as was desired after a good, long life (cf. 1 Kgs 1:21; 11:21, 43), but rather they would die among foreigners in a foreign and hostile land. At the very end, a few would still remain, even fewer than before, but still in an enemy land. Because they sinned, not obeying God's commandments (26:14-15), and because they were descendants of others who had also disobeyed and sinned, this remnant would rot, wasting away in exile like decaying flesh (Hos 5:12; Zech 14:12). Even so, they were not yet dead; there was still a glimmer of hope, as the next section shows.

◆   ## 3. The covenant remembered (26:40-46)

⁴⁰"But at last my people will confess their sins and the sins of their ancestors for betraying me and being hostile toward me. ⁴¹When I have turned their hostility back on them and brought them to the land of their enemies, then at last their stubborn hearts will be humbled, and they will pay for their sins. ⁴²Then I will remember my covenant with Jacob and my covenant with Isaac and my covenant with Abraham, and I will remember the land. ⁴³For the land must be abandoned to enjoy its years of Sabbath rest as it lies deserted. At last the people will pay for their sins,

for they have continually rejected my regulations and despised my decrees.

⁴⁴"But despite all this, I will not utterly
reject or despise them while they are in
exile in the land of their enemies. I will
not cancel my covenant with them by
wiping them out, for I am the LORD their
God. ⁴⁵For their sakes I will remember
my ancient covenant with their ancestors,

whom I brought out of the land of Egypt
in the sight of all the nations, that I might
be their God. I am the LORD."

⁴⁶These are the decrees, regulations, and
instructions that the LORD gave through
Moses on Mount Sinai as evidence of the
relationship between himself and the Israelites.

NOTES

26:40 *at last my people will confess their sins.* This statement, which introduces the final
section of ch 26, has been viewed in two ways: as conditional, something that might
happen—"if my people will confess their sins" (KJV, NASB, NIV, NRSV); or as indicative
and hence predictive, something that will indeed happen (so NLT, TEV). From the point of
view of the original readers, the former is preferable, since two options still remained open
for them. From a later perspective, whereby one knows "the rest of the story," the latter
option also works well.

26:44-46 The last section anticipated a time in the yet distant future since the text was
presented as being revealed to Israel at Mount Sinai (26:46; cf. 7:38; 25:1; 27:34). The
people had yet to settle into the land, let alone live there long enough to have neglected
its Sabbaths. They had not yet been exiled, and certainly had not yet wasted away there.
Some think these verses were added by a later scribe who, having experienced the Exile,
saw it as a fulfillment of the warning God gave here to his people. This does not preclude
divine inspiration of the scribe, since biblical literature was still being given by God
during the Exile (e.g., Ezekiel) and after it (e.g., Haggai, Zechariah). This is similar to
preachers today who, reading Scripture that was written for an earlier occasion, find
contemporary relevance to their own day and apply the text to the current situation. It
also could have been an insightful anticipation of what, based on fallen human nature,
would happen among God's people who had already, while still at Sinai, showed signs
of apostasy (Exod 32).

COMMENTARY

In spite of the bleak picture painted in 26:14-39, all was not lost. After all, the punishments were conditional, happening only "if" Israel made a decision against God
rather than for him. Though we know by looking back on the life of Israel that the
conditional might better be read as "when" rather than "if" since Israel did disobey,
from the point of view of Moses and his audience, the choice still lay before them.
Even if they were to choose wrongly, God still provided hope for restoration (cf.
Deut 30:1-20). There were two parties to the covenant: Israel and God. If one of the
parties broke the covenant, that did not invalidate it if the other saw it as still valid.
That was ultimately what God did. He remembered the earlier covenant that he had
made with the patriarchs, a covenant in which he made promises without obligation. He also remembered his promises to Israel at Sinai given before he had laid
stipulations upon them (Exod 20:2), promises he could keep even in the face of
their covenant unfaithfulness.

The nature of Israel's sin is described in two ways: betrayal of one's legal obligations and hostility (see 26:40). God himself would act as he said at the beginning of

the punishment section (26:16). He would show his own hostility as he had promised (26:24, 28), bringing them to an enemy land (26:36), but not for their ultimate destruction. Rather, his goal was to drive them to a desire to repent, humbling their stubborn (lit., "uncircumcised") hearts enough to say they were wrong and return to God, paying for their sins by accepting the punishment spelled out earlier in the chapter. When they remembered their covenant obligations, and how they had not met them, God himself would remember and act upon his covenant (26:42), the one with Jacob (Gen 35:9-12), Isaac (Gen 17:19), and Abraham (Gen 15:18-21; 17:4-8; 22:17-18), a covenant in which he promised them blessing. He would also remember the land, that it needed rest, and that through Israel's disobedience (26:15) and subsequent exile, though not meant for good by Israel's enemies, the land would benefit (26:43)

Even in awareness of all of Israel's disobedience, God did not treat her as she had treated him (26:15, 43). She had disavowed the covenant by breaking it (26:15), but God would not do the same. The reason for keeping the covenant is related to the common formula (26:44) by which God identifies himself. He is Yahweh, Israel's God, who neither lies nor changes his mind (1 Sam 15:29; Titus 1:2; Heb 6:18). He also would remember the later, Mosaic covenant, in preparation for which he saved the people from Egypt and committed himself as their God. All this happened in front of the nations, the very ones to whom Israel had been exiled (26:33) and who had seen her terrible punishment (26:38). They would also witness that Israel's God was a covenant keeping God, whose name is Yahweh (Deut 28:10; Mic 7:10), just as he was at the Exodus (Exod 7:5; 8:22; 14:4).

A concluding summary in 26:46 refers to all of the regulations, including the ritual instructions (6:2-4, 7, 18; 7:1, 11), similar in form and content to the conclusion in 7:37-38, where the messenger, Moses, and location, Mount Sinai, are also mentioned. Here, unlike there, the divine–human relationship is especially highlighted. Law and command are important, but they were ultimately given to establish and maintain the relationship.

Promises of good and punishment, blessings and curses, are not exclusive to the Old Testament, but also find a place in the New Testament. Jesus uttered blessings (e.g., Matt 5:2-12), but also pronounced punishments (cf. Matt 11:21-24; 24–25; Mark 13; Luke 21). God is long-suffering, but he is also just, so wrongdoing will eventually be severely dealt with (John 9:39; 16:8-11; Acts 17:30-31; 2 Cor 5:10) if there is not repentance and restoration.

◆ **L. Holiness of Oaths (27:1-34)**
   1. Pledging people (27:1-8)

The LORD said to Moses, [2]"Give the following instructions to the people of Israel. If anyone makes a special vow to dedicate someone to the LORD by paying the value of that person, [3]here is the scale of values to be used. A man between the ages of twenty and sixty is valued at fifty shekels* of silver, as measured by the sanctuary shekel. [4]A woman of that age is valued at thirty shekels* of silver. [5]A boy between the ages of five and twenty is valued at twenty shekels of silver; a girl of that age is valued at ten shekels* of silver. ⁶A boy between the ages of one month and five years is valued at five shekels of silver; a girl of that age is valued at three shekels* of silver. ⁷A man older than sixty is valued

at fifteen shekels of silver; a woman of that age is valued at ten shekels* of silver. ⁸If you desire to make such a vow but cannot afford to pay the required amount, take the person to the priest. He will determine the amount for you to pay based on what you can afford.

27:3 Or *20 ounces* [570 grams]. **27:4** Or *12 ounces* [342 grams]. **27:5** Or *A boy . . . 8 ounces* [228 grams] *of silver; a girl . . . 4 ounces* [114 grams]. **27:6** Or *A boy . . . 2 ounces* [57 grams] *of silver; a girl . . . 1.2 ounces* [34 grams]. **27:7** Or *A man . . . 6 ounces* [171 grams] *of silver; a woman . . . 4 ounces* [114 grams].

NOTES

27:1-2a *The LORD said to Moses, "Give the following instructions to the people of Israel."* A revelation formula opens this new section. God again speaks through his intermediary Moses to all of the Israelites, since the regulations were national (cf. 1:2; 4:2; 7:23, 29) and not limited to the priests (see 6:9, 25; 9:7).

27:2b *If anyone makes a special vow to dedicate someone to the LORD by paying the value of that person.* A conditional particle opens the new section, as is common in Leviticus (e.g., 15:2, 16; 19:20; 22:14; 27:14). It concerns any person (*'ish* [TH376, ZH408] in this case not specifically meaning "male"; cf. Job 38:26), male or female, who made a voluntary vow or promise to God (22:21; cf. 7:16) that a person, whether another or themselves, would be his. Both men and women could make such promises (Num 6:2; 1 Sam 1:11). People could be dedicated to God's service. Some were in this service due to the family into which they were born, such as priests and Levites. Others could be dedicated by parents or others (e.g., Samuel, 1 Sam 1:11; Samson, Judg 13:3-5). These volunteers became Nazirites, usually a temporary, special dedication, though some became Nazirites permanently (Num 6:1-21).

COMMENTARY

This chapter is thematically linked with chapters 25-26 by the concept of redemption, and also to 7:16, where vows and freewill offerings were introduced. It thus brings the book to a close by providing a small retrospective, reminding the people that holiness is ultimately a personal, voluntary choice.

This chapter discusses various things that could be dedicated to God (cf. 7:16), whether people (27:1-8), animals (27:9-13), real estate (27:14-25), or other special dedications (27:26-33). Anything could be dedicated to God, but not everything could be used directly in his service. These things could be evaluated and their worth paid in cash. The same could happen when a dedication was made and the owner later changed his mind. In such a case, cash compensation could be arranged. The value was determined by an objective party so that the dedicator could not make a personal, arbitrary decision regarding things belonging to God.

Valuation was based on a specific measure, a standard "sanctuary shekel" (27:25). Since there was no Bureau of Standards in ancient Israel, there needed to be some commonly agreed upon measures to guard against fraud (Amos 8:5) This was especially important regarding taxes paid to a central authority. These, in the case of Israel, were the sanctuary (5:15; Exod 30:13; 38:24-26; Num 3:47-50) and the palace, with its "royal weight" (2 Sam 14:26). The shekel (though of an unspecified standard) was also used for everyday transactions or measurements that were not under the purview of either of these institutions (e.g., Abraham's purchase of a burial cave, Gen 23:15-16; food prices under a siege, 2 Kgs 7:1, 16-18).

Those dedicated to the Lord received a fixed evaluation by which they were to be redeemed. The valuation of people, determined by age and gender, is laid out in the following table:

AGE	MALE, IN SILVER SHEKELS	FEMALE, IN SILVER SHEKELS
Over 60 years	15	10
20–60 years	50	30
5–20 years	20	10
1 month–5 years	5	3

Age 20 was when men could be called to military duty (cf. Num 1:3), and this age was viewed as starting the prime working years, as reflected by its higher value. Younger people represented potential earning power, so were valued less. Infants were valued least of all since the infant mortality rate was relatively high. The elderly were evaluated lower than most since they had residual rather than potential worth. Value relative to the genders always placed the male higher, most probably based on the physical labor possible. The ratio of value between male and female was greater at ages 5–20, the latter years of which were her peak for childbearing, with its dangers, and child rearing, decreasing her ability for extra work. This was only an economic valuation of human potential, not a statement on intrinsic worth, since everyone was created in God's image and given his creation mandate (Gen 1:27-28) and since everyone was viewed as equal in an earlier assessment made upon Israel (Exod 30:11-16).

The only departure from the set value of persons was in the case of a pledge by a poor person who couldn't afford the valuation. There still needed to be compensation, but the priest had discretion to set a lowered price for this person, showing God's continued grace to the poor (cf. 1:14-17; 5:7; 12:8; 14:21-32).

◆   2. Pledging animals (27:9-13)

9"If your vow involves giving an animal that is acceptable as an offering to the LORD, any gift to the LORD will be considered holy. 10You may not exchange or substitute it for another animal—neither a good animal for a bad one nor a bad animal for a good one. But if you do exchange one animal for another, then both the original animal and its substitute will be considered holy. 11If your vow involves an unclean animal—one that is not acceptable as an offering to the LORD—then you must bring the animal to the priest. 12He will assess its value, and his assessment will be final, whether high or low. 13If you want to buy back the animal, you must pay the value set by the priest, plus 20 percent.

COMMENTARY

Animals were a subcategory of living things that could be dedicated to God. Some were clean and suitable for sacrifice (cattle, sheep, and goats), while others were not (cf. ch 11). Each needed different regulations. There were three different possibilities concerning these animals: They could be sacrificed, they could be substituted for another animal, or they could be compensated for by a cash payment. Each possibility needed some regulation.

Dedicated clean animals were reserved for sanctuary use as either burnt (Num 15:3) or peace (7:16; 22:21) offerings, the latter being available for the priest to eat. The Israelite was not to exchange the dedicated animal for one of another species (i.e., a sheep for a bull), nor were they to substitute an animal for another of the same species (27:33; cf. Ezek 48:14). The former was completely banned, possibly because the various acceptable animal species had already been established earlier (chs 1-7). The latter seems to have been allowed, since it would not be enforceable apart from the honesty of the offerer (cf. Mal 1:13-14, addressing this type of fraud). If one wanted to make a substitute, possibly of a better or unblemished animal for a blemished one, one could do so, though at the cost of having them both taken for divine use.

An unclean animal, one not fit for some sacrificial use, might also have been dedicated. This could have been one from the list in chapter 11, or it could be a blemished animal. The latter were apparently acceptable for some offerings and could be eaten (11:40), but could not be used in fulfilling a vow (22:21), which is the case here. In this situation, their worth was determined by the priest, whose decision was final. This value plus a 20 percent surcharge for removing the animal from divine ownership was given to the priest in compensation for the food provision of which he was deprived.

◆   3. Pledging property (27:14-25)

¹⁴"If someone dedicates a house to the LORD, the priest will come to assess its value. The priest's assessment will be final, whether high or low. ¹⁵If the person who dedicated the house wants to buy it back, he must pay the value set by the priest, plus 20 percent. Then the house will again be his.

¹⁶"If someone dedicates to the LORD a piece of his family property, its value will be assessed according to the amount of seed required to plant it—fifty shekels of silver for a field planted with five bushels of barley seed.* ¹⁷If the field is dedicated to the LORD in the Year of Jubilee, then the entire assessment will apply. ¹⁸But if the field is dedicated after the Year of Jubilee, the priest will assess the land's value in proportion to the number of years left until the next Year of Jubilee. Its assessed value is reduced each year. ¹⁹If the person who dedicated the field wants to buy it back, he must pay the value set by the priest, plus 20 percent. Then the field will again be legally his. ²⁰But if he does not want to buy it back, and it is sold to someone else, the field can no longer be bought back. ²¹When the field is released in the Year of Jubilee, it will be holy, a field specially set apart* for the LORD. It will become the property of the priests.

²²"If someone dedicates to the LORD a

field he has purchased but which is not part of his family property, ²³the priest will assess its value based on the number of years left until the next Year of Jubilee. On that day he must give the assessed value of the land as a sacred donation to the LORD.

²⁴In the Year of Jubilee the field must be returned to the person from whom he purchased it, the one who inherited it as family property. ²⁵(All the payments must be measured by the weight of the sanctuary shekel,* which equals twenty gerahs.)

27:16 Hebrew *50 shekels* [20 ounces, or 570 grams] *of silver for a homer* [182 liters] *of barley seed.*
27:21 The Hebrew term used here refers to the complete consecration of things or people to the LORD, either by destroying them or by giving them as an offering; also in 27:28, 29.   27:25 Each shekel was about 0.4 ounces [11 grams] in weight.

NOTES

27:14 *If someone dedicates a house to the LORD.* This new section begins with a new conditional marker (*ki* [TH3588, ZH3954]), referring to a situation where someone might have dedicated (*qadash* [TH6942, ZH7727]) a house. The terminology differs from that of a "vow" (*neder* [TH5088, ZH5624]), which was something promised ahead of time that would be given at some time in the future, while a dedication took effect as soon as it was spoken; it immediately belonged to God (22:2-3; Exod 28:38).

27:25 *the sanctuary shekel.* All of the financial calculations were based on the "sanctuary shekel" (cf. 27:3). This was explained for the uninitiated as being equivalent to 20 *gerah* [TH1626, ZH1743] (Exod 30:13; Num 3:47; 18:16; Ezek 45:12), with a *gerah* equal to approximately 0.5 grams.

COMMENTARY

Another possession of economic value that could be dedicated to God was real property, either a house (27:14-15) or agricultural land (27:16-25). The latter fell into two categories, one's own family property (27:16-21) and property bought from another family (27:22-25). Since each would be treated differently at jubilee, each needed separate regulations.

The property was to be evaluated by the priest, and his valuation was nonnegotiable (27:14). Redemption was allowed, at the valuation price plus the 20 percent surcharge. There was no mention of what would happen if the house was not usable by a priest. It probably would have been sold (cf. 27:20), with the proceeds, though probably without a surcharge, going to the priest.

Land dedicated to divine use had a stipulation not relevant in the case of houses (27:16): It would revert to its original owner at the Year of Jubilee (25:8-25). The laws thus needed to be more detailed in order to take this into consideration. The first option was for land that was a family holding (cf. 25:10, 13) being consecrated to God. The assessment of its value had numerous steps. First its size was determined, based not on a measure of physical area as we might measure today, but on the amount of grain it took to sow the field (27:16). The full price of a field of a size seedable with three to five bushels was reckoned at 50 shekels. Thus, larger or smaller holdings could be calculated in relation to it. This was a more certain way of reckoning advance payment, since a determination of what actual field production would be, which was the basis of an actual sale (25:24-27), would be only a guess. If the dedication should correspond exactly with the jubilee year, a time of celebration in which property was expected to change hands anyway, the entire value would be set, plus the 20 percent surcharge, if one wanted to redeem it. At any other time, the value of the land would be determined by counting the number of years left until the next jubilee and making a payment of one shekel for each remaining year—still using the special "sanctuary shekel" (27:25). After the payment, the land immediately reverted to its ancestral owner (27:19).

An owner might have been unable or unwilling to redeem his dedicated land (27:20). If so, it could be sold to someone else at the established price but without a surcharge. However, since it had been consecrated to divine use and had not been redeemed, it would not revert to the original owner at jubilee. The purchaser would lose it, and it stayed permanently under the control of the priesthood, just as if it had been made an exclusive and irreversible dedication in the first place (27:20-21).

A natural progression from the last law, which touched on land sale, was to ask about bought land that was then consecrated to God (27:22-24). What would happen to it at the jubilee? It was to be given a valuation by the priest proportionate to the number of years until the next jubilee, and payment was to be made based on the value determined at that time, if the owner (possibly either the original one or the one who subsequently bought it) wanted to redeem it. At jubilee, it would not stay in the hand of the priesthood, but would return to its original owner, who had not made the dedication himself and therefore would not suffer loss because of it.

◆   ## 4. Special pledges (27:26-34)

26"You may not dedicate a firstborn animal to the LORD, for the firstborn of your cattle, sheep, and goats already belong to him. 27However, you may buy back the firstborn of a ceremonially unclean animal by paying the priest's assessment of its worth, plus 20 percent. If you do not buy it back, the priest will sell it at its assessed value.

28"However, anything specially set apart for the LORD—whether a person, an animal, or family property—must never be sold or bought back. Anything devoted in this way has been set apart as holy, and it belongs to the LORD. 29No person specially set apart for destruction may be bought back. Such a person must be put to death.

30"One tenth of the produce of the land, whether grain from the fields or fruit from the trees, belongs to the LORD and must be set apart to him as holy. 31If you want to buy back the LORD's tenth of the grain or fruit, you must pay its value, plus 20 percent. 32Count off every tenth animal from your herds and flocks and set them apart for the LORD as holy. 33You may not pick and choose between good and bad animals, and you may not substitute one for another. But if you do exchange one animal for another, then both the original animal and its substitute will be considered holy and cannot be bought back."

34These are the commands that the LORD gave through Moses on Mount Sinai for the Israelites.

NOTES
27:26 In the Hebrew text, a new section begins here with a restrictive particle, "however" (so NASB, NIV, NRSV; cf. 27:28, NLT). It is followed by a statement telling the Israelites that there were some exceptions to the previous regulations.

27:28 However. This is marked as another subsection by means of the same restrictive particle as occurred in 27:26 (left untranslated in the NLT).

COMMENTARY

Some things that might be dedicated to divine use needed special consideration for various reasons. These special cases close the book of Leviticus. The first case pertained to firstborn animals and humans (27:26), which already belonged to God (Exod 13:2; 22:30; Num 3:13), just like the first of the crops did (23:17). Since they were not the property of the owner of the parent animals, they could not be especially dedicated to God since he already owned them (cf. Exod 34:19-20). Firstborn unclean, and thus non-sacrificeable, animals could be bought back through paying a cash assessment plus a 20 percent surcharge sale to someone else, or by substituting an animal acceptable for sacrifice (27:27; cf. Exod 13:13). Some of them, such as the mule or camel, even though not allowed as sacrifice, could still be of service to the sanctuary, as draft animals, for instance.

Some things were permanently reserved for God's use. They, unlike the firstborn unclean animals, could not be redeemed or bought back (27:28). These could be in any of the categories already mentioned: human, animal, or family holding (lumping together houses and lands). To make this exclusivity irrevocable, a person or animal so dedicated was to be put to death as a kind of burnt offering to God (cf. Deut 13:16-17; Judg 19–20). The restriction of things for God's use alone is clear, but its application to humans is more problematic, at least based on the amount of information available within the text itself. In Exodus 22:20, Israelites who turned in worship to gods other than the Lord were to suffer this fate. This could well be the same understanding here in Leviticus, though it is not specifically spelled out. Israel was not to use human sacrifice (cf. Deut 12:29-31; Isa 57:3-6; 66:3), but capital punishment was allowed. This suggests that dedication of humans to God leading to their death in the context of Leviticus fits into this latter category.

This was done numerous times in war, destroying the captives and all they had (e.g., Deut 13:16-17). The only time in the Bible when this occurred outside the context of war was in Ezra 10:8, where possessions were destroyed, but the people were banished rather than killed. Since this was such a serious step, and so little mention was made of it, this special kind of completely setting people apart for God must have been carried out very rarely, especially in light of God's abhorrence of human sacrifice. Property and livestock were more readily handled in this way (cf. 2 Sam 8:10-11).

A much more easily realizable practice is the tithe, setting apart one-tenth of the field produce for God (27:30-33). It could be redeemed for full value plus the 20 percent surcharge, which the priests could use to obtain their own food supplies elsewhere. The same held true for animals eligible to sacrifice, herds (cattle) and flocks (sheep and goats). A tenth of these belonged to God, and a way was given to ensure that the choice of these was arbitrary, not rigged in favor of either the sanctuary or the owner. A person's animals would be made to pass before him (lit., "under [the shepherd's] staff"; cf. Jer 33:13; Ezek 20:37), and he would count off every tenth animal as it passed, no matter what its condition—hardy or frail, whole or maimed. Substitution would again prove ineffective, since both the original and the substitute were liable for sacrifice.

Dedication of a tenth—the tithe—was not a new idea (Gen 14:18-20; 28:22); it was expected in addition to the customary and regular offerings (Deut 12:6, 11). Since it was a visible act, it became a touchstone to determine one's spirituality, eventually turning a good regulation into legalism (cf. Matt 23:23). The same misuse developed for that which could be placed permanently under God's control (27:28). Some people used this as an excuse not to meet their own fundamental duty of honoring their parents (Matt 15:5-6).

The chapter, and the book, closes with a summary statement (27:34), harking back to that in 26:46. Moses was again the intermediary between God and his people, Israel on Mount Sinai. Supplementing the earlier mentioned "decrees, regulations, and instructions," the author here adds "commands" (cf. the use of the verb in the Hebrew of 6:9 [2]; 7:36-38), thereby providing a full description of the nature of the entire revelation of God's will in the book of Leviticus. The entire book is comprised of covenant stipulations concerning how to live as a holy people in correct relationship with a holy God. It is here concluded by its own colophon (see the earlier discussion of 7:37-38).

BIBLIOGRAPHY

Baker, David W.
1980 Further Examples of the *waw explicativum*. *Vetus Testamentum* 30:129-136.
1986 Biblical Colophons: Gevaryahu and Beyond. Pp. 29-61 in *Studies in the Succession Narrative: OTWSA 27 (1984) and OTWSA (1985): Old Testament Essays.* Editor, W. C. van Wyk. Pretoria, South Africa: Ou-Testamentiese Werkgemeenskap in Suid-Afrika.
1987 Leviticus 1-7 and the Punic Tariffs: A Form Critical Comparison. *Zeitschrift für die alttestamentliche Wissenschaft* 99:188-198.
2006 *Joel, Obadiah, Malachi.* New International Version Application Commentary. Grand Rapids: Zondervan.

Bright, John
1967 *The Authority of the Old Testament.* Nashville: Abingdon.

Budd, Philip J.
1996 *Leviticus.* New Century Bible Commentary. Grand Rapids: Eerdmans.

Carmichael, Calum M.
1997 *Law, Legend, and Incest in the Bible: Leviticus 18-20.* Ithaca: Cornell University Press.

Cohen, Mark E.
1993 *The Cultic Calendars of the Ancient Near East.* Bethesda: CDL Press.

Day, John
1989 *Molech: A God of Human Sacrifice in the Old Testament.* Cambridge: Cambridge University Press.

Demarest, Gary W.
1990 *Leviticus.* The Communicator's Commentary. Dallas: Word.

Douglas, Mary
2000 *Leviticus as Literature.* Oxford: Oxford University Press.

Fleming, Daniel E.
1992 *The Installation of Baal's High Priestess at Emar.* Harvard Semitic Studies 42. Atlanta: Scholars Press.
2000 *Time at Emar: The Cultic Calendar and the Rituals from the Diviner's Archive.* Winona Lake: Eisenbrauns.

Gagnon, Robert A. J.
2001 *The Bible and Homosexual Practice: Texts and Hermeneutics.* Nashville: Abingdon.

Gerstenberger, Erhard S.
1996 *Leviticus.* Translator, Douglas W. Stott. Old Testament Library. Louisville: Westminster/John Knox.

Goldingay, John
2003 *Old Testament Theology: Israel's Gospel,* vol. 1. Downers Grove: InterVarsity.

Harris, R. Laird
1990 Leviticus in *The Expositor's Bible Commentary,* vol. 2. Editor, Frank E. Gaebelein. Grand Rapids: Zondervan.

Harrison, R. K.
1980 *Leviticus: An Introduction and Commentary.* Tyndale Old Testament Commentary. Downers Grove: InterVarsity.

Hartley, John E.
1992 *Leviticus.* Word Biblical Commentary 4. Dallas: Word.

Hulse, E. V.
1975 The Nature of Biblical 'Leprosy' and the Use of Alternative Medical Terms in Modern Translations of the Bible. *Palestine Exploration Quarterly* 107:87-105.

Kidner, Derek
1971 *Leviticus, Numbers, Deuteronomy.* Scripture Union Bible Study Books. Grand Rapids: Eerdmans.

King, Philip J., and Lawrence E. Stager
2001 *Life in Biblical Israel.* Louisville: Westminster/John Knox.

Kitchen, K. A.
2003 *On the Reliability of the Old Testament.* Grand Rapids: Eerdmans.

Kiuchi, N.
1987 *The Purification Offering in the Priestly Literature.* Sheffield: Journal for the Study of the Old Testament Press.

2007 *Leviticus.* Apollos Old Testament Commentary. Downers Grove: InterVarsity.

Lawrence of the Resurrection, Brother
1999 *The Practice of the Presence of God.* Nashville: Thomas Nelson.

LaSor, William Sanford, D. A. Hubbard, and F. W. Bush
1996 *Old Testament Survey: The Message, Form, and Background of the Old Testament,* 2nd ed. Grand Rapids: Eerdmans.

Levine, Baruch A.
1989 *Leviticus.* The JPS Torah Commentary. Philadelphia: Jewish Publication Society.

Lewis, C. S.
1970 The Humanitarian Theory of Punishment. Pp. 287–294 in *God in the Dock: Essays on Theology and Ethics.* Editor, Walter Hooper. Grand Rapids: Eerdmans.

Milgrom, Jacob
1991 *Leviticus 1-16: A New Translation with Introduction and Commentary.* Anchor Bible 3. New York: Doubleday.

2000 *Leviticus 17-22: A New Translation with Introduction and Commentary.* Anchor Bible 3. New York: Doubleday.

2001 *Leviticus 23-27: A New Translation with Introduction and Commentary.* Anchor Bible 3. New York: Doubleday.

Moon, Gary W.
1997 *Homesick for Eden: A Soul's Journey to Joy.* Ann Arbor: Vine.

Mulholland, M. Robert
1985 *Shaped by the Word: The Power of Scripture in Spiritual Formation.* Nashville: Upper Room.

Nihan, Christophe
2003 The Death of Nadab and Abihu and the Priestly Legislation on Perfume Offering: Leviticus 10 in the Context of the Final Editing of Leviticus. Paper presented at the annual meeting of the Society of Biblical Literature, Biblical Law section. Atlanta, GA, 2003.

Noordtzij, A.
1982 *Leviticus.* Bible Student's Commentary. Translator, Raymond Togtman. Grand Rapids: Zondervan.

North, Gary
1994 *Leviticus: An Economic Commentary.* Tyler, TX: Institute for Christian Economics.

Noth, Martin
1965 *Leviticus: A Commentary.* Old Testament Library. Philadelphia: Westminster.

Ostrer, B. S.
2003 Birds of Leper: Statistical Assessment of Two Commentaries. *Zeitschrift für die alttestamentliche Wissenschaft* 115:348-361.

Perdue, Leo G.
1997 *Families in Ancient Israel.* Louisville: Westminster/John Knox.

Péter-Contesse, René, and John Ellington
1990 *A Translator's Handbook on Leviticus.* New York: United Bible Societies.

Rooker, Mark F.
2000 *Leviticus.* New American Commentary. Nashville: Broadman & Holman.

Ross, Allen P.
2002 *Holiness to the Lord: A Guide to the Exposition of the Book of Leviticus.* Grand Rapids: Baker.

Ruane, Nicole J.
2005 Male without Blemish: Sacrifice and Gender Ideologies in Priestly Law. Ph.D. diss., Union Theological Seminary.

Smith, D. E.
2003 *From Symposium to Eucharist: The Banquet in the Early Christian World.* Minneapolis: Fortress.

Speiser, E. A.
1967 *Oriental and Biblical Studies: Collected Writings of E. A. Speiser.* Editors, J. J. Finkelstein and Moshe Greenberg. Philadelphia: University of Pennsylvania Press.

Swartley, Willard
1983 *Slavery, Sabbath, War, and Women: Case Issues in Biblical Interpretation.* Scottdale, PA: Herald.

Toorn, Karel van der
1999 *Dictionary of Deities and Demons in the Bible.* 2nd ed. Grand Rapids: Eerdmans.

Waltke, Bruce K., and Michael O'Connor
1990 *An Introduction to Biblical Hebrew Syntax.* Winona Lake, IN: Eisenbrauns.

Warning, Wilfried
1999 *Literary Artistry in Leviticus.* Leiden: Brill.

Webb, William J.
2001 *Slaves, Women & Homosexuals: Exploring the Hermeneutics of Cultural Analysis.* Downers Grove: InterVarsity.

Wenham, Gordon J.
1979 *The Book of Leviticus.* New International Commentary on the Old Testament. Grand Rapids: Eerdmans.

Wiersbe, Warren
1994 *Be Holy.* Wheaton: Scripture Books.

Numbers

DALE A. BRUEGGEMANN

INTRODUCTION TO
Numbers

NUMBERS TELLS A STORY that should never have happened, a story that warns against the rejection of God's plans. Nonetheless, the story reveals that God remains faithful to his gracious promise, even when his people neglect the means and aims of grace.

AUTHOR

Repeated references say that God spoke to Moses.[1] With regard to the stages of the journey we even read that Moses "kept a *written* record" (33:2, emphasis mine). In addition to eyewitness material, Numbers makes use of identifiable sources, such as *The Book of the Wars of the* LORD (21:14-15), an Amorite song (21:27-30), and the Balaam oracles (chs 23–24). Finally, just as we see in Deuteronomy, Numbers includes some material that most likely comes from a later hand: It's unlikely that Moses took a long look back at his own death and burial (Deut 34, especially v. 10) or that Moses personally described himself as superior to all men in humility (12:3). Settling questions as to how much material and organization comes from "another hand" is not an aim of this commentary, which follows the New Testament in referring to material from the Pentateuch as Mosaic (e.g., Matt 8:4; 19:7; Luke 16:29, 31; 24:27, 44; John 1:17, 45; 5:45).

DATE AND OCCASION OF WRITING

The traditional view of Mosaic authorship puts the production of the book—or at least its substance—in the mid-second millennium BC, but the literary diversity in Numbers puts it under the source critic's lens. In the late 1800s, J. Wellhausen set out a hypothesis that identified documentary or literary sources that had been combined together into the Pentateuch. He labeled the sources J, E, D, and P as shorthand for their differing literary characteristics: "J" for the source that speaks early and often of the name Yahweh (*Jahweh* in German); "E" for the source that uses the title Elohim (that is, "God") more than it uses Yahweh; "D" for the Deuteronomist, which seemed different in style on the whole; and "P" for Priestly, referring to material that seemed to reflect the concerns of the priesthood, including details about religious ritual and the Aaronic line. Thus, the source-critical consensus speaks of a book that got its final shape and perhaps even its substance in the postexilic period, though some date even the supposedly late "P" as preexilic (Hurvitz 1974;

Kaufmann 1961:153-211; Milgrom 1983:65-81; Milgrom 1989:xxxii-xxxv). Rejecting this fragmentation, Rendtorff and Noth see the Pentateuch's development in
terms of larger blocks of traditions passed along as self-contained entities:[2] the
twelve-tribe system (Noth 1930; Noth 1968), ordering the camp (Kuschke 1961),
Levitical traditions (Möhlenbrink 1934; Gunneweg 1965), murmuring traditions
(Coats 1968; Fritz 1970), the Balaam cycle (Gross 1974; Mowinckel 1930), allotment of the land (Alt 1953; Noth 1972; Weippert 1973), and the conquest
traditions (Weippert 1971). E. W. Davies sees so many connections between
diverse elements that he even wonders if they *ever* had an independent existence
(1995b:xlvii).

   All of these suggested self-contained entities directly relate to the situation that
would have prevailed during Moses's leadership in the wilderness; conversely, many
of them would have become irrelevant anachronisms for the postexilic community
if they were only learning of them for the first time, rather than remembering them
as a part of their nation's spotty history of covenant faithfulness. We should not go
far wrong in identifying Moses as the predominant author of the Pentateuchal
material, estimating that this material would have been combined into the five
books by the time of the monarchy, and characterizing any subsequent work
(e.g., 12:3; Deut 34) as editorial rather than authorial.

AUDIENCE

For the community of Israel facing the promise and demands of the conquest, this
message about their predecessors would have prompted them to stay with God's
well-ordered plan, to follow his chosen leaders, and to count on his protection and
blessing. The wilderness complaints and wanderings, followed by the death of a
whole generation of would-be conquerors, should have been a potent warning
against repeating that generation's folly. That generation became the Old Testament
byword for failing to enter rest because of unbelief (Ps 95:8-11). And that generation's story still names us as its audience for both its warnings and encouragement
(Heb 3:8-11; 4:3-7).

CANONICITY AND TEXTUAL HISTORY

The Masoretic Hebrew text is mostly problem free. Uncertainty arises only in a few
poetic portions of chapter 21 and in the Balaam oracles of chapters 23–24. The Septuagint variants tend to be name spellings, although there are a few changes in verse
order.[3] The Qumran texts yield little in the way of variant readings, and when they
do, they show an affinity for the Septuagint or the expansionistic and harmonistic
Samaritan Pentateuch.[4] The Masoretic Text generally has the preferred reading.

   All Masoretic texts divide the Torah into five books, and the Talmud speaks of the
five books of the Torah.[5] Numbers itself is sometimes called "the Fifth regarding the
Musterings" for its place among the five and for its focus on registering the military
and Levitical corps. Olson suggests that the varied length of these books indicates
that they did not result from a division to split the Pentateuch into even units for

fitting them on scrolls.[6] Indeed, the books generally include something like an introduction and conclusion.[7]

The place of Numbers in the Pentateuch assured it of unquestioned canonical recognition. The New Testament puts forth the principle that all Scripture is useful to teach, correct, and equip (2 Tim 3:16-17). Accordingly, Paul used Israel's sins in the wilderness to warn against immorality and grumbling (Rom 15:4; 1 Cor 10:1-11), and the writer of Hebrews used the wilderness story as a warning to Christians (Heb 3:6-4:13). At least one commentator has voiced a sad epitaph for the first generation in the wilderness: "Numbers is a book that need not have been!" (Philip 1993:23). May we read this book with profit, so that its wandering message of doom need not be written over our own failures in walking with the Lord.

LITERARY STYLE

Title. The title *Numbers* (cf. LXX *Arithmoi* and Vulgate *Numeri*) reflects the book's many itemized lists (1:20-46; 3:15-51; 7:10-83; 16:49; 25:9; 26:5-51; 28:1-29:40; 31:32-52; 34:1-29). Hebrew traditions title it *bemidbar* [TH871.2/4057, ZH928/4497] ("in the wilderness"), from the book's geography; *wayedaber* [TH2050.1/1696, ZH2256/1819] ("and he said"), from the book's first words; and *khomesh hapequdim* [TH6485, ZH7212] ("the fifth regarding the registered ones"), denoting the book's inclusion as "one fifth" of the five "books" of the Torah and referring to its military and Levitical counts.

Narrative Structure. If there's any book in the Pentateuch that displays narrative tension, it is the book of Numbers. The very fact of its starting off with a military registration injects some degree of tension into the narrative. The repeated warnings against unauthorized encroachment on the holy things add to it. The book sets up the people for what looks to be a successful journey to conquer their Promised Land. But complications arise, as does conflict between the people and their leaders—and thus with the God who appointed those leaders (chs 11-20). This meant death for that first generation. The book also ends with a note of tension regarding whether the new generation will obey and inherit the land or repeat their fathers' sins and failure.

Characterization. The Lord and his servant Moses are the two dominant characters. The Lord's dominant action in Numbers is speech, which is nearly always to Moses, to whom he provides instruction for the nation. He backs up that speech with judgment when the people disobey, but he also follows through with repeated responses to Moses's intercession by mitigating his initial plans for judgment and forgiving the people.

Moses's character receives the narrator's strong affirmation in many ways: The narrator records God's own approval of his servant (12:7), which he prefaces with a note that Moses was "more humble than any other person on earth" (12:3). He repeatedly records Moses's obedience to the divine command[8] and emphasizes Moses's indispensable role as intercessor.[9] Second only to the the words of the Lord himself, Moses's speech dominates the book. Nonetheless, the book allows us a glimpse of Moses's failure (20:1-13; 27:12-14; cf. Deut 3:23-26).

The people's character is ambiguous. They start out with ready and exact obedience, although even then the golden calf incident is looming in the recent background. But then they lapse into chronic grumbling, which dooms them. Nonetheless, a second generation arises, who once again look like a redeemable people.

MAJOR THEMES

God's Justice and Mercy. God lived among his people in fiery, smoking pillars of glory (9:15-23). When his people sinned, he disciplined them (11:1-3; 21:6; 25:1-5, 6-13), including their leaders: Miriam (12:10), the scouts (14:36-38), the Levites (ch 16), Aaron, and even Moses (20:12). But God's merciful purpose prevailed, both in response to Moses's repeated intercession and as the goal of his unchanging purpose for Israel (32:10-12).

Rebellion and Faithlessness. Israel started out as an army marching on the Promised Land, but rebellion turned them into a wandering rabble who shuffled off to desert graves. This established a warning for the rest of Israel's history. Sometimes the warning might contain a positive note about Israel's response to God in those years (Jer 2:2), but more often the emphasis would fall on God's faithfulness contrasted to Israel's faithlessness (Pss 78:18; 95:8-10; 106; Ezek 20).

Priests and Levites. Exodus refers to Aaron as a Levite and to the Levites as priests (Exod 4:14; 6:16-25; 32:25-29), only hinting at a Levitical order (Exod 38:21-31). Even this hint presupposes Ithamar's appointment as head of the Levites, which surfaces only in Numbers (4:28). In Numbers, the priests remain on top of the hierarchy, with Levites functioning as auxiliary personnel (1:47-54; 3:1-4:49; 16:1-18:32; 35:1-8).

Moses as the Prophet Par Excellence. Moses's significance is hard to overestimate, even though he was flesh and blood—in fact, sometimes all too human (20:8-13). He was the matchless prophet with regard to the immediacy and quality of revelation he mediated (12:6-8), and he was the vital interceding prophet.[10] In spite of this, Moses did not reserve a sole claim on the prophetic gift; rather, he wished for a democratization of it (11:25-29; cf. Joel 2:28-32; Acts 2:17-21).

Large Numbers in the Book. The traditional approach has been to take the large numbers in the book of Numbers at face value. But most recent commentators think these numbers improbable, referring to both extrabiblical evidence and intra-biblical tensions with such large population figures. The figures of over 600,000 fighting men (1:46; 26:51) could indicate a total wilderness population in excess of two million. The objection that it would be impossible to feed that many people in the wilderness might be answered by the quite biblical assertion, "It took a miracle." Notes that camping and marching arrangements for that many would be impossible bear more weight, given the impossibility of squeezing millions of people into some of the oases mentioned in the itinerary. Indeed, commentators estimating Israel's population say these figures are considerably larger than those reached even during Israel's late monarchy (E. W. Davies 1995a:449 n. 3 citing Gottwald 1979:51).

Gleason Archer disputes archaeological arguments that Canaan never supported such a large population that early, and he maintains that armies were indeed this large in the ancient Near East.[11] If we look to later population figures, past archaeologists have estimated eighth-century Judah's population at about 250,000 (Albright 1963a:105 n. 118), suggesting a population in both kingdoms of less than one million (de Vaux 1961:66); and other figures estimate Palestine's population in the second half of the Iron Age as less than 500,000 (McCown 1947; Broshi and Finkelstein 1992). These lower population figures derive from estimates of the available water and land resources and of habitable floor space (Wilkinson 1974; Zorn 1994). Still, a conservative response might insist that we reassess the ancient Near Eastern evidence, giving more weight to the statistics in ancient written records—especially the biblical record, which gives higher population counts to Israel, not only during the Exodus and wilderness wanderings (1:46; 26:51; Exod 12:37; 38:26), but during the monarchy as well (2 Sam 24:9; 1 Chr 21:5; 2 Chr 13:3; 17:14-18).

There is another set of problems with these large numbers that reinterpreting archaeological assessments can't change: These large numbers also cause tension with intra-biblical data.

1. E. W. Davies (1995a:167) wonders how a small clan of 70 (Gen 46:27; Exod 1:5) would have grown so dramatically in around 400 years. He thinks growth to about 10,000 would be more reasonable. But Whitelaw calculates that if Jacob's sons and grandsons had four male descendants each, they would have grown to 835,584 in seven generations (1939:4.2166), fulfilling Deuteronomy 10:22.

2. How could only two midwives have served such a large population (Exod 1:15)? But this isn't a problem if Shiphrah and Puah spoke before the pharaoh on behalf of a full cadre of midwives. For that matter, the view that there were only two functioning midwives would remain a problem even for the much reduced population figures that various solutions suggest (e.g., 10,000–140,000).

3. How do such large figures square with other known army and population counts in the biblical record itself? The Transjordan tribes of Reuben, Gad, and half of Manasseh together contributed only 40,000 to conquest efforts west of the Jordan, although their combined military strength in the final count in Numbers ran to 110,580 (26:5-51; Josh 4:12-13). But this may indicate that their entire force wasn't tasked to this fight, either because only elite shock troops went (see note on 32:17) or because these tribes showed less than wholesome enthusiasm for their commitment to help the conquest west of the Jordan (see commentary at 32:28-32).

Early in the period of the judges, Dan looked for new territory. So they first sent out a group of five scouts (Judg 18), then a group of 600 to capture the territory

(Judg 18:16), although their last wilderness count gave them 64,000 troops (26:43). But this was probably a limited response from just those clans (Judg 18:11) that planned to move away from their tribal allotment (Block 1999:493-515).

Counts for Benjamin, Ephraim, Manasseh, Naphtali, Zebulun, and Issachar total 301,000 in the last Numbers census but 40,000 in Judges (ch 26; Judg 5:8). But unlike Numbers, the number in Judges doesn't purport to be a subset of any troop count; indeed, it's in the richly figurative song of Deborah and Barak.

4. The total number of firstborn children (cf. Num 3:43) appears too small for the overall figures. The number of males over age twenty, 603,550, divided by the 22,273 firstborn equals 27 sons per father, even without the large number who would have been under the age of twenty or not "able to go to war" (1:3). If you add the female offspring in this same age category, assuming a number equal to that of the males, you get 54 children per father. The average does decrease if we think in terms of a polygamous society and count every firstborn of a *woman* (3:12) instead of the firstborn from the male head of the larger polygamous household. If there were 44,546 mothers[12] among the Israelites, and there were approximately the same number of women over twenty as there were men over twenty (i.e., 600,000), that would imply the unlikely conclusion that only one in fourteen women of marriageable age had any children.

5. The high count doesn't fit the description of Israel as too few to conquer and hold a land (Exod 23:29; Deut 7:7, 22). One might reassess ancient Near Eastern evidence and conclude that even though Israel fielded 600,000 troops, the nations Israel faced fielded even larger armies. But surely 600,000 troops drawn from a population of over two million ought to have been able to keep the land from becoming "desolate" and handle any dangers that "wild animals" posed (Exod 23:29; Deut 7:22).

Suggestions for solutions to this population question include rhetorical explanations, historical explanations, and philological explanations. Three rhetorical explanations show up in discussions of these large numbers:

A. A century ago, Holzinger tried to explain the totals in 1:46 and 26:51 as gematria—the use of Hebrew letters as representative of numbers and vice versa. For 603,550 in Numbers 1, he said the number represented by the Hebrew letters used in "community of Israel" (1:2) added up to 603. He suggested similar but more complex and highly doubtful possibilities for the number 550.[13] For 601,730 (26:51), he claimed that 601 derived from the letters in "all the ringleaders" (25:4) and that 730 represented another phrase, which he conjectured.[14] Few scholars have accepted this approach.[15] Indeed, the problems are many. E. W. Davies mentions three: It doesn't explain the numbers for each tribe, the ways of calculating 550 and 730 are "particularly arbitrary," and "it is by no means certain that a system of *gematria* was known in Israel prior to the Hellenistic period" (E. W. Davies 1995a:453, citing Noth 1930:131-132). To that, I would add, we would need the same kind of explanation for numbers elsewhere in the Exodus–Wilderness narrative,[16] but this would undoubtedly lead only to more conjecture.

B. Thirty years ago, Barnouin constructed some numerical correspondences with various celestial movements. He concluded that the census numbers present "the people of Israel as 'armies of the LORD' (Exod 12:41; cf. Exod 7:4) corresponding to astral bodies, the Lord's celestial armies (Gen 2:1; Deut 17:3)" (Milgrom 1989:338, summarizing Barnouin 1977). E. W. Davies (1995a:457-460) thinks this takes too much "numerical juggling" and ends up looking "arbitrary and artificial" with its selective use of planetary periods.

C. Others have suggested that the numbers function as hyperbole. For example, Allen notes that the numbers are all rounded to the tens and suggests that they're the result of multiplying by a factor of 10 for "rhetorical exaggeration." He says the resulting army of about 60,000 and population of 250,000–300,000 "seems to fit the requirements of the social, geographical, and political realities without diminishing at all the sense of the miraculous and providential care of God" (Allen 1990:688-691). E. W. Davies rejects any attempt to fit them into history and says they were "purely fictitious," exaggerated numbers used for rhetorical effect. He notes that outside the Bible, Shalmaneser I claimed to have blinded 14,400 captives and deported 28,800, and Sennacherib boasted of taking 200,150 captives (ANET 288).[17] He cites other places in the Old Testament where this kind of exaggeration emphasized "the invincible power of Yahweh's people" (E. W. Davies 1995a:467, citing Judg 20:1-2; 1 Sam 15:4; 2 Chr 13:3; 14:8; 17:14-19). Davies says this same dynamic was incorporated into Numbers to display the fulfillment of the promise to the patriarchs (Gen 12:1-3) and show the prosperity of Jacob's sons (Gen 46): "The essence of that message was that a nation which seemed small and insignificant at the beginning of its existence could increase out of all proportion as a result of Yahweh's blessing and in fulfillment of his promise to the patriarchs" (1995a:468).

It's one thing to think of Moses's "ten thousand thousands of Israel" (10:36, NRSV) or the 600,000 (11:21; Exod 12:37) as potential hyperbole, but quite another to think of 603,550 as hyperbole (1:46). Similarly, 50,000 may be a potential hyperbole, but what of Naphtali's 53,400 (1:43)? Conversely, it's not hard to think of 600,000 (11:21; Exod 12:37) as a rounded figure for 601,730 (26:51). More importantly, this would be an ill-considered use of hyperbole, because it would tend to undermine the point that God's power defeated Egypt in the Exodus and that the people were too few to fight and occupy a new land without God's providential care over their slow pattern of development.

This leaves us with two other explanations, both suggesting misunderstandings by the book's author, editors, or copyists:

A. Albright thought the Priestly editor obtained a list that had passed through the hands of many scribes, which produced the two versions of the census that we have in Numbers 1 and 26. He said they had a historical basis, but the figures came from the period of the monarchy (Albright 1925; Albright 1957:222, 253; see also Dillmann and Knobel 1886:7). He noted comparable figures, such as the following: 800,000 warriors in Israel and 500,000 in Judah (2 Sam 24:9), or 1,300,000 in all; and the 1,100,000 warriors in Israel and 470,000 in Judah, or 1,570,000 in all, even excluding Levi and Benjamin (1 Chr 21:5). Albright thought the editor in Numbers got these numbers confused and so applied the rounded-off 500,000 from Judah to all twelve tribes in Numbers. He said this confusion is noticeable in that when you add the 600,000 from Numbers with the 500,000 from 2 Samuel, you come up with the 1,100,000 of 1 Chronicles. E. W. Davies (1995a:456-457) thinks this solution "contrived and unnecessarily complicated," and notes that it involves "unwarranted tinkering with the numbers" in the two military counts.[18] More to the point, he thinks the 500,000 figure is also too high because Israel during the monarchy would have had about one million in population, not two and a half million. I would suggest that whatever solution we find in Numbers might be presumed to explain the numbers in Chronicles as well.[19]

B. The second suggestion of a misunderstanding rests on the potential to translate *'elep* to mean "chieftain," "family/tent group," or "troop" instead of "thousand." This attempt to solve the tensions has gained ascendancy, although, just like all the other suggested solutions, it has its own complications. Clearly, the term *'elep* [TH505, ZH547] most often means "thousand" (e.g., Judg 20:2; Amos 5:3); however, it can also refer to a related group that is smaller than a tribe but larger than a family.

Petrie introduced this idea, arguing that *'elep*, or "thousand," could also be translated "clan" or "tent group," and *me'ot* [TH3967, ZH4395] (hundreds) would indicate the approximate number of fighting men in each tribe; he came up with a total population of about 20,000 (Petrie 1906:207-221; Petrie 1923:42-46). Mendenhall agreed with the approach, suggesting that *'elep* referred to a clan-based *military* unit (Mendenhall 1958), or as Gottwald called it, a *"mishpakhah* in arms" (1979:242-291, especially 270; cf. *mishpakhah* [TH4940, ZH5476], "family"), and that *me'ot* numbered the contingents each tribe sent to war. So for Reuben's 46,500, we should read 46 units comprising 500 contingents. Wenham argued that this idea broke down: If the two parts were two ways of numbering the same thing, we should expect a correspondence between the numbers labeled with *'elep* and the numbers labeled with *me'ot.* "Alas, there is no such correspondence" (J. W. Wenham 1967:29). Reuben has 46 *'elep* and 5 *me'ot*, and Simeon has 59 *'elep* and 3 *me'ot*, rather than something higher than 5. Similarly, Judah has 74 *'elep* and 6 *me'ot*, while Dan has 62 *'elep* and 7 *me'ot* rather than something lower than 6.

J. W. Wenham (1967:29, following Clark 1955:82-92) links *'lp* with *'allup* [TH441B, ZH477], a term for tribal or clan "chieftain" (e.g., Gen 36:15, etc.).[20] Wenham suggests that each of these "captains of thousands" might have seven or eight *me'ot* of 75 men under his command, for a fighting force of about 18,000 men and a total population, including noncombatants, of about 72,000.[21]

More recently, Colin Humphreys has picked up the problem of the large numbers. He notes that *'lp* has been vocalized three ways: *'elep* to mean "thousand" (e.g., 3:50; Gen 20:16), *'allup* to mean "leader" (chief, captain, chiliarch, etc.; e.g., Gen 36:15; Ps 55:13), and *'elep* to mean "group" (family, clan, etc.; e.g., Judg 6:15; 1 Sam 10:19). He concludes that the present biblical text is the product of scribes misinterpreting *'elep* in the census counts to mean "thousand" rather than "troops," as they should have; a later scribe misunderstood and ran together the two *'lp* figures (598 + 5) to get 603,000 (Humphreys 1998:207).

Humphreys rejects the figures of Wenham and Clark as "inconsistent with the key figure of 273," the number of firstborn sons that exceeded the Levites and needed redemption (3:46). He makes that number the starting point for recalculating (Humphreys 1998:206). He believes that number is "likely to be correct [i.e., precisely accurate] because redemption was involved, which would be taken very seriously." Indeed, the ransom figures that follow check out exactly (Humphreys 1998:201). He assumes that the Levites represent a normal tribal population, so he uses their figures to build a table that establishes potential ratios for male population in each tribe, firstborn, and percentage over age 20. From this he concludes that the original list recorded 598 troops (units), totaling about 5,550 men, with an average of 9.3 men per troop. His results generally support the above-mentioned theory of Mendenhall (Humphreys 1998:211). He finds these figures consistent with known information about ancient Near Eastern troop size (Humphreys 1998:204).[22]

Humphreys responds in his 1998 article to several objections of E. W. Davies' (1995a) to this type of approach. Among other things, Davies objects that to be valid such an approach should work on similarly high numbers elsewhere in the Old Testament (e.g., 1 Chr 12:23-40)—Humphreys does not show that his approach does and responds that each number problem should be considered in its own context.[23] Davies also objects to the assumption that the numbers should even be interpreted in historical terms. But Humphreys thinks it incredible that the Priestly writer would simply invent high numbers and work up something that was logical and coherent with those numbers (Humphreys 1998:207-210; contra E. W. Davies 1995a:463-466).

Additionally, Humphreys' approach has been challenged by Milgrom, who denies that the numbers add up (Milgrom 1999:131-132) and suggests that careless bookkeeping would be inconsistent with record-keeping practices exemplified in Exodus 38:24-30 and Numbers 7:84-88, where numbers for each item are given separately and again as totals; and McEntire, who objects to Humphreys' assumption that the Levites were an average-sized tribe—if they were not, it would skew all of Humphreys' figures (McEntire 1999:263).[24] Humphreys' responses to these arguments can be found in his 2000 article.

In his interaction with these arguments, Rendesburg (2001:392) accepts Davies' argument that the biblical record could use numeric hyperbole, but he sees that as more befitting the rounded 600,000 figure of Exodus 12:37 than the detailed figures of 603,550 and 601,730. He says, "Epic tradition called for the army to be described in exaggerated numbers, whether it be the 600,000 of Israel or the 3,000,000 of Ugarit" (Rendesburg 2001:393). Even so, Rendesburg also accepts the argument that *'lp* should be translated as something other than "thousand." He notes that Humphreys' approach shows historical veracity in regard to what we know of ancient populations and also clan troop sizes: It produces none with a clan fighting unit around the too-small size of 100 and none with the too-large size of 800 or 900 (Rendesburg 2001:394).

In summary: Arguments from the ancient Near Eastern data can be circular, from either side of the debate. One view summons them as evidence for large numbers in military units (cf. endnote 11); others summon them as evidence that hyperbole was common in such figures. Supporters of the traditional view of these numbers will certainly want to see the ancient Near Eastern archaeological data reinterpreted to bring it in line with these larger numbers. Many are finding Humphreys' approach attractive, but serious problems remain. Any solution should work for the high numbers elsewhere in the Bible, especially analogous numbers (e.g., military counts), and a conservative doctrine of Scripture makes it very hard for this commentator to make room for the necessary element of Humphreys' argument that the editorial or scribal tradition that gave us these large numbers was mistaken.

OUTLINE

Various outlines have been suggested, some thematic,[25] some chronological,[26] and many of them geographical.[27] The two counts of the people structure a story that revolves around two distinct generations (chs 1–4 and 26). The first rebelled and complained, was gradually extinguished during its wanderings, and was decisively terminated by the plague at the end of that period (25:9). The second count specifies that none of the first generation survived, except Joshua and Caleb (26:64-65). The end of the book shows Israel's new generation displaying great, but still unrealized, promise; it is not a settled matter whether they will continue in obedience and receive the Promised Land.

I. Death of the Old Generation (1:1–25:18)
  A. At Sinai: Preparing for the Journey to the Promised Land (1:1–10:10)
    1. The first count (1:1–4:49; cf. 26:1-65)
      a. Mustering Israel's warriors (1:1-54)
      b. Arranging the camp by tribes (2:1-31)
      c. Summary of the first census (2:32-34)
      d. Levites appointed for service (3:1-13)
      e. Counting the Levites by clans (3:14-39)
      f. Redeeming the firstborn sons (3:40-51)
      g. Enlisting the Levites (4:1-49)
    2. Commands for holiness in Israel (5:1–10:10)
      a. Removing the unclean from the community (5:1-4)
      b. Holiness and restitution for sin (5:5-10)
      c. Holiness and the test for suspicions (5:11-31)
      d. Holiness and the Nazirite vow (6:1-21)
      e. Priestly blessing for the community (6:22-27)

C. Settlement Arrangements for the Transjordan (31:1–32:42)
  1. Defeating Midian (31:1-54)
  2. Transjordan tribes: Reuben and Gad (32:1-42)
D. Reprise of Wilderness Itinerary (33:1-49)
E. Laws about the Promised Land (33:50–36:13)
  1. Orders for occupying the Promised Land (33:50-56)
  2. Borders of the Promised Land (34:1-15)
  3. Appointed officials (34:16-29)
  4. Levitical holdings in the Promised Land (35:1-34)
  5. Inheritance of Zelophehad's daughters (36:1-13; cf. 27:1-11)

ENDNOTES

1. 1:1; 2:1; 3:1, 5, 11, 14, 40, 44; 4:1, 17, 21; 5:1, 5, 11; 6:1, 22; 7:4; 8:1, 5, 23; 9:1, 9; 10:1; 11:16, 23; 12:4; 13:1; 14:11, 20, 26; 15:1, 17, 37; 16:36, 44; 17:1, 10; 18:25; 19:1; 20:7, 12, 23; 21:8, 34; 25:4, 10, 16; 26:52; 27:6, 12, 18; 28:1; 31:1, 25; 34:1, 16; 35:1, 9.
2. Rendtorff 1977:1-28, 70-74, 147-173; see his summary on 160-163; Noth 1972:5-62.
3. LXX 1:24-37 = MT 1:26-37, 24-25; LXX 6:22-26 = MT 6:22-23, 27, 24-26, 27; and LXX 26:15-47 = MT 26:19-27, 15-18, 44-47, 28-43 (a different order of tribes).
4. The Samaritan Pentateuch is a sectarian recension, which differs from the MT about 6,000 times, about 1,600 times in agreement with the LXX. However, it tends to expand the text, incorporating parallel materials from Deuteronomy to harmonize the parallel accounts, e.g., Num 10:10 has Deut 1:6-8 after it; Num 12:16 has Deut 1:20-23a after it; Num 21 adds various interpolations from Deut 2.
5. *b. Sanhedrin* 44a; *b. Hagigah* 14a.
6. Olson uses the Masoretic data to show that the books are decidedly uneven in percentage of the Pentateuch's entire text (1985:52): Genesis = 1,534 verses (26%), Exodus = 1,209 (21%), Leviticus = 859 (15%), Numbers = 1,288 (22%), and Deuteronomy = 955 (16%). This argument may lack force, however, since the group of scrolls found at Qumran seem to show that scroll length varied noticeably.
7. I.e., 1:1; 36:13; Gen 1:1; 50:26; Exod 1:1-7; 40:38?; Lev 1:1-2?; 27:34; Deut 1:1; 34:9-12. Even though Exod 40:38 and Lev 1:1-2 don't sound much like conclusion and introduction, we do see a major shift in the move from the narrative of Exodus to the cultic legislation of Leviticus.
8. 1:17, 19; 3:16, 42, 49-51; 4:34-37; 8:20; 17:6, 11; 20:9, 27; 27:22-23; 30:1; 31:1-54; 36:5.
9. 11:2; 12:13; 14:13-19; 16:4, 22; 17:10; 20:6; 21:8-9, 16.
10. Moses, the Old Testament prophet par excellence, interceded four times when Pharaoh sought relief from the plagues (Exod 8:8-14; 8:28-31; 9:27-34; 10:16-19). In chs 14–20, he repeatedly interceded before God when divine wrath flared up against the grumbling Hebrew people. See other occasions of prophetic intercession (Gen 18:17-32; 20:1-17; Isa 37:1-7; Amos 7:1-9). God even had to warn Jeremiah not to intercede, so bent on intercession were true prophets (Jer 7:16; 11:14; 14:11-12; 15:1).
11. Archer 1982:132-134. He notes that the Egyptian King Pepi I sent "an army of many ten thousands" against the Asians (ANET 228), the Assyrian King Sennacherib claimed to have taken 20,150 prisoners from Judah's walled cities (ANET 288), and Herodotus said the Persian troops invading Greece numbered 1,700,000 infantry plus 40,000 cavalry (Archer 1982:134, citing Anthon 1871:107).
12. The number 44,546 is double the number of firstborn sons, and assumes a roughly equal number of firstborn girls and one mother for each firstborn (male or female).
13. E. W. Davies 1995a:452, citing Holzinger 1903:5-6, 134. The use of the Hebrew letters to represent numbers is common in medieval writings and occurs in ancient documents

as well. A similar use of letters is found in ancient Greek. The first 10 letters represent 1–10; the next group, 20–90; the next letters, values of 100 and more. The numeric values derived from the letters in *bene yisra'el* ("sons of Israel," 1:2), for example, does add up to 603. But the gematria for 550 is more complex and highly problematic: Holzinger's selection (1) adds up to 551, (2) requires taking some words from 1:2 and others from 1:45, and (3) adjusts one letter in the MT's phrase from 1:45.

14. The text at 25:4 reads *kl-r'shy* ("all the leaders of . . ."), but Holzinger used *kl-r'shym* ("all the leaders") to get 601: $k = 20 + l = 30 + r = 200 + ' = 1 + sh = 300 + y = 10 + m = 40$. He got his 730 from *wkl-pqwdy 'dt* ("and all the number of the assembly"), which doesn't actually occur as a phrase anywhere in the book of Numbers (cf. similar combinations in 1:45; 2:32; 3:39; 14:29).

15. E. W. Davies 1995a:453 n. 3 cites Bentzen 1948–1949:2.34 and Sellin 1933:200, which is also in English (Fohrer 1968:184).

16. E.g., 600,000 in Exod 12:37; Num 11:21. I suppose it might be easier to rate those rounded numbers as hyperbole, except that they are so close to the calculated totals in the two census counts in Num 1 and 26.

17. E. W. Davies 1995a:467, citing Woolley 1928:21-26; see also Fouts 1997, who cites ancient Near Eastern parallels to defend the hyperbolic interpretation.

18. E. W. Davies 1995a:455. He notes that if we look at the military count for just the nine tribes that later split from Judah, the totals come to 434,000 (ch 1) and 457,430 (ch 26), neither of which fits the 470,000; besides, it was the Judah tribes that were given that number. If we look at the overall military count, the 603,550 and 501,730 seem far off the count from 470,000—and too exact.

19. E.g., 1 Chr 12:33, 36-37; 18:5; 19:7, 18; 21:5, 14; 23:3; 2 Chr 2:2; 13:3, 17; 14:8; 17:14, 16-17; 25:5-6, 11; 28:6, 8.

20. Clark subdivides the numbering, thinking there were a certain number of *'allupim* and a certain number of *me'ot*, which always exceeded 10. So instead of 59,300 for Simeon, we should understand 57 *'allupim* and 23 *me'ot* (rather than 59 and 3). Following that pattern, the reading could reconstruct a set of figures that did show correspondence between the *'allupim* and *me'ot*. Following this pattern, Clark came up with a total population of about 140,000.

21. Wenham worked it out to 479 *'allupim* and 226.3 *me'ot* for the final census; cf. 601,730 (J. W. Wenham 1967:31).

22. He cites Knudtzon 1964:1.564-565, pointing out that in the El-Amarna tablets, King Rib-Addi of Byblos asked the king of Egypt for a contingent of troops of 20 men each (108:66-70), and on another occasion for a troop of 10 from Nubia (133:15-18).

23. Humphreys 1998:204-205, 213 (Table 3); citing the 93 gatekeepers of 1 Chr 26:1-12.

24. Heinzerling 2000 cites the arguments of Milgrom 1999 and McEntire 1999 and adds some additional arguments, including that since the numbers in chapters 1 and 2 are closely connected with those in chapters 3 and 4, we should apply the same reading, which yields a striking inconsistency in that the numbers of Levites aged between 30 and 50 years ends up larger than the total number of Levites (Heinzerling 2000:250). He suggests that Humphreys' method implies the unlikely case that "a scribe had a notation of the numbers before him that clearly required two different meanings of *'lp* and *still* misunderstood" (Heinzerling 2000:251).

25. One might draw on the categories of Walter Brueggemann and John Goldingay:
    ORIENTATION 1:1–10:10
    Transitional travel section 10:11–12:16
    DISORIENTATION 13:1–19:22
    Transitional travel section 20:1–22:1
    NEW ORIENTATION 22:1–36:13
    The problems are twofold: Its two transitional travel sections omit much of the frequent travel, which led them to 42 camping sites in 40 years, and its "New Orientation" runs over the major division that the second census constitutes (ch 26).

26. The book's many chronological indicators are an unlikely source for structuring the book (1:1; 7:1; 9:1, 5; 10:11; 20:1; 33:3, 38). Numbers 7:1 and 9:1 are chronological dislocations, and chronology is totally lacking from the middle 38 years of wandering (10:11–20:22).

27. These outlines are structured around Sinai, Kadesh, and the Plains of Moab; however, agreement breaks down after the Sinai section (1:1–10:10). For Sinai to Kadesh, commentators suggest units such as 10:11–20:12, or 10:11–21:19, or 10:11–22:1. And if geography really ruled, we might just as well produce a 42-point outline, listing each campsite.

COMMENTARY ON
Numbers

◆ **I. Death of the Old Generation (1:1–25:18)**
  A. At Sinai: Preparing for the Journey to the Promised Land (1:1–10:10)
    1. The first count (1:1–4:49, cf. 26:1-65)
      a. Mustering Israel's warriors (1:1-54)

A year after Israel's departure from Egypt, the LORD spoke to Moses in the Tabernacle* in the wilderness of Sinai. On the first day of the second month* of that year he said, ²"From the whole community of Israel, record the names of all the warriors by their clans and families. List all the men ³twenty years old or older who are able to go to war. You and Aaron must register the troops, ⁴and you will be assisted by one family leader from each tribe.

⁵"These are the tribes and the names of the leaders who will assist you:

Tribe	Leader
Reuben	Elizur son of Shedeur
⁶Simeon	Shelumiel son of Zurishaddai
⁷Judah	Nahshon son of Amminadab
⁸Issachar	Nethanel son of Zuar
⁹Zebulun	Eliab son of Helon
¹⁰Ephraim son of Joseph	Elishama son of Ammihud
Manasseh son of Joseph	Gamaliel son of Pedahzur
¹¹Benjamin	Abidan son of Gideoni
¹²Dan	Ahiezer son of Ammishaddai
¹³Asher	Pagiel son of Ocran
¹⁴Gad	Eliasaph son of Deuel
¹⁵Naphtali	Ahira son of Enan

¹⁶These are the chosen leaders of the community, the leaders of their ancestral tribes, the heads of the clans of Israel."

¹⁷So Moses and Aaron called together these chosen leaders, ¹⁸and they assembled the whole community of Israel on that very day.* All the people were registered according to their ancestry by their clans and families. The men of Israel who were twenty years old or older were listed one by one, ¹⁹just as the LORD had commanded Moses. So Moses recorded their names in the wilderness of Sinai.

²⁰⁻²¹This is the number of men twenty years old or older who were able to go to war, as their names were listed in the records of their clans and families*:

Tribe	Number
Reuben (Jacob's* oldest son)	46,500
²²⁻²³Simeon	59,300
²⁴⁻²⁵Gad	45,650
²⁶⁻²⁷Judah	74,600
²⁸⁻²⁹Issachar	54,400
³⁰⁻³¹Zebulun	57,400
³²⁻³³Ephraim son of Joseph	40,500
³⁴⁻³⁵Manasseh son of Joseph	32,200
³⁶⁻³⁷Benjamin	35,400
³⁸⁻³⁹Dan	62,700
⁴⁰⁻⁴¹Asher	41,500
⁴²⁻⁴³Naphtali	53,400

⁴⁴These were the men registered by Moses and Aaron and the twelve leaders of Israel, all listed according to their ancestral descent. ⁴⁵They were registered by families—all the men of Israel who were twenty years old or older and able to go to war. ⁴⁶The total number was 603,550.

⁴⁷But this total did not include the

Levites. [48]For the LORD had said to Moses, [49]"Do not include the tribe of Levi in the registration; do not count them with the rest of the Israelites. [50]Put the Levites in charge of the Tabernacle of the Covenant,* along with all its furnishings and equipment. They must carry the Tabernacle and all its furnishings as you travel, and they must take care of it and camp around it. [51]Whenever it is time for the Tabernacle to move, the Levites will take it down. And when it is time to stop, they will set it up again. But any unauthorized person who goes too near the Tabernacle must be put to death. [52]Each tribe of Israel will camp in a designated area with its own family banner. [53]But the Levites will camp around the Tabernacle of the Covenant to protect the community of Israel from the LORD's anger. The Levites are responsible to stand guard around the Tabernacle."

[54]So the Israelites did everything just as the LORD had commanded Moses.

1:1a Hebrew the *Tent of Meeting.* **1:1b** This day in the ancient Hebrew lunar calendar occurred in April or May. **1:18** Hebrew *on the first day of the second month;* see 1:1. **1:20-21a** In the Hebrew text, this sentence (*This is the number of men twenty years old or older who were able to go to war, as their names were listed in the records of their clans and families*) is repeated in 1:22, 24, 26, 28, 30, 32, 34, 36, 38, 40, 42. **1:20-21b** Hebrew *Israel's.* The names "Jacob" and "Israel" are often interchanged throughout the Old Testament, referring sometimes to the individual patriarch and sometimes to the nation. **1:50** Or *Tabernacle of the Testimony;* also in 1:53.

NOTES

1:1 *Tabernacle.* In the ancient Near East portable shrines were pitched in the center of a camp as a place for the kings and priests to meet with their gods while on campaign (Harrison 1990:32). Since Yahweh was Israel's battle chief, the closer parallel is the Egyptian practice of placing their commander's tent in the middle of a rectangular camp and surrounding it with his officers. This is well illustrated in the military camp of Rameses II (Kitchen 1960:11; Milgrom 1989:11; Yadin 1963:264; see note at 2:2).

1:2 *record the names.* Lit., "to lift the head" (cf. 26:2; Exod 30:12), which is combined with "by their skulls," speaking of a headcount (1:2, 18, 20, 22; 3:47).

by their clans and families. Lit., "by their clans, by the house of their fathers." Terminology for Israel's subdivisions is inexact, especially the "paternal household" (*beth 'aboth* [TH1004/1, ZH1074/3]), which is understood variously as a synonym for the whole nation (Ps 45:10[?]; NLT, "family"), a tribe (Josh 22:14; 1 Kgs 8:1), a tribal grouping of multiple clans (Hirsch 1971:2-3; Levine 1993:131-133), a synonym for "clan" (Milgrom 1989:5), a subdivision of the clans (Gray 1903:4-6), or a nuclear family (Exod 12:3; Ps 45:10[?]). Allowing for flexibility and overlapping terminology, the general hierarchy was this: All Israel was divided into 12 tribes, which were subdivided into clans, then into patriarchal houses (i.e., an extended family under a paternal grandfather's authority), and finally into nuclear families (cf. analogous references in Josh 7:14; Judg 6:15; 1 Sam 10:21; 1 Chr 23:11).

1:3 *register the troops.* Milgrom notes, "The Akkadian term for 'muster the troops,' is the exact cognate of the Hebrew *paqad tsaba'"* [TH6485/6635, ZH7212/7372] (1989:4, citing Dossin and Parrot 1950:3.19).

1:6-15 The order of the tribes is listed by order of birth (Gen 29–30), minus Levi, but grouped by mother: Leah (Reuben–Zebulun), then Rachel (Ephraim–Benjamin), then the concubines Bilhah and Zilpah (Dan–Naphtali).

1:14 *Deuel.* This follows the Hebrew (also at 7:42, 47; 10:20); cf. "Reuel" (LXX and Syriac). Elsewhere the Hebrew has "Reuel" (*re'u'el* [TH7467, ZH8294]): Once for this same man (a copyist's error at 2:14, mistaking the initial Daleth [ד] for Resh [ר]), but otherwise for a son of Esau, an ancestor of an Edomite clan (Gen 36:4, 10, 13, 17; 1 Chr 1:35, 37), for Moses's father-in-law (10:29; Exod 2:18), and for a returning Benjamite exile (1 Chr 9:8).

1:50 *take care of it.* The Hebrew is *sharath* [TH8334, ZH9250], a term referring to service like that of an administrative assistant (e.g., Exod 24:13; 1 Kgs 19:21; Ps 103:21). In the cult, it was used for priestly and for non-priestly attendants (e.g., 1:50; 3:31).

1:50, 51, 53 Here we have a cluster of Tabernacle terms: "Tabernacle" (*mishkan* [TH4908, ZH5438], four times) and "Tabernacle of the Covenant" (*mishkan ha'eduth* [TH5715, ZH6343], three times). The *mishkan* was God's camp tent, making good on his covenantal promise to dwell among his people (Exod 25:8; 29:45; Lev 26:11). The *mishkan ha'eduth*, "Tabernacle of the Testimony/Covenant," was so called because it housed the Ark of the Testimony (cf. 4:5 mg; 7:89 mg; Exod 25:22 mg), or Ark of the Covenant (10:33; 14:44; Deut 10:8; Heb 9:4), which held the tablets that testified to God's covenant with Israel (Exod 25:16, 21; 40:20).

1:51 *unauthorized person.* Lit., "a stranger." Here, this refers to anyone other than the Levitical and priestly servants of the Tabernacle (3:10, 38; 18:4, 7; Lev 22:10-12).

C O M M E N T A R Y

At Sinai, Israel fell into idolatry and debauchery (Exod 32:1-6); nonetheless, the Lord sustained his covenant with them. So Numbers 1–10 picks up the account, recording initial high hopes and ready obedience in the people's first steps from slavery to landed nationhood.

Selecting the Officials (1:1-16). Fourteen months after Israel's departure from Egypt (1:1), God told Moses to register potential men of arms, marking a transition from a band of freed slaves to an organized military camp on its way to becoming a great nation (1:1–4:49). Here the narrator makes no complaint about this standard feature of battle plans and assessment. Later leaders instituted counts not so much for enlisting servants of God and Torah as for measuring the military assets of king and country (2 Sam 24:1-2; 1 Chr 21:1). The ancient Near Eastern counts generally focus on the militarily fit (as do 2 Sam 24:9; 2 Chr 14:8), but for this all-important expedition there was no exemption from military service (Deut 20:5-8; 28:30). *The Legend of King Keret* describes a summons that allowed none of the expected deferments:

> The only son must shut up his house,
> > the widow hire someone (to go).
> The invalid must take up his bed,
> > the blind man must grope his way along.
> The newly-wed must go forth,
> > entrusting his wife to someone else,
> > his beloved to someone unrelated.[1]

This entire, all-inclusive troop enlistment of Israel's young men died in the wilderness without advancing on the Promised Land, an appalling miscarriage of national purpose.

Counting the Fighting Men; Exempting the Levites (1:17-53). Earlier, Moses had ascended Sinai to meet God. Thereafter, he came to the Tent of Meeting, which had been pitched outside the camp (Exod 33:7-11). Once the Tabernacle complex sited the sacred tent at camp center, the Levites formed a protective cordon between it and the camps of Israel's twelve tribes (1:53).

The Lord had exempted the Levites from the military draft (1:48-53), but not from national service. They were to help the priests and to serve the Tabernacle as attendants in camp (1:50a), as porters when on the move (1:50b-51a), and as "militaristic defenders of the cult and its cultic centers" (Spencer 1998:546; 1:51b-53). In the last role, they were to "put to death" anyone engaged in unauthorized cultic activity (1:51; cf. 3:10, 38; 18:7).

God dwelled in the camp with his people. The incarnation of Christ would further manifest this promise to dwell among his people (John 1:1-18). Even when Jesus went away, he promised the continuation of that presence (Matt 18:20; 28:20). For that reason, the New Testament can speak of the corporate body of believers (1 Cor 3:16; Eph 2:21-22; 1 Pet 2:5), and even of the individual believer's body (1 Cor 6:19), as God's dwelling place. And this sanctuary, too, must be protected against defilement (Matt 18:17; Acts 5:1-11; Rom 16:17; 1 Cor 5; 11:27-34; 2 Thess 3:6, 14; 1 Tim 1:20; 2 John 1:10). One day, full realization of the promise of his presence will be found in the New Jerusalem (Rev 21:1-4).

A Note of Compliance (1:54). The first chapter ends on a note of obedience, a recurring note early on in the book, although in the subsequent period, we seldom hear of orders being obeyed until the second generation.[2]

Order		Obedience
1:1-3	Moses conducts the survey	1:17-19
1:3-4	Moses and Aaron and the tribal leaders conduct the survey	1:44
1:3	Israel conducts a military registration	1:20a
1:2	The count is organized by tribe, clan, and family	1:20b

Israel's lists always number twelve tribes, no matter how they arrive at that number. This count balances Levi's omission by giving the Joseph tribes a double portion (1:10, 32-35; cf. Gen 49:22-26; Deut 33:13-17). The list retains the same ordering principle at work in verses 5-15, but partially adapted to the arrangement of the camp. The troop total of 603,550 accords with other accounts concerning the number of males who left Egypt (1:46; 11:21; Exod 12:37; 38:26). Including women and children, this would have constituted a camp of two to three million, demonstrating fulfillment of the promise to Abraham (Gen 17:1-8).

ENDNOTES
1. Cited from COS 1.102:334; also found in ANET 143-144.
2. Early mention (1:19, 54; 2:33-34; 3:16, 39, 42, 51; 4:37, 41, 45, 49; 5:4; 8:3-4, 20-22; 9:5, 8, 18, 20, 23); during rebellion (10:13; 17:11; 20:9, 27); second generation (26:4; 27:11, 22-23; 31:7, 31, 41, 47; 32:25; 36:5, 10).

b. Arranging the camp by tribes (2:1-31)

Then the LORD gave these instructions to Moses and Aaron: 2"When the Israelites set up camp, each tribe will be assigned its own area. The tribal divisions will camp beneath their family banners on all four sides of the Tabernacle,* but at some distance from it.

3-4"The divisions of Judah, Issachar, and Zebulun are to camp toward the sunrise on the east side of the Tabernacle, beneath their family banners. These are the names of the tribes, their leaders, and the numbers of their registered troops:

	Tribe	Leader	Number
	Judah	Nahshon son of Amminadab	74,600
5-6	Issachar	Nethanel son of Zuar	54,400
7-8	Zebulun	Eliab son of Helon	57,400

9So the total of all the troops on Judah's side of the camp is 186,400. These three tribes are to lead the way whenever the Israelites travel to a new campsite.

10-11"The divisions of Reuben, Simeon, and Gad are to camp on the south side of the Tabernacle, beneath their family banners. These are the names of the tribes, their leaders, and the numbers of their registered troops:

	Tribe	Leader	Number
	Reuben	Elizur son of Shedeur	46,500
12-13	Simeon	Shelumiel son of Zurishaddai	59,300
14-15	Gad	Eliasaph son of Deuel*	45,650

16So the total of all the troops on Reuben's side of the camp is 151,450. These three tribes will be second in line whenever the Israelites travel.

17"Then the Tabernacle, carried by the Levites, will set out from the middle of the camp. All the tribes are to travel in the same order that they camp, each in position under the appropriate family banner.

18-19"The divisions of Ephraim, Manasseh, and Benjamin are to camp on the west side of the Tabernacle, beneath their family banners. These are the names of the tribes, their leaders, and the numbers of their registered troops:

	Tribe	Leader	Number
	Ephraim	Elishama son of Ammihud	40,500
20-21	Manasseh	Gamaliel son of Pedahzur	32,200
22-23	Benjamin	Abidan son of Gideoni	35,400

24So the total of all the troops on Ephraim's side of the camp is 108,100. These three tribes will be third in line whenever the Israelites travel.

25-26"The divisions of Dan, Asher, and Naphtali are to camp on the north side of the Tabernacle, beneath their family banners. These are the names of the tribes, their leaders, and the numbers of their registered troops:

	Tribe	Leader	Number
	Dan	Ahiezer son of Ammishaddai	62,700
27-28	Asher	Pagiel son of Ocran	41,500
29-30	Naphtali	Ahira son of Enan	53,400

31So the total of all the troops on Dan's side of the camp is 157,600. These three tribes will be last, marching under their banners whenever the Israelites travel."

2:2 Hebrew the Tent of Meeting; also in 2:17.   2:14-15 As in many Hebrew manuscripts, Samaritan Pentateuch, and Latin Vulgate (see also 1:14); most Hebrew manuscripts read son of Reuel.

NOTES

2:2 The tribal divisions will camp beneath their family banners. Lit., "each with/under his division/banner" ('ish 'al-diglo [TH376/1714, ZH408/1840]) "and with his paternal household sign" (be'othoth lebeth 'abotham [TH1004/1, ZH1074/3]). Jewish tradition says each divisional banner displayed a figure: Judah's a lion, Reuben's a man, Ephraim's an ox, and Dan's an eagle (Cohen 1983:798; see 1:52; cf. Ezek 1:10; Rev 4:7), and each tribe's banner matched the color of its stone on the high priest's chestpiece (*Numbers Rabbah* 2:7; cf. Exod 39:14). Levine and Milgrom draw on Persian parallels to describe the *degel* [TH1714, ZH1840] as a "sociomilitary unit" (Levine 1993:147-148) or as a garrison of about 1,000 men living together with their families (Milgrom 1989:11). Yadin has shown this same three-tribe divisional plan in the Qumran War Scroll (1962:168-181). The *'oth* [TH226, ZH253] was an ensign or banner. For the expression "their paternal house," see note on 1:2. The order for camping and marching in ch 2 differs somewhat from that of the military census (ch 1). In ch 1, the count began with Reuben, the firstborn; in ch 2, the camp arrangement and marching order begins with the preeminent tribe of Judah. Even so, the ordering of the subgroups that this chapter forms into larger, three-tribe groups remains the same.

four sides of the Tabernacle. The Egyptian army of Rameses (thirteenth century BC) camped in a square with the royal tent in the middle, with the officers' tents placed round it for protection, like the Levites here (Kitchen 1960:11; Milgrom 1989:11; Yadin 1963:264).

at some distance from it. The term *neged* [TH5048, ZH5584] can mean "in front of" (RSV, NRSV); however, here it means "at a distance" (NLT, also KJV, NASB, NIV). The rabbis figured 2,000 cubits (i.e., 3,000 feet) for this distance; it was the limit for walking on the Sabbath (*b. Sotah* 5:3), and it was the distance by which the Ark led Israel when crossing the Jordan (Josh 3:4).

2:3-4 *divisions of Judah, Issachar, and Zebulun.* Lit., "the division of the camp of Judah," that is, "the Judah division," comprising the tribes of Judah, Issachar, and Zebulun. The same formula is followed for the other three-tribe divisions: Reuben (2:10-11), Ephraim (2:18-19), and Dan (2:25-26).

Nahshon. This was Aaron's brother-in-law (Exod 6:23), his marriage perhaps forming a covenantal link between Aaron's priestly line and the royal line of Judah (Milgrom 1989:300 n. 8; Galil 1985).

2:10 *south side.* Lit., "right," or what is on the right as one faces east.

2:14-15 *Deuel.* The Hebrew has *Re'u'el* [TH7467, ZH8294] (see note on 1:14).

2:17 *Tabernacle, carried by the Levites, will set out.* Lit., "when the Tent of Meeting sets out, the camp of the Levites." "The Tabernacle" is in apposition to "the camp of the Levites," defining them as the Tent of Meeting division.

2:31 *These three tribes . . . under their banners.* The last phrase is better understood as not referring to the Danite division marching under its divisional banner (1:52; 2:2, 3, 10, 17, 18, 25, 31, 34) but to all four three-tribe divisions marching under their divisional banners (Dillmann and Knobel 1886:13).

COMMENTARY

These instructions came to both Moses and Aaron (2:1; see also 1:3, 17, 44), which is unusual; however, it is supported by a pattern of Moses's coleadership with his brother, the priest (Exod 4:14-16). God positioned the twelve tribes in four military divisions on the compass points around the Tabernacle. Inside that ring, the Levites formed a cordon between the Tabernacle and the flanking tribes.

Reuben and Gad, who later settled in the east, camped to the south. The southern tribe of Judah camped on the east with Issachar and Zebulun, who later settled in the north. Benjamin, whose names means "southerner," camped to the west. And so it went, with no attention to the subsequent tribal geography. Instead, symmetry, lines of authority, and concentric holiness ruled how the camp was distributed. Dispersal around the four compass points made for a symmetrical camp. The listing of a tribal leader for each tribe and a lead tribe for each three-tribe division laid out lines of authority, a continuing motif throughout Numbers. And the concentric camp displayed concentric holiness, with holiness increasing as one worked from the boundaries of Israel's tribal camps into the inner cordon of Levites, the Tabernacle walls, and finally all the way into the Ark inside the Holiest Place.

Hoffmeier mounts a spirited offense against dating the camp and Tabernacle description as late as a documentary hypothesis would (2005:202-208). He says, "The plan of Ramesses II's camp, which unquestionably dates to the mid-thirteenth century, is the closest analogue to the wilderness Tabernacle as described in Exodus 25ff" (2005:208). Locating the Tabernacle in the center of a rectangular camp is especially similar to Rameses II's camp at Kadesh, with the pharaoh's own tent camp located at the center of the armies' camps (Hoffmeier 2005:206; Gressmann 1913:240-242; Homan 2000; Homan 2002:ch 7; Kitchen 2003:275-283).

We recognize in the symmetry the same beauty and order that characterized Genesis 1 (Allen 1990:713). This, in turn, formed a prototype for the new Temple (Ezek 40–48), with its primacy of the eastern side (Ezek 47:1a), centrality of the divine presence (Ezek 48:8-20), and inner court walls doing what the Levites did in the wilderness and the other court walls doing what the four three-tribe divisions did (E. W. Davies 1995b:19). Finally, this points us to the new creation's foursquare "scheme for the new Jerusalem" (Snaith 1969:123; see also G. J. Wenham 1981:68; see Rev 21:10–22:5).

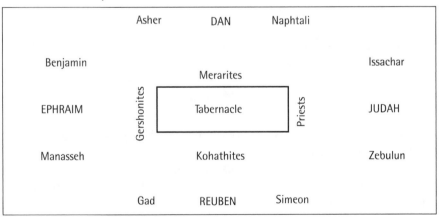

Eastern Tribes (2:1-9). The royal tribe of Judah (Gen 49:8-10) led the largest three-tribe division (2:9, cf. 2:16, 24, 31). They posted up to the east of the Tabernacle (2:3), an honored position at its entrance, and they led the way on the march (2:9). In the ancient Near East, the east was the primary direction, the front, the direction of the dawn. Eden had been sited "in the east" (Gen 2:8); therefore, although the east could also be a place of threat and exile, hope grew that God's redemption would come from the east, from the place of Paradise Lost (Sailhamer 1992:371; see

Ezek 43:2-4; Zech 14:4; Matt 24:27). Judah's leadership here foreshadows Judah's future military leadership through its lionlike Davidic kings (Gen 49:8-9), a status which extends even to John's exclamation, "Look, the Lion of the tribe of Judah, the heir to David's throne, has won the victory" (Rev 5:5).

Southern Tribes (2:10-16). Reuben led a medium-sized division (2:16, cf. 2:9, 24, 31), which camped to the south (2:10) and marched second (2:16). Sherwood says the south was a place of dishonor (Douglas 1993:175-179). It was the place for (1) Kohathites (3:28-29), from whom the Levitical rebel Korah would come (16:1); (2) Reuben, whom his father Jacob had cursed for having sexual relations with Jacob's concubine Bilhah (Gen 35:22; 49:3-4); (3) Simeon, who was rebuked for excessive violence in avenging Dinah's rape (Gen 34:30); and (4) Gad, with low status as a son of Leah's servant, Zilpah (Gen 30:9-11). One might better argue that the south was the prime location after the east (Gray 1903:16-18): (1) It is mentioned first after the east in this sequence; (2) Reuben and Simeon were also sons of Leah, Judah's mother (Gen 46:8-15); (3) the Kohathites were the premier Levitical clan, the clan of Moses and Aaron and the clan that carried the Tabernacle's most holy furnishings; and (4) the right-hand side (which, relative to Judah's position in the east, is the south) is a place of prominence.

Central Tribe: Levites (2:17). The Levites formed an interior cordon to shield the sanctuary from violation by intruders (1:51; 2:17). The Levites' movement in their protected position in the column is described as the Tabernacle's movement (2:17). The four tribal divisions (cf. 3:23-39; the Aaronites [and Moses], the Kohathites, the Gershonites, and the Merarites) served as the Tabernacle's vanguard and rearguard, each marching under its three-tribe divisional banner.

Western Tribes (2:18-24). Ephraim led the smallest division (2:24, cf. 2:9, 16, 31), comprising the three smallest tribes (2:18-23; cf. 2:3-8, 10-15, 25-30). The Ephraim division camped to the west (2:18) and moved third in the line of march (2:24), following not only the two divisions of Judah and Reuben, but also the Levitical Tabernacle division (2:9, 16).

Northern Tribes (2:25-31). Dan led a medium-sized tribal division (2:31; cf. 2:9, 16, 24), which camped north of the Tabernacle. It marched at the tail of the column (2:31). Dan, as the firstborn of Jacob's children from his concubines (Gen 30:3-6), led the concubines' offspring, except for Gad, which was incorporated into Reuben's division (2:10).

◆   ### c. Summary of the first census (2:32-34)

[32]In summary, the troops of Israel listed by their families totaled 603,550. [33]But as the LORD had commanded, the Levites were not included in this registration. [34]So the people of Israel did everything as the LORD had commanded Moses. Each clan and family set up camp and marched under their banners exactly as the LORD had instructed them.

COMMENTARY

The military registration of chapter 1 recorded each tribe's figures individually and then gave a grand troop count of 603,550. Chapter 2 records the same individual tribal counts and grand total, but it includes subtotals for each three-tribe division (2:9, 16, 24, 31). The summary gives us a triple note of obedience: (1) The Levites were excused from the military count, "as the LORD had commanded" (2:33; cf. 1:47); (2) "the people of Israel did everything as the LORD had commanded Moses" (2:34a); and (3) they camped and marched "exactly as the LORD had instructed them" (2:34b). They camped and marched in four three-tribe divisions, perhaps further subdivided by clan and paternal house (see note on 1:2).

◆   ### d. Levites appointed for service (3:1-13)

This is the family line of Aaron and Moses as it was recorded when the LORD spoke to Moses on Mount Sinai: ²The names of Aaron's sons were Nadab (the oldest), Abihu, Eleazar, and Ithamar. ³These sons of Aaron were anointed and ordained to minister as priests. ⁴But Nadab and Abihu died in the LORD's presence in the wilderness of Sinai when they burned before the LORD the wrong kind of fire, different than he had commanded. Since they had no sons, this left only Eleazar and Ithamar to serve as priests with their father, Aaron.

⁵Then the LORD said to Moses, ⁶"Call forward the tribe of Levi, and present them to Aaron the priest to serve as his assistants. ⁷They will serve Aaron and the whole community, performing their sacred duties in and around the Tabernacle.*

⁸They will also maintain all the furnishings of the sacred tent,* serving in the Tabernacle on behalf of all the Israelites. ⁹Assign the Levites to Aaron and his sons. They have been given from among all the people of Israel to serve as their assistants. ¹⁰Appoint Aaron and his sons to carry out the duties of the priesthood. But any unauthorized person who goes too near the sanctuary must be put to death."

¹¹And the LORD said to Moses, ¹²"Look, I have chosen the Levites from among the Israelites to serve as substitutes for all the firstborn sons of the people of Israel. The Levites belong to me, ¹³for all the firstborn males are mine. On the day I struck down all the firstborn sons of the Egyptians, I set apart for myself all the firstborn in Israel, both of people and of animals. They are mine; I am the LORD."

3:7 Hebrew *around the Tent of Meeting, doing service at the Tabernacle.*   3:8 Hebrew *the Tent of Meeting;* also in 3:25.

NOTES

3:1 *the family line of Aaron and Moses.* Harrison (1990:61-63) thinks this "family line" (*toledoth* [TH8435, ZH9352]) is a colophon for ch 2, looking back to 2:1. But ch 3 does describe the family of Aaron, and Milgrom notes that Aaron is listed first only in genealogical texts (1989:15, citing 3:1; 26:59; Exod 6:20; 1 Chr 6:3 [5:29]; 23:13).

3:3 *ordained to minister as priests.* Lit., "filled the hand to be a priest." Akkadian equivalents to "filling the hand" hint that some symbol of office was placed in the person's hands (Milgrom 1989:300 n. 1).

3:4 *the wrong kind of fire, different than he had commanded.* Lit., "strange [*zar*] fire," (cf. Lev 10:1-2), like the *zar* [TH2114A, ZH2424] (NLT, "unauthorized person") intruding on holy space around the Tabernacle (1:51; 3:10, 38).

Eleazar and Ithamar to serve as priests with their father, Aaron. Lit., "and Eleazar and Ithamar served as priests before/in the presence of Aaron their father." Levine translates with a temporal, "during the lifetime of" (Levine 1993:156, citing Gen 11:28); see also NIV, NASB, RSV, NRSV, ESV. But it is most likely a locative, "before," i.e., "under the oversight of" (see Deut 25:2; 1 Sam 3:1).

3:7 *in and around the Tabernacle.* Lit., "before the Tent of Meeting, performing the duties of the Tabernacle" (cf. NLT mg). Milgrom notes that the Hittite "Instructions for the Temple Officials" permits/requires the keepers to enter the temple precinct on the following conditions: when accompanying a layperson coming to perform a rite (e.g., 16:9) or when hunting or pursuing an intruder (Milgrom 1989:16; see ANET 209 or COS 1.83:219-220).

3:10 *Appoint.* The Hebrew is *paqad* [TH6485, ZH7212], the same term used for "registering troops" (1:3, 19; 2:4, etc.).

unauthorized person. The Hebrew term *zar* [TH2114A, ZH2424] has already been used to describe the "wrong kind of fire, different than he had commanded" offered by Nadab and Abihu (3:4), and for the intruder into sacred space (1:51); it would also include a non-Levite trying to perform Levitical tasks (1:51; 3:38; 18:4) or a non-Aaronite Levite trying to serve at the altar (3:10; 16:40; 18:7).

3:12 *I have chosen.* Heb., *wa'ani hinneh laqakhti* [TH3947, ZH4374]. Two things highlight God's sovereign choice here: (1) Starting the clause with the first-person pronoun *'ani* [TH589, ZH638], rather than using the typical verb-subject order, emphasizes the subject— "*I myself* have chosen"; (2) inserting the interjection *hinneh* [TH2009, ZH2180] after that pronoun stresses the subject of the following verb, hence, "and, *as for me, I myself* have chosen" (Waltke and O'Connor 1990:300 n. 9).

substitutes. The Hebrew *takhath* [TH8478A, ZH9393] sometimes expresses recompense (Gen 30:15; 44:4; Ps 38:20); however, here it means substituting "in the place of" (e.g., Gen 4:25; 22:13; Lev 16:32).

firstborn sons. Lit., "firstborn who open a womb."

3:13 *set apart.* This is the Hiphil of *qadash* [TH6942, ZH7727]. It denotes designating or declaring someone (8:17; Jer 1:5) or something (1 Kgs 9:3, 7) to be holy or consecrated.

COMMENTARY

The note about a "family line" (*toledoth* [TH8435, ZH9352]; 3:1) serves multiple narrative functions: (1) It provides a unifying link to a common pentateuchal motif that organizes the story line around this term;[1] (2) it follows the pattern already used to number the tribes in chapter 1;[2] and (3) it relates the narrower line to the broader covenant community by the substitution motif. All of Abraham's offspring are dedicated to the Lord's service; however, priests and Levites are specifically consecrated to his service (cf. 1 Pet 2:9).

The Death of Aaron's Sons (3:2-4). These verses set the tone for chapters 3 and 4, with their recurring mention of the Lord's potentially lethal presence. The Levites were to put to death any *zar* [TH2114A, ZH2424] who intruded on the Tabernacle (1:51). Since Levites couldn't police their priestly superiors, the Lord himself did so, killing even legitimate priests, including the firstborn (3:2), when they burned *zar* fire while on priestly duty (3:4; cf. Lev 10). Commentators offer a range of suggestions to explain the death of Aaron's priestly sons: (1) They may have been drunk, which prompted the prohibition of wine for serving priests (Allen

1990:721; see Lev 10:1-2, 8-9; cf. Num 3:8-11); however, we get no mention of that here; (2) apostasy (E. W. Davies 1995b:27; Robinson 1978); (3) they may have failed to take the correct precautions (Lev 16:12-13) or even taken presumptuous actions like Uzziah's (2 Chr 26:16); (4) they may have burned the wrong incense mixture (Chapman and Streane 1914:54; Levine 1993:156; Exod 30:9, 34-38); and (5) they may have used poor timing (Chapman and Streane 1914:54; Snijders 1954; Elliger 1966:136-139; Lev 10:16-20). If it were because of presumption, one would expect that point to be made; and if it were about timing, like the offense of Eleazar and Ithamar, we might expect similar lenient treatment. But the point is its "strangeness," and it is the fire, not the incense, that is unauthorized; therefore, the text is best understood to speak of fire not taken from the altar (Haran 1960).

The deaths of Aaron's sons had later parallels with those who proved negligent around holy things:

The deaths of Eli's poorly supervised priestly sons (1 Sam 2:12-36, especially vv. 25, 31-34; 4:11)
The deaths of 70 people for looking into the Ark (1 Sam 6:19)
The rejection of Saul for neglecting the full obligation of *kherem* [TH2764, ZH3051] warfare (1 Sam 15)
The death of Uzzah for touching the Ark (2 Sam 6:6-7)
Uzziah's leprosy because of presumption in offering incense (2 Kgs 15:5; 2 Chr 26:16-21)
The hellish expulsion of the wedding guest who dishonors his host with inappropriate dress (Matt 22:11-13)
The deaths of Ananias and Sapphira (Acts 5:1-11)
The deaths of certain Corinthians who abused the Lord's Supper (1 Cor 11:27-34)

Assigning the Levites to Aaron and His Sons (3:5-13). In the ancient Near East the firstborn was expected to provide for the burial of deceased parents, to inherit the family gods and cultic objects, and care for the ancestral spirits, thereby keeping their name alive to act on behalf of the family (Milgrom 1989:17-18). The rabbis even maintained that the firstborn originally enjoyed priestly status:

And he sent the firstborn of the sons of Israel—for until that hour the firstborn had the (office of performing) worship, the tabernacle of ordinance not (as yet) being made, nor the priesthood given unto Aaron; and they offered burnt offerings and consecrated oblations of oxen before the Lord. (*Targum Pseudo-Jonathan*, Exod 24:5)

Substitution plays a fundamental role in Levitical theology in Numbers. God had claimed Israel's firstborn as his own on Passover night. By sparing Israel's firstborn, the Lord acquired them (Exod 13:1-2, 11-16), a principle that God reiterated (Exod 22:29-30; 34:19-20). After the golden calf incident, the Levites were substituted without formal statute (Exod 32:25-29), and this text formalized the arrangement. So the Levites should have been a constant reminder of God's claim on the firstborn, all the more so since Israel was itself God's firstborn (Exod 4:22). Old

Testament Israel existed as the world's priestly people (Gen 12:1-3; Exod 19:6)—and, indeed, the church today serves that purpose (Gal 3:6-7; 1 Pet 2:5-7; Rev 1:6; 5:10; 20:6).

This camp regulation channeled Levitical militarism into protection of the cult (1:51; 3:10, 38).[3] Like the cherubim who guarded the way back into Eden (Gen 3:24), and like the ancient Near Eastern *sadin* who guarded pagan shrines (de Vaux 1961:348), the Levites were the forerunners of the gatekeepers of the Solomonic Temple, who protected the Temple from defilement by stray animals, unclean persons, and pagan intruders (e.g., 2 Kgs 22:4; 1 Chr 9:19; 26:13-19). Later, Nehemiah had them shut the gates to keep the Sabbath holy (Neh 13:19, 22).

The purpose of summary execution for intruders was to prevent God's punishing the whole people for an individual's transgression (see 1:53; 16:1–17:13; cf. 25:8). G. J. Wenham (1981:71-72) says this Levitical obligation to kill encroachers foreshadowed the New Testament obligation of elders to correct erring brethren (see Matt 18:15-18; Acts 18:26; Gal 2:11; 6:1; 1 Thess 5:12-14; 1 Tim 5:19-20; Jas 5:19-20). Perhaps better connections would be the deaths of Ananias and Sapphira (Acts 5:1-10), the note that some are dead because they failed to recognize the Lord's Table (1 Cor 11:27-30), and the eschatological exclusion of the wicked from God's presence (Rev 21:8, 27; 22:15).

ENDNOTES

1. Gen 2:4; 5:1; 6:9; 10:1, 32; 11:10, 27; 25:12, 19; 36:1, 9; 37:2; Exod 6:16, 19; 28:10.
2. 1:20, 22, 24, 26, 28, 30, 32, 34, 36, 38, 40, 42.
3. Genesis depicts Levi as a bloodthirsty man/tribe, who joined with Simeon in avenging Dinah's rape on the men of Shechem (Gen 34; 49:5-7). Moses called on them to kill 3,000 idolaters at the golden calf incident (Exod 32:25-29; cf. Num 25:7-12). Later the high priest also had them guard young king Joash against Athaliah (2 Chr 23:7).

◆   ### e. Counting the Levites by clans (3:14-39)

[14]The LORD spoke again to Moses in the wilderness of Sinai. He said, [15]"Record the names of the members of the tribe of Levi by their families and clans. List every male who is one month old or older." [16]So Moses listed them, just as the LORD had commanded.

[17]Levi had three sons, whose names were Gershon, Kohath, and Merari.
[18]The clans descended from Gershon were named after two of his descendants, Libni and Shimei.
[19]The clans descended from Kohath were named after four of his descendants, Amram, Izhar, Hebron, and Uzziel.
[20]The clans descended from Merari were named after two of his descendants, Mahli and Mushi.

These were the Levite clans, listed according to their family groups.

[21]The descendants of Gershon were composed of the clans descended from Libni and Shimei. [22]There were 7,500 males one month old or older among these Gershonite clans. [23]They were assigned the area to the west of the Tabernacle for their camp. [24]The leader of the Gershonite clans was Eliasaph son of Lael. [25]These two clans were responsible to care for the Tabernacle, including the sacred

tent with its layers of coverings, the curtain at its entrance, ²⁶the curtains of the courtyard that surrounded the Tabernacle and altar, the curtain at the courtyard entrance, the ropes, and all the equipment related to their use.

²⁷The descendants of Kohath were composed of the clans descended from Amram, Izhar, Hebron, and Uzziel. ²⁸There were 8,600* males one month old or older among these Kohathite clans. They were responsible for the care of the sanctuary, ²⁹and they were assigned the area south of the Tabernacle for their camp. ³⁰The leader of the Kohathite clans was Elizaphan son of Uzziel. ³¹These four clans were responsible for the care of the Ark, the table, the lampstand, the altars, the various articles used in the sanctuary, the inner curtain, and all the equipment related to their use. ³²Eleazar, son of Aaron the priest, was the chief administrator over all the Levites, with special responsibility for the oversight of the sanctuary.

³³The descendants of Merari were composed of the clans descended from Mahli and Mushi. ³⁴There were 6,200 males one month old or older among these Merarite clans. ³⁵They were assigned the area north of the Tabernacle for their camp. The leader of the Merarite clans was Zuriel son of Abihail. ³⁶These two clans were responsible for the care of the frames supporting the Tabernacle, the crossbars, the pillars, the bases, and all the equipment related to their use. ³⁷They were also responsible for the posts of the courtyard and all their bases, pegs, and ropes.

³⁸The area in front of the Tabernacle, in the east toward the sunrise,* was reserved for the tents of Moses and of Aaron and his sons, who had the final responsibility for the sanctuary on behalf of the people of Israel. Anyone other than a priest or Levite who went too near the sanctuary was to be put to death.

³⁹When Moses and Aaron counted the Levite clans at the LORD's command, the total number was 22,000 males one month old or older.

3:28 Some Greek manuscripts read *8,300;* see total in 3:39.   3:38 Hebrew *toward the sunrise, in front of the Tent of Meeting.*

NOTES

3:15 one month old or older. Perhaps this was considered to be the age of viability (18:16; Lev 27:6). Milgrom says that with the high infant mortality rate, a child younger than 30 days was not yet considered a person; thus, even today Jewish practice maintains no mourning rites for such an infant (Milgrom 1989:23, citing, on nonpersonhood, Lev 27:6 and *Tosefta Shabbat* 15{16}:7; on mortality, *Tanhuma* Num 21; and for no rites being said, *b. Mo'ed Qatan* 24b).

3:17-20 This list corresponds with the list in Exod 6:16-19 but has its background in Gen 46:11. See also 1 Chr 6:16-19; 23:6-7, 12, 21; cf. Num 26:58.

3:28 8,600. The Lucianic revision of the LXX reads "8,300," which accommodates the grand total of 22,000 (3:39) instead of resulting in 22,300. Scribal error could play a role in either reading, since there is only a one-letter difference in Hebrew between "8,600" and "8,300."

responsible for the care of the sanctuary. Heb., *shomre mishmereth haqqodesh* [TH6944, ZH7731]. The verb *shamar* [TH8104, ZH9068] refers to guarding, keeping a watch over, as does the related noun *mishmereth* [TH4931, ZH5466], a frequent description of Levitical duty (1:53; 3:7, 25, 28, 31, 36, 38; 4:27, 31; 8:26; 9:19, 23; 18:3, 8; 19:9; 31:30, 47).

3:30 Kohathite clans. Lit., "paternal house of the Kohathite clans." In this case, it appears that "paternal house" is the larger group, comprising multiple clans (see note on 1:2).

3:31 inner curtain. This is also called the "veil" (Exod 26:31-33; 35:12), "veil of the screen" (4:5; Exod 35:12; 39:34; 40:21), or "veil of testimony" (Lev 24:3); however, for clarity the NLT regularly uses "inner curtain."

3:32 *responsibility.* The Hebrew is *pequddath* [TH6486, ZH7213], a noun related to the verb *paqad* [TH6485, ZH7212], referring to a commission, appointment, or office (also 3:36).

3:37 *ropes.* This is the framework's guylines (Exod 26:15-30; 27:10-18).

3:38 *final responsibility.* Heb., *shomerim mishmereth* [TH8104/4931, ZH9068/5466] (see note on 3:28).

sanctuary. Heb., *hammiqdash* [TH1886.1/4720, ZH2021/5219]. This refers to the entire Tabernacle complex, everything inside the Levitical inner cordon (1:53).

Anyone other than a priest or Levite. See note on 3:10.

3:39 *Moses and Aaron counted.* The verb is *paqad* [TH6485, ZH7212]. This is the same verb used for "appointing" (3:10) and for registering troops (see note on 1:3). Since the verb is singular, the scribes placed dots over "Aaron," indicating doubt whether his name should be included there with Moses's. Some Hebrew manuscripts lack it, as do the Samaritan Pentateuch and the Syriac. His name is omitted at 3:14 and 16, so perhaps it was later added here to harmonize with the command, which included him (1:3).

22,000. The numbers given in this section of the Hebrew text add up to 22,300. But the Hebrew text of 3:39 records 22,000 as the total. The discrepancy cannot be from rounding off the numbers, because the figures in 3:43 and 3:46 show that the numbers here are not rounded off. The rabbis ingeniously suggested that the totals from verses 22, 28, and 34 included "Levite" firstborn, who could not therefore redeem others. More likely, the number of Kohathites should read "8,300" (see note on 3:28).

Clan	MT	LXX	Suggested Totals
Gershonites	7,500	7,500	7,500
Kohathites	8,600	[1]8,600	8,300
Merarites	6,200	[2]6,050	6,200
Calculated Totals	*22,300*	*22,150*	*22,000*
Recorded Totals	*22,000*	*22,000*	*22,000*

ENDNOTES
1. The Lucianic revision of LXX contains *triakosioi* (300) rather than *hexakosioi* (600), which helps to produce the *stated* total of 22,000 in the Hebrew and LXX.
2. For unknown reasons, the LXX supports the reading *hexakischilioi kai pentēkonta* (6,050).

COMMENTARY

Chapter 3 briefly mentions each Levitical family's responsibilities, but that issue is largely left aside until chapter 4. The real concern of chapter 3 is the Levites' substitutionary role. The Lord told Moses to count and list the names of "every male who is one month old or older" among the Levites (3:15), which he would later correlate with the firstborn males of that same age from the rest of the tribes (3:40-51). As has been the case so far in Numbers, the people promptly obeyed the Lord (3:16).

Levi's Three Sons (3:17-20). These verses trace the Levitical clans back to Levi's three sons, who appear to be listed in birth order (Gen 46:11) rather than in their order of prominence, as chapter 4 treats them (cf. also 26:58). In Exodus the concern was to establish the lineage of Moses and Aaron (Exod 6:26); therefore, the same list (Exod 6:16-19a; cf. Num 3:17-20) preceded a more detailed genealogy (Exod 6:19b-25). But genealogy is not the concern here, so we get only an abbreviated clan breakdown repeated at the head of each family section (3:17-20, cf. 3:21, 27, 33).

Gershonite Clans (3:21-26). The two-clan family of Gershonites formed the inner cordon's western quadrant (3:23). Led by Eliasaph son of Lael (3:24), they cared for all of the Tabernacle's fabric and leather coverings: the "ten curtains of finely woven linen," each 42 feet by 6 feet (Exod 26:1-6); the "eleven curtains of goat-hair cloth," each 45 feet by 6 feet (Exod 26:7-13); the layers of "tanned ram skins" and "fine goat-skin leather" (4:6-14; Exod 26:14); and the embroidered linen curtains used as the entrance to the tent (Exod 26:36) and to enclose the courtyard (Exod 27:9, 16). Note that the more holy "inner curtain" was under the care of the Kohathites (3:31), and it covered the Ark when on the march (4:5). The Gershonite responsibilities also included all the ropes for tying all the curtains and coverings together, plus the equipment for handling and maintaining it, but not the structural guylines (4:24-26). The number of their males who were one month old or older was 7,500.

Kohathite Clans (3:27-32). The four-clan family of the Kohathites formed the inner cordon's southern quadrant (v. 29). Led by Elizaphan son of Uzziel (v. 30), they cared for the Tabernacle's furnishings and utensils (4:4-20). Since they could not actually handle these utensils and furniture, the priests first packaged them for portage (4:5-20). The Kohathites then carried all of this on their own shoulders, rather than with oxcarts like the Gershonites and Merarites had for their heavier and less-sacred loads of fabrics and framework. Kohathites had the inner curtain in their care, along with other sacred objects (4:7, 9, 14; Exod 25:29, 38; 27:3). In fact, this curtain always hid God's throne-chariot, the Ark. It hung over the entrance to the Holiest Place and was draped over the Ark when it traveled. This curtain was the forerunner of the one that was torn from top to bottom upon Jesus' death (Matt 27:51; Mark 15:38; Luke 23:45), which now opens up bold access to God's royal presence (Heb 4:16). The largest of the Levitical families, the Kohathites numbered 8,300 (or 8,600; see note and NLT mg at 3:28) males one month old or older (3:28).

Merarite Clans (3:33-37). The two-clan family of Merarites formed the inner cordon's northern quadrant (3:35). Led by Zuriel son of Abihail, they cared for the Tabernacle's framework: its uprights and their bases, the crossbeams, and the guylines and their pegs (4:31). The smallest Levitical family, they numbered 6,200 males one month old or older.

Summary (3:38-39). Moses, Aaron, and his sons descended from Levi. This family formed an honor guard at the Tabernacle's entrance to the east. The priests were responsible for the whole Tabernacle, supervising the Levites in all their duties (4:16, 27, 33). The Levite males one month old or older were enough to serve as substitutes for 22,000 of Israel's firstborn males, which was the purpose of this count (3:11-12); however, the following verses show that an additional provision was required for any firstborn sons over the 22,000 the Levites redeemed.

◆   ### f. Redeeming the firstborn sons (3:40-51)

⁴⁰Then the LORD said to Moses, "Now count all the firstborn sons in Israel who are one month old or older, and make a list of their names. ⁴¹The Levites must be reserved for me as substitutes for the firstborn sons of Israel; I am the LORD. And the Levites' livestock must be reserved for me as substitutes for the firstborn livestock of the whole nation of Israel."

⁴²So Moses counted the firstborn sons of the people of Israel, just as the LORD had commanded. ⁴³The number of firstborn sons who were one month old or older was 22,273.

⁴⁴Then the LORD said to Moses, ⁴⁵"Take the Levites as substitutes for the firstborn sons of the people of Israel. And take the livestock of the Levites as substitutes for the firstborn livestock of the people of Israel. The Levites belong to me; I am the LORD. ⁴⁶There are 273 more firstborn sons of Israel than there are Levites. To redeem these extra firstborn sons, ⁴⁷collect five pieces of silver* for each of them (each piece weighing the same as the sanctuary shekel, which equals twenty gerahs). ⁴⁸Give the silver to Aaron and his sons as the redemption price for the extra firstborn sons."

⁴⁹So Moses collected the silver for redeeming the firstborn sons of Israel who exceeded the number of Levites. ⁵⁰He collected 1,365 pieces of silver* on behalf of these firstborn sons of Israel (each piece weighing the same as the sanctuary shekel). ⁵¹And Moses gave the silver for the redemption to Aaron and his sons, just as the LORD had commanded.

3:47 Hebrew *5 shekels* [2 ounces or 57 grams].   3:50 Hebrew *1,365 shekels* [34 pounds or 15.5 kilograms].

NOTES

3:40 *count.* Heb., *paqad* [TH6485, ZH7212] (see note on 1:3).

make a list of their names. Lit., "lift up the record of their names" (also 1 Chr 27:23), synonymous with the parallel expressions, "lift up the head" (1:2; 4:2; 26:2; 31:26) and "register" (1:3; Exod 30:12).

3:43 22,273. It is difficult to reconcile this number of firstborn sons with the total of 603,550 Israelite fighting men (1:46). This figure would mean that each Israelite family would have about 27 males—and that would be for each woman (see Introduction, "Large Numbers in the Book").

3:46, 48, 51 *redeem . . . redemption.* The Hebrew is the noun *peduyim* [TH6302, ZH7012], which means "redemption price" or "ransom." See the related term *pidyom* [TH6306, ZH7017] (3:49), used when redeeming property (Exod 21:30) or ransoming a life (Ps 49:8).

COMMENTARY

After completing the count of males one month old or older among the Levites (3:21-39), Moses counted the twelve tribes' firstborn. The 273 left unredeemed by a Levite substitute were each redeemed with silver. It is not clear who paid the redemption price, whether it was collected from the Levites themselves, from all Israel, or from those who were determined to be as yet unredeemed. Traditional Jewish exegesis assumes the last option and suggests the 273 who had to pay were identified by lot, as noted in the following:

Moses said: what should I do with the firstborns of Israel? How can I make any of them pay five shekels? If I say to one of them: "Give me your redemption money and go," He will say to me: "A Levite has already redeemed me!" What did Moses do? He brought 22,000 lots on which he wrote "Levite," and 273 lots on which he wrote "five shekels." He mixed the lots and put them in a box. Moses said to the firstborns: "Take your lots." To one who drew a lot on which it was written "Levite," he said: "A Levite has already redeemed you." To one who drew a lot on which it was written "Five shekels," he said: "Give your redemption money and go." (*b. Sanhedrin* 17a)

According to Milgrom (1989:19), God designated the 273 who were not yet redeemed by means of an oracle. In any case, this ransom depicted the slave price, given as a sign of bond servitude to the Lord rather than to Pharaoh or to the gods of the nations (G. J. Wenham 1981:71; contra Harrison 1990:78). The price of five silver shekels each was not only equivalent to a month's wages, it was the price at which a boy from one month to five years old was valued (Lev 27:6). This continued thereafter to be the price of redemption for the firstborn son (18:16).

In the same way, the firstborn of the Levites' livestock were substituted for the firstborn of Israel's stock. Since the firstborn of pure animals already belonged to the Lord (18:15, 17), the rabbis concluded that the redeemed animals must have been impure animals not eligible for the altar and therefore redeemable (*b. Bekhorot* 4b; so also Dillmann and Knobel 1886:19). But the text doesn't limit it to unclean animals. Critical scholars think this was a late addition providing for redemption of firstborn livestock when sacrificing all these animals no longer seemed practical (E. W. Davies 1995b:35; McNeile 1911:18; Sturdy 1976:33). This is not necessary; it is better to see this exchange as a one-off instance from the wilderness period: All future firstborn livestock would still belong to the Lord and thus be sacrificed.

Payment went to the priests (3:51). Throughout the Old Testament, this provided an ongoing depiction of the principle of firstfruits, which in turn depicted the principle of substitution. This acknowledged that "the earth is the LORD's, and everything in it" (1 Cor 10:26, quoting Ps 24:1). Under the new covenant, redemption is no longer with silver and gold, whether freeing a man from lifelong lameness (Acts 3:1-8) or from an "empty life" (1 Pet 1:18). Now we're reminded, "God paid a high price for you": Therefore, "don't be enslaved by the world" (1 Cor 7:23), but rather "honor God with your body" (1 Cor 6:20).

◆   ### g. Enlisting the Levites (4:1-49)

Then the LORD said to Moses and Aaron, 2"Record the names of the members of the clans and families of the Kohathite division of the tribe of Levi. 3List all the men between the ages of thirty and fifty who are eligible to serve in the Tabernacle.*

4"The duties of the Kohathites at the Tabernacle will relate to the most sacred objects. ⁵When the camp moves, Aaron and his sons must enter the Tabernacle first to take down the inner curtain and cover the Ark of the Covenant* with it. ⁶Then they must cover the inner curtain with fine goatskin leather and spread over that a single piece of blue cloth. Finally, they must put the carrying poles of the Ark in place.

⁷"Next they must spread a blue cloth over the table where the Bread of the Presence is displayed, and on the cloth they will place the bowls, pans, jars, pitchers, and the special bread. ⁸They must spread a scarlet cloth over all of this, and finally a covering of fine goatskin leather on top of the scarlet cloth. Then they must insert the carrying poles into the table.

⁹"Next they must cover the lampstand with a blue cloth, along with its lamps, lamp snuffers, trays, and special jars of olive oil. ¹⁰Then they must cover the lampstand and its accessories with fine goatskin leather and place the bundle on a carrying frame.

¹¹"Next they must spread a blue cloth over the gold incense altar and cover this cloth with fine goatskin leather. Then they must attach the carrying poles to the altar. ¹²They must take all the remaining furnishings of the sanctuary and wrap them in a blue cloth, cover them with fine goatskin leather, and place them on the carrying frame.

¹³"They must remove the ashes from the altar for sacrifices and cover the altar with a purple cloth. ¹⁴All the altar utensils—the firepans, meat forks, shovels, basins, and all the containers—must be placed on the cloth, and a covering of fine goatskin leather must be spread over them. Finally, they must put the carrying poles in place. ¹⁵The camp will be ready to move when Aaron and his sons have finished covering the sanctuary and all the sacred articles. The Kohathites will come and carry these things to the next destination. But they must not touch the sacred objects, or they will die. So these

are the things from the Tabernacle that the Kohathites must carry.

¹⁶"Eleazar son of Aaron the priest will be responsible for the oil of the lampstand, the fragrant incense, the daily grain offering, and the anointing oil. In fact, Eleazar will be responsible for the entire Tabernacle and everything in it, including the sanctuary and its furnishings."

¹⁷Then the LORD said to Moses and Aaron, ¹⁸"Do not let the Kohathite clans be destroyed from among the Levites! ¹⁹This is what you must do so they will live and not die when they approach the most sacred objects. Aaron and his sons must always go in with them and assign a specific duty or load to each person. ²⁰The Kohathites must never enter the sanctuary to look at the sacred objects for even a moment, or they will die."

²¹And the LORD said to Moses, ²²"Record the names of the members of the clans and families of the Gershonite division of the tribe of Levi. ²³List all the men between the ages of thirty and fifty who are eligible to serve in the Tabernacle.

²⁴"These Gershonite clans will be responsible for general service and carrying loads. ²⁵They must carry the curtains of the Tabernacle, the Tabernacle itself with its coverings, the outer covering of fine goatskin leather, and the curtain for the Tabernacle entrance. ²⁶They are also to carry the curtains for the courtyard walls that surround the Tabernacle and altar, the curtain across the courtyard entrance, the ropes, and all the equipment related to their use. The Gershonites are responsible for all these items. ²⁷Aaron and his sons will direct the Gershonites regarding all their duties, whether it involves moving the equipment or doing other work. They must assign the Gershonites responsibility for the loads they are to carry. ²⁸So these are the duties assigned to the Gershonite clans at the Tabernacle. They will be directly responsible to Ithamar son of Aaron the priest.

²⁹"Now record the names of the members of the clans and families of the Merarite division of the tribe of Levi. ³⁰List all the men between the ages of thirty and fifty who are eligible to serve in the Tabernacle.

³¹"Their only duty at the Tabernacle will be to carry loads. They will carry the frames of the Tabernacle, the crossbars, the posts, and the bases; ³²also the posts for the courtyard walls with their bases, pegs, and ropes; and all the accessories and everything else related to their use. Assign the various loads to each man by name. ³³So these are the duties of the Merarite clans at the Tabernacle. They are directly responsible to Ithamar son of Aaron the priest."

³⁴So Moses, Aaron, and the other leaders of the community listed the members of the Kohathite division by their clans and families. ³⁵The list included all the men between thirty and fifty years of age who were eligible for service in the Tabernacle, ³⁶and the total number came to 2,750. ³⁷So this was the total of all those from the Kohathite clans who were eligible to serve at the Tabernacle. Moses and Aaron listed them, just as the LORD had commanded through Moses.

³⁸The Gershonite division was also listed by its clans and families. ³⁹The list included all the men between thirty and fifty years of age who were eligible for service in the Tabernacle, ⁴⁰and the total number came to 2,630. ⁴¹So this was the total of all those from the Gershonite clans who were eligible to serve at the Tabernacle. Moses and Aaron listed them, just as the LORD had commanded.

⁴²The Merarite division was also listed by its clans and families. ⁴³The list included all the men between thirty and fifty years of age who were eligible for service in the Tabernacle, ⁴⁴and the total number came to 3,200. ⁴⁵So this was the total of all those from the Merarite clans who were eligible for service. Moses and Aaron listed them, just as the LORD had commanded through Moses.

⁴⁶So Moses, Aaron, and the leaders of Israel listed all the Levites by their clans and families. ⁴⁷All the men between thirty and fifty years of age who were eligible for service in the Tabernacle and for its transportation ⁴⁸numbered 8,580. ⁴⁹When their names were recorded, as the LORD had commanded through Moses, each man was assigned his task and told what to carry.

And so the registration was completed, just as the LORD had commanded Moses.

4:3 Hebrew *the Tent of Meeting;* also in 4:4, 15, 23, 25, 28, 30, 31, 33, 35, 37, 39, 41, 43, 47.   4:5 Or *Ark of the Testimony.*

NOTES

4:2 *Record the names.* Lit., "lift up the head" (also at 4:22); see note on 1:2.

clans and families. Lit., "clans and paternal houses"; see note on 1:2.

4:3 *eligible to serve.* Heb., *ba' latsaba' la'asoth mela'kah* (lit., "going into the army/host to do work"). *Tsaba'* [TH6635, ZH7372] often refers to military service; here it is adapted for non-military service to the cult. The term *mela'kah* [TH4399, ZH4856] may refer to skilled labor, as opposed to general physical labor (*'abodah* [TH5656, ZH6275]; 4:4), the term used more generally for the Levitical tasks (Milgrom 1989:24; Milgrom 1970:77-82).

4:4 *most sacred objects.* Lit., "holy of holies." This generally refers to the Most Holy Place (Exod 26:33; 1 Kgs 8:6; 1 Chr 6:49; 2 Chr 3:8, 10; 5:7; Ezek 41:4), but here and in 4:19 it refers to the most sacred furniture and utensils.

4:5 *Ark of the Covenant.* Lit., "Ark of the Testimony" (7:89; Exod 25:21; 26:33-34; 30:6, 26; 31:7; 39:35; 40:3, 5, 21; Josh 4:16). The NLT uses "Ark of the Covenant" regularly for both expressions. More frequent is "Ark of the LORD's Covenant" (10:33; 14:44; Deut 10:8; 31:9, 25-26; Josh 3:3 [cf. v. 11], 17; 4:7, 18; 6:8; 8:33; 1 Sam 4:3-5; 1 Kgs 3:15; 6:19; 8:1, 6;

1 Chr 15:25-26, 28-29; 16:37; 17:1; 22:19; 28:2, 18; 2 Chr 5:2, 7; Jer 3:16). The Ark served as the repository for covenant documents (Exod 25:16, 21; 40:20). It was a box of acacia wood covered with gold inside and out, which measured 27 inches by 45 inches (Exod 25:10).

4:6 fine goatskin leather. Heb., *takhash* [TH8476, ZH9391] (also at 4:8, 10-12, 14, 25). There are many possibilities for translating this: "badger skins" (KJV, NKJV), "porpoise skin" (NASB), "narwhale skin" (I. Aharoni 1938:462-463), "goatskin" (RSV, NLT), "sealskin" (ASV, JPS), "hides of sea cows" (NIV, following Dillmann and Knobel 1886), or "dolphin skin" (NJPS) or "dugong skin" because of a connection with the Arabic *d/tukhas* (KBL; Holladay 1971), perhaps even "something of fine quality." Milgrom suggests "yellow-orange" (1989:25). Hoffmeier goes back to Robinson's discovering that the Bedouin made their sandals from "the thick skin of a fish." Robinson had noted that rather than being something fine and luxurious, "The skin is clumsy and coarse, and might answer very well for the external covering of the Tabernacle" (Hoffmeier 2005:213, citing Robinson 1841:1.171).

single piece of blue cloth. Heb., *beged-kelil tekeleth*. The MT connects *kelil* [TH3632B, ZH4003] (single) with *beged* [TH899A, ZH955] (cloth), i.e., a one-piece covering, like a robe. However, *kelil* may modify the color (*tekeleth*), i.e., entirely blue. *Tekeleth* [TH8504, ZH9418] is a bluish-purple or violet color produced from the secretions of the murex snail, particularly the *murex brandaris*, which is known as the fiery-horned snail or the Turk's blood snail. Milgrom (1989:412) notes that it took about 12,000 snails to produce 0.05 oz of the dye, which would have made it a precious commodity, available only to the most wealthy, hence its royal association.

put the carrying poles of the Ark in place. The gold-covered acacia wood poles were inserted through rings attached to the Ark's legs (Exod 25:13-15; 35:12; 37:4-5; 40:20) and left in place even in the Tabernacle (Exod 25:15); therefore, this must refer either to adjusting them (Harrison 1990:83; Hirsch 1971:42) or to reinserting them after temporary removal for packing (Noordtzij 1983:44).

4:7 table where the Bread of the Presence is displayed. Lit., "Table of the Presence." This is an abbreviation for "Table of the Bread of the Presence" (Exod 25:23-30). It was a gold-rimmed and gold-covered table about 3 feet long and 1.5 feet wide on which on every Sabbath 12 loaves were laid out on the north side of the Holy Place (Lev 24:5-9). Here the Samaritan Pentateuch and LXX include the outer court's bronze washbasin (Exod 30:17-21) because it was also anointed with oil (Exod 30:26-28; 40:11) and was therefore holy (Lev 8:11).

special bread. Lit., "the bread [displayed] continuously," like the flame that was kept blazing on the altar (Lev 6:9) or menorah that was kept burning each night (Exod 27:20-21; Lev 24:2-4). This was the "Bread of the Presence" (Exod 25:30; 35:13; 39:36; 1 Sam 21:6; 1 Kgs 7:48; 2 Chr 4:19).

4:8 scarlet cloth. Heb., *beged tola'ath* [TH899A/8438A, ZH955/9357], a royal color ranging from purple to crimson to scarlet, possibly dyed from the *coccus ilicis* (BDB 1068).

4:9 lampstand. Heb., *menorath hamma'or* [TH4501/1886.1/3974, ZH4963/2021/4401], meaning "lampstand for the lighting." Its function was to light the holy place, but its symbolic significance was as a stylized tree of life (see comments on 8:1-4).

lamp snuffers. The Hebrew is a dual form, indicating a two-part utensil, either the scissor-like snuffer (NLT, ASV, NASB, RSV, NRSV, NJB) or a pair of tongs (KJV, ESV, JPS, NJPS).

trays. It is some kind of small pan connected with the Menorah, so "trays" fits well (NLT, RSV, NRSV); cf. "fire pans" (NJPS) or "snuffdishes" (KJV, ASV, JPS). See the same term used for "firepans" for the altar (Exod 27:3; 38:3) or for embers from the offering of incense (16:6; Lev 16:12).

4:10 carrying frame. Heb., *mot* [TH4132, ZH4573], the term used for carrying the huge cluster of Eschol grapes (13:23). Related to the verb for "totter," perhaps *mot* depicts springy poles used as a yoke on someone's shoulders or used to carry a frame between two men walking single file.

4:11 gold incense altar. Lit., "altar of gold," known elsewhere as the incense altar (Exod 31:8). It sat in the Holy Place right in front of the curtain that concealed the Most Holy Place. It was acacia wood overlaid with gold and stood about 36 inches high and was 18 inches square (Exod 30:2). Like the Ark and Table for the Bread, it was fitted with rings for carrying poles. Perhaps its utensils were among those listed in 4:14.

4:13 remove the ashes. This is an expression for fattening, but it is used here for clearing away the fatty soot, i.e., "de-sooting" (Waltke and O'Connor 1990:413 §24.4.f.7).

purple cloth. The word for this color is *'argaman* [TH713, ZH763]. It is another royal color of purple to reddish-purple. This is its only occurrence in Numbers, but it is elsewhere used in describing the Tabernacle curtains (Exod 26, 35–36, 38) and the priests' clothes (Exod 28, 39).

4:14 firepans. Heb., *makhtah* [TH4289, ZH4746]. The KJV has "censers"; however, these were probably used for removing ashes after the sacrifice was consumed (Lev 6:10).

meat forks. Heb., *mazleg* [TH4207, ZH4657]; also translated "hooks" (KJV, ASV, JPS, NJPS), used to manipulate the sacrifice so that it would be completely consumed.

shovels. Or "scoops" or "scrapers" (NJPS) to clean the altar after use.

basins. These were used for splashing sacrificial blood against the altar (Exod 27:3; 38:3).

4:15 The verse repeats the term for "holy," emphasizing the point that wrongful contact with it led to death: "sanctuary" (*haqqodesh* [TH6944, ZH7731]), the *holy* place; "sacred articles" (*kele haqqodesh* [TH3627, ZH3998]), the utensils of the *holy* place.

4:16 Eleazar son of Aaron the priest will be responsible for. This put the Kohathites under Eleazar's supervision; cf. Ithamar supervising the Gershonites and Merarites (4:28, 33). See the Hittite "Instructions to Temple Officials" for the practice of two classes of personnel tending a temple, one guarding it under the supervision of the other (ANET 207-210; COS 1.83).

daily grain offering. Heb., *minkhath hattamid.* The word *tamid* [TH8548, ZH9458] is understood to mean "daily" or "regular" here. Noordtzij (1983:46) says this is the daily burnt offering (Exod 29:38) described as "burnt offerings . . . made each day" (Exod 29:42; or "daily burnt offering," Num 28–29). This was not always called *'olah* [TH5930, ZH6592] as it is in Lev 6:13 [5]; Neh 10:33 [34], but rather *minkhah* [TH4503, ZH4966], because this term used of grain offering (Lev 2) was originally a general term for offering.

4:18 destroyed from among the Levites. Lit., "cut off from" (see note on 9:13).

4:20 enter the sanctuary to look at. The ancient Near East knew of lethal viewings of sacred objects. In the Sumerian "Curse of Agade," the city was cursed because "the Akkadians saw the holy vessels of the gods" (ANET 649). And the "Lamentation over the Destruction of Sumer and Ur" relates that Ur was destroyed because "the holy kettles that no one [was permitted] to look upon, the enemy looked upon" (ANET 618).

for even a moment. Heb., *keballa'* [TH3509.1/1104, ZH3869/1180] (to swallow). JPS and NJPS take the metaphor of being swallowed or engulfed as a metaphor for packaging, i.e., "while they are being covered"; however, most translations take this as a figure of speech for something *momentary* (cf. swallowing spit, Job 7:19), as an ancient Near Eastern equivalent to the blink of an eye. Sherwood (2002:144) suggests that the term might have been "chosen to foreshadow 16:32, where the earth swallows up Korah (a Kohathite) and his followers."

4:23 all . . . eligible. Heb., *kol-habba' litsbo' tsaba'* [TH3807.1/935, ZH4200/995] (all who enter for service); cf. the parallel expression "all who are able to go to war" (1:3, 20, 45; *kol-yotse' tsaba'* [TH3318, ZH3655]); see note on 1:3.

4:26 all the equipment related to their use. Lit., "all the vessels/utensils/fittings for their service." Milgrom thinks they are work tools (1989:30).

4:27 They must assign. This is literally "you [pl.] must assign" and may indicate that both Moses and Aaron gave these assignments or, more probably, that Aaron and his sons gave these assignments, as implied in the NLT.

4:31 The Hebrew has all three terms for Levitical work: *mishmereth* [TH4931, ZH5466] (guard duty), *massa'* [TH4853, ZH5362] (portage, burden), and *'abodah* [TH5656, ZH6275] (common labor).

frames. These were 48 vertical boards (15 feet by 27 inches) of gold-covered acacia wood (Exod 26:15-25) that ran around the courtyard (150 feet by 75 feet). Each had gold rings through which 15 "crossbars" made of gold-covered acacia wood were inserted horizontally (Exod 26:26-29).

posts. These were made of gold-covered acacia wood, which were set in silver bases; they divided the Holy Place from the Most Holy Place (Exod 26:32-33).

4:32 posts for the courtyard walls. These were 60 posts for the outer courtyard, set in their bronze bases (Exod 27:9-19).

pegs. These were used for guying the pillars (Exod 27:19).

ropes. These were used for running from the posts to the pegs (Exod 27:19).

Assign the various loads to each man by name. The assignments may have been by the name of the *carrier*, emphasizing individual responsibility (NEB, NJB; see Harrison 1990), or they may have been by the name of the *object*, emphasizing attention to detail (KJV, NIV, JPS, NJPS; see Hirsch 1971:48; Milgrom 1989:31). Since the text indeed names the objects, I think the latter is the case.

4:34 leaders . . . listed. See note on 1:3. This listing was from the earlier count (1:5-17, 44).

clans and families. Lit., "clans and paternal houses"; see note on 1:2.

4:35, 39, 47 all . . . eligible. See note on 4:23.

COMMENTARY

Just as Moses numbered the men of military age (1:16-45), so also he numbered the Levites of working age. This second Levitical count enrolls "men between the ages of thirty and fifty who are eligible to serve in the Tabernacle" (4:3) and to care for its "sacred objects" (4:4). Elsewhere the Levites are said to serve from ages 25 to 50 (8:24-25) or starting at 20 years (1 Chr 23:24; 2 Chr 31:17; Ezra 3:8). The rabbis harmonize this by positing an apprenticeship beginning at 20–25, with full service starting at 30 (Hertz 1977:607; citing *Sifre Numbers* §62); this would parallel the community at Qumran, where five years' training preceded full service (1QS^a 1:12-19; 1QM 7:3). Ashley suggests the age was raised to 30 because of the deaths of an immature Nadab and Abihu (1993:176). Perhaps this reflects three different historical settings: (1) age 30 for wilderness transport and service (ch 4), (2) age 25 for service in the Tent of Meeting, and (3) age 20 when there was no longer a need for transporting the Tabernacle (Harrison 1990:156-157; Noordtzij 1983:81).

Kohathite Work (4:4-20). The Kohathites' duties "relate to the most sacred objects" (4:4), so they were warned that "they must not touch the sacred objects, or they will die" (4:15). In fact, they could not "enter the sanctuary to look at the sacred objects for even a moment, or they will die" (4:20). So "Aaron and his sons must enter the Tabernacle" and prepare everything for Kohathite portage (4:5a).

Working outward through decreasing degrees of holiness, the priests packaged the holy things for Levitical portage. First, the priest entered the Most Holy Place and prepared the Ark (4:5b-6). They covered it with the "inner curtain," which closed off the Most Holy Place, then with a protective covering of leather, and finally with a blue covering over that. Finally, they adjusted or reinserted the Ark's carrying poles, which were generally left in their attaching rings (Exod 25:15; 38:5).

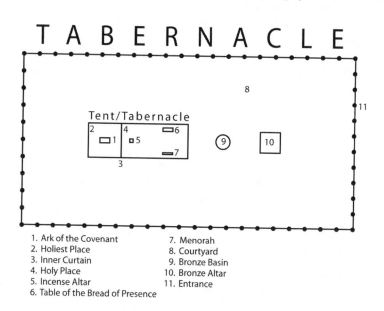

1. Ark of the Covenant
2. Holiest Place
3. Inner Curtain
4. Holy Place
5. Incense Altar
6. Table of the Bread of Presence
7. Menorah
8. Courtyard
9. Bronze Basin
10. Bronze Altar
11. Entrance

Second, the priests prepared the Holy Place's furnishings (4:7-12): the table where the Bread of the Presence was displayed (4:7), the lampstand (4:9), the incense altar (4:11), and the remaining furnishings (4:12). In each case, they first bundled the items in a blue cloth and finally covered it all with a protective leather covering. In the case of the table, they added a layer of scarlet cloth before the protective leather cover. Both the table and the incense altar had their own carrying poles (4:8, 11); the other items were packed on carrying frames (4:10, 12).

Third, they turned to the outer court (4:13-15). The priests prepared the bronze altar: They removed the soot and ashes, then covered the altar with a purple cloth (4:13). Then they laid the altar utensils on that cloth. Next, as was done with the furnishings inside the Tent itself, they laid over that a protective leather covering. Finally, they inserted the carrying poles, as they had with the Ark, table, and incense altar in the Tent. It is interesting to note that no mention is made of the bronze washbasin that was also in the outer court (Exod 30:28).

With that done, the Kohathites could take charge of their loads for the march without risking their lives (4:15). The priests never turned over the specially sanctified lamp oil, incense, grain offering, or anointing oil for Kohathite portage; rather, they carried that themselves (4:16). Only under the leadership of the priest Eleazar could the Kohathites handle the sanctuary and its furnishings (4:16). Every possible priestly precaution was to be taken to avoid a death like Aaron's two oldest sons had already experienced (3:1-4) and like what would happen at Beth-shemesh ("the LORD killed seventy men from Beth-shemesh because they looked into the Ark of the LORD"; 1 Sam 6:19) and to Uzzah, when the Lord "struck him dead because he had laid his hand on the Ark" (1 Chr 13:10; cf. 2 Sam 6:3-7).

We now have bold access to the Lord's presence (Eph 3:12; Heb 4:16; 10:19), and eventually the Most Holy Place will stand wide open to human view (Rev 11:19). Just as with the varied Levitical duties of old, in the New Testament age, "there are different kinds of spiritual gifts . . . service" (1 Cor 12:4-6), and each member of the congregation must work according to the gifts and calling that God sovereignly distributes (Rom 12:6; Eph 4:7).

Gershonite Work (4:21–28). The Gershonites began their responsibilities at the mature age of 30, and they were excused from their heavy lifting at the age of 50 (4:23). They were assigned the Tabernacle coverings (4:25), both the multiple layers of the Tent itself (4:25) and the curtains that formed the surrounding courtyard enclosing the Tent and the space around the altar (4:26). Even though their loads didn't require the same intense priestly intervention that the Kohathite loads required, even the Gershonites carried loads assigned by the priests and remained accountable to "Ithamar son of Aaron the priest" (4:28).

Merarite Work (4:29–33). The Merarites began their responsibilities at the mature age of 30, and they were excused from their heavy lifting at the age of 50 (4:30). Their loads comprised the Tabernacle framework: "the crossbars, the posts, and the bases" of the Tent itself (4:31), and the posts, bases, and guylines and pegs for its outer courtyard walls (4:32). Their loads didn't require the intense priestly intervention that the Kohathite loads required, but like the Gershonites, they carried loads assigned by the priests and remained accountable to the priest Ithamar (4:33, cf. 4:28).

Summary of the Levitical Census Work (4:34–49). The registration in chapter 3 had been for substitutionary purposes, and it listed a Levitical leader for each of the three clans (3:24, 30, 35), though with a reminder of priestly supervision (3:32). Chapter 4 ignored the Levitical clan leaders to focus on priestly oversight for all the Levitical Tabernacle work (4:16, 19, 27, 33). Of course, it is likely that the leaders mentioned in chapter 3 still played a role in the chain of command for managing the Levitical work assignments.

Following the usual practice throughout the early chapters of Numbers, registration was by tribe, clan, and name (4:34, 38, 42, 46, 49). And as with the other counts, we get reminders of the purpose of the count (4:37, 41, 45, 47) and a note that the count went forward "just as the LORD had commanded" (4:37, 41, 45, 49). For the Kohathites, the number eligible for Tabernacle service came to 2,750 (4:36), for the Gershonites, 2,630 (4:40), and for the Merarites, 3,200 (4:44). This came to a total Levitical workforce of 8,580 (4:48).

◆   **2. Commands for holiness in Israel (5:1–10:10)**
         a. Removing the unclean from the community (5:1-4)

The LORD gave these instructions to Moses: ²"Command the people of Israel to remove from the camp anyone who has a skin disease* or a discharge, or who has become ceremonially unclean by touching a dead person. ³This command applies to men and women alike. Remove them so they will not defile the camp in which I live among them." ⁴So the Israelites did as the LORD had commanded Moses and removed such people from the camp.

5:2 Traditionally rendered *leprosy*. The Hebrew word used here describes various skin diseases.

NOTES

5:2 skin disease. This is not the traditional "leprosy" (Hansen's disease, contra Harrison 1990:101); rather, it is a term for various skin diseases on people (Lev 13–14) or for something like mold, mildew, or dry rot when it appears on objects (Hulse 1975; see Lev 13:47, 51-53, 59).

dead person. The Hebrew is *nepesh* [TH5315, ZH5883], used as the opposite of *nepesh khayyah* [TH2416A, ZH2645], "living soul" (e.g., Gen 1:30; 2:7, 19). Here the word that is often translated "soul" does not indicate a ghost (i.e., something incorporeal, like a "soul") but rather a corpse (see TWOT 2.587-591).

5:3 men. This is *zakar* [TH2145, ZH2351], a specific term for "male," as opposed to *'adam* [TH120, ZH132], the general term for humanity.

women. This is *neqebah* [TH5347, ZH5922], a specific term for female, as opposed to *'ishah* [TH802, ZH851] for wife/woman.

COMMENTARY

Now the book of Numbers turns to various regulations for sustaining a holy camp (5:1–10:10). At first, the concern is cleansing the camp (5:1–6:27), then dedicating the altar (7:1-89), and then dedicating the Levites (8:1-26). Following regulations for the second Passover (9:1-14), the section closes with a command to follow the cloud (9:15-23) when alerted by the signaling trumpets (10:1-10).

This section deals with protecting the camp from ritual defilement (5:1-4) and moral defilement by wrongs left without restitution (5:5-10) or by unjustified jealousy or marital infidelity (5:11-31). Then the next chapter deals with the intensified purity required to fulfill a Nazirite's vow (6:1-27).

God ordered the removal of anyone defiling the camp (5:2-3). God himself dwelt with his people (5:3b), fulfilling the central covenantal promise (Lev

26:11; Ezek 37:27; 2 Cor 6:16; Rev 21:3). Because of God's holy presence among them, the people had to remain ceremonially pure. Skin disease, bodily emissions, or contact with corpses caused ceremonial defilement (5:2). Short-term defilement could be caused by bodily discharges, such as those associated with copulation (Lev 15:16-18; cf. Exod 19:15; 1 Sam 21:4), menstruation (Lev 15:19, 24), afterbirth (Lev 12:2-5), or venereal disease (Lev 15:2, 25). People could also be defiled by contact with animal carcasses (Lev 11:24; 17:15). Long-term defilement by skin disease required isolation, whether outside the camp (5:3; 12:14; cf. Lev 13:46) or city (2 Kgs 7:3-11) or by quarantine (2 Kgs 15:5). This was to avoid defiling God's holy camp (5:3), especially his Tabernacle (19:13; Lev 15:31; 2 Kgs 23:16; Ezek 9:7).

Jesus adopted a new approach to physical defilement when he healed the woman suffering from chronic bleeding (Matt 9:20; Mark 5:25; Luke 8:43). So, too, with ceremonial defilement from unclean foods (Acts 10:11-15), not washing (Mark 7:2), or association with Gentiles (John 18:28; Acts 11:3; 21:28; cf. Ps 79:1; Lam 1:10). In fact, the New Testament gives three key examples of language explicitly announcing an onward move from old ideas of ceremonial defilement: Jesus "declared that every kind of food is acceptable in God's eyes" (Mark 7:19; cf. Matt 15:11, 20; Col 2:20-23); Peter was warned, "Do not call something unclean if God has made it clean" (Acts 10:15); and Paul declared, "all foods are acceptable" (Rom 14:20). The New Testament warns against ethical and spiritual defilement, however (Matt 15:11, 18-20; Mark 7:20-23; 1 Cor 8:7; Titus 1:15; Heb 12:15; Jas 3:6; Rev 3:4; 14:4).

◆   ## b. Holiness and restitution for sin (5:5-10)

⁵Then the LORD said to Moses, ⁶"Give the following instructions to the people of Israel: If any of the people—men or women—betray the LORD by doing wrong to another person, they are guilty. ⁷They must confess their sin and make full restitution for what they have done, adding an additional 20 percent and returning it to the person who was wronged. ⁸But if the person who was wronged is dead, and there are no near relatives to whom restitution can be made, the payment belongs to the LORD and must be given to the priest. Those who are guilty must also bring a ram as a sacrifice, and they will be purified and made right with the LORD.* ⁹All the sacred offerings that the Israelites bring to a priest will belong to him. ¹⁰Each priest may keep all the sacred donations that he receives."

5:8 Or bring a ram for atonement, which will make atonement for them.

NOTES

5:6 are guilty. The nepesh [TH5315, ZH5883] ("soul"; see 5:2) of that person incurs "guilt" ('asham). The term 'asham [TH816, ZH870] doesn't appear to refer to a subjective realization of guilt (contra Milgrom 1989:35, ESV, NJPS); rather, it refers to an objective condition of guilt: "are guilty" (NLT) or "incurs guilt," "is found guilty" (ASV, NASB, RSV, NRSV, NJB).

5:7 make full restitution. Lit., "he shall return the reparations on its head," understanding "head" to mean valuing things at their top or total value.

5:8 *But if the person who was wronged is dead.* Though not in the Hebrew, this is supplied in the NLT to make it clear that v. 8 is a secondary provision in case of one's inability to accomplish what is stipulated in v. 7.

near relatives. Heb., *go'el* [TH1350B, ZH1457]. The nearest male relative, called a *go'el*, functioned as an "avenger" to avenge wrongful death in the family (35:12; Deut 19:6, 12) or as a "redeemer" to restore from deprivation (Lev 25:25, 48; Ruth 2:20; 4:9).

COMMENTARY

Because the Lord lived with his people (5:1-4), one could also "betray the LORD by doing wrong to another person" (5:6). Failure in debt repayment was "an act of treachery towards God, who is the guarantor and pledge in transactions between man and man" (Hirsch 1971:56). Restitution for this betrayal was paid to the victim, including a penalty of 20 percent (5:7). The normal restitution was double the value of the stolen article (Exod 22:3-4), or more if it were livestock (Exod 22:1), so perhaps "the intent of the sharp reduction of this penalty here to 20 percent is to encourage the voluntary surrender of the theft" (Milgrom 1989:35). This complemented earlier laws (Exod 22:1-15; Lev 6:1-7), adding a provision for repayment if the person wronged no longer lived (5:8). A kinsman-redeemer could accept restitution for the family member who had suffered the loss (5:8a). If restitution couldn't even be made that way, then restitution went to the Lord through his representatives the priests, but was accompanied by a sacrifice (5:8b). The priests could accept and keep such offerings as part of their own priestly income. This modest requirement of restitution makes Zacchaeus's pledge of fourfold restoration to those he had cheated on taxes seem superabundant (Luke 19:8).

◆   ### c. Holiness and the test for suspicions (5:11-31)

[11]And the LORD said to Moses, [12]"Give the following instructions to the people of Israel.

"Suppose a man's wife goes astray, and she is unfaithful to her husband [13]and has sex with another man, but neither her husband nor anyone else knows about it. She has defiled herself, even though there was no witness and she was not caught in the act. [14]If her husband becomes jealous and is suspicious of his wife and needs to know whether or not she has defiled herself, [15]the husband must bring his wife to the priest. He must also bring an offering of two quarts* of barley flour to be presented on her behalf. Do not mix it with olive oil or frankincense, for it is a jealousy offering—an offering to prove whether or not she is guilty.

[16]"The priest will then present her to stand trial before the LORD. [17]He must take some holy water in a clay jar and pour into it dust he has taken from the Tabernacle floor. [18]When the priest has presented the woman before the LORD, he must unbind her hair and place in her hands the offering of proof—the jealousy offering to determine whether her husband's suspicions are justified. The priest will stand before her, holding the jar of bitter water that brings a curse to those who are guilty. [19]The priest will then put the woman under oath and say to her, 'If no other man has had sex with you, and you have not gone astray and defiled yourself while under your husband's authority, may you be immune from the effects of this bitter water that brings on

the curse. ²⁰But if you have gone astray by being unfaithful to your husband, and have defiled yourself by having sex with another man—'

²¹"At this point the priest must put the woman under oath by saying, 'May the people know that the LORD's curse is upon you when he makes you infertile, causing your womb to shrivel* and your abdomen to swell. ²²Now may this water that brings the curse enter your body and cause your abdomen to swell and your womb to shrivel.*' And the woman will be required to say, 'Yes, let it be so.' ²³And the priest will write these curses on a piece of leather and wash them off into the bitter water. ²⁴He will make the woman drink the bitter water that brings on the curse. When the water enters her body, it will cause bitter suffering if she is guilty.

²⁵"The priest will take the jealousy offering from the woman's hand, lift it up before the LORD, and carry it to the altar.

²⁶He will take a handful of the flour as a token portion and burn it on the altar, and he will require the woman to drink the water. ²⁷If she has defiled herself by being unfaithful to her husband, the water that brings on the curse will cause bitter suffering. Her abdomen will swell and her womb will shrink,* and her name will become a curse among her people. ²⁸But if she has not defiled herself and is pure, then she will be unharmed and will still be able to have children.

²⁹"This is the ritual law for dealing with suspicion. If a woman goes astray and defiles herself while under her husband's authority, ³⁰or if a man becomes jealous and is suspicious that his wife has been unfaithful, the husband must present his wife before the LORD, and the priest will apply this entire ritual law to her. ³¹The husband will be innocent of any guilt in this matter, but his wife will be held accountable for her sin."

5:15 Hebrew ¹/₁₀ of an ephah [2.2 liters].   5:21 Hebrew when he causes your thigh to waste away.
5:22 Hebrew and your thigh to waste away.   5:27 Hebrew and her thigh will waste away.

NOTES

5:12 goes astray. This verb, from the root *satah,* was used by the rabbis (cf. *m. Nashim* and *b. Sotah*) to refer to the woman who goes astray (the *sotah*) and this law in particular.

5:13 defiled herself. This is a Niphal form of *tame'* [TH2930, ZH3237]; if read as a passive, it is "she is defiled" (KJV, ASV, JPS). It is more likely reflexive, however, "she defiled herself" (NLT, NKJV, NASB, NJB, NJPS, ESV).

5:15 offering . . . on her behalf. The Hebrew (*qorban* [TH7133, ZH7933], "offering"; + the fem. sg. suffix) refers to an "offering of her"; this may be an offering "required of her" (ESV) or "offered on her behalf" (NLT, KJV, ASV, NASB, JPS, NJPS). The *qorban* is the least common but most general expression for a gift or sacrifice.

two quarts. The standard measure for a grain offering (15:4; 28:5, 13, 21; Exod 29:40).

Do not mix it with olive oil or frankincense. This is plainer than grain offerings (Lev 2:1, 15; 6:15).

jealousy offering. Lit., "grain offering of jealousies." The rabbis said the plural (jealousies) indicated double jealousy, that of God in addition to that of the husband (Snaith 1969:129), but more likely it is an intensive plural.

an offering to prove whether or not she is guilty. Lit., "a remembrance offering" (*minkhath zikkaron* [TH2146, ZH2355]), "bringing to mind the guilt" (*mazkereth 'awon* [TH2142, ZH2349]), the second expression explaining the first. Reminders are significant in Numbers (10:10; 16:36-38; 17:10; 31:54).

5:17 holy water. Heb., *mayim qedoshim* [TH6918, ZH7705]. Levine (1993:195) translates "holy water," but says it probably means "pure water" (*mayim tehorim* [TH2889, ZH3196]; e.g., Ezek 36:25) or even "running water" (*mayim khayyim* [TH2416A, ZH2645]; e.g., 19:17). That's how the LXX translates it, with its *hudōr katharon zōn* [ᵀᴳ5204/2513/2198, ᶻᴳ5623/2754/2409] (pure living water). This water was for *demonstrating* defilement, not *cleansing* it, so it was probably not the water of purification that was used with sacrificial ashes and hyssop (19:17-19; Lev 14:49-52; Heb 9:19). More likely, it was from the bronze basin where on-duty priests washed (Exod 30:17-21, 29).

pour. Heb., *nathan* [ᵀᴴ5414, ᶻᴴ5989], a word for "putting," not "pouring." It is likely that only a "pinch" of this dust was used in this recipe.

5:18 *he must unbind her hair.* The word "hair" isn't in the Hebrew, but translations like "unbind," "dishevel," "unbraid," or "let down" imply hair (NLT, JPS, ASV, NASB), or perhaps "uncovering/baring her head" (KJV, ESV, NAB, NJPS). It appears to have been a mark of shame over impurity (Lev 13:45; cf. Lam 4:15) or of remorse (Lev 10:6; 21:10; Ezek 24:17).

jar of bitter water that brings a curse to those who are guilty. Lit., "waters of bitterness, which make bitter." The NLT adds "jar" and explains the idiom "which make bitter."

5:21 *May the people know that the LORD's curse is upon you.* Lit., "May the LORD make you into a curse (*'alah* [ᵀᴴ423, ᶻᴴ460]) and an oath (*shebu'ah* [ᵀᴴ7621, ᶻᴴ8652]) in the midst of your people." People would employ her name in a curse, for example, by saying, "May your life end up like that of so-and-so" (cf. Isa 65:15; Jer 29:22; language and examples cited by Milgrom 1989:41).

when he makes you infertile. The NLT adds this phrase to explain the meaning of the two following expressions: (1) "when the LORD makes your *yarek* to collapse/shrivel"—the *yarek* [ᵀᴴ3409, ᶻᴴ3751] is the pelvic region, from the hips to the thighs; (2) "your abdomen to swell," perhaps alluding to a false pregnancy, which would be "featured by distended belly, cessation of the menses and incapacity to conceive" (Brichto 1975:66 n. 10), or to "a prolapsed uterus" (Frymer-Kensky 1984:18, 20-21).

5:22 *Yes, let it be so.* Lit., "Amen, amen!"—that is, "Amen, that I did not defile myself; and if I did, in fact, defile myself, may the water enter me [to do me harm]!" (Levine 1993:198).

5:24 *drink.* Drinking can be seen as a metaphor for "receiving one's destiny from the Hand of God" (Hirsch 1971:73; see Ps 75:8; Jer 25:15, 27-29; 49:12; Obad 1:16).

5:25 *lift it up.* This is the Hiphil of *nup* [ᵀᴴ5130, ᶻᴴ5677], a verb for wielding something like a rod or a tool (Deut 23:25; 27:5; Josh 8:31; Isa 10:15), hence the common translation "wave offering," which probably means to elevate it or "make a gesture of offering" (NJB).

5:26 *as a token portion.* Lit., "as a memorial" (see last note on 5:15).

5:28 *still be able to have children.* Lit., "and she will be seeded with seed," which forms an inclusio with *zera'* [ᵀᴴ2233, ᶻᴴ2446] (seed) in 5:13.

5:31 *The husband will be innocent of any guilt in this matter.* The rabbis interpreted this to mean the husband himself had to be innocent if this matter were to proceed (cf. Hos 4:14).

COMMENTARY

A jealous husband was to take his wife to the priests to determine whether a basis for his suspicions existed, and she was innocent until proven guilty. In fact, only a miracle could convict her. This two-stage process followed other examples of leaving it to God to reveal guilt or innocence and to implement the penalty (16:6; Exod 22:8¹; 1 Kgs 8:31-32). In stage one, the husband was to take his wife to the priest, symbolizing taking her before the Lord. There the priest would administer her self-maledictory oath (5:16-22). In stage two, the priest would activate the oath by writing it on a scroll, which was washed into water that the woman then drank. To that was added a pinch of dust from the Tabernacle floor. If she was guilty, God would sabotage her reproductive organs; if she was innocent, nothing would happen, which would declare her innocence (5:23-31).

Hints of an ordeal, the use of a potion, and the public humiliation of a potentially innocent wife combine to make this a troubling passage, all the more so if the husband retained his innocence whether his jealousy proved well-founded or false (5:31). Nonetheless, we cannot interrogate this passage as though it were an endorsement for inhumane practice. The Lord himself prescribed the ritual (5:12) and was guarantor of its outcome (5:21). So this was more than just a mere case of toned-down borrowing of an ancient Near Eastern practice like two laws (131 and 132) found in the *Code of Hammurabi* (ANET 171):

> 131. If a man's wife is accused by her husband, but she was not caught
>   while lying with another man, she shall make an oath by the god
>   and return home.
> 132. If a finger has been pointed at a man's wife because of another
>   man, but she has not been caught while lying with the other man,
>   she shall leap into the River for the sake of her husband.

On the one hand, Law 131 is parallel, though lacking a means for demonstrating guilt or innocence. On the other hand, Law 132 is precisely what the biblical law is *not* about: "in the case of trial by ordeal the accused is guilty unless proven innocent; whereas in the case of the suspected *sotah* [see note on 5:12], the accused is innocent unless proven guilty" (Brichto 1975:65-66). Allen calls the potion used here "holy dust added to holy water" (1990:745), not to make it poisonous but to symbolize its *holiness*. So "it has a harmful effect—it becomes consequentially 'bitter'—only in the event the water ultimately encounters guilt in the woman's innards" (Levine 1993:209).

I doubt if we should see this as a case where a husband "wishes to vindicate his wife" so he can avoid divorce (Hirsch 1971:66). "Perhaps we should imagine the consequences on a woman rightly or falsely charged with adultery by an angry husband in a context in which there was no provision for her guilt or innocence to be demonstrated. That she was taken to the priest is finally an act of mercy" (Allen 1990:743-744). This required a jealous husband to go before the Lord and "put up or shut up" (Brichto 1975:67).

Frymer-Kensky notes that the outcome was left to God. If the ritual proved the woman guilty, pregnancy would become impossible. If the ritual proved her innocent, conception would be possible. She doubts that the penalty for proven guilt was a divinely instigated abortion, but she does suggest that the reward for innocence might even initiate a pregnancy (Frymer-Kensky 1984:18-23, especially 19). She concludes,

> It should be obvious that to call this procedure a "trial by ordeal" is
> unwarranted and misleading. Judicial ordeals are distinguished by two
> important and interrelated aspects: the god's decision is manifest imme-
> diately, and the result of the trial is not itself the penalty for the offense.

To use modern terminology, the god is the "jury" that gives a "verdict" of guilt or innocence during the ordeal, and the judge then imposes a "sentence" in accord with this "verdict." Here in Numbers 5, God is judge and jury. (Frymer-Kensky 1984:24)

It is interesting to note that there is no biblical record of this trial ever being implemented, though rabbinical tradition talked about it:

> Bemidbar [Numbers] *Rabbah* records an *aggadah* (Naso 9) that illustrates the magical or divine nature of the bitter water, which can discern the difference between a good woman and an evil one. Two married sisters look very much alike but live in different towns. The one who lives in Jerusalem is "clean," the other is "defiled," and goes to her good sister and pleads with her to take her place in the ritual of the bitter water. The good sister agrees, drinks the water, and is unharmed. Returning home, her sister, who has played the harlot, comes out to embrace her. As they kiss, "the harlot smelled the bitter water and instantly died." (Bach 1994:42)

This rabbinical tradition has the flavor of a fairy tale rather than the ring of a historical narrative treating a legal situation; nonetheless, it catches the notion of how the potion worked. And rabbinic tradition extends the idea with expansive *lex talionis:*

> She painted her eyes for his sake, and so her eyes bulge. She braided her hair for his sake, and so the priest dishevels her hair. She beckoned to him with her fingers and so her fingernails fall off. She put on a fine girdle for his sake, and so the priest brings a common rope and ties it above her breasts. She extended her thigh to him and therefore her thigh falls away. She received him upon her womb, and therefore her belly swells. She fed him with the finest dainties; her offering is therefore the food of cattle. She gave him to drink choice wine in elegant flagons, therefore the priest gives her to drink the water of bitterness in a piece of earthenware. (Bach 1994:44, citing *Numbers Rabbah* 9:24)

Shortly after the destruction of the Second Temple, Rabbi Johanan ben Zakkai abolished the ordeal in favor of divorce (*m. Sotah* 9:9, citing Hos 4:14).

This passage in Numbers warns us of two things that are highlighted elsewhere: (1) "Have nothing to do with sexual immorality, impurity, lust, and evil desires" (Col 3:5); (2) "Watch out that no poisonous root of bitterness grows up to trouble you, corrupting many" (Heb 12:15). This passage also tells us that God will judge between us and our accusers, so we should leave our case in God's hands (1 Pet 2:23), remembering that God hates either acquitting the guilty or condemning the innocent (Prov 17:15).

ENDNOTE
1. The NLT translates *'elohim* as "God"; however, some translations understand this as a reference to "judges" (Geneva Bible, KJV, NKJV, NASB, NIV, NET).

◆   ### d. Holiness and the Nazirite Vow (6:1-21)

Then the LORD said to Moses, "Give the following instructions to the people of Israel.

2"If any of the people, either men or women, take the special vow of a Nazirite, setting themselves apart to the LORD in a special way, 3they must give up wine and other alcoholic drinks. They must not use vinegar made from wine or from other alcoholic drinks, they must not drink fresh grape juice, and they must not eat grapes or raisins. 4As long as they are bound by their Nazirite vow, they are not allowed to eat or drink anything that comes from a grapevine—not even the grape seeds or skins.

5"They must never cut their hair throughout the time of their vow, for they are holy and set apart to the LORD. Until the time of their vow has been fulfilled, they must let their hair grow long. 6And they must not go near a dead body during the entire period of their vow to the LORD. 7Even if the dead person is their own father, mother, brother, or sister, they must not defile themselves, for the hair on their head is the symbol of their separation to God. 8This requirement applies as long as they are set apart to the LORD.

9"If someone falls dead beside them, the hair they have dedicated will be defiled. They must wait for seven days and then shave their heads. Then they will be cleansed from their defilement. 10On the eighth day they must bring two turtledoves or two young pigeons to the priest at the entrance of the Tabernacle.* 11The priest will offer one of the birds for a sin offering and the other for a burnt offering. In this way, he will purify them* from the guilt they incurred through contact with the dead body. Then they must reaffirm their commitment and let their hair begin to grow again. 12The days of their vow that were completed before their defilement no longer count. They must rededicate themselves to the LORD as a Nazirite for the full term of their vow, and each must bring a one-year-old male lamb for a guilt offering.

13"This is the ritual law for Nazirites. At the conclusion of their time of separation as Nazirites, they must each go to the entrance of the Tabernacle 14and offer their sacrifices to the LORD: a one-year-old male lamb without defect for a burnt offering, a one-year-old female lamb without defect for a sin offering, a ram without defect for a peace offering, 15a basket of bread made without yeast—cakes of choice flour mixed with olive oil and wafers spread with olive oil—along with their prescribed grain offerings and liquid offerings. 16The priest will present these offerings before the LORD: first the sin offering and the burnt offering; 17then the ram for a peace offering, along with the basket of bread made without yeast. The priest must also present the prescribed grain offering and liquid offering to the LORD.

18"Then the Nazirites will shave their heads at the entrance of the Tabernacle. They will take the hair that had been dedicated and place it on the fire beneath the peace-offering sacrifice. 19After the Nazirite's head has been shaved, the priest will take for each of them the boiled shoulder of the ram, and he will take from the basket a cake and a wafer made without yeast. He will put them all into the Nazirite's hands. 20Then the priest will lift them up as a special offering before the LORD. These are holy portions for the priest, along with the breast of the special offering and the thigh of the sacred offering that are lifted up before the LORD. After this ceremony the Nazirites may again drink wine.

21"This is the ritual law of the Nazirites, who vow to bring these offerings to the LORD. They may also bring additional offerings if they can afford it. And they must be careful to do whatever they vowed when they set themselves apart as Nazirites."

6:10 Hebrew *the Tent of Meeting;* also in 6:13, 18.   6:11 Or *make atonement for them.*

NOTES

6:2 take the special vow of a Nazirite. Heb., *ki yapli' lindor neder nazir* [TH5139B, ZH5687].
The term *pala'* [TH6381, ZH7098] can denote the formal articulation of the vow in public
(HALOT); here it refers to a "special, arduous, extraordinary" vow (6:2; 15:3, 8; Lev 22:21;
27:2; BDB 810). The terms built on the root *nzr* are terms for "consecration" or "office"—
e.g., a royal crown (2 Sam 1:10; 2 Kgs 11:12, etc.), the high priest's diadem/turban (Exod
29:6; 39:30; Lev 8:9), anointing oil (Lev 21:12), or the act or state of consecration itself
(Jer 7:29; Hos 9:10; Zech 7:3).

6:3 they. The plural used in the English in this passage does not imply that the vow was
taken in groups; rather, it results from the use of plurals for a gender-neutral translation,
as required by the notice that either a man or a woman could take this vow (6:2).

give up. This is the verb *nazar* [TH5144A, ZH5693], meaning "to live as a Nazirite," "separating
oneself/abstaining from" what follows in the verse.

alcoholic drinks. Heb., *shekar* [TH7941, ZH8911], meaning "intoxicating drink," from a root
frequently employed for "drunkard" (e.g., Ps 107:27; Prov 26:9; Joel 1:5). It's a general term
for various alcoholic drinks (cf. 1 Sam 1:15), often referring to alcohol made from grain
(i.e., beer), or to alcohol made stronger by addition of honey, dates, or fruit and perhaps
spices, but not distilled alcohol.

vinegar made from wine. Heb., *khomets yayin* [TH2558/3196, ZH2810/3516], "sour wine," a
cheap drink like what was offered to Jesus (Matt 27:48).

other alcoholic drinks. Heb., *khomets shekar*, meaning "some other vinegar/cider."

fresh grape juice. Heb., *mishrat 'anabim* "juice/extract of the grape." Since *mishrat* comes
from *sherah* [TH8281, ZH9223] (to release), this juice may have been infused from grapes by
leaving squeezed-out grapes to steep in water. See "anything in which grapes have been
steeped" (NJPS).

grapes or raisins. Whether moist or dried, they were in clusters (1 Sam 30:12; 2 Sam 16:1)
or cakes (2 Sam 6:19; 1 Chr 16:3; Hos 3:1 mg).

6:4 grape seeds. The Heb., *khartsan* [TH2785, ZH3079] can also be rendered "unripe grapes"
(NAB, NJB) or "pressed grapes" (JPS).

skins. This (*zag* [TH2085, ZH2293]) refers to "some comparatively insignificant product of the
vine" (BDB 260).

6:7 for the hair on their head is the symbol of their separation to God. Lit., "for the *nezer*
[TH5145, ZH5694] to his God is on his head" (see note on 6:2).

6:8 This requirement applies as long as they are set apart. Lit., "all the days of his *nezer*"
(see note on 6:2).

set apart. The word *qadosh* [TH6918, ZH7705] (holy) explains the purpose of *nezer* (consecrated).

6:9 the hair they have dedicated will be defiled. Lit., "the head of his *nezer* is defiled"
(see note on 6:2).

wait for seven days. This is the period of cleansing required for ordination (Exod 29:35;
Lev 8:33), purification after childbirth (Lev 12:2), healing from skin diseases (Lev 14:8;
cf. Lev 13:4-5, 21), and accidental defilement from discharges (Lev 15:13-28).

then shave their heads. The legislation gives no indication of what was to be done with
this defiled hair; possibly it was burnt, though probably not on the altar, as was the case at
the successful conclusion of his vow, when the hair remained *nezer* [TH5145, ZH5694] (6:18;
see note on 6:2).

6:10 turtledoves or . . . pigeons. These two birds are often found together for sacrifices (Lev
1:14; 5:7, 11; 12:6, 8; 14:22, 30; 15:14, 29; cf. Luke 2:24). The turtledove could be used in

burnt offerings (Lev 1:14) and, when poverty made it necessary, even as an inexpensive option for a sin offering (Lev 5:7). Here they are used for purification, as in the case following childbirth (Lev 12:6), leprosy (Lev 14:22, 30), or bodily discharge (Lev 15:14). The Nazirite was not given the least expensive option of bringing a flour offering, which was allowed of the layman who accidentally prolonged his impurity (Lev 5:3, 11-13).

6:11 *purify them.* Lit., "make atonement for himself"—i.e., for the Nazirite.

guilt they incurred through contact with the dead body. Lit., "guilt over the *nepesh* [TH5315, ZH5883]." This speaks not of their own guilty "soul," but defilement from touching a corpse (see note on 5:2).

Then they must reaffirm their commitment and let their hair begin to grow again. Lit., "Then he must consecrate" (using *qadash* [TH6942, ZH7727], not *nazar* [TH5144A, ZH5693]) "his head on that day," i.e., restart the hair growth.

6:14 *female lamb.* In sin offerings, a female lamb was required (Lev 4:32; 5:6).

ram. The ram was slain for peace offerings (Lev 9:4, 18, 19).

peace offering. The word *shelem* [TH8002, ZH8968] can also be rendered as "salvation offering." The animal offerings for the successfully completed and abortive Nazirite period are the same, but now "the *'asham* [TH817, ZH871] for desecration has been replaced by the *shelamim* for joy" (Milgrom 1989:48).

6:18 This appears to be the background for Acts 18:18; 21:24.

Then the Nazirites will shave their heads. Lit., "then the Nazirite will shave . . . the head of his *nezer* [TH5145, ZH5694]" (see notes on 6:2, 3).

beneath the peace-offering. The hair is not so much offered to God (contra Gray 1903:68) as destroyed because it is holy and must not be defiled by use in merely common ways (de Vaux 1961:436; Noth 1968:57; cf. the uneaten portion of peace offerings in Lev 7:17; 19:6, 8). This would follow the same principle observed in the total destruction of things considered *kherem* [TH2764, ZH3051] ("specially set apart"; Lev 27:28; Josh 6:17 mg).

6:19 *shoulder of the ram.* This was the priest's portion (Lev 7:30-33). In the ancient Near East, the right thigh was the choice portion for presentation to deities. See the *Epic of Gilgamesh* 6:160-167 (ANET 85) and the Hittite "Purification Ritual Engaging the Help of Protective Demons" (ANET 348).

6:20 *lift them up as a special offering before the LORD.* See note on 5:25.

6:21 *if they can afford it.* The rabbis derived from this that the community or patrons could help a poor Nazirite discharge these vows (*Temurah* 10a), as some royal patrons did during Roman times (Milgrom 1989:50, 305, citing *m. Nazir* 2:5; *Sifre Zuta* on 6:13; *y. Nazir* 5:3; Josephus *Antiquities* 19. 6.1 [19.293-294]; Acts 21:24).

COMMENTARY

The Nazirite vow was not mandatory: It was a "special vow" of consecration to the Lord (6:2). But if the vow was made, the vow had to be kept, from start to finish (6:9-12). The Nazirites we see in Scripture were all men, and all were subject to lifelong vows made by their parents before birth (Judg 13:7; 16:1; 1 Sam 1:11; Luke 1:15). But a woman could take the vow (6:2), though she would need consent from her father or husband, as with other vows (30:3-13). In fact, many women did, hence the term *nezirah* and laws about her status (e.g., *m. Nazir* 4:1ff). Helena, the queen of Abiabene, took a seven-year vow on the condition that her son return safely from war, and her Nazirite period actually lasted twice or thrice that long (*m. Nazir* 3:6). Bernice, sister of King Agrippa II, took a 30-day vow after she had recovered from illness, which Josephus described as "a custom" (*Wars* 2.15.1 [2.313]). These extrabiblical examples assume that the vow tended to be temporary rather than lifelong, and the apostle Paul appears to have been among those who took such temporary vows.[1]

The Nazirites and the Vine. Like the on-duty priest (Lev 10:9; Ezek 44:21), the Nazirite had to avoid wine for the duration of the vow. This didn't indicate that wine was sinful, any more than trimming one's hair or burying one's dead was sinful; it was rather an extraordinary provision of ritual purity (6:20). And the exclusion of even the obviously nonintoxicating juice, grapes, raisins, seeds, and skins emphasized that extraordinary measures were taken. Perhaps this Recabite-like vow protested the decadence that wine depicted (Jer 35); however, its more likely connection is to the consecration required of on-duty priests, especially the high priest, who was always on duty. Note that pushing a Nazirite to drink was as serious an offense as forbidding a prophet to prophesy (Amos 2:12).

The Nazirites and Their Hair. In the Old Testament, shaving the head was practiced in times of mourning (Job 1:20; Isa 3:24; 22:12; Jer 7:29; 16:6; Ezek 7:18; Amos 8:10; Mic 1:16), though never for priests (Lev 21:5; Ezek 44:20).[2] It was this priestly prohibition that is parallel to the Nazirite vow, during which the hair was not to be trimmed at all. Cutting it off in mourning for the dead would have meant employing something dedicated to the living God as a memorial to the dead, which would be a profanation. Only at the conclusion of the vow was the hair to be cut off; then it was burnt as something dedicated to the Lord.

The Nazirites and Contact with the Dead. The Nazirite vow banned proximity with death, even for burying close family. The Nazirite's hair was dedicated to the living God, so it could not even come into contact with death (6:7). The same degree of purity was demanded of the high priest (Lev 21:11), which is higher than for the regular priests, who could at least mourn and bury their immediate family (Lev 21:1-2; Ezek 44:25). Perhaps it is this Old Testament legislation of radical consecration that lies behind Jesus' call to discipleship: "Follow me, and let the dead bury their own dead" (Matt 8:22, NET). Taken with the wine prohibition, this hair regulation displayed a calling that allowed even laypeople to symbolize total dedication to Israel's national priestly calling (Exod 19:6; 1 Pet 2:9; Rev 1:6; 5:10; 20:6).

Verses 3-6 detail what a Nazirite abstained from to symbolize total dedication: wine and other grape products, haircuts, and contact with death. Verses 9-12 deal with accidental defilement—only the death regulations applied because the other causes were avoidable. The detailed intent of the regulation may be complex, but the overall point is clear: If defiled during the vow, Nazirites must purify themselves and restart the vow.

First, the Nazirite was to sit through a seven-day waiting period, such as was common in cases requiring ritual purification; then, the hair was cut off (6:9). On the eighth day, when they were again considered free of ritual defilement, they were to bring a sin offering and a burnt offering (6:11), which purified them from the guilt incurred when contact with the dead interrupted their vow. Finally, they reaffirmed their vow and restarted their hair growth, setting the clock at zero on the period of the vow originally consecrated to the Lord. To solemnize this, they brought a guilt offering (6:12).

The normal practice for discharging the Nazirite vow would have been to avoid defilement and complete the "time of separation as Nazirites," whereupon they would bring a series of offerings (6:13-15), which the priest would then present to the Lord (6:16-17). Then the Nazirites would shave off their dedicated hair and burn it on the altar (6:18), participate with the priest in a series of offerings (6:19-20a), and then return to normal life (6:20b).

The purification offerings for restarting an interrupted vow were a sin offering, a burnt offering, and a guilt offering (6:11-13). To close out a successful vow, the Nazirite brought a burnt offering, a sin offering, a peace offering, and a combination offering of grain prepared as bread, cakes, and wafers, and liquid, probably wine (6:14-15). Then the decommissioned Nazirite could return to normal life, drinking wine again (6:20) and presumably trimming unruly hair as desired and burying family members as necessary.

Verse 21 forms an inclusio with verse 13. Nazirites were to bring the offerings noted in verses 13-15, and if they could "afford it," they could bring additional offerings. But the core requirements were sacrosanct: The Nazirites had to "be careful to do whatever they vowed" (6:21), a caution about vows that was embedded in the law (30:2; Deut 23:21-23) and in wisdom literature (Prov 20:25; Eccl 5:4-5) and continued in the New Testament (Acts 5:4).

The total dedication that the Nazirite vow prefigured is still the goal of discipleship (Matt 8:22; Luke 14:26), and it should be a lifelong commitment, rather than a passing emphasis to be laid aside in favor of normal life.

ENDNOTES

1. Acts 18:18; 21:23; cf. Josephus *Antiquities* 19.6.1 [19.292-296]; *m. Nazir* 1:3-7; 3:1-7.
2. Sometimes it was linked with the occult (see commentary on Lev 19:27 and Deut 14:1; cf. also Isa 15:2; Jer 48:37).

◆   ### e. Priestly blessing for the community (6:22-27)

²²Then the LORD said to Moses, ²³"Tell Aaron and his sons to bless the people of Israel with this special blessing:

²⁴'May the LORD bless you
    and protect you.
²⁵May the LORD smile on you
    and be gracious to you.
²⁶May the LORD show you his favor
    and give you his peace.'

²⁷Whenever Aaron and his sons bless the people of Israel in my name, I myself will bless them."

NOTES

6:27 In the LXX, this verse follows 6:23, thereby expressing God's command in a single statement before giving the language of the blessing itself.

bless the people of Israel in my name. Lit., "they will put my name upon the children of Israel," or, "they will link my name with Israel" (Milgrom 1989:52).

COMMENTARY
God alone had the power to bestow blessing; in fact, those who were wrongly related to him could neither bless (Mal 2:2) nor be blessed (Deut 28). Kings like David (2 Sam 6:18) and Solomon (1 Kgs 8:14, 55) sometimes assumed that responsibility; however, the main locus of formal blessing was in the Tabernacle, with priests making such pronouncements over arriving (Ps 118:26) or departing worshipers (Lev 9:22).

The priestly blessing comprises three verses, each with poetically parallel expressions. This blessing may have provided the form and content for Malachi's diatribe against the priests (Fishbane 1983, citing Mal 1:6–2:9). Ashley even suggests that the Songs of Ascent (Pss 120–134) were composed with a view to the terminology in this blessing.[1] Two miniature silver scrolls inscribed with this blessing were discovered in a tomb in the Hinnom valley outside Jerusalem and have been dated to the end of the seventh century BC,[2] which puts this some four centuries earlier than the earliest Qumran scrolls.

Let us examine this blessing line by line:

"May the LORD bless you" (6:24a). In the Old Testament, God's blessing comprised material bounty like those included in the positive side of covenant sanctions (Deut 28:3-14): wealth (Gen 24:35), posterity (Gen 28:3; Deut 1:11), land (Gen 35:12; 48:3-4), fertility, health, and victory (Deut 7:12-16), and strength and peace (Ps 29:11). The New Testament focuses the expectation of blessing on those who demonstrate an eschatological kingdom lifestyle (Matt 5:3-12), and that blessing rests first on the pious "poor" (Luke 4:18; 6:20).

"May the LORD . . . protect you" (6:24b). This was the hope that God would guard his people against anything that worked against the blessing (Ps 121). Jesus himself taught his disciples to pray, "rescue us from the evil one" (Matt 6:13), and he himself prayed that way for them (John 17:15).

"May the LORD smile on you" or "make his face shine on you" (6:25a; see Pss 31:16; 67:1; 80:3, 7, 19; 119:135; Dan 9:17). When used figuratively, this verb for the sunrise speaks of the action of a superior who shows his pleasure toward a subject. It is nearly synonymous with the next three expressions.

"May the LORD . . . be gracious to you" (6:25b). This expresses a hope that God would respond to entreaties, saving his people from enemies, sickness, and sin (Pss 4:1; 6:2; 41:4; 51:1). "'Grace' denotes the attitude that issues in kindly action of a superior toward an inferior in which the inferior has no claim on the superior" (Ashley 1993:152). In fact, it may even hint at reprieve from "justified 'displeasure'" (Noth 1968:59).

"May the LORD show you his favor" or "lift up his face to you" (6:26a). This means the Lord would "take into consideration" or "show clemency" (Gen 19:21; Deut 28:50;

1 Sam 25:35). This would certainly be the opposite of hiding his face in anger (Deut 31:17) or of letting one's face fall (Gen 4:5-6; Jer 3:12).

"May the LORD . . . give you his peace" (6:26b). Just as the term "bless" (6:24a) expresses the entire hope of verses 24-26, so does the term "peace" (6:26b). Peace is not just freedom from disaster (Lev 26:6); in a positive sense, it implies prosperity (Deut 23:6; Prov 3:2), good health (Ps 38:3), friendship (Jer 20:10; 38:22), and general well-being (1 Sam 16:4; 2 Sam 18:28). Angels announced Christ's birth saying, "Peace on earth to those with whom God is pleased" (Luke 2:14). Jesus came saying "go in peace" after his acts of forgiveness (Luke 7:50) and healing (Mark 5:34; Luke 8:48). He told his disciples to say "may God's peace be on this house" wherever they found hospitality (Luke 10:5). The resurrected Lord kept offering peace to his followers (Luke 24:36; John 20:19, 21, 26), a peace with God (Acts 10:36; Rom 5:1) the world couldn't give (John 14:27). Small wonder the apostles tended to open and close their communications with a blessing of "peace."[3]

Closely associated with the Tabernacle and Temple, this blessing linked God's name with his people (6:27); however, that didn't make it a uniquely Jewish blessing. Even the Old Testament indicates that the Lord's blessings were to be extended to the nations. That was the purpose statement for Abraham's call (Gen 12:1-3) and the vocational function of Hebrew nationhood (Exod 19:6; Deut 4:6-8; Isa 61:6). The Temple's own hymnbook adapted the language of this priestly blessing with a view to the nations (Ps 67). The New Testament sees this blessing fulfilled in Jesus Christ, who is Lord (Rom 10:9), and through the Holy Spirit, who is Lord (2 Cor 3:17). And the principle embodied in Abraham's call applies today: The people of God are to bless the nations (Gal 3:8), taking the gospel to the nations (Matt 24:14; Mark 13:10; Luke 24:47).

ENDNOTES
1. I.e., "bless" (Pss 128:5; 133:3; 134:3), "keep" (Ps 121; NLT "watch over"), "be gracious" (Pss 123, 130), and "peace" (Pss 122:6-8; 128:5-6) (Ashley 1993:151, citing Liebreich 1955 and Delitzsch 1884–1889:3.282, 287, 321).
2. See E. W. Davies 1995b:66 for a full account of the discovery, referring us to Barkay 1983. The two carefully unrolled scrolls measure about 4" × 1" and about 1.5" × 0.5". See also Hoffmeier 2005:234; Barkay et al. 2004.
3. Rom 1:7; 15:13, 33; 1 Cor 1:3; 2 Cor 1:2; 13:11; Gal 1:3; 6:16; Eph 1:2; 6:23; Phil 1:2; 4:7, 9; Col 1:2; 1 Thess 1:1; 5:23; 2 Thess 1:2; 3:16; 1 Tim 1:2; 2 Tim 1:2; Titus 1:4; Phlm 1:3; Heb 13:20; 1 Pet 1:2; 5:14; 2 Pet 1:2; 2 John 1:3; 3 John 1:15; Jude 1:2; Rev 1:4.

◆   f. Dedicating the altar with tribal offerings (7:1-89)

On the day Moses set up the Tabernacle, he anointed it and set it apart as holy. He also anointed and set apart all its furnishings and the altar with its utensils. ²Then the leaders of Israel—the tribal leaders who had registered the troops—came and brought their offerings. ³Together they brought six large wagons and twelve oxen. There was a wagon for every two leaders and an ox for each leader. They presented these to the LORD in front of the Tabernacle.

⁴Then the LORD said to Moses, ⁵"Receive their gifts, and use these oxen and wagons for transporting the Tabernacle.* Distribute them among the Levites according to the work they have to do." ⁶So Moses took the wagons and oxen and presented them to the Levites. ⁷He gave two wagons and four oxen to the Gershonite division for their work, ⁸and he gave four wagons and eight oxen to the Merarite division for their work. All their work was done under the leadership of Ithamar son of Aaron the priest. ⁹But he gave none of the wagons or oxen to the Kohathite division, since they were required to carry the sacred objects of the Tabernacle on their shoulders.

¹⁰The leaders also presented dedication gifts for the altar at the time it was anointed. They each placed their gifts before the altar. ¹¹The LORD said to Moses, "Let one leader bring his gift each day for the dedication of the altar."

¹²On the first day Nahshon son of Amminadab, leader of the tribe of Judah, presented his offering.

¹³His offering consisted of a silver platter weighing 3¼ pounds and a silver basin weighing 1¾ pounds* (as measured by the weight of the sanctuary shekel). These were both filled with grain offerings of choice flour moistened with olive oil. ¹⁴He also brought a gold container weighing four ounces,* which was filled with incense. ¹⁵He brought a young bull, a ram, and a one-year-old male lamb for a burnt offering, ¹⁶and a male goat for a sin offering. ¹⁷For a peace offering he brought two bulls, five rams, five male goats, and five one-year-old male lambs. This was the offering brought by Nahshon son of Amminadab.

¹⁸On the second day Nethanel son of Zuar, leader of the tribe of Issachar, presented his offering.

¹⁹His offering consisted of a silver platter weighing 3¼ pounds and a silver basin weighing 1¾ pounds (as measured by the weight of the sanctuary shekel). These were both filled with grain offerings of choice flour moistened with olive oil. ²⁰He also brought a gold container weighing four ounces, which was filled with incense. ²¹He brought a young bull, a ram, and a one-year-old male lamb for a burnt offering, ²²and a male goat for a sin offering. ²³For a peace offering he brought two bulls, five rams, five male goats, and five one-year-old male lambs. This was the offering brought by Nethanel son of Zuar.

²⁴On the third day Eliab son of Helon, leader of the tribe of Zebulun, presented his offering.

²⁵His offering consisted of a silver platter weighing 3¼ pounds and a silver basin weighing 1¾ pounds (as measured by the weight of the sanctuary shekel). These were both filled with grain offerings of choice flour moistened with olive oil. ²⁶He also brought a gold container weighing four ounces, which was filled with incense. ²⁷He brought a young bull, a ram, and a one-year-old male lamb for a burnt offering, ²⁸and a male goat for a sin offering. ²⁹For a peace offering he brought two bulls, five rams, five male goats, and five one-year-old male lambs. This was the offering brought by Eliab son of Helon.

³⁰On the fourth day Elizur son of Shedeur, leader of the tribe of Reuben, presented his offering.

³¹His offering consisted of a silver platter weighing 3¼ pounds and a silver basin weighing 1¾ pounds (as measured by the weight of the sanctuary shekel). These were both filled with grain offerings of choice flour moistened with olive oil. ³²He

also brought a gold container weighing four ounces, which was filled with incense. ³³He brought a young bull, a ram, and a one-year-old male lamb for a burnt offering, ³⁴and a male goat for a sin offering. ³⁵For a peace offering he brought two bulls, five rams, five male goats, and five one-year-old male lambs. This was the offering brought by Elizur son of Shedeur.

³⁶On the fifth day Shelumiel son of Zurishaddai, leader of the tribe of Simeon, presented his offering.

³⁷His offering consisted of a silver platter weighing 3¼ pounds and a silver basin weighing 1¾ pounds (as measured by the weight of the sanctuary shekel). These were both filled with grain offerings of choice flour moistened with olive oil. ³⁸He also brought a gold container weighing four ounces, which was filled with incense. ³⁹He brought a young bull, a ram, and a one-year-old male lamb for a burnt offering, ⁴⁰and a male goat for a sin offering. ⁴¹For a peace offering he brought two bulls, five rams, five male goats, and five one-year-old male lambs. This was the offering brought by Shelumiel son of Zurishaddai.

⁴²On the sixth day Eliasaph son of Deuel, leader of the tribe of Gad, presented his offering.

⁴³His offering consisted of a silver platter weighing 3¼ pounds and a silver basin weighing 1¾ pounds (as measured by the weight of the sanctuary shekel). These were both filled with grain offerings of choice flour moistened with olive oil. ⁴⁴He also brought a gold container weighing four ounces, which was filled with incense. ⁴⁵He brought a young bull, a ram, and a one-year-old male lamb for a burnt offering, ⁴⁶and a male goat for a sin offering. ⁴⁷For a

peace offering he brought two bulls, five rams, five male goats, and five one-year-old male lambs. This was the offering brought by Eliasaph son of Deuel.

⁴⁸On the seventh day Elishama son of Ammihud, leader of the tribe of Ephraim, presented his offering.

⁴⁹His offering consisted of a silver platter weighing 3¼ pounds and a silver basin weighing 1¾ pounds (as measured by the weight of the sanctuary shekel). These were both filled with grain offerings of choice flour moistened with olive oil. ⁵⁰He also brought a gold container weighing four ounces, which was filled with incense. ⁵¹He brought a young bull, a ram, and a one-year-old male lamb for a burnt offering, ⁵²and a male goat for a sin offering. ⁵³For a peace offering he brought two bulls, five rams, five male goats, and five one-year-old male lambs. This was the offering brought by Elishama son of Ammihud.

⁵⁴On the eighth day Gamaliel son of Pedahzur, leader of the tribe of Manasseh, presented his offering.

⁵⁵His offering consisted of a silver platter weighing 3¼ pounds and a silver basin weighing 1¾ pounds (as measured by the weight of the sanctuary shekel). These were both filled with grain offerings of choice flour moistened with olive oil. ⁵⁶He also brought a gold container weighing four ounces, which was filled with incense. ⁵⁷He brought a young bull, a ram, and a one-year-old male lamb for a burnt offering, ⁵⁸and a male goat for a sin offering. ⁵⁹For a peace offering he brought two bulls, five rams, five male goats, and five one-year-old male lambs. This was the offering brought by Gamaliel son of Pedahzur.

⁶⁰On the ninth day Abidan son of Gideoni, leader of the tribe of Benjamin, presented his offering.

⁶¹His offering consisted of a silver platter weighing 3¼ pounds and a silver basin weighing 1¾ pounds (as measured by the weight of the sanctuary shekel). These were both filled with grain offerings of choice flour moistened with olive oil. ⁶²He also brought a gold container weighing four ounces, which was filled with incense. ⁶³He brought a young bull, a ram, and a one-year-old male lamb for a burnt offering, ⁶⁴and a male goat for a sin offering. ⁶⁵For a peace offering he brought two bulls, five rams, five male goats, and five one-year-old male lambs. This was the offering brought by Abidan son of Gideoni.

⁶⁶On the tenth day Ahiezer son of Ammishaddai, leader of the tribe of Dan, presented his offering.

⁶⁷His offering consisted of a silver platter weighing 3¼ pounds and a silver basin weighing 1¾ pounds (as measured by the weight of the sanctuary shekel). These were both filled with grain offerings of choice flour moistened with olive oil. ⁶⁸He also brought a gold container weighing four ounces, which was filled with incense. ⁶⁹He brought a young bull, a ram, and a one-year-old male lamb for a burnt offering, ⁷⁰and a male goat for a sin offering. ⁷¹For a peace offering he brought two bulls, five rams, five male goats, and five one-year-old male lambs. This was the offering brought by Ahiezer son of Ammishaddai.

⁷²On the eleventh day Pagiel son of Ocran, leader of the tribe of Asher, presented his offering.

⁷³His offering consisted of a silver platter weighing 3¼ pounds and a silver basin weighing 1¾ pounds (as measured by the weight of the sanctuary shekel). These were both filled with grain offerings of choice flour moistened with olive oil. ⁷⁴He also brought a gold container weighing four ounces, which was filled with incense. ⁷⁵He brought a young bull, a ram, and a one-year-old male lamb for a burnt offering, ⁷⁶and a male goat for a sin offering. ⁷⁷For a peace offering he brought two bulls, five rams, five male goats, and five one-year-old male lambs. This was the offering brought by Pagiel son of Ocran.

⁷⁸On the twelfth day Ahira son of Enan, leader of the tribe of Naphtali, presented his offering.

⁷⁹His offering consisted of a silver platter weighing 3¼ pounds and a silver basin weighing 1¾ pounds (as measured by the weight of the sanctuary shekel). These were both filled with grain offerings of choice flour moistened with olive oil. ⁸⁰He also brought a gold container weighing four ounces, which was filled with incense. ⁸¹He brought a young bull, a ram, and a one-year-old male lamb for a burnt offering, ⁸²and a male goat for a sin offering. ⁸³For a peace offering he brought two bulls, five rams, five male goats, and five one-year-old male lambs. This was the offering brought by Ahira son of Enan.

⁸⁴So this was the dedication offering brought by the leaders of Israel at the time the altar was anointed: twelve silver platters, twelve silver basins, and twelve gold incense containers. ⁸⁵Each silver platter weighed 3¼ pounds, and each silver basin weighed 1¾ pounds. The total weight of the silver was 60 pounds* (as measured by the weight of the sanctuary shekel). ⁸⁶Each of the twelve gold containers that was filled with incense weighed four ounces (as measured by the weight of the sanctuary shekel). The total weight of the gold was three pounds.* ⁸⁷Twelve young bulls, twelve rams, and twelve one-year-old male lambs were donated for the burnt

offerings, along with their prescribed grain offerings. Twelve male goats were brought for the sin offerings. 88Twenty-four bulls, sixty rams, sixty male goats, and sixty one-year-old male lambs were donated for the peace offerings. This was the dedication offering for the altar after it was anointed.

89Whenever Moses went into the Tabernacle to speak with the LORD, he heard the voice speaking to him from between the two cherubim above the Ark's cover—the place of atonement—that rests on the Ark of the Covenant.* The LORD spoke to him from there.

7:5 Hebrew *the Tent of Meeting;* also in 7:89.   7:13 Hebrew *silver platter weighing 130 shekels* [1.5 kilograms] *and a silver basin weighing 70 shekels* [800 grams]; also in 7:19, 25, 31, 37, 43, 49, 55, 61, 67, 73, 79, 85. 7:14 Hebrew *10 shekels* [114 grams]; also in 7:20, 26, 32, 38, 44, 50, 56, 62, 68, 74, 80, 86.   7:85 Hebrew *2,400 shekels* [27.6 kilograms].   7:86 Hebrew *120 shekels* [1.4 kilograms].   7:89 Or *Ark of the Testimony.*

NOTES

7:1 *On the day Moses set up the Tabernacle.* This occurred on the first day of the *first* month of the second year (Exod 40:17), so the narrative has just backtracked one month from the book's beginning on the first day of the *second* month of the second year (1:1). Nonetheless, the narration appears to be ordered this way purposely: tribal leaders are named (ch 7), but their appointment was announced earlier in the narrative (ch 1), and the tribal order of march is stated (ch 7), but the logic was given earlier in the narrative (ch 1).

7:3 *large wagons.* Heb., *'egloth tsab:* an *'agalah* [TH5699, ZH6322] is a cart or wagon. A *tsab* [TH6632, ZH7369] also seems to be some kind of a cart or wagon, although the early versions translated it "covered" (LXX, Vulgate, *Targum Onqelos*). These could either be two-wheeled carts or four-wheeled wagons that were suitable for light freight and pulled by a pair of oxen (IDB 1.540; ISBE 3.69-71; NBD 178; Hoffmeier 2005:221 and fig. 43).

oxen. Heb., *baqar* [TH1241, ZH1330], literally "cow," but used as a pack or draft animal.

ox. Heb., *shor* [TH7794, ZH8802]. The *baqar* stands for the collective and the *shor* for the single animal without indication of sex or age (Péter 1975:493, 496).

7:5 *for transporting.* Lit., "for doing the work/service" (*'abodath* [TH5656, ZH6275]), which, for these animals, implies transport rather than sacrifice.

work they have to do. Lit., "each man according to his work/service" (*'abodatho*), i.e., according to each man's load.

7:10 *dedication gifts.* Heb., *khanukkah* [TH2598, ZH2853]. See also dedication ceremonies for homes (Deut 20:5) and city walls (Neh 12:27). The festival known as Hanukkah celebrates the Maccabees' purification and rededication of the altar.

7:12 *Nahshon . . . leader of the tribe.* This follows the LXX, but if we follow the MT's omission of "leader" in the phrase "leader of the tribe," we might like the rabbis' explanation: He is the only one of the 12 tribal chieftains who is not explicitly called a chieftain, "so if he should ever feel tempted to lord it over the other chieftains by saying, 'I am your king, since I was the first to present the offering,' they could retort by saying, 'You are no more than a commoner, for every one of the others is called a chieftain while you are not described as a chieftain'" (Milgrom 1989:54, quoting *Numbers Rabbah* 13:17).

7:13 *platter.* Heb., *qe'arah* [TH7086, ZH7883], meaning "dish," "bowl," or "platter," probably for dry goods.

basin. Heb., *mizraq* [TH4219, ZH4670], meaning "bowl" or "basin," generally for liquids (see previous note). It is related to *zaraq* [TH2236, ZH2450] (to toss), hence a possible connection with tossing or sprinkling liquids. See Lev 1:5, 11; 3:2, 8, where *zaraq* is used to describe this action (BDB 284b).

7:14 *container.* Heb., *kap* [TH3709, ZH4090], related to the "palm" of a hand, so perhaps this was a utensil formed in the shape of an upturned palm (Levine 1993:257), perhaps a spoon (KJV, ASV), pan (NKJV, NASB, JPS), ladle (NJPS), or dish (NIV, RSV, NRSV, ESV).

7:15 *a young bull.* Heb., *'ekhad ben-baqar* [TH1121/1241, ZH1201/1330], meaning "one bull, a son of the cattle," i.e., a "domesticated bull," because wild animals were precluded from the altar (Milgrom 1989:55).

7:16 *male goat.* Heb., *se'ir-'izzim*, lit., "a he-goat" (*se'ir* [TH8163A, ZH8538]) "of she-goats" (*'izzim* [TH5795, ZH6436]). This construction occurs elsewhere for the goat used to bloody Joseph's coat (Gen 37:31) or as an atoning offering at the Festival of Harvest (28:30). Otherwise, it always refers to the sin offering (7:16, 22, 28, 34, 40, 46, 52, 58, 64, 70, 76, 82; 15:24; 28:15; 29:11, 16, 19, 25; Lev 4:23; 9:3; 23:19; Ezek 43:22; 45:23).

7:17 *bulls.* Heb., *baqar* [TH1241, ZH1330], meaning "bulls" (NLT, NET, NJB), not the castrated "oxen" (JPS, NJPS, ASV, NASB, RSV, NRSV, ESV, NKJV), which would have been forbidden in sacrifice (Milgrom 1989:55; see Lev 22:20).

7:42 *Deuel.* See note on 2:14.

7:48 *seventh day.* Rabbinic tradition says this was a Sabbath, on which individual offerings were prohibited, so an exception was made for the chieftain from Ephraim (Milgrom 1989:57, citing *Sifre Numbers* §51; *Numbers Rabbah* 14:1, 2).

7:89 *speaking to him.* Heb., *middabber 'elayw* [TH1696, ZH1819]. Some say this Hithpael verb's reflexive force means "speaking to himself" and note that it has no antecedent; others suggest reading it as a Piel instead (a slight change in vowel pointing). Waltke keeps the Hithpael and calls the action "reciprocal," i.e., "conversing with him" (Waltke and O'Connor 1990:431).

cherubim. They were the first guardians of holy space (Gen 3:24), and representations of them in the Tabernacle served as reminders that this was inviolable holy space, especially as their wings folded over the top of the Ark. The biblical description is not complete enough to construct their appearance; however, they appear to be some kind of composite creature with human faces, wings, and perhaps a quadruped's body (Ezek 1:5-7; 10:8). Perhaps the term *cherub* comes from an Akkadian term for a being making gestures of adoration or from the verbal form for "adorer"; hence, they have outstretched arms/wings and sometimes uplifted faces (Levine 1993:259; see Exod 25:20; 1 Kgs 6:23-28). In biblical accounts, "their faces were turned downward toward the lid itself, probably to avoid facing God, who was present above them" (Steinmann 2002:112; see Exod 25:20; 37:9).

the Ark's cover. Heb., *kapporeth* [TH3727, ZH4114], which is on or above the Ark of Testimony (see ISBE 3.323-324). The term *kapporeth* is variously translated: "mercy seat" (KJV, ASV, RSV, NRSV, ESV, NJB), "atonement cover" (NIV), "propitiatory" (NAB). Indeed, it is a place of propitiation; however, rather than taking "cover" in its metaphorical sense of "atonement," NLT joins JPS and NJPS in understanding it in its prosaic sense of cover. The Ark is God's footstool, and the lid is his throne (1 Chr 28:2; Ps 99:5).

Ark of the Covenant. See note on 4:5.

COMMENTARY

A month before the military registration of chapter 1, the Tabernacle was consecrated with anointing oil and blood-sprinkling rites. Leaders from each of the twelve tribes brought identical dedication offerings (7:12-83), and together they contributed six carts, each to be pulled by a pair of oxen. Moses distributed the oxen and carts to the Levitical clans, according to what they carried, which chapters 3 and 4 set out.

Clan	Carts	Oxen	Loads
Gershonites	2	4	Heavy Tabernacle coverings (3:25-26; 4:24-26)
Merarites	4	8	Heavier Tabernacle framing (3:36-37; 4:31-32)
Kohathites	—	—	Holy things, carried on the shoulder (4:4-15)

Modern readers groan at formulaic repetition of material that would now be placed in a table or chart. In fact, Levine notes, "In cuneiform tablets we often find lines for columns actually incised on the clay, with headings that provide various kinds of information: names of disbursing and receiving agencies and of individuals, commodities, dates, and quantities," much as we have in 7:12-88 (Levine 1993:261). Whatever the case, the material follows this formula: (1) day of presentation; (2) identity of the tribe's representative, noting that he's a leader (except 7:12); (3) vessel offerings (platters and basins); (4) sacrificial offerings (grain offerings, gold containers of incense, and animals); and (5) inclusio repeating the tribe leader's name. The names match those of 1:5-15, but the order is the camping and marching order (2:3-30).

Tribal Gifts (7:12-83). The formulaic repetition of the pattern for twelve iterations lets us know that each tribe brought one silver platter (130 shekels), one silver basin (70 shekels), one gold ladle (10 shekels), and 21 animals for sacrificial offerings: one young bull, one ram, one year-old male lamb (burnt offerings), one male goat (a sin offering), two bulls, five rams, five male goats, and five year-old male lambs (peace offerings). This gave a total of 2,400 shekels of silver ("60 pounds," NLT), 120 shekels of gold ("three pounds," NLT), and 252 animals for sacrifice (cf. 7:84-88).

The list makes several things obvious. First, the offerings brought over the course of twelve days would have provided lavishly for the required and voluntary sacrifices. Each of the animals was specifically described as a burnt, sin, or peace offering. It is not clear whether they were all offered up in a succession of twelve days of dedication; perhaps they were "contributed to the sacrificial store" (Milgrom 1989:55).

Second, the twelve tribal gifts were each identical. Rather than following a tithing principle that would permit giving according to their ability,[1] the smaller tribes brought the same offerings that the larger tribes brought. Each tribe had an equal responsibility to the Tabernacle, as well as an equal share (cf. 31:4).

Third, the animals provided for peace offerings were two to five times more in number than those provided for burnt and sin offerings. Perhaps that should be a reminder that God desires fellowship with his people above all else.

Fourth, the giving was abundant. This record would have driven home to subsequent generations how generous their forefathers had been with God's work, thereby teaching disciples of any time that disciplined and generous giving is necessary if the Lord's work is to flourish. And it should remind us individually and corporately that God not only records sin and guilt (Col 2:14), but gladly records the names and deeds of those who fear and honor him (Mal 3:16).

The possibility of giving pleasure to God by our glad thank-offerings and worship may be a somewhat remote thought in the minds of Christians, but if so it is a measure of how much the church has lost sight of the real heart of Christian experience, which is fellowship with the Father and Son through the Spirit (1 John 1:3). How should we suppose, if this fellowship is real, that God is indifferent to it from his side? If our chief end is "to enjoy him," should it be thought strange or improbable that he takes pleasure in his people? (Ps 149:4). (Philip 1993:101)

Summary of Dedication of the Altar (7:84-89). The final verses summarize the totals given in the twelve tribal offerings (7:84-88), and they repeat that these offerings were given when Moses anointed the altar (7:84, 89, cf. 7:1). At that time Moses had heard God speaking from his throne/chariot. This was a fulfillment of God's earlier promise (Exod 25:22). From then on, instead of going out to the edge of the camp to a Tent of Meeting, Moses could enter the Tabernacle "to speak with the LORD" (7:89).

ENDNOTE

1. Ezra 2:69; cf. Acts 11:29; 1 Cor 16:2; 2 Cor 8:2-4, 12-14.

◆ ### g. Dedicating the Levites (8:1-26)

The LORD said to Moses, [2]"Give Aaron the following instructions: When you set up the seven lamps in the lampstand, place them so their light shines forward in front of the lampstand." [3]So Aaron did this. He set up the seven lamps so they reflected their light forward, just as the LORD had commanded Moses. [4]The entire lampstand, from its base to its decorative blossoms, was made of beaten gold. It was built according to the exact design the LORD had shown Moses.

[5]Then the LORD said to Moses, [6]"Now set the Levites apart from the rest of the people of Israel and make them ceremonially clean. [7]Do this by sprinkling them with the water of purification, and have them shave their entire body and wash their clothing. Then they will be ceremonially clean. [8]Have them bring a young bull and a grain offering of choice flour moistened with olive oil, along with a second young bull for a sin offering. [9]Then assemble the whole community of Israel, and present the Levites at the entrance of the Tabernacle.* [10]When you present the Levites before the LORD, the people of Israel must lay their hands on them. [11]Raising his hands, Aaron must then present the Levites to the LORD as a special offering from the people of Israel, thus dedicating them to the LORD's service.

[12]"Next the Levites will lay their hands on the heads of the young bulls. Present one as a sin offering and the other as a burnt offering to the LORD, to purify the Levites and make them right with the LORD.* [13]Then have the Levites stand in front of Aaron and his sons, and raise your hands and present them as a special offering to the LORD. [14]In this way, you will set the Levites apart from the rest of the people of Israel, and the Levites will

belong to me. ¹⁵After this, they may go into the Tabernacle to do their work, because you have purified them and presented them as a special offering.

¹⁶"Of all the people of Israel, the Levites are reserved for me. I have claimed them for myself in place of all the firstborn sons of the Israelites; I have taken the Levites as their substitutes. ¹⁷For all the firstborn males among the people of Israel are mine, both of people and of animals. I set them apart for myself on the day I struck down all the firstborn sons of the Egyptians. ¹⁸Yes, I have claimed the Levites in place of all the firstborn sons of Israel. ¹⁹And of all the Israelites, I have assigned the Levites to Aaron and his sons. They will serve in the Tabernacle on behalf of the Israelites and make sacrifices to purify* the people so no plague will strike them when they approach the sanctuary."

²⁰So Moses, Aaron, and the whole community of Israel dedicated the Levites, carefully following all the LORD's instructions to Moses. ²¹The Levites purified themselves from sin and washed their clothes, and Aaron lifted them up and presented them to the LORD as a special offering. He then offered a sacrifice to purify them and make them right with the LORD.* ²²After that the Levites went into the Tabernacle to perform their duties, assisting Aaron and his sons. So they carried out all the commands that the LORD gave Moses concerning the Levites.

²³The LORD also instructed Moses, ²⁴"This is the rule the Levites must follow: They must begin serving in the Tabernacle at the age of twenty-five, ²⁵and they must retire at the age of fifty. ²⁶After retirement they may assist their fellow Levites by serving as guards at the Tabernacle, but they may not officiate in the service. This is how you must assign duties to the Levites."

8:9 Hebrew *the Tent of Meeting;* also in 8:15, 19, 22, 24, 26.   **8:12** Or *to make atonement for the Levites.*
8:19 Or *make atonement for.*   **8:21** Or *then made atonement for them to purify them.*

NOTES

8:2 *set up.* Heb., Hiphil of *'alah* [ᵀᴴ5927, ᶻᴴ6590]; some suggest it means "kindle" or "light" (Milgrom 1989:60, citing *Targum Onqelos, Targum Pseudo-Jonathan,* and Rashi; cf. KJV, ASV, JPS), since it can refer to both the positioning and lighting (see Exod 25:37; 27:20; 30:8; 40:4; Lev 24:2). Most newer translations opt for "set up," "mount," "arrange" (NLT, NIV, RSV, NRSV, ESV, NASB, NJPS, NKJV, NET).

8:4 *entire lampstand.* The entire 75-pound menorah was hammered goldwork (Exod 25:39); other sacred objects were gold-plated wood (Exod 25:10-30; 30:3-5). The design corresponds with Late Bronze Age designs (fifteenth to thirteenth centuries BC) according to Meyers (1976:182-184). For pictures of individual lamps and the Roman depiction of the one they looted in AD 70, see IDB 3.63-71.

base. Heb., *yarek* [ᵀᴴ3409, ᶻᴴ3751], the word for "shaft" (Exod 25:31; 37:17) or "thigh/side" (e.g., Exod 28:42; 40:22, 24). It could be a collective singular reference to the seven stems upon which the lamps were mounted; cf. Vulgate *ductili,* and LXX *kaulos,* which is used for the stalk of a plant (Aristophanes *Knights* 824, 894), quill of a feather (Plato *Phaedrus* 251b), or the duct of the bladder (Crane 2004). However, a bottom-up description elsewhere locates the *yarek* at the base, then moves up through the central shaft, branches, cups, buds, and blossoms (Exod 25:31-36).

beaten gold. This was shaped by a hammer over a model (Meyers 1976:31-33). The ancient Egyptians had developed this technique (Hoffmeier 2005:211-212).

8:7 *sprinkling.* Heb., *nazah* [ᵀᴴ5137A, ᶻᴴ5684], meaning "splatter" or "sprinkle," a term generally used with blood rites (Exod 29:21; Lev 4:6) and a couple of times with oil (Lev 14:16, 27). This time the sprinkling is with water (also 19:18, 21; cf. blood and water, Lev 14:51).

water of purification. Lit., "waters of sin," i.e., "water for removing sin." Commentators differ over its identity: (1) the ash-water mixture for purification ceremonies ("waters for impurity," 19:13, 20; 31:23—so the medieval commentators and Gray 1903:79; Milgrom 1989:61; contra Levine 1993:274; Noordtzij 1983:77); (2) holy waters (5:17); (3) water from the bronze washbasin (Exod 30:17-21; so Harrison 1990:152); or (4) ordinary water (Exod 29:4; Lev 8:6).

shave their entire body. Herodotus said Egyptian priests did this every other day (*Histories* 2.37).

8:8 *young bull.* Heb., *par ben-baqar* [TH6499/1121/1241, ZH7228/1201/1330] (see note on 7:15).

moistened with. This is a frequent phrase used with the grain offerings. The verb is often translated as "mixed with" (KJV, RSV, NASB, NIV).

olive oil. Heb., *shemen* [TH8081, ZH9043], literally, "oil," which can be the oil of myrrh (Esth 2:12) or even fat (Isa 25:6); however, when unmodified, it generally means olive oil. In fact, the full term for olive oil (*shemen zayit* [TH2132, ZH2339]) occurs only three times (Exod 27:20; 30:24; Lev 24:2).

8:11 *Raising his hands, Aaron must then present the Levites to the LORD as a special offering from the people of Israel.* Lit., "and Aaron must wave the Levites as a wave offering before the LORD from the sons of Israel" (see note on 5:25; cf. 6:20). This would have been done symbolically, perhaps "as parallel ranks of Levites moved forward then stepped back in unison in the Tabernacle court near the altar" (Harrison 1990:154). The "waved offering" was part of the peace offering (Lev 3:1-17; 7:11-36); it was "the priest's portion being presented to the LORD with a waving motion before it became the property of the officiating priest" (Harrison 1990:153). So, too, the Levites belonged to God, who in turn assigned them to the priests with the same motion.

8:12 *to purify the Levites and make them right with the LORD.* Lit., "to make expiation/ atonement for the Levites."

8:16 *reserved for me.* Heb., *netunim netunim hemmah li* [TH5414, ZH5989], meaning "formally assigned, dedicated, transferred to" (see comments on 3:5-13). The repetition is emphatic.

in place of . . . as their substitutes. See note on 3:12.

all the firstborn sons of the Israelites. Lit., "the ones who open every womb, all the first-born of the sons of Israel."

8:17 *set them apart.* Heb., *qadash* [TH6942, ZH7727], meaning "consecrate, sanctify." Though they were consecrated for their service, they still lacked the sacred status of priest (cf. 3:9; 8:16).

all the firstborn sons of the Egyptians. Lit., "all the firstborn in the land of Egypt," including animals (Exod 12:29).

8:19 *make sacrifices to purify the people.* Lit., "atone for the sons of Israel." "Atone" rather than "make sacrifices" would be preferable since the Levites did not make sacrifices; rather, by their Tabernacle service they were a living sacrifice to "'cover' the people . . . a kind of buffer" (Riggans 1983:66), "screen" (E. W. Davies 1995b:78), "spiritual lightning rod" (G. J. Wenham 1981:143; Milgrom 1989:371; Milgrom 1970:31; Cole 2000:278), or "insulators who protected the Israelites from the force of God's wrath" (Harrison 1990:247 n. 60).

sanctuary. Heb., *haqqodesh* [TH6944, ZH7731], the term for the Tabernacle that pointed to its sacred *status* rather than to its *function*, either as meeting place (*'ohel mo'ed* [TH168/4150, ZH185/4595], "Tent of Meeting"), repository for the covenant documents (*mishkan ha'eduth* [TH4908/5715, ZH5438/6343], "Tabernacle of the Covenant"), or dwelling place for the Lord (*mishkan*, "Tabernacle"). See note on 1:50.

8:22 *assisting Aaron and his sons.* Lit., "before Aaron and before his sons" (see note on 3:4).

8:24 *must begin serving . . . at the age of twenty-five.* Compare this age to the age of 30 noted in 4:3, 23, 30 (also 1 Chr 23:3) and the age of 20 in 1 Chr 23:24, 27 (cf. 2 Chr 31:17; Ezra 3:8). The LXX eliminates the contradiction between chs 4 and 8, using 25 in both places (e.g., 4:3, 23, 30). See commentary on 4:1-3.

8:25 *at the age of fifty.* In contrast to the priests, "age, not bodily defects, disqualifies Levites" (Milgrom 1989:66, quoting *Sifre Numbers* §62; *Sifre Zuta* on Numbers 8:23).

8:26 *may assist.* Heb., *sharath* [TH8334, ZH9250], meaning "serve" or "minister." Older translations have "shall minister" (KJV, ASV, NAB, JPS); the newer read "may serve" (NASB, RSV, NRSV, NJPS).

serving as guards. See note on 3:28.

may not officiate in the service. Lit., "but he may not serve." They *never* officiated.

COMMENTARY

Preparing the Lamps (8:1-4).

It was Aaron's responsibility (8:2; Exod 30:8; Lev 24:2) to set up the seven-branched lampstand exactly as God had commanded. This was a seven-branched rendition of the tree of life (Gen 2:9; 3:22), which in the Temple was accompanied by other Edenic imagery (1 Kgs 6:18, 29, 35; 2 Chr 3:5). It stood on the left-hand side as the priest entered the Holy Place, positioned so that it lit the room and its other two furnishings—the table for the Bread of the Presence, which was opposite the lamp, and the gold incense altar, which stood before the entrance to the Most Holy Place. It shined the light of God's continual presence upon the bread, which symbolized the Provider's presence (Exod 40:22-25), and it shined upon the way into his glorious presence. This light was regularly lit and then tended from evening until morning (Exod 27:21; 30:7; Lev 24:1-4).

Jesus is the light of the world (John 8:12a; 9:5; cf. John 1:9; 3:19; 12:46), and in turn so are his disciples individually (John 8:12b) and collectively (Matt 5:14-16; Eph 5:8-14). Thus, seven golden lampstands echo the menorah in John's vision of the seven churches of Asia Minor (Rev 1:12-20).

Consecrating the Levites (8:5-26).

The ritual of consecrating the Levites assumes chapters 1-4 as background, even repeating 4:5-13. The Levites' consecration is described in two terms: (1) They were "set apart . . . from the rest of the people of Israel," and (2) they were made "ceremonially clean" by sprinkling, shaving, and washing. It is interesting to compare and contrast this with the priestly ritual of Leviticus 8:

Priests	Levites
Washed (Lev 8:6)	Sprinkled (8:7)
Put on new garments (Lev 8:13)	Washed their clothes (8:21)
Had blood applied to their right ear, thumb, and toe (Exod 29:20; Lev 8:23; 14:14, 17, 25, 28)	—
Made the priests "holy"	Made them "clean" (8:6)

Verses 8-22 describe a substitutionary ceremony. The people of Israel laid hands on the Levites (8:10), designating them as substitutes for all of Israel's first-born males as "a special offering to the LORD" (8:13). This substitutionary arrangement involved all the Levites and their livestock, who served as substitutes for the firstborn males in all Israel, thereby fulfilling God's claim on the firstborn, established when he preserved Israel's firstborn while destroying those of Egypt (8:16-18). In turn, the Lord gave them to the priests as helpers at the Tabernacle (8:19a) and as living sacrifices doing spiritual service in place of all Israel (8:19b).

In the New Testament, the laying on of hands signified transfer of blessing: on children (Matt 19:13), for healing (Mark 6:5; Luke 4:40; Acts 9:12, 17; 28:8), at baptism (Acts 9:17; 19:5-6; cf. Heb 6:2), or at ordination for ministry (Acts 6:6; 13:3; 1 Tim 4:14; 2 Tim 1:6).

Since their wilderness duties involved heavy portage, full duty was confined to their prime years between the ages of 25 and 50; however, after that they might still assist in light duty guarding the Tabernacle (8:23-26).

◆   ## h. Observing the second Passover (9:1-14)

A year after Israel's departure from Egypt, the LORD spoke to Moses in the wilderness of Sinai. In the first month* of that year he said, 2"Tell the Israelites to celebrate the Passover at the prescribed time, 3at twilight on the fourteenth day of the first month.* Be sure to follow all my decrees and regulations concerning this celebration."

4So Moses told the people to celebrate the Passover 5in the wilderness of Sinai as twilight fell on the fourteenth day of the month. And they celebrated the festival there, just as the LORD had commanded Moses. 6But some of the men had been ceremonially defiled by touching a dead body, so they could not celebrate the Passover that day. They came to Moses and Aaron that day 7and said, "We have become ceremonially unclean by touching a dead body. But why should we be prevented from presenting the LORD's offering at the proper time with the rest of the Israelites?"

8Moses answered, "Wait here until I have received instructions for you from the LORD."

9This was the LORD's reply to Moses.

10"Give the following instructions to the people of Israel: If any of the people now or in future generations are ceremonially unclean at Passover time because of touching a dead body, or if they are on a journey and cannot be present at the ceremony, they may still celebrate the LORD's Passover. 11They must offer the Passover sacrifice one month later, at twilight on the fourteenth day of the second month.* They must eat the Passover lamb at that time with bitter salad greens and bread made without yeast. 12They must not leave any of the lamb until the next morning, and they must not break any of its bones. They must follow all the normal regulations concerning the Passover.

13"But those who neglect to celebrate the Passover at the regular time, even though they are ceremonially clean and not away on a trip, will be cut off from the community of Israel. If they fail to present the LORD's offering at the proper time, they will suffer the consequences of their guilt. 14And if foreigners living among you want to celebrate the Passover to the

LORD, they must follow these same de-   apply both to native-born Israelites and
crees and regulations. The same laws   to the foreigners living among you."

9:1 The first month of the ancient Hebrew lunar calendar usually occurs within the months of March and April.
9:3 This day in the ancient Hebrew lunar calendar occurred in late March, April, or early May.   9:11 This day in
the ancient Hebrew lunar calendar occurred in late April, May, or early June.

N O T E S

9:1 *A year after Israel's departure from Egypt.* See 7:1; 9:5; 10:11; 20:1; 33:3, 38.

In the first month. This was one month before the date on which the book opens (1:1).

9:2 *prescribed time.* Heb., *mo'ed* [TH4150, ZH4595], the same term used for Tent of "Meeting"
('*ohel mo'ed* [TH168, ZH185]), but now referring not to an appointed *place*, but rather to an
appointed *time* (Exod 12:6, 14; Lev 23:5).

9:3 *twilight.* Heb., *ben ha'arbayim* [TH6153, ZH6847], "between the two evenings," i.e.,
between sunset and nightfall, the end of one day and the beginning of the next.

9:6 *dead body.* Heb., *nepesh 'adam* [TH120, ZH132]; here again *nepesh* [TH5315, ZH5883] refers
not to a "ghost" or "soul" but to a corpse (see note on 5:2). Leviticus 21:1-12 instituted
this law for the priests; subsequent legislation applied the principle more broadly (5:1-4;
6:6-7, 9-12; 19:1-22).

9:10 *because of touching a dead body.* Lit., "if he is unclean for a *nepesh* [TH5315, ZH5883]"
(see notes on 5:2; 9:6).

9:11 *one month later.* Lit., "in the second month"; cf. "first month" (9:1, 3).

bitter salad greens. Heb., *maror* [TH4844, ZH5353], meaning "bitter thing," with something
like "herbs" understood. The LXX uses *pikris*, which could be endive or chicory; the Vulgate
has *lactucis agrestibus*, meaning "wild lettuce."

9:12 *not break any of its bones.* Lit., "not break any of it," with "bones" understood from
the prior instructions in Exod 12:46. This assured that the lamb was not sectioned but
roasted whole and intact.

9:13 *will be cut off from the community of Israel.* Lit., "that *nepesh* [TH5315, ZH5883] will be
cut off from the people." Milgrom notes that being "cut off" was the punishment for five
categories of offense: violating (1) sacred time (9:13; Exod 12:15, 19; 31:14; Lev 23:29),
(2) sacred substance (15:30; 18:3; Exod 30:33, 38; Lev 7:18, 20, 25, 27; 19:8), (3) purification rituals (19:13-20; Gen 17:14), (4) performing illicit worship (Lev 17:4, 9; 20:2-6; Ezek
14:4-8), or (5) illicit sex (Lev 18:27-29) (Milgrom 1989:406). It is not clear whether the
cutting off meant: (1) excommunication from the community (19:20; Exod 12:15; 31:14;
see de Vaulx 1972:125; Budd 1984:98); (2) execution by the community (Gray 1903:84-85;
Noordtzij 1983:84), or (3) execution by God himself (Lev 17:10; 20:3, 6; Isa 48:19; 56:5;
see McNeile 1911:48). Some say that in the wilderness the effect of either of the first two
would be the same: "excommunication from the community . . . virtually amounted to
a sentence of death" (von Rad 1962:1.268; see Budd 1984:98; Cole 2000:109; Hyatt
1980:135). Hertz rules out the first two: "not by a human tribunal" (Hertz 1977:609), as
do others (G. J. Wenham 1981:99; Levine 1993:241-242). In Egypt, the consequence of failure to follow the Passover ritual was death at the hands of the "death angel" (Exod 12:23),
which might inform our understanding of "cut off" here. Taken together, the phrases "cut
off" and "bear their guilt" "indicate that the one so punished lost Yahweh's protection and,
in essence, operated outside the sphere of the covenant relationship" (Ashley 1993:181).

9:14 *foreigners living among you.* Heb., *yagur 'ittekem ger* [TH1481, ZH1591], meaning
"sojourner sojourning with you." The *ger* [TH1616, ZH1731] left the home village, tribe, or
country to rely on ancient Near Eastern hospitality for shelter from war (2 Sam 4:3; Isa

16:4), famine (Ruth 1:1), or other hardship, but we need not identify these as "fugitives" or "refugees." Generally, their rights to hold property, marry, and participate in judicial and cultic activities were curtailed. The *ger* was similar to but distinguished from the foreigner (*ben-nekar* [TH1121/5236, ZH1201/5797]), the visitor (*toshab* [TH3427, ZH3782]; NLT, "temporary resident"), and the hired worker (*sakir* [TH7916, ZH8502]; NLT, "hired servants"), all of whom were forbidden to observe the Passover in Exod 12:43-45 (Ashley 1993:181; E. W. Davies 1995b:84).

COMMENTARY

God gave Moses this regulation a month before the events with which this book opened (9:1; cf. 1:1) to prepare the people for their first Passover outside of Egypt. God had Moses remind them of the necessary timing and ritual requirements (9:2), and they obeyed (9:5). But accidental ritual defilement kept some from celebrating the Passover; therefore, they came asking how they could participate (9:6).

God's response addressed two things that would keep an Israelite from celebrating the Passover on its correct date: accidental defilement and being on a journey (9:9-13). The one who missed the real Passover date could celebrate it one month later, carefully following the same ritual (9:11); however, this was not a mere optional date for Passover. Participating while unclean or abstention for no good reason were both wrong and would result in being "cut off" so the offenders "suffer the consequences of their guilt" (9:13). This indicates a punitive result targeting the perpetrator rather than a purifying act on behalf of the community, and it meant the victim's death by the hand of God or his agents. These provisions applied equally to the native Israelite and to any foreigner who chose to live with Israel (9:14; see note).

From a Christian perspective, Jesus is the true Passover Lamb, "who takes away the sin of the world" (John 1:29; 1 Cor 5:7). At his crucifixion, none of his bones were broken, perhaps in fulfillment of the Passover requirement (John 19:36; cf. Num 9:12), although this may be just as likely a fulfillment of Psalm 34:20—or perhaps both (Brueggemann 2005:271). Abuse of the Lord's Table, which celebrates the true Passover, can also result in being "cut off" by the sleep of premature death (1 Cor 11:28-30).

◆   i. Following the cloud (9:15-23)

15On the day the Tabernacle was set up, the cloud covered it.* But from evening until morning the cloud over the Tabernacle looked like a pillar of fire. 16This was the regular pattern—at night the cloud that covered the Tabernacle had the appearance of fire. 17Whenever the cloud lifted from over the sacred tent, the people of Israel would break camp and follow it. And wherever the cloud settled, the people of Israel would set up camp. 18In this way, they traveled and camped at the LORD's command wherever he told them to go. Then they remained in their camp as long as the cloud stayed over the Tabernacle. 19If the cloud remained over the Tabernacle for a long time, the Israelites stayed and performed their duty to the LORD. 20Sometimes the cloud would stay over the Tabernacle for only a few days, so the people would stay for only a few days, as the LORD commanded. Then at the

LORD's command they would break camp and move on. ²¹Sometimes the cloud stayed only overnight and lifted the next morning. But day or night, when the cloud lifted, the people broke camp and moved on. ²²Whether the cloud stayed above the Tabernacle for two days, a month, or a year, the people of Israel stayed in camp and did not move on. But as soon as it lifted, they broke camp and moved on. ²³So they camped or traveled at the LORD's command, and they did whatever the LORD told them through Moses.

9:15 Hebrew *covered the Tabernacle, the Tent of the Testimony.*

NOTES

9:16 *at night the cloud that covered the Tabernacle.* The LXX reads, "the cloud covered it by day, and the appearance of fire by night," followed by KJV, ASV, NASB, RSV, NRSV, ESV, JPS; however, the MT has the more difficult reading, followed by NLT and NJPS.

9:22 *a year.* Heb., *yamim* [TH3117, ZH3427] (days). Most modern translations render it "a year" (NLT, NASB, JPS, NJPS; see Snaith 1969:221; Binns 1927:56). Gray called that rendering "quite unjustifiable . . . not to be defended by a reference to Lev 25:29," where *year* and *days* are parallel. He said, "It means simply an indefinite period" (Gray 1903:87; cf. Gen 40:4; 1 Kgs 17:15; Neh 1:4 for that use of *yom*). Levine thinks the parallel in Lev 25:29 does show that it can mean year (Levine 1993:299). North (1961) suggests that it is a technical term for a four-month season. It might be better to have "for two days or a month or longer" (HALOT; cf. NAB, RSV, NRSV, ESV) or "any number of days" (Ashley 1993:182).

COMMENTARY

The initial fiery cloud signaled God's initial presence at the Tabernacle (9:15; Exod 40:34), which set the subsequent pattern: The cloud lifted and the people moved; the cloud settled and the people camped (9:17), whether for lengthy encampments (9:19) or stays of only a few days (9:20) or even overnight (9:21). As Milgrom (1989:75) puts it, "Israel's movements are generated solely by the Lord. He leads Israel to the land He has promised (10:29), moves it (9:15-23; 10:11), retards it (12:14-15; 14:26-35; 20:27-28), and causes it to detour (14:25)."

In the New Testament, the theophanic cloud image conveys particular manifestations of God's presence (Luke 9:34; Acts 1:9), and the Tabernacle image speaks of God's presence in Christ, in believers, and in his body, the church (John 1:14; 1 Cor 3:16; 6:19; 2 Cor 6:16; Eph 2:21-22; 1 Pet 2:5). God's presence in the Spirit not only indwells, God's spiritual presence also leads and guides. In the New Testament, Jesus himself was led by the Spirit (Matt 4:1; Luke 4:1), as was the apostolic community (Acts 8:29; 10:9-13; 11:12), and as are all of God's children (Rom 8:5, 9, 14; Gal 4:6; 5:16, 18).

◆   ## j. Signaling with trumpets (10:1-10)

Now the LORD said to Moses, ²"Make two trumpets of hammered silver for calling the community to assemble and for signaling the breaking of camp. ³When both trumpets are blown, everyone must gather before you at the entrance of the Tabernacle.* ⁴But if only one trumpet is blown, then only the leaders—the heads of the clans of Israel—must present themselves to you.

⁵"When you sound the signal to move on, the tribes camped on the east side of the Tabernacle must break camp and move forward. ⁶When you sound the signal a second time, the tribes camped on the south will follow. You must sound short blasts as the signal for moving on. ⁷But when you call the people to an assembly, blow the trumpets with a different signal. ⁸Only the priests, Aaron's descendants, are allowed to blow the trumpets. This is a permanent law for you, to be observed from generation to generation.

⁹"When you arrive in your own land and go to war against your enemies who attack you, sound the alarm with the trumpets. Then the LORD your God will remember you and rescue you from your enemies. ¹⁰Blow the trumpets in times of gladness, too, sounding them at your annual festivals and at the beginning of each month. And blow the trumpets over your burnt offerings and peace offerings. The trumpets will remind the LORD your God of his covenant with you. I am the LORD your God."

10:3 Hebrew *Tent of Meeting.*

NOTES

10:2 *trumpets.* Heb., *khatsotseroth* [TH2689, ZH2956], perhaps from a word meaning "to be narrow, stretched, to form a stalk, tube," indicating a long, straight instrument. This is not the *shopar* [TH7782, ZH8795] (e.g., Exod 19:16, 19) or *yobel* [TH3104, ZH3413] (Josh 6:4-8), which were made from rams' horns. Josephus describes these trumpets, and the arch of Titus depicts them as 1.5 feet to 2 feet long with flared bells (illustration in Best and Hutter 1975:323; IDB 3.473, illus. 87; IBD 3.1038). Hoffmeier notes Hickman's classic work on trumpets in ancient Egypt and describes many illustrations of trumpets in Egyptian military scenes (Hoffmeier 2005:221 and fig. 41, citing Hickman 1946:3-5; Cooney 1965:69; Naville 1908:plate clv).

hammered silver. The trumpets were formed by hammering a sheet of silver over a trumpet-shaped form. Hoffmeier notes that Tutankhamen's tomb (c. 1325 BC) contained two trumpets, one of an alloy and the other silver, both with the wooden cores around which they were shaped (Hoffmeier 2005:221 and fig. 42).

signaling. The Qumran War Scroll expands upon this regulation with "trumpets of rallying," "alarm," "ambush," "pursuit," "reassembly," "enlisting," "famous men," "camps," "pulling out," and "battle formations" (1QM [1Q33] 3:1-6), found in García Martínez 1994:96-97; García Martínez and Tigchelaar 1997:1.117; Vermes 1998:127).

10:3 *blown.* Heb., *taqa'.* Perhaps this is an example of sound mimicry; indeed, this is exactly the sound advised for rapid double-tonguing of a brass instrument today. The NLT follows the Jewish tradition, which takes this to indicate long blasts to signal the people to gather to Moses, to the Tent of Meeting, and to worship and understands staccato blasts (*taqa' teru'ah* [TH8628/8643, ZH9546/9558]; see 10:5) for battle or the march (Milgrom 1989:74). Some understand the long and staccato blasts the other way around, *taqa'* indicating the short blast and *taqa' teru'ah* indicating a sustained blast (Dillmann and Knobel 1886:49).

10:4 *clans.* Rather than *mishpakhah* [TH4940, ZH5476], here it is *'elep* [TH504A, ZH548], a word that can indicate either one thousand or a clan-based fighting unit (see 10:36).

10:5 *sound the signal to move on.* Heb., *taqa' teru'ah* (see note on 10:3).

10:6 *south.* The LXX adds third and fourth blasts for the camps on the west and north, which some suggest as the original text (Budd 1984:105 n. 6b, citing Paterson 1900:47); others suggest that the first two were representative of the pattern, which had already been already established in 2:3-31, and this was meant to be understood but left unstated thereafter (Harrison 1990:170). The Vulgate has, "and according to this manner shall the rest do." On the other hand, Ibn Ezra points out that the priests, who blew the horns (10:8), would already have moved on with the cultic objects (2:17; 10:21).

sound short blasts as the signal for moving on. Lit., "blow the *teru'ah* for breaking camp" (see note on 10:3).

10:7 blow the trumpets with a different signal. Lit., "sound them, but don't sound the *teru'ah* signal" (*lo' tari'u* [TH7321, ZH8131]; see note on 10:3).

10:8 This is a permanent law for you. Heb., *lekhuqqath 'olam* [TH2708/5769, ZH2978/6409], an expression used mostly for continuity of priestly concerns (15:15; 18:23; 19:10, 21; Exod 12:14, 17; 27:21; 28:43; 29:9; Lev 3:17; 7:36; 10:9; 16:29, 31, 34; 17:7; 23:14, 21, 31, 41; 24:3).

COMMENTARY

God ordered the fabrication of signaling trumpets, which would be used for the wilderness march (10:2-8) and later in the land (10:9-10). While on the march they were for calling assemblies (10:2-3) and signaling the break of camp (10:2, 5). One call would start the Judah corps on the move (10:5), then a second would signal the Reuben corps to move out (10:6). No further signals are mentioned for the three Levitical families (2:17), Ephraimites (2:18-24), or Danites (2:25-31), though the pattern of calls already established may have simply continued. Only the priests could blow these trumpets (10:8), whether on the march (10:2-8) or in the land (10:9-10). One might have expected civil or at least military leaders to blow these signaling trumpets. But priests were an integral part of warfare, addressing the warriors before battle (Deut 20:2-4), giving them God's battle guidance (27:18-21; Judg 20:26-28; 1 Sam 23:9; 30:7), and carrying the Ark and blowing the trumpets for battle (10:33-36; Josh 6; 1 Sam 4; 2 Sam 11:11).

In the land, the trumpets would be blown "in times of gladness" (10:10), which might be coronation days (e.g., 2 Kgs 11:14; 1 Chr 29:22), victory celebrations (10:9; Esth 8:17; 9:17), or the annual festivals (2 Chr 30:21, 23, 26; Ezra 6:22; Neh 8:17). The trumpets would also be blown "over . . . burnt offerings" (10:10, mentioned only here and at 2 Chr 29:26-30).

"The trumpet blasts serve also as a prayer" (Milgrom 1989:75; cf. 2 Chr 13:12-16). Any time the trumpet sounded, the people would have heard a note of reminder, "I am the LORD your God" (10:10),[1] and God would have heard Israel's testimony that they were his people. That was God's central covenant promise (Lev 26:12), which was echoed by the prophets (Jer 7:23; 11:4; 30:22; Ezek 34:31; 36:28; Joel 2:27) and apostles (2 Cor 6:16; Rev 21:3). Reminders are an important motif in Numbers (5:15; 16:36-38; 17:10; 31:54).

ENDNOTE

1. This is a common formula (10:10; 15:41; Exod 6:7; 16:12; Lev 11:44; 18:2, 4, 30; 19:2-4, 10, 25, 31, 34, 36; 20:7, 24; 23:22, 43; 24:22; 25:17, 38, 55; 26:1, 13; Deut 29:6; Judg 6:10; Ezek 20:5, 7, 19-20; Joel 3:17 [4:17]); cf. Numbers references with "I am the LORD" (3:13, 41, 45; 10:10; 14:35; 15:41; 35:34).

◆ B. In the Wilderness (10:11-21:35)
   1. Moving from Sinai to Kadesh (10:11-12:16)
      a. Departing in battle order (10:11-36)

¹¹In the second year after Israel's departure from Egypt—on the twentieth day of the second month*—the cloud lifted from the Tabernacle of the Covenant.* ¹²So the Israelites set out from the wilderness of Sinai and traveled on from place to place until the cloud stopped in the wilderness of Paran.

¹³When the people set out for the first time, following the instructions the LORD had given through Moses, ¹⁴Judah's troops led the way. They marched behind their banner, and their leader was Nahshon son of Amminadab. ¹⁵They were joined by the troops of the tribe of Issachar, led by Nethanel son of Zuar, ¹⁶and the troops of the tribe of Zebulun, led by Eliab son of Helon.

¹⁷Then the Tabernacle was taken down, and the Gershonite and Merarite divisions of the Levites were next in the line of march, carrying the Tabernacle with them. ¹⁸Reuben's troops went next, marching behind their banner. Their leader was Elizur son of Shedeur. ¹⁹They were joined by the troops of the tribe of Simeon, led by Shelumiel son of Zurishaddai, ²⁰and the troops of the tribe of Gad, led by Eliasaph son of Deuel.

²¹Next came the Kohathite division of the Levites, carrying the sacred objects from the Tabernacle. Before they arrived at the next camp, the Tabernacle would already be set up at its new location. ²²Ephraim's troops went next, marching behind their banner. Their leader was Elishama son of Ammihud. ²³They were joined by the troops of the tribe of Manasseh, led by Gamaliel son of Pedahzur,

²⁴and the troops of the tribe of Benjamin, led by Abidan son of Gideoni.

²⁵Dan's troops went last, marching behind their banner and serving as the rear guard for all the tribal camps. Their leader was Ahiezer son of Ammishaddai. ²⁶They were joined by the troops of the tribe of Asher, led by Pagiel son of Ocran, ²⁷and the troops of the tribe of Naphtali, led by Ahira son of Enan.

²⁸This was the order in which the Israelites marched, division by division.

²⁹One day Moses said to his brother-in-law, Hobab son of Reuel the Midianite, "We are on our way to the place the LORD promised us, for he said, 'I will give it to you.' Come with us and we will treat you well, for the LORD has promised wonderful blessings for Israel!"

³⁰But Hobab replied, "No, I will not go. I must return to my own land and family."

³¹"Please don't leave us," Moses pleaded. "You know the places in the wilderness where we should camp. Come, be our guide. ³²If you do, we'll share with you all the blessings the LORD gives us."

³³They marched for three days after leaving the mountain of the LORD, with the Ark of the LORD's Covenant moving ahead of them to show them where to stop and rest. ³⁴As they moved on each day, the cloud of the LORD hovered over them. ³⁵And whenever the Ark set out, Moses would shout, "Arise, O LORD, and let your enemies be scattered! Let them flee before you!" ³⁶And when the Ark was set down, he would say, "Return, O LORD, to the countless thousands of Israel!"

10:11a This day in the ancient Hebrew lunar calendar occurred in late April, May, or early June.   10:11b Or *Tabernacle of the Testimony.*

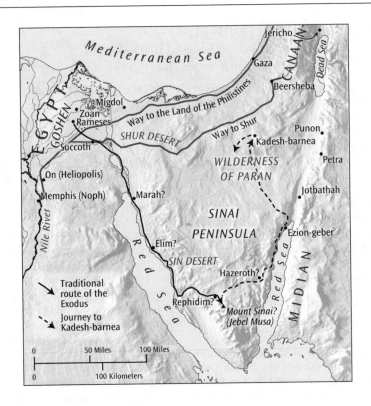

NOTES

10:11 *In the second year.* See Exod 40:17; cf. Num 1:1; 7:1; 9:1, 5; 20:1; 33:3, 38.

10:12 *stopped.* Heb., *shakan* [TH7931, ZH8905], meaning "settled" or "abode." This is a term referring to God's covenantal promise of abiding presence (Exod 29:45; 2 Cor 6:16; Rev 21:3), whether the subject is God himself (5:3; 35:34), his Tabernacle (*mishkan* [TH4908, ZH5438]; Josh 22:19), or this glory-cloud (Exod 40:35).

Paran. This was "not a station but is the general name for the northern half of the Sinai Peninsula" (Milgrom 1989:76). Several campsites were in the region (10:12; 12:16; 13:3, 26; Deut 1:1; 33:2).

10:14 *Judah's troops led the way. They marched behind their banner.* Lit., "the *degel* of the sons of Judah set out at the head, according to their armies." On *degel* [TH1714, ZH1840], see note on 2:2, where it appears to be a three-tribe division (2:2-4, 10, 17, 25, 31, 34). In 1:52, it appears to be a divisional insignia (Hertz 1977:572; Unger 1966:315).

10:20 *Deuel.* The LXX renders this as *Ragouēl* (i.e., *Reuel*); see note on 1:14.

10:21 *carrying the sacred objects from the Tabernacle.* Lit., "carrying the *miqdash* [TH4720, ZH5219]," which is most often the sanctuary, but here it must refer to the holy things (Milgrom 1970:23-24 n. 78; see 4:4-20), perhaps by metonymy (Harrison 1990:174; Keil and Delitzsch 1884:3.559).

10:28 *marched, division by division.* The phrase forms an inclusio with 10:12. The term "divisions" or "hosts" reminds us that God is the Lord of armies, which refers sometimes to heavenly armies (1 Sam 17:45a; Ps 148:2; Isa 6:1-3) and sometimes to the earthly armies of Israel (Exod 7:4; 12:41, 51; 1 Sam 17:45b; Ps 60:10).

10:29 brother-in-law, Hobab son of Reuel. The Hebrew reads, "Hobab, son of Reuel, the *khoten* of Moses." Translating this is complicated by difficulty in identifying and distinguishing between Hobab, Reuel, and Jethro. Each is identified as Moses's *khoten* [TH2859A, ZH3162], which is generally translated "father-in-law" (HALOT; see Exod 3:1; 4:18; 18:1-27; Judg 1:16; 4:11; 19:4-9). Hobab is identified as Moses's *khoten* here and in Judg 1:16 and 4:11, but that role is assigned elsewhere to Reuel (Exod 2:18) or Jethro (Exod 18). If we don't just ascribe this confusion to conflicting source material (Noth 1968:77-78), the possibilities boil down to these: (1) identify Hobab with Jethro as a son of Reuel; (2) identify Jethro, the elder sage, with Reuel as the father of Hobab, the vigorous desert scout (Albright 1963b:7); or (3) take this to be one person with three names (Gray 1903:93). Most translations render *khoten* as "father-in-law" (KJV, RSV, NRSV, NASB, NIV, JPS, NJPS). The NLT reflects the possibility that *khoten* is a term for any male related through a bride from his family (Mitchell 1969), a father-in-law in the case of Jethro/Reuel (Exod 2:18) or brother-in-law in the case of Hobab (Judg 4:11). For more on this, see Hughes 2002:469; Budd 1984:113-14; Milgrom 1989:78-79; Cole 2000:175-77.

Midianite. Elsewhere Hobab is called a Kenite (Judg 1:16; 4:11). Midian is probably the name of a confederation of peoples (Dumbrell 1975), which included the Kenites, who were perhaps smiths who had worked the mines in the Sinai or Midian (24:21).

10:33 They marched for three days. Armies and caravans traveled about 15 miles per day; therefore, the trip was about 40-50 miles (Cole 2000:178).

mountain of the LORD. Lit., "mountain of Yahweh." This was clearly Sinai, even though everywhere else Sinai is called the mountain of *'elohim* [TH430, ZH466] (Exod 3:1; 4:27; 18:5; 24:13; 1 Kgs 19:8), and "mountain of Yahweh" refers to Jerusalem's Mount Zion (Ps 24:3; Isa 2:3; 30:29; Mic 4:2; Zech 8:3; cf. Gen 22:14; 2 Sam 21:6, LXX).

moving ahead of them. Lit., "before them on a journey of three days." If we take it that the Ark moved along three days ahead of them, it would be useless as a guide and comfort. Suggested solutions include the following: (1) The Syriac changes the text to "one day," giving it a lead that would still allow the people to follow by sight. (2) This could be a scribal error of repetition of the formula from earlier in the verse (Levine 1996:316; Noth 1968:78; Snaith 1969:139). (3) The NLT follows Ashley (1993:198-99) in understanding this as a temporal phrase indicating that during the whole three-day journey, the Ark went "before (*lipne* [TH3807.1/6440, ZH4200/7156) the people."

The Pentateuch identifies Israel's divinely designated guidance variously: as a cloud-encased fire (9:15-23; 14:14; Deut 1:33), as the Ark (10:33; Josh 3:3, 6, 11), or as an angel (Exod 14:19a; 23:20-23). Those traditions are harmonizable; however, the contradiction of 10:21 with 2:17 is more difficult to explain. Suggested interpretations include: (1) Only on this particular occasion did the Ark go first rather than in the middle of the camp, either because this was an unusually inhospitable region for marching and camping (MacRae 1953:175) or to provide a picture of divine leadership at the start of this journey (Harrison 1990:179; Noordtzij 1983:94; Hertz 1977:613). (2) We should understand "before them" (*lipnehem*) as meaning "in their presence" (Deut 3:28, "he will cross over before this people"; 10:11; 31:3; cf. Philip 1993:131).

show. Heb., *tur* [TH8446, ZH9365], meaning "to reconnoiter, to scout"; the same term was used for the actions of the men who were commissioned to explore the land (13:2, 16).

10:33-36 The LXX has the verses in the order 33, 35, 36, 34, keeping the verses about the Ark together; however, MT, Targum, Vulgate, and Syriac all have the order as 33, 34, 35, 36.

10:35 Arise. This is a frequent battle cry (von Rad 1966b:109-15, 123), picturing the Lord as seated on his throne/chariot, the Ark, and arising to ride it into battle.

10:36 *when the Ark was set down.* Lit., "when the Ark came to a rest," the Ark being the subject of an active verb, not passive.

Return, O LORD. This is the opposite of "to turn away from, abandon." Some suggest repointing to *shebah* [TH3427, ZH3782] (sit, rest) for an antithetical parallel with the opening words of 10:35 (Noordtzij 1983:96; von Rad 1962:1.237); however, that lacks any versional support.

countless thousands. Lit., "ten thousands of thousands." The two clauses could be in apposition: "Return, O LORD, you who are Israel's myriads of thousands!" (Ehrlich 1968–1969:1.255; Hertz 1977:613; Plaut 1979:103; NJPS). This would be understood in one of two ways: (1) Just as Elijah and Elisha are "the chariots and charioteers of Israel" (2 Kgs 2:12; 13:14), so too God is Israel's most potent military asset. "So in Egypt, King Sesostris III is praised: 'He alone is a million'; and the victory of Rameses II after the battle of Kaesh reads: 'Amun is worth more to me than millions of foot-soldiers, and hundreds of thousands of chariots'" (Milgrom 1989:81). (2) It could read "O LORD of countless thousands" (Sturdy 1976:78; NEB), which would make Israel's "countless thousands" the earthly counterpart of the Lord's celestial armies (Josh 5:14), including the sun, moon, and stars (e.g., Deut 4:19), which warred on Israel's side (Josh 10:12; Judg 5:20). One could compare this to such phrases as "God of Israel" (Isa 21:10; Zeph 2:9), "Mighty One of Israel" (Isa 1:24), and "the God of the armies of Israel" (1 Sam 17:45).

COMMENTARY

So far in the story, the people had been at Sinai, but now they began a three-stage journey: from Sinai to Kadesh (10:11–12:16), the 40 years near Kadesh (13:1–19:22), and finally the move from Kadesh to Moab (20:1–21:35). Up until this point in Numbers, they have demonstrated exemplary obedience, but now anarchy breaks out. The people (11:1-8), and even Miriam and Aaron (12:1-5), complain about Moses. Eventually it degenerates into mutiny as the people refuse to enter the Promised Land (14:1-10), and it also degenerates into Levitical anarchy as Korah refuses to acknowledge priestly leadership (16:1-30). The result is that the whole mutinous generation was consigned to death in the desert rather than life in the land (21:21-35).

Verse 12 summarizes 10:1–12:16: the stages of the journey were Taberah (11:1-3), Kibroth-hattaavah (11:4-35), and Hazeroth (12:1-16a).[1] Describing each of the four tribal divisions as "troops," the narrator puts the Israelites on the march toward conquest. Once the cloud lifted, their marching order was to be as follows:

⋏
ARK
(10:33-36)
⋏
JUDAH
Issachar, Zebulun
(10:13-16)
⋏
TABERNACLE
Gershonites, Merarites
(10:17)
⋏
REUBEN
Simeon, Gad
(10:18-20)
⋏
SACRA
carried by Kohathites
(10:21)
⋏
EPHRAIM
Manasseh, Benjamin
(10:22-24)
⋏
DAN
Asher, Naphtali
(10:25-27)

The Ark, carried on the shoulders of priests, led the way as Israel marched out "division by division" (10:28). Judah, the preeminent tribe both by virtue of size (2:5-15) and royal promise (Gen 49:8-10), led the first three-tribe division. The Tabernacle division marched second. Using their wagons, the Gershonites carried its fabric coverings, and the Merarites carried its framework. They moved ahead of the Kohathites so that when the third Levitical group arrived in camp, the Tabernacle was ready to house their shoulder-borne holy things (10:21). Earlier the Levites were said to march in the middle (2:17; see note on 10:33), after Reuben's division (2:16) and before Ephraim's division (2:24), which included Benjamin and Manasseh.[2] But here, we have the Kohathites alone in this line of march before the Ephraim division. Finally, the Dan division marched in rear guard.

Moses Asks for Hobab's Help (10:29-32). Moses asked for Hobab's help in setting up wilderness camping sites. Hobab initially declined the invitation, so Moses made the case by promising that Hobab could share in Israel's divine blessings if he came along. Hobab's reply isn't given; however, a positive reply is implied in that his Kenite descendants lived in the Promised Land (Judg 1:16; 4:11). Perhaps his affirmation of the agreement is omitted so that his descendants lack a scriptural basis for claiming the same rights as the twelve tribes in the land (Licht 1985). However, "it is more likely due to the conviction that Israel's safe journey through the wilderness was due to the guidance of the Ark, not of Hobab" (Milgrom 1989:80).

There is no need to interpret Moses's recruitment of Hobab as a lack of trust in God's leadership; looking to the leadership of the apostles did not signify that to the early church, and the continued leadership of pastors and elders today similarly signifies no lack of trust. The Bible frequently incorporates what Milgrom (1989:79) labels "double causality," giving the following examples: "Jacob's prosperity is attributed to both his cunning (Gen 30:32ff) and God's directives (31:10-12); Joseph's enslavement is attributed to his brother's designs (37:18ff) and divine design (45:5-8; 50:20)."

The Ark (10:33-36). Verses 35-36 are bracketed by inverted Nuns in the MT, indicating a scribal opinion that they belonged somewhere else or form a separate entity (Milgrom 1989:375-376). Some suggest they came from *The Book of the Wars of the Lord* (21:14) or from the apocryphal book of Eldad and Medad, as suggested by medieval rabbinic sources.[3]

It is possible to read verses 33-36 as a temporary provision for the three-day journey described here, with the Ark normally moving along in the middle of the line of march with the Kohathites (10:21). However, the priests, rather than the Kohathites, carried the Ark, and verses 33-35 seem to indicate a regular wilderness pattern. The narrator describes the Ark as an active agent moving out ahead of the troops as a forward scout; thus, it moved out to the war cry, "Arise, O LORD, and let your enemies be scattered!" (10:35), a phrase repeated almost verbatim in Psalm 68:1 [2]. The Ark was scouting out temporary resting places that would do until the nation finally came to rest in the Promised Land (Deut 12:9; Ps 95:11). And this rest would come not just because the weary march had ended for a time, but because the Lord would "return . . . to the countless thousands of Israel," settling down to dwell among his people (10:36; cf. Pss 6:4; 90:13; 126:4; Isa 44:22; Hos 14:1). This foreshadowed the rest in the Promised Land (e.g., Deut 12:9; Ps 95:11), the Ark's resting place in the Temple (Ps 132:8-18), and the eschatological rest for God's people (Isa 32:18; Matt 11:28; Heb 4:9).

ENDNOTES
1. The final summary of stages (33:16-17) omits Taberah; therefore, some propose that Taberah and Kibroth-hattaavah are the same place (Keil and Delitzsch 1884:3.64-65).
2. Taken with 10:36, that position may have informed the psalmist's petition, "Appear, You who are enthroned on the cherubim, at the head of Ephraim, Benjamin, and Manasseh! Rouse Your might and come to our help!" (Ps 80:2, NJPS) (Philip 1993:128).
3. E. W. Davies 1995b:97, citing, but rejecting as "purely conjectural," the proposal by Leiman 1974 and Levine 1976.

◆   b. Wilderness complaints and God's response (11:1-35)

Soon the people began to complain about their hardship, and the LORD heard everything they said. Then the LORD's anger blazed against them, and he sent a fire to rage among them, and he destroyed some of the people in the outskirts of the camp. ²Then the people screamed to Moses for help, and when he prayed to the LORD, the fire stopped. ³After that, the area was known as Taberah (which means "the place of burning"), because fire from the LORD had burned among them there.

⁴Then the foreign rabble who were traveling with the Israelites began to crave the good things of Egypt. And the people of Israel also began to complain. "Oh, for some meat!" they exclaimed. ⁵"We remember the fish we used to eat for free in Egypt. And we had all the cucumbers, melons, leeks, onions, and garlic we wanted. ⁶But now our appetites are gone. All we ever see is this manna!"

⁷The manna looked like small coriander seeds, and it was pale yellow like gum resin. ⁸The people would go out and gather it from the ground. They made flour by grinding it with hand mills or pounding it in mortars. Then they boiled it in a pot and made it into flat cakes. These

cakes tasted like pastries baked with olive oil. ⁹The manna came down on the camp with the dew during the night.

¹⁰Moses heard all the families standing in the doorways of their tents whining, and the LORD became extremely angry. Moses was also very aggravated. ¹¹And Moses said to the LORD, "Why are you treating me, your servant, so harshly? Have mercy on me! What did I do to deserve the burden of all these people? ¹²Did I give birth to them? Did I bring them into the world? Why did you tell me to carry them in my arms like a mother carries a nursing baby? How can I carry them to the land you swore to give their ancestors? ¹³Where am I supposed to get meat for all these people? They keep whining to me, saying, 'Give us meat to eat!' ¹⁴I can't carry all these people by myself! The load is far too heavy! ¹⁵If this is how you intend to treat me, just go ahead and kill me. Do me a favor and spare me this misery!"

¹⁶Then the LORD said to Moses, "Gather before me seventy men who are recognized as elders and leaders of Israel. Bring them to the Tabernacle* to stand there with you. ¹⁷I will come down and talk to you there. I will take some of the Spirit

that is upon you, and I will put the Spirit upon them also. They will bear the burden of the people along with you, so you will not have to carry it alone.

¹⁸"And say to the people, 'Purify yourselves, for tomorrow you will have meat to eat. You were whining, and the LORD heard you when you cried, "Oh, for some meat! We were better off in Egypt!" Now the LORD will give you meat, and you will have to eat it. ¹⁹And it won't be for just a day or two, or for five or ten or even twenty. ²⁰You will eat it for a whole month until you gag and are sick of it. For you have rejected the LORD, who is here among you, and you have whined to him, saying, "Why did we ever leave Egypt?"'"

²¹But Moses responded to the LORD, "There are 600,000 foot soldiers here with me, and yet you say, 'I will give them meat for a whole month!' ²²Even if we butchered all our flocks and herds, would that satisfy them? Even if we caught all the fish in the sea, would that be enough?"

²³Then the LORD said to Moses, "Has my arm lost its power? Now you will see whether or not my word comes true!"

²⁴So Moses went out and reported the LORD's words to the people. He gathered the seventy elders and stationed them around the Tabernacle.* ²⁵And the LORD came down in the cloud and spoke to Moses. Then he gave the seventy elders the same Spirit that was upon Moses. And when the Spirit rested upon them, they prophesied. But this never happened again.

²⁶Two men, Eldad and Medad, had stayed behind in the camp. They were listed among the elders, but they had not gone out to the Tabernacle. Yet the Spirit rested upon them as well, so they prophesied there in the camp. ²⁷A young man ran and reported to Moses, "Eldad and Medad are prophesying in the camp!"

²⁸Joshua son of Nun, who had been Moses' assistant since his youth, protested, "Moses, my master, make them stop!"

²⁹But Moses replied, "Are you jealous for my sake? I wish that all the LORD's people were prophets and that the LORD would put his Spirit upon them all!" ³⁰Then Moses returned to the camp with the elders of Israel.

³¹Now the LORD sent a wind that brought quail from the sea and let them fall all around the camp. For miles in every direction there were quail flying about three feet above the ground.* ³²So the people went out and caught quail all that day and throughout the night and all the next day, too. No one gathered less than fifty bushels*! They spread the quail all around the camp to dry. ³³But while they were gorging themselves on the meat—while it was still in their mouths—the anger of the LORD blazed against the people, and he struck them with a severe plague. ³⁴So that place was called Kibroth-hattaavah (which means "graves of gluttony") because there they buried the people who had craved meat from Egypt. ³⁵From Kibroth-hattaavah the Israelites traveled to Hazeroth, where they stayed for some time.

11:16 Hebrew *the Tent of Meeting.*   11:24 Hebrew *the tent;* also in 11:26.   11:31 Or *there were quail 3 feet* [2 cubits or 92 centimeters] *deep on the ground.*   11:32 Hebrew *10 homers* [1.8 kiloliters].

NOTES

11:4 *foreign rabble.* Heb., *ha'sapsup* [TH628, ZH671], a reduplicative form of *'asap* [TH622, ZH665] (to collect), referring to the "riff-raff" (NJPS), "bunch of vagabonds" (HALOT), or "rabble" (BDB) that followed Israel from Egypt (Exod 12:38; Lev 24:10; Deut 29:11; Josh 8:35).

good things of Egypt. This language is implied by 11:5 but is not actually present in this verse.

11:6 *our appetites are gone.* Heb., *napshenu yebeshah* [TH3002, ZH3313], a complaint that nothing could whet their appetites (BDB 660b; Dillmann and Knobel 1886:57; Snaith

1969:227; so NASB, NIV, NLT; cf. 11:8). Some translations understand *nepesh* [TH5315, ZH5883] as a reference to the throat/gullet, e.g., "our gullets are shriveled" (NJPS) or "throats are dry" (Noth 1968:86; so NEB) or "we are dehydrated" (Cole 2000:185) or "our strength is dried up" (RSV, NRSV, ESV). Perhaps the KJV did best by referring to a psychological or spiritual complaint like that of the psalmist (Ashley 1993:208-209; KJV, ASV, JPS; cf. Ps 22:15; 90:6; 102:4, 11; 129:6).

11:7 *pale yellow like gum resin.* Lit., "a fragrant, yellowish gum that crystallizes on surfaces" (cf. LXX, *krustallos* [TG2930, ZG3223]), a fine "flaky substance" (Exod 16:14). Commentators refer to a variety of naturally occurring phenomena in the Sinai, from fungi and lichens to secretions from insects or from such plants as the Tamarisk tree (*Tamarix gallica*). But only a miracle provided the recurring, reliably large quantities and the double-helping before each Sabbath (Exod 16:22-23).

11:8 *hand mills.* In Hebrew this is a dual form, indicating a pair of stones, one working against the other.

like pastries baked with olive oil. Lit., "like the butter of the oil," i.e., "the upper layer of the first pressing of the olive oil" (Milgrom 1989:84).

11:10 *Moses was also very aggravated.* Lit., "in the eyes of Moses it was evil." The "it" could refer to the people's complaint (Hirsch 1971:174), the Lord's angry response to Israel (Milgrom 1989:85; Noordtzij 1983:99), or his demand that Moses lead and provide for this people.

11:11 *Why . . . ?* This is a common question in laments (e.g., Pss 2:1; 10:1; 22:1; 42:9; Lam 5:20; Joel 2:17; Hab 1:3, 13).

these people. Lit., "this people" (11:12, 14; Exod 32:9; 33:12), rather than "my people" (Exod 9:27) or even "your people" (Exod 33:13).

11:12 *Did I give birth to them?* Lit., "Did I conceive this entire people?" The word order emphasizes the subject, Moses.

Did I bring them into the world? The word order again emphasizes the subject, Moses.

mother. Heb., *'omen* [TH539B, ZH587], better rendered as "guardian" (Esth 2:7) or "attendant" (2 Sam 4:4; NLT, "nurse"), e.g., the caretakers of children in wealthy families (2 Kgs 10:5). Here it might well connote the pejorative-sounding "babysitter."

11:13 *They keep whining to me.* Heb., *yibku 'alay,* understanding the imperfect of *bakah* [TH1058, ZH1134] as repeated action, which Milgrom (1989:86) characterizes as "nagging," like what Samson's wife did (Judg 14:16-17). Perhaps the *'al* [TH5921, ZH6584] should be understood as an adversative (Ashley 1993:204 n. 10): "crying out *against* me."

11:16 *who are recognized as elders and leaders of Israel.* Lit., "from the elders of Israel, whom you know as elders of the people, and officers." The verb is active ("you know/ acknowledge"); and *you* is singular; therefore, Moses does the acknowledging; it is not via a plebiscite.

leaders. Heb., *shoter* [TH7860, ZH8854] (official, officer). The LXX reads *grammateis* [TG1122, ZG1208] (scribes), but it is unlikely that these officials functioned solely in that capacity. The term was used to refer to the Israelite "foremen" who reported to Egyptian slave drivers (Exod 5:6, 10, 14-15, 19) and to Israel's administrative leadership (Deut 1:15; 16:18; 20:5, 8-9; 29:10; 31:28; Josh 1:10; 3:2; 8:33; 23:2; 24:1; 1 Chr 23:4; 26:29; 27:1; 2 Chr 19:11; 26:11; 34:13; Prov 6:7).

11:17 *talk to you.* The pronoun is singular, i.e., to Moses.

I will take some of the Spirit that is upon you. The expression "take" means "to reserve, set aside" (HALOT), "lay aside, reserve, withdraw, withhold" (BDB, TWOT).

11:18 *Purify.* Heb., *qadash* [TH6942, ZH7727] (sanctify, consecrate), not the term *taher* [TH2891, ZH3197] used for ritual cleansing (8:21; 19:12, 19) or the Piel of *khata'* [TH2398, ZH2627] used for atonement rituals (Lev 8:15; 14:49).

and you will have to eat it. Lit., "and you will eat." It is too early in the passage to recognize the threat; here it still sounds like a cornucopian bonanza, as had been the case with manna (Exod 16:4, 12).

11:20 *a whole month.* Lit., "a month of days" (also 11:21), completing the series of numbers of days in 11:19.

until you gag. Lit., "until it comes out of your nose." "For causing God's anger (lit., 'his nose to flare'), the stench from the meat will fill the people's noses—a fitting punishment" (Milgrom 1989:88).

11:25 *never happened again.* This is sometimes rendered "did not cease" (KJV, Vulgate, *Targum Pseudo-Jonathan, Targum Onqelos,* Luther); however, the LXX and nearly all English translations have "did not continue" or "did not do so again."

11:26 *listed among the elders.* Lit., "among [the names] that had been written down." There are several ways of understanding this: (1) They were written down in a count of elders like the military counts of chs 1–2 from whom the 70 were chosen, though they were not among the 70 themselves (Gray 1903:114). (2) They were listed among the 70 though only 68 went out to the Tent (Cole 2000:194). Snaith conjectures that they were among the 70 chosen, but were ritually impure at the time (Snaith 1969:259); some rabbis think they declined to come out because of feelings of inadequacy (*Targum Pseudo-Jonathan; Sifre Numbers* §95; *b. Sanhedrin* 17a). (3) They were included in an original count of 72 though 70 went to the Tent (Noth 1968:90). Milgrom cites the following speculative but interesting explanation from Jewish tradition:

> Some say: they (e.g., their names) remained in the urn. For when the Holy One, Blessed Be He, said to Moses: "Gather for Me 70 of Israel's elders," Moses said (to himself): "How shall I do it" (11:16); if I select five (from each tribe) then it will be wanting. If, on the other hand, I chose six out of one and five out of another, I shall cause jealousy among the tribes. What shall I do?" He selected six men (out of each tribe), and brought 72 slips, on 70 of which he wrote the word "elder," leaving the other two blank. He then mixed them all up, deposited them in an urn, and said to them, "Come and draw your slips." To each who drew a slip bearing the word "elder," he said, "Heaven has already consecrated you." To him who drew a blank, he said, "Heaven has rejected you, what can I do?" (Milgrom 1989:90, quoting *b. Sanhedrin* 17a).

gone out to the Tabernacle. Cole and Ashley reject the idea that the Tent was outside the camp rather than at camp center as Numbers has it; rather, they take "going out" to mean leaving their own tents, not the camp (Ashley 1993:215; Cole 2000:194).

11:31 *Now the LORD sent a wind.* Lit., "now a wind proceeded [*ruakh nasa'*] from the LORD." The *ruakh* [TH7307, ZH8120] is the subject, not the object of the verb, and *nasa'* [TH5265, ZH5825] is the same verb used to describe the Ark and the Israelites breaking camp and moving out (e.g., 1:51), e.g., "a [theophanic] wind sallied forth from the LORD."

quail. These are *coturnix communis,* which migrate north from Arabia and Africa in the spring and return south in August, following a route through Egypt, Sinai, and Palestine (Hoffmeier 2005:173-174). The fat little birds fly poorly, so they're easily netted in their low-flying fatigue (Aristotle *History of Animals* 8.597b). In the late nineteenth and early twentieth century, Arabs in the northern Sinai would net one to two million of them during their fall migration (Gispen 1959:186-187).

let them fall. Heb., *natash* [TH5203, ZH5759], meaning "left, abandoned, forsook," which implies that they fell to the ground; see below on depth/height.

all around the camp. The manna fell *inside* the camp (11:9); however, the quail fell outside the camp, "in the zone associated with uncleanness and death" (G. J. Wenham 1981:109).

For miles in every direction. Lit., "for a day's journey in this direction, and a day's journey in that direction surrounding the camp," i.e., 15–18 miles. Hoffmeier says, "a day's journey represents a fixed and understood distance" of 14–20 miles (Hoffmeier 2005:120-124).

flying about three feet above the ground. Lit., "two cubits over the face/surface of the earth," with no term for *flying.* Some interpret this as flying over the camp at the height of three feet (Vulgate, *Targum Pseudo Jonathan,* Rashi, NAB, NEB, NLT, NIV mg; see Ashley 1993:218; Budd 1984:129; Harrison 1990:190-191; Hertz 1977:617; Noordtzij 1983:105; Snaith 1969:144), but it seems that we should interpret this as a lying on the ground to the depth of about three feet (most English translations, e.g., KJV, NASB, NRSV, JPS,NJPS, NJB, NLT mg, *Targum Onqelos;* see Cole 2000:197; Levine 1993:314; Milgrom 1989:92; G. J. Wenham 1981:109).

11:32 caught. The actual meaning is "collect" or "gather," which implies that they were laying on the ground (see note about depth/height on 11:31).

11:34 the people who had craved meat from Egypt. Lit., "the people who had the craving." The Hebrew makes no mention of Egypt here. The "meat" is also an addition borrowed from 11:5, which mentions "fish."

COMMENTARY

So far in Numbers we have seen nothing but expressions of agreement with God's direction, obedience, and a high sense of expectancy. But the first three verses of chapter 11 introduce elements that were to become regular features of the subsequent wilderness experience: (1) complaint (11:4-5; 12:1-2; 14:1-4; 16:1-3, 41; 20:3-5; 21:5); (2) divine punishment (11:33; 12:9-10; 14:20-37; 16:32, 45-49; 17:10-13; 21:6); (3) Moses's intercession, which brings a measure of relief (11:2; 12:13; 16:22, 46-49; 21:7); and (4) memorializing the incident by giving a name to the site (11:34; 20:13; cf. Exod 15:23; 17:7).

Complaints had been tolerated earlier (Exod 15:24; 16:2; 17:3), but henceforth God would judge it (11:4, 19, 33; 14:2; 16:3; 20:3; 21:5), and that would require Moses's intercession. First, the people grumbled about general conditions (11:1-3), then troublemakers carped about their reliable—and therefore repetitious—diet of manna (11:4-9). Moses chimed in, moaning about his impossible responsibilities (11:10-15). Miriam and Aaron protested Moses's prophetic leadership (12:1-16). Sniveling reached an unforgivable crescendo when the people rejected not only their daily provisions but even their very salvation in the Promised Land (14:1-4). It continued with Korah's anarchy (ch 16).

Complaint about Food (11:4-9). When the "foreign rabble" stirred up Israel, they took a fond look back to Egypt, where they had enjoyed "free" meat and vegetables (11:5), something they had already done once before (Exod 16:3). Indeed, the waters of Egypt brimmed with fish, so even slaves could eat well (cf. Exod 7:21; Isa 19:8), and its gardens produced a bounty of "cucumbers, melons, leeks, onions, and garlic" (11:5), condiments that garnished the staple diet of even the poor in Egypt. This wish fits well with the traditional dating for this book, as opposed to suggestions that it reflects a later "Priestly" agenda. Hoffmeier notes that the foods listed here "reflect a genuine familiarity with Egyptian diet. . . . These five food items seem out of place in Canaan or Israel and hardly seem to reflect the dietary passions of an exilic or postexilic community" (Hoffmeier 2005:175). Herodotus said the pyramid workmen were given "radishes, onions, and garlics" (*Histories* 2.125). The Egyptian diet of the late nineteenth and early twentieth centuries included the following: "bread (made of millet or of maize), milk, new cheese, eggs, small salted fish, cucumbers and melons, and gourds of a great variety of kinds, onions and leeks, beans, chick-peas, lupins, the fruit of the black egg-plant, lentils, etc., dates (both fresh and dried), and pickles" (Milgrom 1989:83).

But, given the harsh conditions under which Israel had labored in Egypt, their food there was hardly "free." And Israel hadn't complained of irregular provisions threatening starvation, but of having no appetite for God's regular provision. They were complaining that their dietary staple, their "daily bread," was all too reliable (11:6; cf. Matt 6:11; Luke 11:3). And it was "bread from heaven . . . the food of angels" (Ps 78:24-25)!

Loathing manna meant turning up their nose at God's provision, and longing for Egypt meant abandoning God's deliverance. They were effectively repudiating the very basis of their covenant relation with God.[1] They were showing signs of the same spirit that rejected the true bread from heaven, Jesus Christ, who gives eternal life (John 6:32-58).

Moses Complains about his Load (11:10-15). The ubiquitous moaning not only infuriated the Lord (11:1-9), it also aggravated Moses (11:10). We might have thought Moses would take this out on the people, but instead he took it to the Lord (11:11). He didn't reproach God for treating the people shabbily; rather, the one whom we come to know as the intercessor par excellence complained on his own behalf. He probably brooded some on his reluctance to take the job in the first place (Exod 3:1–4:17), then descended to sarcastic questions: Am *I* their father (11:12)? Or maybe you think *I'm* their mother? Is that why you have told me to carry them in my arms? My load is far too heavy (11:12, 14)! Then Moses turned to the people's own incessant complaint, wondering, "Where am I supposed to get meat for all these people?" (11:13), perhaps foreshadowing his dangerous query, "Must we bring you water from this rock?" (20:10). This was a sharp turnaround from bragging about how well God was treating Israel (10:32). Other faithful servants experienced crises of faith (1 Kgs 19:4-18; Job 3:11; 6:9; Matt 11:2-3; 26:69-75); nonetheless, Moses's melodramatic suicide wish (11:15) looks like a shabby parody of Paul's sentiments (Rom 9:3).

God Responds to Moses's Complaint (11:16-25). The Lord told Moses to assemble 70 respected leaders, which could have been the advisory council of elders at Sinai (Exod 18:25-26; 24:9) or a newly selected group. That such a body already existed should have reminded Moses that he was not doing this by himself (11:14). Seventy seems to be a number signifying a full council. We read of 70 nations (Gen 10; cf. LXX = 72), 70 descendants of Jacob (Exod 1:5; Deut 10:22), 70 elders of Israel (Exod

24:1, 9; Ezek 8:11), 70 humiliated kings (Judg 1:7), 70 who were struck by the Lord (1 Sam 6:19), 70 sons or brothers of a judge or king who likely served as royal counsel (Judg 8:30; 12:14; 2 Kgs 10:1-7), and eventually the 70-member Sanhedrin (Mark 14:53-55; Acts 4:3-6; Josephus *Antiquities* 14.168-170, 15.173). The pattern of 70 culminated in the 70 that Jesus sent out with authority to preach the gospel (Luke 10:1-10),[2] and the Spirit-anointed helpers for Moses set the pattern for selecting deacons who were "full of the Spirit" to help the apostles (Acts 6:3).

Rather than just advise Moses that he should make increased use of the 70, the Lord told Moses, "bring them to the Tabernacle" (11:16), indicating that the leadership problem would be solved in communion with the Lord (11:17). God promised that those who led with Moses would have a share of the same Spirit that empowered Moses. Here the Spirit is described in quantitative terms (cf. being "filled" with the Spirit).[3] So some commentators suggest that God rebuked Moses's complaint with a diminution or dilution of his Spirit. For example, Calvin said, "this division comprehends punishment in it" (Calvin 1993:4.25), and Noordtzij said, "Moses will no longer be the old Moses: part of the Lord's Spirit will be taken from him and divided among the seventy" (Noordtzij 1983:101). But this was not to cause a lessening of the Spirit on Moses, such as when the Spirit of the Lord was withdrawn from Saul and given to David (1 Sam 16:13). Nor was it an outright succession, where the anointing passed from one to another, as with Elijah to Elisha (2 Kgs 2:9-15). Rather, it was to be a distribution of the same Spirit to the 70, although not in the same measure (cf. ch 12). It would imply "no diminution of the spiritual power of Moses, 'even as a light that kindles other lights is not thereby dimmed'" (Hertz 1977:615, quoting *Sifre*). Like the tongues of fire that rested on the 120 at Pentecost (Acts 2:3), this was to be a fresh outpouring in broader measure than before.

Then God turned to the people's complaint about food. He commanded the people to "purify" themselves in preparation for the meat they sought (11:18), indicating that "tomorrow" was going to be about something more than the merely mundane matter of diet. The people might have thought they were about to experience straightforward blessing, but ominous talk of griping and gagging undercut that. The people didn't like manna every day; therefore, God was going to force meat on them day after day, until they gagged on it. The reason for this wrathful cuisine was that "you have rejected the LORD" (11:20). That promise of superabundance prompted incredulity. Moses contemplated the impossibility of relief by means of the available resources (11:22), which would fail although they were vast (32:1; Exod 12:38). But God turned from national reserves to divine intervention, throwing down the gauntlet: "Now you will see whether or not my word comes true" (11:23).

The Lord gave the 70 elders a portion of the Mosaic Spirit as promised (11:25; cf. 11:17), and they "prophesied" as observable evidence of the gift they had received (11:25; cf. Joel 2:28-32; Acts 2:17-21). This was not intelligible, authoritative proclamation; rather, the Hithpael of *naba'* [TH5012, ZH5547] here refers to ecstatic utterances or the behavior of spiritual ecstasy.[4] And it "never happened again" (11:25). This did not mean the Spirit departed from them or that their role as Moses's helpers was temporary; rather, ecstatic prophesying served as initial evidence of an ongoing anointing and function.

Eldad and Medad (11:26-29). The prophetic outburst among the unnamed 70 was accompanied by the same sign among two elders who "had not gone out to the Tabernacle" (11:26-29). Moses's response contrasted sharply with Joshua's, and probably with what the reader's initial response might have been, given this book's sharp protection of Mosaic prerogatives. When Joshua wanted this stopped (11:28), Moses asked, "Are you jealous for my sake?" (11:29). A candid Joshua might have responded that he was jealous for his own sake, as his position as Moses's aide-de-camp was being diluted by the addition of 70 others—now 72! Then Moses expressed the hope: "I wish that all the LORD's people were prophets, and that the LORD would put his Spirit upon them all!" (11:29). Moses's yearning was surely a godly wish. Joel echoed it in his promise of a democratized outpouring of the Spirit (Joel 2:28-32), and Peter's Pentecost sermon spoke of its implementation (Acts 2:17-21). The same sentiment drove Paul's wish that all would speak in tongues (1 Cor 14:5) and that all should eagerly desire the greater gifts, especially prophecy (1 Cor 12:27-31; 14:1-5). Just as Moses chided Joshua, so, too, Paul cautioned the early church: "Do not stifle the Holy Spirit" (1 Thess 5:19).

God Responds to the People's Complaint by Sending Quail (11:30-35). God responded to the food "crisis" just as he had threatened. The description of plentitude is expansive, even more so than the threat would have prepared the reader to hear (11:19-20). While the people had gathered manna daily *within* the camp, they would gather meat *outside* the camp, for 10-15 miles in every direction (11:31). This was not their daily food gathered in the measure of "two quarts" (Exod 16:16); rather, they gathered it "all that day and throughout the night and all the next day . . . fifty bushels" (11:32). Sated, they stared around the camp; scattered everywhere was a fearsome glut. And before they could pick their teeth, the Lord "struck them with a severe plague" (11:33). Once again, a negative memorial was established (cf. 11:3); that place got called Glutton's Cemetery (11:34). "He gave them their desire: but he sent leanness into their soul" (Ps 106:15, Geneva Bible).

ENDNOTES
1. Exod 20:2; Deut 5:6, 15; Judg 6:8; 1 Kgs 8:16; 9:9; Jer 7:22; 11:4; 32:21; 34:13; Ezek 20:4-22.
2. The Greek mss evidence for "70" (cf. KJV, ASV, NASB, RSV, NRSV) and "72" (NLT, NIV, NJB, ESV, NET) in Luke 10 is about evenly divided. Since 70 is such a frequent symbolic number in the OT, 70 would be unsurprising in Luke 10:1, 17. I wonder if the charismatic Luke went for 72 to reflect the democratization of Spirit-anointing that Eldad and Medad represented in addition to the 70 who went out to the Tent of Meeting (11:25-27).
3. Exod 28:3; 31:3; 35:31; Mic 3:8; Luke 1:15, 41, 67; Acts 2:4; 4:8, 31; 5:3; 9:17; 13:9, 52; Rom 15:13; Eph 5:18.
4. Levine 1993:313, 325; Gray 1903:113; Hertz 1977:616; Noth 1968:89; Snaith 1969:143; Young 1952:70; contra Harrison 1990:189.

◆   ## c. Miriam and Aaron complain about Moses (12:1-16)

While they were at Hazeroth, Miriam and Aaron criticized Moses because he had married a Cushite woman. ²They said, "Has the LORD spoken only through Moses? Hasn't he spoken through us, too?" But the LORD heard them. ³(Now Moses was very humble—more humble than any other person on earth.)

⁴So immediately the LORD called to Moses, Aaron, and Miriam and said, "Go out to the Tabernacle,* all three of you!" Sothe three of them went to the Tabernacle. ⁵Then the LORD descended in the pillar of cloud and stood at the entrance of the Tabernacle.* "Aaron and Miriam!" he called, and they stepped forward. ⁶And the LORD said to them, "Now listen to what I say:

"If there were prophets among you,
    I, the LORD, would reveal myself
        in visions.
    I would speak to them in dreams.
⁷But not with my servant Moses.
    Of all my house, he is the one
        I trust.
⁸I speak to him face to face,
    clearly, and not in riddles!

He sees the LORD as he is.
    So why were you not afraid
        to criticize my servant Moses?"

⁹The LORD was very angry with them, and he departed. ¹⁰As the cloud moved from above the Tabernacle, there stood Miriam, her skin as white as snow from leprosy.* When Aaron saw what had happened to her, ¹¹he cried out to Moses, "Oh, my master! Please don't punish us for this sin we have so foolishly committed. ¹²Don't let her be like a stillborn baby, already decayed at birth."

¹³So Moses cried out to the LORD, "O God, I beg you, please heal her!"

¹⁴But the LORD said to Moses, "If her father had done nothing more than spit in her face, wouldn't she be defiled for seven days? So keep her outside the camp for seven days, and after that she may be accepted back."

¹⁵So Miriam was kept outside the camp for seven days, and the people waited until she was brought back before they traveled again. ¹⁶Then they left Hazeroth and camped in the wilderness of Paran.

12:4 Hebrew *the Tent of Meeting.* 12:5 Hebrew *the tent;* also in 12:10. 12:10 Or *with a skin disease.* The Hebrew word used here can describe various skin diseases.

NOTES

12:1 *While they were at Hazeroth.* Though not in the Hebrew text, this is implied by 12:16.

Miriam and Aaron criticized Moses. The verb in Hebrew is feminine singular, so it was Miriam, joined by Aaron, who criticized Moses.

Cushite woman. Elsewhere, the NLT has "Ethiopian" for Cushite as does the LXX (Jer 38:7; Dan 11:43; Amos 9:7; cf. Acts 8:27). This might identify this wife as someone other than the Midianite Zipporah; however, in the Old Testament, *kush* [TH3569, ZH3934] can refer not only to a Nubian,¹ but also to the Midianite inhabitants of Cushan.² Commentators are divided, some favoring identification with Zipporah (Binns 1927:75-76; Sturdy 1976:89-90; de Vaulx 1972:159), others favoring another identification (Budd 1984:136; Gray 1903:106-107; Noordtzij 1983:121-122; G. J. Wenham 1981:110-111), and some crediting the two stories to conflicting sources (Noth 1968:94; Snaith 1969:145). If this was Zipporah, the newfound hostility to this long-standing marriage must have been because she was just rejoining Moses after being left behind when he returned to Egypt (Exod 18:5). If this was a Nubian, she was a second wife taken either after Zipporah's unrecorded death or after a divorce, which some identify from the note that Moses "sent his wife away" (Exod 18:2; cf. Deut 24:1, 3; Isa 50:1; Jer 3:8). And if this Cushite were black, the punishment that turned Miriam's skin white could have been an ironic application of the *lex talionis.*³

12:2 *spoken through us, too.* Perhaps they were claiming to be a prophetic family like the priestly families (Milgrom 1989:94; cf. Exod 4:16; 15:20; Mic 6:4).

12:3 *humble.* Heb., *'anaw* [TH6035, ZH6705]. The term can refer to (1) humiliation of victims bowed beneath the proud and powerful (Job 24:4; Prov 16:19; Isa 32:7; Amos 2:7; 8:4), (2) commendable humility (Pss 9:12; 10:12; 22:26; 25:9; 34:2; 37:11; 69:32; 76:9; 147:6; 149:4; Prov 3:34; Isa 11:4; 29:19; 61:1; Zeph 2:3), or possibly (3) dejection (12:3; HALOT). It is possible that the sense here is "dejected," "self-pitying," or "miserable" in the light of Moses's reaction to the troubles in the previous chapter (Rogers 1986). The record shows us a Moses given to anger, self-pity, frustration, and impulsiveness, but not necessarily to self-effacement (Allen 1990:798-799). However, it is difficult to think this says Moses was more dejected than any other man. The LXX has *praüs* [TG4239, ZG4558], meaning "meek" or "humble," which English versions follow. If we follow that understanding, we will see this echoed in the description of Jesus (Matt 11:29).

12:4 *immediately.* Heb., *pit'om* [TH6597, ZH7328]. All but 1 of 25 uses of *pit'om* introduce disaster or judgment (Daube 1964:1-8).

12:6 *If there were prophets among you, I, the LORD.* Since the Hebrew reads, "if your prophet were the LORD," some suggest that a Mem has dropped out and that it would have read, "if there were a prophet *from* the LORD." The NLT (cf. KJV, NASB, NRSV et al.) follows an emendation suggested in BHS that changes *nebi'akem* (your prophet) to *nabi' bakem* [TH5030, ZH5566] (a prophet among you); however, Ashley defends reading "prophet of the LORD among you" (NIV, NJPS) without emending the MT (Ashley 1993:220-221 n. 7, citing GKC §130; Freedman 1972).

12:7 *my servant.* This title was also given to Abraham (Gen 26:24), Caleb (14:24), Joshua (Josh 24:29), David (2 Sam 7:5, etc.[4]), Elijah (2 Kgs 10:10), the prophets (2 Kgs 9:7; 17:13; Jer 7:25; Ezek 38:17; Zech 1:6), and even all Israel (Isa 41:8), but above all to the servant of the Lord (Isa 42–53, especially the servant songs in Isa 42:1-4; 49:1-7; 52:13–53:12).

Of all my house, he is the one I trust. The English translations try various possibilities, such as "he is entrusted with all my house" (RSV, NRSV) or "he is trusted" (JPS, NAB) or he is "faithful in all my house" (KJV, ASV, NASB, NIV); but the NLT fits the context well: "Of all of God's household, Moses is the most trusted; he alone has direct access to the Deity and obtains an audience with him at will" (Milgrom 1989:96; also Levine 1993:331).

12:8 *face to face.* Without following Noth (1968:96) in seeing this as the address of equals, friendship is probably in view here (Exod 33:11; Deut 34:10). "The image is that of a royal house in which only the most trusted servant has regular access to the monarch. Such ones are literally called 'those who see the face of the king.'"[5]

12:10 *leprosy.* See note on 5:2.

12:11 *we have so foolishly committed.* The LXX reads, "which we committed in ignorance," i.e., not committed with malice aforethought and thus expiable by intercession (cf. 15:22-30; Lev 4:2; 5:15, 17; Ezek 45:20).

12:14 *done nothing more than spit in her face.* This is a gesture of legal rejection (Deut 25:9) or of public humiliation (Job 30:10; Isa 50:6; cf. Matt 26:67; 27:30).

defiled. This is the Niphal of *kalam* [TH3637, ZH4007], not *tame'* [TH2930, ZH3237], the normal word for ritual defilement. Rather, here we have a term for shame and disgrace (as in Isa 41:11; 45:16; Jer 22:22).

ENDNOTES

1. I.e., Ethiopia on the Nile (LXX, *Aithiopissan* [TG128, ZG134]; Isa 18:1; cf. Ezek 29:10) at Egypt's southern border (Esth 1:1). Josephus says, "The Ethiopians are called Cushites" and says an Ethiopian princess name Tharbis married Moses (*Antiquities* 1.131; 2.252-253).

2. *Kushan,* which parallels Midian (Hab 3:7); however, this parallel may not indicate identity but some other relation.
3. So Cross 1973:204, but Olson notes that racial prejudice against someone with black skin is "a more modern European prejudice" (1996:71, citing Felder 1989:ch 3).
4. 2 Sam 3:18; 7:5, 8; 1 Kgs 11:13, 32, 34, 36, 38; 14:8; 2 Kgs 19:34; 1 Chr 17:4, 7; Ps 89:3, 20; Isa 37:35; Jer 33:21-22, 26; Ezek 34:23-24; 37:24.
5. Milgrom 1989:96, citing "five of those who see the king's face" (2 Kgs 25:19; NLT, "five of the king's personal advisers").

C O M M E N T A R Y

The litany of complaint continued. "Miriam and Aaron criticized Moses because he had married a Cushite woman" (12:1). This was a bit of peevish cover for the real complaint, which followed: "Has the LORD spoken only through Moses? Hasn't he spoken through us, too?" (12:2). The Lord had indeed spoken through them (e.g., Exod 15:21); however, Moses was the prophet par excellence. The siblings rejected Moses's prophetic supremacy, and "the LORD heard them" (12:2), an ominous note.

A quick editorial aside notes, "Moses was . . . more humble than any other person" (12:3; see note). God summoned all three siblings to appear before him as litigants (12:4). Although the pillar of cloud was always there displaying God's presence, here it manifested a more particular presence as "the LORD descended in the pillar of cloud" (12:5). The Lord "stood at the entrance of the Tabernacle," not as a host greeting company but as a judge grilling defendants (12:5).

God defended Moses's prophetic supremacy (12:6-9), not over against false prophets, but over against true—but ordinary—prophets. The ordinary prophet had access only to enigmatic forms of communication like "visions" and "dreams" (12:6). Dreams (*khalom* [TH2472, ZH2706]) were sometimes enigmatic vehicles of revelation, especially to kings (Gen 20:3-7; 31:10-13; 41; 1 Kgs 3:5-14; Dan 2 and 4). True prophets might even get revelation that might be classified as "riddles" (12:8). With Moses, it was clear, face-to-face communication (12:8), which made Moses unique among all the servants of God's household (12:7). God asked, "Why were you not afraid to criticize [him]?" (12:8). Miriam and Aaron were out of line, and the Lord went away "angry with them" (12:9). How much worse for those who reject the *Logos* made flesh (John 1:1, 14)—those who oppose the one who is "entrusted with God's entire house" (Heb 3:2-6).

Miriam and Aaron had both criticized Moses, and the Lord had summoned them both for the rebuke (12:1, 5); however, divine punishment fell on Miriam. Aaron was spared, but he saw "Miriam, her skin as white as snow from leprosy" (12:10). This not only constituted a near death sentence, it also constituted an apparent elimination of any possibility of continuing in the covenant community, let alone playing the larger role she envisioned. Perhaps Aaron was spared only because his high-priestly role was essential (G. J. Wenham 1981:113). As a priest, his diagnosis would confirm her leprosy (Lev 13:2-17). Aaron cried out, acknowledging both Moses's authority and their sin: "Oh, my master! Please don't punish us for this sin we have so foolishly committed" (12:11).

Moses did not gloat over the punishment that had hit his challenger; he immediately interceded for his presumptuous sister (12:13). Milgrom thinks the prayer's brevity indicates that Moses's heart wasn't in it (1989:98); however, I think it reflected urgency. The Lord immediately healed her, so she experienced only seven days of isolation outside the camp (12:15) and not the full 14-day isolation used to establish the fact of healing and then demonstrate freedom from defilement (Lev 13:5, 21, 26, 31-34). Mercifully, God held the camp in place until Miriam could rejoin the travelers (12:15; cf. 9:15-23).

The New Testament still commands honor for those to whom honor is due (1 Thess 5:12; 1 Tim 5:17; Heb 13:17). And like the humble Moses, leaders must show tender care (1 Thess 5:14), not a despotic spirit (1 Pet 5:2-3). Paul warned that those who wouldn't acknowledge his apostolic authority ought to be publicly shamed (2 Thess 3:14). The ignominy may serve as a public example (1 Tim 5:20); however, it must aim for restoration (1 Cor 11:32; Gal 6:1; Jas 5:19-20; 1 John 5:16), trying to rescue while remaining aware of sin that defiles (Jude 1:22).

We don't hear that the cloud lifted to signal the break of camp, although it had lifted to reveal God's judgment on Miriam (12:10). Given the provisions of 9:15-23, the cloud must have moved on, so they moved on from Hazeroth to the wilderness of Paran (12:16).

◆   2. Forty years near Kadesh (13:1–19:22)
         a. Sending scouts into the Promised Land (13:1-33)

The LORD now said to Moses, [2]"Send out men to explore the land of Canaan, the land I am giving to the Israelites. Send one leader from each of the twelve ancestral tribes." [3]So Moses did as the LORD commanded him. He sent out twelve men, all tribal leaders of Israel, from their camp in the wilderness of Paran. [4]These were the tribes and the names of their leaders:

Tribe	Leader
Reuben.......	Shammua son of Zaccur
[5]Simeon	Shaphat son of Hori
[6]Judah	Caleb son of Jephunneh
[7]Issachar	Igal son of Joseph
[8]Ephraim	Hoshea son of Nun
[9]Benjamin.........	Palti son of Raphu
[10]Zebulun	Gaddiel son of Sodi
[11]Manasseh son of Joseph	Gaddi son of Susi
[12]Dan..........	Ammiel son of Gemalli
[13]Asher.........	Sethur son of Michael
[14]Naphtali	Nahbi son of Vophsi
[15]Gad	Geuel son of Maki

[16]These are the names of the men Moses sent out to explore the land. (Moses called Hoshea son of Nun by the name Joshua.)

[17]Moses gave the men these instructions as he sent them out to explore the land: "Go north through the Negev into the hill country. [18]See what the land is like, and find out whether the people living there are strong or weak, few or many. [19]See what kind of land they live in. Is it good or bad? Do their towns have walls, or are they unprotected like open camps? [20]Is the soil fertile or poor? Are there many trees? Do your best to bring back samples of the crops you see." (It happened to be the season for harvesting the first ripe grapes.)

[21]So they went up and explored the land from the wilderness of Zin as far as Rehob, near Lebo-hamath. [22]Going north, they passed through the Negev and arrived at Hebron, where Ahiman, Sheshai, and Talmai—all descendants of Anak—lived.

(The ancient town of Hebron was founded seven years before the Egyptian city of Zoan.) ²³When they came to the valley of Eshcol, they cut down a branch with a single cluster of grapes so large that it took two of them to carry it on a pole between them! They also brought back samples of the pomegranates and figs. ²⁴That place was called the valley of Eshcol (which means "cluster"), because of the cluster of grapes the Israelite men cut there.

²⁵After exploring the land for forty days, the men returned ²⁶to Moses, Aaron, and the whole community of Israel at Kadesh in the wilderness of Paran. They reported to the whole community what they had seen and showed them the fruit they had taken from the land. ²⁷This was their report to Moses: "We entered the land you sent us to explore, and it is indeed a bountiful country—a land flowing with milk and honey. Here is the kind of fruit it produces. ²⁸But the people living there are powerful, and their towns are large and fortified. We even saw giants there, the descendants of Anak! ²⁹The Amalekites live in the Negev, and the Hittites, Jebusites, and Amorites live in the hill country. The Canaanites live along the coast of the Mediterranean Sea* and along the Jordan Valley."

³⁰But Caleb tried to quiet the people as they stood before Moses. "Let's go at once to take the land," he said. "We can certainly conquer it!"

³¹But the other men who had explored the land with him disagreed. "We can't go up against them! They are stronger than we are!" ³²So they spread this bad report about the land among the Israelites: "The land we traveled through and explored will devour anyone who goes to live there. All the people we saw were huge. ³³We even saw giants* there, the descendants of Anak. Next to them we felt like grasshoppers, and that's what they thought, too!"

13:29 Hebrew *the sea.*   13:33 Hebrew *nephilim.*

NOTES

13:1 *The LORD now said.* Numbers attributes the following idea to the Lord, whereas Deut 1:22-27 attributes it to the people and skips the bad report. The Samaritan Pentateuch conflates the two traditions, placing Deut 1:20-23 here before Num 13:1 and Deut 1:27-33 after Num 13:33. Philip (1993:154) says Moses put Israel's idea to the Lord, who told him how to proceed, and Noordtzij (1983:114) says "Numbers focuses on the 'first cause,' while Deuteronomy describes the secondary cause."

13:4 *These were . . . the names.* Many of the names are at least implicitly theophoric (i.e., their etymology is a sentence involving the name of a god), but none of them uses the *Yah* element that became common later in Israel's history (e.g., Hezekiah = "Yahweh strengthens").

13:6 *Caleb.* The name means "dog," which may have been part of a theophoric name indicating that he was the loyal friend or servant of that deity. "A number of Akkadian names are composites of Kalbu (= Caleb), followed by the name of a god, meaning 'dog [= priest] of god X'" (Noordtzij 1983:114, similar to a suggestion by Milgrom 1989:101).

son of Jephunneh. Here Caleb is a leader of Judah and Jephunneh's son; elsewhere, he's called a Kenizzite (32:12; Josh 14:6, 14; 1 Chr 4:15) and Hezron's son (1 Chr 2:9, 18). The Kenizzites descended from Eliphaz, Esau's oldest son (Gen 36:10), but Judah absorbed them (Josh 14:6) into the clan of Hezron (Josh 15:17; Judg 1:13); therefore, Caleb could be called Hezron's "son" (i.e., descendant) in clan structure (1 Chr 2:9, 18) and yet as "son of Jephunneh" serve as a leader of Judah in tribal structure (Noordtzij 1983:114).

13:16 *explore.* Heb., *tur* [TH8446, ZH9365]; see note on 10:33.

Land allotted to Israel in Numbers 34

Town   Town mentioned in Numbers 13:17-29

Mount Hor?
Lebo-hamath
REHOB
Sidon
Damascus
Tyre
Abel-beth-maacah
Acco   Hazor   Sea of Galilee
BASHAN
Megiddo
Edrei
Beth-shan   GILEAD
Shechem   Jabbok River
Joppa
Jericho   AMMON
Jerusalem
Ashkelon   Heshbon
Gaza
Hebron
Dibon
Beersheba   Arad
Hormah?   MOAB   Arnon River
NEGEV   Kir-haresheth
Zered Brook
Punon
Kadesh-barnea   EDOM

0   25   50 Mi
0   50 Km

Mediterranean Sea
Jordan River
Dead Sea

Joshua. The LXX reads *Iēsous* [TG2424, ZG2652], changing the name from Hoshea, meaning "salvation, rescue" (13:8, 16; 2 Kgs 15:30; 17:1, 3-4, 6; 18:1, 9-10; 1 Chr 27:20; Neh 10:23) to Joshua, meaning "Yah[weh] saves."

13:17 the land. Lit., "the land of Canaan," which comprised a region controlled by Egypt at that time (Y. Aharoni 1966:61-70) in what are now Israel, Lebanon, and southern Syria.

Go north through the Negev. Lit., "Go up there through the Negev." Negev means "parched" or "arid," but it became a geographical term for the southern part of Judah below the central mountain range, i.e., between Beersheba and the Sinai Peninsula (21:1; Gen 20:1; 24:62). So it came to mean "south" (e.g., 35:5; Josh 11:2), just as "the sea" came to mean "west"; therefore, some translations mistakenly translate "south" (e.g., KJV, JPS, ASV).

13:20 the first ripe grapes. Lit., "the firstfruits of the grapes," which puts this in July or August, two or three months after leaving Sinai (10:11).

13:21 Zin. This is the southern border of the Promised Land (34:3; Josh 15:1, 3), not to be confused with the wilderness of Sin (33:11-12; Exod 16:1; 17:1). Kadesh-barnea is sometimes said to be in the desert of Zin (20:1; 27:14; 33:36; Deut 32:51) and sometimes in the Desert of Paran; it must have sat astride their border (13:26).

Rehob. This is not the site in Asher's territory (Josh 19:28; Judg 1:31), but probably Beth-rehob (Judg 18:28; 2 Sam 10:6, 8) in Dan's territory in the north.

Lebo-hamath. Those who take this as a proper noun regard it as a city on Hamath's southern border, which represented the Promised Land's northern boundary (34:7-9; Josh 13:5; Judg 3:3; Ezek 48:1), as it was under David and Solomon (1 Kgs 8:65) and Jeroboam II (2 Kgs 14:25; Amos 6:14) (Y. Aharoni 1966:65-66; Milgrom 1989:103; Sturdy 1976:95). It is probably the same as "the great city of Hamath" (Amos 6:2), which was on the Orontes (Ashley 1993:237; Sturdy 1976:95; G. J. Wenham 1981:231). Some favor translating the words, yielding "entrance of Hamath" (cf. KJV, ASV, JPS, NKJV, NET), which they identify with a pass between Hermon and Lebanon (Binns 1927:83-84; McNeile 1911:70; Noordtzij 1983:116); however, "the place is a Canaanite, not a Syrian site, and is therefore best identified with the modern Libweh, about fourteen miles north-northeast of Baalbek" (Harrison 1990:204-205, citing ISBE 2.602-603; see also Y. Aharoni, Avi-Yonah, Rainey, and Safrai 2002:47, map 51).

13:22 Hebron. This means "association," "league" (BDB 289), "place of alliance" (HALOT), or "league, confederacy, center" (Noordtzij 1983:117). It was the place where God promised Abraham the land (Gen 13:14-18), the base from which he launched the strike that defeated the coalition of kings (Gen 14:13-16), and the patriarchal burial ground (Gen 23; 25:9; 35:27-29; 50:13). It ended up under the control of Caleb and his clan (Josh 14:13; 15:13; Judg 1:20). It eventually became the capital of the tribe of Judah, from which David first reigned (2 Sam 2:11; 5:5) and which Absalom sought to seize (2 Sam 15:9-10).

descendants of Anak. Lit., "neck." Noth suggests they were necklace people, perhaps for military decoration (Noth 1968:105). E. W. Davies tentatively concludes that it was an idiom for tall, long-necked, lanky people, which became associated with giants (E. W. Davies 1995b:136, citing BDB 778b, similar to a suggestion by Noordtzij 1983:117). Feared for their size (13:33, LXX *gigantas*), they were known as Anakites (Deut 2:10-11, 21; Josh 11:21-22; 14:12, 15), the "sons of the Anakim" (Deut 1:28; 9:2, KJV), "sons of Anak" (Josh 15:14), or as *repa'im* [TH7497, ZH8328] (Deut 2:11). Some suggest that rather than "descendant," the term *yalid* [TH3211A, ZH3535] here means "dependant" or "serf," referring to those who had given up their freedom and become a professional class of soldiers, hence the corps of Anak or of Raphah (de Vaux 1961:219; L'Heureux 1976; MacLaurin 1965; see 2 Sam 21:16, 18). They are mentioned only in Numbers—Judges, frequently in the neighborhood of Hebron (Josh 11:21; 14:12-15; 15:13-14; 21:11; Judg 1:20), but also scattered over Canaan's hill country (Josh 11:21-22). Joshua rooted them out of the hill country, but they survived in the Philistine coastal areas (Josh 11:21-22). David's warriors killed four of them (2 Sam 21:18-22), and David himself killed their famous representative Goliath (1 Sam 17).

before . . . Zoan. Cf. Ps 78:12, 43; Isa 19:11-13; 30:4; Ezek 30:14. This statment enhances the reputation of David's first capital city, Hebron (2 Sam 2:1-4, 11), by making it even older than Zoan (= Dja'net = Tanis = Avaris), the capital of the Hyksos pharaohs (Milgrom 1989:103; Snaith 1969:148), which appears to have been established about 1720 BC (ANET 252-253; Gardiner 1961:165), when Abraham lived in the area (Gen 12–15; Harrison 1990:206).

13:26 Kadesh. This was also known as Kadesh-barnea (32:8; 34:4), Meribah (20:13), Meribath-kadesh (27:14; Deut 32:51), or En-mishpat (Gen 14:7). "Wandering tribes favored settling their judicial disputes at the sanctuary at Kadesh—hence the name En-Mishpat, 'Fountain of Judgment,' for Kadesh in Genesis 14:7" (Noordtzij 1983:113). On the border between the wildernesses of Paran (13:26) and Zin (20:1; 27:14), it marked the Promised Land's southern boundary (34:4). The site is generally identified with a group of oases 50 miles south of Beersheba, one of which is still called 'Ain Qadeis, although some identify it with the nearby 'Ain el-Qudeirat (Y. Aharoni 1966:65).

13:27 flowing with milk and honey. This is an ancient Near Eastern expression of abundance (Job 20:17), used in Egyptian (ANET 18-25) and Ugaritic (ANET 140) sources, and frequently used to describe the Promised Land as paradise (Exod 3:8, 17; Jer 11:5; 32:22; Ezek 20:6, 15, etc.). The Egyptian Sinuhe says of Canaan:

> A beautiful land called Yaa. There were figs and grapes, and more wine than water. Honey was there in abundance and its olive trees were numerous, and all kinds of fruit hung on the trees. There was barley and wheat, and various herds without number. . . . I had bread as my daily food and wine as my daily drink, boiled meat and roasted geese; and also game from the desert. (Noordtzij 1983:118, quoting from Gressmann, Ebeling, Ranke, and Rhodokanakis 1926:55-61; also found in ANET 18-22)

Harrison thinks the honey was that of wild bees (Deut 32:13; Judg 14:8), though he notes some possibility of later domestication since it was given as firstfruits (Harrison 1990:211, citing 2 Chr 31:5). Or it could refer to cattle raising and agriculture, with the "honey" (*debash* [TH1706, ZH1831]) being from grapes, dates, or figs rather than bees, or "milk and sap" (Levine 1993:356; cf. Isa 55:1; Joel 3:18). A fall 2007 discovery of an industrial-scale apiary of potentially a hundred hives that date to around the tenth century BC lends new weight to the idea that the honey in these cases was bee honey, and even domesticated rather than wild honey (Hebrew University News Release 2007).

13:28 large and fortified. Canaanites fortified their cities with walls 30 feet to 50 feet high and up to 15 feet thick (Milgrom 1989:105; Noordtzij 1983:119).

giants . . . the descendants of Anak. NLT adds the explanatory "giants" (see note on 13:22).

13:29 On the following peoples, see relevant articles in Bible dictionaries, and in Wiseman 1973:

Amalekites. They descended from Amalek, the offspring of Eliphaz son of Esau by the concubine Timna (Gen 36:12). They ranged across nearly the entire Exodus route (14:25). They attacked Israel at Rephidim on the way to Sinai (Exod 17:8-16) and kept attacking stragglers all the way through the wilderness (Deut 25:17-19). Saul tried unsuccessfully to destroy them, and Samuel had to finish off their king, Agag (1 Sam 15). David decisively defeated them (1 Sam 30:17-19), leaving only remnants at Mount Seir in Transjordan, who were wiped out during Hezekiah's reign (1 Chr 4:41-43).

Hittites. These were an originally non-Semitic people of Asia Minor (1650–1200 BC), some of whom had settled in Canaan (Van Seters 1975:45-46; Josh 1:4; Ezek 16:3). Some lived in the Hebron region, possibly ruling there (Gen 23:3).

Jebusites. These were descendants of Canaan's third son (Gen 10:16). They were the original inhabitants of Jebus/Jerusalem (Josh 18:28; Judg 19:10; 1 Chr 11:4) and were there for most of the Bronze Age (2000–1550 BC). They survived Israelite raids until David took the city as his own, allowing survivors to remain in the city (Josh 15:63; Judg 1:8; 2 Sam 5:5-9).

Amorites. They had entered Canaan from Mesopotamia (Liverani 1973), where they had established powerful dynasties in the early second millennium BC; for example, Hammurabi was an Amorite. In Akkadian, *Amurru* means "west," and by the mid-third millennium the term designated the West-Semitic herdsmen and their territory on the Syrian steppes west of the Euphrates (Van Seters 1975:43-45). By the eighteenth century, Mari texts speak of them in central Syria. Fourteenth and thirteenth century Egyptian and Mesopotamian correspondence (the Amarna letters) defines their area as stretching from the Mediterranean to the Orontes and to Canaan on the south. In the annals of Sennacherib, the kings of the Amurru were those of Phoenicia, Philistia, Ammon, Edom, and Moab (ANET 287), so the Babylonians called the whole land Amurru. Like "Canaanite," "Amorite" ended up serving as a general term for the populace of Canaan during the Bronze Age (Gen 14:7; 48:22; Deut 3:8).

Canaanites. They lived along the sea coast and in the Jordan Valley and gave their name to the whole area (Milgrom 1989:119; Van Seters 1975:46-51). The term "Canaanite" could refer to any inhabitant of the province stretching from Egypt's own border to the Hittite border on the Orontes, i.e., Lebo-hamath (e.g., Gen 12:6; 50:11), or to one of the various peoples living there. It's impossible to establish their origins, whether they descended from ancient inhabitants of the region or migrated from elsewhere, and if so, when this migration occurred. The diversity of opinion and their uncertain origins complicates any effort to identify them with the Canaan that Noah cursed after the flood (Gen 9:25); however, the Genesis record seems to point in that direction (Gen 10:6) and thus provides a rationale for why Israel should dispossess the Canaanites from their lands. See Millard 1973 and Schoville 1994. Later the term came to refer to "merchants" (Prov 31:24; Zech 14:21).

Negev . . . hill country . . . coast . . . Jordan Valley. These are the four major geographical divisions of the Promised Land.

13:32 land . . . will devour. This is an image that sometimes described an infertile or hostile environment (Lev 26:38; Ezek 36:13), even one like Sheol (McEvenue 1971:135-136);

however, here it refers to the land's high quality and location as a land bridge between Asia and Africa (Noordtzij 1983:120), which would keep it perpetually at war and generate a warlike people.

13:33 giants . . . descendants of Anak. Lit., "sons of Anak, who come from the fallen ones" (*hannepilim* [TH5303, ZH5872]). This is probably a reference to the legendary product of marriages between angels and mortal women (Gen 6:4; see note on 13:22).

and that's what they thought, too. Heb., *weken hayinu be'enehem* [TH3651A, ZH4027], "and indeed we were so in their eyes," taking *ken* to mean "thus, so." It is tempting to follow the commentators who recommend translating *ken* [TH3654, ZH4031] as another insect, paralleled with "grasshoppers" (cf. Isa 51:6), i.e., "and in their eyes, we were like gnats" (Snaith 1969:260; Maarsingh 1987:47).

COMMENTARY

This section begins the turn from complaint to outright mutiny, which doomed the entire first generation to a slow death in the wilderness. But revelation would not be put on hold, so what follows is not only wandering itinerary, but also a record of sundry cultic laws (15:1-41), priestly regulations (18:1-32), and cleansing rites (19:1-22). Though it is not throwaway filler, it surely constitutes an exasperating rupture in the narrative that had put the nation on the move toward the Promised Land. But then, they had been on the threshold of the land and would not enter. They were left with nothing but regulation—and waiting to die—a well-regulated death for the rebellious generation.

Selecting the Scouts and Sending Them Out (13:1-24). The rebellion in this account did not consist in sending the scouts in to explore Canaan, for God had assigned this sortie (13:1). The problem was that they undertook the mission in unbelief and made their report in rebellion. Just as the organization of the earlier census counts had involved leaders from each tribe (1:1-4:4), this band of scouts included "one leader from each of the twelve ancestral tribes" (13:2).

The list differs in tribal order and in leaders' names from the records of the polls (1:5-15) and of the gifts to dedicate the Tabernacle (2:4-30). The order change can't be explained, but the leaders were probably a younger group, more fit for the rigors of this reconnaissance mission.

Moses sent them out "to explore the land" (13:17), starting from the Negev and moving up through the hill country as they worked their way north. They were to check out the agricultural and military situation: They were told (13:18-20), "See what the land is like":

Agricultural concerns	Military concerns
"Is it good or bad? . . . Is the soil fertile or poor? Are there many trees? Do your best to bring back samples of the crops you see." (It happened to be the season for harvesting the first ripe grapes.)	"Find out whether the people living there are strong or weak, few or many. . . . Do their towns have walls, or are they unprotected like open camps?

The scouts began in "the wilderness of Zin," and followed a northward path through the hill country until they came to "Rehob, near Lebo-hamath" (13:21). First they moved through the Negev to the ancient city of Hebron, Abraham's old territory, which had become giants' territory (13:22). At Eschol they took the requested crop samples from vineyards, and somewhere along the line they also took samples of orchard crops. We don't get a detailed itinerary of reconnaissance, just a sampling of what they saw while "exploring the land for forty days" (13:25). When they returned and offered a bad report of the good land, the resulting rebellion condemned the people to 40 years of wandering in the wilderness, one nomadic year for every day the scouts spent compiling their report (14:34).

Report from the Scouts (13:26-33). Imagine the tension that simmered while the camp watched for the returning scouts. And excitement would have soared as they informally "reported to the whole community what they had seen and showed them the fruit they had taken from the land" (13:26). The positive tone continued as they started their official report to Moses: "It is indeed a bountiful country—a land flowing with milk and honey" (13:27). But so much for the positive report—they quickly went on to complain of invincible enemies living in fortified cities (13:28), and they even reported that they had come upon giant "descendants of Anak" (13:22, 28). And the land was already fully occupied, from the Negev to the hill country to the coastal plains (13:29). Conquest and settlement would be doomed from the start.

But Caleb, Judah's representative on the scouting mission, exhorted the people, "We can certainly conquer it!" (13:30). Would that this had put some steel into the Israelites, but the other spies objected, "We can't go up against them!" (13:31). They ignored the presence of the Lord of Heaven's Armies, whose powerful presence they announced every time they moved out (10:35). "So they spread this bad report" (13:32). No more mention of "milk and honey"; instead of giant clusters of grapes, all they saw were giants (13:32). They protested, "Next to them we felt like grasshoppers, and that's what they thought, too!" (13:33).

God's reaction is conjectured by the midrash:

> I take no objection to your saying: "we looked like grasshoppers to ourselves" but I take offense when you say "so we must have looked to them." How do you know how I made you look to them? Perhaps you appeared to them as angels? (Milgrom 1989:107, citing *Numbers Rabbah* 16:11; *Tanhuma B. Numbers* 66)

When Caleb said, "We can certainly conquer it" (13:30), they should have prayed to God: "In your strength I can crush an army; with my God I can scale any wall" (2 Sam 22:30; also Ps 18:29). If they saw giants walking, they should have seen Goliaths collapsing (1 Sam 17).

Believers today need to stir up the same sentiments: If we think ourselves weak, we should know that God's power works best through unpretentious human weakness (2 Cor 12:9). Because our Lord Jesus has defeated all powers (Col 2:15), we can be strong in his power (Eph 6:10-13), joining in his victorious rule (Rev 3:21).

b. Rebellion over the Promised Land (14:1-45)

Then the whole community began weeping aloud, and they cried all night. ²Their voices rose in a great chorus of protest against Moses and Aaron. "If only we had died in Egypt, or even here in the wilderness!" they complained. ³"Why is the LORD taking us to this country only to have us die in battle? Our wives and our little ones will be carried off as plunder! Wouldn't it be better for us to return to Egypt?" ⁴Then they plotted among themselves, "Let's choose a new leader and go back to Egypt!"

⁵Then Moses and Aaron fell face down on the ground before the whole community of Israel. ⁶Two of the men who had explored the land, Joshua son of Nun and Caleb son of Jephunneh, tore their clothing. ⁷They said to all the people of Israel, "The land we traveled through and explored is a wonderful land! ⁸And if the LORD is pleased with us, he will bring us safely into that land and give it to us. It is a rich land flowing with milk and honey. ⁹Do not rebel against the LORD, and don't be afraid of the people of the land. They are only helpless prey to us! They have no protection, but the LORD is with us! Don't be afraid of them!"

¹⁰But the whole community began to talk about stoning Joshua and Caleb. Then the glorious presence of the LORD appeared to all the Israelites at the Tabernacle.* ¹¹And the LORD said to Moses, "How long will these people treat me with contempt? Will they never believe me, even after all the miraculous signs I have done among them? ¹²I will disown them and destroy them with a plague. Then I will make you into a nation greater and mightier than they are!"

¹³But Moses objected. "What will the Egyptians think when they hear about it?" he asked the LORD. "They know full well the power you displayed in rescuing your people from Egypt. ¹⁴Now if you destroy them, the Egyptians will send a report to the inhabitants of this land, who have already heard that you live among your people. They know, LORD, that you have appeared to your people face to face and that your pillar of cloud hovers over them. They know that you go before them in the pillar of cloud by day and the pillar of fire by night. ¹⁵Now if you slaughter all these people with a single blow, the nations that have heard of your fame will say, ¹⁶'The LORD was not able to bring them into the land he swore to give them, so he killed them in the wilderness.'

¹⁷"Please, Lord, prove that your power is as great as you have claimed. For you said, ¹⁸'The LORD is slow to anger and filled with unfailing love, forgiving every kind of sin and rebellion. But he does not excuse the guilty. He lays the sins of the parents upon their children; the entire family is affected—even children in the third and fourth generations.' ¹⁹In keeping with your magnificent, unfailing love, please pardon the sins of this people, just as you have forgiven them ever since they left Egypt."

²⁰Then the LORD said, "I will pardon them as you have requested. ²¹But as surely as I live, and as surely as the earth is filled with the LORD's glory, ²²not one of these people will ever enter that land. They have all seen my glorious presence and the miraculous signs I performed both in Egypt and in the wilderness, but again and again they have tested me by refusing to listen to my voice. ²³They will never even see the land I swore to give their ancestors. None of those who have treated me with contempt will ever see it. ²⁴But my servant Caleb has a different attitude than the others have. He has remained loyal to me, so I will bring him into the land he explored. His descendants will possess their full share of that land. ²⁵Now turn around, and don't go on toward the land where the Amalekites and Canaanites live. Tomorrow you must set out for the wilderness in the direction of the Red Sea.*'"

²⁶Then the LORD said to Moses and Aaron, ²⁷"How long must I put up with this wicked community and its complaints about me? Yes, I have heard the complaints the Israelites are making against me. ²⁸Now tell them this: 'As surely as I live, declares the LORD, I will do to you the very things I heard you say. ²⁹You will all drop dead in this wilderness! Because you complained against me, every one of you who is twenty years old or older and was included in the registration will die. ³⁰You will not enter and occupy the land I swore to give you. The only exceptions will be Caleb son of Jephunneh and Joshua son of Nun.

³¹"'You said your children would be carried off as plunder. Well, I will bring them safely into the land, and they will enjoy what you have despised. ³²But as for you, you will drop dead in this wilderness. ³³And your children will be like shepherds, wandering in the wilderness for forty years. In this way, they will pay for your faithlessness, until the last of you lies dead in the wilderness.

³⁴"'Because your men explored the land for forty days, you must wander in the wilderness for forty years—a year for each day, suffering the consequences of your sins. Then you will discover what it is like to have me for an enemy.' ³⁵I, the LORD, have spoken! I will certainly do these things to every member of the community

who has conspired against me. They will be destroyed here in this wilderness, and here they will die!"

³⁶The ten men Moses had sent to explore the land—the ones who incited rebellion against the LORD with their bad report—³⁷were struck dead with a plague before the LORD. ³⁸Of the twelve who had explored the land, only Joshua and Caleb remained alive.

³⁹When Moses reported the LORD's words to all the Israelites, the people were filled with grief. ⁴⁰Then they got up early the next morning and went to the top of the range of hills. "Let's go," they said. "We realize that we have sinned, but now we are ready to enter the land the LORD has promised us."

⁴¹But Moses said, "Why are you now disobeying the LORD's orders to return to the wilderness? It won't work. ⁴²Do not go up into the land now. You will only be crushed by your enemies because the LORD is not with you. ⁴³When you face the Amalekites and Canaanites in battle, you will be slaughtered. The LORD will abandon you because you have abandoned the LORD."

⁴⁴But the people defiantly pushed ahead toward the hill country, even though neither Moses nor the Ark of the LORD's Covenant left the camp. ⁴⁵Then the Amalekites and the Canaanites who lived in those hills came down and attacked them and chased them back as far as Hormah.

14:10 Hebrew *the Tent of Meeting.* 14:25 Hebrew *sea of reeds.*

NOTES

14:3 *little ones.* Heb., *tap* [TH2945, ZH3251], a term that may be related to quick little steps (Budd 1984:155, citing Snaith 1969:150; cf. 31:17-18; Deut 2:34); hence, "toddlers." But it appears to be more widely applied to children, women, and the elderly (HALOT, citing Gen 34:29; 43:8; 45:19; 47:24; 50:8, 21; Deut 2:34; 3:6, 19; 2 Chr 20:13; 31:18, etc.).

14:4 *choose a new leader.* Heb., *nittenah ro'sh* [TH7218, ZH8031], "let us set a head." An ambiguous expression, it may be the equivalent of (1) *natan leb* [TH3820, ZH4213], "set the heart" or "decide"; (2) "turn about," to "*head* back for Egypt" (NJPS); or (3) "appoint a head" to replace Moses. Milgrom (1989:108) prefers a combination of the first two, and Levine prefers the second (1993:363), but most English translations opt for the third.

14:5 *fell face down on the ground.* This is an expression used 25 times in the Old Testament. It expresses deference of the lesser to the greater, sometimes to a human (e.g., 2 Sam 9:6; 14:4; 1 Kgs 18:7). When done before God, it expresses holy awe (Gen 17:3; Lev 9:24;

Josh 5:14; 1 Kgs 18:39; Ezek 1:28; 3:23) and often accompanies a petition against divine punishment (16:22, 45; Josh 7:6).

before the whole community of Israel. This suggests prostration before God (see previous note); however, the meaning of doing it before the community is less clear: It may reflect resignation, despair (Hirsch 1971:208), or fear for their lives (Ashley 1993:247; Milgrom 1989:108; de Vaulx 1972:175); however, Moses and Aaron plead not for their own lives but for the people (14:13-19). Alternatively, it may indicate passivity before divine judgment (Coats 1968:173); however, that is exactly the *opposite* of the attitude that Moses takes when he falls prostrate. Finally, it may mean intercession (Allen 1990:817; Ashley 1993:248; Budd 1984:156; G. J. Wenham 1981:121). In my opinion, they fell before the Lord, but it was a public act that rebuked the people even as it sought God's mercies for the people.

14:7 *a wonderful land.* Heb., *tobah ha'arets me'od me'od* [TH2896, ZH3202], meaning "a very very *good* land," as opposed to the bad report on the land (13:32) and the *good* of returning to Egypt (14:3). For other instances of the emphatic doubling of *me'od* [TH3966, ZH4394], see 14:7; Gen 7:19; 17:2, 6, 20; 30:43; Exod 1:7; 1 Kgs 7:47; 2 Kgs 10:4; Ezek 9:9; 16:13; 37:10.

14:8 *milk and honey.* See note on 13:27.

14:9 *prey.* Heb., *lekhem* [TH3899, ZH4312], "bread."

protection. Heb., *tsel* [TH6738, ZH7498] (shade, shadow). The life-threatening desert sun generated a metaphor for patronage as "shade" afforded by deities or kings (Ps 121:5; Isa 25:4). "It is even expressed in personal names, such as *Si-lu-ush Dagan*, 'Into-the-Protection-of-Dagan'" (Levine 1993:364). This may also be related to the "mother-hen language" of some passages (Allen 1990:816, citing Ps 17:8; cf. Matt 23:37; Luke 13:34).

14:14 *face to face.* Lit., "eye to eye." Ironically, this phrase is parallel to the "face to face" way God revealed himself to Moses (12:8; Exod 33:11; Deut 5:4; 34:10).

14:16 *the land he swore to give them.* This is an oath given to their forefathers, especially Abraham (Gen 12:7; 13:15-17; 15:18; 26:3; Exod 6:8; Deut 19:8).

14:17 *Lord.* Heb., *'adonay* [TH136, ZH151], not *yhwh* [TH3068, ZH3378].

14:18 *The LORD is slow to anger.* This is a shorter version of Exod 34:6-7, a liturgical formula echoed throughout the OT (e.g., Neh 9:17, 19, 31; Pss 78:38; 103:8; Jer 32:18; Jonah 4:2).

unfailing love. Heb., *rab-khesed*, or "great in" *khesed* [TH2617, ZH2876]. Some understand *khesed* as mercy or kindness (TWOT), and some as loyalty or covenant faithfulness (Ashley 1993:258; Budd 1984:158; HALOT). It is God's bountiful and freely given *love, mercy,* and *goodness,* which sustains his redemptive covenant with his people.

forgiving . . . sin. Heb., *nose' 'awon* [TH5771/5375, ZH6411/5951], meaning "to lift/bear/carry sin," implying the removal of punishment due for sin. When *nasa' 'awon* is used with a human subject, the meaning is usually that the person will bear the penalty of divine punishment. Can one say here that God has himself borne the penalty for sin or has taken it away? One cannot be certain of the dynamics of divine forgiveness, but a meaning such as this may not be wide of the mark (Ashley 1993:258).

rebellion. Heb., *pasha'* [TH6588, ZH7322], not "transgression" (most English versions), but "rebellion" (NLT, NIV), since opposition to a person rather than infringement of rules is the point (Snaith 1969:158).

third and fourth generations. This embraces all living members of a family, the maximum alive at any time (E. W. Davies 1995b:144).

14:21 *as surely as I live.* Man swears by the Lord's life or name (Judg 8:19; 1 Sam 14:39), though not always (Gen 42:15; 2 Sam 15:21; 2 Kgs 2:2). God, however, can swear by none greater than himself (Isa 49:18; Jer 22:24; cf. Heb 6:13).

14:22 *again and again they have tested me.* Lit., "They tested me these ten times," or as we might say, "a dozen times." Some have suggested that it refers to the 10 rebellious spies, but most commentators think the "ten times" refers to an indefinitely large number (Binns 1927:95; Budd 1984:158; Dillmann and Knobel 1886:97; Gray 1903:158; Noordtzij 1983:126; Snaith 1969:152; Sturdy 1976:260). Alternatively, rabbinic tradition actually counted 10 tests in the wilderness (*b. Arakhin* 15a, b): (1) at the Red Sea as they feared being run down by Pharaoh (Exod 14:11); (2) at Marah where they found only bitter water (Exod 15:23-24); (3) in the wilderness of Sin when they were hungry (Exod 16:1-3); (4) at Kadesh when they ignored the directive to store manna for the Sabbath (Exod 16:19-20); (5) at Kadesh when they ignored the prohibition against gathering manna on Sabbath (Exod 16:26-28); (6) at Rephidim where they complained about water (Exod 17:1); (7) at Sinai when Aaron supervised the making of a golden calf (Exod 32:1); (8) at Taberah as general complaint against the Lord (11:1); (9) at Kibroth-hattaavah when they wanted some meat instead of manna (11:4); (10) at Kadesh when they listened to the evil report rather than the report generated by faith and thus refused to enter Canaan (chs 13-14).

14:24 *attitude.* Heb., *ruakh* [TH7307, ZH8120] (spirit), with a psychological connotation, "a different motivating force" (Noordtzij 1983:126).

remained loyal to me. Lit., "he is fully after me." See this same testimony in Deut 1:36; Josh 14:8.

14:25 *the land where the Amalekites and Canaanites live.* Lit., "the Amalekites and Canaanites are living in the valleys/plains" (*'emeq* [TH6010, ZH6677]). An *'emeq* is "a plain between two mountain ridges, or between a mountain and the water" (HALOT). Canaanites lived along the maritime *'emeq* (Judg 1:19, 34; cf. Josh 5:1; 11:3), and the Amalekites lived in the southern reaches of the Jordan *'emeq*, which reached down into the Negev (14:45; Josh 13:19, 27).

Tomorrow. This should not be taken in its usual literal sense, since they stayed in Kadesh "many days" (Deut 1:46), apparently 38 years (Deut 2:14). So it should be translated, "in time to come" or "in the future" (Noordtzij 1983:127; cf. Gen 30:33; Exod 13:14; Deut 6:20; Josh 4:6, 21; 22:24, 27; Isa 22:13).

the Red Sea. Lit., "the Sea of Reeds" (*yam sup* [TH3220/5488A, ZH3542/6068]), which could refer to the sea on either side of the Sinai Peninsula. Some think the direction ordered was southwest, toward the Gulf of Suez (Noordtzij 1983:127; cf. 33:10-11; Exod 10:19); others think southeast toward the Gulf of Aqabah/Elath, one of the recognized north-south routes across the Sinai Peninsula (E. W. Davies 1995b:145; G. I. Davies 1979:42, 77; Levine 1993:368; Noth 1968:110; cf. 21:4 and 1 Kgs 9:26). Either way, the course heading was "threatening to nullify the great victory secured at the Sea (Exod 14:1-15:21)" (Budd 1984:159).

14:26 *Moses and Aaron.* The Hebrew continues in 14:28, 39 with singular verbs; it is addressed just to Moses.

14:28 *As surely as I live.* See note on 14:21.

declares the LORD. Heb., *ne'um-yhwh* [TH5002/3068, ZH5536/3378]. This is a frequent formula in the OT (267 times), but occurs only one other place in the Pentateuch, there also with an oath (Gen 22:16).

14:29 *You will all drop dead.* Lit., "Your carcasses will fall in this wilderness, even all who were registered and all who were numbered," i.e., all your registered divisions (14:32). So this is particularly targeted at the registered military troops. The term used here (*peger*) generally refers to the human corpse fallen after battle (e.g., Amos 8:3), but it can refer to animal carcasses as well (Gen 15:11), or to a mixture of animal and human remains (Jer 31:40); it is used here with a contemptuous ring (cf. Lev 26:30; Ezek 6:5).

14:30 I swore. Lit., "I lifted up my hand," a conventional stance for taking an oath (Gen 14:22; Exod 6:8; Ezek 20:5, 15, 23, 28, 42).

14:33 be like shepherds. This does not emphasize pastoral care for sheep but life as landless nomads (Ashley 1993:265; de Vaulx 1972:174).

pay for your faithlessness. Lit., "bear your harlotry," a frequent metaphor for idolatry (Exod 34:16) or any defection from proper relationship with God (15:39) to venerate other gods (Jer 3:2, 9; 13:27; Ezek 23:27; 43:7, 9; Hos 6:10).

14:34 you will discover what it is like to have me for an enemy. Lit., "they will know my frustration." It could be God being frustrated by Israel, or it could be Israel being frustrated by God. Loewe concludes that the best translation is "what it means to thwart me" (1968:142, adopting the translation of NJPS).

14:44 defiantly. Heb., *'apal* [TH6075A, ZH6753] (Hiphil), a term for insolent, reckless action; cf. the parallel account, "thinking it would be easy to attack the hill country" (Deut 1:41).

14:45 Hormah. Because *khormah* [TH2767, ZH3055] has the definite article here, some want to translate it as a generic noun meaning "destruction," or "place devoted to the ban"; however, everywhere else in the OT, it is a proper noun referring to the town, though possibly with that meaning as historical background (21:3). Hormah must have been located somewhere in the north-central Negev; likely, Tell el-Meshash, about 10 miles east of it (Y. Aharoni 1966:184-185; Budd 1984:160; Noth 1968:111), though other suggestions exist, such as Tell esh-Sheri'ah, about 12 miles northwest of Beersheba (Albright 1924:6) or Tell el-Milh (Mazar 1965:298-299).

COMMENTARY

Complaining Because of the Scouts' Report (14:1-10). Instead of bellowing midnight war cries for morning battles, the people "cried all night" (14:1), rebelling "against Moses and Aaron" (14:2). Earlier they had complained that Moses had led them out of the paradise of Egypt (11:4); now they say, "If only we had died in Egypt" (14:2)—which the Egyptians had been trying to arrange before they were delivered. Earlier, they had complained that Moses had led them into the wilderness to die; now they said, "If only we had died . . . here in the wilderness" (14:2). They were thinking that Canaanite giants and fortified cities could only mean their death in battle and the loss of their women and children as slaves (14:3). Unbelief was pushing them back toward slavery in Egypt, and not just as an idle whim: "They plotted among themselves, 'Let's choose a new leader and go back to Egypt'" (14:4). Usually when Moses fell on his face, he was interceding before God, seeking relief from divine wrath against Israel, but here he was begging the people to quit this lunacy (14:5).

Joshua joined Caleb's protest, siding with Moses and Aaron in a gesture of mourning (14:6). They reminded the people that the Promised Land was "wonderful" (14:7) and described the conditions of victory: "If the LORD is pleased with us" he will give us this pleasant land (14:8); however, we must not displease him by rebelling against him and rejecting his gift of the land (14:9). The unbelieving scouts had fretted about formidable foes and forts; Joshua and Caleb said, "They are only helpless prey to us! They have no protection" (14:9).

Like they had with Moses and Aaron, "the whole community" turned on Joshua and Caleb and talked of stoning them (14:10). Wenham says the community attempted to act with judicial authority;[1] however, it was more like a lynch mob, with parallels in the mutinies against the rule of David and Jeroboam (1 Sam 30:6; 1 Kgs 12:18).[2] God's response to this general rejection of every single leader who urged them to do God's will was a display of theophanic power (14:10).

God's Threat of Punishment (14:11-38). God complained, "They never believe me" (14:11). This was not disbelief in God as an axiom of doctrine; rather, they wouldn't sustain a level of commitment that demonstrated that they actually found God credible and trusted him (Heb 11:6). In a divine act of quid pro quo, God proposed to answer Israel's rejection of him (14:11) by rejecting them and starting over with Moses as a new Abraham, a new father of a great nation (14:12; cf. Exod 32:10). This would have been consistent with the remnant principle, wherein God's judgment sometimes eliminated all but a faithful remnant, then passed along the covenant promise through the renewed people who descended from that remnant. So Moses might well have acquiesced, "I am the Lord's servant. May everything you have said about me come true" (Luke 1:38). Instead, he interceded for the rebellious people. Moses could find little from within Israel as a basis for appeal to the Lord, so he didn't even start a bidding campaign based on 50, 20, or 10 righteous in the camp (Gen 18:26-32). Instead, he argued, "What will the Egyptians think?" (14:13). One might wonder why God should be interested in Egypt's opinion about anything, especially since he had so recently humbled them and their gods. But they still had a public voice in the ancient Near East, and they would tell this to the people of this land. Although Israel was ripe for judgment, the nations wouldn't do well by the testimony that Israel's destruction would imply (14:15-16). Then Moses pled, "Prove that your power is as great as you have claimed" by continuing their deliverance (14:17), and prove that your mercy is as great as you say by pardoning this people (14:18). Although it threatened to undo his carefully woven argument, Moses appealed to the Lord's consistent pattern of forgiveness: "Just as you have forgiven them ever since they left Egypt" (14:19).

Moses's intercession won the day (14:20), but there were conditions. Moses had contemplated judgment that did not annihilate, although it might persist for generations (14:18); however, the Lord's plan was extermination of the sinful generation with optimism for the coming generation. Earlier the Lord had proposed killing all of Israel and beginning anew with Moses's descendants; now he said he would annihilate the rebellious generation, beginning anew with the next generation (14:22). Just as Moses had appealed to God's glory, so the Lord himself appealed to it in his own oath (14:21). Israel was without excuse in this unbelieving fear of Canaan's inhabitants, for they had seen God's glorious deeds (14:22) and still discounted God's power. Caleb was "different . . . than the others" in that he "remained loyal" to God; therefore, he would inherit the land (14:24).

Thus far, the movement had always been toward the Promised Land. But now God had them turn around and get away from the land he was going to give them: "set out for the wilderness" (14:25). God warned that he had heard their complaints and wondered how long they would continue (14:27). Elsewhere in the book when God "hears" of sinful behavior, it is a precursor to judgment. In this case, too, the Lord threatened judgment with an oath: "As surely as I live, declares the LORD" (14:28). The judgment would come in the very terms of their libelous complaints about God (14:27-28). They had complained that they had been led out to die in the wilderness; therefore, that is what would happen (14:29). God would wipe out every military man age 20 and up, except the faithful Caleb and Joshua (14:29-30). But their libel wouldn't poison the hopes of the next generation. They had complained that their children would be captured; however, God would bring the next generation into the land so they could enjoy what their fathers had despised (14:31). The only effect on the children would be years of wandering in the wilderness, waiting for their mutinous parents to die off (14:32, 35). That would require 40 years, a year for each day of rebellious reconnaissance, a period when they learned the frustrating consequences of rebelling against God's plans (14:34).

As is the case elsewhere in this book, the parties most to blame for the sin received concentrated judgment. Here it was "the ones who incited rebellion" with their evil reports (14:36). They were not left to die out gradually; instead, they "were struck dead with a plague before the LORD" (14:37). But the two faithful scouts "remained alive" (14:38).

Israelites Experience Defeat (14:39-45). God's verdict led "the people [to be] filled with grief" (14:39), but not repentant sorrow leading to renewed obedience (cf. 2 Cor 7:10). It was mere discontent for things lost, which refused to accept the finality of the curse upon their generation. They conceded, "We have sinned" (14:40); however, it was sorrow come too late (cf. Heb 12:17). Rather than seeking God's will and promising a new obedience, they presumptuously said, "We are ready to enter the land" (14:40b). Now, rather than the whine of the scouts, it was the warning of Moses: "It won't work. . . . You will only be crushed by your enemies" (14:41-42). Again, it was *lex talionis:* "The LORD will abandon you because you have abandoned the LORD" (14:43). The people pushed on anyway (14:44), and their enemies ran them down.

ENDNOTES
1. "Joshua and Caleb have accused them of rebelling against the LORD (14:9); the congregation rejects this charge as false and proposes to exact the appropriate penalty for false witness" (G. J. Wenham 1981:122). But Joshua and Caleb's "do not rebel" (14:9) was not a formal accusation, and the punishment for false witness was not a death penalty; rather, the penalty varied according to *lex talionis* (Deut 19:16-21; Ashley 1993:251).
2. Ashley 1993:250-251; E. W. Davies 1995b:142. For stoning as an expression of public fury, see Exod 17:4; 1 Sam 30:6; 1 Kgs 12:18; 2 Chr 10:18.

◆   ## c. Miscellaneous cultic laws (15:1-41)

Then the LORD told Moses, 2"Give the following instructions to the people of Israel.

"When you finally settle in the land I am giving you, 3you will offer special gifts as a pleasing aroma to the LORD. These gifts may take the form of a burnt offering, a sacrifice to fulfill a vow, a voluntary offering, or an offering at any of your annual festivals, and they may be taken from your herds of cattle or your flocks of sheep and goats. 4When you present these offerings, you must also give the LORD a grain offering of two quarts* of choice flour mixed with one quart* of olive oil. 5For each lamb offered as a burnt offering or a special sacrifice, you must also present one quart of wine as a liquid offering.

6"If the sacrifice is a ram, give a grain offering of four quarts* of choice flour mixed with a third of a gallon* of olive oil, 7and give a third of a gallon of wine as a liquid offering. This will be a pleasing aroma to the LORD.

8"When you present a young bull as a burnt offering or as a sacrifice to fulfill a vow or as a peace offering to the LORD, 9you must also give a grain offering of six quarts* of choice flour mixed with two quarts* of olive oil, 10and give two quarts of wine as a liquid offering. This will be a special gift, a pleasing aroma to the LORD.

11"Each sacrifice of a bull, ram, lamb, or young goat should be prepared in this way. 12Follow these instructions with each offering you present. 13All of you native-born Israelites must follow these instructions when you offer a special gift as a pleasing aroma to the LORD. 14And if any foreigners visit you or live among you and want to present a special gift as a pleasing aroma to the LORD, they must follow these same procedures. 15Native-born Israelites and foreigners are equal before the LORD and are subject to the same decrees. This is a permanent law for you, to be observed from generation to generation. 16The same instructions and regulations will apply both to you and to the foreigners living among you."

17Then the LORD said to Moses, 18"Give the following instructions to the people of Israel.

"When you arrive in the land where I am taking you, 19and you eat the crops that grow there, you must set some aside as a sacred offering to the LORD. 20Present a cake from the first of the flour you grind, and set it aside as a sacred offering, as you do with the first grain from the threshing floor. 21Throughout the generations to come, you are to present a sacred offering to the LORD each year from the first of your ground flour.

22"But suppose you unintentionally fail to carry out all these commands that the LORD has given you through Moses. 23And suppose your descendants in the future fail to do everything the LORD has commanded through Moses. 24If the mistake was made unintentionally, and the community was unaware of it, the whole community must present a young bull for a burnt offering as a pleasing aroma to the LORD. It must be offered along with its prescribed grain offering and liquid offering and with one male goat for a sin offering. 25With it the priest will purify the whole community of Israel, making them right with the LORD,* and they will be forgiven. For it was an unintentional sin, and they have corrected it with their offerings to the LORD—the special gift and the sin offering. 26The whole community of Israel will be forgiven, including the foreigners living among you, for all the people were involved in the sin.

27"If one individual commits an unintentional sin, the guilty person must bring a one-year-old female goat for a sin offering. 28The priest will sacrifice it to purify* the guilty person before the LORD, and that person will be forgiven. 29These same instructions apply both to native-born Israelites and to the foreigners living among you.

³⁰"But those who brazenly violate the LORD's will, whether native-born Israelites or foreigners, have blasphemed the LORD, and they must be cut off from the community. ³¹Since they have treated the LORD's word with contempt and deliberately disobeyed his command, they must be completely cut off and suffer the punishment for their guilt."

³²One day while the people of Israel were in the wilderness, they discovered a man gathering wood on the Sabbath day. ³³The people who found him doing this took him before Moses, Aaron, and the rest of the community. ³⁴They held him in custody because they did not know what to do with him. ³⁵Then the LORD said to Moses, "The man must be put to death! The whole community must stone him outside the camp." ³⁶So the whole community took the man outside the camp and stoned him to death, just as the LORD had commanded Moses.

³⁷Then the LORD said to Moses, ³⁸"Give the following instructions to the people of Israel: Throughout the generations to come you must make tassels for the hems of your clothing and attach them with a blue cord. ³⁹When you see the tassels, you will remember and obey all the commands of the LORD instead of following your own desires and defiling yourselves, as you are prone to do. ⁴⁰The tassels will help you remember that you must obey all my commands and be holy to your God. ⁴¹I am the LORD your God who brought you out of the land of Egypt that I might be your God. I am the LORD your God!"

15:4a Hebrew *1/10 of an ephah* [2.2 liters]. 15:4b Hebrew *1/4 of a hin* [1 liter]; also in 15:5. 15:6a Hebrew *2/10 of an ephah* [4.4 liters]. 15:6b Hebrew *1/3 of a hin* [1.3 liters]; also in 15:7. 15:9a Hebrew *3/10 of an ephah* [6.6 liters]. 15:9b Hebrew *1/2 of a hin* [2 liters]; also in 15:10. 15:25 Or *will make atonement for the whole community of Israel.* 15:28 Or *to make atonement for.*

NOTES

15:3 *special gifts.* Heb., *'isheh.* The NLT opts for a general term of offering, as do some commentators (Milgrom 1989:118; Noordtzij 1983:134); however, most translations follow the lead of the LXX (*holokautōmata* [TG3646, ZG3906]) and key lexicons in understanding this to derive from *'esh* [TH784, ZH836] (fire) and therefore refer to an offering made by fire (BDB, HALOT).

a pleasing aroma to the LORD. This indicates that the sacrifice was acceptable to the Lord and therefore efficacious (Lev 1:9, 13, 17; 2:2, 9, 12; 3:5, 16). The Gilgamesh Epic employs the same image:

> Upon their pot-stands I heaped cane, cedar wood, and myrtle.
> The gods smelled the savor,
> The gods smelled the sweet savor,
> The gods crowded like flies around the sacrificer. (ANET 95)

As was the case throughout the ancient Near East, Israel's worship incorporated aromatic substances, such as the cedar and hyssop thrown on the fire when they offered the red heifer, the daily incense offerings (Exod 30:7-10, 32-33), and the aromatic substances used with grain offerings (Lev 2).

to fulfill a vow . . . or an offering at any of your annual festivals. It is not clear whether this phrase applies to both the "burnt offering" and the "sacrifice" (Ashley 1993:279; Noordtzij 1983:134-135) or just to the "sacrifice" (Gray 1903:172-173; McNeile 1911:79-80). It probably applies to both because peace offerings were offered when fulfilling a vow (Lev 7:15-16), and both burnt offerings and peace offerings were given at the annual festivals (29:39; Lev 23:4, 18, 37).

15:7 *liquid offering.* By NT times, the wine was poured into a bowl on the southwest corner of the top of the altar; from there it flowed through an opening into the base of the altar (*m. Zevahim* 6:2; Hirsch 1971:225, citing *b. Sukkah* 48b and 49b), or was perhaps just poured around the base of the altar (Sir 50:14; Josephus *Antiquities* 3.234 [3.9.4]), as was the blood of certain offerings (Lev 4:7, 18, 25, 30, 34). But since the OT describes the wine as also a "pleasing aroma," perhaps it was originally dribbled on the burning offering to sizzle and send its aroma heavenward.

15:8 *peace offering.* This is variously translated as (1) "peace offering" (KJV, ASV, JPS, NKJV, ESV, NET); (2) "offering of well-being" (NRSV, NJPS); (3) "fellowship offering" (NIV); (4) "communion sacrifice" (NJB); (5) "community offering" (HALOT); and (6) following the LXX (*holokautōma . . . eis sōtērion* [TG3646/4992A, ZG3906/5402]), "salvation offering." The NLT does well to stay with the KJV tradition on this.

15:13 *native-born Israelites.* These are noted as compared to the "rabble of non-Israelites" that tagged along during the exodus from Egypt (11:4; Exod 12:38; Neh 13:3).

15:14 *visit you or live among you.* Lit., "if a sojourner sojourns with you, or whoever is in your midst throughout your generations." The resident aliens (*ger* [TH1616, ZH1731]; see Milgrom 1989:398-402) were treated "like native-born Israelites" (Lev 19:34), sharing most civil rights and obligations. They were to be protected from racist abuse (Exod 23:9; Lev 19:33; Deut 10:19), and they were to observe Israel's laws and rituals, such as ritual purification (9:6-13), Passover (9:14; Exod 12:43), and circumcision (Josh 5:2-11). Of course, they wouldn't have inherited land, which was to pass down within the 12 ancestral tribes (26:55; 33:54; 34:13).

15:20 *flour you grind.* Heb., *'arisotekem* [TH6182, ZH6881]. Almost all translations go with the product of grain (flour, dough, or bread); however, it could refer to the vessel in which it was winnowed, ground, kneaded, or baked, as in Levine's rendering "bread-baking utensils" (1993:394).

15:22 *unintentionally.* This term (along with the cognate noun that appears in 15:24-25, 27-29) has the sense of wandering or going astray. NJPS has "unwittingly" (e.g., Lev 4-5). It is the opposite of "premeditated" or "with a high hand" (cf. 15:30, "brazenly").

15:25 *they will be forgiven.* Milgrom (1989:123-124) prefers "may be forgiven" to avoid any idea that forgiveness is an automatic effect inherent in the priestly ritual, rather than being dependent upon the free grace of God. But a language change is not needed here any more than it is needed in other places where a promise is baldly stated (Matt 17:20; Jas 5:14-16). Compare the prophetic use of "perhaps," "maybe," and "who knows?" in reference to divine sovereignty (Exod 32:30; 1 Sam 6:5; 14:6; 2 Sam 12:22; Jer 51:8; Dan 4:27; Joel 2:13-14; Amos 5:15; Jonah 3:9; Zeph 2:3; Acts 8:22; 2 Tim 2:25).

15:30 *brazenly.* Lit., "with an upraised hand." It is not so much that the sin is deliberate as that it is defiant (Snaith 1969:155), as in shaking one's fist or "thumbing his nose at God" (Allen 1990:831).

blasphemed the Lord. This is a Piel of *gadap* [TH1442, ZH1552], meaning "revile, blaspheme," with "the Lord" in the emphatic position, emphasizing the seriousness of the offense.

cut off from the community. See note on 9:13.

15:35 *stone him.* Stoning was to be imposed for the following: for an ox that kills a person (Exod 21:28-32), child sacrifice (Lev 20:2-5), divination (Lev 20:27), blasphemy (Lev 24:15, 23), Sabbath breaking (15:32-36), adultery (Deut 22:21-24), inducement to worship other gods (Deut 13:6-10), detestable religious practices (Deut 17:1-5), insubordination by a son (Deut 21:18-21), and violation of the sacred ban (Josh 7:25). Executions occurred outside the camp (Lev 24:14, 23) or city (1 Kgs 21:10, 13) so as to avoid profaning the holy camp or city with a corpse.

15:38 *tassels.* Heb., *tsitsith* [TH6734, ZH7492], which could also be rendered "fringes." Ancient Near Eastern background shows magical tendencies for decorations like these, but that sense is not present in this text; rather, the pedagogical verbal series "see . . . remember . . . obey . . . remember . . . obey" (15:39-40) sets the purpose of the tassels.

15:39 *instead of following your own desires and defiling yourselves, as you are prone to do.* Lit., "instead of following (*tur* [TH8446, ZH9365]) after your own heart and your own eyes, after which you are inclined to whore (*zanah* [TH2181, ZH2388])." The term *tur* is the same one used of the Ark scouting out resting places (10:33) and the Lord himself scouting out campsites (Deut 1:33). More to the point in this context, it is used of the rebellious scouts doing reconnaissance of the land (13:2, 16, 21, 25, 32; 14:6-7, 34, 36, 38). The term *zanah* is a metaphor that speaks of illegitimate relations with other gods (Exod 34:15; Ezek 6:9).

COMMENTARY

Instead of the hoped-for record of initial conquest, we have a record of cultic matters like we saw in the preparatory chapters (5:1–10:10). Still, this forward-looking legislation assured the people that they would one day inherit the land. The section prescribes offerings (15:1-31), punishment for Sabbath violation (15:32-36), and tassels of remembrance (15:37-41).

This legislation followed the rejection of the Promised Land, which had been premeditated rebellion. One law and one example dealt with the unforgivable nature of premeditated sins (15:30-36). This fixed the principle that the first generation's sin was unforgivable and that they had been condemned to die in the wilderness. But the legislation actually opens with a forward look, noting that the laws concern "when you finally settle in the land" (15:2). This fixed the principle that God would follow through on his promise to bring Israel to the land of Canaan. The careful provision for sacrifice for "unintentional" sins sustained hopes that things could be kept right with God. Indeed, these sacrifices would be a "pleasing aroma to the LORD" (15:3, 7).

This section treats grain, oil, and wine offerings that were to accompany a variety of animal sacrifices. It provides minimal procedural direction, probably because they followed steps that had already been established (Lev 1:1–3:17; 6:8-23; 7:11-27). But here for the first time they heard the measure of grain and drink that was to accompany each offering:

	Grain	Oil	Wine
Lamb	$\frac{1}{10}$ ephah	$\frac{1}{4}$ hin	$\frac{1}{4}$ hin
Ram	$\frac{2}{10}$ ephah	$\frac{1}{3}$ hin	$\frac{1}{3}$ hin
Bull	$\frac{3}{10}$ ephah	$\frac{1}{2}$ hin	$\frac{1}{2}$ hin

These commodities comprised the main agricultural products with which God would bless Israel when they settled in Canaan.

The same law applied to a full citizen and to an alien; anyone enjoying God's rich provision in Canaan was to follow this practice. Even if the offering itself was freewill, the prescribed method indicated that the land flowing with milk and honey was "no place for human arbitrariness or self-willed religion" (Noordtzij 1983:136). The general pattern was that the more valuable the animal offered, the larger the accompanying grain, oil, and wine offerings. G. J. Wenham points out how this informs New Testament discipleship: "Early Christian commentators asked what offerings could match the Lamb of God. They pointed to Paul's remarks about his sufferings, filling up Christ's afflictions, and his life being poured out as a libation (Phil 2:17; Col 1:24; 2 Tim 4:6), a path which all Christ's disciples must follow, at least figuratively" (1981:128-129).

Grain Offering (15:17–21). By offering their firstfruits, Israel acknowledged that they owed it all to God's largesse, whether agricultural products offered in their natural state (e.g., grain, fruit) or after processing (e.g., oil, flour, dough) or after preparation (e.g., bread). After offering the firstfruits (18:12; Exod 23:19; Deut 26:2-13; Neh 10:35, 37), Israel was free to use the rest. Levine titles this section "Desacralizing the Dough" (1993:393), but we would do better to speak of *sacralizing* the dough. As Paul said, "The entire batch of dough is holy because the portion given as an offering is holy" (Rom 11:16). If the offering was coarse-ground grain, the emphasis would have fallen on "immediacy," on offering the earliest agricultural product, even before refining (Allen 1990:828). If it was dough or bread, the emphasis fell on first domestic use of the agricultural product. That is what the postexilic community made of it, as the woman put a handful of her dough into the fire, "making every hearth an altar and every kitchen a house of God" (G. J. Wenham 1981:129). That is what later Judaism also made of it, giving the first of the dough made in the land from grain grown outside the land, but not of dough kneaded outside the land from grain grown in the land (Hirsch 1971:238, citing *m. Hallah* 2:1). The firstfruits embodied a faith that what God had begun he would finish with abundance. The firstfruits could be safely offered up to God rather than stored up against an as yet uncertain harvest. It spoke of Israel's confidence in God's bounty.

This principle of the firstfruits applies just as much in the spiritual realm as in the material. Paul drew the implication that the patriarchal covenant's firstfruits work through Israel (Jer 2:3), which he applied to the new covenant as well (Rom 11:16) and its resurrection benefits (Rom 8:23; 1 Cor 15:20, 23; 2 Thess 2:13). This was preeminently manifest through the resurrection of Jesus Christ (1 Cor 15:20, 23) and then began to be manifest among the earliest Christians (2 Thess 2:13; Jas 1:18; Rev 14:4).

Offerings for Inadvertent Offenses (15:22–31). This section contrasts inadvertent sins (15:22-29) with brazen sins (15:30-31), dealing first with the general idea of unintentional sins (15:22), then with unintentional sins of the community (15:24-26) and the individual (15:27). Then come brazen sins (15:30), followed by the example of a brazen Sabbath breaker (15:32-36).

Leviticus 4:14 prescribes a bull for the sin offering, but here the bull is for a burnt offering (15:24), and a young goat is for the sin offering. Leviticus also allows a goat or lamb for an individual, whereas Numbers mentions only a goat. To explain this difference, some suggest that Leviticus was dealing with sins of commission while Numbers dealt with sins of omission (Levine 1993:395, citing 15:22; Lev 4:2, 13, 22, 27; 5:2, 17). The key distinction, however, is not between sins of commission and omission but between unintentional and defiant sins (15:30). The passage explicitly talks of something done unintentionally (15:24). Therefore, G. J. Wenham thinks Numbers is modifying the Leviticus law, as happens elsewhere in the Torah as well (1981:131; e.g., Exod 13:2 and Num 3:12; Lev 7:34 and Deut 18:3; and Lev 11:39 and Deut 14:21). In fact, chapter 15 makes clarifications and additions. It adds a whole burnt offering for the individual (15:24), extends application of the law to the sojourner (15:26, 29), and explicitly denies expiation for defiant sins (15:30).

Leviticus 6:1-7 allows for sacrificial atonement for sins when they *realize* their guilt (Lev 6:4, NRSV). Those who despised the Lord and his very word (15:31) cut themselves off from any ability to acknowledge guilt. Cutting themselves off from their Maker, they were to be cut off from the community of his people, wherein he dwelled. The New Testament warns against "a sin that leads to death" (1 John 5:16) and of the impossibility of forgiveness for blasphemy against the Spirit (Mark 3:29) and apostasy (Heb 6:4-6; 10:26-31, referring to Deut 17:2-6). But it is also interesting to note that Jesus treated some very serious sins as things done in ignorance and called for their forgiveness (Luke 23:34), as did Peter (Acts 3:17). Then there is the forgivable ignorance of those who haven't heard the gospel (Rom 10:14), to say nothing of Paul's ignorant blasphemy (1 Tim 1:13). However, ignorance is reprehensible when people "deliberately forget" what God has done, required, or promised (2 Pet 3:5).

Law on Gathering Sticks on the Sabbath (15:32–36). Biblical law spoke of incarceration only as a temporary measure to wait for counsel on "what to do" (15:34; also Lev 24:12).[1] Israel already knew that lighting a fire violated the Sabbath (Exod 35:2-3) and that Sabbath-breaking warranted the death penalty (Exod 31:15). This deliberation would have been to determine whether this sin might be covered by an offering so they didn't have to execute the man or if it was a brazen sin for which no offering was possible. Since gathering wood showed premeditated intent to light a Sabbath fire, it came under the strictures of brazen sin (15:30). So the whole community took the offender outside the camp for execution by stoning.

Law on Tassels of Remembrance (15:37–41). Prevention is better than cure, and the first generation couldn't seem to remember much longer than three days (11:1-3; Allen 1990:828), so the Lord gave Israel an item of decoration on their clothing that would remind them of their sacred office and duty. Every time they glanced down and saw a tassel swinging from their clothes, they should have been reminded of the law and been urged to explore its implications. Swinging in silent exhortation, "Be holy to your God" (15:40), the tassels reminded the people that they were a national priesthood (Exod 19:6). It's decidedly less than "certain that the 'tassels' . . . originally had a magic, apotropaic significance" that was later modified to signify remembering (Noth 1968:117). If anything, the biblical record runs in the opposite order: A godly mandate may have subsided into godless magic. Eventually, the tassels came to be seen as symbols of the power of the wearer, which explains how serious David's offense seemed to him after he had cut them off Saul's robe (1 Sam 24:1-7; cf. 1 Sam 15:24-31). Status- conscious Jews of Jesus' time liked to wear "extra long tassels" (Matt 23:5), and perhaps some magical significance drove sick people to attempt to touch Jesus' tassels (Matt 9:18-21; 14:36). Such people "are not to be thought of, then, as approaching [Jesus] in deep humility, seeking only to touch an insignificant part of his costume, but as seeking to avail themselves of his power by the surest method they knew" (Stephens 1931:69; see also Bertman 1961).

ENDNOTE
1. Other OT records of Israelite leaders imprisoning Israelites portray actions that were obviously against God's will (1 Kgs 22:27; Jer 37:15, 21).

◆   ### d. Korah leads a rebellion against Moses and Aaron (16:1-50)

One day Korah son of Izhar, a descendant of Kohath son of Levi, conspired with Dathan and Abiram, the sons of Eliab, and On son of Peleth, from the tribe of Reuben. [2]They incited a rebellion against Moses, along with 250 other leaders of the community, all prominent members of the assembly. [3]They united against Moses and Aaron and said, "You have gone too far! The whole community of Israel has been set apart by the LORD, and he is with all of us. What right do you have to act as though you are greater than the rest of the LORD's people?"

[4]When Moses heard what they were saying, he fell face down on the ground. [5]Then he said to Korah and his followers, "Tomorrow morning the LORD will show us who belongs to him* and who is holy. The LORD will allow only those whom he selects to enter his own presence. [6]Korah, you and all your followers must prepare your incense burners. [7]Light fires in them tomorrow, and burn incense before the LORD. Then we will see whom the LORD chooses as his holy one. You Levites are the ones who have gone too far!"

[8]Then Moses spoke again to Korah: "Now listen, you Levites! [9]Does it seem insignificant to you that the God of Israel has chosen you from among all the community of Israel to be near him so you can serve in the LORD's Tabernacle and stand before the people to minister to them? [10]Korah, he has already given this special ministry to you and your fellow Levites. Are you now demanding the priesthood as well? [11]The LORD is the one you and your followers are really revolting against! For who is Aaron that you are complaining about him?"

[12]Then Moses summoned Dathan and Abiram, the sons of Eliab, but they replied, "We refuse to come before you! [13]Isn't it enough that you brought us out of Egypt, a land flowing with milk and honey, to kill us here in this wilderness, and that you now treat us like your subjects? [14]What's more, you haven't brought us into another land flowing with milk and honey. You haven't given us a new homeland with fields and vineyards. Are you trying to fool these men?* We will not come."

[15]Then Moses became very angry and said to the LORD, "Do not accept their grain offerings! I have not taken so much as a donkey from them, and I have never hurt a single one of them." [16]And Moses

said to Korah, "You and all your followers must come here tomorrow and present yourselves before the LORD. Aaron will also be here. ¹⁷You and each of your 250 followers must prepare an incense burner and put incense on it, so you can all present them before the LORD. Aaron will also bring his incense burner."

¹⁸So each of these men prepared an incense burner, lit the fire, and placed incense on it. Then they all stood at the entrance of the Tabernacle* with Moses and Aaron. ¹⁹Meanwhile, Korah had stirred up the entire community against Moses and Aaron, and they all gathered at the Tabernacle entrance. Then the glorious presence of the LORD appeared to the whole community, ²⁰and the LORD said to Moses and Aaron, ²¹"Get away from all these people so that I may instantly destroy them!"

²²But Moses and Aaron fell face down on the ground. "O God," they pleaded, "you are the God who gives breath to all creatures. Must you be angry with all the people when only one man sins?"

²³And the LORD said to Moses, ²⁴"Then tell all the people to get away from the tents of Korah, Dathan, and Abiram."

²⁵So Moses got up and rushed over to the tents of Dathan and Abiram, followed by the elders of Israel. ²⁶"Quick!" he told the people. "Get away from the tents of these wicked men, and don't touch anything that belongs to them. If you do, you will be destroyed for their sins." ²⁷So all the people stood back from the tents of Korah, Dathan, and Abiram. Then Dathan and Abiram came out and stood at the entrances of their tents, together with their wives and children and little ones.

²⁸And Moses said, "This is how you will know that the LORD has sent me to do all these things that I have done—for I have not done them on my own. ²⁹If these men die a natural death, or if nothing unusual happens, then the LORD has not sent me. ³⁰But if the LORD does something entirely new and the ground opens its mouth and

swallows them and all their belongings, and they go down alive into the grave,* then you will know that these men have shown contempt for the LORD."

³¹He had hardly finished speaking the words when the ground suddenly split open beneath them. ³²The earth opened its mouth and swallowed the men, along with their households and all their followers who were standing with them, and everything they owned. ³³So they went down alive into the grave, along with all their belongings. The earth closed over them, and they all vanished from among the people of Israel. ³⁴All the people around them fled when they heard their screams. "The earth will swallow us, too!" they cried. ³⁵Then fire blazed forth from the LORD and burned up the 250 men who were offering incense.

³⁶*And the LORD said to Moses, ³⁷"Tell Eleazar son of Aaron the priest to pull all the incense burners from the fire, for they are holy. Also tell him to scatter the burning coals. ³⁸Take the incense burners of these men who have sinned at the cost of their lives, and hammer the metal into a thin sheet to overlay the altar. Since these burners were used in the LORD's presence, they have become holy. Let them serve as a warning to the people of Israel."

³⁹So Eleazar the priest collected the 250 bronze incense burners that had been used by the men who died in the fire, and he hammered them into a thin sheet to overlay the altar. ⁴⁰This would warn the Israelites that no unauthorized person—no one who was not a descendant of Aaron—should ever enter the LORD's presence to burn incense. If anyone did, the same thing would happen to him as happened to Korah and his followers. So the LORD's instructions to Moses were carried out.

⁴¹But the very next morning the whole community of Israel began muttering again against Moses and Aaron, saying, "You have killed the LORD's people!" ⁴²As the community gathered to protest against Moses and Aaron, they turned

toward the Tabernacle and saw that the cloud had covered it, and the glorious presence of the LORD appeared.

⁴³Moses and Aaron came and stood in front of the Tabernacle, ⁴⁴and the LORD said to Moses, ⁴⁵"Get away from all these people so that I can instantly destroy them!" But Moses and Aaron fell face down on the ground.

⁴⁶And Moses said to Aaron, "Quick, take an incense burner and place burning coals on it from the altar. Lay incense on it, and carry it out among the people to purify them and make them right with the LORD.*

The LORD's anger is blazing against them—the plague has already begun."

⁴⁷Aaron did as Moses told him and ran out among the people. The plague had already begun to strike down the people, but Aaron burned the incense and purified* the people. ⁴⁸He stood between the dead and the living, and the plague stopped. ⁴⁹But 14,700 people died in that plague, in addition to those who had died in the affair involving Korah. ⁵⁰Then because the plague had stopped, Aaron returned to Moses at the entrance of the Tabernacle.

16:5 Greek version reads *God has visited and knows those who are his.* Compare 2 Tim 2:19.   16:14 Hebrew *Are you trying to put out the eyes of these men?*   16:18 Hebrew *the Tent of Meeting;* also in 16:19, 42, 43, 50.   16:30 Hebrew *into Sheol;* also in 16:33.   16:36 Verses 16:36-50 are numbered 17:1-15 in Hebrew text.   16:46 Or *to make atonement for them.*   16:47 Or *and made atonement for.*

NOTES

16:1 conspired. Heb., *wayyiqqakh* [TH3947, ZH4374], meaning "took," and lacking the object needed for the transitive verb. The NLT follows the traditional understanding, "took men," i.e., "assembled followers" (Harrison 1990:231, 241, defending the rendering in KJV, ASV, RSV, JPS, ESV). Others suggest emending *wayyiqqakh* to read *wayyaqom* [TH6965, ZH7756] ("and he arose") (Dillmann and Knobel 1886:89-90; Paterson 1900:51). Origen translated it *hyperēphaneuthē* ("he became arrogant"), which commentators think may have represented *wayyoqakh* [TH3354.1, ZH3689] ("and he was bold, insolent"; Ashley 1993:298; Budd 1984:180; Noth 1968:123; Snaith 1969:255-256; de Vaulx 1972:188).

On. Joseph's wife, Asenath, was the daughter of a priest of On (Gen 41:45, 50; 46:20). Hoffmeier says, "This, then, represents a direct connection between the Hebrews and the cult center at On and may explain why a man with the same name who was not a Levite would join a conspiracy against Aaron the priest" (2005:230).

16:5 his followers. Lit., "his congregation," as though he were "attempting to set up a rival 'Israel'" (Sherwood 2002:164, citing Budd 1984:186-187; Magonet 1982:17), a "parody of the real community" (Ashley 1993:306).

Tomorrow. This is a term that "accompanies announcements of decisive acts of Yahweh; *today* is the day of preparation, *tomorrow* is the day of performance, action, or judgment" (Ashley 1993:308).

16:12 come before you. Lit., "come up," a term for appearing before a superior (Gen 46:31; Deut 25:7; Judg 4:5).

16:14 Are you trying to fool these men? Lit., "Will you gouge out the eyes of these men?" This was a punishment for runaway slaves, rebellious vassals, or prisoners of war (Judg 16:21; 2 Kgs 25:4-7; Jer 39:4-7; 52:7-11), but here, "this idiom means 'hoodwink' and corresponds to the modern idiom 'throw dust in the eyes' (Gray 1903:201) or 'pull the wool over the eyes'" (Milgrom 1989:134). In Deut 16:19, taking a bribe blinds the eyes of officials and judges. If Moses understood the accusation in this way, that might explain his answer, "I have not taken so much as a donkey from them" (16:15).

16:24 tents. Heb., *mishkan* [TH4908, ZH5438] (singular), meaning "tent, dwelling." This doesn't indicate that Korah had set up a rival shrine (contra Budd 1984:181, 183;

L'Heureux 1976:86); rather, it is a collective singular referring to their own dwellings, although it is perhaps used as an ironic contrast to the "Tent of the LORD," since *mishkan* in the singular is otherwise reserved for the Tabernacle of the Lord.

16:29 The verse literally reads, "If these men die the death of all men, and if the visitation (*pequddah* [TH6486, ZH7213]) of all men is visited (cf. verb *paqad* [TH6485, ZH7212]) upon them." This was often the visitation of punishment sent from a higher person to a subject (e.g., Isa 10:3; Mic 7:4); here it was God's destiny for all men (cf. note on 3:32).

16:30 *does something entirely new.* Lit., "creates a creation." Milgrom (1989:137) prefers a reading "makes a great chasm," which results in the following parallel:

Verse 30	Verses 31b–33a
1. But if the LORD makes a great chasm,	1. The ground under them burst asunder.
2. so that the ground opens its mouth,	2. The earth opened its mouth,
3. and swallows them up with all that belongs to them,	3. and swallowed them up with their household.
4. and they go down alive into Sheol . . .	4. They went down alive into Sheol.

The Piel of *bara'* [TH1254B, ZH1343/5] means "to cut, hew down" (Josh 17:15, 18), and cognates have the idea of cutting or hewing (BDB 135a); however, the overwhelming evidence of OT usage of the Qal stem shows that it means "create, fashion, shape." English translations nearly universally go with something like the NLT. This meant (1) the event about to occur was completely unexpected and unprecedented, comparable to the awesome deeds of creation (Snaith 1969:260; cf. Exod 34:10; Isa 48:6-7; Jer 31:22) or (2) the retribution that Yahweh would impose on the rebels would be as phenomenal as the work of creation (E. W. Davies 1995b:177; Noth 1968:128).

go down. Because Dathan and Abiram refused to "go up" (*'alah* [TH5927, ZH6590]; 16:12, 14) they will "go down" (*yarad* [TH3381, ZH3718]; 16:30, 33). For complaining that Moses "brought us up" (*he'elithanu* [TH5927, ZH6590]; 16:13) from Egypt to "have us die (*lahamithenu* [TH4191, ZH4637]) in the wilderness" (16:13), they will not "die (*yemuthun*) as all men do" (16:29) but will "go down alive (*weyaredu khayyim* [TH2416A, ZH2645]; 16:30, 33) in Sheol" (Milgrom 1989:137).

grave. Heb., *she'ol* [TH7585, ZH8619], the abode of the dead (Isa 14:9-11), especially the wicked (Pss 9:17; 31:17), to which the most wicked go down alive (Ps 55:15), whereas the righteous ascend heavenward (Prov 15:24). This may reflect the idea of *maweth* [TH4194, ZH4638] ("death"; Ugaritic, *mot*) awaiting the wicked with a gaping mouth to swallow them (Prov 1:12; Isa 5:14; Hab 2:5). Also called "the pit" (Job 33:18; Ps 28:1) and "Abaddon" (Job 26:6), it has the following characteristics: (a) oblivion (Ps 88:12); (b) inability to experience God's presence (Ps 88:5); (c) inability to praise God (Pss 6:5; 30:9; 115:17; Isa 38:18); (d) location beneath the earth (here; Job 26:5; Jonah 2:6); (e) weariness (Job 3:17); (f) attenuation (Ps 88:4); (g) thirst (Isa 5:13); (h) awful silence (Pss 94:17; 115:17); (i) darkness (Job 10:21-22). Cf. Riggans 1983:135.

you will know. This is a recognition formula consequent upon judgment (16:30; Exod 6:7; 11:7; 16:12; 1 Kgs 20:13; Isa 49:23; 60:16; Ezek 7:4, 9; Joel 2:27; 3:17; Zech 2:9; 4:9).

16:38 [17:3] *thin sheet to overlay the altar.* The altar was already bronze plated (Exod 27:2; 38:2); the LXX harmonizes by saying Bezalel made the altar from these censers (Exod 38:22, LXX); however, that is chronologically impossible. More likely, the plating needed periodic renewal. The Egyptians had developed the technique of hammering out plate metal to cover wooden objects; the Hebrews had borrowed the word *pakh* [TH6341A, ZH7063] (plate of metal) from the Egyptians (Hoffmeier 2005:211-212).

16:46 [17:11] *incense . . . to . . . make them right with the LORD.* Lit., "to make *kapar* for them." The term *kapar* [TH3722, ZH4105] means "to cover, atone." Usually blood was required for atonement; however, here Aaron burned the same incense that caused destruction when mishandled.

COMMENTARY

The Rebellion (16:1–27). Korah was a Levite from the Kohathite clan, from which Moses and Aaron themselves descended, and Dathan and Abiram descended from Israel's firstborn, Reuben. The two rebellions were essentially contradictory, as Korah wanted primacy through the priesthood (16:10), and the Reubenites wanted primacy through civil authority. But enemies can often make common cause in opposition to the work of God. (E.g., the Pharisees and Sadducees making common cause against Jesus [Matt 16:1], and Pilate and Herod changing from bitter enemies to fast friends in their joint abuse of Jesus [Luke 23:12].)

Korah came from the clan of Kohathites, which was the one closest to leadership: They were the clan of Moses and Aaron, and thus of the priests. He conspired with a significant portion of Israel's elite (16:2), whipping them up with egalitarian vitriol that sounded a lot like Miriam and Aaron's earlier complaint against Moses's unique prophetic role (16:3; cf. 12:2). Moses's response was to throw himself face down on the ground and call God to arbitrate (16:4). He told Korah to make preparations to engage in priest-like incense burning (16:6), warning that the outcome would show who had "gone too far" (16:7).

Moses reminded the rebel Levites of their own special standing before God and Israel, which they were degrading by their demand for priesthood (16:9). Since the offices and authority of Moses, Aaron, and even the Levites came from God, they were challenging God (16:11), a principle restated in the New Testament by Jesus and Paul (John 19:11; Rom 13:1-2).

After dealing specifically with the priestly pretensions of the Levites, Moses turned to the general rebellion that had spread to many of Israel's elite. Their ringleaders refused Moses's judicial summons (16:12, 14). They idealized their existence in Egypt as though it were paradise and libeled Moses as a murderous overlord (16:13), a tedious refrain in the wilderness complaints (14:2; 20:4; 21:5; Exod 14:11; 16:2; 17:3). The very people who had refused conquest now complained, "You haven't brought us into another land flowing with milk and honey" (16:14; cf. Exod 3:8, 17). When they called Egypt "a land flowing with milk and honey" (16:13), they spoke literal truth (Gen 45:16-20; 47:6) but theological lies (11:5; 14:4; Exod 14:11; 16:3; 17:3). Isaiah's words are fitting here: "What sorrow for those who say . . . bitter is sweet and sweet is bitter" (Isa 5:20). They were early forerunners of those whom Jesus judged with these words: "God's light came into the world, but people loved the darkness more than the light" (John 3:19). No wonder Moses "became very angry" and acted as an anti-intercessor. Protesting his own innocence and classifying their sins as belligerent rather than unintentional, he pled with God, "Do not accept their grain offerings!" (16:15).

This should not be conceived of as a trial by ordeal (contra Coats 1968:171); it was more like the power encounter between Elijah and the Baal prophets (1 Kgs 18:20-40). If Korah's group were really "holy" like he claimed, they would successfully offer their incense. But the moment they lit their censers, even though Moses had commanded it (16:17), they would have been guilty of offering "unauthorized fire" like that of Nadab and Abihu (Lev 10:1-2), which should have given them pause. At this point, "the glorious presence of the LORD appeared to the whole community," a theophanic manifestation of judgment (16:19). God told Moses and Aaron to remove themselves from the community so God could strike the whole camp of rebels. Instead, Moses and Aaron interceded. Although God was threatening death, they looked to him as the source of all life (16:22); although the rebellion was widespread, they said, don't "be angry with all the people when only one man sins" (16:22).

God concurred but told Moses and Aaron to stand back (16:21) and to clear the ground around the "tents of Korah, Dathan, and Abiram" (16:25-27). Dathan and Abiram stood their ground before their tents, dragging "their wives and children and little ones" into this showdown with God (16:27).

Punishment of Rebels (16:28–35). Although Moses was defending Aaron's priesthood, he first defended his own prophetic office. He prophesied and then proposed a test that resonated with one of the tests of a true prophet (Deut 18:21-22): If my prophecy doesn't come to pass, then "the LORD has not sent me" (16:29). But if the ground swallows them alive, as I prophesy, then "the LORD sent me to do all these things" and "these men have shown contempt for the LORD" (16:28, 30). This narrative emphasizes the immediacy and miraculous nature of the rebels' punishment; Moses "had hardly finished speaking the words when the ground suddenly split open beneath them," swallowing the rebels alive along with their households and their belongings (16:31-33). This sounds like the total destruction provisions of *kherem* [TH2764, ZH3051] warfare (e.g., Deut 2:34; 3:6; 13:15, 17; Josh 6:17; 7:15). As the rebel leadership suddenly disappeared, screaming their way down into the open maw of the earth, the camp shrank back in terror that the earth might swallow them, too (16:34). Although they shared some guilt in this widespread rebellion, they should have stood their ground with Moses, who had already moved them away from judgment to a place of safety. Next God's own fire "burned up the 250 men who were offering incense" (16:35; see note on 3:4). This killed Korah's followers, but not his sons, who survived to father the Temple musicians (26:10; 1 Chr 6:33; Pss 42; 44–49; 84; 85; 87; 88).

Aftermath of the Rebellion (16:36–50). God directed "Eleazar son of Aaron the priest to pull all the incense burners from the fire . . . [and] scatter the burning coals" (16:37). The rebels' incense burners were dubious implements for genuine priestly offerings; however, they could no longer be used for common purposes, either, because they had been "used in the LORD's presence" (16:38). So the Lord directed that they should be hammered into plates for re-covering the altar. Just as the tassels were a positive reminder of Israel's holiness (15:38), these plates could serve as a negative *aide-mémoire* (16:40; cf. 5:15; 10:10; 17:10; 31:54).

"The very next morning the whole community of Israel began muttering" (16:41). In spite of the obviously divine nature of this twofold judgment, the people blamed Moses and Aaron: "*You* have killed the LORD's people!" (16:41, emphasis added). As the demonstration gathered steam, "the glorious presence of the LORD appeared" (16:42), not in beaming approval, but in blazing fury.

Moses and Aaron took up a judicial stance "in front of the Tabernacle" (16:43). The Lord echoed his warning that had preceded the earth's opening to ingest Korah, Dathan, and Abiram and the fiery judgment on the 250 rebel incense burners (16:26): "Get away from all these people so that I can instantly destroy them!" (16:45). Instead, "Moses and Aaron fell face down on the ground," a regular posture of intercession throughout Numbers (14:5; 16:4, 22, 45; 20:6). Moses certainly couldn't claim that only one man had sinned this time (cf. 16:22). But rather than having Aaron get away from the people that God was judging, Moses directed him to carry burning incense "out among the people" as a covering act (16:46); "he stood between the dead and the living" (16:48; *Targum Neofiti*). Whether this was Moses's own initiative or his response to God's unrecorded directive, it mitigated the punishment that had already broken out. Only "14,700 died in that plague" (16:49), a small percentage of the people (cf. 2:32) rather than all of them.

◆   e. A sign for the rebels (17:1-13)

[1]*Then the LORD said to Moses, [2]"Tell the people of Israel to bring you twelve wooden staffs, one from each leader of Israel's ancestral tribes, and inscribe each leader's name on his staff. [3]Inscribe Aaron's name on the staff of the tribe of Levi, for there must be one staff for the leader of each ancestral tribe. [4]Place these staffs in the Tabernacle in front of the Ark containing the tablets of the Covenant,* where I meet with you. [5]Buds will sprout on the staff belonging to the man I choose. Then I will finally put an end to the people's murmuring and complaining against you."

[6]So Moses gave the instructions to the people of Israel, and each of the twelve tribal leaders, including Aaron, brought Moses a staff. [7]Moses placed the staffs in the LORD's presence in the Tabernacle of the Covenant.* [8]When he went into Tabernacle of the Covenant the next day, he found that Aaron's staff, representing the tribe of Levi, had sprouted, budded, blossomed, and produced ripe almonds!

[9]When Moses brought all the staffs out from the LORD's presence, he showed them to the people. Each man claimed his own staff. [10]And the LORD said to Moses: "Place Aaron's staff permanently before the Ark of the Covenant* to serve as a warning to rebels. This should put an end to their complaints against me and prevent any further deaths." [11]So Moses did as the LORD commanded him.

[12]Then the people of Israel said to

Moses, "Look, we are doomed! We are   comes close to the Tabernacle of the LORD
dead! We are ruined! ¹³Everyone who even   dies. Are we all doomed to die?"

17:1 Verses 17:1-13 are numbered 17:16-28 in Hebrew text.   17:4 Hebrew *in the Tent of Meeting before the
Testimony.* The Hebrew word for "testimony" refers to the terms of the LORD's covenant with Israel as written
on stone tablets, which were kept in the Ark, and also to the covenant itself.   17:7 Or *Tabernacle of the
Testimony;* also in 17:8.   17:10 Hebrew *before the Testimony;* see note on 17:4.

NOTES

17:1-13 [16-28] In the Hebrew this section is 17:16-28, keeping this story of Aaron's
budding staff connected with the rebellion of ch 16.

17:2 [17] *twelve.* This makes for a total of 13 when the Levites' staff was placed among
them (see note on 17:6).

staffs. Heb., *matteh* [TH4294, ZH4751], which can mean "staff" or "tribe." These may be the
"bare branches" used for everyday walking sticks (Noth 1968:131; Gray 1903:215; see
1 Sam 14:43); more likely, they were symbols of position (Budd 1984:197; Noordtzij
1983:157; Sturdy 1976:124; see 21:18; Gen 38:18, 25; 49:10).

17:4, 7, 10 [19, 22, 25] *in front of the Ark containing the tablets of the Covenant.* Heb.,
lipne ha'eduth [TH5715, ZH6343], meaning, "before the Covenant" (17:4, 10; see note on 4:5).
The term *ha'eduth* sometimes refers only to the tablets (Exod 31:18; 32:15; 34:29), which
were placed inside the Ark (Exod 16:34; 25:16, 21; 40:20), but it sometimes refers to the
Ark itself, which contained them (17:4, 10; Exod 27:21; 30:36; Lev 16:13; 24:3). These
staffs may have been placed inside the Most Holy Place in front of the Ark (Cole
2000:274); however, since that place was accessible to the high priest only on the Day of
Atonement, perhaps they were instead placed right before the curtain separating the Most
Holy Place from the rest of the Tabernacle. As E. W. Davies says, "there is no evidence that
Aaron's rod was actually deposited in the temple" (1995b:182; cf. Heb 9:4); only the two
tablets were in the Ark by the time the Temple was dedicated (1 Kgs 8:9).

17:6 [21] *each of the twelve tribal leaders, including Aaron, brought Moses a staff.* Lit.,
"and all their leaders gave one staff per leader, a staff per leader for each paternal house,
twelve staffs; and Aaron's staff was among their staffs." This makes a total of 13 staffs
(Levine 1993:422) unless there was a single staff for the Joseph tribes, Ephraim and
Manasseh (Budd 1984:195; Cole 2000:274), which is unlikely. The Vulgate makes this
explicit: "12 staffs besides the staff of Aaron" (*virgae duodecim absque virga Aaron*).

COMMENTARY

The Lord told Moses to collect a staff from the leader of each of Israel's twelve tribes,
then to lay Aaron's staff for the tribe of Levi among them, "as it were, in the 'lap' of
God" (Allen 1990:847; cf. Prov 16:33). God told Moses, "Buds will sprout on the
staff belonging to the man I choose" (17:5). At the least, the test would have
required God's providential superintendence so the correct staff budded. But when
Moses checked the very next day, not only had Aaron's rod sprouted, it had run full
cycle from buds to blossoms and to ripe almonds (17:8). With the outcome mani-
festly imprinted with God's own green thumb, Moses brought out the staffs so the
people could see the sign (17:9). "Each man claimed his own staff," noting that his
hadn't sprouted (17:9). This was added to a growing list of reminders/warnings and
negative memorials (5:15; 10:10; 16:38; 31:54), so Moses put Aaron's staff in front
of the Ark, near the Ten Commandments (17:10; Heb 9:4).

Seeing this, the people of Israel protested, "Everyone who even comes close to the Tabernacle of the LORD dies" (17:13). This stretched the law against unauthorized approach, just as Eve had exaggerated the law against eating from the forbidden tree (Gen 3:3). They asked, "Are we all doomed to die?" The answer for this rebellious generation was yes, certainly and comprehensively. But this was not for disobediently entering God's presence; rather, it was for refusing to enter his presence in his new paradise, the Promised Land.

Aaron's vindicated priesthood prefigured that of Christ (Heb 4–10), which God vindicated by raising him from the dead (Acts 17:31; Rom 1:4). The New Testament refers to the placement of Aaron's sprouting staff in the Ark (Heb 9:4), outlining the superiority of Jesus' priesthood in that he gives bold, general, and ongoing access rather than the limited access accorded only the high priest (Heb 10:19-21). No wonder Jesus said, "I am the way" (John 14:6). The principle still applies. As the rebels had said, all of God's people are indeed holy; however, God gives special authority to some, to Christ and his apostles and to their successors as leaders and elders of the church. With that authority comes the necessity of providing an exemplary standard of holiness.

◆   ## f. Regulations for the priests (18:1-32)

Then the LORD said to Aaron: "You, your sons, and your relatives from the tribe of Levi will be held responsible for any offenses related to the sanctuary. But you and your sons alone will be held responsible for violations connected with the priesthood.

2"Bring your relatives of the tribe of Levi—your ancestral tribe—to assist you and your sons as you perform the sacred duties in front of the Tabernacle of the Covenant.* 3But as the Levites go about all their assigned duties at the Tabernacle, they must be careful not to go near any of the sacred objects or the altar. If they do, both you and they will die. 4The Levites must join you in fulfilling their responsibilities for the care and maintenance of the Tabernacle,* but no unauthorized person may assist you.

5"You yourselves must perform the sacred duties inside the sanctuary and at the altar. If you follow these instructions, the LORD's anger will never again blaze against the people of Israel. 6I myself have chosen your fellow Levites from among the Israelites to be your special assistants. They are a gift to you, dedicated to the LORD for service in the Tabernacle. 7But you and your sons, the priests, must personally handle all the priestly rituals associated with the altar and with everything behind the inner curtain. I am giving you the priesthood as your special privilege of service. Any unauthorized person who comes too near the sanctuary will be put to death."

8The LORD gave these further instructions to Aaron: "I myself have put you in charge of all the holy offerings that are brought to me by the people of Israel. I have given all these consecrated offerings to you and your sons as your permanent share. 9You are allotted the portion of the most holy offerings that is not burned on the fire. This portion of all the most holy offerings—including the grain offerings, sin offerings, and guilt offerings—will be most holy, and it belongs to you and your sons. 10You must eat it as a most holy offering. All the males may eat of it, and you must treat it as most holy.

¹¹"All the sacred offerings and special offerings presented to me when the Israelites lift them up before the altar also belong to you. I have given them to you and to your sons and daughters as your permanent share. Any member of your family who is ceremonially clean may eat of these offerings.

¹²"I also give you the harvest gifts brought by the people as offerings to the LORD—the best of the olive oil, new wine, and grain. ¹³All the first crops of their land that the people present to the LORD belong to you. Any member of your family who is ceremonially clean may eat this food.

¹⁴"Everything in Israel that is specially set apart for the LORD* also belongs to you.

¹⁵"The firstborn of every mother, whether human or animal, that is offered to the LORD will be yours. But you must always redeem your firstborn sons and the firstborn of ceremonially unclean animals. ¹⁶Redeem them when they are one month old. The redemption price is five pieces of silver* (as measured by the weight of the sanctuary shekel, which equals twenty gerahs).

¹⁷"However, you may not redeem the firstborn of cattle, sheep, or goats. They are holy and have been set apart for the LORD. Sprinkle their blood on the altar, and burn their fat as a special gift, a pleasing aroma to the LORD. ¹⁸The meat of these animals will be yours, just like the breast and right thigh that are presented by lifting them up as a special offering before the altar. ¹⁹Yes, I am giving you all these holy offerings that the people of Israel bring to the LORD. They are for you and your sons and daughters, to be eaten as your permanent share. This is an eternal and unbreakable covenant* between the LORD and you, and it also applies to your descendants."

²⁰And the LORD said to Aaron, "You priests will receive no allotment of land or share of property among the people of Israel. I am your share and your allotment. ²¹As for the tribe of Levi, your relatives, I will compensate them for their service in the Tabernacle. Instead of an allotment of land, I will give them the tithes from the entire land of Israel.

²²"From now on, no Israelites except priests or Levites may approach the Tabernacle. If they come too near, they will be judged guilty and will die. ²³Only the Levites may serve at the Tabernacle, and they will be held responsible for any offenses against it. This is a permanent law for you, to be observed from generation to generation. The Levites will receive no allotment of land among the Israelites, ²⁴because I have given them the Israelites' tithes, which have been presented as sacred offerings to the LORD. This will be the Levites' share. That is why I said they would receive no allotment of land among the Israelites."

²⁵The LORD also told Moses, ²⁶"Give these instructions to the Levites: When you receive from the people of Israel the tithes I have assigned as your allotment, give a tenth of the tithes you receive—a tithe of the tithe—to the LORD as a sacred offering. ²⁷The LORD will consider this offering to be your harvest offering, as though it were the first grain from your own threshing floor or wine from your own winepress. ²⁸You must present one-tenth of the tithe received from the Israelites as a sacred offering to the LORD. This is the LORD's sacred portion, and you must present it to Aaron the priest. ²⁹Be sure to give to the LORD the best portions of the gifts given to you.

³⁰"Also, give these instructions to the Levites: When you present the best part as your offering, it will be considered as though it came from your own threshing floor or winepress. ³¹You Levites and your families may eat this food anywhere you wish, for it is your compensation for serving in the Tabernacle. ³²You will not be considered guilty for accepting the LORD's tithes if you give the best portion to the

priests. But be careful not to treat the   though they were common. If you do, you
holy gifts of the people of Israel as   will die."

18:2 Or *Tabernacle of the Testimony.*   **18:4** Hebrew *the Tent of Meeting;* also in 18:6, 21, 22, 23, 31.
18:14 The Hebrew term used here refers to the complete consecration of things or people to the LORD, either by
destroying them or by giving them as an offering.   **18:16** Hebrew *5 shekels* [2 ounces or 57 grams] *of silver.*
18:19 Hebrew *a covenant of salt.*

NOTES

18:1 *to Aaron.* Only in this chapter (18:1, 8, 20) and in Lev 10:8 does God give directions
directly to Aaron; generally, Moses relayed them to Aaron (18:25; e.g., 6:22; 8:1; Lev 8:1;
16:2; 21:1).

relatives from the tribe of Levi. Lit., "your brothers from the house of your fathers." The
NLT refers this to the entire Levitical clan as do some commentators (G. J. Wenham
1981:143). However, others think it refers only to the clan of Kohath (Ashley 1993:339;
Milgrom 1989:146, citing Rashi and Ibn Ezra).

offenses related to the sanctuary. Heb., *'eth-'awon hammiqdash* [TH5771, ZH6411]. The *miqdash*
[TH4720, ZH5219] can refer either to the sacred area (Lev 12:4) or to sacred objects (10:21).
The English translations apply it to the sacred space, in which case "house of your fathers"
means the entire Levitical tribe with their general Tabernacle responsibilities; however,
some commentators think "sacred objects" is meant here (Ashley 1993:338; Milgrom
1989:146), in which case "house of your fathers" refers only to the Kohathites, who carried
the sacred objects (see previous note).

18:2 *the tribe of Levi . . . to assist you.* Lit., "tribe of Levi (*lewi* [TH3878, ZH4290]) . . . they
will be joined/join themselves (*lawah* [TH3867, ZH4277]) with you," a play on the words for
the priestly hierarchy and the name of the tribe.

18:5 *perform the sacred duties inside the sanctuary.* Lit., "you must guard the service of
haqqodesh." The *qodesh* [TH6944, ZH7731] can refer to the holy objects inside the sanctuary
(Ashley 1993:338, 342; JPS; see notes on 18:1), or to the sacred area itself, as is the traditional understanding (KJV, ASV, NASB, RSV, NRSV, ESV, NJB, NJPS, NLT).

18:8 *in charge of all the holy offerings that are brought to me.* Heb., *'eth-mishmereth
terumothay.* The term *mishmereth* [TH4931, ZH5466] can refer to *guarding* things, as NLT has it,
or it can refer to *reserved* things, i.e., "those gifts kept back from the altar as perquisites for
the priests" (Milgrom 1989:149). So Snaith prefers, "I have given you all that is reserved
(*mishmereth,* "kept, kept back") of the offerings made to me" (1969:163). This would be
parallel to the first sentence of the following verse.

18:10 *You must eat it as a most holy offering.* Heb., *beqodesh haqqodashim to'kalennu.*
The most natural translation of *beqodesh haqqodashim* [TH6944, ZH7731] is "in the Holy of
Holies." However, since only the high priest could enter that, and only on the Day of
Atonement, that is not possible here. That leaves two possibilities, either (1) an inexact
reference to sacred space within the Tabernacle courtyard (E. W. Davies 1995b:88;
Noordtzij 1983:162; Riggans 1983:143; KJV, RSV, ESV, JPS; cf. Lev 6:16, 26) or (2) a refer-
ence to how the sacrifices are to be viewed, i.e., "as very holy" (Ashley 1993:348; Milgrom
1989:150; G. J. Wenham 1981:143; ASV, NASB, NRSV, NJB, NJPS, NLT, NET).

18:11 *your sons and daughters.* Lit., "your sons and your daughters who are with you,"
thereby excluding married daughters who have joined their husbands' households (Lev
22:12).

Any member of your family who is ceremonially clean. Lit., "all the pure of your household," including slaves (Lev 22:11) but not hired laborers maintaining their own households (Lev 10:10).

18:12 best. This represents two different terms: "fat" (*kheleb* [TH2459, ZH2693]), like "cream of the crop," and "the first (*re'shith* [TH7225, ZH8040]) of what they give," referring either to *first*fruits or to *first* quality.

18:14 specially set apart. Heb., *kherem* [TH2764, ZH3051], a technical term for an ultimate form of dedication, which once given to the Lord could not be redeemed (de Vaux 1961:260-261; NIDOTTE 2.276-277; TWOT 1.324-325). It was solely God's (Lev 27:28), whether annihilated as a war offering (Josh 6:21; 1 Sam 15), entirely burned as a Tabernacle offering (Josh 6:17-21), or reserved for permanent use in the sanctuary (Josh 6:19).

18:15 firstborn of every mother. The firstborn is assumed to be male (3:40; Exod 13:2, 12, 15). The redemption price is the five-shekel price of a male, with no mention of the three-shekel price for a female (Lev 27:6).

redeem. Heb., *padah* [TH6299, ZH7009], meaning "to get by payment what was not originally yours," whereas *ga'al* [TH1350, ZH1457] is "to get back your own possession" (Budd 1984:206 n. 15, citing Snaith 1969:268).

18:19 eternal and unbreakable covenant. Lit., "an eternal covenant of salt" (Lev 2:13; 2 Chr 13:5). Salt was the food preservative par excellence in antiquity. Its use was required for all sacrifices (Lev 2:13; Ezek 43:24), and it stands in contrast to leaven and other fermentatives, whose use is forbidden on the altar (Lev 2:11). Thus salt is a symbol of permanence, and a "salt covenant," therefore, means an unbreakable covenant—the wave offerings would always belong to the priests. Salt likely played a central role at the solemn meal that sealed a covenant (as in Gen 26:30; 31:54; Exod 24:11). A Neo-Babylonian letter speaks of "all who have tasted the salt of the Jakin tribe," referring to the tribe's covenanted allies. Loyalty to the Persian monarch was claimed by having tasted the "salt of the palace" in Ezra 4:14. And Arabic *milkhat*—a derivative of *malakha*, "to salt"—means "a treaty" (Milgrom 1989:154). Snaith also refers to the Arabic idiom, "to eat a man's salt," which signified creating a lasting bond of fellowship between host and guest (Snaith 1969). "It is therefore inviolable, because between the Lord's priests and Israel is 'salt' (Lev 2:13) and the Lord is witness" (Noordtzij 1983:164).

18:23 they will be held responsible for any offenses against it. Lit., "they will bear their guilt." To understand this, we need to identify the antecedent(s) of "they" and "their." Ashley lists four possibilities, which I represent by making the antecedent explicit (1993:356-357): (1) The *Israelites* will bear the *Levites'* guilt, which is "patently absurd in the context" (Ashley 1993:356). (2) Otherwise, *the Israelites* would bear *their own* guilt; however, that doesn't answer the panic of 17:12-13. Perhaps "others would incur guilt" (NJPS) is a variation of this. (3) The *Levites* will bear *their own* guilt, which is the most common exegesis (Allen 1990:856; Dillmann and Knobel 1886:102-103; Gray 1903:234-235; Noordtzij 1983:166; e.g., NIV). (4) The *Levites* will bear the *Israelites'* guilt, meaning the Levites would answer for Israelite encroachment, rather than putting the whole nation in danger (Milgrom 1989:155; e.g., NLT). In my view, the choice lies between the last two options, and the NLT's rendering fits the last option.

COMMENTARY

This chapter builds on the established priestly hierarchy (1:47-54; 3:1–4:49), which had just been threatened (ch 16) and then defended (ch 17). The regulations stipulated in this chapter applied to Aaron and his "father's family," which the NLT takes to mean his "relatives from the tribe of Levi" (18:1). They were responsible for the Tabernacle, the holiness of which is emphasized by calling it *hammiqdash* [TH4720, ZH5219], the "sacred place." The Levites dealt with unlawful intrusion by members of the laity, but only priests could deal with violations of the priesthood itself (18:1). Under Aaron's supervision, the Levites were warned "not to go near any of the sacred objects or the altar" (18:3a). A double sanction backed this: If violation occurred, the priests would die for their passive failure to preserve holiness against incursion, and the Levites would die for their active sin in violating God's holiness (18:3). Only the priests could conduct the sacred duties that occurred at the altar and inside the tent itself (18:5). The Levites were "spiritual lightning rods" (G. J. Wenham 1981:143; cf. Milgrom 1989:371; Milgrom 1970:31; Cole 2000:278) or "insulators who protected the Israelites from the force of God's wrath" (Harrison 1990:247 n. 60). Their obedience meant the Lord's fury would "never again blaze against the people of Israel" (18:5). The "never again" harkened back to the wrath that had already fallen on the people when factions overreached their cultic or civic aspirations (chs 12 and 16). God had chosen the Levites and assigned them to serve the priests at the Tabernacle (18:5; cf. 3:5-13). The same was the case for the priests (17:1-10; Heb 5:4).

Jesus told his apostles, "You didn't choose me. I chose you" (John 15:16; see Luke 6:13; John 6:70; Acts 1:24; 9:15; 10:41; Rom 9:11-16, 21; 1 Cor 9:16-18). The same holds true for disciples (1 John 4:10, 19), so none of us should usurp; we should remain within our callings (1 Cor 7:20-24).

Sacrificial Portions for the Priests (18:8-19). The Lord put the priests "in charge of all the holy offerings" that people brought to the Tabernacle, some of which became the priests' "permanent share" (18:8), as follows:

1. The "portion of the most holy offerings that is not burned on the fire . . . the grain offerings, sin offerings, and guilt offerings" (18:9). God granted it to the priests rather than requiring that altar flames consume it, but the food was still consecrated and could not be eaten as common food, any more than the church is to partake of the bread and wine without discerning the Lord's body (1 Cor 11:27-29). They were to "eat it as a most holy offering . . . treat it as most holy" (18:10); therefore, only ceremonially clean male members of the priestly families could eat these offering portions (18:9; cf. Lev 6:16, 26; 7:6).
2. The "sacred offerings and special offerings" (18:11). Numbers demonstrates the principle of graduated holiness, which extended even to the people's offerings. After describing the offerings that were "most holy," the legislation turned to other offerings, which were less holy, but still consecrated to the Lord (18:11). These were permitted to the whole priestly household, including women and resident servants, unless they were ceremonially unclean (18:11b; cf. Lev 7:31-34; 15:1-33; 22:3-8; 1 Sam 21:4). They were to eat them in a place that was ceremonially clean, though not in a "holy" place.
3. The "first crops," which would include "the best of the olive oil, new wine, and grain," a common merism for all the products of the soil (18:12-13; Exod 23:16-19; Lev 2:14; 23:17; Deut 18:4; 26:1-11). These, too, could be eaten by any ceremonially clean member of the priestly household (18:13).

4. "Everything in Israel that is specially set apart for the LORD" (18:14; cf. Lev 27:21, 28), things irretrievably dedicated to the Lord but not burnt as an offering.

5. The "firstborn of every mother, whether human or animal" (18:15-19; cf. 3:40-51; Exod 13:2, 12-15; 22:29; 34:19; Lev 27:1-13; Deut 12:17; 15:19-23). In theory, it would have been possible that each mother would dedicate her firstborn son, as Samuel's mother did; however, God made other arrangements. After being observed for a month to determine if they were viable (18:16), the firstborn sons were redeemed at a set rate (3:47; 18:16; Lev 27:6). The firstborn of clean animals could not be redeemed (18:17); they belonged to the priests. The priests splattered the blood at the altar and burned the fat to make "a pleasing aroma to the LORD" (18:17). Because they were not sin or guilt offerings, it will probably not do to consider this language of soothing or quieting as an indication of quieting God's wrath; instead, it is better to see in this the pleasure that God takes in fellowship with his people, who are eating in his presence. The meat was theirs to be shared with the entire priestly household (18:18). God described this as their "permanent share" (18:8), guaranteed by a lasting covenant with them and their descendants (18:19). It illustrates a permanent principle, which Paul cited as a basis for supporting those who preach the gospel (1 Cor 9:13).

Responsibilities of Levites (18:20-24). This section gives the reason for the privileges described in verses 8-19. The priests received no territorial tribal land allotment (18:20, 24). Instead, they were given 48 cities with some surrounding pasture, which were scattered throughout the other tribes' territories (34:16–35:34; Josh 13–21). God said, "I am your share and your allotment" (18:20), not that the priests and Levites "owned" the Lord, but in the sense the psalmist described: "LORD, you alone are my inheritance, my cup of blessing" (Ps 16:5; see also Pss 73:26; 142:5; Lam 3:24).

The Levites were paid with the "tithes from the entire land of Israel" (18:21). This text concerns a tithe of the field.[1] Some texts speak of the tithe of the field (or its monetary equivalent) being brought to be enjoyed in God's presence along with the Levites (Deut 12:6, 11, 17-19; 14:22-27). And every third year this tithe was to be distributed locally among the Levites, aliens, fatherless, and widows (Deut 14:28; 26:12).

Tithes were given as a sign of respect to God's priest (Gen 14:20) or as a gift to God (Gen 28:22); actually, the principle of both occasions was the same. It applied to everything and was based on the idea that Israel was God's tenant on the land (Lev 25:23). After captivity, the tithe became a Temple tax (Neh 10:38; 13:5, 10). Actually, it has that tone in this text (18:21), but under a monarchy, this could quickly degenerate into a royal tax (1 Sam 8:17).

The triple notice that the Levites had "no allotment of land" (18:20, 23, 24) finds its parallel in the New Testament reminder that early believers looked for a "heavenly homeland" (Heb 11:16) rather than an earthly citizenship.

Levites and the Wave Offerings (18:25-32). Verses 25-32 treat the Levitical obligations to the priesthood. They received a tithe from all the Israelites, and in turn, they gave a tithe to the priests, as though it were produce from their own fields and vineyards (18:26). The remainder belonged to the Levites. Their families could eat it anywhere they wanted, not just at the Tabernacle. Rather than being an expressly cultic meal, it was their "compensation" for Tabernacle service (18:31). They were "not [to] be considered guilty" for eating food offered to the Lord; nonetheless, they were to remain "careful not to treat the holy gifts of the people of Israel as though they were common" (18:32). The sanction against violating this holiness required death (18:32). The Israelites' offerings were to be without blemish; in turn, the Levites' offerings were to be "the best portions of the gifts" that Israel gave them (18:29). Postexilic failure to meet this requirement led to punishment (Mal 1:6-8).

Jesus and Paul expected that those who received spiritual ministry should pay the ministers properly (Matt 10:9-10; 1 Cor 9:3-10). For the earliest gospel preachers, having the Lord as their portion meant depending upon the hospitality of those who would receive the message as from the Lord (Matt 10:11; Luke 10:7) and living from resources drawn to their ministry (1 Cor 9:13; 1 Tim 5:18).

E N D N O T E
1. For tithe of the field, see 18:20-24, 27, 30; Deut 14:22-29; 26:12-15; Neh 10:37, 39; 13:5-12. Cf. tithe of the fields and flocks, Lev 27:30-33; 2 Chr 31:6.

◆   ## g. Two rituals for cleansing (19:1-22)

The LORD said to Moses and Aaron, [2]"Here is another legal requirement commanded by the LORD: Tell the people of Israel to bring you a red heifer, a perfect animal that has no defects and has never been yoked to a plow. [3]Give it to Eleazar the priest, and it will be taken outside the camp and slaughtered in his presence. [4]Eleazar will take some of its blood on his finger and sprinkle it seven times toward the front of the Tabernacle.* [5]As Eleazar watches, the heifer must be burned—its hide, meat, blood, and dung. [6]Eleazar the priest must then take a stick of cedar,* a hyssop branch, and some scarlet yarn and throw them into the fire where the heifer is burning.

[7]"Then the priest must wash his clothes and bathe himself in water. Afterward he may return to the camp, though he will remain ceremonially unclean until evening. [8]The man who burns the animal must also wash his clothes and bathe himself in water, and he, too, will remain unclean until evening. [9]Then someone who is ceremonially clean will gather up the ashes of the heifer and deposit them in a purified place outside the camp. They will be kept there for the community of Israel to use in the water for the purification ceremony. This ceremony is performed for the removal of sin. [10]The man who gathers up the ashes of the heifer must also wash his clothes, and he will remain ceremonially unclean until evening. This is a permanent law for the people of Israel and any foreigners who live among them.

[11]"All those who touch a dead human body will be ceremonially unclean for seven days. [12]They must purify themselves on the third and seventh days with the water of purification; then they will be purified. But if they do not do this on the third and

seventh days, they will continue to be unclean even after the seventh day. ¹³All those who touch a dead body and do not purify themselves in the proper way defile the LORD's Tabernacle, and they will be cut off from the community of Israel. Since the water of purification was not sprinkled on them, their defilement continues.

¹⁴"This is the ritual law that applies when someone dies inside a tent: All those who enter that tent and those who were inside when the death occurred will be ceremonially unclean for seven days. ¹⁵Any open container in the tent that was not covered with a lid is also defiled. ¹⁶And if someone in an open field touches the corpse of someone who was killed with a sword or who died a natural death, or if someone touches a human bone or a grave, that person will be defiled for seven days.

¹⁷"To remove the defilement, put some of the ashes from the burnt purification offering in a jar, and pour fresh water over them. ¹⁸Then someone who is ceremonially clean must take a hyssop branch and dip it into the water. That person

19:4 Hebrew *the Tent of Meeting.*   19:6 Or *juniper.*

must sprinkle the water on the tent, on all the furnishings in the tent, and on the people who were in the tent; also on the person who touched a human bone, or touched someone who was killed or who died naturally, or touched a grave. ¹⁹On the third and seventh days the person who is ceremonially clean must sprinkle the water on those who are defiled. Then on the seventh day the people being cleansed must wash their clothes and bathe themselves, and that evening they will be cleansed of their defilement.

²⁰"But those who become defiled and do not purify themselves will be cut off from the community, for they have defiled the sanctuary of the LORD. Since the water of purification has not been sprinkled on them, they remain defiled. ²¹This is a permanent law for the people. Those who sprinkle the water of purification must afterward wash their clothes, and anyone who then touches the water used for purification will remain defiled until evening. ²²Anything and anyone that a defiled person touches will be ceremonially unclean until evening."

NOTES

19:1 *Moses and Aaron.* The words "and Aaron" are lacking in some manuscripts, because "tell" and "you" (19:2) are singular, referring to Moses. The LXX and some Vulgate mss have singulars in 19:3 as well, supporting the idea that "and Aaron" was originally lacking.

19:2 *heifer.* Heb., *parah* [TH6510, ZH7239]. A *parah* may have had a calf and thus no longer be a heifer (1 Sam 6:7), so "cow" is more accurate (e.g., NJPS). Most English translations use "heifer," following the LXX (*damalis* [TG1151, ZG1239]), probably because the animal was young enough to have never been yoked.

no defects. Lit., "perfect [*temimah*], which has in her no defect [*mum*]." The term *temimah* [TH8549, ZH9459] means "whole, unscathed, free of blemish" (e.g., Exod 12:5; 29:1; Lev 1:3, 10), and *mum* [TH3971, ZH4583] means "spot, blemish, injury" (Lev 21:17, 21, 23).

19:6 *hyssop.* Heb., *'ezob* [TH231, ZH257]. "It may have been a designation of several labiate plants such as thyme (*Thymus capitatus* L.), sage (*Salvia tribola* L.), or marjoram (*Origanum maru* L.)" (Harrison 1990:256). Its hairy surface retained liquid, which made it ideal for sprinkling in cleansing rituals (19:18; Exod 12:22; Lev 14:4, 6, 49, 51).

scarlet yarn. Lit., "the red of worms," i.e., a dye from a crimson worm, so "scarlet stuff."

19:9 *ashes.* Heb., *'eper* [TH665, ZH709] (cf. *'apar* [TH6083, ZH6760], 19:17), indicating dust-like ashes, not the heavy ash from the altar (Snaith 1969:272).

water for the purification ceremony. Heb., *me niddah* [TH4325/5079, ZH4784/5614], meaning "water of impurity," perhaps "derived from a privative Piel, 'remove impurity'" (Milgrom 1989:160), hence "de-impurifying" (Budd 1984:213).

This ceremony is performed for the removal of sin. This phrase is parallel with *me niddah*, i.e., water to "de-defile" and to "de-sin."

19:12 *purify themselves.* Lit., "cleanse himself" (singular), not emphasizing masculinity but individual responsibility.

19:13 *cut off.* See note on 9:13.

19:17 *ashes.* Heb., *'apar* [TH6083, ZH6760] (dust); see note on *'eper* [TH665, ZH709] (ashes) at 19:9.

COMMENTARY

Leviticus speaks of two ways of purification: washing and then waiting until evening (Lev 11:28, 39; 15:16-18), or for more serious cases, waiting seven days and offering a sacrifice (Lev 14:10-20; 15:13-15, 28-30). Here we get purification "with a concoction of water that contains all the ingredients of a sin offering" (G. J. Wenham 1981:146). It seems like this legislation resolving contact with the dead would have fit better with Leviticus 11–15. Some suggest that it appears here because of the large numbers of dead in the judgment on Korah and his followers (Budd 1984:211-212); however, this passage concerns contact with the dead in everyday circumstances rather than during instances of divine judgment (E. W. Davies 1995b:194).

Red Heifer Ritual (19:1-10). As with nearly any sacrificial animal, the cow for this ritual was to be unblemished. It would not yet have been put to any common use (Levine 1993:461); therefore, it would have been "as close to virginal purity as one could expect in an animal" (Harrison 1990:255). It was brought to the priest Eleazar, which kept Aaron, the high priest, from being contaminated.[1] This process defiled everyone associated with concocting the purification water. So the production of this cleansing water was moved "outside the camp" (19:3), to the realm of uncleanness where persons defiled by skin diseases and other infirmities were sent. The Septuagint adds "to a clean place," a requirement that may seem oxymoronic given its location outside the camp, but one also required for burnt purification offerings (Lev 4:12). Levine explains why this happened in the wilderness rather than in the Tabernacle:

> This rite was not sacrificial, in the usual sense, but it bore a similarity to certain major expiatory sacrifices in which the element of riddance was operative. Rites of riddance were normally enacted outside the camp, for the obvious reason that the objective was to eliminate impurity through its distancing and destruction. Furthermore, . . . riddance implies the transfer of sinfulness and impurity to the victim, in this case, to the red cow. Wherever such transferal occurs, we are dealing with a contaminated object, and it would make little sense to retain such contamination inside the encampment. (1993:461)

The rabbis wondered how this cleaning water "'purifies the impure, and at the same time renders the pure impure'! So inscrutable was its nature—they said—that even King Solomon in his wisdom despaired of learning the meaning of the Red Heifer regulations" (Hertz 1977:652). The best we can say is that this rite is parallel with the scapegoat, as well as with the burnt offerings. Those who prepared what would be used as a purifying agent became defiled for the day, the same period of defilement experienced by the one who carried the remainder of a sin offering outside the camp to burn it (Lev 16:28). The participants may have experienced different levels of defilement—the supervising priest and the man who burned the cow had to wash their bodies and garments (19:7); however, the man who gathered the ashes this produced had only to wash his clothes (19:10).[2]

Sprinkling some of the blood "seven times" (19:4) symbolized dedication of the blood, and thus consecrating the whole animal (Noth 1968:140, citing Lev 4:6). This gesture from the outskirts of the camp was directed "toward the front of the Tabernacle" (19:4), visually linking the ritual to the sanctuary. Burning the blood, which was "the most potent cleansing and sanctifying agent," is unique here to the Old Testament (G. J. Wenham 1981:146). The "stick of cedar, a hyssop branch, and some scarlet" added materials that were also used in a purification rite for lepers (Lev 14), the only other place these three elements were combined. There, they were bundled and used as a sprinkler; here they are burnt to ashes. The aromatic cedar and hyssop may have been burnt as a pleasing aroma to the Lord, and the red suggests both fire and blood, both of which were purifying agents. Commentators commonly associate the cow's redness with blood, which was necessary for cleansing in Israel's rites (Cole 2000:306; E. W. Davies 1995b:197; Levine 1993:460; Milgrom 1989:440; Noordtzij 1983:168; Sturdy 1976:134).

A large bovine provided for the maximum amount of ashes (Ashley 1993:364; Cole 2000:306; Milgrom 1981:440). Once the animal, including its blood, was reduced to "the ultimate biodegradable condition" of a living being (Levine 1993:471), its ashes were deposited in a "purified place outside the camp," which almost seems like an oxymoron, since being outside the camp is generally associated with defilement. These ashes, when mixed with water, could subsequently function as "an instant sin offering"; however, its de-defiling and de-sinning properties were activated upon use, not during the preparation process, which defiled its agents. Offering a sin offering was difficult and expensive; mourners needing purification after contact with their recently dead family member had in this "an alternate remedy which marked the seriousness of the pollution caused by death, yet dealt with it without the cost and inconvenience of sacrifice" (G. J. Wenham 1981:146). E. W. Davies wonders whether Israel ever practiced this ritual on a regular basis, musing if perhaps the more general practice was washing in plain water to remove contamination incurred by contact with the dead (Lev 11:24-32; 22:4-6): "The Mishneh records that only seven or nine heifers were slain in all—one by Moses, one by Ezra, and the others at a later period (*Parah* 3.5). However, there is evidence to suggest that some such rite was performed by the Essenes at Qumran in an effort to uphold the proper standards of Levitical purity" (1995b:193-194, citing Bowman 1958 on 1QS 3:4-10). Nonetheless, the text calls it "a permanent law" (19:21), so we must think it was integral to purification practices.

This Old Testament provision for de-defiling and de-sinning foreshadowed the time when a fountain would be opened to cleanse the people from their impurities and sins (Zech 13:1). This was the psalmist's hope (Ps 51:2, 7), Isaiah's exhortation (Isa 1:16-18), and Ezekiel's promise (Ezek 36:25). Its fulfillment under the new covenant comes not by animal blood and water (Heb 9:13-14) but rather by Jesus' shed blood (1 John 1:7; 5:6; Rev 7:14). This cleansing is received by faith (Acts 15:9; 22:16; Heb 10:22) as a washing of the word (Eph 5:25-27) and cleansing by the Spirit (Titus 3:5). It is applied to the person who obeys the truth of the gospel (1 Pet 1:22).

Purification from Uncleanness (19:11-22). Contact with animal carcasses caused only a one-day impurity (Lev 11:24-40); however, contact with a human corpse caused a seven-day impurity (19:11). Other seven-day impurity situations required only a sin offering on the eighth day: a new mother (Lev 12:2), a person with gonorrhea (Lev 15:13, 28), or a recovered leper (Lev 14:10). But contamination by a corpse was more severe, and thus it required sin offerings on the third and seventh days (19:12).

It is interesting to note that no priestly involvement was required, only the help of "someone who is ceremonially clean" (19:18). Also a bit surprising is the silence about being banished from the camp during the temporary period of uncleanness. Perhaps the banishment is presupposed here (Noordtzij 1983:172); however, the Nazirite who was defiled in this same manner wasn't banished either (6:9-12).

The person's neglect or refusal of the purification ritual was a high-handed sin for which sacrifice was no longer possible, since they had refused the means of grace. Those who refused this water of purification would "defile the LORD's Tabernacle," so they were to be "cut off from the community of Israel" (19:13, 20). This defilement was contagious: Anything a defiled person touched became defiled (19:22). Exposure to a human corpse defiled anyone in the tent where death occurred (19:14) or even an open container in that tent (19:15). Touching even a bone or grave defiled (19:16), so graves were whitewashed, to help people avoid inadvertent contact with them (Matt 23:27; Luke 11:44). But God provided a means of cleansing, even from serious defilement.

This causes us to think of the New Testament warning against defiling the temple of the Lord, whether our physical body (1 Cor 3:16; 6:19; 2 Cor 6:16) or the church body (Eph 2:21-22; 1 Pet 2:5). The new covenant means of purification, by the blood of Jesus Christ, protects us from that defilement.

ENDNOTES
1. Budd thinks it may have been because Aaron was confined to the sanctuary (1984:212, citing Lev 21:10-12); however, Lev 21 doesn't so much confine the high priest to the Tabernacle as forbid him to attend to a dead body. Some rabbis suggest

that Aaron's involvement with the golden calf incident excluded him: "because the prosecuting counsel cannot become the defending counsel"; i.e., Aaron, who had caused the sin, was not the fitting person to atone for it (Hertz 1977:652, citing Moses Haddarshan, quote by Rashi).
2. Some commentators think bathing was also implied for the one who gathered the ashes (cf. 19:7), which is possible though unstated in 19:10 (Cole 2000:308, following Milgrom 1989:160).

3. Moving from Kadesh to Moab (20:1–21:35)
a. Moses strikes the rock (20:1-13)

In the first month of the year,* the whole community of Israel arrived in the wilderness of Zin and camped at Kadesh. While they were there, Miriam died and was buried.

2There was no water for the people to drink at that place, so they rebelled against Moses and Aaron. 3The people blamed Moses and said, "If only we had died in the LORD's presence with our brothers! 4Why have you brought the congregation of the LORD's people into this wilderness to die, along with all our livestock? 5Why did you make us leave Egypt and bring us here to this terrible place? This land has no grain, no figs, no grapes, no pomegranates, and no water to drink!"

6Moses and Aaron turned away from the people and went to the entrance of the Tabernacle,* where they fell face down on the ground. Then the glorious presence of the LORD appeared to them, 7and the LORD said to Moses, 8"You and Aaron must take the staff and assemble the entire community. As the people watch, speak to the rock over there, and it will pour out its water. You will provide enough water from the rock to satisfy the whole community and their livestock."

9So Moses did as he was told. He took the staff from the place where it was kept before the LORD. 10Then he and Aaron summoned the people to come and gather at the rock. "Listen, you rebels!" he shouted. "Must we bring you water from this rock?" 11Then Moses raised his hand and struck the rock twice with the staff, and water gushed out. So the entire community and their livestock drank their fill.

12But the LORD said to Moses and Aaron, "Because you did not trust me enough to demonstrate my holiness to the people of Israel, you will not lead them into the land I am giving them!" 13This place was known as the waters of Meribah (which means "arguing") because there the people of Israel argued with the LORD, and there he demonstrated his holiness among them.

20:1 The first month of the ancient Hebrew lunar calendar usually occurs within the months of March and April. The number of years since leaving Egypt is not specified. 20:6 Hebrew the Tent of Meeting.

NOTES

20:1 *the first month of the year.* Lit., "the first new moon" (Exod 19:1; cf. Num 1:1; 7:1; 9:1, 5; 10:11; 33:3, 38). The unstated year must be the fortieth, since the summary of Israel's itinerary places Kadesh right before the stop where Aaron died in the fifth month of the fortieth year (33:38).

wilderness of Zin. This was an area comprising the drainage area of the Nahal Zin (13:21), between the Sinai desert and Judah to the west of the southern end of the Dead Sea.

Kadesh. This was also known as Kadesh-barnea (32:8; 34:4; Deut 1:2, 19; 2:14; 9:23; Josh 10:41; 14:6; 15:3), the principal oasis in the wilderness of Zin (13:26). Wenham suggests that Kadesh-barnea referred to a group of wells, one of which retains *Kadesh* in its name to this day, i.e., 'Ain Qadeis (G. J. Wenham 1981:150 n. 1). It is now more common to identify Kadesh-barnea with 'Ain Qudeirat (Y. Aharoni, Avi-Yonah, Rainey, and Safrai 2002; Har-El 1983:217).

20:4-5 *Why? . . . Why?* This is a common and acceptable term in biblical laments (Pss 2:1; 10:1; 22:1; 42:9; 43:2; 44:23-24; 74:1, 11; 79:10; 80:12; 88:14; 115:2); however, in Numbers it is Israel's rebellious "why?" that we encounter primarily.

20:9 *the staff.* The reference to "the staff" (lit., "his staff," 20:11) favors Moses's staff (Hirsch 1971:366-367; Levine 1993:489; Milgrom 1989:165; Noth 1968:145). The mention of its being "kept before the LORD" (20:9), however, favor's Aaron's staff (Ashley 1993:382; Budd 1984:218; Harrison 1990:264; Noordtzij 1983:176; G. J. Wenham 1981:149). So "his" probably indicates that Moses had Aaron's staff in his possession for this incident. Since Moses placed Aaron's rod before the Lord, he could take it up again (Budd 1984:218).

20:10 *Must we.* Translation options include the following: (1) "Shall we?" (ASV, NASB, RSV, NRSV, ESV, NJB, NJPS), indicating Moses's hesitation about whether it was right to do so; (2) "Must we?" (Ashley 1993:384; Noordtzij 1983:177; KJV, NLT, NET), indicating reluctance; (3) "Can we?" indicating doubt about the possibility; or perhaps (4) a taunt: "Do you disbelieving rebels think we can really bring forth water for you from this rock?" (Levine 1993:490). I incline toward a view that the statement taunts Israel, "Are we going to have to do this to shut you up?" This taunt included "the fatal pronoun [i.e., 'we'] by which Moses ascribes the miracle to himself and to Aaron" (Milgrom 1989:165).

COMMENTARY

Here begins the last of the three travel narratives of Exodus—Numbers: Red Sea to Sinai (Exod 13-19), Sinai to Kadesh (Num 10:11-12:16), and Kadesh to the Transjordan (Num 20-21). G. J. Wenham notes that all three narratives share certain motifs (1981:148): (1) battles with enemies (14:45; 21:1-35; Exod 14; 17:8-16), (2) complaints about lack of food and water and divine provision (ch 11; 20:2-13; Exod 16-17), (3) the need for faith (14:11; 20:12; Exod 14:31), and (4) the role of Moses, Aaron, and Miriam (ch 12; 20:1; Exod 15:20). But before the travel narrative resumes, we get the notice that all the highest members of Israel's first-generation leadership are excluded from entering the land. The details of the deaths of Miriam (20:1) and Aaron (20:22-29) bracket Moses's disobedience, which excludes him as well (20:8-13).

In the anniversary month of Israel's deliverance from Egypt (20:1; see Exod 12:1-2), the people arrived back at Kadesh, where the unbelieving scouts had misled a rebellious people into rejecting their Promised Land (13:26). Here, a terse note tells us that "Miriam died and was buried" (20:1). Next we encounter another murmuring story about water, reminiscent of an earlier occasion at Rephidim in the wilderness of Sin (Exod 17:1-7). Israel arrived back at Kadesh-barnea, where the water sources had been depleted, perhaps by their on-and-off encampment there. So Israel moaned about lacking water and even had the brass to complain, "no figs, no grapes, no pomegranates" (20:5). Of course, they could have had this in profusion, but for their rebellion (13:23).

When Moses heard this renewed complaint, he fell into his typical intercessory stance, "face down on the ground" (20:6; cf. 14:5; 16:4, 22). God told Moses to "speak to the rock" before the assembly of Israel (20:8). Instead Moses took "the staff" from the Ark (20:9, 11; cf. 17:10; Heb 9:4) and lashed out verbally at the people and physically at the rock. He raged that they were rebels (20:10; cf. 17:10). He adopted "the fatal pronoun" *we* (Milgrom 1989:165), forgetting that he was only God's instrument, not the performer of the miracle. Milgrom's survey of the medieval Jewish commentators' definitions of Moses's sin is representative:

1. Moses's action in striking the rock: (a) that he struck it instead of speaking (Rashi, Rashbam, Arama, Shadal, Malbim); (b) that he chose it although the people wanted another rock (Orah Hayyim, Yalqut, Lekakh Tov); (c) that he struck it twice instead of once (*Targum Pseudo-Jonathan*, Ibn Ezra).
2. His character, shown by (a) his blazing temper (Maimonides, Ibn Ezra, Tanhuma B. 4:210); (b) his cowardice (in fleeing to the sanctuary; 20:6; Albo, Biur); (c) his callousness (in mourning for Miriam while his people died of thirst; Yalqut, Lekakh Tov).
3. His words, (a) which in the form of a question were misconstrued as doubting God (Meir ha-Kohen, Ramban); (b) which actually doubted God (Tanhuma B. 4:121-122; *Deuteronomy Rabbah* 19:13-14); (c) calling Israel "rebels" (Ibn Ezra); (d) *notsi'*, "shall we draw forth . . ." (Hananel, Ramban). (Milgrom 1989:448)

Ruling out the other choices and focusing on arguments against 1a and 1c, Milgrom (1989:452) opts for 3d: "Moses and Aaron might be interpreted as having put themselves forth as God." Perhaps a little of all three of these undermined God's holiness in front of Israel.

Occasional disobedience chips away at faith even as a little leaven can permeate a whole lump of dough (1 Cor 5:6). Despite Moses's long and faithful service (12:7; Heb 3:2, 5), at nearly the last moment, he, too, was excluded from the Promised Land (20:12). Moses blamed Israel for provoking him into this behavior (Deut 1:37; 3:26; 4:21), an explanation the psalmist accepted (Ps 106:32). But here God blamed Moses: inwardly—"you did not trust me"—and outwardly—you did not "demonstrate my holiness to the people of Israel" (20:12). Moses failed to reach the very destination to which he successfully led the nation. Perhaps this story lay behind Paul's apprehension, "I fear that after preaching to others I myself might be disqualified" (1 Cor 9:27). Certainly it demonstrates the principle that from him to whom much is given, much is required (Luke 12:48), which is why teachers are judged more strictly (Jas 3:1).

So this place got another negative memorializing place name; because they had "argued with the LORD," it was named "Meribah," or "Quarrelsville" (20:13). They quarreled with Moses (20:3), but as always, that implied a quarrel with God, whether both were mentioned (21:5) or not (14:2-4, 9, 27). Moses publicly failed to demonstrate it (20:12), so God himself "demonstrated his holiness among them" (20:13), both by imposing a public sentence upon Moses and by maintaining his people despite Moses's fuming, faithless disobedience.

◆   ### b. Journey around Edom (20:14-21)

¹⁴While Moses was at Kadesh, he sent ambassadors to the king of Edom with this message:

"This is what your relatives, the people of Israel, say: You know all the hardships we have been through. ¹⁵Our ancestors went down to Egypt, and we lived there a long time, and we and our ancestors were brutally mistreated by the Egyptians. ¹⁶But when we cried out to the LORD, he heard us and sent an angel who brought us out of Egypt. Now we are camped at Kadesh, a town on the border of your land. ¹⁷Please let us travel through your land. We will be careful not to go through your fields and vineyards. We won't even drink water from your wells. We will stay on the king's road and never leave it until we have passed through your territory."

¹⁸But the king of Edom said, "Stay out of my land, or I will meet you with an army!"

¹⁹The Israelites answered, "We will stay on the main road. If our livestock drink your water, we will pay for it. Just let us pass through your country. That's all we ask."

²⁰But the king of Edom replied, "Stay out! You may not pass through our land." With that he mobilized his army and marched out against them with an imposing force. ²¹Because Edom refused to allow Israel to pass through their country, Israel was forced to turn around.

NOTES

20:16 *angel*. Heb., *mal'ak* [TH4397, ZH4855]. Some suggest a connection between "messenger" (*mal'ak*) and "prophet/messenger" (*nabi'* [TH5030, ZH5566]), since elsewhere we read that the Lord led and guarded the people "by a prophet" (Hos 12:13). Hertz refers "to Moses, the God-sent liberator and guide" (1977:657); however, it is more likely that Moses was claiming that an angel of the Lord led them (cf. Exod 14:19; 23:20; 32:34; 33:2), phrasing designed to impress the Edomites (Ashley 1993:39).

20:17 *king's road*. Fortresses from the Bronze Age through the Iron Age (2200–1000 BC) have been discovered at intervals along this trade route on the ridge east of the Jordan River, between Damascus and the Gulf of Aqaba (Ashley 1993:391-392; Harrison 1990:270).

20:19 *main road*. Heb., *mesillah* [TH4546, ZH5019], "a track firmed with stones or fill" (HALOT). Some mss of the Samaritan Pentateuch read *mesulla'*, "rocky road," and the LXX reads, "through the mountains," implying an alternative, more difficult route.

COMMENTARY

Earlier the Israelites had failed to enter Canaan from the south (14:40-45); now they would try from the east, across the Jordan. The route from their base at Kadesh to the Jordan River would take them through the eastern Arabah, which was Edomite territory. So Moses sent a note that followed a common ancient Near Eastern pattern for diplomatic exchanges, like we see in the Amarna letters (ANET 482-490; Harrison 1990:270; G. J. Wenham 1981:153): (1) recipient = "king of Edom" (20:14), (2) sender and his status = "your relatives, the people of Israel" (20:14), (3) circumstances prompting the petition = "hardships we have been through" (20:14-16), and (4) petition = "let us travel through your land" (20:17).

Moses played on every theme that could help Israel's case. First he addressed the monarchial ego (20:14a). We read of 14 "clan leaders" (Gen 36:15-19) and eight kings ruling Edom (Gen 36:31-39). A diplomatic dispatch addressed "'to the king of Edom' could not fail in stroking the ego of a petty ruler in that territory" (Ashley 1993:389). Then Moses spoke of brotherly ties (20:14b-15a). A brother-nation relationship between Israel and Edom went back to Jacob and Esau, although it was mostly a negative relationship from Jacob's trickery on through Edom's unrelenting hostility (Amos 1:11; Obad 1:10, 12). Moses mentioned their hardship in Egypt, which became a staple of Israel's confession when bringing firstfruits to the Tabernacle (Deut 26:5-10). Then Moses spoke of divine support (20:16). Without elaborating on the power of Egypt, of which Edom was of course well aware, Moses hastened to impress on Edom the power of Israel's God: The sending of his "angel" or "messenger" was sufficient to break Egypt's resistance and to liberate Israel. Moses thus implied that Israel was backed by a strong God and that Edom should think twice before refusing its request (Noordtzij 1983:181-182). Moses then spoke of peaceful intentions (20:17, 19). Moses pledged that Israel was only in transit; they wouldn't disrupt agriculture (20:17a), use up resources (20:17b), or wander around the countryside (20:17c).

But Edom responded, "Stay out" and threatened a military response for any move into its territory (20:18). So Moses added further reassurances to put to rest any worries about any potential military or economic threat (20:19). The answer was still "stay out" (20:20), which forced Israel "to turn around" (20:21), heading south to bypass Edom's territory even though they were trying to move north for a Jordan crossing.

◆   ### c. The death of Aaron (20:22-29)

22The whole community of Israel left Kadesh and arrived at Mount Hor. 23There, on the border of the land of Edom, the LORD said to Moses and Aaron, 24"The time has come for Aaron to join his ancestors in death. He will not enter the land I am giving the people of Israel, because the two of you rebelled against my instructions concerning the water at Meribah. 25Now take Aaron and his son Eleazar up Mount Hor. 26There you will remove Aaron's priestly garments and put them on Eleazar, his son. Aaron will die there and join his ancestors."

27So Moses did as the LORD commanded. The three of them went up Mount Hor together as the whole community watched. 28At the summit, Moses removed the priestly garments from Aaron and put them on Eleazar, Aaron's son. Then Aaron died there on top of the mountain, and Moses and Eleazar went back down. 29When the people realized that Aaron had died, all Israel mourned for him thirty days.

NOTES

20:22 *Mount Hor.* This was Aaron's death site (33:38; Deut 32:50), although another report says he died at Moserah, which was six stages before Mount Hor (Deut 10:6; cf. Num 33:30). Harrison (1990:272) eliminates any conflict in place names, saying the name *moserah* [TH4147A/4149, ZH4593/4594] (chastisement) was applied to the event of the death itself, not to the location of Aaron's death. The traditional site, Jebel Nabi Harun, "the Mount of the prophet Aaron" is near Petra and thus in the heart of Edom, far from its border (Milgrom 1989:169; see also Josephus *Antiquities* 4.82-84). Aharoni tentatively suggests 'Imaret el-Khureishe (Y. Aharoni, Avi-Yonah, Rainey, and Safrai 2002).

20:24 *join his ancestors in death.* Like the phrases "gather to one's fathers" or "sleeping with one's fathers" (Judg 2:10; 1 Kgs 1:21; 14:31; 2 Kgs 22:20, NASB), this refers literally to an honorable burial in the family tomb, which signified being reunited with ancestors in the afterlife in Sheol, the opposite of being "cut off" from one's ancestors (Jer 8:2; 25:33; Ezek 29:5). Of course, neither Aaron nor Moses were buried in an ancestral grave, so we shouldn't make too much of the literal sense (Ashley 1993:395).

20:26 *remove Aaron's priestly garments.* The sense of the verb is to "strip," often with the idea of punishment or degradation (Gen 37:23; 1 Sam 31:9-10; 1 Chr 10:9; Ezek 16:39; 23:26; Hos 2:3; Mic 3:3). "In no case does this stripping happen with the permission of the one stripped"; therefore, perhaps it shows some sense of demotion in favor of another's elevation (Milgrom 1989:170). See the regulations about garment transferring from one person to another (Exod 29:29).

COMMENTARY

Aaron's death merits only a low-key report, though it parallels the story of Moses's subsequent death: (1) Both occurred on a mountain (20:22-28; Deut 34:1-4); (2) neither was allowed to enter the land (20:24; Deut 34:4); (3) mourning lasted for 30 days (20:29; Deut 34:8); and (4) a transfer of leadership was effected (20:28; Deut 34:9). One difference was that Moses at least got to overlook the Promised Land (Deut 3:27; 34:1-4). Despite Aaron's mostly faithful service as Moses's "prophet" (Exod 7:1), Aaron had joined Moses in the intolerable offense at Meribah (20:10). So it came time to transfer the office from Aaron to his son Eleazar. Removing Aaron's priestly garb and enrobing Eleazar with it not only commissioned Eleazar; it also decommissioned Aaron. This may be compared with Moses laying his hands on Joshua as his successor (27:20), or even more with the transfer from Elijah to Elisha, which was symbolized by a transfer of a garment (1 Kgs 19:19; 2 Kgs 2:13). This ceremony was something that "the whole community watched," not necessarily because they could see what was happening on the mountain, but because they had watched Aaron leave robed as the priest and saw Eleazar return enrobed—without Aaron. The people extended mourning beyond the usual seven-day mourning period (Gen 50:10; 1 Sam 31:13; 1 Chr 10:12). Instead they mourned for 30 days (20:29), as they later would for Moses (Deut 34:8).

The New Testament sees Aaron's blemished priesthood as being an antitype of the perfect priesthood of Christ, who made the old priesthood obsolete (Heb 4:14–10:18). Christ, our great high priest, intercedes for us (Heb 9:7-15); he entered the heavenly temple once for all (Heb 9:24), as Aaron entered the Most Holy Place on each Day of Atonement (Lev 16:12).

◆   ## d. Trouble on the way to Moab (21:1-35)

The Canaanite king of Arad, who lived in the Negev, heard that the Israelites were approaching on the road through Atharim. So he attacked the Israelites and took some of them as prisoners. ²Then the people of Israel made this vow to the LORD: "If you will hand these people over to us, we will completely destroy* all their towns." ³The LORD heard the Israelites' request and gave them victory over the Canaanites. The Israelites completely destroyed them and their towns, and the place has been called Hormah* ever since.

⁴Then the people of Israel set out from Mount Hor, taking the road to the Red Sea* to go around the land of Edom. But the people grew impatient with the long journey, ⁵and they began to speak against God and Moses. "Why have you brought us out of Egypt to die here in the wilderness?" they complained. "There is nothing to eat here and nothing to drink. And we hate this horrible manna!"

⁶So the LORD sent poisonous snakes among the people, and many were bitten and died. ⁷Then the people came to Moses and cried out, "We have sinned by speaking against the LORD and against you. Pray that the LORD will take away the snakes." So Moses prayed for the people.

⁸Then the LORD told him, "Make a replica of a poisonous snake and attach it to a pole. All who are bitten will live if they simply look at it!" ⁹So Moses made a snake out of bronze and attached it to a pole. Then anyone who was bitten by a snake could look at the bronze snake and be healed!

¹⁰The Israelites traveled next to Oboth and camped there. ¹¹Then they went on to Iye-abarim, in the wilderness on the eastern border of Moab. ¹²From there they traveled to the valley of Zered Brook and set up camp. ¹³Then they moved out and camped on the far side of the Arnon River, in the wilderness adjacent to the territory of the Amorites. The Arnon is the boundary line between the Moabites and the Amorites. ¹⁴For this reason The Book of the Wars of the LORD speaks of "the town of Waheb in the area of Suphah, and the ravines of the Arnon River, ¹⁵and the ravines that extend as far as the settlement of Ar on the border of Moab."

¹⁶From there the Israelites traveled to Beer,* which is the well where the LORD said to Moses, "Assemble the people, and I will give them water." ¹⁷There the Israelites sang this song:

"Spring up, O well!
    Yes, sing its praises!
¹⁸ Sing of this well,
    which princes dug,
which great leaders hollowed out
    with their scepters and staffs."

Then the Israelites left the wilderness and proceeded on through Mattanah, ¹⁹Nahaliel, and Bamoth. ²⁰After that they went to the valley in Moab where Pisgah Peak overlooks the wasteland.*

²¹The Israelites sent ambassadors to King Sihon of the Amorites with this message:

²²"Let us travel through your land. We will be careful not to go through your fields and vineyards. We won't even drink water from your wells. We will stay on the king's road until we have passed through your territory."

²³But King Sihon refused to let them cross his territory. Instead, he mobilized his entire army and attacked Israel in the wilderness, engaging them in battle at Jahaz. ²⁴But the Israelites slaughtered them with their swords and occupied their land from the Arnon River to the Jabbok River. They went only as far as the Ammonite border because the boundary of the Ammonites was fortified.*

²⁵So Israel captured all the towns of the Amorites and settled in them, including the city of Heshbon and its surrounding villages. ²⁶Heshbon had been the capital of King Sihon of the Amorites. He had defeated a former Moabite king and seized

all his land as far as the Arnon River. ²⁷Therefore, the ancient poets wrote this about him:

"Come to Heshbon and let it be rebuilt!
    Let the city of Sihon be restored.
²⁸A fire flamed forth from Heshbon,
    a blaze from the city of Sihon.
It burned the city of Ar in Moab;
    it destroyed the rulers of the Arnon heights.
²⁹What sorrow awaits you, O people of Moab!
You are finished, O worshipers of Chemosh!
Chemosh has left his sons as refugees,
    his daughters as captives of Sihon,
    the Amorite king.
³⁰We have utterly destroyed them,
    from Heshbon to Dibon.

We have completely wiped them out
    as far away as Nophah and
    Medeba.*"

³¹So the people of Israel occupied the territory of the Amorites. ³²After Moses sent men to explore the Jazer area, they captured all the towns in the region and drove out the Amorites who lived there. ³³Then they turned and marched up the road to Bashan, but King Og of Bashan and all his people attacked them at Edrei. ³⁴The LORD said to Moses, "Do not be afraid of him, for I have handed him over to you, along with all his people and his land. Do the same to him as you did to King Sihon of the Amorites, who ruled in Heshbon." ³⁵And Israel killed King Og, his sons, and all his subjects; not a single survivor remained. Then Israel occupied their land.

21:2 The Hebrew term used here refers to the complete consecration of things or people to the LORD, either by destroying them or by giving them as an offering; also in 21:3.   21:3 *Hormah* means "destruction."   21:4 Hebrew *sea of reeds.*   21:16 *Beer* means "well."   21:20 Or *overlooks Jeshimon.*   21:24 Or *because the terrain of the Ammonite frontier was rugged;* Hebrew reads *because the boundary of the Ammonites was strong.*   21:30 Or *until fire spread to Medeba.* The meaning of the Hebrew is uncertain.

NOTES

21:1 *Arad.* This is the name of an important city in the early Bronze Age. But it was destroyed about 2650 BC and unoccupied when the conquest happened (Y. Aharoni, Amiran, and M. Aharoni 1993), i.e., lacking "Canaanite settlements" (Budd 1984:230). So perhaps it is another site or even the name of the region, which may have had its capital at Hormah (Cole 2000:344; G. J. Wenham 1981:155), although Josh 12:14 distinguishes Arad from Hormah.

road through Atharim. Heb., *'atharim* [TH871, ZH926], a designation that confused the ancient versions, which omitted a character to speak of the "way of the spies" (*tarim;* cf. *tur* [TH8446, ZH9365]), i.e., the path taken earlier by the scouts (e.g., *Targum Onkelos,* Peshitta, Vulgate, KJV, ASV mg); however, it is hard to see how *tarim* would be expanded to the enigmatic *'atharim* (Cole 2000:345).

21:5 *horrible manna.* This term (*qeloqel* [TH7052, ZH7848]) may refer to "lightness" (from *qalal* [TH7043, ZH7837], i.e., to something *insubstantial*); however, it might be related to *qelalah* [TH7045, ZH7839], "to curse" (e.g., Gen 27:13; Deut 28:15, 45, etc.). Earlier English translations understood the term *qeloqel* to be related to *qalal* and went for "light" bread (KJV, ASV, JPS) or "meager" fare (NJB); however, most English translations now contain something like "worthless" (NKJV, RSV, ESV, NET) or "miserable" (NASB, NRSV, NIV, NEB, REB, NJPS). Even more in line with understanding the term *qeloqel* as related to *qelalah,* Snaith says, "Almost any derogatory word will do" (1969:280).

21:6 *poisonous snakes.* Heb., *hannekhashim hasserapim.* Lit., "fiery snakes." Some think it refers to their appearance, i.e., copper-red colored (Budd 1984:234; Coats 1968:117 n. 51) or fire-breathing, like those known in Egyptian lore (Joines 1974:44-45). The term is also the term used for the angels around the Lord's throne (Isa 6:2, 6) and possibly for flying serpents (Isa 14:29; 30:6, KJV); however, these snakes don't engage people in mythological terms of fire-breathing dragons flying through the air but rather like hissing snakes writhing in the dust. The LXX rendering "deadly snakes" (*opheis tous thanatountas* [TG3789/2289, ZG4058/2506]) is more to the point. It focuses on the venomous bite, which causes fiery inflammation. Indeed, the term *sarap* [TH8314, ZH8597] (poisonous) can be listed alongside *nakhash* [TH5175, ZH5729] (snake) and *'aqrab* [TH6137, ZH6832] (scorpion); see Deut 8:15.

21:9 bronze. This was either a copper alloy hardened with other metals (Snaith 1969:172), as it undoubtedly means in some places (1 Sam 17:5; 1 Kgs 4:13), or copper itself (Ashley 1993:405; Budd 1984:234; Gray 1903:278; G. J. Wenham 1981:157). Note the lexical similarity between "copper" (*nekhoshet* [TH5178, ZH5733]) and "serpent" (*nakhash* [TH5175, ZH5729])—the Hebrew for "bronze snake" is an alliterative wordplay. The camp would have been near Timna, a copper production region at the northern end of the Gulf of Aqabah, where archaeologists have found a tent-shrine with the remains of a five-inch copper serpent with a gilded head (Rothenberg 1972:129-132, 152, 183-184). Bronze serpent images have been discovered at Gezer, Hazor, Megiddo, and Beth-shemesh (Joines 1968; Joines 1974:62ff.).

21:11 Iye-abarim. Lit., "the ruins on the far side," i.e., in the Transjordan.

21:12 Zered Brook. This flows from the east into the southern end of the Dead Sea.

21:14 speaks of "the town of Waheb in the area of Suphah." Many commentators assume something is missing, such as a verb for traveling in that area; however, perhaps it is just an ellipsis. The KJV followed the Vulgate in changing *supah* to *yam sup* ("what he did in the Red Sea"). Christensen (1974) proposes emending *'eth-waheb* [TH2052, ZH2259] to *'athah yhwh* [TH857/3068, ZH910/3378], "the LORD came to," thus providing a verb for the place names. The Samaritan Pentateuch reads "Waheb on the Reed Sea," and LXX reads "he has set Zoob aflame."

21:15 settlement of Ar. Or "seat of Ar" (E. W. Davies 1995b:221), probably Moab's ancient capital (Deut 2:9, 18; Isa 15:1), which was Ar of Moab (21:28).

21:16 Beer. Lit., "well"; a common part of place names: "Beer" (Judg 9:21), "Beeroth" ("wells," 2 Sam 4:2), and "Beer-elim" in Moab (Isa 15:8).

21:19 Nahaliel. This means "river of God" or perhaps "mighty river," taking *'el* [TH410, ZH445] not as "God" but as an adjective for powerful.

Bamoth. This was probably Bamoth-baal, located between Dibon and Beth-baal-meon (Josh 13:17). Some identify it with the Beth-bamoth of the Moabite Stone (line 27; ANET 320-321; COS 2.23:138).

21:21 Amorites. This term has various references: Canaanites in general (Gen 15:16), peoples living west of the Jordan (Josh 5:1), inhabitants of the region of Judah (Josh 10:5), inhabitants of the Negev and area south of the Dead Sea (Gen 14:7). Here it is the inhabitants of the land east of the Dead Sea, stretching from the Arnon Gorge in the south to the Wadi Jabbok in the north (21:24), having a capital in Heshbon.

21:23 Jahaz. This is possibly Khirbet el-Medeiyineh. It is mentioned in the Moabite Stone (lines 18-21; ANET 320-321; COS 2.23:138) as occupied by the Israelite king Omri (885-873 BC) when he was fighting the Moabite ruler Mesha, though it later reverted to Moabite control (2 Kgs 3:4-27).

21:24 the boundary of the Ammonites was fortified. This is the reading of the MT; this border was not likely that imposing. The LXX (cf. NASB, RSV) reads "the boundary of the Ammonites was Iazer" (cf. Jazer, 21:32), a reading which some scholars follow (Budd 1984:242), indicating a site east of the Jordan, probably Khirbet es-Sar.

21:28 rulers of the Arnon heights. Lit., "lords (*ba'ale* [TH1167, ZH1251]) of the high places/ heights of Arnon," perhaps a reference to the officiating priests at cultic shrines (E. W. Davies 1995b:232), though Ashley (1993:425) thinks not: "The Targum took 'heights' (*bamoth* [TH1116, ZH1195]) in the sense of 'high places,' i.e., Canaanite shrines, and the 'lords' (in MT) to be Canaanite priests. But *bamoth* here probably means only 'hill country' (Mic 3:12; Jer 26:18; Ezek 36:2), or perhaps 'strategic places' (i.e., 'the high ground'; Deut 32:13; Isa 58:14)." This is probably not a proper noun, such as Bamoth-Arnon (de Vaulx 1972:246) or Bamoth by the Arnon (NJPS). Some even suggest reading *bala'* [TH1104, ZH1180], i.e., "swallowed" (cf. LXX, *katepien* [TG2666, ZG2927]), which makes a nice parallel with "burned" (LXX, *katephagen* [TG2719, ZG2983]) (Ashley 1993:416, 425; Budd 1984:242; Snaith 1969:174; G. J. Wenham 1981:162 n. 3).

21:29 *Chemosh has left his sons as refugees, his daughters as captives of Sihon.* The Moabite Stone has King Mesha saying, "Chemosh was angry with his land" and so he let Israel oppress Moab "many days" under Omri and Ahab (ANET 320-321; COS 2.23).

21:30 *as far away as Nophah and Medeba.* Heb., *'ad-nopakh 'asher 'ad-medeba'.* Lit., "unto Nophah, which is unto Medeba." The MT has a point over the Resh (r) in *'asher* [TH834, ZH889] (which), indicating doubt about it, and indeed the Samaritan Pentateuch and LXX omit the Resh, reading *'esh* [TH784, ZH836], i.e., "*fire* as far as Medeba" (Budd 1984:242; NAB, NEB, NJB, RSV, NRSV, ESV).

21:32 *Jazer.* This was a boundary of the Ammonites (21:24), probably Khirbet es-Sar (Y. Aharoni, Avi-Yonah, Rainey, and Safrai 2002:48, map 52).

21:33 *Edrei.* This is modern Dera.

COMMENTARY

Chapter 21 has four units: (1) victory at Hormah (21:1-3); (2) the plague of fiery serpents (21:4-9); (3) the approach to Moab (21:10-20); and (4) victory over Sihon and Og (21:21-35).

Victory at Hormah (21:1-3). Earlier, Israel had been clobbered and chased all the way to Hormah (14:45). At the same place, God now granted Israel a total reversal of that thorough defeat. If we take the place name *khormah* [TH2767, ZH3055] as an alliterative hint at *kherem* [TH2764, ZH3051] warfare, we may see here a reference to the total-war policy endorsed by Deuteronomy's treatment of Yahweh war (Deut 7).

The Plague of Fiery Serpents (21:4-9). Reversing their journey to avoid Edom (20:21), Israel took "the road to the Red Sea" (21:4). They got cranky and whined about food one last time (cf. 11:4-6; Exod 16). Even speaking against Moses implied a complaint against God (14:27, 29, 35; 16:11; Exod 16:7). But here, for the first time, the record explicitly charges them with finding fault with God. Why had God and Moses brought them "out of Egypt to die . . . in the wilderness" (21:5)—as though they any longer had a choice in this matter (cf. 11:4-6; 14:2-4). Their "daily bread" revolted them (Matt 6:11; Luke 11:3) though it was angel's food (Ps 78:25). "When a person's heart is intent on rebellion and beset by discontent, even the best of gifts from the Lord can lose their savor; nothing will fully satisfy until the heart is made right" (Cole 2000:347).

That brought on a plague of venomous snakes, and judgment always aroused Moses's intercession. Surprisingly, God's response was to tell Moses, "make a replica of a poisonous snake" to put on a pole. In the ancient Near East, snakes were often symbols of life and fertility, and in Egypt, snake images might have been used to ward off snake bites; however, in the Old Testament they symbolized death, sin, and the curse (Gen 3; Lev 11:41). And it was the latter rather than the former use that Moses drew on. "Just as in the ordinary sacrifices, the participant had to identify with the sacrifice by laying his hand on the animal's head, so in this instance with the bronze serpent, 'looking at it' was the equivalent of manual contact" (Philip 1993:232, citing G. J. Wenham 1981:157-158).

The story certainly lends itself to figurative interpretation, which might make the point well: Those who had been bitten "received a symbol of deliverance to remind them of [the] law's command. For the one who turned toward it was saved, not by the thing that was beheld, but by you, the Savior of all" (Wis 16:6-7, NRSV). Or such interpretation might wander off into detailed and speculative allegorization (e.g., Philo *Allegorical Interpretation* 1:20 and *On Planting* 20). In fact, the New Testament itself presents a figurative interpretation:

> Just as the serpent brought deliverance when raised on a pole for all to see, so He, who was made sin for us (2 Cor 5:21), would be raised on a cross to deliver mankind from the penalty of wickedness (John 12:32). In the same way that the ancient Israelite was required to look in faith at the bronze serpent to be saved from death, so the modern sinner must also look in faith at the crucified Christ to receive the healing of the new birth (John 3:14-16). (Harrison 1990:279)

The Approach to Moab (21:10-20). Verses 10-20 describe the journey from Mount Hor up to the Transjordan. They "set out from Mount Hor," aiming to skirt the land of Edom (21:4) and "traveled next to Oboth" (21:10). The fiery serpent event intervened, perhaps at Punon (21:5-9; see commentary at 33:42-43).

As Israel traveled on through Moab's capital (21:15, 28) they came to a town named "Well" (21:16; see note on "Beer"), where they sang of a well that princes had commissioned or dedicated with the symbols of their office (21:18). The narrative quotes a short bit of a song from *The Book of the Wars of the LORD* (21:14). Like *The Book of Jashar* (Josh 10:13; 2 Sam 1:18), this was probably an ancient book of popular songs celebrating Israel's struggle to possess Canaan. This could have been a work song for men digging the well (Eissfeldt 1965:88) or celebrating its completion (Ashley 1993:413). For Israel it expressed their joy at God's repeated provision of water (Exod 15:22-25; 17:1-7). If the ancients sang of a well in the sand, how much more fitting it is to sing of Jesus' Spirit that springs up in our souls (John 7:37-39) and of drinking of Christ (1 Cor 10:4), never to thirst again (John 4:10-15).

From there they passed through Mattanah, "River of God" (Nahaliel) and Bamoth, to Pisgah Peak looking back over the wilderness (21:18b-20). Now it was time to look ahead to the beginnings of conquest, first in the Transjordan (21:22-35) and soon in Canaan proper.

Victory over Sihon and Og (21:21-35). Pisgah Peak was where Balaam later overlooked the camp and attempted to curse Israel (23:14), and it was where Moses would overlook Canaan and die (Deut 3:17; 34:1-5). At this point Israel overlooked

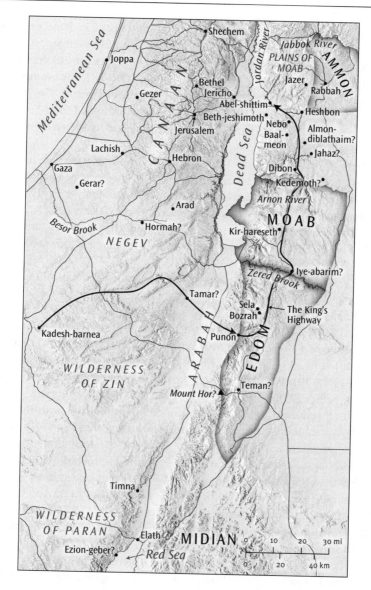

the Amorite territory, which blocked the route through the Transjordan, just as Edom had earlier blocked the route through the Arabah. Verses 21-35 describe Israel's defeat of the two kings in the Transjordan, the Amorite king Sihon (21:21-30) and Og, king of Bashan (21:31-35).

Moses dispatched a diplomatic request for the right of transit, using virtually the same language he had earlier with the king of Edom (20:14-17). Israel had detoured to steer clear of war with their brother nation Edom. But no brotherly constraint inhibited fighting the Amorites. Besides, they could hardly bypass its territory if they were to enter Canaan from the east. King Sihon turned down the appeal for transit rights and directly adopted a combat stance (21:23). Israel's troops took the day, conquered "all the towns of the Amorites" (21:25), even Sihon's royal city of Heshbon, which he had earlier seized from the Moabites (21:26). Israel's victory was comprehensive (21:25, 30; Deut 2:24-27; Judg 11:19-22). For two reasons they didn't carry the battle beyond the Jabbok, into Ammonite territory. First, the border was fortified (21:24). Second, the Ammonites were descended from Lot and were therefore remote relations of Israel (Gen 19:38), and God had given them their own territory (Deut 2:9, 19).

The narrator throws back into the Amorites' faces one of their own ballads with which they had taunted the Moabites (21:27-30). The Amorites had sung ditties to the Moabites about how they had rebuilt a captured Moabite city (21:27), then used it as a base from which to conquer Moab's own royal city (21:28a). They had sung of mastering the Moabite god Chemosh by seizing his cultic shrines (21:28b) and had taunted his worshipers as worshipers of a god who was a loser (21:29).

Next, Og of Bashan, the "last survivor of the giant Rephaites," attacked Israel (21:33; Deut 3:11). Like Goliath, Og was famous for his massive weapons (1 Sam 17:4-7; 2 Sam 21:16, 18, 20, 22) and for his jumbo bedstead (Deut 3:11).[1] God encouraged Moses, "Do not be afraid of him" and promised the same sweeping victory that he had already given over Sihon of the Amorites (21:34). The ensuing victory put the lie to Caleb's fellow scouts, who had fretted over invincible giant warriors (13:28-29). No wonder later writers celebrated these victories in song (Josh 2:10; Neh 9:22; Pss 135:11; 136:17-22).

The church is also to put on God's armor to fight, but not with the sword or against flesh and blood—the battle is against spiritual powers (Eph 6:11-18). In victories more sweeping and significant than Israel's march through the Transjordan, God "continues to lead us along in Christ's triumphal procession" (2 Cor 2:14a). And rather than the *kherem*-inspired [TH2764, ZH3051] scent of death, we "spread the knowledge of Christ everywhere, like a sweet perfume" (2 Cor 2:14b). Our victorious lives are a Christlike fragrance rising up to God. Here we may have a parallel with the *kherem*-produced riches that were offered to God and brought into the Temple in some cases (e.g., Josh 6:19) or used in support of the cult (18:14; Ezek 44:29). Of course, "this fragrance is perceived differently by those who are being saved and by those who are perishing. To those who are perishing, we are a dreadful smell of death and doom. But to those who are being saved, we are a life-giving perfume" (2 Cor 2:15). Such would have been the case with the *kherem* warfare that Israel waged, too.

ENDNOTE

1. "Bedstead" (KJV, NKJV, ASV, NASB, RSV, JPS, NJPS); "bed" (NAB, NIV, NJB, NRSV, NLT). Some suggest "sarcophagus" (Ashley 1993:430 n. 55; NIV mg; NET, NEB,TEV), but the term *'eres* means "couch," "divan," or "platform to on which to sleep" (HALOT); see also Job 7:13; Pss 6:6 [7]; 41:3 [4]; 132:3; Prov 7:16; Song 1:16; Amos 3:12; 6:4.

◆   C. On the Plains of Moab: Preparing to Enter the Promised Land
      (22:1-25:18)
      1. The Balaam story (22:1-24:25)
         a. Balaam hired to curse Israel (22:1-41)

Then the people of Israel traveled to the plains of Moab and camped east of the Jordan River, across from Jericho. ²Balak son of Zippor, the Moabite king, had seen everything the Israelites did to the Amorites. ³And when the people of Moab saw how many Israelites there were, they were terrified. ⁴The king of Moab said to the elders of Midian, "This mob will devour everything in sight, like an ox devours grass in the field!"

So Balak, king of Moab, ⁵sent messengers to call Balaam son of Beor, who was living in his native land of Pethor* near the Euphrates River.* His message said:

"Look, a vast horde of people has arrived from Egypt. They cover the face of the earth and are threatening me. ⁶Please come and curse these people for me because they are too powerful for me. Then perhaps I will be able to conquer them and drive them from the land. I know that blessings fall on any people you bless, and curses fall on people you curse."

⁷Balak's messengers, who were elders of Moab and Midian, set out with money to pay Balaam to place a curse upon Israel.* They went to Balaam and delivered Balak's message to him. ⁸"Stay here overnight," Balaam said. "In the morning I will tell you whatever the LORD directs me to say." So the officials from Moab stayed there with Balaam.

⁹That night God came to Balaam and asked him, "Who are these men visiting you?"

¹⁰Balaam said to God, "Balak son of Zippor, king of Moab, has sent me this message: ¹¹'Look, a vast horde of people has arrived from Egypt, and they cover the face of the earth. Come and curse these people for me. Then perhaps I will be able to stand up to them and drive them from the land.'"

¹²But God told Balaam, "Do not go with them. You are not to curse these people, for they have been blessed!"

¹³The next morning Balaam got up and told Balak's officials, "Go on home! The LORD will not let me go with you."

¹⁴So the Moabite officials returned to King Balak and reported, "Balaam refused to come with us." ¹⁵Then Balak tried again. This time he sent a larger number of even more distinguished officials than those he had sent the first time. ¹⁶They went to Balaam and delivered this message to him:

"This is what Balak son of Zippor says: Please don't let anything stop you from coming to help me. ¹⁷I will pay you very well and do whatever you tell me. Just come and curse these people for me!"

¹⁸But Balaam responded to Balak's messengers, "Even if Balak were to give me his palace filled with silver and gold, I would be powerless to do anything against the will of the LORD my God. ¹⁹But stay here one more night, and I will see if the LORD has anything else to say to me."

²⁰That night God came to Balaam and told him, "Since these men have come for you, get up and go with them. But do only what I tell you to do."

²¹So the next morning Balaam got up, saddled his donkey, and started off with the Moabite officials. ²²But God was angry that Balaam was going, so he sent the angel of the LORD to stand in the road to block his way. As Balaam and two servants were riding along, ²³Balaam's donkey saw the angel of the LORD standing in the road with a drawn sword in his hand. The donkey bolted off the road into a

field, but Balaam beat it and turned it back onto the road. ²⁴Then the angel of the LORD stood at a place where the road narrowed between two vineyard walls. ²⁵When the donkey saw the angel of the LORD, it tried to squeeze by and crushed Balaam's foot against the wall. So Balaam beat the donkey again. ²⁶Then the angel of the LORD moved farther down the road and stood in a place too narrow for the donkey to get by at all. ²⁷This time when the donkey saw the angel, it lay down under Balaam. In a fit of rage Balaam beat the animal again with his staff.

²⁸Then the LORD gave the donkey the ability to speak. "What have I done to you that deserves your beating me three times?" it asked Balaam.

²⁹"You have made me look like a fool!" Balaam shouted. "If I had a sword with me, I would kill you!"

³⁰"But I am the same donkey you have ridden all your life," the donkey answered. "Have I ever done anything like this before?"

"No," Balaam admitted.

³¹Then the LORD opened Balaam's eyes, and he saw the angel of the LORD standing in the roadway with a drawn sword in his hand. Balaam bowed his head and fell face down on the ground before him.

³²"Why did you beat your donkey those three times?" the angel of the LORD demanded. "Look, I have come to block your way because you are stubbornly resisting me. ³³Three times the donkey saw me and shied away; otherwise, I would certainly have killed you by now and spared the donkey."

³⁴Then Balaam confessed to the angel of the LORD, "I have sinned. I didn't realize you were standing in the road to block my way. I will return home if you are against my going."

³⁵But the angel of the LORD told Balaam, "Go with these men, but say only what I tell you to say." So Balaam went on with Balak's officials. ³⁶When King Balak heard that Balaam was on the way, he went out to meet him at a Moabite town on the Arnon River at the farthest border of his land.

³⁷"Didn't I send you an urgent invitation? Why didn't you come right away?" Balak asked Balaam. "Didn't you believe me when I said I would reward you richly?"

³⁸Balaam replied, "Look, now I have come, but I have no power to say whatever I want. I will speak only the message that God puts in my mouth." ³⁹Then Balaam accompanied Balak to Kiriath-huzoth, ⁴⁰where the king sacrificed cattle and sheep. He sent portions of the meat to Balaam and the officials who were with him. ⁴¹The next morning Balak took Balaam up to Bamoth-baal. From there he could see some of the people of Israel spread out below him.

22:5a Or *who was at Pethor in the land of the Amavites.* **22:5b** Hebrew *the river.* **22:7** Hebrew *set out with the money of divination in their hand.*

NOTES

22:5 *in his native land of Pethor near the Euphrates River.* Lit., "Pethor, which is near the River, the land of the sons of his people" (Heb., *'erets bene-'ammo* [TH776, ZH824]). The KJV and ASV follow the LXX, which reads, "by the river of the land of the sons of his people." BHS proposes reading, "land of the sons/people of Amaw" (*'erets bene-'amaw*), which was located between Aleppo and Carchemish (Yahuda 1945; followed by RSV, TEV, NEB). The Samaritan Pentateuch, Vulgate, and Syriac read "Ammon" (*'ammon* [TH5983A, ZH6648]), which would put him close to Moab, although that would confuse the location of Pethor (Albright 1915).

Pethor. This is probably Pitru, on the west bank of the Euphrates about 12 miles south of Carchemish.

22:7 *with money to pay Balaam to place a curse upon Israel.* Lit., "with their 'divinations' in their hand." This could refer to (1) being handy with or "versed in divination" (NJPS),

(2) the paraphernalia used in the practice (Hirsch 1971:393; Moore 1990:98 n. 8; *Tanhuma B. Numbers* 135; *Numbers Rabbah* 20:8, followed by Rashi, Sforno, Ramban, Abravanel), or (3) the fees involved, as nearly all English translations have it (Harrison 1990:295; Noordtzij 1983:203; Sturdy 1976:163).

22:15 *even more distinguished.* Heb., *kabed* [TH3513, ZH3877], which may connote "wealthier" (see next note).

22:17 *I will pay you very well.* Lit., "I will honor (*kabed* [TH3513, ZH3877]) you greatly," a euphemism for monetary rewards, as the next verse makes explicit (Milgrom 1989:188).

22:21 *donkey.* Heb., *'athon* [TH860, ZH912] (a jenny), a female donkey, making her the more pitied for the rough treatment Balaam dished out.

22:22 *to block his way.* Heb., *lesatan lo.* Lit., "as his adversary." Here it is a common noun rather than the proper name "Satan" (*satan* [TH7854A, ZH8477]; cf. 1 Chr 21:1; Job 1–2; Zech 3:1).

22:28 *gave the donkey the ability to speak.* Lit., "opened the donkey's mouth" (see Ezek 3:27; 33:22).

22:41 *Bamoth-baal.* Lit., "high places of Baal," i.e., "the cultic platform of Baal" (Milgrom 1989:193, citing the LXX, "stele of Baal").

see some of the people. Lit., "the end/edge [*qatseh*] of the people." The term *qatseh* [TH7097, ZH7895] may mean "the full extent of" Israel (cf. Vulgate's *extremam partem populi*; followed by Noordtzij 1983:214, KJV, ASV, JPS). However, subsequent shifts for another view incline me to understand it as "some of the people" (so LXX, *meros ti tou laou* [TG3313/5100/2992, ZG3538/5516/3295]; followed by NLT, NAB, NASB, NIV, NJPS, ESV).

COMMENTARY

An inscription written on a plastered wall at Deir 'Alla in modern Jordan speaks of "Balaam son of Beor," who was esteemed as a seer who specialized in curses (Hackett 1986b; Kaiser 1996; Lamaire 1985; Thompson 1986; Zeron 1991). It has been dated anywhere from the ninth century BC to the Persian period (Ashley 1993:438). That doesn't prove that Balaam was a known *historical* character, but it does show that he was at least a known *literary* character in the Transjordan, within a few miles of where the biblical account is set. The accounts in Deir 'Alla and the book of Numbers show striking correspondences (Ashley 1993:439-440): (1) both depict Balaam as a diviner or seer and an exorcist or *baru* prophet rather than a Hebrew prophet; (2) both use the divine names in pretty much the same way, including even Shaddai;[1] and (3) in both, Balaam receives his revelation by night (cf. 22:20).

Origen and Jerome thought Balaam was a good prophet who went bad and then struggled to curse Israel. Others depict him as a bad prophet whom God coerced into blessing Israel. Ambrose and Augustine depict him as entirely bad, which certainly fits the overall canonical assessment. Nonetheless, it is best to start with this passage itself rather than later judgments and note that this story is replete with irony and ambivalence (Lutzky 1999). Balaam is initially portrayed as an obedient servant of Yahweh (22:1-21, 31-41; 23:1–24:25); however, this role is juxtaposed alongside a satirical view of him as "blind seer," quite unable to "see" Yahweh's angel standing directly in his path (22:22-30), unable to see what any ass can see

(Moore 1990:1). Then as the canonical record develops, ambivalence dissolves into general condemnation (31:8, 16; Deut 23:3-6; Josh 13:22; 24:9; Judg 11:23-25; Neh 13:1-3; 2 Pet 2:15; Jude 1:11; Rev 2:14).

Balaam himself claimed to speak the words of the Lord and disclaimed any ability to say anything other than what the Lord allowed. But the canonical judgment doesn't allow him the title "prophet," just one "who used magic to tell the future" (Josh 13:22). Spiritual manifestations do not necessarily establish justification or sanctification. Egyptian magicians matched Moses sign for sign at first (Exod 7:22; 8:7; cf. Exod 8:18). False prophets may mislead with predictions and miracles (Deut 13:1-2). King Saul prophesied, even after his rejection and during his concerted attempts to kill the anointed king (1 Sam 19:23-24). Caiaphas prophesied Jesus' death (John 11:51-52). Jewish exorcists cast out demons in Jesus' name without believing in him (Mark 9:38-39; cf. Acts 19:13-16). The Corinthians reveled in charismatic experience but fell short on faith, hope, and love. False messiahs, men of lawlessness, and "beasts" can perform signs and wonders (Matt 24:24; Mark 13:22; 2 Thess 2:9; Rev 13:11-15; 18:23). So Jesus warned,

> Not everyone who calls out to me, "Lord! Lord!" will enter the Kingdom
> of Heaven. Only those who actually do the will of my Father in heaven
> will enter. On judgment day many will say to me, "Lord! Lord! We
> prophesied in your name and cast out demons in your name and
> performed many miracles in your name." But I will reply, "I never knew
> you. Get away from me, you who break God's laws." (Matt 7:21-23)

Balak Sends for Balaam (22:1-14). "The taunt song of 21:27-30 must have been particularly galling to Moab" (Allen 1990:886). Israel appeared to be "stronger than Sihon, and thus a fortiori stronger than Moab" (Noordtzij 1983:197). So Balak, whose name means "devastator," fell into a "gut-wrenching fear" (Allen 1990:886) that he couldn't live up to his name. His fear of Israel's great numbers made him a "Pharaoh redivivus" and an ironic mirror image of the spies (Sherwood 2002:174, citing 13:31; Exod 1:8-12). Moab and Midian attempted to make common cause against Israel, despite their long-standing enmity for each other (Gen 36:35). "It is like the case of two dogs that were fighting with one another. A wolf attacked one of them. The other thought: If I do not come to his aid the wolf will kill him today, and tomorrow he will attack me. For a similar reason Moab joined with Midian" (Milgrom 1989:186, citing *Numbers Rabbah* 20:4; cf. Josephus *Antiquities* 4.100-102; *Sifre Numbers* §157; *Sanhedrin* 105a; *Tanhuma B. Numbers* 134).

Balak's solution was to hire a curse master to manipulate the will of the gods. He sent generous offers to Balaam, whose greed for payment became the basis for the New Testament judgment on him (2 Pet 2:15; Jude 1:11; Rev 2:14). On the first bid, Balaam told Balak's messengers to wait overnight, and he pronounced the first of his several warnings that he could only report "whatever the LORD directs me to say" (22:8; see 22:18, 38; 23:12, 20, 26; 24:13). Perhaps Balaam was only invoking Yahweh's name before this Moabite delegation to increase their confidence in his access to where it counted so they might pay accordingly, but his statement proved to be true—despite Balaam's pecuniary aspirations.

God subjected Balaam to a bit of judicial cross-examination about what he was up to, just as he had done with the perpetrators of the first sin and the first murder (Gen 3:9-14; 4:9). In this one of four occasions where we read of God using dreams to warn non-Israelites not to proceed with their plans, God told Balaam, "Do not go" (22:12; cf. Gen 20:3; 31:24; Matt 2:1, 12). When he got up, Balaam lamented, "The LORD will not let me go with you" (22:13), omitting the reason: It would be futile to accredit a mission to curse a nation that God had blessed since the times of the patriarchs (Gen 12:1-3; 27:33).

Balaam Accepts Balak's Second Offer (22:15-21). Balak couldn't take seriously Balaam's protestation that he could only pronounce "whatever the LORD directs me to say" (22:8). "After all, what good was he as a sorcerer if he could not manipulate the gods to do or decree as he wanted?" (Sherwood 2002:175). Thinking Balaam was negotiating for a better offer, Balak told Balaam, "I will pay you very well" and even promised, "I will . . . do whatever you tell me" (22:17).

Balaam's response spoke of "Yahweh my God" (22:18). It is possible that this was an actual confession of loyal faith in Israel's God; at this early stage in the story that is the most natural reading of it. But that statement must have sounded bizarre to this story's first readers—it came from a pagan! Of course, the larger narrative and subsequent canonical context undermines his confession. "Since he professed allegiance to and intimacy with Israel's God, he would have had a better chance of convincing Him to curse His people Israel" (Milgrom 1989:188). Indeed, rather than tell Balak that what he was seeking was impossible, Balaam put the king into a holding pattern, hoping the Lord might have something "else to say" if he kept trying (22:19). Indeed, the Lord reversed his early prohibition and allowed Balaam to accompany Balak's delegation (22:20). This introduces narrative tension: Does this mean he might also "change his mind and permit Balaam to curse this nation he had punished in times past?" (Cole 2000:387). After all, Israel had recently been complaining again, so perhaps this was going to be another story of how God punished Israel's incessant complaining. But we soon get the first hint that God may relent with Balaam but not with his basic intent for Israel's blessing in the statement about God's anger being aroused because Balaam took the commission (22:22). Still, Balaam set off with at least some faint hope of pocketing a big paycheck.

God Opposes Balaam (22:22-35). Levine calls these verses "a picturesque fable mocking the reputed clairvoyance of diviners" (Levine 2000:138). The story makes us wonder: First, will Balaam, the "seer," be able to "see" the danger in front of his own nose? His donkey does! Second, will Balaam, the "oracle reciter" so famous for conveying divine answers to divinatory requests in the past, have a "word" placed in his mouth? To our astonishment, he does.

God grew just as angry and frustrated with Balaam as Balaam got with his donkey. Some wonder at God's anger at Balaam for doing what he had already permitted. But God knew that "he was hankering after the reward" (Hertz 1977:672, following the Jewish tradition of *Targum Onqelos*, Rashi, Rashbam, Tosafot). Like the cherubim blocking the way back into Eden (Gen 3:24), the Lord seeking to kill Moses as he set out to return to Egypt (Exod 4:24), and the angel sent to destroy Jerusalem and confront David (1 Chr 21:14-17), God's agent became Balaam's militaristic adversary.

The pitiful jenny saw what Balaam the "seer" (24:4, 16) couldn't see. We shouldn't think of her seeing as an example of animal premonition; it only reminds us that God sometimes chooses "things the world considers foolish in order to shame those who think they are wise" (1 Cor 1:27). But Balaam was not to be put off in his search for the big payday. Three times he beat the jenny, the third time using his "staff" (*maqqel* [TH4731, ZH5234]; 22:23, 25, 27). Perhaps this was just his "riding stick" (Ashley 1993:452); however, if rhabdomancy (divination by use of a rod) was among Balaam's arsenal of divining techniques (Ashley 1993:457; see Hos 4:12), we may be "supposed to conclude that this specialist is not only 'blind' but also incompetent: he does not know how to use his *maqqel* properly" (Moore 1990:72).

Just as God had opened the donkey's eyes, so he opened the donkey's mouth (22:28; Ezek 3:27; 33:22), and why not—who makes a mouth, who decides who can or cannot speak, who can see or cannot see (Exod 4:11)? We shouldn't make too much of this. "The donkey did not give a prophetic oracle; she merely said what a mistreated animal might say to an abusive master if given the chance. There was no preaching from the donkey!" (Allen 1990:893).

Balaam's response was to wish for a sword rather than a staff (22:29). The Midrash scoffs: "At this, the ass laughed. He was intent on destroying the whole people by word of mouth, and to slay a poor ass he requires a sword" (Hertz 1977:672). Indeed, "There was a sword very near, but the object was not about to be the donkey! (22:23, 31-33)" (*Zohar Balak*; cf. *Numbers Rabbah* 20:14; the same idea is in Allen 1990:894). Balaam, the internationally famous seer and curse expert, couldn't even hold his own with a donkey (22:30).

Finally, "the LORD opened Balaam's eyes" (22:31), which makes for sweet irony when Balaam later advertises himself as an ecstatic seer who falls prostrate with eyes wide open (24:4, 16), especially if we remember that this is the same language used of the donkey's previous "vision" (22:23). God himself joined the donkey's case against the serial jenny-beater (22:32). God accused Balaam of being perverse (22:32b) and echoed Balaam's own threat against his donkey, "I would certainly have killed you" but for the donkey, which you wanted to kill (22:33; cf. 22:29). Eventually, Balaam realized the error of his ways (22:34), whether confessing willful transgression of God's will or just a blunder.

Balaam Tells Balak of His Inability to Curse Israel (22:36-41). With the power struggle between Balaam and God settled on the side of God's controlling things, a new power struggle began. King Balak took offense at Balaam's cavalier attitude toward the royal summons and financial offers: "Why didn't you come right away?"

(22:37). Balaam retorted, "Look, now, I have come," then got down to business: "I will speak only the message that God puts in my mouth" (22:38). Balak should have immediately cancelled the contract when he first heard that vital stipulation. Balaam kept insisting that he was a *seer* who could recite only what the Lord gave him to say, but Balak kept hoping that Balaam might function as a *sorcerer*, hatching up effective curses that could force the hand of the gods.

Nonetheless, Balaam accompanied Balak and accepted his sacrificial offers of hospitality, which he probably saw as a wonderful start in the direction of greater rewards (22:39-40). Unlike the sacrifices that Balaam later mandated as part of his divining rites, the sacrifice served the purposes of hospitality more than the purposes of religion. Sacrificial meals were "a regular means of fêting holy men" (G. J. Wenham 1981:171, citing 1 Sam 9:12-13; 16:2-13; also E. W. Davies 1995b:252). Then Balak took Balaam to one of his cultic high places to give him a vantage point for doing his curse business. In case the whole majestic camp of Israel might put Balaam off, Balak showed Balaam only "some of the people of Israel" (22:41).

ENDNOTE

1. Not the uncompromising monotheistic document that the biblical account is, the inscription has '*el* as the divine council's presiding god (I.2), who has a consort with whom he satisfies himself with lovemaking (II.a). And '*l[h]n* (I.2, 14; cf. elohin) probably refers to gods, the *šdyn* (cf. *shaddayin*) refers either to demons (Deut 32:17) or to Shadday-gods (I.12, 14), and other gods are named, e.g., the goddess Shagar (I.15, 29, 39) and Ishtar (I.29, 39) (Levine 1993:243-263).

◆   ## b. Balaam's first ritual and prophecy (23:1-12)

Then Balaam said to King Balak, "Build me seven altars here, and prepare seven young bulls and seven rams for me to sacrifice." [2]Balak followed his instructions, and the two of them sacrificed a young bull and a ram on each altar.

[3]Then Balaam said to Balak, "Stand here by your burnt offerings, and I will go to see if the LORD will respond to me. Then I will tell you whatever he reveals to me." So Balaam went alone to the top of a bare hill, [4]and God met him there. Balaam said to him, "I have prepared seven altars and have sacrificed a young bull and a ram on each altar."

[5]The LORD gave Balaam a message for King Balak. Then he said, "Go back to Balak and give him my message."

[6]So Balaam returned and found the king standing beside his burnt offerings with all the officials of Moab. [7]This was the message Balaam delivered:

"Balak summoned me to come from
    Aram;
the king of Moab brought me from
    the eastern hills.
'Come,' he said, 'curse Jacob for me!
Come and announce Israel's doom!'
[8]But how can I curse those
    whom God has not cursed?
How can I condemn those
    whom the LORD has not condemned?
[9]I see them from the cliff tops;
    I watch them from the hills.
I see a people who live by themselves,
    set apart from other nations.
[10]Who can count Jacob's descendants,
    as numerous as dust?
Who can count even a fourth of
    Israel's people?

Let me die like the righteous;
let my life end like theirs."

¹¹Then King Balak demanded of Balaam, "What have you done to me? I brought you to curse my enemies. Instead, you have blessed them!"

¹²But Balaam replied, "I will speak only the message that the LORD puts in my mouth."

NOTES

23:4 *seven.* This was an important sacred number in the ancient Near East in general (NBD 834) and in Israel's own cultic calendar and ritual prescriptions (ch 29; Lev 8:11; 14:7, 16; 16:14, 19; 25:1-55).

23:5 *The LORD gave Balaam a message.* Lit., "the LORD put a word in the mouth of Balaam."

23:7 *message.* Heb., *mashal* [TH4912, ZH5442], a term referring more to form than content (Ashley 1993:469), used of apothegms (1 Sam 10:12; 24:13 [14]), proverbs (Ezek 12:22; 18:2-3), and lamentations (Isa 14:4; Mic 2:4). The term is used to classify Balaam's pronouncements (23:7, 18; 24:3, 15, 20, 23); however, it is never used for the discourses of Israel's prophets. This may imply that Balaam should not be placed among the prophets (Milgrom 1989:196; Noordtzij 1983:216).

23:9 *a people who live by themselves.* This could be a lonely, unprotected condition (Jer 49:31; Mic 7:14), with "no allies nearby" (Judg 18:28); however, this is in parallel with "set apart from other nations" (lit., "and among the nations is not reckoned"), which makes it sound more like the privilege of election (Ashley 1993:471; G. J. Wenham 1981:173-174, citing Exod 19:5; Deut 7:6; 10:14; 14:2). Others think "alone" refers to Israel's strength and security, noting that this figure of speech is used of God (Deut 32:12) and of Israel (Deut 33:28; Jer 49:31; Gray 1903:346; Milgrom 1989:197).

23:10 *Who can count . . . Israel's people?* Lit., "Who can count the dust of Jacob and who can number a fourth of Israel?" Like their "countless thousands" (10:36), this is an echo of the patriarchal promise (Gen 13:16; 28:14). Some slightly emend the word translated "a fourth" to get an exact parallel between "dust of Jacob" and "dust cloud of Jacob" (HALOT, NRSV).

23:11 *you have blessed them.* In Hebrew this is emphatic: you have "altogether" blessed them (KJV, ASV, JPS) or "only blessed them" (NET), "done nothing but bless them" (RSV, NRSV, ESV).

COMMENTARY

Verses 1-12 set out Balaam's first ritual (23:1-6a), prophecy (23:6b-10), and Balak's disappointment with the result (23:11-12). In the ritual (23:1-6a) Balaam called for "seven altars" (23:1) and ordered king Balak, "Stand here by your burnt offerings" (23:3). Might this be the narrator working a parody of Moses's saying, "Don't be afraid. Just stand still and watch the LORD rescue you today" (Exod 14:13; cf. 1 Sam 12:7, 16), or perhaps a parody of prayerful waiting (Hab 2:1)? In a parody of Moses's Sinai experience, Balaam went off alone to practice his divinatory rites (cf. 24:1). He reported to God that he had gotten Balak to offer sacrifices (23:4), which implies that he thought they would be acceptable to the Lord. Balaam could have understood the sacrifices as incubation for a revelatory dream, so he promised king Balak, "I will tell you whatever [the LORD] reveals to me" (23:3). To the reader's surprise, "the LORD gave Balaam a message" (23:5).

The resulting "message" wasn't Israel's doom (23:7); rather, it protested the impossibility of any such thing. When he asked, "Who can count Jacob's descendants?" (23:10), he echoed the patriarchal promise of numerous offspring (Gen 13:16; 28:14), like the earlier mention of "countless thousands" (10:36). When he asked, "Who can count even a fourth of Israel's people?" (23:10), it is possible that his vantage point over part of Israel gave him a view of one of the four tribal divisions camped at each of the four compass points around the Tabernacle (ch 2; see 22:41; 23:13). Instead of cursing Israel, Balaam blessed himself by Israel, "let my life end like theirs" (23:10), an ancient Near Eastern idiom that perhaps also expresses a desire for inclusion in the blessing promised to Abraham, "All the families on earth will be blessed through you" (Gen 12:3)—though this may also be translated "blessing themselves by you" (RSV, NJB, NJPS, NET).

King Balak complained, "You have blessed them!" (23:11). As Milgrom notes, "Ostensibly there is no blessing in Balaam's first oracle, only praise" (Milgrom 1989:197). Balaam's mantra was that he couldn't say anything but what God put in his mouth (23:12; see 22:18, 38; 23:20, 26, 27; 24:13).

◆   ### c. Balaam's second ritual and prophecy (23:13-26)

¹³Then King Balak told him, "Come with me to another place. There you will see another part of the nation of Israel, but not all of them. Curse at least that many!" ¹⁴So Balak took Balaam to the plateau of Zophim on Pisgah Peak. He built seven altars there and offered a young bull and a ram on each altar.

¹⁵Then Balaam said to the king, "Stand here by your burnt offerings while I go over there to meet the LORD."

¹⁶And the LORD met Balaam and gave him a message. Then he said, "Go back to Balak and give him my message."

¹⁷So Balaam returned and found the king standing beside his burnt offerings with all the officials of Moab. "What did the LORD say?" Balak asked eagerly.

¹⁸This was the message Balaam delivered:

"Rise up, Balak, and listen!
Hear me, son of Zippor.
¹⁹God is not a man, so he does not lie.
He is not human, so he does not
change his mind.
Has he ever spoken and failed to act?
Has he ever promised and not
carried it through?

²⁰Listen, I received a command to bless;
God has blessed, and I cannot
reverse it!
²¹No misfortune is in his plan for Jacob;
no trouble is in store for Israel.
For the LORD their God is with them;
he has been proclaimed their king.
²²God brought them out of Egypt;
for them he is as strong as a
wild ox.
²³No curse can touch Jacob;
no magic has any power against
Israel.
For now it will be said of Jacob,
'What wonders God has done
for Israel!'
²⁴These people rise up like a lioness,
like a majestic lion rousing itself.
They refuse to rest
until they have feasted on prey,
drinking the blood of the
slaughtered!"

²⁵Then Balak said to Balaam, "Fine, but if you won't curse them, at least don't bless them!"
²⁶But Balaam replied to Balak, "Didn't I tell you that I can do only what the LORD tells me?"

NOTES

23:14 plateau of Zophim. Lit., "Peak of Watchers," which might have been an occultic site for seeking omens, such as by observing the stars or the flight of birds, or it could just have meant something like "Lookout Point."

23:21 proclaimed their king. Heb., *teru'ah* [TH8643, ZH9558], the term used earlier for trumpet calls (10:5); here, it is used in celebrating Yahweh as Israel's king (Exod 15:18; Deut 33:5; Judg 8:23; 1 Sam 8:7; 12:12; Pss 47; 98:6; Isa 33:22). This is the first place in the OT that the Lord is called "king," although there was an earlier mention that he "will reign forever" (Exod 15:18).

23:22 for them he is as strong as a wild ox. Lit., "like the horns (*keto'apoth* [TH8443, ZH9361]) of the wild ox (*re'em* [TH7214, ZH8028]) are to/for him" (cf. same expression in 24:8). The versions don't know what to make of *keto'apoth*: the LXX has *hōs doxa* [TG5613/1391, ZG6055/1518] (like glory), the Targums have "in strength," and the Vulgate goes with *fortitudo similis est rinocerotis* (his strength resembles that of the rhinoceros). HALOT goes with "horns" in this verse, reflecting the *re'em*, the bull-like wild aurochs. The extinct aurochs served as an almost mythical figure of strength (24:8; Deut 33:17; Job 39:9; Pss 22:21; 29:6; 92:10; Isa 34:7). Even the horn itself was a symbol of strength and vitality (Deut 33:17; 2 Sam 22:3; Ps 18:2), might and dignity (1 Sam 2:1, 10; Pss 89:17, 24; 92:10; 112:9; 132:17; Lam 2:17), and sometimes arrogance (Ps 75:4-6). It is not clear whether the *lo* [TH3807.1/2050.2, ZH4200/2257] (to him) attributes this intimidating power to Israel's God or to the lionlike nation of Israel (cf. 23:25). "Perhaps, however, the distinction is more apparent than real, for the writer would clearly have understood Yahweh's strength and indomitable power to be manifest in the military prowess of Israel" (E. W. Davies 1995b:263).

23:23 No curse can touch Jacob; no magic has any power against Israel. Lit., "There is no enchantment in/against Jacob, no divination in/against Israel." Some take this to mean none is permitted in Israel (Binns 1927:165; Dillmann and Knobel 1886:154; Gray 1903:355-356; McNeile 1911:134; i.e., ASV, JPS, NJPS, LXX); however, saying that no magic is effective against Israel fits this context better (Ashley 1993:481; Budd 1984:268; Noordtzij 1983:222; Noth 1968:187; Sherwood 2002:179; de Vaulx 1972:280; G. J. Wenham 1981:176; i.e., NLT, KJV, RSV, NRSV, NASB, NJB, NIV, NAB, NET).

COMMENTARY

We see a bit of comedy in the notion that a change of location might make for a change of luck, even if it overlooked another quarter of the camp (23:13) or was a more auspicious occult lookout (23:14). Once again God "gave him a message" (23:16), a phrase stressed in the first two messages (23:1-24) but not for his last two messages, when the Spirit came on him (23:25–24:25). At this point, Balak seemed to acknowledge Balaam's claim to be a seer rather than a sorcerer, asking, "What did the LORD say?" (23:17).

When Balaam exclaimed, "God . . . does not lie. . . . he does not change his mind" (23:19), he wasn't stating a theological absolute about God's unchanging will. Certainly the Bible has language about God not changing (1 Sam 15:29; Mal 3:6; Rom 11:29; Heb 13:8; Jas 1:17); however, it also freely uses language about God changing his mind, often in response to prophetic intervention (e.g., Exod 32:9-14; Amos 7:3, 6) and human repentance (Jonah 3:10; 4:2). But here Balaam was challenging king Balak's notion that sacrificial bribes or repetitive applications of magical pressure could get God to "change his mind" (23:19): "God has blessed, and I cannot reverse it!" was his point (23:20).

Balaam had to report that in spite of his fondest wishes to succeed as a highly paid curse specialist, "no misfortune" was headed Israel's way (23:21a). Why? "The LORD their God is with them" (23:21b). God lives "in the high and holy place," but he also makes his home "with those whose spirits are contrite and humble" (Isa 57:15), whether in Israel, among the church (2 Cor 6:16), or in eternity (Rev 21:3). This was the key covenant promise (Exod 25:8; 29:45; Ps 135:21). And he was their king (23:21)—proclaimed as an enthronement shout echoed over Israel's camp (see Exod 15:18; Deut 33:5; Judg 8:23; 1 Sam 8:7; 12:12; Isa 33:22).

Balaam reported, "God brought them out of Egypt" (23:22). Balaam spoke of Israel as a powerful aurochs (23:22; 24:8) or lion (23:24), roaring while it bulled its way through the wilderness. No international curse expert was going to lay a glove—or tongue—on them. Disgusted, Balak told Balaam not to curse or bless them; however, bless was all that God would let Balaam do when he turned his eyes on Israel (23:26). That may have put his life at risk among King Balak's retinue—but then Balaam had insisted on accepting this commission.

◆　　　### d. Balaam's third ritual and prophecy (23:27–24:13)

[27]Then King Balak said to Balaam, "Come, I will take you to one more place. Perhaps it will please God to let you curse them from there."

[28]So Balak took Balaam to the top of Mount Peor, overlooking the wasteland.* [29]Balaam again told Balak, "Build me seven altars, and prepare seven young bulls and seven rams for me to sacrifice." [30]So Balak did as Balaam ordered and offered a young bull and a ram on each altar.

CHAPTER 24
By now Balaam realized that the LORD was determined to bless Israel, so he did not resort to divination as before. Instead, he turned and looked out toward the wilderness, [2]where he saw the people of Israel camped, tribe by tribe. Then the Spirit of God came upon him, [3]and this is the message he delivered:

"This is the message of Balaam son of Beor,
　the message of the man whose eyes see clearly,
[4]the message of one who hears the words of God,

who sees a vision from the Almighty, who bows down with eyes wide open:
[5]How beautiful are your tents, O Jacob;
　how lovely are your homes, O Israel!
[6]They spread before me like palm groves,*
　like gardens by the riverside.
They are like tall trees planted by the LORD,
　like cedars beside the waters.
[7]Water will flow from their buckets;
　their offspring have all they need.
Their king will be greater than Agag;
　their kingdom will be exalted.
[8]God brought them out of Egypt;
　for them he is as strong as a wild ox.
He devours all the nations that oppose him,
　breaking their bones in pieces,
　shooting them with arrows.
[9]Like a lion, Israel crouches and lies down;
　like a lioness, who dares to arouse her?
Blessed is everyone who blesses you, O Israel,
　and cursed is everyone who curses you."

¹⁰King Balak flew into a rage against Balaam. He angrily clapped his hands and shouted, "I called you to curse my enemies! Instead, you have blessed them three times. ¹¹Now get out of here! Go back home! I promised to reward you richly, but the LORD has kept you from your reward."

¹²Balaam told Balak, "Don't you remember what I told your messengers? I said, ¹³'Even if Balak were to give me his palace filled with silver and gold, I would be powerless to do anything against the will of the LORD. I told you that I could say only what the LORD says!'

23:28 Or *overlooking Jeshimon.*   24:6 Or *like a majestic valley.*

NOTES

23:28 *Mount Peor.* This was perhaps in the vicinity of Beth-peor (cf. Deut 3:29; 4:46; 34:6; Josh 13:20), which was a little north of Mount Nebo. It was likely a sanctuary of Baal of Peor (25:3, 5, 18; Hos 9:10).

24:1 *did not resort to divination as before.* Heb., *welo' halak kepa'am-bepa'am* [TH5173, ZH5728]. The expression *kepa'am-bepa'am* [TH6471, ZH7193] could mean "at times in the past" or "customarily" (e.g., 1 Sam 20:25, cf. BDB 822a); however, here it more likely refers to "the immediately preceding times" (Ashley 1993:486).

24:3 *whose eyes see clearly.* Lit., "whose eye is opened/uncovered" (cf. 24:4); cf. LXX, *ho alēthinōs horōn* [TG230/3708, ZG242/3972], the one whose "eye/sight is true."

24:4 *the message.* Heb., *ne'um* [TH5002, ZH5536], or "declaration, utterance, oracle." Ashley notes that it is used with a human subject only here and 24:15-16 and a few other times (2 Sam 23:1; Ps 36:1; Prov 30:1); rather, it is almost always used of the Lord's words in prophetic oracles (Isa 14:22; Ezek 13:6; Hos 2:13, 16, 21; Mic 4:6).

Almighty. *Shadday* [TH7706, ZH8724] was the patriarchs' ancient name for Israel's God (Exod 6:3; cf. Gen 17:1; 28:3; 35:11). In Canaanite texts such as the Deir 'Alla inscription, the *shaddayin* are the gods (*'lhn*) in El's council (for the text, see Hackett 1986a), so perhaps the title applies to God in his role as head of the divine council (Ashley 1993:488, citing Hackett 1986b:86-87).

bows down. Lit., "falls down." Some think this refers to ecstatic trance (Budd 1984:269; Noth 1968:190) or to a state of sleep to receive a dream, as the LXX understands it; however, Milgrom thinks it merely refers to homage to God (Milgrom 1989:203), as the NLT takes it.

24:6 *like palm groves.* Heb., *kinekhalim* [TH3509.1/5158/5158A, ZH3869/5707/5708]. Earlier translations understood the term to refer to something like a valley or wadi (HALOT *nkhl* I, e.g., KJV, RSV, NIV, JPS, as some still do (NET). Indeed, the LXX (*napai*) refers to wooded vales, dells, or glens, perhaps understanding the Hebrew to be referring to a wadi or brook. But now it's more likely to be translated "palm groves," which makes for more consistent imagery throughout the verse (HALOT *nkhl* II, e.g., NLT, NRSV, NJPS, ESV, NET mg).

like tall trees. Heb., *ka'ahalim* [TH3509.1/174, ZH3869/193], a wordplay on *'ohaleka* [TH168, ZH185], "tents" (24:5). Traditionally, these were aloes or perhaps cardamom (BDB), but commentators suggest various things: "ice-plant, forming lush grassland *Mesembrianthemum nodiflorum*" (HALOT) or the aromatic eaglewood tree (*Aquilaria agallocha*) found not in Palestine but rather in India and Malaysia (Harrison 1990:318; Snaith 1969:298). If the latter is correct, this would be more a theological comment about Eden-like conditions than a botanical note about the actual location of the plant species.

like cedars beside the waters. This is poetic license, since cedars don't grow along the rivers but on mountainsides.

24:7 *Water will flow from their buckets.* This symbolizes fertility, whether water flowing from twin irrigation buckets hooked on both ends of a carrying pole (Ashley 1993:491; Milgrom 1989:204) or abundant semen (Allen 1990:907). See next comment.

their offspring have all they need. Lit., "his seed is in many waters." The phrase refers to Israel's expanding population (Ashley 1993:492; Harrison 1990:318; Sturdy 1976:176; G. J. Wenham 1981:177).

Their king. Cf. the patriarchal promise (Gen 17:6, 16; 35:11), which focused on Judah (Gen 49:9-10). For Jewish messianic interpretation built on this prediction, see Vermes 1961:159-160.

24:8 *for them he is as strong as a wild ox.* Lit., "like the horns of the wild ox for him" (see note on 23:22).

shooting them with arrows. Lit., "crushing his arrows." The verb *makhats* [TH4272, ZH4730] usually implies a club used for crushing foreheads (24:17; Judg 5:26; Pss 68:21; 110:6; Hab 3:13), loins (Deut 33:11), or feet (Ps 68:21); however, the NLT follows the LXX in understanding this as "striking" enemies with arrows.

24:10 *angrily clapped his hands.* Lit., "clapped his hands," with the explanatory "angrily" supplied by NLT. This was an ancient Near Eastern gesture of contempt, derision, or remorse (Job 27:23; 34:37; Lam 2:15; Ezek 6:11; 21:14, 17; 25:6). The gesture was probably not clapping the hands together but striking the palm against a thigh (Levine 2000:198).

you have blessed them. Heb., *berakta barek* [TH1288A, ZH1385], doubling the verb to intensify its force, i.e., "you have actually blessed" (see 23:11).

24:13 *I would be powerless to do anything against the will of the LORD.* Lit., "I would be unable to transgress the mouth of Yahweh, to do good or bad," a climactic declaration that unifies the whole Balaam cycle (Coats 1973:26; Sherwood 2002:180).

COMMENTARY

Even after telling Balaam "if you won't curse them, at least don't bless them" (23:25), Balak opted for a third attempt from a new location, saying, "Perhaps it will please God to let you curse them from there" (23:27b). Balak took Balaam to Mount Peor, which may have been the abode of Baal of Peor (25:3, 5). Certainly, it takes on horrible associations by chapter 25, so its mention here portends trouble. For a third time, Balaam supervised his seven preparatory ritual offerings (23:29). But this time we see three differences from before: First, "he did not resort to divination as before" (24:1). This could refer to his customary practice as a curse expert; in this context it must surely refer to his practice with the previous messages in chapters 22–23.

> Now the reader learns what it is that Balaam has been doing when he separated himself from Balak: He has been seeking omens (*nekhashim*). Is this information meant to put Balaam's prophetic activity in a new light? Balaam has stated (23:23) that there is no divination (*nakhash* [TH5173, ZH5728]) that is effective against Jacob. Are we to conclude that he learned this the hard way? (Sherwood 2002:179)

Second, Balaam now views *all* "the people of Israel camped, tribe by tribe" (24:2). Once Balaam was set to bless Israel, he abandoned Balak's caution and decided to "view the entire Israelite encampment with impunity" rather than just a portion as before (Milgrom 1989:202; cf. 22:41; 23:13). Third, "the Spirit of God came upon him" (24:2). Earlier God "gave Balaam a message" (23:5, 16), but here we see the language describing a prophetic, ecstatic trance (24:3; cf. 11:25-29) or visionary state (Ashley 1993:487; G. J. Wenham 1981:176; cf. 11:17; 1 Sam 10:5, 10; 11:6; 19:20; 1 Kgs 22:24). Balaam described himself as an ecstatic falling into a visionary trance (Budd 1984:269; Noordtzij 1983:225; Noth 1968:190) or at least falling asleep to receive revelation in a dream, as the Septuagint understands it. When he said his eyes were wide open (24:4), he may have been recalling with irony the uncovering of his eyes so he could finally see the angel that his donkey had been veering away from (22:31).

The content of his revelation is rich with the metaphors of idyllic and imperial prosperity and strength. Israel is prospering "like gardens by the riverside . . . like cedars beside the waters" (24:6). This is Edenic language of luxurious riverside growth, including even cedars, though they grow not there but on craggy hillsides. And the point is that they are "planted by the LORD" (24:6). Israel is like the exotic, pampered garden of a king who can sustain anything he wants to in luxurious growth—and he can do so anywhere he wants to, even on a trek through the wilderness.

Israel and its rapidly multiplying offspring would enjoy abundance: "Water will flow from their buckets" (24:7). This, coupled with the mention of "offspring" experiencing plenty, must refer to Israel's expanding population. The Egyptians had found this intimidating, and Balak had too, which was why he had summoned Balaam. The ancient Near Eastern image is that of a farmer with overflowing supplies of water, which the New Testament adopts as a wonderful image of spiritual supply (John 7:37-39).

The patriarchal promise included royal hopes, which finally focused on Judah (Gen 17:6, 16; 35:11; 49:9-10). Balaam spoke of a future king who would prove "greater than Agag" (24:7b), the Amalekite king in the distant future whom Saul, Israel's first king, would eventually defeat (1 Sam 15:8). What are the options for how to understand this message? The first option is to take it as "a straightforward prophecy of Israel's oldest enemy [i.e., the Amalekites]," which in turn was a promise of Israel's triumph over all its foes (G. J. Wenham 1981:178, citing Exod 17:14-16; also suggested as a distinct possibility by Allen 1990:906). This would make the prophecy a prediction that is more specific than most distant predictions are (Ashley 1993:493). A second option is that this was an earlier Agag who was known to Balaam's hearers, which sounds a bit like special pleading. Or, third, this may have been a throne name (Harrison 1990:319) or recurring title like Pharaoh in Egypt (Keil 1869:189; Noordtzij 1983:228), Abimelech in Philistia, and Ben-Hadad in Syria (Allen 1990:906).

When this future king of Israel would come to power, God, who had "brought them out of Egypt," would make Israel "strong as a wild ox" (24:8; cf. 23:22), "like a lion" (24:9; Gen 49:9). Thus the message continues with the question, "Who dares to arouse her" (24:9a) with attempts to curse, especially when blessings and curses aimed at Israel are God-ordained boomerangs, as the original Abrahamic covenant had said (24:9b; Gen 12:3)? This implied there would be a curse on Moab for commissioning a curse expert. It also implied a blessing on Balaam for refusing to curse and only bless Israel (Coats 1982:72). And surely Balaam could have been as blessed as anyone who attached themselves to Israel, if he had stayed the course of blessing Israel. Consider the mixed multitude at the Exodus, Jethro and Hobab in the wilderness, Rahab and Ruth during the period of Joshua and the judges, and Gentiles who are grafted into the one true vine through Christ (Rom 11:17).

This kingdom would be a powerful international force that "devours all the nations that oppose him" (24:8). Balak, who thought he had hired a qualified curse master, hadn't been listening to Balaam's warnings of his inability to say anything but what God gave him to say (24:13; see 22:20, 35; 23:12, 26). His dissatisfaction with Balaam's messages had begun with mild rebuke (23:11) and progressed to impatience (23:25); now they led to outraged revocation of the contract (24:10). One can imagine Balaam figuring out ways to spend a "palace filled with silver and gold" but frustrated that he was "powerless to do anything" (24:13) to earn it.

◆   e. Balaam's fourth prophecy (24:14-19)

¹⁴Now I am returning to my own people. But first let me tell you what the Israelites will do to your people in the future."

¹⁵This is the message Balaam delivered:

"This is the message of Balaam son of Beor,
   the message of the man whose eyes see clearly,
¹⁶the message of one who hears the words of God,
   who has knowledge from the Most High,
who sees a vision from the Almighty,
   who bows down with eyes wide open:

¹⁷I see him, but not here and now.
   I perceive him, but far in the distant future.
A star will rise from Jacob;
   a scepter will emerge from Israel.
It will crush the foreheads of Moab's people,
   cracking the skulls of the people of Sheth.
¹⁸Edom will be taken over,
   and Seir, its enemy, will be conquered,
   while Israel marches on in triumph.
¹⁹A ruler will rise in Jacob
   who will destroy the survivors of Ir."

NOTES

24:16 the Most High. Heb., *'elyon* [TH5945B, ZH6610]. The adjective *'elyon* combines with other divine titles such as *'el* [TH410A, ZH446] (Gen 14:18-20, 22), *'elohim* [TH430, ZH466] (Pss 57:2; 78:56), and *yhwh* [TH3068, ZH3378] (Pss 7:17; 47:2), and "sons of the Most High" *bene-'elyon* [TH1121, ZH1201] is found in parallel with *'elohim* (Ps 82:6). *'Elyon* may have originally had the notion of the highest god in a pantheon, and perhaps had that connotation for Balaam himself.

24:17 I see him. This is a different kind of seeing from before (22:41; 23:13; 24:2); nonetheless, the verbs for *seeing* constitute a unifying motif for chs 22–24 (Alter 1985:105). The identity of "him" may be corporate Israel (Binns 1927:171-172; Gray 1903:369; McNeile 1911:139); however, it is more likely the individual(s) called the "star" and "scepter" (Dillmann and Knobel 1886:159; Keil 1869:192; Noordtzij 1983:230-231; Noth 1968:192; G. J. Wenham 1981:178-179).

star. The Bible seldom uses this as a royal symbol, as it is here (Isa 14:12; cf. Ezek 32:7; Rev 22:16); and we see no compelling ancient Near Eastern examples (contra Ashley 1993:500, citing Cook and Espin 1871:745 and Binns 1927:171-172).

scepter. Heb., *shebet* [TH7626, ZH8657], a royal insignia (Ps 45:6; Amos 1:5, 8), which harkens back to a patriarchal royal promise (Gen 49:10). Some suggest that *shebet* also means "comet" or "meteor," which would maintain a parallel with "star" (Milgrom 1989:208); however, HALOT doesn't list such a meaning, and forcing parallelism makes for poor translation.

cracking the skulls. Lit., "and he will tear down." However, the NLT follows the Samaritan Pentateuch and Jer 48:45, which appears to be using Num 24:17. This reads Daleth (ד) in place of Resh (ר): *qodqod* [TH6936, ZH7721] ("crown of head, skull") rather than *qarqar* [TH6979A/D, ZH7979] ("tear down, shatter"), forming synonymous parallelism with "crushing the foreheads."

people of Sheth. If we take this as "Seth," we have almost the equivalent of the "sons of Adam," indicating that Israel will be at odds with all the rest of mankind, which may shed light on Balaam's earlier comment that Israel lived "by themselves, set apart from other nations" (23:9). If parallelism leads us to see "Moab" and "Sheth" as comparable entities, we have the following choices: (1) Moab and Sheth could be two names for Moab (cf. Jacob/Israel, Edom/Seir), or (2) the *sutu* may have been a neighboring people in Canaan, whose former name and location died out by Jeremiah's time, when he used this text with "sons of tumult" (Jer 48:45, sons of *sha'on* [TH7588A, ZH8623]; NLT, "rebellious people").

24:19 *Ir.* The NLT takes it as a proper noun rather than a common noun meaning "city" ('*ir* [TH5892/5893, ZH6551/6553]), but perhaps it is a reference to Ar-Moab (21:28) or Ir-Moab (22:36). It could also be a collective singular for "Moab's cities."

COMMENTARY

Rather than the sought-for curse on Israel, which implied a blessing for Moab, Balaam progressed from implying a blessing on Israel (23:1-12), to explicit blessing (23:13-26), to threatening Israel's enemies (23:27–24:13), to threatening Moab itself (24:14-19): "Let me tell you what the Israelites will do to your people" (24:14). He began his final message with the same language he used to open his third (24:15; cf. 24:3), but at this point he began speaking of "the future" (24:14, 17). One of the rabbis asks, "How can he know the knowledge of the Most High, when he cannot even read the mind of his ass?" (*b. Sanhedrin* 105b, cited by Vermes 1961:165). But when Balaam said, "I see him" (24:17), he spoke of a spiritual sight that he had lacked before; he now looked into Israel's future and saw a powerful king, which spelled ruin for Israel's foes. As to Edom, who had so mistreated Israel (20:14-21), they would receive their initial judgment when David defeated them (2 Sam 8:14), but they would arise to trouble Israel until their final judgment (Isa 63:1-6; Obadiah).

What are the options for dating "the future . . . far in the distant future" (24:14, 17)? At the least we would not expect to see an immediate fulfillment under the leadership of Moses or even Joshua. Harrison even speaks of "the obvious eschatological tone" of this prophecy (1990:323). Whatever fulfillment Israel experienced early in its history, or even during David's rule, the fullest realization of the message would come with the eschatological messianic kingdom.

The vision spoke of a rising "star" (24:17), a common ancient Near Eastern image for a ruler, with which Old Testament usage resonates. Joseph saw 11 stars symbolizing his brothers, and the sun and moon symbolizing his parents, all bowing down before him (Gen 37:9). The overreaching king of Babylon sought to raise his throne higher than "God's stars" (Isa 14:13) and earned the derisive title "shining star, son of the morning" (Isa 14:12). Finally, the Old Testament uses the starry hosts as a reference to God's heavenly armies (Judg 5:20; Ps 148:2; Isa 40:26). The mention of a "scepter" also foretells a powerful king for Israel (24:17). Naturally, Jewish literature began interpreting Balaam's prophecies messianically: The Qumran community looked to the star and scepter and hoped for the messiahs of Aaron and Israel, i.e., the anointed priest and king (CD 7:18-21). Rabbi Akiba hailed the leader of the second Jewish revolt (AD 132–135) as Bar Kochba, meaning, "son of the Star." *Targum Onkelos* elaborated on the mention of "Cyprus" (or "Kittim") in 24:24 to describe the Romans attacking Mesopotamia (cf. Dan 11:30). Josephus identified "Asshur" (24:22, 24) with the Seleucid Empire of Antiochus Epiphanes (*Antiquities* 13.6.7) and said, "From which completion of all these predictions that he made, one may easily guess that the rest will have their completion in time to come" (*Antiquities* 4.125).

Although intertestamental passages quote Balaam's prophecy as a reference to the coming Messiah, the New Testament never does. So Noordtzij plays down any idea of direct messianic prophecy in favor of referring this to the development of Israel's monarchy. Indeed, David initially fulfilled this prophecy; however, in so doing he foreshadowed the coming of the Messiah. Certainly the New Testament usage of Balaam's imagery (Matt 2:2, 7, 9; Rev 2:28; 22:16) is in keeping with the expectation that Jesus was the ruler whom Balaam promised (Matt 26:63; Mark 14:61; Luke 22:67-70; John 1:20; 4:25). The trajectory set out in Balaam's prophecy is fulfilled when we hear, "The world has now become the Kingdom of our Lord and of his Christ, and he will reign forever and ever" (Rev 11:15).

◆   ### f. Balaam curses Amalek (24:20-25)

20Then Balaam looked over toward the people of Amalek and delivered this message:

"Amalek was the greatest of nations,
   but its destiny is destruction!"

21Then he looked over toward the Kenites and delivered this message:

"Your home is secure;
   your nest is set in the rocks.
22But the Kenites will be destroyed
   when Assyria* takes you captive."

23Balaam concluded his messages by saying:

"Alas, who can survive
   unless God has willed it?
24Ships will come from the coasts of Cyprus*;
   they will oppress Assyria and afflict Eber,
but they, too, will be utterly destroyed."

25Then Balaam and Balak returned to their homes.

24:22 Hebrew *Asshur*; also in 24:24.   24:24 Hebrew *Kittim*.

NOTES

24:20 *Amalek*. A tribe in the Sinai peninsula, they were Israel's implacable enemies (14:43-45; Exod 17:8-16; Judg 6:3, 33).

greatest of nations. Lit., "first (*re'shith* [TH7225, ZH8040]) of the nations." This was the Amalekites' debatable self-assessment (Ashley 1993:506-507), either because of their antiquity (Gen 14:7) or supremacy (cf. Amos 6:1).

its destiny. Heb., *'akharith* [TH319, ZH344]. Lit., "its end," which plays off its antonym, *re'shith* (first); Milgrom 1989:209.

24:22 Kenites. This is the rendering in KJV, NIV, NLT. Others prefer "Kain" (Noordtzij 1983:234; with ASV, NASB, RSV, NRSV, JPS, NJPS). This oracle plays on *qeni* [TH7017, ZH7808] ("Kenite"; 24:21), *qayin* [TH7014A, ZH7804] ("Kain/Kenite"; 24:22), and *qen* [TH7064, ZH7860] ("nest"; 24:21). And if "Kain" is right, it is a proper name substituting for a tribe, like Jacob/Israel = Israelites; Amalek = Amalekites. They were a seminomadic group in the Sinai Peninsula, and they were represented as a subgroup of the Midianites but also as Israelites through Moses's wife and brother-in-law (10:29; Judg 1:16; 4:11). Milgrom says, "The name means 'smith,' implying that they were itinerant craftsmen, a guild of metalworkers who plied their metallurgical skills over a wide area" (1989:209).

Assyria. Heb., *'ashur* [TH805/A, ZH857], probably not Assyria but rather the Ashurites (cf. Asshurites), a tribe in the northern Sinai (Gen 25:3, 18; 2 Sam 2:9; Ps 83:8; cf. Budd 1984:270; Harrison 1990:326; de Vaulx 1972:295). If it were the great imperial power Assyria, they would pose the same threat to the Hebrews that they would to the Kenites. Rather, this tells the Kenites that they will be subdued by their neighbors (G. J. Wenham 1981:181).

24:24 Ships will come from the coasts of Cyprus. Lit., "ships from the hand of Kittim." The term "hand" was a metaphor for the coast, and the "Kittim" are traditionally understood to be the inhabitants of Cyprus (Gen 10:4; cf. Isa 23:1; Jer 2:10; Ezek 27:6). Later, *kittim* [TH3794, ZH4183] came to refer to any western maritime peoples, and eventually to the Romans (e.g., Dan 11:30; LXX *rhōmaioi*; and the Qumran *War Scroll*a [4Q491 f10ii:9; f11ii:1ff; f13:3, 5]).

COMMENTARY

As judgment on Moab and Edom would ensure Israel's future (24:17), so judgment on "Amalek" would help sustain Israel (24:20). A preeminent tribe in the Negev, who had opposed Israel's very birth as a nation-state (cf. Exod 17:8-16), they merited destruction. Saul initiated that destruction, which David, and later Hezekiah, completed (1 Sam 15:18; 30:17; 1 Chr 4:43). It is more surprising to see the "Kenites" as objects of judgment (24:21). They remained on good terms with Israel (Judg 5:24; 1 Sam 30:29). Saul gave them a friendly "heads-up" before attacking their neighbors the Amalekites (1 Sam 15:6), perhaps because descendants of Moses's in-laws were Kenites (Judg 1:16; 4:11). Some Kenites even settled in Judah's southern wilderness (Judg 1:16). That makes us wonder why they should be chosen for doom in an oracle implying blessing for Israel. Ashley notes that this "does not predict that Israel would be involved in the fall of this friendly power"; rather, "it would be *Asshur* that attacked them" (1993:508, citing 24:22).

Balaam closed with a proverbial saying about any nation's ability to resist God's decree. Neither Balak's Moab nor any of Israel's other ancient neighbors such as the Edomites, Amalekites, or Kenites would survive God's decree of destruction. And on the horizon, Balaam saw the Kittim (24:24; NLT, "Cyprus"), which eventually became a generic term for any hostile foreign power, such as the Syrian Seleucids, Egyptian Ptolomies, or Romans. "They, too, will be utterly destroyed" (24:24).

◆   ## 2. National apostasy and divine punishment (25:1-18)

While the Israelites were camped at Acacia Grove,* some of the men defiled themselves by having* sexual relations with local Moabite women. ²These women invited them to attend sacrifices to their gods, so the Israelites feasted with them and worshiped the gods of Moab. ³In this way, Israel joined in the worship of Baal of Peor, causing the LORD's anger to blaze against his people.

⁴The LORD issued the following command to Moses: "Seize all the ringleaders and execute them before the LORD in broad daylight, so his fierce anger will turn away from the people of Israel."

⁵So Moses ordered Israel's judges, "Each of you must put to death the men under your authority who have joined in worshiping Baal of Peor."

⁶Just then one of the Israelite men brought a Midianite woman into his tent, right before the eyes of Moses and all the people, as everyone was weeping at the entrance of the Tabernacle.* ⁷When Phinehas son of Eleazar and grandson of Aaron the priest saw this, he jumped up and left the assembly. He took a spear ⁸and rushed after the man into his tent. Phinehas thrust the spear all the way through the man's body and into the woman's stomach. So the plague against the Israelites was stopped, ⁹but not before 24,000 people had died.

¹⁰Then the LORD said to Moses, ¹¹"Phinehas son of Eleazar and grandson of Aaron the priest has turned my anger away from the Israelites by being as zealous among them as I was. So I stopped destroying all Israel as I had intended to do in my zealous anger. ¹²Now tell him that I am making my special covenant of peace with him. ¹³In this covenant, I give him and his descendants a permanent right to the priesthood, for in his zeal for me, his God, he purified the people of Israel, making them right with me.*"

¹⁴The Israelite man killed with the Midianite woman was named Zimri son of Salu, the leader of a family from the tribe of Simeon. ¹⁵The woman's name was Cozbi; she was the daughter of Zur, the leader of a Midianite clan.

¹⁶Then the LORD said to Moses, ¹⁷"Attack the Midianites and destroy them, ¹⁸because they assaulted you with deceit and tricked you into worshiping Baal of Peor, and because of Cozbi, the daughter of a Midianite leader, who was killed at the time of the plague because of what happened at Peor."

25:1a Hebrew *Shittim.* 25:1b As in Greek version; Hebrew reads *some of the men began having.*
25:6 Hebrew *the Tent of Meeting.* 25:13 Or *he made atonement for the people of Israel.*

NOTES

25:1 *having sexual relations with local Moabite women.* Lit., "playing the harlot with the daughters of Moab." This was in the spiritual as well as the physical sense (Exod 34:15; Deut 31:16; Judg 2:17; 8:33; Jer 5:7; Ezek 16:36; 20:30; 23:35; Hos 4:12; 5:4; 9:1; cf. Rev 2:14). Cultic prostitution was a feature of Canaanite religion (Harrison 1990:337; G. J. Wenham 1981:185; Herodotus 1920:1.199; contra Levine 2000:296, who cites Gruber 1983; Gruber 1986; van der Toorn 1989). This verse speaks of relations with Moabite women, but the story actually recounts a sexual alliance with a Midianite woman (25:4-6). "The Midianites were a mobile group (cf. Jdg 6) who evidently at this time were worshiping at the same shrine as the Moabites, so it should cause no undue tension to read that the slain woman was a Midianite (25:6, 16, 17f.)" (G. J. Wenham 1981:185). We need not consider these verses to be "two unconnected stories, one about promiscuity with Moabite women (25:1-5) and the other with a Midianite woman (25:6-18)" (E. W. Davies 1995b:284); rather, the second is a specific incident of the first.

25:2 *gods of Moab.* Most English translations render the plural *'elohim* [TH430, ZH466] as "gods"; however, since the context indicates that Baal of Peor is intended (25:3, 5), perhaps it should be "Moab's god" (Noordtzij 1983:239; NAB, NJPS), just as the plural *'elohim* is translated "god" when it refers to the pagan god Nisroch (2 Kgs 19:37) or goddess Ashtoreth (1 Kgs 11:5).

25:3 *joined.* Heb., *tsamad* [TH6775, ZH7537]. The verb means "yoked," i.e., becoming adherents of a false god, or perhaps even understood as a double entendre based on the sexual sense of "coupled."

Baal of Peor. This could mean either "the Master of Peor" (i.e., the local chief deity) or "the deity worshiped at a site named *pe'or* [TH6465, ZH7186]" (Levine 2000:284); the two ideas amount to basically the same thing. Other biblical examples are Baal-hermon (Judg 3:3) and Baal-hazor (2 Sam 13:23); extrabiblical examples are Baal-Lebanon, Baal-Tarsus, Baal-Tyre, Baal-Sidon (Ashley 1993:517 n. 22).

25:4 *execute them.* Hiphil of *yaqa'* [TH3363, ZH3697], elsewhere referring to the "dislocation" of Jacob's thigh (Gen 32:25), "execution" of the Gibeonites (2 Sam 21:13), and public "exposure" of Saul at Beth-shan (1 Sam 31:10). Hence, "to display with broken legs and arms (alternatively, to impale, break upon a wheel)" (HALOT). Levine translates, "impale them to YHWH, facing the sun" (2000:285).

25:6 *brought a Midianite woman into his tent.* MT, "brought to his brothers the Midianite," i.e., "to his family" (NIV). Levine translates, "presented the Midianite woman to his kinsmen" (2000:286), perhaps as his new bride (Gray 1903:384). The NLT follows the BHS suggestion to emend from *'ekhayw* [TH251/2050.2, ZH278/2257] (his brothers) to *'oholo* [TH168/2050.2, ZH185/2257] (his tent); see note on 25:8. See note at 25:1 about the Moabite women and the Midianite woman.

25:8 *rushed after the man into his tent.* Lit., "went after the man of Israel to the *qubbah* [TH6898, ZH7688]," a hapax legomenon that is not the usual word for tent. It may even have referred to *her* god's tent-shrine, e.g., a Midianite tent-sanctuary or a domed tent-sanctuary (Budd 1984:274; HALOT). If so, the sex there was not only promiscuous but also a pagan rite (Levine 2000:280).

25:13 *making them right with me.* Lit., "making atonement/paying ransom for the sons of Israel," in this case the sinners themselves dying rather than offering a substitutionary sacrifice.

25:15 *Cozbi.* This name means "deceiver." Lutzky sees a play on two different meanings of the root *kazab: kazab* I means "to lie, deceive, disappoint," whereas *kazab* II means "to be voluptuous." Since in Akkadian *kuzbu* (voluptuousness, sexual vigor) is an attribute of Ishtar and Asherah, Lutzky suggests the possibility that this narrative is directed against the worship of the fertility goddesses. Part of the rhetoric would be in the wordplay on the root of Cozbi's name: "Though the goddess may be alluring and full of promise (*kazab* II), she is no more than a delusion (*kazab* I) to whom all pleas for deliverance would be in vain" (Lutzky 1997:548; see also Niditch 1993:45). The root *kazab* [TH3576, ZH3941] has been heard in 23:19: God is not a man that he should *deceive*, nor a descendant of Adam that he should repent. "Instead of following the God who does not deceive, the people have followed the deceiver" (Sherwood 2002:181-182, citing Lutzky 1997; Niditch 1993).

Zur, the leader of a Midianite clan. Lit., "Zur, the head of some tribes of a paternal house of Midian." He is also called a king (31:8) and a chieftain (Josh 13:21). It appears that Moses had killed Zur earlier (Josh 13:21; cf. Num 21:24-35).

25:18 *Cozbi, the daughter of a Midianite leader.* Lit., "Cozbi, daughter of a chieftain of Midian, their kinswoman," implying the obligation for a kinsman-redeemer-avenger to avenge her death (Milgrom 1989:218).

COMMENTARY

Allen notes, "This chapter presents a formative encounter with Baal worship, a min-iature of the disaster that would one day engulf and destroy the nation." As such, it is both "an end and a beginning. It marks the end of the first generation; it also points to the beginning of a whole new series of wicked acts that will finally lead to Israel's punishment" (Allen 1990:914; see Judg 2:13; 1 Kgs 18; 2 Kgs 17:16; Jer 2:8).

The "fathers" of Moab failed in using Balaam to destroy Israel by a curse; however, Balaam succeeded in using the daughters of Moab to entice Israel into liaisons that would bring on God's curse. Israel's troops may have considered the captured Moabite women fair game for victor's beds after conquering this territory, which the Amorite king Sihon had earlier seized from the Moabites (21:25-26). But this account goes further: The "men defiled themselves" because they began to (literally) "play the harlot with the daughters of Moab" (see 25:1 and note). That the Israelite men rather than the Moabite women were said to "play the harlot" implies that this went beyond physical harlotry to the spiritual whoredom that verse 2 indicates: They "feasted with them and worshiped the gods of Moab" (25:2). Just as the sex may have been cultic, so, too, the meal may have been cultic (cf. meat offered to idols, Acts 15:20, 29; 21:25; 1 Cor 8:4, cf. 1 Cor 10:25). Israel became "coupled" with a false God (25:3a), adher-ents enticed into worship by forbidden coupling with foreign women. One last time in Numbers, "the LORD's anger [blazes] against his people" (25:3b).

God set out to deal with this by publicly executing the guilty ringleaders and partic-ipants in Baal worship (25:4). At that moment, one of the guilty men strutted "right before the eyes of Moses and all the people" (25:6). Commentators give three sugges-tions for identifying the offense: (1) illicit sex (Keil 1869:205), (2) foreign marriage (Baentsch 1903:624-625; Binns 1927:178; Budd 1984:280; Noordtzij 1983:241; Noth 1968:198; Sturdy 1976:184), or (3) cultic offense (Cross 1973:201-203; Levine 2000:280; Milgrom 1989:212, 214, 476-480; de Vaulx 1972:299; G. J. Wenham 1981:187). Ashley concludes, "All three factors seem to apply" (Ashley 1993:520).

For whatever reason, Moses didn't react immediately. The rabbis suggest it was because he himself had a Midianite wife (*Targum Pseudo-Jonathan;* see *Sifre Numbers* §111; *b. Sanhedrin* 82a). But Phinehas, whose father Eleazar and grandfather Aaron had stood between the living and the dead during the rebellion of Korah (16:36-50), now intervened to save many lives. Allen says, "He is typical of Christ the Victor (see Pss 2; 110; Rev 19). He is an early embodiment of 'star' and 'scepter' of 24:17, the smiter of Moab" (1990:920). He killed the pair in the very act (25:8).

What are we to think of this violent deed? As a Levite, Phinehas would have been charged to protect the sanctity of the Tabernacle, even to the point of killing intrud-ers (chs 3-4). This pair was not defiling the Tabernacle itself, however. Phinehas responded in the same way that Moses had ordered the Levites to respond to the golden calf incident (Exod 32:24-29). Some rabbis think Phinehas set a dangerous precedent by taking the law into his own hands. His proverbial zeal (Ps 106:30-31) later motivated the Maccabean fighters (1 Macc 2:23-27) and subsequent Zealots (4 Macc 18:12). God approved of Phinehas's "being as zealous among them as I was" (25:11) and established a "covenant of peace with him" (25:12). Just as God would later grant perpetual kingship to the line of David, God gave Phinehas's line a "permanent right to the priesthood" (25:13). The text here mentions "the priesthood," not "the high priesthood," but it may be that the high priesthood is intended here, or at least that his line, later called Zadokites (Ezek 40:46; 44:15; 48:11) would be exclusive officiants at the Temple.

Jewish tradition has made much of Phinehas's zeal, ranking him third after Moses and Aaron (Sir 45:23). Some Christian commentators treat him as a type of Christ, because he embodied an ideal of Hebrew priesthood and the same zeal that Jesus showed in the Temple (Mark 11:15-17; John 2:13-17; cf. Pss 69:9; 119:139). But the biblical record itself draws a moral rather than a Christological lesson from this account, following Paul's principle that "these things happened as a warning to us" so that we would not repeat their immoral behavior (1 Cor 10:6-8). Micah told Israel to "remember" that event (Mic 6:5), and the New Testament writers compared contemporary false prophets to Balaam's enticements (2 Pet 2:15; Jude 1:11; Rev 2:14).

The quick action of Phinehas had the effect of purifying (lit., "making atonement for") the people of Israel (25:13), assuaging God's wrath by killing the most guilty before God's wrath struck down the whole guilty community. Despite the prompt action of Phinehas, "24,000 people had died" (25:9) by a plague, which exceeded even the 14,700 struck down after Korah's rebellion (16:49). These were the last first-generation corpses that had been doomed to fall in the wilderness (14:29). The census that follows the incident expressly certifies this (26:64).

The story ends by noting that the offenders were from leading families in their two nations. The man from Israel was "the leader of a family from the tribe of Simeon" (25:14), which camped to the south of the Tabernacle. This tribe experienced severe losses in the wilderness, dropping from 59,300 to 22,220; perhaps the losses from plague account for a significant portion of the loss of 37,080 men. The guilty woman from Midian was "Cozbi," daughter of "Zur, the leader of a Midianite clan" (25:15). This execution of one of their princesses would have done little to improve relations between Israel and Midian, who would have felt compelled to avenge it, but the Midianites had maneuvered Israel into a horrible sin for which God's judgment was due. Indeed, conflict continued (Judg 6–8).

◆ II. Birth of the New Generation (26:1–36:13)
   A. The Second Count (26:1-65; cf. 1:1-4:49)

After the plague had ended, the LORD said to Moses and to Eleazar son of Aaron the priest, ²"From the whole community of Israel, record the names of all the warriors by their families. List all the men twenty years old or older who are able to go to war."

³So there on the plains of Moab beside the Jordan River, across from Jericho, Moses and Eleazar the priest issued these instructions to the leaders of Israel: ⁴"List all the men of Israel twenty years old and older, just as the LORD commanded Moses."

This is the record of all the descendants of Israel who came out of Egypt.

⁵These were the clans descended from the sons of Reuben, Jacob's* oldest son:

The Hanochite clan, named after their ancestor Hanoch.

The Palluite clan, named after their ancestor Pallu.

6 The Hezronite clan, named after their ancestor Hezron.

The Carmite clan, named after their ancestor Carmi.

7 These were the clans of Reuben. Their registered troops numbered 43,730.

8 Pallu was the ancestor of Eliab, 9 and Eliab was the father of Nemuel, Dathan, and Abiram. This Dathan and Abiram are the same community leaders who conspired with Korah against Moses and Aaron, rebelling against the LORD. 10 But the earth opened up its mouth and swallowed them with Korah, and fire devoured 250 of their followers. This served as a warning to the entire nation of Israel. 11 However, the sons of Korah did not die that day.

12 These were the clans descended from the sons of Simeon:

The Jemuelite clan, named after their ancestor Jemuel.*

The Jaminite clan, named after their ancestor Jamin.

The Jakinite clan, named after their ancestor Jakin.

13 The Zoharite clan, named after their ancestor Zohar.*

The Shaulite clan, named after their ancestor Shaul.

14 These were the clans of Simeon. Their registered troops numbered 22,200.

15 These were the clans descended from the sons of Gad:

The Zephonite clan, named after their ancestor Zephon.

The Haggite clan, named after their ancestor Haggi.

The Shunite clan, named after their ancestor Shuni.

16 The Oznite clan, named after their ancestor Ozni.

The Erite clan, named after their ancestor Eri.

17 The Arodite clan, named after their ancestor Arodi.*

The Arelite clan, named after their ancestor Areli.

18 These were the clans of Gad. Their registered troops numbered 40,500.

19 Judah had two sons, Er and Onan, who had died in the land of Canaan. 20 These were the clans descended from Judah's surviving sons:

The Shelanite clan, named after their ancestor Shelah.

The Perezite clan, named after their ancestor Perez.

The Zerahite clan, named after their ancestor Zerah.

21 These were the subclans descended from the Perezites:

The Hezronites, named after their ancestor Hezron.

The Hamulites, named after their ancestor Hamul.

22 These were the clans of Judah. Their registered troops numbered 76,500.

23 These were the clans descended from the sons of Issachar:

The Tolaite clan, named after their ancestor Tola.

The Puite clan, named after their ancestor Puah.*

24 The Jashubite clan, named after their ancestor Jashub.

The Shimronite clan, named after their ancestor Shimron.

25 These were the clans of Issachar. Their registered troops numbered 64,300.

26 These were the clans descended from the sons of Zebulun:

The Seredite clan, named after their ancestor Sered.

The Elonite clan, named after their ancestor Elon.

The Jahleelite clan, named after their ancestor Jahleel.

27 These were the clans of Zebulun. Their registered troops numbered 60,500.

28Two clans were descended from Joseph through Manasseh and Ephraim.

29These were the clans descended from Manasseh:

The Makirite clan, named after their ancestor Makir.

The Gileadite clan, named after their ancestor Gilead, Makir's son.

30These were the subclans descended from the Gileadites:

The Iezerites, named after their ancestor Iezer.

The Helekites, named after their ancestor Helek.

31The Asrielites, named after their ancestor Asriel.

The Shechemites, named after their ancestor Shechem.

32The Shemidaites, named after their ancestor Shemida.

The Hepherites, named after their ancestor Hepher.

33(One of Hepher's descendants, Zelophehad, had no sons, but his daughters' names were Mahlah, Noah, Hoglah, Milcah, and Tirzah.)

34These were the clans of Manasseh. Their registered troops numbered 52,700.

35These were the clans descended from the sons of Ephraim:

The Shuthelahite clan, named after their ancestor Shuthelah.

The Bekerite clan, named after their ancestor Beker.

The Tahanite clan, named after their ancestor Tahan.

36This was the subclan descended from the Shuthelahites:

The Eranites, named after their ancestor Eran.

37These were the clans of Ephraim. Their registered troops numbered 32,500.

These clans of Manasseh and Ephraim were all descendants of Joseph.

38These were the clans descended from the sons of Benjamin:

The Belaite clan, named after their ancestor Bela.

The Ashbelite clan, named after their ancestor Ashbel.

The Ahiramite clan, named after their ancestor Ahiram.

39The Shuphamite clan, named after their ancestor Shupham.*

The Huphamite clan, named after their ancestor Hupham.

40These were the subclans descended from the Belaites:

The Ardites, named after their ancestor Ard.*

The Naamites, named after their ancestor Naaman.

41These were the clans of Benjamin. Their registered troops numbered 45,600.

42These were the clans descended from the sons of Dan:

The Shuhamite clan, named after their ancestor Shuham.

43These were the Shuhamite clans of Dan. Their registered troops numbered 64,400.

44These were the clans descended from the sons of Asher:

The Imnite clan, named after their ancestor Imnah.

The Ishvite clan, named after their ancestor Ishvi.

The Beriite clan, named after their ancestor Beriah.

45These were the subclans descended from the Beriites:

The Heberites, named after their ancestor Heber.

The Malkielites, named after their ancestor Malkiel.

46Asher also had a daughter named Serah.

47These were the clans of Asher. Their registered troops numbered 53,400.

48These were the clans descended from the sons of Naphtali:

The Jahzeelite clan, named after their ancestor Jahzeel.

The Gunite clan, named after their ancestor Guni.

⁴⁹The Jezerite clan, named after their ancestor Jezer.

The Shillemite clan, named after their ancestor Shillem.

⁵⁰These were the clans of Naphtali. Their registered troops numbered 45,400.

⁵¹In summary, the registered troops of all Israel numbered 601,730.

⁵²Then the LORD said to Moses, ⁵³"Divide the land among the tribes, and distribute the grants of land in proportion to the tribes' populations, as indicated by the number of names on the list. ⁵⁴Give the larger tribes more land and the smaller tribes less land, each group receiving a grant in proportion to the size of its population. ⁵⁵But you must assign the land by lot, and give land to each ancestral tribe according to the number of names on the list. ⁵⁶Each grant of land must be assigned by lot among the larger and smaller tribal groups."

⁵⁷This is the record of the Levites who were counted according to their clans:

The Gershonite clan, named after their ancestor Gershon.

The Kohathite clan, named after their ancestor Kohath.

The Merarite clan, named after their ancestor Merari.

⁵⁸The Libnites, the Hebronites, the Mahlites, the Mushites, and the Korahites were all subclans of the Levites.

Now Kohath was the ancestor of Amram, ⁵⁹and Amram's wife was named Jochebed. She also was a descendant of Levi, born among the Levites in the land of Egypt. Amram and Jochebed became the parents of Aaron, Moses, and their sister, Miriam. ⁶⁰To Aaron were born Nadab, Abihu, Eleazar, and Ithamar. ⁶¹But Nadab and Abihu died when they burned before the LORD the wrong kind of fire, different than he had commanded.

⁶²The men from the Levite clans who were one month old or older numbered 23,000. But the Levites were not included in the registration of the rest of the people of Israel because they were not given an allotment of land when it was divided among the Israelites.

⁶³So these are the results of the registration of the people of Israel as conducted by Moses and Eleazar the priest on the plains of Moab beside the Jordan River, across from Jericho. ⁶⁴Not one person on this list had been among those listed in the previous registration taken by Moses and Aaron in the wilderness of Sinai. ⁶⁵For the LORD had said of them, "They will all die in the wilderness." Not one of them survived except Caleb son of Jephunneh and Joshua son of Nun.

26:5 Hebrew *Israel's;* see note on 1:20-21b. 26:12 As in Syriac version (see also Gen 46:10; Exod 6:15); Hebrew reads *Nemuelite . . . Nemuel.* 26:13 As in parallel texts at Gen 46:10 and Exod 6:15; Hebrew reads *Zerahite . . . Zerah.* 26:17 As in Samaritan Pentateuch and Greek and Syriac versions (see also Gen 46:16); Hebrew reads *Arod.* 26:23 As in Samaritan Pentateuch, Greek and Syriac versions, and Latin Vulgate (see also 1 Chr 7:1); Hebrew reads *The Punite clan, named after its ancestor Puvah.* 26:39 As in some Hebrew manuscripts, Samaritan Pentateuch, Greek and Syriac versions, and Latin Vulgate; most Hebrew manuscripts read *Shephupham.* 26:40 As in Samaritan Pentateuch, some Greek manuscripts, and Latin Vulgate; Hebrew lacks *named after their ancestor Ard.*

NOTES

26:1a *After the plague had ended.* The Masoretes marked a major break at the end of 26:1a which is not shown in most English versions; however, this is a temporal clause that clearly goes with the rest of 26:1 and the following verses.

26:9 *Nemuel.* This is omitted elsewhere (16:1, 12; Deut 11:6). Some ask whether it was accidentally written here because of its occurrence in 26:12 (E. W. Davies 1995b:293).

26:12 *Jemuel.* The NLT harmonizes with Gen 46:10 and Exod 6:15, as does the Syriac. The Hebrew reads "Nemuel" (cf. NLT mg).

26:13 Zohar. Heb., *zerakh* [TH2226/2227, ZH2438/2439]. NLT harmonizes what is probably a variant spelling with Gen 46:10 and Exod 6:15. Zerah was one of the chief clans of Judah (Gen 46:12), but since Simeon was absorbed into Judah, it is plausible to conjecture that representatives of this Simeonite clan became linked to both tribes (Milgrom 1989:222). Compare the lists of Simeon's sons:

Gen 46:10	Exod 6:15	Num 26:12-13
Jemuel	Jemuel	*Nemuel* (cf. NLT mg), possibly a variant spelling
Jamin	Jamin	Jamin
Ohad	Ohad	*Omitted*, possibly because he did not found a family, perhaps dying in childhood
Jakin	Jakin	Jakin
Zohar	Zohar	*Zerah* (cf. NLT mg), possibly a variant spelling
Shaul	Shaul	Shaul

26:15 Zephon. Cf. Ziphion (Gen 46:16 mg).

26:16 Ozni. Cf. Ezbon (Gen 46:16).

26:23 Puah. This follows the reading *pu'ah* [TH6312, ZH7025] (LXX, Samaritan Pentateuch, Peshitta, and 1 Chr 7:1). The Hebrew reads "Puvah" (so NLT mg), the clan of the judge Tola (Judg 10:1-2).

26:30 Iezer. This is "synonymous with Abiezer (Josh 17:2), the clan of the judge Gideon (Judg 6:11, 24, 34)" (Milgrom 1989:224). He is the first-named son of Gilead but may have been the son of his sister Hammoleketh, who was regarded as his "son" for genealogical purposes (1 Chr 7:18).

26:35 Beker. He is elsewhere called a son of Benjamin rather than of Ephraim (Gen 46:21; cf. "Bicri," 2 Sam 20:1); this is a difficulty that causes his omission in the LXX. Perhaps this clan changed its tribal identity while in Egypt, or possibly the family lived along the Benjamin–Ephraim border (Milgrom 1989:225).

26:44 Beriah. This was also a clan of Ephraim (1 Chr 7:21-24) and Benjamin (1 Chr 8:13); see previous note.

26:46 Serah. The only female in the genealogical lists, she is also mentioned in Gen 46:17 and 1 Chr 7:30. Ramban cites the Targum on this verse: "the name of the daughter of the wife of Asher" (this is not in the extant Targum texts, however). This suggests that her father died without male offspring. She is therefore in the same category as the daughters of Zelophehad (27:1-11), which explains her being mentioned here. Otherwise, her presence remains a mystery (Milgrom 1989:226).

26:58 Kohath was the ancestor of Amram. Cf. 3:19; Exod 6:14-18.

COMMENTARY

Numbers 26 turns the page on the first generation; the plague of chapter 25 had eliminated them. From here on, occupation of the Promised Land again becomes the focus in Numbers.

God commanded Moses and Aaron's successor, Eleazar, to conduct a count of the new generation (26:1-2). The first counts had determined camp divisions in the wilderness; this count would determine land divisions in the Promised Land, which now lay just across the Jordan (26:3). And in a note that we grew used to hearing in the early part of the book, we read of Moses and Eleazar's prompt and exact obedience (26:3-4). A new count of the liberated people would have spoken volumes about new possibilities for this new generation (26:4b).

The counting of the tribes is arranged almost exactly as it was in the military census of chapter 1 (see note on 1:6-15): Reuben (26:5-11), Simeon (26:12-14), Gad (26:15-18), Judah (26:19-22), Issachar (26:23-25), Zebulun (26:26-27), Manasseh (26:28-34), Ephraim (26:35-37), Benjamin (26:38-41), Dan (26:42-43), Asher (26:44-47), and Naphtali (26:48-50). The list also adheres to the same three-tribe groupings of chapters 1 and 2 (see note at 2:2). Verses 5-51 name each tribe's clans, numbers its able-bodied men, and gives an overall total. For Reuben (26:9-11), Judah (26:19), and Manasseh (26:33), the text provides additional information. The resulting count may be compared with the first count as follows:

Tribes	Census (year 2)	Census (year 40)	Decrease	Increase	Percentage
Reuben	46,500	43,730	2,770		-6%
Simeon	59,300	22,200	37,100		-63%
Gad	45,650	40,500	5,150		-11%
Judah	74,600	76,500		1,900	+3%
Issachar	54,400	64,300		9,900	+18%
Zebulun	57,400	60,500		3,100	+5%
Ephraim	40,500	32,500	8,000		-20%
Manasseh	32,200	52,700		20,500	+64%
Benjamin	35,400	45,600		10,200	+29%
Dan	62,700	64,400		1,700	+3%
Asher	41,500	53,400		11,900	+29%
Naphtali	53,400	45,400	8,000		-15%
TOTAL	603,550	601,730	1,820		-0.3%

The major changes are the sharp decline in Simeon, which was soon absorbed by Judah (Josh 19:1; Judg 1:3), and the marked increase in Manasseh, which soon expanded beyond its settled territory (Josh 17:11, 16) and came to dominate events during the judgeships of two of its sons, Gideon and Abimelech (Judg 6–9; 12:1-6).

Reuben suffered small losses (26:5-11); indeed, the account includes a supplementary note that neither the Reubenites nor the Korahites died out, despite their involvement in the rebellion (26:8-11). The Korahites continued into the postexilic period as Temple singers (Pss 42–49, 84, 85, 87, 88) and guards (1 Chr 9:19; 26:1-19). Nonetheless, they are mentioned here as a "warning." Simeon lost nearly two-thirds of its soldiery (26:12-14), which foreboded their absorption into the tribe of Judah, fulfilling Jacob's last words to the violent brothers Levi and Simeon (Gen 49:5-7). Gad suffered about a 10 percent loss (26:15-18). The royal tribe of Judah, already the largest tribe, enjoyed a slight increase (26:19-22). Verse 19 notes the absence of Er and Onan from the clan lists (cf. Gen 46:12). From Judah's line, Perez is the only grandson noted (Gen 46:12), indicating a precedence befitting the line from which king David would come (Ruth 4:18-22), and thus from which Jesus would come (Matt 1:3; Luke 3:33). Issachar experienced about 20 percent growth (26:23-26), and Zebulun experienced modest growth (26:26-27).

Since Levi is omitted from the count to determine land allotments, the Joseph tribes (26:28) of Manasseh (26:29-34) and Ephraim (26:35-37) are listed separately. In the first count, Ephraim had been listed first, as the larger tribe enjoying the preeminence foretold in Jacob's blessing (Gen 48:19). In this count, the brothers are listed in birth order, Manasseh before Ephraim (Gen 46:20). Ephraim had been larger in the first census, but it suffered a 20 percent decrease to become the second-smallest tribe; meanwhile, Manasseh had enjoyed an increase of over 60 percent, approximately double the growth of even the growing tribes of Issachar, Benjamin, and Asher. Manasseh produced the "Makirite clan" (26:29a), which continued through "Gilead, Makir's son," and subdivided into five subclans (26:29b-32). The narrator brought this up to the sixth and seventh generations to mention Zelophehad and his daughters in anticipation of their inheritance and the related laws (26:33; see 27:1-11; 36:1-13). Parallel lists of Benjamin clans differ (26:38-41; cf. Gen 46:21; 1 Chr 7:6). Allen (1990:935-936) gives the following potential explanations for the differences:

1. The name Beker may have been misunderstood in 1 Chronicles 8:1 as *bekoro* [TH1060/2050.2, ZH1147/2257], "his firstborn," leading to the unusual list of ordinals in the rest of the names of that listing.

2. The name Ahiram in 26:38 (= Aharah of 1 Chr 8:1) may be identified with Ehi of Genesis 46:21; alternatively, perhaps there is a confusion of the two names Ehi and Rosh of Genesis 46:21 in the name Ahiram.

3. Shuphupham (= Shupham of Samaritan Pentateuch, Vulgate, Syriac) is confused perhaps with Muppim of Genesis 46:21.

4. Hupham of 26:39 may equal Huppim of Genesis 46:21; but he may be a descendant, not a direct son (see 1 Chr 7:12; yet 1 Chr 7:12 may list descendants who have similar names as their forebears; this issue is complex).

5. Ard in 26:40 is listed as a son of Bela, along with Naaman. Perhaps these men were not born at the time recorded in Genesis 46.

In any case, Benjamin experienced about a 30 percent growth, while Dan held steady in population and ranked second only to Judah in both counts (26:42-43). Since there is only one clan listed here and no evidence elsewhere for any other clans, this one family group must have been most fruitful. Asher experienced 30 percent growth (26:44-47), and Naphtali experienced a 15 percent loss (26:48-50).

The final twelve-tribe troop count of 601,730 constituted a negligible loss after the rigors of 40 years in the wilderness (26:51). It sustained the reality of the patriarchal promise of numerous offspring, as more than half of the tribes grew, and despite the judgments of the wilderness, the overall population remained stable. As G. J. Wenham (1981:190) concludes, "God's promises to the patriarchs may be delayed by human sin, but they are not ultimately frustrated by it (cf. Rom 11)."

With the recount completed, attention turned to the division of the land (26:52-62), with treatment of the method for allotting it (26:52-56) and the concerns of the Levitical clans (26:57-62). The size of the tribe was supposed to determine the *size* of its area (26:53), and casting lots was to determine its *location* (26:55).[1] Earlier the Levites were listed separately because they were exempted from military duty and set apart for cultic duty at the Tabernacle. Here they are listed separately because they are not entitled to a land allotment (26:62; see 18:23). Rather than listing just the three Levitical clans listed earlier (3:21-37), this account lists five Levitical clans: four clans named not for Levi's sons but for some of his grandsons (Libni, Hebron, Mahli, and Mushi) and one named for a great-grandson, Korah (whose sons lived on, 26:10-11; cf. ch 16).

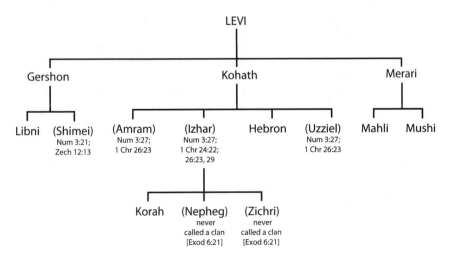

The chart that follows shows the clans that descended from Levi. Those in parentheses are not included in the list of Numbers 26; however, they are found in clan lists elsewhere (Gen 46:11; Exod 6:16-25; Num 3:17-39; 1 Chr 6:1-29; 23:6-23; 24:20-30). There are also some variations in the lists in Chronicles which are not represented in the chart: "Ladan and Shimei, the sons of Gershon" (1 Chr 23:7 mg); "the descendants of Kohath included Amminadab, Korah, Assir," etc. (1 Chr 6:22-24), and "the descendants of Merari included Mahli, Libni, Shimei," etc. (1 Chr 6:29-30). This may hint that these clans died out or were cut off in the wilderness.

Verses 63-65 form a postscript, summarizing the results of the two troop counts and recapitulating the point of the census. The outcome demonstrated that the entire first generation of wilderness wanderers had perished, just as God had threatened (14:23-38).

ENDNOTE

1. The lot reflected God's will (Prov 16:33) in decision making (Ezek 21:18-23; Mic 2:5), deciding disputes (Prov 18:18), dividing spoils (Ps 22:18; Prov 1:14; Joel 3:3), or selecting persons (Judg 20:9; 1 Sam 10:19-21; Neh 11:1; Nah 3:10). Priests used it to set the priestly and Levitical courses (1 Chr 24:5; 26:13-18), to establish the sequence of wood-offering contributions (Neh 10:34), and to select the scapegoat on Yom Kippur (Lev 16:8).

◆   B. Laws about Land, Offerings, and Vows (27:1–30:16)
     1. Inheritance of Zelophehad's daughters (27:1-11; cf. 36:1-13)

One day a petition was presented by the daughters of Zelophehad—Mahlah, Noah, Hoglah, Milcah, and Tirzah. Their father, Zelophehad, was a descendant of Hepher son of Gilead, son of Makir, son of Manasseh, son of Joseph. ²These women stood before Moses, Eleazar the priest, the tribal leaders, and the entire community at the entrance of the Tabernacle.* ³"Our father died in the wilderness," they said. "He was not among Korah's followers, who rebelled against the LORD; he died because of his own sin. But he had no sons. ⁴Why should the name of our father disappear from his clan just because he had no sons? Give us property along with the rest of our relatives."

⁵So Moses brought their case before the LORD. ⁶And the LORD replied to Moses, ⁷"The claim of the daughters of Zelophehad is legitimate. You must give them a grant of land along with their father's relatives. Assign them the property that would have been given to their father.

⁸"And give the following instructions to the people of Israel: If a man dies and has no son, then give his inheritance to his daughters. ⁹And if he has no daughter either, transfer his inheritance to his brothers. ¹⁰If he has no brothers, give his inheritance to his father's brothers. ¹¹But if his father has no brothers, give his inheritance to the nearest relative in his clan. This is a legal requirement for the people of Israel, just as the LORD commanded Moses."

27:2 Hebrew *the Tent of Meeting.*

NOTES

27:5 *their case.* The MT enlarges the final Nun, which serves as a feminine plural suffix, emphasizing this feminine request for land.

27:7 *give them.* This is masculine plural, although we would expect feminine. It was probably a scribal mistake, given how common the masculine plural is compared to the feminine plural (Allen 1990:943-944), though Harrison suggests it was to put the woman on the same footing as male heirs (1990:360).

Assign them. This is the expected feminine plural.

COMMENTARY

Chapters 27–30 deal with matters preparatory to occupying the land. With the foresight of faith, Zelophehad's daughters sought to protect their family's inheritance even though only daughters remained (27:1-11; cf. 36:1-13). Then Moses commissioned Joshua (27:12-23) before setting out various regulations for offerings (28:1-31), festivals (29:1-40), and vows (30:1-16).

Two assumptions drive the story of Zelophehad's daughters: First, the land belongs to the Lord (Lev 25:23); second, males inherit property and perpetuate the family (Deut 21:15-17). The first assumption was never to be challenged (1 Kgs 21:16-19; Mic 2:1-5); however, driven by the foresight of faith, Zelophehad's daughters challenged the second assumption. So they came to the Tabernacle and petitioned Israel's leaders (27:2). They noted that their father had not been among Korah's followers, whose families might well be excluded from land ownership in Canaan; rather, he died because of the guilt shared by everyone in the first generation over the scout episode (27:3b; see ch 14). The problem was not his death, but that he left no sons (27:3c). "In contradistinction to their men who feared to invade Canaan and wished to return to Egypt (14:1-4), they boldly stepped forward and demanded an inheritance in the promised land" (Milgrom 1989:230, citing *Sifre Numbers* §133; *Sifre Zuta* on 27:1; *Numbers Rabbah* 21:10).

Apparently levirate marriage was not an option since Zelophehad's wife would also have died off with the rest of the first generation, as any of his surviving brothers would have (see Gen 38:1-26; Deut 25:5-10; Ruth 3:1-13). And the daughters must not have been married yet, or any land they received would have passed to the clans of their husbands rather than keeping their father's name alive (cf. 36:3). Zelophehad's daughters didn't end up changing the patrilineal pattern, but they did open the way for daughters to keep the father's name alive in the absence of sons. Thus, "the daughter does not really inherit; she transfers the inheritance from father to grandson and thereby keeps the ancestral land in the father's line" (Milgrom 1989:232). So God told Moses to give them their father's land (27:7). Then the law was generalized, but with qualifications aimed at keeping the land in the family and clan (27:9-11; cf. 36:1-13). If a man had no sons, then his land went to his daughters (27:8); if no daughters, then to his brothers (27:9); if no brothers, then to his paternal uncles (27:10).

◆   2. Commissioning of Joshua (27:12-23)

¹²One day the LORD said to Moses, "Climb one of the mountains east of the river,* and look out over the land I have given the people of Israel. ¹³After you have seen it, you will die like your brother, Aaron, ¹⁴for you both rebelled against my instructions in the wilderness of Zin. When the people of Israel rebelled, you failed to demonstrate my holiness to them at the waters." (These are the waters of Meribah at Kadesh* in the wilderness of Zin.)

¹⁵Then Moses said to the LORD, ¹⁶"O LORD, you are the God who gives breath to all creatures. Please appoint a new man as leader for the community. ¹⁷Give them someone who will guide them wherever they go and will lead them into battle, so the community of the LORD will not be like sheep without a shepherd."

¹⁸The LORD replied, "Take Joshua son of Nun, who has the Spirit in him, and lay your hands on him. ¹⁹Present him to Eleazar the priest before the whole community, and publicly commission him to lead the people. ²⁰Transfer some of your authority to him so the whole community of Israel will obey him. ²¹When direction from the LORD is needed, Joshua will stand before Eleazar the priest, who will use the Urim—one of the sacred lots cast before the LORD—to determine his will. This is how Joshua and the rest of the community of Israel will determine everything they should do."

²²So Moses did as the LORD commanded. He presented Joshua to Eleazar the priest and the whole community. ²³Moses laid his hands on him and commissioned him to lead the people, just as the LORD had commanded through Moses.

27:12 Or *the mountains of Abarim.*   27:14 Hebrew *waters of Meribath-kadesh.*

NOTES

27:17 *who will guide them wherever they go and will lead them into battle.* Lit., "who can go out before them and come in before them and lead them out and lead them in." This has a military connotation, which the NLT makes explicit.

like sheep without a shepherd. This was an image widely used of royalty in the ancient Near East. It was used for David, Israel's shepherd-king and for the Lord himself (Ps 23), and it was quoted in Matt 9:36 and Mark 6:34, as well as echoed in John 10:3-4, 9.

27:21 *the Urim—one of the sacred lots cast before the LORD.* Lit., "the Urim before the LORD." This is short for Urim and Thummim, as in 1 Sam 28:6.

COMMENTARY

Why does the author tell this story here, when it could have been left until Deuteronomy's postscript (Deut 34)—especially since Moses still had so many laws (chs 28–36) and a lengthy testament (Deut 1–33) to deliver? Here it drives home the point about judgment eliminating all the first generation in the wilderness—even the great leader, because of his own sin. That is the first point made in the story (27:12-14), which later notes recount (Deut 3:21-29; 32:48-52; 34:1-8).

Like Aaron when his office passed to Eleazar, Moses was told to climb a mountain (27:12; see 20:24-28; 33:38; Deut 32:50). Unlike Aaron with Eleazar, Moses's commissioning of his successor was not followed immediately by his death. From the mount he could view the Promised Land, which he was not going to enter (27:12). Like Abraham he would live to a ripe old age and then "[join] his ancestors" (Gen 25:8; Deut 32:50), in his case 120 years (Deut 34:7). However, like

Miriam and Aaron before him, he would die without the pleasure of leading the people into the long-promised land (27:13; see 20:24-28; 33:38). Like the rest of the rebellious first generation, his grave would be in the wilderness. It is interesting to note that God didn't even allow for the possibility that his bones might later be reburied in Canaan (cf. Gen 47:29-31; 50:5, 25). This resulted from Moses and Aaron's tarnishing God's holiness at Meribah (27:14).

On the one hand, Moses was not set aside in the sense that Paul spoke of (being disqualified; 1 Cor 9:27), especially if taken in the sense of Jesus' words about losing one's soul (Mark 8:36; Luke 9:25). Happily, "there was another Land of Promise from which Moses was not excluded by his offense" (Binns 1927:189). His presence at the Transfiguration demonstrates that (Matt 17:3; Mark 9:4; Luke 9:30). On the other hand, as Binns also notes, "A lifetime of faithful service is apparently wiped out by a single lapse" (1927:189). The account in Deuteronomy shows Moses pleading for God to relent; however, God cut off that plea, much as he cut off Paul's plea for relief from the thorn in the flesh (Deut 3:23-27; 2 Cor 12:8-9). In the face of the one who sovereignly determines who has breath (27:16), Moses resigned himself to his punishment. He only asked, "Please appoint a new . . . leader for the community" (27:16). His main concern was for someone to lead them in the conquest; without such a leader, they would be left like "sheep without a shepherd" (27:17). They would fail as an army, be scattered as a people, and fall prey in the wild.

The Lord responded with directions (27:18-21). He chose Joshua, because even before his commissioning he had "the Spirit in him" (27:18).[1] This must have been evidenced during Joshua's already long record of service (11:26-30; 13:1–14:38; Exod 17:8-16; 24:13; 32:15-20; 33:7-11). The commissioning was to effect a transfer of some of Moses's "authority" to Joshua so the community would acknowledge him as their leader (27:20). The public nature of this commissioning ritual, over which Moses himself officiated, would have lent Joshua an "aura that commands awe and respect" (Levine 2000:351). This didn't make Joshua Moses's equal, since he received only "some" of Moses's gravitas (27:20). He wouldn't enjoy Moses's direct link with God (12:6-8); Joshua was told that he would have to take recourse to the priestly Urim (27:21). However, it's interesting to note that we hear of no use of the Urim and Thummim in the book of Joshua; rather, we hear that the Lord spoke with Joshua (Noordtzij 1983:257, citing Josh 1:1; 3:7; 4:1; 5:2). Displaying a ready obedience, Moses commissioned Joshua (27:22-23).

This succession narrative shows various connections to other texts: (1) There is much in the events that parallels the transfer from Aaron to Eleazar (20:22-29). The differences are that priestly succession involved divestiture and investiture, passing along the sacred vestments; in the transfer from Moses to Joshua, the "authority" is passed on. (2) The succession of Elijah to Elisha involved a transfer of a cloak, like the priestly succession of Aaron to Eleazar, and the transfer of charismatic power, like the succession from Moses to Joshua. (3) The apostolic succession from Jesus involved an even greater transfer of power and authority, which "clothes" a person with power, like a priestly garment or royal robe might (Luke 24:49). This allows those so anointed to expand the messianic work beyond even what the Christ did during his earthly ministry (John 14:12) and gives them kingdom authority to rule (Dan 7:18, 22, 27; Matt 19:28; Luke 22:29; 1 Cor 6:3; Rev 2:26).

ENDNOTE

1. Later, this "Spirit of wisdom" (*ruakh khokmah*) is attributed to Moses's commissioning him (Deut 34:9).

◆   ### 3.   Regulations for offerings (28:1–29:40)

The LORD said to Moses, [2]"Give these instructions to the people of Israel: The offerings you present as special gifts are a pleasing aroma to me; they are my food. See to it that they are brought at the appointed times and offered according to my instructions.

[3]"Say to the people: This is the special gift you must present to the LORD as your daily burnt offering. You must offer two one-year-old male lambs with no defects. [4]Sacrifice one lamb in the morning and the other in the evening. [5]With each lamb you must offer a grain offering of two quarts* of choice flour mixed with one quart* of pure oil of pressed olives. [6]This is the regular burnt offering instituted at Mount Sinai as a special gift, a pleasing aroma to the LORD. [7]Along with it you must present the proper liquid offering of one quart of alcoholic drink with each lamb, poured out in the Holy Place as an offering to the LORD. [8]Offer the second lamb in the evening with the same grain offering and liquid offering. It, too, is a special gift, a pleasing aroma to the LORD.

[9]"On the Sabbath day, sacrifice two one-year-old male lambs with no defects. They must be accompanied by a grain offering of four quarts* of choice flour moistened with olive oil, and a liquid offering. [10]This is the burnt offering to be presented each Sabbath day, in addition to the regular burnt offering and its accompanying liquid offering.

[11]"On the first day of each month, present an extra burnt offering to the LORD of two young bulls, one ram, and seven one-year-old male lambs, all with no defects. [12]These must be accompanied by grain offerings of choice flour moistened with olive oil—six quarts* with each bull, four quarts with the ram, [13]and two quarts with each lamb. This burnt offering will be a special gift, a pleasing aroma to the LORD. [14]You must also present a liquid offering with each sacrifice: two quarts* of wine for each bull, a third of a gallon* for the ram, and one quart* for each lamb. Present this monthly burnt offering on the first day of each month throughout the year.

[15]"On the first day of each month, you must also offer one male goat for a sin offering to the LORD. This is in addition to the regular burnt offering and its accompanying liquid offering.

[16]"On the fourteenth day of the first month,* you must celebrate the LORD's Passover. [17]On the following day—the fifteenth day of the month—a joyous, seven-day festival will begin, but no bread made with yeast may be eaten. [18]The first day of the festival will be an official day for holy assembly, and no ordinary work may be done on that day. [19]As a special gift you must present a burnt offering to the LORD—two young bulls, one ram, and seven one-year-old male lambs, all with no defects. [20]These will be accompanied by grain offerings of choice flour moistened with olive oil—six quarts with each bull, four quarts with the ram, [21]and two quarts with each of the seven lambs. [22]You must also offer a male goat as a sin offering to purify yourselves and make yourselves right with the LORD.* [23]Present these offerings in

addition to your regular morning burnt offering. ²⁴On each of the seven days of the festival, this is how you must prepare the food offering that is presented as a special gift, a pleasing aroma to the LORD. These will be offered in addition to the regular burnt offerings and liquid offerings. ²⁵The seventh day of the festival will be another official day for holy assembly, and no ordinary work may be done on that day.

²⁶"At the Festival of Harvest,* when you present the first of your new grain to the LORD, you must call an official day for holy assembly, and you may do no ordinary work on that day. ²⁷Present a special burnt offering on that day as a pleasing aroma to the LORD. It will consist of two young bulls, one ram, and seven one-year-old male lambs. ²⁸These will be accompanied by grain offerings of choice flour moistened with olive oil—six quarts with each bull, four quarts with the ram, ²⁹and two quarts with each of the seven lambs. ³⁰Also, offer one male goat to purify yourselves and make yourselves right with the LORD. ³¹Prepare these special burnt offerings, along with their liquid offerings, in addition to the regular burnt offering and its accompanying grain offering. Be sure that all the animals you sacrifice have no defects.

CHAPTER 29

"Celebrate the Festival of Trumpets each year on the first day of the appointed month in early autumn.* You must call an official day for holy assembly, and you may do no ordinary work. ²On that day you must present a burnt offering as a pleasing aroma to the LORD. It will consist of one young bull, one ram, and seven one-year-old male lambs, all with no defects. ³These must be accompanied by grain offerings of choice flour moistened with olive oil—six quarts* with the bull, four quarts* with the ram, ⁴and two quarts* with each of the seven lambs. ⁵In addition, you must sacrifice a male goat as a sin offering to purify yourselves and make yourselves right with the LORD.* ⁶These special

sacrifices are in addition to your regular monthly and daily burnt offerings, and they must be given with their prescribed grain offerings and liquid offerings. These offerings are given as a special gift to the LORD, a pleasing aroma to him.

⁷"Ten days later, on the tenth day of the same month,* you must call another holy assembly. On that day, the Day of Atonement, the people must go without food and must do no ordinary work. ⁸You must present a burnt offering as a pleasing aroma to the LORD. It will consist of one young bull, one ram, and seven one-year-old male lambs, all with no defects. ⁹These offerings must be accompanied by the prescribed grain offerings of choice flour moistened with olive oil—six quarts of choice flour with the bull, four quarts of choice flour with the ram, ¹⁰and two quarts of choice flour with each of the seven lambs. ¹¹You must also sacrifice one male goat for a sin offering. This is in addition to the sin offering of atonement and the regular daily burnt offering with its grain offering, and their accompanying liquid offerings.

¹²"Five days later, on the fifteenth day of the same month,* you must call another holy assembly of all the people, and you may do no ordinary work on that day. It is the beginning of the Festival of Shelters,* a seven-day festival to the LORD. ¹³On the first day of the festival, you must present a burnt offering as a special gift, a pleasing aroma to the LORD. It will consist of thirteen young bulls, two rams, and fourteen one-year-old male lambs, all with no defects. ¹⁴Each of these offerings must be accompanied by a grain offering of choice flour moistened with olive oil—six quarts for each of the thirteen bulls, four quarts for each of the two rams, ¹⁵and two quarts for each of the fourteen lambs. ¹⁶You must also sacrifice a male goat as a sin offering, in addition to the regular burnt offering with its accompanying grain offering and liquid offering.

¹⁷"On the second day of this seven-day

festival, sacrifice twelve young bulls, two rams, and fourteen one-year-old male lambs, all with no defects. ¹⁸Each of these offerings of bulls, rams, and lambs must be accompanied by its prescribed grain offering and liquid offering. ¹⁹You must also sacrifice a male goat as a sin offering, in addition to the regular burnt offering with its accompanying grain offering and liquid offering.

²⁰"On the third day of the festival, sacrifice eleven young bulls, two rams, and fourteen one-year-old male lambs, all with no defects. ²¹Each of these offerings of bulls, rams, and lambs must be accompanied by its prescribed grain offering and liquid offering. ²²You must also sacrifice a male goat as a sin offering, in addition to the regular burnt offering with its accompanying grain offering and liquid offering.

²³"On the fourth day of the festival, sacrifice ten young bulls, two rams, and fourteen one-year-old male lambs, all with no defects. ²⁴Each of these offerings of bulls, rams, and lambs must be accompanied by its prescribed grain offering and liquid offering. ²⁵You must also sacrifice a male goat as a sin offering, in addition to the regular burnt offering with its accompanying grain offering and liquid offering.

²⁶"On the fifth day of the festival, sacrifice nine young bulls, two rams, and fourteen one-year-old male lambs, all with no defects. ²⁷Each of these offerings of bulls, rams, and lambs must be accompanied by its prescribed grain offering and liquid offering. ²⁸You must also sacrifice a male goat as a sin offering, in addition to the regular burnt offering with its accompanying grain offering and liquid offering.

²⁹"On the sixth day of the festival, sacrifice eight young bulls, two rams, and four-teen one-year-old male lambs, all with no defects. ³⁰Each of these offerings of bulls, rams, and lambs must be accompanied by its prescribed grain offering and liquid offering. ³¹You must also sacrifice a male goat as a sin offering, in addition to the regular burnt offering with its accompanying grain offering and liquid offering.

³²"On the seventh day of the festival, sacrifice seven young bulls, two rams, and fourteen one-year-old male lambs, all with no defects. ³³Each of these offerings of bulls, rams, and lambs must be accompanied by its prescribed grain offering and liquid offering. ³⁴You must also sacrifice one male goat as a sin offering, in addition to the regular burnt offering with its accompanying grain offering and liquid offering.

³⁵"On the eighth day of the festival, proclaim another holy day. You must do no ordinary work on that day. ³⁶You must present a burnt offering as a special gift, a pleasing aroma to the LORD. It will consist of one young bull, one ram, and seven one-year-old male lambs, all with no defects. ³⁷Each of these offerings must be accompanied by its prescribed grain offering and liquid offering. ³⁸You must also sacrifice one male goat as a sin offering, in addition to the regular burnt offering with its accompanying grain offering and liquid offering.

³⁹"You must present these offerings to the LORD at your annual festivals. These are in addition to the sacrifices and offerings you present in connection with vows, or as voluntary offerings, burnt offerings, grain offerings, liquid offerings, or peace offerings."

⁴⁰*So Moses gave all of these instructions to the people of Israel as the LORD had commanded him.

28:5a Hebrew ¹/₁₀ *of an ephah* [2.2 liters]; also in 28:13, 21, 29. 28:5b Hebrew ¹/₄ *of a hin* [1 liter]; also in 28:7. 28:9 Hebrew ²/₁₀ *of an ephah* [4.4 liters]; also in 28:12, 20, 28 28:12 Hebrew ³/₁₀ *of an ephah* [6.6 liters]; also in 28:20, 28. 28:14a Hebrew ¹/₂ *of a hin* [2 liters]. 28:14b Hebrew ¹/₃ *of a hin* [1.3 liters]. 28:14c Hebrew ¹/₄ *of a hin* [1 liter]. 28:16 This day in the ancient Hebrew lunar calendar occurred in late March, April, or early May. 28:22 Or *to make atonement for yourselves;* also in 28:30. 28:26 Hebrew *Festival of Weeks.* This was later called the Festival of Pentecost (see Acts 2:1). It is celebrated today as Shavuot (or Shabuoth). 29:1 Hebrew *the first day of the seventh month.* This day in the ancient Hebrew lunar calendar occurred in September or October. This festival is celebrated today as Rosh Hashanah, the Jewish new year.

29:3a Hebrew *3/10 of an ephah* [6.6 liters]; also in 29:9, 14.   29:3b Hebrew *2/10 of an ephah* [4.4 liters]; also
in 29:9, 14.   29:4 Hebrew *1/10 of an ephah* [2.2 liters]; also in 29:10, 15.   29:5 Or *to make atonement for
yourselves.*   29:7 Hebrew *On the tenth day of the seventh month;* see 29:1 and the note there. This day in
the ancient Hebrew lunar calendar occurred in September or October. It is celebrated today as Yom Kippur.
29:12a Hebrew *On the fifteenth day of the seventh month;* see 29:1, 7 and the notes there. This day in the
ancient Hebrew lunar calendar occurred in late September, October, or early November.   29:12b Or *Festival
of Booths,* or *Festival of Tabernacles.* This was earlier called the Festival of the Final Harvest or Festival of
Ingathering (see Exod 23:16b). It is celebrated today as Sukkot (or Succoth).   29:40 Verse 29:40 is numbered
30:1 in Hebrew text.

NOTES

28:5 With each lamb you must offer. The phrase "with each lamb" is only implied in the
Hebrew (see 28:4).

**28:7 Along with it you must present the proper liquid offering of one quart of alcoholic
drink with each lamb, poured out in the Holy Place as an offering to the LORD.** Lit., "and
of its libation, a fourth of a hin for one lamb; in the Sanctuary pour out a libation of *shekar*
to the LORD." On *shekar* [TH7941, ZH8911], see note at 6:3.

28:9 On the Sabbath day, sacrifice two. Lit., "and on the Sabbath day, two," with no verb
following. The NLT adds "sacrifice," as do the LXX, Vulgate, and Temple Scroll (11QTemple
13:17).

four quarts of choice flour. This doubles what was offered daily but without mention of
increase in the amount of olive oil. Yet it is probably implied as a necessary increase to
moisten the flour.

28:26 At the Festival of Harvest, when you present the first of your new grain. Lit.,
"And on the Day of Firstfruits when you present the new grain/meal offering."

29:1 Festival of Trumpets. The word "trumpets" is not in the Hebrew, but it is implied
by the verb, which is used for trumpet calls (10:1-10), including those blown the first of
every month (10:10). As early as the third century BC, this feast was connected with Rosh
Hashanah, or the New Year, an identity that Allen accepts (1990:953). More likely, the OT
evidence favors a New Year in the spring rather than autumn; in fact, the OT itself has no
evidence of a New Year festival within Judaism (Ashley 1993:569 n. 35; Kraus 1966:61-66;
Mowinckel 1992:2.94-95; Ringgren 1970:185-200). "The Festival of the Final Harvest"
is connected to "the end of the harvest season" (*betse'th hashanah* [TH3318, ZH3655]; Exod
23:16), or the "turn of the year" (*tequpath hashanah* [TH8622A, ZH9543]; Exod 34:22), which
might then be identified with this festival. However, Block (ISBE 3.529-532) says it is likely
that *betse'th hashanah* means "springtime," as does *ba' shanah* [TH935, ZH995]; cf. 2 Kgs 13:20.
He concludes that Israel's fall festivals were harvest festivals, not New Year festivals; they
lacked all reference to creation, primordial monsters, sacred marriage of the king, or other
ancient Near Eastern imagery generally associated with New Year rituals (ISBE 3.532).

29:6 special gift to the LORD. Cf. ESV, "a food offering to the LORD." Lexicons have "offer-
ing(s) made by fire" (BDB 78; HALOT 93) for the word *'isheh* [TH801, ZH852], so this is perhaps better rendered as, "a fire offering to the LORD."

29:7 the Day of Atonement. Though the technical term *yom hakkippurim* [TH3725, ZH4113] is
not used in these verses, the ritual described here is clearly the one described in detail elsewhere as the Day of Atonement (Lev 16; 23:26-32).

the people must go without food. Lit., "and there shall be for you affliction of your souls,"
which is generally interpreted in terms of fasting (Ps 35:13; Isa 58:3, 5). It may also refer to
wearing sackcloth or to refraining from various foods or drinks, bathing, or sexual intercourse.

do no ordinary work. Lit., "all work you shall not do," the same strict restriction used for
the Sabbath (Lev 23:3), which was more restrictive than for other festivals.

29:11 *sin offering of atonement.* This probably included the goat that was the purification offering for the people's sins (Lev 16:7-9, 15-19) and possibly the bull offering for the priest's own household (Lev 16:6, 11-14).

29:12 *Festival of Shelters.* This is how it was commonly known (*sukkoth* [TH5521, ZH6109]; Lev 23:34; Deut 16:13; Ezra 3:4; Zech 14:16-18; 2 Macc 10:6), but it was also known as "the Festival of the LORD" (Lev 23:39; Judg 21:19), or even "the Festival," that is, the *outstanding* festival (e.g., 1 Kgs 8:2, 65; 2 Chr 5:3; 7:8-9; Neh 8:14; Ezek 45:23, 25).

29:35 *On the eighth day of the festival.* Lit., "on the eighth day," which was "the last day, the climax of the festival" (John 7:37).

COMMENTARY

After he had commissioned Joshua, Moses received the next task for the Israelites— to set up the cultic calendar that the people would follow in the land. Chapters 28– 29 also deal with offerings, overlapping Leviticus 23 and developing it further. Similar but less complete and systematic festal calendars are found elsewhere (Exod 23:14-17; 34:18-24; Lev 23; Deut 16:1-17; Ezek 45:18–46:15).

God described the offerings as "special gifts," a "pleasing aroma to me," and "my food" (28:1-2). Figurative expressions sometimes have God eating and drinking; however, the Bible ridicules those who actually believe that God eats and drinks of the sacrifices (Deut 32:38; Ps 50:7-15). These expressions indicate the pleasure that God would take in the offerings of his children. But these "gifts" were not to be brought only at the whim of the worshiper. God warned, "See to it that they are brought at the appointed times and offered according to my instructions" (28:2).

The treatment of the sacrificial calendar works from the most frequent events to the least frequent: the daily (28:1-8), weekly (28:9-10), monthly (28:11-15), and annual offerings. The latter are treated in calendar order: Passover and Unleavened Bread (28:16-25), Harvest (28:26-31), Trumpets (29:1-6), Day of Atonement (29:7-11), and Shelters (29:12-39). The offerings were cumulative, so that the Sabbath offering was added to the daily offering (28:10) and likewise with the annual offerings (28:10, 15, 24, 31; 29:16, 19, 22, 25, 28, 31, 34, 38).

Milgrom (1989:237-238) details the prominence of the number seven and its multiples in the cultic system:

> In addition to the frequency of the number seven (and its multiple fourteen) in the above table, there are other occurrences of seven: the seven festivals (including the paschal observance, 28:16, and excluding Sabbaths and new moons); the seven-day Unleavened Bread and Sukkot festivals; the preponderance of festivals in the seventh month (New Year, Yom Kippur, Sukkot, Atzereth); the seven festival days, in addition to the Sabbath, on which work is prohibited, listed in 28:18, 25, 26; 29:1, 7, 12, 35; the bulls required for Sukkot add up to seventy; the total number of animals offered on this seven-day festival is $7 \times 7 \times 2$ lambs, 7×2 rams, 7×10 bulls, and 7 goats.

Occasion	Lambs	Rams	Bulls	Goats
Each day (28:3-8)	2	–	–	–
Each Sabbath (28:9-10)	2	–	–	–
Each new moon (28:11-15)	7	1	2	1
Each Day of Unleavened Bread (28:16-25)	7	1	2	1
Feast of Weeks (28:26-31)	7	1	2	1
Feast of Trumpets (29:1-6)	7	1	1	1
Yom Kippur (29:7-11)	7	1	1	1
1st of Sukkot (29:12-16)	14	2	13	1
2nd of Sukkot (29:17-19)	14	2	12	1
3rd of Sukkot (29:20-22)	14	2	11	1
4th of Sukkot (29:23-25)	14	2	10	1
5th of Sukkot (29:26-28)	14	2	9	1
6th of Sukkot (29:29-31)	14	2	8	1
7th of Sukkot (29:32-34)	14	2	7	1
8th day, Shemini Atzereth (29:35-38)	7	1	1	1

Each animal offering was accompanied by oil-moistened grain offerings, and a liquid offering as follows:

		Grain		Drink
Daily (morning & evening)	*Lamb*	1/10 ephah moistened with 1/4 hin oil (28:5)		1/4 hin (28:7)
Weekly	*Lamb* (28:9)	2/10 ephah with oil (28:9)		1/2 hin (28:14)
Monthly & Annual Festivals	*Bull* *Ram* *Lamb*	3/10 ephah with oil (28:12, 20, 28; 29:3, 9, 14) 2/10 ephah with oil (28:12, 20, 28; 29:3, 9) 1/10 ephah with oil (28:13, 21, 29; 29:4, 10)		1/3 hin (28:14) 1/4 hin (28:14) 1/4 hin (28:14)

The amount of grain used for the lamb was doubled for the weekly offering, though not for each lamb in the monthly offering. We might suppose the amount of oil remained proportionate to the size of the grain offerings, since the amount is only listed for the offering of 1/10 ephah (28:5 mg). The drink offerings for the bulls, rams, and lambs for all the annual festivals must have remained the same as those recorded for the monthly festival, since grain offerings stayed the same for each (28:14; see 29:6, 18, 21, 24, 27, 30, 33, 37).

Daily Offerings (28:3–8). The daily offering "constituted the basis of the whole sacrificial system in Israel" (E. W. Davies 1995b:308). Offered both morning and evening, it consisted of a burnt offering of a lamb together with its grain and wine offerings (28:3-8). A parenthetical note describes this as a *tamid* [TH8548, ZH9458] offering, a perpetual offering prescribed at Sinai itself (28:6). The grain offering consisted of 1/10 ephah of choice flour mixed with a quarter hin of the best olive oil (28:5). In addition, a drink offering of a quarter hin of "alcoholic drink" accompanied each lamb (28:7). Although wine and alcohol were forbidden to priests while on duty (Lev 10:9), they were used in Israel's joyous festive meals (Deut 14:26) and recommended to the tired and weak (Prov 31:6). As an offering, wine and stronger drinks were poured out at the bronze altar upon which the lamb was burnt (Sir 50:15; Josephus *Antiquities* 3.234 [3.9.4]).

Jesus became "the Lamb of God who takes away the sin of the world" (John 1:29); in fact, he died at the time of the evening sacrifice, whereupon sacrifice became obsolete (G. J. Wenham 1981:199-200). Nonetheless, Jewish and Christian commentators have always regarded the daily burnt offerings as a model of worship for all time. Prayer should be offered at least every morning and evening; indeed, the whole of life is to be dedicated to God through repeated acts of praise and thanksgiving (Rom 12:1; 1 Thess 5:16-18).

Weekly Offerings (28:9–10). The weekly Sabbath offering included two lambs but doubled the amount of grain used, which probably implies a doubled amount of oil used to moisten it. This was in addition to the daily offering (28:10), which would continue on the Sabbath as on every other day.

The worshiper rested on the Sabbath, imitating the Creator, whose image he bears (Exod 20:8-11), and recalling the Lord as his redeemer from slavery (Deut 5:12-15). Jesus and the apostles honored the Sabbath by attending synagogue (Luke 4:16; Acts 13:42), but they rejected many of the rabbinic traditions about how to observe it (John 5:9-11; Col 2:16) because Jesus was Lord of the Sabbath (Matt 12:8; Luke 6:5). He reasserted the principle that Sabbath was made for man, not man for the Sabbath (Mark 2:27; cf. Exod 23:12; Deut 5:14). So, too, the church has celebrated its redemption by congregating and sharing in the Lord's Table once a week (Acts 20:7), though now on the first day of the week rather than the Sabbath (Matt 28:1; 1 Cor 16:2; Rev 1:10), knowing that Jesus is our Sabbath (Heb 4:1-5).

Monthly Offerings (28:11–15). The quantities for the sacrificial supplements have already been given (15:2-12). Like the daily and Sabbath offerings, lambs were offered, but now seven of them. In addition, the offering included a ram and two bulls (28:11). Each of those included a prescribed grain (28:12) and liquid offering (28:13). The lamb had the same grain offering and drink offering as the daily lamb offering; the ram had twice the grain offering. Finally, there was the "goat for a sin offering," which was not included in the daily or Sabbath offerings but was repeated in the annual festivals (28:15, 22; 29:5, 11, 16, 19, 22, 25, 28, 31, 34, 38).

All of this was in addition to the prescribed daily offering (28:15). The offering amounts are the same as those required on the Festivals of Passover and Unleavened Bread (28:16-25) and Harvest (28:26-31) and similar to the requirements for the Festival of Trumpets (29:1-6) and the Day of Atonement (29:7-11). Only the repetitive doubled offerings of the Festival of Shelters exceeded this monthly offering (29:12-38). This established the new moon as a dominant Sabbath-like festival that provided a monthly opportunity for family worship (1 Sam 20:5; 2 Kgs 4:23).

Amos complained that no one wanted to stop trading on the Sabbath (Amos 8:5), and Isaiah complained that the new moons had become "sinful and false" (Isa 1:13). Because of that, Hosea even called for an end to them (Hos 2:11). In this New Covenant age, one should think oneself neither favored nor condemned for participating or not participating in new moon festivities, which were only shadows pointing forward to Christ (Gal 4:10; Col 2:16-17).

Passover and Unleavened Bread (28:16–25). The spring Festival of Passover was celebrated at home rather than as a public celebration (Exod 12:3-14), and its practices were already laid down (Exod 12:14-20; Lev 23:4-8; also Deut 16:1-8). No more regulation was needed, so the next verse goes right to the weeklong Festival of Unleavened Bread, with which it was associated (Exod 12:15; 34:18; Lev 23:4-8; Deut 16:16).

This was a week away from job-related work (28:18), though it allowed the normal domestic labors that the stricter laws prohibited for the Sabbath (Lev 23:3) and Day of Atonement (29:7). Each day of the Festival of Unleavened Bread a series of offerings were made, which were the same as those already described for the Festival of the New Moon (28:19-25).

From the start, this festival was a matter of faith (Heb 11:28); Jesus observed it (Matt 26:17; Mark 14:12-16; John 2:13) and was crucified at Passover time (John 11:55), considering his own death his "exodus" (Luke 9:31). He died as our Passover lamb, so we are to remove all the "yeast" (i.e., wickedness) from our lives (1 Cor 5:7).

Firstfruits (28:26–31). Better known as the Festival of Harvest (Exod 23:16) or Festival of Weeks (Exod 34:22 mg; Deut 16:10 mg), the Festival of Harvest celebrated the conclusion of the barley harvest seven weeks after the first cutting of grain (28:26-31; cf. Exod 23:16; Lev 23:15-21; Deut 16:9-12). Later Jewish tradition connected it also with the giving of the law at Sinai in the third month after leaving Egypt (Exod 19:1; 2 Chr 15:10-15). Because it was timed seven weeks (50 days) after Passover and Unleavened Bread (Lev 23:9-22), it came to be called Pentecost, a term well-known from a foundational event for the New Testament church (Acts 2). It appears that Paul gladly celebrated this festival (Acts 20:16; 1 Cor 16:8).

Day for Blowing Trumpets (29:1-6). Chapter 29 continues the list of annual festivals that started in chapter 28 with the Festival of Passover and Unleavened Bread (28:16-25) and the Festival of Harvest (28:26-31). Now we have the festivals that fall in "the seventh, and most sacred, month of the Hebrew calendar" (Ashley 1993:568): the Festival of Trumpets (29:1-6), the Day of Atonement (29:7-11), and the Festival of Shelters (29:12-40).

The first day of the seventh month was the Festival of Trumpets (29:1-6). This was celebrated as a day off from regular work, a day for a holy convocation at which a series of offerings were made. These offerings were the same as those offered at the annual festivals already mentioned in chapter 28, with the exception that only one bull was offered, instead of the two used in those festivals (29:2; cf. 28:11, 19, 27). Verse six notes that the special offerings for the Festival of Trumpets were compiled with the new moon offerings (28:9) and daily offerings (28:3-8): 16 lambs, 2 rams, 3 bulls, and 2 goats, each with whatever was prescribed by way of accompanying oil-moistened grain offerings and liquid offerings.

Day of Atonement (29:7-11). The Day of Atonement fell on the tenth day of the seventh month. Whereas the other annual occasions were festive, this holy convocation was a day to "practice self-affliction" (Levine 2000:388). This was to symbolize penitence (30:13; Ps 35:13; Isa 58:3-5; Heb 9:7-12, 23-28). That meant a strict prohibition of work, during which the same offerings presented at the first of the month (29:1-7) were repeated (29:8-11).

Harrison's summary of the Christian meaning of this is strong. He points out that this solemn day was the Old Testament's answer to the problem of universal sinfulness (Rom 3:23), which would lead to death without God's provision of forgiveness (Rom 6:23). By its repetition, it foreshadowed God's final provision; however, the blood of bulls and goats could not actually cleanse (Heb 10:4). Only the Lamb of God could do that (2 Cor 5:19). So Jesus became our High Priest (Heb 7:24), who did not need first to offer a sacrifice for his own sin, and whose blood redeems (Eph 1:7; 1 Pet 1:18-19), justifies (Rom 5:9), brings peace with God (Col 1:20), pardons (Eph 1:7), and sanctifies (Heb 13:12; 1 John 1:7) (Harrison 1990:371).

Festival of Shelters (29:12-39). The Festival of Shelters was an extended celebration marking the end of the agricultural year. It ran from the fifteenth to the twenty-first of the seventh month (29:12-34), with an "eighth day" for a closing assembly (29:35-38). Massive daily offerings were made, doubling the number of lambs and rams offered in other annual festivals, and repeating it for seven days. Rather than offering the 70 bulls at the rate of 10 per day, the festival started out with 13 (29:13), then 12 (29:17), and so forth each day until the count worked its way down to seven bulls offered on the seventh day (29:32). I see no reason to think this indicates a decline in intensity of joy as the festival went on (Noth 1968:223; Sturdy 1976:207) or to connect it in some way to the waning moon (Binns 1927:198-199); rather, it was probably to arrive at the number seven by the final day (Keil 1869:222), "a number that insinuates itself into the entirety of this cultic calendar" (Milgrom 1989:248).

The "eighth day" closed out the festival (1 Kgs 8:66; 2 Chr 7:9) with the stricter Sabbath-like work restrictions (29:35) and with offerings that no longer followed the seven-day succession but were like those offered at the Festival of Trumpets on the first of this month (29:1-6) and on the Day of Atonement on the tenth of this month (29:7-11).

A carnival-like festival developed over time, especially after the return from exile. The seven-day succession of offerings continued (29:12-34; Lev 23:33-36), and each celebrant gathered branches to construct a *sukkah* [TH5521, ZH6109] in which to sleep and eat meals throughout the festival (Lev 23:40-42; Neh 8:13-18). Scraps of these branches were bound together and waved in an act of rejoicing as the people joined in the daily *hallel* [TH1984A, ZH2146] (Pss 113–118; cf. John 12:13; Rev 7:9). Eventually, water and light rituals became important to the festival. By the time of Jesus it seems that the first day of the festival included a procession that the priests led down to the Pool of Siloam to draw out a supply of water, which was to last for the whole festival. This water was carried in joyous procession, with shouts, "Save us, O LORD" or "Hosanna" (*hoshi'ah nna'* [TH3467, ZH3828]; Ps 118:25; cf. 2 Kgs 19:19; Matt 21:9-11; Mark 11:8-10). At night, "Four huge Menorahs fitted out with wicks made from the worn-out garments of the priests illumined the entire temple area. Under them the celebrants danced a torch dance to the accompaniment of flute playing, and the Levites chanted the Psalms of Ascent (120–134)" (IDB 456).

The Gospel of John mentions this festival. The festival's water ritual was accompanied by the words of the prophet Isaiah: "With joy you will drink deeply from the fountain of salvation!" (Isa 12:3; cf. Pss 41:1; 63:1; 143:6), a promise that Jesus fulfilled: "Anyone who is thirsty may come to me!" (John 7:37; cf. John 4:10; 6:35; Rev 21:6; 22:1, 17). In addition, at a particular point, the Temple precincts were flooded with light, a symbolism he also fulfilled: "I am the light of the world. If you follow me, you won't have to walk in darkness, because you will have the light that leads to life" (John 8:12).

The passage closes with a refreshing return to the ready obedience that characterized the response of Moses and the people recorded earlier in the book (29:40).

◆   ## 4. Regulations for vows (30:1-16)

¹*Then Moses summoned the leaders of the tribes of Israel and told them, "This is what the LORD has commanded: ²A man who makes a vow to the LORD or makes a pledge under oath must never break it. He must do exactly what he said he would do.

³"If a young woman makes a vow to the LORD or a pledge under oath while she is still living at her father's home, ⁴and her father hears of the vow or pledge and does not object to it, then all her vows and pledges will stand. ⁵But if her father refuses to let her fulfill the vow or pledge on the day he hears of it, then all her vows and pledges will become invalid. The LORD will forgive her because her father would not let her fulfill them.

⁶"Now suppose a young woman makes a vow or binds herself with an impulsive pledge and later marries. ⁷If her husband

learns of her vow or pledge and does not object on the day he hears of it, her vows and pledges will stand. ⁸But if her husband refuses to accept her vow or impulsive pledge on the day he hears of it, he nullifies her commitments, and the LORD will forgive her. ⁹If, however, a woman is a widow or is divorced, she must fulfill all her vows and pledges.

¹⁰"But suppose a woman is married and living in her husband's home when she makes a vow or binds herself with a pledge. ¹¹If her husband hears of it and does not object to it, her vow or pledge will stand. ¹²But if her husband refuses to accept it on the day he hears of it, her vow or pledge will be nullified, and the LORD will forgive her. ¹³So her husband may either confirm or nullify any vows or pledges she makes to deny herself. ¹⁴But if he does not object on the day he hears of it, then he is agreeing to all her vows and pledges. ¹⁵If he waits more than a day and then tries to nullify a vow or pledge, he will be punished for her guilt."

¹⁶These are the regulations the LORD gave Moses concerning relationships between a man and his wife, and between a father and a young daughter who still lives at home.

30:1 Verses 30:1-16 are numbered 30:2-17 in Hebrew text.

NOTES

30:2 [3] *a man.* Heb., *'ish* [TH376, ZH408], which can refer to people generally (e.g., Judg 9:49; Isa 2:9, 11, 17), but here it is "man" in contrast with "women" (*'ishah* [TH802, ZH851]; 30:3-15).

vow. Heb., *neder* [TH5088, ZH5624], in this chapter a vow to do something positive, such as offering a sacrifice; however, outside of this chapter, the term can refer to either vows of positive action or of abstinence.

a pledge under oath. Lit., "has sworn an oath to bind a bond on his soul." It is a "binding obligation, a vow of abstinence" (HALOT), e.g., a self-imposed fast (30:13; see 1 Sam 14:24) or abstinence from sleep (Ps 132:2-5).

30:4 [5] *does not object.* Lit., "made himself deaf to her," i.e., he kept silent about it. This condition allowed no passive "pocket veto" of her vow; the man must speak if he would forbid it.

30:6 [7] *and later marries.* Lit., "if a woman belongs to a man," whether by espousal (Budd 1984:323; Snaith 1969:193; Sturdy 1976:210) or marriage (Ashley 1993:579). The KJV and traditional interpretation understood this to mean the woman was already espoused or married when taking the vow, even though this would be redundant with the next section (30:10-12). Perhaps a future tense is implied, i.e., "if a woman comes to belong to a man," but still hasn't fulfilled the vow (see Ashley 1993:580; E. W. Davies 1995b:318; Noordtzij 1983:268; G. J. Wenham 1981:208). Newer translations refer to getting married after coming under the vow (NAB, NASB, NRSV, ESV, NJB, NJPS).

30:15 [16] *he will be punished for her guilt.* Lit., "he shall bear her guilt/punishment." Either the husband has forced her to break her vow/oath or he has deceived her into believing that he had annulled her vow/oath as soon as he was informed of it (Rashbam). In such a case, it is as if he has taken over her vow and has violated it (Ramban; see Milgrom 1989:254).

COMMENTARY

Vows were a common part of ancient Near Eastern religion (Beyerlin 1978:30-35, 228-237). The material could have come to Moses any time, perhaps at the same time as the material on the Nazirite vow (ch 6); however, it fits well here. Commentators suggest various connections, which are summarized by G. J. Wenham (1981:206-207):

> Vows were accompanied by sacrifice, perhaps to begin it and then in thanks when the prayer was answered (Lev 7:16; Ps 50:14); and this would be most possible at the feast times when worshipers went to the Temple in Jerusalem.
>
> Vows were frequent in wartime (Num 21:2; Judg 11:30; 21:1-7), and Israel was now facing its wars of conquest (Num 21, 31–32). Not only that, but wives would be left behind for battle (Num 32:26), and returning husbands might not want the family bound by vows their wives had made in their absence.
>
> Including vows here heightens the parallel with the Sinaitic legislation, which also contains material on vows (Lev 27; Num 6).
>
> Israel had already made a vow that they would annihilate the Canaanites (Num 21:2), and this material might be confirming that vow as an acceptable program for conquest.

Vows were strictly voluntary, but once made, they were binding. Scripture pays more attention to the matter than we do, from the psalmist's promise (Ps 116:12-14), to Moses and Qoheleth's warnings (Deut 12:11; 23:21; Eccl 5:4; cf. Eccl 1:1 mg). It arranges for redeeming vowed property (Deut 23:21-23). It even speaks of wicked vows, such as those made to the Queen of Heaven (Jer 44:25) or with fees from prostitution (Deut 23:18; cf. Prov 7:14). It lays out guidelines for making vows of property to the Lord (Lev 27). And it warns people to confess their sin if they "make a foolish vow of any kind" (Lev 5:4-6).

The New Testament says less about vows: Herod's vow to dancing Herodias (Mark 6:23), Paul's Nazirite vow (Acts 18:18), and the one he funded (Acts 21:23) are about all we hear of. Jesus opposed the use of vows to evade responsibilities to one's parents (Matt 15:3-9). As in this text, wives were expected to be subject to their husbands (Eph 5:22-24; Titus 2:5; 1 Pet 3:1-7), although mutual consent had become a strong consideration (1 Cor 7:4). Perhaps James's warning about the tongue also applies here (Jas 5:12). If the vow involved an oath, Jesus thought it better to avoid them (Matt 5:33-37); a simple yes or no without a vow was better (Jas 5:12).

Vows Made by Men (30:1-2). The general principle is this: A grown man must keep his word, whether it is a *vow* to do something positive, such as bringing an offering or sacrifice, or a *pledge* to forgo something, such as sleep (Ps 132:2-5) or food (1 Sam 14:24). A vow might be made in the crisis of sickness, military threat, or the like (e.g., 21:2; Gen 28:20-22); however, once the crisis was passed, the man must do "exactly what he said" (30:2). Some among Judaism thought this meant a vow was binding even if it did not correctly represent the speaker's intention, like Isaac's blessing of Jacob into which he was tricked (Gen 27:33-35). Later Judaism taught that "no utterance is binding unless the mouth and the heart agree" (E. W. Davies 1995b:317, quoting *m. Terumot* 3:8), even though that could certainly be abused with dishonest equivocation. But Ashley (1993:578 n. 24) cites vows that were binding no matter what: Isaac's blessing of Jacob (Gen 27) and Jephthah's foolish and tragic vow (Judg 11:35).

Vows Made by Women (30:3-16). Numbers 30:3-16 rounds off chapters 27–30 with an inclusio that returns to the issue of women's rights, which began the section (27:1-11) (Ashley 1993:576; Budd 1984:324). Verses 3-16 set out the matter for women of various classes: a daughter with her father (30:3-5), a woman who is getting married (30:6-8), a woman who has been widowed or divorced (30:9), and a wife and her husband (30:10-12). Then it makes a generalization about women and vows (30:13-15) and closes with a summary (30:16). The section assumes that fathers and husbands assume responsibility for vows made by their daughters and wives, probably because of reasons of authority over their women and control over all family wealth.

Case One (30:3-5). If a father opposes the vow of a girl living at home, it is abrogated. Philip suggests that this is about rash vows, which the father could disallow (1993:304), or a vow that is "to her detriment." But this verse makes no such qualification of which vows the father might disallow. It was left to his own discretion, with no requirement that he justify his decision (E. W. Davies 1995b:317; Noth 1968:225); perhaps he would annul them if they were to *his* detriment. For that matter, the only biblical example we have of a father, an unmarried daughter, and a rash vow is that of Jephthah's own rash vow about his daughter (Judg 11)! It doesn't seem that rashness constituted justifiable grounds for exemption from fulfilling the obligation (Noordtzij 1983:268), as various texts show (Ashley 1993:574, citing 30:6, 8; Gen 27; Lev 5:4). This verse is not so much about protecting the girl against rash vows, but about protecting her from God's judgment if her father wouldn't allow her to fulfill them, i.e., "the LORD will forgive her" (30:5), not "she will be rescued from a rash vow." It also implies that "neither wives nor children may substitute self-imposed religious obligations for God-given duties" (G. J. Wenham 1981:208). For example, a vow of *qorban* that keeps one from taking care of one's parents is abrogated (Mark 7:10-13).

Case Two (30:6-8). If a new husband doesn't intend to back his fiancée's vows, her vow is abrogated. Proverbs warns, "Don't trap yourself by making a rash promise to God and only later counting the cost" (Prov 20:25). So perhaps what is "impulsive" (30:6) is the very fact of taking a long-term pledge while expecting to marry soon (Noth 1968:226). A young husband might find the provisions of the vow too burdensome, even if they had been an acceptable burden to his bride's economically better-established father. As is the case elsewhere for men with women under their authority, there is no pocket veto of the vow. The new husband must accept or revoke the vow "on the day he hears of it" (30:7-8a). Again, if the man abrogates the vow, the woman remains guiltless (30:8b; cf. 30:5).

Case Three (30:9). A widowed or divorced woman who returned to her father's house remained responsible for her vows. She might seek help from her father, brothers, or sons; however, she remained accountable for the vow and could not return to her premarital status.[1]

Case Four (30:10-12). A husband can veto his wife's vows if he does so as soon as he knows about it, even if the vows are made after they are married; however, he can't have second thoughts later. The best example of this is Hannah's vow (1 Sam 1:11), against which her husband took no action and which she and her husband together implemented (1 Sam 1:22-25), implying his concurrence with her vow (1 Sam 1:23). In fact, perhaps Hannah's vow (1 Sam 1:11) is later called her husband's vow (1 Sam 1:21),[2] "because having not objected to it, he is obligated to fulfill it" (Milgrom 1989:254).

A Generalization (30:13-15). Each of the cases shifted blame for not fulfilling the vow off the woman if her man abrogated it. If the man did so immediately, no penalty accrued to the woman or to himself; however, if he delayed in abrogating the vow, the man assumed the guilt the woman would have carried for refusing to fulfill her vow (Ashley 1993:582; de Vaulx 1972:347-348).

Summary: Vows Made by Women under Authority (30:16; cf. 30:3-8, 10-15). The final verse summarizes the matter of women and their vows when under a man's authority, which is probably why the issues of widows and divorcées (30:9) are not included here.

ENDNOTES
1. This verse is a bit of a parenthetical aside, which the summation (30:16) doesn't mention.
2. "To offer to the LORD the yearly sacrifice and to pay his vow" (ESV).

◆   **C. Settlement Arrangements for the Transjordan (31:1–32:42)**
    1. Defeating Midian (31:1–54)

Then the LORD said to Moses, [2]"On behalf of the people of Israel, take revenge on the Midianites for leading them into idolatry. After that, you will die and join your ancestors."

[3]So Moses said to the people, "Choose some men, and arm them to fight the LORD's war of revenge against Midian. [4]From each tribe of Israel, send 1,000 men into battle." [5]So they chose 1,000 men from each tribe of Israel, a total of 12,000 men armed for battle. [6]Then Moses sent them out, 1,000 men from each tribe, and Phinehas son of Eleazar the priest led them into battle. They carried along the holy objects of the sanctuary and the trumpets for sounding the charge. [7]They attacked Midian as the LORD had commanded Moses, and they killed all the men. [8]All five of the Midianite kings—Evi, Rekem, Zur, Hur, and Reba—died in the battle. They also killed Balaam son of Beor with the sword.

[9]Then the Israelite army captured the Midianite women and children and seized their cattle and flocks and all their wealth as plunder. [10]They burned all the towns and villages where the Midianites had lived. [11]After they had gathered the plunder and captives, both people and animals, [12]they brought them all to Moses and Eleazar the priest, and to the whole

community of Israel, which was camped on the plains of Moab beside the Jordan River, across from Jericho. ¹³Moses, Eleazar the priest, and all the leaders of the community went to meet them outside the camp. ¹⁴But Moses was furious with all the generals and captains* who had returned from the battle.

¹⁵"Why have you let all the women live?" he demanded. ¹⁶"These are the very ones who followed Balaam's advice and caused the people of Israel to rebel against the LORD at Mount Peor. They are the ones who caused the plague to strike the LORD's people. ¹⁷So kill all the boys and all the women who have had intercourse with a man. ¹⁸Only the young girls who are virgins may live; you may keep them for yourselves. ¹⁹And all of you who have killed anyone or touched a dead body must stay outside the camp for seven days. You must purify yourselves and your captives on the third and seventh days. ²⁰Purify all your clothing, too, and everything made of leather, goat hair, or wood."

²¹Then Eleazar the priest said to the men who were in the battle, "The LORD has given Moses this legal requirement: ²²Anything made of gold, silver, bronze, iron, tin, or lead—²³that is, all metals that do not burn—must be passed through fire in order to be made ceremonially pure. These metal objects must then be further purified with the water of purification. But everything that burns must be purified by the water alone. ²⁴On the seventh day you must wash your clothes and be purified. Then you may return to the camp."

²⁵And the LORD said to Moses, ²⁶"You and Eleazar the priest and the family leaders of each tribe are to make a list of all the plunder taken in the battle, including the people and animals. ²⁷Then divide the plunder into two parts, and give half to the men who fought the battle and half to the rest of the people. ²⁸From the army's portion, first give the LORD his share of the plunder—one of every 500 of the prisoners and of the cattle, donkeys, sheep, and goats. ²⁹Give this share of the army's half to Eleazar the priest as an offering to the LORD. ³⁰From the half that belongs to the people of Israel, take one of every fifty of the prisoners and of the cattle, donkeys, sheep, goats, and other animals. Give this share to the Levites, who are in charge of maintaining the LORD's Tabernacle." ³¹So Moses and Eleazar the priest did as the LORD commanded Moses.

³²The plunder remaining from everything the fighting men had taken totaled 675,000 sheep and goats, ³³72,000 cattle, ³⁴61,000 donkeys, ³⁵and 32,000 virgin girls.

³⁶Half of the plunder was given to the fighting men. It totaled 337,500 sheep and goats, ³⁷of which 675 were the LORD's share; ³⁸36,000 cattle, of which 72 were the LORD's share; ³⁹30,500 donkeys, of which 61 were the LORD's share; ⁴⁰and 16,000 virgin girls, of whom 32 were the LORD's share. ⁴¹Moses gave all the LORD's share to Eleazar the priest, just as the LORD had directed him.

⁴²Half of the plunder belonged to the people of Israel, and Moses separated it from the half belonging to the fighting men. ⁴³It totaled 337,500 sheep and goats, ⁴⁴36,000 cattle, ⁴⁵30,500 donkeys, ⁴⁶and 16,000 virgin girls. ⁴⁷From the half-share given to the people, Moses took one of every fifty prisoners and animals and gave them to the Levites, who maintained the LORD's Tabernacle. All this was done as the LORD had commanded Moses.

⁴⁸Then all the generals and captains came to Moses ⁴⁹and said, "We, your servants, have accounted for all the men who went out to battle under our command; not one of us is missing! ⁵⁰So we are presenting the items of gold we captured as an offering to the LORD from our share of the plunder—armbands, bracelets, rings, earrings, and necklaces. This will purify our lives before the LORD and make us right with him.*"

⁵¹So Moses and Eleazar the priest received the gold from all the military commanders—all kinds of jewelry and crafted objects. ⁵²In all, the gold that the generals and captains presented as a gift to the LORD weighed about 420 pounds.* ⁵³All the fighting men had taken some of the plunder for themselves. ⁵⁴So Moses and Eleazar the priest accepted the gifts from the generals and captains and brought the gold to the Tabernacle* as a reminder to the LORD that the people of Israel belong to him.

31:14 Hebrew *the commanders of thousands, and the commanders of hundreds;* also in 31:48, 52, 54.
31:50 Or *will make atonement for our lives before the LORD.*   31:52 Hebrew *16,750 shekels* [191 kilograms].
31:54 Hebrew *the Tent of Meeting.*

NOTES

31:3 *Choose.* Niphal of *khalats* [TH2502/2502A, ZH2740/2741]; BDB and HALOT note two potential senses: (1) "draw off/out, withdraw," i.e., "select, choose" (Snaith 1969:324-325; NLT, NAB, NJPS), or "deploy" or "detach" (Levine 2000:447, 450); or (2) "equip," i.e., "arm" as LXX *exoplizō* reads it (Budd 1984:325; KJV, NKJV, ASV, NASB, RSV, NRSV, ESV, JPS, NIV, NET). The second is related to terms for "belt" (*khalitsah* [TH2488, ZH2723]) and "loins" (*khalatsayim* [TH2504, ZH2743]), i.e., associated with *girding* or strapping on equipment for battle.

31:6 *holy objects of the sanctuary.* Heb., *kele haqqodesh* [TH3627/6944, ZH3998/7731]. The most common meaning of this expression is the sanctuary furniture or utensils (3:31; 4:15; 18:3; 1 Kgs 8:4; 1 Chr 9:29; 2 Chr 5:5), perhaps taking the place of the Ark (Budd 1984:330, citing 10:35-36; 14:44; 1 Sam 4:4) or being used in addition to it (Noth 1968:229). Others suggest it refers to (1) just the Ark (Ashley 1993:592; Snaith 1969:194-195), though the term is plural here rather than singular (10:35; 14:44; Josh 6:6; 1 Sam 4); (2) the signaling trumpets, reading the expression in apposition to the trumpets (E. W. Davies 1995b:323; Harrison 1990:383; Keil 1869:225-226; see 10:1-10; Josh 6), although since they were not anointed, some doubt that they could qualify as holy objects (Ashley 1993:592; Milgrom 1970:1.49 n. 186); (3) the priestly garments, an unusual use of *keli*, though possible (Dillmann and Knobel 1886:189; Gray 1903:420; see Deut 22:5); or (4) the Urim and Thummim (*Targum Pseudo-Jonathan* and Noordtzij 1983:271; Milgrom 1989:257; and perhaps Levine 2000:452), which the priest would consult during war (e.g., 1 Sam 14:18, "ephod," following the LXX rather than the MT's "Ark of God"; cf. 1 Sam 23:1-6), but note that the high priest kept control of them (Ashley 1993:592; Dillmann and Knobel 1886:189; McNeile 1911:164), and that in this case no decision about battle was required (Harrison 1990:383).

31:8 *All five of the Midianite kings . . . died in the battle.* Lit., "they killed the Midianite kings," plus the expression *'al-khalelehem* [TH2490A, ZH2726]. Some see this as a reference to being put on/upon the *khalal*, i.e., impaling stake, gibbet (Allen 1990:966).

31:9 *children.* Heb., *tap* [TH2945, ZH3251] (see note on 14:3).

31:11 This verse uses two roughly synonymous terms: "plunder" (*shalal* [TH7998, ZH8965]), "booty, spoil, goods that have been plundered" (HALOT), and "captives" (*maleqoakh* [TH4455, ZH4917]), the animate spoils of war, such as the livestock and captives (31:11, 12, 26, 32; Isa 49:24).

31:18 *young girls.* Lit., "the *tap* [TH2945, ZH3251] among the women" (see note on 14:3).

31:23 *water of purification.* Heb., *me niddah* [TH4325/5079, ZH4784/5614] (lit., "waters of impurity"; cf. 19:9, 13, 17-20).

must be purified by the water alone. Heb., *ta'abiru bammayim* [TH5674/4325, ZH6296/4784] ("must pass through the waters"). E. W. Davies takes the article in *bammayim* to be generic

(1995b:326, citing GKC §126n and Wright 1985:218-219), referring to ordinary water rather than to the antecedent "waters of impurity" (*me niddah* [TH4325/5079, ZH4784/5614]); however, Ashley thinks something like "living or running waters" would have been used if the author didn't mean to refer back to *me niddah* (Ashley 1993:596).

31:27 *plunder.* Heb., *malqoakh* [TH4455, ZH4917] (see note on 31:11).

31:28 *donkeys.* Modern readers might expect camels here, but camels were not used for caravanning until the end of the Late Bronze or Early Iron Age (Albright 1970). Camels are mentioned in the Bible for only a few ancient journeys (cf. Gen 24:10-64; 31:17, 34; 37:25; Exod 9:3), a fact that corresponds nicely with extrabiblical data (Kitchen 2003:338).

31:40 *16,000 virgin girls.* Lit., "and the human souls were 16,000," i.e., half of the 32,000 virgins kept alive after killing "all the boys and all the women who have had intercourse" (31:17, 35).

31:50 *armbands.* Heb., *'ets'ada* [TH685, ZH731]. Most English translations have "anklets"; see HALOT, "walking-chain (stretching from ankle to ankle) . . . [or] a band, bracelet."

bracelets. Heb., *tsamid* [TH6781, ZH7543]; cf. Ezek 16:11 and 23:42: "*tsemidim* on your hands," i.e., "wrists."

necklaces. Heb., *kumaz* [TH3558, ZH3921], an "ornament for neck and breasts" (HALOT, citing 31:50; Exod 35:22).

purify our lives before the LORD. Lit., "to make atonement/pay a ransom for our souls before the LORD." Commentators suggest various rationales for this offering: Some say (1) thanksgiving for God's favor during the war (Sturdy 1976:217); (2) ransom/expiation (NJB, NJPS) from "corpse defilement" or even to deal with "guilt feelings at the slaughter of the Midianites, whereas their own company had escaped unscathed" (Harrison 1990:391); or (3) atoning for their disregard of the ban during the war (Noordtzij 1983:276), which has the advantage of fitting the context (31:14-20). But most commentators think it was (4) guilt over the census of 31:48-49 (Ashley 1993:599-600; Binns 1927:207; Budd 1984:332; Dillmann and Knobel 1886:192; Gray 1903:425; Noth 1968:232; Snaith 1969:196; G. J. Wenham 1981:212). "Only census taking that was done in response to direct instruction from God was permissible, as were those described in chapters 1 and 26" (Cole 2000:504).

COMMENTARY

Numbers 31 picks up many loose ends from earlier in the narrative[1] but primarily looks forward. Defeating the Midianites (31:1-54) set the stage for the settlement arrangements of the Transjordan tribes (32:1-42). The Midianites descended from Abraham through his concubine Keturah (Gen 25:2-4). They had moved away from Isaac and settled in the east (Gen 25:6), where they became a traveling merchant people (Gen 37:25-28). Some of them, such as Moses's in-laws (Exod 2:15–3:1; 4:18-20), stayed on good terms with Israel. But some followed Balaam's advice to seduce the Israelites into the licentious rites of Baal-peor (25:17-18).

Israel Mobilized (31:1-5). For wooing Israel away from their true husband at the Baal-peor incident (ch 25), these Midianites earned the death penalty for adultery (Harrison 1990:382, citing Lev 20:10; Deut 22:22).[2] This punitive vindication took up the task of the kinsman-redeemer to avenge Midian's seduction (Mendenhall 1973:99). God said the task was to "take revenge on the Midianites for leading [the Israelites] into idolatry" (31:2); Moses said it was "to fight the LORD's war of revenge against Midian" (31:3). In other words, the supreme commander of "the LORD's army" (Josh 5:15; 1 Sam 1:3) declared war to defend his own honor as God of Israel, and thus to defend Israel's honor as the people of God. By divine decree, revenge was to be Moses's last act before he died (31:2; cf. 1 Kgs 2:5, 8).

Israel chose 1,000 from each tribe, a figure often regarded as "unrealistic" (Sturdy 1976:216) or "purely schematic and artificial" (E. W. Davies 1995b:322). But this followed the same principle as each tribe offering exactly the same altar dedication gifts, regardless of population (ch 7). Small tribes bore a disproportionate military burden, which meant gaining a disproportionate gain in plunder.

The Battle (31:6-13). Phinehas the priest led them into battle for a holy war (G. J. Wenham 1981:211, citing Deut 20:2-4). As was the case earlier (25:6-8), he was "acting as the antidote to Balaam" (Cole 2000:495). The priests took "the holy objects of the sanctuary" and the priestly "trumpets for sounding the charge" (31:6), further emphasizing that this was holy war. So they took the field and killed every Midianite who battled against them (31:7), including all five Midianite chieftains (31:8).

Chapters 22–24 may have left us a bit ambivalent about Balaam. But here we find him as an executed member of the coalition against whom God had commissioned a war of vengeance (31:8). Next we hear him called an augur, or one "who used magic to tell the future" (Josh 13:22). Eventually, we read the judgment that he had wished to curse Israel, though God wouldn't let him (Neh 13:2). After burning the Midianite towns and camps (31:10), Israel's victorious troops returned with Midianite cattle, flocks, and captives (31:9).

The Issue of Captive Women (31:14-18). The general law commanded death for the men in enemy armies; however, victors could carry away "all the women, children, livestock, and other plunder" (Deut 20:14). But after this battle, Moses raged, "Why have you let all the women live?" (31:15). These women were covered in guilt over the very matter that prompted the war of vengeance: sexual seduction that led to spiritual apostasy and thus to the plague at Baal-peor (31:16; see ch 25). Moses ordered, "Kill all the boys" (31:17a), who were "the future Midian, a potential danger and peril for Israel if allowed to grow up" (Philip 1993:313). He also ordered the death of "all the women who have had intercourse" (31:17b). Only the young virgins could be left alive to be taken as wives or concubines, after mourning their parents (Deut 21:10-14). "By this they could be brought under the umbrella of the covenant community of faith" (Cole 2000:499), made "part of the redeemed community. . . . mothers in Israel" (Allen 1990:971).

This slaughter was not the result of "collateral damage" in the heat of battle, or even an outrage committed in the heat of war's bloodlust. It was purposeful judicial slaughter after the battle was already over. In fact, this action fits the modern definition of ethnic cleansing or possibly even genocide. The conquest was a holy war aimed at driving out an entire human population from Canaan (33:50-53), annihilating everyone there to purge idolatry and remove its temptations (Deut 20:16-18). It was a divine act against a people who had filled up their cup of wrath (cf. Gen

15:16), as at the flood and in Sodom (Gen 6; 19). And it should be noted that the Lord threatened the same against Israel if she mimicked their sins (Lev 18:24-30; 20:22; Deut 18:12). Allen (1990:967) notes that this ties in with eschatological judgment, which will exceed the scope of anything like the losses that Midian suffered that day.

Purification of the Nation (31:19-24). Even glorious battles fought and won with God's blessing cause death, which doesn't belong in the presence of the God of the living. Purification was therefore necessary, following the ritual laid down earlier (19:9-20; Lev 13:49-59). The returning army and its captives stayed outside the camp for seven days (19:16; Lev 13:5, 21, 26, 32-34), undergoing ritual purification on the third and seventh days (19:12; 31:19). They washed their clothes (19:19) and anything made of hides (Lev 13:47-59), goat hair (cf. 1 Sam 19:13, 16), or wood. Where possible, they purified things with fire and the "water of purification" (31:22-23). Things that were not fireproof they "purified by the water alone" (31:23). This use of fire and water mimicked what we would now recognize as good hygienic procedure; however, it was actually about reconstituting the community's ritual purity. It was an older baptism, which foretold deeper cleansings with water and fire (Matt 3:11; Luke 3:16; cf. Mark 1:8; John 1:26; Acts 1:4-8; 11:16; Eph 5:26; Heb 10:22; 1 Pet 3:21).

Distribution of the Spoils (31:25-54). Moses, Eleazar, and the clan heads supervised the division of spoils and captives (31:26), dividing it all into two parts, half for the combatants and half for the noncombatants (31:27). Perhaps Moses and Eleazar supervised distribution among the priests and the clan leaders supervised distribution among the laity. This record provided later generations of warriors the rationale for carrying away plunder (e.g., Judg 8:24-27; 1 Sam 15:20; 2 Sam 8:9-12; 1 Chr 26:26-28).

The Lord's share was 1/500 of the combatants' half of the plunder and captives (31:28), or 1/1000 of the total. This was given to "Eleazar the priest as an offering to the LORD" (31:29). The Levites' share was 1/50 of the noncombatants' half of the plunder and captives, or 1/100 of the total. Perhaps the relation of this 1/100 and 1/1000 was a tithe-like 10 percent. Thus the 675,000 sheep and goats, 72,000 cattle, 61,000 donkeys, and 32,000 virgins were divided in half—one half went to the army and the other half to the civilians. The army then gave a tribute to the Lord of 675 sheep and goats, 72 cattle, 61 donkeys, and 32 virgins. The civilians, on the other hand, were required to give the Levites 6,750 sheep and goats, 720 cattle, 610 donkeys, and 320 virgins.

These large numbers are consistent with all the other large numbers in the book. Since it would be difficult to reinterpret 'elep [TH505, ZH547] as "clan" or "military unit" when used of livestock and virgins, the likelihood that the authors used 'elep to mean "thousand" in the population counts seems high. And like the case with population figures, the math works out with "thousands": As mentioned, the combatant's half of "675,000 sheep and goats" (31:32) came to 337,500, of which a 1/500 share meant "675 were the LORD's share" (31:37), and so on with the 72 cattle

(31:38), 61 donkeys (31:39), and 32 virgins (31:40). The virgins would have been assigned to the priests as household servants or perhaps to work at the entrance to the Tent of Meeting (Exod 38:8; 1 Sam 2:22).

Half of the plunder belonged to the noncombatants (31:42), a principle later followed by Joshua and David (Josh 22:8; 1 Sam 30:24). From that they had to contribute a 1/50 share to the Levites (31:47). If this provided "the standard for coming campaigns" (Cole 2000:501), "the people should have been thinking, *If we received this much booty in a punitive war, just think how much will be our portion when we are on the campaign of conquest!*" (Allen 1990:970).

After defeating Midian, the officers rejoiced that they had suffered no battle casualties (31:48-49). This post-battle testimony is common in ancient Near Eastern battle reports (Ashley 1993:589 n. 25). They volunteered an offering of the gold jewelry they had captured, saying, "This will purify our lives before the LORD and make us right with him" (31:50). Moses accepted the offering as "a reminder to the LORD that the people of Israel belong to him" (31:54). The question is whether this was to remind Israel of the incident or to remind the Lord so that he would not forget Israel. "Perhaps the two alternatives are not mutually exclusive, for the offerings may have been designed to ensure both that Yahweh would constantly remember his people (cf. 10:10), and that the Israelites would continually direct their thoughts to him" (E. W. Davies 1995b:328-329; so, too, Ashley 1993:601).

ENDNOTES
1. Vengeance on Midian (31:2-3; cf. 25:16-18), Moses's coming death (31:2; cf. 27:13), the trumpets (31:6; cf. 10:2-10), Zur the Midianite (31:8; cf. 25:15), Balaam (31:8, 16; cf. chs 22-24), the incident of Baal-peor (31:16; cf. 25:6-9, 14-15), purification after contact with the dead (31:19-24; cf. 19:11-19 [also Lev 11:32]), care for priests and Levites (31:28-47; cf. 18:8-32), costly offerings (31:48-54, cf. chs 7, 28-29). In addition, the counting or mustering that takes place in 31:3-5, 26, 32-47 reflects the theme of chs 1-4, 26 (Ashley 1993:587).
2. G. J. Wenham notes that this sentence against Midian was in line with the severe punishment that Israel experienced for her own sins in the wilderness inasmuch as the entire first generation died off under judgment. The same principle governs judgment on Israel or the nations (1981:210-211, citing Gen 6:7ff.; Amos 1-2; Rom 2:9; 1 Pet 4:17).

◆   ## 2. Transjordan tribes: Reuben and Gad (32:1-42)

The tribes of Reuben and Gad owned vast numbers of livestock. So when they saw that the lands of Jazer and Gilead were ideally suited for their flocks and herds, ²they came to Moses, Eleazar the priest, and the other leaders of the community. They said, ³"Notice the towns of Ataroth, Dibon, Jazer, Nimrah, Heshbon, Elealeh, Sibmah,* Nebo, and Beon. ⁴The LORD has conquered this whole area for the community of Israel, and it is ideally suited for all our livestock. ⁵If we have found favor with you, please let us have this land as our property instead of giving us land across the Jordan River."

⁶"Do you intend to stay here while your

brothers go across and do all the fighting?" Moses asked the men of Gad and Reuben. ⁷"Why do you want to discourage the rest of the people of Israel from going across to the land the LORD has given them? ⁸Your ancestors did the same thing when I sent them from Kadesh-barnea to explore the land. ⁹After they went up to the valley of Eshcol and explored the land, they discouraged the people of Israel from entering the land the LORD was giving them. ¹⁰Then the LORD was very angry with them, and he vowed, ¹¹'Of all those I rescued from Egypt, no one who is twenty years old or older will ever see the land I swore to give to Abraham, Isaac, and Jacob, for they have not obeyed me wholeheartedly. ¹²The only exceptions are Caleb son of Jephunneh the Kenizzite and Joshua son of Nun, for they have wholeheartedly followed the LORD.'

¹³"The LORD was angry with Israel and made them wander in the wilderness for forty years until the entire generation that sinned in the LORD's sight had died. ¹⁴But here you are, a brood of sinners, doing exactly the same thing! You are making the LORD even angrier with Israel. ¹⁵If you turn away from him like this and he abandons them again in the wilderness, you will be responsible for destroying this entire nation!"

¹⁶But they approached Moses and said, "We simply want to build pens for our livestock and fortified towns for our wives and children. ¹⁷Then we will arm ourselves and lead our fellow Israelites into battle until we have brought them safely to their land. Meanwhile, our families will stay in the fortified towns we build here, so they will be safe from any attacks by the local people. ¹⁸We will not return to our homes until all the people of Israel have received their portions of land. ¹⁹But we do not claim any of the land on the other side of the Jordan. We would rather live here on the east side and accept this as our grant of land."

²⁰Then Moses said, "If you keep your word and arm yourselves for the LORD's battles, ²¹and if your troops cross the Jordan and keep fighting until the LORD has driven out his enemies, ²²then you may return when the LORD has conquered the land. You will have fulfilled your duty to the LORD and to the rest of the people of Israel. And the land on the east side of the Jordan will be your property from the LORD. ²³But if you fail to keep your word, then you will have sinned against the LORD, and you may be sure that your sin will find you out. ²⁴Go ahead and build towns for your families and pens for your flocks, but do everything you have promised."

²⁵Then the men of Gad and Reuben replied, "We, your servants, will follow your instructions exactly. ²⁶Our children, wives, flocks, and cattle will stay here in the towns of Gilead. ²⁷But all who are able to bear arms will cross over to fight for the LORD, just as you have said."

²⁸So Moses gave orders to Eleazar the priest, Joshua son of Nun, and the leaders of the clans of Israel. ²⁹He said, "The men of Gad and Reuben who are armed for battle must cross the Jordan with you to fight for the LORD. If they do, give them the land of Gilead as their property when the land is conquered. ³⁰But if they refuse to arm themselves and cross over with you, then they must accept land with the rest of you in the land of Canaan."

³¹The tribes of Gad and Reuben said again, "We are your servants, and we will do as the LORD has commanded! ³²We will cross the Jordan into Canaan fully armed to fight for the LORD, but our property will be here on this side of the Jordan."

³³So Moses assigned land to the tribes of Gad, Reuben, and half the tribe of Manasseh son of Joseph. He gave them the territory of King Sihon of the Amorites and the land of King Og of Bashan—the whole land with its cities and surrounding lands.

³⁴The descendants of Gad built the towns of Dibon, Ataroth, Aroer, ³⁵Atrothshophan, Jazer, Jogbehah, ³⁶Beth-nimrah, and Beth-haran. These were all fortified towns with pens for their flocks.

³⁷The descendants of Reuben built the towns of Heshbon, Elealeh, Kiriathaim, ³⁸Nebo, Baal-meon, and Sibmah. They changed the names of some of the towns they conquered and rebuilt.

³⁹Then the descendants of Makir of the tribe of Manasseh went to Gilead and conquered it, and they drove out the Amorites living there. ⁴⁰So Moses gave Gilead to the Makirites, descendants of Manasseh, and they settled there. ⁴¹The people of Jair, another clan of the tribe of Manasseh, captured many of the towns in Gilead and changed the name of that region to the Towns of Jair.* ⁴²Meanwhile, a man named Nobah captured the town of Kenath and its surrounding villages, and he renamed that area Nobah after himself.

32:3 As in Samaritan Pentateuch and Greek version (see also 32:38); Hebrew reads *Sebam.* 32:41 Hebrew *Havvoth-jair.*

NOTES
32:1 *Reuben and Gad.* The Samaritan Pentateuch adds "and the half-tribe of Manasseh" to harmonize with 32:33 (also added at 32:2, 6, 25, 29, 31).

Gilead. This is a fluid term, here referring to the hilly Transjordan district south of the Jabbok, but sometimes referring to the entire Transjordan (Deut 3:12-17; Josh 12:2, 5; 13:31; 22:9, 13).

32:3 Most of these cities can be located with fair certainty. Nine towns are mentioned in vv. 34-38, where the first four are assigned to Gad and the remainder to Reuben. They also occur in Isa 15–16 and in Jer 48, where they belong to Moab.

Ataroth. This is Khirbet 'Attarus, 10 miles northwest of Dibon and mentioned in the Moabite Stone as a Gadite site.

Dibon. Dhiban is 3 miles north of the Arnon. Gad's settlement there is confirmed by its alternate name Dibon-gad (33:45) and its attribution to Gad in the Moabite Stone (lines 10ff., in ANET 320). It may have become a Reubenite town at a later date (Josh 13:17).

Jazer. This is perhaps Khirbet es-Sar.

Nimrah. Beth-nimrah (32:36), probably located at Tell el-Bleibil, about 12 miles north of the Dead Sea on Wadi Sha'ib (cf. "waters of Nimrim," Isa 15:6; Jer 48:34). The name is still preserved in Tell Nimrim, south-southwest of Tell Beleibil.

Heshbon. Hisban, 13 miles east of the Dead Sea's northern tip.

Elealeh. El-'Al, northwest of Heshbon.

Sibmah. Sebam (32:3 mg), Khirbet Cam el-Kibsh between Heshbon and Nebo.

Nebo. Possibly Khirbet 'Ayun Musa. The inscription of King Mesha of Moab (lines 14-18, in ANET 320) shows that this location was a center for Yahweh worship in the period before 850 BC.

Beon. Ma'in, 4.5 miles southwest of Madaba. Perhaps an altered form of Baal-meon (Ashley 1993:616; Budd 1984:345; Harrison 1990:399-400; Ezek 25:9); cf. Beth-baal-meon (Josh 13:17) or Beth-meon (Jer 48:23).

32:5 *instead of giving us land across the Jordan River.* Lit., "do not make us cross the Jordan."

32:12 *Kenizzite.* See Josh 14:6, 14; Judg 1:13. The Kenizzites were some of Canaan's original occupants; however, their land was promised to Abram (Gen 15:19). To this clan belonged Jephunneh, the father of Caleb (32:12; Josh 14:6, 14). It had evidently been absorbed by the tribe of Judah, so he could also be classified as a Judahite (13:6; 34:19).

32:17 *we will arm ourselves and lead our fellow Israelites into battle.* Lit., "we will *khalats* ourselves and *khush* before the sons of Israel." On *khalats* [TH2502A, ZH2741], see note at 31:3. The term *khush* [TH2363, ZH2590] denotes swiftness, whether escaping (Ps 55:8), attacking (Judg 20:37), or coming to the aid of someone (Pss 22:19; 38:22; 71:12); however, many commentators doubt that it makes sense here. The LXX has *prophulakē* (advance guard), so commentators sometimes talk of "advance troops" (Levine 2000:490), "shock-troops" (NJPS), or a "vanguard" (Milgrom 1989:270), perhaps "select," i.e., elite troops (cf. 31:5). Some follow the BHS suggestion to emend *khushim* to *khamushim* [TH2567, ZH2821], "arrayed in groups of fifty" (HALOT), i.e., "in battle array" (BDB 332b, citing 32:17; Exod 13:18; Josh 1:14; Judg 7:11). Commentaries following this idea describe an army divided into five parts with vanguard, rear guard, main body, and two flanking groups (Allen 1990:980; Budd 1984:344; Gray 1903:432; Snaith 1969:197-198).

32:34 descendants of Gad. They were to take the central region of Sihon's former kingdom (Josh 13:24-28). Joshua actually made different allotments, which is evidence of changing circumstances, not contradictory sources (Ashley 1993:615; contra Gray 1903:433-444; McNeile 1911:174; Noth 1968:240).

Ataroth. Khirbet 'Attarus. The Moabite Stone says, "The men of Gad. . . . had been living in the land of Ataroth from ancient times" (line 10; see in COS 2.23:137-138; ANET 320-321).

Aroer. 'Ara'ir, just north of the Arnon and thus belonging to the southern group of Gadite towns; however, it was later absorbed by Reuben (Josh 13:15-16). It was of strategic importance because the King's Highway ran past it (Milgrom 1989:274-275).

32:35 Atroth-shophan. This is mentioned only here, probably associated with Ataroth.

Jazer. See the note on 21:32.

Jogbehah. Khirbet el-Jubeihat, 7 miles northwest of Amman, making it the northernmost Gadite site listed in this chapter. It is mentioned once more, together with Nobah (Judg 8:11; cf. Num 32:42).

32:36 Beth-nimrah. This is equivalent to Nimrah (see 32:3).

Beth-haran. Tell Iktanu, just west of Heshbon. This town's name is spelled Beth-haram in Josh 13:27.

32:42 Nobah. This man is mentioned only here, with no tribe or clan listed, although he is implied to be from Manasseh by the context of the preceding verse. If the town (cf. Judg 8:11), which he named after himself, is identified with Kenath, then it is located in the eastern Bashan and is the only settlement north of the Yarmuk recorded in this chapter.

Kenath. Qanawat, 55 miles east of the Sea of Galilee.

COMMENTARY

Reuben and Gad asked for a land distribution from this victory in addition to the other plunder. Moses rejected their first proposal (32:1-15) but accepted a compromise proposal (32:17-27). Interpreters are divided over whether this request was motivated by faith or greed, and whether the outcome was good or bad. On the one hand, the promise to Abraham was for Canaan, land west of the Jordan.[1] So the request echoed the earlier rejection of the land, which was exactly Moses's charge (32:6-15; cf. chs 13-14). G. J. Wenham even points out various parallels in terminology that chapter 32 shares with chapters 13-14 (1981:213 n. 1). On the other hand, Allen likens the request of Reuben and Gad to that of Zelophehad's daughters. He thinks it possible to see this in a positive light once all conditions were met: "Transjordan, too, was a gift of God won by conquest" (Deut 2:24, 31; 3:2, 16, 18; cf. Deut 2:9, 18, 37). Once things are understood, "There is no lack of faith, only an alternate plan" (Allen 1990:980). Harrison actually makes a military boon of this proposal: "This proposal could be of tactical importance for the nation, since it would afford protection for Israel's eastern flank once the other tribes had possessed Canaan" (1990:396). Nonetheless, their vulnerable position on the wrong side of the Jordan rift meant that they got hit first and most often.[2] Later records do not question the legitimacy of the Transjordan tribes when they settle there (Josh 22:1-9).

Later Christian commentators have likened the proposal of Gad and Reuben to those who gave excuses for ignoring the call of Christ (Luke 14:18-20; 16:10-31), although that must be based upon their first proposal rather than the actual compromise agreement. Verses 1-5 report Reuben and Gad's first proposal for settling in the Transjordan: They herded "vast numbers of livestock" (32:1) throughout the wilderness journey (Exod 12:38; 17:3; 34:3) and augmented them with plunder from the Amorites and Midianites (31:9-12, 26). Together with Simeon, Reuben and Gad formed a division that marched and camped together (2:10). Reuben was the firstborn; however, Jacob said, "You are as unruly as a flood, and you will be first no longer" (Gen 49:4). In fact, after verse 1, Gad takes first place even in this narrative (32:2, 6, 25, 29, 31, 33).[3] By the time Moses gave his parting blessings to the tribes, there was concern that Reuben might even die out (Deut 33:6), but Gad was vigorous and expanding (Deut 33:20-21). Reuben is conspicuously absent from the geographical notes in Samuel—Kings.[4] The Moabite leader, Mesha, mentioned Gad but not Reuben in the Moabite Stone of the ninth century BC (Beyerlin 1978:239; ANET 320; Thomas 1961:196).

Just as Lot chose apparent prosperity in the southern Transjordan (Gen 13), Reuben and Gad chose the Transjordan "lands of Jazer and Gilead" (32:1). These highlands overlooking the Jordan were blessed with fertile soil, sufficient rainfall, and streams like the Yarmuk, Jabbok, and Arnon. Ticking off a list of its towns (32:3), they said, "The LORD has conquered this whole area for the community of Israel" (32:4), which indeed reflected God's promise to Moses (Exod 23:31; Deut 2:24, 31; 3:2, 16, 18), for which they later praised the Lord (Ps 136:17-22). So they asked, "Let us have this land . . . instead of giving us land across the Jordan River" (32:5).

Moses accused them of once again rejecting the Promised Land (32:6-15; cf. chs 13–14). The accusation of discouraging the rest of the people (32:7) reminds readers of the rebellious scouts (chs 13–14), a story with which there are many connections.[5] Later, the Song of Deborah echoes these words against Reuben and Gad, implying that these two tribes showed a continuing disregard for Israel's unity (Judg 5:15-17).

Moses launched into a homily covering their national history. The divine oath to Abraham, Isaac, and Jacob[6] had been diverted by another divine oath, which had excluded an entire unbelieving and disobedient generation from the land (32:11; see 14:30). The only exceptions would be faithful Caleb and Joshua (32:12). Verse 13 summarizes the threat of 14:33-35, and Moses told this second generation, "Here you are . . . doing exactly the same thing!" (32:14). He called them a "brood of sinners," imagery later used by John the Baptist and Jesus about their opponents among the Pharisees and Sadducees (Matt 3:7; 12:34). One generation had already been destroyed by this attitude; now Moses said, if this continues, "you will be responsible for destroying this entire nation!" (32:15).

Moses Accepts Compromise Petition (32:16-27). Verses 16-27 recount a compromise proposal, which Moses accepted. Their first request was "Let us have this land . . . instead of giving us land across the Jordan River" (32:5); this time they told Moses that they would build facilities to protect their livestock and dependents while they were away at war (32:16-17), then they would lead the charge into Canaan proper (32:17) and stick with it for the duration (32:18). Moses accepted this, codifying it as a binding covenant, with appropriate threats and curses: "If you keep your word . . . , then . . ." (32:20-22); however, "If you fail to keep your word, then . . ." (32:23). They were bound to fulfill their "duty to the LORD and to the rest of the people of Israel" if they wanted the Transjordan (32:22). Otherwise, "Your sin will find you out" (32:23), a phrase personifying sin (cf. Gen 4:7) and meaning there would be no escaping God the Judge. Reuben and Gad agreed, adopting the language that Moses had added about arming themselves to fight for the Lord (32:27).

Ratification of Proposal to Settle Transjordan (32:28-32). Knowing that he was near the end of his life, Moses passed this agreement along to Eleazar and Joshua, who would succeed him, and to the tribal leaders (32:28). He added that failure to adhere to the agreement would mean a revocation of approval for a Transjordan allotment, and these two tribes would have to settle in Canaan with the rest of the tribes (32:30). Gad and Reuben ratified their acceptance, adopting the language of ready obedience like we saw early in the book (32:31). In fact, the Transjordan tribes ended up sending 40,000 (Josh 4:12-13), about one-third of their number from the second military count (26:7, 18, 37). Apparently the other two-thirds remained behind to protect their women and children from any Amorites, Ammonites, or Moabites still operating in this recently conquered region. Perhaps that explains the lingering irritation with these two tribes in the Song of Deborah (Judg 5).

Land Allotments in Transjordan (32:33-42). Verses 33-42 describe the agreement that allocated cities in the Transjordan to Gad, Reuben, and the half-tribe of Manasseh. This list differs from a later and fuller account (Josh 13:15-32), where Reuben settled east of the Dead Sea, Gad settled between the Dead Sea and Galilee, and Manasseh settled in northern Gilead. Here we see Gad rebuilding Dibon and Aroer, which later fell in Reuben's territory (32:34; cf. Josh 13:16-17), and Reuben occupying Heshbon, which later belonged to Gad (32:37; cf. Josh 21:39). Perhaps they ranged widely throughout the Transjordan with their vast flocks (Miller and Hayes 1986:102-103), or perhaps "over the years Reuben was assimilated into Gad, as also happened to Simeon and Judah" (Noordtzij 1983:284). "Moses assigned land" (32:33), with no mention of using lots, by which Canaan proper was to be distributed (26:55; 33:54; 34:13; 36:2).

Verses 34-38 list 14 towns that Gad and Reuben built or rebuilt. Gad took eight cities that comprised the central part of the former kingdom of Sihon the Amorite (32:34-36; Josh 13:24-28). Reuben took six cities lying to the south of Gad (32:37-38). In some cases, they planned to change the names, probably to rid the names of pagan references like Nebo and Baal (32:38).

Verses 39-42 record the actions of three Manassite clans in the Upper Transjordan: Makir, Jair, and Nobah (cf. Josh 1). The "half-tribe of Manasseh," a newly dominant tribe, horned in on the deal brokered by Reuben and Gad. Manasseh's forces did most of the fighting in the Transjordan, so later, their descendants are described as having "a great reputation as mighty warriors" (1 Chr 5:23-24). No battles are listed for Gad and Reuben, or, for that matter, the rest of Israel! We've already heard of Amorite defeats (21:33-35); however, here we see the Makirites taking Gilead, Transjordan territory that was north of the Jabbok and therefore north of Gad, stretching from Gilead into Bashan and the Golan (32:39). Similarly, we see various other clans of Manasseh conquering their Transjordan territory (32:40-42).

ENDNOTES

1. 32:11; 34:2-12; see Gen 12:5-9; 13:12-15; 28:13-15; Exod 33:1; Deut 1:8; 6:10; 30:20; Ps 105:9-12.
2. Deut 33:6; Judg 3:12; 10:8, 17; 1 Kgs 22:3; 2 Kgs 10:32-33; 15:29; 1 Chr 5:26.
3. The names occur in the birth order (Reuben before Gad) in the LXX (in 32:2, 25, 29, 31), Samaritan Pentateuch (in 32:6, 25, 29, 31, 33) and consistently in the Peshitta throughout the rest of the chapter (32:2, 6, 25, 29, 31, 33).
4. The Transjordan is called the land of Gad and Gilead (1 Sam 13:7).
5. G. J. Wenham 1981:214 n. 2. Milgrom (1989:268) notes, "The relationship with the scout episode (ch 14) is actually reversed: There, two (scouts) were positive and ten were negative; here, two (tribes) are negative and ten are positive."
6. Gen 15:18; 26:3; 28:13; 35:12; Exod 6:8; 32:13; 33:1; Deut 1:8; 6:10; 9:5; 30:20; 34:4.

◆ **D. Reprise of Wilderness Itinerary (33:1-49)**

This is the route the Israelites followed as they marched out of Egypt under the leadership of Moses and Aaron. ²At the LORD's direction, Moses kept a written record of their progress. These are the stages of their march, identified by the different places where they stopped along the way.

³They set out from the city of Rameses in early spring—on the fifteenth day of the first month*—on the morning after the first Passover celebration. The people of Israel left defiantly, in full view of all the Egyptians. ⁴Meanwhile, the Egyptians were burying all their firstborn sons, whom the LORD had killed the night before. The LORD had defeated the gods of Egypt that night with great acts of judgment!

⁵After leaving Rameses, the Israelites set up camp at Succoth.

⁶Then they left Succoth and camped at Etham on the edge of the wilderness.

⁷They left Etham and turned back toward Pi-hahiroth, opposite Baal-zephon, and camped near Migdol.

⁸They left Pi-hahiroth and crossed the Red Sea* into the wilderness beyond. Then they traveled for three days into the Etham wilderness and camped at Marah.

⁹They left Marah and camped at Elim, where there were twelve springs of water and seventy palm trees.
¹⁰They left Elim and camped beside the Red Sea.*
¹¹They left the Red Sea and camped in the wilderness of Sin.*
¹²They left the wilderness of Sin and camped at Dophkah.
¹³They left Dophkah and camped at Alush.
¹⁴They left Alush and camped at Rephidim, where there was no water for the people to drink.
¹⁵They left Rephidim and camped in the wilderness of Sinai.
¹⁶They left the wilderness of Sinai and camped at Kibroth-hattaavah.
¹⁷They left Kibroth-hattaavah and camped at Hazeroth.
¹⁸They left Hazeroth and camped at Rithmah.
¹⁹They left Rithmah and camped at Rimmon-perez.
²⁰They left Rimmon-perez and camped at Libnah.
²¹They left Libnah and camped at Rissah.
²²They left Rissah and camped at Kehelathah.
²³They left Kehelathah and camped at Mount Shepher.
²⁴They left Mount Shepher and camped at Haradah.
²⁵They left Haradah and camped at Makheloth.
²⁶They left Makheloth and camped at Tahath.
²⁷They left Tahath and camped at Terah.
²⁸They left Terah and camped at Mithcah.
²⁹They left Mithcah and camped at Hashmonah.
³⁰They left Hashmonah and camped at Moseroth.
³¹They left Moseroth and camped at Bene-jaakan.

³²They left Bene-jaakan and camped at Hor-haggidgad.
³³They left Hor-haggidgad and camped at Jotbathah.
³⁴They left Jotbathah and camped at Abronah.
³⁵They left Abronah and camped at Ezion-geber.
³⁶They left Ezion-geber and camped at Kadesh in the wilderness of Zin.
³⁷They left Kadesh and camped at Mount Hor, at the border of Edom. ³⁸While they were at the foot of Mount Hor, Aaron the priest was directed by the LORD to go up the mountain, and there he died. This happened in midsummer, on the first day of the fifth month* of the fortieth year after Israel's departure from Egypt. ³⁹Aaron was 123 years old when he died there on Mount Hor.
⁴⁰At that time the Canaanite king of Arad, who lived in the Negev in the land of Canaan, heard that the people of Israel were approaching his land.
⁴¹Meanwhile, the Israelites left Mount Hor and camped at Zalmonah.
⁴²Then they left Zalmonah and camped at Punon.
⁴³They left Punon and camped at Oboth.
⁴⁴They left Oboth and camped at Iye-abarim on the border of Moab.
⁴⁵They left Iye-abarim* and camped at Dibon-gad.
⁴⁶They left Dibon-gad and camped at Almon-diblathaim.
⁴⁷They left Almon-diblathaim and camped in the mountains east of the river,* near Mount Nebo.
⁴⁸They left the mountains east of the river and camped on the plains of Moab beside the Jordan River, across from Jericho. ⁴⁹Along the Jordan River they camped from Beth-jeshimoth as far as the meadows of Acacia* on the plains of Moab.

33:3 This day in the ancient Hebrew lunar calendar occurred in late March, April, or early May. 33:8 Hebrew *the sea.* 33:10 Hebrew *sea of reeds;* also in 33:11. 33:11 The geographical name *Sin* is related to *Sinai* and should not be confused with the English word *sin.* 33:38 This day in the ancient Hebrew lunar calendar occurred in July or August. 33:45 As in 33:44; Hebrew reads *Iyim,* another name for Iye-abarim. 33:47 Or *the mountains of Abarim;* also in 33:48. 33:49 Hebrew *as far as Abel-shittim.*

NOTES

33:3 Cf. 1:1; 7:1; 9:1, 5; 10:10; 20:1; 33:38.

33:4 *The Lord had defeated the gods of Egypt that night.* Lit., "On their gods the Lord had done judgments" (cf. Exod 12:12), lacking "that night." Thus, the defeat of or judgment against the gods of Egypt may be better understood as having occurred throughout the plague cycle.

33:38 Cf. 1:1; 7:1; 9:1, 5; 10:11; 20:1; 33:3. Numbers 20:1 tells us Israel returned to Kadesh "in the first month"; however, no year is given there, so the mention of a year here indicates the end of the wilderness period.

33:39 *Aaron was 123.* Compare his age as 83 at the beginning of the Exodus (Exod 7:7).

COMMENTARY

Chapter 33 reprises the wilderness itinerary of the Israelites: from Egypt to Sinai (33:1-15), the wilderness wanderings (33:16-36), and from Kadesh to Moab (33:27-49). The result is a list of 42 stations from their Egyptian starting point in Rameses to their final encampment at the Jordan.[1] Some commentators omit the first and last sites to arrive at 40 stages, one for each year in the wilderness. But this results in a list where the first stage is still in Egypt but the last is not yet in Canaan; therefore, it does not render 40 stages "in the wilderness." And, of course, there is no question of anything like a stay of one year at each stage.

The whole trip could have been made in about a month if they had been able to proceed directly from Egypt to Sinai (about 230 miles), a 15-day trip,[2] and directly from there to Kadesh on the border with Canaan (about 160 miles), an 11-day trip (Deut 1:2).

The ancient Near East knew of such precise accounts of the stages of a journey, taking the form "and they departed from *x* and encamped at *y*" (IDB 3.57-60, 78-79), especially when such movements were part of a military campaign (Cole 2000:518; e.g., "The Journey of Wen-Amon to Phoenicia," an Egyptian example from the eleventh century BC translated in ANET 25-29). For many of the sites some historical allusion is included (33:6-7, 9, 14, 36-40). As we saw in chapters 1–10, Israel began well, but that didn't continue. It was like what Paul lamented in the Galatian church: "You were running the race so well. Who has held you back from following the truth?" (Gal 5:7). So these verses have the same message that the psalmist has: "I listen carefully to what God the Lord is saying, for he speaks peace to his faithful people. But let them not return to their foolish ways" (Ps 85:8).

The itinerary through 40 grumbling years witnesses to God's gracious sustenance for his people. In fact, the lack of mention of any murmuring is interesting.

> This may be meant to indicate that more important than all the sorry history of sin and failure is the divine provision of grace. When the story is ultimately told, it will be the latter, not the former, that will adorn the permanent record of the pilgrimage. F. B. Meyer, in a comment on this, says, "When we get to heaven and study the way-book, we shall find all the deeds of love and self-denial carefully recorded, though we have forgotten them; and all the sins blotted out, though we remember them." (Philip 1993:336, quoting Meyer 1903:1.150)

A preface gives the nature of the list (33:1), the author (33:2), the time and place for the beginning of the journey (33:3), and the circumstances under which the journey began (33:4). It records the stages of the journey from Egypt to the borders of the Promised Land. "Moses kept a written record of their progress" (33:2)—this is the only bit of Numbers directly said to have been written by Moses, although the whole of it can be described as "of Moses."[3] They started on "the fifteenth day of the first month" (33:3), the day after Passover (Exod 12:6, 18) and the first day of the Festival of Unleavened Bread (Lev 23:6). The addition of "that night" in NLT is potentially misleading (see note on 33:4), especially if we see the multiday sequence of plague signs as a series of victories over Egyptian gods. Indeed, many of the plagues can be understood as judgments against various Egyptian deities as follows (Greenberg 1972; Löwenstamm 1971), although this understanding is more compelling for some than others:

- *Water to blood* (Exod 7:14-25): *Hapi,* the god of the Nile, bringer of fertility; a compelling understanding, given how important the Nile was to Egypt's very existence
- *Frogs* (Exod 8:1-15): *Hekqet,* the frog-headed goddess of fruitfulness
- *Flies* (Exod 8:20-32): *Keper,* in the form of a beetle, symbolizing the daily cycle of the sun across the sky
- *Plague on cattle* (Exod 9:1-7): *Hathor,* a cow-headed goddess or cow-shaped goddess with a human head adorned with horns; *Kenum,* a ram-headed god; *Amon,* a ram-headed king of gods and patron of the pharaohs; *Isis,* queen of the gods who wears cow or ram horns
- *Hail, thunder, and lightning* (Exod 9:13-35): *Nut,* the sky goddess and protector of the dead
- *Locusts* (Exod 10:1-20): *Serapia,* protector of locusts
- *Darkness* (Exod 10:21-29): *Re,* personified sun, king of the gods and father of mankind
- *Death of firstborn* (Exod 11:1–12:36): *Taurt,* goddess of maternity who presided over childbirth and was a protective household deity. Perhaps this last one should rather be seen as an attack on the household (dynasty) of the deified pharaoh himself.

Small wonder the Hebrews pumped their fists as they left Egypt (see 33:3, KJV).

The list of stages does not allow us to identify the route exactly; place names survive through the ages only through continuity of settlement on the same site, which was always unlikely for desert encampments. In addition, the text of this list shows many variants, though they tend to be orthographic errors.[4] Where available, the list will note the occurrence of these place names in the earlier travel narrative as well, although this list mentions many sites not included in the earlier travel narratives. The following is a numbered list of the sites the Israelites traveled to, with what is known about them:

Egypt to the Red Sea (33:5–8).

1. *Rameses* (33:3, 5; see Exod 12:37) was named for the great Pharaoh Rameses II, who lived well after Joseph (Gen 47:11) and even after the Exodus, an example of updating a place name to a more current and recognizable name. "Most scholars are agreed that this is probably to be identified with *Pi-Rameses* of Egyptian texts. This city was undertaken by Seti I and completed by Rameses II and is located at Tanis, Qantir, or perhaps even both sites."[5]

2. *Succoth* (33:5-6; see Exod 12:37; 13:20) is probably Tell Maskhuta near the modern Timsah Lake (Rainey and Notley 2006:119).

3. *Etham* (33:6-8; see Exod 13:20) is perhaps Tell Abu Seifeh, and was the place where the fiery cloud-pillar was first mentioned (Exod 13:21). The name may be related to the Egyptian word *htm*, meaning "fortress" (contra HALOT; contra Rainey and Notley 2006:119, who think that identification phonetically problematic). It may have been an unidentified fortification somewhere along the line of the present Suez Canal. Levine suggests that it may be a variant, abbreviated form of Pithom (2000:516).

4. *Pi-hahiroth* (33:7-8; see Exod 14:2, 9), or "Mouth of the Canals," empties into the Sea of Reeds. It would have been in the eastern part of the Nile Delta region but still west of the Bitter Lakes, so Pharaoh's armies could trap Israel up against their waters. It was "opposite Baal-zephon," which is perhaps modern Mount Casius on the Mediterranean coast (Y. Aharoni, Avi-Yonah, Rainey, and Safrai 2002, map 48). They camped near Migdol, a place-name meaning "watchtower" or "fortress," perhaps Egypt's northernmost frontier town (Ezek 29:10; 30:6).

Red Sea to Sinai (33:8–15).

5. *Marah* (33:8-9; see Exod 15:23, 25, 27) was where bitter waters were made sweet (Exod 15:23). Its location is uncertain. Some have identified it with Ein Hawarah, 47 miles southeast of Suez, but a more likely identification would be Bir el-Murah, 10 miles east of Suez in west-central Sinai, since it would best fit the three-day journey at 20 miles per day (Hoffmeier 2005:161-162). "Although identified as Shur in Exodus 15:22, this need not imply two versions. Etham is simply Egyptian for Hebrew Shur, both meaning 'wall, fortification.' The location probably refers to the defense line built by the Egyptians along the present Suez Canal" (Milgrom 1989:279).

6. *Elim* (33:9-10; see Exod 15:27; 16:1) was perhaps located at Wadi Gharandel, about 75 miles south of the Bitter Lakes, or 55 miles south of Suez. Counting the wells and trees on a piece of property is found in Hittite records (Harrison 1990:405), especially in ancient Near Eastern military itineraries (Milgrom 1989:279). Jewish exegetes connected the 12 springs and 70 palms at this location to the 12 tribes and 70 elders (11:16).

7. *Red Sea* (33:10-11; see 14:25; 21:4; Exod 15) is literally "Sea of Reeds." This was a later encampment on the *eastern* shore of the Suez Gulf (Hoffmeier

2005:164), which *followed* the crossing of Reed Sea, "one of the marshy lakes in the Isthmus of Suez" (Hoffmeier 2005:164). This station is not mentioned in the Exodus record.

8. *Wilderness of Sin* (33:11-12; see Exod 16:1; 17:1) refers to a coastal area of northwest Sinai along the Suez Gulf. Some identify it with Dibbet-er-Rammeleh (Y. Aharoni, Avi-Yonah, Rainey, and Safrai 2002:map 48), which would fit the traditional location for Mount Sinai in the south of the peninsula.

9. *Dophkah* (33:12-13; cf. LXX *Raphaka*) was possibly Serabit el-Khadem (Y. Aharoni, Avi-Yonah, Rainey, and Safrai 2002:map 48), though some consider this identification doubtful (Budd 1984:354; G. I. Davies 1979:84). Hoffmeier thinks Dophkah may be connected linguistically with *mfk't,* an Egyptian word for turquoise, which was mined in the district of Wadi Maghara, about 20 miles inland from the gulf of Suez (Hoffmeier 2005:165-169).

10. *Alush* (33:13-14) is an unknown desert location not mentioned in Exodus, but some suggest Wadi el-'Esh (Snaith 1969:200; Hoffmeier 2005:169), though G. I. Davies doubts it (1979:84) and Budd calls that association "philologically dubious" (1984:355).

11. *Rephidim* (33:14-15; see Exod 17:1, 8; 19:2). If the traditional southern location of Sinai is held, Rephidim is usually identified with Wadi Feiran near the southern tip of the Sinai Peninsula (Harrison 1990:405), though some now identifiy it with Wadi Refayid, about 30 miles north of the southern tip of the Sinai Peninsula (Y. Aharoni, Avi-Yonah, Rainey, and Safrai 2002:map 48; Hoffmeier 2005:170). This was the place where water came from the rock, a phenomenon like the modern Bedouin practice of tapping rock formations for shallow ground water in the southern Sinai (Hoffmeier 2005:170-71).

12. *Wilderness of Sinai* (33:15). This would be located in the south-central portion of the peninsula.

Wilderness Wanderings (33:16–36).

13. *Kibroth-hattaavah* (33:16-17; see 11:34-35), meaning "Graves of Desire" or "Glutton's Cemetery" (11:34; Deut 9:22), was a three-day journey from Sinai (10:33). Some suggest Wadi es-Sudr or upper Wadi Gheidara (Cole 2000:523). Missing from this list of campsites are Taberah (11:3) and later Mattanah, Nahaliel, and Bamoth (21:18-19).

14. *Hazeroth* (33:17-18; see 11:35; 12:16; Deut 1:1) means something like "courtyards, villages, settlements." It is an unknown location, possibly identified with the philologically equivalent Wadi Khudeirat, 22 miles northeast of Jebel Musa, the traditional location of Sinai; however, "Doubts about the latter identification are automatically transferred to the former" (Milgrom 1989:280). Now some suggest 'Ain Khadra, about 40 miles northeast of Jebel Musa (Y. Aharoni, Avi-Yonah, Rainey, and Safrai 2002).

15. *Rithmah* (33:18-19), a name perhaps derived from the broom plant (Gray 1903:445-446), is an otherwise unknown site mentioned only here.

16. *Rimmon-perez* (33:19-20), or perhaps "Pomegranate Gap," is otherwise unknown and mentioned only here.

17. *Libnah* (33:20-21), or "White Place," is perhaps a variant of Liban, located near Hazeroth and Di-zahab (Deut 1:1); otherwise, it is mentioned only here, because Libnah in Joshua 10:29 is clearly recognized as a different place.

18. *Rissah* (33:21-22) is mentioned only here; its location is unknown.

19. *Kehelathah* (33:22-23), or "Gathering Place," an unknown place mentioned only here but is perhaps a duplicate of Makheloth (33:25).

20. *Mount Shepher* (33:23-24), or "Mount of Beauty," is mentioned only here.

21. *Haradah* (33:24-25), or "Frightening" or "Trembling," is mentioned only here and is perhaps another symbolic name like Kibroth-hattaavah (33:16).

22. *Makheloth* (33:25-26), or "Place of Assembly," is an unknown location mentioned only here, unless it is taken as a duplication of Kehelathah (33:22).

23. *Tahath* (33:26-27), or "Foot of the Mountain" (Levine 2000:519), is mentioned only here.

24. *Terah* (33:27-28) is mentioned only here and is otherwise known only as the name of Abraham's father (Gen 11:24-32; Josh 24:2).

25. *Mithcah* (33:28-29), or "Sweetness," is mentioned only here but may be associated with sweet water.

26. *Hashmonah* (33:29-30) is mentioned only here, which makes 12 consecutive place names that are unknown to us. Cf. Heshmon, a town in the Negev of Judah (Josh 15:27).

27. *Moseroth* (33:30-31), or "Reins" or "Band" or "Straps," is another form of Moserah, where Aaron died (Deut 10:6), although Numbers says he died on Mount Hor (33:38). These could be alternate names for the same place or for sites in the same vicinity. It is also possible that this is not so much a place name as a common noun *moserah* [TH4147A, ZH4593], meaning "chastisement," which gives not the place but the reason for Aaron's death (Ashley 1993:630, who cites as "not particularly convincing" this suggestion by Harrison 1969:511).

28. *Bene-jaakan* (33:31-32), or "Sons of Jaakan," is a place in Edom that is elsewhere called Akan (1 Chr 1:42; cf. Gen 36:27) or "the wells of the people of Jaakan" (Deut 10:6).

29. *Hor-haggidgad* (33:32-33), or "Cave of Gidgad," was also called Gudgodah (Deut 10:7). It is an unknown site, tentatively identified with Wadi Ghadhaghedh (Levine 2000:520).

30. *Jotbathah* (33:33-34), or "Pleasantness," was a place with streams of sweet water (Deut 10:7). It is tentatively identified as Tabbeh in southern Arabia (Y. Aharoni, Avi-Yonah, Rainey, and Safrai 2002; Baly 1963:174), that is, 'Ain Tabah, 6 miles south of Elath.

31. *Abronah* (33:34-35), or "Regions Beyond," is mentioned only here. It is
    probably right at the head of the Gulf of Aqabah, possibly just west of Elath
    (Y. Aharoni, Avi-Yonah, Rainey, and Safrai 2002:map 48) or at 'Ain Defiyeh,
    about 7 miles north of Ezion-geber at the head of the Gulf of Aqabah.
32. *Ezion-geber* (33:35-36), or "Mighty Trees," was the oft-mentioned oasis near
    Elath at the north end of the Gulf of Aqabah (Deut 2:8; 1 Kgs 9:26; 22:48;
    2 Chr 8:17; 20:36). Nelson Glueck's identification with Tell el-Kheleifeh at
    Elath has been widely accepted (Y. Aharoni, Avi-Yonah, Rainey, and Safrai
    2002:map 48); however, others have questioned it (Ashley 1993:631-632;
    Levine 2000:520), and an alternative has been suggested at Jezeirat Faraun,
    a small island a couple of miles south of the head of the Gulf of Aqabah
    (G. I. Davies 1979:85-86; Flinder 1989).
33. *Kadesh* (33:36-37; called Kadesh in 13:26; 20:1, 14, 16, 22; 27:14 and
    Kadesh-barnea in 32:8; Deut 1:2; 1:19; 2:14; 9:23), or "Sanctuary" (see note
    on 13:26). In the nineteenth century it was identified with the well-known
    'Ain Qedeis oasis located some 50 to 75 miles from Ezion-geber, which
    would mean that three to five intermediate stops were left unmentioned.
    Various twentieth-century studies have placed it instead at 'Ain Qudeirat. "It
    stands near the junction of a road leading from Suezto Beer-sheba/Hebron,
    the 'way of Shur' (Gen 16:7) and the road branching from the coastal high-
    way, the 'way of the land of the Philistines' (Ex 13:17) near el-'Arîsh, which
    leads to 'Aqabah. This area is now the largest oasis in the northern Sinai and
    has a spring that produces about 40 cubic meters of water per hour" (Rainey
    and Notley 2006:121). It was either "located in" (NLT, NAB, NIV) or "identi-
    fied with" (e.g., KJV, NASB, ESV, JPS, NJPS) "the wilderness of Zin" (33:36).
    Here the people rebelled after hearing the spies' report (chs 13–14), Korah
    led a rebellion (chs 16–17), Miriam died, Moses struck the rock, and Edom
    refused passage to the children of Israel (ch 20).

Kadesh to Moab (33:37–49).

34. *Mount Hor* (33:37-40; see 20:22-23, 25, 27; 21:4 and the note on 20:22),
    where Aaron died at age 123, in the 40th year of wandering (33:38). Deuter-
    onomy 2:14 indicates that the journey from Kadesh to Mount Hor took 38
    years, which means stages 1–33 and 34–40 went quickly. An early tradition
    identified Mount Hor with Nebi Harun near Petra (Josephus *Antiquities*
    4.82-84 [4.4.7]), and later geographers identified it with Jebel Madeirah just
    south of Petra (Cole 2000:625); however, Imaret el-Khureiseh, located 8
    miles north of Kadesh, "deserves some consideration" (Rainey and Notley
    2006:121). The list of stages also makes a brief note to opposition from the
    king of Arad (33:40; cf. 21:1-3).
35. *Zalmonah* (33:41-42), or "Black Place" or "Gloomsville," is an unknown site
    not to be identified with either of the Mount Zalmons mentioned elsewhere
    (Judg 9:48; Ps 68:14). It may have been in the region of Wadi es-Salmaneh
    east of 'Ain Hazeva and 22 miles west of the Dead Sea (Y. Aharoni, Avi-Yonah,

Rainey, and Safrai 2002:map 52; Cole 2000:526). Verses 41-49 give the impression that Israel cut through the territories of Edom and Moab (Deut 2:2-13, 29), although they had turned away from them at first (21:4).

36. *Punon* (33:42-43) is not mentioned in the narrative section of Exodus or Numbers, but it is at this point, before moving to Oboth, that we have the story of the fiery serpents (21:5-9). It's identified with Khirbet Feinan in Wadi Feinan—tentatively by some (e.g., Rasmussen 1989:248) and "surely" by others (e.g., Rainey and Notley 2006:121). This would locate it on the eastern edge of the Arabah and 30 miles south of the Dead Sea, in Edomite country.

37. *Oboth* (33:43-44; see 21:10-11) faced Moab from the east (21:10). It might be identified with 'Ain el-Weieh, just to the north of modern Feinan but before entering the Zered (Rainey and Notley 2006:121); however, G. I. Davies objects that this makes for an inexplicable detour to the west and prefers something north of there (Davies 1979:90); however, Israel *was* "wandering."

38. *Iye-abarim* (33:44-45; see 21:11), or "Ruins of Abarim" or "Ruins of the Passes," faced Moab from the east somewhere in the Zered Gorge (21:11-12), perhaps el-Medeiyineh, (Y. Aharoni, Avi-Yonah, Rainey, and Safrai 2002:map 52; Rainey and Notley 2006:122).

39. *Dibon-gad* (33:45-46; see "Dibon" at 21:30 and note at 32:3) or Dhiban, located four miles north of the Arnon and 13 miles east of the Dead Sea. The "-gad" element denotes the fact that after the conquest Gad rebuilt and fortified this formerly Moabite town (32:34).

40. *Almon-diblathaim* (33:46-47) is probably a variant of Beth-diblathaim, perhaps a conflation of two names: Baal-meon and Beth-diblathaim (Snaith 1969:201). Jeremiah mentions it along with Nebo and Dibon in his oracle against Moab (Jer 48:22; see the Moabite Stone, line 30). It has been tentatively located at Khirbet Deleilat esh-Sherqiyeh, which is near both Medeba and Baal-meon, which Mesha mentions with Beth-diblathaim (Y. Aharoni, Avi-Yonah, Rainey, and Safrai 2002:map 52). This would locate it east of the Dead Sea and 21 miles southeast of Amman.

41. *The mountains east of the river* (33:47-48), or "Mountains of Abarim" (see 21:11; 27:12; 33:47-49), were facing Mount Nebo, which is traditionally identified with a 2,600-foot peak five miles northwest of Madaba. These were in the Plains of Moab facing Jericho, thus providing a view of the land (Deut 32:49).

42. *The Plains of Moab* (33:48-50; see 21:12; 22:1; 26:3, 63; 35:1, 13-14) were located "east of the Jordan River, across from Jericho" (22:1; cf. 34:15; Josh 13:32). The people camped at Beth-jeshimoth, or perhaps "House of the Wilderness" (Josh 12:3; 13:20; Ezek 25:9), which is possibly echoed in the Arabic toponym Khirbet es-Suweimeh (Levine 2000:522), although Glueck identified it with Tell el-'Azeimah 12 miles south of Jericho, on the east side of the Jordan and just north of the Dead Sea (Y. Aharoni, Avi-Yonah, Rainey, and Safrai 2002:map 52).

ENDNOTES

1. Patristic commentators compared these 42 stations to the 42 (3 × 14) generations in Jesus' genealogy, but that doesn't shed any light on ch 33 (G. J. Wenham 1981:217, citing de Vaulx 1972:381, who lists Origen, Ambrose, and Jerome).

2. Some say Sinai was only a three-day journey from Egypt; however, the texts that give that distance don't specify Sinai, only a three-day journey to a place to sacrifice (Exod 5:3; 8:27).

3. Elsewhere the Pentateuch includes other references to Moses's writing (Exod 17:14; 24:4; Deut 31:9, 22-24), and the Pentateuch makes various references to written public documents that God wrote and gave to Moses or that Moses himself wrote (Deut 4:13; 5:22; 9:10; 10:2-4; 31:24-26; cf. 2 Kgs 17:37).

4. E.g., LXX, *Raphaka*/רפקה for דפקה in the MT ("Dophkah," 33:12), *Dessa*/דסה for רסה ("Rissah," 33:21), or *Charadath*/חרדת for חרדה ("Haradah," 33:24).

5. Ashley (1993:626), citing G. I. Davies 1979:79; Kitchen 1966:57-59; G. J. Wenham 1981:224; Budd 1984:354; and noting that Snaith (1969:199) opts for Qantir.

◆ E. Laws about the Promised Land (33:50–36:13)
  1. Orders for occupying the Promised Land (33:50-56)

⁵⁰While they were camped near the Jordan River on the plains of Moab opposite Jericho, the LORD said to Moses, ⁵¹"Give the following instructions to the people of Israel: When you cross the Jordan River into the land of Canaan, ⁵²you must drive out all the people living there. You must destroy all their carved and molten images and demolish all their pagan shrines. ⁵³Take possession of the land and settle in it, because I have given it to you to occupy. ⁵⁴You must distribute the land among the clans by sacred lot and in proportion to their size. A larger portion of land will be allotted to each of the larger clans, and a smaller portion will be allotted to each of the smaller clans. The decision of the sacred lot is final. In this way, the portions of land will be divided among your ancestral tribes. ⁵⁵But if you fail to drive out the people who live in the land, those who remain will be like splinters in your eyes and thorns in your sides. They will harass you in the land where you live. ⁵⁶And I will do to you what I had planned to do to them."

NOTES

33:52 *carved and molten images.* These are *maskith* [TH4906, ZH5381], figures "carved" from stone (Lev 26:1, e.g., "figured stones"; Gray 1903:450), and *massekoth* [TH4541, ZH5011], which are images cast from "molten" metal (Exod 34:17; Lev 19:4).

pagan shrines. Lit., "high places," perhaps referring to cult platforms (Sturdy 1976:231), since they could even be found in a valley such as the valley of Ben-Hinnom (Jer 7:31).

COMMENTARY

The final section of Numbers (33:50–36:13) deals with laws pertaining to life in the Promised Land. Moses gave laws for occupying it (33:50-56), established its borders (34:1-15), appointed officials to distribute it (34:16-29), described the Levitical holdings in it (35:1-34), and returned to the issue of women who might inherit it (36:1-13).

Israel was to drive out the Canaanites and eliminate all vestiges of their religion

(Exod 23:23-33; 34:11-26; Lev 26:1). They were to destroy all the idols and shrines (33:52). To Canaan's ancient inhabitants, this wanton destruction must have looked something like the Taliban's demolition of Buddhist cliff carvings in Afghanistan. The "pagan shrines" (33:52) were probably the hill shrines or cult platforms that are condemned elsewhere (1 Kgs 13:2, 32-34; 2 Kgs 12:3; 14:4; 15:4, 35; 23:5-20). The initial fulfillment of this command came under Joshua (Josh 11:20, 23). Later Judean kings performed poorly on this count (1 Kgs 22:43; 2 Kgs 12:3; 14:4; 15:4, 35), and their attitude toward these shrines determined the Deuteronomistic Historian's evaluation of them (e.g., 1 Kgs 14:22-23).

God had given Israel a land grant, which they were to distribute among the tribes and clans. Lots determined the location of a tribe's holding (26:55), then a lot would determine the same for each clan within those tribal borders (33:54). The Canaanites were to be driven out (33:55; Exod 23:33; 34:11-13; Deut 7:16). God warned that if they failed in this he would do to the Israelites what he had planned to do to these idolatrous nations (33:56). That is, if Israel failed to drive out the "Hivites, Canaanites, and Hittites" (Exod 23:28), God would send invaders to terrify Israel and drive them out of the land (Exod 23:27). Benjamin's failure to expel the Jebusites (Judg 1:21-36) fulfilled the warning that they would be "splinters in your eyes" (33:55). Indeed, like "a snare and a trap . . . [like] brambles in your eyes" (Josh 23:13), the influence of these Canaanite remnants led to Israel's collapse (Ps 106:34-36).

This was an international application of a personal warning against keeping company with the wicked (Pss 1:1; 26:4). Under Old Testament law it meant avoiding intermarriage with pagans (Exod 34:16; Ezra 9-10; Neh 13), and it disallowed treaties with nearby pagan neighbors (Deut 7:2). The same principle carried into the New Testament, which warns, "Bad company corrupts good character" (1 Cor 15:33); "Don't team up with those who are unbelievers. . . . Come out from among unbelievers, and separate yourselves from them" (2 Cor 6:14, 17); and "If you want to be a friend of the world, you make yourself an enemy of God" (Jas 4:4). Peter preached, "Save yourselves from this crooked generation!" (Acts 2:40), and about "Babylon," the heavenly voice still warns, "Come away from her, my people. Do not take part in her sins, or you will be punished with her" (Rev 18:4).

◆   ## 2. Borders of the Promised Land (34:1-15)

Then the LORD said to Moses, ²"Give these instructions to the Israelites: When you come into the land of Canaan, which I am giving you as your special possession, these will be the boundaries. ³The southern portion of your country will extend from the wilderness of Zin, along the edge of Edom. The southern boundary will begin on the east at the Dead Sea.* ⁴It will then run south past Scorpion Pass* in the direction of Zin. Its southernmost point will be Kadesh-barnea, from which it will go to Hazar-addar, and on to Azmon. ⁵From Azmon the boundary will turn toward the Brook of Egypt and end at the Mediterranean Sea.*

⁶"Your western boundary will be the coastline of the Mediterranean Sea.

⁷"Your northern boundary will begin at the Mediterranean Sea and run east to

Mount Hor, ⁸then to Lebo-hamath, and on through Zedad ⁹and Ziphron to Hazar-enan. This will be your northern boundary.

¹⁰"The eastern boundary will start at Hazar-enan and run south to Shepham, ¹¹then down to Riblah on the east side of Ain. From there the boundary will run down along the eastern edge of the Sea of Galilee,* ¹²and then along the Jordan River to the Dead Sea. These are the boundaries of your land."

¹³Then Moses told the Israelites, "This territory is the homeland you are to divide among yourselves by sacred lot. The LORD has commanded that the land be divided among the nine and a half remaining tribes. ¹⁴The families of the tribes of Reuben, Gad, and half the tribe of Manasseh have already received their grants of land ¹⁵on the east side of the Jordan River, across from Jericho toward the sunrise."

34:3 Hebrew *Salt Sea;* also in 34:12.   34:4 Or *the ascent of Akrabbim.*   34:5 Hebrew *the sea;* also in 34:6, 7. 34:11 Hebrew *Sea of Kinnereth.*

NOTES

34:4 *Scorpion Pass.* Lit., "the ascent of *'aqrabbim* [TH6137A, ZH6832] (scorpions)," perhaps the same location as Naqb es-Tsafa.

Hazar-addar. This may be 'Ain Qedis (Y. Aharoni, Avi-Yonah, Rainey, and Safrai 2002:map 51).

Azmon. This may be 'Ain Muweilekh, about 60 miles south of Gaza.

34:5 *Brook of Egypt.* Milgrom identifies this as the modern Wadi el-'Arish, describing it as "a long and deep watercourse that is full only after a substantial rain. It constituted a natural barrier between the Negev and the Sinai Peninsula" (1989:286; see Josh 15:4, 47; 1 Kgs 8:65; 2 Kgs 24:7; 2 Chr 7:8; Isa 27:12).

34:7 *Mount Hor.* This is not the Mount Hor on Edom's border, where Aaron died (20:22-28); rather, this is one of the peaks in the Lebanon range, perhaps Ras Shakkah, about 15 miles north of Byblos.

34:11 *run down along the eastern edge of the Sea of Galilee.* Lit., "and the boundary ran down and *makhah* the *katep* of Kinnereth to the East." For *makhah* [TH4229A, ZH4682], lexicons suggest "strike" (BDB) or "encounter, meet" (HALOT). Levine suggests, "the border 'abutted'" (2000:535). The term *katep* [TH3802, ZH4190] means "shoulder," metaphorically referring to a mountain slope (Josh 15:8-10; 18:12, 16, 18) or a "ridge" (Budd 1984:367).

Galilee. Lit., "Kinnereth," meaning "harp-shaped" (Deut 3:17; Josh 11:2; 12:3; 13:27; 19:35; 1 Kgs 15:20). It is successively known as the Sea of Gennesar (1 Macc 11:67) or Gennesaret (Matt 14:34; Mark 6:53; Luke 5:1 mg), Tiberias (John 6:1; 21:1 mg), and Galilee, as NLT regularly names it.

COMMENTARY

Perhaps the scouts of chapter 13 returned with enough geographical information for Moses to do this mapping. It describes the borders of "Canaan" (34:2) as "congruent with those of the Egyptian province of Canaan during the second half of the second millennium" (Milgrom 1989:285; also Y. Aharoni 1966:68-69; Levine 2000:540). This same sphere of Egyptian hegemony would later be reflected in these words: "Babylon captured the entire area formerly claimed by Egypt—from the Brook of Egypt to the Euphrates River" (2 Kgs 24:7). Sometimes the Promised Land's description was a modest "from Dan in the north to Beersheba in the south" (Judg 20:1), or from Lebo-hamath in the north to the Arabah Valley or the Brook of

Egypt in the south (1 Kgs 8:65). But often descriptions were expansionistic: "as far as you can see in every direction—north and south, east and west" (Gen 13:14; 28:14), "all the way from the border of Egypt to the great Euphrates River" (Gen 15:18), or Egypt to Lebanon and the Mediterranean to the Euphrates (Deut 1:7). In any case, Canaan comprised an area larger than Israel proved able to possess, except during the reigns of David and Solomon.

The southern border is described in 34:1-5. It began at the southern tip of the Dead Sea (34:3) and ran "south past Scorpion Pass" then southeast to its "southern-most point" at "Kadesh-barnea" (34:4). It continued west along the "wilderness of Zin" (see 34:3; cf. 13:21; 33:36), passing through "Hazar-addar" and "Azmon." It then followed the northwestern course of the "Brook of Egypt" to end at the Mediterranean (34:5).

The western border was the Mediterranean coastline (34:6). Its people and territories remained unconquered after the conquest (Josh 13:2-6; Judg 1:19, 27, 29, 31; cf. Judg 3:1-6). Generally, the coastal plains remained occupied by the Philistines in the south and by the Phoenicians in the north (2 Sam 5:17-25; 8:1-14; 2 Chr 2:1-16). Israel remained unable to control Mediterranean ports, with only a few temporary exceptions: (1) Dor may have been an Israelite port during David's time (Levine 2000:540). (2) For a short period, Hezekiah revolted against the Babylonian supremacy and imprisoned Padi of Ekron in Jerusalem, which is not mentioned in the Bible but only in Babylonian tablets (Snaith 1969:340), though it is doubtful whether this actually constituted an occupation, which would have given him control of Padi's Philistine ports (Budd 1984:366). (3) During the time of the Maccabees, Jonathan and Simon seized Joppa for a port (Philip 1993:340; see 1 Macc 10:76; 12:33; 14:5).

The northern border (34:7-9) is the most difficult to define, but it took in much of modern Lebanon, thus reaching further north than the boundaries of Dan, the proverbial northern limit (e.g., Judg 20:1). It began at the Mediterranean Sea; Budd and Snaith place it between Tyre and Sidon (Budd 1984:366; Snaith 1969:340), but Milgrom (1989:286) starts "just north of Byblos, in present-day Lebanon, which marked the northern boundary of the Egyptian province of Canaan according to the peace treaty between Rameses II and the Hittites at the beginning of the thirteenth century B.C.E." (so also Y. Aharoni, Avi-Yonah, Rainey, and Safrai 2002:map 51). From the Mediterranean, the northern border ran east to Mount Hor, one of the summits of the Lebanese range. From there the northern boundary ran to Lebo-hamath, at the head of the Orontes River (see note on 13:21). The description of the northern border in Joshua 13:4 adds Aphek, or modern Afqa, 15 miles east of Byblos. From there it ran to Zedad, modern Tsada east of the Sirion (the Anti-Lebanon Range), about 35 miles northeast of Lebweh (Lebo). From there the northern boundary ran to Ziphron and to Hazar-enan, both of which remain unknown. Milgrom suggests they may be the oases east of Zedad called Hawwarin and Qaryatein (1989:287; so also Cole 2000:537). Harrison suggests locating Hazar-enan at the base of Mount Hermon (1990:413).

The eastern border (34:10-15) is difficult to nail down north of the Sea of Galilee, because Hazar-enan, Shepham, Riblah, and Ain cannot be located; however, south of the Sea of Galilee the Jordan River forms the border. Shepham is mentioned only here and is unknown from any other source. Perhaps Riblah refers to the important ancient Near Eastern site on the Orontes, the location of Egypt's battles with Judah and then Babylon (608 and 588 BC; 2 Kgs 23:33-35; 25:6, 21; Jer 39:5-7; 52:9-11, 27). But some commentators doubt this location because it was so out of the way and because that toponymn was always written without the definite article (Levine 2000:535, citing Gray 1903:461; contrast 34:11, which reads "the Riblah"). The Septuagint has *Arbēla*, which could be Arbela in Galilee just west of the widest part of the Sea of Kinnereth (1 Macc 9:2), near Hermon. The name *'ayin* [TH5871/5869, ZH6526/6524], meaning "spring," would have been as common in ancient Canaan as "Springfield" is in the United States. Gray suggests it may be a mispronunciation of *'iyyon* [TH5859, ZH6510] (1903:461-462, citing 1 Kgs 15:20; 2 Kgs 15:29), which was right at the source of the Jordan. The rest of the eastern border followed southward along "the eastern edge of the Sea of Galilee" (34:11), then "along the Jordan to the Dead Sea" (34:12). Elsewhere the eastern boundary is described solely in terms of the Jordan and Dead Sea (Ezek 47:18).

Verses 13-15 form an inclusio with verse 2 and deal with the "nine and a half remaining tribes" after "Reuben, Gad, and half the tribe of Manasseh" had arranged to settle in the Transjordan. It was a magnificent land grant. "The size of the land and Israel's inability to occupy it all remind us of God's liberality 'who is able to do far more abundantly than all that we ask or think' (Eph 3:20; cf. Rom 8:32; Jas 1:5)" (G. J. Wenham 1981:232).

◆   ## 3. Appointed officials (34:16-29)

¹⁶And the LORD said to Moses, ¹⁷"Eleazar the priest and Joshua son of Nun are the men designated to divide the grants of land among the people. ¹⁸Enlist one leader from each tribe to help them with the task. ¹⁹These are the tribes and the names of the leaders:

Tribe	Leader
Judah	Caleb son of Jephunneh
²⁰Simeon	Shemuel son of Ammihud
²¹Benjamin	Elidad son of Kislon
²²Dan	Bukki son of Jogli
²³Manasseh son of Joseph	Hanniel son of Ephod
²⁴Ephraim son of Joseph	Kemuel son of Shiphtan
²⁵Zebulun	Elizaphan son of Parnach
²⁶Issachar	Paltiel son of Azzan
²⁷Asher	Ahihud son of Shelomi
²⁸Naphtali	Pedahel son of Ammihud

²⁹These are the men the LORD has appointed to divide the grants of land in Canaan among the Israelites."

COMMENTARY

Gad and Reuben settled in the Transjordan, so only 10 tribal leaders were appointed to deal with the nine and one-half tribes settling within Canaan proper. They were chosen on the same principle as those chosen to supervise the earlier census (1:1-15); however, Joshua and Eleazar (34:17) replaced Moses and Aaron as overall supervisors (34:17; cf. 1:3). The 10 tribes are listed in a geographical order, moving from south to north, but with Judah being given precedence in the south, rather than Simeon. It is a list "fitting for a new beginning" (Ashley 1993:644).

The southern tribes (34:19-22) comprised Judah, Simeon, Benjamin, and Dan. Though Dan originally settled in the south, the tribe later migrated to the north (Josh 19:40-48; Judg 18). The central tribes (34:23-24) comprised the two Joseph tribes, Ephraim and the half-tribe of Manasseh. The northern tribes (34:25-28) comprised Zebulun, Issachar, Asher, and Naphtali.

◆   ## 4. Levitical holdings in the Promised Land (35:1-34)

While Israel was camped beside the Jordan on the plains of Moab across from Jericho, the LORD said to Moses, [2]"Command the people of Israel to give to the Levites from their property certain towns to live in, along with the surrounding pasturelands. [3]These towns will be for the Levites to live in, and the surrounding lands will provide pasture for their cattle, flocks, and other livestock. [4]The pastureland assigned to the Levites around these towns will extend 1,500 feet* from the town walls in every direction. [5]Measure off 3,000 feet* outside the town walls in every direction—east, south, west, north—with the town at the center. This area will serve as the larger pastureland for the towns.

[6]"Six of the towns you give the Levites will be cities of refuge, where a person who has accidentally killed someone can flee for safety. In addition, give them forty-two other towns. [7]In all, forty-eight towns with the surrounding pastureland will be given to the Levites. [8]These towns will come from the property of the people of Israel. The larger tribes will give more towns to the Levites, while the smaller tribes will give fewer. Each tribe will give property in proportion to the size of its land."

[9]The LORD said to Moses, [10]"Give the following instructions to the people of Israel.

"When you cross the Jordan into the land of Canaan, [11]designate cities of refuge to which people can flee if they have killed someone accidentally. [12]These cities will be places of protection from a dead person's relatives who want to avenge the death. The slayer must not be put to death before being tried by the community. [13]Designate six cities of refuge for yourselves, [14]three on the east side of the Jordan River and three on the west in the land of Canaan. [15]These cities are for the protection of Israelites, foreigners living among you, and traveling merchants. Anyone who accidentally kills someone may flee there for safety.

[16]"But if someone strikes and kills another person with a piece of iron, it is murder, and the murderer must be executed. [17]Or if someone with a stone in his hand strikes and kills another person, it is murder, and the murderer must be put to death. [18]Or if someone strikes and kills another person with a wooden object, it is murder, and the murderer must be put to death. [19]The victim's nearest relative is responsible for putting the murderer to death. When they meet, the avenger must put the murderer to death. [20]So if someone hates another person and pushes him or throws a dangerous object at him and he dies, it is murder. [21]Or if someone hates another person and hits him with a fist and he dies, it is murder. In such cases, the avenger must put the murderer to death when they meet.

[22]"But suppose someone pushes another person without having shown previous hostility, or throws something that

unintentionally hits another person, ²³or accidentally drops a huge stone on someone, though they were not enemies, and the person dies. ²⁴If this should happen, the community must follow these regulations in making a judgment between the slayer and the avenger, the victim's nearest relative: ²⁵The community must protect the slayer from the avenger and must escort the slayer back to live in the city of refuge to which he fled. There he must remain until the death of the high priest, who was anointed with the sacred oil.

²⁶"But if the slayer ever leaves the limits of the city of refuge, ²⁷and the avenger finds him outside the city and kills him, it will not be considered murder. ²⁸The slayer should have stayed inside the city of refuge until the death of the high priest. But after the death of the high priest, the slayer may return to his own property. ²⁹These are legal requirements for you to observe from generation to generation, wherever you may live.

³⁰"All murderers must be put to death, but only if evidence is presented by more than one witness. No one may be put to death on the testimony of only one witness. ³¹Also, you must never accept a ransom payment for the life of someone judged guilty of murder and subject to execution; murderers must always be put to death. ³²And never accept a ransom payment from someone who has fled to a city of refuge, allowing a slayer to return to his property before the death of the high priest. ³³This will ensure that the land where you live will not be polluted, for murder pollutes the land. And no sacrifice except the execution of the murderer can purify the land from murder.* ³⁴You must not defile the land where you live, for I live there myself. I am the LORD, who lives among the people of Israel."

35:4 Hebrew *1,000 cubits* [460 meters]. 35:5 Hebrew *2,000 cubits* [920 meters]. 35:33 Or *can make atonement for murder.*

NOTES

35:4 *1,500 feet from the town walls in every direction.* This is the "radius" measured from the "town walls" rather than from a theoretical center, because the hamlet was of negligible size.

35:5 *3,000 feet outside the town walls in every direction.* Lit., "from the outside of the city, the east quarter, 2,000 cubits, the south quarter, 2,000 cubits, the west quarter, 2,000 cubits, and the north quarter, 2,000 cubits; and the city is in the midst." This is the perimeter measurement on each quarter (Budd 1984:376). Levine suggests a more complicated design with the town itself being 3,000 feet square and the pastureland extending out from that 1,500 feet for a total area of 6,000 feet squared (Levine 2000:571).

35:11 *accidentally.* Heb., *bishegagah.* The Geneva Bible-KJV-ASV tradition has "unawares"; however, it is better to use a term like "accidentally" (NIV, NKJV, NLT), "without intent" (RSV, NRSV, ESV), or "unintentionally" (NASB, NJPS, NET). The term *shegagah* [TH7684, ZH8705] here and in 35:15 is the same term used elsewhere for unintentional sins (15:24-29).

35:12 *from a dead person's relatives who want to avenge the death.* Heb., *miggo'el,* meaning "from the avenger" (see 35:19). Since the *go'el* [TH1350B, ZH1457] was an individual, "relatives" could be a misleading translation; and since this vengeance is later translated as a responsibility (35:19), the phrase "who *want* to" may also be misleading. In addition to this responsibility, the *go'el* could be responsible to recover money owing to a relative (5:8), to recover family property (Lev 25:25; Ruth 4:1-6; Jer 32:8-12), to redeem a kinsman from slavery (Lev 25:47-49), or even to contract a levirate marriage (Deut 25:5-9; Ruth 3:13; 4:5).

35:15 *foreigners living among you, and traveling merchants.* Lit., "for the *ger* and for the *toshab* among you," possibly a hendiadys, i.e., "for the alien, even the one living among you," e.g., "resident aliens" (Milgrom 1989:292). BDB, which defines the *ger* [TH1616,

ZH1731] as a "temporary dweller, new-comer (no inherited rights), (as opposed to *homeborn*)," then defines the *toshab* [TH8453, ZH9369] as "*sojourner*, apparently of a more temporary and dependent (Lv 22:10; 25:6) kind than the *ger*, (with which it is often joined)." The NLT rather reflects the interpretation that *toshab* describes in economic terms what *ger* describes in legal terms (TDOT 2.439-449).

35:19 the victim's nearest relative is responsible for putting the murderer to death. Lit., "the redeemer (*go'el* [TH1350B, ZH1457]) of blood, he shall kill the murderer."

35:20 pushes. Heb., *hadap* [TH1920, ZH2074]. Older translations followed the Geneva Bible's choice of a "thrusting" movement (KJV, ASV, JPS) or "stab" (RSV); however, newer translations prefer "push" (NLT, NRSV, ESV, NASB, NKJV, NJPS) or "shove" (NIV), like sheep butting (Ezek 34:21), a person shoving someone away (2 Kgs 4:27), knocking them down (Jer 46:15), or driving them out (Deut 9:4; Josh 23:5; Job 18:18). Therefore, it is something like pushing someone off a building or cliff.

throws a dangerous object at him. Lit., "or throws at him"; no object is mentioned, though the LXX has "anything" as an object. More significantly, the Hebrew includes *bitsediyyah* [TH6660, ZH7402] after this phrase, meaning "while lying in wait," i.e., a premeditated ambush, which most translations indicate with a term for ambush (e.g., KJV, RSV, JPS, LXX) or premeditation (NIV, NET, NJPS). The NLT omits this telling qualification, though it's already implied in the preexisting hatred mentioned in the verse.

COMMENTARY

In Numbers, directions about the Levites frequently follow directions for the other tribes: The first census (1:1-46) was followed by a note that the Levites were exempt (1:47-54); camp arrangements (ch 2) were followed by Levitical arrangements (ch 3); and the final census (26:1-56) was followed by a Levitical count (26:57-62). Here, land arrangements for the tribes (ch 34) are followed by allocation of Levitical cities (ch 35).

The tribes of Israel selected and apportioned to the Levites "towns to live in" (35:2), along with each town's surrounding pastureland (35:3). Ranging outward from the town center for 1,500 feet, the surrounding pastureland had a perimeter with 3,000 feet on each side (35:4). Greenberg (1968) suggests that verse 5 is a theoretical conclusion that the frontage on each side would be a minimum of 3,000 feet (this is followed by G. J. Wenham 1981:235, with similar solutions suggested by Budd 1984:378; Keil 1869:259-260; Milgrom 1989:502-504; Noordtzij 1983:296). Since this comprised an area suitable for a small village, rather than a town or city, it is possible that as a city grew, its boundaries pushed out so that the overall dimensions of the pastureland increased proportionately (Allen 1990:1000; Milgrom 1989:502-504; G. J. Wenham 1981:234-235).

Some say the Levites were allowed to *dwell* in these cities and to use the surrounding pastureland, but were not actually given possession of them (Budd 1984:376). That's an unnatural reading of this text. E. W. Davies, however, thinks they probably had possession only of a small quarter in each city, with other people constituting the majority living in them (1995b:358, citing Haran 1978:124, 130-131; Albright 1946:123). Noordtzij notes that we know that some Levitical sites had mixed populations, though they were probably governed by the Levites: Hebron, Shechem,

Libnah, Gibeon, Gezer, Jokneam, Taanach, and Kadesh. He compares this to the Hittite temple cities, which were not populated exclusively by temple personnel but were governed by them (Noordtzij 1983:296).

Each tribe was to "give property in proportion to the size of its land" (35:8), though it appears that the idea of proportionality didn't actually work out in practice (Josh 21). Judah and Simeon contributed nine cities between them. Naphtali gave only three, even though it was larger than Ephraim or Gad, which each contributed four. The even larger tribes of Issachar and Dan didn't give a larger share.

It is interesting to find that neither Jerusalem nor any of the earlier worship centers like Gilgal, Shiloh, or Mizpah were among these, although the patriarchal Hebron was included (Josh 21:11, 13). Mazar (1959, cited by E. W. Davies 1995b:356-357) notes that the Levitical cities sat at the frontiers, and he thinks these areas would have had mixed populations that needed Levites to promulgate Yahweh worship among them (cf. Y. Aharoni 1966:272-273).

Cities of Refuge (35:9-34). Six of the 48 Levitical cities were additionally classified as cities of refuge (Deut 4:43; Josh 20:7-9; 21:13, 21, 27, 32, 36-38; see Josh 20:1-9), where a person who had committed accidental manslaughter could flee for refuge from the act of blood vengeance. They were not for premeditated, deliberate murders (Exod 21:12-14; Deut 19:4-13), which would have been an example of an unforgivable deliberate sin (15:29-31). This extended the principle of finding refuge at the altar of a shrine, Tabernacle, or Temple (Exod 21:12-14; 1 Kgs 1:50-53).

The killer received initial asylum until he could be "tried by the community" (35:12). So that the killer would not have to make the risky flight all the way to the altar at a central sanctuary, the people were told to "designate six cities of refuge" (35:13). Three were to be in the Transjordan (35:14a; Josh 20:8) and three in Canaan proper (35:14b; Josh 20:7). The Transjordan cities were (1) Bezer, possibly the modern Umm el-'Amad, which is about 15 miles east of the mouth of the Jordan; (2) Ramoth-gilead, the modern Tell Ramid, which is about 20 miles east of the Jordan to the southeast of the Sea of Galilee; and (3) Golan, the modern Sakhem el-Jolan, which is 18 miles east of the Sea of Galilee. Those located in Canaan proper were (1) Kedesh in Galilee for the northern region—the modern Tell Qades; (2) Shechem for the central region—the modern Tell Balatah; and (3) Hebron for the south—the modern el-Khalil.

Like other important laws,[1] this law about cities of refuge benefited not only the native Israelites but also any foreigners living or working in Israel (35:15). The law applied to anyone who accidentally killed someone; elsewhere, the law forbade granting protection to the willful offender (Exod 21:14).

First, the text lays out various scenarios defined as murder (35:16-21).[2] The crucial factor was *premeditation*. Had the act come from ongoing hatred, or was it rather the result of a violent surge of anger? One way to tell was if the slayer used a weapon that might indicate purposeful action: iron (35:16), stone (35:17), or wood (35:18). Another way to tell was if the person had lain in wait or already had a reputation for hating someone (35:20); then even if the death was the result of a shove

(35:20) or blow from the fist (35:21), it was murder. Then "the murderer must be put to death" (35:17), and "the victim's nearest relative is responsible" (35:19). There may be the same distinction in the words of Jesus, "Father, forgive them, for they don't know what they are doing" (Luke 23:34), and in Paul telling Timothy, "God had mercy on me because I [acted] in ignorance and unbelief" (1 Tim 1:13). But the better New Testament parallel is Jesus' teaching that connects blame for murder to its motivating hatred (Matt 5:21-22).

Second, the text lays out scenarios defined as accidental homicide (35:22), which was the judgment if the killer had "[not] shown previous hostility" (35:22) and "they were not enemies" (35:23). Absence of premeditation meant accidental homicide, whether the death resulted from a shove (35:22) or from an object like a stone (35:17), whether thrown (35:22b) or dropped on the victim (35:23).

Third, the chapter lays out the procedure for allowing flight to the city of refuge (35:24-34). If community representatives judged that the conditions for accidental homicide applied (35:23) rather than those for first-degree murder (35:16-21), then they were obligated to "protect the slayer from the avenger" while the slayer returned to the city of refuge (35:25). This implies that the investigation or trial took place elsewhere. It could have been outside the city of refuge to which he had fled (Ashley 1993:653; G. J. Wenham 1981:238), whether it was one nearest to his own hometown or the one nearest the place where the slaying occurred (Noordtzij 1983:300).[3] Perhaps the trial was to be at the Tent of Meeting, which eventually meant in Jerusalem (Sturdy 1976:242).

Then the killer had to stay in the city of refuge "until the death of the high priest" (35:25). Noth explains this in terms of royal amnesty, with the priest taking on the role generally reserved for ancient Near Eastern kings, granting amnesty at the end of an era (Wellhausen 1983:150, followed by Noth 1968:255; Noordtzij 1983:302). But E. W. Davies thinks this ignores the law's own focus on the necessity of expiation for the manslayers (1995b:365). Indeed, it was the *death* of the high priest, not the edict of a newly anointed priest, that effected this release. Maimonides thinks that the death of the high priest was an event that moved the entire people so much that no thoughts of vengeance could arise in the avenger of blood. According to the Talmud, the high priest should by the power of prayer have made such a calamity as murder an impossibility in Israel. That he had not succeeded in doing so was a proof that he had failed in his duty. Hence he had to bear the penalty of knowing how welcome his death would be to the man exiled to the city of refuge (Hertz 1977:722). More to the point, G. J. Wenham (1981:228) explains this in terms of substitutionary atonement:

> That it was the high priest's death, not the exile of the manslaughterer, that atoned is confirmed by the mishnaic dictate, "If after the slayer has been sentenced as an accidental homicide the high priest dies, he need not go into exile" and the talmudic comment thereon, "But is it not the exile that expiates? It is not the exile that expiates, but the death of the high priest."

The several other commentators who also interpret it as atonement are surely correct (Keil 1869:265; Budd 1984:384; Harrison 1990:422; Ashley 1993:654; Cole 2000:554). If the avenger caught him away from the city of refuge and killed him, it was not murder (35:27); rather, it was justifiable vengeance—not even homicide.

A guilty murderer was given over to the family go'el [TH1350B, ZH1457] (35:19, 21); however, judgment was reached before a community court (35:24) and required "more than one witness" (35:30), preventing retribution from degenerating into a family blood feud (Deut 17:6; 19:15). This ancient Near Eastern principle of sufficient witness was also written into the Code of Hammurabi (§9-11; ANET 166), and the same Old Testament principle (Heb 10:28) was carried into New Testament church discipline (1 Tim 5:19; cf. Matt 18:16; John 8:17; Rev 11:3).

Neither the go'el [TH1350B, ZH1457] nor the authorities could "accept a ransom payment for the life," whether to forestall execution of the murderer (35:31) or to allow the premature release of a killer who had "fled to a city of refuge" (35:32). This would violate two principles: It would violate the principle of *lex talionis*, and it would violate the principle of equality, favoring the rich over the poor, who could not afford ransom—or bribery. Instead, "Murderers must always be put to death" (35:31), or the death of the high priest must occur before release from the city of refuge (35:32). Human bloodshed must be atoned for by human death (Gen 9:5; Exod 21:12; Lev 24:17; cf. Deut 19:11-13). Because the killer had to stay until this happened, we must see the city of refuge as more than just a place for protective custody; it was *punitive* confinement (Harrison 1990:421) or even a form of banishment (E. W. Davies 1995b:367, citing Josephus *Antiquities* 4.172-173 [4.7.4]; Philo *On Special Laws* 3.123). Levine (2000:570) thinks the fugitives were probably lodged in a specific quarter in the town, perhaps there supervised by Levites, and maybe even put to work like indentured servants.

Finally, the chapter closes out with the religious basis for this regulation (35:33). It was to protect the land from pollution (35:33) and defilement (35:34). God commanded them to keep the land clean because "I live there myself" (35:34), and he is a pure God, who "cannot stand the sight of evil" (Hab 1:13).

Christian application of this legislation will recognize three ideas: First, it affirms the sanctity of human life (Exod 20:13) and the authority of the man made in God's image and likeness to administrate judicial penalties, including a death penalty (Gen 9:5). Second, the cities of refuge foreshadowed Christ, who is the sinner's refuge from the avenger of blood (Philip 1993:351-352, citing Prov 18:10; cf. Ps 18:2 // 2 Sam 22:3; Pss 27:1; 61:3; 91:2; 144:2 on the tower of safety). Third, the high priest anticipated the ministry of Jesus, who not only offered sacrifices and prayer on behalf of the people, but whose own death was atoning (G. J. Wenham 1981:239, citing Heb 4-9).

ENDNOTES
1. Passover (9:14), special offerings (15:15), purification water (19:10), Day of Atonement (Lev 16:29), killing animals in the field (Lev 17:8), eating blood (Lev 17:15), sexual relationships (Lev 18:26), not offering children to Molech (Lev 20:2), blasphemy (Lev 24:16).

2. On murder see Archer 1975; ISBE 3.241, 434-435; IDB 1.738-739.
3. Whether the trial occurred at the town where the death occurred or not, the congregation listened to evidence from the elders of the murderer's hometown (Deut 19:12), and Noordtzij thinks "there 'the voice of the blood' (Gen 4:10) is heard" (Noordtzij 1983:300). This would also fit the directions given to elders and judges in the town nearest a homicide when there is nobody to put on trial (Deut 21:1-9).

◆   5. Inheritance of Zelophehad's daughters (36:1-13; cf. 27:1-11)

Then the heads of the clans of Gilead—descendants of Makir, son of Manasseh, son of Joseph—came to Moses and the family leaders of Israel with a petition. ²They said, "Sir, the LORD instructed you to divide the land by sacred lot among the people of Israel. You were told by the LORD to give the grant of land owned by our brother Zelophehad to his daughters. ³But if they marry men from another tribe, their grants of land will go with them to the tribe into which they marry. In this way, the total area of our tribal land will be reduced. ⁴Then when the Year of Jubilee comes, their portion of land will be added to that of the new tribe, causing it to be lost forever to our ancestral tribe."

⁵So Moses gave the Israelites this command from the LORD: "The claim of the men of the tribe of Joseph is legitimate. ⁶This is what the LORD commands concerning the daughters of Zelophehad: Let them marry anyone they like, as long as it is within their own ancestral tribe. ⁷None of the territorial land may pass from tribe to tribe, for all the land given to each tribe must remain within the tribe to which it was first allotted. ⁸The daughters throughout the tribes of Israel who are in line to inherit property must marry within their tribe, so that all the Israelites will keep their ancestral property. ⁹No grant of land may pass from one tribe to another; each tribe of Israel must keep its allotted portion of land."

¹⁰The daughters of Zelophehad did as the LORD commanded Moses. ¹¹Mahlah, Tirzah, Hoglah, Milcah, and Noah all married cousins on their father's side. ¹²They married into the clans of Manasseh son of Joseph. Thus, their inheritance of land remained within their ancestral tribe.

¹³These are the commands and regulations that the LORD gave to the people of Israel through Moses while they were camped on the plains of Moab beside the Jordan River across from Jericho.

NOTES

36:4 *Jubilee.* This was named for the ram's horn (*yobel* [TH3104, ZH3413]) that ushered in the year (Lev 25:9).

COMMENTARY

To close the book, we get an anticlimactic bit of case law rather than an expression like, "Arise, O LORD, and let your enemies be scattered! Let them flee before you!" (10:35). Numbers 36:1-13 recounts a *clan* appeal against a *family* decision. Without further protections, the right of daughters to inherit would alienate clan property if they married outside it (36:3). Even the Year of Jubilee wouldn't remedy that loss (Lev 25:8-55; Westbrook 1991:38ff.).

The Lord gave further directives for this business of daughters inheriting and then marrying. This was not so much prescribing whom they must marry, but setting limits on whom they could marry. If they weren't heiresses, they could choose husbands from any tribe in Israel; however, with tribal lands in their hands, they had to marry within their tribe. The geographical integrity of each clan's holdings must be sustained (36:7). Zelophehad's daughters were part of the Gileadite segment of Manasseh (36:1; cf. 26:29-33), which took Transjordan territory (32:39-42); however, that was protected inheritance, just as much as any within Canaan proper. Zelophehad's daughters followed this new provision (36:10). In this case the issue was not so much the potential of being unequally yoked (contra Philip 1993:358, citing 2 Cor 6:14), but about joining in a marriage that would cut the family off from specific covenant blessings.

The book closes with a geographical note about "the commands and regulations" coming to Moses "on the plains of Moab" (36:13). It is not clear whether this refers only to chapters 27–36 (Snaith 1969; Sturdy 1976), to the larger corpus of chapters 22–36 (Gray 1903; McNeile 1911; Ashley 1993:659),[1] or to the entire book of Numbers (Binns 1927; Budd 1984:389; Cole 2000:563).[2] Whatever the case, it is a fitting verse to close out the entire book, with its implication of good prospects for Israel if they will obey the Lord's commands.

ENDNOTES
1. Ashley cites parallel summary statements in Leviticus (Lev 7:37; 26:46; 27:34), thus taking Lev 27:34 as a section summary rather than a book summary, as Budd also does.
2. Cole even calls it an envelope with 1:1; Budd compares it with the end of Leviticus (Lev 27:34).

BIBLIOGRAPHY

Aharoni, Israel
1938 *On Some Animals Mentioned in the Bible.* Brugge: Osiris.

Aharoni, Yohanan
1966 *The Land of the Bible: A Historical Geography.* London: Burns & Oates.

Aharoni, Yohanan, Ruth Amiran, and Miriam Aharoni
1993 Arad. Pp. 75-87 in *The New Encyclopedia of Archaeological Excavations in the Holy Land,* vol. 1. Editors, Ephraim Stern, Ayelet Levinzon-Gilbo'a, and Joseph Aviram. Jerusalem: Israel Exploration Society.

Aharoni, Yohanan, Michael Avi-Yonah, Anson F. Rainey, and Ze'ev Safrai
2002 *The Carta Bible Atlas.* 4th ed. Jerusalem: Carta.

Albright, W. F.
1915 The Home of Balaam. *Journal of the American Oriental Society* 35:386-390.

1924 Researches of the School in Western Judea. *Bulletin of the American School of Oriental Research* 15:2-11.

1925 The Administrative Divisions of Israel and Judah. *Journal of the Palestine Oriental Society* 5:20-25.

1944 The Oracles of Balaam. *Journal of Biblical Literature* 63:207-233.

1946 *Archaeology and the Religion of Israel.* 2nd ed. Baltimore: Johns Hopkins University Press.

1957 *From the Stone Age to Christianity.* Garden City: Doubleday.

1963a *The Biblical Period from Abraham to Ezra.* New York: Harper & Row.

1963b Jethro, Hobab, and Reuel in Early Hebrew Tradition. *Catholic Biblical Quarterly* 25:1-11.

1970 Midianite Donkey Caravans. Pp. 197-205 in *Translating and Understanding the Old Testament: Essays in Honor of Herbert Gordon May.* Editors, Harry Thomas Frank, W. L. Reed, and Herbert Gordon May. Nashville: Abingdon.

Allen, Ronald B.
1990 Numbers. *The Expositor's Bible Commentary,* vol. 2. Editor, F. E. Gaebelein. Grand Rapids: Zondervan.

Alt, A.
1953 Das System der Stammesgrenzen im Buche Josua. Pp. 193-202 in *Klein Schriften zur Geschichte des Volkes Israel.* Munich: C. H. Beck.

Alter, Robert
1985 *The Art of Biblical Narrative.* New York: Basic Books.

Anthon, Charles
1871 *A Classical Dictionary, Containing an Account of the Principal Proper Names Mentioned in Ancient Authors and Intended to Elucidate All the Important Points Connected with the Geography, History, Biography, Mythology, and Fine Arts of the Greeks and Romans. Together with an Account of Coins, Weights, and Measures, with Tabular Values of the Same.* New York: Harper.

Archer, Gleason L.
1975 Crimes and Punishment—B.1. Homicide. Pp. 1032-1033 in *Zondervan Pictorial Encyclopedia of the Bible,* vol. 1. Editor, Merrill C. Tenney. Grand Rapids: Zondervan.

1982 *Encyclopedia of Bible Difficulties.* Grand Rapids: Zondervan.

Ashley, Timothy R.
1993 *The Book of Numbers.* New International Commentary on the Old Testament. Grand Rapids: Eerdmans.

Bach, Alice
1994 Good to the Last Drop: Viewing Sotah (Numbers 5:11-31) as the Glass Half Empty and Wondering How to View It as Half Full. Pp. 26-54 in *The New Literary Criticism and the Hebrew Bible.* Editors, J. Cheryl Exum and D. J. A. Clines. Valley Forge: Trinity Press International.

Baentsch, Bruno
1903 *Exodus, Leviticus, Numeri.* Handkommentar Zum Alten Testament. Göttingen: Vandenhoeck & Ruprecht.

Baly, Denis
1963 *Geographical Companion to the Bible.* New York: McGraw-Hill.

Barkay, Gabriel
1983 The Divine Name Found in Jerusalem. *Biblical Archaeology Review* 9/2:14-19.

Barkay, Gabriel, Andrew G. Vaugh, Marilyn J. Lundberg, and Bruce Zuckerman
2004 The Amulets of Ketef Hinnom: A New Addition and Evaluation. *Bulletin of the American Schools of Oriental Research* 334:41-71.

Barnouin, M.
1977 Les recensements du livre des Nombres et l'astronomie babylonienne. *Vetus Testamentum* 27:280-303.

Bentzen, Aage
1948-1949 *Introduction to the Old Testament.* Copenhagen: G. E. C. Gad.

Bertman, S.
1961 Tasselled Garments in the Ancient East Mediterranean. *Biblical Archaeologist* 24/4:119-128.

Best, Harold M., and David K. Hutter
1975 Music: Musical Instruments. Pp. 311-324 in *Zondervan Pictorial Encyclopedia of the Bible,* vol. 4. Editor, Merrill C. Tenney. Grand Rapids: Zondervan.

Beyerlin, Walter
1978 *Near Eastern Religious Texts Relating to the Old Testament.* Religionsgeschichtliches Textbuch zum Alten Testament. Editors, John Bowden et al. Philadelphia: Westminster.

Binns, Leonard Elliott
1927 *The Book of Numbers.* Westminster Commentaries. London: Methuen.

Block, Daniel I.
1999 *Judges, Ruth.* New American Commentary. Nashville: Broadman & Holman.

Bowman, John W.
1958 Did the Qumran Sect Burn the Red Heifer [Num 19]? *Revue de Qumran* 1:73-84.

Brichto, Herbert Chanan
1975 The Case of Sota and a Reconsideration of Biblical Law. *Hebrew Union College Annual* 46:55-70.

Broshi, Magen, and Israel Finkelstein
1992 The Population of Palestine in Iron Age II. *Bulletin of the American Schools of Oriental Research* 287:47-60.

Broshi, Magen, and Ram Gophna
1984 The Settlements and Population of Palestine During the Early Bronze Age II-III. *Bulletin of the American Schools of Oriental Research* 253:41-53.

Brueggemann, Dale A.
2005 The Evangelists and the Psalms. Pp. 263-278 in *Interpreting the Psalms: Issues and Approaches.* Editors, Philip S. Johnston and David G. Firth. Leicester, UK: Apollos/IVP.

Budd, Philip J.
1984 *Numbers.* Word Biblical Commentary. Dallas: Word.

Calvin, John
1993 *Commentaries on the Four Last Books of Moses in the Form of a Harmony.* 4 vols. Translator, Charles W. Bingham. Grand Rapids: Baker.

Chapman, Arthur Thomas, and A. W. Streane
1914 *The Book of Leviticus.* Cambridge Bible for Schools and Colleges. Cambridge: Cambridge University Press.

Christensen, Duane L.
1974 Num 21:14-15 and the Book of the Wars of Yahweh. *Catholic Biblical Quarterly* 36:359-360.

Clark, R. E. D.
1955 The Large Numbers of the Old Testament. *Journal of the Transactions of the Victoria Institute* 87:82-92.

Coats, George W.
1968 *Rebellion in the Wilderness.* Nashville: Abingdon.

1973 Balaam: Sinner or Saint? *Biblical Research* 18:21-29.

1982 The Way of Obedience. *Semeia* 24:53-79.

Cohen, A.
1983 *The Soncino Chumash: The Five Books of Moses with Haphtaroth; Hebrew Text and English Translation with an Exposition Based on the Classical Jewish Commentaries.* Soncino Books of the Bible. Hindhead, Surrey: Soncino.

Cole, R. Dennis
2000 *Numbers: An Exegetical and Theological Exposition of Holy Scripture.* New American Commentary. Nashville: Broadman & Holman.

Cook, F. C., and T. E. Espin
1871 *The Fourth Book of Moses Called Numbers.* London: Murray.

Cooney, John D.
1965 *Amarna Reliefs from Hermopolis in American Collections.* New York: Brooklyn Museum.

Crane, Gregory R., editor
2004 καυλός. In *The Perseus Project.* http://www.perseus.tufts.edu. Accessed August 2004.

Cross, Frank M.
1973 *Canaanite Myth and Hebrew Epic: Essays in the History of the Religion of Israel.* Cambridge, MA: Harvard University Press.

Daube, David
1964 *The Sudden in the Scriptures.* Leiden: Brill.

Davies, Eryl W.
1995a A Mathematical Conundrum: The Problem of the Large Numbers in Numbers I and XXVI. *Vetus Testamentum* 45/4:449-469.

1995b *Numbers.* New Century Bible. Grand Rapids: Eerdmans.

Davies, Graham I.
1974 The Wilderness Itineraries: A Comparative Study. *Tyndale Bulletin* 25:46-81.

1979 *The Way of the Wilderness: A Geographical Study of the Wilderness Itineraries in the Old Testament.* Cambridge: Cambridge University Press.

Delitzsch, Franz
1884–1889 *Biblical Commentary on the Psalms.* 3 vols. Translator, D. Eaton. Rev. ed. Foreign Biblical Library. London: Hodder & Stoughton.

Dillmann, Christian Friedrich August, and August Wilhelm Knobel
1886 *Die Bücher Numeri, Deuteronomium und Josua.* Kurzgefasstes Exegetische Handbuch zum Alten Testament. Leipzig: Hirzel.

Dossin, Georges, and André Parrot, editors and translators
1950 *Archives Royales de Mari 1–9.* 2 vols. Archives royales de Mari. Paris: Imprimerie Nationale.

Douglas, Mary T.
1993 *In the Wilderness: The Doctrine of Defilement in the Book of Numbers.* Sheffield: Journal for the Study of the Old Testament Press.

Dumbrell, William J.
1975 Midian: A Land or a League? *Vetus Testamentum* 25/3:323-337.

Ehrlich, Arnold B.
1968–1969 מקרא כפשוטו. 3 vols. Jerusalem: Magnes.

Eissfeldt, Otto
1965 *The Old Testament: An Introduction.* New York: Harper & Row.

Elliger, Karl
1966 *Leviticus.* Handbuch zum Alten Testament. Tübingen: Mohr/Siebeck.

Felder, Cain Hope
1989 *Troubling Biblical Waters: Race, Class and Family.* Maryknoll, N. Y.: Orbis.

Fishbane, Michael
1983 Form and Reformulation of the Biblical Priestly Blessing. *Journal of the American Oriental Society* 103/1:115-121.

Flinder, Alexander
1989 Is This Solomon's Seaport? *Biblical Archaeology Review* 15/4:30-43.

Fohrer, Georg
1968 *Introduction to the Old Testament.* Maryknoll, N. Y.: Orbis.

Fouts, David M.
1996 The Use of Large Numbers in the Old Testament: With Particular Emphasis on the Use of *'Elep.* Ann Arbor: UMI Dissertation Services.

1997 A Defense of the Hyperbolic Interpretation of the Large Numbers in the Old Testament. *Journal of the Evangelical Theological Society* 40/3:377-387.

Freedman, David N.
1972 The Broken Construct Chain. *Biblica* 53/4:534-536.

Fritz, V.
1970 *Israel in der Wüste: Traditionsgeschichtliche Untersuchung de Wüstenüberlieferung des Jahwisten.* Marburg: N. G. Elwert.

Frymer-Kensky, Tikva
1984 The Strange Case of the Suspected Sôtah (Numbers V.11-31). *Vetus Testamentum* 34:11-26.

Galil, G.
1985 The Sons of Judah and the Sons of Aaron in Biblical Historiography. *Vetus Testamentum* 35:488-495.

García Martínez, Florentino
1994 *The Dead Sea Scrolls Translated.* Translator, Wilfred Watson. Leiden: Brill.

García Martínez, Florentino, and Eibert J. C. Tigchelaar
1997 *The Dead Sea Scrolls Study Edition.* Editor, García-Martínez. Leiden: Brill.

Gardiner, A.
1961 *Egypt of the Pharaohs: An Introduction.* Oxford: Clarendon.

Gesenius, W., and E. Kautzsch
1910 *Gesenius' Hebrew Grammar.* Translator, A. E. Cowley. Oxford: Clarendon.

Gispen, W. H.
1959 *Het Boek Numeri.* Kampen: Kok.

Gottwald, Norman K.
1979 *The Tribes of Yahweh: A Sociology of the Religion of Liberated Israel.* Maryknoll, NY: Orbis.

Gray, George Buchanan
1903 *Numbers.* International Critical Commentary. Edinburgh: T&T Clark.

Greenberg, Moshe
1968 Idealism and Practicality in Numbers 35:4-5 and Ezekiel 48. *Journal of the American Oriental Society* 88:59-66.

1972 Plagues of Egypt. Pp. 604-613 in *Encyclopedia Judaica,* vol. 16. Jerusalem: Keter.

Gressmann, Hugo
1913 *Mose und sein Zeit: Ein Kommentar zu den Mose-Sagen.* Forschungen zur Religion und Literatur des Alten und Neuen Testaments 1. Gottingen: Vandenhoeck & Ruprecht.

Gressmann, Hugo, Erich Ebeling, Hermann Ranke, and Nikolaus Rhodokanakis, editors
1926 *Altorientalische Texte und Bilder zum Alten Testamente.* Berlin: de Gruyter.

Gross, W.
1974 *Bileam: Literar- und Form-Kritische Untersuchung der Prosa in Num 22–24.* Munich: Kösel.

Gruber, M.
1980 *Aspects of Nonverbal Communication in the Ancient Near East.* Rome: Pontifical Biblical Institute.

1983 הקֶרֶשׁ בְּסֵפֶר מְלָכִים וּבַמְקוֹרוֹת אֲחֵרִים. *Tarbiz* 52:167-176.

1986 The *Qedešah* and Her Canaanite Cognates. *Ugarit-Forschungen* 18:133-148.

Gunneweg, A. H. J.
1965 *Leviten und Priester.* Forschungen zur Religion und Literatur des Alten und Neuen Testaments. Göttingen: Vandenhoeck & Ruprecht.

Hackett, Jo Ann
1986a The Balaam Text from Deir 'Alla. *Vetus Testamentum* 36/4:507-508.

1986b Some Observations of the Balaam Tradition at Deir 'Alla. *Biblical Archaeologist* 49:216-222.

Haran, Menahem
1960 The Use of Incense in the Ancient Israelite Ritual. *Vetus Testamentum* 10/2:113-129.
1978 *Temples and Temple Service in Ancient Israel.* Oxford: Clarendon.

Har-El, Menashe
1983 *The Sinai Journeys: The Route of the Exodus.* Mas'e Sinai. Los Angeles: Ridgefield.

Harrison, Roland K.
1969 *Introduction to the Old Testament.* Grand Rapids: Eerdmans.
1990 *Numbers.* Wycliffe Evangelical Commentary. Chicago: Moody.

Hebrew University in Jerusalem
2007 Hebrew University Excavations Reveal First Beehives in Ancient Near East in 'Land of Milk and Honey'. News release, Jerusalem, September 5, 2007. Accessed March 2, 2008 at http:// www.hunews.huji.ac.il/articles.asp?cat=6&artID=814.

Heinzerling, Rüdinger
2000 On the Interpretation of the Census Lists by C. J. Humphreys and G. E. Mendenhall. *Vetus Testamentum* 50/2:250-252.

Herodotus
1920 *Historia.* Translator, A. D. Godley. Loeb Classical Library. Cambridge, MA: Harvard University Press.

Hertz, J. H., editor
1977 *Pentateuch and Haftorahs.* 2nd ed. London: Soncino.

Hickman, H.
1946 *La trompette dans l'Egypte ancienne.* Cairo, Egypt: IFAO.

Hirsch, Samson Raphael
1971 *Pentateuch Translated and Explained,* vol. 4, *Numbers.* 2nd ed. Editor and Translator, Isaac Levy. New York: Judaica. (Orig. pub. 1867–1878.)

Hoffmeier, James K.
2005 *Ancient Israel in Sinai: The Evidence for the Authenticity of the Wilderness Tradition.* New York: Oxford University Press.

Hoffner, H. A.
1973 The Hittites and Hurrians. Pp. 197-228 in *Peoples of Old Testament Times.* Editor, D. J. Wiseman. Oxford: Clarendon.

Holladay, William L.
1971 *A Concise Hebrew and Aramaic Lexicon of the Old Testament.* Grand Rapids: Eerdmans.

Holzinger, H.
1903 *Numeri.* Kurzer Hand-Commentar zum Alten Testament 4. Tübingen: Mohr.

Homan, Michael M.
2000 The Divine Warrior in His Tent: A Military Model for Yahweh's Tabernacle. *Biblical Research* 16:22-26, 28-33, 55.
2002 *To Your Tents, O Israel! The Terminology, Function, Form, and Symbolism of Tents in the Hebrew Bible and the Ancient Near East.* Leiden: Brill.

Hughes, P. E.
2002 Jethro. Pp. 467-469 in *Dictionary of the Old Testament: Pentateuch.* Editors, T. Desmond Alexander and David W. Baker. Downers Grove: InterVarsity.

Hulse, E. V.
1975 The Nature of Biblical 'Leprosy' and the Use of Alternate Medical Terms in Modern Translations of the Bible. *Palestine Exploration Quarterly* 107:87-105.

Humphreys, Colin J.
1998 The Number of People in the Exodus: Decoding Mathematically the Very Large Numbers in Numbers I and XXVI. *Vetus Testamentum* 48:196-213.
2000 The Numbers in the Exodus from Egypt: A Further Appraisal. *Vetus Testamentum* 50:323-328.

Hurvitz, Avi
1974 The Evidence of Language in Dating the Priestly Code. *Revue Biblique* 81:24-57.

Hyatt, J. P.
1980 *Exodus.* New Century Bible Commentary. Grand Rapids: Eerdmans.

Johnson, Aubrey R.
1967 *Sacral Kingship in Ancient Israel.* Cardiff: University of Wales Press.

Joines, Karen Randolph
1968 Bronze Serpent in the Israelite Cult. *Journal of Biblical Literature* 87/3:245-256.

1974 *Serpent Symbolism in the Old Testament: A Linguistic, Archaeological, and Literary Study.* Haddonfield, NJ: Haddonfield.

Kaiser, Walter C., Jr.
1996 Balaam Son of Beor in Light of Deir Alla and Scripture. Saint or Soothsayer? Pp. 95-106 in *Go to the Land I Will Show You.* Editors, Joseph E. Coleson and Victor Matthews. Winona Lake: Eisenbrauns.

Kaufmann, Yigal
1961 *The Religion of Israel.* Translator, Moshe Greenberg. London: Allen & Unwin.

Keil, Carl Friedrich
1869 *The Book of Numbers.* 3 vols. Translator, James Martin. Biblical Commentary on the Old Testament. Edinburgh: T&T Clark.

Keil, Carl Friedrich, and Franz Delitzsch
1884 *Pentateuch.* 3 vols. Translator, James Martin. Biblical Commentary on the Old Testament. Edinburgh: T&T Clark.

Kitchen, Kenneth A.
1960 Some Egyptian Background to the Old Testament. *Tyndale Bulletin* 5-6:7-11.

1966 *Ancient Orient and the Old Testament.* London: Tyndale.

2003 *On the Reliability of the Old Testament.* Grand Rapids: Eerdmans.

Knudtzon, J. A.
1964 *Die el-Amarna-Tafeln, mit Einleitung und Erläuterungen.* 2 vols. Leipzig: Otto Zeller. (Orig. pub. 1915.)

Kraus, Hans-Joachim
1966 *Worship in Israel: A Cultic History of the Old Testament.* Translator, G. Buswell. Richmond: Knox.

Kuschke, A.
1961 Die Lagerverstellung der Priesterschriftlichen Erzählung. *Zeitschrift für die alttestamentliche Wissenschaft* 73:71-77.

Lamaire, André
1985 Fragments from the Book of Balaam Found at Deir Alla. *Biblical Archaeology Review* 11/5:26-39.

Lambdin, Thomas Oden
1971 *Introduction to Biblical Hebrew.* New York: Scribner.

Lane, Edward William
1986 *An Account of the Manners and Customs of the Modern Egyptians, Written in Egypt During the Years 1833-1835.* London: Darf. (Orig. pub. 1896.)

Leiman, Sid Z.
1974 Inverted 'Nuns' at Numbers 10:35-36 and the Book of Eldad and Medad. *Journal of Biblical Literature* 93/3:348-355.

Levenson, Jon D.
1993 *The Death and Resurrection of the Beloved Son: The Transformation of Child Sacrifice in Judaism and Christianity.* New Haven: Yale University Press.

Levine, Baruch A.
1976 More on the Inverted Nuns of Num 10:35-36. *Journal of Biblical Literature* 95/1:122-124.

1993 *Numbers 1-20: A New Translation with Introduction and Commentary.* Anchor Bible. New York: Doubleday.

1996 Offerings Rejected by God: Numbers 16:15 in Comparative Perspective. Pp. 107-116 in *Go to the Land I Will Show You.* Editors, Joseph E. Coleson and Victor Matthews. Winona Lake: Eisenbrauns.

2000 *Numbers 21-36: A New Translation with Introduction and Commentary.* Anchor Bible. New York: Doubleday.

L'Heureux, Conrad E.
1976 The Yelide Harapa': A Cultic Association of Warriors. *Bulletin of the American Schools of Oriental Research* 221:83-85.

Licht, Jacob
1985 *A Commentary on the Book of Numbers (I–X)*. Jerusalem: Magnes.

Licht, Jacob, and Shmuel Ahituv
1985 פירוש על ספר במדבר. 3 vols. Jerusalem: Magnes.

Liebreich, Leon J.
1955 The Songs of Ascent and the Priestly Blessing. *Journal of Biblical Literature* 74/1:33-36.

Liverani, M.
1973 The Amorites. Pp. 100-133 in *Peoples of Old Testament Times*. Editor, D. J. Wiseman. Oxford: Clarendon.

Loewe, Raphael
1968 Divine Frustration Exegetically Frustrated. Pp. 137-158 in *Words and Meanings: Essays Presented to David Winton Thomas on His Retirement from the Regius Professorship of Hebrew in the University of Cambridge*. Editors, Peter R. Ackroyd and Barnabas Lindars. Cambridge: Cambridge University Press.

Löwenstamm, Samuel E.
1971 The Number of Plagues in Psalm 105. *Biblica* 52:34-38.

Lucas, A.
1944 The Number of Israelites at the Time of the Exodus. *Palestine Exploration Quarterly* 76:164-168.

Lutzky, Harriet C.
1997 The Name 'Cozbi' (Numbers XXV 15, 18). *Vetus Testamentum* 47/4:546-549.

1999 Ambivalence Toward Balaam. *Vetus Testamentum* 49/3:421-425.

Maarsingh, B.
1987 *Numbers: A Practical Commentary*. Translator, John Vriend. Grand Rapids: Eerdmans.

MacLaurin, E. C. B.
1965 Anak/Ἀναξ. *Vetus Testamentum* 15/4:468-474.

MacRae, A. A.
1953 Numbers. Pp. 162-194 in *The New Bible Commentary*. Editor, Francis Davidson. London: InterVarsity.

Magonet, Jonathan
1982 The Korah Rebellion. *Journal for the Study of the Old Testament* 24:3-25.

Mazar, Benjamin
1959 The Cities of the Priests and Levites. Pp. 193-205 in *1959 Congress Volume, Oxford*. Vetus Testamentum Supplements 7. Leiden: Brill.

1965 The Sanctuary of Arad and the Family of Hobab the Kenite. *Journal of Near Eastern Studies* 24/3:292-303.

McCarthy, Dennis J.
1972 *Old Testament Covenant: A Survey of Current Opinions*. Translation and adaptation of *Der Gottesbund im Alten Testament* (Stuttgart: Katholisches Bibelwerk, 1966). Growing Points in Theology. Oxford: Blackwell.

McCown, Chester Carlton
1947 The Density of Population in Ancient Palestine. *Journal of Biblical Literature* 66/4:425-436.

McEntire, M.
1999 A Response to Colin J. Humphreys's "The Number of People in the Exodus from Egypt: Decoding Mathematically the Very Large Numbers in Numbers I and XXVI." *Vetus Testamentum* 49:262-264.

McEvenue, S. E.
1971 *The Narrative Style of the Priestly Writer*. Analecta Biblica 50. Rome: Pontifical Biblical Institute.

McNeile, Alan Hugh
1911 *The Book of Numbers, in the Revised Version with Introduction and Notes*. Rev. ed. Cambridge Bible for Schools and Colleges. Cambridge: Cambridge University Press.

Mendenhall, George E.
1958 The Census of Numbers 1 and 26. *Journal of Biblical Literature* 77:52-66.

1973 *The Tenth Generation*. Baltimore: Johns Hopkins University Press.

Meyer, F. B.
1903 *Our Daily Homily: Chapter by Chapter Through the Bible*. 5 vols. London: Marshall, Morgan & Scott.

Meyers, Carol L.

1976 The Tabernacle Menorah: A Synthetic Study of a Symbol from the Biblical Cult. ASOR Dissertation Series 2. Missoula: Scholars Press.

Milgrom, Jacob

1970 *Studies in Levitical Terminology I: The Encroacher and the Levite; the Term 'Aboda.* University of California Publications, Near Eastern Studies 14. Berkeley: University of California Press.

1981 The Paradox of the Red Cow (Num 19). *Vetus Testamentum* 31/1:62-72.

1983 *Studies in Cultic Theology and Terminology.* Studies in Judaism and Late Antiquity 36. Leiden: Brill.

1989 *Numbers.* JPS Torah Commentary. Philadelphia: Jewish Publication Society.

1999 On Decoding Very Large Numbers. *Vetus Testamentum* 49:131-132.

Millard, A. R.

1973 The Canaanites. Pp. 29-52 in *Peoples of Old Testament Times.* Editor, D. J. Wiseman. Oxford: Clarendon.

Miller, J. Maxwell, and John H. Hayes

1986 *A History of Ancient Israel and Judah.* London: SCM.

Mitchell, T. C.

1969 The Meaning of the Noun חתן in the Old Testament. *Vetus Testamentum* 19/1:93-112.

Möhlenbrink, K.

1934 Die Levitischen Überlieferungen des Alten Testaments. *Zeitschrift für die alttestamentliche Wissenschaft* 52:184-231.

Moore, Michael S.

1990 *The Balaam Tradition: Their Character and Development.* SBL Dissertation Series 113. Atlanta: Scholars Press.

Mowinckel, Sigmund

1930 Der Ursprung der Bileamsage. *Zeitschrift für die alttestamentliche Wissenschaft* 49:233-271.

1992 *The Psalms in Israel's Worship.* 2 vols. in one. Translator, D. R. Ap-Thomas. Sheffield: Sheffield Academic.

Naville, E.

1908 *The Temple of Deir el-Bahri VI.* London: Egypt Exploration Society.

Niditch, Susan

1993 War, Women, and Defilement in Numbers 31. *Semeia* 61:39-57.

Noordtzij, A.

1983 *Numbers.* Translator, Ed van der Maas. Bible Student's Commentary. Grand Rapids: Zondervan.

North, Francis Sparling

1961 Four Month Seasons of the Hebrew Bible. *Vetus Testamentum* 11:446-448.

Noth, Martin

1930 *Das System der Zwölf Stämme Israels.* Beiträge zur Wissenschaft vom Neuen Testament. Stuttgart: Kohlhammer.

1960 *The History of Israel.* Rev. ed. New York: Harper & Row.

1968 *Numbers.* Old Testament Library. Philadelphia: Westminster.

1972 *A History of the Pentateuchal Tradition.* Translator, Bernard W. Anderson. Englewood Cliffs, NJ: Prentice-Hall. (Orig. pub. 1948.)

Olson, Dennis T.

1985 *The Death of the Old and the Birth of the New: The Framework of the Book of Numbers and the Pentateuch.* Brown Judaic Studies. Chico, CA: Scholars Press.

1996 *Numbers.* Interpretation. Louisville: Knox.

Paterson, J. A.

1900 *The Book of Numbers: Critical Ed. of the Hebrew Text Printed in Colors Exhibiting the Composite Structure of the Book.* Sacred Books of the Old Testament. Leipzig: Hinrichs.

Péter, René

1975 Par et Sor. *Vetus Testamentum* 25/3:496.

Petrie, W. M. Flinders

1906 *Researches in Sinai.* New York: E. P. Dutton.

1923 *Egypt and Israel.* New York: Macmillan.

Philip, James
1993 *Numbers.* Mastering the Old Testament. Dallas: Word.

Plaut, W. Gunther
1979 *Numbers Commentary.* New York: Jewish Publication Society.

Rad, Gerhard von
1962 *Old Testament Theology.* 2 vols. Translator, D. M. G. Stalker. New York: Harper & Row.

1966a The Form-Critical Problem of the Hexateuch. Pp. 1–78 in *The Problem of the Hexateuch and Other Essays.* Translator, E. W. Trueman Dicken. London: Oliver & Boyd.

1966b The Tent and the Ark. Pp. 103–124 in *The Problem of the Hexateuch and Other Essays.* Translator, E. W. Trueman Dicken. London: Oliver & Boyd.

Rainey, Anson F., and R. Steven Notley
2006 *The Sacred Bridge: Carta's Atlas of the Biblical World.* With contributions by J. Uzziel, I. Shai, and B. Schults. Jerusalem: Carta.

Rasmussen, Carl G.
1989 *Zondervan NIV Atlas of the Bible.* Regency Reference Library. Maps by Carta (Jerusalem). Grand Rapids: Zondervan.

Rendesburg, Gary A.
2001 An Additional Note on Two Recent Articles on the Number of the People in the Exodus from Egypt and the Large Numbers in Numbers i and xxvi. *Vetus Testamentum* 51/3:392–396.

Rendtorff, Rudolph
1977 *Das Überlieferungsgeschichtliche Problem des Pentateuch.* Beihefte zur Zeitschrift für die alttestamentliche Wissenschaft. Berlin: de Gruyter.

Riggans, Walter
1983 *Numbers.* Daily Study Bible. Philadelphia: Westminster.

Ringgren, Helmer
1970 *Israelite Religion.* Translator, D. E. Green. Philadelphia: Fortress.

Robinson, Gnana
1978 The Prohibition of Strange Fire in Ancient Israel: A New Look at the Case of Gathering Wood and Kindling Fire on the Sabbath. *Vetus Testamentum* 28/3:301–317.

Rogers, Cleon
1986 Moses: Meek or Miserable? *Journal of the Evangelical Theological Society* 29/3:257–263.

Rothenberg, Benno
1972 *Timna: Valley of the Biblical Copper Mines.* London: Thames & Hudson.

Sailhamer, John H.
1992 *The Pentateuch as Narrative: A Biblical-Theological Commentary.* Library of Biblical Interpretation. Grand Rapids: Zondervan.

Schoville, Keith N.
1994 Canaanites and Amorites. Pp. 157–182 in *Peoples of the Old Testament World.* Editors, Alfred J. Hoerth, Gerald L. Mattingly, and Edwin M. Yamauchi. Grand Rapids: Baker.

Sellin, Ernst von
1933 *Theologie des Alten Testaments.* Alttestamentliche Theologie auf religionsgeschischtlicher Grundlage. Leipzig: Quelle & Meyer.

Sherwood, Stephen K.
2002 *Leviticus, Numbers, Deuteronomy.* Berit Olam. Collegeville, MN: Liturgical Press.

Smith, W. Robertson
1901 *The Religion of the Semites.* London: Black.

Snaith, Norman H.
1949 *The Jewish New Year Festival: Its Origin and Development.* London: SPCK.

1969 *Leviticus and Numbers.* New Century Bible. Greenwood, SC: Attic.

Snijders, L. A.
1954 The Meaning of 'Zar' in the Old Testament. *Oudtestamentische Studiën* 10:1–154.

Spencer, John R.
1998 PQD, the Levites, and Numbers 1–4. *Zeitschrift für die alttestamentliche Wissenschaft* 110:535–546.

Steinmann, A. E.
2002 Cherubim. Pp. 112-113 in *Dictionary of the Old Testament: Pentateuch.* Editors, T. Desmond Alexander and David W. Baker. Downers Grove: InterVarsity.

Stephens, Ferris J.
1931 The Ancient Significance of Sîsîth. *Journal of Biblical Literature* 50/2:59-70.

Stern, Ephraim
1994 *Dor, Ruler of the Seas: Twelve Years of Excavations at the Israelite-Phoenician Harbor Town on the Carmel Coast.* Jerusalem: Israel Exploration Society. University of Cambridge.
1995 *The Explorations at Dor: A Preliminary Report.* Jerusalem: Israel Exploration Society.

Stern, Ephraim, and John Berg
1995 *Dor: Final Report.* Qedem Reports. Jerusalem: The Institute of Archaeology, Hebrew University of Jerusalem, in cooperation with The Israel Exploration Society.

Sturdy, John
1976 *Numbers.* Cambridge Bible Commentary. Cambridge: Cambridge University Press.

Thomas, David Winton, editor
1961 *Documents from Old Testament Times. Translated with introductions and notes by members of the Society for Old Testament.* New York: Harper.

Thompson, Henry O.
1986 Balaam in the Bible and at Deir 'Alla. *Biblical Archaeologist* 49:218-219.

Toorn, K. van der
1989 Female Prostitution in Payment of Vows in Ancient Israel. *Journal of Biblical Literature* 108:193-205.

Unger, Merrill F.
1966 *Unger's Bible Dictionary.* Chicago: Moody.

Van Seters, John
1975 *Abraham in History and Tradition.* New Haven: Yale University Press.

Vaulx, Jean de
1972 *Les Nombres.* Sources Bibliques. Paris: J. Gabalda.

Vaux, Roland de
1961 *Ancient Israel: Its Life and Institutions.* Translator, John McHugh. London: Darton, Longman & Todd.

Vermes, Geza
1961 *Scripture and Tradition in Judaism.* Leiden: Brill.
1998 *The Complete Dead Sea Scrolls in English.* Revised and extended 4th ed. London: Penguin.

Waltke, Bruce K., and Michael O'Connor
1990 *An Introduction to Biblical Hebrew Syntax.* Winona Lake: Eisenbrauns.

Weippert, H.
1971 *The Settlement of the Israelite Tribes in Palestine.* Studies in Biblical Theology. London: SCM.
1973 Das Geographische System der Stämme Israels. *Vetus Testamentum* 23:76-89.

Wellhausen, Julius
1983 *Prolegomena to the History of Ancient Israel.* Rev. ed. Translator, J. Sutherland Black and Allan Menzies. New York: Meridian. (Orig. pub. 1878.)

Wenham, Gordon J.
1978 Leviticus 22:2-8 and the Price of Slaves. *Zeitschrift für die alttestamentliche Wissenschaft* 90:254-265.
1981 *Numbers.* Tyndale Old Testament Commentary. Downers Grove: InterVarsity.

Wenham, John W.
1967 Large Numbers in the Old Testament. *Tyndale Bulletin* 18:19-53.

Westbrook, Raymond
1991 *Property and the Family in Biblical Law.* Journal for the Study of the Old Testament Supplement 113. Sheffield: Journal for the Study of the Old Testament Press.

Whitelaw, T.
1939 Numbers, Book of. Pp. 216-370 in *International Standard Bible Encyclopedia,* vol. 4. Editors, James Orr et al. Grand Rapids: Zondervan.

Wilkinson, John
1974 Ancient Jerusalem: Its Water Supply and Population. *Palestine Exploration Quarterly* 106:33-51.

Wiseman, Donald J.
1972 Flying Serpents? *Tyndale Bulletin* 23:108-110.

1973 *Peoples of Old Testament Times.* Oxford: Clarendon.

Woolley, C. Leonard
1928 *The Sumerians.* Oxford: Clarendon.

Wright, David Pearson
1985 Purification from Corpse-Contamination in Numbers XXXI:19-24. *Vetus Testamentum* 35/2:213-223.

Yadin, Yigael
1962 *The Scroll of the War of the Sons of Light against the Sons of Darkness.* Translators, B. Rabin and C. Rabin. Oxford: Oxford University Press.

1963 *The Art of Warfare in Biblical Lands in the Light of Archaeological Discovery.* London: Weidenfeld and Nicolson.

Yahuda, Abraham S.
1945 The Name of Balaam's Homeland. *Journal of Biblical Literature* 64/4:547-551.

Young, Edward J.
1952 *My Servants the Prophets.* Grand Rapids: Eerdmans.

1965–1967 *The Book of Isaiah.* 3 vols. Grand Rapids: Eerdmans.

Zeron, A.
1991 Pseudo-Philonic Parallels to the Inscriptions of Deir-Alla. *Vetus Testamentum* 41/2:186-191.

Zorn, Jeffrey R.
1994 Estimating the Population Size of Ancient Settlements: Methods, Problems, Solutions, and a Case Study. *Bulletin of the American Schools of Oriental Research* 295:31-48.

Deuteronomy

EUGENE H. MERRILL

INTRODUCTION TO
Deuteronomy

DEUTERONOMY is sometimes called "the theology book of the Old Testament" because it summarizes the teachings of Moses in the rest of the Pentateuch and lays the foundation for the messages of the poets and prophets who followed him. In content, it consists of Moses's farewell address to the nation of Israel, and in form, it is largely a covenant document reminding the people of God's gracious act of calling them to be his special community and of their responsibility to fulfill that calling by representing him before all the nations.When tempted in the desert, Jesus quoted from Deuteronomy, and the writers of the New Testament cite it more than any other Old Testament book except Isaiah and Psalms. Careful reading and study of its great theological themes will inevitably lead one to a fuller understanding of God's saving grace through Jesus Christ.

AUTHOR

Until the advent of the European Enlightenment in the seventeenth and eighteenth centuries, there was continuous and nearly unanimous consensus among Jews and Christians alike that Moses was the author of Deuteronomy (Eissfeldt 1965:155-159). This conviction arose from the tradition that Moses wrote the entire Torah (or Pentateuch, the fifth book of which is Deuteronomy) and from the internal evidence of the book itself as to its authorship (29:1; 31:9, 22, 24; 32:45). Further confirmation was based on the later Old Testament record (Josh 1:7, 13; 8:31-35; 23:6; 1 Kgs 2:3; 2 Kgs 14:6; 21:8; 23:25; 2 Chr 23:18; 25:4; 33:8; 34:14; Ezra 3:2; Neh 9:14; 10:29; 13:1; Dan 9:13), the New Testament (Matt 19:7-8; 22:24; Mark 12:19; Acts 3:22; Rom 10:19; 1 Cor 9:9; Rev 15:3), and extracanonical Jewish literature such as the Apocrypha (Prologue to Ben Sirach), the Talmud (*b. Baba Batra* 14b), and the apologetic works of Josephus (*Against Apion* 1.8 [1.38-39]).

For the Christian, the testimony of Jesus on the matter is particularly compelling. For example, when the Pharisees raised the issue of divorce, they cited a text from Deuteronomy (24:1-4), which they attributed to Moses. In his response, Jesus did not correct their connecting the passage to Moses; in fact, he said, "Moses permitted divorce only as a concession to your hard hearts" (Matt 19:7-8). Likewise, when his critics challenged Jesus about the failure of his disciples to observe the oral traditions, he alluded to Deuteronomy 5:16 (found also in Exod 20:12): "Moses gave you this law from God: 'Honor your father and mother'" (Mark 7:10). His statement was designed to show that whereas the Pharisees were quick to honor human traditions, they were slow to obey the clear word of God. Thus, Jesus clearly associated Deuteronomy with Moses himself (cf. also Mark 12:18-24).

Despite this authoritative endorsement, the prevailing view in Old Testament scholarship today is that Moses did not write Deuteronomy and that, in fact, the book did not originate until 700 years after his death. Admittedly, *b. Baba Batra* 14b had suggested that the very end of the book—the account of Moses's death and burial (Deut 34:5-12)—was from another pen, probably Joshua's. Apart from this, hardly a single question was raised until the post-Renaissance period and the development of the so-called historical-critical method.

This approach, linked with such names as Simon, Hobbes, Spinoza, and Eichhorn, argued on the basis of the varying uses of divine names; evidence of repetitions, contradictions, and doublets; varying literary styles and vocabulary; and different theological and ideological perspectives that the Pentateuch was a composite of sources, none of which was as early as Moses (Eissfeldt 1965:159-162). These sources came to be known as J (standing for "Yahweh" or "the Yahwist"— both start with J in German), E ("Elohim" or "Elohist"), D (Deuteronomy), and P (the Priestly source). W. M. L. de Wette, in an 1805 dissertation, proposed that the J and E materials (most of Genesis through Numbers) were post-Mosaic and that Deuteronomy presupposed both of those alleged sources, thus making Deuteronomy later still (Rogerson 1992:40-42). He then went on to suggest that the scroll found in the Jerusalem Temple during Josiah's reformation of 622 BC (see 2 Kgs 22:8–23:3; 2 Chr 34:14-33) was none other than Deuteronomy and that it had only recently been composed and placed in the Temple. The effect of this hypothesis is to deny Moses any hand whatsoever in the authorship of the book.[1]

This point of view dominates the field of modern critical scholarship, though certain recent discoveries—such as the formal resemblance of Deuteronomy to Late Bronze Age (1550–1200 BC) treaty texts—have forced some scholars to reassess the situation and to look more positively at possible Mosaic input (Mendenhall 1954). Some are willing to go so far as to concede that the core religious content of Deuteronomy may go back to Moses, at least in oral form, but few are prepared to accept the ancient tradition of full Mosaic authorship (Nicholson 1967:121). On balance, however, it must be said that there is absolutely no objective evidence that compels a late provenance for the book; in fact, the available data point more strongly than ever to Moses as the author not only of Deuteronomy, but of the entire Pentateuch (Wolf 1991:78).[2]

DATE AND OCCASION OF WRITING

Mosaic authorship of Deuteronomy obviously necessitates its Mosaic milieu. That is, the date of the book is linked to the date(s) of the man himself. Specifically, the writing is said to have taken place at the very end of Moses's life, just before he ascended Mount Nebo to view the Land of Promise, to which he had been denied access (cf. 31:1, 9, 24-29; 32:44-52). This raises the need to determine, if possible, the date of Moses's death, a matter of some uncertainty even among those who take seriously the historicity of the event.

It is impossible here to rehearse the whole debate about Old Testament chronology, especially for the pre-monarchy period. I myself and others have done so at great length elsewhere (Merrill 2008:83-96). However, those facts necessary to the matter at hand must be addressed, as well as the chronological and historiographical assumptions upon which they are based. A straightforward reading and interpretation of the Masoretic chronological tradition puts beyond doubt the datum that the exodus of Israel from Egypt took place exactly 480 years prior to the commencement of the building of Solomon's Temple (1 Kgs 6:1). This latter date—967/966 BC—is virtually certain according to the best means of computation. The Exodus, then, occurred in 1446. Moses died 40 years after the Exodus (2:7; 31:1-2; 34:7; Exod 7:7), in 1406 BC. Archaeologically speaking, this was in the Late Bronze Age, specifically Late Bronze II.

Such information might appear to settle the case once and for all but there is another—perhaps majority—view that dates the Exodus to the mid-thirteenth century (c. 1250 BC) and Moses's death 40 years after that. This date for the Exodus appears to find support in the archaeological record, which seems to give evidence of massive destruction in late-thirteenth-century Canaan, a destruction attributed to the conquest under Joshua. This reading necessitates the assumption that 1 Kings 6:1 is a symbolic number (12 x 40—that is, 12 generations of a symbolic 40 years each; see Bright 1981:123), and it also disregards the clear biblical witness that the conquest, while bloody, was virtually without violence against physical structures, thus leaving no archaeological record (6:10-15; 19:1; cf. Josh 24:13; see Merrill 1982:107-121). Only the cities of Jericho, Ai, and Hazor are said to have been destroyed by Israel (Josh 6:24; 8:28; 11:13). The ravages of undisciplined archaeological method and natural erosion have left the Jericho evidence ambiguous at best, Ai has yet to be identified with certainty, and Hazor yields more than one interpretation.[3] The attested destruction of earlier sites and the eruption of scores of highland villages in the late thirteenth century can be explained by the tumultuous times of the judges of that period (Judg 4:3; 5:6-7; 6:1-6; 9:40-55) just as well as by a late conquest by Israel. On the whole, the case for an early Exodus and thus a 1400 BC date for Moses's death and the writing of Deuteronomy has the most in its favor.

Few books of the Bible have a more clearly articulated occasion than Deuteronomy. The opening statement declares that "these are the words that Moses spoke to all the people of Israel while they were in the wilderness east of the Jordan River" (1:1). To this setting is added the explanation that "forty years after the Israelites left Egypt, on the first day of the eleventh month, Moses addressed the people of Israel, telling them everything the LORD had commanded him to say" (1:3). Thus, the geographical setting is the Transjordan, the chronological setting is 40 years after the Exodus and the giving of the law at Sinai, and the purpose of the writing is to communicate what God revealed to Moses at the plains of Moab.

That revelation consisted of a review of God's dealings with the nation from the Exodus to the time of Moses's speech (chs 1–4), the setting forth of a covenant-renewal text (chs 5–28), and a concluding series of exhortations, warnings, promises, instructions, and narratives (chs 29–34). The similarities between the contents of the covenant section of Deuteronomy and various parts of Exodus, Leviticus, and Numbers have led many readers to the rather facile conclusion that Deuteronomy is nothing but a repetition of the earlier Sinaitic covenant. In fact, the title itself feeds this misunderstanding about Deuteronomy's intent and purpose. The word derives from the Latin Vulgate's *deuteronomium,* itself a transliteration of the Greek (LXX) version's title of the book, *deuteronomion* ("second law"), a title that dates from about 250–200 BC. The notion that Deuteronomy was a "second law" (second to the Sinai law) resulted from a faulty understanding of 17:18, in which the book is called *mishneh hattorah hazzo't* [TH4932/8451, ZH5467/9368] ("a copy of this law"; *to deuteronomion touto* in LXX). The intent of the phrase is to suggest not that Deuteronomy is just a repetition of previous legal texts, but that the book itself should be copied and preserved for future generations.

In any event, a close scrutiny of Deuteronomy's contents makes clear the significant differences between it and the earlier legislation. It is true, the Sinai covenant is presupposed by Deuteronomy and, in fact, forms its underpinnings and *raison d'etre.* But the covenant content of Deuteronomy is much more expansive and goes far beyond the clearly limited intent of the Sinai revelation. That intent was (1) to establish the fact that Israel was a redeemed people called to a divine mission and (2) to outline the basic principles by which that mission was to be carried out in the immediate future. Forty years had passed, however, and a new generation was about to embark on a new adventure—the conquest and occupation of the Promised Land. No longer would Israel be a nomadic people en route to its permanent home. They would now become a settled, domestic, urbanized community. With that radical shift of nature and prospect arose the need for a radically different version of the covenant, one suitable to a new generation in a new place and time (Longman and Dillard 2006:92-93).

Deuteronomy, then, is in its most basic form the text of that revised and expanded covenant. The Sinai generation had all but passed from the scene because of its disobedience (cf. Num 14:26-35), and now the new generation was called upon to renew its covenant commitment to Yahweh. In principle, the Deuteronomic covenant was identical to the Sinaitic; in detailed exposition and practical application, it was a considerable advancement.

AUDIENCE
The immediate audience of the book of Deuteronomy was literally that—an audience—because the book appears to consist of a series of messages first delivered orally by Moses (cf. 1:1; 5:1; 27:1, 9, 11; 29:2; 31:1, 30). Scholars have pointed out the sermonic nature of the material and, in fact, have spoken of the whole collection as Moses's farewell address (Keil and Delitzsch n.d.:276). I have already proposed

that Moses was addressing the younger generation of Israelites, those who had survived the rigors and judgment of the desert wanderings and who were on the threshold of entering the land promised to their patriarchal ancestors. But the message was not for them alone, or it would never have been put into writing and enshrined within the canonical collection as sacred Scripture. In fact, the book itself refers regularly to the need to write down its teachings precisely so they could be preserved and transmitted to future generations (cf. 28:58; 29:20; 30:10; 31:19, 22, 24).

The audience also reached far beyond Israel and embraced the church as well. Next to Isaiah and Psalms, Deuteronomy is cited or alluded to more times in the New Testament than any other Old Testament writing, well over 100 times. Clearly Jesus, the apostles, and the early church recognized the ongoing theological significance and authority of the book and appreciated the enlargement of its horizons as going beyond the masses gathered in the plains of Moab to include men and women of faith for all time. The message as delivered by Moses may have had its most specific and immediate relevance to those who heard him, but they could not and did not exhaust its theological and practical significance.

CANONICITY AND TEXTUAL HISTORY

Deuteronomy, as a part of the Mosaic Torah, was never subject to debate regarding its canonicity. Its very association with the inspired lawgiver guaranteed its insulation against challenges to its authenticity or authority. Its constant citation throughout the Old and New Testaments testifies to its canonical status. Rabbinical controversy regarding the canonicity of certain Old Testament books never gave a hint of concern about Deuteronomy. Finally, every ancient list of the canonical books includes Deuteronomy, and it is always listed as a constituent part of the Mosaic literature.

The text of Deuteronomy is remarkably well-preserved and uncontested in terms of both its Hebrew manuscript tradition and its relationship to the ancient versions (Tigay 1996:xi). The evidence from Qumran is quite ample and supports, for the most part, the best-attested Masoretic readings (Ulrich 1995). Its variations from the major versions such as the Septuagint and the Samaritan Pentateuch are usually because of the typical aversion of the latter two to the anthropomorphisms of Hebrew thought and language, their occasional dependence on non-Masoretic sources, and other such factors (Wevers 1977:498-505). Of special interest are the places where the Samaritan Pentateuch's Deuteronomy goes against the Masoretic Text in order to justify the claims of the Samaritan community with regard to the proper place and mode of community worship. For example, where the Masoretic Text reads "Mount Ebal" in 27:4, the Samaritan Pentateuch has "Mount Gerizim," the place where the later Samaritan temple stood. Such changes are so obviously ideological in nature that they confirm the authenticity of the Masoretic Text (Tov 1992:94-95).

LITERARY STYLE

Were one to attempt to encapsulate the entire book of Deuteronomy within one literary rubric, the most appropriate term might be valedictory. The book clearly presents itself as Moses's farewell address to his people on the eve of his impending death, and indeed, older scholarship primarily understood it in this way. Despite the enormous variety of forms, genres, and structures that the writing exhibits, all of them form elements of a great sermon delivered by the greatest of the Old Testament prophets. More particularly, the sermon consists of a series of exhortations, or what more recent scholarship calls "paraeneses." From beginning to end, Moses urges, commands, threatens, entreats, pleads, and otherwise invokes his powers of persuasion to induce his congregation either to a positive course of action or to the avoidance of a negative tendency. These paraenetic formulas introduce, intersperse, or conclude sections of the book, which reflects a wide variety of literary types, thus showing the possibility of communicating virtually any kind of message in any kind of mode, all within one sustained address.

Typical of the hortatory style is the use of the imperative (e.g., 4:1, 9, 15) in the context of attitude or action about to be demonstrated or undertaken. Over and over, Moses commands the assembly to listen to the covenant requirements and to determine to carry them out. The Ten Commandments are, of course, the most famous of these injunctions (Deut 5:1-21), and the so-called Shema ("Listen!"; 6:4-5) expresses the very heart of what Israel is to believe and do with respect to Yahweh and the covenant. Given that Deuteronomy on the whole is in the form of a treaty text, it is not surprising that paraenesis should be so dominant, for it is in the very nature of the covenant relationship—particularly of the so-called suzerain–vassal type—that commandments, statutes, and ordinances should be reiterated, along with the constant reminders to obey them.

The covenant themes and overtones of Deuteronomy have been recognized from the beginning, but only in recent decades has it become clear that it not only contains covenant language but is in itself a massive covenant text. This new appraisal is the result of the recovery of a cache of tablets from the Turkish city Boghazkeui, a place identified as the ancient Hittite capital city Hattusha (Hoffner 1994:134-136). Among the tablets were a number of treaty texts of two major kinds: those between the Hittite kings and their foreign equals, notably Egyptian pharaohs, and those between these same kings and the rulers of smaller nearby states brought under Hittite domination (Hoffner 1994:144-146). The former are known popularly as parity treaties and the latter suzerain–vassal treaties. In each case, there were certain sections and clauses that were sine qua non to their form and classification. Before long, Bible scholars took note of these findings and drew attention to the remarkable similarities in form (and even wording at times) between them and certain biblical texts, particularly Exodus 20–23 and the entire book of Deuteronomy (Mendenhall 1954; Kitchen 1970:1-24). Specifically, these Old Testament passages resembled the suzerain–vassal type, in which the Great King (in this case, Yahweh) graciously brought a servant people (in this case, Israel) into covenant fellowship with himself.

An important adjunct to this association was the objective evidence it brought to the matter of Deuteronomy's date and, indirectly at least, its authorship. The Hittite tablets originated in the Late Bronze Age, primarily in the 1300s BC. This means they postdated the traditional date of Moses's authorship of Deuteronomy by only a half century or so. Thus, it appeared that Deuteronomy's early provenance could be well established or, at the very least, that its redactors had cast it in a form prevalent 600 years earlier. This latter option seems to be without serious merit for two reasons. First, how could (or even why should) the precise form have been preserved centuries after the Hittite empire had fallen from historical remembrance? Second, what purpose would be served in composing Deuteronomy in such an archaic pattern, when other patterns were ready at hand? These other treaty patterns are exemplified in Neo-Assyrian documents from the seventh-century reigns of Kings Sennacherib and Esarhaddon (Wiseman 1958). Even though they bear striking correspondence in form to both the Hittite and biblical examples, they lack certain features and exaggerate others that are characteristic of these latter. Specifically, they fail to include a historical prologue and a list of blessings for those who obey the covenant terms. The closer affinities between Deuteronomy and the Hittite texts provide *prima facie* evidence of Deuteronomy's early date.

Both the Hittite and Neo-Assyrian treaty texts contain, at times, as many as a dozen different sections or elements, but the following six are found invariably in all the Hittite examples as well as in Deuteronomy:

1. Preamble
2. Historical prologue
3. General stipulations
4. Specific stipulations
5. Blessings and curses
6. Witnesses

It is possible to outline Deuteronomy according to this pattern, though there are parts of the book that cannot readily be accommodated to it. A full outline incorporating this structure appears later in this Introduction, but for now it is useful to see how Deuteronomy is arranged with respect to these essential elements of the standard Hittite form:

1. The preamble (1:1-5). This section provides information about the contracting parties (Yahweh and Israel) and the geographical and historical setting in which the covenant arrangement is taking place.

2. The historical prologue and call to obedience (1:6–4:49). The purpose of this section in general is to trace the history of the past relationship of the covenant partners or of their ancestors. In this case, Yahweh, through Moses, recounts his faithfulness to Israel in calling and redeeming them from Egypt. Moses draws special attention to God's having met them at Sinai to give them their assignment as his special servant people. He then reviews the long and tedious journey through the desert, a journey made difficult by the disobedience of the people, despite Yahweh's constant, gracious care (1:6–3:29). Finally, he introduces the stipulations yet to come by exhorting the people to obedience in contrast to their past behavior

(4:1-49). The upshot is that, despite Israel's waywardness, Yahweh, the Great King, has proved to be reliable.

3. The general stipulations (5:1-11:32). Every covenant or treaty arrangement must have a body of clearly spelled-out requirements to which the respective signatories pledge themselves. In the case of parity treaties, these were reciprocal or mutual, but in the suzerain–vassal variety, the greater party would simply guarantee to the subordinate party protection from hostility and provision of security from want. The vassal must pledge his undivided loyalty and regular payment of both ceremonial honor and material tribute. These chapters of Deuteronomy focus on the Decalogue (5:6-21), which forms, in this instance, a statement of broad principle.

4. The specific stipulations (12:1-26:15). Because of the principial nature of the general stipulations, it was necessary to know how to apply the broad requirements to everyday life and particular situations. This leads to the nature of the laws in each case, a matter to be addressed subsequently. For now, it is useful to observe that the structure of this section suggests that it follows the order of the Ten Commandments point by point and thus, in effect, provides examples as to how the commandments were to be construed in various situations (Kaufman 1978–1979:105-158).

5. The blessings and curses (27:1-28:68). Hittite suzerain–vassal treaties typically promised special benefits to subordinate rulers who were scrupulous to abide by their terms. Conversely, those who failed in this respect could expect punishment. This is precisely what Deuteronomy holds out to Israel. To obey Yahweh is to guarantee his favor; to disobey is to invite his severe displeasure, even to the extent of the termination of Israel's national identity and the deportation of her citizens.

6. The witnesses (30:19; 31:19; 32:1-43). As a legal document, a treaty text had to be sworn to in the presence of witnesses who could certify its validity and testify to its having been drawn up in a proper manner. Ancient Near Eastern examples show the gods of the respective parties in this role. Obviously, this was impossible in the case of Yahweh's covenant with Israel, for only Yahweh was God. Nonetheless, to sustain the formal appearance and to underscore the seriousness of the transaction implied by the document, an appeal was made to creation itself to give attention.

Traditionally, the Pentateuch as a whole has been characterized as "the law"—the implication of which is that "law" in the sense of codified statutes constitutes its essence. This has come from a misunderstanding of the term *torah* itself, a misunderstanding that results in a serious misplacement of emphasis, and also one that has to some extent generated the "law-versus-grace" debate regarding the relationship of the Old and New Testaments. Recognition of the covenant character of the laws of the Pentateuch has at last helped put the matter in proper perspective. It is now clear that the laws are in fact the stipulation sections of the covenant document that attests to the Yahweh–Israel relationship.

This perception of the law helps clarify its function contextually as one limited to Old Testament Israel and not inclusive of the church or the whole human race. The covenant at Sinai, reiterated and expanded in Moab, was with a select people for a specific purpose, and therefore its stipulations—the "laws" regulating its implementation—are time- and theology-bound to that people. This does not preclude the relevance of the law in principle from application beyond Israel, for the law fundamentally is an expression of the nature and foundational purposes of God himself. Moreover, the Decalogue, at least, finds its roots in pre-Mosaic times, indeed, in a setting embracing the whole human race.

A great deal of attention has been paid in the last half-century to the formal, literary character of Old Testament law and the resulting implications for its meaning (Clark 1974:99-139; Patrick 1985:13-27). Basically, these studies have underscored the differences between apodictic and casuistic law, the former having to do with law as an expression of fundamental norms of attitude and behavior and the latter with examples of these in everyday experience. Formally, apodictic law consists of an injunction or prohibition without a statement of qualification or consequence. Casuistic law, on the other hand, usually contains a dependent clause (a protasis) indicating a particular circumstance (e.g., if X does such and such) followed, perhaps, by a series of sub-circumstances (e.g., while here or there, or in connection with this or that), and concluding with an independent clause (an apodosis) stating the penalty (e.g., then this is what is to be done).

Laws of the casuistic type are characteristic of the great law codes of the ancient Near East such as the famous Code of Hammurabi. Apodictic law is uncommon in these collections. The reason for this is that apodictic law is nearly always indigenous to covenant texts—that is, it is the form taken by the stipulations of these documents (Mendenhall 1970:7-9). This is particularly true of the so-called "general stipulations," in which the superior party in suzerain–vassal treaties lays out the standards of behavior he expects of his lesser partner. Thus, apodictic is a feature of the Late Bronze Hittite documents after which Deuteronomy appears to be modeled. It is not surprising, then, that Deuteronomy contains apodictic law, especially in the "general stipulation" section, chapters 5–11. Furthermore, chapters 12–26, the "specific stipulation" section, consist of law primarily in casuistic form, the form found in Hittite and other ancient Near Eastern law codes.

Other literary genres of Deuteronomy are itinerary texts, modified by the intrusion of "editorial" comment and other observations (1:19–3:29); poetry, notably the "Song of Moses" (ch 32) and "Blessing of Moses" (33:2-29); and narratives (e.g., 4:41-43; 31:1-30; 32:44-52; 34:1-8). In addition, a host of smaller units within some of these, as well as apart from them, have been identified by intensive form-critical analysis. These will all receive attention at the appropriate place in the commentary to follow.

Finally, I shall note two remaining features in the literature of Deuteronomy, one of a source-critical nature and the other quite the opposite. Though source critics almost universally have agreed that there are no evidences of the Yahwist or Elohist in Deuteronomy (though many argue for a P redaction), most concur that the book is a composite of a number of sources that are difficult to isolate and identify separately. A clear criterion for identification to some analysts, however, has been the alternation of the second person singular with the second person plural pronouns in direct address (Minette de Tillesse 1962:29-78). To such scholars this has provided indisputable evidence of twin traditions, one that preferred to refer to Israel collectively (the singular) and the other that addressed the nation as individuals (the plural). Superficially, this appears to raise genuine problems for the original unity of the book's authorship, but, in fact, the opposite is true. Such a view fails to take into account the ambivalence attendant to Israel's nature as the covenant people (a singular, "corporate" personality consisting of thousands of people) (Weinfeld 1991:15-16), an ambivalence seen also, for example, in the fluctuation of the Isaiah servant passages where the servant is seen sometimes as an individual and sometimes as Israel itself. Furthermore, it is impossible to explain why a redactor interested in blending or homogenizing his sources would fail to do such an easy thing as to achieve consistency in the grammatical number of pronouns.

In opposition to the hypothesis of source distinctions is the increasingly apparent evidence for unity of authorship as demonstrated by recent application of new literary (or rhetorical) analysis. Such devices as *inclusios,* chiasms, key words, and thematic connections have revealed that what were thought to be disparate, unrelated texts are, in fact, components of larger compositions and that the omission of any one of them would destroy the overall literary architecture (Christensen 1991:xlix-lxii). These structural indicators appear in very brief segments of text and, in some analyses, across the entire book of Deuteronomy. One could argue, of course, that the magnificent symmetries and cohesions evident in rhetorical study of the book could have come about through the creative genius of redactors, but it seems *prima facie* that it is much easier to account for them as the product of a single mind and pen writing from the start.

MAJOR THEMES

Themes and theology are difficult to separate, particularly in such a theologically rich book as Deuteronomy, in which every statement and theme is of theological import. Nevertheless, the following list constitutes major ideas in Deuteronomy that will receive full theological treatment either separately or integratedly in the next section and in the commentary proper. For now, it is helpful just to identify them and briefly trace their occurrence throughout the book.

The Covenant. In a composition whose very structure is in the form of a covenant document, one should not be surprised that the covenant idea is a dominant one. The word "covenant" (*berith* [TH1285, ZH1382]) occurs about 25 times in Deuteronomy, 13 of those times in chapters 29, 31, and 33. Apart from this is the plethora of technical terms related to "covenant" such as "commandment," "statute," "ordinance," and the like. On a number of occasions, "covenant" refers back to Sinai (or Horeb) as a reminder of God's initial act of bringing Israel into a servitude designed to effect universal redemption (4:13, 23, 31; 5:2, 3; 8:18; 9:9-15; 10:8). The remaining occurrences refer to the renewal of the covenant, which is the central subject of the book (29:1, 9, 12, 14, 25; 31:16, 20; 33:9).

Eschatological Hope. From the divine perspective, an inherent element of the covenant was the recognition that Israel would be unable or unwilling to keep it and would therefore be brought to judgment. But God's covenant promises are unshakable—they will be kept and will achieve their desired ends no matter what path Israel might take. This act, whereby a recalcitrant servant people could and would be redeemed and reinstated, is a major motif in the eschatological unfolding of God's purposes. This is particularly clear in the "curses and blessings" section of the book (chs 27 and 28), as well as at the end of the "Song of Moses" (32:36-43), and here and there in Moses's blessing of the tribes (33:17, 26-29).

God's Faithfulness in the Past. A basis for eschatological hope is God's faithfulness to his people in history. One of the features of the suzerain–vassal treaty form is the historical prologue, a section devoted to recounting the past relationship of the contracting parties or their ancestors. I have already noted that 1:6–4:40 is such a section. Careful reading of the passage, largely itinerary literature, reveals several appeals to the past as grounds for present hope (cf. 1:30-31; 2:7, 9-12, 16-25; 3:2-3; 4:3-4, 32-40). The theme of God's dependability is epitomized in 4:34: "Has any other god dared to take a nation for himself out of another nation by means of trials, miraculous signs, wonders, war, a strong hand, a powerful arm, and terrifying acts? Yet that is what the LORD your God did for you in Egypt, right before your eyes."

The Fear and Love of God. At first blush, it might seem that fear and love are mutually exclusive terms. As part of stock covenant terminology, however, these are mutually informing ideas, two sides of the same coin. Throughout the Old Testament, the fear of God almost always suggests not terror but profound reverence. It is a natural concomitant of a close, personal relationship with him. In fact, it is precisely because the sinner does not know God that he also does not fear him (cf. Pss 36:1; 55:19; Prov 1:29; Eccl 8:13). By contrast, love in the covenant context especially speaks of choice (NIDOTTE 1.279-280). For God to elect one to salvation and service is tantamount to God having loved him first (cf. Neh 13:26; Ps 78:68; Hos 11:1; Eph 1:4). Both fear and love are expected of God's people toward him. If he loved them, they must love (i.e., choose, obey) him. These ideas are common in Deuteronomy (cf. 4:10; 5:29; 6:2, 5, 13; 7:9; 10:12, 20; 11:1, 13, 22; 13:3, 4; 14:23; 30:6, 16, 20; 31:12, 13).

Holiness. The central idea of holiness in the Bible is that of separation, especially for a distinctive and usually sacred purpose. A secondary but important nuance has moral or ethical overtones. That is, God is holy not only because he is distinct, but also because he is pure and without fault or defect. Likewise, men and women can be set apart as vessels for God's glory, but that setting apart hopes for—in fact, demands—moral integrity. In Deuteronomy, the point is often made that Israel is a holy people because they belong to Yahweh; the converse, of course, is also true:

They belong to Yahweh because they have become holy—that is, set apart for God (7:6; 14:2, 21; 26:19; 28:9).

Idolatry and Apostasy. This theme is especially prominent in Deuteronomy because the call to covenant loyalty is always set against the backdrop of competing inducements. That is, the issue in the book is whether Israel is going to become and remain a devoted servant of Yahweh or become a slave to the idolatrous Canaanite social and religious system about to be encountered. To fall to that system is not just a matter of spiritual apostasy, as deplorable as that might be. In the context of covenant, such defection is a renunciation of the covenant claims of the Great King himself, a challenge to his authority that can result only in unmitigated disaster. Thus, Deuteronomy's message is laced with warnings against lapsing into idolatry (cf. 4:15-24; 5:7-10; 7:1-5; 13:1-18) and promises of judgment, should those warnings be ignored (4:25-31; 8:19-20; 11:16-17; 27:15; 28:20-46; 29:14-21).

Promises to the Patriarchs. Despite the centrality of the so-called Mosaic covenant in Deuteronomy, Moses himself insists that this covenant is based on antecedent covenants and promises to the patriarchal ancestors. Abraham had been called to establish a special people (Gen 12:1-3), one charged with the task of channeling the message of redemptive grace to the whole world (Gen 17:1-8). A major feature of the Abrahamic covenant was the promise of land, a geographical arena in which the ministry of universal reconciliation could be proclaimed and exhibited. That land was none other than Canaan, the land to which God had led Abraham at the very outset (Gen 12:1, 4-5) and which he promised to grant to Abraham's offspring as their inheritance (Gen 13:14-18; 15:12-21; 17:8; cf. Gen 26:4; 46:4). Now, on the very eve of conquest, Moses recapitulated these promises as justification for Israel's impending occupation of the land (1:8, 35; 6:3, 10, 18, 23; 7:13; 8:1; 10:11; 11:9, 21; 26:3, 15; 28:11; 30:20; 31:7, 20). The very covenant relationship with Yahweh into which Israel had entered was the fruit of the ancient promises he had made with the fathers of the nation.

True and False Prophets. The chief function of a prophet is to speak on behalf of the deity whom he represents. Moses, the prophet of Yahweh, was the greatest of them all (34:10-12) and was the prototype of others who would follow, individuals like Samuel, Elijah, Nathan, and the "canonical prophets" who authored the books bearing their names. Like any office or ministry, however, that of the prophet could be prostituted or counterfeited, and it could become an instrument drawing God's people away from him and their covenant responsibilities. The Old Testament describes two kinds of false prophets—those who represented the gods of the nations and those in Israel who falsely claimed to be spokesmen of Yahweh. Both kinds were to be exposed and dealt with harshly, for they would instigate covenant disloyalty and thus rupture the relationship the covenant had established. Moses warns against prophets from within Israel who would betray their true colors by advocating the worship of other gods, a message whose "authenticity" would be bolstered by their ability to work supernatural signs (13:1-5). Such prophets must be eradicated (13:6-11). Sorcerers, diviners, and witches of Canaan must also be extirpated (18:9-14), so that those prophets whom God would raise up and whose genuineness could be tested by the fulfillment of their prophecies might stand unchallenged (18:20-22).

Remembrance. A significant element of covenant-keeping is the responsibility of the contracting parties to remember what they have pledged themselves to. Covenant demands commitment, and commitment presupposes remembrance. In Deuteronomy, there is the remarkable plea by Moses to Yahweh that he might remember Israel and all that he has brought to the covenant arrangement with them (9:27-29). Far more common is the injunction that Israel should remember Yahweh and his expectations of them (4:20, 39; 5:15; 7:18-19; 8:2; 16:12; 24:18, 22; 29:16; 32:7). In the case of Yahweh remembering, it is obvious that more is meant than simply recollection. The omniscient God cannot forget, so it is unnecessary to encourage him to remember. The idea is that he would act upon what is in his mind (NIDOTTE 1.1102). Moses's prayer, then, is that Yahweh will not ignore his people and that he will focus his attention on them for their good. This also is the thrust behind the command to Israel to remember Yahweh and the covenant. To remember him is to make him the focal point of Israel's faith and action.

Social Responsibility. When Jesus was asked to name the greatest commandment, he quoted the Shema of Deuteronomy 6:4-5 (to love God with all one's being), but he added to that a command that he said was equally important: "Love your neighbor as yourself" (Matt 22:38-39). This second finds precise verbal expression in Leviticus 19:18, but its truth pervades the book of Deuteronomy. In texts too numerous to list here, the principle is articulated that the covenant between Yahweh and Israel also has horizontal dimensions. To love God is to love God's people, no matter their rank or station. Moreover, love of this kind is not an abstract emotion. Its reality must be seen in its application, its sense of social concern, and the alleviation of human need. A key theme of the book, then, is not just the enunciation of a broad principle of social welfare within the theocratic community but specific instruction as to how this can be fleshed out on behalf of the orphan, the widow, the poor, the stranger, and all others in Israel who would suffer deprivation (14:28-29; 15:7-18; 23:15-16; 24:14-15, 17-18, 19-22; 26:12-15).

War. A major ethical issue in biblical studies is not only the existence of war in ancient Israel but its divine sanction. The fact of war is not particularly problematic because the human race in its fallenness is selfish, greedy, ambitious, and arrogant—characteristics that, whether in individuals or nations, inevitably lead to conflict. Israel was no different, for it was a nation that exhibited these tendencies from time to time despite its uniqueness as a chosen people. Moreover, Israel, from the Deuteronomic perspective, had already engaged hostile peoples in the Transjordan such as Moabites, Ammonites, and Amorites and would encounter even more in Canaan. In fact, it was already clear that the occupation of Canaan would necessitate war, for the indigenous peoples would not surrender it voluntarily (cf. 1:20-21;

2:24-25, 31-37; 3:1-11; 7:1-5, 17-26). War, then, was authorized by Yahweh in pursuit of the acquisition of the land promised to the patriarchs. A subset of war in general is the principle of so-called "holy war" or "Yahweh war." This was directed against the Canaanites and their allies who lived in Canaan proper and whose character and prospects were such as to prove them irremedially beyond redemption. No terms of accommodation could be offered them. They must be completely annihilated, put to the "ban" (Heb., *hakharem takharim* [TH2764/2763, ZH3051/3049]), so as to remove them from the land and preclude their leading Israel astray (cf. 7:2; 13:15; 20:17; all of which employ this term *kharam* [TH2763, ZH3049]). The fuller theological ramifications of war in the Old Testament must await discussion later as must its justification in light of the New Testament ethic.

Worship. Worship, in general, is the recognition of and the proper (liturgical) response to the deity. It has emotional, intellectual, and spiritual dimensions often manifested in physical acts and events. In Deuteronomy, however, worship emerges as something more—it is Israel's confession of the sovereignty of Yahweh and their obedient response to the covenant obligations inherent in and mandated by that sovereignty. In other words, Israel's life before God is worship—in the broadest sense. More narrowly, the worship theme in Deuteronomy centers around the notion of tribute, the people's presentation to the Great King of prescribed offerings on regular, stipulated occasions. This is in line with the ancient Near Eastern tradition according to which vassal rulers tendered their homage to their lord as a sign of their unwavering loyalty. To the notion of worship as acts and attitudes of reverence, then, Deuteronomy adds that of worship as compliance with proper protocol in the framework of covenant relationship (cf. 12:6-14; 15:19-23; 16:1-17).

THEOLOGICAL CONCERNS

The rich tapestry of Deuteronomic theology, though consisting of hundreds of colorful theological strands, is woven together around three principal themes—God, Israel, and covenant (Merrill 1991:62-86). The last, already apparent from the very structure and atmosphere of the book, necessitates the other two. Even superficial scanning of the text makes clear that the whole thrust of Deuteronomy is the insistence that God, having elected Israel from among all the nations of the earth, created a formal forensic instrument—the covenant—by which he brought this people to a position of responsibility and through which he offered the potential of unlimited blessing. It is instructive to view each of these separately but even more so to observe how they are creatively integrated to present a full picture of God's redemptive design.

God in Deuteronomy. In light of the fact that Deuteronomy is a covenant text, the presentation of God that emerges from it is one sensitive to that particular reality. The book makes no attempt to develop a theology proper but is satisfied to reveal God in his covenant-making and covenant-keeping capacity. As a result, God appears preeminently as sovereign, deliverer, covenant-maker, warrior, and provider.

God as sovereign. As a composition modeled after ancient Near Eastern suzerain–vassal treaty texts, it is not surprising that Deuteronomy portrays Yahweh in the role of a Great King, one who by creation and sovereign choice exercises dominion over all things. Thus, he always takes the initiative in calling and equipping his people, and he provides supernatural enablement for the accomplishment of his purposes through them. Moses speaks only what Yahweh commands (1:3), he leads the people toward the Land of Promise by divine direction (1:19), and he recognizes that the land he journeys toward is a land God has already given to Israel, though other people live there (1:25).

The very notion of promise is indicative of God's sovereignty, for only a God who manages the universe could presume not only to forecast the future but to arrange circumstances so as to bring his pledges to pass. He had promised the patriarchal fathers that he would multiply Israel as the stars of heaven (1:10), deliver them from Egyptian bondage (7:8), and bring them to the very borders of their inheritance (26:9), all of which had transpired before their very eyes. In light of all these displays of wisdom and power, it is understandable that Moses could assert that "he showed you these things so you would know that the LORD is God and there is no other" (4:35).

In fact, few writings of the Old Testament are more insistent in their proclamation of Yahweh as the one and only God, the one to whom praise, worship, and total obedience are due. The Shema (6:4-5) is instructive in its declaration: "Listen, O Israel! The LORD is our God, the LORD alone. And you must love the LORD your God with all your heart, all your soul, and all your strength." This pithy but profound confession describes both who Yahweh is and how he must be regarded. He is the sovereign before whom all creation submits in fear and surrender. Elsewhere in Deuteronomy this sovereignty is seen in God's distribution of the earth to the various nations (2:9-25), his destruction of Israel's enemies (3:1-11), his redemption of his chosen ones from Egypt (4:32-38), and his provision of all their physical, material, and spiritual needs (6:10-15; 7:12-16; 8:1-20; 11:8-15).

God as deliverer. Perhaps the mightiest manifestation of God's sovereignty was the Exodus deliverance of his chosen people. This was not merely a sign of his dominion over nature—the plagues and parting of the sea—but at its heart the conquest of a competing political and religious system, the awesome power and glory of Egypt. In a very real sense, Egypt represented the anti-God forces of the world that keep mankind in the prison-house of sin and death. It is that realm from which there is no escape apart from divine intervention. Historically, Israel found itself in that plight, but at last, the promised day of release came, and all the forces of Pharaoh and his hosts were powerless to prevent the outworking of redemptive grace.

Deuteronomy gives much attention to this aspect of God's mighty acts. Moses describes the deliverance of Israel in terms of God's having "rescued you from the iron-smelting furnace of Egypt" (4:20), and he reminds his people that "we were Pharaoh's slaves in Egypt, but the LORD brought us out of Egypt with his strong hand" (6:21). In astonishment Moses asks, "Has any other god dared to take a nation for himself out of another nation by means of trials, miraculous signs, wonders, war, a strong hand, a powerful arm, and terrifying acts? Yet that is what the LORD your God did for you in Egypt, right before your eyes" (4:34). The answer clearly is that only Yahweh is such a deliverer.

God as covenant-maker. Deuteronomy makes the point over and over again that Yahweh delivered his people from Egypt in order to make a covenant with them (4:20; 6:23-25; 7:6-11). This covenant was predicated on earlier ones made to the ancestors (e.g., 7:7-8), but it differed from those in significant ways. The earlier covenants were promissory and unconditional, but this one was subsidiary and, in its historical outworking, conditional. God had called the patriarchs to be his people, the founders of a nation through which he would redemptively bless the whole world. That nation proved to be Israel, whose existence was a manifestation of God's unconditional promise to the fathers.

God's covenant with Israel, then, was not to make them his people, for they already were by virtue of their descent from Abraham, Isaac, and Jacob. Rather, it was to offer to the nation an opportunity to be precisely what God had promised Abraham—the means by which he would reconcile the world to himself (Gen 12:1-3; 22:17-18). This offer was made at Sinai and in unmistakably conditional terms: "Now if you will obey me and keep my covenant, you will be my own special treasure from among all the peoples on earth; for all the earth belongs to me. And you will be my kingdom of priests, my holy nation" (Exod 19:5-6). In short, Israel was the product of an unconditional promise, while her call to serve and the effectiveness of that service were a matter of her own obedience to the offer and conditions God presented to her as the covenant-maker.

God as warrior. From the very beginning of history, the creating and redeeming purposes of God have met with unrelenting opposition from the hostile forces of evil, human and demonic, visible and invisible. Every move forward engenders countermoves, designed to sabotage God's intentions to bring about universal perfection. In short, world history at its deepest core is a history of war, a conflict waged in the spiritual realm but with earthly, physical manifestation.

With this in mind, it should be no surprise that the Bible is filled with militaristic imagery. The Exodus deliverance is viewed as a battle in which Yahweh prevails over the Egyptians and, in fact, over the Red Sea as emblematic of more transcendent powers of wickedness (Exod 15:1-3, 6, 9). Then, as Deuteronomy points out, the desert wanderings and the anticipated conquest of Canaan are achieved only as Yahweh, the warrior, leads his people to victory (1:4; 3:21-22; 7:17-24; 20:1-18).

God as provider. The Lord provided for the redeemed people he called into covenant partnership with him. Their needs had already been met in lavish ways in the desert (8:1-10), and now they could anticipate a continuation of God's supply in the land of milk and honey (7:12-15; 11:8-12). But they would be tempted to take credit for their own success, to claim that their prosperity was a fruit of their own energy and cleverness (8:11-17). Such temptation must be resisted for, as Moses pointed out, "the LORD your God . . . is the one who gives you power to be successful" (8:18). Worse still, some would attribute the blessings of life to the gods of the land, to the "baals" who were thought by the Canaanites to be responsible for fertility and other aspects of the natural world. This would be not only a wrong perception but also a violation of the covenant principle that there is only one God and that in him alone is success and happiness. Deuteronomy makes much of this polemic against the imagined gods of the nations and the utter futility of depending on them (3:24; 4:25-28; 8:19-20; 12:29-31; 29:14-18).

Israel in Deuteronomy. In the book of Deuteronomy, Israel is depicted as a people in transition. No longer an amorphous multitude of slaves in Egypt but not yet an organized nation, Israel in the interim of desert life constituted a coalition of tribes, a seminomadic community en route to a more permanent home and status. More particularly, Israel should be viewed as heirs of ancient promises, as the "son" of Yahweh, as the servant of Yahweh, and as a community of faith.

Israel as the heirs of promises. Fundamental to an explanation of Israel's historical reality is the recognition that it existed as a direct fulfillment of God's promises to the Hebrew ancestors. God had told Abraham that he would make his descendants into a great nation (Gen 12:2), one that would grow and be nurtured in a foreign land for 400 years (Gen 15:13) but that would come forth in a mighty act of deliverance (Exod 3:6-8). Deuteronomy recounts those promises and deeds and identifies Israel as the nation long foretold (1:10-11; 4:37-38; 6:23; 10:15). Paramount in this whole process is the elective grace of God who not only chose Abraham in the beginning but also Israel as Abraham's seed and God's people. This idea is best captured in 7:7-8: "The LORD did not set his heart on you and choose you because you were more numerous than other nations. . . . Rather, it was simply that the LORD loves you, and he was keeping the oath he had sworn to your ancestors."

Israel as the son of Yahweh. One of the most startling metaphors in the Bible describes Israel as God's son (Exod 4:22-23). The occasion for doing so was explicitly the impending tenth plague in which the firstborn of every unprotected family in Egypt would be put to death (Exod 11:4-5; 12:12-13, 29). Since Pharaoh would not release God's son, God would destroy Pharaoh's son. Such a term of endearment speaks powerfully of the love of God for Israel and the intimacy of relationship presupposed by his having chosen them for service. The same tenderness is carried over into the New Testament, where believers are described as "God's children" (1 John 3:2). Deuteronomy never uses the term "son" for Israel directly, but the statement that God cared for Israel in the wilderness "just as a father cares for his child" (1:31) and Moses's question, "Isn't he your Father who created you?" (32:6), certainly make the same point. There is more to the covenant relationship than a mere business arrangement. God initiated the covenant precisely because Israel was his beloved one.

Israel as the servant of Yahweh. The concept of Israel as a servant people, a notion that finds its fullest theological development in Isaiah's "Servant Songs" (Isa 49:1-4; cf. Isa 41:8; 43:10; 44:1-2), is self-evident in the fact that Deuteronomy presents itself as a suzerain–vassal treaty text—that is, God is the sovereign (suzerain) and Israel the servant (vassal). Beyond this, the book constantly draws attention to Israel's responsibility within the covenant framework—that of carrying out the mandate consistent with Israel's election.

That mandate is epitomized in the task of bearing witness to Yahweh's exclusiveness in such a manner as to attract the nations to him. Moses says that if Israel is faithful to the covenant, "you [Israel] will display your wisdom and intelligence among the surrounding nations. When they hear all these decrees, they will exclaim, 'How wise and prudent are the people of this great nation!'" (4:6). Israel did not exist for her own sake alone, but for the sake of the nations that needed to hear of the true and living God.

Israel as a community of faith. Israel was chosen for covenant partnership not only to *do* something but to *be* something, namely, the people of God in the midst of a world of unbelief. By its very uniqueness, Israel could and should demonstrate microcosmically God's intentions for all mankind. She was paradigmatically to instruct the whole world as to what it means to live in a right relationship with God; she was to recover something of Eden.

This point, as suggested above, is made in 4:6-8. When the nations observe Israel's life and faith, they will irresistibly be drawn to the questions, "What makes these people different?" and "Who is their God?" The same idea appears in 26:19 where Moses teaches that if Israel is faithful to live in holiness before the world, Israel will receive praise, honor, and renown from those who take note of her.

Covenant in Deuteronomy. The relationship between Yahweh and Israel, though based purely and simply on God's elective grace, is symbolized by and attested to in a formal manner by a covenant arrangement. This instrument quite obviously was for Israel's benefit, not the Lord's, for Israel needed constant and tangible reminders of her privileges and responsibilities as God's servant people. In Deuteronomy, the covenant serves primarily as a vehicle of relationship, an instrument of responsibility, and a pledge of God's promise fulfillments.

The covenant as a vehicle of relationship. Though Israel was the people of God by promise to their ancestors, that relationship found historical expression in the Sinai and Moab (Deuteronomic) covenants. By this mutually accepted arrangement, Israel came to know more concretely that what had been pledged to the patriarchs was at long last a reality. Thus, at the point of receiving the Ten Commandments, Moses could say, "The LORD our God made a covenant with us at Mount Sinai. The LORD did not make this covenant with our ancestors, but with all of us who are alive today" (5:2-3). That is, a new relationship was then underway, one in which Israel would be able to validate its role as the promised seed.

The covenant as an instrument of responsibility. Beyond merely attesting to Israel's relationship to God, the covenant in Deuteronomy was to be understood as a commitment made by Israel to undertake certain specified obligations. These are pervasive throughout the book, particularly in the "stipulation" sections (chs 5–11, 12–26). The point is that covenant privilege (being God's people) inevitably calls for covenant responsibility (being God's servant).

The covenant as a pledge of God's promise fulfillments. Not to be overlooked in secular suzerain–vassal treaty arrangements was the self-imposed obligation of the Great King toward his subordinates. This involved protection, provision in times of want, assurance of friendship, and the like. Since these were promises made by human rulers, as often as not, they were either ignored or proved impossible to keep.

Yahweh likewise had made promises to the Hebrew patriarchs, pledges he renewed to Israel as an element of his covenant participation. These included victory over their foes (9:3), inheritance of Canaan (1:21; 6:18, 23), prosperity of spiritual and physical life (12:20; 13:17; 15:6), and, most important of all, his loyalty and faithfulness to them forever (7:12; 26:18; 28:9). The promises of Yahweh in the context of a formal covenant document were not to remind him of his commitments, as goes without saying, but to remind Israel that the God who cannot lie had staked his own reputation on his covenant with them, enshrined in a written text.

OUTLINE
  I. The Covenant Setting (1:1-5)
 II. The Historical Review and Mosaic Exhortation (1:6-4:40)
     A. The Past Dealings of Yahweh with Israel (1:6-3:29)
         1. Events at Sinai (1:6-18)
         2. Instructions at Kadesh-barnea (1:19-25)
         3. Disobedience at Kadesh-barnea (1:26-33)
         4. Judgment at Kadesh-barnea (1:34-40)
         5. Unsuccessful attempt at conquest (1:41-46)
         6. Instructions concerning Edom (2:1-8a)
         7. Instructions concerning Moab (2:8b-15)
         8. Instruction concerning Ammon (2:16-25)
         9. Defeat of Sihon, king of Heshbon (2:26-37)
        10. Defeat of Og, king of Bashan (3:1-11)
        11. Distribution of the Transjordanian allotments (3:12-17)
        12. Instructions to the Transjordanian tribes (3:18-22)
        13. Moses denied the Promised Land (3:23-29)
     B. The Exhortation of Moses (4:1-40)
         1. The privileges of the covenant (4:1-8)
         2. Reminder of the Horeb covenant (4:9-14)
         3. The nature of Israel's God (4:15-24)
         4. Threats and blessings (4:25-31)
         5. The uniqueness of Israel's God (4:32-40)
III. The Preparation for the Covenant Text (4:41-49)
     A. The Narrative concerning Cities of Refuge (4:41-43)
     B. The Setting and Introduction (4:44-49)

IV. The Principles of the Covenant (5:1–11:32)
    A. The Opening Exhortation (5:1-5)
    B. The Ten Commandments (5:6-21)
        1. Commandments pertaining to one's relationship with God (5:6-15)
        2. Commandments pertaining to the people's relationships with one another (5:16-21)
    C. The Narrative Relating the Sinai Revelation and Israel's Response (5:22-33)
    D. The Nature of the Principles (6:1-25)
        1. Exhortation to obey the covenant principles (6:1-3)
        2. The essence of the covenant principles (6:4-5)
        3. Exhortation to teach the covenant stipulations (6:6-9)
        4. Exhortation to give Yahweh exclusive obedience (6:10-19)
        5. Exhortation to remember the past (6:20-25)
    E. The Content of the Principles (7:1–11:32)
        1. Driving out the nations (7:1-26)
            a. Exhortation to holiness (7:1-6)
            b. The basis of Israel's election (7:7-11)
            c. Promises of blessing for covenant obedience (7:12-15)
            d. Exhortation to destroy Canaanite paganism (7:16-26)
        2. Yahweh as the source of blessing (8:1-20)
            a. Yahweh's provision in the wilderness (8:1-10)
            b. Exhortation to remember that blessing comes from God (8:11-20)
        3. Blessing as a product of grace (9:1–10:11)
            a. Victory by God's grace (9:1-6)
            b. A history of Israel's stubbornness (9:7-24)
            c. Moses's plea on behalf of Yahweh's reputation (9:25-29)
            d. The opportunity to begin again (10:1-5)
            e. Conclusion of the historical résumé (10:6-11)
        4. Love of Yahweh and love of people (10:12-22)
        5. Obedience and disobedience and their rewards (11:1-32)
            a. Reiteration of the call to obedience (11:1-7)
            b. The bounties of the Land of Promise (11:8-15)
            c. Exhortation to instruction and obedience (11:16-25)
            d. Anticipation of a blessing and cursing ceremony (11:26-32)
V. The Specific Stipulations of the Covenant (12:1–26:15)
    A. The Exclusiveness of Yahweh and His Worship (12:1–16:17)
        1. The central sanctuary (12:1-14)
        2. The sanctity of blood (12:15-19)

ENDNOTES

1. For a convenient review of alternative hypotheses, see Tigay 1996:xxii-xxiv. Tigay holds a view—widely espoused—that Deuteronomy arose within prophetic circles in the northern kingdom, perhaps under Hosea in the eighth century BC.
2. K. A. Kitchen, *On the Reliability of the Old Testament* (Grand Rapids: Eerdmans, 2003), 299.
3. Bryant G. Wood, "From Rameses to Shiloh: Archaeological Discoveries Bearing on the Exodus-Judges Period," in *Giving the Sense: Understanding and Using Old Testament Historical Texts,* ed. David M. Howard, Jr. and Michael A. Grisanti, 262-268 (Grand Rapids: Kregel, 2003).

COMMENTARY ON

Deuteronomy

◆ I. The Covenant Setting (1:1-5)

These are the words that Moses spoke to all the people of Israel while they were in the wilderness east of the Jordan River. They were camped in the Jordan Valley* near Suph, between Paran on one side and Tophel, Laban, Hazeroth, and Di-zahab on the other.

²Normally it takes only eleven days to travel from Mount Sinai* to Kadesh-barnea, going by way of Mount Seir. ³But forty years after the Israelites left Egypt, on the first day of the eleventh month,* Moses addressed the people of Israel, telling them everything the LORD had commanded him to say. ⁴This took place after he had defeated King Sihon of the Amorites, who had ruled in Heshbon, and King Og of Bashan, who had ruled in Ashtaroth and Edrei.

⁵While the Israelites were in the land of Moab east of the Jordan River, Moses carefully explained the LORD's instructions as follows.

1:1 Hebrew *the Arabah;* also in 1:7.   1:2 Hebrew *Horeb,* another name for Sinai; also in 1:6, 19.   1:3 Hebrew *In the fortieth year, on the first day of the eleventh month.* This day in the ancient Hebrew lunar calendar occurred in January or February.

NOTES

1:1 *east of the Jordan River.* Lit., "on the other side of the river." Obviously, if Moses wrote Deuteronomy in the land of Moab, "the other side of the river" would ordinarily refer to Canaan to the west. However, the possibility exists that among the indigenous peoples of Canaan this was a technical term for the eastern region. For a modern example, until the formation of the Hashemite Kingdom of Jordan in 1946, the region was called the Emirate of Transjordan (1921–1946), even by those who lived there.

Jordan Valley. The Hebrew is *the Arabah* (see NLT mg), which means "wasteland." Though it sometimes includes the depression between the Dead Sea and the Red Sea (cf. 2:8), here it refers to the deep valley between the Sea of Galilee and the Dead Sea.

1:2 *Mount Sinai.* NLT interprets the name Horeb (see NLT mg) here to be Mount Sinai, a correct assumption. Deuteronomy favors the name Horeb for the place of covenant (1:6, 19; 4:10, 15; 5:2; 9:8; 18:16; 29:1, NASB). Sinai occurs only in 33:2, a poetic piece.

1:3 *the first day of the eleventh month.* By the Hebrew calendar this would be Shebat 1, corresponding to a date in January/February on the modern Gregorian calendar (cf. NLT mg).

COMMENTARY

Deuteronomy, as a composition shaped largely on the model of an ancient Near Eastern treaty text (see Introduction), contains all the literary elements common to those texts. These treaty texts invariably begin with what some scholars call a "preamble," a brief section introducing the parties to the agreement, the setting in which the agreement was implemented, and other such preliminary incidentals. The first five verses of Deuteronomy serve this function.

The setting is an assembly of all the people of Israel in the Transjordan, preparatory to the conquest of Canaan to the west. The purpose of the assembly is for Moses to outline in detail the renewal of the covenant originally made with Israel at Mount Sinai (Exod 19–24). The generation with whom that covenant had been made had, for the most part, died off (Num 26:63-65) because of their incessant and unrepentant rebellion against Yahweh (Num 14:20-24). Only Joshua, Caleb, and those under 20 years old survived to see the Land of Promise (Num 14:26-35; cf. Deut 1:34-40).

The phrase "all the people of Israel" (1:1) need not mean that every individual was there or could hear, for the word *kol* [TH3605, ZH3972] (all) also means "as a whole." That is, the words of covenant were intended for the nation as a collective entity. The specific location of the encampment is unclear because the place names of 1:1 refer to camping places in the Sinai northward to the Transjordan (Tigay 1996:3-4, 417-422). What is certain from the narrative is that the conclave took place in the lower Jordan Valley not far north of the Dead Sea.

By referring to the ordinarily short time of 11 days to travel from Sinai to Kadesh-barnea (1:2), Moses was already drawing attention to the rebellious spirit of his people, which had caused 11 days to stretch into nearly 40 years (1:3; cf. 2:7; 8:2, 4; 29:5). The journey of faith may be difficult, but it is direct. The journey of unbelief is interminable. As well as describing literal periods of time (as here), the number 40 is also of unusual symbolic value in the Bible, its main significance having to do with trials or testings (see 25:3; Gen 7:12, 17; Num 13:25; 14:33, 34; 1 Sam 17:16; 1 Kgs 19:8; Ps 95:10; Ezek 29:12, 13; Jonah 3:4; Matt 4:2; Mark 1:13). It is also a way of describing an era, a generation, or a time of reigning, perhaps the ideal in these cases (Gen 25:20; 26:34; Exod 24:18; Josh 14:7; Judg 3:11; 5:31; 8:28; 13:1; 1 Sam 4:18; 2 Sam 2:10; 5:4; 1 Kgs 2:11; 11:42).

The setting of Moses's address is further specified as having occurred after Israel had defeated King Sihon of the Amorites and King Og of Bashan (1:4). A full account of these campaigns appears in Numbers 21:21-35, and Moses reiterates them in Deuteronomy 2:26–3:11. For now, the intent is simply to note that all the Transjordan was under Israel's domination—from Bashan in the north to the Amorite territory in the south—and that the stage is now set for the conquest of Canaan and possession of the Promised Land.

◆ II. The Historical Review and Mosaic Exhortation (1:6–4:40)
    A. The Past Dealings of Yahweh with Israel (1:6–3:29)
        1. Events at Sinai (1:6-18)

⁶"When we were at Mount Sinai, the LORD our God said to us, 'You have stayed at this mountain long enough. ⁷It is time to break camp and move on. Go to the hill

country of the Amorites and to all the neighboring regions—the Jordan Valley, the hill country, the western foothills,* the Negev, and the coastal plain. Go to the land of the Canaanites and to Lebanon, and all the way to the great Euphrates River. ⁸Look, I am giving all this land to you! Go in and occupy it, for it is the land the LORD swore to give to your ancestors Abraham, Isaac, and Jacob, and to all their descendants.' "

⁹Moses continued, "At that time I told you, 'You are too great a burden for me to carry all by myself. ¹⁰The LORD your God has increased your population, making you as numerous as the stars! ¹¹And may the LORD, the God of your ancestors, multiply you a thousand times more and bless you as he promised! ¹²But you are such a heavy load to carry! How can I deal with all your problems and bickering? ¹³Choose some well-respected men from each tribe who are known for their wisdom and understanding, and I will appoint them as your leaders.'

¹⁴"Then you responded, 'Your plan is a good one.' ¹⁵So I took the wise and respected men you had selected from your tribes and appointed them to serve as judges and officials over you. Some were responsible for a thousand people, some for a hundred, some for fifty, and some for ten.

¹⁶"At that time I instructed the judges, 'You must hear the cases of your fellow Israelites and the foreigners living among you. Be perfectly fair in your decisions ¹⁷and impartial in your judgments. Hear the cases of those who are poor as well as those who are rich. Don't be afraid of anyone's anger, for the decision you make is God's decision. Bring me any cases that are too difficult for you, and I will handle them.'

¹⁸"At that time I gave you instructions about everything you were to do.

1:7 Hebrew *the Shephelah.*

NOTES

1:7 *the hill country of the Amorites.* This refers to the great central part of Canaan, the series of mountain ranges extending from the Jezreel Valley in the north to the Negev in the south. The OT tradition (not in any way contradicted by archaeological evidence) is that the hill country at that time (c. 1400 BC, the Late Bronze Age) was populated by Amorites, whereas the valleys and plains were home to the Canaanites. Thus, Moses pointed out elsewhere that in patriarchal times, this hill country was inhabited by Canaanites (Gen 12:6; cf. Gen 13:7). He was even more precise in recording the report of the 12 spies that "[the] Amorites live in the hill country. The Canaanites live along the coast of the Mediterranean Sea and along the Jordan Valley" (Num 13:29). Clearly a change had occurred between Abraham's time and Moses's, the Canaanites evidently having been displaced in the hill country by the Amorites.

the land of the Canaanites. Both the historical facts (see previous note) and the grammar support a translation here of "the coastal plain, the land of the Canaanites" (Thompson 1974:85; Tigay 1996:9).

Euphrates River. The command to occupy the land as far as the Euphrates is in line with the promises to the patriarchs (Gen 15:18) and Moses's previous statements to Israel (Exod 23:31; cf. also Deut 11:24; Josh 1:4). Historically, David may have controlled Aram as far as the Euphrates (2 Sam 8:3), and Solomon certainly did (1 Kgs 4:21, 24; 2 Chr 9:26; Ps 72:8). Eschatological texts speak of Messiah's dominion extending to the Euphrates (Zech 9:10). The territorial assignments of the tribes under Joshua are, however, limited to Palestine proper (Josh 13:8–19:48), and Israel in the end times also seems to find its primary locus there (Ezek 47:13–48:29). Palestine, thus, will be the center of a future messianic kingdom, which will extend secondarily as far as the Euphrates.

1:10 *as numerous as the stars.* From the standpoint of modern astronomy, this is obviously hyperbole, for there appear to be hundreds of millions of stars. However, from the phenomenological viewpoint of Moses's time, the statement is most understandable.

1:17 *the decision you make is God's decision.* Lit., "for the judgment is God's." Since this is so, human judges were not to make decisions based on their own prejudices, in response to bribes or other pressures, or without careful thought. They must depend on God and realize that they represent him to the people (see Exod 4:16; 7:1).

COMMENTARY

The second major element of standard ancient Near Eastern treaty documents was the historical prologue, a section describing the past relationship of the covenant partners and their forebears. This appears in Deuteronomy as well, consisting of 1:6–4:40. Here Moses recounts Israel's history from the time of the giving of the law at Sinai to the present moment, the reaffirmation of the covenant in Moab. This historical review is divided into two parts: the past dealings of Yahweh with Israel (1:6–3:29) and Moses's exhortation (4:1-40).

The first of these encounters of Yahweh with his people was at Sinai (1:6-18). Moses did not rehearse the story of God's appearance (the theophany) and bestowal of the covenant law at this point (see 4:9-14; 5:22-33); his interest was in the series of events that brought the nation to its present place. The Lord had told them that they had stayed at Sinai long enough; it was time to move on (1:6-7). They had arrived there two months after the Exodus (Exod 19:1) and departed for Canaan on the twentieth day of the second month (called Ziv or Iyyar = April/May) of the second year (Num 10:11). In all, they had been at Sinai for a little over a year.

Their destination was clear: They had to go to the land promised to their patriarchal ancestors (1:8). This land was comprised of a number of regions: the hill country (see notes on 1:7), the Jordan Valley (lit., "the Arabah"), the foothills (modern Shephelah), the Negev (lit., "the south"—namely, the desert land from Beersheba southward), and the coastal plain—that is, the area along the Mediterranean Sea. The order is from east to west, a pattern that makes best sense when viewed from the perspective of a group camped on the east side of the Jordan. Beyond the immediate land of Palestine, God's promises extended to the conquest of Lebanon and the territories to the north and east as far as the Euphrates River (see notes on 1:7).

Occupation of the land was not an option but an edict. In two staccato-like commands, Yahweh had said "go in" and "occupy"! Justification for the people's taking this mandatory action was the fact that the land was already theirs by promise to the patriarchs (Gen 15:18-21; 17:9; 26:3-4). No permission was needed from its occupants nor was any apology to them expected as a result of conquest, for they were squatters on land already belonging to Israel by divine oath (1:8).

God's blessing of Israel proved to be a two-edged sword to Moses. He rejoiced at how God had multiplied the people until they had become as numerous as the stars (1:10). And he prayed that this might be only the beginning, that they might become a thousand times as populous (1:11)! But since he had taken the responsibility to be their judge, as well as theocratic mediator, Moses found himself overwhelmed by their needs. Using a verb commonly employed to suggest onerous, back-breaking labor (1:9; *nasa'* [TH5375, ZH5951], "lift up, carry"), Moses complained that he could not sustain the people by himself. In this comment, Moses is referring to the days when he acted as a one-man judicial system for the whole nation (Exod 18:13-26). Seeing his exhaustion, his father-in-law, Jethro, had advised him to set up a system whereby lower courts would hear ordinary cases and only those beyond their capacity to judge would be appealed to Moses. This particular solution was put into place but was never mentioned again in the record. Presumably, it had flaws or deficiencies in actual implementation and so it quickly died out.

In the Deuteronomy version, Moses says that he had urged the people to "choose" candidates as judges, and he would appoint them to their office (1:13). The Exodus account says that Moses himself chose them (Exod 18:25). Technically, the Hebrew verb in Deuteronomy is the imperative *habu* [TH3051, ZH2035], a word that means "get" (KBL 223). The verb in Exodus 18:25 is *bakhar* [TH977, ZH1047], the meaning of which is "choose" or "elect" (KBL 117-118). A simple harmony of the passages is that Moses asked the people to get a slate of candidates (1:13), from which he would choose (Exod 18:25) the best.

The qualifications were that they be well-respected men of wisdom and understanding (1:13). All of these are summarized in the Exodus narrative as "capable" (Exod 18:25). In the Old Testament, "wise" (*khakam* [TH2450, ZH2682]) is more descriptive of godliness than of intellect (Knierim 1995:283-285). "Understanding" (*nebonim* [TH995, ZH1067]) has more to do with discernment and discretion. And "well-respected" is the translation of *widu'im* (the conjunction and Qal passive participle of *yada'* [TH3045, ZH3359], "to know"). Literally, then, these were "known men" or, in the modern idiom, "known quantities." There were no secrets here, no coverups that someday would be exposed. They were solid citizens.

Still recounting the past, Moses said the people liked his plan (1:14). Actually, the overall idea was Jethro's (Exod 18:14), but the revelation of that plan to the people and the means of carrying it out were Moses's. The qualified men were then appointed (lit., "given") to serve as judges and officials (1:15). The text reads literally, "I took the heads of your tribes . . . and gave them to be heads over you, leaders of thousands." The idea is that men already known for leadership skills—as well as being wise, discerning, and of good reputation—became leaders in a different capacity. Leadership is not an office; it's a gift.

The leaders (*sar* [TH8269, ZH8569], generic for any kind of leader; KBL 929) of the different groupings are also called "officials" (*shoter* [TH7860, ZH8854]) in 1:15. Although the two terms are parallel here, "officials" derives from a root having to do with writing or record keeping and seems to focus more on the need for careful documentation of legal proceedings. In 1:16 these same officials are called "judges" (*shopet* [TH8199A, ZH9149]). Hence *sar* and *shoter* and also *shopet* appear to be interchangeable ways of describing these men and their functions.

Above all else, Moses told them, the judges must render their verdicts fairly, no matter who the parties to the dispute might be (1:16). The principle is that they must act righteously. The fundamental idea of the word *tsedeq* [TH6664, ZH7406] and its various cognate forms (cf. [TH6659/6662/6663/6666, ZH7401/7404/7405/7407]) is adherence to a norm, in this case to the divine standard (NIDOTTE 3.746). To be fair is to be true to God's own character and expectations as revealed in his covenant law. An evidence of fairness is a refusal to be partial (1:17). The Hebrew idiom here for "to be partial" is "to recognize faces." That is, when a judge holds court, he is not to say, "Oh, I know him, so I must treat him with special favor." Rather, as the Hebrew so pungently puts it, "As the small, so the great" (1:17, lit.). In God's community the ground is level at the courthouse.

Frequently, the application of righteous justice brings negative and fearful repercussions, especially from people of power and influence. Moses says, however, that such people are not to be feared (1:17). If they have a complaint, they should take it up with God himself, for the human judge is simply his instrument (see note on 1:17). But God is a difficult target, so it is the way of the world to attack more visible targets such as the men and women who try to represent and serve him—Moses was such a man. Nonetheless, with great sensitivity and courage, Moses urged the judges to pass on to him the difficult cases they could not handle. A sign of compassionate leadership is the willingness to "take the heat," as Moses did here.

Moses then summarized the section by reminding his listeners that the bottom line of what the experience at Sinai was about was instruction in the things Israel was to do. The Hebrew is a little stronger than the NLT, asserting "At that time I commanded you" (1:18). We should be reminded that God gave the Ten Commandments and not the Ten Suggestions.

◆   2. Instructions at Kadesh-barnea (1:19-25)

¹⁹"Then, just as the LORD our God commanded us, we left Mount Sinai and traveled through the great and terrifying wilderness, as you yourselves remember, and headed toward the hill country of the Amorites. When we arrived at Kadesh-barnea, ²⁰I said to you, 'You have now reached the hill country of the Amorites that the LORD our God is giving us. ²¹Look! He has placed the land in front of you. Go and occupy it as the LORD, the God of your ancestors, has promised you. Don't be afraid! Don't be discouraged!'

²²"But you all came to me and said, 'First, let's send out scouts to explore the land for us. They will advise us on the best route to take and which towns we should enter.'

²³"This seemed like a good idea to me, so I chose twelve scouts, one from each of your tribes. ²⁴They headed for the hill country and came to the valley of Eshcol and explored it. ²⁵They picked some of its fruit and brought it back to us. And they reported, 'The land the LORD our God has given us is indeed a good land.'

NOTES

1:20 *is giving us.* This translates a participle, a verb form commonly used (as here) as a *futur instans*—that is, it communicates that something is about to happen or to become a reality: "is about to give us."

COMMENTARY

The account of the journey from Sinai to Kadesh-barnea is greatly truncated here, as compared to the version in Numbers, which occupies 77 verses (Num 10:11–12:16). However, Moses's present purpose is not to repeat but to recapitulate, to review those items of the past that highlight God's dealings with his people in a special way. Thus, in one verse (1:19), the whole itinerary is summed up as taking place in a "great and terrifying wilderness." "Wilderness" (*midbar* [TH4057, ZH4497]) should not be understood as a sandy desert or impenetrable thicket. Rather, it describes a steppe-land where some pasturage is usually possible (see 1 Sam 17:28, NASB; cf. Jer 2:2; 3:2). However, compared to the lush garden spot of the Egyptian delta from which they had come, the Israelites viewed the interior of the Sinai Peninsula as great and terrifying.

Kadesh-barnea is a large oasis about 140 miles due north of Mount Sinai and 55–60 miles south of Beersheba. Now known as 'Ain Qudeirat, the site is large enough to have accommodated many thousands of nomadic people, just as the Israelites were at that time (Cohen 1981:93-107). This place would have been the center of settlement from which the shepherds and herdsmen would have moved out to find more distant pasture. Deuteronomy omits here the information that Israel remained at Kadesh-barnea for 38 years in all (see 2:14; Num 14:33).

Kadesh-barnea marked a major port of entry into Canaan to the north, so Moses could say, "You have now reached the hill country of the Amorites that the LORD our God is giving us" (1:20). Then with two sharp commands, he said, "Go and occupy" (1:21). As in 1:8, the justification for such drastic action is the promise of Yahweh to the patriarchs. God's protection and assurance of success are seen in the two vetitives (i.e., wishes that something not happen), "Don't be afraid! Don't be discouraged!" With verbs of this kind, imperatives are, in the nature of the case, of little use, for one can hardly be commanded not to fear. The idea, then, is that of entreaty or urging: "Please stop fearing and being discouraged, for God has promised ultimate success."

One might criticize the people's response as a lack of faith. They were open to the idea of entering the land but not before they could spy it out to determine what they were up against (1:22). Moses, however, defended their cautious approach and decided, at their suggestion, to send out scouts. Mosaic sanction of such a strategy lends support to the idea that wise planning is not inimical to God's will. Sometimes God may, indeed, demand precipitous action; usually, however, he also incorporates human preparation.

A man from each of the 12 tribes was selected in order to make this a truly unified and nationwide program (1:23). In Numbers they are named, with Joshua and Caleb being prominent (Num 13:1-16). The Numbers account also gives a much more detailed description of the route they took to see the land (Num 13:21-24). It covered the area from Zin in the south (where they were) to Rehob in the north (a region north of Galilee in the lower Beqaa Valley; see Josh 13:5). On the way back, they passed through the valley of Eshcol ('*eshkol* [TH811A, ZH865], "cluster"), from which they picked some fruit and took it back to Kadesh-barnea (1:25). Numbers says it was one cluster of grapes, a bunch so large that it took two men to carry it on a pole suspended between them (Num 13:23)! The consensus of the spies was that the land was "indeed a good land" (1:25).

◆　　## 3. Disobedience at Kadesh-barnea (1:26-33)

26"But you rebelled against the command of the LORD your God and refused to go in. 27You complained in your tents and said, 'The LORD must hate us. That's why he has brought us here from Egypt—to hand us over to the Amorites to be slaughtered. 28Where can we go? Our brothers have demoralized us with their report. They tell us, "The people of the land are taller and more powerful than we are, and their towns are large, with walls rising high into the sky! We even saw giants there— the descendants of Anak!"'

29"But I said to you, 'Don't be shocked or afraid of them! 30The LORD your God is going ahead of you. He will fight for you, just as you saw him do in Egypt. 31And you saw how the LORD your God cared for you all along the way as you traveled through the wilderness, just as a father cares for his child. Now he has brought you to this place.'

32"But even after all he did, you refused to trust the LORD your God, 33who goes before you looking for the best places to camp, guiding you with a pillar of fire by night and a pillar of cloud by day.

NOTES

1:27 *The LORD must hate us.* The word "hate" (*sin'ah* [TH8135, ZH8534]), in covenant contexts such as this, means not so much to harbor negative emotional feelings as to express rejection (NIDOTTE 3.1257; cf. Moran 1963). "To love" indicates choice, acceptance, and election, whereas "to hate" suggests non-choice (cf. 7:6-11; Mal 1:2-3; Rom 9:13). Israel here interprets Yahweh's command to go up into the land as tantamount to facing certain annihilation; therefore, they thought, he must not have chosen them to be his people after all.

1:28 *descendants of Anak.* Anak, a descendant of Arba for whom the city of Kiriath-arba was named (Josh 14:15), is otherwise unknown except that from him sprang a line of giants. Among these were the Nephilim, the fearsome people encountered by the spies according to the Numbers narrative (Num 13:33; cf. NLT mg). The Anakites came to symbolize or typify any giant people (2:10) and remained a problem to Israel for years to come. Goliath of Gath may, in fact, have been an Anakite (see Josh 11:21-22; cf. 1 Sam 17:4).

1:33 *places to camp, guiding you.* The LXX reads "your goings" for the MT's "your camps." This seems preferable in light of the reference to guiding. See also Exod 13:21, where the same idea occurs, this time with the verb *nakhah* [TH5148, ZH5697] (guide) instead of *khanah* [TH2583, ZH2837] (encamp). There appears to be a clear case of metathesis (the interchange of two letters, here represented in *kh* and *n*) in the Deuteronomy passage.

COMMENTARY

Although Canaan was indeed a good land (1:25), Numbers records how 10 of the 12 scouts gave the negative report that the obstacles standing in the way of conquest were too great (Num 13:25-29). Only Caleb and Joshua thought otherwise (Num

14:6-10; cf. Deut 1:36, 38). Because of the discouraging report of the majority of the scouts, the people rebelled against Yahweh and Moses and refused to move forward (1:26). The allusion to "tents" (1:27) suggests that the murmuring was at first private, within families and small groups, and then more public and general. In a gross misunderstanding of the Lord and his perfect purposes, they charged him with hating them (see note on 1:27) and bringing them to this point only to destroy them. How easy it is to interpret the difficulties of life as a sign of God's displeasure or even his rejection.

The major difficulty was that gigantic people occupied the hill country and lived in cities with unscalable and impenetrable walls (1:28). Though laced with exaggeration, the scouts' perception was not altogether false. Archaeological research has uncovered evidence of strongly fortified cities in that area in the Late Bronze Age (1550-1200 BC), the time of the conquest (Mazar 1990:243; Ahlström 1993:218). To cap off their plea of inadequacy, the people noted the existence of Anakites in the land, giants of legendary size and strength (see note on 1:28).

Again Moses said, "Don't be . . . afraid" (1:29). This word of assurance occurs in this form (lo'-thire'un [TH3372, ZH3707]) or its vetitive (e.g., 'al-tira' [TH3372, ZH3707]) many times in Deuteronomy to provide encouragement in difficult circumstances (e.g., 1:21; 3:2, 22; 7:18; 20:1, 3; 31:6, 8). Moses's call for assurance was based on history—that which God had done for Israel in Egypt and throughout the desert journeys (1:30-31). He had fought for Israel and (lit.) "carried them along as a man carries his son." These tender words are later picked up by Hosea, who said, "I [Yahweh] myself taught Israel how to walk, leading him along by the hand. . . . I led Israel along with my ropes of kindness and love. I lifted the yoke from his neck, and I myself stooped to feed him" (Hos 11:3-4). What God had done in the past, Moses said, he could also do in the future. But Israel had already spurned his grace, despite his leading them night and day (1:33). Would they do so now, on the eve of a new challenge?

◆   ## 4. Judgment at Kadesh-barnea (1:34-40)

34"When the LORD heard your complaining, he became very angry. So he solemnly swore, 35'Not one of you from this wicked generation will live to see the good land I swore to give your ancestors, 36except Caleb son of Jephunneh. He will see this land because he has followed the LORD completely. I will give to him and his descendants some of the very land he explored during his scouting mission.'

37"And the LORD was also angry with me because of you. He said to me, 'Moses, not even you will enter the Promised Land! 38Instead, your assistant, Joshua son of Nun, will lead the people into the land. Encourage him, for he will lead Israel as they take possession of it. 39I will give the land to your little ones—your innocent children. You were afraid they would be captured, but they will be the ones who occupy it. 40As for you, turn around now and go on back through the wilderness toward the Red Sea.*'

1:40 Hebrew sea of reeds.

NOTES

1:35 *Not one of you from this wicked generation will live to see the good land I swore to give your ancestors.* Verse 34 states that God swore, and 1:35 records the vow. However, the Hebrew formula for this (and other) oaths is much stronger than the translation here. It begins with the conjunction "if" (*'im* [TH518, ZH561]), which introduces a protasis ("If anyone among these people of this wicked generation," etc.), but gives no apodosis (that is, there is no "then" clause) because what Yahweh threatens is so unthinkable it is incapable of articulation (cf. Waltke and O'Connor 1990:679).

1:36 *he explored.* The verb *darak* [TH1869, ZH2005] (walked) sometimes (as here) conveys the notion of real or anticipated ownership. It means literally "to tread upon," the treading being symbolic of dominion, usually by force (NIDOTTE 1.992). Other examples are 11:24-25; Isa 63:3; Hab 3:19; Zech 9:13 (in Hebrew).

1:40 *Red Sea.* The sea referred to here (*yam-sup* [TH3220/5488A, ZH3542/6068] lit., "Reed Sea") is not the one crossed by Israel in the Exodus but the eastern branch of that sea now called the Gulf of Eilat or the Gulf of Aqaba.

COMMENTARY

Israel's rebellion upon hearing the report of the spies was the last straw for God. With patience, he had brought them out of Egypt and provided for them along the way, but at every step they had complained and become obstinate. Now the whole nation would be condemned to remain in the desert, with that generation never to see the Land of Promise. Caleb, a scout from the tribe of Judah (Num 13:6), would be an exception, as also Joshua the Ephraimite (1:38; cf. Num 13:8).

Caleb's credential was that "he . . . followed the LORD completely" (1:36). The MT says literally, "he was full (of being) after Yahweh." With his whole mind, heart, and soul, Caleb determined to do the will of God. Nothing else mattered to him. This commendation is used only of Caleb and Joshua (Num 14:24; 32:11, 12; Josh 14:8, 9, 14) and of David (1 Kgs 11:6). Caleb and his descendants would take ownership of the land he had already claimed by walking over it (see note on 1:36). Those who step out in faith and claim the victory in the name of the Lord have every right to have hope in him.

Shockingly, Moses also would be precluded from entering the land (1:37). It was, as he says, "because of you [people]" that he could not do so. The incident that triggered this harsh sentence was his intemperate striking of the rock in the desert, a blow of rage because of the incessant carping and complaining of the people (Num 20:12). The principle is clear: "When someone has been given much, much will be required in return" (Luke 12:48). As the leader of the covenant community, Moses was most expected to attain to its highest standards of expectation. This is true of leaders of the church as well.

Joshua would succeed Moses and lead the people in. Preparation for this transfer of leadership had already begun (Num 14:30); later in Deuteronomy it is validated by a public ceremony (31:14-23). The background to the reference to the children in 1:39 is somewhat unclear since neither the account in Numbers nor the one in Deuteronomy says anything about the people's fear that their children would be captured. It is possible, of course, that this was part of a longer report not fully recorded in the text. In any case, there was no use thinking about continuing north to enter Canaan, for Yahweh had closed that door. What they had to do now was head south toward the Red Sea (see note on 1:40).

◆   5. Unsuccessful attempt at conquest (1:41-46)

⁴¹"Then you confessed, 'We have sinned against the LORD! We will go into the land and fight for it, as the LORD our God has commanded us.' So your men strapped on their weapons, thinking it would be easy to attack the hill country.

⁴²"But the LORD told me to tell you, 'Do not attack, for I am not with you. If you go ahead on your own, you will be crushed by your enemies.'

⁴³"This is what I told you, but you would not listen. Instead, you again rebelled against the LORD's command and arrogantly went into the hill country to fight. ⁴⁴But the Amorites who lived there came out against you like a swarm of bees. They chased and battered you all the way from Seir to Hormah. ⁴⁵Then you returned and wept before the LORD, but he refused to listen. ⁴⁶So you stayed there at Kadesh for a long time.

NOTES

1:44 *Seir to Hormah.* Seir refers to the land otherwise known as Edom, southeast of the Dead Sea. Hormah was the name the Israelites gave to a city near Beersheba and Arad (Num 21:1; 33:40) after they destroyed it in Num 21:3 (*khormah* [TH2767, ZH3055], from the verb *kharam* [TH2763, ZH3049], "to destroy"). It is difficult to trace the route of this campaign from the sparse information given. Probably Israel headed east from Kadesh-barnea toward the Arabah, hoping to penetrate Canaan from that direction. Having been intercepted by the Amorites, they fled to the northwest, where they suffered defeat, and then returned to Kadesh-barnea.

COMMENTARY

True to human nature, when God forbade Israel to undertake the conquest because of their previous refusal to do so, they decided that that was precisely what they would do. Their warriors, thinking it to be an easy matter, armed themselves and setout for the hill country (1:41). Their confessions of sin were hollow and self-serving, something certainly known to Yahweh, so he told them that if they went they would go without him and would experience defeat (1:42). The conquest would only come as the result of holy war (or Yahweh war), as carried out by God's direction (see 2:26-37). In holy war, the priests would accompany the troops bearing the symbol of God's presence, the Ark of the Covenant (20:3-4; Josh 6:1-7). Yahweh's refusal to go left them on their own, for it was now carnal conflict and not holy war.

Moses reminded his hearers that he had given them God's warnings; nevertheless, they set out (1:43). They went arrogantly, that is, presumptuously (*zid* [TH2102, ZH2326]; 1:43), as though the presence of God made no difference to the outcome. They soon found out the folly of attempting to do God's work without God's power. The Amorites came against them "like a swarm of bees"; they were innumerable, inflicting inescapable pain (1:44). Relentlessly, they pursued Israel from Seir to Hormah to Kadesh-barnea (see note on 1:44).

The tears of repentance at the end of the tragic episode were to no avail, for the die had been cast (1:45). Even the patience and grace of God can expire, especially when he knows the human heart to be hopelessly hardened against him (see Exod 9:12). The end of the dismal tale is that Israel stayed at Kadesh "a long time"— 38 years, in fact (2:14).

♦ ## 6. Instructions concerning Edom (2:1-8a)

"Then we turned around and headed back across the wilderness toward the Red Sea,* just as the LORD had instructed me, and we wandered around in the region of Mount Seir for a long time.

²"Then at last the LORD said to me, ³'You have been wandering around in this hill country long enough; turn to the north. ⁴Give these orders to the people: "You will pass through the country belonging to your relatives the Edomites, the descendants of Esau, who live in Seir. The Edomites will feel threatened, so be careful. ⁵Do not bother them, for I have given them all the hill country around Mount Seir as their property, and I will not give you even one square foot of their land. ⁶If you need food to eat or water to drink, pay them for it. ⁷For the LORD your God has blessed you in everything you have done. He has watched your every step through this great wilderness. During these forty years, the LORD your God has been with you, and you have lacked nothing."'

⁸"So we bypassed the territory of our relatives, the descendants of Esau, who live in Seir.

2:1 Hebrew *sea of reeds.*

NOTES

2:1 *Red Sea.* The term *yam-sup* [TH3220/5488A, ZH3542/6068] means "Reed Sea" (cf. NLT mg). The LXX translates it as *thalassan eruthran* [TG2281/2063, ZG2498/2261], "Red Sea," referring to both the Gulf of Suez and the Gulf of Aqaba, probably because of the reddish mud of the Suez area.

Mount Seir. This is another name for the land of Edom, south and southeast of the Dead Sea. The area was inhabited by Horites (perhaps Semitic "Hurrians"; de Vaux 1978:136-138; Speiser 1964:282-283) who were displaced by the descendants of Esau (2:12; cf. Gen 14:6; 36:1-43; Josh 24:4). Later, the region was known as Nabataea, its capital being the famous city of Petra.

2:7 *forty years.* Israel was en route to and then at Sinai for over a year (see 1:3) and at Kadesh-barnea for 38 years (2:14), making a total of about 40.

2:8 *bypassed the territory of our relatives.* The Edomites were descendants of Esau, brother of Jacob (Gen 36:1). The route here went east of Edom, along the desert highway.

COMMENTARY

The itinerary at this point is somewhat difficult to trace. According to Numbers, the Israelites made a second, more successful penetration of Canaan from the south, defeating the king of Arad at Hormah, near Beersheba (Num 21:1-3). However, they did not follow this up but proceeded from Mount Hor (where Aaron had died; Num 20:28) toward the Red Sea, that is, the Gulf of Aqaba (Num 21:4 = Deut 2:1). They evidently crossed the Arabah south of the Dead Sea (see 1:1) and bypassed

Edom on the east (2:8a). At first, they had sought permission from the king of
Edom to take the most direct route, the so-called King's Highway, offering to pay for
food and water along the way and promising not to leave the main route (Num
20:14-19). The king refused to grant this permission (Num 20:20-21), so Israel had
to take the alternative, more difficult route (Num 21:4-20).

After traveling south to circumvent Edom, the Lord told Israel to turn north (2:3).
They were now on the desert route and, though on the fringes of the desert, were
still in Edomite territory (2:4a). Moses thus cautioned them not to antagonize their
Edomite brothers, who were actually afraid of them and for this reason had denied
them access to the King's Highway (2:4b). Furthermore, God had given this land to
Edom every bit as much as he had given Canaan to Israel (2:5; cf. 2:12).

The idea that God had given an inheritance to Edom as well as to Israel (cf. also
2:9, 19, 22, 23) is of great theological significance, for it stresses the universal nature
of God's purposes and grace. He had indeed chosen Israel to be his "own special
treasure from among all the peoples on earth" and to be a "kingdom of priests" and
a "holy nation" (Exod 19:5-6), but this was for the purpose of using Israel as a servant people to make known the message of redemption. He had also set apart the
other nations, assigning them their places and responsibilities (cf. 32:8-9; Acts
17:26-28).

The freedom of Edom from Israelite domination is clear from the Hebrew underlying the phrase "one square foot of their land" (2:5). It says literally, "even to treading of the sole of [your] foot." As noted above with reference to Caleb's "treading
upon the land" of his inheritance (see note on 1:36), the image of placing the foot
on the land, especially with the verb used here, is suggestive of dominion. Israel
must respect Edom's independence. Furthermore, Israel must not be dependent on
Edom for handouts of food and drink (2:6). God, not Edom, would meet all her
needs, just as he had done for the past 40 years (2:7).

Heeding Moses's advice, the people bypassed their Edomite brothers. As noted
already (2:1), rather than taking the King's Highway, the direct route through the
Arabah Valley, they took the desert route to the east and thence went northward.
Elath and Ezion-geber (2:8a) were cities on the Gulf of Aqaba, at the southern
end of the Arabah. They had passed through that area years before on their way
from Sinai to Kadesh-barnea (Num 33:35-36). The modern name of Elath is
Eilat, Israel's Red Sea port on the Gulf of Aqaba (also known to Israel as the Gulf
of Eilat).

♦   ## 7. Instructions concerning Moab (2:8b-15)

We avoided the road through the Arabah
Valley that comes up from Elath and
Ezion-geber.
    "Then as we turned north along the
desert route through Moab, 9the LORD

warned us, 'Do not bother the Moabites,
the descendants of Lot, or start a war with
them. I have given them Ar as their property, and I will not give you any of their
land!'"

¹⁰(A race of giants called the Emites had once lived in the area of Ar. They were as strong and numerous and tall as the Anakites, another race of giants. ¹¹Both the Emites and the Anakites are also known as the Rephaites, though the Moabites call them Emites. ¹²In earlier times the Horites had lived in Seir, but they were driven out and displaced by the descendants of Esau, just as Israel drove out the people of Canaan when the LORD gave Israel their land.)

¹³Moses continued, "Then the LORD said to us, 'Get moving. Cross the Zered Brook.' So we crossed the brook.

¹⁴"Thirty-eight years passed from the time we first left Kadesh-barnea until we finally crossed the Zered Brook! By then, all the men old enough to fight in battle had died in the wilderness, as the LORD had vowed would happen. ¹⁵The LORD struck them down until they had all been eliminated from the community.

NOTES

2:9 Ar. Usually this refers to a city by this name located near the Arnon River (Num 21:28). Sometimes (as here) it is synonymous with Moab as a whole. Quite likely it is a dialectal variant of the Hebrew word meaning "city" (*'ir* [TH5892, ZH6551]), and it may also be a short form of the name Aroer (as in LXX; cf. 2:36). See also Weinfeld 1991:161.

2:11 the Rephaites. These people (*repa'im* [TH7497, ZH8328]) once lived throughout the Canaan/Transjordan area, being identified by the Moabites as Emites (as here) and by the Ammonites as Zamzummites (2:20). They first appear in the account of the conquest of the cities of the plain (Gen 14:5) as contemporary with Abraham (Gen 15:20). King Og of Bashan was considered to be the last of the Rephaites (3:11, 13). Their identification is complicated by the fact that *repa'im* [TH7496, ZH8327] refers also to dead spirits, mysterious dwellers of Sheol (KBL 903-904; cf. Job 26:5; Prov 9:18; Isa 14:9). Perhaps the giant size of the Rephaites led to their being associated with these underworld beings.

2:12 just as Israel drove out the people of Canaan. The MT reads "just as Israel did to the land of its possession." This most likely refers to the conquest of the Transjordan that had already taken place (Num 32:33-42) because the conquest of Canaan still lay in the future. If the reference were to be construed as a post-Mosaic gloss, the main conquest of Canaan would be in view.

2:13 Zered Brook. There are four rivers or wadis (*nakhal* [TH5158, ZH5707]) that flow west into the Jordan River or Dead Sea from the Transjordanian plateaus. From north to south they are the Yarmuk, Jabbok, Arnon, and Zered. The Zered empties into the south end of the Dead Sea. At times, it marked the border between Moab to the north and Edom to the south.

COMMENTARY

The desert highway on the eastern edge of Edom continued north toward Moab. The NLT here (2:8b) should be understood in that sense and not as though the Israelites were already in Moab. The actual crossing into Moabite territory took place only after the Zered Brook was crossed, an event recorded in 2:13.

The same instructions that Yahweh gave concerning the Edomites (2:5) he also gave concerning the Moabites: Do not bother them (2:9). The implicit reason for such a policy is the same in each instance. Edom was populated by the descendants of Esau, brother of Jacob (or Israel), and thus to attack Edom would amount to internecine warfare. Long before, Esau, though he sold his birthright and lost the primary blessing of his father, was promised that he would serve his brother for a time but then be freed from him (Gen 27:40). Furthermore, the land Edom possessed was a gift of God and could not be occupied by Israel (2:5).

Moab was a son of Lot by Lot's incestuous relationship with one of his daughters (Gen 19:37). Since Lot was Abraham's nephew, Moab also enjoyed family connections with Israel. And Moab's land, too, had come as a divine bestowment. This precluded Israel's seizure and occupation of Moabite territory, at least for the time. Ar (that is, Moab; cf. note on 2:9) was off limits to Israel, just as Edom was. In later times, both Edom and Moab fell under Israelite jurisdiction, as did Ammon (2:19) and all of the Transjordan. Both David (2 Sam 8:2, 14) and Solomon (1 Kgs 9:26; 11:14) ruled over this region; throughout the history of the divided monarchy, there were alternating times of subjugation and independence for these lands.

Verses 10-12 are somewhat a digression from Moses's historical summary. Having mentioned Ar, he decided to provide the background to Moab's settlement there and to mention Edom's earlier history also. The Emites, he said, once lived there (2:10). They, like the Anakites (cf. 1:28), were a giant people. Their name ('emim [TH368, ZH400]) appears to be derived from a root meaning "frighten" (KBL 38; Tigay 1996:27). The Emites were a frightful, terror-inspiring race.

Sometimes, Moses said, the Emites (and the Anakites) were called Rephaites, but the Moabites preferred the term Emites (2:11). "Rephaites" describes many gigantic peoples (see note on 2:11); it is a word used also to refer to inhabitants of the netherworld who exist as spirits or ghosts (Talmon 1983). Perhaps the frightening size and behavior of certain races of giants called to mind the underworld spirits who thus gave them their name. It is difficult to know, therefore, whether Rephaites was the actual ethnic name of a people or an epithet loosely applied to giants because they were so frightening.

Continuing with his discourse, Moses related that the indigenous population of Mount Seir (another name for Edom; see note on 1:44) had been Horite. The Horites are sometimes identified with a well-known people of the ancient Near East known as Hurrians (see note on 2:1). Esau's descendants expelled the Horites (2:12) and replaced them. To make clear that God's purposes for Moab and Edom were somehow linked to his plan for Israel, Moses said that these two nations had driven out the original populations just as Israel did. The expulsion of the Canaanite people was only a prospect from that historical vantage-point, however, so Moses must have had in mind Israel's conquest of the Transjordan that had recently taken place (see note on 2:12).

The next turning point in the itinerary to the Land of Promise was the crossing of the Zered Brook (2:13), a milestone that occurred 38 years after Israel had first settled in Kadesh-barnea (2:14). More significant, by that time all the warriors of the Exodus generation had died, making possible the advance into Canaan. That generation included men who were 20 years old and older at the time of Israel's rebellion at the beginning of the sojourn at Kadesh-barnea (Num 14:26-35). Since this was 38 years earlier, the youngest of them would be 58. They and all those who were older passed from the scene because "the LORD had lifted his hand against them" (2:15, lit.). In Hebrew metaphor, the hand symbolized power. God had exercised his power, not to bless and heal, but to destroy.

♦   8. Instruction concerning Ammon (2:16-25)

16"When all the men of fighting age had died, 17the LORD said to me, 18"Today you will cross the border of Moab at Ar 19and enter the land of the Ammonites, the descendants of Lot. But do not bother them or start a war with them. I have given the land of Ammon to them as their property, and I will not give you any of their land.' "

20(That area was once considered the land of the Rephaites, who had lived there, though the Ammonites call them Zamzummites. 21They were also as strong and numerous and tall as the Anakites. But the LORD destroyed them so the Ammonites could occupy their land. 22He had done the same for the descendants of Esau who lived in Seir, for he destroyed the Horites so they could settle there in their place. The descendants of Esau live there to this day. 23A similar thing happened when the Caphtorites from Crete* invaded and destroyed the Avvites, who had lived in villages in the area of Gaza.)

24Moses continued, "Then the LORD said, 'Now get moving! Cross the Arnon Gorge. Look, I will hand over to you Sihon the Amorite, king of Heshbon, and I will give you his land. Attack him and begin to occupy the land. 25Beginning today I will make people throughout the earth terrified because of you. When they hear reports about you, they will tremble with dread and fear.' "

2:23 Hebrew *from Caphtor.*

NOTES

2:18 border of Moab. At that time, Moab's southern border with Edom was the Zered Brook (see note on 2:13). The northern border (so this passage) was at Ar, otherwise called Aroer (see note on 2:9). The ruins of the site (known today as Ara'ir) are on the northern edge of the great Arnon Valley, which actually formed the border between Moab and Ammon. In other texts the Arnon (now Wadi Mujib) is said to have separated Moab from the Amorites (see Num 21:13). Both descriptions are correct because Ammon lay east of Amorite territory, both having a common border with Moab.

2:20 Zamzummites. The Rephaites, whom the Moabites called Emites (2:11), were called Zamzummites by the Ammonites. If the name is related to the Arabic root *zamam,* "to murmur," this could be a way of referring to the Rephaites as "murmurers," that is, as barbarians—those whose language is unintelligible and thus inferior (KBL 259; cf. BDB 273). The name occurs only here.

2:23 Crete. As the NLT mg indicates, the text reads Caphtor, the identity of which is without doubt the island of Crete. The location of the Caphtorites here "in the area of Gaza" points clearly to their being early Philistines, that is, Philistines who preceded those who 300 years later caused difficulty for Samson, Samuel, and then Saul and David (Merrill 1987:41-42). The Table of Nations links the Philistines and Caphtorites (Gen 10:14). Jeremiah 47:4 describes the Philistines as colonists from Crete (Caphtor), and Amos 9:7 categorically affirms that Yahweh "brought the Philistines from Crete [Caphtor]."

villages in the area of Gaza. The LXX (B) reads here *Asēdōth* (Ashdod) for the MT's *khatserim* [TH2691, ZH2958] (villages). Other LXX witnesses read *Hasērōth* (Hazeroth), a city name. The MT and NLT's "villages" appears suitable.

2:24 Heshbon. Now known as Hesban, this important site is in modern Jordan, about 15 miles SSW of Amman.

COMMENTARY

As though the death of the last remaining warriors was a signal (see 2:14), Yahweh instructed Moses to cross the Arnon Valley in the vicinity of Ar (Aroer) and enter Ammon (2:16-19a). Since Ammon extended a long way east into the Syro-Arabian desert, there was no way Israel could circumvent Ammonite territory in that direction. To try to do so by going around the western side would bring Israel into the land of the Amorites. They must, then, go straight through Ammon, but as with Edom (2:5) and Moab (2:9), they must leave the Ammonites alone. They were kinfolk to Israel, and Yahweh had also given them their land as an inviolable trust (2:19).

Moab was one son of Lot by a daughter (2:9; Gen 19:37), and Ammon was another son by a second daughter (Gen 19:38). Even this unsavory origin placed Ammon in special relationship to Israel and so, as "members of the family," they must not be harmed. Again, as with Edom and Moab, however, Ammon from time to time was later brought under Israelite military and political domination (1 Sam 11:11; 2 Sam 8:12; 2 Chr 27:5).

In another digression, Moses reflected on an earlier time and recollected that the land of Ammon had once been occupied by Rephaites, as had Moab (2:20). The Ammonites called them Zamzummites, however, perhaps because they were impressed by their barbarity (see note on 2:20). They were a giant people like the Anakites (cf. 2:10), but Yahweh had destroyed them so that the Ammonites could have their land (2:21). He had done the same for Esau's descendants in Mount Seir (Edom), expelling the indigenous Horites (2:22), and for that matter had even paved the way for the Caphtorites to invade the Mediterranean coastal area and drive out the Avvites (2:23). What is remarkable is that Israel's conquest of Canaan was not absolutely unique. Yahweh, the God of all the nations, moved others about as well, according to his sovereign pleasure.

The Caphtorites were early Philistines (see note on 2:23) who settled in and about Gaza, on the lower Mediterranean coast. The Avvites, whom they displaced, are otherwise unknown (cf. Josh 13:3; 18:23; 2 Kgs 17:31). These Philistines were the same stock as those encountered by Abraham and Isaac (Gen 21:32; 26:1, 8, 14, 18); they must be distinguished from those who later encountered the judges and kings of Israel (see note on 2:23).

Resuming the main narrative, Moses harkened back to the day Israel crossed the Arnon and prepared to do battle with the Amorite king, Sihon of Heshbon (2:24). The Amorites were a Semitic people who originated in what is now Syria and who appear to have migrated in large numbers to Canaan around 2200–2000 BC. When Abraham came to Canaan, he found the Canaanites living throughout the land, but by Moses's time the Canaanites had been forced out by the Amorites and restricted to the valleys and plains (see note on 1:7). They obviously were occupying the high plateaus of Transjordan, at least in the region just north and east of the Dead Sea (Schoville 1994:164-167).

Not being related to Israel, the Amorites were not under Yahweh's protection; therefore, their land could be taken by Israel. Moses gave the command to attack

Sihon and seize his lands (2:24). Success in this venture, he said, would reverberate throughout the region, and all who heard would become terrified of Israel (2:25). Later, Rahab of Jericho would testify to the panic that had set in among the Canaanites when they heard that Israel was about to undertake the conquest (Josh 2:9).

◆   ## 9. Defeat of Sihon, king of Heshbon (2:26-37)

26Moses continued, "From the wilderness of Kedemoth I sent ambassadors to King Sihon of Heshbon with this proposal of peace:

27'Let us travel through your land. We will stay on the main road and won't turn off into the fields on either side. 28Sell us food to eat and water to drink, and we will pay for it. All we want is permission to pass through your land. 29The descendants of Esau who live in Seir allowed us to go through their country, and so did the Moabites, who live in Ar. Let us pass through until we cross the Jordan into the land the LORD our God is giving us.'

30"But King Sihon of Heshbon refused to allow us to pass through, because the LORD your God made Sihon stubborn and defiant so he could help you defeat him, as he has now done.

31"Then the LORD said to me, 'Look, I have begun to hand King Sihon and his land over to you. Begin now to conquer and occupy his land.'

32"Then King Sihon declared war on us and mobilized his forces at Jahaz. 33But the LORD our God handed him over to us, and we crushed him, his sons, and all his people. 34We conquered all his towns andcompletely destroyed* everyone—men, women, and children. Not a single person was spared. 35We took all the livestock as plunder for ourselves, along with anything of value from the towns we ransacked.

36"The LORD our God also helped us conquer Aroer on the edge of the Arnon Gorge, and the town in the gorge, and the whole area as far as Gilead. No town had walls too strong for us. 37However, we avoided the land of the Ammonites all along the Jabbok River and the towns in the hill country—all the places the LORD our God had commanded us to leave alone.

2:34 The Hebrew term used here refers to the complete consecration of things or people to the LORD, either by destroying them or by giving them as an offering.

NOTES

2:27 *stay on the main road.* The MT reads literally "by the way, by the way" (*badderek badderek* [TH1870, ZH2006]). The LXX omits the repetition, and the notes in BHS suggest a scribal error occurred (homoeoteleuton), preferring to read the phrase as *badderek hammelek* ("by the King's Highway"), in light of the wording of the original narrative (Num 21:22). While this makes good sense, the textual evidence supporting the MT is strong, and the Hebrew use of doubling for emphasis is quite common (see 7:22; 14:22; 15:20; 25:13; and Waltke and O'Connor 1990:115-116).

2:30 *stubborn and defiant.* The MT reads "hardened his spirit and hardened his heart [= mind]." The verbs are different (*qashah* [TH7185, ZH7996], "harden"; and *'amets* [TH553, ZH599] "make obstinate"; respectively) but synonymous, meaning "to make stubborn" (as in NLT). "Spirit" (*ruakh* [TH7307, ZH8120]) and "heart" (*lebab* [TH3824, ZH4222]) are also commonly synonymous (KBL 878b), so the overall effect here is emphasis: Yahweh made Sihon "extremely stubborn," or the like. The causative nuance (Hiphil stem) is theologically significant. Sihon was an instrument in God's hand, whose stubbornness, brought on by God (probably because of Sihon's own impenitence), became the occasion for Israel's victory over him. The verb *qashah* [TH7185, ZH7996] is used the same way to describe the hardening of the pharaoh's heart (Exod 7:3).

2:34 completely destroyed. The verb form here (a Hiphil of *kharam* [TH2763, ZH3049]) is a technical term to describe annihilation ordered by the Lord and done on his behalf. Sometimes it is rendered "place under the ban," meaning to give over to the Lord whoever or whatever has become the object of his wrath and judgment (NIDOTTE 2.276-277). The concept is tied closely to that of so-called holy war (e.g., 3:6; 7:2; 13:15 [16]; 20:17).

2:37 Jabbok River. This river, about halfway between the Sea of Galilee and the Dead Sea, flows into the Jordan River from the east. It marked the traditional border between the Ammonites to the south and the kingdom of Bashan to the north (Num 21:24) and between Israel's eastern tribes and Ammon (3:16; Josh 12:2). It is now known as Nahr ez-Zerqa.

COMMENTARY

Still reviewing the past, Moses recounts how he had sent a delegation to King Sihon seeking a peaceful resolution to their impending confrontation (2:26). Moses was at Kedemoth at that time (perhaps modern 'Aleiyan, less than five miles north of Aroer; see note on 2:9). He offered "words of peace" (thus MT), a technical term for making a treaty. "If we can pass through your land," he said, "we will stick straight to the roadway and will pay for all supplies we need" (2:27-28).

With some exaggeration, perhaps, Moses says that his request is not unreasonable, for a precedent had already been set: Both Edom and Moab had allowed Israel to traverse their territories (2:29). It is true that Israel had passed through the eastern edges of those respective lands (see 2:8), but it is a little misleading to imply that they had traveled by the King's Highway through Edom and Moab as they were requesting to do (see note on 2:27). If Moses was guilty of stretching the truth here, it is important to remember that there is no divine sanction for it (anywhere at anytime), nor does this suggest a pattern of morality to be followed by others. Moses was simply a human being like the rest of us, and he had the same tendency to cut ethical corners at times.

All his appeals fell on deaf ears anyway; Moses soon learned of Sihon's denial of the request. Added to Sihon's natural disinclination to allow Israel to pass through his land was Yahweh's supernatural intervention. He made Sihon to become stubborn (see note on 2:30) precisely so he would be noncompliant and thus bring disaster on himself. God's purpose was for Israel to occupy Amorite land, an occupation that presupposed Sihon's defeat and annihilation.

Once Sihon's intransigence was apparent, Yahweh instructed Moses to begin the battle—for Yahweh had already commenced to deliver Sihon over to Israel (2:31). This was done by hardening his heart so that he would immediately begin to resist. Moses had to take the initiative and to do so quickly. The Hebrew of 2:31 makes this especially clear: "Begin! Take the possession!"

The battle site was Jahaz, possibly a site about 12 miles north of Aroer (see Josh 13:18; 21:36; Isa 15:4). The outcome was no contest: Yahweh, commander of Israel's armies, brought about the defeat of the Amorites (2:33). The hardening of Sihon, the command to Moses to launch the battle, and the devastating results for the Amorites—all are clues that this is "holy war" (sometimes called "Yahweh war"). This was battle for the purpose of asserting Yahweh's dominion over hostile and irremedially unrepentant forces of evil that would attempt to interdict that lordship (Craigie 1978:45-54). It was particularly directed against the inhabitants of the Promised Land such as the Amorites and Canaanites (see 7:1; 20:16-18).

The result of holy war, if properly prosecuted, was the complete destruction of its targets. Sometimes (as here) this was limited to the people only (2:34), but at other times livestock and even material objects such as buildings and city walls were razed to the ground. Jericho, Ai, and Hazor are the only examples in the Old Testament of the full implementation of such war (see, respectively, Josh 6:21-24; 8:24-29; 11:10-15). The verb invariably employed to speak of the waging of holy war is *kharam* [TH2763, ZH3049], usually in its causative (Hiphil) form (see note on 2:34). It means to deliver something over to Yahweh for destruction or for his exclusive use. In this instance, the livestock were not under the ban, nor were valuables that were seized from the various Amorite settlements (2:35).

The concept of holy war (and for that matter, war in general) is repugnant to many people who find it incompatible with the message of the gospel. However, the gospel also speaks of severe divine judgment against all who spurn the overtures of God's grace (e.g., John 3:36; cf. Rev 20:11-15). The judgment reserved to an eschatological age in the New Testament often found more immediate, historical expression in the Old Testament. The principle is exactly the same in both: A holy God has no recourse in the face of hopeless unrepentance but to destroy such wickedness from his presence. This included even "innocent" children (2:34) because these people, God foreknew, would also never embrace the true and living one but, to the contrary, would become a trap ensnaring God's own people in idolatry and apostasy (7:16).

Moses summarized the Amorite campaign by describing the conquest and occupation of all the land from Aroer (see 2:16-19) to Gilead—that is, to the Jabbok River (see note on 2:37). Eventually, this was assigned to the tribes of Reuben and Gad (3:12; Num 32:28-33). However, the Israelites stayed clear of the Ammonites who lived to the north and east of the Jabbok, because their land was to be left to them by divine command (2:37; cf. 2:19). The "hill country" referred to here is not that in Canaan, which was commonly so described. Rather, it pertains to the high elevations of the Transjordan regions.

◆   ## 10. Defeat of Og, king of Bashan (3:1-11)

"Next we turned and headed for the land of Bashan, where King Og and his entire army attacked us at Edrei. ²But the LORD told me, 'Do not be afraid of him, for I have given you victory over Og and his entire army, and I will give you all his land. Treat him just as you treated King Sihon of the Amorites, who ruled in Heshbon.'

³"So the LORD our God handed King Og and all his people over to us, and we killed them all. Not a single person survived. ⁴We conquered all sixty of his towns—the entire Argob region in his kingdom of Bashan. Not a single town escaped our conquest. ⁵These towns were all fortified with high walls and barred gates. We also took

many unwalled villages at the same time. ⁶We completely destroyed* the kingdom of Bashan, just as we had destroyed King Sihon of Heshbon. We destroyed all the people in every town we conquered—men, women, and children alike. ⁷But we kept all the livestock for ourselves and took plunder from all the towns.

⁸"So we took the land of the two Amorite kings east of the Jordan River—all the way from the Arnon Gorge to Mount Hermon. ⁹(Mount Hermon is called Sirion by the Sidonians, and the Amorites call it Senir.) ¹⁰We had now conquered all the cities on the plateau and all Gilead and Bashan, as far as the towns of Salecah and Edrei, which were part of Og's kingdom in Bashan. ¹¹(King Og of Bashan was the last survivor of the giant Rephaites. His bed was made of iron and was more than thirteen feet long and six feet wide.* It can still be seen in the Ammonite city of Rabbah.)

3:6 The Hebrew term used here refers to the complete consecration of things or people to the LORD, either by destroying them or by giving them as an offering. Also in 3:6b.   3:11 Hebrew *9 cubits* [4.1 meters] *long and 4 cubits* [1.8 meters] *wide.*

NOTES

3:1 *Edrei.* Now usually identified with Der'a in modern Syria, this city lay on the upper Yarmuk Valley, about six miles northeast of Ramoth-gilead (Bimson 1995:107). It was later assigned to the allotment of the tribe of Manasseh (Josh 13:31). In Moses's time, it was a capital of Og's kingdom (1:4).

3:4 *Argob region.* Most scholars locate this area in the upper Bashan, east of the Jordan River and south of Mount Hermon. It shared the Golan Heights with ancient Geshur (Bimson 1995:36; cf. 1 Kgs 4:13).

3:9 *Sirion . . . Senir.* These alternative names for the Anti-Lebanon mountains in general or Mount Hermon in particular illustrate the difficulties of ancient toponymy (Noth 1966:60). Hermon is so dominant (over 9,000 feet high) that it can be seen from many different vantage points in surrounding nations. Each area, then, would tend to lend its name to the mountain. The name Sirion was given it by the Sidonians, a Phoenician people. It is worth noting that David employs this name for Hermon in Psalm 29:6, a psalm believed to have many Phoenician (or Ugaritic) connections. Senir, the Amorite designation, occurs also in the OT as a poetic name for Hermon (Song 4:8).

3:11 *bed.* The word *'eres* [TH6210, ZH6911], usually translated "bed," has long been problematic since the word actually refers more generically to a framework of some kind (KBL 739). Among other options, it has been suggested that Og's final resting place was a basalt sarcophagus, described as iron because its color is sometimes iron-like (Millard 1988:481-492).

COMMENTARY

The third of the three campaigns in the Transjordan designed to claim the region for Israelite occupation was directed against Bashan and its king Og. The Bashanites are ethnically identified later as Amorites (3:8), and they suffered the same policy of extermination of the Amorites that had already been set in motion against Sihon (2:34). Bashan was located between the Yarmuk River (not mentioned by name in the OT) to the south and Mount Hermon to the north and east of the Great Rift Valley. Its capital was Edrei (see note on 3:1).

Yahweh had already granted great success in war against Sihon of Heshbon, so Israel needed have no fear in confronting Og (3:2). Furthermore, Og was to be dealt with as Sihon had been—that is, by holy war. Armed with this assurance, Israel went forth, defeated Og, and occupied all of Bashan, including Argob (see note on 3:4).

The latter consisted of 60 "cities," a translation of the term 'ir [TH5892, ZH6551] that may be somewhat grandiose in terms of modern sociology (Frick 1977:30-39). Perhaps "settlements" is preferable in most cases, though usually an 'ir at least had defensive walls. Here the 60 settlements meet the criterion of city status because of their fortifications (3:5). In addition, many unwalled villages were taken. All were put to the ban (see NLT note on 3:6), but as in the earlier Amorite battles, only the people were destroyed (3:6). Livestock and valuables were preserved and distributed (3:7).

In sum, Moses said that by then the whole Transjordan had fallen to Israel, at least that part ruled by Sihon and Og (3:8). This vast area extended from the Arnon to Mount Hermon, a distance from south to north of about 150 miles. The parenthetical information about Hermon's other names may be for the purpose of drawing attention to the height and massiveness of this famous peak (see note on 3:9). More specifically, Moses said, all the cities of the "plateau" (mishor [TH4334, ZH4793], a term especially used of the Transjordan plateaus; cf. 4:43; Josh 13:9, 16-20; 20:8; Aharoni 1979:39) and all of Gilead and Bashan had been taken. The extent of Bashan is described as extending to Edrei (cf. 3:1) and Salecah (3:10). The latter place (also spelled Salcah; modern Salkhad; Bimson 1995:267) is about 30 miles east of Edrei, deep in the Hauran desert. These would be on a line marking Bashan's southern boundary.

Finally, and with King Og still in mind, a bit of historical information appears, which is most likely a post-Mosaic insertion (3:11). Almost legendary to the historian, Og is described as the last of the Rephaites (see note on 2:11). So huge was he that his bed (or sarcophagus; see note on 3:11) was nine cubits long and four cubits wide (or about 13 x 6 feet, as in NLT). Any skeptic could look for himself by going to Rabbah, the capital city of Ammon (modern Amman, Jordan). There the artifact was still on view, perhaps in a museum. Since Rabbah was not the Ammonite capital until the time of David or a little earlier, this verse must have originated around that time.

◆   ## 11. Distribution of the Transjordanian allotments (3:12-17)

¹²"When we took possession of this land, I gave to the tribes of Reuben and Gad the territory beyond Aroer along the Arnon Gorge, plus half of the hill country of Gilead with its towns. ¹³Then I gave the rest of Gilead and all of Bashan—Og's former kingdom—to the half-tribe of Manasseh. (This entire Argob region of Bashan used to be known as the land of the Rephaites. ¹⁴Jair, a leader from the tribe of Manasseh, conquered the whole Argob region in Bashan, all the way to the border of the Geshurites and Maacathites. Jair renamed this region after himself, calling it the Towns of Jair,* as it is still known today.) ¹⁵I gave Gilead to the clan of Makir. ¹⁶But I also gave part of Gilead to the tribes of Reuben and Gad. The area I gave them extended from the middle of the Arnon Gorge in the south to the Jabbok River on the Ammonite frontier. ¹⁷They also received the Jordan Valley, all the way from the Sea of Galilee down to the Dead Sea,* with the Jordan River serving as the western boundary. To the east were the slopes of Pisgah.

3:14 Hebrew Havvoth-jair.   3:17 Hebrew from Kinnereth to the Sea of the Arabah, the Salt Sea.

NOTES

3:14 Geshurites and Maacathites. Geshur was an area east of the upper Jordan Valley, likely somewhat west of Argob. Maacah was north of Geshur, not far from Dan and Mount Hermon. In David's time, Maacah was an ally with Ammon in a war with Israel (2 Sam 10:6-8).

Towns of Jair. The word translated "towns" (*khawwoth* [TH2333, ZH2557]) should perhaps be simply transliterated as "Havvoth." The region then would be known as Havvoth-jair [TH2334, ZH2596] (Weinfeld 1991:185; see NLT mg).

as it is still known today. The reference to "Towns of Jair" is probably a later inspired editorial comment.

3:15 Makir. According to Num 32:39, Makir was a son of Manasseh (cf. also Gen 50:23; Num 26:29; 27:1; Josh 13:31; etc.). Since the tribe of Manasseh had two allotments, one east of the Jordan and the other west, various Manasseh clans settled in each. Makir claimed Gilead, while Manasseh's remaining descendants (see the list in Josh 17:2) occupied land in the west.

3:17 Pisgah. This may be another name for Mount Nebo, but more likely it is a lower peak of the same range of which Nebo is the highest (Bimson 1995:254; see 3:27; cf. 34:1).

COMMENTARY

At the time of the conquest of the Transjordan, the tribes of Reuben, Gad, and half of Manasseh had requested of Moses that they be allowed to remain in and settle that region rather than cross the river to Canaan (see Num 32:1-32). After establishing certain guidelines and qualifications, Moses granted the request and then set about allocating their various territories (3:12). Reuben and Gad received land from (not "beyond," as in NLT) Aroer; it and the Arnon Valley established their southern boundary. Moab, of course, was south of the Arnon and was not to be displaced (see 2:8b).

In brief, Moses says that he had split Gilead between Reuben and Gad to the south and Manasseh to the north (3:12-13). The lines of demarcation between Reuben and Gad are not clear (Ashley 1993:615-616). In fact, the account in Numbers suggests that Reubenites lived between Gadite elements (Num 32:33-38). What is clear is that no part of either Gad or Reuben extended north of the Jabbok River. Joshua presents the situation somewhat differently, locating all of Reuben to the south and in possession of all the former kingdom of Sihon (Josh 13:21). Gad, again, was to the north. The accounts are different perhaps because although Moses made the assignments, the implementation of the allotments under Joshua may have taken another form.

Manasseh received "Og's former kingdom" (3:13), which included northern Gilead and all of Bashan. The southernmost boundary was Mahanaim, a town on the Jabbok River (Josh 13:30), and the northern boundary stretched as far as Mount Hermon (cf. 3:8). The two small principalities of Geshur and Maacah, both north and east of the Sea of Galilee, were excluded (see note on 3:14). The main part of Bashan was known as Argob (3:13; cf. note on 3:4). Jair, a Manassehite, located himself there and changed the name of the area to Havvoth-jair (see note on 3:14).

Only half the tribe of Manasseh elected to remain in the Transjordan, a half consisting of the clan of Makir (3:15 and note). They settled in Gilead, that is, the part of Gilead south of Bashan all the way to the Jabbok (cf. 3:13). The remainder of Gilead fell to Reuben and Gad, a vast area from the Arnon to the Jabbok. This time Jabbok must refer to the south–north section of that river, for the Ammonites lived mainly east of the Jabbok (3:16). The river has its source near modern Amman, flows north for about 20 miles, and then flows west to the Jordan. It thus provided the boundary between Ammon and Reuben/Gad on the one hand and between Reuben/Gad and Manasseh on the other.

All three tribes (so 3:17 should be understood) were bordered by the Jordan River on the west, all the way from the Sea of Galilee to the Dead Sea. The "slopes of Pisgah" probably provides a reference point to the southern terminus of that border.

◆   ## 12. Instructions to the Transjordanian tribes (3:18-22)

18"At that time I gave this command to the tribes that would live east of the Jordan: 'Although the LORD your God has given you this land as your property, all your fighting men must cross the Jordan ahead of your Israelite relatives, armed and ready to assist them. 19Your wives, children, and numerous livestock, however, may stay behind in the towns I have given you. 20When the LORD has given security to the rest of the Israelites, as he has to you, and when they occupy the land the LORD your God is giving them across the Jordan River, then you may all return here to the land I have given you.'

21"At that time I gave Joshua this charge: 'You have seen for yourself everything the LORD your God has done to these two kings. He will do the same to all the kingdoms on the west side of the Jordan. 22Do not be afraid of the nations there, for the LORD your God will fight for you.'

NOTES

3:22 *Do not be afraid.* A number of mss and versions suggest a singular form of the verb here since Joshua is the subject addressed in 3:21. However, v. 22 closes with a plural pronoun suffix ("for you"), which supports the plurality of the opening verb. Besides, 3:22 seems to be a summary statement addressed not just to Joshua but to the whole community.

COMMENTARY

Once Moses had finished his allotment of the Transjordan to the two and a half eastern tribes, he responded to their request to settle there permanently by reminding them that they must send their warriors to Canaan with the rest of the tribes to assist them in their conquest (3:18; cf. Num 32:1-27). The rest of the people could remain behind in their protected cities (most likely the meaning of *'ir* [TH5892, ZH6551] here, 3:19) until their soldiers returned. This would be possible once the Canaanite enemies had been defeated, their lands appropriated, and the Israelites had settled in (3:20). The Transjordanian tribes could not return immediately thereafter, however, for their brethren must be "given security" by the Lord. This was one of the pledges that Yahweh had given Moses about the Land of Promise: "I will personally go with you, Moses, and I will give you rest—everything will be fine for you" (Exod 33:14; cf. Heb 4:1-11).

Turning to Joshua, Moses encouraged him about the upcoming conquest by teaching him through history. Just as Sihon and Og (the two kings of 3:21) had been defeated, so would the kings of the west be. The God who proved himself to be faithful and powerful in the past could be trusted to meet every need of the future. There was no need to be afraid (3:22), for the battle was not Israel's but God's. This was to be holy war, a crusade on Yahweh's behalf and one that he directed as commander in chief.

◆   ### 13. Moses denied the Promised Land (3:23-29)

²³"At that time I pleaded with the LORD and said, ²⁴'O Sovereign LORD, you have only begun to show your greatness and the strength of your hand to me, your servant. Is there any god in heaven or on earth who can perform such great and mighty deeds as you do? ²⁵Please let me cross the Jordan to see the wonderful land on the other side, the beautiful hill country and the Lebanon mountains.'

²⁶"But the LORD was angry with me because of you, and he would not listen to me. 'That's enough!' he declared. 'Speak of it no more. ²⁷But go up to Pisgah Peak, and look over the land in every direction. Take a good look, but you may not cross the Jordan River. ²⁸Instead, commission Joshua and encourage and strengthen him, for he will lead the people across the Jordan. He will give them all the land you now see before you as their possession.' ²⁹So we stayed in the valley near Beth-peor.

NOTES

3:24 *O Sovereign LORD*. This highly exalted epithet translates *'adonay yhwh* [TH136/3068, ZH151/3378] (Lord, the LORD). In such cases where Adonai and Yahweh are juxtaposed, the MT's *yhwh* is pointed with the vowels of Elohim (God), and the Qere (oral tradition) suggests reading it as *'elohim* [TH430, ZH466]. Thus, many English versions translate here "O LORD God." NLT better reflects the intention of the written text itself.

3:25 *Lebanon*. This does not refer to the nation Lebanon (which did not exist then) but, as in the NLT, to the Lebanon mountains, the northernmost extremity of the Promised Land.

3:29 *Beth-peor*. This site, about six miles west of Heshbon and the same distance northwest of Nebo, was the place where Israel experimented with the Canaanite cult of Baal-peor (Num 25:1-3). Ironically, Moses was buried in a valley nearby this same place (34:6).

COMMENTARY

Because Moses had struck the rock in the desert rather than merely speaking to it to provide water (see Num 20:2-13), Yahweh had forbidden him to enter Canaan (cf. 1:37-38). Moses could not easily resign himself to that verdict, so he pleaded with God to relent. Addressing him in the most respectful terms, with language displaying his recognition of God's absolute sovereignty (see note on 3:24), Moses cast himself on God's mercy and grace. He declared God's omnipotence—he had power unequalled by any other god (3:24). Moses's reference to another god (*'el* [TH410A, ZH446]) should not lead to the inference that he was not monotheistic. All Moses was saying is that in that pagan world, in which all the surrounding peoples boasted in their pantheons of deities, none of them could claim a god as powerful as Yahweh, God of Israel.

Moses made this appeal to the power of Yahweh in the hope that this power could overturn God's own condemnatory sentence against him. What Moses needed to understand, however, was that this was not a matter of ability but will. God clearly could have reversed himself under certain conditions, but Moses's sin in discrediting the Lord as well as himself would not, in this instance, go unpunished. Moses was surely forgiven—yes, indeed—but the consequences of his sin must remain as a testimony to God's high and holy expectations of men and women whom he places in leadership. The plea to "cross the Jordan to see the wonderful land on the other side" (3:25) would be to no avail, but God would graciously condescend to grant the latter part of the request—that Moses might view the land.

In anger Yahweh told Moses to desist from his entreaties because the matter was settled. The verb expressing the divine displeasure (a Hithpael of 'abar [TH5674A, ZH6297]) is one of the strongest in the Hebrew language. In the Hithpael stem it suggests the idea of displaying fury (KBL 676), almost rage, the vehemence of which sent Moses the clear signal that to beg further would invite disaster. Perhaps to remind the people of their culpability in this turn of events, Moses once more said that his sin in the first place had been "because of you" (cf. 1:37). Close examination of the original episode (Num 20:2-13) reveals that the real reason for Moses's punishment was his failure to communicate to the people the holiness of God (Num 20:12). Rather than the altogether Exalted One who condescended to respond to a word spoken in prayer, the Lord had become in Israel's eyes a mere runner of errands who, like a robot, reacted to the striking of a stone (Harrison 1990:266-267).

Yahweh, nevertheless, conceded to Moses the privilege of viewing the land from afar. "Go up to Pisgah Peak," he said. From that vantage point, Moses could see all the Land of Promise (3:27; see note on 3:17). As for the people, Joshua would lead them across; through him God would grant the conquest and occupation of the land (3:28; cf. 1:38-39).

Thus the historical résumé comes to an end. Moses turns next to exhortation. In light of what had happened, it was important for Israel to know what God expected in the days just ahead.

◆ B. The Exhortation of Moses (4:1-40)
   1. The privileges of the covenant (4:1-8)

"And now, Israel, listen carefully to these decrees and regulations that I am about to teach you. Obey them so that you may live, so you may enter and occupy the land that the LORD, the God of your ancestors, is giving you. ²Do not add to or subtract from these commands I am giving you. Just obey the commands of the LORD your God that I am giving you.

³"You saw for yourself what the LORD did to you at Baal-peor. There the LORD your God destroyed everyone who had worshiped Baal, the god of Peor. ⁴But all of you who were faithful to the LORD

your God are still alive today—every one of you.

⁵"Look, I now teach you these decrees and regulations just as the LORD my God commanded me, so that you may obey them in the land you are about to enter and occupy. ⁶Obey them completely, and you will display your wisdom and intelligence among the surrounding nations. When they hear all these decrees, they will exclaim, 'How wise and prudent are the people of this great nation!' ⁷For what great nation has a god as near to them as the LORD our God is near to us whenever we call on him? ⁸And what great nation has decrees and regulations as righteous and fair as this body of instructions that I am giving you today?

NOTES

4:1 decrees and regulations. These terms translate *khuqqim* [TH2706, ZH2976] and *mishpatim* [TH4941, ZH5477] respectively, terms (with others to be noted below) that are characteristic of OT covenant literature, especially in Deuteronomy. In this section alone, *khuqqim* occurs in 4:1, 5, 6, 8; and *mishpatim* in 4:1, 5, 8. The former derives from the root *khaqaq* [TH2710, ZH2980], having to do with engraving or inscribing. The latter is related to the verb *shapat* [TH8199, ZH9149] (to judge). In Deuteronomy they are essentially synonymous, and they appear interchangeably throughout the OT (TDOT 5.142-143). They are used in covenant contexts as technical terms to speak of covenant stipulations.

4:8 body of instructions. The NLT correctly understands the Hebrew *kol hatorah* [TH8451, ZH9368] here to refer to the collection of stipulations described above as "decrees and regulations" (4:1). In other settings *torah* is synonymous with the five books of Moses or, in its etymological sense, simply means "instruction" (NIDOTTE 4.893).

COMMENTARY

The second major part of Moses's historical review is the lengthy exhortation of 4:1-40. Having recited Yahweh's past dealings with Israel (1:6–3:29), he now urges actions and attitudes based on those experiences. The focus is primarily on the nature (4:15-24) and uniqueness (4:32-40) of God, the one who made covenant with Israel at Horeb (4:9-14) and who will bring judgment (4:25-29) followed by blessing (4:30-31) on those who disobey its mandates.

The exhortation begins with a direct address (Israel) and the imperative verb "listen" (*shama'* [TH8085, ZH9048]), which occurs regularly in Deuteronomy to express the urgency of the covenant requirements (cf. 5:1; 6:4; 9:1; 20:3; 27:9). In Hebrew, the connotation of this verb is not merely to hear but to act upon what is heard, that is, to obey. What is to be obeyed in this instance are the "decrees and regulations" (see note on 4:1) that Yahweh is about to teach the assembly through Moses. Obedience to them will allow the people to live (as opposed to their parents who died in the desert; cf. 1:34-36). Their survival would result in their successful entry into and conquest of the Promised Land (4:1).

The obedience, moreover, must be precisely according to Yahweh's instructions, no more and no less (4:2). It must conform to his commands. This third technical term (*mitswoth* [TH4687, ZH5184], from *tsawah* [TH6680, ZH7422], "command"; KBL 797), along with "decrees" and "regulations," also refers to the whole body of covenant stipulations (cf. 4:40; 5:10, 29, 31; 6:1, 2, 17, 25; 7:9, 11; 8:1, 2, 6, 11; 10:13). As an example of what happens when the covenant is violated, Moses cited the incident at Baal-peor

(4:3), the full account of which is narrated in Numbers 25. Peor is a place name (see note on 3:29) referring to an area in Moab where the god Baal was worshiped. "Baal" is technically a term meaning "lord" and so is not a proper name (Ringgren 1973:131). Frequently, the term "baal" is part of place names where local deities were enshrined, in the case of Baal-peor probably Chemosh, head of the Moabite pantheon (cf. Num 21:29; Judg 11:24; 1 Kgs 11:33; 2 Kgs 23:13; Jer 48:13). Early in Israel's occupation of Moab, they had become involved in the Baal rituals at Peor, an act of apostasy that led to the death of thousands of them (Num 25:9). Those who had not succumbed were still alive, a testimony to the blessing of obedience (4:4).

So as to impress upon the assembly the need for obedience, Moses virtually repeated the exhortation of 4:1 and underscored the authority of the decrees and regulations by alluding to their divine origin (4:5). The past tense ("commanded") might suggest the first giving of the covenant at Sinai, but more likely Moses was relating a revelation just given him recently, namely, the covenant renewal text of Deuteronomy itself.

Obedience to the covenant demands would result in Israel's wisdom and understanding being manifest to the world (4:6). "Wisdom" (khokmah [TH2451, ZH2683]) pertains to a knowledge of and relationship to God (cf. 1:13; Ps 111:10; Prov 9:10). "Understanding" (binah [TH998, ZH1069]) is frequently synonymous, though its meaning usually has a more "practical" bent—wisdom applied (TDOT 2.103). Admiration of Israel's spiritual sagacity should naturally elicit the admiration of God, the source of such wisdom, especially in his immanence or relatedness (4:7). The holy and transcendent one is at the same time the God who hears and answers prayer. But another mark of his intimacy with his people is his revelation to them of the body of laws (see note on 4:8) he is about to share with them, laws described as righteous. Righteous law is law that sets a standard of behavior expectation, one commensurate with God's own holy character.

◆ ## 2. Reminder of the Horeb covenant (4:9-14)

9"But watch out! Be careful never to forget what you yourself have seen. Do not let these memories escape from your mind as long as you live! And be sure to pass them on to your children and grandchildren. 10Never forget the day when you stood before the LORD your God at Mount Sinai,* where he told me, 'Summon the people before me, and I will personally instruct them. Then they will learn to fear me as long as they live, and they will teach their children to fear me also.'

11"You came near and stood at the foot of the mountain, while flames from the mountain shot into the sky. The mountain was shrouded in black clouds and deep darkness. 12And the LORD spoke to you from the heart of the fire. You heard the sound of his words but didn't see his form; there was only a voice. 13He proclaimed his covenant—the Ten Commandments*—which he commanded you to keep, and which he wrote on two stone tablets. 14It was at that time that the LORD commanded me to teach you his decrees and regulations so you would obey them in the land you are about to enter and occupy.

4:10 Hebrew Horeb, another name for Sinai; also in 4:15.   4:13 Hebrew the ten words.

NOTES

4:13 *covenant.* Though the covenant idea is dominant in Deuteronomy, this is the first occurrence of the word translated "covenant" (*berith* [TH1285, ZH1382]). Hereafter it occurs commonly in the book (4:23, 31; 5:2, 3; 7:9, 12; 8:18; 9:9, 11, 15; 10:8; 17:2; 29:1, 9, 12, 14, 15, 18, 21, 25; 31:9, 16, 20, 25, 26; 33:9). Its etymology and fundamental meaning have to do with the idea of linking or yoking together (TDOT 2.253). For a discussion of the nature of the covenant in Deuteronomy, see the Introduction.

COMMENTARY

The urgency of covenant commitment finds expression again in the pointed language of this text: "Watch out! Be careful never to forget what you yourself have seen" (4:9). The people must never forget what they had seen and learned; moreover, they must transmit what they knew to the generations to come (cf. 6:4-9, 20-25). A nation that forgets its past is doomed to repeat its failures, and a people that fails to pass on its righteous principles has no right to expect a continuation of those principles in the life and experience of its descendants.

The most important thing for Israel to remember was the decisive moment when Yahweh made covenant with them at Horeb (or Sinai; see note on 1:2). This was decisive because in this experience Israel learned two important lessons: To fear God and to know his will (4:10). To fear God primarily communicates the notion of reverence and not stark terror, but here both ideas come into view. Instruction in the covenant would instill a proper regard for the awesomeness and holiness of God (lit., "I will make them hear . . . so that they will learn to fear me," 4:10), but the encounter at Sinai was itself a cause of overwhelming terror (4:11), a point clearly made in the original narrative (Exod 19:16). The awful display of celestial and terrestrial upheaval testified to both God's transcendence and his immanence (Barth 1991:120-122).

The remoteness of the Lord was seen in the cloud and his nearness in the fire. From the fire he spoke, just as he had spoken to Moses from the burning bush (Exod 3:1-6), but his openness to the people was balanced by his hiddenness. As Moses recalled it, they saw no form of God but only heard a voice (4:12). This tension of divine accessibility and inaccessibility is a major theme of biblical theology (cf. Exod 33:17-23; 1 Kgs 19:9-14), one that reaches its climax in the incarnation of our Lord who, as the God-man, bridged the two ideas.

The voice from the fire proclaimed the covenant message, a revelation epitomized in the Ten Commandments and inscribed on two stone tablets (4:13). It is likely, as some scholars argue, that the tablets were duplicates, one copy for Israel and the other, as it were, for Yahweh (Kline 1972:117-121). As in any legal transaction, both parties to the arrangement should have a copy of the instruments of agreement for future reference.

Still reflecting on the Sinai experience, Moses recalls that in addition to the Ten Commandments (Exod 20:1-17), God had revealed "decrees and regulations" (cf. 4:1) that Israel must learn and obey. These were the stipulations of the Sinai covenant, a section commonly described as the "Book of the Covenant" (Exod 20:22–23:33).

The use of that pair of words prepared the way for Moses's introduction of the renewal of the covenant, a matter he addresses at the end of this chapter (4:44-45).

◆ ## 3. The nature of Israel's God (4:15-24)

¹⁵"But be very careful! You did not see the LORD's form on the day he spoke to you from the heart of the fire at Mount Sinai. ¹⁶So do not corrupt yourselves by making an idol in any form—whether of a man or a woman, ¹⁷an animal on the ground, a bird in the sky, ¹⁸a small animal that scurries along the ground, or a fish in the deepest sea. ¹⁹And when you look up into the sky and see the sun, moon, and stars—all the forces of heaven—don't be seduced into worshiping them. The LORD your God gave them to all the peoples of the earth. ²⁰Remember that the LORD rescued you from the iron-smelting furnace of Egypt in order to make you his very own people and his special possession, which is what you are today.

²¹"But the LORD was angry with me because of you. He vowed that I would not cross the Jordan River into the good land the LORD your God is giving you as your special possession. ²²You will cross the Jordan to occupy the land, but I will not. Instead, I will die here on the east side of the river. ²³So be careful not to break the covenant the LORD your God has made with you. Do not make idols of any shape or form, for the LORD your God has forbidden this. ²⁴The LORD your God is a devouring fire; he is a jealous God.

NOTES

4:16 *idol.* This word, *pesel* [TH6459, ZH7181], is related to the verb *pasal* [TH6458, ZH7180], "carve" or "hew" (KBL 769-770). This kind of image, then, is one manufactured from wood, stone, or even metal. The "form" of God mentioned in 4:15 (cf. also 4:12) is much more generic, pertaining to any kind of representation, whether divine, human, or animal.

4:20 *furnace.* The word *kur* [TH3564, ZH3929] is cognate to Akkadian *kuru* and, like it, refers not to a source of heat but to a crucible in which precious metals were melted down and freed of their impurities (CAD 8.571). Egypt was such a crucible, a place God used to purify his people and make them more fit for servanthood (cf. Gen 15:13-16; 50:19-21; 1 Kgs 8:50-51).

4:21 *I would not cross . . . into the good land.* The NLT smooths over the MT which reads "going into" (participle) instead of the expected "I would go." The LXX and its dependent versions correct MT *bo'* [TH935, ZH995] to *bo'i* in line with the preceding perfect and preterite tense forms.

COMMENTARY

The exhortation continues with essentially the same literary formula as in 4:9: "Be careful." The note of urgency could hardly be more emphatic. This time the warning is about idolatry, a direct violation of the first two commandments (4:16-19; cf. 5:7-10). Moses's argument is *a fortiori:* Since the people of Israel saw no form (*temunah* [TH8544, ZH9454]) of God in his most glorious self-revelation at Sinai (4:15), why should they think they could capture his essence in any kind of image (*pesel* [TH6459, ZH7181]; cf. note on 4:16)?

The warning here is not about the worship of other gods but about the misguided attempt to represent Yahweh himself by means of forms or statues. The order in which Moses lists the possibilities of divine representation is descending—from humankind through the lowest life forms (4:16b-18) and even to inanimate creation (4:19a). All these are physical, material, and created. How can they possibly capture the essence of the invisible, ineffable Creator? Thus, all creation—whether terrestrial or celestial—is off limits in terms of making likenesses for worship. In fact, the heavenly bodies, rather than being objects of worship, were created to serve the human race (4:19b). The creation narrative itself reveals their purpose: "Let lights appear in the sky to separate the day from the night. Let them be signs to mark the seasons, days, and years" (Gen 1:14; cf. Deut 4:19). The human tendency always is to worship the creature rather than the Creator, a tendency that, if unchecked, leads to every kind of moral and spiritual debauchery (Rom 1:21-32). Moses here says that if the people engage in idolatry, they will corrupt themselves (4:16).

Even before Jacob and his family settled in Egypt, they had begun to be tainted by the Canaanite environment in which they lived (see Gen 35:22; 38:1-30). Yahweh had caused them to go to Egypt, which, because it was a crucible (see note on 4:20), became to them a place of purification. The dross of their pagan predispositions was burned away, and they became a people suitable for servanthood. As the text puts it, Israel had come out of the iron furnace as a people qualified to enjoy the inheritance God had prepared for them (4:20).

Once more, however, Moses lamented his inability to participate in that inheritance. Because the Lord was angry with him for unadvisedly striking the rock to get water for the people (cf. 1:37; 3:26), Moses would not enter the Land of Promise (4:21). Instead, he would die where he was, in the Transjordan (4:22). This third reference to his exclusion from the land underscores the indescribable disappointment and regret Moses must have felt. So near and yet so far! But sin, though forgiven, always leaves some scar, some reminder of its abhorrence to a holy God and the price that must be paid as a result.

Moses used his experience as a warning to the people (4:23). As he had disobeyed God by striking the rock, they could do so by breaking the covenant that he had made with them. Most particular and most serious was the prospect of breaking the underlying principle of the covenant—the uniqueness and exclusiveness of Yahweh. The verb translated "break" (4:23) is *shakakh* [TH7911, ZH8894], meaning "to forget." One can become idolatrous, then, merely by benign neglect, simply by forgetting the Lord and all his benefits; for when one forgets God, he or she must fill the void with someone or something else. Even if the void is filled with representations of God, these are so inadequate and limiting as to become substitutes for him. Hence, they become idolatrous.

The intolerable nature of idolatry—even the kind that professes it is done in worship of the true God—is graphically portrayed in the ominous warning of Moses that Yahweh "is a devouring fire; he is a jealous God" (4:24). The words fire (*'esh* [TH784, ZH836]) and jealous (*qanna'* [TH7067, ZH7862]) provide a significant juxtaposition, for 6:15 describes the Lord as a jealous God whose anger flares up like a destructive flame. To practice idolatry is to invite certain and devastating retribution.

◆   ## 4. Threats and blessings (4:25-31)

²⁵"In the future, when you have children and grandchildren and have lived in the land a long time, do not corrupt yourselves by making idols of any kind. This is evil in the sight of the LORD your God and will arouse his anger.

²⁶"Today I call on heaven and earth as witnesses against you. If you break my covenant, you will quickly disappear from the land you are crossing the Jordan to occupy. You will live there only a short time; then you will be utterly destroyed. ²⁷For the LORD will scatter you among the nations, where only a few of you will survive. ²⁸There, in a foreign land, you will worship idols made from wood and stone—gods that neither see nor hear nor eat nor smell. ²⁹But from there you will search again for the LORD your God. And if you search for him with all your heart and soul, you will find him.

³⁰"In the distant future, when you are suffering all these things, you will finally return to the LORD your God and listen to what he tells you. ³¹For the LORD your God is a merciful God; he will not abandon you or destroy you or forget the solemn covenant he made with your ancestors.

NOTES

4:26 *I call on heaven and earth as witnesses*. This phrase anticipates a later literary pattern or form known as a *rib* (controversy). It occurs more fully in other settings that are clearly forensic or judicial in nature and usually in contexts of covenant violation (Limburg 1969:303-304; see, e.g., 30:19; Isa 1:2; 3:13; Jer 2:9). The court setting is implicit here with the adducing of heaven and earth as witnesses. The collocation of heaven and earth is a merism suggesting all of creation.

COMMENTARY

Following up his warning about idolatry (4:15-24), Moses restates the warning and points out again how this most heinous of all sins evokes God's wrath (4:25). His wrath, in turn, will impel him to bring Israel to trial on the charge of breach of (covenant) contract. The whole creation (see note on 4:26), having witnessed the establishment of the covenant in the first place (cf. 30:19), will testify with one voice to Israel's perfidy. If convicted—as surely she will be, given such testimony—Israel will be sentenced to utter ruin and absolute destruction. The intensity suggested by the use of synonymous verbs and their infinitives is overpowering. God's judgment for idolatry will be swift and awful (4:26).

Literal annihilation of all Israel is not in view, however, for the judgment will result primarily in exile, an exile that will nonetheless reduce the nation to only a few in number (4:27). This found fulfillment in later Old Testament times with the Assyrian conquest of Israel in 722 BC and the Babylonian deportation of Judah in 586 BC. The reason for the former is particularly poignant in light of Moses's threats: "They [Israel] did not turn from these sins until the LORD finally swept them away from his presence, just as all his prophets had warned" (2 Kgs 17:22b-23a).

Israel's exile would not immediately cure her of idolatry. In fact, Moses said, it would intensify and take even more reprobate form, for no longer would the lifeless idols of wood and stone represent Yahweh, but they would take his place (4:28).

Presupposed here are the pantheons of deities of the pagan world that were worshiped in the guise of images made by human hands. Their pathetic impotence is seen clearly in their inability to exhibit even the human abilities of hearing, eating, and smelling (cf. Ps 115:4-8; Isa 44:9-17; Jer 10:6-16). But that would not mean the end for Israel, as hopeless as her apostasy might seem to be. In a remarkable linkage of divine initiative and human responsibility, Moses declares flatly, "You will search again for the LORD your God" (4:29)—a statement with no strings attached (cf. Lev 26:40-41a). Yet that seeking must be done sincerely, with the whole being (4:29). This brings human will to bear (cf. Lev 26:41b). The prompting of God to seek him must be followed by one's willingness to do so.

The outcome of this linkage of God's call and Israel's response is left in no doubt, however. At the end of the day, in the age of God's ultimate eschatological triumph (cf. 31:29; Gen 49:1; Num 24:14; Isa 2:2; Ezek 38:16; Dan 10:14; Mic 4:1), Israel unequivocally will return to Yahweh in covenant faithfulness (4:30). The basis for this certainty is not Israel's predictability or Godward tendency—far from it, for Israel's history was one of unremitting defection from the Lord. Rather, Israel's hope would be in Yahweh's mercy (4:31). The tender term used here (*rakhum* [TH7349, ZH8157]) is cognate to the Hebrew word for "womb" (*rekhem* [TH7358, ZH8167]; NIDOTTE 3.1093). The maternal concern Yahweh expresses here for Israel—concern founded on his covenant commitments—is echoed later by Isaiah: "Can a mother forget her nursing child? Can she feel no love for the child she has borne? But even if that were possible, I would not forget you!" (Isa 49:15).

◆   ## 5. The uniqueness of Israel's God (4:32-40)

32"Now search all of history, from the time God created people on the earth until now, and search from one end of the heavens to the other. Has anything as great as this ever been seen or heard before? 33Has any nation ever heard the voice of God* speaking from fire—as you did—and survived? 34Has any other god dared to take a nation for himself out of another nation by means of trials, miraculous signs, wonders, war, a strong hand, a powerful arm, and terrifying acts? Yet that is what the LORD your God did for you in Egypt, right before your eyes.

35"He showed you these things so you would know that the LORD is God and there is no other. 36He let you hear his voice from heaven so he could instruct you. He let you see his great fire here on earth so he could speak to you from it. 37Because he loved your ancestors, he chose to bless their descendants, and he personally brought you out of Egypt with a great display of power. 38He drove out nations far greater than you, so he could bring you in and give you their land as your special possession, as it is today.

39"So remember this and keep it firmly in mind: The LORD is God both in heaven and on earth, and there is no other. 40If you obey all the decrees and commands I am giving you today, all will be well with you and your children. I am giving you these instructions so you will enjoy a long life in the land the LORD your God is giving you for all time."

4:33 Or *voice of a god.*

NOTES

4:32 *people.* Heb., *'adam* [TH120, ZH132], which could refer to Adam as an individual.

4:37 *Because he loved your ancestors.* Though the word for love is the one for ordinary interpersonal affection (*'ahab* [TH157, ZH170]), in the covenant context of Deuteronomy it usually is a synonym for "choose" or "elect" (*bakhar* [TH977, ZH1047]). That is, for God to love Israel is tantamount to saying that he elected Israel as his special people (TDOT 1.114-116). The passage that best demonstrates this connection, perhaps, is 7:7-8: "The LORD did not set his heart on you and choose you because you were more numerous than other nations. . . . Rather, it was simply that the LORD loves (*'ahab* [TH157, ZH170]) you." The difficult idea that God loved Jacob but hated Esau (Mal 1:2-3) is alleviated by understanding love to be choosing and hate to be not choosing.

COMMENTARY

As noted already (4:31), Israel's hope of restoration would be based on Yahweh's covenant faithfulness, the evidence for which is his record throughout history. That record, Moses says, begins with creation itself and ends with him and the people assembled before him. It thus spans all time. In addition, there is a spatial dimension. All of creation—from one horizon to the other (lit., "the edge of the heavens")—likewise offers proof of God's constancy. Whenever or wherever one looks, there is abundant testimony to his power and grace. But the moment at hand, that which commenced at Sinai and continued to the present hour, was of special significance. It was a moment of unprecedented divine activity (4:32).

The whole could be summarized under two headings: what God said (his verbal revelation) and what he did (his revelation in acts and deeds). In a rhetorical question, Moses challenged Israel to think of another occasion in which a god (or, in line with 5:26, God) revealed himself from the midst of fire with no fatal aftereffects (4:33). The reference, of course, is to the Sinai revelation (Exod 19:18-19), an absolutely unique event in the history of the world. Some might dare to challenge this assertion, for it could not easily be publicly documented one way or another. But what is one to say about historical events that had already become widely known?

The events in question are those associated with the Exodus, that mighty act by which God extricated his people from Egypt, the dominant world power of the time (4:34). The list of "terrifying acts" describes the plagues (Exod 7:1–12:30) and attendant events that not only Israel but Egypt also witnessed. Even beyond Egypt the surrounding peoples learned of the awesome glory, grace, and power of Israel's God, and on hearing of them trembled at their implications (cf. 2:25; Exod 18:1; Josh 2:9-10). But the important thing is that Yahweh did these deeds for Israel and in Israel's view so that they could have no doubt as to his elective grace and enabling power.

The reason for this display of word and work was pedagogical, to teach Israel that only Yahweh was God and none other (4:35). The verbal revelation was to provide instruction as to his covenant purposes for Israel, and the visual revelation was to attest to the authenticity of the instruction and to the power of the God who could make such declarations. The reference to fire, again, is to evoke something of the awesome glory and holiness of God, his remoteness from the human and mundane (see 4:11). But the fact that he spoke from the fire teaches his desire to communicate, to bring himself near (4:12).

Foundational to both kinds of revelation was God's choice of Israel in the first place. Israel did not become the people of Yahweh at Sinai; rather, it was because they already were his people that he brought them into the covenant of servanthood. This is the theological message of 4:37. God had loved (i.e., chosen; see note on 4:37) the patriarchal ancestors, and from that love issued the redemption of their descendants, the nation Israel. That such a blessing would take place had already been communicated to Abraham some 600 years earlier (Gen 15:13-16). And when Moses was called to lead Israel out of Egypt, Yahweh called them by such relational terms as "my people" (Exod 3:7, 10; 5:1) and, even more striking, "my firstborn son" (Exod 4:22).

A major element of the ancient Abrahamic covenant was the promise of land. God had told Abraham to "go to the land that I will show you" (Gen 12:1), the land of Canaan, as it turned out. There the Lord instructed the patriarch to "go and walk through the land in every direction, for I am giving it to you" (Gen 13:17). Finally, God told Abraham in unmistakable terms, "I have given this land to your descendants, all the way from the border of Egypt to the great Euphrates River" (Gen 15:18). The Exodus deliverance now made it possible for that aspect of the promise to come to fruition. Already, powerful nations (the Amorites and their kinsmen; cf. 2:31-3:11) had been defeated and their lands possessed by Israel (4:38; cf. 3:12-17).

All of this—the promises and fulfillments—testify to one overriding truth: Yahweh and only Yahweh is God! This truth needed to become deeply engraved in the hearts and minds of the people because the battle was not over yet. The conquest of Canaan lay ahead, and only when that had successfully been completed would the promises of land find their full consummation. But again, it was precisely because Yahweh had proved himself in the past that Israel had grounds for hope in the future.

The call to servanthood carried with it heavy responsibility as well as privilege. The responsibility, already partially spelled out in the Sinai covenant, would find full exposition in the Deuteronomic covenant stipulations about to be revealed. These are the "decrees and commands" already referred to earlier (4:1-2) and mentioned again here (4:40). Obedience to these would be prerequisite to enjoying long life in the land with all its attendant blessings. By implication, of course, one could understand that disobedience would result in severe judgment, even to the extent of deportation to far-flung places (cf. 4:26-28).

◆ III. The Preparation for the Covenant Text (4:41-49)
   A. The Narrative concerning Cities of Refuge (4:41-43)

⁴¹Then Moses set apart three cities of refuge east of the Jordan River. ⁴²Anyone who killed another person unintentionally, without previous hostility, could flee there to live in safety. ⁴³These were the cities: Bezer on the wilderness plateau for the tribe of Reuben; Ramoth in Gilead for the tribe of Gad; Golan in Bashan for the tribe of Manasseh.

NOTES

4:41 *east of the Jordan River.* The Hebrew here (*be'eber* [TH5676, ZH6298] *hayyarden*) means literally "on the other side of the Jordan." However, the phrase became a fixed form meaning Transjordan, even to those Israelites who lived on the east side (see note on 1:1).

COMMENTARY

This section of narrative, itself divided between Moses's allocation of the cities of refuge (4:41-43) and a very brief recapitulation of recent history (4:44-49), is clearly not an element of the covenant text proper, a point noted by virtually all scholars. It is sections like this that should guard one against the tendency to view Deuteronomy as a treaty text in its purest form. It is of such a character, but one generously interspersed with hortatory, narrative, poetic, and other literary genres. Yet these "interruptive" texts are usually so brief and widely distributed as to leave unchallenged the idea that Deuteronomy as a whole is a treaty document (see Introduction).

The cities of refuge are mentioned here perhaps because of the reference in the previous passage to enjoying a long life in the land (4:40). In certain circumstances, one of which is alluded to here, life could be difficult without ameliorating safeguards. The situation in view is that of accidental or unpremeditated homicide. The Hebrew calls it *bibli-da'ath* [TH1847, ZH1981], literally, "without knowledge" (4:42)— that is, in legal terms there was no malice aforethought. The procedures to be carried out in such cases are developed in detail in 19:2-13 (cf. also Num 35:9-29), so they need not be described here.

Eventually, there were to be six cities set apart, three on each side of the river (Josh 20:7-9). Moses's immediate concern was with the Transjordan, so he limited his list to the eastern cities only (Tigay 1996:418-421). They were Bezer (perhaps Bozrah, now Umm el-'Amad, 6 miles east of Heshbon) of Reuben, Ramoth (modern Tel Ramith, 35 miles east of Beth-shan) in Gilead, and Golan (al-Jawlan, about 20 miles east of the Sea of Galilee) in Bashan (4:43). They were distributed in such a way as to provide reasonable access to at least one of them from any place in the Transjordan.

◆   B. The Setting and Introduction (4:44-49)

⁴⁴This is the body of instruction that Moses presented to the Israelites. ⁴⁵These are the laws, decrees, and regulations that Moses gave to the people of Israel when they left Egypt, ⁴⁶and as they camped in the valley near Beth-peor east of the Jordan River. (This land was formerly occupied by the Amorites under King Sihon, who ruled from Heshbon. But Moses and the Israelites destroyed him and his people when they came up from Egypt. ⁴⁷Israel took possession of his land and that of King Og of Bashan—the two Amorite kings east of the Jordan. ⁴⁸So Israel conquered the entire area from Aroer at the edge of the Arnon Gorge all the way to Mount Sirion,* also called Mount Hermon. ⁴⁹And they conquered the eastern bank of the Jordan River as far south as the Dead Sea,* below the slopes of Pisgah.)

4:48 As in Syriac version (see also 3:9); Hebrew reads *Mount Sion.*   4:49 Hebrew *took the Arabah on the east side of the Jordan as far as the sea of the Arabah.*

NOTES

4:48 Mount Sirion. As the NLT mg notes, this follows the Syriac version (cf. ESV, NRSV, GNB). The MT reads "Mount Sion" (*si'on* [TH7865, ZH8481]). This is not to be confused with Mount Zion, which in Hebrew is *tsiyyon* [TH6726, ZH7482]. In 3:9, Mount Hermon was said to be named Sirion (*siryon* [TH8303, ZH8590] by the Sidonians and Senir by the Amorites. There is no textual evidence of a misreading in the MT, so it is likely that "Sion" is just another name, among the others cited, for the imposing Mount Hermon (Bimson 1995:287).

COMMENTARY

The third-person narrative ("Moses" or "he" rather than "I") continues with the summary statement that Moses presented the law (*torah* [TH8451, ZH9368]; 4:44) to Israel, which is a corpus consisting of "laws, decrees, and regulations" (4:45). These terms, as noted already (see 4:1), are heavy with covenant connotation. The structure of 4:44-45 ("This is the body of instruction. . . . These are the laws, decrees, and regulations") is such that one could understand *torah* here as meaning the collection of these elements (Craigie 1976:146).

The reference to the Exodus (4:45b) should not be understood to mean that the Sinai covenant is exclusively in view here, because the ongoing context makes it clear that Moses was also speaking of the so-called Deuteronomic covenant, the one given "near Beth-peor east of the Jordan River" (4:46). The continuing comments about the location of Beth-peor and the historical circumstances that delivered the land over to Israel suggest that this pericope was written later, in post-Mosaic times, so as to provide an explanation as to the occasion for the making of the covenant. All the material in 4:46b-49 is recapitulative of the much more extensive account of the Transjordan conquest found in 2:31–3:11 (cf. also 1:4).

This observation by no means proves the hypothesis of many scholars that the core of Deuteronomy was chapters 5–26, to which were added enveloping prelude and postlude texts, designed to tie the book into the corpus known as the "Deuteronomistic history." It does suggest, however, that inspired redactional activity was occasionally at work to provide retrospective interpretation of crucial historical moments for the benefit of later generations. This section (and perhaps 4:41-43) could be such an example inasmuch as 4:40 leads very naturally into chapter 5.

◆ IV. The Principles of the Covenant (5:1–11:32)
   A. The Opening Exhortation (5:1-5)

Moses called all the people of Israel together and said, "Listen carefully, Israel. Hear the decrees and regulations I am giving you today, so you may learn them and obey them!

²"The LORD our God made a covenant with us at Mount Sinai.* ³The LORD did not make this covenant with our ancestors, but with all of us who are alive today. ⁴At the mountain the LORD spoke to you face to face from the heart of the fire. ⁵I stood as an intermediary between you and the LORD, for you were afraid of the fire and did not want to approach the mountain. He spoke to me, and I passed his words on to you. This is what he said:

5:2 Hebrew *Horeb*, another name for Sinai.

NOTES

5:1 *decrees and regulations.* These technical terms (*khuqqim* [TH2706, ZH2976] and *mishpatim* [TH4941, ZH5477]), are freighted with theological content, drawing attention to the covenant nature of the following discourse. A nearly identical formula introduces Moses's exhortation in 4:1 (cf. also 6:4-6).

5:2 *Mount Sinai.* The MT has Horeb, another name for Sinai (see NLT mg), a name favored in Deuteronomy (9 times; cf. "Sinai," 1 time) but occurring also in Exodus (3 times). There is nothing to support the idea that the alternate names are indicative of source distinctions (e.g., Mayes 1979:115).

COMMENTARY

An indispensable feature of covenant texts is a body of stipulations outlining the responsibilities of the contracting parties. The ancient Near Eastern models relevant to Deuteronomy have (like Deuteronomy) a bifid pattern—a section of general principles followed by extensive examples of cases to which the principles apply (see Introduction). The general principles are set forth in 5:6–11:32, and the specific stipulations in 12:1–26:15. The whole is prefaced by the brief introduction of 5:1-5 (and perhaps 4:44-49).

A noteworthy feature of Hebrew narrative literature is repetition either in whole or in part. The present passage is very much illustrative of this technique. Here Moses has assembled the people together in order to present the terms of the covenant to which they have already assented and to urge upon them the need to learn and obey them (5:1). He then briefly reviewed their history from Sinai to the present moment (5:2-5). The same pattern was elaborated at the beginning of the book with the gathering of the people (1:1-5) to hear "everything the LORD had commanded him to say" (1:3)—that is, the terms of the covenant. Then he presented a lengthy account of the nation's history since the Sinai covenant encounter (1:6–3:29). A much shorter example is that of the apparently later gloss of 4:44-49, where the presentation of the stipulations (4:44-46a) is followed by a brief historical résumé (4:46b-49).

Elements new to the exhortation of 5:1-5 are Moses's observation that the Sinai covenant was a new one—that is, one not known to the patriarchs (5:3)—and his mention of his special mediatorial role (5:5). He had played down that role in the other accounts (4:11-14, 33, 36), though the Exodus narrative makes much of it (Exod 19:3, 20-25; 24:2, 12-13).

◆   **B. The Ten Commandments (5:6-21)**
       1. Commandments pertaining to one's relationship with God (5:6-15)

⁶"I am the LORD your God, who rescued you from the land of Egypt, the place of your slavery.

⁷"You must not have any other god but me.

⁸"You must not make for yourself an idol of any kind, or an image of anything in the heavens or on the earth or in the sea. ⁹You must not bow down to them or worship them, for I, the LORD your God, am a jealous God who will not tolerate your affection for any

other gods. I lay the sins of the parents upon their children; the entire family is affected—even children in the third and fourth generations of those who reject me. ¹⁰But I lavish unfailing love for a thousand generations on those* who love me and obey my commands.

¹¹"You must not misuse the name of the LORD your God. The LORD will not let you go unpunished if you misuse his name.

¹²"Observe the Sabbath day by keeping it holy, as the LORD your God has commanded you. ¹³You have six days each week for your ordinary work,

¹⁴but the seventh day is a Sabbath day of rest dedicated to the LORD your God. On that day no one in your household may do any work. This includes you, your sons and daughters, your male and female servants, your oxen and donkeys and other livestock, and any foreigners living among you. All your male and female servants must rest as you do. ¹⁵Remember that you were once slaves in Egypt, but the LORD your God brought you out with his strong hand and powerful arm. That is why the LORD your God has commanded you to rest on the Sabbath day.

5:10 Hebrew *for thousands of those.*

NOTES

5:8 *an idol of any kind.* The MT reads "an image, any likeness," thus equating "image" *pesel* [TH6459, ZH7181] (anything carved or molded; cf. 4:16) and "likeness." The Qumran mss, Samaritan Pentateuch, and many versions presuppose (with Exod 20:4) "an image and/or any likeness," making some distinction. The LXX suggests "or any likeness," again indicating a difference. It seems best, in light of a similar construction in 4:16, 23, to view "image" and "likeness" as appositives, the second clarifying the meaning of the first. Thus, an image is not an object of worship *per se,* but is the likeness of a deity that is worshiped (NIDOTTE 4.717).

COMMENTARY

Scholars have long noted that the Ten Commandments can be divided into two main themes: (1) those that speak to the relationship between human beings and God (the first four commandments, 5:6-15) and (2) those that address human beings' relationships to each other (the last six commandments, 5:16-21). Another way to put it is that the commandments have either a vertical dimension or a horizontal one. In the very nature of the suzerain–vassal treaty arrangement, vassals have responsibility to both the liege lord and to one another. This is certainly self-evident in a study of the Old Testament examples.

Some debate exists as to the structure of the Decalogue, primarily as to whether 5:6 and 5:7 are one or two commandments and, likewise, whether 5:21 is one or two (Weinfeld 1991:243-245). The grammatical pattern of all but commandments four and five clearly favors the view that the first commandment is that prohibiting polytheism (5:7), a commandment based on Yahweh's redemptive work on Israel's behalf (5:6). In other words, it is the fiat declaration that Yahweh, Israel's God, brought them out of bondage to Egypt that constitutes his right to exclusive worship by them. While this text does not assert absolute monotheism (in fact, it might even appear to concede the existence of other gods), the practical result is the same: Only Yahweh is to be acknowledged as God.

The pagan nations surrounding Israel represented their gods with idols, but such representation by material means implicitly limited how these deities could be perceived (see note on 5:8). A god capable of being circumscribed physically was a god too small and weak to be worthy of authentic worship. Thus, according to the second commandment, Yahweh could not be "manufactured" in any form. The exact form was irrelevant because all images were creaturely. The result of making an image was the futile and blasphemous act of fashioning the creature and setting it up in the place of the Creator (cf. 4:15-19, 23-24, 28, 35).

Should Israel worship or bow down to idols—even images of Yahweh—they would invite his severest displeasure (5:9). He is a "jealous God" (cf. 4:24), one who brooks no rivals, real or imaginary, and who punishes those who fail to appreciate his unique claims to worship. These he classifies as the ones who "hate" him (that is, reject him; cf. 7:10), the covenant-breakers. The aftereffects of their apostate insubordination would reverberate for generations to come.

Those who refrained from such misguided attempts to create God in their own image and who showed that by loving him (that is, by keeping covenant) could expect his reciprocal loyalty and blessing (5:10). The term here (*khesed* [TH2617, ZH2876], translated "unfailing love" by NLT) describes God's unconditional grace, his unremitting and everlasting fealty toward those to whom he has committed himself (NIDOTTE 2.213-217). Those who show their undivided submission to God's sovereignty can expect the overflow of his abundant love for not just three or four generations, but for a thousand. (These numbers should not be taken literally. Their intent is to show that God's mercy is incomparably richer than his anger.)

The third commandment (5:11) shares much in common with the first two because it also addresses the "cheapening" of God, the attempt to use (or misuse) him for mundane purposes. The Hebrew states literally, "You may not take up the name of Yahweh your God vainly" (KBL 951). The idea is a prohibition against using the divine name as a charm or talisman so as to produce or preclude a certain result. In such a situation, God, represented by his name, becomes a genie invoked to human service. This reversal of roles is blasphemous because, like idolatry, it robs God of his sovereignty.

The fourth commandment (5:12-15) differs from the first three in its form (infinitive absolute of *shamar* [TH8104, ZH9068] without particle of negation) and its inclusion of a motive clause (5:15b: "That is why" *'al-ken* [TH5921/3651A, ZH6584/4027]). It also marks the transition from the vertical to the horizontal thrust of the Decalogue inasmuch as both divine and human relationships are in view. However, its place here as a logical and theological sequel to what precedes is clear: God and God alone must be worshiped (5:6-7); as such, he cannot be concretized in any creaturely form (5:8-10). Nor can his name be profaned, for the name is just a cipher for who God is in his fullness (5:11). God as sovereign, recognized through his attributes and works to enjoy that exclusive claim, must have special times set apart when he can be worshiped.

The commandment specifies that one such occasion must be the Sabbath day

(5:12). Though linked to the seventh day (5:14), Sabbath comes not from the root related to "seventh" (*shebi'i* [TH7637, ZH8668]), but from one meaning "rest" or "cessation" (*shabath* [TH7673, ZH8697]). This day was to be set apart—that is, made holy. The Exodus version of the Decalogue specifies that the seventh day was chosen as Sabbath because God made everything in six days and rested on the seventh (Exod 20:11; cf. Gen 2:1-3). Echoes of that rationale exist here in the oblique reference to the day being "dedicated to the LORD" (lit., "a Sabbath to Yahweh"), as well as in the injunction to prohibit all members of one's household from work on the Sabbath (5:14). As I have noted, Exodus 20:11 explicitly links human cessation from labor with God's own rest from his work of creation. That idea is here as well.

In the forefront, however, is a significant theological advancement, one occasioned by the passing of 40 years and the opportunity for more acute historical reflection. The motive here in Deuteronomy for setting aside the Sabbath to Yahweh is his mighty and gracious act of redemption, not his work of creation. It is not that creation is no longer worthy of celebration but that the "re-creation" of a people (in a sense their resurrection from death in Egypt) has come to supersede that primal event as the one most packed with theological (and historical) significance (Dumbrell 1984:122-123). God's granting of rest from Egyptian slavery is justification aplenty for human overseers to give rest to themselves and all who work with and for them. In this manner, Yahweh is glorified. Moreover, if the Deuteronomy Decalogue enjoins rest for Exodus redemption, how much more should those redeemed from eternal bondage to death rejoice in the resurrection of Jesus Christ on the first day of the week and therefore hallow that day as one of utmost importance.

◆   ## 2. Commandments pertaining to the people's relationships with one another (5:16-21)

¹⁶"Honor your father and mother, as the LORD your God commanded you. Then you will live a long, full life in the land the LORD your God is giving you.
¹⁷"You must not murder.
¹⁸"You must not commit adultery.
¹⁹"You must not steal.

²⁰"You must not testify falsely against your neighbor.
²¹"You must not covet your neighbor's wife. You must not covet your neighbor's house or land, male or female servant, ox or donkey, or anything else that belongs to your neighbor.

NOTES
5:16 *Honor.* Lit., "regard as heavy" (*kabed* [TH3513, ZH3877]), that is, ascribe importance to.

COMMENTARY
The fifth commandment (5:16), like the fourth, lacks a prohibition and forms somewhat of a transition between the first three (which focus exclusively on Yahweh) and the last five, where interpersonal human relationships are at the fore. Parents are subjects of special respect and obedience because in the divine hierarchy

they stand next to God himself—that is, in the administration of his kingdom polity. This is strongly hinted at already in the summary statement of God's creation of the human race in Genesis 5. "When God created human beings," so reads the text, "he made them to be like himself. . . . When Adam was 130 years old, he became the father of a son who was just like him—in his very image" (Gen 5:1, 3). The parent thus stands as the image of God to the child and is worthy of the reverence that entails (Wenham 1987:126-127).

Paul reflected on this commandment in a discussion of parental respect and observed that this is the first of the Ten Commandments that ends with a promise (Eph 6:2). That promise is one of long life in the Land of Promise, a word of hope for individuals but surely for the nation as well.

The familiar pattern of prohibition (lo' [TH3808, ZH4202]) resumes in the sixth commandment, which deals with homicide (5:17). The word "homicide" is appropriate as a literal translation of the Hebrew ratsakh [TH7523, ZH8357], but the NLT is correct in understanding the idea here as murder—that is, a premeditated, intentional, and unlawful killing. Killing in war, for capital punishment, and for other similar reasons was, of course, permissible and even demanded (see 13:5, 9; 20:13, 16-17). Murder, however, must be punished in kind, by the death penalty (see Gen 9:6; Num 35:33). Such severe redressing flows from the idea of image just stated above. In fact, the Noahic covenant, which authorizes capital punishment for murder, does so precisely because "God made human beings in his own image" (Gen 9:6).

The prohibition against adultery (5:18) is designed to protect the sanctity of the family and to safeguard the vows inherent in the covenant of marriage. This leads to a further theological consideration, that of human marriage as a metaphor of the divine–human relationship (NIDOTTE 3.3). This image is common in both the Old Testament (Isa 54:6-8; 62:4-5; Jer 2:2; 3:6, 20; Ezek 16:32; Hos 2:2-5, 19) and the New Testament (2 Cor 11:2; Eph 5:23; Rev 19:7; 21:2, 9), and just as infidelity between man and wife is severely condemned, so is the unfaithfulness of those who claim to be covenantally bound to the Lord.

In a sense, adultery is theft, for it robs people of something very precious to them. Not surprisingly, then, the commandment "Do not steal" comes next in the list (5:19). In terms of the covenant context, the issue is the misappropriation of goods or properties that God has sovereignly bestowed according to his own pleasure. To steal is to show discontent with what one has as a result of divine disposition (cf. 1 Tim 6:8).

Bearing false testimony (5:20) is closely related to theft because it robs people of their good reputations. Literally, the command says, "You must not testify against your neighbor with an empty (or vain) witness." That is, accusations must have substance—they must be grounded in fact. Technically, the law here has to do with court cases in which testimony is given (Mayes 1979:171), but misrepresentation of truth in general is certainly implicit (Kaiser 1983:228).

Finally (and yet again in the area of stealing) comes the commandment against coveting (5:21). The verb used to speak of coveting the wife (khamad [TH2530, ZH2773]) is different in Deuteronomy from that pertaining to properties (*'awah* [TH183, ZH203]; though Exodus uses the more generic *khamad* in both places), because there is a slightly different nuance in the respective kinds of desire. The former certainly has overtones of sexual lust (cf. Song 2:3), whereas the latter is more materialistic. This is why some lists of the Ten Commandments divide the tenth command into two. However, there is good reason to retain the traditional breakdown, because this commandment, unlike all the others, has to do with interior intent or desire rather than external action. And yet the one can lead to the other—in fact, they are virtually the same—as Jesus made clear in speaking of anger and lust as tantamount to murder and adultery (Matt 5:21-22, 27-28).

◆   **C. The Narrative Relating the Sinai Revelation and Israel's Response (5:22-33)**

22"The LORD spoke these words to all of you assembled there at the foot of the mountain. He spoke with a loud voice from the heart of the fire, surrounded by clouds and deep darkness. This was all he said at that time, and he wrote his words on two stone tablets and gave them to me.

23"But when you heard the voice from the heart of the darkness, while the mountain was blazing with fire, all your tribal leaders and elders came to me. 24They said, 'Look, the LORD our God has shown us his glory and greatness, and we have heard his voice from the heart of the fire. Today we have seen that God can speak to us humans, and yet we live! 25But now, why should we risk death again? If the LORD our God speaks to us again, we will certainly die and be consumed by this awesome fire. 26Can any living thing hear the voice of the living God from the heart of the fire as we did and yet survive? 27Go yourself and listen to what the LORD our

God says. Then come and tell us everything he tells you, and we will listen and obey.'

28"The LORD heard the request you made to me. And he said, 'I have heard what the people said to you, and they are right. 29Oh, that they would always have hearts like this, that they might fear me and obey all my commands! If they did, they and their descendants would prosper forever. 30Go and tell them, "Return to your tents." 31But you stand here with me so I can give you all my commands, decrees, and regulations. You must teach them to the people so they can obey them in the land I am giving them as their possession.' "

32So Moses told the people, "You must be careful to obey all the commands of the LORD your God, following his instructions in every detail. 33Stay on the path that the LORD your God has commanded you to follow. Then you will live long and prosperous lives in the land you are about to enter and occupy.

NOTES

5:31 [27] *commands, decrees, and regulations.* This collocation of terms points to the introduction of covenant stipulations. The MT reads as a *singular mitswah* [TH4687, ZH5184], "command." This singular suggests that what follows the "command" (the *khuqqim* [TH2706, ZH2976], "decrees," and *mishpatim* [TH4941, ZH5477], "regulations") is in apposition to *mitswah*, functioning descriptively, thus: "the entire command, that is, the decrees and regulations." If this is the case, *mitswah* serves as a functional equivalent to *torah* [TH8451, ZH9368], "law, instruction" (Tigay 1996:74).

COMMENTARY

Once again, Moses reflected on events leading up to the present moment of covenant renewal. He presented the Ten Commandments as having come from Sinai at a former time (5:22; cf. 4:11-14, 32-36; 5:4-5; Exod 19:16-20), though, of course, the wording was not precisely the same as the present rendition. To previous descriptions of Israel's awesome encounter with Yahweh Moses adds the information that in their terror they pleaded with him to become their intermediary, their vehicle through whom Yahweh could reveal himself (5:27; cf. Exod 20:18-20). They were amazed that they had lived through the experience of encountering God's awesome glory and greatness in the darkness and the fire (5:23-24). This may have been a fluke, they reasoned; they could not count on it happening a second time (5:25). It was axiomatic to them that mere mortals could not have such confrontations with God and come away alive (5:26). Indeed, Moses had already pointed out to them this unlikelihood when he asked, "Has any nation ever heard the voice of God speaking from fire—as you did—and survived?" (4:33).

This brief recapitulation was designed to prepare the people for a second presentation of God's covenant stipulations. There is no evidence that this presentation in Moab was accompanied by such a glorious theophany as was seen at the first, but it was nonetheless with the same God, that very one who had shaken heaven and earth in his awesome displays of majestic power and sovereignty.

Then, beginning with 5:28, Moses blends narrative with paraenesis. He continued to look back to Sinai but with an eye to covenant renewal. A generation earlier, God had granted the people's plea that Moses be their mediator because of their terror. And Moses had communicated God's desire that the reverential awe he inspired in the past might be retained by Israel in the future, for if it were, it would guarantee their success forever (5:28-29). Once the people had left the sacred place (5:30), God had revealed the law with all its stipulations (see note on 5:31). Their purpose was to provide guidelines for successful covenant life in the Land of Promise (5:31).

In light of that past disclosure, Israel, on the eve of conquest and occupation of that land, had to make a commitment to obey all that Yahweh had commanded. They must not deviate to the right or the left (5:32, so in Hebrew) but stay on the pathway of God's perfect will. This would bring quantitative and qualitative blessing to life in the land. The image of life as a journey on a pathway is one common to both the Old Testament and the New Testament (NIDOTTE 1.989-990; cf. 9:16; 31:29; Judg 2:17; Job 19:8; Pss 1:6; 5:8; 17:5; 119:105; Gal 6:1; 2 Tim 2:18; Heb 12:13). God's blessings accompany those who choose to follow God.

◆ ## D. The Nature of the Principles (6:1-25)
1. Exhortation to obey the covenant principles (6:1-3)

"These are the commands, decrees, and regulations that the LORD your God commanded me to teach you. You must obey them in the land you are about to enter and occupy, [2]and you and your children and grandchildren must fear the LORD your God as long as you live. If you obey all his decrees and commands, you will enjoy a long life. ³Listen closely, Israel, and be careful to obey. Then all will go well with you, and you will have many children in the land flowing with milk and honey, just as the LORD, the God of your ancestors, promised you.

NOTES

6:1 commands. See note on 5:31 regarding *mitswah*.

6:2 decrees and commands. These are *khuqqoth* [TH2708, ZH2978] and *mitswoth* [TH4687, ZH5184], respectively, suggesting the latitude with which such terms, especially *mitswah*, are used. Here it clearly refers to single stipulations, as opposed to 6:1, where it is synonymous with *torah* [TH8451, ZH9368].

6:3 milk and honey. This is shorthand for productivity in both domesticated and undomesticated endeavors (cf. Exod 3:8, 17; 13:5; 33:3; Lev 20:24; Num 13:27; 14:8; 16:13, 14).

COMMENTARY

Having prepared the way for the announcement of the covenant stipulations, Moses employed a technical formula ("commands, decrees, and regulations," 6:1; cf. 5:31) to speak of them again and to urge Israel's compliance with them. Inculcation of these principles would instill a godly fear that encourages obedience. Obedience, in turn, would be prerequisite to long life in the land, both for the community and the individual (6:2).

Amplifying his urgency, Moses spoke directly to Israel by name, calling upon them to hear and to be careful (6:3), verbs commonly found together in paraenetic address (NIDOTTE 4.175-181; cf. 5:1; 13:18 [19]; 15:5; 28:1, 13, 15, 45; 30:10). The combined effect communicates the idea, "Pay attention and do it!" There are no options here, nor are there ever any in doing the will of God. It is always "his way or no way," for he is Lord. Full obedience to him brings fullness of blessing. In Israel's case, they would have a multiplied population in a land of unlimited natural resources (6:3).

◆   ## 2. The essence of the covenant principles (6:4-5)

⁴"Listen, O Israel! The LORD is our God, the LORD alone.* ⁵And you must love the LORD your God with all your heart, all your soul, and all your strength.

6:4 Or *The LORD our God is one LORD;* or *The LORD our God, the LORD is one;* or *The LORD is our God, the LORD is one.*

NOTES

6:4 alone. Other translations render the word *'ekhad* [TH259, ZH285] as "one," thereby stressing the unity of Yahweh rather than his uniqueness in Israel's monotheistic faith. The construction of the clause is so terse that it is open to a variety of interpretations, as is displayed in the translations in the NLT mg. Moreover, *'ekhad* can embrace both meanings (Merrill 1990:123-124). In this covenant setting, in which claims are being made for Yahweh's exclusiveness, the NLT's rendering is preferable. However, from a macro-theological standpoint, the notion of Yahweh's oneness—in the sense of unity—has much in its favor as preparation for the NT truth of the divine Trinity.

COMMENTARY

Deuteronomy 6:4-5, commonly called the Shema after its first word (*shema'* [TH8085, ZH9048]), constitutes the very heart of the Old Testament and Jewish faith. It is Israel's doctrinal confession in its most essential form. From a covenant perspective, it is the cardinal principle of which all else is interpretive. When Jesus was asked what is the most important commandment, he replied, "'You must love the LORD your God with all your heart, all your soul, and all your mind.' This is the first and greatest commandment" (Matt 22:37-38). The absence of rebuttal from his critics suggests that what Jesus said was commonly accepted.

The command to love (that is, in covenant terms, to obey) is predicated on the declaration of who Yahweh is. Moses said, "Yahweh is our God," that is, the God of no other people and the only God for Israel. The phrase "the LORD alone" (see note on 6:4) affirms this conviction that only Yahweh is Israel's God. This is not a tacit admission of the existence of other gods; rather, it is a declaration that Yahweh alone is worthy of worship (von Rad 1966a:63). In light of that indisputable fact, Israel must love him fully and unreservedly (6:5). In this theological context, love has to do with loyalty, commitment, and obedience (cf. 5:10; 7:7, 9; 10:12; 11:1, 13, 22; 13:3; 19:9; 30:6, 16, 20), not just affection.

The fullness of such love is seen in its comprehensive expression—the whole heart, the whole soul, the full strength (Wolff 1974:53). "Heart" (*lebab* [TH3824, ZH4222]; cf. *leb* [TH3820, ZH4213]) in Old Testament physiology refers to the mind or will, the center of the intellect. "Soul" (*nepesh* [TH5315, ZH5883]) describes the person himself or herself, the essential being, especially the desires or longings. "Strength" (*me'od* [TH3966, ZH4394], lit., "muchness") is not an element of one's being, but of human activity, what one does. Thus, the command is to be obedient to God with fullness of being and totality of effort. The New Testament variations on this formula (cf. Matt 22:37-39; Mark 12:29-30; Luke 10:27) agree on the fundamental truths being propounded; the differences in wording may be explained by explanatory glosses in the Septuagint (Bock 1996:1025), made necessary in a more Hellenistic environment.

◆ 3. Exhortation to teach the covenant stipulations (6:6-9)

⁶And you must commit yourselves wholeheartedly to these commands that I am giving you today. ⁷Repeat them again and again to your children. Talk about them when you are at home and when you are on the road, when you are going to bed and when you are getting up. ⁸Tie them to your hands and wear them on your forehead as reminders. ⁹Write them on the doorposts of your house and on your gates.

NOTES

6:7 *Repeat.* This verb form may come from a root meaning "sharpen" (*shanan* I [TH8150, ZH9111]) or from one meaning "repeat" (*shanan* II [TH8150A, ZH9112], so KBL). BDB suggests "to teach incisively" (based on the Piel of *shanan* I). Either meaning is appropriate here.

6:8 *wear them on your forehead.* More literally, "they will be for phylacteries [a kind of headdress] on your forehead" (Tigay 1996:441-444). In the course of time, these objects became tiny boxes (called "tefillin") tied to the forehead and divided into four compartments, each containing a Scripture passage (6:5-9; 11:13-21; Exod 13:1-10, 11-16). The third of these texts included the Shema itself.

6:9 *doorposts.* The word *mezuzoth* [TH4201, ZH4647] refers in the Old Testament to doorposts (Exod 12:7, 22, 23; Judg 16:3; 1 Sam 1:9; 1 Kgs 6:33) but also, by postbiblical times, to the tiny plaques attached to the doorposts, which contained Deut 6:4-9; 11:13-21 and sometimes the Decalogue and other texts.

COMMENTARY

Since to love God is to obey him, it is essential that Israel take these commandments (lit., "words"; *debarim* [TH1697, ZH1821]; 6:6) to heart (lit., "upon your heart," that is, firmly in mind). They should be committed to memory and then taught to the children over and over (see note on 6:7) until they are deeply ingrained. In a series of merisms (opposites juxtaposed to suggest totality), Moses commanded that this instruction be unremitting and made part of everyday life (6:7). And then as a visual reminder, they should be tied to the hands and forehead (see note on 6:8) and engraved on the doorposts of their houses and towns (6:8-9).

Whether these latter instructions were to be taken literally or not (today they are taken literally by the most conservative Jewish communities), their intent was to encourage every means possible to ensure knowledge of and compliance with the covenant principles upon which national and family life were to be based. Both inwardly and outwardly, the faithful of Israel must demonstrate that they were God's people, fully committed to serving him.

◆   ## 4. Exhortation to give Yahweh exclusive obedience (6:10-19)

10"The LORD your God will soon bring you into the land he swore to give you when he made a vow to your ancestors Abraham, Isaac, and Jacob. It is a land with large, prosperous cities that you did not build. 11The houses will be richly stocked with goods you did not produce. You will draw water from cisterns you did not dig, and you will eat from vineyards and olive trees you did not plant. When you have eaten your fill in this land, 12be careful not to forget the LORD, who rescued you from slavery in the land of Egypt. 13You must fear the LORD your God and serve him. When you take an oath, you must use only his name. 14"You must not worship any of the gods of neighboring nations, 15for the LORD your God, who lives among you, is a jealous God. His anger will flare up against you, and he will wipe you from the face of the earth. 16You must not test the LORD your God as you did when you complained at Massah. 17You must diligently obey the commands of the LORD your God—all the laws and decrees he has given you. 18Do what is right and good in the LORD's sight, so all will go well with you. Then you will enter and occupy the good land that the LORD swore to give your ancestors. 19You will drive out all the enemies living in the land, just as the LORD said you would.

NOTES

6:16 *Massah.* This refers to the place in the Sinai Peninsula where Moses accused the people of testing (*nasah* [TH5254, ZH5814], "test" or "try") Yahweh by complaining about the lack of water (Exod 17:1-2). Yahweh granted their request by having Moses strike a rock from which water gushed out. The site was then named Massah (*massah* [TH4532/4531, ZH5001/4999]) as a reminder of that experience (Exod 17:7; cf. also Deut 9:22; 33:8).

COMMENTARY

Once more an exhortation is based on Yahweh's faithfulness in the past (6:12) and (here at least) on his promises concerning the future. The ancient oath in which God had sworn to give land to the patriarchs and their descendants was about to find reality in the present (6:10; cf. 1:8). This turn of events both testified to the faithfulness of God and provided persuasive justification for Israel to obey him in the days to come. An advance over previous revelation concerning the land is that Israel would take intact already existing cities, houses with their contents, cisterns, and fruit trees (6:10-11). This presupposes a conquest in which there would be only minimal physical damage, though the populations themselves would largely be decimated. As it turns out, this was precisely the pattern and strategy that Joshua followed. In his farewell address to postconquest Israel he said, "I gave you land you had not worked on, and I gave you towns you did not build—the towns where you are now living. I gave you vineyards and olive groves for food, though you did not plant them" (Josh 24:13).

Close study of the conquest narratives reveals that only Jericho, Ai, and Hazor are said to have been destroyed, the rest of the cities having been left on their mounds, at least in the case of the northern campaign (Josh 11:13). Efforts to find archaeological evidence of Joshua's conquest of Canaan are misguided, since it was Moses's prophecy and Joshua's policy to save cities and houses for Israel's own use (Merrill 1982:109-111). This blessing—truly an evidence of God's grace—might, however, be taken for granted. Moses therefore urged his audience not to forget that it was Yahweh who had redeemed them and brought them to this happy state of affairs (6:12). For this, they owed him total allegiance and recognition as their one and only God (6:13).

This insistence on single-minded devotion to Yahweh leads to the logical corollary of the rejection of other gods (6:14). Whether individual Israelites actually believed that such gods existed or not, idolatry would be a temptation, because in its essence idolatry is attributing success or blessing to something other than God. The nature cults of Canaan were especially alluring, for the bounties of the land "flowing with milk and honey" (6:3) were thought to be linked to certain myths and rituals that, when enacted properly, guaranteed their continuance (Gaster 1961:124-129).

Should Israel succumb to these enticements, they could expect the wrath of Yahweh, the "jealous God" (cf. 4:24; 5:9), who tolerates no rivals, even those concocted by depraved imagination (6:15). They must not test God's patience, as they did at Massah (see note on 6:16); rather, they must make every effort to comply with Yahweh's commandments—that is, the stipulations and laws that constitute the covenant relationship (6:16-17).

Put succinctly, they must do what is right and good according to God's standard. The former term connotes the idea of measuring up to something that is straight— something construed as a norm of proper behavior. In context, this suggests adherence to the divine standard of Torah. If and when this is done, blessing inevitably follows. They would conquer and occupy the Land of Promise (6:18), having expelled from it those who unjustly made claim to it (6:19).

◆   5.   Exhortation to remember the past (6:20-25)

20"In the future your children will ask you, 'What is the meaning of these laws, decrees, and regulations that the LORD our God has commanded us to obey?'

21"Then you must tell them, 'We were Pharaoh's slaves in Egypt, but the LORD brought us out of Egypt with his strong hand. 22The LORD did miraculous signs and wonders before our eyes, dealing terrifying blows against Egypt and Pharaoh and all his people. 23He brought us out of Egypt so he could give us this land he had sworn to give our ancestors. 24And the LORD our God commanded us to obey all these decrees and to fear him so he can continue to bless us and preserve our lives, as he has done to this day. 25For we will be counted as righteous when we obey all the commands the LORD our God has given us.'

NOTES

6:21 *with his strong hand.* This imagery is in line with a role Yahweh plays frequently in Deuteronomy, that of Divine Warrior (cf. 5:15; 7:8; 9:26; 26:8).

COMMENTARY

The pericope here is in the form of a creed or confession, one that accounts for present belief on the basis of historical events, in this case, events God performed on behalf of Israel. The time would come when children would ask their parents about the significance of the covenant stipulations (6:20). Why do we believe what we do? What is the history that has given rise to our religious traditions?

The answer is cast in the form of a brief recital of sacred history, one consisting of several stages or turning points. Israel must remember that they (1) were slaves to Pharaoh and (2) had been delivered by God, their champion (3) by a series of signs and wonders so that (4) he could bring them into the Land of Promise (6:21-23). This was Israel's "gospel" message, one of salvation and blessing. This is what must be remembered, repeated, and passed on from one generation to the next (cf. 6:6-9). Paul's brief summation of the gospel in 1 Corinthians 15:3-4 is reminiscent of this in Deuteronomy in both its thrust and its brevity.

The "signs and wonders" (6:22) were designed not only to bring about supernatural results but to testify to the nature of the God who could perform them. That is, like the signs (Greek *sēmeia* [TG4592, ZG4956]) that often accompanied the ministry of Jesus (see John 2:11; 4:54; 6:14; 11:47; 12:37) to authenticate his messianic claims, those performed by Yahweh attested to his incomparability and sovereignty (TDOT 1.177-178). The impact would be powerful indeed (cf. 4:34; 7:19; 26:8; 29:2; 34:11; Exod 7:3; Neh 9:10; Ps 135:9; Isa 8:18; Jer 32:20, 21).

The recollection of God's mighty saving acts must result in regular recommitment to obey the covenant to which they pointed (6:24). God had delivered them, not just to display his power, but to declare that Israel was his elect nation, a declaration that expected a reciprocal response of loyal service. Faithfulness in this regard would result in prosperity (lit., "our good") and well-being (lit., "keep us alive"), a condition they were enjoying even as Moses spoke (6:24). More importantly, covenant commitment brings a state of righteousness before God. The word *tsedaqah* [TH6662, ZH7404] (cf. NLT, "righteous") speaks of adherence to a standard, in this case the standard of belief and behavior inherent in and mandated by the covenant stipulations (6:25).

◆ **E. The Content of the Principles (7:1–11:32)**
    1. Driving out the nations (7:1–26)
        a. Exhortation to holiness (7:1–6)

"When the LORD your God brings you into the land you are about to enter and occupy, he will clear away many nations ahead of you: the Hittites, Girgashites, Amorites, Canaanites, Perizzites, Hivites, and Jebusites. These seven nations are greater and more numerous than you. ²When the LORD your God hands these nations over to you and you conquer them, you must completely destroy* them. Make no treaties with them and show them no mercy. ³You must not intermarry with them. Do not let your daughters and sons marry their sons and daughters, ⁴for they will lead your children away from me to worship other gods. Then the anger of the LORD will burn against you, and he will quickly destroy you. ⁵This is what you must do. You must break down their pagan altars and shatter their sacred pillars. Cut down their Asherah poles and burn their idols. ⁶For you are a holy people, who belong to the LORD your God. Of all the people on earth, the LORD your God has chosen you to be his own special treasure.

7:2 The Hebrew term used here refers to the complete consecration of things or people to the LORD, either by destroying them or by giving them as an offering; also in 7:26.

NOTES

7:1 *Hittites, Girgashites, Amorites, Canaanites, Perizzites, Hivites, and Jebusites.* This list appears to be somewhat stylized, in this case including seven nations in all, the number seven perhaps indicating completeness—that is, all the inhabitants of the land. The same seven do not always occur in other lists describing the population of Canaan (Exod 3:8 lists six; Exod 13:5, five; Exod 23:23, six; Exod 23:28, three; Exod 33:2, six; Exod 34:11, six; Deut 20:17, six; Josh 3:10, all seven; Josh 9:1, six; Josh 24:11, all seven). Usually the Girgashites are lacking in the shorter lists. The Hittites are related to the great Hittite Empire of Anatolia (central Turkey) that flourished in the Late Bronze Age (c. 1500–1200 BC). The Girgashites cannot be ethnically identified. The Amorites were descendants of seminomadic immigrants to Canaan from Aram (Syria), who may have settled there in patriarchal times (c. 2200 BC; cf. 1:4, 7, 19, 27, 44; 3:2, 9; 4:46). The Canaanites were indigenous to Canaan, their existence there going back probably as early as 3000 BC. The Perizzites are linked with the Canaanites in ancient times (Gen 13:7; 34:30), probably being a Canaanite clan. The Hivites are usually identified with the famous Hurrians of ancient Near Eastern texts. Finally, the Jebusites were located, with Hittites and Amorites, in the hill country of Canaan (Num 13:29), especially in the vicinity of Jerusalem (Josh 15:8; cf. Josh 15:63; 18:16). In fact, by David's time Jerusalem was regarded as a Jebusite city (2 Sam 5:6; 24:16). The Table of Nations (Gen 10:15-19) adds the information that all of these nations (except the Perizzites) were descendants of Canaan—that is, they were all linked sociologically and perhaps politically to the Canaanites. Clearly, the intent in Deuteronomy is not to suggest a variety of ethnically distinct people but to speak of tribes or clans in Canaan by these various terms (Ishida 1979:461-490).

greater and more numerous. The Hebrew phrase *rabbim wa'atsumim* [TH7227/6099, ZH8041/6786] is better understood as a hendiadys meaning "much stronger" and not as two separate adjectives meaning "greater and stronger" or the like.

7:5 sacred pillars . . . Asherah poles. These objects, though technically not images or idols, usually represented the presence of pagan (specifically Canaanite) deities. The pillar (*matsebah* [TH4676, ZH5167]) was a stela erected at or near a shrine to memorialize some manifestation or act of a deity (NIDOTTE 3.135). Sometimes they were set up for non-cultic and even secular purposes—and by Israelites—to recall covenant arrangements (Gen 31:45), mark grave sites, or memorialize persons (Gen 35:20; 2 Sam 18:18). Also, the appearances of Yahweh himself were sometimes recalled by such monuments (Gen 28:18, 22; 31:13; 35:14; Exod 24:4). Generally, however, they had pagan associations and so were forbidden (cf. 12:3; Exod 23:24; 34:13; 1 Kgs 14:23; 2 Kgs 17:10; Jer 43:13; Hos 3:4; 10:1). The Asherah poles (*'asherah* [TH842A, ZH895]) took their name from the Canaanite deity who was wife or sister of El and goddess of fertility (TDOT 1.441-443). She was commonly associated with clusters of evergreen trees or, in their scarcity, by a wooden pole representative of life and abundance. Her worship also was strongly proscribed, and the poles reminiscent of her powers were to be burned or cut down (12:3; 16:21; Judg 6:25, 28, 30; 2 Kgs 18:4; 23:6, 14, 15).

COMMENTARY

Once Yahweh the Warrior (cf. 1:29-30) brought Israel into Canaan, he would rid the land of the seven enemies that awaited them there (see note on 7:1), enemies Moses said were much more powerful than they. Once delivered over to Israel, they must be annihilated (7:2; i.e., put under God's wrath, *hakharem takharim* [TH2763, ZH3049]; cf. note on 2:34). In any case, Israel must not enter into any kind of legal or social relationship with the Canaanites (7:2-3) because such affiliations would tend to draw God's people away from him and toward other gods, a violation of the very essence of the covenant (7:4a; cf. 5:6-7; 6:4-5). This in turn would result in Yahweh's swift retaliatory judgment (7:4b).

Rather than yielding to Canaanite allurements, Israel must demolish them, particularly the altars, sacred pillars (see note on 7:5), Asherah poles (see note on 7:5), and idols. The commands against making idols (see notes on 4:16; 5:8; cf. 4:23, 25; Exod 20:4) associate the root of the word for idols here with the idea of a "likeness" (*temunah* [TH8544, ZH9454]), suggesting that such an object was an attempt to represent deity in some kind of anthropomorphic or zoomorphic (i.e., humanlike or animallike) form.

Among other reasons for this drastic action is the fact that Israel was a "holy people," that is, a people chosen by Yahweh from among all people to be his "special
treasure." This verse virtually repeats the classic text that first presented Yahweh's
offer of a covenant to Israel (Exod 19:4-6). To put these sublime theological ideas
together more tightly, one could say: God chose Israel, setting them apart for divine
service, thereby making them the special object of his affection (7:6). To be
Yahweh's "special treasure" (*segullah* [TH5459, ZH6035]) meant being the central jewel
in his royal diadem (Greenberg 1951:172-174; cf. 14:2; 26:18; 1 Chr 29:3; Ps 135:4;
Eccl 2:8; Mal 3:17).

◆   ## b. The basis of Israel's election (7:7-11)

7"The LORD did not set his heart on you
and choose you because you were more
numerous than other nations, for you
were the smallest of all nations! 8Rather,
it was simply that the LORD loves you, and
he was keeping the oath he had sworn to
your ancestors. That is why the LORD rescued you with such a strong hand from
your slavery and from the oppressive
hand of Pharaoh, king of Egypt. 9Under-
stand, therefore, that the LORD your God is
indeed God. He is the faithful God who
keeps his covenant for a thousand generations and lavishes his unfailing love on
those who love him and obey his commands. 10But he does not hesitate to
punish and destroy those who reject him.
11Therefore, you must obey all these
commands, decrees, and regulations I am
giving you today.

NOTES

7:8 *rescued*. Here NLT compresses two verbs (*yatsa'* [TH3318, ZH3655], "bring out," and *padah*
[TH6299, ZH7009], "redeem") into one, and in the process, the idea of the deliverance from
Egypt as a redemptive act is attenuated. The verb *padah* has at its core the idea of ransom,
the payment by one party for the release of another in bondage or captivity (NIDOTTE
3.578). At the Exodus, the ransom, symbolized by the slaughter of the Passover lamb, was
actually the release of the firstborn sons of Israel to serve God in perpetuity (cf. Exod 12:1-
14, 29; 13:2, 13-16). That is, they became the ransom on behalf of the whole nation. Later,
the tribe of Levi assumed the role of ransom, taking the place of the eldest sons of the
other tribes (Num 3:11-13). All of this prefigured the ministry of Jesus Christ, who, by his
own testimony, came "to give his life as a ransom for many" (Matt 20:28; cf. 1 Pet 1:18).

7:9-10 *keeps his covenant*. The Hebrew has "covenant and loyalty"; the grammatical construction favors a translation something like, "who keeps covenant with unwavering loyalty" (Mayes 1979:186).

***love . . . reject*.** For the use of these terms in covenant context to mean covenant fidelity
and infidelity respectively, see the note on 4:37 and other texts cited there.

COMMENTARY

The sense of pride Israel might have felt in having been chosen by Yahweh out of all
possible options is deflated here by the unmistakable assertion that election is a
work of grace. There was not an inherent, redeeming quality in Israel that prompted
Yahweh to become "attracted to" (*khashaq* [TH2836, ZH3137]; NLT, "set his heart on")
Israel, thus choosing her (TDOT 1.99-118). And it certainly was not because Israel

was impressive in population, for to the contrary, Israel was smallest among the nations (7:7). Since, in fact, Israel numbered more than 600,000 men alone at the time of the Exodus—making her larger than any nation in Canaan—the reference here must be to the 70 that first descended into Egypt (Exod 1:5). By promise, God had already selected that small band to be his servant people (cf. Mal 1:3-4).

This seems clear from 7:8, which asserts that Yahweh's choice of Israel issued from his covenantal love and the honoring of the promise he had made to the patriarchal ancestors when they were "few in number" (26:5). God chose Israel in order to bring them into covenant fellowship, an act that necessitated their deliverance from Egyptian slavery. The Exodus itself, then, was another expression of elective grace (7:8).

God's choice of such an unlikely vehicle through which to demonstrate his power and glory could lead to only one conclusion—Yahweh your God, he is the God (7:9)! But he is not God in some deistic fashion, for he is the one upon whom Israel could lean. He is the faithful one, in whom they could have absolute confidence that he would keep his covenant. The benefits of that covenant grace are applicable only to those who love (that is, choose or favorably respond to) God—to those who show they are committed to keep his commands in all its parts (7:9). Those who reject him can expect his retribution. He will confront them with their disloyalty and exact full payment from them. These promises and threats ought to have provided sufficient reason for keeping the commands, the whole *torah* [TH8451, ZH9368], with its various laws and regulations.

◆   c. Promises of blessing for covenant obedience (7:12-15)

12"If you listen to these regulations and faithfully obey them, the LORD your God will keep his covenant of unfailing love with you, as he promised with an oath to your ancestors. 13He will love you and bless you, and he will give you many children. He will give fertility to your land and your animals. When you arrive in the land he swore to give your ancestors, you will have large harvests of grain, new wine, and olive oil, and great herds of cattle, sheep, and goats. 14You will be blessed above all the nations of the earth. None of your men or women will be childless, and all your livestock will bear young. 15And the LORD will protect you from all sickness. He will not let you suffer from the terrible diseases you knew in Egypt, but he will inflict them on all your enemies!

NOTES

7:12 *covenant of unfailing love.* The MT reads "the covenant and the faithfulness" (*khesed* [TH2617, ZH2876]), but, as in 7:9, the construction should be understood as a hendiadys with a meaning such as that proposed by the NLT.

COMMENTARY

Moses reiterates the conditional nature of covenant blessing (cf. 7:9), stressing that adherence to Yahweh's regulations will result in ongoing displays of his covenant loyalty (see note on 7:12). According to the promises made to the patriarchs, God will multiply the nation (cf. Gen 17:2; 22:17), grant abundant offspring to man and beast, and fructify the soil so that it will yield great increase (7:13). In fact, Israel will be blessed more than any other people on earth in terms of human and animal progeny. In somewhat hyperbolic terms, Moses goes so far as to say that no man, woman, or livestock would ever go barren (7:14). This overstatement is perhaps designed to offset the barrenness characteristic of the ancestral mothers of the nation such as Sarah (Gen 11:30), Rebekah (Gen 25:21), and Rachel (Gen 29:31), all of whom are described as 'aqarah [TH6135, ZH6829], the adjective for barrenness used here.

Moreover, Israel will escape all illnesses, particularly those they had known about in Egypt (7:15). It is likely, of course, that diseases of all kinds afflicted Israel in the centuries of their life in Egypt, but the record is silent about this. What Moses has in view here, then, is the plagues that afflicted the Egyptians but left the Israelites unharmed (Weinfeld 1991:374; cf. Exod 9:1-12). They "knew" these diseases but only in the sense of having witnessed their devastating effects on others. They would be free of them in the future as well, if they remained true to the covenant. Their enemies, however, would, like the Egyptians, suffer all these things.

◆   ### d. Exhortation to destroy Canaanite paganism (7:16-26)

16"You must destroy all the nations the LORD your God hands over to you. Show them no mercy, and do not worship their gods, or they will trap you. 17Perhaps you will think to yourselves, 'How can we ever conquer these nations that are so much more powerful than we are?' 18But don't be afraid of them! Just remember what the LORD your God did to Pharaoh and to all the land of Egypt. 19Remember the great terrors the LORD your God sent against them. You saw it all with your own eyes! And remember the miraculous signs and wonders, and the strong hand and powerful arm with which he brought you out of Egypt. The LORD your God will use this same power against all the people you fear. 20And then the LORD your God will send terror* to drive out the few survivors still hiding from you!

21"No, do not be afraid of those nations, for the LORD your God is among you, and he is a great and awesome God. 22The LORD your God will drive those nations out ahead of you little by little. You will not clear them away all at once, otherwise the wild animals would multiply too quickly for you. 23But the LORD your God will hand them over to you. He will throw them into complete confusion until they are destroyed. 24He will put their kings in your power, and you will erase their names from the face of the earth. No one will be able to stand against you, and you will destroy them all.

25"You must burn their idols in fire, and you must not covet the silver or gold that covers them. You must not take it or it will become a trap to you, for it is detestable to the LORD your God. 26Do not bring any detestable objects into your home, for then you will be destroyed, just like them. You must utterly detest such things, for they are set apart for destruction.

7:20 Often rendered *the hornet*. The meaning of the Hebrew is uncertain.

NOTES
7:20 *terror.* The meaning of the word *tsir'ah* [TH6880, ZH7667] here is much disputed (Tigay 1996:90) and uncertain (see NLT mg). Though such translations as "depression, discouragement" (KBL 817), and "hornets" (BDB 864) are proposed, it is also possible that the

word is linked to *tsara'ath* [TH6883, ZH7669] (leprosy). A major difficulty with this (or anything like disease or discouragement) is its unsuitability with the verb used here (*shalakh* [TH7971, ZH8938], "send"). See also Exod 23:28; Josh 24:12.

7:25 *detestable*. The word *to'ebah* [TH8441, ZH9359] speaks of anything abominable to Yahweh, that is, altogether inconsistent with his nature and purposes (NIDOTTE 4.315). Frequently, objects that are so described are consigned to utter annihilation lest they contaminate anyone or anything with which they come in contact (cf. 13:17; 20:17-18).

7:26 *detest*. The verb here (*shaqats* [TH8262, ZH9210]) is different from the one implied by *to'ebah* [TH8441, ZH9359] in the previous verse (which is *ta'ab* [TH8581, ZH9493]). Though the two are used synonymously, *shaqats* appears to be more narrow in focus, having to do primarily with persons or things that are cultically reprehensible (Milgrom 1991:656-659; cf. Lev 11:11, 13; Ps 22:24 [25]).

COMMENTARY

The following injunctions are among the most morally and theologically perplexing in the Bible, for in effect Yahweh is authorizing here a policy of genocide, an "ethnic cleansing" as it were. What must constantly be borne in mind, however, is that God, who knows all hearts and all prospects, viewed the Canaanites as hopelessly degraded and unrepentant. They had in effect "sinned away their day of grace." All that remained was their destruction, a course of action that was morally justifiable as well as practically necessary lest Israel be subverted by them (Kaiser 1983:266-269).

This latter point is patent in the text. Israel must destroy all these people, showing no compassion for them, lest they and their corrupt religious practices lead to Israel's undoing (7:16). Given the apparent superiority of these peoples (cf. 1:26-28; 7:1), the Israelites might despair of success against them (7:17). As he had done numerous times before, Moses exhorted the assembly to learn from history (cf. 4:3-4, 9-14, 32-34; 6:21-25). Moses emphatically urged them to bring to mind what Yahweh had done in Egypt (7:18; cf. 1:30; 4:20, 34; 5:6, 15; 6:12, 21; 7:8)— how he had brought testings (7:19; *massah* [TH4531, ZH4999]; not "terrors" as NLT) against the Egyptians, which proved their impotence (cf. Exod 8:19; 10:7). Israel had seen all this firsthand.

These testings all together were comprised of signs and wonders (cf. comments on 6:21)—that is, the ten plagues, as well as the powerful arm of Yahweh the Warrior, by which he delivered them from bondage (7:19). As he had done to Egypt in the past, so he would do to the Canaanite peoples in the future. By a barrage of unimaginable terrors (see note on 7:20), God's awesome strength would destroy the remnant that survived the conquest as a whole.

For extra assurance, Moses repeated his admonition not to fear. There was no need for terror because Yahweh, the "great and awesome" (7:21; *nora'* [TH3372, ZH3707], "the fear-inspiring") God, would be among them. This juxtaposition of the ideas of not fearing man and of recognizing the fear-inspiring presence of God is theologically and practically instructive (cf. Matt 10:28).

At this point, a caveat is introduced. In pursuing a policy of annihilation and expulsion, the people must not act precipitously. Yahweh would set the example by clearing the land of its inhabitants a little at a time, and Israel must do likewise, lest wild animals overrun the vacated countryside (7:22). In any case, it is Yahweh who would take the initiative to destroy the enemy. He would bring about circumstances (7:23; *hamam mehumah* [TH2000/4103, ZH2169/4539], "he will stir discomfiture") that would immobilize them to the point of their destruction. Their kings would surrender, and their very memory (lit., "names") would perish forever. No one would survive (7:24).

Turning now to the matter of "detestable things" (cf. notes on 7:25, 26), namely, idols and other cultic objects, Moses sternly commanded that they be burned. The precious metals with which these images were overlaid (cf. Jer 10:3-5) must also be put to the flames and melted down. In any case, they could not be kept as spoils because, as "detestable" things (7:25; *to'abath* [TH8441, ZH9359], "abominations"), they had to be surrendered over to the Lord in destruction. Should there be disobedience in this matter—particularly if such objects were kept as personal goods—those who sinned in this respect would themselves suffer destruction (7:26; *kherem* [TH2764, ZH3051], "be put to the ban"; cf. 3:6; 7:2; 20:17; Josh 6:18). Just as God detested these things and the practices they represented, so must his people.

◆   ## 2. Yahweh as the source of blessing (8:1-20)
a. Yahweh's provision in the wilderness (8:1-10)

"Be careful to obey all the commands I am giving you today. Then you will live and multiply, and you will enter and occupy the land the LORD swore to give your ancestors. ²Remember how the LORD your God led you through the wilderness for these forty years, humbling you and testing you to prove your character, and to find out whether or not you would obey his commands. ³Yes, he humbled you by letting you go hungry and then feeding you with manna, a food previously unknown to you and your ancestors. He did it to teach you that people do not live by bread alone; rather, we live by every word that comes from the mouth of the LORD. ⁴For all these forty years your clothes didn't wear out, and your feet didn't blister or swell. ⁵Think about it: Just as a parent disciplines a child, the LORD your God disciplines you for your own good.

⁶"So obey the commands of the LORD your God by walking in his ways and fearing him. ⁷For the LORD your God is bringing you into a good land of flowing streams and pools of water, with fountains and springs that gush out in the valleys and hills. ⁸It is a land of wheat and barley; of grapevines, fig trees, and pomegranates; of olive oil and honey. ⁹It is a land where food is plentiful and nothing is lacking. It is a land where iron is as common as stone, and copper is abundant in the hills. ¹⁰When you have eaten your fill, be sure to praise the LORD your God for the good land he has given you.

NOTES

8:1 *commands.* The MT has the singular (*mitswah* [TH4687, ZH5184]) here as a way of incorporating the whole covenant text, i.e., the Torah (for other examples of this usage, see the MT in 5:31; 6:1, 25; 7:11; 11:8, 22; 15:5; 17:20; 19:9; 27:1; 30:11; 31:5). The plural of the same word (*mitswoth*) describes particular stipulations (as in 8:2, 6 in this section).

8:3 *manna.* The popular etymology of this word derives from a play on the phrase *man hu'* [TH4478A/1931, ZH4943/2085], "What is it?" (Exod 16:15). This is what the Israelites asked

Moses when they first saw this "flaky substance as fine as frost" that covered the ground
(Exod 16:14). Another description is that "it was white like coriander seed, and it tasted
like honey wafers" (Exod 16:31; cf. Num 11:7). Those who understand manna apart from
a special act of creation propose such sources as the excretion of an insect that attaches
itself to a tamarisk tree (*Tamarix nilotica*), known to the Arabs as *mann es-Sama* ("heavenly
manna"), or a lichen (*Lecanora esculenta*) that grows on limestone in desert regions (Hepper
1992:63). However, the fact that this was a food unknown to Israel's ancestors (8:3, 16)
suggests that God created it especially for Israel in the desert (cf. also Josh 5:12).

COMMENTARY

The hortatory character of the covenant address continues in this passage, a hallmark of which is the formula, familiar by now, "be careful to obey" (cf. 5:32; 6:3,
25; 11:32; 12:1, 32 [13:1]; 15:5; 17:10; 24:8; 28:15, 58; 31:12; 32:46). What must be
obeyed is the whole covenant text (see note on 8:1), adherence to which will ensure
abundant life and possession of the Land of Promise (cf. 4:1; 5:33). To undergird
the promise, Moses again turned to the past, to the historical record of God's faithfulness. Yahweh had led Israel through the desert for 40 years; during all that time
he had "humbled" (8:2; *'anah* [TH6031, ZH6700]) and "tested" (*nasah* [TH5254, ZH5814])
them in order to know their motives (lit., "what was in [their] heart") and to determine the degree to which they would keep the covenant (8:2).

The point, of course, is not that Yahweh could not have otherwise known these
things, but that the people themselves might know how committed they were and
to acknowledge how dependent they must be on God. Testing frequently comes to
God's children so that they can mature in faith as they confront it and, by God's
grace, overcome it (cf. Job 1:12; Pss 26:2; 139:23; 1 Tim 3:10; Jas 1:3, 12; 1 Pet 1:7).
In Israel's case, the testing took the form of famine followed by a miraculous supply
of manna (see note on 8:3). Lack of food would certainly be challenging, but so
would the unexpected and totally gratuitous provision, for it was supplied a day at a
time and in amounts sufficient only for that day (Exod 16:16-30). Yesterday's faith
would not be efficacious for today's needs. Every day was exam day, so every day
demanded fresh confidence in a wonder-working God.

Beyond this provision for physical need was a more profound truth—namely,
that spiritual benefits are immeasurably more important than physical ones. The
bread that came from heaven (that is, from God) symbolized something much
more satisfying, the revelatory word by which God communicates his nature and
purposes to humankind. Physical life is sustained by the fruit of the earth. Spiritual
life is sustained by that which (like manna) comes from above (8:3). Jesus, when
tempted by the devil to satisfy his hunger by turning stones into bread, expounded
the meaning of this text by retorting that "people do not live by bread alone, but by
every word that comes from the mouth of God" (Matt 4:4; cf. Luke 4:4).

Divine grace in the wilderness was not confined to food alone. Moses reflected on
the miracle of durable clothing and maintenance of physical capacity. Illustrative of
good bodily health was the amazing fact that in all the years of walking the rough
terrain of Sinai the people's feet had not swollen (8:4). Deuteronomy 29:5, referring
to the same events, reads, "Your clothes and sandals did not wear out." The ideas are

obviously complementary because swollen feet would not have fit one's sandals, and worn-out sandals would lead to swollen feet. The point to Moses's argument here is that the God who sustained the people miraculously in the past is well able to do so in the future precisely because he can bypass the normal and mundane.

The purpose for the humbling and testing was pedagogical. Israel must learn that nations, like children, cannot grow up to maturity without discipline (8:5). The word rendered "disciplines" (*yasar* [TH3256, ZH3579]) bears a primary meaning of correction, but correction with a view to instruction. God did not set out to punish his people in this instance but to allow them to suffer and then to witness his gracious provision so that they might learn more of him and, at the same time, more about themselves.

Choosing another idiom for obedience, Moses urged the people to walk (8:6; *halak* [TH1980, ZH2143]) in God's ways—that is, to live as God lives (NIDOTTE 1.1033). This new way of life—impossible as it was, humanly speaking—was appropriate for life in a new land (8:7). There would no longer be scarcity requiring heavenly manna and water gushing from rocks (cf. 8:15; Exod 17:6; Num 20:11). Rather, water would be available from wadis, springs, and artesian wells that erupt from both valleys and hills (8:7). Wadis are streams that flow in times of rainfall but whose waters can be stored for irrigation in dry times. Springs and artesian wells are essentially the same, the latter being distinguished because their streams issue from the very depths of the earth, from the subterranean oceans as it were (cf. Gen 1:2; 49:25; Pss 77:17; 78:15; 135:6; 148:7).

These ideal environmental conditions made possible a variety of edible plant life—grains, fruits, and even honey (8:8), all in abundance (8:9a). The land was rich in mineral wealth as well. With some poetic license, Moses described the stone as iron and remarked on the plentiful stores of copper (8:9b). Perhaps (as in NLT) he compared iron to stones in abundance, or (more likely) he is referring to iron ore mined from the earth as opposed to meteorite iron that was more commonly known. Both iron and copper deposits exist in the region, the former especially in the Transjordan and the latter in the Arabah region of the Negev (Noth 1966:43-45).

Israel's response to all this bounty must be praise to Yahweh, the one who must be recognized as the author of all such blessings (8:10).

◆ ## b. Exhortation to remember that blessing comes from God (8:11-20)

11"But that is the time to be careful! Beware that in your plenty you do not forget the LORD your God and disobey his commands, regulations, and decrees that I am giving you today. 12For when you have become full and prosperous and have built fine homes to live in, 13and when your flocks and herds have become very large and your silver and gold have multiplied along with everything else, be careful! 14Do not become proud at that time and forget the LORD your God, who rescued you from slavery in the land of Egypt. 15Do not forget that he led you through the great and terrifying wilderness with its poisonous snakes and scorpions, where it was so hot and dry. He gave you water from the rock! ¹⁶He fed you with manna in the wilderness, a food unknown to your ancestors. He did this to humble you and test you for your own good. ¹⁷He did all this so you would never say to yourself, 'I have achieved this wealth with my own strength and energy.' ¹⁸Remember the LORD your God. He is the one who gives you power to be successful, in order to fulfill the covenant he confirmed to your ancestors with an oath.

¹⁹"But I assure you of this: If you ever forget the LORD your God and follow other gods, worshiping and bowing down to them, you will certainly be destroyed. ²⁰Just as the LORD has destroyed other nations in your path, you also will be destroyed if you refuse to obey the LORD your God.

NOTES

8:18 *ancestors.* The Samaritan Pentateuch and the Lucianic edition of the LXX add here the names "Abraham, Isaac, and Jacob," a reading seen in almost stereotypical use elsewhere (cf. in 1:8; 6:10; 9:5, 27; 29:13; 30:20; 34:4). However, the sparseness of the MT text suggests that it is original.

COMMENTARY

Besides the use of phrases such as "be careful" (8:11), the intense collocation of words for "remembering" and "not forgetting" lends to this section a highly paraenetic (i.e., hortatory) character. In the midst of prosperity, Moses warned, it will be easy to take credit for one's own success. Israel must therefore not forget Yahweh and the covenant. Full bellies, beautiful houses, large herds and flocks, abundant material resources, and the like—all these would be conducive to corrosive and false ideas of self-sufficiency (8:12-13).

Far from believing that all is well in these circumstances, one should be wary that such blessing has within it the sting of gravest danger. Dependence on God in former times of need can easily give way to pride (lit., "your heart be lifted up," 8:14) when all is going well. Israel must never forget Yahweh and the Exodus deliverance with all its concomitant evidences of grace. In a mini-review of sacred history, Moses recalled such events as the deliverance from venomous (lit., "fiery," probably figurative for "poisonous") serpents and scorpions, unbearable heat, lack of water, and such limited food supplies as to require supernatural provision of manna (8:15-16a; cf. note on 8:3). All this, Moses said, was to humble and discipline the people for their own good (cf. 8:2, 5).

The purpose of such deprivation and hardship on the one hand and divine provision on the other was to underscore the fact that all good things come from God. Or, as James later puts it so well, "Whatever is good and perfect comes down to us from God our Father" (Jas 1:17). One form of idolatry is overweening pride and independence. Those who feel they do not need God because they can get by on their own are as guilty of paganism as the Israelites were at Beth-peor. Therefore, it was incumbent on Israel (as it is on us) to remember (*zakar* [ᵀᴴ2142, ᶻᴴ2349], 8:18; cf. 5:15; 7:18; 8:2; 9:7; 15:15; 16:3, 12; 24:18, 22; 32:7) that Yahweh was the power behind their success. And to put things in even clearer perspective and priority, it must be remembered that God's blessing was not an end in itself but was granted in response to his ancient promises to the patriarchal ancestors (8:18). God blesses for our good, but ultimately he does so for his own great glory.

Conversely, those who forget Yahweh—the most glaring and self-evident proof of which is idolatry—must expect certain and inescapable destruction (*'abad* [TH6, ZH6]; 8:19). The verb employed is the same one commonly used to describe the eradication of God's enemies (as in 8:20). When it comes to the violation of the fundamental premise of the covenant—that there is one God and only he must be worshiped (cf. 5:6-7; 6:4-5)—being an Israelite or not makes no difference. One could even say that being an Israelite makes one even more culpable in this case. He, the jealous God, must and will avenge such disloyalty for his name's sake.

◆   ## 3. Blessing as a product of grace (9:1–10:11)
a. Victory by God's grace (9:1-6)

"Listen, O Israel! Today you are about to cross the Jordan River to take over the land belonging to nations much greater and more powerful than you. They live in cities with walls that reach to the sky! ²The people are strong and tall—descendants of the famous Anakite giants. You've heard the saying, 'Who can stand up to the Anakites?' ³But recognize today that the LORD your God is the one who will cross over ahead of you like a devouring fire to destroy them. He will subdue them so that you will quickly conquer them and drive them out, just as the LORD has promised.

⁴"After the LORD your God has done this for you, don't say in your hearts, 'The LORD has given us this land because we are such good people!' No, it is because of the wickedness of the other nations that he is pushing them out of your way. ⁵It is not because you are so good or have such integrity that you are about to occupy their land. The LORD your God will drive these nations out ahead of you only because of their wickedness, and to fulfill the oath he swore to your ancestors Abraham, Isaac, and Jacob. ⁶You must recognize that the LORD your God is not giving you this good land because you are good, for you are not—you are a stubborn people.

NOTES

9:6 *stubborn.* Lit., "hard-necked." The idea is that of a draft animal that is so unbroken as to refuse to turn its head right or left in response to a command, an animal that is unsubmissive to the yoke. This is an apt and quite common description of rebellious Israel (cf. 9:13; Exod 32:9; 33:3, 5; 34:9).

COMMENTARY

A major break in Moses's address is evident here with the call for attention (*shema'* [TH8085, ZH9048]; 9:1; cf. 4:1; 5:1; 6:4). The theme is the same as that of chapter 8—the imminence of the conquest—but the emphasis is different. Here the point is not so much that Israel's anticipated success will not be a function of their efforts but that it may be erringly appraised as something deserved. In the previous passage, Moses's concern was that the people would forget Yahweh and take credit for their own prosperity. In this text, the issue is not the likelihood that Yahweh will be forgotten but that Israel will attribute whatever good he does for Israel to their own worthiness (von Rad 1966a:74). In a sense, chapter 8 deals with salvation by works and chapter 9 with salvation by self-righteousness. Neither mindset is cognizant of the need for divine grace.

In language reminiscent of the report of the twelve Israelite spies and his response to it (1:22-33), Moses enjoined the people to prepare to cross over into Canaan and to dispossess the populations there (9:1). They may be much more powerful (cf. 7:1), their cities may have unscalable walls (cf. 1:28), and the people themselves may be Anakite giants (cf. 2:10), but God could give victory. The proverbial question, "Who can stand up to the Anakites?" would be answered by Yahweh who, like a raging inferno (lit., "devouring fire"), would bring them to ruin (9:3). The Divine Warrior imagery (cf. 1:30; 3:22; 7:17-24) continues with Yahweh's threat to destroy and dispossess all who stand in his way.

The very success of this course of events would, as in the case of Israel's material prosperity in the land (cf. 8:11-18), give rise to improper interpretations as to how and why it happened. The tendency would be for Israel to be self-congratulatory and say, "The LORD has given us this land because we are such good people!" (9:4). This is inevitably the conclusion of people who have no comprehension of the profundity of their sin or of the magnificence and necessity of God's grace. Like Israel, we want to relish the thought that good things happen to us because we are good.

The truth, however, is not that good things always happen to good people; rather, it is that bad things happen to all people who rely on their own righteousness. Israel would not conquer and occupy Canaan as a reward for good behavior. Instead, the indigenous peoples would be destroyed and expelled for their moral and spiritual rebellion against a holy God, an act and attitude so deeply ingrained and of such irreparable character as to be past remediation.

In a sense, Israel was no better than those they would dispossess. Surely it was not because of some commendable feature or potential that Yahweh was about to give them the land (9:5a). Their qualification lay in the elective grace of their God, who had called their patriarchal ancestors into covenant with himself and who had promised to them a seed and a land (9:5b). The time had finally come for the strands of that promise—seed and land—to come together. Thus, Israel's claims rested exclusively on divine promise, and any success in the land must be attributed to divine grace. To underscore this truth, Moses reiterated the point that the Israelites, of all people, were undeserving of the blessing of the land. Far from being righteous, they were stubborn—an intractable people who resisted the will of God at every turn (9:6; see note).

◆   ### b. A history of Israel's stubbornness (9:7-24)

⁷"Remember and never forget how angry you made the LORD your God out in the wilderness. From the day you left Egypt until now, you have been constantly rebelling against him. ⁸Even at Mount Sinai* you made the LORD so angry he was ready to destroy you. ⁹This happened when I was on the mountain receiving the tablets of stone inscribed with the words of the covenant that the LORD had made with you.

I was there for forty days and forty nights, and all that time I ate no food and drank no water. ¹⁰The LORD gave me the two tablets on which God had written with his own finger all the words he had spoken to you from the heart of the fire when you were assembled at the mountain.

¹¹"At the end of the forty days and nights, the LORD handed me the two stone tablets inscribed with the words of the covenant. ¹²Then the LORD said to me, 'Get up! Go down immediately, for the people you brought out of Egypt have corrupted themselves. How quickly they have turned away from the way I commanded them to live! They have melted gold and made an idol for themselves!'

¹³"The LORD also said to me, 'I have seen how stubborn and rebellious these people are. ¹⁴Leave me alone so I may destroy them and erase their name from under heaven. Then I will make a mighty nation of your descendants, a nation larger and more powerful than they are.'

¹⁵"So while the mountain was blazing with fire I turned and came down, holding in my hands the two stone tablets inscribed with the terms of the covenant. ¹⁶There below me I could see that you had sinned against the LORD your God. You had melted gold and made a calf idol for yourselves. How quickly you had turned away from the path the LORD had commanded you to follow! ¹⁷So I took the stone tablets and threw them to the ground, smashing them before your eyes.

¹⁸"Then, as before, I threw myself down before the LORD for forty days and nights. I ate no bread and drank no water because of the great sin you had committed by doing what the LORD hated, provoking him to anger. ¹⁹I feared that the furious anger of the LORD, which turned him against you, would drive him to destroy you. But again he listened to me. ²⁰The LORD was so angry with Aaron that he wanted to destroy him, too. But I prayed for Aaron, and the LORD spared him. ²¹I took your sin—the calf you had made—and I melted it down in the fire and ground it into fine dust. Then I threw the dust into the stream that flows down the mountain.

²²"You also made the LORD angry at Taberah,* Massah,* and Kibroth-hattaavah.* ²³And at Kadesh-barnea the LORD sent you out with this command: 'Go up and take over the land I have given you.' But you rebelled against the command of the LORD your God and refused to put your trust in him or obey him. ²⁴Yes, you have been rebelling against the LORD as long as I have known you.

9:8 Hebrew *Horeb*, another name for Sinai.   9:22a *Taberah* means "place of burning." See Num 11:1-3. 9:22b *Massah* means "place of testing." See Exod 17:1-7.   9:22c *Kibroth-hattaavah* means "graves of gluttony." See Num 11:31-34.

NOTES

9:7 *Remember and never forget.* The intensity of Moses's admonition here is conveyed by the collocation of the words *zekor 'al-tishkakh*, which uses the verbs *zakar* [TH2142, ZH2349] (remember) and *shakakh* [TH7911, ZH8894] (forget) to say, "Remember—do not forget!" These antonymous terms used together bespeak the highest urgency (TDOT 4.65). For other occurrences of the verbs together, see Gen 40:23; 1 Sam 1:11; Job 11:16; Pss 9:12; 74:18-19; 77:9-11; Prov 31:7; Isa 17:10; 54:4, NASB.

9:12 *an idol.* The MT reads only *massekah* [TH4541, ZH5011], "a cast thing." Some mss and the Samaritan Pentateuch supply *'egel* [TH5695, ZH6319] (calf)—thus, "a molten calf" or the like (cf. Exod 32:8). However, the omission may be deliberate by Moses to communicate his (or the Lord's) utter contempt for this "cast thing," so much so as not to name it.

9:21 *your sin.* By the use of metonymy (in this case, the effect standing for the cause), Moses says he threw Israel's sin into the fire and melted it down. He does, of course, explain his own figure by identifying the sin (the effect) with the golden calf (the cause).

COMMENTARY

Having just reminded Israel that their prospects for entering and occupying Canaan were based not on their righteousness but on God's love and grace, Moses turned to history once more to document that Israel was undeserving. It is easy for all of God's people to forget how refractory and wholly unworthy they are and to suppose that God must see and act upon at least some small praiseworthy element in their lives. It is not spiritually healthy to dwell constantly on the sinful past and to flagellate oneself endlessly for waywardness already forgiven. But it is beneficial to recall over and over that present blessing is always to be disconnected from any commendable past behavior. Who we are and what we enjoy are fruits of divine largess, not rewards for self-righteousness.

This passage should be studied against the background of the books of Exodus and Numbers, where the history in view is greatly elaborated. Moses said that the whole period from the Exodus deliverance to the present moment was character- ized by rebellion against God (9:7). Even at Sinai, at the very time Moses was on the mountain receiving the terms of the covenant, the people down below were in defi- ant apostasy. Having remained in divine audience for 40 days and nights, Moses, in the opinion of the people, had disappeared—with no likelihood of his return (cf. Exod 32:1). They therefore melted down their gold earrings, molded the material into the image of a calf, and proceeded to indulge in pagan revelry (Exod 32:2-6). This so incited the wrath of Yahweh that he was ready to annihilate the nation and begin all over again with Moses (9:8; cf. Exod 32:10).

The reference to Moses's fast from food and water for the 40 days (9:9) contrasts ironically with the behavior of the Israelites, who, according to the Exodus account, "celebrated with feasting and drinking" (Exod 32:6). Instead of remaining prayerful and expectant before a holy God, they entered into unbridled sensuality and license as they began to worship the creature rather than the Creator (Exod 32:8; cf. Rom 1:25). A further striking inconcinnity is that while the people were abandoning themselves to blatant paganism, Yahweh was in the process of inscribing on stone tablets the words of his covenant with them (9:9-10). His personal love for and vital interest in his chosen people is reflected in the unparalleled manner in which the covenant (specifically, the Ten Commandments; cf. Exod 34:28) was inscribed. The NLT reads "the two tablets on which God had written with his own finger" (9:10). The intent seems to be to underscore not only the importance of the Decalogue but Yahweh's intense involvement in imparting it to Israel (Weinfeld 1991:408).

Continuing his recital of history, Moses described his descent down the moun- tain following the 40 days of encounter with Yahweh (9:11). Even before he left, he knew something of what was transpiring below. The people had become corrupt, Yahweh said, and had turned aside from the covenant to make an idol of gold (lit., "a cast thing"; see note on 9:12). This was in direct violation of the first two com- mandments (5:6-10), adherence to which is the major idea of this entire section of Deuteronomy (the so-called general stipulations, chs 5-11).

This egregious act of betrayal prompted Yahweh to threaten to break his covenant with Israel. They were so intractable (lit., "hard of neck"; see note on 9:6) that he would give up on them. More than that, he was about to utterly obliterate them so that their very existence would pass from human memory (9:13-14a). To destroy them was serious and final enough, but to "erase their name" was to expunge from the annals of history any evidence that there had ever been an Israel (NIDOTTE 2.913-914). The verb for "erase" (*makhah* [TH4229, ZH4681]) is elsewhere employed of wiping the mouth (Prov 30:20), drying up tears (Isa 25:8), or drying a dish (2 Kgs 21:13). Like a great sponge, Yahweh's wrath would soak up Israel leaving no residue behind (cf. 29:19; 2 Kgs 14:27; Ps 9:6). The same verb was employed in a dialogue in Exodus 32 (omitted in the Deuteronomy narrative), in which Moses intercedes for sinful Israel and begs God to forgive his people. If God would not do this, then Moses asked God, "Erase my name from the record you have written!" (Exod 32:32). Yahweh's response was that only the memory of those who sinned would be expunged (Exod 32:33). The passage teaches, among other things, that people are responsible and must be punished for their own sins. That is, one person cannot substitute or atone for another. God in Christ alone is able to do this (cf. Isa 53:4-6).

God's threat to eradicate Israel is followed by his overture to Moses to make him the founder of a new chosen people (9:14b; cf. Exod 32:10). Since this did not happen, both the threat and the overture are moot points. However, the theological dilemma they raise can hardly be ignored. The promises made to the patriarchs were unconditional, secured by divine oath (cf. Gen 22:16-17). Moreover, the line of transmission of the messianic dimensions of the promises had also been set. It was to pass through Isaac, not Ishmael (Gen 17:19-21); through Jacob, not Esau (Gen 25:23; 27:33); and, most particularly, through Judah, not Levi or one of the other sons of Jacob (Gen 49:10). How could God abrogate his promise to the Judahites in favor of one of the Levites, a move necessary if Moses the Levite were to found a new nation?

The resolution of the dilemma resides perhaps in recognizing that it was Moses, not Yahweh, who was being tested (Jacob 1992:944). Rising to the occasion, Moses reminded Yahweh of his covenant commitments and of the irreparable damage to his reputation should he abandon his people for another (Exod 32:11-14; cf. Deut 9:25-29). The situation is akin to that in which Yahweh commanded Abraham to offer Isaac as a burnt offering, a command in direct contradiction to the promise that Isaac would be the covenant son, and a commandment inconsistent with the nature of Yahweh himself, a God to whom human sacrifice was abhorrent. Again, it was not Yahweh who was under scrutiny, but Abraham. It was he who had to learn new and deeper ways of trusting God (Gen 22:1, 12). And so it was with Moses. God's threat to destroy Israel and to begin again with Moses challenged Moses's faith and revealed to Moses, as a result, that God was sufficient for him and for his people.

Resuming his recollection, Moses spoke of having descended the mountain with the two stone tablets (cf. comments on 4:13) and seeing the gold calf the people had made. The Hebrew word *'egel* [TH5695, ZH6319], translated "calf" (9:16), is better rendered "young bull" (KBL 679). Since the bull was a universally recognized symbol of fertility, there is no doubt that Israel viewed the image the same way (Weinfeld 1991:424-426). It is difficult to know whether they were harking back to the Apis bull of Egyptian myth; anticipating the Canaanite deity Baal, often represented as or associated with bovine features; or worshiping Yahweh in the guise of a bull or, perhaps, as standing invisibly on the back of a bull. In any case, what they did was idolatrous and therefore an act of reprehensible covenant disloyalty (cf. 5:6-7). Filled with uncontrollable righteous indignation, Moses dashed the stone tablets to the earth, where they were shattered beyond repair (9:17).

Exercising his role as covenant mediator, Moses interceded before Yahweh on behalf of the nation, pleading that God's wrath might be overcome by his mercy (9:18). Amazingly, he reported, "he listened to me" (9:19). There is no greater theological mystery than the mystery of efficacious prayer. How can it be that the sovereign God, whose ways are perfect and established from eternity past, would be moved to a course of action by human petition? Though the answer is elusive, the fact remains that God does listen.

The anger of Yahweh was directed particularly against Aaron, the high priest and leader of Israel's priests (9:20). Despite his disclaimer that he was forced by public pressure to participate in the making of the image and in its attendant festivities (cf. Exod 32:21-24), Aaron was fully culpable and therefore subject to divine discipline. With urgent intercession, Moses prayed for him and, just as God had listened before and had spared the people, so he relented and permitted Aaron to live (9:20).

Finally, Moses took the gold bull ("the sin," as he described it; see note on 9:21), melted it down (lit., "burned it with fire"), crushed it thoroughly, and ground it into dust (9:21). He then threw the dust into a mountain stream and, as the Exodus narrative adds, forced the Israelites to drink the water containing the dust (Exod 32:20). To drink the residue of the idol was to suggest its total and complete disappearance (Childs 1974:569). The bull, far from being a god who brought the Israelites out of Egypt (Exod 32:8), proved to be illusory, ephemeral, able to be digested and deposited as waste.

Though the "golden calf" incident was the most famous example of Israel's stubbornness (cf. 9:6), it was not by any means the only one. In a wearisome litany, Moses recounted one episode after another in which Israel had demonstrated perfidious rebellion. So as never to forget those times and places, Moses had given them names, all reminiscent of the kind of behavior that had prompted the naming.

The first of these was Taberah (9:22), a name that by popular etymology is linked to the verb *ba'ar* [TH1197, ZH1277] ("to burn"; see KBL 140) and means "burning." The incident in question was the outburst of God's fiery wrath against the murmurers of Israel who complained incessantly about their trek through the Sinai deserts (Num 11:1-3). The precise location of the place cannot presently be determined.

The second place name is Massah, so called because of the people's testing God (*massah* [TH4531, ZH4999], from the verb *nasah* [TH5254, ZH5814], "to test, to try"). Moses had already alluded to this as the prototypical instance of Israel's putting God to trial by their demand for water in the desert place (6:16; cf. Exod 17:1-7). Rather than waiting quietly and expectantly for God to supply in his own time and in his own manner, the people had raised the surly question, "Is the LORD here with us or not?" (Exod 17:7). To demand anything of God is to act insubordinately. It is to make him as a servant to respond to the beck and call of those who should rather wait in patience before him.

Moses's third example of a place named for rebellion is Kibroth-hattaavah (9:22). The phrase means literally "burial places of appetite"; the grammatical structure (genitive of instrument; Waltke and O'Connor 1990:144) suggests the idea of graves (that is, death) that resulted from inordinate craving. The allusion is to the gluttonous response of the Israelites to the quail that God had provided to alleviate their hunger (Num 11:31-35). Besides the demand for food (Num 11:4)—an entirely inappropriate stance to take in regard to Yahweh's lordship—there is no evidence that having gotten it the people thanked him for it. Indeed, the record is clear that they began to stuff themselves like animals (Num 11:33), lusting for physical things while ignoring things of the spirit.

Finally, Moses brought to mind the episode at Kadesh-barnea, where God had instructed the people to begin their conquest of Canaan, but in vain (9:23; cf. Num 13:1-2). As in all the other instances, the people rebelled (9:24; *marah* [TH4784, ZH5286]) against God, would not trust (9:23; *'aman* [TH539, ZH586]) God, and refused to obey (*shama'* [TH8085, ZH9048]) him. In sum, Moses said, "You have been rebelling against the LORD as long as I have known you."

◆   ## c. Moses's plea on behalf of Yahweh's reputation (9:25–29)

25"That is why I threw myself down before the LORD for forty days and nights—for the LORD said he would destroy you. 26I prayed to the LORD and said, 'O Sovereign LORD, do not destroy them. They are your own people. They are your special possession, whom you redeemed from Egypt by your mighty power and your strong hand. 27Please overlook the stubbornness and the awful sin of these people, and remember instead your servants Abraham, Isaac, and Jacob. 28If you destroy these people, the Egyptians will say, "The Israelites died because the LORD wasn't able to bring them to the land he had promised to give them." Or they might say, "He destroyed them because he hated them; he deliberately took them into the wilderness to slaughter them." 29But they are your people and your special possession, whom you brought out of Egypt by your great strength and powerful arm.'

NOTES

9:25 *threw myself down.* The force of the verb (Hithpael of *napal* [TH5307, ZH5877]) is to the effect that Moses threw himself down or prostrated himself. This lends greater intensity to Moses's intercession.

9:28 *the Egyptians.* This is an interpretation of the awkward MT, "the land from which you brought us out." The Samaritan Pentateuch supplies "people" (*'am* [TH5971A, ZH6639]), thus, "the people of the land," whereas the LXX and its dependent versions read "the inhabitants of the land." The MT is suitable as it stands, since "land" is clearly elliptical for "people of the land."

COMMENTARY

Israel's history of rebellion was so blatant and their future so much in jeopardy as a result that Moses felt compelled to implore God with all his heart and soul for mercy and forgiveness. As he had been in the presence of Yahweh for 40 days of glorious theophany (cf. 9:9), so also he had fallen prostrate before the Lord for 40 days of abject humiliation (see note on 9:25). Fully cognizant of his own unworthiness and of God's transcendent glory, he had addressed him as "Sovereign LORD" (9:26; 'adonay yhwh [TH136/3068, ZH151/3378], "lord Yahweh"), an epithet altogether appropriate in this covenant connection. Those who know they are addressing the God of the universe find it easy—indeed, necessary—to fall on their faces before him.

In that posture, one does not demand but only implores. Moses used an optative verb form here: "May you not [or, please do not] destroy your [own] people" (9:26, lit.). The basis of Moses's plea was that Israel was God's possession or property, an entity of priceless value since they were ransomed by Yahweh at the cost of every firstborn of Egypt (cf. Exod 13:11-16). Such "effort" (lit., "by your strong hand") by Yahweh would, in a sense, go to waste should Israel go by the board.

The translation "overlook" (9:27) is perhaps too strong. Moses did not pray that God would ignore Israel's sin—for he could not—but he prayed that he would not be so preoccupied by it as to forget the covenant he made with the patriarchs. He asked, "May you not look at Israel's hardness and sin, but instead remember the faithfulness of their fathers of days gone by."

Most important is the reputation of Israel's God, the one who committed himself by covenant pledge. Should God destroy Israel, the Egyptians (see note on 9:28), among others, could draw at least two conclusions: (1) God, having brought his people out of Egypt, was powerless to see them all the way to Canaan; or (2) with cruel treachery he brought them out, all the while planning to destroy them. The one deduction would reflect negatively on God's power, the other on his character. To Moses's way of thinking, neither was a tolerable prospect. To sum up as well as to reemphasize the heart of his argument, Moses "reminded" Yahweh that the people whose plight was so tenuous in light of the impending divine wrath were, after all, God's people, the ones he had redeemed at great price (9:29).

◆   ### d. The opportunity to begin again (10:1-5)

"At that time the LORD said to me, 'Chisel out two stone tablets like the first ones. Also make a wooden Ark—a sacred chest to store them in. Come up to me on the mountain, ²and I will write on the tablets the same words that were on the ones you smashed. Then place the tablets in the Ark.'

³"So I made an Ark of acacia wood and cut two stone tablets like the first two. Then I went up the mountain with the tablets in my hand. ⁴Once again the LORD wrote the Ten Commandments* on the tablets and gave them to me. They were the same words the LORD had spoken to you from the heart of the fire on the day you were assembled at the foot of the mountain. ⁵Then I turned and came down

the mountain and placed the tablets in the Ark of the Covenant, which I had made, just as the LORD commanded me. And the tablets are still there in the Ark."

10:4 Hebrew *the ten words.*

NOTES

10:1 *Chisel out.* The word *pasal* [TH6458, ZH7180] means to carve or shape (cf. *pesel* [TH6459, ZH7181], a carved image; see note on 4:16). The original stone tablets appear to have been divinely fabricated (cf. Exod 24:12; 31:18; 32:16), whereas now Moses is told to make two more himself. Perhaps because he shattered those God had made (Exod 32:19), it became his responsibility to make their replacements (cf. Exod 34:1).

COMMENTARY

The effectiveness of Moses's intercession is apparent: The Lord told him to make two more tablets (10:1). These tablets, unlike the first two, must be made by Moses himself (see note on 10:1), and in addition, he must build a chest (*'aron* [TH727, ZH778], commonly translated "ark") in which to house them. In the Exodus account, the instruction to build the sacred chest immediately follows the account of Moses's ascent up Mount Sinai to receive the tablets (Exod 25:10-22; cf. Exod 24:12). Here it seems that the command to build the chest follows Moses's descent from the mountain and the shattering of the tablets. The best resolution of the apparent difference is to view the Exodus instruction as only that and not as a record of work done (Keil and Delitzsch n.d.:340). In fact, the Ark appears not to have been built until sometime after the golden calf incident, and then by Bezalel (Exod 37:1). The instruction to Moses here to make the chest (10:1) and his apparent compliance (10:3) need not be pressed to mean that he did it with his own hands but only that he had it done.

As for the stone tablets, Yahweh made it clear that he himself would inscribe them with the Ten Commandments, just as he had the originals (10:2). This remarkable statement suggests that the Decalogue, at least, was not penned initially by human hands but, as Exodus 31:18 puts it, by the very "finger of God" (cf. 4:13; Exod 32:15-16; 34:1, 28). This does not make it more inspired than the rest of Scripture, but it certainly attests to the significance of this text to the overall theology of the Bible. Furthermore, the words God said he would write would be "the same words" as those on the shattered tablets. The revelation of the mind of God would extend, then, beyond mere ideas to the very words themselves (Merrill 1998:110-111).

The purpose for placing the tablets in the sacred chest was to preserve them as a record of the covenant transaction between Yahweh and Israel (10:2; cf. Exod 25:16). God, as partner in the relationship, had his copy, as did Israel (hence, two stone tablets; cf. comments on 4:13). And since the Ark represented the royal throne on which Yahweh sat invisibly, it was appropriate that the covenant text be located there (cf. 1 Sam 4:4; 2 Sam 6:2; Isa 37:16). This was not to remind Yahweh of his obligations but to symbolize to Israel the certainty of his faithfulness. Israel's copy of the text, located perhaps in the royal palace later on (cf. 17:18-20), was to be kept ready at hand as a witness to their obligation before God to maintain covenant faithfulness.

Continuing the narrative, Moses recounted how Yahweh had revealed himself to Israel from the midst of the fire (cf. 4:12), declaring the Ten Commandments orally and then inscribing them on stone tablets (10:4; cf. Exod 20:22). The very same words of those tablets were repeated on the new tablets Moses had made following the debacle of the golden calf. Having received these new tablets, written by God himself (cf. 10:2), Moses had descended to the assembly below and, when it was finished, had placed them in the sacred Ark. There they had remained through all the years of desert sojourn until the time of Moses's speech (10:5).

◆　　　　　### e. Conclusion of the historical résumé (10:6-11)

⁶(The people of Israel set out from the wells of the people of Jaakan* and traveled to Moserah, where Aaron died and was buried. His son Eleazar ministered as high priest in his place. ⁷Then they journeyed to Gudgodah, and from there to Jotbathah, a land with many brooks and streams. ⁸At that time the LORD set apart the tribe of Levi to carry the Ark of the LORD's Covenant, and to stand before the LORD as his ministers, and to pronounce blessings in his name. These are their duties to this day. ⁹That is why the Levites have no share of property or possession of land among the other Israelite tribes. The LORD himself is their special possession, as the LORD your God told them.)

¹⁰"As for me, I stayed on the mountain in the LORD's presence for forty days and nights, as I had done the first time. And once again the LORD listened to my pleas and agreed not to destroy you. ¹¹Then the LORD said to me, 'Get up and resume the journey, and lead the people to the land I swore to give to their ancestors, so they may take possession of it.'

10:6 Or *set out from Beeroth of Bene-jaakan.*

NOTES

10:6 *wells of the people of Jaakan.* Perhaps the Hebrew should be simply transliterated to reflect a place name: Beeroth Bene-jaakan (Tigay 1996:418; so NASB et al.). By contrast, the Samaritan Pentateuch reads, "From Moseroth they encamped at Bene-jaakan," substituting Moseroth for Beeroth. Such a reading is in line with the itinerary of Num 33:31.

Moserah, where Aaron died. According to both Num 20:28 and 33:38, Aaron died on Mount Hor, not at Moserah. However, since the precise location of Moserah cannot be determined, it is possible that Hor was in or near that place (Bimson 1995:220).

10:7 *Gudgodah . . . Jotbathah.* The Gudgodah here, since it is linked with Jotbathah, must be the same as Hor-haggidgad of Num 33:33, which is similarly listed with Jotbathah. These places were probably in the northern west Arabah region (Bimson 1995:148).

10:8 *At that time.* The period in view depends on the exact extent of the parenthetical material. (Note the NLT opens the parenthesis at v. 6 and closes it in v. 9.) If it includes all of 10:6-9 (Mayes 1979:205), "at that time" should (contra Mayes 1979:206) refer to the events surrounding Aaron's death (10:6). However, if the parenthesis is only 10:6-7 (Cairns 1992:108-109), the reference is to the original affirmation of the Levites, following the apostasy regarding the golden calf (Exod 32:25-29; cf. Deut 10:5). Unless one posits a non-Mosaic interpolation in 10:6-7 (for which there is no objective evidence), "at that time" most naturally relates to the events of those verses.

COMMENTARY

The rationale for placing this pericope where it stands is not clear. It does complete the abbreviated itinerary begun in 9:7, but since, unlike the rest, it does not focus on Israel's rebellion, its mere conclusion of Moses's historical résumé seems not to be its intent. More likely, the introduction of the stone tablets and the Ark of the Covenant (10:1-5) prompted Moses to comment on the role of the priests and Levites vis-à-vis these and other related matters (Weinfeld 1991:419).

The death of Aaron and his burial at Mount Hor (see note on 10:6) is a somber way to bring to attention the operation of the priesthood. This note is necessary, however, to explain succession to the office of high priest and to point out how this called for a new definition of the duties of the Levites. The office of high priest, like that of the later Davidic monarchy, was hereditary. Aaron, therefore, was succeeded by Eleazar, his third but eldest surviving son (cf. Num 3:1-4; 20:25-28).

After further travel (see note on 10:7), the tribe of Levi was set apart (10:8; *badal* [TH914, ZH976], "separate off") to perform at least three duties: (1) to carry the Ark, (2) to minister before Yahweh (lit., "to stand before Yahweh to serve him"), and (3) to bless in his name (10:8). Such a role for Levi had already been described years before (cf. Num 3:11-13; 8:12-26), but now, with Aaron's death, it seemed important to reiterate these duties as if to say the worship of Yahweh goes forward, despite the death of his servants.

The privilege of carrying the Ark was assigned specifically to the Levitical clan of Kohath (cf. Num 4:1-6), the clan from which Aaron and Moses sprang (Exod 6:18, 20). They and the others served Yahweh by facilitating the whole process of community worship. To bless "in [Yahweh's] name" is to invoke Yahweh to be or do something on someone's behalf that otherwise would be unlikely or impossible (NIDOTTE 1.761-762). The most famous example of a priestly blessing formula is that of Numbers 6:24-26:

> May the LORD bless you and protect you. May the LORD smile on you
> and be gracious to you. May the LORD show you his favor and give you
> his peace.

Since the Levites were to be wholly concerned with—indeed, consumed by—the service of Yahweh, they had no land inheritance. Yahweh was their inheritance, their preoccupation. Just as the other tribes were to devote themselves entirely to proper stewardship of the land God had given them, so Levi must unstintingly serve and live for Yahweh, who, in some mysterious and profound sense, belonged especially to that tribe (cf. Num 18:20-24).

His parenthetical comments about priestly and Levitical matters at an end (see note on 10:8), Moses returned to the scene at Sinai, where, because of Israel's apostasy relative to the golden calf (cf. 9:12), God had threatened to destroy them. Moses's prayerful intervention had stayed the hand of divine wrath, however, and Israel had been allowed to live (10:10). More than this, they were permitted to pick up the pieces and to go on to the Land of Promise under Moses's direction (10:11).

◆   ## 4. Love of Yahweh and love of people (10:12-22)

¹²"And now, Israel, what does the LORD your God require of you? He requires only that you fear the LORD your God, and live in a way that pleases him, and love him and serve him with all your heart and soul. ¹³And you must always obey the LORD's commands and decrees that I am giving you today for your own good.

¹⁴"Look, the highest heavens and the earth and everything in it all belong to the LORD your God. ¹⁵Yet the LORD chose your ancestors as the objects of his love. And he chose you, their descendants, above all other nations, as is evident today. ¹⁶Therefore, change your hearts* and stop being stubborn.

¹⁷"For the LORD your God is the God of gods and Lord of lords. He is the great God, the mighty and awesome God, who shows no partiality and cannot be bribed. ¹⁸He ensures that orphans and widows receive justice. He shows love to the foreigners living among you and gives them food and clothing. ¹⁹So you, too, must show love to foreigners, for you yourselves were once foreigners in the land of Egypt. ²⁰You must fear the LORD your God and worship him and cling to him. Your oaths must be in his name alone. ²¹He alone is your God, the only one who is worthy of your praise, the one who has done these mighty miracles that you have seen with your own eyes. ²²When your ancestors went down into Egypt, there were only seventy of them. But now the LORD your God has made you as numerous as the stars in the sky!

10:16 Hebrew *circumcise the foreskin of your hearts.*

NOTES

10:13 *And you must always obey.* The MT lacks the coordinate conjunction "and" (though the Samaritan Pentateuch, Syriac, and Vulgate attest it), and no doubt rightly so, for 10:13 is best understood as a summary of the ideas expressed by the four verbs of 10:12.

10:16 *change your hearts.* The text reads literally, "Circumcise the foreskin of your hearts." This highly allusive image recollects the so-called Abrahamic covenant, in which circumcision symbolized entrance into that covenant (Gen 17:9-14). Just as the removal of that flesh testified to obedience and covenant allegiance, so circumcision of the heart reflects an internal commitment to belong to and serve Yahweh unreservedly (cf. 30:6; Jer 4:4; 9:26).

COMMENTARY

This magnificent discourse is an elaboration on the Shema (6:4-5)—the core of Deuteronomy's theology and of Israel's faith—and on the law that Jesus associated with the Shema, namely, to love our neighbors as ourselves (cf. Lev 19:18; Matt 19:19). The former is the theme of 10:12-16, 20-22, and the latter is the theme of 10:17-19. The passage also introduces the great, climactic conclusion of the general stipulations section of the Deuteronomic covenant text—that is, chapter 11. It will be recalled that these stipulations centered on the first two commandments (5:6-8), which, in turn, are encapsulated in the Shema (see Introduction).

The injunctions to acknowledge only Yahweh as God and to refrain from idolatry are very much at the fore here. Moses asks, "What does Yahweh want?" The answer is fourfold: to fear, to live (lit., "walk"), to love, and to serve (10:12). To fear God is simply to recognize him as such and to hold him in reverential awe (cf. 4:10; 5:29; 6:2, 13). To "walk in all his ways" (or "live in a way that pleases him," NLT) suggests a lifestyle patterned after that of God himself, one completely characterized by righteousness (cf. 5:33; 8:6; 11:22; 13:4, 5; 19:9). To love God means, in the context of covenant language, to choose to worship and serve him exclusively, to be absolutely loyal to him (cf. 6:5; 7:9; 11:1, 13, 22; 13:3; 19:9). To serve God is, in plainest terms, to be his slave. But the verb "serve" (10:12; 'abad [TH5647, ZH6268]) also carries the meaning of "worship" (cf. 6:13; Exod 3:12; Josh 23:7; Judg 2:7).

These four requirements that God makes of his people may be summarized in one: "Obey the LORD's commands and decrees" (10:13). Though some ancient witnesses join this verse to the previous four (see note on 10:13), it seems best grammatically and theologically to view this demand as a distillation of the others. People show their fear, godliness, love, and service (or worship) when they obey God's covenant mandates. To profess these things while living in disobedience is the height of hypocrisy (cf. John 14:15, 21).

Yahweh's right to make such demands rests on (1) his unquestioned sovereignty (10:14) and (2) his choice of Israel to be his people (10:15). Again, the text is packed with covenant terminology. Literally it reads, "Yahweh delighted to love (le'ahabah [TH157, ZH170]) them [the ancestors] and he chose (wayyibkhar [TH977, ZH1047]) their descendants." To love and to choose are hallmarks of Old Testament covenant texts (see note on 4:37). As Creator and covenant-maker, then, Yahweh has every basis on which to call his people to account. Thus, any defection from his standards of expectation calls for repentance and renewal (see note on 10:16).

The command to love one another (10:19) is also predicated on an assertion of Yahweh's sovereignty (10:17). He is supreme over all gods, real or imaginary (cf. 5:7), and over all lords, divine or human. He is great, mighty, and awe-inspiring, but most important to the exhortation Moses is leading up to, he is impartial and uninfluenced by inducements designed to curry his favor. Yahweh cannot be bought! Illustrative of his evenhandedness is God's special attention to those least able to offer bribes—orphans, widows, and foreigners (10:18; ger [TH1616, ZH1731], a "sojourner, newcomer," KBL 192). He delights to care for those from whom he can expect nothing in return (cf. Craigie 1976:206-207).

This heavenly example provides a springboard for asserting right human behavior. If God loves, so must we. In Israel's case, unconcern for the foreigner should be unthinkable in light of Israel's prior status as a stranger in Egypt, a status from which Yahweh graciously delivered them (10:19; cf. 23:7; Exod 22:21; 23:9; Lev 19:34). In fact, Jesus said it is impossible to separate love for God from love for one another when he taught that the command to love your neighbor is equally as important as the command to love God (Mark 12:31). John adds to this the convicting observation that "if we don't love people we can see, how can we love God, whom we cannot see?" (1 John 4:20; cf. Jas 2:1-9).

Moses rounded out his present exhortation by returning to the thought of 10:12—the people need to fear, serve, and hold fast to Yahweh (10:20). This is the essence of the first two commandments (5:6-8). To complete the trilogy, Moses alluded to the third by enjoining the people to swear by Yahweh's name alone. To do so is to use his name rightly (cf. 5:11; 6:13). To swear by his name is to invoke his authority, an authority derivative of his intrinsic worthiness and his mighty acts on behalf of his people (10:21). Most particularly, his claims to unrivaled praise and worship find substance in Israel itself. Once a meager people of only 70 individuals, they had become (in the interim of Egyptian sojourn) a mighty nation, so numerous, said Moses, as to vie with the very stars of the sky (10:22). One cannot escape the overtones of covenant fulfillment—Abraham had been told that his offspring would reach such stupendous proportions (Gen 15:5; 22:17; cf. Deut 1:10; 26:5).

◆ 5. Obedience and disobedience and their rewards (11:1-32)
a. Reiteration of the call to obedience (11:1-7)

"You must love the LORD your God and obey all his requirements, decrees, regulations, and commands. ²Keep in mind that I am not talking now to your children, who have never experienced the discipline of the LORD your God or seen his greatness and his strong hand and powerful arm. ³They didn't see the miraculous signs and wonders he performed in Egypt against Pharaoh and all his land. ⁴They didn't see what the LORD did to the armies of Egypt and to their horses and chariots—how he drowned them in the Red Sea* as they were chasing you. He destroyed them, and they have not recovered to this very day! ⁵"Your children didn't see how the LORD cared for you in the wilderness until you arrived here. ⁶They didn't see what he did to Dathan and Abiram (the sons of Eliab, a descendant of Reuben) when the earth opened its mouth in the Israelite camp and swallowed them, along with their households and tents and every living thing that belonged to them. ⁷But you have seen the LORD perform all these mighty deeds with your own eyes!

11:4 Hebrew *sea of reeds*.

NOTES

11:1 *requirements.* This noun form, derived from the verb *shamar* [TH8104, ZH9068] (to watch, be careful), means literally "the things pertaining to him [Yahweh] that need to be observed" (KBL 578)—i.e., the following three kinds of covenant stipulations: decrees (*khuqqoth* [TH2708, ZH2978]), regulations (*mishpatim* [TH4941, ZH5477]), and commands (*mitswoth* [TH4687, ZH5184]). It is not another category, but a generic expression encompassing the whole covenant requirement (cf. 10:13).

COMMENTARY

Moses's insistent exhortation to covenant fidelity continues here in a statement that by now has become almost cliche (6:5; 10:12). They must love Yahweh and do everything he commands (Thompson 1974:152). They must live by all the stipulations of the covenant so far revealed and yet to be revealed (see note on 11:1). And this word is for the adult generation, those in living memory of the plagues against Egypt, the Exodus deliverance, and the difficult experiences of the desert wanderings (11:2). These people must first be challenged because they have the advantage of learning from history. It was they who made up the leadership of their time and had the task of transmitting God's requirements to the generation to come.

The youth were uninstructed by the discipline of the past and had not had the life-changing experience of witnessing God's "signs and wonders" (see 4:34; 6:22; 7:19). These, of course, were the plagues (cf. Exod 7:3; Pss 78:43; 135:9) that devastated Egypt but brought great glory to God (11:3). Moreover, the young were not there to see the drowning of Pharaoh's army, a destruction from which Egypt had not recovered to that very day, 40 years later (11:4; see Merrill 1987:99).

The events of the 38 years of desert sojourn were also not fully known to Israel's most recent sons and daughters. They had missed both the experience of God's miraculous provision (cf. 8:1-5) and the outpouring of his wrath on the disobedient. A striking example of the latter was the supernatural decease of Dathan and Abiram, Reubenites who had challenged the leadership of Moses and Aaron (Num 16:1-3). Collaborating with certain Levites, Dathan and Abiram argued that since all God's people were equally set apart, Moses and Aaron had no right to claim a special status. Perhaps because Dathan and Abiram descended from Reuben, Jacob's eldest son, they felt they had some privilege based on primogeniture (Harrison 1990:232). In any event, their challenge to God-appointed leadership was subversive of God's sovereignty. Therefore, they and all that was precious to them were swallowed up in a great crevice in the earth (11:6; cf. Num 16:31-35). The adults had seen all this for themselves; as a result, they should be all the more attentive to love and serve God in the future (11:7).

◆   ## b. The bounties of the Land of Promise (11:8-15)

8"Therefore, be careful to obey every command I am giving you today, so you may have strength to go in and take over the land you are about to enter. 9If you obey, you will enjoy a long life in the land the LORD swore to give to your ancestors and to you, their descendants—a land flowing with milk and honey! 10For the land you are about to enter and take over is not like the land of Egypt from which you came, where you planted your seed and made irrigation ditches with your foot as in a vegetable garden. 11Rather, the land you will soon take over is a land of hills and valleys with plenty of rain— 12a land that the LORD your God cares for. He watches over it through each season of the year!

13"If you carefully obey all the commands I am giving you today, and if you love the LORD your God and serve him with all your heart and soul, 14then he will send the rains in their proper seasons— the early and late rains—so you can bring in your harvests of grain, new wine, and olive oil. 15He will give you lush pastureland for your livestock, and you yourselves will have all you want to eat.

NOTES

11:8 every command. The singular (*mitswah* [TH4687, ZH5184], "command") is here more likely a way of speaking of the whole corpus of covenant stipulations (cf. 6:1, 25; 7:11; 8:1). A translation like "the whole command" is to be preferred.

COMMENTARY

Instructive experiences of the past should prepare one for the challenges of tomorrow. Moses thus urged obedience to the covenant principles (see note on 11:8)—

something all too frequently ignored until then—so that Israel's entrance to and occupation of the land of Canaan would be unhindered (11:8). Compliance with the provisions of the covenant would bring long life in the land and many amenities with it (11:9). The long life in question seems most immediately to refer to individual longevity, but the plural used throughout could also suggest long national existence (cf. 4:40; 5:16, 33).

Moses had already provided a brief description of the land to which they were headed, one he called "a good land" (8:7-10). Here he employs the formulaic "flowing with milk and honey" (cf. 6:3; 26:9, 15; 27:3; 31:20; Exod 3:8, 17; 13:5; 33:3; Josh 5:6), a hyperbole followed by a contrast drawn between Canaan and Egypt. In Egypt, he said, irrigation was by foot (11:10). The idea is not so much digging with the foot but the operation of irrigation machinery by pedal-power, something practiced in modern times in parts of Egypt (Driver 1902:129). Canaan would be vastly different and much easier than Egypt, however. In Canaan, Yahweh would provide the irrigation in the form of rainfall that runs down the hills and through the valleys (11:11). Such provision testifies to a remarkable relationship to the land—Yahweh "cares for" it (11:12), so much so that he watches it (lit., "his eyes are upon it") all year long. The Hebrew text states the concern of Yahweh for the land even more forcefully: "It is a land Yahweh your God constantly seeks after." That is, it is the focus of his attention and the thing with which he is intensely preoccupied. This emphasis on the land is, of course, very much in line with the centrality of the land to the promises made to the patriarchs (cf. Gen 12:1, 7; 13:15; 15:7, 16, 18; 17:8; 26:3).

But, as in the case here, covenant blessings are always conditional (though the covenant relationship itself is not). Once more, strict obedience to the whole covenant, especially as it is epitomized in the injunction of the Shema ("all your heart and soul"; cf. 6:5), would assure God's favor, in this instance bountiful and timely rain (lit., "former and latter rain"; cf. Baly 1957:49-52) that would eventuate in plentiful harvest of all kinds of produce (11:13-14). Man and beast alike would have all the food they need (11:15).

◆   **c. Exhortation to instruction and obedience (11:16-25)**

[16]"But be careful. Don't let your heart be deceived so that you turn away from the LORD and serve and worship other gods. [17]If you do, the LORD's anger will burn against you. He will shut up the sky and hold back the rain, and the ground will fail to produce its harvests. Then you will quickly die in that good land the LORD is giving you.

[18]"So commit yourselves wholeheartedly to these words of mine. Tie them to your hands and wear them on your forehead as reminders. [19]Teach them to your children. Talk about them when you are at home and when you are on the road, when you are going to bed and when you are getting up. [20]Write them on the doorposts of your house and on your gates, [21]so that as long as the sky remains above the earth, you and your children may flourish in the land the LORD swore to give your ancestors.

²²"Be careful to obey all these commands I am giving you. Show love to the LORD your God by walking in his ways and holding tightly to him. ²³Then the LORD will drive out all the nations ahead of you, though they are much greater and stronger than you, and you will take over their land. ²⁴Wherever you set foot, that land will be yours. Your frontiers will stretch from the wilderness in the south to Lebanon in the north, and from the Euphrates River in the east to the Mediterranean Sea in the west.* ²⁵No one will be able to stand against you, for the LORD your God will cause the people to fear and dread you, as he promised, wherever you go in the whole land.

11:24 Hebrew *to the western sea.*

NOTES

11:16 *Don't let your heart be deceived.* The MT reads, "lest your heart be deceived and you turn away." This fuller rendition is important in light of the ensuing instructions about education. The verb translated "deceived" (*patah* [TH6601, ZH7331]) reflects a root idea of being simple or uninformed (KBL 786). The admonition, then, is a plea for sound instruction in covenant truth.

COMMENTARY

If obedience brings blessing in the framework of covenant relationship, then disobedience brings quite the opposite. Again, the epitome of covenant transgression is disloyalty to Yahweh and the "worship" (11:16; *'abad* [TH5647, ZH6268], "to serve") of other gods. Only solid instruction in truth can preclude this from happening (see note on 11:16). The price of such defection was to be the reversal of the blessings just listed (for "curse" as exact counterpart to "blessing," see 28:1-6, 15-19). God would shut off the rain, the land would become sterile, and the people would surely die (11:17).

The antidote to apostasy is commitment to the Word of God. "Set these words upon your heart and mind," the text literally reads (11:18). And to assist the process of internalizing these things, Moses enjoins the people to bind them upon their hands and foreheads (for an explanation of the objects used and their significance, see the comments on 6:4-9). Whenever they looked at these outer reminders, they would bring to mind the need for loyal adherence to the covenant requirements. Thus, they could continue to enjoy God's blessings.

The connection of this text to the Shema (6:4ff) and its consequent instructions is clear again from the exhortation for parents to instruct their children in all the elements of the covenant. This learning should not simply occur in a time set apart for formal education. Rather, it must be lifestyle learning, the kind gained by watching as well as listening. As noted above (6:7), this embraces every waking moment and extends to every kind of activity (11:19). Even the entryways to houses and villages must be display areas where texts of Scripture can be publicly seen as reminders to keep the whole Torah (11:20; cf. 6:9). If all this is done faithfully, the nation will enjoy life in the land forever (11:21).

With painstaking repetition, Moses continues his exhortation to be most careful to observe the whole law, evidence of which is covenant loyalty (11:22; *'ahab* [TH157, ZH170], "love"), adherence to Yahweh's standards of righteousness, and such undivided attachment to him (thus *dabaq* [TH1692, ZH1815], "hold tightly to"; TDOT

3.81-82; cf. 10:20; 13:4; 30:20), as to leave no doubt as to whom Israel belongs and whom they serve. The exhortation of 11:13, couched in essentially the same literary formula, had promised abundant life in Canaan should it be heeded (11:14-15). Now the promise is the dispossession of all the nations that occupy the land (11:23; cf. 6:19; 7:20, 22; 9:3, 5; 12:2, 29; 18:12) and establishment of Israelite control. This is put in terms of treading upon the land (11:24; cf. *darak* [TH1869, ZH2005] + *regel* [TH7272, ZH8079]), using a technical expression denoting conquest and dominion (cf. 1:36 and comments there).

The extent of the dominion is described here as embracing the territory from "the steppe-land" (*hammidbar* [TH4057, ZH4497]; "wilderness," NLT), "and the Lebanon, from the river, the river Euphrates, and as far as the back (i.e., Western) sea" (11:24). This rather awkward way of referring to the directions and perimeters of the land makes precision most difficult, and, indeed, the intention is to list only the farthest extremes (Tigay 1996:115). The western border clearly is the Mediterranean Sea (western sea) and the northeastern border is the Euphrates River. Very likely the "steppe-land" is to the south, that is, the Negev and Arabah, so the northern extent would be the Lebanon mountains. For other descriptions see 1:7-8; Genesis 15:18; Exodus 23:31.

With Yahweh as leader, there would be no question as to the outcome of the conquest. The enemy would be unable to withstand the onslaught of the hosts of Yahweh because, as the Divine Warrior (see 7:17-24), he would so empower his people that everyone would be filled with fear of them (11:25; *pakhdekem* [TH6343, ZH7065]) and the dread of them (*mora'akem* [TH4172, ZH4616]), the two terms perhaps forming a hendiadys meaning "absolutely terrified of them" or the like. It is not so much that the Canaanites will tremble before Yahweh as before his people Israel (cf. also Rahab's testimony in Josh 2:9). As those whom the Lord has called into covenant partnership with him exercise all the powers and privileges that come with that relationship, they take on the very invincibility of God himself. Israel can take the land because they are God's powerful and fearsome instrument (11:25).

◆　　### d. Anticipation of a blessing and cursing ceremony (11:26-32)

26"Look, today I am giving you the choice between a blessing and a curse! 27You will be blessed if you obey the commands of the LORD your God that I am giving you today. 28But you will be cursed if you reject the commands of the LORD your God and turn away from him and worship gods you have not known before.

29"When the LORD your God brings you into the land and helps you take possession of it, you must pronounce the blessing at Mount Gerizim and the curse at Mount Ebal. 30(These two mountains are west of the Jordan River in the land of the Canaanites who live in the Jordan Valley,* near the town of Gilgal, not far from the oaks of Moreh.) 31For you are about to cross the Jordan River to take over the land the LORD your God is giving you. When you take that land and are living in it, 32you must be careful to obey all the decrees and regulations I am giving you today.

11:30 Hebrew *the Arabah.*

NOTES

11:27 commands. The word *mitswoth* [TH4687, ZH5184] is used here as a term summarizing the content of the covenant stipulations, particularly the so-called general stipulations of chs 5–11. Two other terms (*khuqqim* [TH2706, ZH2976] and *mishpatim* [TH4941, ZH5477]) occur in 11:32 to express the same thing, suggesting, perhaps, that *mitswoth* is a more generic term for covenant law as a whole.

11:30 oaks of Moreh. Instead of the MT's *'elone* [TH436, ZH471] ("oaks," plural), many Greek mss have the singular "oak," a reading supported by the only other occurrence of the place name (Gen 12:6). The Samaritan Pentateuch has *mwr'* for the MT's *moreh* [TH4176, ZH4622] and adds *mul shekem* [TH7927, ZH8901], "near Shechem." This suggests that the Samaritan Pentateuch has confused Moreh with Mamre (*mamre'* [TH4471, ZH4934]), a reading attested in the Syriac and Targum Pseudo-Jonathan. There is a locale called "Oaks of Mamre" near Hebron, where Abram settled for awhile (Gen 13:18); close to this was his burial site, the cave at Machpelah (Gen 23:17-19; 49:30; 50:13). To preclude this as the place in view in our text, the Samaritan Pentateuch adds the qualifier "near Shechem," as though there were two Mamres (or Morehs).

COMMENTARY

The large section I have designated "general stipulations" (chs 5–11) closes, not surprisingly, with reference to blessings and curses. In virtually every ancient Near Eastern treaty text (the pattern after which Deuteronomy is modeled), there are lists of blessings promised to those who faithfully keep the covenant requirements; conversely, there are sanctions against those who do not. At this point, these sections and their ritualistic application are mentioned almost in passing, but at the end of the full stipulations section there is extensive enumeration of these positive and negative consequences of interacting with the covenant (27:1–28:68).

Moses said that on that very day he was setting before Israel a choice: They could opt for either a blessing or a curse (11:26). This did not mean that the people had reached a crisis point where such a choice had to be made right then and there (as they did in Joshua's offer of a similar kind; Josh 24:15), but it was not too early for them to understand that a decision would have to be made formally and collectively in the near future. Therefore, it was appropriate to get in the mode of covenant compliance in the present so that the right choice could more easily be made when the time came.

The blessing, quite naturally, was a concomitant of obedience to the whole covenant arrangement (see note on 11:27) that Yahweh had made with Israel. The "curse" (11:28; *qelalah* [TH7045, ZH7839]), however, would ensue in the event of disobedience (lit., "not hearing") to the covenant, specifically in turning aside from its injunctions by pursuing a course of life inimical to Yahweh's expectations. Such rebellion is epitomized by breaking the first commandment—that is, by worshiping (lit., "walking after" or "following the course of life of") other gods (cf. 5:6-7). I noted above that the general stipulations section of Deuteronomy is an expanded commentary on the first and second commandments, so it is not surprising that Moses equated covenant infidelity in general with the violation of that fundamental principle on which the covenant is based, namely, the uniqueness and exclusiveness of Yahweh, the God of Israel.

The nation's choice of blessings or cursings was to be expressed in a ceremony of covenant commitment, some details of which are elaborated here. A formal convocation would be gathered at a place long sacralized by divine visitation to Abraham, a place nearby a settlement known as Shechem (see Gen 12:4-7). This was the first site occupied by the patriarch according to the record (Gen 12:6) and the first to have witnessed the appearance of Yahweh to him (Gen 12:7). Abraham had built an altar there to commemorate that theophany; from then on, Shechem had come to symbolize most profoundly the Abrahamic covenant and its implications (see Gen 33:18-20; 35:4; cf. Josh 24:1, 25).

Besides its hallowed tradition, Shechem provided a most suitable location for mass assembly, being located in a great valley between Mount Gerizim and Mount Ebal. The setting was like an amphitheater with the principal actors on the stage below, surrounded by the population above on the mountainsides. The detailed instructions of 27:1-14 required that half the tribes gather on one mountain and half on the other, those on Gerizim representing the choral response to the blessings to be read out and those on Ebal the curses (11:29).

The information concerning the location of the place (11:30) could have originated either with Moses (as the phrase "on the other side of the Jordan" would suggest) or with some later editor who wanted to make sure that everyone understood where this momentous event took place. Mosaic origination has the most to commend it inasmuch as later generations could hardly have misunderstood where Gerizim and Ebal were located. Moses's own contemporaries, however, could well have been ignorant of such things.

From the Transjordan perspective (where Moses and the people were), the designated place was to the west (lit., "the way of the going [down] of the sun"), in the land of the Canaanites "who live in the Jordan Valley" (11:30), near Gilgal, and not far from the "oaks of Moreh" (see note on 11:30). This rather complicated description can best be understood as directional—that is, as providing an itinerary (Thompson 1974:158; Tigay 1996:116-117). The starting point is where they are, at Shittim, and by traveling northwest to Shechem, they would pass through Gilgal in the Arabah (i.e., the Jordan Valley) and end up at the mountains Gerizim and Ebal.

All of this was imminent, for Israel was on the verge of conquest and occupation of the Promised Land (11:31). In light of that imminence, Moses could do no less than impress upon the nation the absolute necessity of obedience to the covenant mandates they were in process of receiving (11:32).

◆ V. The Specific Stipulations of the Covenant (12:1–26:15)
　　A. The Exclusiveness of Yahweh and His Worship (12:1–16:17)
　　　　1. The central sanctuary (12:1-14)

"These are the decrees and regulations you must be careful to obey when you live in the land that the LORD, the God of your ancestors, is giving you. You must obey them as long as you live.

2"When you drive out the nations that

live there, you must destroy all the places where they worship their gods—high on the mountains, up on the hills, and under every green tree. ³Break down their altars and smash their sacred pillars. Burn their Asherah poles and cut down their carved idols. Completely erase the names of their gods!

⁴"Do not worship the LORD your God in the way these pagan peoples worship their gods. ⁵Rather, you must seek the LORD your God at the place of worship he himself will choose from among all the tribes—the place where his name will be honored. ⁶There you will bring your burnt offerings, your sacrifices, your tithes, your sacred offerings, your offerings to fulfill a vow, your voluntary offerings, and your offerings of the firstborn animals of your herds and flocks. ⁷There you and your families will feast in the presence of the LORD your God, and you will rejoice in all you have accomplished because the LORD your God has blessed you.

⁸"Your pattern of worship will change. Today all of you are doing as you please,

⁹because you have not yet arrived at the place of rest, the land the LORD your God is giving you as your special possession. ¹⁰But you will soon cross the Jordan River and live in the land the LORD your God is giving you. When he gives you rest from all your enemies and you're living safely in the land, ¹¹you must bring everything I command you—your burnt offerings, your sacrifices, your tithes, your sacred offerings, and your offerings to fulfill a vow—to the designated place of worship, the place the LORD your God chooses for his name to be honored.

¹²"You must celebrate there in the presence of the LORD your God with your sons and daughters and all your servants. And remember to include the Levites who live in your towns, for they will receive no allotment of land among you. ¹³Be careful not to sacrifice your burnt offerings just anywhere you like. ¹⁴You may do so only at the place the LORD will choose within one of your tribal territories. There you must offer your burnt offerings and do everything I command you.

NOTES

12:1 *your ancestors . . . you.* A major issue in biblical scholarship, one not observable in English translations, emerges here (and elsewhere; cf. 6:3, 13-19; 7:4) with reference to the alternating use of singular and plural pronouns and pronominal suffixes (see Introduction). By and large, plural forms dominate in 12:1-12 and singular ones in 12:13-28. This exchange in number (called *Numeruswechsel* in German scholarship) has led many critics to conclude that ch 12 and certain other passages exhibit redactional activity in which sources that preferred the plural form were integrated with those that used the singular (see Begg 1979). Such a conclusion, besides lacking any ancient manuscript evidence, betrays insensitivity to the important theological idea that Israel was considered both plural—a collection of individuals—and singular—a corporate entity (Mayes 1979:35-36). There may also be metrical/stylistic factors in view (Christensen 1993). It is true, however, that the ancient versions (LXX, Syriac, Targum) have the plural throughout 12:1 (and generally elsewhere in the chapter) to bring the pronouns into consistency with the predicate ("you [plural] must obey") and the independent pronoun ("you [plural] live").

12:7 *feast in the presence of the LORD.* This feasting indicates that the occasions especially in view here are those times of covenant renewal or reaffirmation centered particularly on the three annual festivals, Passover, Pentecost, and Tabernacles—matters addressed fully in ch 16.

12:9 *you . . . your.* In the Hebrew, the first "you" is plural, while the later second person pronouns are singular; this has prompted many ancient versions to read "your (plural) God" and "giving you" (plural), whereas others read "our" or "us" respectively. For the issue of alternation in grammatical number, see note on 12:1.

12:13 *just anywhere.* The MT's anarthrous form *bekol maqom* [TH4725, ZH5226] means "in any place." Many major ancient versions presuppose the articular form *bekol hammaqom*, meaning "in the whole place" or "in all the place." The meaning, however, is essentially the same in this context.

COMMENTARY

This passage introduces the next major section in the covenant code of Deuteronomy—namely, the specific stipulations (12:1–26:15). These laws elaborate on the basic principles of the previous section (chs 5–11), providing particular examples of case law that are illustrative of the principles. In general, an argument can be made that this whole section is developed according to the order of the Ten Commandments, which are, of course, the foundation of the covenant relationship (see Introduction).

Within this large section, attention is paid first to the theologically dominant idea of the exclusiveness of Yahweh and his worship (12:1–16:17), an idea that necessitates a central place in the Land of Promise where Yahweh will choose to dwell among his people and to which they must resort as a community (12:1–14). This whole subsection clearly relates to the first four commandments and most particularly to the first two: the exclusiveness of Yahweh and prohibition against idolatry (5:7-10).

That this is a major break in the book is clear from the formulaic introduction of 12:1, in which Israel is solemnly charged to obey the "decrees and regulations" (cf. 4:1; 5:1; 6:1; 11:1). By and large, the community is addressed in the plural here (cf. note on 12:1), perhaps to stress the importance of individual responsibility. The first thing they must do in Canaan in the interest of asserting the uniqueness and exclusiveness of Yahweh is to destroy the religious systems already prevailing there (12:2-3). They had already been enjoined to do this in another context, one in which the holiness of the people themselves was at stake (7:1-6). Now the focus was on the holiness of God, an attribute incompatible with idolatry.

The command thus was to destroy the high places on which the indigenous peoples had worshiped their gods. The "green tree" (12:2) refers to various heavily leafed species that, by their very luxuriance, symbolized fertility in the Baal cult (de Vaux 1965:278-279). In later times, the prophets chided the people for participating in the orgiastic rites that accompanied such nature religions (cf. 1 Kgs 14:23-24; 2 Kgs 16:4; 17:10-13). All the paraphernalia of those pagan shrines—altars, sacred pillars (cf. 7:5), Asherah poles (7:5; Judg 3:7; 6:25-30), and carved idols—must be eradicated and the very names of the gods removed from memory (12:3). The significance of remembering and forgetting names is a leading idea in the passage (cf. 12:5, 11, 21).

Yahweh must be worshiped in ways radically contradictory to those just mentioned (12:4). He would not be approached just anywhere, at "all the places where they worship their gods" (12:2), but only at the place he would choose to locate his name (12:5). God was not suggesting that he was limited spatially to one spot or was inaccessible to those who wished to commune with him wherever they were.

The point being made in this context was that the covenant community as a holistic entity could not worship wherever they pleased, thus putting themselves in danger of succumbing to Canaanite ideas of places especially vested with chthonic powers. To preserve the notion of their oneness, they must meet as one and at one place only, the place of Yahweh's own earthly dwelling.

It is, of course, impossible for the infinite God—he who transcends creation itself—to be encapsulated within a tabernacle or temple, a point Solomon was to make most emphatically (1 Kgs 8:27-30). By a figure of speech (metonymy), then, Yahweh was said to dwell among his people through his name. Though largely lost to the modern West, the idea of a name representing the being thus named was well understood in the ancient Near East. Moreover, names, whether of deities or human beings, were usually descriptive of the nature, character, or even anticipated prospects for the individual (NIDOTTE 4.147). Thus, Moses insisted that the names of the pagan gods be obliterated (12:3) and that, instead, the name of Yahweh be remembered. To aid in this process, Yahweh's name would inhabit a place that forever after would be linked to it: the Temple of Yahweh on Mount Zion.

To this central place, the community must gather on stated occasions to offer homage to its God (12:6). It is important to recall that in terms of the covenant ideology of Deuteronomy, Yahweh was the Great King and Israel was the vassal upon whom it was incumbent to offer tribute to their Lord as acknowledgment of his sovereignty (see "Literary Style" and "Theological Themes" in the Introduction). This is the fundamental significance of the sacrifices and other offerings listed here.

Contrary to the policy that existed throughout Israel's history up to the point of the eve of conquest, Israel must adopt a new pattern of worship in Canaan, one exclusively centered on a single sanctuary of God's choosing. Individuals would have no choice in the matter as to where the whole community must assemble to pay homage to Yahweh (12:8-9). Once their enemies had been defeated or expelled and peace prevailed, the chosen people must appear at the "dwelling place" of Yahweh, the site that his name would occupy (12:10-11; cf. 12:5). Inasmuch as the kind of peace anticipated here did not come to pass until the reign of David, the centrality of the sanctuary remained more an ideal than a reality in the pre-monarchic period.

In the past, as the sacred record makes clear, individuals and families could erect altars and worship God wherever they encountered him (cf. Gen 8:20; 12:7; 13:18; 22:9; 26:25; 35:1, 3, 7; Exod 17:15). Even after the Sinai revelation, worship, though largely confined to the Tabernacle, was carried out wherever the Tabernacle was located at any given time. Moreover, provision was made even at Sinai for stone altars to be erected and used in the future in whatever places God would be memorialized (Exod 20:24-26; Childs 1974:466-467). The record again is replete with examples of such local shrines where individuals or small congregations could worship God with his full endorsement and blessing (cf. 16:21; Judg 6:24-27; 13:19-20; 1 Sam 7:17; 10:5, 13; 2 Sam 24:18-25; 1 Kgs 18:30).

The thrust of this text, however, is the centralizing of community worship at one place only and then for an extended time. This would be the pattern in Canaan; the theocratic community, conceived as a corporate entity for the purpose of covenant relationship, must recognize and dramatize that fact by appearing regularly before Yahweh at his dwelling place (see 12:7). The corporate nature of worship at the central sanctuary is made quite explicit in 12:12, where families, servants, and Levites are included. It seems all are to come from their villages with their tribute for the Great King and tribute for whatever the Levites lack, inasmuch as they have no means of food production but still must enter into proper worship of Yahweh. Numbers 18 outlines the provisions for the priests and Levites. They would have no land holdings in Canaan and thus could not farm and otherwise provide food for their families (Num 18:8-32). Their needs must be met by the tithes of the offerings made to the sanctuary (18:1-8). Such worship could not be practiced in their home villages (see note on 12:13), but only in "the place the LORD will choose" (12:14)— that is, in the one designated place in one of the tribal allotments.

Critical scholarship that asserts a late, non-Mosaic authorship of Deuteronomy is forced to surmise that the exact location of the sanctuary is unmentioned in order to lend the appearance that the text is indeed Mosaic and preconquest (de Vaux 1965:338). The traditional view is much more satisfying here: Moses did not designate the place or even in what tribal territory it would be located precisely because he did not know! In fact, several decades passed before the Tabernacle was set up in its first "permanent" location in Canaan, namely, in Shiloh, a site in Ephraim (Josh 18:1). Before that, it was rather unsettled, Gilgal being its principal location (Josh 4:19; 5:10-12; 9:6; 10:6-15, 43). Shiloh remained the home of the Tabernacle from about 1350–1100 BC, at which time Shiloh was destroyed, and the worship center moved elsewhere (1 Sam 4–6), probably to Nob (1 Sam 21:1-6) and then to Gibeon (1 Chr 16:39). Eventually, of course, the Mosaic Tabernacle gave way to one built by David on Mount Zion (2 Sam 6:16-19) and then to Solomon's Temple (1 Kgs 6:1). Jerusalem remained the site of the central sanctuary for about 365 years (951–586 BC), until the Temple and city were demolished by the Babylonians (2 Kgs 25:9).

◆   ## 2. The sanctity of blood (12:15-19)

[15]"But you may butcher your animals and eat their meat in any town whenever you want. You may freely eat the animals with which the LORD your God blesses you. All of you, whether ceremonially clean or unclean, may eat that meat, just as you now eat gazelle and deer. [16]But you must not consume the blood. You must pour it out on the ground like water.

[17]"But you may not eat your offerings in your hometown—neither the tithe of your grain and new wine and olive oil, nor the firstborn of your flocks and herds, nor any offering to fulfill a vow, nor your voluntary offerings, nor your sacred offerings. [18]You must eat these in the presence of the LORD your God at the place he will choose. Eat them there with your children, your servants, and the Levites who live in your towns, celebrating in the presence of the LORD your God in all you do. [19]And be very careful never to neglect the Levites as long as you live in your land.

NOTES

12:16 *You must pour.* The MT has the plural verb form instead of the expected singular. Such fluctuation occurs regularly in this section (see note on 12:1).

COMMENTARY

Still in line with the broad theme of centralized worship, Moses now deals with a nuancing of that theme by addressing the issue of animal slaughter in general, not just that done in a religious context. Quite clearly Israelites who lived many days' journey from the central sanctuary—as thousands would once the land was occupied—could hardly be expected to make such a trek every time they wanted to butcher animals for food. And yet, in a culture such as Israel's, in which distinctions between the sacred and the profane were blurred or nonexistent, even slaughter for human consumption involved the spilling of blood, an element invested with great sanctity (cf. Gen 9:4; Lev 17:11).

Moses, therefore, provided instruction that would safeguard both proper practicality and holiness. The people could slaughter wherever they wished, domesticated animals as well as wild game—even if they were not ceremonially purified (12:15; cf. Lev 15; 17-19). However, the blood was taboo. It could not be eaten or put to any other use. Hence, it must be spilled out on the ground (12:16; cf. Lev 3:17; 7:26-27).

The tithes of all produce, including flocks and herds, could not be consumed in local villages but must be taken to the central sanctuary, no matter how far it might be (12:17). The phrase "at the place he will choose" (12:18) is clearly speaking of the future dwelling place of Yahweh. These tithes would accompany the three annual festivals, at which adult males, at least, were expected to be in attendance (cf. 12:6-7; 16:1-17). The rejoicing or celebrating associated with these festivals suggests the covenant nature of these gatherings; invariably, covenant affirmation included fellowship meals in which Yahweh and Israel broke bread together in great joy (12:18; cf. 14:26; 16:11, 14-15). Again, however, they must remember the Levites in all their celebrating because the Levites depended on the community for their well-being (12:19; cf. 12:12).

◆   ### 3. The problem of distance (12:20-28)

[20]"When the LORD your God expands your territory as he has promised, and you have the urge to eat meat, you may freely eat meat whenever you want. [21]It might happen that the designated place of worship—the place the LORD your God chooses for his name to be honored—is a long way from your home. If so, you may butcher any of the cattle, sheep, or goats the LORD has given you, and you may freely eat the meat in your hometown, as I have commanded you. [22]Anyone, whether ceremonially clean or unclean, may eat that meat, just as you do now with gazelle and deer. [23]But never consume the blood, for the blood is the life, and you must not consume the lifeblood with the meat. [24]Instead, pour out the blood on the ground like water. [25]Do not consume the blood, so that all may go well with you and your children after you, because you will be doing what pleases the LORD.

[26]"Take your sacred gifts and your offerings given to fulfill a vow to the place

the LORD chooses. ²⁷You must offer the meat and blood of your burnt offerings on the altar of the LORD your God. The blood of your other sacrifices must be poured out on the altar of the LORD your God, but you may eat the meat. ²⁸Be careful to obey all my commands, so that all will go well with you and your children after you, because you will be doing what is good and pleasing to the LORD your God.

NOTES

12:25 the LORD. The LXX reads, "the Lord your God." This seems to be an attempt to bring the epithet in line with its common occurrence otherwise in the passage (vv. 20, 21, 27 [twice], 28). However, this forces the text into an artificial straitjacket (note other exceptions in vv. 21, 26).

12:26 chooses. The MT ends with "the place Yahweh chooses," but to bring 12:26 into line with a similar idea in 12:11, the LXX adds "your God will choose to place his name there." While this brings consistency, it forces the passage to conform too rigidly to a pattern that was probably never intended and for which there is no other evidence.

COMMENTARY

There is much repetition between this section and the last (12:15-19), but a new idea explicitly articulated here is the practical problem of distance. If community worship was to be carried out only at the central sanctuary, what would be the plight of those who lived too far from that sacred place to be able to worship there regularly? Clearly some way had to be found to resolve the impasse between the command to worship Yahweh at a specific place and the practical impossibility of doing so more than the three times mandated for the nation as a whole (see 12:17). This is an issue that continues to perplex scholars to this day.

Moses anticipated the problem when he noted that the geographical enlargement of the nation would preclude ordinary slaughter from being carried out at the central sanctuary alone (12:20; cf. 12:15). Thus, such procedures could be undertaken in local villages, provided the sanctity of blood was recognized and rigorously protected (12:21-24; cf. 12:16). By no means could it be eaten because blood was essentially equivalent to life itself, and thus its consumption was treading upon the realm of the sacred (12:25).

The Mosaic law, though not expressly teaching it, made allowance for limited individual worship at local shrines (Driver 1902:136-138; NIDOTTE 2.895-897). This in no way contradicts the requirement of "sole sanctuary" (vv. 1-14) because the issue there was the community as a collective entity. The present passage deals with the exigencies caused by population distribution and the practical necessity of family worship in scattered places. The precise modes and forms of such worship are elusive, but the existence of Yahweh altars at various sites where sacrifice and other cultic activities took place without criticism is sufficient to show that worship could be and was undertaken apart from the central sanctuary (cf. Judg 6:19-24; 1 Sam 7:17; 9:11-14; 2 Sam 24:18-25; 1 Kgs 18:30). Whatever the case, it is unthinkable that God would demand that all worship whatsoever be limited to a single central place and, at the same time, insist that his chosen people conquer and occupy the whole land from Dan to Beersheba. What is clear is that distance notwithstanding, all Israel had to make pilgrimage to Yahweh's earthly dwelling place at least three times a year—for there and there only could the community give God obedient homage. The journeys of Joseph, Mary, and Jesus from Nazareth to Jerusalem at festival times illustrate the tenacity of this tradition (cf. Luke 2:41).

The "sacred gifts" and "offerings" of 12:26 are spoken of in reference to these festival times. The rituals of the worship place would include burnt offerings (12:27; 'oloth [TH5930, ZH6592], "the things rising up") as well as other kinds. Burnt offerings—those sometimes called "holocaust" offerings because the whole thing was consumed—required that every part of the animal be devoted to God, meat and blood alike. The reason is that sins and trespasses were atoned for with such sacrifices (cf. Lev 1:3-4), and therefore it would be most untoward for the offerer to materially benefit from any part of it.

The "other sacrifices" (12:27b)—those such as the thanksgiving and fellowship offerings—followed a different procedure. The blood of these kinds must be poured out on the ground, but the meat could be eaten, at least in part (Lev 3; 7:11-14, 19-21). The rest was "eaten" by Yahweh—that is, offered up to him. The whole ceremony was viewed as a banquet at which Yahweh sat at table with the offerer, his family, his friends, and frequently the Levites and others dependent on such fare for their physical sustenance (Lev 7:28-36; 10:12-15).

The section on centralization of worship ends very much like it began, with a strong exhortation to obey everything (here, "all my commands") that Yahweh had commanded (12:28). This is prerequisite to the abiding blessing of God in the land and to enjoying his approval. Unless and until the people do what is good, they cannot expect that things will go well. This is the conditional side to the covenant relationship.

◆   ## 4. The abomination of pagan gods (12:29-31)

29"When the LORD your God goes ahead of you and destroys the nations and you drive them out and live in their land, 30do not fall into the trap of following their customs and worshiping their gods. Do not inquire about their gods, saying, 'How do these nations worship their gods? I want to follow their example!' 31You must not worship the LORD your God the way the other nations worship their gods, for they perform for their gods every detestable act that the LORD hates. They even burn their sons and daughters as sacrifices to their gods.

COMMENTARY

In a passage reminiscent of a previous warning about the Canaanite cult and its gods (7:4-5; cf. 12:4), Moses here anticipates Yahweh's expulsion of the native populations (12:29) and the Israelites' temptation, at the same time, to worship the Canaanite gods (12:30a). In other words, Israel could well enjoy military victory and experience spiritual defeat. Despite the power and goodness of their God in giving them success, they would find the religious systems of Canaan alluring—with all their fascinating mythology and elaborate ritual. The sensuality of it all and its apparent and immediate connection to the world of nature would make the Canaanite religious expression a matter of intense curiosity at best and the occasion for wholesale apostasy from Yahweh at worst. Israel must not inquire as to the character of these pagan ways and must desist from any desire to emulate them (12:30b).

To embrace paganism was to reject Yahwism, as well as to violate the very heart and soul of the covenant relationship. Both the first two commandments (5:6-10) and the Shema (6:4-5) enjoined single-minded allegiance to Yahweh without which covenant was impossible. The worship of other gods was treasonous under any circumstances, but the worship of Canaanite deities was particularly odious because of their very nature. Every act of their religious expression was detestable, reaching the most abhorrent form in human sacrifice (12:31).

◆   ## 5. The evil of false prophets (12:32–13:11)

32*"So be careful to obey all the commands I give you. You must not add anything to them or subtract anything from them.

CHAPTER 13

1*"Suppose there are prophets among you or those who dream dreams about the future, and they promise you signs or miracles, 2and the predicted signs or miracles occur. If they then say, 'Come, let us worship other gods'—gods you have not known before—3do not listen to them. The LORD your God is testing you to see if you truly love him with all your heart and soul. 4Serve only the LORD your God and fear him alone. Obey his commands, listen to his voice, and cling to him. 5The false prophets or visionaries who try to lead you astray must be put to death, for they encourage rebellion against the LORD your God, who redeemed you from slavery and brought you out of the land of Egypt. Since they try to lead you astray from the way the LORD your God commanded you to live, you must put them to death. In this way you will purge the evil from among you.

6"Suppose someone secretly entices you—even your brother, your son or daughter, your beloved wife, or your closest friend—and says, 'Let us go worship other gods'—gods that neither you nor your ancestors have known. 7They might suggest that you worship the gods of peoples who live nearby or who come from the ends of the earth. 8But do not give in or listen. Have no pity, and do not spare or protect them. 9You must put them to death! Strike the first blow yourself, and then all the people must join in. 10Stone the guilty ones to death because they have tried to draw you away from the LORD your God, who rescued you from the land of Egypt, the place of slavery. 11Then all Israel will hear about it and be afraid, and no one will act so wickedly again.

12:32 Verse 12:32 is numbered 13:1 in Hebrew text.   13:1 Verses 13:1-18 are numbered 13:2-19 in Hebrew text.

NOTES

12:32 [13:1] *the commands I give you. You must.* Attention has already been drawn to the alternation of singular and plural Hebrew pronouns (see note on 12:1) and the resulting tendency by scholars to make wholesale emendations to achieve greater consistency. This verse provides a good example of the problem and suggested solutions, both ancient and modern. It reads, "Everything I am commanding you [plural] you [plural] must be careful to do; you [singular] must not add to it nor should you [singular] subtract from it." The Samaritan Pentateuch, LXX, Syriac, and Vulgate suggest the singular for the first two, but a few Samaritan Pentateuch mss have plural for the last two. The former is favored because of the preponderance of the singular in the ensuing context. However, a sensitive theological reading of the text negates any need for harmonization because the purpose clearly is to view Israel as both a collective (singular) and a body made up of many individuals (plural).

13:9 [10] *You must put them to death.* The LXX reads, "You must expose him," that is, bring him to public attention. This reading clearly has in mind the last statement of 13:8, "do not conceal him." Such a reading is unattested in the Hebrew tradition and is unnecessary in the context (Tigay 1996:132-133).

COMMENTARY

This pericope begins with 12:32, which is more appropriately numbered 13:1 in the Hebrew text. The starting point is evident from the injunction to "be careful to obey," a formula that is repeatedly used in Deuteronomy to introduce a new section (cf. 8:1; 12:1; 18:9; 26:16; 28:1), as well as close one, as here (13:18; cf. 6:24-25; 11:32). Thus, 12:32 and 13:18 form an *inclusio* embracing the topic of false prophets. An addition to the exhortation to obedience is the prohibition against tampering with the text by adding to or deleting from it (12:32). This not only is a warning about the inspiration of the received instructions, but it is also an indication of a process of canonization already at work (Merrill 1998:114; Vasholz 1990:84-86). God not only dictates the content of his word but also its extent (cf. 4:2; Rev 22:18-19).

This caution was in order because of the existence of false prophets who might profess to have extracanonical revelation—that is, a message from God beyond that of Moses, his authorized spokesman. These could be either prophets who spoke on behalf of other gods (ch 13) or those who falsely professed to speak on behalf of Yahweh (18:15-22). The former are in view here. They are the "prophet" (13:1; *nabi'* [TH5030, ZH5566]) and the "dreamer" (*kholem* [TH2492A, ZH2731]) from within or among Israel itself and not foreigners. This is what would make them so subtle and dangerous. By definition, a prophet is a spokesman, a mouth, as it were, for another person (cf. Exod 4:14-17; 7:1). The term thus speaks of an office (NIDOTTE 4.1068). By contrast, a dreamer was a prophet who specialized in dream revelation. The emphasis in this case is on the means and not the office.

In the hypothetical situation envisioned here, there would be prophets in Israel who would attempt to authenticate their message by performing miraculous signs (13:1). Such signs (*'oth* [TH226, ZH253] and *mopeth* [TH4159, ZH4603]) ordinarily attested to a genuine work of God in the Old Testament (cf. 28:46; Isa 20:3), just as they confirmed the work and message of Jesus in the New Testament (Gr., *sēmeion* [TG4592, ZG4956]; cf. Matt 12:38-39; John 2:11, 18; 20:30-31). However, they could be counterfeited or even given by God to false prophets (as here) in order to accomplish some divine objective. The point is that signs and wonders do not automatically point to the genuine work of the Holy Spirit or to the credibility of those who practice them.

Here the signs would be accompanied by the enticement to worship other gods (13:2). Clearly, such a message and messenger cannot be from God, signs and wonders notwithstanding. In fact, Moses said that the Lord would allow such miracles as a means of testing the loyalty of his people at the very core of their confession: Do they love him with all their being (13:3; cf. 6:4-5)? The theological point is that the message without confirming signs is more important than signs without the sanctioning message. The response to such a duplicitous prophet is prescribed in a rapid-fire succession of six verbs (13:4): *walk* (after Yahweh), *fear* (him), *keep* (his commandment), *obey* (his voice), *serve* (him), and *cling to* (him). Such a collocation of terms in service of covenant loyalty is unparalleled in the Old Testament.

As for false prophets, they must be put to death for the crime of high treason, for they have rebelled against God and enticed others to do the same (13:5). He is the one who freed them from the dominion of Pharaoh to make them his own special people. To advocate leaving Yahweh now and follow after other masters would be to devalue his redemptive grace and obstinately spurn his rightful claims to sovereignty. Though such remedy as the execution of false prophets is inappropriate in the modern, non-theocratic, secular world, their danger is no less diminished, nor is the fearful judgment that awaits them.

One might withstand the temptation to follow a misleading prophet in spite of his signs and wonders. But what about the urgings of a loved one who advocates the worship of other gods (13:6)? They may be gods with whom the community is familiar (such as those in Canaan), or they may be others yet to be encountered from distant lands. Even if the well-known gods are rejected because of their recognized impotence or even falseness, what about more appealing gods that Israel might someday encounter?

Moses's answer to such real and imagined contingencies is clear: No matter what or where they are, such gods are not to be worshiped, and those who promote them for such must suffer the consequences. As heart-wrenching as it might be, family members who collaborate in idolatry must be exposed to the public (13:8) and publicly executed (13:9). In fact, the kinsman who reveals the perpetrator must be the first to strike a blow against him.

The reason for this sequence may be twofold: (1) to test the level of commitment to Yahweh of the one being tempted to idolatry and (2) to be absolutely certain of the validity of the charge. The accuser must love God more than his guilty loved one, but he also must refrain from acting with undue haste in the heat of emotion. In a similar situation, Jesus is said to have agreed with the letter of the Old Testament law in the matter of the stoning of the woman taken in adultery, but with this proviso: "Let the one who has never sinned throw the first stone" (John 8:7). Moreover, the application of grace led him to say that he did not condemn her (v. 11). With this challenge ringing in their ears, her accusers slunk away, for none was qualified. In the context of our passage, the point is simply that the allegations must have a sound basis, the accuser must have Yahweh's interests in view above all others, and the accuser must demonstrate his own integrity and concern by initiating the penalty.

Stoning was the most common means of capital punishment in the Old Testament (21:21; 22:21; Lev 24:14; Num 15:35; Josh 7:25), probably because it afforded community participation (Mayes 1981:255). The accuser would begin the execution, but others would join in so that the result was a corporate act of vengeance. Israel's actions as an entity in these cases were to preclude private vindictiveness. Even in modern times, capital punishment is enacted in the name of the people and not on behalf of an individual.

Such harsh measures were appropriate because, as in the previous instance (13:5), solicitation to idolatry is tantamount to high treason against Yahweh (13:10). Nothing short of death is suitable for such an egregious sin. More than that, however, is the deterrent effect. Once false prophets pay with their lives, it is much less likely that others will be inclined to emulate their example. Israel will hear and fear (13:11), a response that elsewhere results from Yahweh's righteous wrath (17:13; 19:20; 21:21). Those who challenge the notion of punishment as a deterrent fail to understand the full import of this text.

◆   ## 6. Punishment of community idolatry (13:12-18)

12"When you begin living in the towns the LORD your God is giving you, you may hear 13that scoundrels among you are leading their fellow citizens astray by saying, 'Let us go worship other gods'—gods you have not known before. 14In such cases, you must examine the facts carefully. If you find that the report is true and such a detestable act has been committed among you, 15you must attack that town and completely destroy* all its inhabitants, as well as all the livestock. 16Then you must pile all the plunder in the middle of the open square and burn it. Burn the entire town as a burnt offering to the LORD your God. That town must remain a ruin forever; it may never be rebuilt. 17Keep none of the plunder that has been set apart for destruction. Then the LORD will turn from his fierce anger and be merciful to you. He will have compassion on you and make you a large nation, just as he swore to your ancestors.

18"The LORD your God will be merciful only if you listen to his voice and keep all his commands that I am giving you today, doing what pleases him.

13:15 The Hebrew term used here refers to the complete consecration of things or people to the LORD, either by destroying them or by giving them as an offering; similarly in 13:17.

NOTES

13:14 [15] *among you.* Theodotion (an ancient Greek version) reads "in Israel," perhaps to suggest that the deed has national and not just local implications. However, "among you" is consistent in all mss in 13:13, which describes the same situation.

13:18 [19] *pleases him.* Lit., "is pleasing." To this, the Samaritan Pentateuch and the LXX add "and good" to complete the stereotypical phrase found elsewhere (cf. 6:18; Josh 9:25; 2 Kgs 10:3; 2 Chr 14:2 [1]; 31:20; Jer 26:14). Such slavishness to form, however, is unjustified in light of the well-known practice of broken stereotypes. See also W. G. E. Watson, *Classical Hebrew Poetry.* (Sheffield: Journal for the Study of the Old Testament Supplement 26, 1986), 328-332.

COMMENTARY

Having dealt with the punishment of false prophets exposed as such (13:5, 9-10), Moses turned to the possibility of whole towns guilty either of practicing idolatry or at least harboring those who do so (13:12-13). The instigators of such a movement (described as "scoundrels" or "worthless ones"; TDOT 2.132-133) do exactly the same as the false prophets already mentioned: They foment disloyalty to and rebellion against Yahweh in pursuit of other gods (13:13; cf. 13:2, 6).

Because such a thing is alleged in a place distant from Israel's leadership, they must take great care in determining the facts of the case and following proper legal procedure (13:14). If, indeed, the charges are borne out, not only the ringleaders but the whole community must be annihilated (13:15). The verb employed here to describe the destruction is *kharam* [TH2763, ZH3049], a technical term commonly translated "put under the ban." This was the policy to be followed in the destruction of Canaanite places and peoples because of their irremediable stance toward Yahweh and his grace (cf. 3:6; 7:2; 20:17; Josh 2:10; 6:18; 8:26), but it is rarely applied to Israel as here (cf. Judg 21:11; TDOT 5.194). The fact that idolatry in Israel could evoke such response from Yahweh—one normally reserved for the heathen—points to the heinousness of this sin in his eyes.

Typical of situations involving such a ban (*kherem* [TH2764, ZH3051]) is the total conflagration of material things (13:16) and the warning that the place must be left in ruins, never to be rebuilt (cf. Josh 6:26). Nothing whatsoever could be kept by the destroyers for themselves because it all belonged to Yahweh as a kind of burnt offering—it was to be burned entirely (*kalil* [TH3632B, ZH4003]), as something entirely devoted to God. The sad account of rapacious Achan most effectively documents the fate of those who keep for themselves what belongs to God alone (Josh 7).

If this prescription for detecting and punishing apostasy in Israel is followed to the letter, Israel can expect God's unstinted mercy (13:17). Literally, the text says, "He will give you mercy and make you the object of his mercy." No more powerful way could be found to underscore the divine compassion which, while not ignoring sin, is ever available to those who deal with sin in a proper, biblical way. Ultimately, that mercy will result in national blessing conforming to the ancient promises to the fathers (13:17b). Conditions must be met, then, in carrying out the will of God. Only those who live in covenant obedience can expect to reap the benefits of covenant blessing (13:18).

♦   ## 7. The distinction between clean and unclean animals (14:1-21)

"Since you are the people of the LORD your God, never cut yourselves or shave the hair above your foreheads in mourning for the dead. ²You have been set apart as holy to the LORD your God, and he has chosen you from all the nations of the earth to be his own special treasure.

³"You must not eat any detestable animals that are ceremonially unclean. ⁴These are the animals* you may eat: the ox, the sheep, the goat, ⁵the deer, the gazelle, the roe deer, the wild goat, the addax, the antelope, and the mountain sheep.

⁶"You may eat any animal that has

completely split hooves and chews the cud, ⁷but if the animal doesn't have both, it may not be eaten. So you may not eat the camel, the hare, or the hyrax.* They chew the cud but do not have split hooves, so they are ceremonially unclean for you. ⁸And you may not eat the pig. It has split hooves but does not chew the cud, so it is ceremonially unclean for you. You may not eat the meat of these animals or even touch their carcasses.

⁹"Of all the marine animals, you may eat whatever has both fins and scales. ¹⁰You may not, however, eat marine animals that do not have both fins and scales. They are ceremonially unclean for you.

¹¹"You may eat any bird that is ceremonially clean. ¹²These are the birds you may not eat: the griffon vulture, the bearded vulture, the black vulture, ¹³the kite, the falcon, buzzards of all kinds, ¹⁴ravens of all kinds, ¹⁵the eagle owl, the short-eared owl, the seagull, hawks of all kinds, ¹⁶the little owl, the great owl, the barn owl, ¹⁷the desert owl, the Egyptian vulture, the cormorant, ¹⁸the stork, herons of all kinds, the hoopoe, and the bat.

¹⁹"All winged insects that walk along the ground are ceremonially unclean for you and may not be eaten. ²⁰But you may eat any winged bird or insect that is ceremonially clean.

²¹"You must not eat anything that has died a natural death. You may give it to a foreigner living in your town, or you may sell it to a stranger. But do not eat it yourselves, for you are set apart as holy to the LORD your God.

"You must not cook a young goat in its mother's milk.

14:4 The identification of some of the animals and birds listed in this chapter is uncertain. 14:7 Or coney, or rock badger.

NOTES

14:3 You. Rather than the expected plural pronoun found elsewhere in the context (cf. 14:4), the MT has the singular, an anomaly adjusted in most ancient versions. Though I have noted the common interchange of grammatical number elsewhere (see note on 12:1), a case can be made here for a faulty MT reading.

14:8 split hooves. A comparison of this verse to its otherwise exact parallel, Lev 11:7, indicates that a scribal lapse (haplography) has occurred in which the words "and is clovenfooted" (*weshosa' shesa' parsah* [ᵀᴴ8156/8157, ᶻᴴ9117/9118]) were accidentally omitted. The Samaritan Pentateuch and LXX both attest the longer reading.

14:19 may not be eaten. The MT reads a passive verb here (Niphal stem), whereas one would expect the Qal "you (pl.) must not eat," as is found in the Samaritan Pentateuch and LXX. However, the *lectio difficilior* (the more difficult reading) is to be preferred—that is, the passive.

COMMENTARY

The general theme of this part of Deuteronomy (12:1–16:17)—the exclusiveness of Yahweh and his worship—continues with attention to the idea of the holiness of Israel and what that implies for behavior, specifically, in the text at hand, dietary regulations. A leading Old Testament theological motif is that God is holy and anyone or anything associated with him must also be holy—that is, set apart from the mundane and, in the case of persons, exhibiting a moral and ethical lifestyle commensurate with that relationship (Dyrness 1979:51-53). Only holy ones are qualified to appear before a holy God to tender the worship and praise that are due him.

The list of animals forbidden for human consumption is preceded by a statement of rationale for the prohibition (14:1-2). Precisely because Israel is Yahweh's people, they must be recognizable as such in both appearance and practice. Contrary to pagan custom they cannot, for example, mutilate themselves or otherwise display heathen mourning rites. While the original purpose for such behavior can no longer be determined, the Old Testament is replete with examples of its being done (1 Kgs 18:28; Jer 16:6; 41:5; 47:5), as well as stern warnings against it (Lev 21:5; Jer 16:5). The reason is simple: Israel has been set apart (*bakhar* [TH977, ZH1047], "chosen") to be a "special treasure" (*segullah* [TH5459, ZH6035]) for Yahweh (14:2). The covenant overtones of this statement are unmistakable and clearly reminiscent of Exodus 19:4-6, the text central to Israel's calling and role as a servant nation (cf. also 7:6; 26:18; Ps 135:4; Mal 3:17; Titus 2:14; 1 Pet 2:9).

One way of distinguishing Israel from all other peoples was its adherence to a specified diet. There appear to be no vegetarian restrictions, but the menu of animal offerings was carefully regulated. Many scholars have attempted (unsuccessfully, in my view) to account for the criteria by which forbidden animals were distinguished from those permitted (Jenson 1992:75-83). Apart from some obvious reasons of health dictated by the inherently toxic nature and habits of certain life forms (e.g., swine, shellfish, carrion-eating birds), the main part of the list appears quite arbitrary. In fact, it is likely that the arbitrariness itself is the key to understanding the dietary guidelines. Things are clean or unclean simply because God declares them to be. Peter learned this when he objected to eating what the Lord commanded him to eat on the grounds that it was ceremonially unclean. "Do not call something unclean if God has made it clean," said the voice from heaven (Acts 10:15). The point to be made, of course, is that Israel itself was holy not because of some innate quality but because of God's elective grace that made it so (Milgrom 1991:724-725). This act of divine and arbitrary choice had already been a subject of Moses's instruction (see 7:6-11).

The list here begins with animals, concerning which there is no question as to their suitability (14:3-5). It continues with the criterion by which larger land animals may be judged to be clean or unclean in terms of cultic or ceremonial standards (14:6-8). Very simply, clean animals must have divided hooves and chew the cud. This precludes such well-known (to Israel) creatures as the camel, hare, hyrax (see 14:7 NLT mg), and pig. While they may have one or the other characteristic, they are ineligible without both. They are so unclean that one must refuse even to touch their carcasses (14:8b). This prohibition clearly shows that the uncleanness has more to do with cultic purity than with the physical animal per se.

The criteria applied to aquatic creatures are very plain: They must have fins and scales (14:9-10). Lack of one or the other disqualifies them from the dinner table because it marked them as unclean. The health benefits of this prohibition are particularly obvious since unrefrigerated shellfish are notoriously prone to carry and transmit all kinds of noxious disease. Even so, their "uncleanness" is not so much related to the issue of the deleterious effect of their consumption but, as noted with regard to other creatures, to God's own arbitrary lines of distinction.

Because birds were so prolific and diverse, it was impossible to separate the clean from the unclean by simple application of the kind of criteria already noted with other creatures. Therefore, the forbidden—21 in all—are merely listed. Their technical, scientific classification or name is a matter of some disagreement, but by and large, these winged animals are scavengers whose own dietary habits are repulsive if not potentially injurious to human health.

Winged insects that walk along the ground are taboo (14:19). Other winged insects are acceptable tablefare (14:20). Then, as a general and blanket restriction, God forbade the Israelites from eating any creature that had died naturally. Whereas the foreigner may do so, God's people must demonstrate their distinctiveness by eating only that which they slaughter for food. This, Moses says, is another hallmark of their being a holy people of Yahweh (14:21a).

The passage closes with an admonition about boiling a young goat in its mother's milk, a message that, at first glance, seems peculiarly out of place here (14:21b). This is far from the case, however, from a number of standpoints (Mayes 1979:243). First, the unit as a whole begins with an appeal not to emulate pagan mourning rites (14:1); this last injunction forbids a practice (possibly ritualistic) pertaining to birth and infancy. Second, in the other two places where this command appears, Exodus 23:19 and 34:26, it serves to conclude major sections known respectively as the Book of the Covenant (Exod 20:22–23:19) and the Ritual Decalogue (Exod 34:10-26). This favors the possibility that it closes the Deuteronomy passage as well. Third, a stipulation about the propriety or impropriety of eating certain things is an appropriate climax to the whole section that has addressed precisely this issue.

The meaning of the practice that gave rise to this prohibition is not altogether clear. Some scholars suggest that such a custom has been attested at Ugarit and other places as part of an elaborate fertility ritual. The evidence for this, however, is sparse or nonexistent (Craigie 1976:232-233). More likely is the view that there is something morally abhorrent about taking the life of a suckling and, ironically, making its own mother a "collaborator" in its preparation for a meal. This prohibition provides the basis for the Jewish kosher tradition of not mixing meat and dairy at all and using separate vessels for storing, cooking, and eating dairy and meat products. The tradition followed to this day has roots as ancient as Second Temple times (cf. Jacob Neusner, *The Mishnah. A New Translation.* [New Haven: Yale University Press, 1988], 559, citing tractate *Hullin* 8:4).

◆   ## 8. Tribute to the sovereign (14:22-29)

22"You must set aside a tithe of your crops—one-tenth of all the crops you harvest each year. 23Bring this tithe to the designated place of worship—the place the LORD your God chooses for his name to be honored—and eat it there in his presence. This applies to your tithes of grain, new wine, olive oil, and the first-born males of your flocks and herds. Doing this will teach you always to fear the LORD your God.

24"Now when the LORD your God blesses you with a good harvest, the place of worship he chooses for his name to be honored might be too far for you to bring the tithe. ²⁵If so, you may sell the tithe portion of your crops and herds, put the money in a pouch, and go to the place the LORD your God has chosen. ²⁶When you arrive, you may use the money to buy any kind of food you want—cattle, sheep, goats, wine, or other alcoholic drink. Then feast there in the presence of the LORD your God and celebrate with your household. ²⁷And do not neglect the Levites in your town, for they will receive no allotment of land among you.

²⁸"At the end of every third year, bring the entire tithe of that year's harvest and store it in the nearest town. ²⁹Give it to the Levites, who will receive no allotment of land among you, as well as to the foreigners living among you, the orphans, and the widows in your towns, so they can eat and be satisfied. Then the LORD your God will bless you in all your work.

NOTES

14:29 *all your work.* The MT has the usual formula, "all the work of your hand(s)," a reading suggested by a number of Hebrew mss, LXX, Hexapla, Syriac, and Vulgate (cf. 2:7; 16:15; 24:19; 27:15; 28:12; 30:9). However, a shorter form is also attested (15:10), one that corresponds to the NLT here.

COMMENTARY

Ancient Near Eastern covenant protocol called for vassal states to pay regular monetary tribute at stated (at least annual) intervals as a sign of their loyalty to the Great King and as compensation for his protection and other benefits (Mendenhall 1955:33). This is no less true for Israel *vis-à-vis* Yahweh. In the Old Testament, the tribute consisted primarily of the tithe of all produce and other revenues, all of which must be brought to Yahweh at his earthly dwelling place, the central sanctuary. Such an expression of submission was designed not only to honor Israel's God but, as a practical measure, was a means of providing for the priests and the needy of the nation.

The instruction here is unequivocal: Bring to Yahweh a tenth of all harvests each year (14:22). Likewise, the destination is clear. The tribute must be taken to the "palace" of King Yahweh, that is, to the Tabernacle or Temple (14:23). The occasion is essentially one of covenant renewal or reaffirmation, the celebration of which included a common meal shared by all parties (Exod 24:3-11). Yahweh's participation was symbolized by the people's offering to him those parts of sacrificial animals and produce of greatest value (Lev 3; 7:11-14) with the rest going to the offerer and others whom he had invited. Pilgrimage to the central sanctuary was to be undertaken three times a year—at Passover, Pentecost, and Tabernacles—and each time Yahweh must be presented with the tithe of the harvest of that season (12:6-7; cf. 16:1-7; Exod 23:14-19; Lev 23:5-21; Num 28:16-31; 29:12-39).

The fundamental purpose of presenting tribute to Yahweh in such a manner was to "teach you always to fear the LORD your God" (14:23). In other words, true submission to the sovereignty of Israel's God would be most effectively and dramatically symbolized by the sacrificial presentation of themselves and their productivity to him who sat enthroned among them. "Fear," in this context, is an entirely appropriate way in which to describe the awe one should feel in the presence of God.

As a matter of practicality, it would not be possible for Israelites living far from the central sanctuary to transport their tithes of animals and grains there (14:24; cf. 12:20-28). This being the case, the tithes could be sold, the silver (*kesep* [TH3701, ZH4084]; NLT, "money") taken to the sanctuary, and local animals and goods purchased there as offerings (14:25-26a). This practice continued on into New Testament times, as the account of Jesus and the money changers so dramatically highlights (Matt 21:12-16). The festive nature of the gatherings there is indicative, again, of the joy to be found in recognition and celebration of Yahweh's kingship (14:26; cf. 12:12). In the midst of personal celebration, however, the Israelite must not forget the needs of others, particularly the Levites, who had no means of production and were therefore dependent on the goodwill of their brother Israelites. They, too, must be invited to share in the bounties of the land and have the means of tendering their own offerings to their God (14:27; cf. 12:19).

His reference to the Levites prompts Moses to a fuller expostulation concerning their welfare and the means of securing it. At the end of every third year—presumably at the end of the fall harvest—the tithes, rather than going directly to Yahweh, must be stored up in local villages where the Levites might have access to them (14:28). This remarkable provision demonstrates not only that God's servants are worthy of support by God's people but that God himself relinquishes what is his in order to care for those who serve him in special ways (Thompson 1974:185). Moreover, in this way the two greatest commandments, namely, to love God with all the heart, soul, and strength, and the neighbor as oneself, are fleshed out in practical terms. As Israel cared for the Levites, they were caring for God in the finest sense (cf. Matt 10:42).

In ancient Israelite society, the Levite was not alone in his need of public assistance. Foreigners (*ger* [TH1616, ZH1731], "sojourner"), orphans, and widows alike were vulnerable, defenseless, and usually with little or no opportunity to fend for themselves. Ruth is a classic example of this, inasmuch as she, with her mother-in-law Naomi, was forced to find sustenance from a kinsman, Boaz, who recognized not only his duty under the law but relished the opportunity it provided to serve God at the same time (Ruth 2:11-13). To provide for the least among these oft-marginalized people was to meet the conditions for continued blessing and success (14:29; Matt 10:42).

◆   ## 9. Release for debtors (15:1-6)

"At the end of every seventh year you must cancel the debts of everyone who owes you money. ²This is how it must be done. Everyone must cancel the loans they have made to their fellow Israelites. They must not demand payment from their neighbors or relatives, for the LORD's time of release has arrived. ³This release from debt, however, applies only to your fellow Israelites—not to the foreigners living among you.

⁴"There should be no poor among you, for the LORD your God will greatly bless you in the land he is giving you as a special possession. ⁵You will receive this blessing if you are careful to obey all the

commands of the LORD your God that I am
giving you today. ⁶The LORD your God will
bless you as he has promised. You will
lend money to many nations but will
never need to borrow. You will rule many
nations, but they will not rule over you.

NOTES

15:2 *This is how . . . Everyone must cancel.* Lit., "This is the procedure of loosing (*hashmittah* [TH8058, ZH9023]): Every creditor must release" (*shamot* [TH8059, ZH9024]).

15:4 *the LORD your God.* The MT omits "your God" after this instance of "LORD," but many Hebrew mss and the major versions supply it in the interest of completing the standard epithet "Yahweh your God."

COMMENTARY

The theme of providing for the destitute in Israel (14:28-29) continues in this section with its instructions about debt cancellation. This could follow one of two procedures—simple "cash" loans or personal indenture. The former is addressed in 15:1-6 and the latter in 15:12-18. The appeal to be generous in any case and to see to it that the needs of the poor are met is the focus of 15:7-11. There was no state welfare system in ancient Israel, so the responsibility for those who fell on hard times devolved upon their friends and neighbors. They had a moral obligation to provide interest-free loans (cf. Lev 25:35-38) or to allow the debtor to work off his encumbrance. In any case, the arrangement was mutually terminated at the end of a seven-year period (the so-called "Sabbatical Year"; Lev 25:1-7), at which time the debtor was released from further compensation (15:1), or, at least, he need make no payment on the seventh year (Craigie 1976:236-237).

The procedure to be followed is that the creditor must, at the stated time, cancel all debts, for Yahweh's time of cancellation (*shemittah;* NIDOTTE 4.155-160) has arrived (see note on 15:2). This is not a blanket release, however, for it applies only to the "brother," that is, to a fellow Israelite. All others were expected to make payment in full (15:3; Wright 1990:167-173).

Though the text (here and elsewhere) is silent on the matter, it is reasonable to assume that safeguards must have been in place to protect the interests of the lender. Otherwise, lazy and irresponsible people could simply demand financial assistance, wait out the seven-year period, and then go scot-free. Such a policy would encourage freeloading and would erode any sense of pride or initiative in work and self-reliance. Presumably there were ways and means of "qualifying" loans and putting in place mechanisms that would demand good faith of and provide some securities for both parties.

The ideal is that there be no poverty at all, nor should there be, says Moses, in view of the abundant provision promised by Yahweh in the land they were about to possess (15:4). This possibility is not at odds with Jesus' observation that "you will always have the poor among you" (Mark 14:7; cf. Deut 15:11); the harsh reality is that human sin breeds poverty on the one hand and callous indifference to it on the other. This contingency is spelled out in our text in the reminder that material blessing, like any other kind in the framework of covenant, depends on total and unqualified obedience to the command (*mitswah* [ᵀᴴ4687, ᶻᴴ5184], that is, the whole covenant; see note on 5:31) of Yahweh (15:5).

To obey is to enjoy prosperity; to disobey is to invite abject material and spiritual poverty. When the conditions are met, God pours out his promised blessings. In what may be somewhat utopian or hyperbolic terms, Moses said that Israel, like the wealthy benefactors already described (15:2), would be in a position to be of aid to their impoverished neighbor states and would never have to borrow from them (cf. 28:12-13). Even more astounding and significant than this, Israel would dominate other nations but never suffer the imperialism of others (15:6).

Rarely was the ideal of this scenario lived out in Israel's subsequent historical experience (see, however, 2 Sam 8:1-14; 2 Kgs 14:23-29). Instead, the violation of the law and receipt of its curses was all too common, particularly in the Assyrian (2 Kgs 17:1-6) and Babylonian (2 Kgs 25) conquests. Only in the eschaton at the end of the ages, when Yahweh himself exercises his universal dominion, will Israel, fully redeemed and in full covenant compliance, take up this promise and enjoy the headship intended from the beginning (28:1; Isa 2:2-4; Dan 7:27-28; Zech 14:9-11, 16-21).

◆   ## 10. The spirit of liberality (15:7-11)

⁷"But if there are any poor Israelites in your towns when you arrive in the land the LORD your God is giving you, do not be hard-hearted or tightfisted toward them. ⁸Instead, be generous and lend them whatever they need. ⁹Do not be mean-spirited and refuse someone a loan because the year for canceling debts is close at hand. If you refuse to make the loan and the needy person cries out to the LORD, you will be considered guilty of sin. ¹⁰Give generously to the poor, not grudgingly, for the LORD your God will bless you in everything you do. ¹¹There will always be some in the land who are poor. That is why I am commanding you to share freely with the poor and with other Israelites in need.

NOTES

15:10 *not grudgingly.* In light of a similar formula in 15:8, the LXX of Origen adds "you shall surely lend to him sufficient for his need." Such slavish adherence to stock phrases is unwarranted.

COMMENTARY

Having dispensed with the ideal of a society free of poverty (15:4), Moses set forth the attitude that must prevail in redressing the problem when it would, in fact, exist in Canaan. There must be more than a mere perfunctory display of generosity. It must be heartfelt and lead to openhandedness (15:7). The temptation might be to defer making loans because of the nearness of the Sabbatical Year and, thus, to minimize the need of the destitute person. Surely he or she can make it a little longer! Moreover, to make a loan at the last minute might jeopardize the chances of being repaid. But this temptation must be overcome, because to neglect the truly needy is to sin against God (15:9). Conversely, to give under less than favorable economic circumstances is to put oneself in a position to enjoy God's abundant blessing (15:10).

Finally, Moses faced the undeniable fact that poverty is endemic to human existence (Kaiser 1983:212). He, therefore, rose above the theoretical or hypothetical and cast his instruction in the form of a command (*tsawah* [TH6680, ZH7422], "covenant law"): Open your hand (15:11)! To meet the needs of the poor and helpless is, then, not an option but an edict. And those who do so with unrestrained compassion and generosity are thereby serving God as well (Matt 10:40-42).

◆   ## 11. Release of debtors (15:12-18)

¹²"If a fellow Hebrew sells himself or herself to be your servant* and serves you for six years, in the seventh year you must set that servant free.

¹³"When you release a male servant, do not send him away empty-handed. ¹⁴Give him a generous farewell gift from your flock, your threshing floor, and your winepress. Share with him some of the bounty with which the LORD your God has blessed you. ¹⁵Remember that you were once slaves in the land of Egypt and the LORD your God redeemed you! That is why I am giving you this command.

¹⁶"But suppose your servant says, 'I will not leave you,' because he loves you and your family, and he has done well with you. ¹⁷In that case, take an awl and push it through his earlobe into the door. After that, he will be your servant for life. And do the same for your female servants.

¹⁸"You must not consider it a hardship when you release your servants. Remember that for six years they have given you services worth double the wages of hired workers, and the LORD your God will bless you in all you do.

15:12 Or *If a Hebrew man or woman is sold to you.*

NOTES

15:15 *I am giving you this command.* The MT lacks the expected infinitive construction *la'asoth* [TH6213, ZH6913] (to do), an omission rectified by certain Greek and Targumic mss and some from Qumran. These are probably efforts to smooth out an otherwise awkward syntax.

COMMENTARY

Besides taking loans with full intention and expectation of repayment, the poor could also hire themselves out to a creditor and thus work off their loans. These latter would likely be so debt-ridden or unlikely to make repayment that they had no choice but to indenture themselves. In both Exodus 21:2-6 and in this text, the person submitting to such an arrangement is called a "Hebrew" (15:12; *'ibri* [TH5680, ZH6303]) and not an Israelite as is usually the case (cf. 15:2; 17:15; 22:19; 23:20; 24:14). That fact, coupled with the description of the person released from such servitude as "free" (*khopshi* [TH2670, ZH2930], 15:12), has convinced some scholars that fellow Israelites are not in view here but perhaps classes of persons known variously as *habiru, 'apiru,* and the like (Gottwald 1979:769). These groups appear frequently in a wide variety of ancient Near Eastern texts and possibly in such biblical passages as 1 Samuel 14:11, 21. The suggestion is that the *'apiru* who have served their time and been released should become free, even though their social status is low.

While this interpretation is attractive in some respects, it is difficult to account for a whole set of regulations relevant to a people who were so few or marginal as to find little or no reference elsewhere. More likely the term "Hebrew" occurs to conjure up the memory of bondage in Egypt where the enslaved people were known not as Israelites but Hebrews (cf. Exod 1:15-16, 19; 2:6-7, 11, 13; 3:18; 5:3; 7:16; 9:1, 13; 10:3). To indenture oneself is, in a sense, to put oneself back under the onerous conditions of Egyptian slavery.

Whatever the identity of the "Hebrew" here, a person reduced to such drastic measures must be released free of debt in the Sabbatical Year (15:12). Furthermore, he or she must be given a "stake," and a liberal one at that, lest they have no opportunity for fiscal recovery and thus fall back into penury (15:13-14). The incentive to show mercy and latitude was the recollection of Israel's own years in Egyptian bondage (15:15). How could creditors, whose ancestors or who themselves experienced God's redemptive grace in freeing them from Egypt, refuse to do the same for their less fortunate brothers and sisters? Allusion to that experience strengthens the case that *'ibri* [TH5680, ZH6303] (15:12) means "Hebrew" (i.e., "Israelite").

Every society has citizens who will not or cannot care for themselves and who must, therefore, depend on welfare programs of one kind or another. This would have been true in Israel as well. One available safety net was the security found in perpetuating the creditor–debtor relationship just described. And sometimes bonds of mutual affection would be forged, emotional ties so strong that the bondservant would beg not to be released but retained as almost a part of his patron's family (15:16). Should this be the case by mutual agreement, the servant would participate in a formal, public ceremony in which his ear was, in effect, "nailed" to a door, probably the door of his master's house. The pierced ear would testify forever to the voluntary submission the man or woman had made to the erstwhile creditor (15:17).

Lest some should consider such an arrangement as indenture to be a one-sided or unfair transaction, Moses reminded them that they will have gotten more than their money's worth. The servant has provided six years of labor and at a rate of compensation that would equal only half that of hired employees. The term translated "double" (*mishneh* [TH4932, ZH5467], 15:18) is somewhat problematic. Very possibly it means "equivalent to" (so Craigie 1976:239), but it seems that Moses was trying to say that the master got not just a good deal but an excellent one. The reason might be that the servant in such a situation was full-time, day and night, whereas a hired worker would put in only the hours of his shift (Tigay 1996:150). But the greater incentive was not monetary. It was the promise of God's blessing (15:18). Those who honor God by showing compassion to the weak and defenseless have every expectation of enjoying the benefits of his responsive grace.

◆   12. Giving God the best (15:19-23)

¹⁹"You must set aside for the LORD your God all the firstborn males from your flocks and herds. Do not use the firstborn of your herds to work your fields, and do not shear the firstborn of your flocks. ²⁰Instead, you and your family must eat these animals in the presence of the LORD your God each year at the place he chooses. ²¹But if this firstborn animal has any defect, such as lameness or blindness, or if anything else is wrong with it, you must not sacrifice it to the LORD your God. ²²Instead, use it for food for your family in your hometown. Anyone, whether ceremonially clean or unclean, may eat it, just as anyone may eat a gazelle or deer. ²³But you must not consume the blood. You must pour it out on the ground like water.

NOTES

15:22 clean or unclean. Various LXX recensions add *en soi* (among you) here to make it clear that the "clean or unclean" refers not to the animals but to the persons. Though the antecedent to the adjectives is ambiguous, the context leaves no doubt that unclean people, not animals, are intended (cf. 12:15, 22).

COMMENTARY

Because Yahweh had spared the firstborn sons of all the households of Israel in the tenth plague, he mandated that they therefore belonged to him, perhaps as "living sacrifices" (cf. Exod 11:4-8; 12:12-14; 13:1-2, 11-16; 22:29; Rom 12:1-2). Likewise, the firstborn of the flocks and herds were to be dedicated to him as a peace offering at festival times (15:19-20). They could not be used for personal gain (15:19) and must be the finest specimen, without defect (15:21; cf. Lev 22:17-25). The principle, of course, is that God deserves the best that one has and not the castoffs or rejects. Malachi excoriated the Jewish people of his own time who presented to Yahweh animals that were blind, crippled, and diseased. And he challenged them to "try giving gifts like that to your governor, and see how pleased he is!" (Mal 1:8). If a mere human ruler would be offended by such self-serving, despicable overtures, how much more the King of kings.

Such defective animals could be butchered for food and with no need for ritualistic preparation (see note on 15:22). They would be considered in the class of wild game, which, though conforming to such criteria as cloven hooves and chewing the cud (14:4-6), were disqualified because they were not domesticated and, hence, represented no labor value to the offerer. Imperfect domesticated animals did, indeed, have commercial worth, but their very imperfections precluded their being suitable to a holy God (cf. Lev 20:25-26).

In all instances, however, blood must not be eaten with the meat but poured out on the ground. The very frequency of this prohibition throughout the Torah underscores its theological centrality and importance (cf. 12:16, 23, 25; Lev 3:17; 7:26; 17:10, 12, 14; 19:26).

◆   13. The Passover and the Festival of Unleavened Bread (16:1-8)

"In honor of the LORD your God, celebrate the Passover each year in the early spring, in the month of Abib,* for that was the month in which the LORD your God brought you out of Egypt by night. ²Your Passover sacrifice may be from either the flock or the herd, and it must be sacrificed to the LORD your God at the designated place of worship—the place he chooses for his name to be honored. ³Eat it with bread made without yeast. For seven days the bread you eat must be made without yeast, as when you escaped from Egypt in such a hurry. Eat this bread—the bread of suffering—so that as long as you live you will remember the day you departed from Egypt. ⁴Let no yeast be found in any house throughout your land for those seven days. And when you sacrifice the Passover lamb on the evening of the first day, do not let any of the meat remain until the next morning.

⁵"You may not sacrifice the Passover in just any of the towns that the LORD your God is giving you. ⁶You must offer it only at the designated place of worship—the place the LORD your God chooses for his name to be honored. Sacrifice it there in the evening as the sun goes down on the anniversary of your exodus from Egypt. ⁷Roast the lamb and eat it in the place the LORD your God chooses. Then you may go back to your tents the next morning. ⁸For the next six days you may not eat any bread made with yeast. On the seventh day proclaim another holy day in honor of the LORD your God, and no work may be done on that day.

16:1 Hebrew *Observe the month of Abib, and keep the Passover unto the LORD your God.* Abib, the first month of the ancient Hebrew lunar calendar, usually occurs within the months of March and April.

NOTES

16:4 the Passover lamb. Lit., "the meat that you sacrifice on the first day." Here, the wording of Exod 12:6, "between the evenings" ("at twilight," NLT) is not found in the Hebrew. The Samaritan Pentateuch adds the words from the parallel Exodus passage but in doing so betrays a tendency to harmonize similar texts when no need exists to do so.

16:6 the place. The MT has *'el-hammaqom* [TH413/4725, ZH448/5226] ("*at* the place"). But the preposition *'el* should probably be replaced with the preposition *ba-* [TH871.2, ZH928], yielding *bammaqom* ("*in* the place"), as is found in the Samaritan Pentateuch, Syriac, Targums, and Vulgate. This provides a better parallel with "in any of your villages" in 16:5, to which this is a contrast.

there. The Samaritan Pentateuch and certain Greek recensions add another "there" in this verse, reading "to place his name there; there you shall sacrifice." It is possible, however, that the single *sham* [TH8033, ZH9004] in the MT is doing double duty to avoid an undesirable sound repetition (for "double duty" or "gapping," see Waltke and O'Connor 1990: §11.4.2b).

COMMENTARY

The following extended passage (16:1-17) deals with the three great annual festivals of the religious year, a topic already introduced briefly and almost incidentally from time to time (12:4-7; 14:22-27). Here the purpose, meaning, and general guidelines for their observance are systematically developed. The linkage to the larger context is most apparent (Braulik 1993:322). Moses has spoken of the importance of a central sanctuary (12:1-14), the nature of the worship to be carried out there (12:15–13:18), proper offerings (14:1-27) and care of the dependent (14:28–15:11), release of slaves in the seventh year (15:12-18), and the dedication of the firstborn to Yahweh, a requirement especially associated with the Passover (15:19-23). Now Moses addresses the Passover and, naturally, the other festivals that follow.

The first of the three national, annual festivals is Passover, and it is tied to the month Abib (see NLT note) because in that month God had redeemed Israel from Egyptian bondage (16:1). This event was so important that Abib (later called Nisan) was designated as the first month of the cultic calendar (Exod 12:2). The ritual required the sacrifice of an animal from either the flock (sheep) or herd (cattle) and specifically the firstborn (15:19-23; cf. Exod 13:2, 11-16). And as long as there was a Tabernacle or Temple, the festival must be celebrated there or in its environs (16:2). In the times of Jewish diaspora later on, Passover (and all the festivals) became family or at least local affairs (Schiffman 1991:163).

Passover proper—celebrated on the 14th of Abib (Exod 12:6)—was from the beginning connected to the Festival of Unleavened Bread, which commenced on Abib 15 and continued for seven days (Exod 12:15-20). Its purpose was to remember the haste in which Israel fled from Egypt (16:3). The two observances together were considered a single festival, one of the three requiring attendance by every Israelite adult male (16:16; cf. Exod 23:17). All three festivals marked critical historical turning points, but they also coincided with certain seasonal agricultural events, especially the second and third. In fact, Passover and Unleavened Bread are associated primarily with livestock, which would have produced offspring in and about the month of Abib (de Vaux 1965:489).

The absence of yeast in the bread does not so much use yeast as a symbol of sin (though that is legitimate in certain contexts, especially in the NT; cf. Matt 16:6, 11; Gal 5:9) but as an example of something that takes time to do its work of causing dough to rise (the Exodus had been sudden, with no time for bread to rise). Moses also called it the "bread of suffering" (16:3; 'oni [TH6040, ZH6715], "oppression"), a reminder of the severity of Israel's bondage in Egypt. Yeast must be thoroughly removed from every house lest there be a temptation to make leavened bread and thus be detained. And no part of the Passover animal could be left overnight because that, too, might be an inducement to remain the next day to enjoy one more meal (16:4).

Moses continued his emphasis on the central sanctuary as the only legitimate place of corporate (national) worship by forbidding the observance of the Passover at local shrines or even in the home (see comment on 16:2). It must be celebrated only at the place where Yahweh would cause his name to dwell, that is, the Tabernacle or Temple. Otherwise the Passover must follow the practice at its very inauguration in Egypt. The Passover animal must be sacrificed in the evening, at the setting of the sun (the usual Hebrew formula is "between the evenings," that is, at twilight; see note on 16:4; cf. Exod 12:6). And it must also occur "at the time when you went out of Egypt," that is, on the 14th of Abib (see comment on 16:1). Once the communal meal was over, the people could return to their tents (16:7). Though "tents" is a regular way to speak of homes in the Old Testament (cf. Gen 26:25; Judg 19:9; Ps 132:3; Jer 30:18), here it means a temporary encampment on the outskirts of the area housing the sanctuary. This is evident from the fact that the Festival of Unleavened Bread immediately follows (16:8). This part could not have taken place in distant villages. Furthermore, the whole festival is climaxed by a massive assembly, which again presupposes the continuation of the people at the festival site.

◆   14. The Festival of Harvest (16:9-12)

9"Count off seven weeks from when you first begin to cut the grain at the time of harvest. 10Then celebrate the Festival of Harvest* to honor the LORD your God. Bring him a voluntary offering in proportion to the blessings you have received from him. 11This is a time to celebrate before the LORD your God at the designated place of worship he will choose for his name to be honored. Celebrate with your sons and daughters, your male and female servants, the Levites from your towns, and the foreigners, orphans, and widows who live among you. 12Remember that you were once slaves in Egypt, so be careful to obey all these decrees.

16:10 Hebrew *Festival of Weeks;* also in 16:16. This was later called the Festival of Pentecost (see Acts 2:1). It is celebrated today as Shavuot (or Shabuoth).

COMMENTARY

In Palestine the wheat begins to ripen as early as Passover time, usually in April, but the full harvest is gathered in late May or early June, about seven weeks later (Matthews 1991:51). The second universal festival celebrates the goodness of God in providing for his people with abundant crops of grain. Since seven weeks pass between the end of the Passover and Unleavened Bread Festivals and the gathering of the grain, the harvest festival is called Weeks (16:10; *shabu'oth* [TH7620, ZH8651]) or simply Harvest (*qatsir* [TH7105, ZH7907]; Exod 23:16). The actual celebration was to take place on the fiftieth day, which would be the first day of the week following the seventh Sabbath (Lev 23:15-16)—that is, the day we call Sunday. (Second Temple Pharisaic Judaism altered the biblical tradition by counting the 50 days from the first day of Pesach no matter what day of the week that might be; cf. *m. Hagigah* 2:4; *m. Menahot* 10:1-3). The Septuagint translates "fiftieth" as *pentēkostos* (cf. Lev 25:10-11; 2 Macc 12:32, LXX), from whence comes the Christian name for the holy day of Pentecost, which marks the descent of the Holy Spirit 50 days after Jesus' resurrection (cf. Acts 2:1). The redemptive work of Christ is thus closely tied to this period of the Jewish calendar. Furthermore, Jesus' postresurrection appearances and his ascent would have occurred in this period as well.

The beginning of the harvest (lit., "sickle of the standing grain") is somewhat arbitrarily linked to the end of the Festival of Unleavened Bread. It was marked by the waving of a sheaf of the new grain before Yahweh on the day after the Sabbath of the Passover/Unleavened Bread ceremony (Lev 23:9-11). From that day, 49 days must be counted until the Harvest festival—that is, 50 days from the Sabbath of Unleavened Bread (16:9).

The ritual for the Harvest festival included the presentation of a freewill offering (16:10; *nedabah* [TH5071, ZH5607]), which, according to the more detailed instructions of Leviticus 23, consisted of two loaves of bread, seven yearling lambs, one bull, two rams, and appropriate grain and drink offerings (Lev 23:17-18). The festivities must be carried out at the central sanctuary because this was a community festival (16:11). Families must participate and share with the Levites and others dependent upon such occasions for their well-being (cf. 12:7). The ceremonies would commemorate especially the bondage in Egypt and Yahweh's blessing in delivering them to freedom and, in later tradition, with the giving of the covenant at Sinai (de Vaux 1965:494). The particular practical linkage here was that Jews were to care for the destitute who also yearned for deliverance from economic bondage (16:12).

◆ 15. The Festival of Shelters (16:13-17)

13"You must observe the Festival of Shelters* for seven days at the end of the harvest season, after the grain has been threshed and the grapes have been pressed. 14This festival will be a happy time of celebrating with your sons and daughters, your male and female servants, and the Levites, foreigners, orphans, and widows from your towns. 15For seven days you must celebrate this festival to honor the LORD your God at the place he chooses, for it is he who blesses you with bountiful harvests and gives you success in all your work. This festival will be a time of great joy for all.

16"Each year every man in Israel must celebrate these three festivals: the Festival of Unleavened Bread, the Festival of Harvest, and the Festival of Shelters. On each of these occasions, all men must appear before the LORD your God at the place he chooses, but they must not appear before the LORD without a gift for him. 17All must give as they are able, according to the blessings given to them by the LORD your God.

16:13 Or *Festival of Booths*, or *Festival of Tabernacles;* also in 16:16. This was earlier called the Festival of the Final Harvest or Festival of Ingathering (see Exod 23:16b). It is celebrated today as Sukkot (or Succoth).

COMMENTARY

The third and final national festival was to be that of Shelters. The Hebrew name, *sukkoth* [TH5521, ZH6109] (16:13), describes the temporary shelters to be erected in memory of the nomadic lifestyle of the Israelites in the Sinai wanderings (cf. Lev 23:42-43). It was also another harvest festival, the last of the year, celebrating the ingathering of remaining crops of grain, fruits, and products of the vine (Lev 23:39-40). For this reason, it is also called the Festival of Ingathering (*'asip* [TH614, ZH658]; Exod 23:16; 34:22; cf. NLT "Final Harvest"). This was to commence on the fifteenth day of the seventh month (Tishri) and continue for seven days (16:13; cf. Lev 23:34, 39).

Like the other two community festivals, this one was a time for great joy and sharing (cf. 12:18; 14:26; 16:11; 27:7). But it was also (and primarily) an opportunity for the vassal people Israel to pay tribute to their great and beneficent God who had lavished such good things upon them (16:15). For a solid week, Yahweh and his people could enter into a unique fellowship, one celebrating the covenant relationship that bound them together.

The three special occasions just elaborated—Passover, Pentecost, and Shelters—must be observed by every Israelite male (16:16), though women were also welcome to attend (cf. 16:11, 14). And the reason is most emphatically and clearly stated: to appear before Yahweh (16:16) at his "residence," that is, the place he has chosen (i.e., the central sanctuary) in order to proffer their tribute. The principle of giving is almost identical with that of the New Testament: Each must give "according to the gift of his hand," that is, as much as his physical strength enabled him to produce. And each must give as God had blessed him. Proper stewardship, then, consists of responding generously to the goodness of God and recognizing also that it is he "who gives you power to be successful" (8:18; cf. 2 Cor 8:1-15).

◆   B. Kingdom Officials (16:18–18:22)
        1. Judges and officers (16:18–17:13)
           a. Provision for the offices (16:18-20)

¹⁸"Appoint judges and officials for yourselves from each of your tribes in all the towns the LORD your God is giving you. They must judge the people fairly. ¹⁹You must never twist justice or show partiality. Never accept a bribe, for bribes blind the eyes of the wise and corrupt the decisions of the godly. ²⁰Let true justice prevail, so you may live and occupy the land that the LORD your God is giving you.

COMMENTARY

After the great section on the exclusiveness of Yahweh and his worship (12:1–16:17), Moses addressed the matter of human officials who, under Yahweh, must administer the affairs of the nation (16:18–18:22). The underlying principle of rule must be justice, so the office and responsibility of judges are brought to the fore. First of all, their own character must be circumspect, for unless judges can be trusted as persons, their disposition of legal cases is always open to question.

For ease of access to the legal system, judges and "officials" (16:18; *shoterim* [TH7860, ZH8854]) were to be distributed throughout the land. The term "official" is generic, signifying public officials as a whole, but in this context, the term probably refers to either the judges themselves or other court-related personnel such as bailiffs (Craigie 1976:247). The most important criterion to mark their qualifications would be fairness. The literal rendering is that "they must judge the people with a righteous judgment" (*mishpat tsedeq* [TH4941/6664, ZH5477/7406]). The Hebrew lexeme *tsedeq* (righteous) refers ultimately to a standard or norm against which attitudes and actions must be measured (NIDOTTE 3.750). It is one established by God himself and in line with his character. Israel's judges must render verdicts, then, not according to some personal whim or even a community consensus about right and wrong. Rather, they must do so in line with God's divinely revealed and objective bench marks (16:18).

Consistent and rigorous attention to this ideal would preclude any display of judicial corruption. Thus, the administration of justice would be unaffected by public or private pressure (i.e., not twisted) and would abstemiously refuse to show partiality (lit., "recognize faces"—that is, differentiate according to class or status). Even inducements to do otherwise—such as offers of bribes—must not deter the judge from doing the right thing. In the language of proverbial wisdom, Moses noted that bribes blind the eyes of the wise and distort the dealings of the righteous. That is, judges who otherwise would have clear insight into right and wrong and who exercise integrity in their application of justice can be (and often are) drawn into compromises that betray the sacred trust of their office (cf. 10:17; 1 Sam 8:3; Prov 17:23; Isa 5:23).

To underscore the importance of the standard of justice, Moses concluded by admonishing "justice, justice you must pursue" (16:20, literal rendering). Only unalloyed (or, as in NLT, "true") justice is acceptable, that untainted by fear or favor. This is one of the conditions for long and happy life in the Land of Promise.

◆ b. Examples of legal cases (16:21–17:1)

²¹"You must never set up a wooden Asherah pole beside the altar you build for the LORD your God. ²²And never set up sacred pillars for worship, for the LORD your God hates them.

CHAPTER 17

"Never sacrifice sick or defective cattle, sheep, or goats to the LORD your God, for he detests such gifts.

COMMENTARY

Illustrations are powerful ways of clarifying abstractions. Thus, Moses drew attention to certain acts of covenant violation that would likely occur in Canaan (16:21–17:1) and how they must be adjudicated (17:2-7). The examples he chose are singularly appropriate because they relate to the very heart of the covenant relationship—the exclusiveness of Yahweh and how he must be worshiped.

An Asherah (pole) was a stylized version of a shade tree, the symbol of the Canaanite fertility goddess Asherah (cf. 7:5). In the interest of a syncretistic cult that would embrace the "best" elements of both Baalism and Yahwism, the temptation would be to worship both Yahweh and the gods of Canaan (16:21). But Yahwism cannot coexist with paganism. He hates such superstitions and the trappings, such as "sacred" pillars (cf. 7:5), that accompany them (16:22). Fundamentally at issue here is adherence to the first two commandments—do not worship any other gods and do not make idols of any kind (5:7-8). There could be no greater crime than this and, hence, no greater need for application of true justice.

The second example pertains to proper modes and materials of worship, a theme generally embodied in the third and fourth commandments (5:11-15). Specifically, Moses says, offerings made to Yahweh must be worthy of him, for he is the Great King, who, according to covenant protocol, has just claim upon everything and everyone. This being the case, nothing could be more abhorrent and deserving of divine displeasure than offering him despicable and discarded tribute (17:1; cf. 15:21). In the strongest possible terms, Moses described such an affront as an abomination to God.

◆ c. Judgment for idolatry (17:2-7)

²"When you begin living in the towns the LORD your God is giving you, a man or woman among you might do evil in the sight of the LORD your God and violate the covenant. ³For instance, they might serve other gods or worship the sun, the moon, or any of the stars—the forces of heaven—which I have strictly forbidden. ⁴When you hear about it, investigate the matter thoroughly. If it is true that this detestable

thing has been done in Israel, [5]then the man or woman who has committed such an evil act must be taken to the gates of the town and stoned to death. [6]But never put a person to death on the testimony of only one witness. There must always be two or three witnesses. [7]The witnesses must throw the first stones, and then all the people may join in. In this way, you will purge the evil from among you.

NOTES

17:3 the sun. The MT reads "and to the sun" for the expected "or to the sun" (so Theodotion, Lucian). The meaning is not essentially different, though the MT suggests that the sun, moon, and stars are gods, as opposed to alternatives to them (Tigay 1996:162).

COMMENTARY

The prohibitions of 16:21-22 are now put in the setting of the legal procedures to be followed in redressing their violation. The typical form of case law ("suppose a man or woman . . .") is followed in presenting a hypothetical situation in which an Israelite breaks the covenant by doing something "evil" (17:2; *ra'* [TH7451, ZH8273]), that is, something offensive to Yahweh. The evil thing here is the denial of Yahweh's claim to exclusive worship and the veneration of other gods or even the heavenly luminaries (see note on 17:3). Only the Deuteronomic law refers to the latter, but under its influence, prophets throughout subsequent centuries drew attention to this pernicious practice in which the creature was worshiped rather than the Creator (cf. 2 Kgs 23:5, 11; Ezek 8:16; Zeph 1:5; Rom 1:25).

Should such a thing be exposed, it must be carefully investigated (lit., "you must seek after [it] well") and, if the report is found to be accurate, the community must exercise its collective responsibility to administer justice—capital punishment in such a case (17:4-5; cf. 13:6-11). The gates (17:5) refer to the square or plaza of a town, usually just inside the main gateway. This was the usual place of holding court as well as public execution (cf. 22:24; Ps 127:5; Jer 17:19-23; Mic 1:12).

To preclude personal animosity or misinterpretation, the law required more than one witness to testify (17:6). Collusion would still be possible, but the testimony of several persons who concurred would certainly inject an element of credibility that might otherwise be lacking (cf. 19:15; Matt 18:16; 2 Cor 13:1). A further safeguard against miscarriage of justice was the requirement that the witnesses themselves initiate the execution (17:7). Psychologically speaking, false witnesses would be greatly constrained if they knew they would compound their perjury with murder. Persons tempted to bear false witness would think twice under this proviso. Moreover, the law elsewhere mandates that a false witness, if discovered to be such, must suffer the penalty that would have befallen the falsely accused (19:18-19).

◆   ### d. Appeal to a higher court (17:8-13)

[8]"Suppose a case arises in a local court that is too hard for you to decide—for instance, whether someone is guilty of murder or only of manslaughter, or a difficult lawsuit, or a case involving different kinds of assault. Take such legal cases to the

place the LORD your God will choose, ⁹and present them to the Levitical priests or the judge on duty at that time. They will hear the case and declare the verdict. ¹⁰You must carry out the verdict they announce and the sentence they prescribe at the place the LORD chooses. You must do exactly what they say. ¹¹After they have interpreted the law and declared their verdict, the sentence they impose must be fully executed; do not modify it in any way. ¹²Anyone arrogant enough to reject the verdict of the judge or of the priest who represents the LORD your God must die. In this way you will purge the evil from Israel. ¹³Then everyone else will hear about it and be afraid to act so arrogantly.

NOTES

17:8 *God will choose.* Several Greek recensions add "to place his name there" in order to complete the usual formula (cf. also 17:10). The added phrase suggests that the central sanctuary is in view. In the larger context, however, the MT favors the idea that local, Levitical cities are the places of judgment.

17:11 *interpreted the law.* The MT reads more literally, "according to the law that they will teach you." Many Greek readings presuppose the Hebrew root *'wr* [TH215, ZH239] (light) for the MT verbal form *yoruka* [TH3384E, ZH3723] ("they will teach you") and render "they will enlighten you," or the like. The meaning is essentially the same.

17:12 *represents the LORD.* Lit., "to serve there the Lord." The LXX suggests a transposition of *sham* [TH8033, ZH9004] (there) and *'et* [TH853, ZH906] (accusative) and a repointing to read, "to serve (in) the name of (*'et-shem* [TH8034, ZH9005]) Yahweh."

COMMENTARY

Legal cases are never identically complex or easy of resolution, and most legal systems have provisions for appeal to higher legal jurisdictions. This was the case in ancient Israel, even prior to the revelation of the law (cf. Exod 18:21-22). Given such circumstances, if matters arose concerning homicide (lit., "between blood and blood"), civil law ("between judgment and judgment"), or bodily harm ("between blow and blow"), and these were contested in the local courts (lit., "in your gates") without satisfactory adjudication, the case would be carried to a higher court at a place chosen by Yahweh (17:8).

The verb "choose" (17:8; *bakhar* [TH977, ZH1047]), usually used in connection with the central sanctuary (cf. 12:5, 11, 14, 18; 16:6), may refer here to the selection of a number of places where courts of appeal would be located. The fact that the officiants at such places are called Levites (lit., "the priests, the Levites") argues presumptively for these sites being the 48 Levitical towns that were to be allocated once the land was conquered. Included among these were six cities of asylum in which persons accused of homicide could find refuge pending trial (19:1-13; cf. 4:41-43; Num 35:1-28; Josh 20). It is likely that in these cities the Levites served as courts of appeal. The "supreme" court, of course, was to be located at the central sanctuary, eventually Jerusalem.

Perhaps one of the Levites is meant by the technical term "judge" (*shopet* [TH8199A, ZH9149]) in 17:9, but it is worth noting that as part of King Jehoshaphat's reformation he scattered judges through the nation, probably to restore the very system in view in Deuteronomy (2 Chr 19:5-11). And since these officials are not called Levites in that setting, it is likely that the judge here was also not a Levite but a layman who worked in cooperation with them. In any event, these judges constituted a court of appeal (17:10). Their verdict was final and their recommended punishment must be meted out exactly as it was handed down. There was no loophole of nuancing or equivocation (17:11). Anyone presumptuous enough to alter the verdict or its sentence must die, for he has flaunted not just the laws of a court but the sovereignty of God himself (17:12). Such harsh measures were designed to inculcate a healthy respect for Yahweh and his covenant expectations (17:13).

Not to be overlooked is the qualification of 17:11 that all legal matters must be addressed in light of the Torah. No matter how innovative, insightful, compassionate, or experienced a judge might be, his only guide and authority for decision-making was the law of the Covenant Code itself. In other words, he was not a neutral party beholden to no one but himself, nor was he to be a hireling to be bought and sold in the marketplace of special-interest groups. In the final analysis, he was an interpreter of the Mosaic law who humbly but authoritatively applied it in service to the King of kings.

◆   ## 2. Kings (17:14–20)

14"You are about to enter the land the LORD your God is giving you. When you take it over and settle there, you may think, 'We should select a king to rule over us like the other nations around us.' 15If this happens, be sure to select as king the man the LORD your God chooses. You must appoint a fellow Israelite; he may not be a foreigner.

16"The king must not build up a large stable of horses for himself or send his people to Egypt to buy horses, for the LORD has told you, 'You must never return to Egypt.' 17The king must not take many wives for himself, because they will turn his heart away from the LORD. And he must not accumulate large amounts of wealth in silver and gold for himself.

18"When he sits on the throne as king, he must copy for himself this body of instruction on a scroll in the presence of the Levitical priests. 19He must always keep that copy with him and read it daily as long as he lives. That way he will learn to fear the LORD his God by obeying all the terms of these instructions and decrees. 20This regular reading will prevent him from becoming proud and acting as if he is above his fellow citizens. It will also prevent him from turning away from these commands in the smallest way. And it will ensure that he and his descendants will reign for many generations in Israel.

NOTES

17:18 copy . . . this body of instruction. This text is particularly interesting because the name Deuteronomy is based on the LXX rendition of it: *to deuteronomion touto* (lit., "this second law") for MT's *mishneh hattorah hazzo'th* [TH4932, ZH5467] ("copy of this law").

17:20 will reign. The MT reads, "in order that he might lengthen (his) days upon his kingship." The Samaritan Pentateuch supplies *kisse'* [TH3678, ZH4058] (throne), thus, "upon the throne of his kingship." This overliteralizes what is already a clearly intended meaning.

COMMENTARY

The second of four kingdom "offices" regulated in Deuteronomy is the monarchy or kingship (the others are judges, priests, and prophets). Its appearance in the

Mosaic literature 400 years before its actual historical emergence under Saul appears to provide support to those who view Deuteronomy as a seventh-century composition falsely attributed to Moses (see Introduction). However, most advanced societies in the Late Bronze Age were monarchic, so there is no reason that Moses, even unaided by revelation, could not have anticipated that this would some day be Israel's form of government. Indeed, the promise was already made that Sarah would be the mother of kings (Gen 17:16), and kings of Edom are said to have reigned "before any king ruled over the Israelites" (Gen 36:31). And kingship is also implicit in Jacob's blessing of Judah, about whom it is said, "The scepter will not depart from Judah, nor the ruler's staff from his descendants, until the coming of the one to whom it belongs" (Gen 49:10). Clearly the impression throughout is that kingship is an established fact (Wenham 1994:22) and what was needed in Deuteronomy was not a promise of its future reality but regulations as to its deportment (Craigie 1976:253).

The divine impetus for kingship was theological, but as it turned out, the human drive was political, based on a desire to keep in step with all the neighboring nations (17:14; cf. 1 Sam 8:1-9, 19-20). Once this happened (and it surely would), it would not be forbidden, but the selection of a candidate must be careful indeed. He must be chosen by God, and he must not be a foreigner (17:15). Even Saul met these qualifications, for even though it turned out that he was not the "man after [God's] own heart" (1 Sam 13:14), he was an Israelite and one anointed by Samuel at Yahweh's behest (1 Sam 10:1).

Once in place, the king must strictly observe certain well-defined guidelines, all of which were designed to help him keep things in proper perspective. First, in the realm of military might, he must remember that Yahweh, not horses, is the source of strength and success (17:16; cf. Ps 20:7). Therefore, he is not to be a horse trader, particularly with the Egyptians (cf. 1 Kgs 10:29). Second, in his domestic or family life, he must refrain from excessive polygamy, for wives taken especially for political purposes would exert pressure on him to adopt their religious systems and forsake Yahweh (17:17). Third, he must not become overly materialistic because great wealth tends to breed great self-sufficiency and corresponding apathy with respect to the need for God (cf. 8:11-18).

These instructions for royal behavior seem tailor-made for Solomon. He had a virtual monopoly on the horse market and owned thousands of the animals himself (1 Kgs 10:26-29); he had an enormous harem of wives and concubines who caused his heart to turn from Yahweh (1 Kgs 11:1-8); and he was fabulously wealthy, more so than anyone else in the known world (1 Kgs 10:14-23). In fact, many scholars argue that the Deuteronomic standards were drawn up after Solomon's time precisely to warn against the kind of profligate monarchy that Solomon exhibited (Driver 1902:211-212). In objection to this, it must be noted that the passage presents itself as a Mosaic, preconquest composition (17:14). Only a hypothesis that ignores or rejects the text's own testimony can gainsay its pre-Solomonic setting. Furthermore, Samuel the prophet also warned of the impending abuses of kingship (in this case, that of Saul) in advance of its actual inauguration (1 Sam 8:10-18). Again, the only recourse to those who are disinclined to see this as an advance warning is to assume that these words were put into Samuel's mouth long after the fact.

To safeguard against untoward behavior by Israel's future kings, Moses commanded that a copy of "this Torah" must be made by the king (probably actually on his behalf) from a text in the custody of the Levites (17:18). At the minimum, this document would consist of 17:15-17, but much more likely would include the entire book as it currently exists. Evidence of this is the technical language that follows. Future kings must read from their copy of the law all their lives so that they might fear Yahweh (17:19; cf. 4:10; 5:29; 6:2, 13, 24; 10:12) and obey "this Torah" and its stipulations. This terminology elsewhere is virtually synonymous with the whole content of Deuteronomy (cf. 4:1, 6; 5:1; 6:1, 24; 7:11; 11:32; 12:1; 16:12).

Faithful adherence to this policy should (1) humble future kings, (2) prevent them from turning aside from "the commandment" (*hammitswah* [TH4687, ZH5184]); and (3) guarantee longevity of reign for themselves and their dynastic successors (17:20). Tragically, the history of Israel's kingship as it unfolded provided all too few examples of obedience to the Mosaic prescription.

◆　　　## 3. Priests and Levites (18:1-8)

"Remember that the Levitical priests—that is, the whole of the tribe of Levi—will receive no allotment of land among the other tribes in Israel. Instead, the priests and Levites will eat from the special gifts given to the LORD, for that is their share. ²They will have no land of their own among the Israelites. The LORD himself is their special possession, just as he promised them.

³"These are the parts the priests may claim as their share from the cattle, sheep, and goats that the people bring as offerings: the shoulder, the cheeks, and the stomach. ⁴You must also give to the priests the first share of the grain, the new wine, the olive oil, and the wool at shearing time. ⁵For the LORD your God chose the tribe of Levi out of all your tribes to minister in the LORD's name forever.

⁶"Suppose a Levite chooses to move from his town in Israel, wherever he is living, to the place the LORD chooses for worship. ⁷He may minister there in the name of the LORD his God, just like all his fellow Levites who are serving the LORD there. ⁸He may eat his share of the sacrifices and offerings, even if he also receives support from his family.

NOTES

18:1 *Levitical priests.* The Syriac distinguishes between the priests and Levites by rendering the phrase "to the priest and to the Levite." The MT reads "to the priests, the Levites," suggesting (as in NLT) by the apposition that the priests in view are Levitical priests—that is, they are legitimate because they are from the tribe of Levi.

18:5 *to minister.* Reflecting priestly roles elsewhere (cf. 10:8; 21:5), the Samaritan Pentateuch and certain LXX recensions add here "and to bless" (in the name of Yahweh).

COMMENTARY

Having dealt with the more "secular" offices of judge and king, Moses turned to those more obviously "spiritual" or cultic ones, namely, the priest and the prophet (18:9-22). Such distinctions are, of course, meaningless in terms of ancient Israel's theocratic, covenant community, in which there was no such bifurcation. Nonetheless, there is a more explicit religious connotation to these two functions, especially that of the priests and Levites.

Deuteronomy is marked by its pervasive description of Israel's cultic personnel as "the priests, the Levites," or, more accurately, "the Levitical priests" (see note on 18:1; cf. 17:9, 18; 21:5; 24:8; 27:9; Josh 3:3; 8:33; 2 Chr 5:5; 23:18; 30:27; Jer 33:18; Ezek 43:19; 44:15). The precise meaning of this phrase is a matter of some debate (see articles by Abba 1977; Emerton 1962; Wright 1954), but in the light of 18:1 it seems clear that the intention is not to designate priests as opposed to Levites but to equate Levites with priests—that is, as having priestly privileges and responsibilities. One could understand the verse as saying, "the Levitical priests, that is, the whole tribe of Levi."

In actual fact, the priests of Israel were a subset of the Levites, for all priests were to be descendants of Aaron (one family of the tribe of Levi; cf. Exod 6:16-20; 28:1; Num 3:1-20). Since all priests must be able to trace their lineage to Aaron, Levites who could not do so were technically disqualified from holding that office. However, they could function in priestly matters and so, in a generic sense at least, could be (as here) designated as priests. The distinction Moses wanted to make was between nature and function (Tigay 1996:169-170). The point here is that since Levi was to be given no tribal territory, the tribe must be allowed to share in the fellowship offerings of God's people so as to provide for themselves and their families (18:1; cf.12:12, 18, 19; 14:27, 29; 16:11, 14; 26:11-13). Yahweh himself was their inheritance, a compensation immeasurably greater than any bestowment of lands and properties (18:2; cf. 10:9; Lev 25:33).

Beginning with 18:3, Moses appears to be speaking of the priests only and not the Levites because the items listed in 18:3-4 as offerings designated for the priests are mentioned elsewhere as emoluments for the descendants of Aaron—that is, priests in the strict sense (cf. Lev 7:31-36; Num 18:8-11). The statement in 18:5 provides the rationale for this provision: Yahweh had chosen the priest (lit., "him"; not the "tribe of Levi," as in NLT) to serve him in a special way forever. In exchange for this service—a service to the whole nation as well—God's faithful ministers could expect his abundant supply.

The Levites of 18:6-8, in view of the previous observation, should be understood in precise terms as officiants separate and distinct from the priests. The interesting regulation here has to do with occupational mobility, the freedom of a Levite to move about in his ministry responsibilities. Specifically, if a Levite should choose to leave a local sanctuary (presumably in one of the 48 Levitical towns; cf. 17:8-13) in order to serve at the central sanctuary, he must be allowed to (18:6). Furthermore, he must not suffer discrimination; rather, he should enjoy all the rights and privileges of Levites already there (18:7). Even though he is far from home—where his physical and material needs would ordinarily be met—he must be included in the same benefits at the Tabernacle or Temple. Moreover, whatever he owned by way of disposition of family properties (*mimkarayw* [TH4465, ZH4928] *'al-ha'aboth*, "his selling according to the fathers") could not be counted against him and thus deprive him of his just due (18:8).

◆   ## 4. Prophets (18:9-22)

9"When you enter the land the LORD your God is giving you, be very careful not to imitate the detestable customs of the nations living there. 10For example, never sacrifice your son or daughter as a burnt offering.* And do not let your people practice fortune-telling, or use sorcery, or interpret omens, or engage in witchcraft, 11or cast spells, or function as mediums or psychics, or call forth the spirits of the dead. 12Anyone who does these things is detestable to the LORD. It is because the other nations have done these detestable things that the LORD your God will drive them out ahead of you. 13But you must be blameless before the LORD your God. 14The nations you are about to displace consult sorcerers and fortune-tellers, but the LORD your God forbids you to do such things."

15Moses continued, "The LORD your God will raise up for you a prophet like me from among your fellow Israelites. You must listen to him. 16For this is what you yourselves requested of the LORD your God when you were assembled at Mount Sinai.* You said, 'Don't let us hear the voice of the LORD our God anymore or see this blazing fire, for we will die.'

17"Then the LORD said to me, 'What they have said is right. 18I will raise up a prophet like you from among their fellow Israelites. I will put my words in his mouth, and he will tell the people everything I command him. 19I will personally deal with anyone who will not listen to the messages the prophet proclaims on my behalf. 20But any prophet who falsely claims to speak in my name or who speaks in the name of another god must die.'

21"But you may wonder, 'How will we know whether or not a prophecy is from the LORD?' 22If the prophet speaks in the LORD's name but his prediction does not happen or come true, you will know that the LORD did not give that message. That prophet has spoken without my authority and need not be feared.

18:10 Or *never make your son or daughter pass through the fire.* 18:16 Hebrew *Horeb,* another name for Sinai.

NOTES

18:15 *from among your fellow Israelites.* The MT has "from among you, from your brothers," an expansion of the more common formula, "from among your brethren" (cf. 17:15; 18:18), a formula attested by the Samaritan Pentateuch and a number of Greek readings. However, the expansion seems designed to emphasize the fact that the prophet to be raised up will be not only from Israel but a full-blooded Israelite.

18:19 *the prophet.* MT lacks "the prophet" here, but the DSS and a few Greek minuscules attest to it, thereby providing clarity of antecedent.

18:21 *we know.* To harmonize the plural predicate with the singular subject of the MT ("if you [singular] say, 'How can we know'"), the Samaritan Pentateuch reads Niphal singular ("how can it be known"), thus achieving the desired compatibility. Certain LXX recensions and their derivatives (Syriac, Vulgate) suggest first-person singular ("how can I know"), but this requires alteration of the consonants.

COMMENTARY

The final "office" of theocratic community would differ greatly from the previous two (king and priest) in its being not hereditary but *ad hoc*, or, as some scholars suggest, charismatic. That is, a prophet could be called by God from any family at any time; one could not be a prophet just because his father was. Also, the prophetic gift was bestowed upon women as well as men (cf. Exod 15:20; Judg 4:4; 2 Kgs 22:14; 2 Chr 34:22; Neh 6:14).

Moses introduces the topic of prophetism by ruling out pagan or fraudulent manifestations of it (18:9-14). He had already dealt with false prophets who would arise from among the Israelites themselves (ch 13). Now he addresses those who would be encountered in Canaan and thereby warns his people not to practice the abominable things they would find there (18:9). Most heinous of all, perhaps, was the Canaanite ritual of having their children "pass through the fire" (18:10; see NLT mg). There is general agreement that this refers, somewhat euphemistically, to human sacrifice, a practice already severely condemned (12:31). Its relevance to false prophetism is not altogether clear, but it may be that certain divination or apotropaic rituals included such horrendous means (de Vaux 1965:444-446).

Some of the following technical terms—and thus the practices associated with them—defy easy explanation. The first two ("fortune-telling" and "sorcery" in NLT) appear to involve divination—that is, the ability to determine the plans and purposes of the gods through the observation of various natural phenomena such as animal entrails, flights of birds, and the like (NIDOTTE 3.945-951). The third (NLT, "interpret omens") has also to do with divination (Gen 44:5, 15) but, in some texts, with incantation, the uttering of powerful curses (Num 23:23; 24:1). The fourth (NLT, "witchcraft") deals with signs done to ward off evil (NIDOTTE 2.735-738). Spell casters (18:11) specialized in uttering powerful curses to bring things under their control (TDOT 4.195). A medium professed to communicate with the dead (necromancy), as did the spiritist (NLT, "psychics"; NIDOTTE 1.303-304). Finally, those who "call forth the spirits of the dead" appears to be generic for anyone who by any means attempts to communicate with the netherworld. These would all be in the class of diviner—that is, someone who tries to find out the future so as to take advantage of its opportunities or avoid its calamities.

All of these superstitious and satanic practices are described as abominations to Yahweh. They are reprehensible to him, so much so that he would expel from the land of Canaan all the nations that engage in them (18:12). The Israelites must be radically different. Rather than being abominable in his sight, they must be blameless (*tamim* [TH8549, ZH9459], "upright"; 18:13) before him. The pagans might be characterized by such sinful and foolish behavior, but Yahweh has destined better things for his people (18:14).

One of those better things would be a Moses-like prophet, one raised up from Israel and not from the land of Canaan (18:15). Though the singular (*nabi'* [TH5030, ZH5566]) is used to describe that prophet, the context (especially 18:20) supports the idea that a line of prophets is intended. Hitherto, prophets had randomly and rarely appeared (cf. Gen 20:7; Exod 7:1; 15:20; Num 11:29; 12:6), but in the future they would become numerous, common, and almost institutionalized. Samuel is generally regarded as the first of that illustrious line, a line of prophets brought to its grand and glorious climax in Jesus Christ (Merrill 1994:27-32; 1 Sam 3:15–4:1; Acts 3:17-23). Indeed, Jesus himself understood that he was the ultimate Prophet foreseen by Moses (see John 5:45-47; cf. John 1:21).

The principal task of a prophet was to be a spokesman for God (cf. Exod 4:14-16; 7:1). Moses fulfilled this function at Mount Horeb because of the people's terror in confronting the living God (5:22-27; cf. Exod 20:18-19). From that time onward, Moses was regarded as a prophet, but one of a special order with special access to Yahweh (Num 12:6-8). His uniqueness is celebrated in his epitaph: "There has never been another prophet in Israel like Moses, whom the LORD knew face to face" (34:10).

Responding to the fear of the people at Horeb, Yahweh not only allowed Moses to be a prophetic mediator (18:16), but he promised a line of succession after Moses— spokesmen for God whose mouths would speak only what God commanded (18:17-18). Those who failed to heed the prophetic word must suffer the consequences (18:19). However, others would claim prophetic revelation for themselves and would either speak falsehoods in the name of Yahweh or deliver messages on behalf of other gods. In either case, such prophets must be executed (18:20) because they aid and abet disloyalty and sedition.

The question must inevitably arise, however, as to how true prophets could be distinguished from false (VanGemeren 1990:59-66). In his earlier discourse (ch 13), Moses had said that prophets who urged God's people to defect to other gods were *ipso facto* false (13:2-3, 8). Here (18:21) the test pertains not so much to the content of the message as to its timing: Should a prophet predict a coming event only to have that prediction fail, he or she must be regarded as false. God is the God of truth but also the God of foreknowledge and omnipotence. What he ordains must come to pass and in ways and times of his own choosing. Prophets not in tune with his disclosures can only be false and need not be feared (18:22).

◆   C. Civil Law (19:1–21:23)
     1. Legal provisions for manslaughter (19:1-13)

"When the LORD your God destroys the nations whose land he is giving you, you will take over their land and settle in their towns and homes. ²Then you must set apart three cities of refuge in the land the LORD your God is giving you. ³Survey the territory,* and divide the land the LORD your God is giving you into three districts, with one of these cities in each district. Then anyone who has killed someone can flee to one of the cities of refuge for safety.

⁴"If someone kills another person unintentionally, without previous hostility, the slayer may flee to any of these cities to live in safety. ⁵For example, suppose someone goes into the forest with a neighbor to cut wood. And suppose one of them swings an ax to chop down a tree, and the ax head flies off the handle, kill-

ing the other person. In such cases, the slayer may flee to one of the cities of refuge to live in safety.

⁶"If the distance to the nearest city of refuge is too far, an enraged avenger might be able to chase down and kill the person who caused the death. Then the slayer would die unfairly, since he had never shown hostility toward the person who died. ⁷That is why I am commanding you to set aside three cities of refuge.

⁸"And if the LORD your God enlarges your territory, as he swore to your ancestors, and gives you all the land he promised them, ⁹you must designate three additional cities of refuge. (He will give you this land if you are careful to obey all the commands I have given you—if you

always love the LORD your God and walk in his ways.) ¹⁰That way you will prevent the death of innocent people in the land the LORD your God is giving you as your special possession. You will not be held responsible for the death of innocent people.

¹¹"But suppose someone is hostile toward a neighbor and deliberately ambushes and murders him and then flees to one of the cities of refuge. ¹²In that case, the elders of the murderer's hometown must send agents to the city of refuge to bring him back and hand him over to the dead person's avenger to be put to death. ¹³Do not feel sorry for that murderer! Purge from Israel the guilt of murdering innocent people; then all will go well with you.

19:3 Or *Keep the roads in good repair.*

NOTES

19:9 *walk in his ways.* Many Greek mss add "all" before "ways" to conform to the stereotypical language found otherwise in 10:12; 11:22; and 30:16, LXX. While this clearly adds emphasis to Moses's injunction to total obedience ("all the commands" and "all his ways"), the addition is so patently an attempt to replicate the formula found elsewhere that the MT should be left as it stands.

19:12 *to be put to death.* The MT actually has a Qal stem here ("that he may die"), but the Samaritan Pentateuch, correctly understanding the causative aspect of this death, reads with a Hophal form ("that he might be executed").

COMMENTARY

In anticipation of the coming defeat and displacement of the Canaanite populations, Moses set in motion the allocation of certain cities throughout the land as places of refuge for persons accused of murder or other kinds of homicide. This matter had been addressed briefly before, both in Deuteronomy (4:41-43) and, at greater length, in Numbers 35:9-34. In his previous instruction in this book, however, Moses had limited it to the matter of Transjordanian sites of which there were to be three (see commentary on 4:41-43). Now it was necessary to attend to the three others in Canaan itself.

In passing, it is interesting to note that Israel would "settle in their [the Canaanites'] towns and homes" (19:1), indicating that the conquest would not consist of the destruction of physical or material things on the whole, but only of the people and their cultic paraphernalia (cf. 6:10-11; Josh 24:13). The cities of refuge, then, would simply be taken over and occupied by the Israelites with little or no need of repair. This information supports the notion that the traditional early date for the Exodus and conquest finds confirmation in the absence of archaeological evidence for massive destruction in the early part of the fourteenth century BC.

Once proper roads had been constructed, the land had to be divided into three zones, with each containing a city of refuge (19:3). When Joshua brought this about later on, he selected the cities of Kedesh in the tribal area of Naphtali, Shechem in Ephraim, and Hebron in Judah (Josh 20:7). These were conveniently and accessibly located so that anyone living in the land could reach one of them reasonably easily.

The purpose of these cities was to provide temporary sanctuary to anyone guilty of homicide (Greenberg 1959:125-132). The term "slayer" (*rotseakh* [TH7523, ZH8357]; 19:4, 6), a generic expression that says nothing about motives or methods, affirms only the fact of homicide (Childs 1974:419-421). Because such a deed, accidental or otherwise, was so heinous, the relatives of the victim were not only permitted but expected to initiate clan vengeance. Should it be immediately obvious that premeditated murder had taken place, retribution could be administered without trial or the benefit of sanctuary (Num 35:16-21). If, however, it could be shown that the death was accidental (*beli-da'ath* [TH1097/1847, ZH1172/1981], "with lack of knowledge"; 19:4), the perpetrator must have a place of security beyond the reach of the avenger until the matter could be brought to trial (19:4-5). Human nature being what it is, avengers, filled with rage, might retaliate before the facts were known, thus compounding the problem (19:6). This is why these cities had to be strategically located throughout the land—the accused in such cases should have at least a running chance (19:7).

Should the time come when the population spread or the density was such that the three cities were insufficient, three more should be selected (19:8-9). However, there were conditions to this growth, namely, adherence to the entire covenant code—that is, to Torah itself. The essence of this commitment was twofold: "Love the LORD your God" and "walk in his ways." The former is an abbreviated expression of the Shema, Israel's most fundamental confession (cf. 6:4-5), whereas the latter speaks of a lifetime of fleshing it out. Belief is more than just adherence to theological truths; it must demonstrate its reality in obedience to the requirements of those truths (cf. Jas 2:14-26). Sadly, there is no record in Israel's subsequent history of the establishment of other cities of refuge. The reality is that such were never needed because Israel never reached the limits of its promises. This indictment echoes like a refrain in many lives; the promise is out there to be appropriated, but disobedience, lack of faith, or other interventions preclude what God has in store for those willing to meet the conditions.

The main topic resumes in 19:11 with the hypothetical situation in which an individual has clearly committed murder and yet managed to find his way to a sanctuary. The qualifiers here are that the criminal has already displayed ill will toward his victim (lit., he "hates his neighbor") and has lain in wait to kill him (19:11). In such a case, there can be no sanctuary nor, apparently, even a trial (though, presumably, there must be witnesses). Rather, the murderer must be extradited to the elders of the village from whence he came, and there he must be handed over to the avenger for execution (19:12).

One should note the qualifications again. One is internal, and the other is overt or external. The hating by itself would never kill, though it frequently paves the way to destructive action. Yet lying in wait by itself also could be inconclusive since there might be no witnesses to the act; and even if there were, the act might be susceptible to more than one interpretation. A history of ill will coupled with a violent act would constitute an almost unassailable legal case against the accused. No wonder Jesus said that anger is tantamount to murder, because anger, left unchecked and unremediated, all too often results in physical violence (cf. Matt 5:21-22).

Perhaps the most difficult part of the passage is the injunction not to pity the murderer (19:13). This may seem to go against the New Testament ethic of forgiving those who do us harm (Mark 11:25; Luke 6:37; 17:3-4; Col 3:13), but what must be understood here is that the crime is not fundamentally against a solitary victim but against the entire theocratic community. Failure to punish it in kind (cf. Exod 21:24) would also inculpate the whole community. More than that, it was a sin against the Lord himself, the Ruler of the theocracy. Though the application of justice in such cases in modern societies can and must be different because none can claim theocratic status, the principle of life's sanctity still holds, as does that of God's retributive response.

◆　　### 2. The testimony of witnesses (19:14-21)

14"When you arrive in the land the LORD your God is giving you as your special possession, you must never steal anyone's land by moving the boundary markers your ancestors set up to mark their property.

15"You must not convict anyone of a crime on the testimony of only one witness. The facts of the case must be established by the testimony of two or three witnesses.

16"If a malicious witness comes forward and accuses someone of a crime, 17then both the accuser and accused must appear before the LORD by coming to the priests and judges in office at that time. 18The judges must investigate the case thoroughly. If the accuser has brought false charges against his fellow Israelite, 19you must impose on the accuser the sentence he intended for the other person. In this way, you will purge such evil from among you. 20Then the rest of the people will hear about it and be afraid to do such an evil thing. 21You must show no pity for the guilty! Your rule should be life for life, eye for eye, tooth for tooth, hand for hand, foot for foot.

NOTES

19:17 *appear before the LORD by coming to the priests and judges.* In Hebrew, the appositional construction would yield the literal translation, "before the Lord, before the priests and the judges." The idea, then, is that these public officials represent the Lord. To stand before divinely appointed servants of God is tantamount to standing before him (cf. Rom 13:1-7).

19:19 *purge.* The verb bi'arta [TH1197A, ZH1278] has the idea of "burning out," that is, purging by fire. Like cancer, sin in the community of faith will eat away at the body until it is seriously ill or weakened. Therefore, it must be excised (NIDOTTE 1.687-689; cf. 13:5 [6]; 17:7; 19:13; 21:21; 22:21, 24; 24:7).

COMMENTARY

It is likely that the matter of dividing the land up into sections and the allotment of cities of refuge (19:1-3) provides the rationale for the laws here about the removal of boundary markers (Rofé 1988:271). Since the land was really the Lord's and he had only entrusted it to the patriarchs and their descendants as a stewardship, to move boundary markers between such allocated properties was to flout God's distribution of his own inheritance to the tribes and clans of Israel (cf. Josh 13:9–14:5). Obviously, boundary markers would always be moved to the advantage of the encroacher, so the issue in the final analysis is theft. A famous example of the sanctity of ancestral lands and the need to retain them within families is that of King Ahab's illegal seizure of Naboth's vineyard, a sin for which he and his wife Jezebel later paid dearly (1 Kgs 21:1-29; 22:37-40; 2 Kgs 9:30-37).

The somewhat interruptive (and yet related) reference to boundary markers gives way now to the theme introduced by 19:1-13, namely, proper procedures for determining guilt or innocence in cases of criminal allegation (cf. 17:6-7). At the outset, guilt can never be established on the basis of the testimony of only one witness (19:15). An exchange that pits one person's word against another's demands the impossible ability to assess which of the two opposing parties has the most credibility in any given matter.

For example, should a "malicious" witness (lit., "a violent witness,"—i.e., one whose objective is to do harm) rise up to testify to a crime (19:16), both he and the accused must appear before the Lord, represented in the covenant community by priests and judges (see note on 19:17; cf. 17:9; Exod 21:6; 22:8-9). Should the witness prove to have perjured himself (19:18; lit., "the lying witness has given a lying witness"), the punishment appropriate to the crime must devolve upon him instead of the intended victim (19:19). Only such measure-for-measure justice could eradicate evil from the body of the community (see note on 19:19). The deterrent effect alone would tend to discourage others from attempting such miscarriage of justice (19:20).

To preclude timidity or reluctance in the application of such stern measures, Moses stated (19:21; cf. 19:13) that no pity must be shown when administering the punishment called for by the crime. The Hebrew says literally, "Your eye should not flow" (19:21), that is, tears of compassion must be restrained (cf. 7:16; 13:9; 25:12; Isa 13:18; Ezek 5:11; 7:4, 9; 8:18; etc.). Surely this does not mean that one can or should stifle human emotion at such a tragic turn of events, but that emotion cannot overturn the need for and execution of proper justice. This kind of justice, in sum, is talionic justice, one in which the punishment fits the crime (19:21b; cf. Exod 21:23-25; Lev 24:20). Quite possibly punishment was seldom if ever meted out in such literal terms (Patrick 1985:76-77). The point here is equity—one should not be punished more or less than he or she deserves for committing any given offense.

◆   3. The Manual of War (20:1-20)

"When you go out to fight your enemies and you face horses and chariots and an army greater than your own, do not be afraid. The LORD your God, who brought you out of the land of Egypt, is with you! ²When you prepare for battle, the priest must come forward to speak to the troops. ³He will say to them, 'Listen to me, all you men of Israel! Do not be afraid as you go out to fight your enemies today! Do not lose heart or panic or tremble before them. ⁴For the LORD your God is going with you! He will fight for you against your enemies, and he will give you victory!'

⁵"Then the officers of the army must address the troops and say, 'Has anyone here just built a new house but not yet dedicated it? If so, you may go home! You might be killed in the battle, and someone else would dedicate your house. ⁶Has anyone here just planted a vineyard but not yet eaten any of its fruit? If so, you may go home! You might die in battle, and someone else would eat the first fruit. ⁷Has anyone here just become engaged to a woman but not yet married her? Well, you may go home and get married! You might die in the battle, and someone else would marry her.'

⁸"Then the officers will also say, 'Is anyone here afraid or worried? If you are, you may go home before you frighten anyone else.' ⁹When the officers have finished speaking to their troops, they will appoint the unit commanders.

¹⁰"As you approach a town to attack it, you must first offer its people terms for peace. ¹¹If they accept your terms and open the gates to you, then all the people inside will serve you in forced labor. ¹²But if they refuse to make peace and prepare to fight, you must attack the town. ¹³When the LORD your God hands the town over to you, use your swords to kill every man in the town. ¹⁴But you may keep for yourselves all the women, children, livestock, and other plunder. You may enjoy the plunder from your enemies that the LORD your God has given you.

¹⁵"But these instructions apply only to distant towns, not to the towns of the nations in the land you will enter. ¹⁶In those towns that the LORD your God is giving you as a special possession, destroy every living thing. ¹⁷You must completely destroy* the Hittites, Amorites, Canaanites, Perizzites, Hivites, and Jebusites, just as the LORD your God has commanded you. ¹⁸This will prevent the people of the land from teaching you to imitate their detestable customs in the worship of their gods, which would cause you to sin deeply against the LORD your God.

¹⁹"When you are attacking a town and the war drags on, you must not cut down the trees with your axes. You may eat the fruit, but do not cut down the trees. Are the trees your enemies, that you should attack them? ²⁰You may only cut down trees that you know are not valuable for food. Use them to make the equipment you need to attack the enemy town until it falls.

20:17 The Hebrew term used here refers to the complete consecration of things or people to the LORD, either by destroying them or by giving them as an offering.

NOTES

20:5 *dedicated.* The verb *khanak* [TH2596, ZH2852] ordinarily has religious connotations (NIDOTTE 2.200-201) and may well have them here (cf. 1 Kgs 8:63; 2 Chr 7:9; Neh 12:27). The better-known noun form, *khanukkah* [TH2598, ZH2853] (e.g., Num 7:10-11), was later applied to the festival of Temple (re)dedication in Maccabean times (1 Macc 4:56-59), giving rise to the popular Jewish holiday known as Hanukkah.

20:8 *before you frighten anyone else.* The MT points the verb as a Niphal ("dissolve, melt") but the syntax requires Hiphil ("cause to melt" or, as in NLT, "frighten"). The causative is also attested in the Samaritan Pentateuch, LXX, Syriac, and Vulgate.

20:17 *completely destroy.* The infinitive absolute pattern of the verb *kharam* [TH2763, ZH3049] used here speaks of total annihilation, a feature of so-called "holy war" when it was directed against God's enemies (and, therefore, Israel's), particularly the Canaanites and their allies (cf. 3:22; 7:2, 18-24).

Jebusites. The LXX adds "Girgashites" after this in order to produce the standard list of seven enemies in the land (cf. 7:1). A variation of this kind of numerical formula—this time with ten nations listed—is Gen 15:19-21.

COMMENTARY

Ever since the Fall, humankind has been hostile to and in rebellion against the Creator, a condition that, if unrepented, leads ultimately to divine retribution and death. In the Old Testament, that conflict was frequently manifested historically by Yahweh's "taking up arms" against his and Israel's implacable foes, those who had so entrenched themselves in moral corruption and spiritual rebellion as to be beyond hope of redemption. This "holy war" (or "Yahweh war"; see Jones 1975) was sometimes executed by Yahweh alone, but more frequently it was implemented through his people Israel (see comments on 2:26-37). In addition, of course, there was "ordinary" war, the kind engaged in by nations over territorial disputes, arms buildups, imperialistic ambition, and a host of other reasons. The present "manual," therefore, deals with both kinds—with "secular" war in 20:10-15 and holy war in 20:16-20. The whole is prefaced by instructions for undertaking battle in general.

Whenever war occurs, especially in the case of holy war, Israel is told not to be afraid, for Yahweh, the Warrior who already proved his might at the Exodus, will go with them (20:1; cf. Exod 15:3-18). The role of the priests was a hallmark of this kind of war; they carried the Ark of the Covenant—the visible symbol of God's presence—and uttered words of comfort and encouragement on his behalf (cf. Num 10:35; Josh 3:1-6; 6:1-14; 1 Sam 4:3-8). The "fear not" formula (*'al-tire'u* [TH3372, ZH3707]) of 20:3 is a stock phrase also associated with Yahweh's leadership in battle (cf. 1:29; 3:2, 22; 7:18; Num 14:9; Josh 10:8; Isa 43:1). The reason Israel can be at peace is that God himself is the one who goes to war and gains the victory (20:4).

The battle was so much in the hand of Yahweh that human participation, though commanded, was hardly necessary. Thus, all kinds of exemptions from military service were allowed. If one had just built a house and had not begun to live in it, he could be exempted (see note on 20:5). Likewise, those who had not yet been able to reap the first harvest of a plot of land (20:6) or who were newly married (20:7) could be released. The reason in each case was the inherent unfairness of being unable to enjoy the benefits of one's labors and relationships. But even the fearful (despite the "fear nots" of 20:1-4) could remain at home, not so much for their sake as for the sake of other soldiers who might lose heart (see note on 20:8) if one of their companions should do so (20:8). Only after all these provisos had been spelled out and acted upon would the various officers be designated (20:9). Presumably these would have been men who most clearly displayed courage and leadership capacity.

Moses then turned his attention to battle strategy as it pertained to "distant towns" (20:15). These would have been outside the territories of the "seven nations" traditionally identified as Israel's (and Yahweh's) mortal enemies (20:17). First, they must have opportunity to surrender (20:10). The "terms for peace" of NLT (and most translations) in 20:10-11 understates the harsh reality that peace (*shalom* [TH7965, ZH8934]) here means unconditional capitulation to bondage, called *mas* [TH4522, ZH4989] in Hebrew, "task-work" (KBL 540). The best known example is the account of the Gibeonites who, having convinced Joshua they had come from afar, were forced into labor bondage once they surrendered and their ruse was discovered (Josh 9:3-27).

Those who refused such terms would become subject to attack and siege (20:12). Once overcome, they would fall victim to a modified *kherem* [TH2764, ZH3051], an annihilation of at least the men. The word used here for "men" (*zekur* [TH2138A, ZH2344]) is normally best rendered "males," but 20:14 clearly exempts children from the ban without gender distinction. The apparent reason for such harsh measures is that the male leadership of recalcitrant cities exhibits the same traits as the Canaanites, namely, a rebellious, unrepentant spirit in the face of a divinely sanctioned military operation. Women, children, and goods could be spared and, in fact, could become the property of the victorious Israelites (20:14).

As for the nations already designated by Yahweh as Israel's inheritance (*nakhalah* [TH5159, ZH5709]; 20:16; cf. 4:20-21; 15:4; 19:10; 21:23; 24:4; 25:19; 26:1), there was to be with them no negotiations, no proffer of covenant relationship, even vassalage. Instead, they must be placed under the ban—that is, they must, as a function of holy war, be totally annihilated (see note on 20:17), all seven (here six; seen note on 20:17) people groups who loosely qualified as Canaanites.

Besides the reasons commonly adduced to explain such uncompromising and merciless judgment—God's holiness, the Canaanites' total corruption, their obstinate incapacity for repentance, and the like—the text here adds the practical point that by example and precept the inhabitants of the land, if left to do so, would infect the people of Israel with their pernicious teachings and practice (20:18). In effect, Israel would become Canaanite, deserving the same outpouring of divine wrath.

Even the ravages of holy war had its limits, however, and the passage ends with an example of its amelioration. Fruit trees, because they supply needed food in times of siege and, more important, because they are "innocent" toward God and humankind, must be spared (20:19). Other trees could be used to provide materials for various kinds of siege works such as stagings, ladders, and platforms (20:20). They, too, were not "enemies," but neither were they essential to life.

This holy war, then, could take a number of forms up to and including the total destruction or divine appropriation of all living as well as inanimate things. Jericho, Ai, and Hazor were examples of places and people devoted wholly to such ends (cf. Josh 6:21-24; 8:26-28; 11:10-12). More often only persons were eradicated, their dwelling places and properties usually falling to Yahweh and his conquering hosts (cf. Josh 11:13-15).

4. Disposition of unsolved murder (21:1-9)

"When you are in the land the LORD your God is giving you, someone may be found murdered in a field, and you don't know who committed the murder. ²In such a case, your elders and judges must measure the distance from the site of the crime to the nearby towns. ³When the nearest town has been determined, that town's elders must select from the herd a young cow that has never been trained or yoked to a plow. ⁴They must lead it down to a valley that has not been plowed or planted and that has a stream running through it. There in the valley they must break the young cow's neck. ⁵Then the Levitical priests must step forward, for the LORD your God has chosen them to minister before him and to pronounce blessings in the LORD's name. They are to decide all legal and criminal cases.

⁶"The elders of the town must wash their hands over the young cow whose neck was broken. ⁷Then they must say, 'Our hands did not shed this person's blood, nor did we see it happen. ⁸O LORD, forgive your people Israel whom you have redeemed. Do not charge your people with the guilt of murdering an innocent person.' Then they will be absolved of the guilt of this person's blood. ⁹By following these instructions, you will do what is right in the LORD's sight and will cleanse the guilt of murder from your community.

NOTES

21:1 murdered. That this person is a victim of homicide and not someone who has died of natural causes is clear from the use of the substantival adjective *khalal* [TH2491, ZH2728], "pierced one," that is, one who has been violently attacked (NIDOTTE 2.151-152; cf. Num 19:16; 23:24; Jer 51:52; Ezek 26:15; 30:24; 31:17-18).

21:7 hands did not shed. The Kethiv yields the unexpected singular verb *shapekah* [TH8210, ZH9161]. The Qere renders this as a plural (*shapeku*) to bring it in line with the plural subject, and this agrees with some Hebrew mss, Samaritan Pentateuch, Targum, and at least one ms from Qumran. No change to the MT is necessary, however, if the subject "hands" is viewed as a collective meaning the community as a whole (Driver 1902:243).

COMMENTARY

On occasion, homicide would take place with no one taking responsibility and with no witnesses. In such a case, there was still culpability, and someone needed to bear the onus of restoring legal and moral equilibrium. Unless and until the perpetrator could be found and brought to justice, that onus fell on the community nearest to the scene of the crime (21:1-2). That is, the community itself, while not collectively guilty of the crime, must disavow any corporate involvement in it and must undertake the necessary rituals and ceremonies of absolution.

This text is one of the most helpful of all in demonstrating the sense and, indeed, the reality of the principle of Israel's corporate solidarity as Yahweh's covenant nation. The nation consisted of thousands of individuals, to be sure, and each of them was personally accountable to God, but each also was part of a collectivity, a body which, as a whole, related to him and functioned in his interests. The New Testament church must be understood in precisely the same way—a single body consisting of millions of parts over 2,000 years (see Rom 12:3-8; 1 Cor 12:12-31; Eph 4:1-16).

Having determined which settlement was closest to the murdered body, Israel's leaders would turn the matter over to local officials who would set in motion the process of exculpation. First, an unbroken heifer would be selected, its very lack of domestication suggesting innocence or purity (21:3). The notion of non-contamination continues with the requirement that the animal be taken to a "valley" that had never been farmed and through which ran a perennial stream (21:4; *nakhal 'ethan* [TH5158/386, ZH5707/419], "everflowing river," as opposed to a seasonally running wadi; Tigay 1996:192). The uninterrupted flow of water symbolizes unending vitality or purificatory efficacy.

The ritual there consisted of the breaking of the heifer's neck, a bloodless means of securing its death—bloodless perhaps because the place of the ritual was not a duly authorized cult center or because this was not so much a sin or trespass offering as it was a redemption (Zevit 1976:383-384). Sin and trespass offerings required the slaughter of sacrificial animals and the application of their blood on an altar (Lev 4:1–5:19), whereas rituals of redemption—where one animal was substituted for another—permitted the breaking of the neck only (Exod 13:13). Why this was a redemptive and not an expiatory act is not clear, though it may partly be that the animal, being unbroken, was disqualified as a sin or trespass offering. The town itself had not committed sin, so a sin offering would be inappropriate. Yet there was need for the community to acknowledge the deed that had cast such a shadow over it. The cultic nature of the ceremony is underscored by the presence of the priests who were there to oversee the proceedings. They must ensure that proper protocol was followed and that the end result was in line with legal precedent in both its assessment of responsibility and application of justice (21:5).

Resuming his description of the ritual, Moses stated that the elders of the town must literally and metaphorically "wash their hands of the whole affair" over the slain heifer (21:6). The water presumably came from the nearby river which, because it ran constantly, most aptly suggested both purity and permanence. The act of washing was to be accompanied by an oral disavowal of collective or community culpability. Just as their hands had been made clean by the pure water, they said, so were they all clean before God. They had neither committed the murder nor had any of them witnessed it (21:7). Yet there was a plea for forgiveness because the sin of one member of the chosen nation was, in some sense at least, the sin of all members (21:8a).

However, the absence of sin or trespass offerings suggests, as I have already proposed, that the community neither viewed itself nor was viewed by the Lord as actually having shed human blood. Their prayer was not that they be forgiven the sin but that they not be charged falsely with having committed it. Until this was done, the people collectively would bear the opprobrium of having done nothing to declare their innocence publicly and thereby to satisfy those who might have lingering doubts. If they did all this, Moses said, they would be declared free (lit., "the [shed] blood will be covered") of all suspicion and culpability (21:8). In fact, the community was to purge (*teba'er* [TH1197A, ZH1278]; 21:9) the innocent blood from their midst—that is, blame for the death of the homicide victim will no longer stay with the community, no matter who the actual culprit might be.

◆ ## 5. Laws concerning captive wives (21:10-14)

¹⁰"Suppose you go out to war against your enemies and the LORD your God hands them over to you, and you take some of them as captives. ¹¹And suppose you see among the captives a beautiful woman, and you are attracted to her and want to marry her. ¹²If this happens, you may take her to your home, where she must shave her head, cut her nails, ¹³and change the clothes she was wearing when she was captured. She will stay in your home, but let her mourn for her father and mother for a full month. Then you may marry her, and you will be her husband and she will be your wife. ¹⁴But if you marry her and she does not please you, you must let her go free. You may not sell her or treat her as a slave, for you have humiliated her.

NOTES

21:11 *want to marry her.* The MT has literally "you take to yourself as a wife," omitting the pronoun "her" with the verb. The Samaritan Pentateuch, LXX, Syriac, and Targum supply the pronoun.

21:14 *let her go free.* The verb *shillakhtah* [TH7971, ZH8938] (with suffix) commonly refers, somewhat euphemistically, to divorce (NIDOTTE 4.120). It has that meaning here as well, but its use with the following adverbial phrase, "as she pleases" (*lenapshah* [TH5315, ZH5883]; cf. NLT, "free"), implies that the woman is no longer a mere possession but a full wife and therefore also has some say in the proceedings, at least in determining somewhat the conditions and qualifications of the divorce (Mayes 1979:303). This is lacking in ordinary divorce law in the OT (cf. 24:1, 3-4).

COMMENTARY

Moses had already addressed the possibility of taking prisoners of war in campaigns against "distant" nations (20:14). He resumed that topic here but with attention especially to the disposition of female captives. Should they fall victim to Israel through God's provision (21:10) and, because of their beauty or other qualities (*khashaqta bah* [TH2836, ZH3137], "you are attracted to her"; 21:11), seem suitable as wives, such an arrangement must be protected by many qualifications. Nowhere is this kind of marriage encouraged—not here or anywhere else in the Old Testament—and, in fact, marriage with aliens was generally frowned upon if not forbidden (cf. 7:3). The present text, then, cannot be used to justify these kinds of relationships but only to provide regulation as to how various parties are to be treated given their reality.

First, though the passage is silent about polygamy (but see 21:15-17), one may assume that the arrangement in view here is monogamous—that is, the Israelite seeking a wife from among the captives was unmarried. Having chosen her, he must take her to his home where she would go through a period of preparation for the upcoming nuptials. This includes shaving her head, cutting her fingernails, changing her clothing, and mourning for her parents (21:12-13). The reasons for these actions are disputed, but most likely these are ways of symbolizing a radical change in life in which old things are put away in anticipation of new loyalties and relationships. Some suggest that in doing these things, the woman would make herself unattractive and thus the man would be motivated to marry on bases other than physical appearance (Tigay 1996:194).

Moreover, once the marriage is *de facto*, should the groom become disenchanted with his wife (lit., "you find no pleasure in her"), he must release her from the marriage if that is what she wishes (21:14). The verb translated "you must let her go" (*shillakhtah* [TH7971, ZH8938]) is the technical term for divorce, but here it is qualified by the fact that the wife also has certain options (lit., "according to her desire"; cf. NLT, "free"). Her freedom, then, is not so much that she is released from the authority of her husband but that she has the choice to pursue whatever kind of life she wants thereafter (see note on 21:14). In any event, she cannot be disposed of like so much property (lit., "you may not be tyrannical over her"), for she has been humiliated. The verb here (*'anah* [TH6031, ZH6700]) in the piel stem frequently describes rape (KBL 719; cf. Gen 34:2; Judg 19:24; 2 Sam 13:12). Though technically this has not occurred here, the fact that it was a coerced marriage of a captive woman means that the woman was forced into sexual relations and now, by virtue of losing her virginity, has become undesirable (cf. 22:24, 29).

◆   ## 6. Laws concerning children (21:15-21)

15"Suppose a man has two wives, but he loves one and not the other, and both have given him sons. And suppose the firstborn son is the son of the wife he does not love. 16When the man divides his inheritance, he may not give the larger inheritance to his younger son, the son of the wife he loves, as if he were the firstborn son. 17He must recognize the rights of his oldest son, the son of the wife he does not love, by giving him a double portion. He is the first son of his father's virility, and the rights of the firstborn belong to him.

18"Suppose a man has a stubborn and rebellious son who will not obey his father or mother, even though they discipline him. 19In such a case, the father and mother must take the son to the elders as they hold court at the town gate. 20The parents must say to the elders, 'This son of ours is stubborn and rebellious and refuses to obey. He is a glutton and a drunkard.' 21Then all the men of his town must stone him to death. In this way, you will purge this evil from among you, and all Israel will hear about it and be afraid.

NOTES

21:15 *not the other.* Lit., "the other hated" (*senu'ah* [TH8130, ZH8533]). Here, to hate means to reject or to love less (see Gen 29:31, 33; Mal 1:2-3; see also note on 1:27).

21:17 *double portion.* The phrase *pi shenayim* [TH6310/8147, ZH7023/9109] means literally "measure of two," that is, two-thirds: The elder gets two parts and the younger one part. This was true of Isaac's blessing of Jacob (Gen 25:31-34) and Jacob's blessing of Ephraim (Gen 48:8-22; cf. also 2 Kgs 2:9; Zech 13:8).

21:20 *to the elders.* This reading of the MT is altered by the Samaritan Pentateuch and LXX to "to the men," to bring the phrase in line with 21:21. Elders normally carried out such judicial proceedings, however, so the MT is preferred (cf. 19:12; 21:3, 6; 25:7-8).

COMMENTARY

The next example begins with the typical case-law formula, "Suppose a man . . .";
that is, it is neither sanctioning nor condemning a given reality but only attempting
to provide guidelines for its proper regulation. The case here is one concerning a
bigamous relationship involving sons by both wives (21:15). Besides the inherent
and well-attested problems associated with polygamy (see Gen 16:1-6; 29:31–
30:24; 1 Sam 1:1-8), the tension is exacerbated here by the fact that the man's firstborn son, and thus principal heir, has been born to the wife whom he loves less (see
note on 21:15).

In such a situation, when the time comes for the disposition of his estate, he
must abide by custom and ancient tradition and not bestow the inheritance of the
elder son upon the younger despite his feelings toward their respective mothers
(21:16). Instead, he must give the double portion (see note on 21:17) to the elder
son, to whom it rightly belongs both on account of the custom and because he
represents the strength of his father's virility (21:17). The Hebrew (*re'shith 'ono*
[TH7225/202, ZH8040/226]) means, literally, "the beginning of his generative power,"
that is, the first evidence of the man's procreative ability (Fohrer 1968:99). The
fact that the boy is the offspring of the rejected wife is irrelevant to the issue of
inheritance rights.

Moses continued his topic of child rearing and relationships by adducing the
hypothetical case of a disobedient son (*sorer umoreh* [TH5637/4784, ZH6253/5286] "rebellious and disobedient"; probably a hendiadys meaning "incurably rebellious").
Despite every effort to teach him (*yasar* [TH3256, ZH3579]) otherwise, he remained
beyond parental control (21:18). Clearly this was not a matter of preadolescent discipline, for the ensuing measures are much too severe and "legal" for that. The situation in the home had reached the point that the whole community must take a
hand in its resolution. The lad is thus to be presented to the town elders (21:19),
who will be informed by the parents, in a legal setting, that they can no longer control their wayward son (21:20).

The specific allegation is that the youth is "a glutton and a drunkard." The
Hebrew here (*zolel wesobe'* [TH2151A/5433, ZH2361/6010]) suggests almost a cliche for
laziness and a generally undisciplined manner of life (NIDOTTE 3.219; cf. Prov
23:20-21; Matt 11:19). The Wisdom Literature of the Old Testament severely con-
demns this kind of antisocial behavior (cf. Prov 10:4; 12:27; 26:15; Eccl 10:18), as
does the Torah—as our present text makes clear. Once the facts of the case have
been presented and the charges against the youth proved, the wheels of justice
turn to punishment, in this case to public execution. What was a scandal only in
the family had become a cancer in the body of the community, and so the community as a whole must effect the cure, namely, removal of the offending parts by
death (21:21). This astounding course of action underscores the sanctity of the
parent in the theocratic scheme of hierarchical authority and elicits a deterrent
effect: "All Israel will hear about it and be afraid" (21:21; cf. 13:11; 17:13; 19:20).

◆   ## 7. Disposition of a criminal's remains (21:22-23)

²²"If someone has committed a crime worthy of death and is executed and hung on a tree,* ²³the body must not remain hanging from the tree overnight. You must bury the body that same day, for anyone who is hung* is cursed in the sight of God. In this way, you will prevent the defilement of the land the LORD your God is giving you as your special posses-sion.

21:22 Or *impaled on a pole;* similarly in 21:23.   21:23 Greek version reads *for everyone who is hung on a tree.* Compare Gal 3:13.

NOTES

21:22 *a tree.* For the MT's "a tree," the Samaritan Pentateuch, Targum, and some Greek minuscules have "the tree," suggesting, perhaps, a designated tree (or post) where execu-tions were carried out.

COMMENTARY

Having just dealt with the matter of capital punishment (21:18-21), Moses turned, logically enough, to the matter of the treatment of the remains of an executed felon. The hypothetical case here is different from others so far addressed in that the crimi-nal is first put to death (*humath* [TH4191, ZH4637]) and after that is "hanged on a tree" (21:22). That is, the hanging does not produce the death but accomplishes the pur-pose of publicly displaying the corpse of the offender, probably to serve as a deter-rent to others (Craigie 1976:285). The revenge David allowed against certain descendants of Saul who had broken Israel's covenant with the Gibeonites was sim-ilar to this—they were executed and publicly displayed (2 Sam 21:1-9; cf. Josh 9:3, 15-20).

The hanging in 21:22 undoubtedly refers not to suspension by a rope but impalement on a sharp post (*'ets* [TH6086, ZH6770] means pole as well as tree), a prac-tice well attested in ancient Near Eastern texts and illustrations (Grayson 1976:124, 135, 139, 145; Curtis and Reade 1995:61). Moreover, there may have been a single post designated for this purpose, a kind of community "death cham-ber" (see note on 21:22). The text does not say that subjects of execution must be treated in this manner—in fact, the evidence usually points to the absence of such practice—but it says only that should the carcass be hanged, a proper protocol must be adhered to.

That proviso was the removal of the body from the post and its burial before sun-set for, literally, "a hanged (one) is cursed of God" (21:23; cf. Josh 8:29; 10:26-27). The idea seems not to be that the hanging made one the object of God's curse but precisely because he was cursed by God he was hung up in public view (Mayes 1979:305). There were crimes or sins so evil as to invoke God's special wrath. The punishment for these (as in this hypothetical case) was execution and impalement. Support for this understanding is found in the punishment of Saul's kinsmen who were "executed [lit., "hanged"] . . . on the mountain before the LORD" (2 Sam 21:9). To be "hanged before the Lord" is a way of speaking of having been cursed by him. To leave the body of the cursed one on the tree, however, would corrupt the land, so the body must be buried before sundown. The linkage of the dead man to his community is thus most clear.

The theological ramifications of this practice are far-reaching because Jesus, Paul said, "rescued us from the curse pronounced by the law. When he was hung on the cross, he took upon himself the curse for our wrongdoing" (Gal 3:13). The apostle then went on to cite Deuteronomy 21:23 as the legal basis on which the divine curse was applied. The curse of God that should have resulted in our death and impalement was instead inflicted upon the Savior, who, therefore, was "cursed by God."

◆ D. Laws of Purity (22:1–23:18)
   1. Laws concerning preservation of life (22:1-8)

"If you see your neighbor's ox or sheep or goat wandering away, don't ignore your responsibility.* Take it back to its owner. ²If its owner does not live nearby or you don't know who the owner is, take it to your place and keep it until the owner comes looking for it. Then you must return it. ³Do the same if you find your neighbor's donkey, clothing, or anything else your neighbor loses. Don't ignore your responsibility.

⁴"If you see that your neighbor's donkey or ox has collapsed on the road, do not look the other way. Go and help your neighbor get it back on its feet!

⁵"A woman must not put on men's cloth-ing, and a man must not wear women's clothing. Anyone who does this is detestable in the sight of the LORD your God.

⁶"If you happen to find a bird's nest in a tree or on the ground, and there are young ones or eggs in it with the mother sitting in the nest, do not take the mother with the young. ⁷You may take the young, but let the mother go, so that you may prosper and enjoy a long life.

⁸"When you build a new house, you must build a railing around the edge of its flat roof. That way you will not be considered guilty of murder if someone falls from the roof.

22:1 Hebrew *don't hide yourself*; similarly in 22:3.

NOTES
22:1 *ox or sheep.* The Samaritan Pentateuch adds "or any other of his animals," an addition that, while no doubt stating the intent of the regulation, is unnecessary in light of 22:3 and 4.

22:4 *donkey or ox.* Most MT mss lack the sign of the accusative before *shoro* [TH7794, ZH8802] (his ox), but it is supplied in the Samaritan Pentateuch and Targum. The *'eth-* [TH853, ZH906] before *khamor* [TH2543, ZH2789] (donkey) does double duty in the MT, however, thus obviating the need for its repetition (cf. note on 16:6).

COMMENTARY
The juxtaposition of this passage on preserving life with the previous section, which deals with taking life, is most striking and, at the same time, informative as to the literary composition of this part of the book. Yet there are aspects of the passage (especially 22:5) that seem at first glance to be out of place in terms of the material as a whole. These apparent incongruences require some attention.

Lost animals stood a great risk of either being permanently separated from their owners (and thus dead, for all practical purposes) or actually perishing from lack of care. Since they were also indispensable to an owner's livelihood or even his very survival, they must, if found away from home, be returned to their owner (22:1). To fail to do so would, at the least, be theft. Moreover, the finder could not relinquish his responsibility merely by his ignorance of the owner's identity. Instead, he must corral the animal, keep up its care, and then return it once ownership had been established (22:2). The same procedures must be followed no matter what is lost, even inanimate possessions like clothing (22:3). To punctuate the point he was making, Moses exhorted (lit.): "You must not hide yourself"—that is, you must not withdraw from the scene as though you were oblivious to the problem.

Still pursuing the theme of preservation, Moses offered a "for instance" that speaks not of lost animals but incapacitated ones. Should one see another man's animal unable to stand even with its owner's assistance, that observer must not "hide himself" (see 22:3), but instead he should help him raise it up (22:4). The principle here in 22:1-4 is not just common neighborliness but an assertion of community solidarity: What hurts you hurts me; your losses are my losses. To ignore this principle is to put the whole community in jeopardy.

The stipulation prohibiting transvestism, which follows next (22:5), is suitable to its literary context both by the enveloping structure of 22:5-12 (dress, 22:5, 11-12; animals, 22:6-7, 10; house, 22:8; field, 22:9) and by the idea of separation—that of male and female in 22:5 and that of a mother bird and her chick in 22:6-7 (Kaufman 1978–1979:136). Undergirding it all (22:1-8) is the theme of preservation of life, because to practice transvestism is to invite God's severest displeasure (22:5; it is *to'abath* [TH8441, ZH9359], "detestable"; cf. 7:25-26; 12:31; 14:3; 17:1; 18:12). The covenant framework of these stipulations suggests, no doubt, a cross-dressing typical of pagan fertility cults (cf. Mayes 1981:307; cf. also Gaster 1969:316-318), one commonly associated with homosexuality (cf. 23:17-18) or with ritual and curse forms to affect the sexual potency of oneself or one's enemy (Hoffner 1966:333-334).

Preservation of life is clearly the issue in 22:6-7, and life at a comparatively primitive level. Should one find a bird incubating her eggs or chicks, he or she may take these offspring, but the mother must be left alive. This regulation provides a means of balancing between the need for human preservation, namely, the acquisition of food, and the need to guarantee the survival of the avian species. When carried out properly, this ecologically sound measure would enable both humankind and nature to live together in prosperity.

Finally, Moses spoke of the commonsense need to protect oneself and others from harmful or even fatal accidents. Should one build a house, he said, that person should erect a wall around the perimeter of the roof to prevent people from falling off (22:8). Failure to do this leaves the owner liable for any negative consequences that might follow. This again underscores the notion that no Israelite was an island unto himself. What he or she did or did not do had community reverberations. To bless one was to bless all. To hurt one was to hurt the whole body.

◆ 2. Illustrations of principles of purity (22:9-12)

⁹"You must not plant any other crop between the rows of your vineyard. If you do, you are forbidden to use either the grapes from the vineyard or the other crop.

¹⁰"You must not plow with an ox and a donkey harnessed together.

¹¹"You must not wear clothing made of wool and linen woven together.

¹²"You must put four tassels on the hem of the cloak with which you cover yourself—on the front, back, and sides.

NOTES

22:11 *clothing.* The kind of garment or material here is not altogether clear. The Hebrew term *sha'atnez* [TH8162, ZH9122] occurs only here and in Lev 19:19. Suggested meanings are "stuff of large meshes" (KBL 1000) or "mixed stuff" (BDB 1043).

COMMENTARY

The next large block of covenant stipulations (22:9–23:18) pertains to personal (moral) and cultic purity. To illustrate the principle in view, Moses cited a number of random examples from work and fashion. The first prohibits the planting of mixed crops, specifically the sowing of a vineyard with seed of another kind, probably a grain such as wheat or barley. To do so would render both grape and grain inappropriate for human consumption (22:9; *tiqdash* [TH6942, ZH7727], "you will put it into a state of holiness, that is, of inviolability," NIDOTTE 3.884). The point is not that vines and field crops cannot botanically coexist but that their separation should symbolize Israel's own need for separation from moral and cultic impurity. The same is true of yoking together different animal species such as the ox and donkey.

Another apparently harmless pursuit—the wearing of a garment of mixed fabric (see note on 22:11)—also violates the purity principle and must be abjured (22:11). Again, the point is not that such a mixture violates commonly accepted textile tradition but that abstinence from it will be a constant reminder to Israel to be separate from the world of nations so as to bear witness to Yahweh's own purity. Instead of wearing mingled fabrics, the Israelite should adorn his garments with tassels (*gedilim* [TH1434, ZH1544], "twisted threads") to serve as reminders of the need for covenant fidelity (22:12; cf. Num 15:38), a kind of ancient "tying a string around the finger" to diminish one's forgetfulness.

◆ 3. Purity in the marriage relationship (22:13-30)

¹³"Suppose a man marries a woman, but after sleeping with her, he turns against her ¹⁴and publicly accuses her of shameful conduct, saying, 'When I married this woman, I discovered she was not a virgin.' ¹⁵Then the woman's father and mother must bring the proof of her virginity to the elders as they hold court at the town gate. ¹⁶Her father must say to them, 'I gave my daughter to this man to be his wife, and now he has turned against her. ¹⁷He has accused her of shameful conduct, saying, "I discovered that your daughter was not a virgin." But here is the proof of my daughter's virginity.' Then they must spread her bed sheet before the elders. ¹⁸The elders must then take the man and punish him. ¹⁹They must also

fine him 100 pieces of silver,* which he must pay to the woman's father because he publicly accused a virgin of Israel of shameful conduct. The woman will then remain the man's wife, and he may never divorce her.

²⁰"But suppose the man's accusations are true, and he can show that she was not a virgin. ²¹The woman must be taken to the door of her father's home, and there the men of the town must stone her to death, for she has committed a disgraceful crime in Israel by being promiscuous while living in her parents' home. In this way, you will purge this evil from among you.

²²"If a man is discovered committing adultery, both he and the woman must die. In this way, you will purge Israel of such evil.

²³"Suppose a man meets a young woman, a virgin who is engaged to be married, and he has sexual intercourse with her. If this happens within a town, ²⁴you must take both of them to the gates of that town and stone them to death. The woman is guilty because she did not scream for help. The man must die because he violated another man's wife. In this way, you will purge this evil from among you.

²⁵"But if the man meets the engaged woman out in the country, and he rapes her, then only the man must die. ²⁶Do nothing to the young woman; she has committed no crime worthy of death. She is as innocent as a murder victim. ²⁷Since the man raped her out in the country, it must be assumed that she screamed, but there was no one to rescue her.

²⁸"Suppose a man has intercourse with a young woman who is a virgin but is not engaged to be married. If they are discovered, ²⁹he must pay her father fifty pieces of silver.* Then he must marry the young woman because he violated her, and he may never divorce her as long as he lives.

³⁰*"A man must not marry his father's former wife, for this would violate his father.

22:19 Hebrew *100 shekels of silver*, about 2.5 pounds or 1.1 kilograms in weight.   22:29 Hebrew *50 shekels of silver*, about 1.25 pounds or 570 grams in weight.   22:30 Verse 22:30 is numbered 23:1 in Hebrew text.

NOTES

22:17 accused her. The MT lacks the pronoun, an ellipsis rectified by some Cairo mss, LXX, Syriac, and Vulgate by the addition of "against her."

22:21 being promiscuous. For the MT's Qal, "being a harlot," the Samaritan Pentateuch and LXX suggest Hiphil, "bring about harlotry" (or the like), thus making connection with the phrase "her parents' home." The idea is that the girl's action has tainted not only her own reputation but also brought shame to her family.

COMMENTARY

The relative importance of sexuality and, particularly, of sexual purity in Israel is apparent in the extensive attention devoted to it here (22:13-30). Among other reasons for this, of course, is the imagery or symbolism of marriage as a metaphor for the relationship between God and his covenant partner Israel, a theme pervasive throughout the Old Testament (Isa 54:5-6; Jer 3:14, 20; 31:32; Hos 2:16). Also, the sexual perversions of the Canaanites necessitated clear instruction and strong warnings to the Israelite people about to embark on Canaanite conquest.

The first matter has to do with a man who, having taken a bride, subsequently suspects her of not being a virgin at the time of marriage (22:13-21). The allegation forms the protasis of a lengthy sentence (22:13-14), which deals with the following points: (1) the marriage, (2) sexual relations, (3) a change of attitude (*sene'ah*

[TH8130, ZH8533], "he hates her"), (4) an accusation of infidelity, (5) public disclosure of charges against her, and (6) the wording of the allegations. The apodosis (22:15) is the parents' response to the allegation: They present proof of her virginity.

The order of events seems quite clear, but the reason for the man's unexpected hatred of his new bride is not at all transparent. The two main interpretations are (1) that he came to detest her for unspecified reasons and then fabricated the charge of infidelity in order to establish grounds for divorce (Keil and Delitzsch n.d.:410-411), or (2) that he discovered evidence of her infidelity on the wedding night and thus undertook divorce proceedings (Thompson 1974:235-236). There is no justification for the commonly held view that the man "slanders her" (so NIV) because all that the Hebrew *wesam lah 'aliloth debarim* [TH5949/1697, ZH6613/1821] means in 22:14 is "accusation of evil deeds" (KBL 708), which may or may not actually be true. A better rendition might be "recklessly accuses her"—that is, he does so without adequate proof. On the whole, it is more likely that his dislike of his bride leads to the allegations of her infidelity, charges he hopes can be sustained in court.

The response of her parents is more empirical than verbal—they produce the blood-stained cloth (22:17; *simlah* [TH8071, ZH8529], "garment") that must have been kept following initial intercourse on the wedding night. After inspecting it and presumably being convinced of its authenticity, the elders of the village would exonerate the woman of these baseless charges and would instead convict the man of perjury (22:18). His punishment must be a flogging (*yasar* [TH3256, ZH3579]; cf. TDOT 6.130) and a fine of 100 shekels, about 40 ounces of silver. This would be paid to the woman's father. Moreover, the husband, contrary to normal practice, could never initiate divorce proceedings against his wife (22:19). It is likely, however, that she could leave him, because he had publicly humiliated and defamed her (cf. 21:14 and comments).

The husband's accusation could, of course, have substance, based not only on his testimony but on the inability of his wife's parents to produce the evidence of her virginity (22:20; *bethulim* [TH1331, ZH1436], "state of virginity"; TDOT 2.342; KBL 160). This being the case, she must be publicly executed, not at the village gate as usual (cf. 21:19-21), but by the door of her father's house (22:21). This is because she had lost her virginity while under her parents' authority and oversight and also, no doubt, because her parents collaborated with her in producing false evidence, that is, a blood-stained cloth that they themselves had improvised (so Nelson 2002:271). The harshness of the penalty is because the girl has "committed foolishness"—that foolishness being harlotry, a serious offense indeed, for it struck right at the heart of the covenant principles of purity and loyalty (cf. 23:17; Lev 19:29; 21:9).

The second example of impurity in the marriage relationship is the sin of adultery, one singled out explicitly in the Decalogue itself (22:22; cf. 5:18). Should a man be caught in the act of intercourse with a married woman, both persons must die in order to "purge" (*ba'ar* [TH1197/1197A, ZH1277/1278], "burn out"; 22:22) such evil things from Israel. Execution of the pair would not only eliminate them as moral cancers from the theocratic body, but it would serve as a stern and graphic warning to others who might be tempted along those lines. The difference between the behavior of this woman and that of the woman in the previous example (22:21) is that this one, being married, commits adultery (na'ap [TH5003, ZH5537]), whereas the other committed fornication (zanah [TH2181, ZH2388]; 22:21) before she got married (though she was perhaps already betrothed). The guilt and punishment are, however, exactly the same.

The third example (22:23-27) deals with fornication but in a case in which the woman is betrothed. She was a virgin (bethulah [TH1330, ZH1435]; 22:23) until she encountered a man with whom she had sexual relations but under highly nuanced conditions. In one scenario the act took place in an urban area, so, once discovered, both parties must be stoned to death in a community execution (22:24). The rationale is that an innocent victim of sexual coercion would surely have called for help, a call that in the closely packed environs of the cities of ancient Israel could not help being heard. Her guilt is therefore established in the negative. The man involved was patently culpable, and because he had violated another man's fiancée, he had in effect committed adultery and was therefore open to its prescribed penalty (22:24; cf. 22:22).

However, should the act take place in the open countryside, the presumption would be that it was rape and that the woman had cried out but in vain (22:25-27). The text, in fact, says the man "seized her" (hekheziq-bah [TH2388, ZH2616]; 22:25), a clear indication that this was something forced on the young woman. It is possible, of course, that this was a consensual relationship after all and that the woman, caught in the act, could claim rape if she wished to avoid the ordinary penalty for voluntary fornication (22:24). This law does not address that possibility, however, but proceeds on the presumption of her innocence absent any evidence to the contrary.

The fourth case pertains to the rape of a woman who is neither married nor engaged (22:28-29). This time she, in effect, becomes betrothed by virtue of the sexual encounter, and therefore her attacker/fiancée must pay her father 50 shekels (about 20 ounces) of silver, the ordinary rate of the mohar [TH4119, ZH4558] or bride-price (de Vaux 1965:26-27; cf. Gen 34:12; Exod 22:16; 1 Sam 18:25). In addition, because he publicly humiliated her ('innah [TH6031, ZH6700]; cf. 21:14), he can never divorce her. Clearly, a young man in such circumstances had better be sure of his love for the girl before he committed an act that would result in his spending a lifetime with her.

The final example is particularly abhorrent because though the deed is not adulterous, it is at least quasi-incestuous (22:30 [23:1]). The "father's wife" in question is, of course, not the man's own mother, for she would be called that. What is in view here is the marriage (thus, laqakh [TH3947, ZH4374]) of a man to his stepmother, his father having either divorced her or left her a widow. To have such intimacy with a woman who had been intimate with his father would "uncover his father's nakedness" (cf. Lev 18:7, 8; 20:11)—that is, it would permit him to violate his own father's unique prerogatives (Tigay 1996:209; cf. Gen 9:20-24).

◆ ## 4. Purity in worship (23:1-8)

1*"If a man's testicles are crushed or his penis is cut off, he may not be admitted to the assembly of the LORD.

2"If a person is illegitimate by birth, neither he nor his descendants for ten generations may be admitted to the assembly of the LORD.

3"No Ammonite or Moabite or any of their descendants for ten generations may be admitted to the assembly of the LORD. 4These nations did not welcome you with food and water when you came out of Egypt. Instead, they hired Balaam son of Beor from Pethor in distant Aram-naharaim to curse you. 5But the LORD your God refused to listen to Balaam. He turned the intended curse into a blessing because the LORD your God loves you. 6As long as you live, you must never promote the welfare and prosperity of the Ammonites or Moabites.

7"Do not detest the Edomites or the Egyptians, because the Edomites are your relatives and you lived as foreigners among the Egyptians. 8The third generation of Edomites and Egyptians may enter the assembly of the LORD.

23:1 Verses 23:1-25 are numbered 23:2-26 in Hebrew text.

NOTES

23:2 [3] *illegitimate by birth.* The term *mamzer* [TH4464, ZH4927] occurs in only one other place in the OT (Zech 9:6), and there, like here, it refers to some kind of corrupt product issuing from an unnatural mixture. In the larger context of this passage, where incest is very much the issue (22:30; 23:3-7), it is likely that the offspring of incestuous relationships are in view and not illegitimate children in general.

COMMENTARY

The principal issue in this passage is who may or may not enter "the assembly of the LORD" (23:1, 2, 3, 8). Though the term "assembly" (*qahal* [TH6951, ZH7736]; 23:1) can mean the community of Israel as a whole, that is, the nation (cf. 31:30; Num 16:3; 20:4; Josh 8:33-35), or, more narrowly, the levy of free men (von Rad 1966a:146), the meaning here is the community gathered for worship and festival (Craigie 1976:296). This is clear from the use of the verb "enter" (*bo'* [TH935, ZH995]; cf. "be admitted," NLT) to speak of access to the assembly. Clearly, these alienated people were already present in Israel, having (in the case of the Egyptians, 23:8) been part of the nation since the Exodus. They had already "entered." Could they, however, enjoy full access to the covenant presence and blessing of Yahweh?

Persons of reproductive or genetic deficiency are mentioned first because the previous section dealt with these and similar matters (22:13-30). Emasculated men must be precluded from the assembly gathered for community worship (23:1), as must children conceived in incest (see note on 23:2). In the former instance, the disbarment may be because of the man's inability to contribute to the continuation of the community throughout future generations, or, more likely, because physical impairment of this kind symbolized spiritual impairment and disqualification (cf. Lev 21:16-24). As for the "illegitimate," the circumstances of their conception—particularly if they were the product of incest (NIDOTTE 2.971)—were so corrupt and counter to standards of sexual purity that they, too, would symbolize a deeper spiritual perversion. The fact that in both cases, and especially the latter, the persons might be innocent had nothing to do with the fact that they physically represented elements of cultic impurity that would offend a holy God. And this exclusion would be for "ten generations," that is, forever. That this meant permanent exclusion for him and his descendants is clear from 23:3 [4], which reads *'ad-'olam* [TH5704/5769, ZH6330/6409], "until forever" (Tigay 1996:211).

Among descendants of incest were the Ammonites and Moabites, both of whose eponymous ancestors issued from sexual contact between Lot and his daughters (Gen 19:30-38). This did not prohibit persons of those nations from becoming Israelites and even worshipers of Yahweh, a point made poignantly clear in the case of Ruth the Moabite (cf. Ruth 1:16-18; 4:9-12). However, even proselyte status appears not to have opened the doors to full covenant privilege. The following reminder of the past hostility of these peoples (23:4-6) seems not to be part of the reason for their rejection. Rather, the intent is to highlight the baseness of their character, something to be attributed perhaps to the nature of their national origins (for the documentation of these acts and attitudes see Num 22:5-6; 23:5-12, 26; 24:13).

As for Edomites, they were a "brother" people because of their descent from Jacob's brother Esau (Gen 36:9), a descent unmarked by any moral taint, though originating in struggle and strife (cf. Gen 25:24-26). The Egyptians, having provided an incubus for Israel for more than 400 years (Exod 12:40; cf. Gen 15:13-16), must also, with the Edomites, be denied access to the worshiping community of Israel, but for only three generations (23:7-8). Whether to be taken literally or figuratively, "three generations" (as opposed to ten) was a word of grace and hope.

The theological assessment of all this is that God's holiness demands holiness of those who would approach him in fellowship and worship. Israel's understanding of reality was one in which the outer and inner life could not be bifurcated. Outward appearance was indicative of inward disposition. Thus, impurity of origin, deficiency or deformity of body, and similar physical elements symbolized spiritual dysfunction and disqualification. Even in those times and circumstances, however, there must have been a recognition by the spiritually enlightened that God was no respecter of persons. What might prevent access to the corporate worship ceremonies could not impair access to the love and grace of God himself. This is the message of the gospel, the redemptive word known and embraced by believers of both Testaments, no matter their ancestry or outwardly perceived liabilities (cf. Gal 3:23-29; Col 3:11).

◆   ## 5. Purity in personal hygiene (23:9-14)

9"When you go to war against your enemies, be sure to stay away from anything that is impure.

10"Any man who becomes ceremonially defiled because of a nocturnal emission must leave the camp and stay away all day. 11Toward evening he must bathe himself, and at sunset he may return to the camp.

12"You must have a designated area outside the camp where you can go to relieve yourself. 13Each of you must have a

spade as part of your equipment. When- moves around in your camp to protect you
ever you relieve yourself, dig a hole with and to defeat your enemies. He must not
the spade and cover the excrement. ¹⁴The see any shameful thing among you, or he
camp must be holy, for the LORD your God will turn away from you.

NOTES

23:10 [11] *ceremonially defiled because of a nocturnal emission.* The Hebrew reads
literally "impure because of a night happening" (*miqqereh-laylah* [TH7137/3915A, ZH7937/
4326])—that is, accidentally. The NLT is correct in understanding the euphemism as it
does.

23:14 [15] *shameful thing.* The Hebrew *'erwath dabar* [TH6172/1697, ZH6872/1821] (lit.,
"nakedness of a thing") usually (as here) refers to the genitals (cf. Gen 9:22; Lev 18:7-17;
20:11, 17; 1 Sam 20:30) or, by extension, sexual intercourse or any other function of the
genitals (NIDOTTE 3.528). Such intimate aspects of life and behavior are too private for
public view; even Yahweh is "embarrassed" by it.

COMMENTARY

Impurity is not only a concern of cult and worship but, in a theocratic community, a
concern of the whole life. Even in the heat and danger of war, there are certain minimal standards of propriety that must be maintained in these areas. For example,
should a soldier have an accidental emission in the night (see note on 23:10), he
must leave the camp, undergo ritual cleansing, and only afterwards return at sunset
(23:11). "Non-accidental" bodily discharges must be cared for outside the camp in
a designated area which, by virtue of its purpose, would become unclean (23:12,
14). Human waste must not be allowed to lie exposed, so each man would carry an
implement (*yathed* [TH3489, ZH3845], usually rendered "tent-peg") with which to dig a
pit and bury it (23:13 [14]).

The reason for this fastidiousness is that "the LORD your God moves around in
your camp" (23:14). This statement and the rest of the verse ("to protect, to
defeat," etc.) are highly suggestive of so-called holy war (cf. 7:1-6) but not exclusively so, because whenever God's people undertook military operations in his
name and under his direction, he was in their midst (cf. 20:1, 4). No matter the
nature of the war, the theocratic community must subscribe to principles of holiness and purity.

Given this reality, "indecencies" such as bodily emissions must be strictly regulated as to their occurrence and their aftermath. The text describes such matters as a
"shameful thing" (see note on 23:14), not because they are inherently so but
because of their intensely private nature and their association with the genitals, the
symbol of procreative power with all of its mysteries. Contrary to modern times
when public display of private parts and intimate behavior is becoming increasingly permitted and even endorsed, the standards of Yahweh in respect to such
things must be understood and publicly proclaimed if we are to avoid offending the
Holy One himself any more than we have already done, and thus have him "turn
away from" us (23:14).

◆   6. Purity in the treatment of escaped slaves (23:15-16)

¹⁵"If slaves should escape from their   ters. ¹⁶Let them live among you in any
masters and take refuge with you, you   town they choose, and do not oppress
must not hand them over to their mas-   them.

COMMENTARY

The location of the brief stipulation about escaped slaves in this context may be
explained by the previous discussion of military camps, implying the possibility of
runaway slaves from the enemy side, and by the following legislation concerning
the exaction of interest, a practice tantamount to theft (23:19-20). The reason for
providing haven for the escaped slave is that Israel, as an escaped slave people, had
found refuge in Yahweh (cf. 5:6).

To grace they should add even more grace by allowing such refugees to live wherever they chose. Failure to follow this policy—both by returning slaves to their masters and by forbidding them to live where they wish—would be to oppress them.
The slaves' latter condition would then be worse than their former, because they
would receive severe punishment from their masters.

◆   7. Purity in worship practice (23:17-18)

¹⁷"No Israelite, whether man or woman,   the LORD your God any offering from the
may become a temple prostitute. ¹⁸When   earnings of a prostitute, whether a man*
you are bringing an offering to fulfill a   or a woman, for both are detestable to the
vow, you must not bring to the house of   LORD your God.

23:18 Hebrew *a dog.*

NOTES

23:17 [18] *temple prostitute.* Heb., *qedeshah* [ᵀᴴ6945, ᶻᴴ7728] (fem.) and *qadesh* [ᵀᴴ6945,
ᶻᴴ7728] (masc.) refer to persons set apart in pagan temple ritual for the purpose of engaging
in so-called "sacred prostitution" (Ringgren 1973:80-81, 167). The purpose of such practice
was to induce the fertility deities to render the livestock and fields productive. The root
qadash [ᵀᴴ6942, ᶻᴴ7727] suggests here not moral separation but a priestly caste dedicated to
this decidedly immoral superstition (cf. Gen 38:21-22; 1 Kgs 14:24; 15:12; 22:46; 2 Kgs 23:7;
Hos 4:14). The term for a "secular" female prostitute is *zonah* [ᵀᴴ2181B, ᶻᴴ2390] (cf. 22:21),
whereas the male sodomite bears the derogatory label "dog" (*keleb* [ᵀᴴ3611, ᶻᴴ3978]; 23:18).

COMMENTARY

The statute of 23:17-18 consists of two parts: (1) not participating in pagan fertility
rites and (2) not presenting to Yahweh income derived from prostitution. The former
has to do with "sacred" prostitution, the latter with the "secular" or street variety (see
note on 23:17). Both were reprehensible to Yahweh because both violated standards
of purity in both literal and metaphorical ways. Sexual purity in Israel should stand in
stark contrast to the rampant degeneracy of Canaanite life and worship vis-à-vis sexuality. It, therefore, would function polemically as a counter-exhibition of how life

ought to be lived. More importantly, it would speak volumes about Israel's relationship to Yahweh, one that must be characterized above all by holiness.

The prohibition about submitting income from prostitution as a votive offering to Yahweh is most instructive in both its Old Testament and contemporary ramifications. The idea that any offering—no matter its nature or its source—is pleasing to Yahweh is clearly insupportable biblically. God does not need human assets, and though he enjoins their presentation as an act of true worship (cf. 12:5-6, 11; 14:22-29; Lev 27:30-33; Num 18:21-32; Mal 3:10), their kind and the motives behind the giving of them are of overriding importance in determining their efficacy (cf. 2 Sam 24:24).

◆ E. Laws of Interpersonal Relationships (23:19–25:19)
1. Respect for others' property (23:19–24:7)

¹⁹"Do not charge interest on the loans you make to a fellow Israelite, whether you loan money, or food, or anything else. ²⁰You may charge interest to foreigners, but you may not charge interest to Israelites, so that the LORD your God may bless you in everything you do in the land you are about to enter and occupy.

²¹"When you make a vow to the LORD your God, be prompt in fulfilling whatever you promised him. For the LORD your God demands that you promptly fulfill all your vows, or you will be guilty of sin. ²²However, it is not a sin to refrain from making a vow. ²³But once you have voluntarily made a vow, be careful to fulfill your promise to the LORD your God.

²⁴"When you enter your neighbor's vineyard, you may eat your fill of grapes, but you must not carry any away in a basket. ²⁵And when you enter your neighbor's field of grain, you may pluck the heads of grain with your hand, but you must not harvest it with a sickle.

CHAPTER 24
"Suppose a man marries a woman but she does not please him. Having discovered something wrong with her, he writes her a letter of divorce, hands it to her, and sends her away from his house. ²When she leaves his house, she is free to marry another man. ³But if the second husband also turns against her and divorces her, or if he dies, ⁴the first husband may not marry her again, for she has been defiled. That would be detestable to the LORD. You must not bring guilt upon the land the LORD your God is giving you as a special possession.

⁵"A newly married man must not be drafted into the army or be given any other official responsibilities. He must be free to spend one year at home, bringing happiness to the wife he has married.

⁶"It is wrong to take a set of millstones, or even just the upper millstone, as security for a loan, for the owner uses it to make a living.

⁷"If anyone kidnaps a fellow Israelite and treats him as a slave or sells him, the kidnapper must die. In this way, you will purge the evil from among you.

NOTES
23:20 [21] *everything you do.* This translation, which is more in line with the LXX (*pasi tois ergois sou* [TG2041, ZG2240], "in your works") than with the MT (*kol mishlakh yadeka* [TH4916A/3027, ZH5448/3338], "put your hand to"), is broader in scope and probably better contextually than the more limited "put your hand to" of the NIV and other renditions.

24:1 *something wrong with her.* The Hebrew *bah 'erwath dabar* [TH6172/1697, ZH6872/1821] (as in 23:14) suggests something to do with the shameful exposure of the private parts. Here, however, as in a number of other texts (cf. Lev 18:6-18; 20:11, 17, 20-21; Ezek 22:10; 23:29; Hos 2:10), the reference is to illicit sexual behavior such as adultery. This apparently is what Jesus had in mind when he cited this passage as the only basis for divorce, i.e., marital unfaithfulness including adultery (Gr., *porneia* [TG4202, ZG4518] Matt 5:31-32; 19:7-9; Blomberg 1992:110-111).

letter of divorce. The formality of the divorce proceedings, which required an official document (*seper kerithuth* [TH5612/3748, ZH6219/4135], lit., "writing of cutting off"), presupposes also certificates of marriage (de Vaux 1965:33; cf. Mal 2:14). Marriage, though a human institution, must be viewed as a solemn act or relationship reflective of the covenant relationship between God and his people. Divorce, then, must be tightly regulated and permitted under only the most extenuating circumstances.

24:5 *bringing happiness to the wife.* The Syriac represents a Qal (*samakh* [TH8055, ZH8523], "enjoy") instead of the MT's Piel (*simmakh* [TH8055, ZH8523], "bring joy to"). Either is possible, and both were the objective of the statute.

COMMENTARY

This section on respect for others' property introduces a longer one dealing in general with interpersonal relationships (23:19–25:19), the penultimate collection of specific stipulations in Deuteronomy. Others' property includes that belonging to other persons or even to the Lord, and it ranges from extraction of interest from a fellow citizen to proper treatment of a divorced wife.

First of all, it was illegal to demand interest on a loan made to a fellow Israelite (23:19-20). Though this was acceptable in the case of foreigners, the overriding sense of community oneness made it unthinkable to "put the bite on" (thus the literal Hebrew) a member of one's own body. The stipulation here lacks a motive clause, but in Leviticus 25:35-38 the reason for refraining from usury is in the divine assertion, "I am the LORD your God, who brought you out of the land of Egypt to give you the land of Canaan and to be your God." That is, since God's actions toward his people were gracious and generous, so must his elect nation relate and react graciously to one another. If they act in this manner, they can expect his blessing in the land (23:20b).

When it came to making vows to Yahweh, such pledges must be carried out lest the one making the vow incur sin. Such promises, usually rendered to God in gratitude for or in anticipation of some blessing from him, were strictly voluntary (23:22), but once made, must be kept at any cost (23:23). Clearly, one would want to count the cost before making rash commitments—as Jephthah, for example, discovered to his sorrow (Judg 11)—for failure to follow through was the same as robbing God. The making and keeping of Spirit-guided vows could be a means of great spiritual fulfillment (cf. 12:11-12).

True to the principle that Yahweh was the owner of the land and that Israel was only his steward, individuals could freely trespass each other's properties and in doing so could help themselves to whatever produce they could pluck with the hand en route (23:24-25). However, to do so with a harvest basket and sickle would suggest that the trespasser had more in mind than merely snacking along the way. Therefore, anyone taking a shortcut through a neighbor's vineyard or grain field must do so empty-handed. Such legislation taught the virtue of generosity and also the concept of divine ownership of all things, but it also conveyed the idea that one could not sponge on his or her neighbor but must be self-reliant.

In a broad, nontechnical sense a wife "belonged" to her husband in ancient Israel. The very term *ba'al* [TH1167, ZH1251], frequently translated "husband," also means "owner" or "lord" (KBL 137-138). One should not read too much into this terminology, as though the wife was property or chattel. However, there was a "belongingness" that goes beyond modern Western understandings of the marriage relationship. It is proper, therefore, that the law on divorce and remarriage be addressed at this point in the book of Deuteronomy (24:1-4).

The hypothetical case is one in which a man, having found something shameful about his wife, divorces her. Should she remarry and then divorce again or become widowed, she could not remarry her original husband (24:1-4). The grounds for divorce are not made clear, but they must have to do with sexual matters (see note on 24:1; cf. note on 23:14). This, however, is almost incidental to the case at hand, as is the divorce itself. With no judgment as to the propriety or impropriety of divorce, all that is said here is that a divorce document (see note on 24:1) is drawn up and he sends her away (*shillekhah* [TH7971, ZH8938], "divorce her"), but subsequently remarries (24:2). All is in order to this point, but then the woman becomes free again by virtue of her husband's death or a second divorce (24:3). Her first husband, thinking to remarry her, may not do so because such a thing is detestable (*to'ebah* [TH8441, ZH9359], "an abomination") to Yahweh (24:4).

This passage is frequently used to teach the permissibility of divorce or, at least, its regulation. Neither, in fact, is its primary intent, for though divorce is severely condemned in other places (cf. Mal 2:16) but tolerated in still others because of its reality in sinful society (cf. Matt 19:6-9), the issue here is remarriage of persons once married to each other. That is strictly forbidden because the woman's second marriage had made her adulterous (cf. Matt 5:32b) and therefore disqualified her as a marriage partner. The law thus addresses remarriage of divorced persons to each other and not divorce per se (Thompson 1974:243).

In contrast to the unhappy plight of the divorced couple of the previous passage is that of the newlywed man, who, in order to provide his bride with security and joy early in their marriage, must not be forced into military service or any other compulsory occupation (24:5). The "happiness" brought to the wife (see note on 24:5) through the year of her husband's exemption from other duties might have included pregnancy and childbirth, something that would be endangered should he go off to war (20:7).

Loans by one Israelite to another could be secured by the payment of a pledge to guarantee restitution (24:10-13; Exod 22:25-27). However, items necessary to human survival or even well-being—such as millstones or a widow's garment (24:6, 17)—could not be demanded. What one needed to provide food and clothing was off-limits to the creditor. Sadly, this law (along with most others) was largely ignored in Israel's everyday life (cf. Job 24:3, 9; Ezek 18:16; Amos 2:8). Legal demands should be balanced by merciful compassion.

Finally, it is unnecessary to make the case that kidnapping is a violation of "property" rights, for it is the theft of an individual himself (24:7). No matter whether the victim is dealt with despotically (cf. 21:14) by the thief or sold to another, such a reprehensible attitude toward another human being, especially a fellow Israelite, calls for the death penalty. Only in this way can the cancer of sin be cleansed or purged (ba'ar [TH1197/1197A, ZH1277/1278], "burned out") from the body of the community.

2. Respect for human dignity (24:8-25:4)

8"In all cases involving serious skin diseases,* be careful to follow the instructions of the Levitical priests; obey all the commands I have given them. 9Remember what the LORD your God did to Miriam as you were coming from Egypt.

10"If you lend anything to your neighbor, do not enter his house to pick up the item he is giving as security. 11You must wait outside while he goes in and brings it out to you. 12If your neighbor is poor and gives you his cloak as security for a loan, do not keep the cloak overnight. 13Return the cloak to its owner by sunset so he can stay warm through the night and bless you, and the LORD your God will count you as righteous.

14"Never take advantage of poor and destitute laborers, whether they are fellow Israelites or foreigners living in your towns. 15You must pay them their wages each day before sunset because they are poor and are counting on it. If you don't, they might cry out to the LORD against you, and it would be counted against you as sin.

16"Parents must not be put to death for the sins of their children, nor children for the sins of their parents. Those deserving to die must be put to death for their own crimes.

17"True justice must be given to foreigners living among you and to orphans, and you must never accept a widow's garment as security for her debt. 18Always remember that you were slaves in Egypt and that the LORD your God redeemed you from your slavery. That is why I have given you this command.

19"When you are harvesting your crops and forget to bring in a bundle of grain from your field, don't go back to get it. Leave it for the foreigners, orphans, and widows. Then the LORD your God will bless you in all you do. 20When you beat the olives from your olive trees, don't go over the boughs twice. Leave the remaining olives for the foreigners, orphans, and widows. 21When you gather the grapes in your vineyard, don't glean the vines after they are picked. Leave the remaining grapes for the foreigners, orphans, and widows. 22Remember that you were slaves in the land of Egypt. That is why I am giving you this command.

CHAPTER 25

"Suppose two people take a dispute to court, and the judges declare that one is right and the other is wrong. 2If the person in the wrong is sentenced to be flogged, the judge must command him to lie down and be beaten in his presence with the number of lashes appropriate to the crime. 3But never give more than forty lashes; more than forty lashes would publicly humiliate your neighbor.

4"You must not muzzle an ox to keep it from eating as it treads out the grain.

24:8 Traditionally rendered leprosy. The Hebrew word used here can describe various skin diseases.

NOTES

24:8 *the instructions of the Levitical priests.* The Samaritan Pentateuch and LXX add "according to all the Torah," thus linking priestly instruction unmistakably to the Mosaic revelation. This, however, is presupposed without the direct reference.

24:11 *brings it out to you.* The DSS and Samaritan Pentateuch read a Qal for the Hiphil here: "will come out with you."

24:16 *must not be put to death.* The Samaritan Pentateuch, LXX, Syriac, and Targum represent a transposed vocalization resulting in Qal *yamuthu* [TH4191, ZH4637] (they will die) for Hophal *yumethu* (they will be made to die). This shifts the emphasis (unnecessarily) from death by execution to death by undefined manner as a result of sin.

25:2 *lie down and be beaten in his presence.* LXX (B) suggests "you will throw him down in their presence," a reading more in line with the public nature of such punishment, but one unnecessary in light of the overall context of the judiciary. The beating obviously would have taken place in the presence of both the judge and the assembly.

COMMENTARY

Disfiguring diseases of the skin are not only a cause of extreme embarrassment, but in Old Testament Israel were also symbolic of impurity. Therefore, the Torah has much to say about their symptoms, effects, treatments, and cures, the latter being necessary for full reinstatement to the covenant community (Lev 13–14). The NLT translation "skin diseases" for *tsara'ath* [TH6883, ZH7669] (24:8) is preferable to the common rendition, "leprosy," since the description of the ailment, while indicative at times of true leprosy, often suggests other skin diseases as well (NIDOTTE 3.846). The instruction here refers back to the laws of Leviticus 13–14, measures to be taken in times of plague (thus *benega'-hatsara'ath* [TH5061, ZH5596]; lit., "when the skin disease strikes"). The abhorrent nature of such a malady is seen in the case of Miriam, Moses's sister, who when struck by it was quarantined for a week before she could return to camp (24:9; cf. Num 12:9-15). Another example is King Uzziah, who suffered a skin disease as punishment for his arrogance in offering incense and as a result, had to spend his last few years in a sanitarium (2 Chr 26:16-21).

An Israelite's dignity must be protected also in times of financial straits. If he or she had come to the point of needing a loan (cf. 23:19-20), the requisite security (*'abot* [TH5667, ZH6287], occurring only here) could not be forcibly reclaimed by the creditor's entering the debtor's house and thus violating the sanctuary of the home (24:10). Moreover, if the pledge consisted of a garment, "you may not lie down in his pledge" (thus in Hebrew). That is, the protection and comfort of a poor person could not be sacrificed over the matter of a loan security. The creditor might keep the garment (*salmah* [TH8008, ZH8515], "wrapper"; the usual spelling is *simlah* [TH8071, ZH8529], a metathesized form) during the day, but it must be returned by sunset (24:13). Both the poor man and Yahweh will bless this deed and count it as a righteous thing (*tsedaqah* [TH6666, ZH7407])—that is, a work that, though done to another human being, counts as having been done for God (cf. 6:25; Gen 15:6; Ps 106:31; Isa 1:27).

Contrary to common opinion of an earlier period that personal responsibility and personal consequences (as opposed to corporate or community) arose only late in Israel's understanding (Robinson 1935:30), this next statute (24:16) makes clear that, as Ezekiel puts it, "The person who sins is the one who will die" (Ezek 18:20). It is true, of course, that the aftermath of one's sins may negatively impact unborn generations (so 5:9), but not as punishment per se. Likewise, the sins of children, while heartbreaking to parents, cannot be imputed to parents and result in their being punished. Thus, the principle of covenant solidarity that viewed Israel as a corporate unity must be balanced with the view that the individual in that body had personal accountability before God.

The least privileged in Israel—foreigners, orphans, and widows—must have special protection because of their vulnerability (24:17-18). The justice due them could not be "twisted" (thus *natah* [TH5186, ZH5742])—that is, manipulated by bribery or social considerations. For example, though a garment could ordinarily be used as pledge for a loan (cf. 24:13), this could not be taken from a widow. The reason for such special consideration of these weak ones is that Israel itself was once in the shackles of Egyptian bondage. Those most greatly liberated should exercise greatest grace to others in need (cf. Matt 18:21-35; Luke 7:41-47).

To the need for justice for the disenfranchised of Israel, Moses added a word concerning the need for charity (24:19-22). Given the absence of government welfare programs and social agencies, it was incumbent on citizens themselves to provide safety nets for those who, for whatever reason, could not fend for themselves. But this aid came with strings attached: it was not "welfare" but "workfare." Thus, when farmers harvested their grain, olives, and grapes, they must not try to pick up every scrap, but instead they must leave parts unharvested and parts uncollected so the foreigners, orphans, and widows could gather what was left over. The narrative of Ruth and Boaz provides a touching example of this being implemented. Ruth, both a foreigner and a widow, was allowed not only to glean Boaz's fields but to pick up whole sheaves of grain that his reapers "accidentally" left behind (Ruth 2:3-16). The rationale for such a generous policy was, as in the previous provision (24:18), the poverty from which Yahweh had delivered Israel in the Exodus.

The holiness and integrity of the Lord demanded that justice be rigidly and equitably applied (25:1-3). However, even in its application there must be consideration of human dignity. For example, in the disposition of a legal case in which guilt has been determined and punishment assessed, that punishment must not exceed the limitations of the law. In the case of public flogging, the person to be thus treated (*bin hakkoth* [TH1121/5221, ZH1201/5782]; lit., "a son of flogging," that is, one deserving to be flogged) must be forced to lie on the ground in the presence of the court (see note on 25:2) and receive 40 lashes at the very maximum. More than that would hold the criminal up to public ridicule (thus *qalah* [TH7034, ZH7829], "lightly esteem"). Whatever shred of dignity is left after such punishment must be left intact. An extension of this mercy appears in later practice, where 39 lashes were administered as a maximum to ensure that the number 40 would not be exceeded (cf. 2 Cor 11:24; Carson 1984:119).

In order to drive home the point of human dignity, Moses concludes this section by the remarkable assertion that even animals must be humanely treated (25:4). For example, an ox in process of threshing grain (by treading upon it; cf. 2 Kgs 13:7;

Isa 28:28) must not be muzzled but, rather, must be allowed to eat even the precious product of its master's labor. Paul alluded to this in urging the Corinthians to remunerate Christian workers for their labor in the gospel (1 Cor 9:9-10; cf. 1 Tim 5:18). The result of this *a fortiori* argument in both Moses and Paul is that if animals must receive human respect and favor, how much more should one human being respect another!

◆   ### 3. Respect for the significance of others (25:5-16)

⁵"If two brothers are living together on the same property and one of them dies without a son, his widow may not be married to anyone from outside the family. Instead, her husband's brother should marry her and have intercourse with her to fulfill the duties of a brother-in-law. ⁶The first son she bears to him will be considered the son of the dead brother, so that his name will not be forgotten in Israel.

⁷"But if the man refuses to marry his brother's widow, she must go to the town gate and say to the elders assembled there, 'My husband's brother refuses to preserve his brother's name in Israel—he refuses to fulfill the duties of a brother-in-law by marrying me.' ⁸The elders of the town will then summon him and talk with him. If he still refuses and says, 'I don't want to marry her,' ⁹the widow must walk over to him in the presence of the elders,

pull his sandal from his foot, and spit in his face. Then she must declare, 'This is what happens to a man who refuses to provide his brother with children.' ¹⁰Ever afterward in Israel his family will be referred to as 'the family of the man whose sandal was pulled off'!

¹¹"If two Israelite men get into a fight and the wife of one tries to rescue her husband by grabbing the testicles of the other man, ¹²you must cut off her hand. Show her no pity.

¹³"You must use accurate scales when you weigh out merchandise, ¹⁴and you must use full and honest measures. ¹⁵Yes, always use honest weights and measures, so that you may enjoy a long life in the land the LORD your God is giving you. ¹⁶All who cheat with dishonest weights and measures are detestable to the LORD your God.

NOTES

25:11 *testicles.* The MT has *mebushim* [TH4016, ZH4434], "shameful things" (from the root *bosh* [TH954, ZH1017], "be ashamed") as a reference to the genitalia. The Samaritan Pentateuch reads *basar* [TH1320, ZH1414] (flesh) as a euphemism for penis (cf. Lev 15:2-3; Ezek 16:26).

COMMENTARY

One of the greatest social tragedies for a man in ancient Israel was to die without leaving a male heir to bear his name and thus immortalize it. To preclude this possibility, a surviving, unmarried (suggested by *yeshebu . . . yakhdaw* [TH3427/3162B, ZH3782/3481], "living together"; 25:5) brother had the duty of taking the widow as his own wife and naming the first son of this relationship by his deceased brother's name (25:5-10; cf. Gen 38). This practice, known in modern scholarship as the "levirate" custom (after Latin *levir*, "husband's brother"), existed outside Israel and the Old Testament as well (de Vaux 1965:37-38). For the younger brother to do this, then, is to fulfill "brother-in-law" obligation.

This was not absolutely mandated, however, because it was more of a moral than legal responsibility. The younger brother could refuse (25:7), but if he did the widow could have him arraigned and accused before a hearing of the town elders. They would attempt to persuade him to change his mind, but if he remained obstinate, the widow could publicly humiliate him. She did so by (1) pulling off his sandal, (2) spitting in his face, and (3) cursing him by predicting that from that time on his family would be called "the family of the man whose sandal was pulled off" (25:10).

Removal of the sandal symbolized, perhaps, disconnection from the land or estate of the dead brother (Hubbard 1988:251). A possible example in a narrative context is that of Naomi's next of kin, who, having refused to redeem her property from her creditor, removed his own sandal, thus publicly relinquishing any further claim (Ruth 4:7-8). Spitting in the face, as we see in the incident with Miriam's challenge of Moses's leadership (Num 12:14), was a sign of utter disgust and revulsion (cf. Matt 26:67). In the opinion of the community, one so insensitive to a dead brother as to fail to perpetuate his name deserved to be held up to such ignominious scorn. The last part of the proceedings—the oral curse—ironically renames the brother who refused to provide a name in honor of his own sibling.

Clearly related to the foregoing is the case of two men engaged in a fight (25:11-12). The wife of one, trying to protect her husband, impetuously and shamelessly grabs the other man's genitalia (see note on 25:11). Partially because of her immodesty but primarily because of the possibility of rendering her victim impotent, she must suffer the loss of her offending hand (25:12). Both of these cases highlight the great importance of providing for offspring to carry on the family name.

Finally, respect for others should be manifested in business transactions (25:13-16). Weighing scales in the ancient world were not elaborate, calibrated mechanisms, but merely beams resting evenly on crossbars. On one side were weights of various denominations and on the other the goods to be weighed and paid for (Negev 1980:338-340). The law here is that one must not have in his pouch differing weights ('*eben wa'aben* [TH68, ZH74], lit., "stone and stone," 25:13), that is, one when buying (the heavy one) and one when selling (the light one). The same is true with dry and liquid measures ('*epah we'epah* [TH374, ZH406], lit., "ephah and ephah," 25:14). Weights and measures must be full (*shelemah* [TH8003, ZH8969], "whole") and accurate (*tsedeq* [TH6664, ZH7406], "just"; 25:15). Those who used them, and were otherwise scrupulous in their dealings, would prosper in the Land of Promise. Those who failed to do so were an abomination (*to'ebah* [TH8441, ZH9359]; 25:16; cf. 7:25) to the Lord.

◆　　## 4. Revenge on the Amalekites (25:17-19)

¹⁷"Never forget what the Amalekites did to you as you came from Egypt. ¹⁸They attacked you when you were exhausted and weary, and they struck down those who were straggling behind. They had no fear of God. ¹⁹Therefore, when the LORD your God has given you rest from all your enemies in the land he is giving you as a special possession, you must destroy the Amalekites and erase their memory from under heaven. Never forget this!

NOTES

25:18 *God.* The occurrence of *'elohim* [TH430, ZH466] by itself in the MT of Deuteronomy here is quite exceptional, prompting the LXX and Syriac to put *yhwh* [TH3068, ZH3378] in its place or to add *yhwh*, thus creating "Yahweh your God." While this is understandable from the standpoint of a literary formula, the MT reflects the use of the non-covenantal divine name ("God") when employed with a pagan people such as the Amalekites.

COMMENTARY

The Amalekites, descendants of Esau (Gen 36:12) who lived primarily in what is now the Negev and northwestern Saudi Arabia (ABD 169-171), had attacked Israel's rear flanks in the Sinai desert, thereby invoking God's promise of their complete destruction (Exod 17:14; cf. Num 24:20). By attacking his people, Amalek had, in effect, also attacked God (25:18). The original command to Moses is now more particularized: When Canaan has been brought under Israel's control, Amalek must be destroyed—its very existence erased (*makhah* [TH4229, ZH4681], "blotted out"; 25:19) from human memory. Despite the strong admonition never to forget, Israel did forget—until at last God commanded Saul through Samuel to execute the long-delayed vengeance (1 Sam 15:1-3). Sadly, Saul was not perfect in his compliance, a defect that contributed to the cessation of any dynastic royal hopes (1 Sam 13:13).

◆ **F. Laws of Covenant Celebration and Confirmation (26:1-15)**
   1. The offering of the firstfruits (26:1-11)

"When you enter the land the LORD your God is giving you as a special possession and you have conquered it and settled there, ²put some of the first produce from each crop you harvest into a basket and bring it to the designated place of worship—the place the LORD your God chooses for his name to be honored. ³Go to the priest in charge at that time and say to him, 'With this gift I acknowledge to the LORD your God that I have entered the land he swore to our ancestors he would give us.' ⁴The priest will then take the basket from your hand and set it before the altar of the LORD your God.

⁵"You must then say in the presence of the LORD your God, 'My ancestor Jacob was a wandering Aramean who went to live as a foreigner in Egypt. His family arrived few in number, but in Egypt they became a large and mighty nation. ⁶When the Egyptians oppressed and humiliated us by making us their slaves, ⁷we cried out to the LORD, the God of our ancestors. He heard our cries and saw our hardship, toil, and oppression. ⁸So the LORD brought us out of Egypt with a strong hand and powerful arm, with overwhelming terror, and with miraculous signs and wonders. ⁹He brought us to this place and gave us this land flowing with milk and honey! ¹⁰And now, O LORD, I have brought you the first portion of the harvest you have given me from the ground.' Then place the produce before the LORD your God, and bow to the ground in worship before him. ¹¹Afterward you may go and celebrate because of all the good things the LORD your God has given to you and your household. Remember to include the Levites and the foreigners living among you in the celebration.

NOTES

26:3 the LORD your God. Some LXX recensions read "the Lord my God," a rendition more conducive to the context of personal, individual confession. The MT may reflect dittography (the error of copying the same same thing twice) between the Kaph of the second person suffix *ka* [TH3509.2, ZH3870] (your) and the first letter of the following *ki* [TH3588, ZH3954].

26:5 wandering Aramean. The verb *'abad* [TH6, ZH6] attests ambivalence between "perish" and "go astray, wander" (KBL 2). The LXX ms B reads *apebalen* [TG577, ZG610] (lost), "corrected" perhaps by the metathesis of LXX mss A and Ambrosianus (F) to *apelaben* [TG618, ZG655] (received). Other Greek witnesses offer *kateleipen* [TG2641, ZG2901] (leave, abandon). The NLT seems best to represent the seminomadic implications of the passage—formerly wandering but now domesticated.

26:10 the ground. The LXX adds "a land flowing with milk and honey," an unnecessary repetition of the phrase found in 26:9.

COMMENTARY

This last section of covenant stipulations contains what many scholars call a "credo" or summation of Israel's sacred history (26:5b-9; von Rad 1966b:3-8). Enveloping this, it is said, is a ritual associated with the Festival of Firstfruits, a festival eventually observed on Sivan 15 (roughly May/June on our calendar) to celebrate the conclusion of the wheat harvest (Lev 23:15-16). While on the whole it is proper to view 26:1-11 as an instruction for the annual presentation of grain tithes, and even to understand the litany within it as a kind of confession, the tradition-history presuppositions that underlie most contemporary understandings of the pericope detract from its theological significance as an authentic and important element of Deuteronomy in its traditional preconquest, Mosaic setting.

The ritual outlined here requires the Israelite, having settled in Canaan and having begun to domesticate the land, to present to Yahweh an offering of the first products of his harvest (26:1-2). The technical phrase "first produce" (*mere'shith kol-peri ha'adamah,* "the first [or best] of all the produce of the soil") alludes, as already noted, to the variously named Festival of Harvest (*qatsir* [TH7105, ZH7907]), of Firstfruits (*bikkurim* [TH1061, ZH1137]), or of Weeks (*shabu'oth* [TH7620, ZH8651]). This has already received attention in Deuteronomy (cf. 16:9-12) and is fully elaborated elsewhere (Exod 23:16; Lev 23:15-21; Num 28:26-31). The purpose of the presentation is to dramatize the gratitude of the offerer toward God for having brought him and his people into the Land of Promise (26:3).

The priest will accept the basket of grain and place it on the altar as though handing it to the Lord himself (26:4). Then the words of presentation are solemnly intoned, words of thanksgiving and praise that recite Yahweh's mighty redemptive acts on Israel's behalf from the ancient days of Jacob (the "wandering Aramean"; the actual name is lacking in the MT but supplied by the NLT) through the momentous era of Egyptian bondage and divine deliverance, up to the present times of prosperity in the land of Canaan (26:5-9). The offerer then will declare the purpose of his coming—to present a token (lit., "the first of the fruit of the land") to his beneficent God (26:10). Having said that, he will bow in deepest reverence. The whole ceremony concludes with a celebration involving the whole family as well as dependents such as Levites and foreigners (26:11). The celebrating (*samakh* [TH8055, ZH8523], "rejoice") probably centered on a common meal, a way of acknowledging and enacting the covenant relationship implicit in the elements of the festival itself (Thompson 1974:256-257; see 12:7; cf. 12:18; 14:23, 26; 15:20; 27:7; Exod 24:11).

◆   ## 2. Presentation of the third-year tithe (26:12-15)

12"Every third year you must offer a special tithe of your crops. In this year of the special tithe you must give your tithes to the Levites, foreigners, orphans, and widows, so that they will have enough to eat in your towns. 13Then you must declare in the presence of the LORD your God, 'I have taken the sacred gift from my house and have given it to the Levites, foreigners, orphans, and widows, just as you commanded me. I have not violated or forgotten any of your commands. 14I have not eaten any of it while in mourning; I have not handled it while I was ceremonially unclean; and I have not offered any of it to the dead. I have obeyed the LORD my God and have done everything you commanded me. 15Now look down from your holy dwelling place in heaven and bless your people Israel and the land you swore to our ancestors to give us—a land flowing with milk and honey.'

NOTES
26:12 *year of the special tithe.* For the MT's "year of (*shenath* [TH8141, ZH9102]) the tithe," the LXX reads "a second (*deuteron* [TG1208A, ZG1309]) tithe." This provides a smoother rendition but appears to have been based largely on that consideration. Tov (1981:77) suggests that the intent also was to avoid the notion of a third tithe (as opposed to a third-year tithe; cf. 14:28-29).

COMMENTARY
The previous passage (26:1-11) is thematically linked with the present one (26:12-15), which deals not with direct offerings to Yahweh but with largess to fellow Israelites, especially the poor, the weak, and those otherwise susceptible to hardship and exploitation. The thematic link rests on the biblical idea that to give to God's people who are in need is to give to him as well (Matt 10:40-42).

The third-year tithe (a matter already introduced in 14:28-29), as the term suggests, was one given every three years. It appears not to have been a tithe given in addition to the regular ten percent given to Yahweh—a view endorsed by the LXX and Josephus (*Antiquities* 4.4.4; 4.8.22 [4.69-75; 4.240]) (and perhaps implied by NLT's "special tithe")—but one replacing the usual offering. It was special only because of its recipients and not because of its amount or content. The content, in fact, would have been the livestock and produce usually presented (14:22-27; Lev 27:30-33).

As for the recipients, they include the "standard" list of Israel's most dependent—Levites, foreigners, orphans, and widows (26:12; cf. 10:18; 14:29; 16:11, 14; 24:19-21; 27:19; Pss 94:6; 146:9; Isa 1:17). In the absence of evidence to the contrary, one must assume that the tithes in question were those presented at all the times of the year when they were due. Upon their presentation the giver pronounced before God that he had taken what ordinarily would go to him (*haqqodesh* [TH6944, ZH7731], "the sacred thing"), that is, the thing set apart for Yahweh, and given it to the needy (26:13). Moreover, he proclaims his innocence of covenant violation, particularly in areas associated with paganism. This includes eating any of the offerings while in mourning, handling them while ceremonially unclean, or offering anything to the dead (26:14). The mourning in question refers to pagan rituals designed to evoke the sympathy of the gods (Hos 9:1-4; cf. Ezek 8:14). Offerings to the dead may be an allusion to the heathen notion that deities who were trapped in the netherworld could be kept alive by food supplies surreptitiously provided to them (Craigie 1976:323).

Having affirmed his innocence of all these acts and attitudes, the offerer concludes his litany by a prayer of petitionary intercession (26:15). He pleads that God, in response to the obedience and fervent devotion of his people, will be mindful of them and will continue to bless them with the rich produce of the land, the token of which has been presented to him and to those most dependent on him.

◆ VI. Exhortation and Narrative Interlude (26:16-19)

16"Today the LORD your God has commanded you to obey all these decrees and regulations. So be careful to obey them wholeheartedly. 17You have declared today that the LORD is your God. And you have promised to walk in his ways, and to obey his decrees, commands, and regulations, and to do everything he tells you. 18The LORD has declared today that you are his people, his own special treasure, just as he promised, and that you must obey all his commands. 19And if you do, he will set you high above all the other nations he has made. Then you will receive praise, honor, and renown. You will be a nation that is holy to the LORD your God, just as he promised."

COMMENTARY

Upon completing his presentation and exposition of the general (5:1–11:32) and specific (12:1–26:15) stipulations of the covenant renewal text, Moses inserted a word of paraenesis (exhortation) and promise. The setting and format are clearly those of an originally oral address, which now appears as a brief narrative interlude in the book.

Most urgent, Moses said, is the need to obey the covenant laws (*khuqqim* [TH2706, ZH2976]) and regulations (*mishpatim* [TH4941, ZH5477]), beginning that very day (26:16). Since these technical terms refer to the Deuteronomic covenant as a whole, this is a call to commitment to the relationship expressed thereby. The translation "wholeheartedly" reflects the more literal "with all your heart and with all your being"— the very basis for covenant fellowship expressed in the Shema (6:4-5) and elsewhere (cf. 4:29; 10:12).

Though the text is silent on the matter, Moses must have extended to the assembly the terms of the covenant, terms which he notes they have sworn to uphold (26:17; Tigay 1996:245). Their acceptance of its provisions and requirements would lead to more than mere intellectual assent; it would require also that they "walk in his ways"—that is, that they live lives commensurate with their profession. They had declared Yahweh to be their God (26:17), and he, in an incomprehensible act of grace, reciprocated by promising to embrace them as his people, his "special treasure" (*segullah* [TH5459, ZH6035]; 26:18; cf. 7:6; Exod 19:5). In light of that gracious overture, and by obedient response to it, Israel could expect to be elevated above all other nations, a nation "holy to Yahweh your God."

◆ VII. The Curses and Blessings (27:1–29:1)
    A. The Gathering at Shechem (27:1-13)

Then Moses and the leaders of Israel gave this charge to the people: "Obey all these commands that I am giving you today. ²When you cross the Jordan River and enter the land the LORD your God is giving you, set up some large stones and coat them with plaster. ³Write this whole body of instruction on them when you cross the river to enter the land the LORD your God is giving you—a land flowing with milk and honey, just as the LORD, the God of your ancestors, promised you. ⁴When you cross the Jordan, set up these stones at Mount Ebal and coat them with plaster, as I am commanding you today.

⁵"Then build an altar there to the LORD your God, using natural, uncut stones. You must not shape the stones with an iron tool. ⁶Build the altar of uncut stones, and use it to offer burnt offerings to the LORD your God. ⁷Also sacrifice peace offerings on it, and celebrate by feasting there before the LORD your God. ⁸You must clearly write all these instructions on the stones coated with plaster."

⁹Then Moses and the Levitical priests addressed all Israel as follows: "O Israel, be quiet and listen! Today you have become the people of the LORD your God. ¹⁰So you must obey the LORD your God by keeping all these commands and decrees that I am giving you today."

¹¹That same day Moses also gave this charge to the people: ¹²"When you cross the Jordan River, the tribes of Simeon, Levi, Judah, Issachar, Joseph, and Benjamin must stand on Mount Gerizim to proclaim a blessing over the people. ¹³And the tribes of Reuben, Gad, Asher, Zebulun, Dan, and Naphtali must stand on Mount Ebal to proclaim a curse.

NOTES

27:4 *Mount Ebal.* The Samaritan Pentateuch reads "Mount Gerizim," a clearly ideological emendation intended to justify the location of the postexilic Samaritan temple on Gerizim rather than Ebal. This is what the Samaritan woman had in mind when she pointed to Gerizim and said to Jesus that her ancestors had worshiped "on this mountain" (John 4:20, NLT mg).

27:7 *sacrifice peace offerings.* Various LXX recensions add "to Yahweh" or "to Yahweh your God," additions that, while in line with common formulae, are clearly implicit in the MT's abbreviated form.

COMMENTARY

As a visual symbol and reminder of the terms of the covenant and their pledge to obey it, Israel was to erect a stela in Canaan near Mount Ebal (see note on 27:4), one on which the fundamental precepts of the Deuteronomic text could be inscribed.

Though the precise name Shechem is not explicit, the location of the stela between the twin mountains Ebal and Gerizim (27:12-13) clearly marks Shechem as the place of assembly where the tribes would pledge their fealty to the covenant. Given that Yahweh first appeared to Abram at Shechem, that the patriarch built an altar there (Gen 12:6-7), and that Jacob purchased property and dug a well at Shechem (Gen 33:19-20; John 4:5), the place was logically and theologically appropriate for a ceremony of covenant renewal. Joshua also led Israel in a covenant-renewal ceremony at Shechem in addition to the one specifically commanded here (Josh 24:1, 25; cf. Josh 8:30-35).

The monument itself must consist of large stones laminated with plaster (27:2). This suggests that the text was not engraved but written with a stylus while the plaster was soft or with a pen after it had hardened. Inasmuch as there is no hint as to the size of the stela, one can draw no conclusions as to how much text was to be written. At the minimum, it seems, it would have included Deuteronomy 12–26 (Tigay 1996:248). As long as the pillar stood and its text was legible, the generations of Israel would be reminded of their privileges and responsibilities as the conveyors of God's redemptive design. Alongside the stela, the Israelites must build an altar, one unlike pagan models in that it was to be built of unhewn field stones (27:5-6; cf. Exod 20:22-26). There they must offer sacrifices appropriate to covenant ceremonial ritual and partake of a common meal, another feature characteristic of such occasions (see Exod 24:1-11). The importance of adhering to these instructions may be seen in the highly repetitive nature of the account (27:2, 3, 4, 8) and in Joshua's subsequent care to fulfill them to the letter (Josh 8:30-35).

Joined now by the priests (lit., "the priests, the Levites," i.e., members of the tribe of Levi), Moses proclaimed the remarkable declaration that "today you have become the people of the LORD your God" (27:9). This does not mean that Israel had not previously been Yahweh's people but merely that the act of covenant renewal reaffirmed for the present generation that they, too, then and there, were his own special community (Craigie 1976:329). It is healthy for all believers periodically to review the basis of their status and to reenter, as it were, the experience of being God's elect ones. But such reflection must also call forth fresh obedience because being the people of Yahweh demands a radical commitment to live accordingly (27:10).

Returning to the anticipated conclave at Shechem, Moses commanded that the people, at that future time, should divide into two groups of six tribes each, each group to stand on the slopes of Mount Ebal and Mount Gerizim respectively (27:11-13). As in a natural amphitheater, the two sides would face each other and then participate in an antiphonal chorus of covenant oaths. The rationale for tribal distribution is not at all clear. One should note, however, that Ephraim and Manasseh are not mentioned. The reason is that Levi, the priestly tribe, is included and therefore to avoid having thirteen tribes, Joseph, the "father" of Ephraim and Manasseh, makes up the twelfth. The inclusion of Levi shows the need for them to pledge covenant loyalty despite their "favored," priestly status.

◆   ## B. The Curses That Follow Disobedience (27:14-26)

14"Then the Levites will shout to all the people of Israel:

15'Cursed is anyone who carves or casts an idol and secretly sets it up. These idols, the work of craftsmen, are detestable to the LORD.'
And all the people will reply, 'Amen.'

16'Cursed is anyone who dishonors father or mother.'
And all the people will reply, 'Amen.'

17'Cursed is anyone who steals property from a neighbor by moving a boundary marker.'
And all the people will reply, 'Amen.'

18'Cursed is anyone who leads a blind person astray on the road.'
And all the people will reply, 'Amen.'

19'Cursed is anyone who denies justice to foreigners, orphans, or widows.'
And all the people will reply, 'Amen.'

20'Cursed is anyone who has sexual intercourse with one of his father's wives, for he has violated his father.'
And all the people will reply, 'Amen.'

21'Cursed is anyone who has sexual intercourse with an animal.'
And all the people will reply, 'Amen.'

22'Cursed is anyone who has sexual intercourse with his sister, whether she is the daughter of his father or his mother.'
And all the people will reply, 'Amen.'

23'Cursed is anyone who has sexual intercourse with his mother-in-law.'
And all the people will reply, 'Amen.'

24'Cursed is anyone who attacks a neighbor in secret.'
And all the people will reply, 'Amen.'

25'Cursed is anyone who accepts payment to kill an innocent person.'
And all the people will reply, 'Amen.'

26'Cursed is anyone who does not affirm and obey the terms of these instructions.'
And all the people will reply, 'Amen.'

NOTES

27:16 *dishonors.* For the MT's *maqleh* (Hiphil participle of *qalah* [TH7034, ZH7829]), other mss (with Exod 21:17, a parallel text) read *meqallel* (Piel participle of *qalal* [TH7043, ZH7837]). Both verbs denote viewing or treating someone lightly, thus undervaluing him or her. It is the opposite of honoring, as in the fifth commandment (5:16).

27:22 *sexual intercourse with his sister, whether she is the daughter of his father or his mother.* The NLT translates the MT here. The LXX has "sexual intercourse with the sister of his father or mother," thus toning the case down somewhat by distancing it from such blatant incest as that between brother and sister. The very difficulty of the MT makes it more likely to be original; moreover, these are not full siblings but half- or foster children.

COMMENTARY

Because there are twelve prohibitions and curses in this passage (27:14-26), it is sometimes described as a "dodecalogue" (von Rad 1966a:164). This may be a convenient way of remembering how many there are, but there is no plausible linkage between this list and the "Decalogue," that is, the Ten Commandments, even if 27:15 and 26 are not counted as part of the list. Rather, it seems that there are twelve prohibitions because of the number of tribes (Keil and Delitzsch n.d.:434). Perhaps as each was read a solitary tribe would respond to it in turn.

More important is the fact that all suzerain-vassal treaties (including this one) contained a curse section detailing the consequences of violating the covenant terms (see Introduction, "Literary Style"). The list here is by no means exhaustive of all the covenant stipulations (see chs 5–26), but it is representative of attitudes and practices that Israel must avoid if God's judgment is not to fall. A faint structural pattern may be seen in the fact that curses 1–3 deal with God, persons, and property (as in the Decalogue); curses 4 and 5 match 10 and 11; curses 6–9 have to do with sexual improprieties; and curses 6 and 9 match 7 and 8.

The first curse is directed against anyone who engages in the manufacture and worship of images, a sin described as "detestable" (27:15; to'ebah [TH8441, ZH9359]; cf. 5:8-10). The second addresses disrespect for parents, "making light" of them, a capital offense (cf. Exod 21:17). The third covers theft, with unlawful appropriation of property being the example (27:17; cf. 19:14). Next is the curse for leading the blind astray, a classic case of maltreatment of the disabled (27:18; cf. Lev 19:14). Fifth, those who take advantage of the weak and powerless are subject to divine displeasure (27:19; cf. 24:17-18).

The sexual taboos range from intercourse with one's stepmother (27:20; cf. 22:30), bestiality (27:21; cf. Exod 22:19; Lev 18:23; 20:15), and sibling incest (27:22; see note on 27:22 and cf. Lev 18:6-18), to sexual relations with one's mother-in-law (27:23; cf. Lev 20:14). Such apparently inordinate attention to sexual matters (four out of twelve curses) stems from the perverse practices of the Canaanite fertility cults to which Israel would be so easily attracted (Kalland 1992:164). Moreover, since the covenant relationship between Yahweh and Israel is sometimes viewed under the metaphor of marriage (cf. Isa 54:6; Ezek 16:32; Hos 2:2), the physical purity of the people must be safeguarded as a witness to its spiritual purity.

The tenth curse deals with premeditated murder (27:24; cf. 19:11-13); the eleventh pertains to bribery, especially in aiding and abetting homicide (27:25; cf. 16:19; Exod 23:8); and the last—in a broad and summarizing fashion—promises a curse upon those who violate these and all other conditions of the covenant (27:26). To each of these, the tribes in concert must pledge solemn commitment. By shouting "Amen!" they were, in effect, freeing God to pour out upon them the judgment attendant to covenant disobedience.

◆   ## C. The Blessings That Follow Obedience (28:1-14)

"If you fully obey the LORD your God and carefully keep all his commands that I am giving you today, the LORD your God will set you high above all the nations of the world. ²You will experience all these blessings if you obey the LORD your God:

³Your towns and your fields
  will be blessed.

⁴Your children and your crops
  will be blessed.
The offspring of your herds and flocks
  will be blessed.
⁵Your fruit baskets and breadboards
  will be blessed.
⁶Wherever you go and whatever you do,
  you will be blessed.

⁷"The LORD will conquer your enemies when they attack you. They will attack you from one direction, but they will scatter from you in seven!

⁸"The LORD will guarantee a blessing on everything you do and will fill your storehouses with grain. The LORD your God will bless you in the land he is giving you.

⁹"If you obey the commands of the LORD your God and walk in his ways, the LORD will establish you as his holy people as he swore he would do. ¹⁰Then all the nations of the world will see that you are a people claimed by the LORD, and they will stand in awe of you.

¹¹"The LORD will give you prosperity in the land he swore to your ancestors to give you, blessing you with many children, numerous livestock, and abundant crops. ¹²The LORD will send rain at the proper time from his rich treasury in the heavens and will bless all the work you do. You will lend to many nations, but you will never need to borrow from them. ¹³If you listen to these commands of the LORD your God that I am giving you today, and if you carefully obey them, the LORD will make you the head and not the tail, and you will always be on top and never at the bottom. ¹⁴You must not turn away from any of the commands I am giving you today, nor follow after other gods and worship them.

NOTES

28:4 *crops.* The MT reads after this "and the offspring of your livestock," a phrase lacking in the NLT and also in the LXX. Cf. 28:18, where it is missing in the MT as well. The difficulty of the reading favors its retention in this verse.

28:9 *he swore he would do.* The MT has "swore to you," but since the promise was actually given first to the patriarchs, the LXX seeks to achieve greater precision by reading "to your ancestors."

COMMENTARY

Whereas the section on curses (27:15-26) reveals some loose structural and conceptual affinities with the Decalogue, this present one on blessings (28:1-14) seems not to do so; in fact, it is difficult to detect any clear pattern. The most that can be said in this respect is that the bulk of the blessings have to do with prosperity (particularly agricultural: 28:4, 5, 8, 11, 12) and with Israel's exaltation among the nations (28:7, 9, 10, 13). By way of further contrast, the curses are not defined (that is, the outcome is not stated), but the blessings are highly specific (that is, the outcome is stated). On the other hand, the curses of 28:15-68 are carefully spelled out, and, as we shall see, they are frequently matched antithetically with the blessings of this passage.

The conditions for blessing, as always, are based on covenant loyalty (28:1a). The results would be elevation among the nations (28:1b) and the blessings of life in the land itself (28:2). The first is very general, probably introductory to the whole—blessing in town and country, that is, everywhere in the land (28:3). The second and third promise abundant children, livestock, and agricultural produce (28:4-5). The fourth, like the first, is general. The "coming and going" is a merism, a figure of speech describing all of life's activities by citing two ends of a spectrum (cf. 6:7).

More specifically (and in line with 28:1b), Yahweh will deliver Israel in battle (28:7) and by doing so will make known to the nations that he is Israel's God (28:10). Furthermore, Israel will be so prosperous that she will become a lender and not a borrower in relation to other nations (28:12b), the "head" and not the "tail"

(28:13). This metaphor (cf. 28:44) means that Israel will be at the forefront in a position of leadership and not a lowly rearguard.

Domestic blessings (see 28:3) will consist of riches of family and farm (28:4-6, 11) made possible by the outpouring of life-giving rains at the most beneficial times (28:12a). So abundant will the harvests be that the granaries will overflow with them (28:8). All this will happen as a result of wholehearted commitment to Yahweh and his gracious covenant guidelines, a point that both introduces (28:1a) and concludes (28:14) the unit. This thread ties together the whole skein of the Deuteronomic message (cf. 5:32-33).

◆ D. The Curses That Follow Disobedience of General Stipulations (28:15-68)

1. Curses as reversal of blessings (28:15-19)

¹⁵"But if you refuse to listen to the LORD your God and do not obey all the commands and decrees I am giving you today, all these curses will come and overwhelm you:

¹⁶Your towns and your fields will be cursed.

¹⁷Your fruit baskets and breadboards will be cursed.

¹⁸Your children and your crops will be cursed.

The offspring of your herds and flocks will be cursed.

¹⁹Wherever you go and whatever you do, you will be cursed.

COMMENTARY

The converse of obedience is disobedience, and just as obedience brings blessings, so disobedience invites judgment, or, in covenant terms, curses. The curses of the so-called "dodecalogue" (27:15-26) correspond, as we have seen, to the great principles of the Decalogue—that is, they point out Yahweh's severe displeasure at the breaking of these commandments. These curses, on the other hand, respond tit for tat to the blessings of 28:3-13, particularly in the matching of 28:3-6 with 28:16-19. The first and fourth blessings find their counterpart in the first and fourth curses. Perhaps for variety's sake, the second and third curses (28:17-18) are in reverse order to the second and third blessings (28:4-5).

◆ 2. Curses of disease and drought (28:20-24)

²⁰"The LORD himself will send on you curses, confusion, and frustration in everything you do, until at last you are completely destroyed for doing evil and abandoning me. ²¹The LORD will afflict you with diseases until none of you are left in the land you are about to enter and occupy. ²²The LORD will strike you with wasting diseases, fever, and inflammation, with scorching heat and drought, and with blight and mildew. These disasters will pursue you until you die. ²³The skies above will be as unyielding as bronze, and the earth beneath will be as hard as iron. ²⁴The LORD will change the rain that falls on your land into powder, and dust will pour down from the sky until you are destroyed.

NOTES

28:20 *abandoning me.* The pronoun "me" in this context appears to refer to Moses. The LXX mss therefore read either "the Lord" or "him" (i.e., Yahweh). While this brings grammatical uniformity to the passage, the more problematic MT is probably the original reading.

28:23 *The skies.* The MT has "Your skies," whereas the LXX reads, "The sky will be to you," and Syriac, "The skies." There is no need to correct what is a clearly understood figure in the MT.

COMMENTARY

The curses listed in rapid-fire fashion in 28:16-19 are now elaborated and greatly expanded, though not necessarily in order. The "empty baskets" of 28:17 speak of famine, a situation much in the forefront here, especially in 28:23-24. The rains will not drop water but sand and dust. The stinginess of the sky will be matched by the hardness of the earth. But added to this calamity of meteorological disaster will be plague (*deber* [TH1698, ZH1822]; 28:21), consumption (*shakhepeth* [TH7829, ZH8831]; 28:22), fever (*qaddakhath* [TH6920, ZH7707]), and inflammation (*dalleqeth* [TH1816, ZH1945])—diseases that will relentlessly lead to death.

◆ ## 3. Curses of defeat and deportation (28:25-37)

25"The LORD will cause you to be defeated by your enemies. You will attack your enemies from one direction, but you will scatter from them in seven! You will be an object of horror to all the kingdoms of the earth. 26Your corpses will be food for all the scavenging birds and wild animals, and no one will be there to chase them away.

27"The LORD will afflict you with the boils of Egypt and with tumors, scurvy, and the itch, from which you cannot be cured. 28The LORD will strike you with madness, blindness, and panic. 29You will grope around in broad daylight like a blind person groping in the darkness, but you will not find your way. You will be oppressed and robbed continually, and no one will come to save you.

30"You will be engaged to a woman, but another man will sleep with her. You will build a house, but someone else will live in it. You will plant a vineyard, but you will never enjoy its fruit. 31Your ox will be butchered before your eyes, but you will not eat a single bite of the meat. Your donkey will be taken from you, never to be returned. Your sheep and goats will be given to your enemies, and no one will be there to help you. 32You will watch as your sons and daughters are taken away as slaves. Your heart will break for them, but you won't be able to help them. 33A foreign nation you have never heard about will eat the crops you worked so hard to grow. You will suffer under constant oppression and harsh treatment. 34You will go mad because of all the tragedy you see around you. 35The LORD will cover your knees and legs with incurable boils. In fact, you will be covered from head to foot.

36"The LORD will exile you and your king to a nation unknown to you and your ancestors. There in exile you will worship gods of wood and stone! 37You will become an object of horror, ridicule, and mockery among all the nations to which the LORD sends you.

NOTES

28:27 *tumors.* Instead of the MT's Kethiv (*uba'apalim* [TH6076, ZH6754], "and with boils, tumors"), the MT Qere, along with the Syriac and Targum, reads *ubattekhorim* [TH2914, ZH3224], "and with hemorrhoids," a more precise identification of the tumor.

28:30 *sleep with.* The MT Kethiv reads *shagal* [TH7693, ZH8711], "rape," a term altered in the Qere to *shakab* [TH7901, ZH8886], "lie with," an obvious but unnecessary euphemism. In fact, the context supports a violent act and not one of consensual sex. The euphemism is also attested in the Samaritan Pentateuch, Targum, and Vulgate.

COMMENTARY

The theme of judgment by enemies (28:25-26), the antithesis to the blessing of victory over enemies (28:7), is one picked up later in this passage with greater specificity (28:36-37, 49-57). Here the threat is of destruction so severe that Israel will thereafter epitomize such judgment for the rest of the world. As for the promise of general well-being (28:3), disobedience will bring oppression, all without remedy (28:27-29). Hope for a happy family life (28:4, 11) will be dashed when Israel's apostasy produces rape, loss of property, slavery, and manifold tragedies of all kinds (28:30-35). Most humiliating and unthinkable of all, unrepentant covenant disloyalty will result in exile to a distant land where Israel herself will become a pagan people and, at the same time, a paradigm of what happens when a people forget their God (28:36-37).

The precision of this threat and its fulfillment centuries later in the Assyrian (722 BC) and Babylonian (586 BC) exiles is evidence used by those who advocate a late, even postexilic, date for Deuteronomy's final redaction (Cross 1973:287). Such a position is necessary only to those who cannot or will not countenance predictive prophecy of this kind. The question, then, is theological and not historical or even critical.

◆   ## 4. Curse of reversed status (28:38-48)

38"You will plant much but harvest little, for locusts will eat your crops. 39You will plant vineyards and care for them, but you will not drink the wine or eat the grapes, for worms will destroy the vines. 40You will grow olive trees throughout your land, but you will never use the olive oil, for the fruit will drop before it ripens. 41You will have sons and daughters, but you will lose them, for they will be led away into captivity. 42Swarms of insects will destroy your trees and crops.

43"The foreigners living among you will become stronger and stronger, while you become weaker and weaker. 44They will lend money to you, but you will not lend to them. They will be the head, and you will be the tail!

45"If you refuse to listen to the LORD your God and to obey the commands and decrees he has given you, all these curses will pursue and overtake you until you are destroyed. 46These horrors will serve as a sign and warning among you and your descendants forever. 47If you do not serve the LORD your God with joy and enthusiasm for the abundant benefits you have received, 48you will serve your enemies whom the LORD will send against you. You will be left hungry, thirsty, naked, and lacking in everything. The LORD will put an iron yoke on your neck, oppressing you harshly until he has destroyed you.

NOTES

28:39 *eat*. Instead of the MT's *'agar* [TH103, ZH112] (to gather in), the LXX reads "take delight in it" (cf. 14:26). The NLT's translation of the MT, while not literal, conveys the general sense in the context, providing a good parallel with the verb "drink."

COMMENTARY

The stark pairing and polarity of the blessings and curses already noted (28:3-6, 16-19), while not so striking in 28:38-48, provides the structure here as well. Here, however, the judgment takes the form of a reversal of (potential) blessing. Thus, crops will be grown but insects and disease will devour them (28:38-40, 42; cf. 28:4b-5). Parents will have children only to see them cruelly taken off as prisoners of war (28:41; cf. 28:4a). Foreigners living among them will soon overpower them, and Israel will become no longer lenders, but borrowers, no longer the head, but the tail (28:43-44; cf. 28:12b-13).

These dire consequences and more would inevitably befall the nation if it should persist in violation of the covenant (28:45). They would be "signs and wonders" (*le'oth ulemopeth* [TH226/4159, ZH253/4603]) forever linked to Israel, advertisements of the horrendous price to be paid for disobeying the sovereign Lord (28:46). Having abandoned him and rejected his dominion, Israel would become a slave to other masters, human ones that would reduce her to utmost poverty and shame and, at last, to utter annihilation (28:47-48).

◆ ## 5. Curse of an enemy siege (28:49-57)

⁴⁹"The LORD will bring a distant nation against you from the end of the earth, and it will swoop down on you like a vulture. It is a nation whose language you do not understand, ⁵⁰a fierce and heartless nation that shows no respect for the old and no pity for the young. ⁵¹Its armies will devour your livestock and crops, and you will be destroyed. They will leave you no grain, new wine, olive oil, calves, or lambs, and you will starve to death. ⁵²They will attack your cities until all the fortified walls in your land—the walls you trusted to protect you—are knocked down. They will attack all the towns in the land the LORD your God has given you.

⁵³"The siege and terrible distress of the enemy's attack will be so severe that you will eat the flesh of your own sons and daughters, whom the LORD your God has given you. ⁵⁴The most tenderhearted man among you will have no compassion for his own brother, his beloved wife, and his surviving children. ⁵⁵He will refuse to share with them the flesh he is devouring—the flesh of one of his own children—because he has nothing else to eat during the siege and terrible distress that your enemy will inflict on all your towns. ⁵⁶The most tender and delicate woman among you—so delicate she would not so much as touch the ground with her foot—will be selfish toward the husband she loves and toward her own son or daughter. ⁵⁷She will hide from them the afterbirth and the new baby she has borne, so that she herself can secretly eat them. She will have nothing else to eat during the siege and terrible distress that your enemy will inflict on all your towns.

NOTES

28:57 *all your towns.* The LXX precedes "your towns" with "all" (*pasais* [TG3956, ZG4246]), the regular formula (cf. 28:55) and the one used in the NLT.

COMMENTARY

The curse of foreign conquest alluded to briefly in previous passages (28:25-26, 30-37, 41, 48) is continued in 28:49-57, but with special emphasis on the horrible effects of a long-term siege of Israel's towns by the armies of distant enemies. In the future these curses would find fulfillment in the Assyrians and Babylonians, who from Israel's perspective came from "the end of the earth" and spoke an unintelligible language (28:49). Moses had already alluded to these (28:36) in terms so specific that modern critics, as I have noted, deny the passage (and, indeed, all of Deuteronomy) to Moses and view the "prediction" as a *vaticinium ex eventu* (a prophecy crafted after the event). Such a move, however, can be justified only on presuppositionary and epistemological bases that preclude prediction as a possibility or at least as a biblical modus operandi.

The Assyrians, who destroyed Samaria in 722 BC and exiled much of the population of Israel (cf. 2 Kgs 17:3-23), are well-known for their barbaric treatment of conquered peoples. The description here of a fierce, pitiless, and destructive foe (28:50-51) is true to the character of the Assyrians, as even they themselves document it in their own inscriptions (von Soden 1994:86). The record is replete with texts and reliefs portraying Assyrian sieges of enemy cities, campaigns that usually resulted in the penetration of their defenses and the slaughter of their citizens (28:52; ANET 275-301).

One can hardly imagine the terror of such a circumstance—even in light of this passage, which surely must be one of the most graphic and disturbing in all literature. The siege would be so unrelenting that the Israelites would resort to cannibalism (for an example in Israel's history, see 2 Kgs 6:24-31), even to eating their own children (28:53). Along with such unthinkable callousness, there would be a sense of self-preservation that would drive a man to retain his horrific fare, refusing to share it with even his closest kin (28:54-55). And the women would be no better. Ladies so adverse to social impropriety and indignity as to not place their feet on the ground will be glad to make a meal of their own afterbirth and newborn (28:56-57)—but secretly, thus depriving their families of their "good fortune."

Moses took no delight in painting such a scene, nor, indeed, does Yahweh find joy in judging his people. Sin demands payment, however, and the sin of rebellion against the Lord—the one who though absolutely gracious is also uncompromisingly holy and just—must inevitably result in an outpouring of his wrathful recompense.

◆   ## 6. Curse of covenant termination (28:58-68)

⁵⁸"If you refuse to obey all the words of instruction that are written in this book, and if you do not fear the glorious and awesome name of the LORD your God, ⁵⁹then the LORD will overwhelm you and your children with indescribable plagues. These plagues will be intense and without relief, making you miserable and unbearably

sick. ⁶⁰He will afflict you with all the diseases of Egypt that you feared so much,
and you will have no relief. ⁶¹The LORD will
afflict you with every sickness and plague
there is, even those not mentioned in this
Book of Instruction, until you are destroyed. ⁶²Though you become as numerous as the stars in the sky, few of you will
be left because you would not listen to the
LORD your God.

⁶³"Just as the LORD has found great
pleasure in causing you to prosper and
multiply, the LORD will find pleasure in destroying you. You will be torn from the
land you are about to enter and occupy.
⁶⁴For the LORD will scatter you among all
the nations from one end of the earth to
the other. There you will worship foreign

gods that neither you nor your ancestors
have known, gods made of wood and
stone! ⁶⁵There among those nations you
will find no peace or place to rest. And the
LORD will cause your heart to tremble,
your eyesight to fail, and your soul to despair. ⁶⁶Your life will constantly hang in
the balance. You will live night and day in
fear, unsure if you will survive. ⁶⁷In the
morning you will say, 'If only it were
night!' And in the evening you will say, 'If
only it were morning!' For you will be terrified by the awful horrors you see around
you. ⁶⁸Then the LORD will send you back to
Egypt in ships, to a destination I promised
you would never see again. There you will
offer to sell yourselves to your enemies as
slaves, but no one will buy you."

NOTES

28:63 *You will be torn*. The LXX (B) adds "quickly," an adverb found elsewhere in formulae of threat (cf. 7:4). Its absence here merely shows that stereotypes are commonly broken
in Hebrew prose.

COMMENTARY

If God's mighty and gracious deliverance of Israel from Egypt was a sign of and
necessity to his making a covenant with her at Sinai, then surely Israel's return to
Egypt would signal the undoing or at least suspension of that covenant. This is the
threat that forms the theme of 28:58-68.

Israel was to keep all the terms of the covenant that had just been revealed (lit.,
"this Torah"—i.e., the book of Deuteronomy). Failure to do so would result in affliction in all the ways just described (28:15-57), divine punishments akin to those of
the plagues of Egypt, which, while not experienced by Israel at that time, must have
brought terror to them by merely observing their awesomeness (28:59-60; cf. Exod
7:14–12:36). Such tribulations—and others not even mentioned in "this Book of
Instruction" (i.e., Deuteronomy)—would result in the virtual annihilation of the
covenant nation (28:61-62).

Thus, the ancient promises to the patriarchs that their descendants would be innumerable (Gen 15:5) would suffer a tragic reversal. These same descendants would be
uprooted from the land (28:63) and scattered among the nations where they would
become paganized, no longer people of Yahweh (28:64). Life in these exilic conditions would be harsh indeed, mere existence filled with insecurity, fear, and dissatisfaction (28:65-66). Time would drag by slowly. The terrors of the daytime would
prompt a desire for night, and the fears of night would cause the people to wish for
daylight (28:67). In effect, life in exile would be a return to Egypt, the place of bondage and slavery (28:68). It would be as though no Exodus had ever taken place, no

Reed Sea crossed, no covenant made. Surely, Israel's unrepentant defection from Yahweh's gracious covenant provisions would be a fate worse than death. How could his threats to the assembled community be any more powerful and ominous?

◆ E. Narrative Interlude (29:1)

²These are the terms of the covenant the LORD commanded Moses to make with the Israelites while they were in the land of Moab, in addition to the covenant he had made with them at Mount Sinai.*

29:1a Verse 29:1 is numbered 28:69 in Hebrew text.   29:1b Hebrew *Horeb,* another name for Sinai.

COMMENTARY

Most modern versions of the Bible understand Deuteronomy 29:1 to be the heading or introduction to the next section of Deuteronomy, the "Historical Review." However, the ancient Masoretic tradition of considering it to be the conclusion of the preceding material is much more persuasive (Driver 1902:319). First, the verse matches the viewpoint and even the wording of 1:1-5, the preamble to the covenant text that follows. Thus, this verse serves as a closing parenthesis or *inclusio* to 1:6–28:68. Second, 29:2 is in the form of an introduction, in this case matching 5:1, the beginning of the general stipulation section of the book. It is appropriate that that section as well as the next (29:2–30:20) begin with a very similar formula.

◆ VIII. The Epilogic Historical Review (29:2–30:20)
A. Review of the Exodus, Wandering, and Conquest (29:2–8)

²*Moses summoned all the Israelites and said to them, "You have seen with your own eyes everything the LORD did in the land of Egypt to Pharaoh and to all his servants and to his whole country—³all the great tests of strength, the miraculous signs, and the amazing wonders. ⁴But to this day the LORD has not given you minds that understand, nor eyes that see, nor ears that hear! ⁵For forty years I led you through the wilderness, yet your clothes and sandals did not wear out. ⁶You ate no bread and drank no wine or other alcoholic drink, but he gave you food so you would know that he is the LORD your God.

⁷"When we came here, King Sihon of Heshbon and King Og of Bashan came out to fight against us, but we defeated them. ⁸We took their land and gave it to the tribes of Reuben and Gad and to the half-tribe of Manasseh as their grant of land.

29:2 Verses 29:2-29 are numbered 29:1-28 in Hebrew text.

NOTES

29:5 [4] *I led you.* Because Yahweh appears to be the subject throughout this pericope, the LXX, Syriac, and Vulgate read "he led you." This is obviously an attempt to bring uniformity to the text and for that reason is not likely to reflect the original wording. "I" could refer either to Moses or, by a sudden shift of pronoun, to Yahweh himself (see next note).

29:6 [5] *he is the LORD your God.* Again, the MT reads "I am the Lord your God," emended by the LXX to the reading reflected in the NLT.

COMMENTARY

True to the paraenetic and pedagogical nature of Moses's covenant address, he repeated or recapitulated the most significant points he had already made, especially when he was about to enter into a major new section or topic. Just as the historical prologue (1:6-4:40) had introduced the covenant text proper, so here a truncated version introduces the appendical elements with which the book closes.

Briefly reflecting on Yahweh's signs and wonders, by which he confounded Pharaoh and his hosts in the plagues and Exodus (29:2-3), Moses lamented that it seemed to be a wasted effort since Israel apparently learned nothing life-changing from it (29:4). They ran true to the adage that those who fail to learn from history are bound to repeat it, especially in its harshest forms. But God's power and goodness were not exhausted in the Exodus. He had preserved Israel all through the 40 years of sojourning in the desert, going so far as to clothe and feed them supernaturally (29:5-6; cf. 8:3-4), all to the end that they might see in this display of omnipotent beneficence something of his sovereignty. Beyond this, Yahweh as Divine Warrior had led Israel's armies into battle with Sihon and Og, whom they had conquered and whose Transjordanian territories they occupied (29:7-8; cf. 2:26-3:17).

The point of this résumé is at least twofold: (1) to remind Israel of the faithfulness and grace of Yahweh in the past, attributes worth their emulating; and (2) to provide a basis of hope for the future. What God has done, he can do again. At this new threshold of her national life, Israel could take heart, despite the hard times that lay ahead.

◆ **B. The Present Covenant Setting (29:9-15)**

9"Therefore, obey the terms of this covenant so that you will prosper in everything you do. 10All of you—tribal leaders, elders, officers, all the men of Israel—are standing today in the presence of the LORD your God. 11Your little ones and your wives are with you, as well as the foreigners living among you who chop your wood and carry your water. 12You are standing here today to enter into the covenant of the LORD your God. The LORD is making this covenant, including the curses. 13By entering into the covenant today, he will establish you as his people and confirm that he is your God, just as he promised you and as he swore to your ancestors Abraham, Isaac, and Jacob.

14"But you are not the only ones with whom I am making this covenant with its curses. 15I am making this covenant both with you who stand here today in the presence of the LORD our God, and also with the future generations who are not standing here today.

NOTES

29:10 [9] *tribal leaders.* For the MT's literal "your heads, your tribes," an apposition, the Syriac (followed by others) suggests either "heads of your tribes" (thus NLT, "tribal leaders") or "heads of your judges" (*shopetekem* [TH8199, ZH9149]; cf. the Hebrew for "your tribes," *shibtekem* [TH7626, ZH8657]). The difficulty of the MT reading here makes it likely that it is correct and the Syriac sought to improve the flow of the text in translation.

COMMENTARY

Predicated on God's past performance on Israel's behalf, Moses exhorts the listening community to pay heed in the present and future to the demands of the covenant relationship if they expect to enjoy God's blessings (29:9-15). And this includes everybody—heads of tribes (see note on 29:10), elders, public officials, full citizens (lit., "men of Israel"), children, wives, and even resident foreigners who performed much of the menial work (29:10-11; for the latter class, see Josh 9:22-27). The pledges of their ancestors to obedience are not sufficient for the new generation. This generation, too, must enter into a covenant relationship with Yahweh and swear to uphold its terms, even as Yahweh himself has sworn to do (29:12). This remarkable act of commitment by Yahweh, dramatized in a ceremony of covenant making that is at least implicit in the text (Craigie 1976:356-357), calls for Israel's reciprocation just as it did when Yahweh bound himself to the patriarchs (29:13; cf. Gen 17:9-14) and later to Israel at Sinai (Exod 19:4-8).

The fact that the previous covenant avowals were not efficacious for this generation of Israelites leads to the observation that future generations, while heirs to the potentialities of the Deuteronomic promises, would also have to make fresh commitment to it—that is, the covenant itself was everlasting, but its benefits must be appropriated by every individual and by every generation. The exhortation here, then, was for Israel, on the eve of conquest, to reaffirm its intentions to be the people of God and to assume gladly all the privileges and responsibilities attendant to that sacred resolution.

◆   C. The Cost of Disobedience (29:16-29)

[16]"You remember how we lived in the land of Egypt and how we traveled through the lands of enemy nations as we left. [17]You have seen their detestable practices and their idols* made of wood, stone, silver, and gold. [18]I am making this covenant with you so that no one among you—no man, woman, clan, or tribe—will turn away from the LORD our God to worship these gods of other nations, and so that no root among you bears bitter and poisonous fruit.

[19]"Those who hear the warnings of this curse should not congratulate themselves, thinking, 'I am safe, even though I am following the desires of my own stubborn heart.' This would lead to utter ruin! [20]The LORD will never pardon such people. Instead his anger and jealousy will burn against them. All the curses written in this book will come down on them, and the LORD will erase their names from under heaven. [21]The LORD will separate them from all the tribes of Israel, to pour out on them all the curses of the covenant recorded in this Book of Instruction.

[22]"Then the generations to come, both your own descendants and the foreigners who come from distant lands, will see the devastation of the land and the diseases the LORD inflicts on it. [23]They will exclaim, 'The whole land is devastated by sulfur and salt. It is a wasteland with nothing planted and nothing growing, not even a blade of grass. It is like the cities of Sodom and Gomorrah, Admah and Zeboiim, which the LORD destroyed in his intense anger.'

[24]"And all the surrounding nations will ask, 'Why has the LORD done this to this land? Why was he so angry?'

²⁵"And the answer will be, 'This happened because the people of the land abandoned the covenant that the LORD, the God of their ancestors, made with them when he brought them out of the land of Egypt. ²⁶Instead, they turned away to serve and worship gods they had not known before, gods that were not from the LORD. ²⁷That is why the LORD's anger has burned against this land, bringing down on it every curse recorded in this book. ²⁸In great anger and fury the LORD uprooted his people from their land and banished them to another land, where they still live today!'

²⁹"The LORD our God has secrets known to no one. We are not accountable for them, but we and our children are accountable forever for all that he has revealed to us, so that we may obey all the terms of these instructions.

29:17 The Hebrew term (literally *round things*) probably alludes to dung.

NOTES

29:17 [16] *detestable practices.* The word *shiqquts* [TH8251, ZH9199] is a generic term for anything that is reprehensible to Yahweh because of its nature or effects. It is synonymous with *to'ebah* [TH8441, ZH9359] (usually rendered "abominable, loathsome" or the like), occurring sometimes with it or in its place (NIDOTTE 4.244; cf. 2 Kgs 23:13; Jer 16:18; Ezek 5:11; 7:20; 11:18, 21). The grammar here permits either a distinction between the detestable things and idols or (more likely) an epexegetical construction such as "detestable things, i.e., idols."

29:19 [18] *utter ruin.* The NLT is a paraphrase of the Hebrew, which literally reads, "sweeping away the watered and the parched," that is, everything.

COMMENTARY

Continuing his historical review as a foil against which to warn Israel of the consequences of covenant failure, Moses returns to the Egyptian sojourn and the Exodus, with all the negative memories associated with that period (29:16). In particular he recounts how Israel had been tempted to turn away from Yahweh as they encountered the gods of the various nations with whom they came in contact (29:17). The best-known example of this was Israel's apostasy at Peor in Moab, where many of them worshiped the Baal of that place (Num 25:1-5; cf. Deut 4:3).

The purpose of the covenant renewal, in fact, was to provide opportunity for this new Israelite generation to disavow the idolatry of their fathers and to swear undivided allegiance to Yahweh (cf. 29:14-15). The flagrant exhibition of paganism at Peor had not occurred without precedent. Already at Sinai, Israel had created and bowed down to a golden calf, even while Moses was receiving the Decalogue on the mountain (Exod 32:1-6). Most likely the calf (or bull) was associated with Egyptian myth and ritual, the attractiveness of which may be the "root" that produced the "bitter and poisonous fruit" of the idolatry to which Moses refers (29:18).

Moses then turned to the assembly before him and warned his hearers that they, too, were vulnerable. It would not do to be spiritually smug and outwardly compliant while harboring iniquity within. They needed to be warned not to show an outward and hypocritical facade of righteousness. Should they try this, the covenant curses they had invoked upon themselves would come to pass. Both "the watered and the parched" (i.e., everything; see note on 29:19) would be destroyed. Their very names would be forgotten (cf. 9:14), and they would be excommunicated from the theocratic commonwealth (29:20-21).

While all these judgments pertain to both the individual and the nation as a whole, the emphasis here is clearly on the latter, as the following passage shows. The effect of the curse is too devastating to be limited only to those persons who on their own violate the covenant precepts. They are in view, indeed, as the singular pronoun and attention to individual attitudes and actions make clear (29:18, 19, 21). But it is the cumulative result, the aggregation of personal sins, that would eventually permeate the whole community and bring it to ruin.

In days to come—surely the days after the defeat and deportation of the twin kingdoms already alluded to (cf. 28:25, 36-37, 47-48, 63-68)—the land of Israel would be so utterly devastated and desolate that the nations around it would look in amazement and wonder how such things could be (29:22-24). Even future generations of Israelites would be astounded at what they saw. The books of Ezra and Nehemiah provide glimpses of the reactions of post-exilic Jews to the conditions they found when they returned to their homeland from distant places (cf. Ezra 3:12-13; 9:5-7; Neh 1:3; 2:11-13; 7:4).

The description here seems to go beyond historical dimensions, however, and to assume apocalyptic overtones. The references to "sulfur and salt" and to the cataclysmic destruction of the cities of the plain (29:23-24) find clear correspondence to conditions found in such apocalyptic texts as Ezekiel 37–39, where the prophet views the land as a barren desolation, a place of ruin, plague, and death (cf. Ezek 37:1-2, 11-14; 39:11-16). Only when he speaks the Lord's message to the desiccated bones of his people do they come alive again (Ezek 37:7-10).

Inasmuch as the nations understood that Yahweh was God of Israel, a nation to which he had bound himself by everlasting covenant, the questions that inevitably would be asked in light of such awesome calamity were, "Why has Yahweh done this?" and "Why is he so angry?" (29:24). The answer—clear and unambiguous—is that Israel broke her covenant with Yahweh, the gracious relationship he had established with her following the Exodus deliverance (29:25). The same answer appears in lengthy detail in 2 Kings 17:7-23 to account for the destruction of Samaria and the deportation of the northern kingdom.

Most particularly, Israel, by her idolatry, would violate the first two commandments, the very basis of her claim to be the people of Yahweh. It would be because they had worshiped other gods besides him and made and bowed down to idols that they would suffer such horrendous consequences (29:26; cf. 5:7-21). This is what would provoke the unleashing of his wrath, a holy anger manifest in the curses already spelled out (29:27; cf. 27:15-26; 28:16-68). The culmination would be exile, the uprooting of Israel from the Land of Promise to another place (29:28). The effects would last until "today"—that is, to the time of those future witnesses who would observe and be astounded at the duration of God's anger (cf. 29:24-25, 28).

In another sense, however, the question as to how or why this could happen could not be answered because of human ignorance. This is the sentiment of

29:29. How can it be that God could call a people to himself and, with irrefragable promise, pledge to them an everlasting fidelity, only to write them off, even for a time? Of course, from the standpoint of a total biblical eschatology, no such thing will happen, for God will lead wayward Israel to repentance and full restoration (cf. 30:6-10; Lev 26:40-45; Jer 31:27-37; Ezek 36:22-38; Rom 11:1-24; etc.). However, from Israel's perspective there on the plains of Moab, the apparently contradictory words of election and rejection could not be resolved by human understanding (Craigie 1976:360). Such "secret things" are known only to God. What Israel could know and needed to know was the Torah (law) that Moses was presenting to them and their descendants. And more than this, Israel must obey if she were to have any hope of averting Yahweh's awful judgment.

◆   ## D. The Results of Covenant Disobedience (30:1-10)

"In the future, when you experience all these blessings and curses I have listed for you, and when you are living among the nations to which the LORD your God has exiled you, take to heart all these instructions. ²If at that time you and your children return to the LORD your God, and if you obey with all your heart and all your soul all the commands I have given you today, ³then the LORD your God will restore your fortunes. He will have mercy on you and gather you back from all the nations where he has scattered you. ⁴Even though you are banished to the ends of the earth, the LORD your God will gather you from there and bring you back again. ⁵The LORD your God will return you to the land that belonged to your ancestors, and you will possess that land again. Then he will make you even more prosperous and numerous than your ancestors!

⁶"The LORD your God will change your heart* and the hearts of all your descendants, so that you will love him with all your heart and soul and so you may live! ⁷The LORD your God will inflict all these curses on your enemies and on those who hate and persecute you. ⁸Then you will again obey the LORD and keep all his commands that I am giving you today.

⁹"The LORD your God will then make you successful in everything you do. He will give you many children and numerous livestock, and he will cause your fields to produce abundant harvests, for the LORD will again delight in being good to you as he was to your ancestors. ¹⁰The LORD your God will delight in you if you obey his voice and keep the commands and decrees written in this Book of Instruction, and if you turn to the LORD your God with all your heart and soul.

30:6 Hebrew *circumcise your heart.*

NOTES

30:4 *bring you back again.* Certain LXX recensions add "Yahweh your God" as the subject. This appears to be an unnecessary attempt to provide the full epithet in line with its very common use throughout this passage.

30:8 *the LORD.* The Samaritan Pentateuch, LXX, Syriac, and Vulgate add "your God" (see previous note).

30:10 *written.* Instead of the MT's singular (*hakkethubah*), the Syriac and Targums have the plural (*hakkethubim*) [TH3789, ZH4180], a grammatically more acceptable reading. However, strict grammatical number agreement is frequently disregarded in biblical Hebrew (cf. 29:21 [20], which also uses the singular *hakkethubah* with a plural noun).

COMMENTARY

The "secrets" of the previous verse (29:29) will remain so no longer, because in 30:1-10 Moses reconciles the apparent contradiction between God's unconditional promise that Israel will forever be his people with the possibility that its favored status can be forfeited by her covenant defection. Should that defection occur and the nation experience God's curses—including deportation—they will be able to return (*shub* [TH7725, ZH8740], "repent") to Yahweh in full and complete renewal of faith and commitment (30:1-2). The latter phrase (lit., "with all your heart and with all your being") is reminiscent of how Israel is to love Yahweh according to the Shema (6:5). In short, those who fall away from Yahweh may return to him again and find complete restoration.

Again, even if things go so far as to force Israel into exile, Yahweh will be willing and able to exercise compassion (*rakham* [TH7355, ZH8163]; 30:3) and restore his people to their homeland. Twice in 30:3 the verb *shub* [TH7725, ZH8740] is used to speak of Yahweh's returning or turning, just as it was used in 30:2 to describe Israel's turning or repentance. If sinners turn (i.e., repent), then God turns (i.e., restores). No matter how distant the place of exile might be—even to the far horizons (lit., "edge of the heavens")—Yahweh can find his beloved ones and return them to the land he promised to their patriarchal ancestors. Beyond that, he will prosper them even more than he had those ancient forebears (30:3-5).

The question might remain, however, as to how rebellious covenant breakers make the decision to repent and return. It is at this point that the "secrets" of 29:29 are most brilliantly revealed and God's covenant constancy and his intolerance of sin can be reconciled. The answer lies in grace, an undeserved initiative on God's part, whereby he sovereignly chooses to bring hopeless sinners back to perfect fellowship (Cairns 1992:264).

The text speaks in no uncertain terms: Yahweh *will* cleanse (*mal* [TH4135, ZH4576], "circumcise"; 30:6) the guilty of that and every generation and *will* instill within them a covenant loyalty (*'ahab* [TH157, ZH170], "love") in line with the expectations of the Shema, the very core of Israelite faith and life (cf. 6:5; Jer 31:33-34; 32:39-40; Ezek 11:19; 36:26). What Israel could not do on its own—namely, turn from its wickedness and unbelief—Yahweh will then do for her. This "gospel" of the Old Testament has the same basis and produces the same effects as the gospel of Jesus Christ in the New Testament. It is a message of grace which, acted on by faith, leads to life. The curses that ought to have fallen on such beneficiaries of divine favor will fall instead on those who are enemies of his sovereign intentions (30:7). Along with restoration to fellowship and return to the land will be the ability—again, God-given—to keep the terms of the covenant (30:8). In addition, Israel would prosper as before and even more so as evidence of God's ongoing grace (30:9).

The passage closes with what at first appears to be contrary to the message of grace just announced. Grammatically, 30:10 begins with a conditional clause (*ki* [TH3588, ZH3954], "if") and then goes on to suggest that all the aforementioned blessings will come *if* there is unequivocal obedience to the terms of the covenant (*seper hattorah* [TH5612/8451, ZH6219/9368], "book of the law," clearly referring to the book of Deuteronomy) and *if* the people repent with all their being. There is, however, no conflict here, for it is true that fellowship with God depends on one's faith and obedience, but it is likewise crystal clear from this text that the ability to believe and to obey is an ability that God himself gives (cf. Eph 2:8-9; Titus 3:5).

◆   E. Exhortation to Covenant Obedience (30:11-20)

¹¹"This command I am giving you today is not too difficult for you to understand, and it is not beyond your reach. ¹²It is not kept in heaven, so distant that you must ask, 'Who will go up to heaven and bring it down so we can hear it and obey?' ¹³It is not kept beyond the sea, so far away that you must ask, 'Who will cross the sea to bring it to us so we can hear it and obey?' ¹⁴No, the message is very close at hand; it is on your lips and in your heart so that you can obey it.

¹⁵"Now listen! Today I am giving you a choice between life and death, between prosperity and disaster. ¹⁶For I command you this day to love the LORD your God and to keep his commands, decrees, and regulations by walking in his ways. If you do this, you will live and multiply, and the LORD your God will bless you and the land you are about to enter and occupy.

¹⁷"But if your heart turns away and you refuse to listen, and if you are drawn away to serve and worship other gods, ¹⁸then I warn you now that you will certainly be destroyed. You will not live a long, good life in the land you are crossing the Jordan to occupy.

¹⁹"Today I have given you the choice between life and death, between blessings and curses. Now I call on heaven and earth to witness the choice you make. Oh, that you would choose life, so that you and your descendants might live! ²⁰You can make this choice by loving the LORD your God, obeying him, and committing yourself firmly to him. This* is the key to your life. And if you love and obey the LORD, you will live long in the land the LORD swore to give your ancestors Abraham, Isaac, and Jacob."

30:20 Or *He.*

COMMENTARY

Moses sums up the whole covenant text with the singular word *mitswah* [TH4687, ZH5184] (command), a set of stipulations that are not beyond the people's capacity to obey (30:11). They are not too inscrutable (lit., "wonderful")—that is, transcendent to the point of being intellectually incomprehensible—nor are they so physically distant as to be humanly inaccessible (30:11). One need not traverse the infinite expanse of the heavens to procure them and bring them down to earth so they can be heard and obeyed (30:12); nor are they so geographically remote that one must journey to the other side of the earth (lit., "from across the sea") to bring them back so that God's people can know and do them (30:13). To the contrary, these covenant truths had already become interiorized within the assembly. They lodged firmly within the minds of God's people and therefore could be verbally articulated by them (30:14).

The truth here is precious and profound. The infinite and omniscient God of Israel can reveal and has revealed the mysteries of his saving purposes to a lowly, undeserving, and often hardhearted and unresponsive people. There is no need for any angelic or even human intermediation apart from the inspired prophets, like Moses, through whom the revelation came. The truth is not so obscure or elusive as to require interpretive savants. Israel's opportunities and responsibilities before Yahweh are not so esoteric that they cannot be apprehended and carried out. Rather, they are transparently clear and personalized. The community and all its members have unfettered access to the very mind and plan of the Almighty.

Paul made use of the sentiment of this text when he equated Christ with the covenant word of Deuteronomy (Rom 10:6-8; Hodge 1955:340). Christ, too, did not need to be brought down from heaven or raised up from "the place of the dead" (Gr., *abussos* [TG12, ZG12], "the abyss," that is, the depths of the sea) because he, through the message of the gospel, was already deeply implanted in the minds and on the lips of those to whom Paul had preached and who responded with saving faith (Rom 10:9). The word of redemption is no mystery to those who are open to it (cf. 1 Cor 1:18-21).

But there must be a response to the proffer of grace. Moses therefore called the assembly to make a decision as to how they would respond to this gracious word of revelation. Using a figure of speech (a metonymy), in which the effect stands for the cause, Moses presented the options of life and good or death and disaster (so the Hebrew text)—that is, he extended choices which, when made, will result in one pair or the other. The choices are either to love the Lord or to reject him.

As has been noted in the text time and again (cf. 6:5; 7:9; 10:12; 11:1, 13, 22; 13:3; 19:9; 30:6), to love God is to enter into covenant with him and to obey him fully and unconditionally. The collocation of love and obedience is nowhere brought together more clearly than here (30:15). To choose to do this and to be faithful to such a commitment will result in life and blessing in the land of Canaan (30:16). However, to turn away from the Lord (that is, to hate him) will bring certain and inevitable judgment. The most profound expression of such rejection of the Lord is the worship of other gods, which is a violation of the first two commandments (30:17; cf. 5:7-10).

To underscore the urgency of the need to make a choice and to be prepared to live with its consequences, Moses once more drew attention to the present moment by using the word "today" (30:19). No longer could Israel vacillate; the day of decision had come, the time when the destiny of individuals and, indeed, of the whole covenant community was to be settled one way or another. The options again are presented in bold relief. One can elect obedience to the covenant, a choice that guarantees life and blessing, or one can by default (if by no other means) opt for death and cursing. The formality and finality of the occasion and the people's reaction to it are most apparent in the technical act of invoking witnesses (Thompson 1974:287). "Heaven and earth" suggests totality, that is, all creation. Everyone and everything that God had made would bear witness to Yahweh's gracious offer and Israel's response. Never in the future could Israel deny with any credibility the decision she had made at this moment of truth.

Moses was involved as a member of the community as well as being the mediator between Yahweh and the community. As he had done on past occasions, Moses implored his people to choose wisely, to love and obey Yahweh in order that they might live. In fact, he went so far as to say (lit.), "He [Yahweh] is your life" (30:20). The Lord not only grants life as something outside himself, but he is life in himself. Knowledge of Yahweh brings life, and those who are truly alive testify thereby to the presence of Yahweh in their lives. There could hardly be a clearer statement of the gospel message: "The Word gave life to everything that was created, and his life brought light to everyone" (John 1:4). Choosing to adopt and obey the terms of the covenant would procure blessings far beyond the moment of decision. It would offer hope for descendants yet unborn (30:19b) and the perpetuation of national existence in the land God had promised to the patriarchal ancestors (30:20).

◆ IX. Deposit of the Text and Provision for Its Future Implementation (31:1-29)

A. Joshua's Succession of Moses (31:1-8)

When Moses had finished giving these instructions* to all the people of Israel, ²he said, "I am now 120 years old, and I am no longer able to lead you. The LORD has told me, 'You will not cross the Jordan River.' ³But the LORD your God himself will cross over ahead of you. He will destroy the nations living there, and you will take possession of their land. Joshua will lead you across the river, just as the LORD promised.

⁴"The LORD will destroy the nations living in the land, just as he destroyed Sihon and Og, the kings of the Amorites. ⁵The LORD will hand over to you the people who live there, and you must deal with them as I have commanded you. ⁶So be strong and courageous! Do not be afraid and do not panic before them. For the LORD your God will personally go ahead of you. He will neither fail you nor abandon you."

⁷Then Moses called for Joshua, and as all Israel watched, he said to him, "Be strong and courageous! For you will lead these people into the land that the LORD swore to their ancestors he would give them. You are the one who will divide it among them as their grants of land. ⁸Do not be afraid or discouraged, for the LORD will personally go ahead of you. He will be with you; he will neither fail you nor abandon you."

31:1 As in Dead Sea Scrolls and Greek version; Masoretic Text reads *Moses went and spoke.*

NOTES

31:4 *kings of the Amorites.* The LXX adds "to the two" before this phrase, bringing the text in line with 3:21. The LXX also adds "who were on the other side of the Jordan" to the end of the verse (cf. 3:8; 4:47).

31:7 *you will lead.* This translation reflects the Hiphil of *bo'* [TH935, ZH995], "go," a reading attested by the Samaritan Pentateuch, Syriac, and Vulgate. The MT reads Qal, "you will go with." The difference between the spellings of the two involves only a single letter.

COMMENTARY

Having presented to the assembly of Israel the challenge to commit themselves to covenant obedience, Moses turned to the topic of the conquest of Canaan and the new leadership God would raise up to ensure its success. Moses had already learned and disclosed to his people that he would not personally participate in the triumph of conquest and the blessing of occupation of the Promised Land. He had acted rashly in regard to eliciting water from the rock and for that impetuous reaction was condemned to die and be buried at Nebo in the Transjordan (1:37; cf. Num 20:9-13; 27:12-14). Moreover, he was now 120 years old and, therefore, past the age of effective leadership (31:2).

Tragic as this might be for Moses—and even for Israel—the truth was that Moses was unnecessary to the accomplishment of Yahweh's purposes, for it was Yahweh, not Moses, who was Israel's real leader. Using "holy war" terminology, Moses describes the coming conquest as a work of God. It is he who will lead the way (31:3a, 6; cf. 7:1), he who will destroy the hostile nations (31:3b-5), and he who will never fail nor forsake them (31:6). The guarantee of future success is the accomplishment of the Lord in history past. As he had overcome Sihon and Og in the Transjordan (2:26–3:11; cf. Num 21:21-35), so he would deal with the rulers of the Canaanite states (31:4).

Despite this clear statement of theocratic polity, however, the text insists that God uses human beings to carry out his will on earth. Moses, his initial disclaimers and resistance notwithstanding (cf. Exod 3:11; 4:10), proved to be a mighty instrument in God's hands. Now with Moses's impending demise, steps were underway to secure a successor, another man through whom God could carry out his redemptive program. This man was Joshua (31:3), one who had already been designated in the past (Num 27:15-23), an individual of spiritual sensitivity (Exod 33:11) and courage (1:38; Num 14:30).

Such a momentous change of leadership called for a public ceremony of investiture. Calling for Joshua to stand in the midst of the assembly, Moses exhorted him to be courageous in taking up the mantle of responsibility that had fallen upon him by divine appointment (31:7). The words of Moses's charge to his younger confidant are echoed and expanded upon by Yahweh himself, who, following Moses's death, appeared to Joshua and directly sanctioned the commission first uttered here (Josh 1:1-9). Repeating his assurances of the divine presence (cf. 31:3, 6), Moses addressed Joshua individually with the same promise: "He will be with you; he will neither fail you nor abandon you" (31:8).

The truth more universally applied is that the man or woman whom God calls to leadership or any other task can go forward in the confidence that as God leads the way, he also remains present and available. At the same time, he guarantees success in both the implementation and completion of whatever objective he has for those with whom he enters into partnership.

◆   ## B. The Deposit of the Text (31:9-13)

⁹So Moses wrote this entire body of instruction in a book and gave it to the priests, who carried the Ark of the LORD's Covenant, and to the elders of Israel. ¹⁰Then Moses gave them this command: "At the end of every seventh year, the Year

of Release, during the Festival of Shelters, ¹¹you must read this Book of Instruction to all the people of Israel when they assemble before the LORD your God at the place he chooses. ¹²Call them all together—men, women, children, and the foreigners living in your towns—so they may hear this Book of Instruction and learn to fear the LORD your God and carefully obey all the terms of these instructions. ¹³Do this so that your children who have not known these instructions will hear them and will learn to fear the LORD your God. Do this as long as you live in the land you are crossing the Jordan to occupy."

NOTES

31:11 *assemble before.* Lit., "appear before." In place of the syncopated Niphal infinitive *lera'oth* (usually *lehera'oth*), "to appear," BHS suggests Qal *lir'oth* [TH7200, ZH8011], "to see." (A similar revocalization is suggested in 16:16 but with no grammatical justification.) The NLT translates according to the sense of the MT.

COMMENTARY

In the Introduction, I noted that parties to ancient Near Eastern treaties secured the texts of those agreements by depositing them in a place that was both secure and conveniently accessible for future reference. The Deuteronomic covenant document was to be similarly preserved. Since the Tabernacle would, for the foreseeable future, be the "residence" of the Lord, a dwelling place marked particularly by the Ark of the Covenant, the Lord's copy most logically would be retained there. Absent a political center separate from the Tabernacle, Israel's copy presumably was also deposited there (Kline 1972:121-122). In the later monarchy, there is some evidence that the king kept a copy and was required to read a copy under his direct safekeeping (17:18-20; cf. 2 Chr 29:15).

In the meantime, Moses handed "this entire body of instruction" (lit., "this law") over to the priests (31:9). The writing in view included the stipulations sections of Deuteronomy at least (5:1–26:15) and probably the blessings and curses passages (chs 27–28) as well. The fact that the Ark is mentioned suggests its importance to the deposition of the text. Both it and the text of Deuteronomy were to be housed in the Holy of Holies (cf. 31:26). To remind the nation of the contents of the covenant and their duty to obey it, the priests must read it publicly every seventh year as part of the ritual of the Festival of Tabernacles ("Festival of Shelters" in NLT; 31:10-11). This was appropriate because this festival marked Israel's sojourn in the desert, where God had faithfully provided for them from the time of the Exodus to the Transjordanian conquest (cf. 16:13-15).

That this was more than merely an agricultural festival is clear from the reference to the "Year of Release" (NIDOTTE 4.158). This release of all indentured Israelite debtors (see 15:1-6) would be a proper response to Yahweh's having released Israel itself from Egyptian bondage (15:15). The combination of divine redemption and supernatural provision would, then, be sufficient rationale for the periodic reading of the covenant text. The God who had thus blessed his people had every right to expect their loving obedience to his gracious expectations.

The ceremony of public reading would take place at the worship center—that is, the place the Lord would choose (31:11; cf. 12:4-7). All must assemble there and listen intently to all the provisions and mandates of the covenant (31:12). Faithful adherence to this requirement would ensure that unborn generations of Israelites would hear the word of God and, hopefully, would learn to fear (that is, worship and serve) him (31:13). Sadly enough, subsequent history suggests that the ceremony, if carried out at all, met with less than resounding compliance (cf. perhaps 2 Kgs 23:1-3; Neh 9:5-37). And such indifference is not limited to Old Testament Israel. The history of the church and, indeed, the biographies of individual lives testify to the wide chasm between divine expectation and human performance. But the only safeguard against total and final spiritual amnesia is the regular proclamation of the eternal truths of God's revelation.

◆ ## C. Joshua's Commission (31:14-23)

¹⁴Then the LORD said to Moses, "The time has come for you to die. Call Joshua and present yourselves at the Tabernacle,* so that I may commission him there." So Moses and Joshua went and presented themselves at the Tabernacle. ¹⁵And the LORD appeared to them in a pillar of cloud that stood at the entrance to the sacred tent.

¹⁶The LORD said to Moses, "You are about to die and join your ancestors. After you are gone, these people will begin to worship foreign gods, the gods of the land where they are going. They will abandon me and break my covenant that I have made with them. ¹⁷Then my anger will blaze forth against them. I will abandon them, hiding my face from them, and they will be devoured. Terrible trouble will come down on them, and on that day they will say, 'These disasters have come down on us because God is no longer among us!' ¹⁸At that time I will hide my face from them on account of all the evil they commit by worshiping other gods.

¹⁹"So write down the words of this song, and teach it to the people of Israel. Help them learn it, so it may serve as a witness for me against them. ²⁰For I will bring them into the land I swore to give their ancestors—a land flowing with milk and honey. There they will become prosperous, eat all the food they want, and become fat. But they will begin to worship other gods; they will despise me and break my covenant. ²¹And when great disasters come down on them, this song will stand as evidence against them, for it will never be forgotten by their descendants. I know the intentions of these people, even now before they have entered the land I swore to give them."

²²So that very day Moses wrote down the words of the song and taught it to the Israelites.

²³Then the LORD commissioned Joshua son of Nun with these words: "Be strong and courageous, for you must bring the people of Israel into the land I swore to give them. I will be with you."

31:14 Hebrew *Tent of Meeting;* also in 31:14b.

NOTES

31:14 *the Tabernacle.* The LXX prefixes "at the door of," probably to soften the bold idea of human beings actually entering that holy place (cf. "entrance to the sacred tent" in 31:15).

31:15 *sacred tent.* The LXX and Syriac add "of meeting" in order to supply the usual full name of the structure (cf. 31:14).

31:23 *the LORD commissioned . . . "I will be with you."* By adding "the LORD" as subject at the beginning of the verse, the NLT is able to retain this clause as it stands in the MT. However, the subject of "commissioned" is actually "he" and, by context (see v. 22), Moses. The difficulty with the MT is that it appears that Moses will be with Joshua in Canaan when, in fact, he has already declared that he cannot go there (31:2). The LXX reads "as the Lord promised them, and he will be with you." It is, however, likely that the "he" of "commissioned" in the MT is the Lord, for such unexpected changes of subject are not rare in Hebrew compositions. The changes of subject tend to authenticate the MT as the pristine reading.

COMMENTARY

This passage begins (31:14) and ends (31:23) with information about Joshua's official and public ordination as Moses's theocratic successor. In between are predictions about Israel's defection in days to come and its consequences (31:16-18) and instructions to Moses about composing a song whose message will stand as a witness to indict the nation for its unbelief (31:19-22).

The setting of the commissioning appears to be private, as opposed to the earlier public notice of Joshua's role (31:1-8). Moses and Joshua must go to the Tent of Meeting (*'ohel mo'ed* [TH168/4150, ZH185/4595]; as in NLT note on 31:14). This was not the Tabernacle (*mishkan* [TH4908, ZH5438]), but, as a number of texts point out (Exod 33:7-11; Num 11:16, 24, 26; 12:4), a place where God encountered individuals—especially Moses—for special purposes (Terrien 1978:175-183; Childs 1974:590-593). It was a "meeting place," hence the term "Tent of Meeting." Once there and in the presence of Yahweh (see note on 31:14), Moses and Joshua witnessed the symbol of Yahweh's theophanic glory, a pillar of cloud (31:15; cf. Exod 33:9-11). The cloud served both to obscure the otherwise intolerable brilliance of God's immanence and to reveal the otherwise undetectable hiddenness of his transcendence. Such a display provided undeniable evidence of the presence of Yahweh—to both Moses and Joshua nearby and surely to the assembly from a distance—and it certified that something significant was about to transpire.

The need for Joshua's commissioning becomes apparent in the announcement (once more; cf. 31:2) of Moses's death and the apostasy of Israel that would inevitably follow (31:16). This time it is not "if" the nation becomes unfaithful (cf. 28:15, 45, 58), but "when." It is a foregone conclusion. However, the fact that it was predicted did not mean it was excusable as though it were part of a divine plan. In fact, sin is never a necessity, and it always, as here, invites God's severe wrath and judgment. If Israel leaves him, he will leave them until at last they acknowledge that all their calamities have come because God is no longer among them (31:17). He who now confronts Moses and Joshua openly (31:15) will hide his face from that future generation that breaks covenant by worshiping other gods (31:18; cf. 29:22-28).

Such times as those described here would require Moses-like leadership. But the people would also be in need of constant reminders of both God's grace and his judgment. Secular treaty texts usually contained lists of witnesses to the mutually pledged promises, and a modified example of that appears here. What is unusual in this case is that Israel would become a witness for or against itself as it recited a liturgical song of witness in the ages to come (31:19). That song (the text of which is 32:1-43) would be an adumbration of Israel's sacred history, sung as either a self-affirmation or self-condemnation depending on her adherence or non-adherence to the terms of the covenant (Kline 1972:92-93). The latter will be most likely, it seems, for Israel's experience in the land will be one of increasing idolatry (31:20), followed by God's judgment, a judgment well deserved—as even Israel would confess through its singing of the song of witness (31:21).

Sensing the urgency of his task, Moses set about composing the song and teaching it to the assembly (31:22). Then the Lord himself (see the note on 31:23), and not Moses (cf. 31:7), commissioned (lit., "commanded") Joshua to his upcoming ministry (31:23). He must be courageous (cf. Josh 1:1-9), for only great boldness would equip him for the formidable assignment that lay ahead. But the battle would not be his in the final analysis; it would be Yahweh's. Thus, Yahweh would be with him.

◆   D. Anticipation of Covenant Disloyalty (31:24-29)

24When Moses had finished writing this entire body of instruction in a book, 25he gave this command to the Levites who carried the Ark of the LORD's Covenant: 26"Take this Book of Instruction and place it beside the Ark of the Covenant of the LORD your God, so it may remain there as a witness against the people of Israel. 27For I know how rebellious and stubborn you are. Even now, while I am still alive and am here with you, you have rebelled against the LORD. How much more rebellious will you be after my death!

28"Now summon all the elders and officials of your tribes, so that I can speak to them directly and call heaven and earth to witness against them. 29I know that after my death you will become utterly corrupt and will turn from the way I have commanded you to follow. In the days to come, disaster will come down on you, for you will do what is evil in the LORD's sight, making him very angry with your actions."

NOTES

31:24 book. This term is technically anachronistic since it connotes the modern idea of bound pages. Bound books (codices) did not come into use until the early centuries AD. The word *seper* [TH5612, ZH6219] means simply a "writing" or "inscription," so its form (tablet, scroll, etc.) cannot be ascertained with confidence. In light of the Egyptian scribal practice of composing long texts on papyrus scrolls, Deuteronomy itself may originally have been written in such a medium.

31:28 *all the elders and officials of your tribes.* The LXX has "all your leaders, judges, and officials" (cf. 29:10).

COMMENTARY

Resuming his instructions to the Levitical priests as to their guardianship of the covenant text (cf. 31:9-13), Moses handed the complete document over to them and stipulated that it must be placed in the Holy of Holies beside the Ark of the

Covenant. There it would be a perpetual reminder (witness) to them of the solemn obligations to which they had sworn by entering into covenant with their God (31:24-26). "This entire body of instruction" (31:24) refers to the stipulations section of Deuteronomy (chs 5–26; Mayes 1979:379) and probably also the curses and blessings (chs 27–28; cf. 31:9).

The Ark of the Covenant (31:26) was so named because it contained the stone tablets of the Decalogue that Moses had brought down from Mount Sinai (10:1-5; Exod 25:16; 40:20). The Deuteronomy scroll was not to be put into the Ark but placed beside it, thus juxtaposing the heart of the earlier covenant with its full expression nearly 40 years later. It would function as a witness against Israel both by its silent presence, symbolizing Israel's relationship to Yahweh, and by its public reading at least every seven years (31:10-11).

The need for such a witness was already clear to Moses. Even while he was their theocratic leader, the people unremittingly rebelled against Yahweh. In fact, their entire post-Exodus history was marked more by insurrection than almost any other feature (see Exod 16:1-3; 17:1-7; 32:1-6; Num 11:1-15; 14:1-10; 16:1-50). Moses was not optimistic about their future (31:27). If Israel was bold enough to resist his leadership, despite the evidence of God's sanctioning that role (cf. Num 12:6-8), to what depths of disloyalty to the covenant would they sink once he was gone?

In addition to the witness of the covenant scroll, Moses had composed the "song of witness" as a means whereby Israel would, at unspecified times, invoke judgment upon itself if it lived in unrepentant rebellion (cf. 31:19, 22). This self-imprecation is in view in 31:28, as the phrase "call heaven and earth to witness against them" makes clear. This phrase, in fact, is the essence of the opening verse in the song itself (32:1). "Heaven and earth" is a merism, a figure of speech that by enlisting extreme opposites intends to include all that is between—that is, everything. What Moses was about to enjoin upon the assembly, and the assembly's response, would be witnessed by the whole creation. At the day of reckoning, then, there would be no opportunity for evasion or misrepresentation. With brokenhearted finality, Moses predicted that after his death Israel would become hopelessly corrupt and rebellious. Just as certain—and more so—would be the wrathful consequences of such flagrant flaunting of Yahweh's sovereignty (31:29).

◆ X. The Song of Moses (31:30–32:43)
A. Invocation of Witnesses (31:30–32:4)

30So Moses recited this entire song publicly to the assembly of Israel:

CHAPTER 32

1"Listen, O heavens, and I will speak!
  Hear, O earth, the words that
    I say!
2Let my teaching fall on you like rain;
  let my speech settle like dew.

Let my words fall like rain on tender
    grass,
  like gentle showers on young plants.
3I will proclaim the name of the LORD;
  how glorious is our God!
4He is the Rock; his deeds are perfect.
  Everything he does is just and fair.
  He is a faithful God who does no wrong;
  how just and upright he is!

NOTES

32:3 the name. The Samaritan Pentateuch and Targum read "in the name," an unjustified and misleading alternative.

32:4 the Rock. The LXX, out of deference to the transcendence and ineffability of God, uses *theos* [TG2316, ZG2536] (God) to translate MT's "rock," a term considered too concrete or physical to describe the invisible and all-glorious one.

COMMENTARY

Having composed it, Moses began to proclaim publicly the words of the song of witness and continued until they had all been declared (31:30). Since his purpose was to teach it to them (31:19), he and others may have read it many times or, more likely, made copies for wider distribution and later memorization. The text of the song makes up most of the content of chapter 32.

In terms of literary genre the song of witness opens with what is commonly described as a "*rib*-pattern," that is, a formulaic presentation at home in a court of law (Huffmon 1959:288-289). The setting here has features of such an environment such as invocation of witnesses (32:1-4), the leveling of charges of wrongdoing (32:5-18), and the threat of judgment in historical times or (as in this case) in the eschaton (32:19-43). Ordinarily, of course, witnesses in such trials would be human beings, but in Old Testament covenant contexts (and even in ancient Near Eastern treaty texts) the witnesses are from another realm. In extrabiblical examples they are the various deities of the contracting parties, but since the Old Testament view is that such gods are nonexistent and, furthermore, Yahweh himself is a party to the covenant, the witnesses must be "the heavens and the earth"—a figurative way to include all creation (32:1; cf. 4:26; 31:28; Isa 1:2; Mic 1:2).

Beginning in 32:2, Moses addresses the assembly. His instruction, he says, will be "like rain," a simile designed to speak of its refreshing, renewing properties. In that land of scarce moisture, this was an especially apt metaphor. Moses understood Israel to be like vegetation that, though planted in fertile soil, struggled against the harsh elements of temptation and hostility. He wanted this song (and all his mediation of truth) to fall gently upon his people and to impart fresh hope and energy.

The fundamental message centers on God himself. The very proclamation of his name (32:3-4)—that is, who he is and what he has done and can do—is sufficient because it testifies to his greatness (thus *godel* [TH1433, ZH1542], v. 3), his stability (*tsur* [TH6697, ZH7446], lit., "a boulder," v. 4), the flawlessness (*tamim* [TH8549, ZH9459]) of his works, the propriety of his ways, his unimpeachable dependability (lit., "a God of faithfulness, without injustice"), and his justice (*tsaddiq weyashar* [TH6662/3477, ZH7404/3838]). All Israel needed to know was God, in all his perfections, because knowing him is to know oneself and how one must relate to and obey him. The same sentiment is expressed by Paul who said that "everything else is worthless when compared with the infinite value of knowing Christ Jesus my Lord" (Phil 3:8).

◆ B. The Indictment of God's People (32:5-6)

5 "But they have acted corruptly toward
    him;
when they act so perversely,
are they really his children?*
They are a deceitful and twisted
    generation.

6 Is this the way you repay the LORD,
    you foolish and senseless people?
Isn't he your Father who created
    you?
Has he not made you and
    established you?

32:5 The meaning of the Hebrew is uncertain.

NOTES
32:5 *acted corruptly.* The MT's "he acted corruptly" (*shikheth* [TH7843, ZH8845]) is rendered as a plural of the same root by the Samaritan Pentateuch (*shikhathu*), "they acted corruptly." This second reading is favored by the NLT and supported by the plural suffix on *mum* [TH3971, ZH4583] ("defect"; cf. NLT "perversely") and the plural "his children" (*banayw* [TH1121, ZH1201]).

COMMENTARY
Moses's pointed indictment of Israel comes early in the song of witness (32:5-6): The nation has become corrupt toward Yahweh, so much so that it is difficult to recognize them as his people. This seems to be the best way of understanding the highly elliptical *lo' banayw mumam* [TH3971, ZH4583] (lit., "not his children, their blemish"). Deep flaws in their character and behavior (cf. NLT's "perversely") preclude their being readily identified as members of God's family (Tigay 1996:301). Put succinctly, they are a perverted and twisted generation, one with a totally distorted view of God and life (32:5).

The incredible thing about this is that Israel has turned out this way despite Yahweh's lavish display of parental love (32:6). They have become a nation of absolute fools, a description not so much of their diminished intellectual capacity but of their spiritual status and sensitivity. After all, it is the fool who says within himself, "There is no God" (Ps 14:1). Such children cannot recognize their own Father, the very one who created them and, beyond that, who established them firmly in place as his elect people. This probably alludes to the original choice of the patriarchs and the eventual creation of a covenant with their descendants, a sequence suggested in 32:7-14.

◆ C. Recital of God's Past Benefits (32:7-14)

7 Remember the days of long ago;
    think about the generations past.
Ask your father, and he will inform
    you.
Inquire of your elders, and they will
    tell you.
8 When the Most High assigned lands to
    the nations,

when he divided up the human race,
he established the boundaries of the
    peoples
according to the number in his
    heavenly court.*

9 "For the people of Israel belong to the
    LORD;

Jacob is his special possession.
10 He found them in a desert land,
   in an empty, howling wasteland.
He surrounded them and watched
      over them;
   he guarded them as he would guard
      his own eyes.*
11 Like an eagle that rouses her chicks
      and hovers over her young,
   so he spread his wings to take them up
      and carried them safely on his
      pinions.
12 The LORD alone guided them;
   they followed no foreign gods.

13 He let them ride over the highlands
      and feast on the crops of the fields.
   He nourished them with honey from
      the rock
      and olive oil from the stony
      ground.
14 He fed them yogurt from the herd
      and milk from the flock,
   together with the fat of lambs.
   He gave them choice rams from
      Bashan, and goats,
      together with the choicest wheat.
   You drank the finest wine,
      made from the juice of grapes.

32:8 As in Dead Sea Scrolls, which read *the number of the sons of God*, and Greek version, which reads *the number of the angels of God;* Masoretic Text reads *the number of the sons of Israel.* 32:10 Hebrew *as the pupil of his eye.*

NOTES

32:7 *think about.* For the MT's second person masculine plural (*binu* [TH995, ZH1067]), the Syriac, Targum, and Vulgate have a second person masculine singular (*binah* or *bin*), a reading more amenable to the otherwise consistent use of the singular in this passage.

32:8 *the number in his heavenly court.* The MT has "the sons of Israel," to which the Targum Pseudo-Jonathan adds "70," that is, "70 sons of Israel." This refers, no doubt, to the 70 descendants of Jacob who settled in Egypt (Gen 46:27). The Qumran text 4QDeut^j (=4Q37) has *bene 'el* [TH1121/410A, ZH1201/446] or *bene 'elim*, both best understood as "sons of God" (cf. Ps 29:1). The LXX reads *angelōn theou* [TG32/2316, ZG34/2536] ("angels of God"). It seems best to retain the MT and to understand the couplet (32:8c-d) as describing the favored status of Israel around whose allocation all other nations are arranged.

32:9 *Israel.* The MT reads literally, "For the portion of Yahweh is his people; Jacob is the allotment of his inheritance." The Samaritan Pentateuch and LXX add "Israel" to the second line, and BHS suggests, in line with this: "The Lord's allotment is Jacob; the portion of his inheritance is Israel." The NLT adopts a similar reconstruction. However, the MT displays a chiastic structure in which "Jacob" matches "his people" and "allotment" matches "inheritance." Such a pattern may have overridden the poet's normal concern for parallelism.

COMMENTARY

In order to make his point about Yahweh's goodness to Israel in the past (see 32:6b), Moses provided a brief résumé of sacred history. He went to distant times, even before the patriarchal ancestors of Israel, to establish the fact that God already had Israel in mind when he set about to allocate territories and responsibilities to the nations of the earth. Verification of this, he said, can be obtained by turning to the oral traditions of the ancient among them, which would attest to the truth of what Moses was saying (32:7).

The antiquity of the tradition is underscored by the use of the divine name Elyon ("Most High"), here in its abbreviated form (without El; see elsewhere Num 24:16; 2 Sam 22:14; Isa 14:14; many psalms). God became known to Abraham by this name, as the one especially worshiped by Melchizedek (Gen 14:18). The reference to dividing up the human race (32:8) reminds one of the post-Babel distribution of the nations (Gen 11:8), the result of which is clarified in the so-called "Table of Nations" (Gen 10; cf. Merrill 1997:3-22). There it is clear that the descendants of Shem are central to the divine purpose (Gen 10:21-31; note "Eber" as the root of "Hebrew" in Gen 10:24-25). This is confirmed by a repetition and elaboration of Shem's genealogy in Genesis 11, one leading climactically to Abraham (Gen 11:26–12:1). All of this forms the background to Moses's observation that God had long before distributed the nations of the earth according to the principle of Israel's (see note on 32:8) centrality. That centrality is emphasized again in his following declaration that "the people of Israel belong to the LORD" and that "Jacob is his special possession" (32:9; cf. note).

Moses made the fine (and important) theological distinction between Israel's election through the call of the patriarchs in ancient times and the formation of Israel as a national entity as an aftermath of the Exodus. Israel, God's "son," had become Israel, God's servant nation (cf. Exod 2:24-25; 4:22-23; Isa 63:16-19; 64:8-9; Hos 11:1). Yahweh "found them" in the desert in the sense that they were a helpless and hopeless people who, without him, would surely have perished (cf. Ezek 16:1-14). He took them up in tender love, regarding them as the "pupil of his eye" (32:10; see NLT note; *'ishon 'eno* [TH380/5869, ZH413/6524] means, lit., "little man of his eye," that is, the pupil; cf. Ps 17:8; Prov 7:2).

The imagery of Yahweh's protective care continues under the simile of an eagle that hovers over her chicks to guard them from predators and other harm. Under greater threat, the eagle picks up the young and carries them off to safety (32:11). One thinks of the canopy of security afforded by the pillars of fire and cloud (Exod 13:21-22; 14:19-20; Pss 78:14; 105:39) and especially of Yahweh's having brought Israel to himself in the Exodus redemption and having carried them "on eagles' wings" (Exod 19:4). All of this was done by Yahweh alone, without the assistance of other gods (32:12). This last assertion does not presuppose the existence of other gods (see 32:37-39) but emphatically declares the solitary existence and sovereignty of Israel's God.

The scene shifts in 32:13 and 14, both geographically and historically. The setting is now in the Promised Land itself, and Moses views the future course of Israel's life there. Israel will (the Hebrew preterites following the initial imperfect have a future nuance) easily overcome the hill country of Canaan and there manage to prosper, despite the inhospitable conditions (32:13). The fields will yield abundant crops, the cliffs will contain deposits of honey (cf. Ps 81:16), and olive oil will flow from flint stone. This is an ellipsis for the idea that olive trees will be able to grow even on ledges in the Promised Land.

Domesticated agriculture will also thrive. Curds (lit., "weak butter"), milk, and the fattest of lambs, rams, and goats will be plentiful. The land of Bashan, in the northern Transjordan, was especially famous for its livestock, one reason the tribes of Reuben, Gad, and Manasseh asked Moses to be allowed to settle there (Num

32:1-5; cf. Ps 22:12; Isa 2:13; Ezek 27:6; 39:18). That and all of Canaan would provide bountifully, Moses said, not only meat and dairy products but wheat and wine of highest quality (32:14).

The point being made here is that the God who elected Israel (32:6-9), who rescued them from Egyptian bondage to form them into his own privileged people (32:10-12), and who then provided for their total well-being in the land flowing with milk and honey, had a right to expect them to reciprocate with appreciation, loyalty, and obedience. God's saving grace, though totally without preconditions, certainly deserves grateful response from its recipients. Sadly—as in Israel's case—such grace is met as often as not with indifference at best or outright rebellion and rejection at worst.

◆ D. Israel's Rebellion (32:15-18)

¹⁵ "But Israel* soon became fat and unruly;
   the people grew heavy, plump, and
   stuffed!
Then they abandoned the God who
   had made them;
   they made light of the Rock of their
   salvation.
¹⁶ They stirred up his jealousy by
   worshiping foreign gods;
   they provoked his fury with
   detestable deeds.

¹⁷ They offered sacrifices to demons,
   which are not God,
   to gods they had not known
   before,
   to new gods only recently arrived,
   to gods their ancestors had never
   feared.
¹⁸ You neglected the Rock who had
   fathered you;
   you forgot the God who had given
   you birth.

32:15 Hebrew *Jeshurun*, a term of endearment for Israel.

NOTES
32:15 *the people.* The MT reads "you" (sg.) as subject of the three predicates in this line, a "problem" corrected by the LXX to "he" and understood (correctly) by the NLT as a reference to Israel. However, fluctuations in grammatical person (such as in the MT here) are not uncommon in biblical Hebrew and usually cause no need for emendation.

32:16 *foreign gods.* The MT has only "alien (things)," clearly a reference to illicit deities. The Vulgate, in fact, supplies *diis* (gods).

COMMENTARY
From a description of God's gracious benefits throughout Israel's sacred history, the sentiment of the song shifts radically to Israel's response to the divine favor, a response both unexpected and inexplicable (32:15-18). To underscore the contrast between what the Lord had done and how Israel reciprocated, Moses employed the pet name "Jeshurun" to describe the covenant nation. Not only is it a term of tenderness, but it derives from a root (*yashar* [TH3474, ZH3837]) meaning "to be upright" (TDOT 6.472-477; cf. 33:5, 26; Isa 44:2). The irony is inescapable. The upright people had become anything but that, despite their being recipients of God's bountiful mercy and grace.

Rather than becoming strong and docile in the service of the Lord, Israel had become fat and rebellious (32:15). The image is that of a well-fed animal that refused to pull the load but instead kicked and stomped in rebellion. Like a beast of burden whose energy should have been employed in the service of the farmer but, to the contrary, was converted into self-indulgence, so Israel gave herself up to luxury, indolence, and indifference. Soon the gift became more important than the Giver, and the benefits of grace outweighed the God who had freely bestowed them. The Creator (God) and Redeemer (the Rock, cf. 32:4) was supplanted by his own largess to his ungrateful people.

To compound the tragedy of unrequited love, Israel had attributed all of Yahweh's bounties to other gods, acknowledging their existence and committing abominable things in their honor (32:16). The reference to God's jealousy being aroused as Israel went after foreign gods (see note on 32:16) brings to mind immediately the first two commandments, which, as we have seen, lay at the very foundation of the covenant relationship (cf. 5:7-10). The sacrifice to demons (32:17; *shedim* [TH7700, ZH8717], i.e., vapid, powerless spirits; NIDOTTE 4.48; cf. Ps 106:37)—which Moses called "non-gods" because they were creations of depraved imagination—was an act of the worship of gods Israel had never encountered before. Their ancient ancestors had never heard of such deities, for Israel had only recently come to know them. Who or what these "new" gods were is unclear, but Moses may well have had in mind the golden calf (Exod 32:1-8) or the Baal of Peor (Num 25:1-3). Whatever the case, Israel had embraced these newfound pagan deities and, in doing so, had betrayed the very God who had fathered them, the Rock, who was the foundation of their covenant faith (32:18). The image of God as father—rare in the Old Testament (see 32:6; cf. Exod 4:22; Jer 3:19-20; Hos 11:1-3)—is paired here with the even rarer idea of mothering, as the verb "had given you birth" (*mekholeleka* [TH2342A, ZH2655], "having labor pains," 32:18) makes clear (Brueggemann 1997:245). God thus played the role of both father and mother in bringing Israel into existence, a parental act of love that Israel spurned in her pursuit of other gods.

◆   E. A Promise of Judgment (32:19-25)

19 "The LORD saw this and drew back,
      provoked to anger by his own sons
      and daughters.
20 He said, 'I will abandon them;
      then see what becomes of them.
   For they are a twisted generation,
      children without integrity.
21 They have roused my jealousy by
      worshiping things that are
      notGod;
   they have provoked my anger with
      their useless idols.

Now I will rouse their jealousy through
   people who are not even a people;
I will provoke their anger through
   the foolish Gentiles.
22 For my anger blazes forth like fire
      and burns to the depths of the grave.*
   It devours the earth and all its crops
      and ignites the foundations of the
      mountains.
23 I will heap disasters upon them
      and shoot them down with my
      arrows.

²⁴I will weaken them with famine,
burning fever, and deadly disease.
I will send the fangs of wild beasts
and poisonous snakes that glide in
the dust.

²⁵Outside, the sword will bring death,
and inside, terror will strike
both young men and young
women,
both infants and the aged.

32:22 Hebrew *of Sheol.*

COMMENTARY

The flagrant disloyalty described by Moses would not remain unanswered. The God of bountiful grace is also the God of unimpeachable justice and holiness; when those facets of his character are denigrated and despised, he must—to be true to himself—react in righteous wrath (32:19-25). When these children of his, whom he had brought into the world and nourished, would betray him, they would also set themselves up for parental discipline of the most serious kind. Inflamed by contempt and loathing, the Lord determined to discipline his children with the harshest punishment, even going so far as to turn his back on (lit., "hide his face from") them (32:19-20a). He would let them go their own way and find out for themselves what it is to live without God. They had become a people having no faith in God.

Repeating the accusation of 32:16, Moses (speaking for the Lord) referred to Yahweh's jealousy engendered by Israel's idolatry (32:21). The incident particularly in mind was likely that of the golden calf (cf. Exod 32:1-6), an act of idolatry that roused his jealousy (cf. Exod 34:14) and nearly terminated his covenant relationship with the people (Exod 32:7-14). That incident was only paradigmatic of others that Moses foresaw. The idolatrous behavior that would stir the Lord to jealousy would also make Israel jealous. But the two jealousies are different: The use of the verb *qana'* [TH7065, ZH7861] (NIDOTTE 3.938) cleverly distinguishes between the Lord's jealousy, which springs out of his rightful demand for exclusive worship (cf. 5:9), and Israel's jealousy, which is envy over God's goodness to another people (32:21b). God had been made jealous by Israel's worship of "non-gods" (32:21a); Israel would be made jealous by Yahweh's acceptance of a "non-people" (*lo'-'am* [TH3808/5971A, ZH4202/6639]; 32:21b). These "non-people" would be the Gentile nations, people whom Yahweh would bring within the orbit of his saving grace and call "my people" (*'ammi* [TH5971A, ZH6639]), a prophecy greatly advanced and clarified by Hosea (Hos 2:23; cf. Rom 9:19-26).

This drastic action would be an expression of God's wrath, an anger so profound and universal as to extend to Sheol (or "the grave," as in NLT), the very heart of the earth. Even the dead, as it were, could not escape it (32:22a). Like a fire, it would consume everything in its path, the earth and everything in it (32:22b). Though hyperbolic, these threats were not to be taken lightly. Harmful effects of all kinds would come, shot like arrows from Yahweh's bow of judgment (32:23). There would be famine, plague, and disease, as well as attacks by wild and venomous animals (32:24), the ravages of military conquest, and domestic crime and violence (32:25a). No one would escape—all genders and ages alike would experience Yahweh's awful retributive justice (32:25b).

◆ F. The Impotence of Heathen Gods (32:26–38)

26 I would have annihilated them,
   wiping out even the memory of them.
27 But I feared the taunt of Israel's
   enemy,
   who might misunderstand and say,
   "Our own power has triumphed!
   The LORD had nothing to do with
   this!'"
28 "But Israel is a senseless nation;
   the people are foolish, without
   understanding.
29 Oh, that they were wise and could
   understand this!
   Oh, that they might know their fate!
30 How could one person chase a
   thousand of them,
   and two people put ten thousand to
   flight,
   unless their Rock had sold them,
   unless the LORD had given them up?
31 But the rock of our enemies is not like
   our Rock,
   as even they recognize.*
32 Their vine grows from the vine of
   Sodom,
   from the vineyards of Gomorrah.
   Their grapes are poison,

and their clusters are bitter.
33 Their wine is the venom of serpents,
   the deadly poison of cobras.

34 "The LORD says, 'Am I not storing up
   these things,
   sealing them away in my treasury?
35 I will take revenge; I will pay them
   back.
   In due time their feet will slip.
   Their day of disaster will arrive,
   and their destiny will overtake
   them.'

36 "Indeed, the LORD will give justice to
   his people,
   and he will change his mind about*
   his servants,
   when he sees their strength is gone
   and no one is left, slave or free.
37 Then he will ask, 'Where are their gods,
   the rocks they fled to for refuge?
38 Where now are those gods,
   who ate the fat of their sacrifices
   and drank the wine of their
   offerings?
   Let those gods arise and help you!
   Let them provide you with shelter!

32:31 The meaning of the Hebrew is uncertain. Greek version reads *our enemies are fools.* 32:36 Or *will take revenge for.*

NOTES

32:26 *I would have annihilated.* The MT's *'ap'ehem* (from *pa'ah* [TH6284, ZH6990]) means "I will chop them up," a meaning rejected by the LXX, which presupposes *'apitsem* [TH6327, ZH7046], "I will scatter them." The verb presupposed in the LXX is more in line with standard curse formulae (cf. 4:27; 28:64).

32:29 *Oh.* Instead of the MT's interjection *lu* [TH3863, ZH4273], other Hebrew mss, the Samaritan Pentateuch, and LXX read the negative particle *lo'* [TH3808, ZH4202], "they are not wise."

32:34 *storing.* For the hapax legomenon *kamus* [TH3647, ZH4022] (store up), the Samaritan Pentateuch has *kanus* [TH3664, ZH4043] (gather), a much more commonly attested verb. The rarity of the MT reading is, however, no reason to disqualify it as the original; in fact, it favors it as such.

32:35 *I will pay them back.* The problematic form *shillem* [TH7999, ZH8966], if a finite verb, requires, in this context, the addition of a first person singular pronominal prefix, thus, *'ashallem* [TH7999, ZH8966] (I will recompense). However, by a slight repointing, it could also be construed as an infinitive absolute with the same meaning. BHS suggests a repointing to *shillum* [TH7966, ZH8936], "retribution," a noun found also in Hos 9:7 and Mic 7:3. The meaning is unaffected in any case.

COMMENTARY

As the culmination of Yahweh's judgment against Israel (32:26-38), he would determine to pulverize (see note on 32:26) them so that they no longer existed. Should he do that, however, he would be liable to the charge of his enemies that he was a weak and unreliable God, one unable to keep his promises to his people that he would lead them into their inheritance (32:27). The Lord's "anxiety" over his being misrepresented is, of course, an anthropomorphism, for he has no fear of any human response. Rather, his concern is for his own people's embarrassment at having to concede that maybe their God was, indeed, inferior to those of the nations. Moses had previously used this line of argument with Yahweh when he had threatened to disinherit Israel and prevent them from entering Canaan (9:25-29; cf. Exod 32:7-14).

Israel's tendency to be in awe of the gods of the surrounding nations could be attributed only to her lack of clear direction and spiritual understanding (32:28). They represented the classic definition of a fool: one who denies the existence or at least the significance of the one true God (Ps 14:1). This was not because God had failed to reveal himself to them—in fact, he did so over and over—but because they would not open themselves to that revelation and its demands on their life. With almost tangible pathos, Yahweh laments Israel's folly; in strikingly human terms and tones, he expresses his wish that they might be otherwise—so that they might understand their deplorable spiritual condition and the inevitable judgment that awaits them (32:29).

In a dramatic reversal of the promise that "Five of you [Israelites] will chase a hundred [of the enemy], and a hundred of you will chase ten thousand" (Lev 26:8), the Lord threatens that without his protection Israel's enemies will need only one to chase a thousand of them or two to pursue ten thousand (32:30). They had already been defeated by inferior forces at Hormah, for example (cf. Num 14:39-45), and this was only a portent of future disaster should God, their Rock, deliver them over to other foes in days to come. When that happened, they must acknowledge that it was not because of Yahweh's inability to defend them but because he had abandoned them.

Indeed, the gods of the enemy nations (their rocks) could not even compare to Yahweh, the Rock of Israel, as even their worshipers must acknowledge. These enemies themselves are judges (32:31; thus *pelilim* [TH6414, ZH7130]; NIDOTTE 3.628) of history who, when confronted with the evidence, must render a verdict in Yahweh's favor: Only he is God when it comes to a test of strength (cf. Exod 14:4, 25). The reason for their impotence is that these gods sprang, like a vine, from Sodom and Gomorrah (32:32). This metaphor draws attention to the debauchery of these cities of the Dead Sea plains, the epitome of all that was immoral, reprobate, and anti-God (Gen 19:1-28; cf. Isa 1:10; 3:9; Jer 23:14; Lam 4:6; Ezek 16:44-52; Matt 10:15; 11:23-24). The fruit they produce is poisonous, and their wine is like snake's venom (32:33). Behind the imagery is the reality that those who worship such gods eat and drink damnation to themselves (Driver 1902:372).

The judgment on idolatry may not come all at once or even in the near future. One thing is sure, however: It will come. The Lord speaks again and says that he takes note of Israel's idolatry and other sins and "stores them up"—that is, he retains them in his memory (32:34; cf. note). Moreover, judgment is also reserved in his armory, from whence he will unleash it in the day of reckoning. He will some day consummate all things by the exercise of his retribution (32:35a). The Rock will then slip out from under his rebellious people, and they will totter in the face of onrushing and inescapable disaster. Then he will regret that Israel was ever his people, and when they are at their weakest—so much so that virtually none are left ("slave or free," a merism for the whole people)—he will offer no help (32:36). To the contrary, he will taunt them about the gods they had chosen in preference to him. Having gone after them, Israel in distress should cry out to them for deliverance (32:37).

Such a plea will be in vain, however, for those gods that were so real in times of peace and plenty and to whom they catered by sacrifice and ritual will prove, in the hour of extremity, to be evanescent, without substance or even existence (32:38). When the roof of their idolatrous patterns of life crashes down on them, they will find that their imaginary gods can provide neither solace nor shelter.

◆   ## G. The Lord's Vindication (32:39-43)

39 Look now; I myself am he!
   There is no other god but me!
   I am the one who kills and gives life;
   I am the one who wounds and
      heals;
   no one can be rescued from my
      powerful hand!
40 Now I raise my hand to heaven
   and declare, "As surely as I live,
41 when I sharpen my flashing sword
   and begin to carry out justice,
   I will take revenge on my enemies
   and repay those who reject me.
42 I will make my arrows drunk with
      blood,
   and my sword will devour flesh—

the blood of the slaughtered and the
      captives,
   and the heads of the enemy leaders.'"
43 "Rejoice with him, you heavens,
   and let all of God's angels worship
      him.*
Rejoice with his people, you nations,
   and let all the angels be
      strengthened in him.*
For he will avenge the blood of his
      servants;
   he will take revenge against his
      enemies.
He will repay those who hate him*
   and cleanse the land for his people."

32:43a As in Dead Sea Scrolls and Greek version; Masoretic Text lacks the first two lines. Compare Heb 1:6.
32:43b As in Greek version; Hebrew text lacks this line.   32:43c As in Dead Sea Scrolls and Greek version;
Masoretic Text lacks this line.

NOTES
32:43 As noted in NLT mg, the NLT here follows a DSS manuscript (4QDeutq) and the LXX instead of the MT. This means that the NLT has "heavens" instead of "nations," and includes two lines not found in the MT: "and let all of God's angels worship him" (cf. Heb 1:6) and "He will repay those who hate him."

COMMENTARY

Having shown in unmistakable terms that the gods of the nations that were so attractive to Israel were powerless and, in fact, nonexistent, Yahweh once more presents himself as the one true God, the only one in whom Israel can find deliverance and ultimate restoration (32:39-43). This text—one of the most unambiguous affirmations of monotheism in the Bible (Cairns 1992:288; cf. also Isa 41:4; 43:10; 45:5-6)—not only affirms Yahweh's ontological uniqueness but attributes to him sovereign omnipotence. He kills and gives life, wounds and heals (32:39). The reason for this order (rather than "gives life and kills," etc.) is that Israel in apostate rebellion will be as good as dead and therefore will need virtual resurrection.

The threat of judgment on Israel is tempered by God's irrevocable promises of covenant fidelity. Israel may (and, indeed, will) sin and go into exile, but as surely as Yahweh is God, he will effect a spirit of repentance within them and will restore them to covenant fellowship and obedience (28:1-14; cf. Lev 26:40-45; Jer 31:31-37; Ezek 36:8-31). In a gesture of oath making, he raises his hand and swears by his own eternal existence that he will carry out his purposes of vindication and salvation (32:40).

But before his people can be redeemed, Yahweh must deal with their (and his) enemies. Those very nations whom God would use to carry off his people (cf. 28:25-46) will themselves be condemned and sentenced to death. Typical of them will be Assyria, about whom Isaiah speaks:

> What trouble awaits Assyria, the rod of my anger. I use it as a club to express my anger. I am sending Assyria against a godless nation, against a people with whom I am angry. Assyria will plunder them, trampling them like dirt beneath its feet. But the king of Assyria will not understand that he is my tool; his mind does not work that way. His plan is simply to destroy, to cut down nation after nation. . . . After the Lord has used the king of Assyria to accomplish his purposes on Mount Zion and in Jerusalem, he will turn against the king of Assyria and punish him— for he is proud and arrogant. (Isa 10:5-7, 12)

In grossly graphic terms Yahweh describes his arrows as being intoxicated with blood and his sword gorged on human flesh irrespective of rank (32:42).

Moses concluded the song of witness with an invitation to heaven itself to join in a great anthem of praise to the Lord (32:43). He had begun the song with an appeal to the universe to bear witness to the mutual covenant commitments made by Yahweh and Israel (32:1). He now comes full circle and exhorts it to celebrate God's faithful consummation of all things, a finale marked by vengeance on his enemies and full restoration of his chosen people Israel. The song, dominated in terms of length by Israel's sorry history of unfaithfulness, sounds out at the same time the counter-theme of Yahweh's grace. Israel would surely fail, but this song of witness, which would painfully remind her of her failure, would also testify to the amazing grace of the one who had first called the nation to be a kingdom of priests and a holy nation.

◆ XI. Narrative Interlude (32:44-52)

⁴⁴So Moses came with Joshua* son of Nun and recited all the words of this song to the people.

⁴⁵When Moses had finished reciting all these words to the people of Israel, ⁴⁶he added: "Take to heart all the words of warning I have given you today. Pass them on as a command to your children so they will obey every word of these instructions. ⁴⁷These instructions are not empty words— they are your life! By obeying them you will enjoy a long life in the land you will occupy when you cross the Jordan River."

⁴⁸That same day the LORD said to Moses, ⁴⁹"Go to Moab, to the mountains east of the river,* and climb Mount Nebo, which is across from Jericho. Look out across the land of Canaan, the land I am giving to the people of Israel as their own special possession. ⁵⁰Then you will die there on the mountain. You will join your ancestors, just as Aaron, your brother, died on Mount Hor and joined his ancestors. ⁵¹For both of you betrayed me with the Israelites at the waters of Meribah at Kadesh* in the wilderness of Zin. You failed to demonstrate my holiness to the people of Israel there. ⁵²So you will see the land from a distance, but you may not enter the land I am giving to the people of Israel."

32:44 Hebrew *Hoshea*, a variant name for Joshua.   32:49 Hebrew *the mountains of Abarim*.   32:51 Hebrew *waters of Meribath-kadesh*.

NOTES

32:51 *me.* LXX reads "my word" for "me," thereby diminishing the role of Moses himself as the source of divine authority. The more difficult MT is preferable.

COMMENTARY

Upon the completion of the text of the "Song of Witness" (32:1-43), Moses and Joshua (Hoshea in the Hebrew text) addressed the assembly once more, this time to teach the song to them (32:44; cf. 31:30). Having done so, Moses reiterated to the people the significance of its message, not only in terms of its content but regarding what it symbolized as a document. "Take to heart all the words," he said to them (32:46). The appeal is reminiscent of the command Moses gave the people to let the words of the Shema be upon their hearts—that is, to be part and parcel of who they were (6:6). The comparison of the two occasions extends also to the passing on of the message to future generations (32:46; cf. 6:7). The purpose in each case is to elicit obedience to the full body of covenant requirements (cf. 4:9).

The reason for such intense commitment to both song and Shema is that they are not mere empty shells into which one may pour whatever content he wishes. To the contrary, their divinely originated messages are life itself! That is, they are the channel through which Yahweh reveals the secret of successful life and prosperity. "In this thing," the text literally says, is length of life in the land that the people were about to enter and acquire as the legacy promised to their patriarchs in ancient times (32:47). The "thing," also to be rendered "word," is the whole sum and substance of the covenant document Moses had been proclaiming in their hearing (32:46).

Before that day was over, Yahweh summoned Moses to his long-announced appointment with death (32:48; cf. 3:27; Num 27:12-14). Moses had represented Israel before Pharaoh at the time of the plagues, he had led the way through the sea at the Exodus, he had mediated between Yahweh and Israel at the giving of the Sinaitic covenant, and he had brought them through the deserts to the present moment of assembly near the Jordan River. For one indiscretion, however, that of striking the rock in impatient rage (Num 20:10-13), he would be denied access to Canaan and, instead, would die and be buried in the Transjordan (see comments on 3:23-29).

The severity of that sentence was mitigated somewhat by Moses's opportunity to view the Promised Land from Mount Nebo (32:49). This imposing peak, part of the Abarim range (see NLT note and Num 27:12; 33:47-48), was either equivalent to Mount Pisgah (3:17, 27; Num 21:20; 23:14) or a promontory of a collection of mountains known as Pisgah (4:49; Bimson 1995:225). From Nebo, on a clear day, one can see Mount Hermon to the north, the Mediterranean Sea to the west, and deep into the Negev to the south. The panorama spread before him must have filled Moses with both unbounded delight at the prospects for his people and deep regret and sadness that he could not personally experience what had long been before promised to his ancestors.

Less for Moses's sake than for Israel's (and ours), Yahweh reiterated the pronouncement of Moses's death, comparing it to that of his brother Aaron, who had also been buried on a mountain (10:6; Num 20:28; 33:38) and who had been denied access to Canaan because of his role in Israel's pattern of rebellion against Yahweh (Num 20:12, 24). The sin of both men was not so much that of overt, aggressive deeds of evil but passive failure to manifest Yahweh's glory (32:51; *lo'-qiddashtem 'othi* [TH6942, ZH7727], lit., "you did not sanctify me") in the presence of Israel earlier in the wilderness: The water of life would have gushed forth at the mere speaking of the prophetic word—thus magnifying the powerful provision of Yahweh—but Moses struck the rock to get the precious liquid, drawing attention to himself in the process (Harrison 1990:267; cf. Num 20:8, 11-12).

In somber words of crushing finality, the Lord issued his last invitation and prohibition to Moses: "You will see the land" but "you may not enter" (32:52). The word of judgment tinged with a note of grace makes the point, one made already, that great leadership privilege carries with it awesome leadership responsibility. Failure to discharge that responsibility often results in revocation of the privilege (cf. 3:26-27).

◆ XII. The Blessing of Moses (33:1-29)
A. Introduction to Moses's Blessing of the Tribes (33:1-5)

This is the blessing that Moses, the man of God, gave to the people of Israel before his death:

² "The LORD came from Mount Sinai
   and dawned upon us* from Mount Seir;

he shone forth from Mount Paran
   and came from Meribah-kadesh
   with flaming fire at his right hand.*
³ Indeed, he loves his people;*
   all his holy ones are in his hands.
They follow in his steps
   and accept his teaching.

⁴Moses gave us the LORD's instruction,
    the special possession of the people
    of Israel.*
⁵The LORD became king in Israel*—

when the leaders of the people
    assembled,
when the tribes of Israel gathered
    as one."

33:2a As in Greek and Syriac versions; Hebrew reads *upon them.* 33:2b Or *came from myriads of holy ones, from the south, from his mountain slopes.* The meaning of the Hebrew is uncertain. 33:3 As in Greek version; Hebrew reads *Indeed, lover of the peoples.* 33:4 Hebrew *of Jacob.* The names "Jacob" and "Israel" are often interchanged throughout the Old Testament, referring sometimes to the individual patriarch and sometimes to the nation. 33:5 Hebrew *in Jeshurun,* a term of endearment for Israel.

NOTES

33:2 us. For the MT's *lamo* [TH3807.1/4123.1, ZH4200/4564], "to him," the LXX and its dependents read *hēmin* [TG1473, ZG1609] (to us). Since Israel is clearly the referent in the MT, the singular, viewed as a collective, is quite appropriate in translation.

Meribah-kadesh. This reading requires a slight emendation of *meribeboth qodesh* [TH4480/7233/6944, ZH4946/8047/7731], "ten thousand holy (ones)," to *mimribath qadesh* [TH4809A, ZH5315]. The emended form provides a better parallelism with the place name "Mount Paran," but the context of holy war in which Yahweh leads his heavenly hosts favors the MT: "[He] came with myriads of holy ones [i.e., the angelic host]."

flaming fire at his right hand. The NLT reflects *mimino 'ishedeth* [TH799A, ZH—] ("throwing of fire," i.e., flashes of lightning), a vocalization of the MT suggested by Keil and Delitzsch (n.d.:1008; comments on 33:2). The MT Qere, *'esh dath* [TH784/1881, ZH836/2017] ("a fiery law," KJV), is difficult and perhaps a corruption of *'ashedoth* [TH794, ZH844], "mountain slopes," thus the verse would read, "with the mountain slopes at his right hand." The difficulty has given rise to various suggested emendations such as *mimino 'esh lapidoth* or *mimino 'esh doleqeth* (or *yoqedeth*), speaking of "flaming" or "burning" fires respectively. The LXX (supported by the NT; cf. Acts 7:53; Gal 3:19; Heb 2:2) instead reads "angels with him." The holy war imagery of the passage gives some credence to this latter interpretation. However, on balance the theophanic elements of the verse tilt the meaning toward the NLT rendering.

COMMENTARY

Moses, having heard for the last time that his death was imminent, pronounced a blessing upon his covenant "children," the nation of Israel, just as Jacob had done centuries before as he lay on his deathbed surrounded by his sons, the ancestors of Israel's twelve tribes (33:1; cf. Gen 49:1). In a very real sense, Moses was as much a father to the covenant people as Jacob had been; so, in line with ancient patriarchal tradition, he had the responsibility of outlining to each of the tribes their destined roles and outcomes. This suggests that the blessings were not merely expressions of hope but, in the case of Jacob and Moses, at least, genuine words of prophecy (Thompson 1974:306).

The efficacy of the blessing and its fulfillment lay not in Moses or in any human authority but in Yahweh himself. Thus, the blessing section is prefaced by a description of Yahweh, who, with his innumerable heavenly army (see notes on 33:2), is seen riding in brilliant splendor from Sinai, Seir, and Paran (regarding Meribah-kadesh, see note on 33:2). The poetic nature of this epiphany precludes the need for geographic or directional precision as though God's route was from Sinai in the south to Seir in the northeast and then back to Kadesh via Paran.

Rather, these are all places (perhaps to be understood synonymously; Cross 1973:86) where God revealed himself or displayed his glory in some significant way (cf. Exod 19:16-19; Deut 1:44; Num 14:10, respectively).

The central motif of the passage is the giving of the covenant law. Moses speaks of Yahweh as loving (*khabab* [TH2245, ZH2462]) "(the) people(s)" (33:3), a term in synonymous parallelism with his "holy ones" and thus referring to Israel as the object of divine election. The Septuagint, in fact, reads "his people," removing any possible ambiguity as to the people in view (NIDOTTE 2.3; cf. 7:6-8 and the synonymous verb *'ahab* [TH157, ZH170]). He is also described as keeping them in his protective power. Reciprocally, Israel attentively heard and received the words of covenant relationship (33:3). These words of instruction (*torah* [TH8451, ZH9368]) were revealed to Israel exclusively and became her exclusive possession (33:4). This notion of Israel as a chosen vessel charged with custodial responsibility for God's self-revelation is pervasive in Deuteronomy and, in fact, explains the purpose of the Deuteronomic covenant in the first place (cf. 4:20, 32-40; 7:6-11; 14:2).

The ultimate guarantee of the fulfillment of the blessings that follow is God's sovereignty over the coalition of tribes that, at Sinai, became a solidified entity. When they became a nation, he became enthroned as their king in a formal manner. The covenant text was the document that regulated that newly formulated status. Such blessings may be only wishes in the mouths of even mighty men like Moses. Backed by divine, omnipotent sovereignty, however, these blessings became foregone conclusions.

◆ B. The Blessing of Reuben (33:6)

⁶Moses said this about the tribe of Reuben:*

"Let the tribe of Reuben live and not die out,

though they are few in number."

33:6 Hebrew lacks *Moses said this about the tribe of Reuben.*

COMMENTARY

Appropriately enough, the first tribe singled out for blessing is Reuben, the descendants of Jacob's eldest son (33:6). He also appears first in Jacob's blessing (Gen 49:3-4), but there the word is one of condemnation and disqualification from the rights of the firstborn because of his incestuous relations with one of Jacob's wives. The result was a weakening of Reuben that called now for merciful extension of life.

◆ C. The Blessing of Judah (33:7)

⁷Moses said this about the tribe of Judah:

"O LORD, hear the cry of Judah and bring them together as a people.

Give them strength to defend their cause; help them against their enemies!"

COMMENTARY

In Jacob's blessing, Judah comes fourth in order, following Simeon and Levi (Gen 49:5-12). It seems that the reason for Judah's special significance is that Simeon, Levi, and Reuben, though older than Judah, were disqualified from the place of the eldest son for various kinds of disobedience, thus leaving Judah in the place of primacy. Moses presupposes Simeon and Levi's displacement and elevates Judah above them in the list without comment (33:7). The elevation of Judah also came with an apparent messianic prophecy (Gen 49:10), though that is not reflected in Moses's words here. Anticipating the rupture of the kingdom after Solomon's death, Moses prayed that Judah might survive alone and, at last, might be rejoined to "their people," that is, to united Israel (Driver 1902:396-397).

◆   D. The Blessing of Levi (33:8-11)

8Moses said this about the tribe of Levi:

"O LORD, you have given your
    Thummim and Urim—the sacred
    lots—
to your faithful servants the Levites.*
You put them to the test at Massah
    and struggled with them at the
    waters of Meribah.
9The Levites obeyed your word
    and guarded your covenant.
They were more loyal to you
    than to their own parents.
They ignored their relatives
    and did not acknowledge their
    own children.

10They teach your regulations to
    Jacob;
they give your instructions
    to Israel.
They present incense before you
    and offer whole burnt offerings
    on the altar.
11Bless the ministry of the Levites,
    O LORD,
    and accept all the work of their
    hands.
Hit their enemies where it hurts the
    most;
    strike down their foes so they never
    rise again."

33:8 As in Greek version; Hebrew lacks *the Levites.*

COMMENTARY

The earlier "blessing" of Levi by Jacob was, in fact, no blessing at all because of Levi's violent attack against the Shechemites, an act not divinely sanctioned no matter its apparent justification (Gen 49:5-7; cf. Gen 34:1-31). Simeon also participated in effecting vengeance and, like Levi, received no paternal favor. Moses, however, had the benefit of a fuller history, one in which Levi could be seen in a much better light (33:8-11).

First, Levi had been chosen as the priestly tribe, the one entrusted with the ministry of mediation between the Lord and the whole nation. This involved leadership in the priesthood and its proper operation, the pronouncement of blessing over the people, instruction in Torah, and determination of God's will in critical moments in Israel's life and history. The latter is summed up here in the statement that Yahweh gave the "sacred lots" (i.e., the Urim and Thummim; cf. Exod 28:30; Num 27:21; 1 Sam 28:6) to Levi and thus made this tribe a vehicle of receiving special revelation.

Moreover, at Massah (*massah* [TH4532/5254, ZH5001/5814]), the "testing place," and at Meribah (*meribah* [TH4809/7379, ZH5313/8190]), the "place of contention," Levi was representatively put to the test and proved worthy in the acts of its greatest member, Moses (Exod 17:1-7). It is true that the incident in question—the smiting of the rock to procure water at Rephidim—was one in which God was put on trial and not Levi (Exod 17:7). However, Moses was on the spot, as it were, and he proved his faith and worthiness as a leader by striking the rock and obtaining the water. In Moses, then, Levi demonstrated the ability to stand the test of both public criticism and divine challenge.

Another historical witness to Levi's loyalty to Yahweh is implicit in 33:9. The allusion to the zeal of the tribe in taking vengeance on their own Israelite kinfolk because of their superior devotion to the Lord calls to mind the story of the golden calf (Exod 32:1-29; von Rad 1966a:206). Ironically, Aaron the high priest, and thus a Levite himself, had taken the lead in the idolatry involved (Exod 32:2-4), but when the matter came to a head and God's judgment fell, it was the Levites who volunteered to carry out that judgment (Exod 32:25-29). Moses had said, "Go back and forth from one end of the camp to the other. Kill everyone—even your brothers, friends, and neighbors" (Exod 32:27), a command the Levites carried out to the extent of killing 3,000.

In light of this record of past performance, Moses entreated the Lord to bless Levi by allowing them to continue their ministries of teaching (Lev 10:11; cf. Deut 17:8-13; 31:9-13) and offering sacrifices (33:10; cf. Lev 9:1-24). The whole range of their responsibilities is summed up in the phrase "all the work of their hands" (33:11). The plea continues with Moses's solicitation of God's protection of Levi in the future. In imprecatory language, he urged Yahweh to destroy all who would set themselves up in opposition to the priestly tribe (33:11).

◆   ## E. The Blessing of Benjamin (33:12)

¹²Moses said this about the tribe of Benjamin:

"The people of Benjamin are loved by
    the LORD

and live in safety beside him.
He surrounds them continuously
    and preserves them from every
    harm."

COMMENTARY

Though Benjamin, as Jacob's youngest son, appears last in the list of the brothers in Genesis 49—and furthermore in a negative light—his tribe follows that of Levi in Moses's blessing (33:12). Moreover, Judah and Benjamin, later to make up the two elements of the southern kingdom, are separated also only by Levi. The structure of the blessing in Deuteronomy, then, appears designed not only to list the tribes by priority (except for Reuben; see comments on 33:6) but also in a generally geographical order from south to north. In light of this, the location of Levi in the list may be explained by Levi's principal residence in Jerusalem, right between Judah and Benjamin. In any event, Benjamin appears here as greatly favored by Yahweh (lit., "the beloved of Yahweh"), a people who will enjoy his protective cover. In intimate terms, Moses spoke of Benjamin's dwelling place as, literally, "between [Yahweh's] shoulders," a description reminiscent of the closeness of John the apostle to the Lord Jesus (John 13:23). Strikingly, in that New Testament text, John, like Benjamin, is known as the beloved one.

◆   F. The Blessing of Joseph (33:13-17)

¹³Moses said this about the tribes of Joseph:

"May their land be blessed by the LORD
with the precious gift of dew from the heavens
and water from beneath the earth;
¹⁴with the rich fruit that grows in the sun,
and the rich harvest produced each month;
¹⁵with the finest crops of the ancient mountains,
and the abundance from the everlasting hills;

¹⁶with the best gifts of the earth and its bounty,
and the favor of the one who appeared in the burning bush.
May these blessings rest on Joseph's head,
crowning the brow of the prince among his brothers.
¹⁷Joseph has the majesty of a young bull;
he has the horns of a wild ox.
He will gore distant nations,
driving them to the ends of the earth.
This is my blessing for the multitudes of Ephraim
and the thousands of Manasseh."

NOTES

33:17 *young bull.* The MT reads something like "his firstborn bull" (RSV) or "the firstborn of his ox" (NASB), though the syntax is awkward and hence most versions, like the NLT, do not translate the suffix meaning "his." Though "firstborn" does not inherently mean "young," the strength and vitality of the bull here suggests at least its prime of life.

COMMENTARY

The tribe of Joseph comes next in Moses's list in line with the observation that the order follows a generally south to north pattern (33:13-17). Understandably, Joseph enjoys an inordinately rich expression of blessing from his dying father Jacob (Gen 49:22-26), for, as the ancient narratives consistently attest, Joseph was the favorite son (Gen 37:3; 44:20). The predictions about Joseph reveal a future filled with prosperity and power. Settled in the heart of the Promised Land, the tribe would be the seat of political dominance.

As it turned out, there was no tribe of Joseph per se, for in order to retain a twelve-tribe confederation, Joseph was divided into two clans, Ephraim and Manasseh, to make up for the fact that the tribe of Levi had no territory of its own (cf. 18:1-2; Josh 14:1-5). This was already anticipated in the bestowal of Jacob's private blessing on Joseph's two sons from whom the clans of Ephraim and Manasseh sprang (Gen 48). Between them, these two occupied the entire central hill country of Canaan, from

Benjamin in the south to the plain of Jezreel in the north. In addition, half of Manasseh settled in a vast region in the northern part of the Transjordan (3:13-15; cf. Num 32:33-42).

The lands to be assigned to Joseph were not only expansive but productive. Watered by both rain and springs (33:13), the warmth of its sunshine would guarantee year-round crops (33:14), especially those like grapes and olives that abounded in the hills and valleys of central Canaan (33:15). All these good things—the best the earth could produce—would be testimony to the good pleasure of Yahweh, he who revealed himself (lit., "who dwells") in the (burning) bush. This curious way of referring to the Lord draws attention to the origins of the covenant relationship. It was from the midst of the bush that God had called out to Moses, commanding him to lead Israel from Egyptian bondage and to make a covenant with him at Sinai (Exod 3:1-12; 6:7-8). Furthermore, the "good pleasure" (NLT, "favor") of the Lord toward Joseph (and by extension, all Israel) carries heavy overtones of election, for he chose them as unique recipients of his covenant grace (cf. Isa 60:10; 61:2).

The political eminence of Joseph emerges in 33:16b, which asserts the blessing of coronation. Joseph had long ago predicted that his brothers would bow down to him (cf. Gen 37:5-11; 42:6), and now Moses sees a continuation of Joseph's headship amongst the tribes (Tigay 1996:409, n. 120). After the conquest of Canaan, Shiloh, a site in Ephraim, became the home of the Tabernacle and thus the religious center of the nation, and eventually Samaria of Manasseh was selected as the political capital. The whole presupposes a people of great strength, power described here under the imagery of a mighty bull or a fierce wild ox. Ephraim and Manasseh, representative of the whole northern kingdom, would for a time, at least, be an aggressive and expanding nation, one capable of defeating and dominating many of her surrounding neighbors (e.g., 2 Kgs 3:1-27; 14:23-25). In both domestic prosperity and political and military prowess, then, the Joseph clans, Ephraim and Manasseh, would enjoy God's outpouring of blessing in days to come (33:17).

◆   ### G. The Blessing of Zebulun and Issachar (33:18-19)

[18]Moses said this about the tribes of Zebulun and Issachar*:

"May the people of Zebulun prosper in their travels.
May the people of Issachar prosper at home in their tents.

[19]They summon the people to the mountain
to offer proper sacrifices there.
They benefit from the riches of the sea and the hidden treasures in the sand."

33:18 Hebrew lacks *and Issachar.*

COMMENTARY

Zebulun and Issachar, the two youngest sons of Leah (Gen 30:18-20), appear in Jacob's blessing right after Judah (Gen 49:13-15), whom they immediately followed in the order of Leah's sons. Geographically their descendants settled just to the north of the western half of Manasseh, between the Jordan rift and the Mediterranean Sea.

Their territorial distribution (33:18-19) explains their respective destinies, for Zebulun, along the coast, would become active in maritime industries, whereas Issachar, landlocked, would remain "in the tents"—that is, they would be sedentary and live off the soil. Issachar, in fact, was assigned to the Valley of Jezreel, the breadbasket of both ancient and modern Israel.

The reference to their calling people to "the mountain" to worship there (33:19) is not nearly so clear. The definiteness of the mountain (*the* mountain) and the existence of only one mountain in Jezreel that would best qualify, namely, Mount Tabor (see note in BHS), leads many scholars to view it as the referent here (Mayes 1979:407). It is described here as a place of "sacrifices of righteousness" (*zibkhe-tsedeq* [TH2077/6664, ZH2285/7406]), a phrase better understood (with the NLT) as a place of "proper" or "legitimate" sacrifices (33:19). If it does refer to Tabor and proper worship was carried out there in some ancient time, by the eighth century BC it had become a place of idolatry (Hos 5:1).

To return to the more mundane, Moses concluded this blessing by speaking of the abundance of the seas from which Zebulun would draw (that is, fish and other resources to be found there) and of the sands from which Issachar would extract minerals or even plant life. Life in all its aspects, both spiritual and material, would be good.

◆   H. The Blessing of Gad (33:20-21)

²⁰Moses said this about the tribe of Gad:

"Blessed is the one who enlarges Gad's
   territory!
Gad is poised there like a lion
   to tear off an arm or a head.
²¹The people of Gad took the best land
   for themselves;

a leader's share was assigned to
   them.
When the leaders of the people were
   assembled,
they carried out the LORD's justice
   and obeyed his regulations for
   Israel."

COMMENTARY

In Jacob's blessing of his sons, Dan comes immediately after Zebulun and Issachar, for he was the first of the sons by a concubine (Gen 49:16-19). After Leah had produced six sons, Rachel in desperation begged Jacob to give her a son through Bilhah, that child being Dan (Gen 30:1-6). Moses, however, in line with his more geographical scheme, mentioned Gad next, for that tribe settled in the east, in Gilead (33:20-21), south of the later settlement of Dan. One should also note that Gad was the firstborn of Leah's handmaid, Zilpah (Gen 30:9-12), offsetting in a certain sense the advantage gained by Rachel.

Gad, Moses said, would be like a female lion stealthily crouching to seize for herself the best of whatever came her way. Though God would indeed provide for her abundantly (33:20a), Gad the lioness would be dissatisfied and rapaciously rip off an arm or a head (33:20b). Though the details of this are difficult to discern historically, it is clear that Gilead was a most desirable territory, one Gad had already requested as a place of residence (Num 32:1-5). One might say that Gad had the "lion's share" of the Transjordan, but Moses described it as the "leader's share" (lit., "inscriber's share," that is, the part the allocator of territories would keep for himself; see Thompson 1974:315). As for Gad's role in regulating the application of Yahweh's justice and doing so in line with his covenant commandments, nothing specific can be said in the absence of historical information.

◆ I. The Blessing of Dan (33:22)

²²Moses said this about the tribe of Dan:

"Dan is a lion's cub,
leaping out from Bashan."

COMMENTARY

Dan, Rachel's son by Bilhah, was the first of Jacob's sons born to a maidservant (Gen 30:3-6), so he comes just after Issachar in Jacob's blessing (Gen 49:16-18; see discussion of Deut 33:20-21). Here (33:22) he follows Gad because Moses traced the territorial allotment of the tribes from south to north, viewing Dan not in its original allocation west of Benjamin but in its later settlement north of the Sea of Galilee (cf. Josh 19:40-48). Described as a venomous snake by Jacob (Gen 49:17), Moses called him by the equally unflattering epithet "lion's cub," perhaps because of the previous reference to Gad as a lioness (33:20). Both metaphors allude, no doubt, to Dan's outrageous slaughter of the Leshemites and appropriation of their land (Tigay 1996:332), an attack that may have been launched from Bashan, just to the east of Laish (33:22; cf. Josh 19:47).

◆ J. The Blessing of Naphtali (33:23)

²³Moses said this about the tribe of Naphtali:

"O Naphtali, you are rich in favor
and full of the LORD's blessings;
may you possess the west and
the south."

COMMENTARY

Rachel's second son by proxy, Naphtali appears on Jacob's blessing list unexpectedly after Gad and Asher, Leah's sons by her maidservant (Gen 49:21). It is possible, of course, that these two were, indeed, born before Naphtali and that the Genesis birth accounts (Gen 30:1-13) do not intend to say otherwise. In any case, both Jacob and Moses spoke favorably of Naphtali, the former likening him to a graceful deer and the latter predicting for him the fullness of God's blessings (33:23). Naphtali settled in the upper Galilee, hemmed in by Zebulun to the south and Asher to the west. The prayer that Naphtali might extend in those directions is, therefore, somewhat enigmatic. Perhaps it is to be understood figuratively, along the lines of Isaiah 9:1, which speaks of the areas of Naphtali and Zebulun being filled with glory at the advent of the Messiah.

◆ ## K. The Blessing of Asher (33:24-25)

24Moses said this about the tribe of Asher: may he bathe his feet in olive oil.
"May Asher be blessed above other 25May the bolts of your gates be of iron
sons; and bronze;
may he be esteemed by his brothers; may you be secure all your days."

NOTES
33:25 secure. The Samaritan Pentateuch reads *rbyk* [TH7235, ZH8049], "your greatness," a meaning reflected in LXX "your strength." The MT's *dob'eka* [TH1679, ZH1801], though a hapax legomenon, seems original and makes good sense with the meaning "secure."

COMMENTARY
Asher, Zilpah's second son and thus the youngest of all accounted to Leah, appears just after his brother Gad in Jacob's blessing (Gen 49:20). Moses mentioned this tribe last because it was assigned to the far northwest, on the Mediterranean just beyond Zebulun (33:24-25). Asher, whose very name connotes prosperity (*'asher* [TH836/833A, ZH888/887], "bless"), was seen by Jacob as a source of blessing to others. Moses suggested that the means by which this would be done was Asher's abundant supply of oil—olive oil, to be precise. To this day, the hills of Western Galilee are covered with orchards of productive olive trees. It is likely, however, that Moses was looking beyond mere material provision to some way in which Asher would contribute to Israel's spiritual well-being. All these blessings should be understood as having fulfillment beyond the time of the present text, as the blessing of Judah especially makes clear.

Because of the desirability of its resources, Asher would be the target of avaricious attack and thus would be in need of protection. Moses entreated Yahweh to make her gates impregnable and to give her strength commensurate with her life—that is, may Asher enjoy the protective grace of God as long as she lived.

◆ ## L. Final Praise and Benediction (33:26-29)

26"There is no one like the God of Israel.* prosperous Jacob in security,
He rides across the heavens to in a land of grain and new wine,
help you, while the heavens drop down dew.
across the skies in majestic splendor. 29How blessed you are, O Israel!
27The eternal God is your refuge, Who else is like you, a people saved
and his everlasting arms are under by the LORD?
you. He is your protecting shield
He drives out the enemy before you; and your triumphant sword!
he cries out, 'Destroy them!' Your enemies will cringe before you,
28So Israel will live in safety, and you will stomp on their backs!"

33:26 Hebrew *of Jeshurun*, a term of endearment for Israel.

NOTES
33:29 a people saved. Instead of the anarthrous MT reading, the Samaritan Pentateuch and Targums read, "*the* people saved" so as to draw attention to Israel as the exclusive people of the Lord.

COMMENTARY

In a magnificent, climactic note of praise, Moses speaks of God—his person and his exploits—and of Israel, the beneficiary of all that flows from being related to God (33:26-29). Appealing to the very foundational basis of Israel's faith and confession, namely, the first commandment and the Shema (5:6-7; 6:4-5), the prophet describes the Lord as the incomparable one who rides across the heavens on clouds of glory in order to attend to his people's every need (33:26). Since Baal was also said to be the "rider of the clouds," Moses's intent here is not only to celebrate Yahweh's greatness but to debunk any pretenders to his sovereignty (Cairns 1992:301-302; cf. Ps 68:33-34).

This lordly one, transcendently glorious as he is, also cares for those who know and trust him. He is their shelter (*me'onah* [TH4585, ZH5104], "hiding place") and also their safety net, the God who holds them forever in his mighty arms. Shifting the imagery a bit, Moses portrays the Lord as a warrior, the commander who would go before them to prepare their enemies for destruction (33:27; cf. 7:1-5; 20:4). The result was that the land of Canaan to which they were headed would lie open before Israel. They would live there in security and unmolested (lit., "alone"), savoring the bounty of the earth and the moisture from the heavens that would enable it to sustain them (33:28).

Finally, addressing the assembly, Moses expostulates, "How blessed you are!" Of all the nations of the earth, only they had been chosen by the Lord to be the special recipients of his favor (cf. 4:32-40; 7:6-8; 14:2). Only they had come to know him as shield and sword—that is, as a sure defense and a warrior doing battle on their behalf. Surely they did not need to fear when contemplating the conquest of the Promised Land because the mighty God, their God, would enable them to place their feet triumphantly on the backs of their defeated foes (33:29).

◆ XIII. Narrative Epilogue (34:1-12)
A. The Death of Moses (34:1-8)

Then Moses went up to Mount Nebo from the plains of Moab and climbed Pisgah Peak, which is across from Jericho. And the LORD showed him the whole land, from Gilead as far as Dan; ²all the land of Naphtali; the land of Ephraim and Manasseh; all the land of Judah, extending to the Mediterranean Sea*; ³the Negev; the Jordan Valley with Jericho—the city of palms—as far as Zoar. ⁴Then the LORD said to Moses, "This is the land I promised on oath to Abraham, Isaac, and Jacob when I said, 'I will give it to your descendants.' I have now allowed you to see it with your own eyes, but you will not enter the land."

⁵So Moses, the servant of the LORD, died there in the land of Moab, just as the LORD had said. ⁶The LORD buried him* in a valley near Beth-peor in Moab, but to this day no one knows the exact place. ⁷Moses was 120 years old when he died, yet his eyesight was clear, and he was as strong as ever. ⁸The people of Israel mourned for Moses on the plains of Moab for thirty days, until the customary period of mourning was over.

34:2 Hebrew *the western sea.*   34:6 Hebrew *He buried him;* Samaritan Pentateuch and some Greek manuscripts read *They buried him.*

NOTES

34:1-3 *from Gilead as far as Dan . . . Mediterranean Sea.* In place of these words, the Samaritan Pentateuch reads "from the river of Egypt to the great river, the Euphrates, and to the Mediterranean Sea." This is apparently in order to conform to a more standard formula (Gen 15:18; cf. Deut 1:7; 11:24). The MT is preferable, with Moses viewing the land from where he was (Gilead) and looking in a counterclockwise fashion at some of its major regions and cities, finishing with Jericho on the Jordan plain in v. 3.

34:4 *promised on oath.* The Samaritan Pentateuch and Syriac add "to your fathers."

34:6 *The LORD buried.* Lit., "He buried him" (cf. NLT mg). It is true that the passive in Hebrew ("he was buried") is frequently expressed in an active voice with indefinite subject (Waltke and O'Connor 1990:4.4.2), but the fact that no one knew where he was buried, coupled with the later mysterious tradition about Michael the archangel arguing with Satan about Moses's body (Jude 1:9), appear to favor the idea that God himself entombed the prophet, perhaps to prevent idolatrous veneration of his remains (Craigie 1976:405).

34:7 *strong as ever.* Instead of the MT's *lo'-nas lekhoh* [TH3893/5127, ZH4301/5674], "had not lost his vital strength," the Vulgate reads "had not lost his teeth," something that would have been an impressive feat even for a much younger man in the ancient world. The NLT follows the MT text but phrases the idea as a grammatically positive statement.

COMMENTARY

Having concluded his blessing of the tribes, Moses ascended to the top of Nebo on Mount Pisgah. The relationship between Pisgah and Nebo is not clear. They may be synonymous (thus one could render it, "to Mount Nebo, that is, to Pisgah"), or one or the other may be the name of a group of mountains of which the other was the name of a particular peak. Comparison of all the biblical data seems to favor the idea that Nebo was a promontory on Mount Pisgah (cf. 3:17, 27; 4:49; 32:49; Num 21:20; 23:14; 33:47; Josh 12:3; 13:20). The traditional site is now known as Jebel en-Neba, about six miles southwest of Hesban in modern Jordan (biblical Heshbon; cf. Bimson 1995:225). From there one can view almost all the land of Canaan. Turning first toward the north, Moses overlooked Gilead of the Transjordan and saw the region of Dan on the lower slopes of Mount Hermon (34:1; see note). He then directed his gaze to the northwest and dimly made out the allotment of Naphtali represented perhaps by Mount Carmel. Between his vantage point and Zebulun lay Ephraim and Manasseh, the heartland of Canaan. To his immediate west and southwest Moses saw what would become Judah, and beyond that he could discern the Mediterranean (34:2). Finally he turned toward the south and in the far distance made out the Negev desert. Just below him, on the other side of the Jordan, lay the plain of Jericho, a stretch of flat land extending to Zoar at the south end of the Dead Sea (34:3).

In the midst of Moses's reverie, Yahweh interrupted with the observation that what Moses saw was the land promised to the patriarchs centuries before (cf. Gen 12:7; 26:3; 28:13), but, alas, a land that he himself could never enter (34:4). There was no reason to reiterate the reason why, for Moses knew full well that his own sin had precluded his enjoyment of the culmination of his hopes and dreams (cf. 32:48-52 and passages cited there).

Finally, the narrator—in terms laconically reportorial—recounts Moses's death, noting that it took place just as Yahweh had said it would (34:5). The text then goes on to say "the LORD buried him" (see note on 34:6). This being the case, the narrator can supply the general place of interment, a valley near Beth-peor (34:6), but no more.

Though Moses was 120 years old, the observation is made that he was in generally good health. His eyesight was sound and his bodily systems (lit., "[life]-sap"; NIDOTTE 2.783) vigorous (34:7). The implication is that Moses's death, though he was so old, was premature. He died then and there because it was time for Israel to enter and occupy Canaan without him. They could and would not do so, however, until the customary 30 days of mourning were over (34:8). Surely the length of their lament was not just to conform to tradition. It was deep and heartfelt because they had lost the one who, in many respects, was the father of their country (cf. 1:31).

◆   B. The Epitaph of Moses (34:9-12)

⁹Now Joshua son of Nun was full of the spirit of wisdom, for Moses had laid his hands on him. So the people of Israel obeyed him, doing just as the LORD had commanded Moses.

¹⁰There has never been another prophet in Israel like Moses, whom the LORD knew face to face. ¹¹The LORD sent him to perform all the miraculous signs and wonders in the land of Egypt against Pharaoh, and all his servants, and his entire land. ¹²With mighty power, Moses performed terrifying acts in the sight of all Israel.

COMMENTARY

The transition from Moses to Joshua was smooth because it had been in process for a long time. As far back as the time of the Exodus, Joshua had been singled out as a worthy assistant to the lawgiver, having participated with him in the defeat of the Amalekites (Exod 17:8-16). Later, he became designated as Moses's aide, gaining thereby greater and greater access to the holy things of God (Exod 24:13; 33:11), though sometimes in what seems to be an over-protective manner (Num 11:26-30).

When Moses sent out a team to reconnoiter Canaan, Joshua was among them (Num 13:8). Upon their return he, with Caleb, demonstrated his great courage and faith by urging Moses to go forward with conquest despite the pessimistic majority report to desist (Num 14:4-10). Because of this mark of leadership, Moses informed Joshua that he and Caleb would enter Canaan, though all the other men of their generation would not (Num 14:26-35). In fact, Joshua would succeed Moses and become the leader in conquering and occupying the Promised Land (Num 27:15-23; cf. Deut 1:38; 3:28; 31:3-8). As Moses's death drew near, Joshua's role as successor became formalized by a ceremony of ordination that made it clear to the whole community that Yahweh's imprimatur rested upon him (31:14, 23; cf. 32:44). The whole is summarized here with the observation that Joshua was well prepared for his task because Moses had imparted to him a wise spirit (34:9; cf. Num 27:18). This spirit came from God and, in New Testament theological terms, is the Holy Spirit, the third

Person of the Godhead (cf. Num 11:24-25). Only a Spirit-filled person could accomplish what God had in mind for Joshua in the years ahead.

The death notice about Moses concludes with an epitaph, a brief encapsulation of his life that celebrates who he was and what he did. The narrator described him as a prophet *nonpareil*, the only one whom Yahweh knew "face-to-face," that is, without the mediation of visions and dreams. This uniqueness of Moses as a recipient and dispenser of revelation had already been asserted to Miriam and Aaron on the occasion of their rebellion against the prophetic leadership of their brother. At that time, Yahweh had chided them by the remarkable declaration that "if there were prophets among you, I, the LORD, would reveal myself in visions. I would speak to them in dreams. But not with my servant Moses. Of all my house, he is the one I trust. I speak to him face to face [lit., 'mouth to mouth'], clearly, and not in riddles! He sees the LORD as he is" (Num 12:6-8; cf. Deut 18:15-22).

This prophet par excellence had been Yahweh's instrument of mighty power, as well. He had terrified Pharaoh and all Egypt with the ten plagues (34:11) and, at the same time, had reminded Israel of who God was and what he demanded of them (34:12). Surely nothing more glorious could be said of a servant of God than this: He lived and labored in such a way as to make his God known among his people.

BIBLIOGRAPHY

Abba, Raymond
1977 Priests and Levites in Deuteronomy. *Vetus Testamentum* 27:257-267.

Aharoni, Yohanan
1979 *The Land of the Bible.* Philadelphia: Westminster.

Ahlström, Gösta W.
1993 *The History of Ancient Palestine.* Minneapolis: Fortress.

Ashley, Timothy R.
1993 *The Book of Numbers.* New International Commentary on the Old Testament. Grand Rapids: Eerdmans.

Baly, Denis
1957 *The Geography of the Bible.* New York: Harper.

Barth, Christoph
1991 *God With Us: A Theological Introduction to the Old Testament.* Grand Rapids: Eerdmans.

Begg, Christopher T.
1979 The Significance of the *Numeruswechsel* in Deuteronomy: The "Pre-history" of the Problem. *Ephemerides theologicae lovanienses* 55:116-124.

Bimson, John J., editor
1995 *Baker Encyclopedia of Bible Places.* Grand Rapids: Baker.

Block, Daniel I.
2001 Recovering the Voice of Moses: The Genesis of Deuteronomy. *Journal of the Evangelical Theological Society* 44:385-408.

Blomberg, Craig L.
1992 *Matthew.* Nashville: Broadman & Holman.

Bock, Darrell L.
1996 *Luke. Volume 2 (9:51–24:53).* Grand Rapids: Baker.

Braulik, Georg
1993 The Sequence of the Laws in Deuteronomy 12–26 and in the Decalogue. Pp. 313-335 in *A Song of Power and the Power of Song: Essays on the Book of Deuteronomy.* Editor, Duane L. Christensen. Winona Lake: Eisenbrauns.

Bright, John
1981 *A History of Israel.* 3rd ed. Philadelphia: Westminster.

Brueggemann, Walter
1997 *Theology of the Old Testament.* Minneapolis: Fortress.

Cairns, Ian
1992 *Word and Presence: A Commentary on the Book of Deuteronomy.* Grand Rapids: Eerdmans.

Carson, D. A.
1984 *From Triumphalism to Maturity: An Exposition of 2 Corinthians 10–13.* Grand Rapids: Baker.

Childs, Brevard S.
1974 *The Book of Exodus.* Philadelphia: Westminster.

Christensen, Duane L.
1991 *Deuteronomy 1–11.* Word Biblical Commentary. Dallas: Word.
1993 The *Numeruswechsel* in Deuteronomy 12. Pp. 394-402 in *A Song of Power and the Power of Song: Essays on the Book of Deuteronomy.* Editor, Duane L. Christensen. Winona Lake: Eisenbrauns.

Clark, W. Malcolm
1974 Law. Pp. 99-139 in *Old Testament Form Criticism.* Editor, John H. Hayes. San Antonio: Trinity University Press.

Cohen, Rudolph
1981 The Excavations at Kadesh-barnea (1976-78). *Biblical Archaeologist* 44:93-107.

Craigie, Peter C.
1976 *The Book of Deuteronomy.* New International Commentary on the Old Testament. Grand Rapids: Eerdmans.

1978 *The Problem of War in the Old Testament.* Grand Rapids: Eerdmans.

Cross, Frank Moore
1973 *Canaanite Myth and Hebrew Epic.* Cambridge, MA: Harvard University Press.

Curtis, J. E., and J. E. Reade
1995 *Art and Empire.* New York: The Metropolitan Museum of Art.

Driver, S. R.
1902 *A Critical and Exegetical Commentary on Deuteronomy.* Edinburgh: T&T Clark.

Dumbrell, W. J.
1984 *Covenant and Creation.* Nashville: Thomas Nelson.

Dyrness, William
1979 *Themes in Old Testament Theology.* Downers Grove: InterVarsity.

Eissfeldt, Otto
1965 *The Old Testament: An Introduction.* New York: Harper & Row.

Emerton, J. A.
1962 Priests and Levites in Deuteronomy. *Vetus Testamentum* 12:129-138.

Fohrer, Georg
1968 Twofold Aspects of Hebrew Words. Pp. 95-103 in *Words and Meanings.* Editors, Peter R. Ackroyd and Barnabas Lindars. Cambridge: Cambridge University Press.

Fokkelman, J. P.
1998 *Major Poems of the Hebrew Bible.* Assen: Van Gorcum.

Frick, Frank S.
1977 *The City in Ancient Israel.* Missoula, MT: Scholars Press.

Gaster, Theodor H.
1961 *Thespis. Ritual, Myth, and Drama in the Ancient Near East.* New York: Harper & Row.

1969 *Myth, Legend, and Custom in the Old Testament,* vol. 1. New York: Harper & Row.

Gottwald, Norman K.
1979 *The Tribes of Yahweh.* Maryknoll, NY: Orbis Books.

Grayson, Albert Kirk
1976 *Assyrian Royal Inscriptions.* Vol. 2., *Records of the Ancient Near East.* Wiesbaden: Harrassowitz.

Greenberg, M.
1951 Hebrew *sequlla:* Akkadian *sikiltu. Journal of the American Oriental Society* 71:172-174.

1959 The Biblical Concept of Asylum. *Journal of Biblical Literature* 67:125-132.

Harrison, R. K.
1990 *Numbers.* Chicago: Moody.

Heiser, Michael S.
2001 Deuteronomy 32:8 and the Sons of God. *Bibliotheca sacra* 158:52-74.

Hepper, F. Nigel
1992 *Baker Encyclopedia of Bible Plants.* Grand Rapids: Baker.

Hodge, Charles
1955 *Commentary on the Epistle to the Romans.* Grand Rapids: Eerdmans.

Hoffner, H. A., Jr.
1966 Symbols for Masculinity and Femininity: Their Use in Ancient Near Eastern Sympathetic Magic Rituals. *Journal of Biblical Literature* 85:326-334.

1994 Hittites. Pp. 127-155 in *Peoples of the Old Testament World.* Editors, Alfred J. Hoerth, Gerald L. Mattingly, and Edwin M. Yamauchi. Grand Rapids: Baker.

Hubbard, Robert L., Jr.
1988 *The Book of Ruth.* New International Commentary on the Old Testament. Grand Rapids: Eerdmans.

Huffmon, Herbert B.
1959 The Covenant Lawsuit in the Prophets. *Journal of Biblical Literature* 78:285-295.

Ishida, T.
1979 The Structure and Historical Implications of the Lists of Pre-Israelite Nations. *Biblica* 60:461–490.

Jacob, Benno
1992 *The Second Book of the Bible: Exodus.* Hoboken: KTAV.

Jenson, Philip Peter
1992 *Graded Holiness: A Key to the Priestly Conception of the World.* Journal for the Study of the Old Testament Supplement Series 106. Sheffield: Journal for the Study of the Old Testament Press.

Jones, G. H.
1975 Holy War or Yahweh War? *Vetus Testamentum* 25:642–658.

Kaiser, Walter C., Jr.
1983 *Toward Old Testament Ethics.* Grand Rapids: Zondervan.

Kalland, Earl S.
1992 Deuteronomy. Pp. 3–238 in *The Expositor's Bible Commentary,* vol. 3. Editor, Frank E. Gaebelein. Grand Rapids: Zondervan.

Kaufman, S. A.
1978–1979 The Structure of the Deuteronomic Law. *Maarav* 1/2:105–158.

Keil, C. F., and F. Delitzsch
n.d. *The Pentateuch.* Biblical Commentary on the Old Testament, vol. 3. Translator, James Martin. Grand Rapids: Eerdmans.

Kitchen, Kenneth A.
1970 Ancient Orient, "Deuteronomism," and the Old Testament. Pp. 1–24 in *New Perspectives on the Old Testament.* Editor, J. Barton Payne. Waco: Word.

Kline, Meredith G.
1972 *The Structure of Biblical Authority.* Grand Rapids: Eerdmans.

Knierim, Rolf P.
1995 *The Task of Old Testament Theology.* Grand Rapids: Eerdmans.

Limburg, James
1969 The Root *ryb* and the Prophetic Lawsuit Speeches. *Journal of Biblical Literature* 88:291–304.

Longman, Tremper, III, and Raymond B. Dillard
2006 *An Introduction to the Old Testament.* Grand Rapids: Zondervan.

Matthews, Victor H.
1991 *Manners and Customs in the Bible.* Peabody, MA: Hendrickson.

Mayes, A. D. H.
1979 *Deuteronomy.* Greenwood, SC: Attic.

1981 *Deuteronomy.* Grand Rapids: Eerdmans.

Mazar, Amihai
1990 *Archaeology of the Land of the Bible: 10,000–586 BCE.* New York: Doubleday.

McConville, J. Gordon
1993 *Grace in the End: A Study in Deuteronomic Theology.* Grand Rapids: Zondervan.

Mendenhall, G. E.
1954 Covenant Forms in Israelite Tradition. *Biblical Archaeologist* 17:50–76.

1955 Covenant Forms in Israelite Traditions. Pp. 24–50 in *Law and Covenant in Israel and the Ancient Near East.* Pittsburgh: Biblical Colloquium.

1970 Ancient Oriental and Biblical Law. Pp. 3–24 in *The Biblical Archaeologist Reader,* vol. 3. Editors, Edward F. Campbell Jr. and David Noel Freedman. Garden City: Doubleday.

Merrill, Eugene H.
1982 Palestinian Archaeology and the Date of the Conquest: Do Tells Tell Tales? *Grace Theological Journal* 3/1:107–121.

1987 *Kingdom of Priests. A History of Old Testament Israel.* Grand Rapids: Baker.

1990 Is the Doctrine of the Trinity Implied in the Genesis Creation Account? Pp. 110–129 in *The Genesis Debate.* Editor, Ronald F. Youngblood. Grand Rapids: Baker.

1991 A Theology of the Pentateuch. Pp. 1–87 in *A Biblical Theology of the Old Testament.* Editor, Roy B. Zuck. Chicago: Moody.

1994 Deuteronomy, New Testament Faith, and the Christian Life. Pp. 19-33 in *Integrity of Heart, Skillfulness of Hands*. Editors, Charles H. Dyer and Roy B. Zuck. Grand Rapids: Baker.

1997 The Peoples of the Old Testament according to Genesis 10. *Bibliotheca sacra* 154:3-22.

1998 Internal Evidence for the Inerrancy of the Pentateuch. *The Conservative Theological Journal* 2/5:102-122.

2000 Deuteronomy and History: Anticipation or Reflection? *Faith and Mission* 18/1:57-76.

2008 *Kingdom of Priests: A History of Old Testament Israel*. 2nd ed. Grand Rapids: Baker.

Milgrom, Jacob
1991 *Leviticus 1–16*. Anchor Bible 3. New York: Doubleday.

Millard, A. R.
1988 King Og's Bed and Other Ancient Ironmongery. Pp. 481-492 in *Ascribe to the Lord*. Editors, L. Eslinger and G. Taylor. Journal for the Study of the Old Testament Supplement 67. Sheffield: Journal for the Study of the Old Testament Press.

Miller, Patrick D.
1999 Deuteronomy and Psalms: Evoking a Biblical Conversation. *Journal of Biblical Literature* 118:3-18.

Minette de Tillesse, G.
1962 Sections 'tu' et sections 'vous' dans le Deutéronome. *Vetus Testamentum* 12:29-87.

Moran, W. L.
1963 The Ancient Near Eastern Background of the Love of God in Deuteronomy. *Catholic Biblical Quarterly* 25:77-87.

Negev, Avraham, editor
1980 *Archaeological Encyclopedia of the Holy Land*. Englewood, NJ: SBS.

Nelson, Richard D.
2002 *Deuteronomy*. Louisville: Westminster John Knox.

Nicholson, E. W.
1967 *Deuteronomy and Tradition*. Philadelphia: Fortress.

Noth, Martin
1966 *The Old Testament World*. Philadelphia: Fortress.

Patrick, Dale
1985 *Old Testament Law*. Atlanta: John Knox.

Rad, Gerhard von
1966a *Deuteronomy: A Commentary*. Philadelphia: Westminster.

1966b The Form-Critical Problem of the Hexateuch. Pp. 1-78 in *The Problem of the Hexateuch and Other Essays*. London: SCM. (Orig. pub. 1938.)

Ringgren, Helmer
1973 *Religions of the Ancient Near East*. Philadelphia: Westminster.

Robinson, H. Wheeler
1935 *Corporate Personality in Ancient Israel*. Philadelphia: Fortress.

Rofé, Alexander
1988 The Arrangement of the Laws in Deuteronomy. *Ephemerides theologicae lovanienses* 64:265-287.

Rogerson, John W.
1992 *W. M. L. DeWette: Founder of Modern Biblical Criticism*. Journal for the Study of the Old Testament Supplement Series 126. Sheffield: Journal for the Study of the Old Testament Press.

Schiffman, Lawrence H.
1991 *From Text to Tradition*. Hoboken: KTAV.

Schoville, Keith N.
1994 Canaanites and Amorites. Pp. 157-182 in *Peoples of the Old Testament World*. Editors, Alfred J. Hoerth, Gerald L. Mattingly, and Edwin M. Yamauchi. Grand Rapids: Baker.

Soden, Wolfram von
1994 *The Ancient Orient*. Grand Rapids: Eerdmans.

Speiser, E. A.
1964 *Genesis*. Anchor Bible 1. Garden City: Doubleday.

Talmon, S.

1983 Biblical רְפָאִ֫ים and Ugaritic RPU/I(M). *Hebrew Union College Annual* 7:235-249.

Taylor, J. Glen

1993 *Yahweh and the Sun.* Journal for the Study of the Old Testament Supplement Series 111. Sheffield: Journal for the Study of the Old Testament Press.

Terrien, Samuel

1978 *The Elusive Presence.* San Francisco: Harper & Row.

Thompson, J. A.

1974 *Deuteronomy: An Introduction and Commentary.* Downers Grove: InterVarsity.

Tigay, Jeffrey H.

1996 *Deuteronomy. The JPS Torah Commentary.* Philadelphia: Jewish Publication Society.

Tov, Emanuel

1981 *The Text-Critical Use of the Septuagint in Biblical Research.* Jerusalem: Simor.

1992 *Textual Criticism of the Hebrew Bible.* Minneapolis: Fortress.

Ulrich, Eugene

1995 *Qumran Cave 4. IX: Deuteronomy, Joshua, Judges, Kings.* Discoveries in the Judean Desert XIV. Oxford: Clarendon.

VanGemeren, Willem A.

1990 *Interpreting the Prophetic Word.* Grand Rapids: Zondervan.

Vasholz, Robert I.

1990 *The Old Testament Canon in the Old Testament Church.* Lewiston, NY: Mellen.

Vaux, Roland de

1965 *Ancient Israel.* New York: McGraw-Hill.

1978 *The Early History of Israel.* Philadelphia: Westminster.

Waltke, Bruce K., and M. O'Connor

1990 *An Introduction to Biblical Hebrew Syntax.* Winona Lake: Eisenbrauns.

Weinfeld, Moshe

1991 *Deuteronomy 1–11.* Anchor Bible 5. New York: Doubleday.

Wenham, Gordon J.

1987 *Genesis 1–15.* Word Biblical Commentary 1. Waco: Word.

1994 *Genesis 16–50.* Word Biblical Commentary 2. Dallas: Word.

Wevers, J. W.

1977 Attitudes of the Greek Translator of Deuteronomy towards His Parent Text. Pp. 498–505 in *Beiträge zur Alttestamentlichen Theologie.* Editors, Herbert Donner, Robert Hanhart, and Rudolf Smend. Göttingen: Vandenhoeck & Ruprecht.

Wiseman, D. J.

1958 *The Vassal-Treaties of Esarhaddon.* London: British School of Archaeology in Iraq.

Wolf, Herbert

1991 *An Introduction to the Old Testament Pentateuch.* Chicago: Moody.

Wolff, Hans Walter

1974 *Anthropology of the Old Testament.* Philadelphia: Fortress.

Wright, Christopher J. H.

1990 *God's People in God's Land.* Grand Rapids: Eerdmans.

Wright, G. Ernest

1954 The Levites in Deuteronomy. *Vetus Testamentum* 4:325-330.

Zevit, Z.

1976 The *'eglâ* Ritual of Deuteronomy 21:1-9. *Journal of Biblical Literature* 95:377-390.